HALSBURY'S
Laws of England

FIFTH EDITION
2015

Volume 35

This is volume 35 of the Fifth Edition of Halsbury's Laws of England, containing the first part of the title EDUCATION.

The title EDUCATION replaces the EDUCATION title contained in volumes 35 (2011), 36 (2011).

Volumes 35 (2011), 36 (2011) may now be archived.

For a full list of volumes comprised in a current set of Halsbury's Laws of England please see overleaf.

Fifth Edition volumes:

1 (2008), 2 (2008), 3 (2011), 4 (2011), 5 (2013), 6 (2011), 7 (2015), 8 (2015), 9 (2012), 10 (2012), 11 (2009), 12 (2009), 13 (2009), 14 (2009), 15 (2009), 16 (2011), 17 (2011), 18 (2009), 19 (2011), 20 (2014), 21 (2011), 22 (2012), 23 (2013), 24 (2010), 25 (2010), 26 (2010), 27 (2010), 28 (2010), 29 (2014), 30 (2012), 31 (2012), 32 (2012), 33 (2013), 34 (2011), 35 (2015), 36 (2015), 37 (2013), 38 (2013), 38A (2013), 39 (2014), 40 (2014), 41 (2014), 41A (2014), 42 (2011), 43 (2011), 44 (2011), 45 (2010), 46 (2010), 47 (2014), 47A (2014), 48 (2008), 49 (2008), 49 (2015), 50 (2008), 51 (2013), 52 (2014), 53 (2014), 54 (2008), 55 (2012), 56 (2011), 57 (2012), 58 (2014), 58A (2014), 59 (2014), 59A (2014), 60 (2011), 61 (2010), 62 (2012), 63 (2012), 64 (2012), 65 (2015), 66 (2015), 67 (2008), 68 (2008), 69 (2009), 70 (2012), 71 (2013), 72 (2015), 73 (2015), 74 (2011), 75 (2013), 76 (2013), 77 (2010), 78 (2010), 79 (2014), 80 (2013), 81 (2010), 82 (2010), 83 (2010), 84 (2013), 84A (2013), 85 (2012), 86 (2013), 87 (2012), 88 (2012), 88A (2013), 89 (2011), 90 (2011), 91 (2012), 92 (2010), 93 (2008), 94 (2008), 95 (2013), 96 (2012), 97 (2015), 97A (2014), 98 (2013), 99 (2012), 100 (2009), 101 (2009), 102 (2010), 103 (2010), 104 (2014)

Additional Materials:

Sentencing and Disposition of Offenders (Release and Recall of Prisoners) containing vol **92** (2010) paras 761–820

Consolidated Index and Tables:

2015 Consolidated Index (A–E), 2015 Consolidated Index (F–O), 2015 Consolidated Index (P–Z), 2016 Consolidated Table of Statutes, 2016 Consolidated Table of Statutory Instruments, etc, 2015 Consolidated Table of Cases (A–G), 2015 Consolidated Table of Cases (H–Q), 2015 Consolidated Table of Cases (R–Z, ECJ Cases)

Updating and ancillary materials:

2015 Annual Cumulative Supplement; Monthly Current Service; Annual Abridgments 1974–2014

September 2015

HALSBURY'S
Laws of England

Volume 35

2015

Members of the LexisNexis Group worldwide

United Kingdom	LexisNexis, a Division of Reed Elsevier (UK) Ltd, Lexis House, 30 Farringdon Street, LONDON, EC4A 4HH, and 9–10, St Andrew Square, EDINBURGH, EH2 2AF
Australia	Reed International Books Australia Pty Ltd trading as LexisNexis, Chatswood, New South Wales
Austria	LexisNexis Verlag ARD Orac GmbH & Co KG, Vienna
Benelux	LexisNexis Benelux, Amsterdam
Canada	LexisNexis Canada, Markham, Ontario
China	LexisNexis China, Beijing and Shanghai
France	LexisNexis SA, Paris
Germany	LexisNexis GmbH, Dusseldorf
Hong Kong	LexisNexis Hong Kong, Hong Kong
India	LexisNexis India, New Delhi
Italy	Giuffrè Editore, Milan
Japan	LexisNexis Japan, Tokyo
Malaysia	Malayan Law Journal Sdn Bhd, Kuala Lumpur
New Zealand	LexisNexis New Zealand Ltd, Wellington
Singapore	LexisNexis Singapore, Singapore
South Africa	LexisNexis, Durban
USA	LexisNexis, Dayton, Ohio

FIRST EDITION	*Published in 31 volumes between 1907 and 1917*
SECOND EDITION	*Published in 37 volumes between 1931 and 1942*
THIRD EDITION	*Published in 43 volumes between 1952 and 1964*
FOURTH EDITION	*Published in 56 volumes between 1973 and 1987, with reissues between 1988 and 2008*
FIFTH EDITION	*Published between 2008 and 2014, with reissues from 2014*

A CIP Catalogue record for this book is available from the British Library.

ISBN 13 (complete set, standard binding): 9781405734394

ISBN 13: 9781405798518

ISBN 978-1-4057-9851-8

9 781405 798518

Typeset by Letterpart Limited, Caterham on the Hill, Surrey CR3 5XL
Printed and bound by CPI Group (UK) Ltd, Croydon, CR0 4YY
Visit LexisNexis at www.lexisnexis.co.uk

EDUCATION

Consultant Editor

TANYA CALLMAN, MA (Cantab),

Barrister and Legal Trainer, EduLaw Chambers;

Member of the Honourable Society of the Middle Temple;

Ad Eundem Member of the Honourable Society of the Inner Temple;

Exhibitioner at Peterhouse, Cambridge;

Founder and Former Editor of Education, Public Law and the Individual

The law stated in this volume is in general that in force on 1 August 2015, although subsequent changes have been included wherever possible.

Any future updating material will be found in the Current Service and annual Cumulative Supplement to Halsbury's Laws of England.

TABLE OF CONTENTS

HOW TO USE HALSBURY'S LAWS OF ENGLAND

Volumes

Each text volume of Halsbury's Laws of England contains the law on the titles contained in it as at a date stated at the front of the volume (the operative date).

Information contained in Halsbury's Laws of England may be accessed in several ways.

First, by using the tables of contents.

Each volume contains both a general Table of Contents, and a specific Table of Contents for each title contained in it. From these tables you will be directed to the relevant part of the work.

Readers should note that the current arrangement of titles can be found in the Current Service.

Secondly, by using tables of statutes, statutory instruments, cases or other materials.

If you know the name of the Act, statutory instrument or case with which your research is concerned, you should consult the Consolidated Tables of statutes, cases and so on (published as separate volumes) which will direct you to the relevant volume and paragraph.

(Each individual text volume also includes tables of those materials used as authority in that volume.)

Thirdly, by using the indexes.

If you are uncertain of the general subject area of your research, you should go to the Consolidated Index (published as separate volumes) for reference to the relevant volume(s) and paragraph(s).

(Each individual text volume also includes an index to the material contained therein.)

Updating publications

The text volumes of Halsbury's Laws should be used in conjunction with the annual Cumulative Supplement and the monthly Noter-Up.

The annual Cumulative Supplement

The Supplement gives details of all changes between the operative date of the text volume and the operative date of the Supplement. It is arranged in the same volume, title and paragraph order as the text volumes. Developments affecting particular points of law are noted to the relevant paragraph(s) of the text volumes.

For narrative treatment of material noted in the Cumulative Supplement, go to the Annual Abridgment volume for the relevant year.

Destination Tables

In certain titles in the annual *Cumulative Supplement*, reference is made to Destination Tables showing the destination of consolidated legislation. Those Destination Tables are to be found either at the end of the titles within the annual *Cumulative Supplement*, or in a separate *Destination Tables* booklet provided from time to time with the *Cumulative Supplement*.

The Noter-Up

The Noter-Up is contained in the Current Service Noter-Up booklet, issued monthly and noting changes since the publication of the annual Cumulative Supplement. Also arranged in the same volume, title and paragraph order as the text volumes, the Noter-Up follows the style of the Cumulative Supplement.

For narrative treatment of material noted in the Noter-Up, go to the relevant Monthly Review.

REFERENCES AND ABBREVIATIONS

ACT	Australian Capital Territory
A-G	Attorney General
Admin	Administrative Court
Admlty	Admiralty Court
Adv-Gen	Advocate General
affd	affirmed
affg	affirming
Alta	Alberta
App	Appendix
art	article
Aust	Australia
B	Baron
BC	British Columbia
C	Command Paper (of a series published before 1900)
c	chapter number of an Act
CA	Court of Appeal
CAC	Central Arbitration Committee
CA in Ch	Court of Appeal in Chancery
CB	Chief Baron
CCA	Court of Criminal Appeal
CCR	County Court Rules 1981 (as subsequently amended)
CCR	Court for Crown Cases Reserved
CJEU	Court of Justice of the European Union
C-MAC	Courts-Martial Appeal Court
CO	Crown Office
COD	Crown Office Digest
CPR	Civil Procedure Rules
Can	Canada
Cd	Command Paper (of the series published 1900–18)
Cf	compare
Ch	Chancery Division
ch	chapter
cl	clause
Cm	Command Paper (of the series published 1986 to date)

Cmd	Command Paper (of the series published 1919–56)
Cmnd	Command Paper (of the series published 1956–86)
Comm	Commercial Court
Comr	Commissioner
Court Forms (2nd Edn)	Atkin's Encyclopaedia of Court Forms in Civil Proceedings, 2nd Edn. See note 2 post.
CrimPR	Criminal Procedure Rules
DC	Divisional Court
DPP	Director of Public Prosecutions
EAT	Employment Appeal Tribunal
EC	European Community
ECJ	Court of Justice of the European Community (before the Treaty of Lisbon (OJ C306, 17.12.2007, p 1) came into force on 1 December 2009); European Court of Justice (after the Treaty of Lisbon (OJ C306, 17.12.2007, p 1) came into force on 1 December 2009)
EComHR	European Commission of Human Rights
ECSC	European Coal and Steel Community
ECtHR Rules of Court	Rules of Court of the European Court of Human Rights
EEC	European Economic Community
EFTA	European Free Trade Association
EGC	European General Court
EWCA Civ	Official neutral citation for judgments of the Court of Appeal (Civil Division)
EWCA Crim	Official neutral citation for judgments of the Court of Appeal (Criminal Division)
EWHC	Official neutral citation for judgments of the High Court
Edn	Edition
Euratom	European Atomic Energy Community
EU	European Union
Ex Ch	Court of Exchequer Chamber
ex p	ex parte
Fam	Family Division
Fed	Federal
Forms & Precedents (5th Edn)	Encyclopaedia of Forms and Precedents other than Court Forms, 5th Edn. See note 2 post.
GLC	Greater London Council
HC	High Court
HC	House of Commons

HK	Hong Kong
HL.......................................	House of Lords
IAT	Immigration Appeal Tribunal
ILM.....................................	International Legal Materials
INLR....................................	Immigration and Nationality Law Reports
IRC......................................	Inland Revenue Commissioners
Ind......................................	India
Int Rels................................	International Relations
Ir	Ireland
J..	Justice
JA	Judge of Appeal
Kan......................................	Kansas
LA	Lord Advocate
LC	Lord Chancellor
LCC......................................	London County Council
LCJ......................................	Lord Chief Justice
LJ	Lord Justice of Appeal
LoN......................................	League of Nations
MR.......................................	Master of the Rolls
Man......................................	Manitoba
n..	note
NB.......................................	New Brunswick
NI..	Northern Ireland
NS	Nova Scotia
NSW.....................................	New South Wales
NY	New York
NZ	New Zealand
OHIM	Office for Harmonisation in the Internal Market
OJ..	The Official Journal of the European Community published by the Office for Official Publications of the European Community
Ont......................................	Ontario
P..	President
PC	Judicial Committee of the Privy Council
PEI.......................................	Prince Edward Island
Pat.......................................	Patents Court
q..	question
QB.......................................	Queen's Bench Division
QBD.....................................	Queen's Bench Division of the High Court
Qld......................................	Queensland
Que	Quebec
r..	rule

RDC.......................................	Rural District Council
RPC.......................................	Restrictive Practices Court
RSC.......................................	Rules of the Supreme Court 1965 (as subsequently amended)
reg	regulation
Res	Resolution
revsd.....................................	reversed
Rly..	Railway
s..	section
SA...	South Africa
S Aust...................................	South Australia
SC...	Supreme Court
SI..	Statutory Instruments published by authority
SR & O.................................	Statutory Rules and Orders published by authority
SR & O Rev 1904	Revised Edition comprising all Public and General Statutory Rules and Orders in force on 31 December 1903
SR & O Rev 1948	Revised Edition comprising all Public and General Statutory Rules and Orders and Statutory Instruments in force on 31 December 1948
SRNI	Statutory Rules of Northern Ireland
STI...	Simon's Tax Intelligence (1973–1995); Simon's Weekly Tax Intelligence (1996-current)
Sask	Saskatchewan
Sch..	Schedule
Sess.......................................	Session
Sing	Singapore
TCC	Technology and Construction Court
TS..	Treaty Series
Tanz.......................................	Tanzania
Tas...	Tasmania
UDC	Urban District Council
UKHL.....................................	Official neutral citation for judgments of the House of Lords
UKPC	Official neutral citation for judgments of the Privy Council
UN	United Nations
V-C..	Vice-Chancellor
Vict..	Victoria
W Aust...................................	Western Australia
Zimb	Zimbabwe

NOTE 1. A general list of the abbreviations of law reports and other sources used in this work can be found at the beginning of the Consolidated Table of Cases.

NOTE 2. Where references are made to other publications, the volume number precedes and the page number follows the name of the publication; eg the reference '12 Forms & Precedents (5th Edn) 44' refers to volume 12 of the Encyclopaedia of Forms and Precedents, page 44.

NOTE 3. An English statute is cited by short title or, where there is no short title, by regnal year and chapter number together with the name by which it is commonly known or a description of its subject matter and date. In the case of a foreign statute, the mode of citation generally follows the style of citation in use in the country concerned with the addition, where necessary, of the name of the country in parentheses.

NOTE 4. A statutory instrument is cited by short title, if any, followed by the year and number, or, if unnumbered, the date.

TABLE OF STATUTES

TABLE OF STATUTORY INSTRUMENTS

TABLE OF EUROPEAN
UNION LEGISLATION

TABLE OF CONVENTIONS ETC

TABLE OF CASES

Decisions of the European Court of Justice are listed below numerically. These decisions
are also included in the preceding alphabetical list.

EDUCATION

1. GENERAL FRAMEWORK OF THE EDUCATIONAL SYSTEM

(1) THE LEGAL BASIS OF THE EDUCATIONAL SYSTEM

(i) The Legislation relating to Education

1. Outline of the legislative framework. Education law is contained largely in statute[1], and includes a significant element of secondary legislative provision. For many years, the principal statute was the Education Act 1944, which contained many of the key elements of the modern law of education. It set out the basic statutory system of education based upon the three progressive stages of primary, secondary and further education[2]. It also established the main duties in relation to the provision of education including: (1) the duty of local authorities[3] to ensure that they contribute to the spiritual, moral, mental and physical development of the community by providing efficient primary and secondary education[4], and to ensure that sufficient schools[5] are provided for their areas[6]; (2) the duty of the Secretary of State[7] and local authorities to adhere to the general principle that pupils are to be educated in accordance with the wishes of their parents[8]; and (3) the general duty of parents to ensure that their children who are of compulsory school age[9] receive efficient full-time education[10]. It also contained the system for registration of independent schools[11]. The Education Act 1944 remained largely untouched by reform but in 1996 it was consolidated with much of the then-existing legislation relating to education[12] and, although most of its key elements survived the consolidation, the 1944 Act is now of historical importance only.

Today, the Education Act 1996[13], together with the Education Act 1997, the Education (Schools) Act 1997 and the School Standards and Framework Act 1998, as amended and supplemented by the Education Act 2002, the Education Act 2005, the Education and Inspections Act 2006, the Education and Skills Act 2008, the Apprenticeships, Skills, Children and Learning Act 2009, the Academies Act 2010, the Education Act 2011 and the Children and Families Act 2014, amongst others, establish the current framework for the law governing the provision of nursery education for pre-compulsory school age children[14], and primary and secondary education for children and young persons[15]. In particular, provision is made in relation to school organisation[16], governance, staffing and funding[17], as well as admissions[18], registration and school attendance[19], teachers' disciplinary authority[20] and academy arrangements and academies[21]. Provision is also made in relation to pupils with special educational needs or disabilities[22].

The inspection regime introduced by the School Inspections Act 1996, and the provisions regarding intervention in maintained schools, are superseded by the Education Act 2005, as supplemented and amended by the Education and Inspections Act 2006, the Education and Skills Act 2008 and the Apprenticeships, Skills, Children and Learning Act 2009[23].

New provision is made by the Education and Skills Act 2008 in relation to the education and training of young persons over compulsory school age[24]; and by the Apprenticeships, Skills, Children and Learning Act 2009 in relation to apprenticeships[25].

The consolidation of the earlier legislation in 1996[26] did not affect the provisions on further and higher education in the Education Reform Act 1988 and the Further and Higher Education Act 1992[27]. In relation to further education and training, the Further and Higher Education Act 1992 established a framework for the funding and governance of institutions, including sixth form colleges[28]. This framework was substantially reformed by the Learning and Skills Act 2000, which in turn has been supplemented and amended by the Education and Inspections Act 2006, the Further Education and Training Act 2007 and the Apprenticeships, Skills, Children and Learning Act 2009. The Education Reform Act 1988 and the Further and Higher Education Act 1992 are the principal enactments relating to higher education; they established a single framework for higher education, by removing many of the distinctions between universities, polytechnics and higher education colleges. These Acts also introduced a single funding structure[29]. The Higher Education Act 2004, amongst other things[30], sets out a mechanism imposing conditions for the charging of tuition fees and, if certain requirements relating to 'fair access' are complied with[31], for authorising fees of more than the basic amount[32]. Despite these reforms, many universities have retained distinct structures of governance, and parts of some of the original statutes relating to the oldest established universities remain in force[33].

The Teaching and Higher Education Act 1998, the Education Act 2002 and the Education Act 2005 provided a statutory regime for the registration and qualification requirements for teachers[34], their training and discipline[35]. Provision is made for teachers' pay and conditions[36], and in relation to teachers' pensions[37].

Increasingly, separate provision is being made in legislation to reflect the different education policies operating in England and Wales following the introduction of devolved government in Wales and this trend continued with the Education 2011 and since. In this title, where different provisions exist for England and for Wales they have generally been set out or noted separately; but unless otherwise indicated the provisions set out apply to both England and Wales, although often Welsh provisions are considered in less detail than their English equivalents.

Whilst the domestic legislation outlined above provides the main framework for the law of education, there are also important rights and principles that derive from international and European Union law[38].

1 As to those aspects of education law upon which the common law bears an influence see PARA 2.
2 See the Education Act 1944 s 7 (repealed). This has been re-enacted in the Education Act 1996 s 1(1): see PARA 18.
3 As to the meaning of 'local authority' see PARA 25.
4 See the Education Act 1944 s 7 (repealed). This has been re-enacted in the Education Act 1996 s 13(1): see PARA 27.
5 As to the meaning of 'school' see PARA 91. It should be noted that 'schools' can include certain types of academies (see further PARA 91). As to academies generally see PARA 345 et seq.
6 See the Education Act 1944 s 8 (repealed). This has been re-enacted in the Education Act 1996 s 14(1): see PARA 31.
7 As to the Secretary of State see PARA 58. As to the transfer of certain functions of the Secretary of State, so far as exercisable in relation to Wales, to the Welsh Ministers see PARA 59.
8 See the Education Act 1944 s 76 (repealed). This has been re-enacted in the Education Act 1996 s 9: see PARA 7.
9 As to the meaning of 'compulsory school age' see PARA 19.
10 See the Education Act 1944 s 36 (repealed). This has been re-enacted in the Education Act 1996 s 7: see PARA 435.
11 See the Education Act 1944 ss 70–75 (repealed). As to the regulation of independent schools see PARA 382 et seq. As to independent schools generally see PARA 369 et seq.
12 The consolidation was recommended by the Law Commission in its report entitled *Education Bill: School Inspection Bill: Report on the Consolidation of Certain Enactments Relating to Education* (Law Com no 240) (Cm 3251) (1996). In response to this, the Education Act 1996 and the School Inspections Act 1996 were passed.

The Education Act 1996 consolidated the Education Act 1944, the Education Act 1946, the Education Act (Miscellaneous Provisions) Act 1948, the Education Act (Miscellaneous Provisions) Act 1953, the Education Act 1959, the Education Act 1964, the Education Act 1968, the Education (Handicapped Children) Act 1970, the Education (Work Experience) Act 1973, the Education Act 1975, the Education (School-leaving Dates) Act 1976, the Education Act 1976, the Education Act 1979, the Education Act 1981, the Education (Grants and Awards) Act 1984), and many provisions of various other Acts including the Education Act 1980, the Education (No 2) Act 1986, the Education Reform Act 1988, the Further and Higher Education Act 1992 and the Education Act 1993.

The School Inspections Act 1996 consolidated most of the Education (Schools) Act 1992 and the whole of the Education Act 1993 Pt V (ss 204–228), with amendments to give effect to recommendations of the Law Commission.

13   In the Education Act 1996, the Education Act 1996 with the following Acts are known together as 'the Education Acts': the Education Act 1973; the Education Act 1980; the Education (Fees and Awards) Act 1983; the Further Education Act 1985 (except ss 4 and 5); the Education Act 1986; the Education (No 2) Act 1986; the Education Reform Act 1988; the Further and Higher Education Act 1992; the Education Act 1994; the Education Act 1997; the Education (Schools) Act 1997; the Teaching and Higher Education Act 1998; the School Standards and Framework Act 1998; the Education Act 2002; the Higher Education Act 2004; the Education Act 2005; the Learner Travel (Wales) Measure 2008; the Academies Act 2010; the Education Act 2011; the Education (Wales) Measure 2011; the School Standards and Organisation (Wales) Act 2013; the Children and Families Act 2014 Pt 3 (ss 19–83), s 100; the Education (Wales) Act 2014; the Higher Education (Wales) Act 2015; and the Qualifications Wales Act 2015: see the Education Act 1996 s 578 (amended by the Education Act 1997 s 57(1), Sch 7 para 42; the Education (Schools) Act 1997 s 6(2); the Education (Student Loans) Act 1998 s 6(1); the Teaching and Higher Education Act 1998 s 44, Sch 3 para 15, Sch 4; the School Standards and Framework Act 1998 s 140(1), Sch 30 paras 57, 182; the Education Act 2002 s 215, Sch 21 para 56, Sch 22; the Education Act 2005 ss 61, 123, Sch 9 para 9, Sch 19 Pt 1; the Learner Travel (Wales) Measure 2008 s 29(2); the Academies Act 2010 s 20(2); the Education Act 2002 s 217(2); the Higher Education Act 2004 s 54(2); the Education Act 2005 s 128(2); the Education Act 2011 s 83(2); the Education (Wales) Measure 2011 s 34(2); the School Standards and Organisation (Wales) Act 2013 s 101(2); the Children and Families Act 2014 s 139(1); the Education (Wales) Act 2014 s 45; the Higher Education (Wales) Act 2015 s 60(2); and the Qualifications Wales Act 2015 s 61(2)).

The Audit Commission Act 1998 s 36 (studies at the request of educational bodies: see LOCAL GOVERNMENT vol 69 (2009) PARA 782) was to be construed as one with the Education Act 1996, and references in any enactment to the Education Acts include a reference to the Audit Commission Act 1998 s 36: s 36(6) (s 36 now repealed). As to the reading of Acts together see *Canada Southern Rly Co v International Bridge Co* (1883) 8 App Cas 723 at 727, PC, per Lord Selborne LC; and STATUTES AND LEGISLATIVE PROCESS vol 96 (2012) PARA 1193.

'Enactment' does not include an enactment comprised in, or in an instrument made under, an Act of the Scottish Parliament: Interpretation Act 1978 s 5, Sch 1 (definitions of 'Act' and 'enactment' added by the Scotland Act 1998 s 125, Sch 8 para 16(3)). Where an Act describes or cites a portion of an enactment by referring to words, sections or other parts from or to which (or from and to which) the portion extends, the portion described or cited includes the words, sections or other parts referred to unless the contrary intention appears: Interpretation Act 1978 s 20(1). Where an Act refers to an enactment, the reference, unless the contrary intention appears, is a reference to that enactment as amended, and includes a reference thereto as extended or applied, by or under any other enactment, including any other provision of that Act: s 20(2). 'Act' means an Act of Parliament: Sch 1 (definition as added). As to the Scottish Parliament see CONSTITUTIONAL AND ADMINISTRATIVE LAW vol 20 (2014) PARA 66.

14   As to nursery education see PARAS 95–98.

15   As to primary and secondary education see PARA 99 et seq.

16   As to school organisation see PARA 147 et seq.

17   As to the government of maintained schools see PARA 150 et seq. As to the staffing of maintained schools see PARA 268 et seq. As to the funding of maintained schools see PARA 305 et seq.

18   As to admissions arrangements for maintained schools see PARA 235 et seq.

19   As to registration and school attendance see PARA 435 et seq.

20   As to the statutory responsibility of the governing body and head teacher for discipline and the statutory power of the head teacher to exclude pupils see PARAS 509, 517.

21   As to academy arrangements and academies see PARA 345 et seq.

22   As to special educational needs and disabilities see PARA 941 et seq.

23 As to the inspection of schools see PARA 1127 et seq. As to the inspection of independent schools see PARA 418 et seq.
24 See PARA 725 et seq.
25 See PARA 765 et seq.
26 See note 12.
27 As to further education see PARA 555 et seq; and as to higher education see PARA 619 et seq.
28 As to sixth form college corporations see PARA 577 et seq; as to intervention in relation to sixth form colleges see PARA 1247 et seq.
29 As to the funding of higher education see PARA 691 et seq.
30 The Higher Education Act 2004 also established a student complaints scheme (see PARA 1090 et seq) while limiting the jurisdiction of visitors (see PARAS 630, 1090).
31 To this end, a Director of Fair Access to Higher Education has been created for England: see the Higher Education Act 2004 s 31; and PARA 714. As to fees and access in Wales see PARA 721 et seq.
32 See PARA 715 et seq.
33 See eg the Oxford and Cambridge Act 1571, the Oxford University Act 1854, the Cambridge University Act 1856, the Oxford University Act 1857, the Oxford University Act 1860, the Oxford University Act 1862, the Oxford University, Vinerian Foundation, Act 1865, the Universities Tests Act 1871, the College Charter Act 1871, the Universities of Oxford and Cambridge Act 1877, and the Universities of Oxford and Cambridge Act 1923.
34 See PARA 1047 et seq.
35 Ie including the establishment of the Training and Development Agency for Schools and the General Teaching Council for England (both now abolished) and the General Teaching Council for Wales (reformed and renamed as the Education Workforce Council).
   The Training and Development Agency for Schools (which had previously been known as the Teacher Training Agency) and the provisions relating to it (ie the Education Act 2005 ss 74–84, Sch 13) were abolished by the Education Act 2011 s 14 from 1 April 2012: see PARA 1054. Functions previously exercised by the Agency were transferred to the Secretary of State in regard to England and the Welsh Ministers in regard to Wales: see the Education Act 2002 s 14, the Education Act 2005 ss 84A, 84B; and PARAS 1054–1056. As to the transfer of staff, property, rights and liabilities from the Agency to the Secretary of State see the Education Act 2011 s 17, Sch 6. The National College for Teaching and Leadership and the Education Workforce Council are now the bodies responsible for teacher training: see PARA 1054 et seq. As to the Secretary of State see PARA 58; and as to the Welsh Ministers see PARA 59.
   The General Teaching Council for England was abolished by the Education Act 2011 s 7 from 1 April 2012: see PARA 1066. As to the transfer of staff, rights and liabilities from the Council to the Secretary of State see the Education Act 2011 s 12, Sch 3. The National College for Teaching and Leadership operates as the regulator of the teaching profession on behalf of the Secretary of State: see PARA 1066. As to the regulation of teacher conduct in England see the Education Act 2002 ss 141B–141H, Schs 11A, 11B; and PARA 1066 et seq.
   The relevant provisions about the General Teaching Council for England (ie the Teaching and Higher Education Act 1998 ss 1–7) were effectively merged with the provisions on the General Teaching Council for Wales (ie the Teaching and Higher Education Act 1998 ss 8–15A) to apply to the latter Council only. However the General Teaching Council for Wales was reformed and renamed as the Education Workforce Council by the Education (Wales) Act 2014 s 2, Sch 1 from 18 August 2014 and the relevant Teaching and Higher Education Act 1998 provisions repealed: see PARA 1075. As to the regulation of teacher conduct in Wales see PARA 1075 et seq.
36 See the Education Act 2002 ss 119–130 (which repealed the School Teachers' Pay and Conditions Act 1991 and re-enacted the provisions with little change); and PARA 1076 et seq.
37 See PARA 1081 et seq.
38 See PARAS 3–7.

(ii) The Common Law relating to Education

2. Common law. The law relating to education is substantially statutory[1], but the common law still bears upon some areas of educational practice[2], notably the common law duty of care owed by local authorities and their employees in relation to the care and supervision of pupils, and in fact wider duties of care[3]. In particular, the standard of care expected of a teacher in supervising pupils at school and protecting them from harm has been extensively considered by the courts[4]. Judicial consideration has also been given to the extent of a teacher's disciplinary authority under statute[5], including the degree to which a teacher may legally detain[6] or restrain a pupil, or administer corporal punishment[7]. The question of the vicarious liability (including liability for intentional assaults) of a local authority or private employer has received detailed consideration[8].

The definition of statutory duties and powers by the courts has become increasingly important as a very wide range of such powers and duties underscores educational provision and administration. There have been successful attempts to extend common law negligence to the performance of the statutory duties of teachers, educational psychologists and other professionals employed in the sphere of education[9].

The extent to which decisions made within the education system have a public law dimension has also been considered by the courts. As such decisions have important consequences for parents, children and other interested parties, education has become one of the most active areas of public law, with numerous judicial review judgments, accumulating into a large body of case law[10]. Most such decisions do fall within the realm of public law, but there are exceptions. For example, decisions of independent schools, being bodies whose authority is derived solely from contract or consent of the parties, are not subject to judicial review[11] (save in very limited circumstances[12]).

1 For an outline of the legislative framework see PARA 1.
2 Many cases are in amplification of particular statutory provisions and, accordingly, are cited in the paragraphs containing the relevant legislation.
3 See further PARAS 1087–1088. Note in particular *Phelps v Hillingdon London Borough Council, Anderton v Clwyd County Council, Jarvis v Hampshire County Council, G v Bromley London Borough Council* [2001] 2 AC 619, [2000] 4 All ER 504, [2000] ELR 499, HL, at PARA 1087.
4 See e g the cases relating to teachers' duties cited in PARAS 1087–1088.
5 As to the statutory responsibility of the governing body and head teacher for discipline and the statutory power of the head teacher to exclude pupils see PARAS 509, 517.
6 As to cases considering the legality of detention see PARA 512.
7 As to cases on the legality of corporal punishment see PARAS 3, 545.
8 See PARA 377.
9 This has most notably been considered in the context of the identification of children with special educational needs and the provision of suitable education for them (see PARA 1039), but could equally extend to other areas of education (see PARA 47). For cases considering various aspects of the provision of education for children with special educational needs or disabilities see PARAS 943 et seq, 989 et seq.
10 As to judicial review see JUDICIAL REVIEW vol 61 (2010) PARA 601 et seq.
11 See PARA 425.
12 See PARA 381.

(iii) Rights and Freedoms

3. Convention for the Protection of Human Rights and Fundamental Freedoms. The Convention for the Protection of Human Rights and Fundamental Freedoms[1] which guarantees basic rights and freedoms is given effect in the United Kingdom by the Human Rights Act 1998[2].

Under the First Protocol to the Convention[3], no one may be denied the right to education[4]. However, the right to education calls for regulation by the state, and such regulation will vary in time and place according to particular circumstances[5]. In the exercise of any functions which it assumes in relation to education and to teaching, the state must respect the right of parents to ensure that such education and teaching conforms with their own religious and philosophical convictions[6]. The United Kingdom only accepts this right in so far as it is compatible with the provision of efficient instruction and training, and the avoidance of unreasonable public expenditure[7].

The Convention contains other rights and freedoms which may be capable of application in relation to education. The prohibition of torture or inhuman or degrading treatment or punishment[8] has been held not to outlaw the use of corporal punishment[9]. The right to a fair and public hearing in the determination of civil rights and obligations[10] has been held inapplicable to certain decisions relating to education, on the basis that no civil right is in issue[11]; but subject to qualification the right may be possibly be engaged in disciplinary proceedings against teaching staff where the outcome may have a substantial effect on a person's right to practise his profession[12]. The right to respect for a person's private and family life, his home and his correspondence[13] may also be applicable to certain areas of educational decision-making and practice, but has not been successfully invoked in cases concerning corporal punishment[14], compulsory sex education[15], choice of school[16], school transport[17], exclusion from school[18] or teaching in the language of a parent's choice[19]. Since religious education is part of the curriculum of maintained schools[20], the right to freedom of thought, conscience and religion[21] may be relevant[22]. The right to freedom of expression is also of relevance in relation to education[23].

The rights and fundamental freedoms enshrined in the Convention must be secured without discrimination on any ground such as sex, race, colour, language, religion, political or other opinion, national or social origin, association with a national minority, property, birth or other status[24].

1   Ie the Convention for the Protection of Human Rights and Fundamental Freedoms (Rome, 4 November 1950; TS 71 (1953); Cmd 8969). See generally RIGHTS AND FREEDOMS vol 88A (2013) PARA 88.

2   See the Human Rights Act 1998 s 1(2). As to the Human Rights Act 1998 generally see RIGHTS AND FREEDOMS vol 88A (2013) PARA 14 et seq.

3   Ie the Convention for the Protection of Human Rights and Fundamental Freedoms, First Protocol (Paris, 20 March 1952; TS 46 (1954); Cmd 9221).

4   See the Convention for the Protection of Human Rights and Fundamental Freedoms, First Protocol art 2; Human Rights Act 1998 s 1, Sch 1; and RIGHTS AND FREEDOMS vol 88A (2013) PARA 548 et seq. Although the right to education in the Convention for the Protection of Human Rights and Fundamental Freedoms, First Protocol art 2 is positive, its negative formulation indicates that the contracting states did not see themselves as required to establish at their own expense, or to subsidise, education of any particular type or at any particular level: *Belgian Linguistics Case (No 2)* (1968) 1 EHRR 252, ECtHR. However, in domestic law, there is no doubt that, at least in theory, the Convention for the Protection of Human Rights and Fundamental Freedoms, First Protocol art 2 applies to tertiary education because education is a continuing process and any divisions between primary, secondary, and tertiary are, in a sense, artificial: *R (on the application of Douglas) v North Tyneside Metropolitan Borough Council* [2003] EWCA Civ 1847, [2004] 1 All ER 709, [2004] 1 WLR 2363.

    The right to education includes the right to draw the full benefit from the education received: *Belgian Linguistics Case (No 2)* above. However, the European Commission on Human Rights has commented that it would not be contrary to the Convention for the Protection of Human Rights and Fundamental Freedoms, First Protocol art 2 for pupils to be suspended or expelled, provided that the national regulations did not prevent them from enrolling in another establishment to pursue their studies: Application 14524/89 *Yanasik v Turkey* 74 DR 14 (1993) at 27, EComHR. See also dicta in *R (on the application of S) v Brent London Borough Council, R (on the application of T) v Head Teacher of Wembley High School, R (on the application of P) v Oxfordshire County Council Exclusion Appeals Panel* [2002] EWCA Civ 693 at [9], [2002] ELR 556, [2002] All ER (D) 277 (May). In domestic law, the unlawful exclusion of a pupil from school may give rise to a claim for damages for denial of a Convention right: see *A v Head Teacher and Governors of Lord Grey School* [2004] EWCA Civ 382, [2004] QB 1231, [2004] 4 All ER 628 (revsd as to award of damages but not as to principle of potential claim: *A v Head Teacher and Governors of Lord Grey School* [2006] UKHL 14, [2006] AC 363, sub nom *Ali v Head Teacher and Governors of Lord Grey School* [2006] 2 All ER 457); *A v Essex County*

Council [2008] EWCA Civ 364, [2009] LGR 182, [2008] ELR 321 (affd [2010] UKSC 33, [2011] 1 AC 280, [2010] 4 All ER 199). See also Application 36458/02 *Temel v Turkey* [2009] ELR 301, [2009] ECHR 36458/02, ECtHR (imposition of a disciplinary sanction held to not to be reasonable or proportionate); Application 60856/00 *Eren v Turkey* (2006) 44 EHRR 619, [2006] ELR 155, [2006] ECHR 60856/00, ECtHR (annulment of student's exam results denied him his right to education).

 The general right to education has been held to consist of separate rights (none of which is absolute) which include: (1) right of access to such educational establishments as exist; (2) a right to effective education; and (3) a right to official recognition of academic qualifications: *R (on the application of Holub) v Secretary of State for the Home Department* [2001] 1 WLR 1359 at 1367, sub nom *Holub v Secretary of State for the Home Department* [2001] ELR 401 at 408–409, CA, per Tuckey LJ. Effective education need not be the most effective possible but must reach a minimum standard: *R (on the application of Holub) v Secretary of State for the Home Department* above. The right to education does not guarantee the right to an assisted place at an independent school where public education is available: *R v Secretary of State for Education and Employment, ex p Begbie* [2000] 1 WLR 1115, [2000] ELR 445, CA. See also *Valsamis v Greece* (1996) 24 EHRR 294, [1998] ELR 430, ECtHR. The right is not engaged by the withdrawal of school transport: *R (on the application of R) v Leeds City Council* [2005] EWHC 2495 (Admin), [2006] LGR 579, [2006] ELR 25.

5 *Belgian Linguistics Case (No 2)* (1968) 1 EHRR 252 at 281, ECtHR. Provided such regulation does not injure the substance of the right to education and is 'reasonable', it will not breach the Convention for the Protection of Human Rights and Fundamental Freedoms, First Protocol art 2: *Belgian Linguistics Case (No 2)* (above); *Ali v United Kingdom* [2011] ECHR 40385/06, [2011] ELR 85, 30 BHRC 44; *Campbell and Cosans v United Kingdom* (1982) 4 EHRR 293 at 307, ECtHR. See also *A v Head Teacher and Governors of Lord Grey School* [2006] UKHL 14, [2006] 2 AC 363, sub nom *Ali v Head Teacher and Governors of Lord Grey School* [2006] 2 All ER 457 (decision affd in *Ali v United Kingdom* above); *In the Matter of an Application by 'JR17' for Judicial Review* [2010] UKSC 27, [2010] NI 105, [2010] All ER (D) 186 (Jun); *A v Essex County Council* [2010] UKSC 33, [2010] 4 All ER 199, [2010] 3 WLR 509. In *R (on the application of C) v Brent London Borough Council* [2006] EWCA Civ 728, [2006] ELR 435, [2006] All ER (D) 189 (Apr) it was held that compliance by the local authority with its obligations under the Education Act 1996 s 19 (see PARA 427) was sufficient to comply with the Convention for the Protection of Human Rights and Fundamental Freedoms, First Protocol art 2.

6 Convention for the Protection of Human Rights and Fundamental Freedoms, First Protocol art 2. Respect is only due to convictions on the part of parents which do not conflict with the fundamental right of the child to education: Application 35504/03 *Konrad v Germany* [2007] ELR 435, ECtHR. The views of parents of children with special educational needs should be taken into account, but such children have no absolute right to parity of access with other pupils: Application 14135/88 *PD and LD v United Kingdom* 62 DR 292 (1989), EComHR; Application 14688/89 *Simpson v United Kingdom* 64 DR 188 (1989), EComHR; Application 13887/88 *Graeme v United Kingdom* 64 DR 158 (1990), EComHR. There is no requirement to provide special facilities to accommodate a particular conviction, although the Convention for the Protection of Human Rights and Fundamental Freedoms, First Protocol art 2 may affect the use of existing facilities: Application 25212/94 *Klerks v Netherlands* 82 DR 129 (1995), EComHR. See also Application 10476/83 *W and KL v Sweden* 45 DR 143 (1983), EComHR; Application 14688/89 *Simpson v United Kingdom*; Application 25959/94 *Cohen v United Kingdom* (1996) 21 EHRR CD 104; *L v Hereford and Worcester County Council and Hughes* [2000] ELR 375. The duty to uphold religious and philosophical convictions does not extend to upholding linguistic preferences (*Belgian Linguistics Case (No 2)* (1968) 1 EHRR 252, ECtHR) or to the exemption of pupils from sex education (*Kjeldsen, Busk Masden and Pedersen* (1976) 1 EHRR 711, ECtHR). Philosophical convictions can include the conviction that corporal punishment should not be used with respect to a child: see *Campbell and Cosans v United Kingdom* (1982) 4 EHRR 293, ECtHR; and PARA 545. See also Application 15472/02 *Folgero v Norway* (2007) 23 BHRC 227, ECtHR in which it was held that the refusal of the competent authorities to grant the parents' application for exemption from compulsory attendance at religious instruction for their children violated the parents rights.

7 See the Human Rights Act 1998 s 15, Sch 3 Pt II. This mirrors the conditions attached to the duty under the Education Act 1996 to educate pupils in accordance with the wishes of their parents: see s 9; and PARA 7.

8 See the Convention for the Protection of Human Rights and Fundamental Freedoms art 3; Human Rights Act 1998 s 1, Sch 1; and RIGHTS AND FREEDOMS vol 88A (2013) PARA 158 et seq.

9 Ie provided the corporal punishment is administered within strict limitations concerned with factors such as the nature and context of the punishment, the manner and method of its execution, its duration, its physical and mental effects, and the pupil's age, sex and state of health: see *Costello-Roberts v United Kingdom* (1993) 19 EHRR 112, [1994] ELR 1, ECtHR; *Tyrer v United Kingdom* (1978) 2 EHRR 1, ECtHR. In *Webster v Ridgeway Foundation School* [2010] EWHC 157 (QB), [2010] ELR 694, [2010] All ER (D) 52 (Feb), the court accepted that an attack on a pupil with a hammer on school premises after the end of the school day did attain the minimum degree of severity to constitute the type of treatment within the scope of the Convention for the Protection of Human Rights and Fundamental Freedoms art 3, but dismissed a claim that the school had acted unlawfully in that, in accordance with the positive obligation inherent in art 3 to take steps to prevent a breach of the rights protected by that article, it had failed to take reasonable steps within its powers to protect him from the attack.

10 See the Convention for the Protection of Human Rights and Fundamental Freedoms art 6; Human Rights Act 1998 s 1, Sch 1; and RIGHTS AND FREEDOMS vol 88A (2013) PARA 243 et seq.

11 See Application 14688/89 *Simpson v United Kingdom* 64 DR 188 (1989), EComHR. See also *R v Richmond upon Thames London Borough Council, ex p C* [2001] LGR 146, sub nom *R v Richmond upon Thames London Borough Council, ex p JC* [2001] ELR 21, CA; *Hanuman v United Kingdom* [2000] ELR 685, ECtHR; Application 20027/02 *Herbst v Germany* [2007] ELR 363, [2007] ECHR 20027/02, ECtHR. Neither admission appeal panels nor exclusion appeal panels were considered to be subject to the Convention for the Protection of Human Rights and Fundamental Freedoms art 6 in *R (on the application of B) v Head Teacher of Alperton Community School, R (on the application of T) v Head Teacher of Wembley High School, R (on the application of C) v Governing Body of Cardinal Newman High School* [2001] EWHC (Admin) 229, [2001] ELR 359; *R (on the application of LG) v Independent Appeal Panel for Tom Hood School (Secretary of State for Children, Schools and Families, interested party)* [2010] EWCA Civ 142, [2010] ELR 291, [2010] All ER (D) 292 (Feb). See further PARA 531. Exclusion of a pupil from school for a limited period of 14 days did not engage the right: *R (on the application of B) v Head Teacher of St Michael's Church of England School* [2007] EWHC 2052 (Admin), [2008] ELR 116.

12 See *R (on the application of G) v Governors of X School (Secretary of State for Children, Schools and Families intervening)* [2011] UKSC 30, [2012] 1 AC 167, [2011] 4 All ER 625 (Convention for the Protection of Human Rights and Fundamental Freedoms art 6(1) did not apply to certain proceedings which did not satisfy a 'substantial influence or effect test'). As to the discipline of teachers see further PARA 1068 et seq.

13 See the Convention for the Protection of Human Rights and Fundamental Freedoms art 8; Human Rights Act 1998 s 1, Sch 1; and RIGHTS AND FREEDOMS vol 88A (2013) PARA 317 et seq. The Convention for the Protection of Human Rights and Fundamental Freedoms art 8 was relevant in a case concerning the lawfulness of the disclosure of the non-conviction material relating to alleged sexual misconduct by the claimant teacher: see *R(on the application of AB) v Chief Constable of Hampshire Constabulary* [2015] EWHC 1238 (Admin), [2015] All ER (D) 187 (May).

14 *Costello-Roberts v United Kingdom* (1993) 19 EHRR 112, [1994] ELR 1, ECtHR.

15 *Kjeldsen, Busk Masden and Pedersen v Denmark* (1976) 1 EHRR 711, ECtHR.

16 *R v Richmond upon Thames London Borough Council, ex p C* [2001] LGR 146, sub nom *R v Richmond upon Thames London Borough Council, ex p JC* [2001] ELR 21, CA.

17 *R (on the application of R) v Leeds City Council* [2005] EWHC 2495 (Admin), [2006] LGR 579, [2006] ELR 25.

18 *R (on the application of B) v Head Teacher of Alperton Community School, R (on the application of T) v Head Teacher of Wembley High School, R (on the application of C) v Governing Body of Cardinal Newman High School* [2001] EWHC (Admin) 229, [2001] ELR 359, where it was argued that the exclusion of a child from a mainstream school gave rise to a breach of the Convention for the Protection of Human Rights and Fundamental Freedoms art 8, as the child was deprived of the right to develop a personality in conjunction with others. However, the court did not recognise the existence of such a right in the field of education, and held that a child was not denied the opportunity to develop his personality in conjunction with others simply because he was not in a mainstream school. The point was not pursued on appeal sub nom *R (on the application of S) v Brent London Borough Council, R (on the application of T) v Head Teacher of Wembley High School, R (on the application of P) v Oxfordshire County Council Exclusion Appeals Panel* [2002] EWCA Civ 693, [2002] ELR 556, [2002] All ER (D) 277 (May).

19 See *Belgian Linguistics Case (No 2)* (1968) 1 EHRR 252, ECtHR.

20 See *Valsamis v Greece* (1996) 24 EHRR 294, [1998] ELR 430, ECtHR. If a court's determination of any question arising under the Human Rights Act 1998 might affect the exercise by a religious organisation (itself or its members collectively) of the right to freedom of thought, conscience and religion, the court must have particular regard to the importance of that right: s 13(1). For these purposes, 'court' includes a tribunal: s 13(2). As to the curriculum in England see PARA 856 et seq; and as to the curriculum in Wales see PARA 870 et seq.

21 See the Convention for the Protection of Human Rights and Fundamental Freedoms art 9; Human Rights Act 1998 s 1, Sch 1; and RIGHTS AND FREEDOMS vol 88A (2013) PARA 368 et seq.

22 As to the court's role in identifying a religious belief calling for protection under the Convention for the Protection of Human Rights and Fundamental Freedoms art 9 see *R (on the application of Williamson) v Secretary of State for Education and Employment* [2005] UKHL 15, [2005] 2 AC 246, [2005] 2 All ER 1 (cited in PARA 545 note 9). A school uniform policy which prohibited a pupil from wearing a particular form of Islamic dress did not contravene the Convention for the Protection of Human Rights and Fundamental Freedoms art 9. The court stressed that the case concerned a particular pupil and a particular school in a particular place at a particular time; and that the court was not, and nor could it be, invited to rule whether Islamic dress, or any feature of Islamic dress, should or should not be permitted in schools in the United Kingdom: *R (on the application of Begum) v Headteacher and Governors of Denbigh High School*, sub nom *R (on the application of SB) v Governors of Denbigh High School*, [2006] UKHL 15, [2007] 1 AC 100, [2006] 2 All ER 487. See also *R (on the application of X) v The Headteacher of Y School* [2007] EWHC 298 (Admin), [2008] 1 All ER 249, [2007] LGR 698; Application 27058/05 *Dogru v France* (2008) 49 EHRR 179, [2009] ELR 77, [2008] ECHR 27058/05, ECtHR. The wearing by a female pupil of a ring that signified her belief in abstinence from sexual intercourse before marriage did not engage the Convention for the Protection of Human Rights and Fundamental Freedoms art 9; but, in any event, the school's uniform policy banning the wearing of such rings did not contravene that article if it were engaged: *R (on the application of Playfoot) v Governing Body of Millais School* [2007] EWHC 1698 (Admin), [2007] LGR 851, [2007] 3 FCR 754. See also *R (on the application of Watkins-Singh) v Governing Body of Aberdare Girls' High School* [2008] EWHC 1865 (Admin), [2008] 3 FCR 203, [2008] ELR 561 (in which the claimant, who followed the Sikh religion and was denied the right to wear the Kara (religious bangle) at school, brought her claim, not under the Convention for the Protection of Human Rights and Fundamental Freedoms art 9, but under the provisions relating to unlawful race and religious discrimination under the Race Relations Act 1976 and the Equality Act 2006 (both now repealed)); and PARA 9. School transport decisions do not engage the right: *R (on the application of R) v Leeds City Council* [2005] EWHC 2495 (Admin), [2006] LGR 579, [2006] ELR 25. As to the ability to have a particular haircut see *G (by his litigation friend) v Head Teacher and Governors of St Gregory's Catholic Science College* [2011] EWHC 1452 (Admin), [2011] All ER (D) 113 (Jun) where it was held that the defendants' school uniform policy, which had not permitted the African-Caribbean claimant wearing his hair in cornrows, had had a legitimate aim but that its application to the claimant had, in his circumstances and without justification, been indirectly racially discriminatory.

A local authority must take into account the religious convictions of parents when formulating its admissions policy (see PARA 228): *R (on the application of K) v Newham London Borough Council* [2002] EWHC 405 (Admin), [2002] ELR 390, (2002) Times, 28 February.

23 See the Convention for the Protection of Human Rights and Fundamental Freedoms art 10; Human Rights Act 1998 s 1, Sch 1; and RIGHTS AND FREEDOMS vol 88A (2013) PARA 398 et seq. See Application 8010/77 *X v United Kingdom* 16 DR 101 (1979), EComHR, where a teacher forbidden from wearing religious and anti-abortion stickers to work failed in arguing that his rights under the Convention for the Protection of Human Rights and Fundamental Freedoms art 10 had been violated, and it was held that the school was justified in its ban in view of the need for non-denominational schools to have regard to parents' rights to have their religious and philosophical convictions upheld. See also *Vogt v Germany* (1995) 21 EHRR 205, [1996] ELR 232, ECtHR. As to freedom of speech in universities and further and higher education establishments see also PARA 6.

24 See the Convention for the Protection of Human Rights and Fundamental Freedoms art 14; Human Rights Act 1998 s 1, Sch 1; and RIGHTS AND FREEDOMS vol 88A (2013) PARA 506 et seq. This prohibition against discrimination only arises where another right is first engaged: see further RIGHTS AND FREEDOMS vol 88A (2013) PARA 506. Decisions on art 14 arising in the context of education include: *Belgian Linguistics Case (No 2)* (1968) 1 EHRR 252, ECtHR; Application 7782/77 *X v United Kingdom* 14 DR 179 (1978), EComHR; Application 23419/94 *Verein Gemeinsam Lernen v Austria* 82 DR 41 (1995), EComHR.

4. Development of quality education under European Union law. The European Union (EU) must contribute to the development of quality education by encouraging co-operation between member states and, if necessary, by supporting and supplementing their action, while fully respecting the responsibility of the member states for the content of teaching and the organisation of education systems and their cultural and linguistic diversity[1].

EU action must be aimed at: (1) developing the European dimension in education, particularly through the teaching and dissemination of the languages of the member states; (2) encouraging mobility of students and teachers, by encouraging inter alia, the academic recognition of diplomas and periods of study; (3) promoting cooperation between educational establishments; (4) developing exchanges of information and experience on issues common to the education systems of the member states; (5) encouraging the development of youth exchanges and of exchanges of socio-educational instructors, and encouraging the participation of young people in democratic life in Europe; (6) encouraging the development of distance education; (7) developing the European dimension in sport, by promoting fairness and openness in sporting competitions and cooperation between bodies responsible for sports, and by protecting the physical and moral integrity of sportsmen and sportswomen, especially the youngest sportsmen and sportswomen[2]. The EU and the member states must foster cooperation with third countries and the competent international organisations in the field of education and sport, in particular the Council of Europe[3].

The EU must implement a vocational training policy which must support and supplement the action of the member states, while fully respecting the responsibility of the member states for the content and organisation of vocational training[4]. EU action must aim to: (a) facilitate adaptation to industrial changes, in particular through vocational training and retraining; (b) improve initial and continuing vocational training in order to facilitate vocational integration and reintegration into the labour market; (c) facilitate access to vocational training and encourage mobility of instructors and trainees and particularly young people; (d) stimulate cooperation on training between educational or training establishments and firms; (e) develop exchanges of information and experience on issues common to the training systems of the member states[5]. The EU and the member states must foster cooperation with third countries and the competent international organisations in the sphere of vocational training[6].

There are other provisions which have application to education. A person exercising the right under EU law relating to freedom of movement for workers must have access to training in vocational schools and retraining centres[7]; and the resident children of such a person have a right to be admitted to the host state's general educational and vocational training courses, under the same conditions as nationals[8]. Under the Charter of Fundamental Rights of the European Union[9], everyone has the right to education and the right of access to vocational and continuing training[10]. This includes the possibility to receive free compulsory education[11]. The freedom to found educational establishments with due respect for democratic principles and the right of parents to ensure education and teaching of their children in conformity with their religious, philosophical and pedagogical convictions must be respected in accordance with the national laws governing the exercise of that freedom and right[12].

The Treaty provisions[13] relating to freedom of movement of citizens of the EU preclude a condition in accordance with which, in order to obtain an education or training grant for studies in a member state other than that of which the students applying for such assistance were nationals, those studies had to be a continuation of education or training pursued for at least one year in the member state of origin of those students[14]. National legislation granting tax relief on school fees paid to private schools established in the member state concerned but excluding that possibility in relation to school fees paid to a private school established in another member state has been held to be contrary to EU law[15].

1 Treaty on the Functioning of the European Union (Rome, 25 March 1957; TS 1 (1973); Cmnd 5179) art 165(1). The Treaty was formerly known as the Treaty Establishing the European Community; it was renamed by the Treaty of Lisbon Amending the Treaty Establishing the European Union and the Treaty Establishing the European Community (Lisbon, 13 December 2007, ECS 13 (2007); Cm 7294) and its provisions renumbered by that Treaty and previously by the Treaty of Amsterdam amending the Treaty on European Union, the Treaties establishing the European Communities and Related Acts (OJ C340, 10.11.1997, p 1). As to the Treaty on the Functioning of the European Union see EUROPEAN UNION vol 47A (2014) PARA 6.
   In order to contribute to the achievement of the objectives referred to in the Treaty on the Functioning of the European Union art 165: (1) the European Parliament and the Council, acting in accordance with the ordinary legislative procedure, after consulting the Economic and Social Committee and the Committee of the Regions, must adopt incentive measures, excluding any harmonisation of the laws and regulations of the member states; and (2) the Council, on a proposal from the Commission, must adopt recommendations: art 165(4) (as so renumbered).
   In exercising the power under the Treaty on the Functioning of the European Union arts 165(1), 166(1) (see the text and note 4) as regards the organisation of their education systems and of vocational training, member states must comply with European Union law and in particular the provisions on the freedom to move and reside within the territory of the member states: see Case C-73/08 *Bressol v Gouvernement de la Communaute francaise; Chaverot v same* [2010] ECR I-2735, [2010] 3 CMLR 559. Member states are free to opt for an education system based on free access without restriction on the number of students who may register, or for a system based on controlled access in which the students are selected; but the rules of the chosen system must comply with European Union law and, in particular, the principle of non-discrimination on grounds of nationality. That principle, and the right of freedom of movement, preclude national legislation limiting the number of non-resident students who may enrol in medical and paramedical courses at higher education establishments unless that legislation is justified in the light of the objective of protection of public health: Case C-73/08 *Bressol v Gouvernement de la Communaute francaise; Chaverot v same* above.

2 Treaty on the Functioning of the European Union art 165(2) (as renumbered: see note 1). See also European Parliament and EC Council Decision 50/2002 (OJ L10, 12.1.2002, p 1) establishing a programme of Community action to encourage cooperation between member states to combat social exclusion and which provides that particular attention should be paid to relevant policy developments in various areas including education.

3 Treaty on the Functioning of the European Union art 165(3) (as renumbered: see note 1). As to the Council of Europe see INTERNATIONAL RELATIONS LAW vol 61 (2010) PARA 534.

4 Treaty on the Functioning of the European Union art 166(1) (as renumbered: see note 1). The European Parliament and the Council, acting in accordance with the ordinary legislative procedure and after consulting the Economic and Social Committee and the Committee of the Regions, must adopt measures to contribute to the achievement of the objectives referred to in art 166, excluding any harmonisation of the laws and regulations of the member states, and the Council, on a proposal from the Commission, must adopt recommendations: art 166(4) (as so renumbered).

5 Treaty on the Functioning of the European Union art 166(2) (as renumbered: see note 1).

6 Treaty on the Functioning of the European Union art 166(3) (as renumbered: see note 1).

7 See European Parliament and Council Regulation (EU) 492/2011 (OJ L141, 27.5.2011, p 1) on the freedom of movement for workers within the European Union art 7(3). Generally see Case C-542/09 *EC v Netherlands (Higher Education Funding of Migrant Worker's Children)* [2012] 3 CMLR 643, ECJ.

8 See European Parliament and Council Regulation (EU) 492/2011 (OJ L141, 27.5.2011, p 1) on the freedom of movement for workers within the European Union art 10. Member states must encourage all efforts to enable such children to attend these courses under the best possible

conditions: art 10. However as to the right of a child to complete its education in a host state if the parent is a migrant worker from another EU member state see Case C-480/08: *Teixeira v Lambeth London Borough Council* [2010] ECR I-1107, [2010] ICR 1118, [2010] All ER (D) 249 (Feb).

9   Ie the Charter of Fundamental Rights of the European Union (OJ C303, 14 12 2007, p 1). The Charter of Fundamental Rights is legally binding on the European Union and on member states when implementing EU legislation: see the Treaty on European Union (Maastricht, 7 February 1992; Cm 1934; TS 12 (1994); Cm 2485) art 6 (renumbered by the Treaty of Lisbon Amending the Treaty Establishing the European Union); *Explanatory Memorandum on the Treaty of Lisbon* (Foreign and Commonwealth Office). However, a specific Protocol guarantees that the Charter does not create any greater rights than already applied in European Union law at the time of the signing of the Lisbon Treaty, or extend the powers of any court, European or domestic, to strike down United Kingdom laws: see Consolidated version of the Treaty on European Union Protocols (Protocol (No 30)) on the application of the Charter of Fundamental Rights of the European Union to Poland and to the United Kingdom (OJ C115, 9.5.2008, p 313); *Explanatory Memorandum on the Treaty of Lisbon* (Foreign and Commonwealth Office).

10   European Union Charter of Fundamental Rights (OJ C364, 18.12.2000, p 1) art 14(1).

11   European Union Charter of Fundamental Rights art 14(2).

12   European Union Charter of Fundamental Rights art 14(1).

13   Ie the Treaty on the Functioning of the European Union arts 17, 18 (as renumbered: see note 1).

14   See Cases C-11/06, C-12/06 *Morgan v Bezirksregierung Koln, Bucher v Landrat des Kreises Duren* [2008] All ER (EC) 851, [2007] ECR I-9161, [2009] 1 CMLR 1, ECJ.

15   Cases C-76/05 *Schwarz v Finanzamt Bergisch Gladbach*, C-318/05 *EC v Germany* [2008] All ER (EC) 556, [2007] ECR I-6957, [2007] 3 CMLR 1283, ECJ.

5.   Rights under international treaties.   There are various international treaties which are of relevance to education. These include the United Nations' Universal Declaration of Human Rights[1], the United Nations' Convention on the Rights of the Child[2], the United Nations' International Covenant on Economic, Social and Political Rights[3] and the Council of Europe's European Social Charter[4].

Under the Universal Declaration of Human Rights, everyone has the right to education[5], and education must be directed to the full development of the human personality and to the strengthening of respect for human rights and fundamental freedoms[6]. It must promote understanding, tolerance and friendship among all nations and racial or religious groups, and it must further the activities of the United Nations for the maintenance of peace[7]. Parents have a right to choose the kind of education that is given to their children[8].

Under the Convention on the Rights of the Child, the right of the child to education is recognised, and with a view to achieving this right progressively and on the basis of equal opportunity, signatory states must: (1) make primary education compulsory and available to all; (2) encourage the development of different forms of secondary education (including general and vocational education), make them available and accessible to every child, and take appropriate measures such as introducing free education and offering financial assistance in case of need; (3) make higher education accessible to all on the basis of capacity by every appropriate means; (4) make educational and vocational guidance available and accessible to all children; and (5) take measures to encourage regular attendance at schools and the reduction of drop-out rates[9]. The education of the child must be directed towards: (a) the development of the child's personality, talents and mental and physical abilities to their fullest potential; (b) the development of respect for human rights and fundamental freedoms, and for the principles enshrined in the Charter of the United Nations; (c) the development of respect for the child's parents, for his or her own cultural identity, language and values, for the national values of the country in which the child is living and of the country from which he or she may originate, and for civilisations different from his or her own; (d) the preparation of the child for responsible life in a free society, in the spirit of understanding, peace, tolerance, equality of sexes, and friendship among all peoples and ethnic, national and religious groups and persons of indigenous origin; and (e) the development of respect for the natural environment[10].

The International Covenant on Economic, Social and Political Rights recognises the right of everyone to education[11]. The parties to the Covenant agree that education must be directed to the full development of the human personality and the sense of its dignity, and must strengthen the respect for human rights and fundamental freedoms[12]. They further agree that education must enable all persons to participate effectively in a free society, promote understanding, tolerance and friendship among all nations and all racial, ethnic or religious groups, and further the activities of the United Nations for the maintenance of peace[13]. With a view to achieving the full realisation of that right: (i) primary education must be compulsory and available free to all; (ii) secondary education in its different forms, including technical and vocational secondary education, must be made generally available and accessible to all by every appropriate means, and in particular by the progressive introduction of free education; (iii) higher education must be made equally accessible to all, on the basis of capacity, by every appropriate means, and in particular by the progressive introduction of free education; (iv) fundamental education must be encouraged or intensified as far as possible for those persons who have not received or completed the whole period of their primary education; and (v) the development of a system of schools at all levels must be actively pursued, an adequate fellowship system must be established and the material conditions of teaching staff must be continuously improved[14].

The European Social Charter provides for the right to protection against poverty and social exclusion[15]. With a view to ensuring the effective exercise of this right, the parties, being members of the Council of Europe, undertake: (A) to take measures within the framework of an overall and co-ordinated approach to promote effective access to employment, housing, training, education, culture, and social and medical assistance for persons who live or risk living in a situation of social exclusion or poverty, as well as their families; and (B) to review these measures with a view to their adaptation if necessary[16].

1   Ie the Universal Declaration of Human Rights (Paris, 10 December 1948; UN 2 (1949); Cmd 7662): see the text to notes 5–8. See also the United Nations Declaration on Human Rights Education and Training (A/HRC/RES/16/1; adopted by the UN General Assembly, 11 December 2011) as to which see the website for the Office of the Higher Commissioner for Human Rights.

2   Ie the Convention on the Rights of the Child (20 November 1989; TS 44 (1992); Cm 1976): see the text to notes 9–10. The Convention was signed by the United Kingdom on 19 Apr 1990 and ratified on 16 Dec 1991. See also generally as to the rights of the child the Charter of Fundamental Rights of the European Union (OJ C364, 18.12.2000, p 1) art 24.

3   Ie the International Covenant on Economic, Social and Cultural Rights 1966 (16 December 1966; UN TS 993, p 3): see the text to notes 11–14. The Covenant was signed by the United Kingdom on 16 Sep 1968 and ratified on 20 May 1976.

4   Ie the European Social Charter (Strasbourg, 3 May 1996; ETS 163): see the text to notes 15–16. The Charter was signed by the United Kingdom on 7 November 1997 but has yet to be ratified. As to the Council of Europe see INTERNATIONAL RELATIONS LAW vol 61 (2010) PARA 534.

5   Universal Declaration of Human Rights art 26(1). The Universal Declaration of Human Rights also provides that: (1) education must be free, at least in the elementary and fundamental stages; (2) elementary education must be compulsory; (3) technical and professional education must be made generally available; and (4) higher education must be accessible to all on the basis of merit: art 26(1).

6   Universal Declaration of Human Rights art 26(2).

7   Universal Declaration of Human Rights art 26(2).
8   Universal Declaration of Human Rights art 26(3).
9   Convention on the Rights of the Child art 28(1). As to the administration of discipline see
    art 28(2). As to the promotion of international co-operation see art 28(3).
10 Convention on the Rights of the Child art 29(1). No part of art 29 or art 28 (see the text to
    note 9) may be construed so as to interfere with the liberty of individuals and bodies to establish
    and direct educational institutions, subject always to the observance of the principles set out in
    art 29(1) and to the requirements that the education given in such institutions must conform to
    such minimum standards as may be laid down by the state: art 29(2).
11 International Covenant on Economic, Social and Political Rights art 13(1).
12 International Covenant on Economic, Social and Political Rights art 13(1).
13 International Covenant on Economic, Social and Political Rights art 13(1).
14 International Covenant on Economic, Social and Political Rights art 13(2). Universal free and
    compulsory primary education is to be progressively implemented if not currently available: see
    art 14. The parties undertake to have respect for the liberty of parents and, where applicable,
    legal guardians to choose for their children schools other than those established by public
    authorities, which conform to such minimum educational standards as may be laid down or
    approved by the state, and to ensure the religious and moral education of their children in
    conformity with their own convictions: see art 13(3). No part of art 13 is to be construed so as
    to interfere with the liberty of individuals and bodies to establish and direct educational
    institutions, subject always to the observance of the principles set out in art 13(1) (see the text to
    notes 11–13) and to the requirement that the education given in such institutions must conform
    to such minimum standards as may be laid down by the state: art 13(4).
15 See the European Social Charter Pt II art 30. The Charter also provides for a right to vocational
    guidance (Pt II art 9) and training (Pt II art 10), which is to be without discrimination on the
    grounds of sex (Pt II art 20). All rights guaranteed by the Charter are to be enjoyed without
    discrimination on any ground (Pt V art E).
16 European Social Charter Pt II art 30(a), (b).

6.   Freedom of speech in universities and further and higher education establishments.   Every individual and body of persons concerned in the government of: (1) any university[1]; (2) any institution other than a university within the higher education sector[2]; (3) any establishment of higher or further education[3] which is maintained by a local authority[4]; and (4) any institution within the further education sector[5], must take such steps as are reasonably practicable to ensure that freedom of speech within the law is secured for members, students and employees of the establishment and for visiting speakers[6]. Such a duty includes in particular the duty to ensure, so far as is reasonably practicable, that the use of any of the establishment's premises is not denied to any individual or body of persons on any ground connected with the beliefs or views of that individual or of any member of that body or that body's policy or objectives[7].

With a view to facilitating the discharge of the duty to secure freedom of speech in relation to an establishment, its governing body[8] must issue and keep up to date a code of practice setting out:

(a)   the procedures to be followed by members, students and employees of the establishment in connection with the organisation of meetings which are to be held on premises of the establishment and which fall within any class of meeting specified in the code, and other activities which are to take place on those premises and which fall within any class of activity so specified[9]; and

(b)   the conduct required of such persons in connection with any such meeting or activity[10],

and dealing with such other matters as the governing body considers appropriate[11]. Every individual and body of persons concerned in the government of any such establishment must take such steps as are reasonably practicable, including where appropriate the initiation of disciplinary measures, to secure that the requirements of the establishment's code of practice are complied with[12].

The governing body of every establishment to which the statutory provisions relating both to students' unions[13] and to the freedom of speech in universities and colleges[14] apply must, as regards any students' union for students at the establishment, bring to the attention of all students, at least once a year, the statutory provisions relating to freedom of speech in universities and colleges and any code of practice issued thereunder, relevant to the activities or conduct of the union[15].

1   Education (No 2) Act 1986 s 43(1), (5)(a). 'University' includes a university college and any college, or institution in the nature of a college, in a university: s 43(6). As to universities see PARA 621 et seq.

2   Education (No 2) Act 1986 s 43(1), (5)(aa) (added by the Education Reform Act 1988 s 237, Sch 12 Pt III para 100; and substituted by the Further and Higher Education Act 1992 s 93, Sch 8 para 22). As to references to institutions within the higher education sector see PARA 619.

3   'Establishment of higher or further education' means an institution which provides higher education or further education, or both: Education (No 2) Act 1986 s 65(1) (definition added by the Education Reform Act 1988 Sch 12 Pt III para 105). As to the meaning of 'further education' see PARA 23; and as to the meaning of 'higher education' see PARA 24 (definitions applied by virtue of the Education (No 2) Act 1986 s 67(3) (amended by the Education Act 1996 s 582(1), Sch 37 para 66(3), (4))).

4   Education (No 2) Act 1986 s 43(1), (5)(b) (substituted by the Education Reform Act 1988 Sch 12 Pt III para 100; and amended by SI 2010/1158). Where any establishment falls within the Education (No 2) Act 1986 s 43(5)(b) the local authority, for the purposes of s 43, is to be taken to be concerned in its government: s 43(7) (amended by the Further and Higher Education Act 1992 s 93, Sch 8 Pt I para 22(b), Sch 9; SI 2010/1158). As to the meaning of 'local authority' see PARA 25 (definition applied by the Education (No 2) Act 1986 s 67(3)).

5   Education (No 2) Act 1986 s 43(1), (5)(ba) (added by the Further and Higher Education Act 1992 Sch 8 Pt I para 22). As to references to institutions within the further education sector see PARA 555.

6   Education (No 2) Act 1986 s 43(1). As to the right to freedom of expression see also the Convention for the Protection of Human Rights and Fundamental Freedoms (Rome, 4 November 1950; TS 71 (1953); Cmd 8969) art 10; Human Rights Act 1998 s 1, Sch 1; and RIGHTS AND FREEDOMS vol 88A (2013) PARA 398 et seq. See also PARA 3. See also a House of Commons briefing paper of 20 May 2015 entitled 'Freedom of speech and preventing extremism in UK higher education institutions' which makes the point that while United Kingdom higher education institutions have a statutory duty to uphold freedom of speech in their institutions as far as is practical within the law, this duty is coming under pressure from the government's Prevent Strategy and provisions in the Counter-Terrorism and Security Act 2015. See also 'Protecting children from radicalisation: the prevent duty' (1 July 2015), on the Department for Education's website. See also PARA 8; and CRIMINAL LAW.

7   Education (No 2) Act 1986 s 43(2). It has been held that s 43 may be justiciable by judicial review, but does not give rise to private law rights: see *R v University College London, ex p Riniker* [1995] ELR 213 (in this case, the university did not breach the Education (No 2) Act 1986 s 43 by making it a condition of the contract of a teacher of German that on ceasing to be involved in matters concerning the running of the language centre she should not enter the centre without permission). See also *R v University of Liverpool, ex p Caesar-Gordon* [1991] 1 QB 124, [1990] 3 All ER 821 (where it was held that the university's ban on speeches on campus by members of the South African embassy, on the ground that there was a risk of unrest and disturbance outside its precincts, was unlawful under the Education (No 2) Act 1986 s 43); *R v Thames Valley University Students Union, ex p Ogilvy* [1997] CLY 2149 (where it was held that the exclusion of a student counsellor from the university premises for alleged misconduct did not give rise to a breach of his freedom of speech for the purposes of the Education (No 2) Act 1986 s 43).

8   'Governing body', in relation to any university, means the executive governing body having responsibility for the management and administration of its revenue and property and the conduct of its affairs (ie the body commonly called the council of the university): Education (No 2) Act 1986 s 43(6).

9   Education (No 2) Act 1986 s 43(3)(a). Where a student's union occupies premises which are not
    premises of the establishment in connection with which the union is constituted, any reference in
    s 43 to premises of the establishment is to be taken to include a reference to the premises
    occupied by the students' union: s 43(8). As to students' unions see PARA 1115 et seq.
10 Education (No 2) Act 1986 s 43(3)(b).
11 Education (No 2) Act 1986 s 43(3).
12 Education (No 2) Act 1986 s 43(4).
13 Ie the Education Act 1994 Pt II (ss 20–22).
14 Ie the Education (No 2) Act 1986 s 43: see the text to notes 1–12.
15 See the Education Act 1994 s 22(4)(c); and PARA 1125.

7.   **Pupils to be educated in accordance with parents' wishes.** In exercising or
performing all their respective powers and duties under the Education Acts[1], the
Secretary of State[2], the Welsh Ministers[3] and local authorities[4] must have regard
to the general principle that pupils[5] are to be educated in accordance with the
wishes of their parents[6], so far as that is compatible with the provision of
efficient instruction and training and the avoidance of unreasonable public
expenditure[7].

Parents also have a right under the Universal Declaration of Human Rights[8]
to choose the kind of education that is given to their children[9]. Under the
Convention for the Protection of Human Rights and Fundamental Freedoms[10],
parents have a right to ensure any education and training is in conformity with
their own religious and philosophical convictions[11]. The United Kingdom
affirmed this principle only so far as it is compatible with the provision of
efficient instruction and training, and the avoidance of unreasonable public
expenditure[12].

Parents may request that a pupil of a community, foundation or voluntary
school[13] is wholly or partly excused from receiving religious education given at
the school in accordance with the school's basic curriculum[14], from attendance at
religious worship in the school[15]. Special arrangements may also be made if a
parent of a pupil desires him to receive religious education of a kind which is not
provided in the school during the periods of time the pupil is so excused[16].

If the parent of any pupil in attendance at a maintained school[17] requests that
he may be wholly or partly excused from receiving sex education[18] at the school,
the pupil must, except so far as such education is comprised in the National
Curriculum[19], be so excused accordingly until the request is withdrawn[20].

1   As to the meaning of 'the Education Acts' see PARA 1 note 13.
2   As to the Secretary of State see PARA 58.
3   The functions of the Secretary of State under the Education Act 1996 s 9, in so far as they relate
    to Wales, were transferred to the National Assembly for Wales and are now exercisable by the
    Welsh Ministers: see the National Assembly for Wales (Transfer of Functions) Order 1999,
    SI 1999/672, art 2, Sch 1; Government of Wales Act 2006 s 162(1), Sch 11 paras 30, 32. As to
    the Welsh Ministers see PARA 59.
        'Wales' means the combined area of the counties which were created by the Local
    Government Act 1972 s 20 (as originally enacted) (see LOCAL GOVERNMENT vol 69 (2009)
    PARAS 5, 37), but subject to any alteration made under s 73 (consequential alteration of
    boundary following alteration of watercourse) (see LOCAL GOVERNMENT vol 69 (2009) PARA
    90): Interpretation Act 1978 Sch 1 (definition substituted by the Local Government (Wales)
    Act 1994 s 1(3), Sch 2 para 9). 'England' means, subject to any alteration of boundaries of local
    government areas, the area consisting of the counties established by the Local Government
    Act 1972 s 1 (see LOCAL GOVERNMENT vol 69 (2009) PARAS 5, 22), Greater London and the
    Isles of Scilly: Interpretation Act 1978 s 5, Sch 1. As to local government areas see LOCAL
    GOVERNMENT vol 69 (2009) PARA 22 et seq; and as to boundary changes see LOCAL
    GOVERNMENT vol 69 (2009) PARA 54 et seq. As to Greater London see LONDON GOVERNMENT
    vol 71 (2013) PARA 14. References to 'England' in Acts passed before 1967 include references to
    Wales (see the Interpretation Act 1978 Sch 2 para 5(a)).

4   As to the meaning of 'local authority' see PARA 25.
5   As to the meaning of 'pupil' see PARA 20 note 4.
6   In the Education Act 1996, unless the context otherwise requires, 'parent', in relation to a child
     or young person, includes any person (1) who is not a parent of his but who has parental
     responsibility for him; or (2) who has care of him, except that in s 499(8) (see PARA 56) it only
     includes such a person if he is an individual: s 576(1). 'Parental responsibility' has the same
     meaning as in the Children Act 1989 (see s 3; and CHILDREN AND YOUNG PERSONS vol 9 (2012)
     PARA 151): Education Act 1996 s 576(3). In determining for these purposes whether an
     individual has care of a child or young person, any absence of the child or young person at a
     hospital or boarding school and any other temporary absence must be disregarded: s 576(4).
     'Child' means a person who is not over compulsory school age: s 579(1). 'Young person' means
     a person over compulsory school age but under the age of 18: s 579(1). As to the meaning of
     'compulsory school age' see PARA 19. The time at which a person attains a particular age
     expressed in years is the commencement of the relevant anniversary of the date of his birth: see
     the Family Law Reform Act 1969 s 9; and CHILDREN AND YOUNG PERSONS vol 9 (2012) PARA 2.
     'Person', unless the contrary intention appears, includes a body of persons corporate or
     unincorporate: Interpretation Act 1978 s 5, Sch 1. As to bodies corporate and unincorporate see
     COMPANIES vol 14 (2009) PARAS 2, 3; CORPORATIONS vol 24 (2010) PARA 301 et seq.
        In cases where there is a dispute between parents as to the choice of school and there is no
     parental agreement, the court should reach a decision: *Re P (A Child) (Parental Dispute)* [2002]
     EWCA Civ 1627, [2003] 1 FLR 286, [2002] All ER (D) 80 (Oct).
7   Education Act 1996 s 9 (amended by the School Standards and Framework Act 1998 s 140(1),
     Sch 30 paras 57, 61; and SI 2010/1158). The chief object of the provision as to the avoidance of
     unreasonable public expenditure in the Education Act 1996 s 9 is to prevent parental choice
     placing an undue or disproportionate burden on the education budget. In cases where the
     parental preference is for an independent school over an available state school, it is for the local
     authority to decide whether those cost implications make the expenditure on the independent
     school unreasonable. This means striking a balance between (1) the educational advantages of
     the placement preferred by the parents; and (2) the extra cost of it to the local authority as
     against what it will cost the local authority to place the child in the maintained school: *R (on the
     application of Oxfordshire County Council) v GB* [2001] EWCA Civ 1358, [2002] LGR 279,
     [2002] ELR 8. See also *Ealing London Borough Council v Special Educational Needs and
     Disability Tribunal* [2008] EWHC 193 (Admin), [2008] ELR 183. The Education Act 1996 s 9
     still applies where the choice, based on the parents' preference, is between two schools in the
     maintained sector: *O v Lewisham London Borough Council* [2007] EWHC 2130 (Admin),
     [2008] LGR 765, [2007] All ER (D) 51 (Sep). Expenditure relating to the education of a child
     which would arise regardless of where that child is educated is not relevant when considering
     the cost of educating a child in accordance with parental wishes: *R (on the application of
     Oxfordshire County Council) v GB* above. The precise route by which payment is made out of
     what is ultimately the local authority's budget is immaterial; no distinction can be made between
     payment by the local authority directly from its own pocket and payment by the school under
     delegated arrangements: *Coventry City Council v Special Educational Needs and Disability
     Tribunal* [2007] EWHC 2278 (Admin), [2008] ELR 1, [2007] All ER (D) 60 (Sep). As to school
     delegated budgets see PARA 315 et seq.
        There is judicial disagreement as to what constitutes 'public expenditure' for the purposes of
     the Education Act 1996 s 9. In *S v Somerset County Council* [2002] EWHC 1808 (Admin),
     [2003] ELR 78, [2002] All ER (D) 387 (Jul) it was held that the term refers not to the
     expenditure of the local authority as a whole, but is restricted to the expenditure of the local
     authority. However, in *O v Lewisham London Borough Council* above it was held that the term
     is not confined to the expenditure of the local authority.
        The principle that pupils are to be educated in accordance with parents' wishes is a general
     principle only and, while the relevant persons must have regard to the principle when exercising
     or performing their powers and duties, they are not precluded from taking account of other
     factors as well, and also may make exceptions to the general principle if they think fit to do so:
     Watt v Kesteven County Council [1955] 1 QB 408, [1955] 1 All ER 473, CA (where Denning LJ
     held at 424 and 476 that: 'It cannot therefore be said that a county council is at fault simply
     because it does not see fit to comply with the parent's wishes'). See also *Darling v Ministry of
     Education, Jones v Ministry of Education* (1962) Times, 7 April; *Wood v Ealing London
     Borough Council* [1967] Ch 364, [1966] 3 All ER 514; *Cumings v Birkenhead Corpn* [1972]
     Ch 12, [1971] 2 All ER 881, CA; *Harvey v Strathclyde Regional Council* 1989 SLT 612, HL
     (decided under the equivalent provision in Scotland); *R v Lambeth London Borough Council,
     ex p G* [1994] ELR 207. These cases were mostly decided under the Education Act 1944 s 76
     whose terms were very similar to the Education Act 1996 s 9 which replaced it. The line of

authority they represent has continuing effect despite the fact that they predate the substantial reforms introduced by the Education Act 1996 and other subsequent legislation including the Children and Families Act 2014 (as to which see PARA 1): *T v Special Educational Needs Tribunal and Wiltshire County Council* [2002] EWHC 1474 (Admin) at [38](ii), [2002] ELR 704 per Richards J, citing *Watt v Kesteven County Council* and *Cumings v Birkenhead Corpn* above.

The principle in the Education Act 1996 s 9 may be a particular factor to be considered in conjunction with parental choice of special educational provision and school placement: see *B v Harrow London Borough Council* [2000] 1 All ER 876, [2000] 1 WLR 223, [2000] ELR 109, HL; *S v Dudley Metropolitan Borough Council* [2000] ELR 330; *R v West Sussex County Council, ex p S* [1999] ELR 40. See also *B v Gloucestershire County Council and the Special Educational Needs Tribunal* [1998] ELR 539; *S and S v Bracknell Forest Borough Council and the Special Educational Needs Tribunal* [1999] ELR 51; *W-R v Solihull Metropolitan Borough Council and Wall (Chairman of the Special Educational Needs Tribunal)* [1999] ELR 528; *C v Buckinghamshire County Council and the Special Educational Needs Tribunal* [1999] LGR 321, [1999] ELR 179, CA; *T v Special Educational Needs Tribunal and Wiltshire County Council* above. See also *K&K v The Authority (SEN)* [2013] UKUT 624 (AAC).

See also *EH v Kent County Council* [2011] EWCA Civ 709, [2011] LGR 798 (whether a child's parents' choice of school would be compatible with the avoidance of unreasonable public expenditure was a question of fact to be answered by the tribunal in a commonsense way); *FS (Re T) v Bromley London Borough Council* [2013] UKUT 529 (AAC), [2014] ELR 1 (as to what constituted genuine additional public expenditure in the particular circumstances); and *H v Warrington Borough Council* [2014] EWCA Civ 398, [2014] 3 All ER 747, [2014] LGR 374 (the correct meaning of the words 'public expenditure' in the Education Act 1996 s 9 was expenditure incurred by a public body, as opposed to expenditure by a private body). See also *Cambridgeshire County Council v SF (SEN)* [2015] UKUT (AAC) (about the transition of a boy with autistic spectrum disorder (ASD) and other diagnoses to secondary education. As to the relationship between the Education Act 1996 ss 9 and 316 (as to s 316 see PARA 1014) see *KC v London Borough of Hammersmith and Fulham (SEN)* [2015] UKUT 177 (AAC).

As to parental preferences in relation to admissions to maintained schools see further PARA 228. In relation to special educational needs, the Education Act 1996 s 9 does not apply if Sch 27 para 3 applies: see PARA 1012. As to the duty of parents to secure the education of children of compulsory school age see s 7; and PARA 435. Where an education supervision order is in force in relation to a child, the provisions of s 9 do not apply to the child: see the Children Act 1989 s 36, Sch 3 para 13(2)(b); and PARA 453.

8 Ie the Universal Declaration of Human Rights (Paris, 10 December 1948; UN 2 (1949); Cmd 7662).

9 See the Universal Declaration of Human Rights art 26(3); and PARA 5.

10 Ie the Convention for the Protection of Human Rights and Fundamental Freedoms (Rome, 4 November 1950; TS 71 (1953); Cmd 8969).

11 See the Convention for the Protection of Human Rights and Fundamental Freedoms First Protocol (Paris, 20 March 1952; TS 46 (1954); Cmd 9221) art 2; PARA 3; and RIGHTS AND FREEDOMS vol 88A (2013) PARA 548.

12 See the Human Rights Act 1998 s 15, Sch 3; PARA 3; and RIGHTS AND FREEDOMS vol 88A (2013) PARA 558. The conditions mirror those attached to the duty under the Education Act 1996 s 9: see the text to notes 1–7.

13 As to community, foundation and voluntary schools see PARA 106 et seq. Similar provision may be made by regulations in relation to pupils attending community or foundation special schools: see the School Standards and Framework Act 1998 s 71(7); and PARA 924.

14 See the School Standards and Framework Act 1998 s 71(1); and PARA 924.

15 See the School Standards and Framework Act 1998 s 71(1A); and PARA 924.

16 See the School Standards and Framework Act 1998 s 71(3)–(5), (6); and PARA 924.

17 As to the meaning of 'maintained school', in relation to the curriculum in England, see PARA 856 note 3; and, in relation to the curriculum in Wales, see PARA 870 note 4.

18 As to the meaning of 'sex education' see PARA 857 note 10.

19 'The National Curriculum' (without more) means: (1) in relation to England, the National Curriculum for England; and (2) in relation to Wales, the National Curriculum for Wales: Education Act 1996 s 579(1) (definition added by the Education Act 2002 s 215(1), Sch 21 para 57(b)). As to the meaning of 'England' see PARA 7 note 3. As to the National Curriculum for England see PARA 859 et seq; and as to the National Curriculum for Wales see PARA 873 et seq.

20 Education Act 1996 s 405. See also PARA 907.

(iv) Duty to Prevent People from being Drawn into Terrorism

8.   Duty on authorities involved in providing education.   Part 5 of the Counter-Terrorism and Security Act 2015[1] contains provisions aimed at dealing with the risk of being drawn into terrorism.

Specified authorities[2] must, in the exercise of their functions, have due regard to the need to prevent people from being drawn into terrorism ('the prevent duty')[3]. The Secretary of State may issue and from time to time revise guidance to the specified authorities about the exercise of the prevent duty[4]. The Secretary of State is empowered to issue, and enforce, directions to a specified authority to enforce the performance of the prevent duty[5]. Specified authorities which are universities or similar institutions must have particular regard to their statutory duty to secure freedom of speech when carrying out the prevent duty[6]. A duty is imposed on relevant higher and further education bodies to provide information to a monitoring authority to allow the monitoring authority to assess the bodies' compliance with the prevent duty[7]. The Secretary of State is empowered to give directions to relevant higher and further education bodies where satisfied that they have failed to comply with their duty to provide information to the monitoring authority, and the Secretary of State can enforce any such directions[8]. A failure in respect of any above duty[9] does not constitute a cause of action under private law[10].

Local authorities[11] are required to ensure that a panel is in place for its area for the purposes of assessing the extent to which individuals referred to the panel by the police are vulnerable to being drawn into terrorism, and requires the panel to prepare a support plan in respect of any identified individual whom it considers should be offered support for the purposes of reducing their vulnerability to being drawn into terrorism[12]. Provision is made for the membership of a panel, which must include the responsible local authority and the chief officer of police for that authority's area[13]. The partners of a panel[14] must co-operate with the panel in the carrying out of its functions, and the police in the carrying out of their functions[15]. The Secretary of State may agree to indemnify a person who provides support to an identified individual under a support plan ('a support provider') against any costs and expenses that the support provider reasonably incurs in carrying out functions as a support provider[16].

1   Ie the Counter-Terrorism and Security Act 2015 Pt 5 (ss 26–41). Part 5 Ch 1 (ss 26–35) contains provisions aiming to prevent people being drawn into terrorism and Pt 5 Ch 2 (ss 36–41) contains provisions in regard to support etc for people vulnerable to being drawn into terrorism. As to the Counter-Terrorism and Security Act 2015 Pt 5 see CRIMINAL LAW.
2   Ie in regard to England and Wales listed in the Counter-Terrorism and Security Act 2015 s 26, Sch 6 Pt 1. As far as education is concerned such specified bodies include the following:
    (1)   a person who is authorised by virtue of an order made under the Deregulation and Contracting Out Act 1994 s 70 to exercise a function specified in the Education Act 1996 Sch 36A (see PARA 25);
    (2)   a person with whom arrangements have been made for the provision of education under the Education Act 1996 s 19 (see PARAS 20, 427) or the Education and Inspections Act 2006 s 100 (see PARA 528) (cases of illness, exclusion etc);
    (3)   the proprietor of (a) a school that has been approved under the Education Act 1996 s 342 (see PARAS 919, 1042, 1043); (b) a maintained school within the meaning given by the School Standards and Framework Act 1998 s 20(7) (see PARA 99); (c) a maintained nursery school within the meaning given by s 22(9) (see PARA 99); (d) an independent school registered under the Education Act 2002 s 158 (see PARA 369); (e) an independent educational institution registered under the Education and Skills Act 2008 s 95(1) (see PARA 382); or (f) an alternative provision academy within the meaning given by the Academies Act 2010 s 1C (see PARA 346 note 14);

    (4)   a person who is specified or nominated in a direction made in relation to the exercise of a local authority's functions given by the Secretary of State under the Education Act 1996 s 497A (see PARA 62);

    (5)   the governing body of a qualifying institution within the meaning given by the Higher Education Act 2004 s 11 (see PARA 1090);

    (6)   the provider of education or training (a) to which the Education and Inspections Act 2006 Pt 8 Ch 3 (ss 123–134) applies (see PARA 1261 et seq); and (b) in respect of which funding is provided by, or under arrangements made by, the Secretary of State or the Chief Executive of Skills Funding;

    (7)   a person who is specified in a direction made in relation to the exercise of a local authority's functions given by the Welsh Ministers under the School Standards and Organisation (Wales) Act 2013 s 25 (see PARA 1239);

    (8)   the governing body of an educational establishment maintained by a local authority in Wales (see PARA 195);

    (9)   the governing body or proprietor of an institution (not otherwise listed) at which more than 250 students, excluding students undertaking distance learning courses, are undertaking (a) courses in preparation for examinations related to qualifications regulated by the Office of Qualifications and Examinations Regulation (Ofqual) or the Welsh Government; (b) courses of a description mentioned in the Education Reform Act 1988 Sch 6 (higher education courses) (see PARAS 24, 684).

As from a day to be appointed, the last entry (see head (9) above) is amended by the Qualifications Wales Act 2015 Sch 4 para 11(1), (3) so as to refer to qualifications awarded by bodies in respect of the award of which they are recognised by Qualifications Wales under the Qualifications Wales Act 2015 Pt 3 (ss 4–12) (see PARA 853 et seq), instead of referring to qualifications regulated by the Welsh Government. At the date at which this volume states the law no such day had been appointed. As to the Office of Qualifications and Examinations Regulation generally see PARA 824 et seq.

    The Secretary of State may by regulations amend the Counter-Terrorism and Security Act 2015 Sch 6, but, before adding, amending or removing an entry relating to a Welsh authority, must consult the Welsh Ministers and, before adding, amending or removing an entry relating to a Scottish authority, must consult the Scottish Ministers: see ss 27, 28; and the Counter-Terrorism and Security Act 2015 (Risk of Being Drawn into Terrorism) (Amendment and Guidance) Regulations 2015, SI 2015/928 (made under the Counter-Terrorism and Security Act 2015 s 27(1), (3)). As to the Secretary of State see PARA 58. As to the Welsh Ministers see PARA 59. As to the abolition of the office of the Chief Executive of Skills Funding see PARA 776 note 1. As to the meanings of 'England' and 'Wales' see PARA 7 note 3.

3   See the Counter-Terrorism and Security Act 2015 s 26.

4   See the Counter-Terrorism and Security Act 2015 s 29; and the Counter-Terrorism and Security Act 2015 (Risk of Being Drawn into Terrorism) (Amendment and Guidance) Regulations 2015, SI 2015/928 (made under the Counter-Terrorism and Security Act 2015 s 29(5)). See e g 'Prevent Duty Guidance for England and Wales: Guidance for specified authorities in England and Wales on the duty in the Counter-Terrorism and Security Act 2015 to have due regard to the need to prevent people being drawn into terrorism' (March 2015).

5   See the Counter-Terrorism and Security Act 2015 s 30 (s 30(2) amended by SI 2015/928).

6   See the Counter-Terrorism and Security Act 2015 s 31 (s 31(1)–(5) amended by SI 2015/928).

7   See the Counter-Terrorism and Security Act 2015 s 32. As from a day to be appointed, the definition of 'relevant further education body' in s 32(1) is amended by the Qualifications Wales Act 2015 Sch 4 para 11(1), (2). At the date at which this volume states the law no such day had been appointed.

8   See the Counter-Terrorism and Security Act 2015 s 33.

9   Ie imposed by the Counter-Terrorism and Security Act 2015 Pt 5 Ch 1.

10   See the Counter-Terrorism and Security Act 2015 s 34.

11   As to the meaning of 'local authority' see the Counter-Terrorism and Security Act 2015 s 41. See also note 14.

12   See the Counter-Terrorism and Security Act 2015 s 36.

13   See the Counter-Terrorism and Security Act 2015 s 37.

14   Ie in regard to England and Wales listed in the Counter-Terrorism and Security Act 2015 s 38, Sch 7 Pt 1. As far as education is concerned such persons and bodies include the following:

    (1)   a sixth form college corporation within the meaning given by the Further and Higher Education Act 1992 s 90(1) (see PARA 577 note 7);

    (2)   the governing body of an institution within the further education sector within the meaning given by s 91(3) (see PARA 560 note 6);

(3)   a person who is authorised by virtue of an order made under the Deregulation and Contracting Out Act 1994 s 70 to exercise a function specified in the Education Act 1996 Sch 36A (see PARA 25);

(4)   a person with whom arrangements have been made for the provision of education under the Education Act 1996 s 19 (see PARAS 20, 427) or the Education and Inspections Act 2006 s 100 (see PARA 528) (cases of illness, exclusion etc);

(5)   the proprietor of (a) a school that has been approved under the Education Act 1996 s 342 (see PARAS 919, 1042, 1043);(b) a maintained school within the meaning given by the School Standards and Framework Act 1998 s 20(7) (see PARA 99); (c) a maintained nursery school within the meaning given by s 22(9) (see PARA 99); (d) an independent school registered under the Education Act 2002 s 158 (see PARA 369); (e) an independent educational institution registered under the Education and Skills Act 2008 s 95(1) (see PARA 382); (f) a 16 to 19 academy within the meaning given by the Academies Act 2010 s 1B (see PARA 346 note 13); (g) an alternative provision academy within the meaning given by s 1C (see PARA 346 note 14); or (h) a special post-16 institution within the meaning given by the Children and Families Act 2014 s 83(2) (see PARA 943 note 9);

(6)   a person who is specified or nominated in a direction made in relation to the exercise of a local authority's functions given by the Secretary of State under Education Act 1996 s 497A (see PARA 62);

(7)   the governing body of a qualifying institution within the meaning given by the Higher Education Act 2004 s 11 (see PARA 1090);

(8)   a person who is specified in a direction made in relation to the exercise of a local authority's functions given by the Welsh Ministers under the School Standards and Organisation (Wales) Act 2013 s 25 (see PARA 1239);

(9)   the governing body of an educational establishment maintained by a local authority in Wales (see PARA 195);

(10)   the governing body or proprietor of an institution (not otherwise listed) at which more than 250 students, excluding students undertaking distance learning courses, are undertaking (a) courses in preparation for examinations related to qualifications regulated by the Office of Qualifications and Examinations Regulation or the Welsh Government; (b) courses of a description mentioned in the Education Reform Act 1988 Sch 6 (higher education courses) (see PARAS 24, 684).

As from a day to be appointed, the last entry (see head (10) above) is amended by the Qualifications Wales Act 2015 Sch 4 para 11(1), (3) so as to refer to qualifications awarded by bodies in respect of the award of which they are recognised by Qualifications Wales under the Qualifications Wales Act 2015 Pt 3 (ss 4–12) (see PARA 853 et seq), instead of referring to qualifications regulated by the Welsh Government. At the date at which this volume states the law no such day had been appointed.

    The Secretary of State may by regulations amend the definition of 'local authority' in the Counter-Terrorism and Security Act 2015 s 41 and Sch 7 but, before adding, amending or removing an entry relating to a Welsh authority, must consult the Welsh Ministers and, before adding, amending or removing an entry relating to a Scottish authority, must consult the Scottish Ministers: see s 39; and the Counter-Terrorism and Security Act 2015 (Risk of Being Drawn into Terrorism) (Amendment and Guidance) Regulations 2015, SI 2015/928 (made under the Counter-Terrorism and Security Act 2015 s 29(1), (4)).

15 See the Counter-Terrorism and Security Act 2015 s 38.
16 See the Counter-Terrorism and Security Act 2015 s 40.

(v) Duties under the Equality Act 2010

A. EQUALITY DUTIES IN RELATION TO SCHOOLS

9.   Duty not to discriminate in the provision of education. The responsible body of a school[1] must not discriminate[2] against:

(1)   a person in the arrangements it makes for deciding who is offered admission as a pupil[3];

(2)   a person as to the terms on which it offers to admit the person as a pupil[4];

(3)   a person by not admitting the person as a pupil[5];

(4)   a pupil in the way it provides education for the pupil[6];

(5)   a pupil in the way it affords the pupil access to a benefit, facility or service[7];

(6)   a pupil by not providing education for the pupil[8];

(7)   a pupil by not affording the pupil access to a benefit, facility or service[9];

(8)   a pupil by excluding the pupil from the school[10];

(9)   a pupil by subjecting the pupil to any other detriment[11].

The responsible body of a school must not harass[12] a pupil[13] or a person who has applied for admission as a pupil[14].

The responsible body of a school must not victimise[15]:

(a)   a person in the arrangements it makes for deciding who is offered admission as a pupil[16];

(b)   a person as to the terms on which it offers to admit the person as a pupil[17];

(c)   a person by not admitting the person as a pupil[18];

(d)   a pupil in the way it provides education for the pupil[19];

(e)   a pupil in the way it affords the pupil access to a benefit, facility or service[20];

(f)   a pupil by not providing education for the pupil[21];

(g)   a pupil by not affording the pupil access to a benefit, facility or service[22];

(h)   a pupil by excluding the pupil from the school[23];

(i)   a pupil by subjecting the pupil to any other detriment[24].

A duty to make reasonable adjustments for disabled persons applies to the responsible body of a school[25].

The powers of the Secretary of State[26] and the Welsh Ministers[27] under the Education Act 1996[28] to give directions where a body is in default of its obligations in relation to a school apply to the performance of a duty under the above provisions[29].

Nothing in the above provisions applies to anything done in connection with the content of the curriculum[30].

1   The Equality Act 2010 s 85 applies to: (1) a school maintained by a local authority (s 85(7)(a)); (2) an independent educational institution (other than a special school) (s 85(7)(b)); (3) an alternative provision academy that is not an independent educational institution (s 85(7)(ba) (added by SI 2012/976); and (4) a special school (not maintained by a local authority) (Equality Act 2010 s 85(7)(c)). The 'responsible body' of a school is: (a) if the school is within head (1) above, the local authority or governing body (s 85(9)(a)); (b) if it is within head (2), (3) or (4) above, the proprietor (s 85(9)(b) (amended by SI 2012/976). A reference to a school includes a reference to an independent educational institution in England; and a reference to an independent educational institution in England is to be construed in accordance with the Education and Skills Act 2008 Pt 4 Ch 1 (see PARA 382): Equality Act 2010 s 89(6). A reference to an independent educational institution is a reference to an independent educational institution in England, or an independent school in Wales: s 89(7). 'Independent school', in relation to Wales, has the meaning given in the Education Act 1996 s 463 (see PARA 369): Equality Act 2010 s 89(8)(a). As to the meaning of 'school' see PARA 91 (definition applied by s 89(5)(a)). As to the meaning of 'special school' see PARA 1041 (definition applied by s 89(9)). 'Local authority' means, in relation to England, an English local authority, and, in relation to Wales, a Welsh local authority, within the meanings of the Education and Inspections Act 2006 s 162 (see PARA 26 notes 7, 8): Equality Act 2010 s 89(10). As to the meaning of 'proprietor' see PARA 51 note 4 (definition applied s 89(4)(a)). As to alternative provision academies see PARA 546 note 14. As to the meanings of 'England' and 'Wales' see PARA 7 note 3. As to maintained schools see PARA 99 et seq.

2   As to what amounts to discrimination see the Equality Act 2010 ss 13–19; and DISCRIMINATION vol 33 (2013) PARA 65 et seq. The Equality Act 2010 Pt 6 Ch 1 (ss 84–89) does not apply to the protected characteristics of age or marriage and civil partnership: s 84. As to the interpretation

of terms used in relation to the protected characteristic of age see s 5; and DISCRIMINATION vol 33 (2013) PARA 49. As to the interpretation of terms used in relation to the protected characteristic of marriage and civil partnership see s 8; and DISCRIMINATION vol 33 (2013) PARA 60.

Section 85(1), so far as relating to sex, does not apply in relation to a single-sex school: Sch 11 para 1(1). A 'single-sex school' is a school which admits pupils of one sex only (Sch 11 para 1(2)(a)), or on the basis of the assumption in Sch 11 para 1(3), would be taken to admit pupils of one sex only (Sch 11 para 1(2)(b)). That assumption is that pupils of the opposite sex are to be disregarded if (1) their admission to the school is exceptional (Sch 11 para 1(3)(a)); or (2) their numbers are comparatively small and their admission is confined to particular courses or classes (Sch 11 para 1(3)(b)). In the case of a school which is a single-sex school by virtue of Sch 11 para 1(3)(b), s 85(2)(a)–(d) (see the text to notes 6–9), so far as relating to sex, does not prohibit confining pupils of the same sex to particular courses or classes: Sch 11 para 1(4). As to the meaning of 'pupil' see PARA 20 note 4 (definition applied by s 89(3)(a)). As to the interpretation of terms used in relation to the protected characteristic of sex see s 11; and DISCRIMINATION vol 33 (2013) PARA 63. As to applications in relation to single-sex schools becoming co-educational see PARA 10.

Section 85(1), so far as relating to sex, does not apply in relation to admission as a boarder to a specified school (see Sch 11 para 2(1)); and s 85(2)(a)–(d) (see the text to notes 6–9), so far as relating to sex, does not apply in relation to boarding facilities at a specified school (see Sch 11 para 2(2)). A 'specified school' is a school (other than a single-sex school) which has some pupils as boarders and others as non-boarders and which (a) admits as boarders pupils of one sex only (Sch 11 para 2(3)(a)); or (b) on the basis of the assumption in Sch 11 para 2(4), would be taken to admit as boarders pupils of one sex only (Sch 11 para 2(3)(b)). That assumption is that pupils of the opposite sex admitted as boarders are to be disregarded if their numbers are small compared to the numbers of other pupils admitted as boarders: Sch 11 para 2(4).

The provisions of s 85(1) and (2)(a)–(d), so far as relating to religion or belief, do not apply in relation to: (i) a school designated under the School Standards and Framework Act 1998 s 69(3) (foundation or voluntary school with religious character: see PARA 914) (Equality Act 2010 Sch 11 para 5(a)); (ii) a school (other than an alternative provision academy) listed in the register of independent schools for England or for Wales, if the school's entry in the register records that the school has a religious ethos (Sch 11 para 5(b) (amended by SI 2012/976). As to the registration of independent schools in England see PARA 384 et seq; and in Wales see PARA 416 et seq. The provisions of the Equality Act 2010 s 85(2)(a)–(d), so far as relating to religion or belief, do not apply in relation to anything done in connection with acts of worship or other religious observance organised by or on behalf of a school (whether or not forming part of the curriculum): Sch 11 para 6. A minister of the Crown may by order amend Sch 11 Pt 2 (paras 5–7) so as to add, vary or omit an exception to s 85 (Sch 11 para 7(1)(a)), or so as to make provision about the construction or application of s 19(2)(d) (see DISCRIMINATION vol 33 (2013) PARA 72) in relation to s 85 (Sch 11 para 7(1)(b)). This power is exercisable only in relation to religious or belief-related discrimination: Sch 11 para 7(2). Before making such an order the minister must consult the Welsh Ministers, the Scottish Ministers, and such other persons as the minister thinks appropriate: Sch 11 para 7(3). At the date at which this volume states the law no such order had been made. As to the interpretation of terms used in relation to the protected characteristic of religion or belief, see s 10; and DISCRIMINATION vol 33 (2013) PARA 62. As to ministers of the Crown see CONSTITUTIONAL AND ADMINISTRATIVE LAW vol 20 (2014) PARA 151. As to the Welsh Ministers see PARA 59. As to the Scottish Ministers see CONSTITUTIONAL AND ADMINISTRATIVE LAW vol 20 (2014) PARA 67. As to the meaning of 'person' see PARA 7 note 6.

A person does not contravene s 85(1), so far as relating to disability, only by applying a permitted form of selection: Sch 11 para 8(1). In relation to England and Wales, a permitted form of selection is: (A) in the case of a maintained school which is not designated as a grammar school under the School Standards and Framework Act 1998 s 104 (see PARA 263), a form of selection mentioned in s 99(2) or (4) of that Act (see PARA 258) (Equality Act 2010 Sch 11 para 8(2)(a)); (B) in the case of a maintained school which is so designated, its selective admission arrangements (within the meaning of the School Standards and Framework Act 1998 s 104; see PARA 263) (Equality Act 2010 Sch 11 para 8(2)(b)); (C) in the case of an independent educational institution, arrangements which provide for some or all of its pupils to be selected by reference to general or special ability or aptitude, with a view to admitting only pupils of high ability or aptitude (Equality Act 2010 Sch 11 para 8(2)(c)). 'Maintained school' has the meaning given in the School Standards and Framework Act 1998 s 22 (see PARA 305): Equality Act 2010 Sch 11 para 8(4). As to the interpretation of terms used in relation to the protected characteristic of disability, see s 6, Sch 1; and DISCRIMINATION vol 33 (2013) PARA 50 et seq. Particular note should be taken of positive discrimination provisions in regard to disability as this can be a big issue for schools: generally see s 13(3); and DISCRIMINATION vol 33 (2013) PARA 65.

3   Equality Act 2010 s 85(1)(a). As to school admissions see PARA 224 et seq.

4   Equality Act 2010 s 85(1)(b).

5   Equality Act 2010 s 85(1)(c).

6   Equality Act 2010 s 85(2)(a). See also note 2.

7   Equality Act 2010 s 85(2)(b). See also note 2. A reference (however expressed) to providing or affording access to a benefit, facility or service includes a reference to facilitating access to the benefit, facility or service: s 212(4).

8   Equality Act 2010 s 85(2)(c). See also note 2.

9   Equality Act 2010 s 85(2)(d). See also note 2.

10 Equality Act 2010 s 85(2)(e). As to exclusion of pupils see PARA 517 et seq.

11 Equality Act 2010 s 85(2)(f). 'Detriment' does not, subject to s 212(5), include conduct which amounts to harassment: s 212(1). Where the Equality Act 2010 disapplies a prohibition on harassment in relation to a specified protected characteristic, the disapplication does not prevent conduct relating to that characteristic from amounting to a detriment for the purposes of discrimination within s 13 (see DISCRIMINATION vol 33 (2013) PARAS 65–66) because of that characteristic: s 212(5). The refusal by a school to allow a pupil who followed the Sikh religion the right to wear the Kara (religious bangle) at school amounted to unlawful discrimination on grounds of religion or belief: see *R (on the application of Watkins-Singh) v Governing Body of Aberdare Girls' High School* [2008] EWHC 1865 (Admin), [2008] 3 FCR 203, [2008] ELR 561 (decided under the previous legislation). See more recently *G (by his litigation friend) v Head Teacher and Governors of St Gregory's Catholic Science College* [2011] EWHC 1452 (Admin), [2011] All ER (D) 113 (Jun) (the defendants' school uniform policy, which had not permitted the African-Caribbean claimant wearing his hair in cornrows, was held to have had a legitimate aim but that its application to the claimant had, in his circumstances and without justification, been indirectly racially discriminatory).

12 As to what amounts to harassment see the Equality Act 2010 s 26; and DISCRIMINATION vol 33 (2013) PARA 73. In the application of s 26 for the purposes of s 85(3), none of the following is a relevant protected characteristic: (1) gender reassignment; (2) religion or belief; (3) sexual orientation: s 85(10).

13 Equality Act 2010 s 85(3)(a).

14 Equality Act 2010 s 85(3)(b).

15 As to what amounts to victimisation see the Equality Act 2010 s 27; and DISCRIMINATION vol 33 (2013) PARA 75. As to the application of s 27 in relation to s 85(4), (5) see s 86.

16 Equality Act 2010 s 85(4)(a).

17 Equality Act 2010 s 85(4)(b).

18 Equality Act 2010 s 85(4)(c).

19 Equality Act 2010 s 85(5)(a).

20 Equality Act 2010 s 85(5)(b).

21 Equality Act 2010 s 85(5)(c).

22 Equality Act 2010 s 85(5)(d).

23 Equality Act 2010 s 85(5)(e).

24 Equality Act 2010 s 85(5)(f).

25 See the Equality Act 2010 s 85(6). As to the general duty to make reasonable adjustments see s 20; and DISCRIMINATION vol 33 (2013) PARA 227 et seq. As to the reasonable adjustments with specific reference to education in schools see s 98, Sch 13.

26 As to the Secretary of State see PARA 58.

27 As to the Welsh Ministers see PARA 59.

28 Ie the Education Act 1996 s 496 (see PARA 64) and s 497 (see PARA 65).

29 See the Equality Act 2010 s 87(1). But neither of the Education Act 1996 s 496 and s 497 applies to the performance of a duty under the Equality Act 2010 s 85 by the proprietor of an independent educational institution (other than a special school) or an alternative provision academy that is not an independent educational institution: s 87(2) (amended by SI 2012/976). The Equality Act 2010 s 87(1), (2) does not apply in the case of a school in Wales: s 87(A1) (added by the School Standards and Organisation (Wales) Act 2013 Sch 5 para 11(2)). For provisions specifically about Wales see the Equality Act 2010 s 87(3), (4) (added by the School Standards and Organisation (Wales) Act 2013 Sch 5 para 11(3)). As to the meaning of 'Wales' see PARA 7 note 3.

30 See the Equality Act 2010 s 89(2).

10. Single-sex schools turning co-educational. If the responsible body[1] of a single-sex school[2] decides to alter its admissions arrangements so that the school will cease to be a single-sex school, the body may apply for a transitional exemption order in relation to the school[3]. If the responsible body of a school (other than a single-sex school) which has some pupils[4] as boarders and others as non-boarders and which admits as boarders pupils of one sex only[5] decides to alter its admissions arrangements so that the school will cease to be such a school, the body may apply for a transitional exemption order in relation to the school[6].

A 'transitional exemption order' in relation to a school is an order which, during the period specified in the order as the transitional period, authorises[7]:

(1)   sex discrimination[8] by the responsible body of the school in the arrangements it makes for deciding who is offered admission as a pupil[9];

(2)   the responsible body, in the circumstances specified in the order, not to admit a person as a pupil because of the person's sex[10].

The responsible body of a school does not contravene the Equality Act 2010, so far as relating to sex discrimination, if in accordance with a transitional exemption order[11], or pending the determination of an application for a transitional exemption order in relation to the school[12], it does not admit a person as a pupil because of the person's sex[13].

1   As to the meaning of 'responsible body' see PARA 9 note 1.
2   As to the meaning of 'single-sex school' see PARA 9 note 2.
3   Equality Act 2010 Sch 11 para 3(1).
4   As to the meaning of 'pupil' see PARA 20 note 4 (definition applied by the Equality Act 2010 s 212(1)).
5   Ie a school to which the Equality Act 2010 Sch 11 para 2 applies: see PARA 9 note 2.
6   Equality Act 2010 Sch 11 para 3(2).
7   The Equality Act 2010 Sch 11 para 4 applies in relation to the making of transitional exemption orders: Sch 11 para 3(4). In the case of a maintained school within the meaning given by the Education and Inspections Act 2006 s 32 (see PARA 110 note 1), a transitional exemption order may be made in accordance with such provision as is made in regulations under s 21 of that Act (orders made by local authority or adjudicator in relation to schools in England: see PARA 133): Equality Act 2010 Sch 11 para 4(1). In the case of a school in Wales maintained by a local authority, a transitional exemption order may be made in accordance with the School Standards and Organisation (Wales) Act 2013 s 82 (see PARA 140) or Sch 3 Pt 3 (transitional exemption orders for purposes of Equality Act 2010): Equality Act 2010 Sch 11 para 4(2) (amended by the School Standards and Organisation (Wales) Act 2013 Sch 5 para 28). In the case of a school in England or Wales not coming within the Equality Act 2010 Sch 11 para 4(1), (2) or (4) the responsible body may submit to the Commission for Equality and Human Rights an application for the making of a transitional exemption order (Sch 11 para 4(6)(a)), and the Commission may make the order (Sch 11 para 4(6)(b)). An application under Sch 11 para 4(6) must specify: (1) the period proposed by the responsible body as the transitional period to be specified in the order (Sch 11 para 4(7)(a)); (2) the stages within that period by which the body proposes to move to the position where s 85(1)(a) and (c) (see PARA 9), so far as relating to sex, is complied with (Sch 11 para 4(7)(b)); and (3) any other matters relevant to the terms and operation of the order applied for (Sch 11 para 4(7)(c)). The Commission must not make an order on such an application unless satisfied that the terms of the application are reasonable, having regard to the nature of the school's premises (Sch 11 para 4(8)(a)), the accommodation, equipment and facilities available (Sch 11 para 4(8)(b)), and the responsible body's financial resources (Sch 11 para 4(8)(c)). As to the meanings of 'England' and 'Wales' see PARA 7 note 3. As to the Commission for Equality and Human Rights see DISCRIMINATION vol 33 (2013) PARA 30 et seq.
8   As to what amounts to sex discrimination see the Equality Act 2010 s 25(8); and DISCRIMINATION vol 33 (2013) PARA 70. As to the interpretation of terms used in relation to the protected characteristic of sex see s 11; and DISCRIMINATION vol 33 (2013) PARA 63.
9   Equality Act 2010 Sch 11 para 3(3)(a).
10   Equality Act 2010 Sch 11 para 3(3)(b).

11 Equality Act 2010 Sch 11 para 3(5)(a).
12 Equality Act 2010 Sch 11 para 3(5)(b).
13 Equality Act 2010 Sch 11 para 3(5).

11.   Accessibility strategies and plans for schools. A local authority[1] must, in relation to schools for which it is the responsible body[2], prepare an accessibility strategy[3] and further such strategies at such times as may be prescribed[4]. A local authority must implement its accessibility strategy[5].

The responsible body of a school must prepare an accessibility plan[6] and further such plans at such times as may be prescribed[7]. The responsible body must implement its accessibility plan[8].

If:

(1)   the appropriate authority[9] is satisfied (whether or not on a complaint) that a responsible body has acted or is proposing to act unreasonably in the discharge of a duty under the above provisions[10], or has failed to discharge such a duty[11];

(2)   the appropriate authority is satisfied (whether or not on a complaint) that a responsible body of a school (ie of a non-maintained special school[12], an academy school or an alternative provision academy[13]) has acted or is proposing to act unreasonably in the discharge of a duty the body has in relation to the provision to the authority of copies of the body's accessibility plan or the inspection of that plan[14], or has failed to discharge the duty[15];

(3)   a tribunal has made an order[16] in relation to a claim relating to a disabled pupil and the appropriate authority is satisfied (whether or not on a complaint) that the responsible body concerned has acted or is proposing to act unreasonably in complying with the order[17], or has failed to comply with the order[18],

the appropriate authority may give a responsible body such directions[19] as the authority thinks expedient as to the discharge by the body of the duty[20], or compliance by the body with the order[21]. A direction may be varied or revoked by the appropriate authority[22]; and may be enforced, on the application of the appropriate authority, by a mandatory order[23].

1   'Local authority' means, in relation to England, an English local authority, and, in relation to Wales, a Welsh local authority, within the meanings of the Education and Inspections Act 2006 s 162 (see PARA 26 notes 7, 8): Equality Act 2010 s 89(10). As to the meanings of 'England' and 'Wales' see PARA 7 note 3.

2   'Responsible body' means: (1) in relation to a maintained school or a maintained nursery school, the local authority or governing body (Equality Act 2010 Sch 10 para 6(5)(a)); (2) in relation to a pupil referral unit, the local authority (Sch 10 para 6(5)(b)); (3) in relation to an independent educational institution or an alternative provision academy that is not an independent educational institution, the proprietor (Sch 10 para 6(5)(c) (amended by SI 2012/976)); (4) in relation to a special school not maintained by a local authority, the proprietor (Equality Act 2010 Sch 10 para 6(5)(d)). 'Governing body', in relation to a maintained school, means the body corporate (constituted in accordance with regulations under the Education Act 2002 s 19: see PARAS 150, 195) which the school has as a result of that section: Equality Act 2010 Sch 10 para 6(6). As to the meaning of 'maintained school' see PARA 99; and as to the meaning of 'maintained nursery school' see PARA 99 note 4 (definitions applied by Sch 10 para 6(7)). As to pupil referral units see PARA 427 et seq. As to the meaning of 'independent educational institution' see PARA 382 (definition applied by s 89(6)). As to the meaning of 'proprietor' see PARA 51 note 4 (definition applied s 89(4)(a)). As to the meaning of 'special school' see PARA 1041 (definition applied by s 89(9)). As to alternative provision academies see PARA 346 note 14.

3   Equality Act 2010 Sch 10 para 1(1)(a). An 'accessibility strategy' is a strategy for, over a prescribed period: (1) increasing the extent to which disabled pupils can participate in the

schools' curriculums (Sch 10 para 1(2)(a)); (2) improving the physical environment of the schools for the purpose of increasing the extent to which disabled pupils are able to take advantage of education and benefits, facilities or services provided or offered by the schools (Sch 10 para 1(2)(b)); (3) improving the delivery to disabled pupils of information which is readily accessible to pupils who are not disabled (Sch 10 para 1(2)(c)). The delivery in head (3) must be within a reasonable time (Sch 10 para 1(3)(a)) and in ways which are determined after taking account of the pupils' disabilities and any preferences expressed by them or their parents (Sch 10 para 1(3)(b)). An accessibility strategy must be in writing: Sch 10 para 1(4). As to the meaning of 'writing' see PARA 76 note 8. 'Disabled pupil' includes a disabled person who may be admitted to the school as a pupil: Sch 10 para 6(4). Regulations may prescribe services which are, or are not, to be regarded as being (a) education (Sch 10 para 6(2)(a)); (b) a benefit, facility or service (Sch 10 para 6(2)(b)). The power to make regulations under Sch 10 is exercisable by, in relation to England, a Minister of the Crown, and, in relation to Wales, the Welsh Ministers: Sch 10 para 6(3). As to ministers of the Crown see CONSTITUTIONAL AND ADMINISTRATIVE LAW vol 20 (2014) PARA 151. As to the Welsh Ministers see PARA 59. At the date at which this volume states the law no such regulations had been made.

In preparing its accessibility strategy, a local authority must have regard to the need to allocate adequate resources for implementing the strategy (Sch 10 para 2(1)(a)) and to guidance issued, for England, by a Minister of the Crown, for Wales, by the Welsh Ministers, as the content of an accessibility strategy, the form in which it is to be produced, and persons to be consulted in its preparation (see Sch 10 para 2(1)(b), (3), (4)). A local authority must, if asked, make a copy of its accessibility strategy available for inspection at such reasonable times as it decides: Sch 10 para 2(5). A local authority in England must, if asked by a Minister of the Crown, give the Minister a copy of its accessibility strategy: Sch 10 para 2(6). A local authority in Wales must, if asked by the Welsh Ministers, give them a copy of its accessibility strategy: Sch 10 para 2(7). A local authority must keep its accessibility strategy under review during the period to which it relates and, if necessary, revise it: Sch 10 para 1(6).

4   Equality Act 2010 Sch 10 para 1(1)(b). 'Prescribed' means prescribed by regulations: s 212(1). As to the prescribed times see the Disability Discrimination (Prescribed Periods for Accessibility Strategies and Plans for Schools) (Wales) Regulations 2003, SI 2003/2531; Disability Discrimination (Prescribed Times and Periods for Accessibility Strategies and Plans for Schools) (England) Regulations 2005, SI 2005/3221, both of which have effect by virtue of the Equality Act 2010 (Commencement No 4, Savings, Consequential, Transitional, Transitory and Incidental Provisions and Revocation) Order 2010, SI 2010/2317, art 21(1), Sch 7, as if made under the Equality Act 2010 Sch 10.

5   Equality Act 2010 Sch 10 para 1(5). The authority must have regard to guidance issued, for England, by a Minister of the Crown, and, for Wales, by the Welsh Ministers, as to compliance with Sch 10 para 1(5): Sch 10 para 2(2), (4).

6   Equality Act 2010 Sch 10 para 3(1)(a). An 'accessibility plan' is a plan for, over a prescribed period: (1) increasing the extent to which disabled pupils can participate in the school's curriculum (Sch 10 para 3(2)(a)); (2) improving the physical environment of the school for the purpose of increasing the extent to which disabled pupils are able to take advantage of education and benefits, facilities or services provided or offered by the school (Sch 10 para 3(2)(b)); and (3) improving the delivery to disabled pupils of information which is readily accessible to pupils who are not disabled (Sch 10 para 3(2)(c)). The delivery in head (3) above must be within a reasonable time (Sch 10 para 3(3)(a)) and in ways which are determined after taking account of the pupils' disabilities and any preferences expressed by them or their parents (Sch 10 para 3(3)(b)). An accessibility plan must be in writing: Sch 10 para 3(4). The responsible body must keep its accessibility plan under review during the period to which it relates and, if necessary, revise it: Sch 10 para 3(5).

In preparing an accessibility plan, the responsible body must have regard to the need to allocate adequate resources for implementing the plan: Sch 10 para 4(1). The proprietor of an independent educational institution (other than an academy) must, if asked, make a copy of the school's accessibility plan available for inspection at such reasonable times as the proprietor decides: Sch 10 para 4(2). The proprietor of an independent educational institution in England (other than an academy) must, if asked by a Minister of the Crown, give the Minister a copy of the school's accessibility plan: Sch 10 para 4(3). The proprietor of an independent school in Wales (other than an academy) must, if asked by the Welsh Ministers, give them a copy of the school's accessibility plan: Sch 10 para 4(4). As to academies see PARA 345 et seq.

7   Equality Act 2010 Sch 10 para 3(1)(b). As to the regulations made see note 4.

8   Equality Act 2010 Sch 10 para 3(6). A relevant inspection may extend to the performance by the responsible body of its functions in relation to the preparation, publication, review, revision and implementation of its accessibility plan: Sch 10 para 3(7). A 'relevant inspection' is an inspection

under the Education Act 2005 Pt 1 (ss 5–63) (see PARA 1162 et seq), or the Education and Skills Act 2008 Pt 4 Ch 1 (ss 92–141) (regulation and inspection of independent education provision in England: see PARA 382 et seq): Equality Act 2010 Sch 10 para 3(8).

9 The appropriate authority is, in relation to the responsible body of a school in England, the Secretary of State; and, in relation to the responsible body of a school in Wales, the Welsh Ministers: Equality Act 2010 Sch 10 para 5(10). As to the Secretary of State see PARA 58.

10 Equality Act 2010 Sch 10 para 5(1)(a).

11 Equality Act 2010 Sch 10 para 5(1)(b).

12 Ie a school approved under the Education Act 1996 s 342 (see PARA 1042): Equality Act 2010 Sch 10 para 5(3)(a).

13 Equality Act 2010 Sch 10 para 5(3)(b), (c) (Sch 10 para 5(3)b) substituted and Sch 10 para 5(3)(c) added by the Education Act 2011 Sch 13 para 20(1), (3)). As to academy schools see PARA 346 note 12.

14 Equality Act 2010 Sch 10 para 5(2)(a).

15 Equality Act 2010 Sch 10 para 5(2)(b).

16 Ie under the Equality Act 2010 Sch 17 para 5: see PARA 12.

17 Equality Act 2010 Sch 10 para 5(4)(a).

18 Equality Act 2010 Sch 10 para 5(4)(b).

19 A direction may be given in relation to the Equality Act 2010 Sch 10 para 5(1) or (2) (see heads (1) and (2) in the text) even if the performance of the duty is contingent on the opinion of the responsible body: Sch 10 para 5(6). A direction may not be given to the responsible body of a school in England in respect of a matter:

   (1) that has been complained about to a Local Commissioner in accordance with the Apprenticeships, Skills, Children and Learning Act 2009 Pt 10 Ch 2 (ss 206–224) (parental complaints against governing bodies etc) (repealed) (Equality Act 2010 Sch 10 para 5(7)(a)); or

   (2) that the appropriate authority thinks could have been so complained about (Sch 10 para 5(7)(b)),

   unless the Local Commissioner has made a recommendation to the responsible body under the Apprenticeships, Skills, Children and Learning Act 2009 s 211(4) (statement following investigation) (repealed) in respect of the matter (Equality Act 2010 Sch 10 para 5(8)(a)), and the responsible body has not complied with the recommendation (Sch 10 para 5(8)(b)).

20 Equality Act 2010 Sch 10 para 5(5)(a).

21 Equality Act 2010 Sch 10 para 5(5)(b).

22 Equality Act 2010 Sch 10 para 5(9)(a).

23 Equality Act 2010 Sch 10 para 5(9)(b). The mandatory order referred to is one obtained in accordance with the Senior Courts Act 1981 s 31 (see JUDICIAL REVIEW vol 61 (2010) PARA 703): see the Equality Act 2010 Sch 10 para 5(9)(b).

12. Claim as to contravention of duty not to discriminate because of a person's disability. A claim that a responsible body[1] has contravened the duty not to discriminate in the provision of education at schools[2] because of a person's disability[3] may be made to the English tribunal[4] by the person's parent or, if the person is over compulsory school age, the person or to the Welsh Tribunal by the person's parent[5]. Proceedings on a claim may not be brought after the end of the period of six months[6] starting with the date when the conduct complained of occurred[7].

If the tribunal finds that the contravention has occurred[8] it may make such order as it thinks fit[9]. This power may, in particular, be exercised with a view to obviating or reducing the adverse effect on the person of any matter to which the claim relates[10], but does not include power to order the payment of compensation[11].

If appeal arrangements[12] have been made in relation to admissions decisions[13] a claim that a responsible body has, because of a person's disability, contravened the duty not to discriminate in the provision of education at schools[14] in respect of an admissions decision must be made under the appeal arrangements[15]. The body hearing the claim has the powers it has in relation to an appeal under the appeal arrangements[16].

If appeal arrangements[17] have been made in relation to exclusion decisions that are made in relation to schools in Wales[18] a claim that a responsible body[19] has, because of a person's disability, contravened the duty not to discriminate in the provision of education at schools[20] in respect of an exclusion decision must be made under the appeal arrangements[21]. The body hearing the claim has the powers it has in relation to an appeal under the appeal arrangements[22].

1   As to the meaning of 'responsible body' see PARA 9 note 1 (definition applied by the Equality Act 2010 Sch 17 para 1).

2   Ie has contravened the Equality Act 2010 Pt 6 Ch 1 (ss 84–89): see PARAS 9–11.

3   As to the interpretation of terms used in relation to the protected characteristic of disability, see the Equality Act 2010 s 6, Sch 1; and DISCRIMINATION vol 33 (2013) PARA 50 et seq.

4   'The tribunal' means, in relation to a school in England, the First-tier Tribunal; and, in relation to a school in Wales, the Special Educational Needs Tribunal for Wales: Equality Act 2010 Sch 17 para 1. As to the First-tier Tribunal see COURTS AND TRIBUNALS vol 24 (2010) PARA 874 et seq. As to the Special Educational Needs Tribunal for Wales see PARA 1034. As to the meanings of 'England' and 'Wales' see PARA 7 note 3.

    In relation to the Special Educational Needs Tribunal for Wales the Welsh Ministers may by regulations make provision as to the proceedings on a claim under the Equality Act 2010 Sch 17 para 3 or 3A (Sch 17 para 6(1), (2)(a) (amended by the Education (Wales) Measure 2009 s 11(1), (2)(a)) and the making of a claim (Equality Act 2010 Sch 17 para 6(1), (2)(b)). The regulations may, in particular, include provision: (1) as to the manner in which a claim must be made (Sch 17 para 6(3)(a)); (2) for enabling functions relating to preliminary or incidental matters (including in particular a decision under Sch 17 para 4(3) (see note 6) to be performed by the President or by the person occupying the chair) (Sch 17 para 6(3)(b)); (3) enabling hearings to be conducted in the absence of a member other than the person occupying the chair (Sch 17 para 6(3)(c)); (4) for adding and substituting parties (Sch 17 para 6(3)(ca) (added by the Education (Wales) Measure 2009 s 11(1), (2)(b)); (5) as to persons who may appear on behalf of the parties (Equality Act 2010 Sch 17 para 6(3)(d)); (6) for granting such rights to disclosure or inspection of documents or to further particulars as may be granted by the county court (Sch 17 para 6(3)(e)); (7) requiring persons to attend to give evidence and produce documents (Sch 17 para 6(3)(f)); (8) for authorising the administration of oaths to witnesses (Sch 17 para 6(3)(g)); (9) for deciding claims without a hearing in prescribed circumstances (Sch 17 para 6(3)(h)); (10) as to the withdrawal of claims (Sch 17 para 6(3)(i)); (11) for enabling the tribunal to stay proceedings (Sch 17 para 6(3)(j)); (12) for the award of costs or expenses (Sch 17 para 6(3)(k)); (13) for settling costs or expenses (and, in particular, for enabling costs to be assessed in the county court) (Sch 17 para 6(3)(l)); (14) for the registration and proof of decisions and orders (Sch 17 para 6(3)(m)); (15) for enabling prescribed decisions to be reviewed, or prescribed orders to be varied or revoked, in such circumstances as may be decided in accordance with the regulations (Sch 17 para 6(3)(n)). Proceedings must be held in private, except in prescribed circumstances: Sch 17 para 6(4). The Welsh Ministers may pay such allowances for the purpose of or in connection with the attendance of persons at the tribunal as they may decide: Sch 17 para 6(5). The Arbitration Act 1996 Pt I (ss 1–84) (see ARBITRATION vol 2 (2008) PARA 1209 et seq) does not apply to the proceedings, but regulations may make provision in relation to such proceedings that corresponds to a provision of that Part: Equality Act 2010 Sch 17 para 6(6). The regulations may make provision for a claim to be heard, in prescribed circumstances, with an appeal under the Education Act 1996 Pt IV (ss 311A–349) (special educational needs: see s 332ZA; and PARA 999 et seq) (Part IV only applies in relation to Wales and in relation to England see now the Children and Families Act 2014 Pt 3 (ss 19–83); and PARA 950 et seq): Equality Act 2010 Sch 17 para 6(7). A person commits an offence by failing to comply with (a) a requirement in respect of the disclosure or inspection of documents imposed by virtue of Sch 17 para 6(3)(e) (see head (6) above); or (b) a requirement imposed by virtue of Sch 17 para 6(3)(f) (see head (7) above): Sch 17 para 6(8). A person guilty of the offence is liable on summary conviction to a fine not exceeding level 3 on the standard scale: Sch 17 para 6(9). As to the standard scale see SENTENCING AND DISPOSITION OF OFFENDERS vol 92 (2010) PARA 142. As to the Welsh Ministers see PARA 59. In regard to Wales the provisions of Sch 17 paras 6A–6E (added by the Education (Wales) Measure 2009 ss 12–16) deal with case friends (Equality Act 2010 Sch 17 para 6A); advice and information (Sch 17 para 6B); resolution of disputes (Sch 17 para 6C); independent advocacy services (Sch 17 para 6D) and power of direction (Sch 17 para 6E). As to regulations made see the Special Educational Needs Tribunal for Wales Regulations 2012, SI 2012/322 (made under the Equality Act 2010 Sch 17 paras 6(1)–(5), (7), 6A).

5 Equality Act 2010 Sch 17 para 3 (amended by the Children and Families Act 2014 s 60). As to jurisdiction in Wales see the Equality Act 2010 Sch 17 para 3A (added by the Education (Wales) Measure 2009, s 9(1), (3)) As to the meaning of 'parent' see PARA 7 note 6 (definition applied by the Equality Act 2010 s 212(1)). In relation to any such proceedings, if there are facts from which the tribunal could decide, in the absence of any other explanation, that a person (A) contravened the provision concerned, the tribunal must hold that the contravention occurred: see s 136(1), (2), (6)(d), (e). But this does not apply if A shows that A did not contravene the provision: s 136(3).

6 If, in relation to proceedings or prospective proceedings on a claim under the Equality Act 2010 Sch 17 para 3 or 3A (see note 5), the dispute is referred for resolution in pursuance of arrangements under Sch 17 para 6C (see note 4) before the end of the period of six months mentioned in Sch 17 para 4(1), that period is extended by three months: Sch 17 para 4(2A) (added by the Education (Wales) Measure 2009 s 10). The tribunal may consider a claim which is out of time (Equality Act 2010 Sch 17 para 4(3)) but this does not apply if the tribunal has previously decided under Sch 17 para 4(3) not to consider a claim (Sch 17 para 4(4)). As to the meaning of 'month' see PARA 54 note 26.

7 Equality Act 2010 Sch 17 para 4(1). For these purposes: (1) if the contravention is attributable to a term in a contract, the conduct is to be treated as extending throughout the duration of the contract (Sch 17 para 4(5)(a)); (2) conduct extending over a period is to be treated as occurring at the end of the period (Sch 17 para 4(5)(b)); (3) failure to do something is to be treated as occurring when the person in question decided on it (Sch 17 para 4(5)(c)). In the absence of evidence to the contrary, a person (P) is to be taken to decide on failure to do something (a) when P acts inconsistently with doing it (Sch 17 para 4(6)(a)); or (b) if P does not act inconsistently, on the expiry of the period in which P might reasonably have been expected to do it (Sch 17 para 4(6)(b)).

8 Equality Act 2010 Sch 17 para 5(1).

9 Equality Act 2010 Sch 17 para 5(2).

10 Equality Act 2010 Sch 17 para 5(3)(a).

11 Equality Act 2010 Sch 17 para 5(3)(b).

12 'Appeal arrangements' are arrangements under the School Standards and Framework Act 1998 s 94 (see PARA 251), or academy arrangements (as defined in the Academies Act 2010 s 1: see PARA 346) between the responsible body for an academy and the Secretary of State, enabling an appeal to be made by the person's parent against the decision: Equality Act 2010 Sch 17 para 13(4) (amended by the Education Act 2011 Sch 15 para 2).

13 Equality Act 2010 Sch 17 para 13(1). An 'admissions decision' is a decision of a kind mentioned in the School Standards and Framework Act 1998 s 94(1) or (2) (see PARA 251), or a decision as to the admission of a person to an academy school or an alternative provision academy taken by the responsible body or on its behalf: Equality Act 2010 Sch 17 para 13(5) (amended by the Education Act 2011 para 20(4). See PARA 346.

14 Ie has contravened the Equality Act 2010 Pt 6 Ch 1 (ss 84–89): see PARA 9.

15 Equality Act 2010 Sch 17 para 13(2).

16 Equality Act 2010 Sch 17 para 13(3).

17 'Appeal arrangements' are arrangements under the Education Act 2002 s 52(3) (see PARA 63) enabling an appeal to be made against an exclusion decision: Equality Act 2010 Sch 17 para 14(4) (substituted by the Education Act 2011 Sch 1 paras 11, 13(b)). Appeals are now more commonly called 'reviews'. As to reviews of exclusions see PARA 531 et seq.

18 Equality Act 2010 Sch 17 para 14(1) (amended by the Education Act 2011 Sch 1 paras 11, 13(a)). An 'exclusion decision' is a decision of a kind mentioned in the Education Act 2002 s 52(3) (see PARA 517): Equality Act 2010 Sch 17 para 14(5) (amended by the Education Act 2011 Sch 1 paras 11, 13(c)).

19 'Responsible body', in relation to a maintained school, includes the discipline committee of the governing body if that committee is required to be established as a result of regulations made under the Education Act 2002 s 19 (see PARAS 150, 195): Equality Act 2010 Sch 17 para 14(6). As to the meaning of 'maintained school' see PARA 99 (definition applied by Sch 17 para 14(7)).

20 Ie has contravened the Equality Act 2010 Pt 6 Ch 1 (ss 84–89): see PARA 9.

21 Equality Act 2010 Sch 17 para 14(2). This is a complex area where a parent may have a claim challenging a child's exclusion to a review panel (or independent review panel (IRP)) but also may bring a disability discrimination claim to the First-Tier Tribunal. In terms of timing the two remedies interrelate, and the IRP must address discrimination if it comes in front of it: generally see the guidance on exclusions; and PARA 540. As to the First-Tier Tribunal see COURTS AND TRIBUNALS vol 24 (2010) PARA 876 et seq.

22 Equality Act 2010 Sch 17 para 14(3).

B. EQUALITY DUTIES IN RELATION TO FURTHER AND HIGHER EDUCATION

13. Duty not to discriminate in the provision of further and higher education.
The responsible body[1] of a university, any other institution within the higher education sector, or an institution within the further education sector must not discriminate[2] against:

(1) a person in the arrangements it makes for deciding who is offered admission as a student[3];

(2) a person as to the terms on which it offers to admit the person as a student[4];

(3) a person by not admitting the person as a student[5];

(4) a student in the way it provides education for the student[6];

(5) a student in the way it affords the student access to a benefit, facility or service[7];

(6) a student by not providing education for the student[8];

(7) a student by not affording the student access to a benefit, facility or service[9];

(8) a student by excluding the student[10];

(9) a student by subjecting the student to any other detriment[11].

The responsible body of such an institution must not discriminate[12] against a disabled person[13]: (a) in the arrangements it makes for deciding upon whom to confer a qualification[14]; (b) as to the terms on which it is prepared to confer a qualification on the person[15]; (c) by not conferring a qualification on the person[16]; (d) by withdrawing a qualification from the person or varying the terms on which the person holds it[17].

The responsible body of such an institution must not harass[18] a student[19], a person who has applied for admission as a student[20], or a disabled person who holds or has applied for a qualification conferred by the institution[21].

The responsible body of such an institution must not victimise[22]:

(i) a person in the arrangements it makes for deciding who is offered admission as a student[23];

(ii) a person as to the terms on which it offers to admit the person as a student[24];

(iii) a person by not admitting the person as a student[25];

(iv) a student in the way it provides education for the student[26];

(v) a student in the way it affords the student access to a benefit, facility or service[27];

(vi) a student by not providing education for the student[28];

(vii) a student by not affording the student access to a benefit, facility or service[29];

(viii) a student by excluding the student[30];

(ix) a student by subjecting the student to any other detriment[31].

The responsible body of such an institution must not victimise a disabled person: (A) in the arrangements it makes for deciding upon whom to confer a qualification[32]; (B) as to the terms on which it is prepared to confer a qualification on the person[33]; (C) by not conferring a qualification on the person[34]; (D) by withdrawing a qualification from the person or varying the terms on which the person holds it[35].

A duty to make reasonable adjustments applies to the responsible body of such an institution[36].

Nothing in the above provisions applies to anything done in connection with the content of the curriculum[37].

1 A 'responsible body' is: (1) in the case of a university, any other institution within the higher education sector, or an institution within the further education sector, the governing body (Equality Act 2010 s 91(12)(a)); (2) in the case of an institution within s 91(10)(d) (see DISCRIMINATION vol 33 (2013) PARA 175) (ie a 16 to 19 academy: see PARA 346 note 13), the proprietor (within the meaning of the Education Act 1996: see PARA 51 note 4) (Equality Act 2010 s 91(12)(aa) (added by the Education Act 2011 Sch 13 para 20(2)(b)); (3) in the case of a college of further education under the management of a board of management, the board of management (Equality Act 2010 s 91(12)(c)); (4) in the case of any other college of further education, any board of governors of the college or any person responsible for the management of the college, whether or not formally constituted as a governing body or board of governors (s 91(12)(d)). A reference to a university includes a reference to a university college and a college, school or hall of a university: s 94(4). A reference to an institution within the further or higher education sector is to be construed in accordance with the Further and Higher Education Act 1992 s 91 (see PARAS 555, 619): Equality Act 2010 s 94(5). As to the meaning of 'person' see PARA 7 note 6. As to universities generally see PARA 811 et seq.

2 As to what amounts to discrimination see the Equality Act 2010 ss 13–19; and DISCRIMINATION vol 33 (2013) PARA 65 et seq. The Equality Act 2010 Pt 6 Ch 2 (ss 90–94) does not apply to the protected characteristic of marriage and civil partnership: s 90. As to the interpretation of terms used in relation to the protected characteristic of marriage and civil partnership see s 8; and DISCRIMINATION vol 33 (2013) PARA 60.

Section 91(1), so far as relating to sex, does not apply in relation to a single-sex institution: Sch 12 para 1(1). A 'single-sex institution' is a university, any other institution within the higher education sector, or an institution within the further education sector which (1) admits students of one sex only (Sch 12 para 1(2)(a)); or (2) on the basis of the assumption in Sch 12 para 1(3), would be taken to admit students of one sex only (Sch 12 para 1(2)(b)). That assumption is that students of the opposite sex are to be disregarded if (a) their admission to the institution is exceptional (Sch 12 para 1(3)(a)); or (b) their numbers are comparatively small and their admission is confined to particular courses or classes (Sch 12 para 1(3)(b)). In the case of an institution which is a single-sex institution by virtue of Sch 12 para 1(3)(b), s 91(2)(a)–(d) (see heads (4)–(7) in the text), so far as relating to sex, does not prohibit confining students of the same sex to particular courses or classes: Sch 12 para 1(4). As to the interpretation of terms used in relation to the protected characteristic of sex see s 11; and DISCRIMINATION vol 33 (2013) PARA 63. As to applications for a transitional exemption order by the responsible body of a single-sex institution which decides to alter its admissions arrangements so that the institution will cease to be a single-sex institution see PARA 14.

A person (P) does not contravene s 91(1) or (2) if P shows that P's treatment of another person relates only to training that would help fit that other person for work the offer of which the other person could be refused in reliance on Sch 9 Pt 1 (see DISCRIMINATION vol 33 (2013) PARAS 111 et seq, 153 et seq): Sch 12 para 4.

The responsible body of an institution which is designated for these purposes does not contravene s 91(1), so far as relating to religion or belief, if, in the admission of students to a course at the institution it gives preference to persons of a particular religion or belief (Sch 12 para 5(1)(a)), it does so to preserve the institution's religious ethos (Sch 12 para 5(1)(b)), and the course is not a course of vocational training (Sch 12 para 5(1)(c)). A Minister of the Crown may by order designate an institution if satisfied that the institution has a religious ethos: Sch 12 para 5(2). As to ministers of the Crown see CONSTITUTIONAL AND ADMINISTRATIVE LAW vol 20 (2014) PARA 151. As to the order made see the Equality Act 2010 (Designation of Institutions with a Religious Ethos) (England and Wales) Order 2010, SI 2010/1915. As to the interpretation of terms used in relation to the protected characteristic of religion or belief see the Equality Act 2010 s 10; and DISCRIMINATION vol 33 (2013) PARA 62.

3 Equality Act 2010 s 91(1)(a). A reference to a student, in relation to an institution, is a reference to a person for whom education is provided by the institution: s 94(3).

4 Equality Act 2010 s 91(1)(b).

5 Equality Act 2010 s 91(1)(c).

6 Equality Act 2010 s 91(2)(a). See also note 2.

7 Equality Act 2010 s 91(2)(b). See also note 2. A reference (however expressed) to providing or affording access to a benefit, facility or service includes a reference to facilitating access to the benefit, facility or service: s 212(4). A person does not contravene s 91, so far as relating to sexual orientation, by providing married persons and civil partners (to the exclusion of all other persons) with access to a benefit, facility or service: Sch 12 para 6. As to the interpretation of terms used in relation to the protected characteristic of sexual orientation see s 12; and DISCRIMINATION vol 33 (2013) PARA 64.

A person does not contravene s 91(2)(b) or (d) (see the text to note 9), so far as relating to age, only by providing, or making arrangements for or facilitating the provision of, care for children of a particular age group: Sch 12 para 7(1). Facilitating the provision of care for a child includes: (1) paying for some or all of the cost of the provision (Sch 12 para 7(2)(a)); (2) helping a parent of the child to find a suitable person to provide care for the child (Sch 12 para 7(2)(b)); (3) enabling a parent of the child to spend more time providing care for the child or otherwise assisting the parent with respect to the care that the parent provides for the child (Sch 12 para 7(2)(c)). A child is a person who has not attained the age of 17: Sch 12 para 7(3). A reference to care includes a reference to supervision: Sch 12 para 7(4). As to the time at which a person attains a particular age see PARA 7 note 6. As to the meaning of 'parent' see PARA 7 note 6 (definition applied by s 212(1)). As to the interpretation of terms used in relation to the protected characteristic of age see s 5; and DISCRIMINATION vol 33 (2013) PARA 49.

8   Equality Act 2010 s 91(2)(c). See also note 2.
9   Equality Act 2010 s 91(2)(d). See also notes 2, 7.
10 Equality Act 2010 s 91(2)(e).
11 Equality Act 2010 s 91(2)(f). 'Detriment' does not, subject to s 212(5), include conduct which amounts to harassment: s 212(1). Where the Equality Act 2010 disapplies a prohibition on harassment in relation to a specified protected characteristic, the disapplication does not prevent conduct relating to that characteristic from amounting to a detriment for the purposes of discrimination within s 13 (see DISCRIMINATION vol 33 (2013) PARAS 65–66) because of that characteristic: s 212(5). The decision of a university leading to the exclusion of a pregnant student on academic grounds could not be equated with the dismissal of a pregnant employee for the purposes of the legislation prohibiting discrimination on the grounds of sex: see *R v South Bank University, ex p Coggeran* [2001] ELR 42, [2000] ICR 1342, CA (decided under the Sex Discrimination Act 1975 (repealed)).
12 The Equality Act 2010 s 91(3) applies only to disability discrimination: s 91(4). As to what amounts to disability discrimination see s 25(2); and DISCRIMINATION vol 33 (2013) PARA 83.
13 As to the interpretation of terms used in relation to the protected characteristic of disability see the Equality Act 2010 s 6; and DISCRIMINATION vol 33 (2013) PARAS 50–51.
14 Equality Act 2010 s 91(3)(a). A reference to conferring a qualification includes a reference: (1) to renewing or extending the conferment of a qualification; (2) to authenticating a qualification conferred by another person: s 94(11A) (added by SI 2010/2279).
15 Equality Act 2010 s 91(3)(b).
16 Equality Act 2010 s 91(3)(c).
17 Equality Act 2010 s 91(3)(d).
18 As to what amounts to harassment see the Equality Act 2010 s 26; and DISCRIMINATION vol 33 (2013) PARA 73.
19 Equality Act 2010 s 91(5)(a).
20 Equality Act 2010 s 91(5)(b).
21 Equality Act 2010 s 91(5)(c).
22 As to what amounts to victimisation see the Equality Act 2010 s 27; and DISCRIMINATION vol 33 (2013) PARA 75.
23 Equality Act 2010 s 91(6)(a).
24 Equality Act 2010 s 91(6)(b).
25 Equality Act 2010 s 91(6)(c).
26 Equality Act 2010 s 91(7)(a).
27 Equality Act 2010 s 91(7)(b). See also note 7.
28 Equality Act 2010 s 91(7)(c).
29 Equality Act 2010 s 91(7)(d). See also note 7.
30 Equality Act 2010 s 91(7)(e).
31 Equality Act 2010 s 91(7)(f).
32 Equality Act 2010 s 91(8)(a).
33 Equality Act 2010 s 91(8)(b).
34 Equality Act 2010 s 91(8)(c).
35 Equality Act 2010 s 91(8)(d).
36 Equality Act 2010 s 91(9). As to the general duty to make reasonable adjustments see s 20; and DISCRIMINATION vol 33 (2013) PARA 227 et seq. As to the reasonable adjustments with specific reference to further and higher education see s 98, Sch 13.
37 Equality Act 2010 s 94(2).

14.   Single-sex institutions turning co-educational.   If the responsible body[1] of a single-sex institution[2] decides to alter its admissions arrangements so that the institution will cease to be a single-sex institution, the body may apply for a transitional exemption order in relation to the institution[3]. A 'transitional exemption order' relating to an institution is an order which, during the period specified in the order as the transitional period, authorises[4]:

(1) sex discrimination[5] by the responsible body of the institution in the arrangements it makes for deciding who is offered admission as a student[6];

(2) the responsible body, in the circumstances specified in the order, not to admit a person as a student because of the person's sex[7].

The responsible body of an institution does not contravene the Equality Act 2010, so far as relating to sex discrimination, if in accordance with a transitional exemption order[8], or pending the determination of an application for a transitional exemption order in relation to the institution[9]: (a) it does not admit a person as a student because of the person's sex[10]; or (b) it discriminates in the arrangements it makes for deciding who is offered admission as a student[11].

1   As to the meaning of 'responsible body' see PARA 13 note 1.
2   As to the meaning of 'single-sex institution' see PARA 13 note 2.
3   Equality Act 2010 Sch 12 para 2(1).
4   The Equality Act 2010 Sch 12 para 3 applies in relation to the making of a transitional exemption order: Sch 12 para 2(3). In the case of a single-sex institution its responsible body may submit to the Commission for Equality and Human Rights an application for the making of a transitional exemption order (Sch 12 para 3(1)(a)), and the Commission may make the order (Sch 12 para 3(1)(b)). The application must specify: (1) the period proposed by the responsible body as the transitional period to be specified in the order (Sch 12 para 3(2)(a)); (2) the stages, within that period, by which the body proposes to move to the position where s 91(1)(a) and (c) (see PARA 13), so far as relating to sex, is complied with (Sch 12 para 3(2)(b)); and (3) any other matters relevant to the terms and operation of the order applied for (Sch 12 para 3(2)(c)). The Commission must not make an order on such an application unless satisfied that the terms of the application are reasonable, having regard to: (a) the nature of the institution's premises (Sch 12 para 3(3)(a)); (b) the accommodation, equipment and facilities available (Sch 12 para 3(3)(b)); and (c) the responsible body's financial resources (Sch 12 para 3(3)(c)). As to the Commission for Equality and Human Rights see DISCRIMINATION vol 33 (2013) PARA 30 et seq.
5   As to what amounts to sex discrimination see the Equality Act 2010 s 25(8); and DISCRIMINATION vol 33 (2013) PARA 70. As to the interpretation of terms used in relation to the protected characteristic of sex see s 11; and DISCRIMINATION vol 33 (2013) PARA 63.
6   Equality Act 2010 Sch 12 para 2(2)(a). A reference to a student, in relation to an institution, is a reference to a person for whom education is provided by the institution: s 94(3).
7   Equality Act 2010 Sch 12 para 2(2)(b).
8   See the Equality Act 2010 Sch 12 para 2(4)(a), (5)(a).
9   See the Equality Act 2010 Sch 12 para 2(4)(b), (5)(b).
10 Equality Act 2010 Sch 12 para 2(4).
11 Equality Act 2010 Sch 12 para 2(5).

15.   Duty not to discriminate in the provision of further and higher education courses.   The responsible body[1], in relation to a course of further or higher education secured by a responsible body in England or Wales or a course of education provided[2] by the governing body of a maintained school, must not discriminate[3] against a person: (1) in the arrangements it makes for deciding who is enrolled[4] on the course[5]; (2) as to the terms on which it offers to enrol the person on the course[6]; (3) by not accepting the person's application for enrolment[7]. The responsible body in relation to such a course must not discriminate against a person who is enrolled on the course in the services it provides or offers to provide[8].

The responsible body in relation to such a course must not harass[9] a person who: (a) seeks enrolment on the course[10]; (b) is enrolled on the course[11]; (c) is a user of services provided by the body in relation to the course[12].

The responsible body in relation to such a course must not victimise[13] a person: (i) in the arrangements it makes for deciding who is enrolled on the course[14]; (ii) as to the terms on which it offers to enrol the person on the course[15]; (iii) by not accepting the person's application for enrolment[16]. The responsible body in relation to such a course must not victimise a person who is enrolled on the course in the services it provides or offers to provide[17].

A duty to make reasonable adjustments applies to the responsible body[18].

Nothing in the above provisions applies to anything done in connection with the content of the curriculum[19].

1   A 'responsible body' is: (1) a local authority in England or Wales, for the purposes of a course of further or higher education secured by it (see the Equality Act 2010 s 92(7)(a), (8)(a))); (2) the governing body of a maintained school, for the purposes of a course of education provided by it under the School Standards and Framework Act 1998 s 80 (see PARA 588) (see the Equality Act 2010 s 92(7)(b), (8)(b)). 'Local authority' means, in relation to England, an English local authority and, in relation to Wales, a Welsh local authority, within the meaning of the Education and Inspections Act 2006 s 162 (see PARA 26 notes 7, 8): s 94(10). 'Course', in relation to further education, includes each component part of a course if there is no requirement imposed on persons registered for a component part of the course to register for another component part of the course: s 92(9). As to the meaning of 'further education' see PARA 23 (definition applied by s 94(6)(a)). 'Higher education' means education provided by means of a course of a description mentioned in the Education Reform Act 1988 Sch 6 (see PARA 684): Equality Act 2010 s 94(7)(a). As to the meaning of 'maintained school' see PARA 99 (definition applied by s 92(9)).
2   Ie under the School Standards and Framework Act 1998 s 80: see PARA 588.
3   As to what amounts to discrimination see the Equality Act 2010 ss 13–19; and DISCRIMINATION vol 33 (2013) PARA 65 et seq. The Equality Act 2010 Pt 6 Ch 2 (ss 90–94) does not apply to the protected characteristic of marriage and civil partnership: s 90. As to the interpretation of terms used in relation to the protected characteristic of marriage and civil partnership see s 8; and DISCRIMINATION vol 33 (2013) PARA 60.
4   'Enrolment' includes registration for a component part of a course: Equality Act 2010 s 92(9).
5   Equality Act 2010 s 92(1)(a).
6   Equality Act 2010 s 92(1)(b).
7   Equality Act 2010 s 92(1)(c).
8   Equality Act 2010 s 92(2). 'Services' means services of any description which are provided wholly or mainly for persons enrolled on a course: s 92(9).
9   As to what amounts to harassment see the Equality Act 2010 s 26; and DISCRIMINATION vol 33 (2013) PARA 73.
10   Equality Act 2010 s 92(3)(a).
11   Equality Act 2010 s 92(3)(b).
12   Equality Act 2010 s 92(3)(c).
13   As to what amounts to victimisation see the Equality Act 2010 s 27; and DISCRIMINATION vol 33 (2013) PARA 75.
14   Equality Act 2010 s 92(4)(a).
15   Equality Act 2010 s 92(4)(b).
16   Equality Act 2010 s 92(4)(c).
17   Equality Act 2010 s 92(5).
18   Equality Act 2010 s 92(6). As to the general duty to make reasonable adjustments see s 20; and DISCRIMINATION vol 33 (2013) PARA 227 et seq. As to the reasonable adjustments with specific reference to further and higher education see s 98, Sch 13.
19   Equality Act 2010 s 94(2).

16.   Duty not to discriminate in the provision of recreational and training facilities. The responsible body[1] in relation to recreational and training facilities secured by that body[2] must not discriminate[3] against a person: (1) in the arrangements it makes for deciding who is provided with the facilities[4]; (2) as to the terms on which it offers to provide the facilities to the person[5]; (3) by not accepting the person's application for provision of the facilities[6]. The responsible body in relation to such facilities must not discriminate against a person who is provided with the facilities in the services it provides or offers to provide[7].

The responsible body in relation to such facilities must not harass[8] a person who: (a) seeks to have the facilities provided[9]; (b) is provided with the facilities[10]; (c) is a user of services provided by the body in relation to the facilities[11].

The responsible body in relation to such facilities must not victimise[12] a person: (i) in the arrangements it makes for deciding who is provided with the facilities[13]; (ii) as to the terms on which it offers to provide the facilities to the person[14]; (iii) by not accepting the person's application for provision of the facilities[15]. The responsible body in relation to such facilities must not victimise a person who is provided with the facilities in the services it provides or offers to provide[16].

A duty to make reasonable adjustments applies to the responsible body[17].

Nothing in the above provisions applies to anything done in connection with the content of the curriculum[18].

1 A 'responsible body' is: (1) a local authority in England for the purposes of facilities secured under the Education Act 1996 s 507A (see PARA 503) or s 507B (see PARA 504) (see the Equality Act 2010 s 93(7)(a), (8)(a)); (2) a local authority in Wales, for the purposes of facilities secured under the Education Act 1996 s 508 (see PARA 505) (see the Equality Act 2010 s 93(7)(b), (8)(b)). 'Local authority' means, in relation to England, an English local authority and, in relation to Wales, a Welsh local authority, within the meaning of the Education and Inspections Act 2006 s 162 (see PARA 26 notes 7, 8): s 94(10).

2 Ie facilities secured by a local authority in England under the Education Act 1996 s 507A (see PARA 503) or s 507B (see PARA 504), or facilities secured by a local authority in Wales under s 508 (see PARA 505): see the Equality Act 2010 s 93(1), (7)(a), (b).

3 As to what amounts to discrimination see the Equality Act 2010 ss 13–19; and DISCRIMINATION vol 33 (2013) PARA 65 et seq. The Equality Act 2010 Pt 6 Ch 2 (ss 90–94) does not apply to the protected characteristic of marriage and civil partnership (s 90); and s 93 does not apply to the protected characteristic of age, so far as relating to persons who have not attained the age of 18 (s 93(9)). As to the interpretation of terms used in relation to the protected characteristic of marriage and civil partnership see s 8; and DISCRIMINATION vol 33 (2013) PARA 60. As to the interpretation of terms used in relation to the protected characteristic of age see s 5; and DISCRIMINATION vol 33 (2013) PARA 49. As to the time at which a person attains a particular age see PARA 7 note 6.

4 Equality Act 2010 s 93(1)(a).

5 Equality Act 2010 s 93(1)(b).

6 Equality Act 2010 s 93(1)(c).

7 Equality Act 2010 s 93(2).

8 As to what amounts to harassment see the Equality Act 2010 s 26; and DISCRIMINATION vol 33 (2013) PARA 73.

9 Equality Act 2010 s 93(3)(a).

10 Equality Act 2010 s 93(3)(b).

11 Equality Act 2010 s 93(3)(c).

12 As to what amounts to victimisation see the Equality Act 2010 s 27; and DISCRIMINATION vol 33 (2013) PARA 75.

13 Equality Act 2010 s 93(4)(a).

14 Equality Act 2010 s 93(4)(b).

15 Equality Act 2010 s 93(4)(c).

16 Equality Act 2010 s 93(5).

17 Equality Act 2010 s 93(6). As to the general duty to make reasonable adjustments see s 20; and DISCRIMINATION vol 33 (2013) PARA 227 et seq. As to the reasonable adjustments with specific reference to further and higher education see s 98, Sch 13.

18 Equality Act 2010 s 94(2).

C. EQUALITY DUTIES IN RELATION TO QUALIFICATIONS BODIES

17. Duty of qualifications bodies not to discriminate in relation to the conferment of qualifications. A qualifications body[1] (A) must not discriminate[2] against a person (B): (1) in the arrangements A makes for deciding upon whom to confer a relevant qualification[3]; (2) as to the terms on which it is prepared to confer a relevant qualification on B[4]; (3) by not conferring a relevant qualification on B[5]. A qualifications body (A) must not discriminate against a person (B) upon whom A has conferred a relevant qualification: (a) by withdrawing the qualification from B[6]; (b) by varying the terms on which B holds the qualification[7]; (c) by subjecting B to any other detriment[8].

A qualifications body must not, in relation to conferment by it of a relevant qualification, harass[9] a person who holds the qualification[10], or a person who applies for it[11].

A qualifications body (A) must not victimise[12] a person (B): (i) in the arrangements A makes for deciding upon whom to confer a relevant qualification[13]; (ii) as to the terms on which it is prepared to confer a relevant qualification on B[14]; (iii) by not conferring a relevant qualification on B[15]. A qualifications body (A) must not victimise a person (B) upon whom A has conferred a relevant qualification: (A) by withdrawing the qualification from B[16]; (B) by varying the terms on which B holds the qualification[17]; (C) by subjecting B to any other detriment[18].

A duty to make reasonable adjustments[19] applies to a qualifications body[20].

1   A 'qualifications body' is an authority or body which can confer a relevant qualification: Equality Act 2010 s 97(1), (2). An authority or body is not a qualifications body in so far as: (1) it is the responsible body of a school to which s 85 (see PARA 9) applies (s 97(4)(a)); (2) it is the governing body of an institution to which s 91 (see PARA 13) applies (s 97(4)(b)); (3) it exercises functions under the Education Acts (s 97(4)(c)); or (4) it exercises functions under the Education (Scotland) Act 1980 (Equality Act 2010 s 97(4)(a)). As to the meaning of 'the Education Acts' see PARA 1 note 13 (definition applied by s 212(1)). A qualifications body does not include an authority or body of such description, or in such circumstances, as may be prescribed: s 97(5). 'Prescribed' means prescribed by regulations: s 212(1). At the date at which this volume states the law no regulations had been made under s 97(5). A 'relevant qualification' is an authorisation, qualification, approval or certification of such description as may be prescribed, in relation to conferments in England, by a minister of the Crown (s 97(3)(a)) and, in relation to conferments in Wales, by the Welsh Ministers (s 97(3)(b)). Section 96(11) (see note 20) applies for the purposes of s 97(3) as it applies for the purposes of s 96(10): s 97(8). A reference to conferring a relevant qualification includes a reference (a) to renewing or extending the conferment of a relevant qualification (s 97(6)(a)); (b) to authenticating a relevant qualification conferred by another person (s 97(6)(b)). At the date at which this volume states the law no regulations had been made under s 97(3). As to the meanings of 'England' and 'Wales' see PARA 7 note 3. As to ministers of the Crown see CONSTITUTIONAL AND ADMINISTRATIVE LAW vol 20 (2014) PARA 151. As to the Welsh Ministers see PARA 59.
2   As to what amounts to discrimination see the Equality Act 2010 ss 13–19; and DISCRIMINATION vol 33 (2013) PARA 65 et seq. The Equality Act 2010 Pt 6 Ch 3 (ss 95–97) does not apply to the protected characteristic of marriage and civil partnership: s 95. As to the interpretation of terms used in relation to the protected characteristic of marriage and civil partnership see s 8; and DISCRIMINATION vol 33 (2013) PARA 60.
3   Equality Act 2010 s 96(1)(a).
4   Equality Act 2010 s 96(1)(b).
5   Equality Act 2010 s 96(1)(c).
6   Equality Act 2010 s 96(2)(a).
7   Equality Act 2010 s 96(2)(b).
8   Equality Act 2010 s 96(2)(c).
9   As to what amounts to harassment see the Equality Act 2010 s 26; and DISCRIMINATION vol 33 (2013) PARA 73.
10 Equality Act 2010 s 96(3)(a).

11 Equality Act 2010 s 96(3)(b).
12 As to what amounts to victimisation see the Equality Act 2010 s 27; and DISCRIMINATION vol 33 (2013) PARA 75.
13 Equality Act 2010 s 96(4)(a).
14 Equality Act 2010 s 96(4)(b).
15 Equality Act 2010 s 96(4)(c).
16 Equality Act 2010 s 96(5)(a).
17 Equality Act 2010 s 96(5)(b).
18 Equality Act 2010 s 96(5)(c).
19 As to the general duty to make reasonable adjustments see the Equality Act 2010 s 20; and DISCRIMINATION vol 33 (2013) PARA 227 et seq. As to the reasonable adjustments with specific reference to qualifications bodies see s 98, Sch 13.
20 Equality Act 2010 s 96(6). Section 96(6) does not apply to the body in so far as the appropriate regulator specifies provisions, criteria or practices in relation to which the body: (1) is not subject to a duty to make reasonable adjustments (s 96(7)(a)); (2) is subject to a duty to make reasonable adjustments, but in relation to which such adjustments as the regulator specifies should not be made (s 96(7)(b)). For these purposes the appropriate regulator must have regard to (a) the need to minimise the extent to which disabled persons are disadvantaged in attaining the qualification because of their disabilities (s 96(8)(a)); (b) the need to secure that the qualification gives a reliable indication of the knowledge, skills and understanding of a person upon whom it is conferred (s 96(8)(b)); (c) the need to maintain public confidence in the qualification (s 96(8)(c)). The appropriate regulator must not specify any matter for the purposes of s 96(7) unless it has consulted such persons as it thinks appropriate (s 96(9)(a)); and must publish matters so specified (including the date from which they are to have effect) in such manner as is prescribed (s 96(9)(b)). The appropriate regulator is: (i) in relation to a qualifications body that confers qualifications in England, a person prescribed by a minister of the Crown (s 96(10)(a)); (ii) in relation to a qualifications body that confers qualifications in Wales, a person prescribed by the Welsh Ministers (s 96(10)(b)). For the purposes of s 96(10), a qualification is conferred in a part of Great Britain if there are, or may reasonably be expected to be, persons seeking to obtain the qualification who are or will be assessed for those purposes wholly or mainly in that part: s 96(11). A reference in s 96(8), (10) or (11) to a qualification is a reference to a relevant qualification: s 97(7). As to the regulations made under s 96 see the Equality Act 2010 (General Qualifications Bodies Regulator and Relevant Qualifications) (Wales) Regulations 2010, SI 2010/2217; and the Equality Act 2010 (General Qualifications Bodies) (Appropriate Regulator and Relevant Qualifications) Regulations 2010, SI 2010/2245. As to the interpretation of terms used in relation to the protected characteristic of disability, see s 6, Sch 1; and DISCRIMINATION vol 33 (2013) PARA 50 et seq. As to the meaning of 'person' see PARA 7 note 6.

(2) THE STATUTORY SYSTEM OF EDUCATION

18. The stages of education. The statutory system of public education consists of three progressive stages: primary education[1], secondary education[2] and further education[3]. Part I of the Education Act 1996[4] confers functions[5] on the Secretary of State[6], the Welsh Ministers[7] and local authorities[8] with respect to primary, secondary and further education[9]. Additional provision is made in respect of further education by Part I of the Further and Higher Education Act 1992[10]. Apart from the general duty of the Secretary of State and the Welsh Ministers to promote the education of the people of England and Wales[11], nothing in the Education Act 1996 confers any functions with respect to higher education[12]. Separate provision[13] is made in relation to early years provision and nursery education[14].

1 As to the meaning of 'primary education' see PARA 20.
2 As to the meaning of 'secondary education' see PARA 21.
3 Education Act 1996 s 1(1). As to the meaning of 'further education' see PARA 23.
4 Ie the Education Act 1996 Pt I (ss 1–30).
5 'Functions' includes powers and duties: Education Act 1996 s 579(1).
6 As to the Secretary of State see PARA 58.

7   The functions of the Secretary of State under the Education Act 1996 Pt I (ss 1–29), in so far as
     they relate to Wales, were transferred to the National Assembly for Wales and are now
     exercisable by the Welsh Ministers: see the National Assembly for Wales (Transfer of Functions)
     Order 1999, SI 1999/672, art 2, Sch 1; Government of Wales Act 2006 s 162(1), Sch 11
     paras 30, 32. As to the Welsh Ministers see PARA 59. As to the meaning of 'Wales' see PARA 7
     note 3.
8   As to the meaning of 'local authority' see PARA 25.
9   Education Act 1996 s 1(2)(a) (amended by SI 2010/1158).
10   Education Act 1996 s 1(3) (amended by the Learning and Skills Act 2000 s 149, Sch 9 paras 1,
     51). As to the Further and Higher Education Act 1992 Pt I (ss 15–61A) see PARA 555 et seq.
11   Ie the duty under the Education Act 1996 s 10: see PARA 60. As to the meaning of 'England' see
     PARA 7 note 3.
12   Education Act 1996 s 1(4). However, the Education Act 2002 s 28A gives power to the
     governing body of a maintained school to provide higher education to pupils at the school: see
     PARA 170. As to the meaning of 'higher education' see PARA 24. As to higher education see PARA
     619 et seq.
13   Ie the School Standards and Framework Act 1998 Pt V (ss 117–124).
14   See PARAS 29, 96-97. As to the meanings of 'early years provision' and 'nursery education' see
     PARA 95.

19.   Compulsory education and meaning of 'compulsory school age'. The
parent[1] of every child[2] of compulsory school age must cause him to receive
efficient full-time education suitable to his age, ability and aptitude, and to any
special educational needs[3] he may have, either by regular attendance at school[4]
or otherwise[5].

The following provisions apply to determine for the purposes of any
enactment[6] whether a person is of compulsory school age[7]. A person begins to be
of compulsory school age when he attains the age of five[8], if he attains that age
on a prescribed day[9], and otherwise at the beginning of the prescribed day next
following his attaining that age[10]. A person ceases to be of compulsory school
age at the end of the day which is the school leaving date for any calendar year[11]:
(1) if he attains the age of 16 after that day but before the beginning of the
school year[12] next following[13]; (2) if he attains that age on that day[14]; or (3)
(unless head (1) above applies) if that day is the school leaving date next
following his attaining that age[15].

1   As to the meaning of 'parent' see PARA 7 note 6.
2   As to the meaning of 'child' see PARA 7 note 6.
3   As to the meaning of 'special educational needs' see PARAS 943, 989.
4   As to the meaning of 'school' see PARA 91.
5   Education Act 1996 s 7. As to this duty see also PARA 435. As to the requirement that children
     be educated in accordance with parents' wishes see PARA 7. As to work experience in the last
     year of compulsory schooling see s 560; and CHILDREN AND YOUNG PERSONS vol 10 (2012)
     PARA 706.
6   As to the meaning of 'enactment' see PARA 1 note 13.
7   Education Act 1996 s 8(1).
8   As to the time at which a person attains a particular age see PARA 7 note 6.
9   The Secretary of State or, in relation to Wales, the Welsh Ministers may by order provide that
     such days in the year as are specified in the order are, for each calendar year, prescribed days for
     the purposes of the Education Act 1996 s 8(2): s 8(4)(a) (s 8(4) substituted by the Education
     Act 1997 s 52(1), (3)). The prescribed days are 31 March, 31 August and 31 December:
     Education (Start of Compulsory School Age) Order 1998, SI 1998/1607, art 2 (which applies to
     both England and Wales). The functions of the Secretary of State under the Education Act 1996
     s 8, in so far as they relate to Wales, were transferred to the National Assembly for Wales and
     are now exercisable by the Welsh Ministers: see the National Assembly for Wales (Transfer of
     Functions) Order 1999, SI 1999/672, art 2, Sch 1; Government of Wales Act 2006 s 162(1),
     Sch 11 paras 30, 32. As to the Welsh Ministers see PARA 59. As to the Secretary of State see PARA
     58. As to the meanings of 'England' and 'Wales' see PARA 7 note 3.
10   Education Act 1996 s 8(2) (substituted by the Education Act 1997 s 52(1), (2)). Where the age
     of any person is required to be proved for the purposes the Education Act 1996 or of any

enactment relating to the employment of children or young persons, provision is made for certificates issued by the registrar to be provided at a reduced fee: see the Education Act 1996 s 564; and REGISTRATION CONCERNING THE INDIVIDUAL vol 88 (2012) PARAS 226, 343. Where in any proceedings under the Education Act 1996 the person by whom the proceedings are brought alleges that any person whose age is material to the proceedings is under, of, or over, any age and satisfies the court that, having used all reasonable diligence to obtain evidence as to the age of that person, he has been unable to do so, the court may, unless the contrary is proved, presume that person to be under, of, or, as the case may be, over, the age alleged: s 565(1). This has effect subject to s 445(3), which provides that where a court is obliged by virtue of s 445(2) (see PARAS 446, 447) to presume a child to have been of compulsory school age s 565(1) does not apply: see ss 445(3), 565(2).

11 Education Act 1996 s 8(3). The Secretary of State or, in relation to Wales, the Welsh Ministers may by order determine the day in any calendar year which is to be the school leaving date for that year: s 8(4)(b) (as substituted: see note 9). The school leaving date is the last Friday in June: Education (School Leaving Date) Order 1997, SI 1997/1970, art 2 (which applies to both England And Wales).

12 'School year' in relation to a school, means the period beginning with the first school term to begin after July and ending with the beginning of the first such term to begin after the following July: Education Act 1996 s 579(1) (definition added by the Education Act 1997 s 57(1), Sch 7 para 43).

13 Education Act 1996 s 8(3)(a).

14 Education Act 1996 s 8(3)(b).

15 Education Act 1996 s 8(3)(c).

20. Meaning of 'primary education'. 'Primary education' means:

(1) full-time or part-time education[1] suitable to the requirements of children[2] who have attained the age of two but are under compulsory school age[3];

(2) full-time education suitable to the requirements of junior pupils[4] of compulsory school age who have not attained the age of ten years and six months[5]; and

(3) full-time education suitable to the requirements of junior pupils who have attained that age and whom it is expedient to educate together with junior pupils within head (2) above[6].

1 References to education in the Education Act 1996 s 2 do not include references to higher education: s 2(7). As to the meaning of 'higher education' see PARA 24.

2 As to the meaning of 'child' see PARA 7 note 6.

3 Education Act 1996 s 2(1)(a) (s 2(1) substituted by the Education Act 2002 s 156(2)). As to the meaning of 'compulsory school age' see PARA 19. As to the time at which a person attains a particular age see PARA 7 note 6.

4 'Junior pupil' means a child who has not attained the age of 12: Education Act 1996 s 3(2). 'Pupil' means a person for whom education is being provided at a school, other than:

    (1)   a person who has attained the age of 19 for whom further education is being provided; or

    (2)   a person for whom part-time education suitable to the requirements of persons of any age over compulsory school age is being provided;

and references to pupils in the context of the admission of pupils to, or the exclusion of pupils from, a school are references to persons who following their admission will be, or, as the case may be, before their exclusion were, pupils as defined by this provision: s 3(1) (amended by the Education Act 1997 s 57(1), Sch 7 para 9). However, a person is not for the purposes of the Education Act 1996 to be treated as a pupil at a school merely because any education is provided for him at the school in the exercise of the powers conferred by the Education Act 2002 s 27 (power of governing body of maintained school to provide community facilities etc: see PARA 174): Education Act 1996 s 3(1A) (added by the Education Act 2002 s 215(1), Sch 21 para 34(1), (2)). The Education Act 1996 s 3(1), (1A) also applies, unless the context otherwise requires, for the purposes of any instrument made or having effect as if made under the Education Acts: Education Act 1996 s 3(3) (amended by the Education Act 2002 Sch 21 para 34(1), (3)). As to the meaning of 'school' see PARA 91. As to the meaning of 'further education' see PARA 23. As to the meaning of 'the Education Acts' see PARA 1 note 13. As to school admissions see PARA 224 et seq. As to the exclusion of pupils from school see PARA 517 et seq.

　　Any child for whom education is provided otherwise than at school in pursuance of the Education Act 1996 s 19 (exceptional provision of education in pupil referral units or elsewhere: see PARA 427) and any young person for whom full-time education is so provided in pursuance of s 19, is to be treated for the purposes of the Education Act 1996 as a pupil: s 19(5). As to the meaning of 'young person' see PARA 7 note 6.

5　Education Act 1996 s 2(1)(b) (as substituted: see note 3).
6　Education Act 1996 s 2(1)(c) (as substituted: see note 3).

21.　Meaning of 'secondary education'. 'Secondary education' means:

(1)　full-time education[1] suitable to the requirements of pupils[2] of compulsory school age[3] who are either senior pupils[4], or junior pupils[5] who have attained the age of ten years and six months and whom it is expedient to educate together with senior pupils of compulsory school age[6]; and

(2)　full-time education suitable to the requirements of pupils who are over compulsory school age but under the age of 19 which is provided at a school[7] at which education within head (1) above is also provided[8].

Education is also secondary education for the purposes of the Education Act 1996[9] if it is provided by an institution which: (a) is maintained by a local authority or is an academy[10]; and (b) is principally concerned with the provision of full-time education suitable to the requirements of pupils who are over compulsory school age but under the age of 19[11].

Where:

(i)　a person is in full-time education[12];

(ii)　he receives his education partly at a school and, by virtue of arrangements made by the school, partly at another institution or any other establishment[13]; and

(iii)　the education which he receives at the school would be secondary education if it was full-time education at the school[14],

the person's education, both at the school and at the other institution or establishment, is secondary education for the purposes of the Education Act 1996[15].

1　References to education in the Education Act 1996 s 2 do not include references to higher education: s 2(7). In the context of the definition of 'secondary education', references in s 2 to education include vocational, social, physical and recreational training: s 2(6A) (added by the Education Act 2002 s 177(1), (3)). As to the meaning of 'higher education' see PARA 24.
2　As to the meaning of 'pupil' see PARA 20 note 4.
3　As to the meaning of 'compulsory school age' see PARA 19.
4　'Senior pupil' means a person who has attained the age of 12 but not the age of 19: Education Act 1996 s 3(2). As to the time at which a person attains a particular age see PARA 7 note 6.
5　As to the meaning of 'junior pupil' see PARA 20 note 4.
6　Education Act 1996 s 2(2)(a).
7　As to the meaning of 'school' see PARA 91.
8　Education Act 1996 s 2(2)(b). For the purposes of the Education Act 1996, education provided for persons who have attained the age of 19 is further education not secondary education; but where a person: (1) has begun a particular course of secondary education before attaining the age of 18; and (2) continues to attend that course, the education does not cease to be secondary education by reason of his having attained the age of 19: s 2(5). As to the meaning of 'further education' see PARA 23.
9　Ie subject to the Education Act 1996 s 2(5): see note 8.
10　Education Act 1996 s 2(2A)(a) (s 2(2A) added by the Learning and Skills Act 2000 s 110(1); Education Act 1996 s 2(2A)(a) amended by the Education Act 2002 s 65(3), Sch 7 Pt 2 para 6(1), (2); SI 2010/1158). As to the meaning of 'local authority' see PARA 25. As to academies see PARA 345 et seq.

11 Education Act 1996 s 2(2A)(b) (as added: see note 10). As to the provision of secondary education by the further education sector see PARA 595.

12 Education Act 1996 s 2(2B)(a) (s 2(2B) added by the Learning and Skills Act 2000 s 110(1)).

13 Education Act 1996 s 2(2B)(b) (as added (see note 12); and amended by the Education Act 2002 s 177(1), (2)(a)).

14 Education Act 1996 s 2(2B)(c) (as added: see note 12).

15 Education Act 1996 s 2(2B) (as added (see note 12); and amended by the Education Act 2002 s 177(1), (2)(b)). The Education Act 1996 s 2(2B) is subject to s 2(5) (see note 8): s 2(2B) (as so added and amended). The Education Acts have effect in their application to persons receiving secondary education within s 2(2B) with such modifications as may be specified in an order under the Education Act 2002 s 177(4): s 177(4). The power to make such an order is exercisable: (1) in relation to England, by the Secretary of State (s 177(5)(a)); and (2) in relation to Wales, by the Welsh Ministers (s 177(5)(b)). At the date at which this volume states the law, no such order had been made. As to the meaning of 'the Education Acts' see PARA 1 note 13. 'Modifications' includes additions, alterations and omissions and 'modify' must be construed accordingly: Education Act 1996 s 579(1) (definition applied by the Education Act 2002 s 212(2), (3)). As to the Secretary of State see PARA 58. As to the meanings of 'England' and 'Wales' see PARA 7 note 3. As to the Welsh Ministers see PARA 59. The functions under s 177(5)(b) were originally vested in the National Assembly for Wales and are now exercisable by the Welsh Ministers by virtue of the Government of Wales Act 2006 s 162(1), Sch 11 para 30.

22.   Duty to participate in education or training.   Any person who is resident in England and who has ceased to be of compulsory school age, has not reached the age of 18, and has not attained a level 3 qualification must either be participating in appropriate full-time education or training, or be participating in training in accordance with a contract of apprenticeship or an apprenticeship agreement, or both be in full-time occupation and participate in sufficient relevant training or education[1].

1   See the Education and Skills Act 2008 Pt 1 (ss 1–67); and PARA 725 et seq.

23.   Meaning of 'further education'.   'Further education' means[1]:

(1)   full-time and part-time education[2] suitable to the requirements of persons who are over compulsory school age[3]; and

(2)   organised leisure-time occupation[4] provided in connection with the provision of such education[5].

However, it does not include secondary education[6] or[7] higher education[8].

1   Ie subject to the Education Act 1996 s 2(5): see PARA 21 note 8.

2   References to education in the Education Act 1996 s 2 do not include references to higher education: s 2(7). In the context of the definition of 'further education', references in s 2 to education include vocational, social, physical and recreational training: s 2(6A) (added by the Education Act 2002 s 177(1), (3)). As to the meaning of 'higher education' see PARA 24.

3   Education Act 1996 s 2(3)(a) (amended by the Education Act 2002 s 215(2), Sch 22 Pt 3). As to the meaning of 'compulsory school age' see PARA 19.

4   'Organised leisure-time occupation' means leisure-time occupation, in such organised cultural training and recreative activities as are suited to their requirements, for any persons over compulsory school age who are able and willing to profit by facilities provided for that purpose: Education Act 1996 s 2(6).

5   Education Act 1996 s 2(3)(b).

6   As to the meaning of 'secondary education' see PARA 21.

7   Ie in accordance with the Education Act 1996 s 2(7): see note 2.

8   Education Act 1996 s 2(3). Accordingly, unless it is education within s 2(2)(b) or s 2(2A) (see PARA 21), full-time education suitable to the requirements of persons over compulsory school age who have not attained the age of 19 is further education for the purposes of the Education Act 1996 and not secondary education: s 2(4) (amended by the Education Act 2002 s 215(1), Sch 21 para 33). As to the time at which a person attains a particular age see PARA 7 note 6.

24. Higher education. 'Higher education' means education provided by means of any of the following courses[1]:

(1) a course for the further training of teachers[2] or youth and community workers[3];

(2) a-graduate course (including a higher degree course)[4];

(3) a first degree course[5];

(4) a course for the Diploma of Higher Education[6];

(5) a course for the Higher National Diploma or Higher National Certificate of the Business and Technician Education Council, or the Diploma in Management Studies[7];

(6) a course for the Certificate in Education[8];

(7) a course in preparation for a professional examination at higher level[9];

(8) a course providing education at a higher level (whether or not in preparation for an examination)[10].

1 Education Reform Act 1988 ss 120(1), s 235(1), Sch 6; Education Act 1996 s 579(1). The Secretary of State or, in relation to Wales, the Welsh Ministers may by order amend the Education Reform Act 1988 Sch 6: s 120(10). At the date at which this volume states the law no such order had been made. As to the Secretary of State see PARA 58. The functions of the Secretary of State under the Education Reform Act 1988 s 120(10), in so far as they relate to Wales, were transferred to the National Assembly for Wales and are now exercisable by the Welsh Ministers: see the National Assembly for Wales (Transfer of Functions) Order 1999, SI 1999/672, art 2, Sch 1; Government of Wales Act 2006 s 162(1), Sch 11 paras 30, 32. As to the Welsh Ministers see PARA 59. As to the meaning of 'Wales' see PARA 7 note 3.

2 References in the Education Acts to training, in relation to teachers, include any training or education with a view to fitting persons to be teachers, or better teachers: Education Act 2005 s 96(2). As to the meaning of 'the Education Acts' see PARA 1 note 13.

3 Education Reform Act 1988 Sch 6 para 1(a); Education Act 1996 s 579(1).

4 Education Reform Act 1988 Sch 6 para 1(b); Education Act 1996 s 579(1).

5 Education Reform Act 1988 Sch 6 para 1(c); Education Act 1996 s 579(1).

6 Education Reform Act 1988 Sch 6 para 1(d); Education Act 1996 s 579(1).

7 Education Reform Act 1988 Sch 6 para 1(e); Education Act 1996 s 579(1).

8 Education Reform Act 1988 Sch 6 para 1(f); Education Act 1996 s 579(1).

9 Education Reform Act 1988 Sch 6 para 1(g); Education Act 1996 s 579(1). A professional examination is at higher level if its standard is higher than the standard of examinations at advanced level for the General Certificate of Education or the examination for the National Certificate or the National Diploma of the Business and Technician Education Council: Education Reform Act 1988 Sch 6 para 2.

10 Education Reform Act 1988 Sch 6 para 1(h); Education Act 1996 s 579(1). A course is to be regarded as providing education at a higher level if its standard is higher than the standard of courses providing education in preparation for any of the examinations mentioned in the Education Reform Act 1988 Sch 6 para 2 (see note 9): Sch 6 para 3.

(3) LOCAL AUTHORITIES

(i) General Education Duties and Functions of Local Authorities

A. PROVISION OF EDUCATION

25. Meanings of 'local authority' and 'education functions'. In the Education Act 1996, 'local authority' means a local authority in England and a local authority in Wales[1]. 'Local authority in England' means a county council in England, a metropolitan district council, a non-metropolitan district council for an area for which there is no county council, a London borough council, and the Common Council of the City of London (in its capacity as a local authority)[2]. 'Local authority in Wales' means a county council in Wales and a county borough council[3].

'Education functions' means the functions[4] conferred on a local authority under the Education Acts[5], and various other functions conferred on a local authority under other enactments[6].

1 Education Act 1996 s 579(1) (definition substituted by SI 2010/1158). As to the meanings of 'England' and 'Wales' see PARA 7 note 3.

2 Education Act 1996 s 579(1) (definition added by SI 2010/1158). For the purposes of the Education Act 1996 the area of the Common Council of the City of London must be treated as including the Inner Temple and the Middle Temple: s 579(4A) (added by SI 2010/1158). As to local government areas and authorities in England see LOCAL GOVERNMENT vol 69 (2009) PARA 22 et seq. As to the London boroughs and their councils see LONDON GOVERNMENT vol 71 (2013) PARA 20 et seq. As to the Common Council of the City of London see LONDON GOVERNMENT vol 71 (2013) PARAS 34–38.

As from a day to be appointed, the following is added, that references in the Education Act 1996 to a person who is 'in the area' of a local authority in England do not include a person who is wholly or mainly resident in the area of a local authority in Wales; and references in the Act to a person who is 'in the area' of a local authority in Wales do not include a person who is wholly or mainly resident in the area of a local authority in England: s 579(3A), (3B) (prospectively added by the Children and Families Act 2014 Sch 3 paras 1, 59(d)). At the date at which this volume states the law no such day had been appointed.

3 Education Act 1996 s 579(1) (definition added by SI 2010/1158). As to local government areas and authorities in Wales see LOCAL GOVERNMENT vol 69 (2009) PARA 37 et seq. See note 2.

4 As to the meaning of 'functions' see PARA 18 note 5.

5 Education Act 1996 s 579(1), Sch 36A para 1 (s 579(1) definition added, Sch 36A added, by SI 2010/1158, and Sch). As to the meaning of 'the Education Acts' see PARA 1 note 13.

6 See the Education Act 1996 s 579(1), Sch 36A para 2 (as added: see note 5). The functions are as follows:

(1) Children and Young Persons Act 1933 s 18 (making of byelaws relating to the employment of children: see CHILDREN AND YOUNG PERSONS vol 10 (2012) PARA 709);

(2) Superannuation Act 1972 s 9(5A) (payment of injury benefit to or in respect of teachers: see PARA 1081);

(3) Employment and Training Act 1973 ss 10, 10A (powers and duties relating to careers services: see EMPLOYMENT vol 40 (2014) PARAS 638, 642;

(4) Employment and Training Act 1973 s 12 (duty to provide information to the Secretary of State: see EMPLOYMENT vol 40 (2014) PARAS 634, 637, 643;

(5) Public Passenger Vehicles Act 1981 s 46 (power to use a school bus to carry fare-paying passengers: see ROAD TRAFFIC vol 90 (2011) PARA 936);

(6) Representation of the People Act 1983 Sch 5 para 2 (duty to prepare and revise lists of rooms in school premises which candidates may use: see ELECTIONS AND REFERENDUMS vol 37 (2013) PARA 336);

(7) Disabled Persons (Services, Consultation and Representation) Act 1986 s 5(1)–(4), (6), (8) (duty to require the appropriate officer to give an opinion as to whether a child with an EHC plan or a statement is disabled: see SOCIAL SERVICES AND COMMUNITY CARE vol 95 (2013) PARA 12);

(8) Children Act 1989 s 36 and Sch 3 Pt 3 (paras 12–21) (except para 19(2)) (education supervision orders: see PARAS 453–455).

(9) Learning and Skills Act 2000 s 33J (duty to assist Welsh Ministers in planning the local curriculum: see PARA 899), ss 33K, 33L (duty relating to delivery of local curriculum and joint working in Wales: see PARA 900);

(10) Learning and Skills Act 2000 s 83 (duty of local authority in Wales to provide information to Chief Inspector), s 84 (duties relating to preparation of an action plan following an area inspection in Wales) (see PARA 1275);

(11) Learning and Skills Act 2000 s 96 (see PARA 934), s 101 (see PARA 936), s 102 (see PARA 938) (duties as an 'authorised body' relating to qualifications);

(12) Learning and Skills Act 2000 ss 123–125 (see PARA 813–815) and s 128 (see PARA 1288) (support services for 11 to 25 years olds in Wales);

(13) Learning and Skills Act 2000 s 140(5) (duty to send copy of a statement of special educational needs to the Welsh Ministers if requested: see PARA 998);

(14) Learning and Skills Act 2000 Schs 7 and 7A (repealed) (see now the School Standards and Organisation (Wales) Act 2013 Pt 3 Ch 5 (ss 71–77) (powers for Welsh Ministers to restructure sixth form education: see PARA 1250);

(15)　Local Government Act 2000 Sch A1 paras 6–8, Sch 1 paras 8–9 (duty to include certain persons on overview and scrutiny committee if it relates to education functions: see PARA 55);

(16)　Nationality, Immigration and Asylum Act 2002 s 37 (powers and duties relating to education of a child in an accommodation centre: see IMMIGRATION AND ASYLUM vol 57 (2012) PARA 355);

(17)　Anti-social Behaviour Act 2003 ss 19–21, 22A (powers and duties relating to parenting orders and parenting contracts: see CHILDREN AND YOUNG PERSONS vol 10 (2012) PARA 1283 et seq);

(18)　National Health Service Act 2006 Sch 1 para 5 (duty to make available to the Secretary of State appropriate accommodation for enabling the Secretary of State to arrange for medical inspections in schools: see HEALTH SERVICES vol 54 (2008) PARA 33);

(19)　Equality Act 2010 s 29(7) (duty to make reasonable adjustments for disabled persons: see DISCRIMINATION vol 33 (2013) PARAS 84, 229) in its application to a local authority's functions under the Education Acts; s 85(6) (duty (as responsible body) to make reasonable adjustments for disabled pupils: see PARA 9); s 92(6) (duty (as responsible body) to make reasonable adjustments for disabled persons in further and higher education: see PARA 15); s 93(6) (duty (as responsible body) to make reasonable adjustments for disabled persons in the provision of recreational or training facilities: see PARA 16); Sch 10 para 1 (duty to prepare and implement accessibility strategy: see PARA 11); Sch 10 para 3 (duty (as responsible body) to prepare and implement an accessibility plan: see PARA 11): Education Act 1996 Sch 36A para 2 Table (as so added; and amended by the Equality Act 2010 Sch 26 paras 35, 42, Sch 27 Pt 1; and the Children and Families Act 2014 Sch 3 para 62).

In head (11) above, as from a day to be appointed, the reference to the Learning and Skills Act 2000 s 102 is omitted and the words '(in England)' are added after the word 'qualifications': Education Act 1996 Sch 36A para 2 Table (as so added and amended; prospectively further amended by the Qualifications Wales Act 2015 Sch 4 para 1(1), (3)). At the date at which this volume states the law no such day had been appointed.

26.　Transfer of local education authority functions to local authorities. The Secretary of State[1] may by order[2]:

(1)　make such provision as appears to him to be appropriate for the purpose of repealing any reference in any statutory provision[3] to a local education authority[4] (however expressed) in so far as it relates to such an authority in England or such an authority in Wales[5], or to both[6], and replacing it, where it appears to him to be appropriate, with a reference (however expressed) to, as the case may be, an English local authority[7] or a Welsh local authority[8], or to both[9];

(2)　make such provision as appears to him to be appropriate for the purpose of repealing any reference in any statutory provision to a children's services authority[10] (however expressed) in so far as it relates to a children's services authority in England or a children's services authority in Wales, or to both[11], and replacing it, where it appears to him to be appropriate, with a reference (however expressed) to, as the case may be, an English local authority or a Welsh local authority, or to both[12];

(3)　make such provision as appears to him to be appropriate in consequence of or in connection with any provision made by virtue of head (1) above[13].

Such an order may make provision modifying[14] any enactment[15] whenever passed or made[16], and may, in particular, make provision:

(a)　modifying references (however expressed) in any statutory provision to the functions of a local education authority, or the functions of a local authority (however defined) in its capacity as a local education authority, where the references wholly or partly relate to a local education authority in England or a local education authority in Wales[17];

(b) modifying statutory provisions which consist of or include provision requiring or authorising consultation, co-operation, communication or other action between a local education authority in England and an English local authority or between a local education authority in Wales and a Welsh local authority[18];

(c) modifying statutory provisions which consist of or include provision imposing a duty on a local education authority in England or on a local education authority in Wales where the duty imposed is similar to a duty imposed by that or any other statutory provision on, as the case may be, an English local authority or a Welsh local authority[19];

(d) modifying statutory provisions which consist of or include provision imposing a duty on an English local authority or on a Welsh local authority where the duty imposed is similar to a duty imposed by that or any other statutory provision on, as the case may be, a local education authority in England or a local education authority in Wales[20];

(e) repealing statutory provisions which are spent or have ceased to be of any practical utility[21].

The following powers to make provision by order under the above provisions[22] are exercisable by the Welsh Ministers[23] as well as by the Secretary of State[24]: (i) the power to make provision under head (1) above in relation to any reference in any statutory provision to a local education authority (however expressed) in so far as it relates to such an authority in Wales[25]; (ii) the power to make provision under head (2) above in relation to any reference in any statutory provision to a children's services authority (however expressed) in so far as it relates to a children's services authority in Wales[26], and (iii) the power to make provision under head (3) above in consequence of or in connection with any provision made by virtue of the powers under head (1) or (2) above mentioned in head (i) or (ii) above, or by virtue of both those powers[27].

The Welsh Ministers may by order[28]: (A) make such provision as appears to them to be appropriate for the purpose of repealing any reference in a measure of the National Assembly for Wales to a local education authority (however expressed)[29], and replacing it, where it appears to them to be appropriate, with a reference (however expressed) to a Welsh local authority[30]; and (B) make such provision as appears to them to be appropriate in consequence of or in connection with any provision made by virtue of head (A) above[31].

Finally it should be noted that the Secretary of State also has certain powers and duties in regard to academy arrangements[32].

1   As to the Secretary of State see PARA 58.
2   An order under the Education and Inspections Act 2006 s 162(1) may make provision which is within the legislative competence of the Scottish Parliament only in consequence of provision made under such an order which is outside that competence: s 162(5). As to the Scottish Parliament see CONSTITUTIONAL AND ADMINISTRATIVE LAW vol 20 (2014) PARA 66. As to the orders made under s 162 see the Local Education Authorities and Children's Services Authorities (Integration of Functions) Order 2010, SI 2010/1158; and the Local Education Authorities and Children's Services Authorities (Integration of Functions) (Local and Subordinate Legislation) Order 2010, SI 2010/1172.
3   'Statutory provision' means: (1) any provision of the Education and Inspections Act 2006 or any other Act, including any Act passed after 8 November 2006 (ie the date of the passing of the Education and Inspections Act 2006), and (2) any provision of subordinate legislation, including

any such legislation made under, or after the passing of, the Education and Inspections Act 2006: s 162(6). 'Subordinate legislation' means Orders in Council, orders, rules, regulations, schemes, warrants, byelaws and other instruments made or to be made under any Act: Interpretation Act 1978 s 21(1) (definition applied by the Education and Inspections Act 2006 s 187(1)). As to subordinate legislation generally see STATUTES AND LEGISLATIVE PROCESS vol 96 (2012) PARA 1030 et seq.

4   In the Education Acts and certain other enactments the functions of local education authorities are now vested in local authorities: see PARA 25.

5   As to the meanings of 'England' and 'Wales' see PARA 7 note 3.

6   Education and Inspections Act 2006 s 162(1)(a)(i).

7   'English local authority' means a county council in England, a metropolitan district council, a non-metropolitan district council for an area for which there is no county council, a London borough council, the Common Council of the City of London, or the Council of the Isles of Scilly: Education and Inspections Act 2006 s 162(6). As to local government areas and authorities in England see LOCAL GOVERNMENT vol 69 (2009) PARA 22 et seq. As to the London boroughs and their councils see LONDON GOVERNMENT vol 71 (2013) PARA 20 et seq. As to the Common Council of the City of London see LONDON GOVERNMENT vol 71 (2013) PARAS 34–38. As to the Council of the Isles of Scilly see LOCAL GOVERNMENT vol 69 (2009) PARA 36.

8   'Welsh local authority' means a county council or county borough council in Wales: Education and Inspections Act 2006 s 162(6). As to local government areas and authorities in Wales see LOCAL GOVERNMENT vol 69 (2009) PARA 37 et seq.

9   Education and Inspections Act 2006 s 162(1)(a)(ii).

10 As to children's services authorities see CHILDREN AND YOUNG PERSONS vol 9 (2012) PARA 203 et seq.

11 Education and Inspections Act 2006 s 162(1)(b)(i).

12 Education and Inspections Act 2006 s 162(1)(b)(ii).

13 See the Education and Inspections Act 2006 s 162(1)(c).

14 'Modify' includes amend or repeal: Education and Inspections Act 2006 s 162(6).

15 'Enactment' includes an enactment comprised in subordinate legislation: Education and Inspections Act 2006 s 187(1). As to the meaning of 'enactment' generally see PARA 1 note 13.

16 Ie including the Education and Inspections Act 2006.

17 Education and Inspections Act 2006 s 162(2)(a).

18 Education and Inspections Act 2006 s 162(2)(b).

19 Education and Inspections Act 2006 s 162(2)(c).

20 Education and Inspections Act 2006 s 162(2)(d).

21 Education and Inspections Act 2006 s 162(2)(e).

22 Ie under the Education and Inspections Act 2006 s 162(1): see the text to notes 1–13.

23 The functions under the Education and Inspections Act 2006 s 162(3), (4) (see note 24) were originally vested in the National Assembly for Wales and are now exercisable by the Welsh Ministers by virtue of the Government of Wales Act 2006 s 162(1), Sch 11 paras 30, 32. The Government of Wales Act 2006 Sch 11 paras 33–35 (see CONSTITUTIONAL AND ADMINISTRATIVE LAW vol 20 (2014) PARA 380) make provision about the National Assembly for Wales procedures that apply to any statutory instrument containing regulations or an order made in exercise of functions conferred upon the Assembly by the Education and Inspections Act 2006 that have been transferred to the Welsh Ministers by virtue of the Government of Wales Act 2006 Sch 11 para 30: Education and Inspections Act 2006 s 182A(2) (s 182A added by the Learner Travel (Wales) Measure 2008 s 23(1), (4)). As to the Welsh Ministers see PARA 59.

24 The Secretary of State must not make an order under the Education and Inspections Act 2006 s 162(1) (see the text to notes 1–13), except with the consent of the Welsh Ministers, which contains provision made wholly or partly by virtue of any of the powers to make provision under that provision mentioned in any of s 162(3)(a)–(c) (see the text to notes 25–27): s 162(4).

25 Education and Inspections Act 2006 s 162(3)(a).

26 Education and Inspections Act 2006 s 162(3)(b).

27 Education and Inspections Act 2006 s 162(3)(c).

28 An order under the Education and Inspections Act 2006 s 162(5A) may make provision modifying any enactment whenever passed or made, and may, in particular, make provision of the kind specified in s 162(2)(a)–(e) (see heads (a)–(e) in the text): s 162(5B) (added by the Education (Wales) Measure 2009 s 23, Schedule paras 10, 11). In interpreting the Education and Inspections Act 2006 s 162(2)(a)–(e) for the purposes of s 162(5B), 'statutory provision' (see note 3) also includes any provision of a measure of the National Assembly for Wales, including any measure passed after the Education (Wales) Measure 2009: Education and Inspections Act 2006 s 162(7) (added by the Education (Wales) Measure 2009 s 23, Schedule paras 10, 12).

The Education (Wales) Measure 2009 was passed (ie approved by Her Majesty in Council) on 9 December 2009. As to measures of the National Assembly for Wales see CONSTITUTIONAL AND ADMINISTRATIVE LAW vol 20 (2014) PARA 351 et seq.

Any statutory instrument containing an order made under the Education and Inspections Act 2006 s 162(5A) by the Welsh Ministers may not be made unless a draft of the instrument has been laid before, and approved by a resolution of, the National Assembly for Wales: s 182A(1) (as added: see note 23). As to the orders made see the Local Education Authorities and Children's Services Authorities (Integration of Functions) (Subordinate Legislation) (Wales) Order 2010, SI 2010/1142; and the Local Education Authorities and Children's Services Authorities (Integration of Functions) (Wales) Order 2010, SI 2010/1148.

29 Education and Inspections Act 2006 s 162(5A)(a)(i) (s 162(5A) added by the Learner Travel (Wales) Measure 2008, s 23(1), (2); and substituted by the Education (Wales) Measure 2009 s 23, Schedule paras 10, 11).

30 Education and Inspections Act 2006 s 162(5A)(a)(ii) (as added and substituted: see note 29).

31 See the Education and Inspections Act 2006 s 162(5A)(b) (as added and substituted: see note 29).

32 As to academy arrangements and academies generally see PARA 345 et seq.

27. General responsibility for education.

A local authority[1] must, so far as its powers enable it to do so, contribute towards the spiritual, moral, mental and physical development of the community by securing that efficient primary education[2] and secondary education[3] and, in the case of a local authority in England[4], further education[5], are available to meet the needs of the population of its area[6].

This duty does not extend to matters in respect of which any duty is imposed on the Secretary of State under Part 4 of the Apprenticeships, Skills, Children and Learning Act 2009[7] and the Welsh Ministers[8] under Part 2[9] of the Learning and Skills Act 2000[10], or the Higher Education Funding Councils established[11] under the Further and Higher Education Act 1992[12].

1   As to the meaning of 'local authority' see PARA 25.
2   As to the meaning of 'primary education' see PARA 20.
3   As to the meaning of 'secondary education' see PARA 21.
4   As to the meaning of 'local authority in England' see PARA 25.
5   This reference to further education is to further education for persons who are over compulsory school age but under 19, or who are aged 19 or over and for whom an EHC plan is maintained: Education Act 1996 s 13(3) (s 13(3)–(6) added by the Apprenticeships, Skills, Children and Learning Act 2009 s 59, Sch 2 paras 1, 2(1), (3); and the Education Act 1996 s 13(3) amended and s 13(4), (5) repealed by the Children and Families Act 2014 Sch 3 para 3). As to the meaning of 'further education' see PARA 23. As to the meaning of 'compulsory school age' see PARA 19. As to the time at which a person attains a particular age see PARA 7 note 6. As to the meaning of 'EHC plan' see PARA 958. As to EHC plans (ie education, health and care plans) generally see PARA 958 et seq.
6   Education Act 1996 s 13(1) (amended by the Learning and Skills Act 2000 s 149, Sch 9 paras 1, 52(1), (3); Apprenticeships, Skills, Children and Learning Act 2009 s 59, Sch 2 paras 1, 2(1), (3); and SI 2010/1158).

For the purposes of the Education Act 1996 a person is to be treated as belonging, or as not belonging, to the area of a particular local authority in accordance with regulations; and any question under the regulations must, in the case of a dispute, be determined by the Secretary of State or, in relation to Wales, the Welsh Ministers: see s 579(4) (amended by SI 2010/1158). As to the Secretary of State see PARA 58. As to the Welsh Ministers see PARA 59. As to the meaning of 'Wales' see PARA 7 note 3. As to the regulations made see the Education (Areas to which Pupils and Students Belong) Regulations 1996, SI 1996/615 (amended by SI 1997/597; SI 2009/1301; SI 2009/1338). Persons who are subject to a detention order are to be regarded as part of the population of the area in which they are detained (and not any other area): Education Act 1996 s 13(6) (as added: see note 5). As to when a person is subject to a detention order, and as to the application of the Education Act 1996 to detained persons see PARA 547. As to the provision of education for persons subject to detention orders see PARA 38. A resident of an accommodation centre is not to be treated as part of the population of a local authority's area: see the Nationality, Immigration and Asylum Act 2002 s 36; and IMMIGRATION AND

ASYLUM vol 57 (2012) PARA 355. However, a local authority may arrange for the education of children resident in such centres in certain circumstances: see s 37; and IMMIGRATION AND ASYLUM vol 57 (2012) PARA 355.

It would be inappropriate to seek to enforce the duty under the Education Act 1996 s 13(1) by way of a declaration by judicial review: *R (on the application of Rhodes) v Kingston upon Hull* [2001] ELR 230. The duty under the Education Act 1996 s 13 does not equate to a duty to ensure that all children within the local authority's area receive an education appropriate to their needs and circumstances: see *Hughes v First Secretary of State* [2006] EWCA Civ 838, [2007] ELR 1, [2007] LGR 320.

7   Education Act 1996 s 13(2)(a) (substituted by the Learning and Skills Act 2000 s 149, Sch 9 paras 1, 52(1), (3); and amended by SI 2005/3238; the Apprenticeships, Skills, Children and Learning Act 2009 s 123(2), Sch 6 para 13; and the Deregulation Act 2015 Sch 14 Pt 2 paras 42, 43). The reference in the text is to the Apprenticeships, Skills, Children and Learning Act 2009 Pt 4 (ss 83–121): see PARA 776 et seq.
8   The functions under this provision were originally vested in the National Assembly for Wales and are now exercisable by the Welsh Ministers by virtue of the Government of Wales Act 2006 s 162(1), Sch 11 paras 30, 32.
9   Ie the Learning and Skills Act 2000 Pt 2 (ss 31–41): see PARA 789 et seq.
10   Education Act 1996 s 13(2)(aa) (added by SI 2005/3238).
11   Ie under the Further and Higher Education Act 1992 s 62: see PARA 691 et seq.
12   Education Act 1996 s13(2)(b) (substituted by the Learning and Skills Act 2000 s 149, Sch 9 paras 1, 52(1), (3)).

28.   Duties in relation to the welfare of children.   A local authority[1] must make arrangements for ensuring that its education functions[2] are exercised with a view to safeguarding and promoting the welfare of children[3]. Such an authority must, in considering what arrangements are required to be made by it, have regard to any guidance[4] given from time to time, in relation to England[5], by the Secretary of State[6] or, in relation to Wales[7], by the Welsh Ministers[8].

1   As to the meaning of 'local authority' see PARA 25 (definition applied by the Education Act 2002 s 212(1) (amended by SI 2010/1158)).
2   As to the meaning of 'functions' see PARA 18 note 5 (definition applied by virtue of the Education Act 2002 s 212(2), (3)).
3   Education Act 2002 s 175(1) (amended by SI 2010/1158). For this purpose, 'child' means a person under the age of 18: Education Act 2002 s 175(5). As to the time at which a person attains a particular age see PARA 7 note 6. The duty contained in s 175 is imposed also on the governing body of a maintained school (see PARA 211) and on the governing body of an institution within the further education sector (see PARA 783).
4   As to the publication of such guidance see the Education Act 1996 s 571 (see PARA 60) applied by virtue of the Education Act 2002 s 212(2), (3).
5   As to the meaning of 'England' see PARA 7 note 3.
6   As to the Secretary of State see PARA 58.
7   As to the meaning of 'Wales' see PARA 7 note 3.
8   Education Act 2002 s 175(4). The functions under this provision were originally vested in the National Assembly for Wales and are now exercisable by the Welsh Ministers by virtue of the Government of Wales Act 2006 s 162(1), Sch 11 paras 30, 32. As to the Welsh Ministers see PARA 59. As to the application of the Education Act 2002 s 175(4) to pupil referral units (see PARA 427 et seq) see the Education (Pupil Referral Units) (Application of Enactments) (England) Regulations 2007, SI 2007/2979, Sch 1 Pt 1 para 19A (added by SI 2012/3158).

29.   Functions in respect of establishing, maintaining and assisting nursery schools and securing early years provision and nursery education.   A local authority[1] may: (1) establish nursery schools[2]; (2) maintain nursery schools established by it or by an authority which was[3] a local authority[4]; and (3) assist[5] any nursery school not so established[6].

An English local authority must secure that early years provision[7] is available free of charge, for each young child in its area who is under compulsory school age, and is of such description as may be prescribed[8].

A local authority in Wales must secure that the provision of nursery education, whether or not by it, for children who have not attained compulsory school age but have attained such age as may be prescribed by regulations, is sufficient for its area[9]. Every local authority in Wales must establish for its area a body known as an early years development and childcare partnership[10].

Any local authority providing relevant early years education, and any person employed by such an authority, is under a duty to have regard to the provisions of the relevant code of practice in regard to special educational needs or disabilities[11].

A local authority may also assist with travel arrangements for children receiving nursery education in appropriate circumstances[12].

1   As to the meaning of 'local authority' see PARA 25.

2   Education Act 1996 s 17(1)(a) (amended by SI 2010/1158). As to the meaning of 'nursery school' see PARA 91. As to the duties of a local authority in respect of childcare see PARA 30.

3   Ie within the meaning of any enactment repealed by the Education Act 1944 or an earlier Act: see the Education Act 1996 s 17(1)(b). As to the Education Act 1944 see PARA 1.

4   Education Act 1996 s 17(1)(b) (amended by SI 2010/1158).

5   As to the meaning of 'assist' see PARA 51.

6   Education Act 1996 s 17(1)(c). Section 14(4) (local authority not under any duty to provide sufficient schools in respect of children under compulsory school age: see PARA 31) does not affect a local authority's power under s 16(1) (see PARA 41) to establish, maintain and assist schools at which education is provided both for children under compulsory school age and for older pupils (including schools at which there are nursery classes for children under compulsory school age): s 17(2) (amended by the Education Act 1997 s 57(1), Sch 7 para 13; and SI 2010/1158). As from a day to be appointed, the Education Act 1996 s 17(2) is further amended by the substitution for the words 'establish, maintain and assist' of the words 'establish and maintain': s 17(2) (as so amended; and prospectively amended by the School Standards and Framework Act 1998 s 140(1), Sch 30 paras 57, 65). At the date at which this volume states the law, no such day had been appointed. As to the meaning of 'child' see PARA 7 note 6. As to the meaning of 'compulsory school age' see PARA 19. As to the meaning of 'pupil' see PARA 20 note 4.

7   As to the meaning of 'early years provision' see PARA 95.

8   See the Childcare Act 2006 s 7; PARA 96; and CHILDREN AND YOUNG PERSONS vol 10 (2012) PARA 1083. As to the inspection of early years provision see PARA 1252.

9   See the School Standards and Framework Act 1998 s 118; and PARA 97. As to the meaning of 'nursery education' see PARA 95. As to the inspection of nursery education in Wales see PARA 1253 et seq.

10 See the School Standards and Framework Act 1998 s 119; and PARA 97.

11 See the School Standards and Framework Act 1998 s 123; and PARAS 969, 978, 1019, 1033. The reference in the text to the relevant code of practice in regard to special educational needs or disabilities is a reference to the code of practice under the Children and Families Act 2014 s 77 (in the case of education in England) (see PARA 943) or under the Education Act 1996 s 313 (in the case of education in Wales) (see PARA 1033).

12 See the Education Act 1996 s 509A (see PARA 468); Learner Travel (Wales) Measure 2008 s 8 (see PARA 476).

30.   Functions in respect of provision of childcare.   A local authority in England[1] has a general duty to improve the well-being of young children in its area[2], and specific duties with regard to childcare[3]. A local authority in Wales[4] also has duties in relation to childcare[5].

1   As to the meaning of 'England' see PARA 7 note 3.

2   See the Childcare Act 2006 s 1; and CHILDREN AND YOUNG PERSONS vol 10 (2012) PARA 1078.

3   See the Childcare Act 2006 ss 6–11; and CHILDREN AND YOUNG PERSONS vol 10 (2012) PARA 1082 et seq. As to the local authority's duty to secure early years provision free of charge in England see PARAS 95, 96.

4   As to the meaning of 'Wales' see PARA 7 note 3.

5   See the Childcare Act 2006 ss 22–26; and CHILDREN AND YOUNG PERSONS vol 10 (2012) PARA 1144 et seq. As to the duty of a local authority in Wales in respect of the availability of nursery education see PARA 97.

        Until a day to be appointed, a local authority in Wales must review annually the sufficiency of childcare provision for its area: School Standards and Framework Act 1998 s 118A(1) (s 118A added by the Education Act 2002 s 149(1); and amended by SI 2010/1158). In carrying out such a review, a local authority: may have regard to any facilities which it expects to be available outside its area for providing childcare; and must have regard to any guidance given from time to time by the Welsh Ministers: School Standards and Framework Act 1998 s 118A(2) (as so added and amended). A local authority in Wales must also establish and maintain a service providing information to the public relating to the provision of childcare and related services in its area (s 118A(3) (as so added and amended)); and in relation to the function, form and content of a service so established and maintained, a local authority must have regard to any guidance given from time to time by the Welsh Ministers (s 118A(4) (as so added and amended)). The School Standards and Framework Act 1998 s 118A is repealed by the Childcare Act 2006 s 103, Sch 2 para 31, Sch 3 Pt 2. The repeal is in force, in relation to England: see the Childcare Act 2006 (Commencement No 2 and Savings and Transitional Provisions) Order 2007, SI 2007/1019, art 3. The repeal will come into force in relation to Wales on a day to be appointed: see the Childcare Act 2006 ss 109(2), 110(1), (5)(a), (6)(b). As to the meaning of 'local authority' see PARA 25 (definition applied by the School Standards and Framework Act 1998 s 142(8)). As to the publication of guidance see the Education Act 1996 s 571 (applied by virtue of the School Standards and Framework Act 1998 s 142(8)); and PARA 60. The function under the School Standards and Framework Act 1998 s 118A(4) was originally vested in the Secretary of State. The functions of the Secretary of State under the School Standards and Framework Act 1998 s 118A, so far as exercisable in relation to Wales, were transferred to the National Assembly for Wales (see the National Assembly for Wales (Transfer of Functions) Order 1999, SI 1999/672, art 2, Sch 1) and are now vested in the Welsh Ministers (see the Government of Wales Act 2006 s 162(1), Sch 11 para 30). As to the Welsh Ministers see PARA 59.

31.   Functions in respect of provision of primary and secondary schools. A local authority[1] must secure that sufficient schools[2] for providing:

(1)   primary education[3]; and

(2)   education that is[4] secondary education[5],

are available for its area[6]. The schools available for an area are not to be regarded as sufficient for such purposes unless they are sufficient in number, character and equipment to provide for all pupils[7] the opportunity of appropriate education[8].

    A local authority for an area in Wales[9] may secure that regional schools[10] for providing primary education[11], and education that is[12] secondary education[13], are available for Wales or any part of Wales that includes the area of the authority[14].

    In exercising these functions[15], a local authority must in particular have regard to:

(a)   the need for securing that primary and secondary education are provided in separate schools[16];

(b)   the need for securing that special educational provision[17] is made for pupils who have special educational needs[18]; and

(c)   the expediency of securing the provision of boarding accommodation, in boarding schools or otherwise, for pupils for whom education as boarders[19] is considered by their parents[20] and the authority to be desirable[21].

    A local authority in England[22] must exercise its functions under the above provisions with a view to: (i) securing diversity in the provision of schools[23], and (ii) increasing opportunities for parental choice[24]. Where a local authority in England receives any representation[25] from a parent of a qualifying child[26] as to the exercise by the authority of its functions under the above provisions, the authority must consider the representation and what action (if any) to take in response to it[27], and within a reasonable time provide the parent with a statement setting out any action which the authority propose to take in response to the representation[28], or where the authority are of the opinion that no such action is necessary, their reasons for being of that opinion[29].

1   As to the meaning of 'local authority' see PARA 25.

2   As to the meaning of 'school' see PARA 91. 'Schools' can include certain types of academies (see further PARA 91); and as to academies generally see PARA 345 et seq. As to invitations for proposals for establishment of new schools, including academies see PARA 111. As to new schools see PARA 155.

3   Education Act 1996 s 14(1)(a) (amended by SI 2010/1158). As to the meaning of 'primary education' see PARA 20. A local authority is not, by virtue of the Education Act 1996 s 14(1)(a), under any duty in respect of children under compulsory school age: s 14(4) (amended by the Education Act 1997 s 57(1), Sch 7 para 12; SI 2010/1158). As to the meaning of 'child' see PARA 7 note 6. As to the meaning of 'compulsory school age' see PARA 19.

4   Ie by virtue of the Education Act 1996 s 2(2)(a): see PARA 21.

5   Education Act 1996 s 14(1)(b). As to the meaning of 'secondary education' see PARA 21.

6   Education Act 1996 s 14(1). The duty under s 14 is a target duty which will be met if the local authority is taking all reasonable steps to meet that duty. The duty does not require the local authority to guarantee a particular standard of school: *R (on the application of O) v Hackney London Borough Council* [2006] EWHC 3405 (Admin), [2007] ELR 405, [2006] All ER (D) 36 (Dec) (applying *R v Inner London Education Authority, ex p Ali* below). The cases cited below were decided under the Education Act 1944 s 8 (repealed), the terms of which were very similar to the Education Act 1996 s 14 which replaced it.

    The duty to secure the provision of sufficient schools is a target duty rather than an absolute duty and does not give an individual a cause of action, although a complaint of non-performance may be pursued via the Secretary of State's default powers (see PARA 65): *R v Inner London Education Authority, ex p Ali* (1990) 2 Admin LR 822, 154 LG Rev 852. See also *Watt v Kesteven County Council* [1955] 1 QB 408, [1955] 1 All ER 473, CA; *Bradbury v Enfield London Borough Council* [1967] 3 All ER 434, [1967] 1 WLR 1311, CA; *Meade v Haringey London Borough Council* [1979] 2 All ER 1016, [1979] 1 WLR 637, CA. Local authorities have a broad discretion as to the manner of performance of the duty (*Secretary of State for Education and Science v Tameside Metropolitan Borough Council* [1977] AC 1014, [1976] 3 All ER 665, HL) and they may have regard to financial constraints (see *R v Hereford and Worcester Local Education Authority, ex p Jones* [1981] 1 WLR 768, 79 LGR 490). As to the exercise of discretion generally see CONSTITUTIONAL AND ADMINISTRATIVE LAW vol 20 (2014) PARA 335 et seq.

    When acting in furtherance of its duty, a local authority may not differentiate between applicants living inside and those living outside the area of the authority: *R v Bromley London Borough Council, ex p C* [1992] 1 FLR 174, 156 LG Rev 282; and see PARA 228.

    The following cases were decided before the enactment of the Equality Act 2010 (see PARAS 9–12) but continue to be relevant in relation to the duty of the local authority not to act in a way that constitutes discrimination. See *Birmingham City Council v Equal Opportunities Commission* [1989] AC 1155, sub nom *Equal Opportunities Commission v Birmingham City Council* [1989] 1 All ER 769, HL (where, in aggregate, fewer single sex places for girls were available in the area than there were equivalent places for boys); *R v Secretary of State for Education and Science, ex p Keating* (1985) 84 LGR 469 (where a local authority proposed to close the only single sex school for boys in its area while continuing to maintain two single sex schools for girls); *R v Secretary of State for Education and Science, ex p Malik* [1992] COD 31; *R v Northamptonshire County Council and Secretary of State for Education, ex p K* [1994] ELR 397, CA (where a local authority proposed to close a single sex school for boys which was no longer viable, while maintaining a single sex school for girls). See also *R v Birmingham City Council, ex p Equal Opportunities Commission (No 2)* (1992) 91 LGR 14, [1994] ELR 282, sub nom *Equal Opportunities Commission v Birmingham City Council* [1993] 1 FCR 753, CA (where it was held that, in considering the availability of places for boys and girls, a local authority must take account of other maintained schools in the area, not merely those which it actually maintains).

7   As to the meaning of 'pupil' see PARA 20 note 4.

8   Education Act 1996 s 14(2). For this purpose, 'appropriate education' means education which offers such variety of instruction and training as may be desirable in view of the pupils' different ages, abilities and aptitudes, and the different periods for which they may be expected to remain

at school, including practical instruction and training appropriate to their different needs: s 14(3). The duty under the Education Act 1996 s 14 does not equate to a duty to ensure that all children within the local authority's area receive an education appropriate to their needs and circumstances: see *Hughes v The First Secretary of State* [2006] EWCA Civ 838, [2007] ELR 1, [2007] LGR 320. As to the admission of children as pupils otherwise than at the beginning of a school term see the Education Act 1996 s 433(1); and PARA 224.

The following cases were decided under the Education Act 1944 s 8 (repealed), the terms of which were very similar to the Education Act 1996 s 14 which replaced it. The duty to secure the provision of sufficient schools extends to the adequate provision of staff: *R v Liverpool City Corpn, ex p Ferguson* [1985] IRLR 501. See also *R v Northamptonshire County Council and Secretary of State for Education, ex p K* [1994] ELR 397, CA (local authority could not meet its obligation by keeping open a school whose pupil numbers had declined significantly).

9   As to the meaning of 'Wales' see PARA 7 note 3.
10 For this purpose, a 'regional school', in relation to a local authority, is a school maintained by that authority which provides education to meet both: (1) the needs of pupils with particular special educational needs in its area; and (2) the needs of such pupils in the rest, or any other part, of Wales, whether or not the institution also provides education suitable to the requirements of other pupils: Education Act 1996 s 14(4B) (added by the Education Act 2002 s 194(1); and amended by SI 2010/1158). As to the meaning of 'special educational needs' see PARAS 943, 989.
11 Education Act 1996 s 14(4A)(a) (s 14(4A) added by the Education Act 2002 s 194(1)).
12 Ie by virtue of the Education Act 1996 s 2(2)(a): see PARA 20.
13 Education Act 1996 s 14(4A)(b) (as added: see note 11).
14 Education Act 1996 s 14(4A) (as added (see note 11); and amended by SI 2010/1158). As to the power of the Welsh Ministers to make regional provision for special educational needs see PARA 1024 et seq.
15 Ie its functions under the Education Act 1996 s14: see the text to notes 1–14. As to the meaning of 'functions' generally see PARA 18 note 5.
16 Education Act 1996 s 14(6)(a) (s 14(6) amended by SI 2010/1158). The duty imposed by s 14(6)(a) does not apply in relation to middle schools or special schools: s 14(7). As to the meaning of 'middle school' see PARA 91. As to the meaning of 'special school' see PARA 1041.
17 As to the meaning of 'special educational provision' see PARAS 943, 989.
18 Education Act 1996 s 14(6)(b) (as amended: see note 16).
19 'Boarder' includes a pupil who boards during the week but not at weekends: Education Act 1996 s 579(1).
20 As to the meaning of 'parent' see PARA 7 note 6.
21 Education Act 1996 s 14(6)(c) (as amended: see note 16).
22 As to the meaning of 'England' see PARA 7 note 3.
23 Education Act 1996 s 14(3A)(a) (s 14(3A) added by the Education and Inspections Act 2006 s 2; and amended by SI 2010/1158).
24 Education Act 1996 s 14(3A)(b) (as added and amended: see note 23).
25 The Education Act 1996 s 14A(1) does not apply in relation to any representation which (1) appears to the local authority to be frivolous or vexatious (Education Act 1996 s 14A(3)(a) (s 14A added by the Education and Inspections Act 2006 s 3; and amended by SI 2010/1158)); or (2) is the same as, or similar to, a representation previously received by the authority from the same person (Education Act 1996 s 14A(3)(b) (as so added and amended)).
26 'Qualifying child', in relation to a local authority, means any child in the authority's area who is of or under compulsory school age: Education Act 1996 s 14A(2) (as added and amended: see note 25).
27 Education Act 1996 s 14A(1)(a) (as added and amended: see note 25). In exercising its functions under s 14A, a local authority must have regard to any guidance given from time to time by the Secretary of State: s 14A(4) (as so added and amended). As to the publication of guidance see PARA 60. As to the Secretary of State see PARA 58.
28 Education Act 1996 s 14A(1)(b)(i) (as added: see note 25).
29 Education Act 1996 s 14A(1)(b)(ii) (as added: see note 25).

32. Duty in respect of education and training for persons over compulsory school age in England. A local authority[1] in England[2] must secure that enough suitable education[3] and training[4] is provided to meet the reasonable needs of:

(1)   persons in its area[5] who are over compulsory school age[6] but under 19[7]; and

(2) persons in its area who are aged 19 but for whom an EHC plan is maintained[8].

A local authority may comply with this duty by securing the provision of education or training outside as well as within its area[9]. In deciding whether education or training is suitable to meet persons' reasonable needs, a local authority must (in particular) have regard to: (a) the persons' ages, abilities and aptitudes[10]; (b) any learning difficulties or disabilities the persons may have[11]; (c) the quality of the education or training[12]; (d) the locations and times at which the education or training is provided[13].

In performing the duty imposed by these provisions a local authority must: (i) act with a view to encouraging diversity in the education and training available to persons[14]; (ii) act with a view to increasing opportunities for persons to exercise choice[15]; (iii) act with a view to enabling persons to whom the duty to participate in education or training applies[16] to fulfil that duty[17]; (iv) take account of education and training whose provision the authority thinks might reasonably be secured by other persons[18].

Local authorities in England must co-operate with each other in performing their duties under the above provisions[19]. A local authority in England must also encourage participation in education and training by persons in their area who are within head (1) or (2) above[20], and encourage employers to participate in the provision of education and training for such persons[21].

1   As to the meaning of 'local authority' see PARA 25. In performing the duties imposed by the Education Act 1996 s 15ZA(1) (see the text and notes 1–8), s 15ZB (see the text and note 19) and s 15ZC(1)(b) (see the text and note 21), a local authority in England must have regard to any guidance issued by the Secretary of State: s 15ZD (added by the Education Act 2011 Sch 16 para 11).

2   As to the meaning of 'England' see PARA 7 note 3.

3   'Education' includes full-time and part-time education: Education Act 1996 s 15ZA(8), 15ZC(3) (ss 15ZA, 15ZB added by the Apprenticeships, Skills, Children and Learning Act 2009 s 41; the Education Act 1996 s 15ZC added by the Apprenticeships, Skills, Children and Learning Act 2009 s 42).

4   'Training' includes (1) full-time and part-time training; (2) vocational, social, physical and recreational training; (3) apprenticeship training: Education Act 1996 s 15ZA(8) (as added: see note 3). 'Apprenticeship training' means training provided in connection with: (a) an apprenticeship agreement (within the meaning given in the Apprenticeships, Skills, Children and Learning Act 2009 s 32 (see PARA 766)); (b) any other contract of employment; or (c) any other kind of working in relation to which alternative English completion conditions apply under s 1(5) of that Act (see PARA 760): Education Act 1996 ss 15ZA(8), 15ZC(3) (both as so added). A local authority must, in (i) making any determination as to the provision of apprenticeship training that should be secured under s 15ZA(1); or (ii) securing the provision of any apprenticeship training under that provision, co-operate with the Secretary of State: s 15ZA(5) (as so added; and amended by SI 2010/1158; and the Deregulation Act 2015 Sch 14 Pt 2 paras 42, 44). As to the Secretary of State see PARA 58.

5   As to when a person is treated as belonging to the area of a local authority see PARA 27 note 6.

6   As to the meaning of 'compulsory school age' see PARA 19.

7   Education Act 1996 s 15ZA(1)(a) (as added: see note 3). The duty in s 15ZA(1) does not apply in relation to persons in a local authority's area who are subject to a detention order: s 15ZA(9) (substituted by the Children and Families Act 2014 Sch 3 para 5(1), (5)). As to the time at which a person attains a particular age see PARA 7 note 6. As to when a person is subject to a detention order, and as to the application of the Education Act 1996 to detained persons see PARA 547. As to the provision of education for persons subject to detention orders see PARA 38.

8   Education Act 1996 s 15ZA(1)(b) (as added (see note 3); and amended by SI 2010/1158 and the Children and Families Act 2014 Sch 3 para 5(1), (2)). As to the meaning of 'EHC plan' see PARA 958. As to EHC plans (ie education, health and care plans) generally see PARA 958 et seq.

9   Education Act 1996 s 15ZA(2) (as added (see note 3); and amended by SI 2010/1158).

10 Education Act 1996 s 15ZA(3)(a) (as added (see note 3); and amended by SI 2010/1158).

11 Education Act 1996 s 15ZA(3)(b) (as added (see note 3); and amended by the Children and Families Act 2014 Sch 3 para 5(1), (3)). For these purposes a person has a learning difficulty or disability if: (1) the person has a significantly greater difficulty in learning than the majority of persons of the same age (Education Act 1996 s 15ZA(6)(a) (as so added; and s 15ZA(6) amended by the Children and Families Act 2014 Sch 3 para 5(1), (4))); or (2) the person has a disability which either prevents or hinders the person from making use of facilities of a kind generally provided by institutions providing education or training for persons who are over compulsory school age (Education Act 1996 s 15ZA(6)(b) (as so added)). But a person is not to be taken to have a learning difficulty or disability solely because the language (or form of language) in which the person is or will be taught is different from a language (or form of language) which has at any time been spoken in the person's home (s 15ZA(7) (as so added; and amended by the Children and Families Act 2014 Sch 3 para 5(1), (4))).

12 Education Act 1996 s 15ZA(3)(c) (as added see note 3).

13 Education Act 1996 s 15ZA(3)(d) (as added: see note 3).

14 Education Act 1996 s 15ZA(4)(a) (as added (see note 3); and amended by SI 2010/1158).

15 Education Act 1996 s 15ZA(4)(b) (as added: see note 3).

16 Ie the persons to whom the Education and Skills Act 2008 Pt 1 (ss 1–67) applies: see s 1; and PARA 725.

17 See the Education Act 1996 s 15ZA(4)(c) (as added: see note 3). As to the duty to participate in education or training see the Education and Skills Act 2008 s 2; and PARA 725.

18 Education Act 1996 s 15ZA(4)(d) (as added: see note 3).

19 Education Act 1996 s 15ZB (as added (see note 3); and amended by SI 2010/1158).

20 Education Act 1996 s 15ZC(1)(a) (as added (see note 3); and amended by SI 2010/1158).

21 Education Act 1996 s 15ZC(1)(b) (as added: see note 3). For these purposes, participating in the provision of training includes participating by entering into: (1) an apprenticeship agreement (within the meaning given in the Apprenticeships, Skills, Children and Learning Act 2009 s 32 (see PARA 766)) (Education Act 1996 s 15ZC(2)(a) (as so added)); or (2) any other contract of employment in connection with which training is provided (s 15ZC(2)(b) (as so added)).

33. Work experience for persons over compulsory school age in England. A local authority[1] in England may secure the provision of work experience for persons in their area[2]: (1) who are over compulsory school age[3] but under 19[4]; or (2) who are aged 19 or over and for whom an EHC plan is maintained[5].

A local authority in England must encourage participation in work experience by persons in their area who are within head (1) or (2) above[6], and encourage employers to participate in the provision of work experience for such persons[7].

1   As to the meaning of 'local authority in England' see PARA 25.

2   Education Act 1996 s 560A(1) (s 560A added by the Apprenticeships, Skills, Children and Learning Act 2009 s 47). As to when a person is treated as belonging to the area of a local authority see PARA 27 note 6.

3   As to the meaning of 'compulsory school age' see PARA 19.

4   Education Act 1996 s 560A(1)(a) (as added: see note 2). As to the time at which a person attains a particular age see PARA 7 note 6.

5   Education Act 1996 s 560A(1)(b) (as added (see note 2); and amended by the Children and Families Act 2014 Sch 3 para 54). As to the meaning of 'EHC plan' see PARA 958. As to EHC plans (ie education, health and care plans) generally see PARA 958 et seq.

6   Education Act 1996 s 560A(2)(a) (as added: see note 2).

7   Education Act 1996 s 560A(2)(b) (as added: see note 2).

34. Powers in respect of education and training for 16 to 18-year-olds. A local authority[1] in England[2] may secure the provision for its area of full-time or part-time education suitable to the requirements of persons from other areas who are over compulsory school age[3] but have not attained the age of 19[4]. A local authority in Wales[5] may secure the provision for its area of full-time or part-time education suitable to the requirements of persons over compulsory school age who have not attained the age of 19, including provision for persons from other areas[6].

This power[7] includes the power to secure the provision of[8]: (1) training, including vocational, social, physical and recreational training[9]; and (2) organised leisure-time occupation[10] which is provided in connection with the provision of education or of training within head (1) above[11].

In exercising these functions in respect of secondary education[12], a local authority must in particular have regard to:

(a)   the need for securing that primary and secondary education[13] are provided in separate schools[14];

(b)   the need for securing that special educational provision[15] is made for pupils[16] who have special educational needs[17]; and

(c)   the expediency of securing the provision of boarding accommodation, in boarding schools or otherwise, for pupils for whom education as boarders[18] is considered by their parents[19] and the authority to be desirable[20].

In exercising these functions in respect of further education[21], a local authority in England must in particular have regard to the needs of persons with learning difficulties or disabilities[22].

A local authority may do anything which appears to it to be necessary or expedient for the purposes of or in connection with the exercise of these functions[23].

1   As to the meaning of 'local authority' see PARA 25.
2   As to the meaning of 'England' see PARA 7 note 3.
3   As to the meaning of 'compulsory school age' see PARA 19.
4   Education Act 1996 s 15A(1ZA) (s 15A added by the School Standards and Framework Act 1998 s 140(1), Sch 30 paras 57, 63; the Education Act 1996 s 15A(1ZA) added by the Apprenticeships, Skills, Children and Learning Act 2009 s 59, Sch 2 paras 1, 4(1), (3); and amended by SI 2010/1158). As to the time at which a person attains a particular age see PARA 7 note 6. As to the duty of a local authority in England to secure education and training for persons in its area over compulsory school age see PARA 32. As to the power of such an authority to secure the provision of work experience for persons in its area who are over compulsory school age see PARA 33.
5   As to the meaning of 'Wales' see PARA 7 note 3.
6   Education Act 1996 s 15A(1) (s 15A as added (see note 4); s 15A(1) amended by the Learning and Skills Act 2000 s 149, Sch 9 paras 1, 54(1), (2); the Apprenticeships, Skills, Children and Learning Act 2009 s 59, Sch 2 paras 1, 4(1), (2); and SI 2010/1158).
      A local authority may not continue to maintain an institution which would have become a school on the coming into force of the Learning and Skills Act 2000 s 110(1) (which added the Education Act 1996 s 2(2A), (2B) (see PARA 21)) in pursuance of s 15A: Learning and Skills Act 2000 s 110(2), (4) (amended by SI 2010/1158). The Learning and Skills Act 2000 s 110(1) came into force in relation to Wales on 1 April 2001 (see the Learning and Skills Act 2000 (Commencement No 3 and Transitional Provisions) (Wales) Order 2001, SI 2001/1274), and in relation to England for certain purposes on 1 September 2000 (see the Learning and Skills Act 2000 (Commencement No 1) Order 2000, SI 2000/2114) and for the remaining purposes on 1 April 2001 (see the Learning and Skills Act 2000 (Commencement No 3 and Savings and Transitional Provisions) Order 2001, SI 2001/654).
7   Ie the power under the Education Act 1996 s 15A(1) and (1ZA): see the text to notes 1–6.
8   Education Act 1996 s 15A(1A) (s 15A as added (see note 4); s 15A(1A) added by the Learning and Skills Act 2000 Sch 9 paras 1, 54(1), (3), and amended by the Apprenticeships, Skills, Children and Learning Act 2009 s 59, Sch 2 paras 1, 4(1), (4)).
9   Education Act 1996 s 15A(1A)(a) (as added: see note 8).
10 Ie within the meaning of the Education Act 1996 s 2(6): see PARA 23 note 4.
11 Education Act 1996 s 15A(1A)(b) (as added: see note 8).
12 As to the meaning of 'secondary education' see PARA 21.
13 As to the meaning of 'primary education' see PARA 20.
14 Education Act 1996 ss 14(6)(a), 15A(2) (ss 15A as added (see note 4); s 15A(2) amended by the Learning and Skills Act 2000 Sch 9 paras 1, 54(1), (4); SI 2010/1158). The duty imposed by the Education Act 1996 s 14(6)(a) does not apply in relation to middle schools or special schools:

ss 14(7), 15A(2) (as so added and amended). As to the meaning of 'middle school' see PARA 91. As to the meaning of 'special school' see PARA 1041.

15   As to the meaning of 'special educational provision' see PARAS 943, 989.

16   As to the meaning of 'pupil' see PARA 20 note 4.

17   Education Act 1996 ss 14(6)(b), 15A(2) (as added and amended: see note 14). As to the meaning of 'special educational needs' see PARAS 943, 989.

18   As to the meaning of 'boarder' see PARA 31 note 19.

19   As to the meaning of 'parent' see PARA 7 note 6.

20   Education Act 1996 ss 14(6)(c), 15A(2) (as added and amended: see note 14).

21   As to the meaning of 'further education' see PARA 23.

22   Education Act 1996 s 15A(3)(a) (s 15A as added (see note 5); s 15A(3), (4) added by the Learning and Skills Act 2000 Sch 9 paras 1, 54(1), (5), and the Education Act 1996 s 15A(3) amended by SI 2010/1158; and the Children and Families Act 2014 Sch 3 para 6). The reference in the text to 'learning difficulties or disabilities' is a reference to learning difficulties or disabilities within the Education Act 1996 s 15ZA(6), (7): see PARA 32 note 11. For corresponding provision as to Wales see the Education Act 1996 s 15A(3)(b) (as so added and amended). As to the meaning of 'England' see PARA 7 note 3.

23   Education Act 1996 s 15A(4) (s 15A(4) as added and amended: see note 22).

35. Duties in relation to the core entitlement. As from a day to be appointed the following provisions have effect[1].

A local authority in England[2] must exercise its functions[3] in such a way as to secure that the core entitlement[4] is satisfied in relation to persons in its area who are over compulsory school age[5] but under 19[6].

In exercising its functions as required above, a local authority in England must have regard to any guidance given from time to time by the Secretary of State[7].

1   The Education Act 1996 s 17A is added by the Apprenticeships, Skills, Children and Learning Act 2009 s 45 as from a day to be appointed: see s 269(4). At the date at which this volume states the law no such day had been appointed.

2   As to the meaning of 'local authority in England' see PARA 25.

3   As to the meaning of 'functions' see PARA 18 note 5.

4   As to the meaning of 'the core entitlement' see PARA 724.

5   As to the meaning of 'compulsory school age' see PARA 19.

6   Education Act 1996 s 17A(1) (as added (see note 1); and amended by SI 2010/1158; and the Education Act 2011 s 30(3)(a)). The references in the Education Act 1996 s 17A(1) to persons in a local authority's area who are over compulsory school age but under 19 do not include persons who are subject to a detention order: s 17A(9) (as so added and amended). As to the time at which a person attains a particular age see PARA 7 note 6. As to when a person is subject to a detention order, and as to the application of the Education Act 1996 to detained persons see PARA 547. As to the provision of education for persons subject to detention orders see PARA 38.

7   Education Act 1996 s 17A(6) (as added (see note 1); and amended by SI 2010/1158). As to the publication of guidance see PARA 60.

36. Functions in respect of education for persons over 19. A local authority[1] may secure the provision for its area of full-time or part-time education suitable to the requirements of persons who have attained the age of 19[2], including provision for persons from other areas[3]. This power includes power to secure the provision of: (1) training, including vocational, social, physical and recreational training[4]; and (2) organised leisure-time occupation[5] which is provided in connection with the provision of education or of training within head (1) above[6]. In exercising these functions, a local authority in England must in particular have regard to the needs of persons with learning difficulties or disabilities[7].

A local authority may do anything which appears to it to be necessary or expedient for the purposes of or in connection with the exercise of these functions[8].

None of the provisions described above applies to higher education[9].

1   As to the meaning of 'local authority' see PARA 25.

2 As to the time at which a person attains a particular age see PARA 7 note 6.
3 Education Act 1996 s 15B(1) (s 15B added by the Learning and Skills Act 2000 s 149, Sch 9 paras 1, 55; Education Act 1996 s 15B(1), (3), (4) amended by SI 2010/1158). As to when a person is treated as belonging to the area of a local authority see PARA 27 note 6.
4 Education Act 1996 s 15B(2)(a) (as added: see note 3).
5 Ie within the meaning of the Education Act 1996 s 2(6): see PARA 23 note 4.
6 Education Act 1996 s 15B(2)(b) (as added: see note 3).
7 Education Act 1996 s 15B(3)(a) (as added and amended (see note 3); and s 15B(3) amended by the Children and Families Act 2014 Sch 3 para 7). As to the meaning of 'learning difficulties or disabilities' see the Education Act 1996 s 15ZA(6), (7) (see PARA 32 note 11) (definition applied by s 15B(3) (as so added and amended); and amended by the Apprenticeships, Skills, Children and Learning Act 2009 s 59, Sch 2 paras 1, 5). For corresponding provision as to Wales see the Education Act 1996 s 15B(3)(b) (as so added and amended). As to the meanings of 'England' and 'Wales' see PARA 7 note 3.
8 Education Act 1996 s 15B(4) (as added and amended: see note 3).
9 Education Act 1996 s 15B(5) (as added: see note 3). As to the meaning of 'higher education' see PARA 24.

37. Functions in respect of provision of education in pupil referral units and elsewhere. Each local authority[1] must make arrangements for the provision of suitable education[2] at school[3] or otherwise than at school for those children of compulsory school age[4] who, by reason of illness, exclusion from school[5] or otherwise, may not for any period receive suitable education unless such arrangements are made for them[6].

1 As to the meaning of 'local authority' see PARA 25.
2 As to the meaning of 'suitable education' see PARA 427 note 3.
3 As to the meaning of 'school' see PARA 91.
4 As to the meaning of 'compulsory school age' see PARA 19.
5 As to the exclusion of pupils from school see PARA 517 et seq.
6 See the Education Act 1996 s 19; and PARA 427 et seq.

38. Provision of education for persons subject to youth detention. A local authority[1] must secure that[2]:

(1) enough suitable education is provided to meet the reasonable needs of children[3] subject to youth detention in its area[4];

(2) enough suitable education and training is provided to meet the reasonable needs of persons who are over compulsory school age[5] but under 19[6], and subject to youth detention in their area[7].

In deciding for these purposes whether education or training is suitable to meet persons' reasonable needs, a local authority must (in particular) have regard to: (a) the persons' ages, abilities and aptitudes[8]; (b) any special educational needs[9] the persons may have[10]; (c) in the case of a local authority in England, any learning difficulties or disabilities[11] the persons may have[12]; (d) the desirability of enabling persons to complete programmes of study or training which they have begun[13]; (e) any relevant curriculum[14] and the desirability that education received by persons subject to youth detention should be comparable with education which they could be expected to receive if they were attending a school[15] or institution implementing a relevant curriculum[16]; (f) the desirability of the core entitlement[17] being satisfied in relation to persons over compulsory school age but under 19[18].

Any arrangements made by a local authority[19] for the provision by another person[20] (the 'learning provider') of education or training must require the learning provider, in making any determination as to the education or training to be provided for a particular person, to have regard to any of certain specified information[21].

In performing the duty imposed by these provisions[22], a local authority must have regard to any guidance[23] issued, in the case of a local authority in England, by the Secretary of State[24] or, in the case of a local authority in Wales, by the Welsh Ministers[25].

1   As to the meaning of 'local authority' see PARA 25.

2   Education Act 1996 s 18A(1) (s 18A added by the Apprenticeships, Skills, Children and Learning Act 2009 s 48; and amended by SI 2010/1158). At the date at which this volume states the law the Apprenticeships, Skills, Children and Learning Act 2009 s 48 is in force for England only, to the extent that it inserts the Education Act 1996 s 18A(1), (2)(a)–(d), (3) and (5)–(8), and only in relation to persons who are subject to youth detention (as defined by s 18A(8): see note 4) by virtue of being detained in a relevant young offender institution: see the Apprenticeships, Skills, Children and Learning Act 2009 (Commencement No 2 and Transitional and Saving Provisions) Order 2010, SI 2010/303, art 6, Sch 5. The Education Act 1996 s 18A will come into force in relation to England for remaining purposes, and in relation to Wales, on a day to be appointed: see the Apprenticeships, Skills, Children and Learning Act 2009 s 269(3)(f), (4). At the date at which this volume states the law no such day had been appointed. 'Relevant young offender institution' means a young offender institution in England, or part of such an institution, other than Ashfield Young Offender Institution, South Gloucestershire: Apprenticeships, Skills, Children and Learning Act 2009 (Commencement No 2 and Transitional and Saving Provisions) Order 2010, SI 2010/303, art 1(2). As to the meanings of 'England' and 'Wales' see PARA 7 note 3. As to young offender institutions see PRISONS AND PRISONERS vol 85 (2012) PARA 487 et seq.

3   As to the meaning of 'child' see PARA 7 note 6.

4   Education Act 1996 s 18A(1)(a) (as added: see note 2). A person is subject to youth detention in the area of a local authority if subject to a detention order, and detained in relevant youth accommodation in the area of the authority: s 18A(8) (as so added and amended). As to when a person is subject to a detention order, and as to the meaning of 'relevant youth accommodation', see PARA 46 note 9.

5   As to the meaning of 'compulsory school age' see PARA 19.

6   Education Act 1996 s 18A(1)(b)(i) (as added: see note 2). As to the time at which a person attains a particular age see PARA 7 note 6.

7   Education Act 1996 s 18A(1)(b)(ii) (as added: see note 2).

8   Education Act 1996 s 18A(2)(a) (as added: see note 2).

9   As to the meaning of 'special educational needs' see PARAS 943, 989.

10   Education Act 1996 s 18A(2)(b) (as added (see note 2); and amended by the Children and Families Act 2014 Sch 3 para 8(a)).

11   Ie within the meaning of the Education Act 1996 s 15ZA(6), (7): see PARA 32 note 11.

12   Education Act 1996 s 18A(2)(ba) (s 18A(2) (ba), (bb) added by the Children and Families Act 2014 Sch 3 para 8(b)). For corresponding provision as to Wales see the Education Act 1996 s 18A(2)(bb) (as so added and amended).

13   Education Act 1996 s 18A(2)(c) (as added: see note 2).

14   'Relevant curriculum' means: (1) in relation to a local authority in England, the National Curriculum for England established under the Education Act 2002 s 87 (see PARA 863) as subsisting for the time being (Education Act 1996 s 18A(3)(a) (as added and amended: see note 2)); (2) in relation to a local authority in Wales (a) the National Curriculum for Wales established under the Education Act 2002 s 108 (see PARA 878) as subsisting for the time being (Education Act 1996 s 18A(3)(b)(i) (as so added and amended)); or (b) any local curriculum formed by the authority under the Education Act 2002 s 116A (formation of local curricula for pupils in Key Stage 4: see PARA 885) or for its area under the Learning and Skills Act 2000 s 33A (formation of local curricula for students aged 16 to 18: see PARA 895) (Education Act 1996 s 18A(3)(b)(ii) (as so added)).

15   As to the meaning of 'school' see PARA 91.

16   Education Act 1996 s 18A(2)(d) (as added: see note 2).

17   As to the core entitlement see PARA 35. The Education Act 1996 s 17C (see PARA 724) applies for the purposes of s 18A(2)(e): s 18A(4) (as added (see note 2); and substituted by the Education Act 2011 s 30(7)(b).

18   Education Act 1996 s 18A(2)(e) (as added (see note 2); and amended by the Education Act 2011 s 30(7)(a)).

19   Ie under the Education Act 1996 s 18A(1): see the text to notes 1–7.

20   As to the meaning of 'person' in this context see PARA 7 note 6.

21 See the Education Act 1996 s 18A(5) (as added and amended: see note 2). The specified information is: (1) information provided under s 562F (see PARA 551) by a local authority as to the level of the person's literacy and numeracy skills (see s 18A(6)(a) (as so added and amended)); (2) any other information provided under s 562F by the person's home authority (within the meaning of Pt 10 Ch 5A (ss 562A–562J): see PARA 548 note 3) for the purpose of assisting a determination such as is mentioned in s 18A(5) (see s 18A(6)(b) (as so added)).
22 Ie imposed by the Education Act 1996 s 18A(1): see the text to notes 1–7.
23 As to the publication of guidance see PARA 60.
24 Education Act 1996 s 18A(7)(a) (as added: see note 2). As to the Secretary of State see PARA 58.
25 Education Act 1996 s 18A(7)(b) (as added and amended: see note 2). As to the Welsh Ministers see PARA 59.

39. Functions of local authorities with respect to higher education. A local authority[1] is no longer under a duty to secure the provision for its area of facilities for higher education[2]. However, a local authority does have power to secure the provision for its area of such facilities for higher education as appear to it to be appropriate for meeting the needs of the population of its area and to secure the provision of higher education for persons from other areas, as well as to do anything which appears to it to be necessary or expedient for the purposes of or in connection with such provision[3].

1 As to the meaning of 'local authority' see PARA 25.
2 See the Education Reform Act 1988 s 120(1); and PARA 678.
3 See the Education Reform Act 1988 s 120(3); and PARA 678.

40. Arrangements for the provision of education at non-maintained schools. A local authority[1] may make arrangements for the provision of primary[2] and secondary education[3] for pupils[4] at schools[5] not maintained[6] by it or another local authority[7].

1 As to the meaning of 'local authority' see PARA 25.
2 As to the meaning of 'primary education' see PARA 20.
3 As to the meaning of 'secondary education' see PARA 21.
4 As to the meaning of 'pupil' see PARA 20 note 4.
5 As to the meaning of 'school' see PARA 91.
6 As to maintained schools see PARA 99 et seq.
7 Education Act 1996 s 18 (amended by SI 2010/1158). Any function of a local authority in England which is conferred by or under the Education Act 1996 s 18 may be exercised by, or by employees of, such person as may be authorised in that behalf by the local authority whose function it is: Contracting Out (Local Authority Education Functions) (England) Order 2002, SI 2002/928, art 3, Sch 1 para (a) (art 3 amended by SI 2010/1172). As to the meaning of 'England' see PARA 7 note 3. As to the meaning of 'person' see PARA 7 note 6. As to the payment of fees where arrangements have been made under the Education Act 1996 s 18, see s 517 (amended by SI 1999/2260; SI 2010/1158; and the Children and Families Act 2014 Sch 3 para 51; and repealed, as from a day to be appointed, by the School Standards and Framework Act 1998 s 140(1), (3), Sch 30 para 138, Sch 31). At the date at which this volume states the law no such day had been appointed. Any function of a local authority in England which is conferred by or under the Education Act 1996 s 517 may be exercised by, or by employees of, such person as may be authorised in that behalf by the local authority whose function it is: Contracting Out (Local Authority Education Functions) (England) Order 2002, SI 2002/928, art 3, Sch 1 para (w) (both amended by SI 2010/1172). With the repeal of the Education Act 1996 s 517, a local authority will be required to pay fees only in relation to the provision of special education at non-maintained schools in Wales: see s 348; and PARA 1016.

41. Power to establish primary and secondary schools. For the purpose of fulfilling its functions[1] under the Education Act 1996, a local authority[2] may:

(1) establish primary schools[3] and secondary schools[4];

(2) maintain primary and secondary schools, whether established by it or not[5]; and

(3)   assist[6] any primary or secondary school which is not maintained by it[7].

A local authority may, under these powers, establish, maintain and assist schools outside as well as inside its area[8]. However, it may not, under these powers, establish a school to provide: (a) part-time education suitable to the requirements of persons of any age over compulsory school age[9]; or (b) full-time education suitable to the requirements of persons who have attained the age of 19[10]; and a local authority in England[11] may not establish a school which is principally concerned with the provision of full-time education suitable to the requirements of pupils[12] who are over compulsory school age but under 19[13].

1 As to the meaning of 'functions' see PARA 18 note 5.
2 Education Act 1996 s 16(1) (amended by SI 2010/1158). As to the meaning of 'local authority' see PARA 25. As to the general responsibility of local authorities for education see PARA 27.
3 As to the meaning of 'primary school' see PARA 91.
4 Education Act 1996 s 16(1)(a). As to the meaning of 'secondary school' see PARA 91.
5 Education Act 1996 s 16(1)(b).
6 As to the meaning of 'assist' see PARA 51.
7 Education Act 1996 s 16(1)(c).
8 Education Act 1996 s 16(2) (amended by SI 2010/1158).
9 Education Act 1996 s 16(3)(a). As to the meaning of 'compulsory school age' see PARA 19. As to the time at which a person attains a particular age see PARA 7 note 6.
10 Education Act 1996 s 16(3)(b).
11 As to the meaning of 'local authority in England' see PARA 25.
12 As to the meaning of 'pupil' see PARA 20 note 4.
13 Education Act 1996 s 16(3A) (added by the Apprenticeships, Skills, Children and Learning Act 2009 s 126(1); and amended by SI 2010/1158).

42.   Power to award or authenticate academic and vocational qualifications.
A local authority[1] may award or authenticate academic and vocational qualifications, and may in particular[2]: (1) devise and administer a qualification or a course leading to a qualification[3]; (2) register candidates[4]; (3) set, administer and moderate examinations or other assessments[5]; and (4) require the payment of fees in respect of the exercise of the power[6]. A local authority may secure the exercise by any other person[7] of such of these powers as the authority may specify[8]; and a local authority may exercise its powers under these provisions by forming, or participating in forming, or being a member of, a body corporate[9].

The powers under the above provisions must be regarded as always having been within the powers of a local authority; and the above provisions are without prejudice to the generality of the powers of a local authority[10].

1 As to the meaning of 'local authority' see PARA 25 (definition applied by the Education Act 2002 s 212(1)).
2 Education Act 2002 s 190(1) (amended by SI 2010/1158).
3 Education Act 2002 s 190(1)(a).
4 Education Act 2002 s 190(1)(b).
5 Education Act 2002 s 190(1)(c).
6 Education Act 2002 s 190(1)(d).
7 As to the meaning of 'person' see PARA 7 note 6.
8 Education Act 2002 s 190(2) (amended by SI 2010/1158).
9 Education Act 2002 s 190(3) (amended by SI 2010/1158).
10 Education Act 2002 s 190(4) (amended by SI 2010/1158).

43.   Duty to promote high standards and fulfilment of potential.   A local authority in England[1] must ensure that its relevant education functions[2] and its relevant training functions[3] are (so far as they are capable of being so exercised) exercised by the authority with a view to[4]:

(1)   promoting high standards[5];

(2)   ensuring fair access to opportunity for education and training[6]; and
(3)   promoting the fulfilment of learning potential by every person (a) under
      the age of 20[7], or (b) aged 20 or over and for whom an EHC plan is
      maintained[8].

A local authority in Wales[9] must ensure that its relevant education functions[10]
and its relevant training functions are (so far as they are capable of being so
exercised) exercised by the authority with a view to[11]: (i) promoting high
standards[12], and (ii) promoting the fulfilment of learning potential by every
person under the age of 20[13].

1   As to the meaning of 'local authority in England' see PARA 25.
2   'Relevant education function', in relation to a local authority in England, means a function
    relating to the provision of education for: (1) persons of compulsory school age (whether at
    school or otherwise); (2) persons (whether at school or otherwise) who are over compulsory
    school age and are (a) under the age of 20, or (b) aged 20 or over and for whom an EHC plan
    is maintained; (3) persons who are under compulsory school age and are registered as pupils at
    schools maintained by the authority: see the Education Act 1996 s 13A(2), (5) (s 13A added by
    the School Standards and Framework Act 1998 s 5; substituted by the Education and
    Inspections Act 2006 s 1; and further substituted by the Apprenticeships, Skills, Children and
    Learning Act 2009 s 59, Sch 2 paras 1, 3; the Education Act 1996 s 13A(2) amended by the
    Children and Families Act 2014 Sch 3 para 4; and the Education Act 1996 s 13A(5) amended by
    SI 2010/1158). As to the meaning of 'education' see PARA 32 note 3 (definition applied by the
    Education Act 1996 s 13A(5) (as so added and substituted)). As to the meaning of 'functions' see
    PARA 18 note 5. As to the meaning of 'compulsory school age' see PARA 19. As to the meaning of
    'school' see PARA 91. As to the time at which a person attains a particular age see PARA 7 note 6.
    As to the meaning of 'EHC plan' see PARA 958 and as to EHC plans (ie education, health and
    care plans) generally see PARA 958 et seq. As to the meaning of 'registered' see PARA 437. As to
    the meaning of 'pupil' see PARA 20 note 4.
3   'Relevant training function' means a function relating to the provision of training: Education
    Act 1996 s 13A(5) (as added and substituted: see note 2). As to the meaning of 'training' see
    PARA 32 note 4 (definition applied by the Education Act 1996 s 13A(5) (as so added and
    substituted)).
4   Education Act 1996 s 13A(1) (as added and substituted (see note 2); and amended by
    SI 2010/1158).
5   Education Act 1996 s 13A(1)(a) (as added and substituted: see note 2).
6   Education Act 1996 s 13A(1)(b) (as added and substituted: see note 2).
7   See the Education Act 1996 s 13A(1)(c), (2)(a) (as added and substituted: see note 2).
8   See the Education Act 1996 s 13A(1)(c), (2)(b) (as added, substituted and amended (see note 2).
9   As to the meaning of 'local authority in Wales' see PARA 25.
10 'Relevant education function', in relation to a local authority in Wales, means a function relating
    to the provision of education for: (1) persons of compulsory school age (whether at school or
    otherwise); (2) persons (whether at school or otherwise) who are over compulsory school age
    but under the age of 20; (3) persons who are under compulsory school age and are registered as
    pupils at schools maintained by the authority: Education Act 1996 s 13A(5) (as added,
    substituted and amended: see note 2).
11 Education Act 1996 s 13A(3) (as added and substituted (see note 2); and amended by
    SI 2010/1158).
12 Education Act 1996 s 13A(3)(a) (as added and substituted: see note 2).
13 See the Education Act 1996 s 13A(3)(b), (4) (as added and substituted: see note 2).

44.   Complaints and enforcement in Wales.   Until a day to be appointed the
following provisions have effect[1].

A local authority[2] in Wales[3] must, after consultation with governing bodies[4]
of foundation and voluntary aided schools[5] in Wales, make arrangements for the
consideration and disposal of any specified complaint[6]. A specified complaint is
one which is to the effect that the authority, or the governing body of any
community, foundation or voluntary school[7] maintained by the authority, any
maintained nursery school so maintained[8], or any community so maintained
which is not established in a hospital[9]: (1) has acted or is proposing to act

unreasonably in relation to the exercise of a power conferred on it by or under a relevant enactment[10]; or (2) has acted or is proposing to act unreasonably in relation to the performance of, or has failed to discharge, a duty imposed on it by or under a relevant enactment[11].

1   The Education Act 1996 s 409 is repealed by the Apprenticeships, Skills, Children and Learning Act 2009 ss 223(1)(b), 266, Sch 16 Pt 7. This repeal is in force in relation to schools maintained by specified councils (see the Apprenticeships, Skills, Children and Learning Act 2009 (Commencement No 2 and Transitional and Saving Provisions) Order 2010, SI 2010/303, art 5, Sch 4; Apprenticeships, Skills, Children and Learning Act 2009 (Commencement No 3 and Transitional and Transitory Provisions) and (Commencement No 2 (Amendment)) Order 2010, SI 2010/1151, art 4, Sch 2), and will be brought into force for remaining purposes as from a day to be appointed: see the Apprenticeships, Skills, Children and Learning Act 2009 s 269(3)(h), (4). At the date at which this volume states the law no such day had been appointed.

2   As to the meaning of 'local authority' see PARA 25.

3   As to the meaning of 'Wales' see PARA 7 note 3.

4   As to governing bodies see PARA 150 et seq.

5   As to foundation and voluntary aided schools see PARA 106 et seq.

6   Education Act 1996 s 409(1) (amended by the School Standards and Framework Act 1998 s 140(1), Sch 30 para 107(a); the Education Act 2002 s 215, Sch 21 para 47(1), (2), Sch 22 Pt 3; SI 2010/1158; and the Education Act 2011 s 45(2)(a)).

7   As to community, foundation and voluntary schools see PARA 106 et seq.

8   At the date at which this volume states the law, the words 'any maintained nursery school so maintained' are not yet in force: see the Education Act 1996 s 409(2) (amended by the Education Act 2002 s 215(1), Sch 21 para 47(1), (3)). The amendment will be brought into force as from a day to be appointed by order made under the Education Act 2002 s 216(4). At the date at which this volume states the law no such day had been appointed. 'Maintained nursery school' has the meaning given by the School Standards and Framework Act 1998 s 22(9) (see PARA 99 note 4): Education Act 1996 s 579(1) (definition added by the Education Act 2002 s 215(1), Sch 21 para 57(a)).

9   Education Act 1996 s 409(2) (amended by the School Standards and Framework Act 1998 Sch 30 para 107(b); and the School Standards and Organisation (Wales) Act 2013 Sch 5 Pt 2 paras 17(1), (4)).

10   Education Act 1996 s 409(2)(a). 'Relevant enactment' means: (1) any provision which by virtue of s 408(4) (see PARA 940) is a relevant provision of Pt V (ss 375–409) for the purposes of s 408(1) (see PARA 940); (2) any provision which by virtue of s 408(4A) (see PARA 940) is a relevant provision of the Education Act 2002 for the purposes of the Education Act 1996 s 408(1); and (3) any other enactment, whether contained in Pt V or otherwise, so far as relating to the curriculum for, or religious worship in, maintained schools: s 409(3) (amended by the School Standards and Framework Act 1998 Sch 30 para 107(c), Sch 31; and the Education Act 2002 Sch 21 para 47(1), (4)).

11   Education Act 1996 s 409(2)(b). The Welsh Ministers must not entertain under the School Standards and Organisation (Wales) Act 2013 Pt 2 Ch 1 (ss 2–20) (see PARA 1229 et seq) or Pt 2 Ch 2 (ss 21–31) (see PARA 1235 et seq) (intervention in conduct of maintained schools and local authorities) any complaint to which the Education Act 1996 s 409(2) (see the text to notes 7–9) applies, unless a complaint concerning the same matter has been made and disposed of in accordance with arrangements made under s 409(1) (see the text to notes 2–6): s 409(4) (amended by the Education Act 2011 s 45(2)(a)(ii); and the School Standards and Organisation (Wales) Act 2013 Sch 5 Pt 1 para 2(1), (2)). As to the Welsh Ministers see PARA 59.

45.   Power to secure proper performance of local authorities' functions. If a local authority[1] is failing in any respect to perform its functions[2] which relate to the provision of education to an adequate standard or at all, steps may be taken to secure that the functions are properly performed[3].

1   As to the meaning of 'local authority' see PARA 25.

2   As to the meaning of 'functions' see PARA 18 note 5.

3   See PARA 62.

46.   Persons not covered by the Education Act 1996. No power or duty conferred or imposed by the Education Act 1996 on local authorities[1] is to be construed as relating to any person who is employed by or under the Crown in any service or capacity with respect to which the Secretary of State[2] or, in relation to Wales, the Welsh Ministers[3] certify that, by reason of the arrangements made for the education of children[4] and young persons[5] so employed, the exercise and performance of those powers and duties with respect to such children and young persons is unnecessary[6].

No power or duty conferred or imposed by or under the Education Act 1996 on local authorities[7] is to be construed as relating to any person who is subject to a detention order[8] and is detained in accommodation that is not relevant youth accommodation[9], but a local authority may make arrangements for such a person to receive the benefit of educational facilities provided by the authority[10].

These provisions are applied for the purposes of the School Standards and Framework Act 1998[11] and, with certain exceptions, for the purposes of the Education Act 2002[12], the Education Act 2005[13], the Education and Inspections Act 2006[14], the Education and Skills Act 2008[15] and the Apprenticeships, Skills, Children and Learning Act 2009[16].

1   See the Education Act 1996 s 561(b) (amended by SI 2010/1158). As to the meaning of 'local authority' see PARA 25.
2   As to the Secretary of State see PARA 58.
3   The functions of the Secretary of State under the Education Act 1996 s 561, so far as exercisable in relation to Wales, were transferred to the National Assembly for Wales (see the National Assembly for Wales (Transfer of Functions) Order 1999, SI 1999/672, art 2, Sch 1) and are now vested in the Welsh Ministers (see the Government of Wales Act 2006 s 162(1), Sch 11 para 30). As to the Welsh Ministers see PARA 59. As to the meaning of 'Wales' see PARA 7 note 3.
4   As to the meaning of 'child' see PARA 7 note 6.
5   As to the meaning of 'young person' see PARA 7 note 6.
6   Education Act 1996 s 561.
7   See the Education Act 1996 s 562(1)(b) (amended by SI 2010/1158).
8   A person is subject to a detention order if detained in pursuance of: (1) an order made by a court; or (2) an order of recall made by the Secretary of State: Education Act 1996 s 562(1A)(a) (s 562(1), (2) amended, (1A), (3) added, by the Apprenticeships, Skills, Children and Learning Act 2009 s 49). At the date at which this volume states the law the amendments and additions to the Education Act 1996 s 562 made by the Apprenticeships, Skills, Children and Learning Act 2009 s 49 are in force in relation to England and Wales only and in relation only to persons who are detained in relevant youth accommodation (as defined by the Education Act 1996 s 562(1A): see note 9) by virtue of being detained in a relevant young offender institution: as to England see the Apprenticeships, Skills, Children and Learning Act 2009 (Commencement No 2 and Transitional and Saving Provisions) Order 2010, SI 2010/303, art 6, Sch 5, and as to Wales see the Apprenticeships, Skills, Children and Learning Act 2009 (Commencement No 3) (Wales) Order 2011, SI 2011/829, art 2). The amendments and additions so made will come into force in relation to England and Wales for remaining purposes on a day to be appointed: see the Apprenticeships, Skills, Children and Learning Act 2009 s 269(3)(f), (4). At the date at which this volume states the law no such day had been appointed. As to the meaning of 'relevant young offender institution' see PARA 38 note 2. As to the meaning of 'England' see PARA 7 note 3.
    A child or young person who is being educated as a boarder at a school is not to be regarded for these purposes as detained in pursuance of an order made by a court by reason of the fact that he is required to be at the school (a) by virtue of an order made by a court under the Children and Young Persons Act 1933 (see SENTENCING AND DISPOSITION OF OFFENDERS vol 92 (2010) PARA 10 et seq) or by virtue of anything done under such an order; or (b) by virtue of a requirement of a youth rehabilitation order under the Criminal Justice and Immigration Act 2008 s 1 (see SENTENCING AND DISPOSITION OF OFFENDERS vol 92 (2010) PARA 202 et seq) or by virtue of anything done under such a requirement: Education Act 1996 s 562(2) (amended by the Criminal Justice and Immigration Act 2008 s 6(2), Sch 4 Pt 1 para 47; and as further amended: see above). As to the meaning of 'boarder' see PARA 31 note 19. A child or young person who is being kept in accommodation provided for the purpose of restricting liberty is not to be regarded for these purposes as detained in pursuance of an order made by a court by reason of the fact that a court has authorised the person to be kept in such accommodation

under the Children Act 1989 s 25(4) (use of accommodation for restricting liberty: see CHILDREN AND YOUNG PERSONS vol 10 (2012) PARA 1045): Education Act 1996 s 562(3) (as so added).

9   'Relevant youth accommodation' is accommodation which: (1) is youth detention accommodation (within the meaning given by the Powers of Criminal Courts (Sentencing) Act 2000 s 107(1): see SENTENCING AND DISPOSITION OF OFFENDERS vol 92 (2010) PARA 91), and (2) is not in a young offender institution, or part of such an institution, that is used wholly or mainly for the detention of persons aged 18 and over: Education Act 1996 s 562(1A)(b) (as added: see note 8). As to young offender institutions see PRISONS AND PRISONERS vol 85 (2012) PARA 487 et seq.

10   Education Act 1996 s 562(1) (as amended (see note 8); and further amended by SI 2010/1158). Until a day to be appointed the following provisions have effect in relation to England for those purposes for which the amendments to the Education Act 1996 s 562(1) made by the Apprenticeships, Skills, Children and Learning Act 2009 s 49 are not yet in force, and in relation to Wales (see note 8): No power or duty conferred or imposed by or under the Education Act 1996 on local authorities is to be construed as relating to any person who is detained in pursuance of an order made by a court or of an order of recall made by the Secretary of State, but a local authority may make arrangements for a person who is detained in pursuance of such an order to receive the benefit of educational facilities provided by the authority: Education Act 1996 s 1996 s 562(1) (as originally enacted; and amended by SI 2010/1158).

11   See the School Standards and Framework Act 1998 s 142(8).

12   See the Education Act 2002 s 212(2), (3).

13   See the Education Act 2005 s 122(2), (3).

14   See the Education and Inspections Act 2006 s 187(2), (3) (s 187(3) amended by the Education Act 2011 s 33(2)).

15   See the Education and Skills Act 2008 s 168(2), (3), (5).

16   See the Apprenticeships, Skills, Children and Learning Act 2009 s 264(2)–(4).

47.   Liability of local authorities in failing to provide adequately for children with special educational needs. The failure of local authorities[1] to diagnose learning difficulties or to make suitable education provision for children with special educational needs[2] has been the subject of claims for breach of statutory duty and negligence[3] which have been considered by the House of Lords[4]. While concerned with special educational needs, the potential scope of these rulings may extend to other areas of education as well.

1   As to local authorities and their education functions see PARA 25.

2   As to special educational needs or disabilities see PARAS 950 et seq, 989 et seq.

3   As to the nature of statutory duty see STATUTES AND LEGISLATIVE PROCESS vol 96 (2012) PARA 721 et seq. As to breach of statutory duty see TORT vol 97 (2015) PARA 500 et seq. As to negligence in relation to statutory powers see TORT vol 97 (2015) PARAS 809–810.

4   See *X (Minors) v Bedfordshire County Council, M (A Minor) v Newham London Borough Council, E (A Minor) v Dorset County Council, Christmas v Hampshire County Council, Keating v Bromley London Borough* [1995] 2 AC 633, [1995] 3 All ER 353, HL; *Phelps v Hillingdon London Borough Council, Anderton v Clwyd County Council, Jarvis v Hampshire County Council, G v Bromley London Borough Council* [2001] 2 AC 619, [2000] 4 All ER 504, [2000] ELR 499, HL. See further PARA 1039. As to the replacement of the House of Lords by the Supreme Court see COURTS AND TRIBUNALS vol 24 (2010) PARA 640 et seq.

B. INFORMATION, PLANS AND PROPOSALS

48.   Provision of information by local authorities. A local authority[1] must make such reports and returns to the appropriate national authority[2] and give to the appropriate national authority such information[3], as it may require for the purpose of the exercise of its functions[4] under the Education Act 1996[5].

A local authority must compile such information[6], and make such provision for conducting, or assisting the conduct of, research[7], as may be required for the purpose of providing the appropriate national authority, in such form and at such times as may be prescribed[8], with such information relating to the provision of primary or secondary education[9] in the area of the local authority as may be prescribed[10]. The appropriate national authority must exercise such powers so as to secure, in particular, the provision of information relating to the provision of education for children[11] with special educational needs[12].

A local authority must, at such time or times and in such manner as may be required by regulations, publish such information as may be so required with respect to its policy and arrangements in respect of any matter relating to primary or secondary education[13].

1 As to the meaning of 'local authority' see PARA 25.
2 See the Education Act 1996 s 29(1)(a). The appropriate national authority means the Secretary of State or, in relation to Wales, the Welsh Ministers. As to the Secretary of State see PARA 58. The functions of the Secretary of State under the Education Act 1996 s 29, so far as exercisable in relation to Wales, were transferred to the National Assembly for Wales (see the National Assembly for Wales (Transfer of Functions) Order 1999, SI 1999/672, art 2, Sch 1) and are now vested in the Welsh Ministers (see the Government of Wales Act 2006 s 162(1), Sch 11 para 30). As to the Welsh Ministers see PARA 59. As to the meaning of 'Wales' see PARA 7 note 3.
3 Education Act 1996 s 29(1)(b).
4 As to the meaning of 'functions' see PARA 18 note 5.
5 Education Act 1996 s 29(1) (amended by SI 2010/1158). As to the general powers and duties of the Secretary of State and the Welsh Ministers see PARA 58 et seq.
6 Education Act 1996 s 29(3)(a).
7 Education Act 1996 s 29(3)(b).
8 'Prescribed' means prescribed by regulations made by the Secretary of State or, as appropriate, the Welsh Ministers: see the Education Act 1996 s 579(1).
9 As to the meaning of 'primary education' see PARA 20. As to the meaning of 'secondary education' see PARA 21.
10 Education Act 1996 s 29(3) (amended by the School Standards and Framework Act 1998 s 140(1), (3), Sch 30 para 67, Sch 31; SI 2010/1158). As to the regulations made see the Single Education Plan (Wales) Regulations 2006, SI 2006/877; the Education (School Performance Information) (England) Regulations 2007, SI 2007/2324 (amended by SI 2012/765; SI 2012/1274; SI 2013/1759; SI 2013/3212; SI 2015/902; and SI 2015/1566); the Information as to Provision of Education (England) Regulations 2008, SI 2008/4 (amended by SI 2011/1438; SI 2012/1554; SI 2013/1255; and SI 2013/2149); and the School Performance Information (Wales) Regulations 2011, SI 2011/1963 (amended by SI 2013/437).
11 As to the meaning of 'child' see PARA 7 note 6.
12 Education Act 1996 s 29(4). As to the meaning of 'special educational needs' see PARAS 943, 989. As to information and advice in the context of local offers under the Children and Families Act 2014 s 30 see PARA 951.
13 Education Act 1996 s 29(5) (amended by SI 2010/1158). As to the regulations made see the Education (School Hours and Policies) (Information) Regulations 1989, SI 1989/398; the Education (School Curriculum and Related Information) Regulations 1989, SI 1989/954; the Special Educational Needs (Provision of Information by Local Education Authorities) (England) Regulations 2001, SI 2001/2218 (amended by SI 2013/235); the Special Educational Needs (Provision of Information by Local Education Authorities) (Wales) Regulations 2002, SI 2002/157; the Education (Revocation of Spent Provisions) (England) Regulations 2003, SI 2003/2694; the Single Education Plan (Wales) Regulations 2006, SI 2006/877; the School Information (England) Regulations 2008, SI 2008/3093 (amended by SI 2012/8; SI 2012/979; SI 2012/1124; SI 2013/758; SI 2013/2912; and SI 2015/902). See also the Education (Pupil Referral Units) (Application of Enactments) (England) Regulations 2007, SI 2007/2979 (amended by SI 2012/1201; SI 2012/1825; and SI 2013/1624) which apply, with modifications, various enactments to pupil referral units. As to pupil referral units see PARA 427 et seq. As from a day to be appointed, the School Information (England) Regulations 2008, SI 2008/3093 (see above) are further amended by the Deregulation Act 2015, Sch 16 para 6(5). At the date at which this volume states the law no such day had been appointed.
    As from a day to be appointed, a new provision is added to the Education Act 1996 s 29 to the effect that the Welsh Ministers may, by regulations, require local authorities in Wales to publish prescribed information, at such times and in such manner as may be prescribed, for the purpose of providing information to the public about whether, and if so how, local authority education functions are being exercised to promote the purpose of the Violence against Women, Domestic Abuse and Sexual Violence (Wales) Act 2015 (see s 1): Education Act 1996 s 29(6A)

(prospectively added by the Violence against Women, Domestic Abuse and Sexual Violence (Wales) Act 2015 s 9(1), (2)). At the date at which this volume states the law no such day had been appointed.

49. Annual targets in respect of educational performance in England. The Secretary of State[1] may by regulations[2] require local authorities in England[3] to set annual targets in respect of the educational performance[4]: (1) of pupils[5] at schools[6] maintained by them[7]; and (2) of any persons of compulsory school age[8], whether or not pupils at such schools, who are or have been looked after[9] by them[10]. Such regulations may in particular:

(a) specify the matters in respect of which targets are required to be set[11];

(b) require proposed targets to be notified to the Secretary of State by a prescribed[12] time[13];

(c) authorise the Secretary of State to modify[14] any proposed target notified to him, or to require a local authority to modify the proposed targets and to notify him of the proposed targets as modified[15];

(d) require the targets to be set by a prescribed time[16];

(e) require local authorities to publish, in such manner as may be specified in the regulations, any targets which they set[17].

1 As to the Secretary of State see PARA 58.
2 As to the regulations made see the Education (Local Authority and School Performance Targets) (Revocation and Amendment) (England) Regulations 2010, SI 2010/3014 (amended by SI 2011/937).
3 As to the meaning of 'local authority in England' see PARA 25 (definition applied by the Education Act 2005 s 122(2), (3)).
4 Education Act 2005 s 102(1) (amended by SI 2010/1158). As from a day to be appointed, s 102 is omitted by the Deregulation Act 2015 s 66(3). At the date at which this volume states the law no such day had been appointed.
5 As to the meaning of 'pupil' see PARA 20 note 4 (definition applied by virtue of the Education Act 2005 s 122(2), (3)).
6 As to the meaning of 'school' see PARA 91 (definition applied by virtue of the Education Act 2005 s 122(2), (3)).
7 Education Act 2005 s 102(1)(a). As to maintained schools see PARA 99 et seq. See note 4.
8 As to the meaning of 'compulsory school age' see PARA 19 (definition applied by virtue of the Education Act 2005 s 122(2), (3)).
9 For this purpose, 'looked after' is to be read in accordance with the Children Act 1989 s 22 (see **CHILDREN AND YOUNG PERSONS** vol 10 (2012) PARA 843): Education Act 2005 s 102(3). See note 4.
10 Education Act 2005 s 102(1)(b). See note 4.
11 Education Act 2005 s 102(2)(a). See note 4.
12 'Prescribed' means prescribed by regulations made by the Secretary of State: see the Education Act 1996 s 579(1) (definition applied by virtue of the Education Act 2005 s 122(2), (3)).
13 Education Act 2005 s 102(2)(b). See note 4.
14 As to the meaning of 'modify' see PARA 21 note 15.
15 Education Act 2005 s 102(2)(c) (amended by SI 2010/1158). See note 4.
16 Education Act 2005 s 102(2)(d). See note 4.
17 Education Act 2005 s 102(2)(e) (amended by SI 2010/1158). See note 4.

50. Documentary evidence. In any legal proceedings:

(1) a document purporting to be a document issued by a local authority[1], and to be signed by the clerk of that authority or by the director of children's services (in the case of an authority in England[2]) or the chief education officer (in the case of an authority in Wales[3]) or by any other officer of the authority authorised to sign it[4]; or

(2) a document purporting to be a certificate issued by a medical officer[5] of a local authority, and to be signed by such an officer[6],

is to be received in evidence and treated, without further proof, as the document which it purports to be and as having been signed by the person by whom it purports to have been signed, unless the contrary is proved[7].

1 As to the meaning of 'local authority' see PARA 25.
2 As to the appointment of the director of children's services see PARA 57.
3 As to the appointment of the chief education officer see PARA 57.
4 Education Act 1996 s 566(1)(a) (amended by the Children Act 2004 s 18(9), (10), Sch 2 para 4(1), (3); SI 2010/1158).
5 'Medical officer', in relation to a local authority, means a registered medical practitioner who is employed or engaged, whether regularly or for the purposes of any particular case, by the authority or whose services are made available to the authority by the Secretary of State or, in relation to Wales, the Welsh Ministers: see the Education Act 1996 s 579(1) (definition amended by SI 2010/1158). As to the Secretary of State see PARA 58. The functions of the Secretary of State under the Education Act 1996 were transferred to the National Assembly for Wales (see the National Assembly for Wales (Transfer of Functions) Order 1999, SI 1999/672, art 2, Sch 1) and are now vested in the Welsh Ministers (see the Government of Wales Act 2006 s 162(1), Sch 11 para 30). As to the Welsh Ministers see PARA 59. As to the meaning of 'registered medical practitioner' see MEDICAL PROFESSIONS vol 74 (2011) PARA 176.
6 Education Act 1996 s 566(1)(d) (amended by SI 2010/1158). In any legal proceedings, any such certificate as is mentioned in s 566(1)(d) is evidence of the matters stated in it: see s 566(2).
7 Education Act 1996 s 566(1). As to the evidential effect of certificates admissible by statute see CIVIL PROCEDURE vol 11 (2009) PARA 897.

C. GRANTS AND ALLOWANCES

51. Assistance by local authorities. A school[1] is to be regarded as 'assisted' by a local authority[2] which does not maintain it[3] if the authority makes to its proprietor[4] any grant in respect of the school or any payment in consideration of the provision of educational facilities there[5].

An institution other than a school is to be regarded as 'assisted' by a local authority if the authority makes to the persons responsible for its maintenance any grant in respect of the institution or any payment in consideration of the provision of educational facilities there[6]. However, neither a university[7], nor any institution within the further education sector[8] or within the higher education sector[9] other than a university[10], is to be regarded as 'assisted' by a local authority by virtue of the making by the authority to the persons responsible for the maintenance of the university or institution of any grant in respect of the institution or payment in consideration of the provision of educational facilities there[11].

1 As to the meaning of 'school' see PARA 91.
2 As to the meaning of 'local authority' see PARA 25.
3 As to maintained schools see PARA 99 et seq.
4 'Proprietor', in relation to a school or a 16 to 19 academy, means the person or body of persons responsible for the management of the school or academy (so that, in relation to a community, foundation or voluntary or community or foundation special school, or a maintained nursery school, it means the governing body): Education Act 1996 s 579(1) (definition amended by the School Standards and Framework Act 1998 s 140(1), Sch 30 para 183(a)(iii); SI 2003/2045; SI 2005/2913; and the Education Act 2011 Sch 13 para 9(1), (17)(c)(iii)). As to the meaning of '16 to 19 academy' see PARA 346 note 13. As to the meaning of 'person' see PARA 7 note 6. As to the meanings of references to a community, foundation or voluntary school or a community or foundation special school see PARA 106. As to the meaning of 'maintained nursery school' see PARA 99 note 4. As to governing bodies see PARA 150 et seq.
5 Education Act 1996 s 579(5) (amended by SI 2010/1158). 'Assist', in relation to any school, institution or university, is to be construed in accordance with the Education Act 1996 s 579(5)–(7) (see the text to notes 6–11): see s 579(1) (definition added by the School Standards and Framework Act 1998 s 140(1), Sch 30 para 183(a)(i)). As to universities see PARA 621 et seq.

6   Education Act 1996 s 579(6) (amended by SI 2010/1158).
7   Education Act 1996 s 579(7)(a).
8   As to references to institutions within the further education sector see PARA 555. As to the meaning of 'further education' see PARA 23.
9   As to references to institutions within the higher education sector see PARA 619. As to the meaning of 'higher education' see PARA 24.
10   Education Act 1996 s 579(7)(b).
11   Education Act 1996 s 579(7) (amended by SI 2010/1158).

52.   Travelling and subsistence allowances for governors of schools and further or higher education institutions. A local authority[1] may, in accordance with the provisions of a scheme made by it for these purposes, pay such allowances as may be prescribed[2] to governors[3] of: (1) any community, foundation or voluntary school or community or foundation special school[4] which does not have a delegated budget[5]; and (2) any institution providing higher education[6] or further education[7], or both, which is maintained by a local authority[8]. Such a scheme may make different provision in relation to schools or other institutions of different categories, including provision for allowances not to be paid in respect of certain categories, but must not make different provision in relation to different categories of governor of the same school or institution[9].

A local authority may pay such allowances as may be prescribed to any person appointed to represent it on the governing body of[10] any institution providing higher education or further education, or both, which is not maintained by it[11], or any independent school[12], alternative provision academy[13] which is not an independent school or special school[14] which is not maintained by it[15]. However, a local authority must not pay any such allowance for expenses in respect of which the person incurring them is entitled to reimbursement by any person[16] other than the authority[17]. In addition, a local authority must not pay any such allowance if it has not made any such scheme or if the arrangements under which the allowance would otherwise be payable[18]: (a) provide for allowances which are to any extent more generous than the most generous payable by the authority under any such scheme[19]; or (b) contain any provision which the authority would not have power to include in any such scheme[20].

Regulations may impose a limit on the amount which may be paid by way of any allowance under the above provisions[21].

1   As to the meaning of 'local authority' see PARA 25.
2   'Prescribed' means prescribed by regulations made by the Secretary of State or, in relation to Wales, the Welsh Ministers: see the Education Act 1996 s 579(1). The functions of the Secretary of State under the Education Act 1996 s 519, so far as exercisable in relation to Wales, were transferred to the National Assembly for Wales (see the National Assembly for Wales (Transfer of Functions) Order 1999, SI 1999/672, art 2, Sch 1) and are now vested in the Welsh Ministers (see the Government of Wales Act 2006 s 162(1), Sch 11 para 30). As to the Secretary of State see PARA 58. As to the Welsh Ministers see PARA 59. As to the meaning of 'Wales' see PARA 7 note 3. As to the regulations made under the Education Act 1996 s 519 see the Governor Allowances (Wales) Regulations 2005, SI 2005/2915; and the School Governance (Rules, Procedures and Allowances) (England) Regulations 2013, SI 2013/1624.
3   Education Act 1996 s 519(1) (amended by SI 2010/1158). No allowance may be paid to any governor of a school or institution of the kind mentioned in the Education Act 1996 s 519(1) (see the text to notes 4–8), in respect of the discharge of his functions as such a governor, otherwise than under s 519: s 519(6). As to the meaning of 'school' see PARA 91. As to governing bodies of schools see PARA 150 et seq. As to the meaning of 'functions' see PARA 18 note 5.
4   As to the meanings of references to a community, foundation or voluntary school or a community or foundation special school see PARA 106.
5   Education Act 1996 s 519(1)(a) (amended by the School Standards and Framework Act 1998 s140(1), Sch 30 paras 57, 139(1), (2)). As to the meaning of 'delegated budget' see PARA 323 (definition applied by the Education Act 1996 s 519(1)(a) (as so amended)).

6   As to the meaning of 'higher education' see PARA 24.
7   As to the meaning of 'further education' see PARA 23.
8   Education Act 1996 s 519(1)(b) (amended by SI 2010/1158).
9   Education Act 1996 s 519(2).
10 Education Act 1996 s 519(3) (amended by the School Standards and Framework Act 1998 Sch 30 paras 57, 139(1), (3); SI 2010/1158; and SI 2012/976).
11 Education Act 1996 s 519(3)(a).
12 As to the meaning of 'independent school' see PARA 369.
13 As to the meaning of 'alternative provision academy' see PARA 346 note 14.
14 As to the meaning of 'special school' see PARA 1041.
15 Education Act 1996 s 519(3)(b) (amended by SI 2012/976).
16 As to the meaning of 'person' see PARA 7 note 6.
17 Education Act 1996 s 519(4) (amended by SI 2010/1158).
18 Education Act 1996 s 519(5) (amended by SI 2010/1158).
19 Education Act 1996 s 519(5)(a).
20 Education Act 1996 s 519(5)(b).
21 Education Act 1996 s 519(7) (added by the School Standards and Framework Act 1998 Sch 30 paras 57, 139(1), (4)). As to the regulations made see note 2.

D. EDUCATIONAL RESEARCH AND CONFERENCES

53. Powers as to educational research and conferences. A local authority[1] may make such provision for conducting, or assisting the conduct of, research as appears to it to be desirable for the purpose of improving the educational facilities provided for its area[2].

A local authority may also[3] (1) organise, or participate in the organisation of, conferences for the discussion of questions relating to education[4]; and (2) expend such sums as may be reasonable in paying, or contributing towards, any expenditure incurred in connection with conferences for the discussion of such questions, including the expenses of any person authorised by it to attend such a conference[5].

1   As to the meaning of 'local authority' see PARA 25.
2   Education Act 1996 s 526 (amended by SI 2010/1158). Any function of a local authority in England which is conferred by or under the Education Act 1996 ss 526, 527 (see the text to notes 3–5) may be exercised by, or by employees of, such person as may be authorised in that behalf by the local authority whose function it is: Contracting Out (Local Authority Education Functions) (England) Order 2002, SI 2002/928, art 3, Sch 1 paras (xx), (yy) (art 3 amended by SI 2010/1172). As to the meaning of 'England' see PARA 7 note 3. As to the meaning of 'person' see PARA 7 note 6.
3   Education Act 1996 s 527 (amended by SI 2010/1158).
4   Education Act 1996 s 527(a). See also note 2.
5   Education Act 1996 s 527(b). See also note 2.

E. SUPPLY OF GOODS AND SERVICES

54. Powers of local authorities in relation to the supply of goods and services. Under the Further Education Act 1985, a local authority[1] has power:

(1)   to enter into an agreement for the supply of goods or services (or both) through an institution[2] which is maintained by it and which provides higher education or further education (or both)[3];

(2)   to lend money for the purposes of such an agreement to a body corporate[4] in which it has a holding of not less than 20 per cent of the issued shares comprised in the share capital of the body corporate and carrying rights to vote in all circumstances at general meetings of the body corporate[5].

A local authority also has power to lend money:

(a)   to a higher education corporation[6], further education corporation[7] or sixth form college corporation[8];

(b)   in the case of:

       (i)   an institution within the higher education sector[9] which is not conducted by a higher education corporation[10];

       (ii)   an institution within the further education sector[11] which is not conducted by a further education corporation or a sixth form college corporation[12]; or

       (iii)   an institution which provides higher education or further education and is assisted[13] by a local authority[14],

       to the governing body of the institution or, if it is conducted by a company, to the company[15]; or

(c)   to a body corporate in which such a corporation or company as is mentioned in head (a) or head (b) above has a holding of not less than 20 per cent of the issued shares comprised in the share capital of the body corporate and carrying rights to vote in all circumstances at general meetings of the body corporate[16],

if the loan is for the purposes of an agreement for the supply of goods or services, or both, through the institution conducted by the corporation, company or governing body[17].

Money may be lent under the above provisions for the purposes of an agreement either before the agreement is made or during its currency[18]. Nothing in the above provisions is to be construed as derogating from any powers exercisable by a local authority apart from those above[19].

1   As to the meaning of 'local authority' see PARA 25 (definition applied by the Further Education Act 1985 s 8(3) (amended by the Education Act 1996 s 582(1), Sch 37 para 61)).

2   For the purposes of the Further Education Act 1985 goods are supplied through an institution which provides higher education or further education (or both) if they result: (1) from its educational activities (s 1(1)(a) (s 1(1), (2) amended by the Education Reform Act 1988 s 237, Sch 12 Pt III para 92)); (2) from the use of its facilities and the expertise of persons employed at it in the fields in which they are so employed (Further Education Act 1985 s 1(1)(b)); (3) from ideas of a person employed at it, or of one of its students, arising out of its educational activities (s 1(1)(c)). For the purposes of the Act services are supplied through such an institution: (a) if they are provided by making available its facilities, or the expertise of persons employed at it in the fields in which they are so employed (s 1(2)(a) (as so amended)); (b) if they result from its educational activities or from ideas such as are mentioned in s 1(1)(c) (see head (3) above) (s 1(2)(b) (as so amended)). Educational activities are: (i) the provision of teaching and industrial and vocational training (s 1(3)(a)); (ii) the carrying out of research (s 1(3)(b)); and (iii) any activity incidental or ancillary to any activity mentioned in head (i) or (ii) above (s 1(3)(c)). 'Institution' does not include a school: s 1(4) (added by the Further and Higher Education Act 1992 s 93, Sch 8 Pt I para 20). As to the meaning of 'school' see PARA 91; as to the meaning of 'higher education' see PARA 24; and as to the meaning of 'further education' see PARA 23: definitions applied by the Further Education Act 1985 s 8(3).

3   Further Education Act 1985 s 2(1)(a) (amended by the Education Reform Act 1988 s 237(1), Sch 12 Pt III para 93(2); SI 2010/1158). A local authority may not under an agreement under the Further Education Act 1985 s 2(1)(a) supply goods or services for less than their open market value: s 2(3) (amended by SI 2010/1158). The 'open market value' of goods or services is to be taken to be the amount of the consideration in money that would be payable for the supply by a person standing in no such relationship with any person as would affect that consideration: Further Education Act 1985 s 2(7). As to the meaning of 'person' see PARA 7 note 6. Section 2(3) does not apply to the supply of goods or services: (1) where the goods are produced, or the goods or services are supplied, in the normal course of any of the educational activities mentioned in s 1(3)(a) (see head (i) in note 2) (s 2(4)); or (2) where the supply is for a body which is a research council for the purposes of the Science and Technology Act 1965 (see NATIONAL CULTURAL HERITAGE vol 77 (2010) PARA 967) or for the Arts and Humanities Research Council (as defined by the Higher Education Act 2004 s 1: see NATIONAL CULTURAL HERITAGE vol 77 (2010) PARA 976) (Further Education Act 1985 s 2(4)(a) (amended by the

Higher Education Act 2004 s 49, Sch 6 para 6)) or for a body specified in an order under the Further Education Act 1985 s 2(5) (s 2(4)(b)). The Secretary of State or, in relation to Wales, the Welsh Ministers may by order made by statutory instrument provide that any person who is specified in the order or is of a description so specified, being a person or description of persons appearing to the Secretary of State or, as the case may be, the Welsh Ministers to be exercising functions of a public nature, is to be a public body for the purposes of the Further Education Act 1985: s 2(5). Any such statutory instrument made by the Secretary of State is subject to annulment in pursuance of a resolution of either House of Parliament: see s 2(5). As to the annulment of statutory instruments see STATUTES AND LEGISLATIVE PROCESS vol 96 (2012) PARA 1049. As to the equivalent procedure in relation to subordinate legislation made by the Welsh Ministers see the Government of Wales Act 2006 Sch 11 paras 33–35; and CONSTITUTIONAL AND ADMINISTRATIVE LAW vol 20 (2014) PARA 380. An order made under the Further Education Act 1985 s 2(5) may contain such provisions as the Secretary of State or the Welsh Ministers consider appropriate: (a) for restricting the application of s 2(4)(b) (see head (2) above) to agreements of a description specified in the order (s 2(6)(a)); (b) without prejudice to head (a), for securing the inclusion of terms imposing restrictions in any agreement to which s 2(4)(b) applies and which is made by a body to which the order applies (s 2(6)(b)). At the date at which this volume states the law, no order had been made under s 2(5). As to the meaning of 'functions' see PARA 18 note 5 (definition applied by s 8(3)).

The functions of the Secretary of State under the Further Education Act 1985, so far as exercisable in relation to Wales, were transferred to the National Assembly for Wales (see the National Assembly for Wales (Transfer of Functions) Order 1999, SI 1999/672, art 2, Sch 1) and are now vested in the Welsh Ministers (see the Government of Wales Act 2006 s 162(1), Sch 11 para 30). As to the Secretary of State see PARA 58. As to the Welsh Ministers see PARA 59. As to the meaning of 'Wales' see PARA 7 note 3.

4   As to bodies corporate see COMPANIES vol 14 (2009) PARA 2; CORPORATIONS vol 24 (2010) PARA 301 et seq.

5   Further Education Act 1985 s 2(1)(b), (8) (amended by the Education Reform Act 1988 Sch 12 Pt III para 94(5); and the Further and Higher Education Act 1992 Sch 8 Pt I para 21(2)).

6   As to the meaning of 'higher education corporation' see PARA 645 (definition applied by the Further Education Act 1985 s 2(2)(a)).

7   As to the meaning of 'further education corporation' see PARA 555 note 3 (definition applied by the Further Education Act 1985 s 2(2)(a)).

8   Further Education Act 1985 s 2(2)(a) (s 2(2)(a)–(c) substituted by the Further and Higher Education Act 1992 Sch 8 Pt I para 21; and the Further Education Act 1985 s 2(2)(a), (b) amended by SI 2010/1080). As to the meaning of 'sixth form college corporation' see PARA 577 note 7 (definition applied by the Further Education Act 1985 s 2(2)(a)).

9   As to references to institutions within the higher education sector see PARA 619 (definition applied by the Further Education Act 1985 s 8(3)).

10   Further Education Act 1985 s 2(2)(b)(i) (as substituted: see note 8).

11   As to references to institutions within the further education sector see PARA 555 (definition applied by the Further Education Act 1985 s 8(3)).

12   Further Education Act 1985 s 2(2)(b)(ii) (as substituted and amended: see note 8).

13   As to the meaning of 'assisted' see PARA 51 (definition applied by the Further Education Act 1985 s 8(3)).

14   Further Education Act 1985 s 2(2)(b)(iii) (as substituted (see note 8); and amended by SI 2010/1158).

15   Further Education Act 1985 s 2(2)(b) (as substituted: see note 8).

16   Further Education Act 1985 s 2(2)(b), (8) (s 2(2)(b) as substituted (see note 8); s 2(8) as amended (see note 5)).

17   Further Education Act 1985 s 2(2) (amended by the Education Reform Act 1988 Sch 12 Pt III para 93; SI 2010/1158).

18   Further Education Act 1985 s 2(9).

19   Further Education Act 1985 s 2(10) (amended by SI 2010/1158).

(ii) Committees, Officers, etc with Education Functions

55.   Education functions of overview and scrutiny committees.   Subject to any express provision contained in the Local Government Act 1972, or any subsequent Act, a local authority may arrange for the discharge of any of its functions by a committee, a sub-committee or an officer of the authority, or by any other local authority[1]. Where executive arrangements[2] are in operation, some functions may also be discharged by the executive or individual members of the executive[3].

Executive arrangements by a local authority must include provision for the appointment by the authority of one or more committees of the authority (known as 'overview and scrutiny committees') and must ensure that its overview and scrutiny committee has, or its overview and scrutiny committees have between them, power to review or scrutinise decisions made or other action taken in connection with the discharge of certain functions, and power to make reports or recommendations to the authority or the executive with respect to the discharge of certain functions[4].

Where, in relation to an overview and scrutiny committee of a relevant authority in England[5], or a sub-committee of such an overview and scrutiny committee, the committee's or sub-committee's functions[6] relate wholly or partly to any education functions which are the responsibility of the authority's executive[7], then: (1) in the case of a relevant authority which maintains one or more Church of England schools[8], such an overview and scrutiny committee or sub-committee must include at least one qualifying person[9]; and (2) in the case of a relevant authority which maintains one or more Roman Catholic Church schools[10], such an overview and scrutiny committee or sub-committee must include at least one qualifying person[11]. A member of an overview and scrutiny committee or sub-committee so appointed is entitled to vote at a meeting of the committee or sub-committee on any question which relates to any education functions which are the responsibility of the executive of the authority concerned and which falls to be decided at the meeting[12]. The Secretary of State[13] may by directions to a relevant authority require any of the authority's overview and scrutiny committees or sub-committees to which these provisions apply[14] to include persons who are appointed, in accordance with the directions, as representatives of the persons who appoint foundation governors[15] for the foundation or voluntary schools[16] maintained by the authority which are not Church of England schools or Roman Catholic Church schools but which are specified in the directions[17]. Such directions may make provision with respect to the voting rights of persons appointed in accordance with such directions[18].

The Secretary of State may by regulations require such an overview and scrutiny committee or sub-committee to include one or more persons elected, in accordance with the regulations, as representatives of parent governors at maintained schools which are maintained by the relevant authority concerned[19]. Such regulations may make provision for: (a) the number of persons who are to be elected in the case of any relevant authority[20]; (b) the procedure to be followed in connection with the election of such persons and the persons who are entitled to vote at such an election[21]; (c) the circumstances in which persons are qualified or disqualified for being so elected or for holding office once elected[22]; (d) the term of office of persons so elected and their voting rights[23]; (e) the application to any such committee or sub-committee, with or without any modification, of any enactment (whenever passed or made) relating to committees or, as the case may be, sub-committees of a local authority[24]; (f) such other matters connected with such elections or persons so elected as the Welsh Ministers consider appropriate[25].

Where, in relation to an overview and scrutiny committee of a relevant authority[26] in Wales, or a sub-committee of such an overview and scrutiny committee, the committee's or sub-committee's functions[27] relate wholly or partly to any education functions which are the responsibility of the authority's executive[28], then such an overview and scrutiny committee or sub-committee must include one or more persons appointed as representatives of the persons who appoint foundation governors for the maintained schools[29] which are maintained by the authority concerned and which are specified in directions made by the Welsh Ministers[30] as schools which have a character connected with a particular religion, or particular religious denomination, specified in the directions[31]. A member of an overview and scrutiny committee or sub-committee so appointed is entitled to vote at a meeting of the committee or sub-committee on any question which relates to any education functions which are the responsibility of the executive of the authority concerned, and which falls to be decided at the meeting[32].

Where, in relation to an overview and scrutiny committee of a relevant authority[33], or a sub-committee of such an overview and scrutiny committee, the committee's or sub-committee's functions[34] relate wholly or partly to any education functions which are the responsibility of the authority's executive[35], the Welsh Ministers may by regulations[36] require such an overview and scrutiny committee or sub-committee to include one or more persons elected, in accordance with the regulations, as representatives of parent governors at maintained schools which are maintained by the relevant authority concerned[37]. Such regulations may make provision for: (i) the number of persons who are to be elected in the case of any relevant authority[38]; (ii) the procedure to be followed in connection with the election of such persons and the persons who are entitled to vote at such an election[39]; (iii) the circumstances in which persons are qualified or disqualified for being so elected or for holding office once elected[40]; (iv) the term of office of persons so elected and their voting rights[41]; (v) the application to any such committee or sub-committee, with or without any modification, of any enactment (whenever passed or made) relating to committees or, as the case may be, sub-committees of a local authority[42]; (vi) such other matters connected with such elections or persons so elected as the Secretary of State considers appropriate[43].

1   See the Local Government Act 1972 s 101(1), (2); and LOCAL GOVERNMENT vol 69 (2009) PARA 369 et seq.

2   As to executive arrangements see LOCAL GOVERNMENT vol 69 (2009) PARA 303 et seq.

3   See the Local Government Act 2000 Pt IA (ss 9B–9R), Pt II (ss 10–48A); and LOCAL GOVERNMENT.

4   See the Local Government Act 2000 ss 9F, 21; and LOCAL GOVERNMENT.

5   For these purposes, 'relevant authority' means a local authority which has education functions: Local Government Act 2000 Sch A1 para 6(1) (Sch A1 added by the Localism Act 2011 Sch 2 Pt 2 para 2). The Local Government Act 2000 Sch A1 applies to executive arrangements in England while Sch 1 applies to executive arrangements in Wales and generally has corresponding provisions: see the text to notes 26–43. As to the meanings of 'England' and 'Wales' see PARA 7 note 3. As to the meaning of 'education functions' see PARA 25 (definition applied by the Local Government Act 2000 Sch A1 para 10(2) (as so added). As to local authorities with education functions see PARA 25.

6   Ie under the Local Government Act 2000 ss 9F, 9FA: see LOCAL GOVERNMENT.

7   Local Government Act 2000 Sch A1 para 6(2), (3) (Sch A1 as added: see note 5). The Education Act 1996 s 496 (powers of the Secretary of State to require duties under the Education Act 1996 to be exercised reasonably: see PARA 64) and s 497 (powers of the Secretary of State where local authorities are in default: see PARA 65) apply to the performance of any duty imposed on a local authority by virtue of the Local Government Act 2000 Sch A1 paras 6–8 as they apply to the performance by a local authority of a duty imposed by the Education Act 1996: Local Government Act 2000 Sch A1 para 9 (as so added).

8   As to the meaning of 'Church of England school' see PARA 146 note 12 (definition applied by virtue of the Local Government Act 2000 Sch A1 para 10 (Sch A1 as added: see note 5)).

9 Local Government Act 2000 Sch 1 para 7(1) (Sch A1 as added: see note 5). A person is a qualifying person for these purposes if he is nominated by the diocesan board of education for any Church of England diocese which falls wholly or partly in the area of the authority concerned: Sch A1 para 7(2) (as so added). As to diocesan boards of education see ECCLESIASTICAL LAW vol 34 (2011) PARA 247 et seq.

10 As to the meaning of 'Roman Catholic Church school' see PARA 146 note 12 (definition applied by virtue of the Local Government Act 2000 Sch A1 para 10 (Sch A1 as added: see note 5)).

11 Local Government Act 2000 Sch A1 para 7(3) (Sch A1 as added: see note 5). A person is a qualifying person for these purposes if he is nominated by the bishop of any Roman Catholic diocese which falls wholly or partly in the area of the authority concerned: Sch A1 para 7(4) (as so added).

12 Local Government Act 2000 Sch A1 para 7(5) (Sch A1 as added: see note 5).

13 As to the Secretary of State see PARA 58.

14 Ie committees or sub-committees to which the Local Government Act 2000 Sch A1 para 7 applies: see the text to notes 5–7.

15 As to foundation governors, in relation to England, see PARA 152 et seq.

16 As to foundation or voluntary schools see PARA 106 et seq.

17 Local Government Act 2000 Sch A1 para 7(6) (Sch A1 as added: see note 5).

18 Local Government Act 2000 Sch A1 para 7(7) (Sch A1 as added: see note 5).

19 Local Government Act 2000 Sch A1 para 8(1) (Sch A1 as added: see note 5). Such regulations may also make provision: (1) enabling the Secretary of State to determine, where the Secretary of State considers it expedient to do so in view of the small number of maintained schools which are maintained by a relevant authority, that the requirement imposed on the committee or sub-committee by virtue of Sch A1 para 8(1) is to have effect as if it referred to representatives of parents of registered pupils (rather than representatives of parent governors) at those schools; (2) for any such regulations to have effect, where the Secretary of State makes any such determination, with such modifications as may be prescribed: Local Government Act 2000 Sch A1 para 8(3) (as so added). As to the meaning of 'registered pupil' see PARA 437 (definition applied by virtue of the School Standards and Framework Act 1998 s 142(8); and Local Government Act 2000 Sch A1 para 10(1) (as so added)). At the date at which this volume states the law no regulations have been made under the Local Government Act 2011 Sch A1 but see note 36.

20 Local Government Act 2000 Sch A1 para 8(2)(a) (Sch A1 as added: see note 5).

21 Local Government Act 2000 Sch A1 para 8(2)(b) (Sch A1 as added: see note 5).

22 Local Government Act 2000 Sch A1 para 8(2)(c) (Sch A1 as added: see note 5).

23 Local Government Act 2000 Sch A1 para 8(2)(d) (Sch A1 as added: see note 5).

24 Local Government Act 2000 Sch A1 para 8(2)(e) (Sch A1 as added: see note 5).

25 Local Government Act 2000 Sch A1 para 8(2)(f) (Sch A1 as added: see note 5).

26 For these purposes, 'relevant authority' means a local authority in Wales (see note 5) which has education functions: Local Government Act 2000 Sch 1 para 8(1) (amended by SI 2010/1158; and the Localism Act 2011 paras 8, 72(1), (7), Sch 25 Pt 4).

27 Ie under the Local Government Act 2000 s 21: see LOCAL GOVERNMENT vol 69 (2009) PARA 342 et seq.

28 Local Government Act 2000 Sch 1 para 8(2), (3) (amended by the Localism Act 2011 Sch 3 paras 72(1), (7), Sch 25 Pt 4). See also note 7.

29 As to the meaning of 'maintained school' see PARA 99 (definition applied by virtue of Local Government Act 2000 Sch 1 para 11). As to foundation governors, in relation to Wales, see PARA 230 et seq.

30 The functions under Local Government Act 2000 were originally vested in the National Assembly for Wales and are now exercisable by the Welsh Ministers by virtue of the Government of Wales Act 2006 s 162(1), Sch 11 paras 30, 32. As to the Welsh Ministers see PARA 59.

31 Local Government Act 2000 Sch 1 para 8(4) (amended by the Localism Act 2011 Sch 3 paras 8, 72(1), (7)). The Local Government Act 2011 Sch 1 para 8(4) does not apply if there are no maintained schools which are maintained by the authority concerned and which are specified in directions under that provision: Sch 1 para 8(5). The Welsh Ministers may by directions to a relevant authority require any of the authority's overview and scrutiny committees or sub-committees to which these provisions apply to include persons who are appointed, in accordance with the directions, as representatives of the persons who appoint foundation governors for such of the maintained schools which are maintained by the authority concerned and which are not specified in directions under Sch 1 para 8(4) as may be specified in directions under this provision: Sch 1 para 8(7) (amended by the Localism Act 2011 Sch 3 paras 8, 71(1)

(7)). Directions under the Local Government Act 2000 Sch 1 para 8(7) may make provision with respect to the voting rights of persons appointed in accordance with such directions: Sch 1 para 8(8).

32 Local Government Act 2000 Sch 1 para 8(6).

33 For these purposes, 'relevant authority' means a local authority which has education functions: Local Government Act 2000 Sch 1 para 9(1) (amended by SI 2010/1158).

34 Ie under the Local Government Act 2000 s 21: see LOCAL GOVERNMENT vol 69 (2009) PARA 342 et seq.

35 Local Government Act 2000 Sch 1 para 9(2), (3). See also note 7.

36 As to the regulations which have been so made (but before all the Localism Act 2011 amendments) see the Parent Governor Representatives (England) Regulations 2001, SI 2001/478; and the Parent Governor Representatives and Church Representatives (Wales) Regulations 2001, SI 2001/3711 (amended by SI 2013/3005). See note 19.

37 Local Government Act 2000 Sch 1 para 9(4) (amended by the Localism Act 2011 Sch 3 paras 8, 72(1), (8)). Such regulations may make provision: (1) enabling the Welsh Ministers to determine, where they consider it expedient to do so in view of the small number of maintained schools which are maintained by a relevant authority, that the requirement imposed on the committee or sub-committee by virtue of the Local Government Act 2000 Sch 1 para 9(4) is to have effect as if it referred to representatives of parents of registered pupils (rather than representatives of parent governors) at those schools; and (2) for any regulations under Sch 1 para 9 to have effect, where the Welsh Ministers make any such determination, with such modifications as may be prescribed: Sch 1 para 9(6) (amended by the Localism Act 2011 Sch 3 paras 8, 72(1), (8)). As to the meaning of 'registered pupil' see PARA 437 (definition applied by virtue of the School Standards and Framework Act 1998 s 142(8); and Local Government Act 2000 Sch 1 para 11).

38 Local Government Act 2000 Sch 1 para 9(5)(a).

39 Local Government Act 2000 Sch 1 para 9(5)(b).

40 Local Government Act 2000 Sch 1 para 9(5)(c).

41 Local Government Act 2000 Sch 1 para 9(5)(d).

42 Local Government Act 2000 Sch 1 para 9(5)(e).

43 Local Government Act 2000 Sch 1 para 9(5)(f) (amended by the Localism Act 2011 Sch 3 paras 8, 72(1), (8)).

56. Power to direct appointment of members of education committees. In relation to any local authorities[1] which have appointed any committees[2] wholly or partly for the purpose of discharging any of their education functions[3], the appropriate national authority[4] may by directions[5] to any such local authorities require every such committee, or any such committee of a description specified in the direction, to include persons appointed, in accordance with the directions, for securing the representation on the committee of persons[6] who appoint foundation governors[7] for voluntary schools[8] in the area for which the committee acts[9].

In relation to any two or more local authorities which have appointed any committees[10] wholly or partly for the purpose of discharging any of their education functions[11], the appropriate national authority may by directions to any such local authorities require every such committee, or any such committee of a description specified in the direction, to include persons appointed, in accordance with the directions, for securing the representation on the committee of persons who appoint foundation governors for voluntary schools in the area for which the committee acts or in such area as may be specified in the direction[12].

Regulations[13] may require committees[14] to include one or more persons elected, in accordance with the regulations, as representatives of parent governors[15] at maintained schools[16] in relation to which the committee or sub-committee acts[17]. Regulations may also make provision for[18]:

(1) the number of persons who are to be elected[19] in the case of any local authority[20];

(2) the procedure to be followed in connection with the election of such persons and the persons who are entitled to vote at such an election[21];

(3) the circumstances in which persons are qualified or disqualified for being so elected or for holding office once elected[22];

(4) the term of office of persons so elected and their voting rights[23];

(5) the application to any such committee or sub-committee, with or without any modification, of any provision made by or under any other enactment[24] and relating to committees or, as the case may be, sub-committees of a local authority[25];

(6) such other matters connected with such elections or persons so elected as the appropriate national authority considers appropriate[26].

Regulations may also make provision:

(a) enabling the appropriate national authority to determine, where it considers it expedient to do so in view of the small number of maintained schools in relation to which a committee or sub-committee acts, that the requirement imposed on the committee or sub-committee[27] is to have effect as if it referred to representatives of parents[28] of registered pupils[29] (rather than representatives of parent governors) at those schools[30];

(b) for any regulations under heads (1) to (6) above to have effect, where the appropriate national authority makes any such determination, with such modifications[31] as may be prescribed[32].

1   As to the meaning of 'local authority' see PARA 25.

2   Ie in accordance with the Local Government Act 1972 s 102(1): see LOCAL GOVERNMENT vol 69 (2009) PARA 371.

3   Education Act 1996 s 499(1) (amended by SI 2010/1158). As to the meaning of 'education functions' see PARA 25.

4   The appropriate national authority means the Secretary of State or, in relation to Wales, the Welsh Ministers. The functions of the Secretary of State under the Education Act 1996 s 499, so far as exercisable in relation to Wales, were transferred to the National Assembly for Wales (see the National Assembly for Wales (Transfer of Functions) Order 1999, SI 1999/672, art 2, Sch 1) and are now vested in the Welsh Ministers (see the Government of Wales Act 2006 s 162(1), Sch 11 para 30). As to the Secretary of State see PARA 58. As to the Welsh Ministers see PARA 59. As to the meaning of 'Wales' see PARA 7 note 3.

5   As to directions see PARA 75.

6   As to the meaning of 'person' see PARA 7 note 6.

7   As to schools having foundation governors see PARA 108 et seq.

8   As to voluntary schools see PARA 106 et seq.

9   Education Act 1996 s 499(2). The power of the Secretary of State or the Welsh Ministers to give directions under s 499(2) or s 499(4) (see the text to note 12) is exercisable in relation to any sub-committees which: (1) are appointed by the authorities concerned or any such committee as is mentioned in s 499(2) or s 499(4) (s 499(5)(a)); and (2) are so appointed wholly or partly for the purpose of discharging the authorities' education functions (s 499(5)(b) (amended by SI 2010/1158)).

10 Ie in accordance with the Local Government Act 1972 s 102(1): see LOCAL GOVERNMENT vol 69 (2009) PARA 371.

11 Education Act 1996 s 499(3) (amended by SI 2010/1158).

12 Education Act 1996 s 499(4). See also note 9.

13 Ie regulations made by the Secretary of State or, as appropriate, the Welsh Ministers: see the Education Act 1996 s 579(1). As to the regulations made under s 499 see the Parent Governor Representatives (England) Regulations 2001, SI 2001/478; and the Parent Governor Representatives and Church Representatives (Wales) Regulations 2001, SI 2001/3711 (amended by SI 2013/3005).

14 Ie (1) any such committee as is mentioned in the Education Act 1996 s 499(1) (see the text to notes 1–3) or s 499(3) (see the text to notes 10–11) (s 499(6)(a) (s 499(6) added by the School Standards and Framework Act 1998 s 9)); and (2) any sub-committee appointed by any

authorities within s 499(1) or s 499(3), or by any committee within head (1), for the purpose of discharging the authorities' functions as mentioned in s 499(1), (3) (s 499(6)(b) (as so added)).

15 For these purposes, 'parent governor' means a governor elected or appointed as a parent governor under regulations made under the Education Act 2002 s 19 (see PARA 150): Education Act 1996 s 499(9)(b) (s 499(9) added by the School Standards and Framework Act 1998 s 9; and substituted by the Education Act 2002 s 215(1), Sch 21 para 50).

As to transitional provisions, which allow parent governors appointed or elected to a governing body constituted under the School Standards and Framework Act 1998 s 36 (repealed), as well as parent governors of governing bodies constituted under regulations made under the Education Act 2002 s 19, to be treated as parent governors for the purposes of the Education Act 1996 s 499(6), (8), see the Education Act 2002 (Commencement No 7 and Transitional Provision) Order 2003, SI 2003/2071, art 2(2). In relation to Wales, despite the substitution of the Education Act 1996 s 499(9)(b) made by the Education Act 2002 Sch 21 para 50, a parent governor appointed or elected to a governing body constituted under the School Standards and Framework Act 1998 s 36 (repealed) is also to be treated as a parent governor for the purposes of the Education Act 1996 s 499(6), (8): see the Education Act 2002 (Transitional Provisions and Consequential Amendments) (Wales) Regulations 2005, SI 2005/2913, reg 9.

16 For these purposes, 'maintained school' means a community, foundation or voluntary school, a community or foundation special school or a maintained nursery school: Education Act 1996 s 499(9)(a) (as added and substituted: see note 15). As to the meanings of references to a community, foundation or voluntary school or a community or foundation special school see PARA 106. As to the meaning of 'maintained nursery school' see PARA 99 note 4.

17 Education Act 1996 s 499(6) (as added: see note 14). Any function of a local authority in England which is conferred by or under the Education Act 1996 s 499(6)–(9) (see also the text to notes 18–32) may be exercised by, or by employees of, such person as may be authorised in that behalf by the local authority whose function it is: Contracting Out (Local Authority Education Functions) (England) Order 2002, SI 2002/928, art 3, Sch 1 para (nn) (both amended by SI 2010/1172).

18 Education Act 1996 s 499(7) (s 499(7) added by the School Standards and Framework Act 1998 s 9). See also note 17.

19 Ie for the purposes of the Education Act 1996 s 499(6): see the text to notes 13–17.

20 Education Act 1996 s 499(7)(a) (as added (see note 18); and amended by SI 2010/1158).

21 Education Act 1996 s 499(7)(b) (as added: see note 18).

22 Education Act 1996 s 499(7)(c) (as added: see note 18).

23 Education Act 1996 s 499(7)(d) (as added: see note 18). As to the scope of parent governor voting rights under the Education Act 1996 s 499 and regulations made thereunder see *R (on the application of Transport and General Workers Union) v Walsall Metropolitan Borough Council* [2001] EWHC 452 (Admin), [2002] ELR 329, [2001] All ER (D) 85 (Jun) (decided under the Education (Parent Governor Representatives) Regulations 1999, SI 1999/1949, reg 10 (revoked)).

24 As to the meaning of 'enactment' see PARA 1 note 13.

25 Education Act 1996 s 499(7)(e) (as added: see note 18).

26 Education Act 1996 s 499(7)(f) (as added: see note 18).

27 Ie by virtue of the Education Act 1996 s 499(6): see the text to notes 13–17.

28 As to the meaning of 'parent' see PARA 7 note 6.

29 As to the meaning of 'registered pupil' see PARA 437.

30 Education Act 1996 s 499(8)(a) (s 499(8) added by the School Standards and Framework Act 1998 s 9). See also note 17.

31 As to the meaning of 'modifications' see PARA 21 note 15.

32 Education Act 1996 s 499(8)(b) (as added: see note 30). See also note 17. 'Prescribed' means prescribed by regulations made by the Secretary of State or, as appropriate, the Welsh Ministers: see the Education Act 1996 s 579(1). As to the regulations made see note 13.

57. Appointment of director of children's services and chief education officer.

A local authority in England[1] must appoint an officer, known as its 'director of children's services', for purposes including education functions[2] conferred on or exercisable by the authority[3].

The duties of a local authority in Wales[4] under the Local Government Act 1972 with respect to the appointment of officers include[5] the duty of appointing a fit person to be the chief education officer of the authority[6].

1   As to the meaning of 'local authority' see PARA 25. As to the meaning of 'England' see PARA 7 note 3.
2   As to the meaning of 'education functions' see PARA 25 (definition applied by the Children Act 2004 s 18(10) (substituted by SI 2010/1158)).
3   See the Children Act 2004 s 18; and CHILDREN AND YOUNG PERSONS vol 9 (2012) PARA 207.
4   As to the meaning of 'local authority in Wales' see PARA 25.
5   Ie without prejudice to the generality of the provisions of the Local Government Act 1972. As to the appointment of officers under the Local Government Act 1972 generally see LOCAL GOVERNMENT vol 69 (2009) PARA 425 et seq.
6   Education Act 1996 s 532 (amended by the Children Act 2004 s 18(9), (10), Sch 2 para 4(1), (2); SI 2010/1158).

(4) THE SECRETARY OF STATE AND THE WELSH MINISTERS

(i) General Duties and Functions relating to Education

58. The Secretary of State. A Minister of Education was appointed in 1944[1], when the Ministry of Education was created in succession to the Board of Education[2], which itself had taken over the functions of the Education Department[3]. In 1964, the functions of the Minister of Education were transferred to the Secretary of State and became the responsibility of the Secretary of State for Education and Science[4]. As a result of subsequent reorganisations and transfers of functions, the Secretary of State for Education and Science became the Secretary of State for Education[5], later the Secretary of State for Education and Employment[6], the Secretary of State for Education and Skills[7], and the Secretary of State for Children, Schools and Families[8]. In 2010 the functions of the Secretary of State for Children, Schools and Families were transferred to the Secretary of State for Education[9].

Some earlier legislation mentions the Education Department, the Board of Education or the minister[10], but modern statutes generally refer simply to the 'Secretary of State'. In any enactment, 'Secretary of State' means one of Her Majesty's principal Secretaries of State[11]. The office of Secretary of State is a unified office, and generally in law each Secretary of State is capable of performing the functions of all or any of them[12]. In practice, however, functions relating to education in England[13] generally belong to the Secretary of State for Education[14].

In relation to Wales[15], many functions of the Secretary of State relating to education are now exercisable by the Welsh Ministers[16].

1   See the Education Act 1944 s 1(1) (repealed); and the Education (Date of Appointment of Minister) Order 1944, SR & O 1944/937.
2   See the Education Act 1944 s 2(1) (repealed).
3   See the Board of Education Act 1899 ss 1, 2(1) (both repealed).
4   See the Secretary of State for Education and Science Order 1964, SI 1964/490.
5   See the Transfer of Functions (Science) Order 1992, SI 1992/1296.
6   See the Transfer of Functions (Education and Employment) Order 1995, SI 1995/2986.
7   See the Secretaries of State for Education and Skills and for Work and Pensions Order 2002, SI 2002/1397.
8   See the Secretaries of State for Children, Schools and Families, for Innovation, Universities and Skills and for Business, Enterprise and Regulatory Reform Order 2007, SI 2007/3224.
9   See the Secretary of State for Education Order 2010, SI 2010/1836. The Department for Education works with various agencies and public bodies in carrying out its functions, one of which is the Education Funding Agency, which is an executive agency of the Department. It is responsible for (1) funding education for learners between the ages of 3 and 19, and those with learning difficulties and disabilities between the ages of 3 and 25; (2) funding and monitoring

academies, university technical colleges, studio schools, and free schools; (3) building maintenance programmes for schools and sixth-form colleges; (4) allocating funds to local authorities for maintained schools, and voluntary-aided schools: see the Government website. There is also a Skills Funding Agency, which funds skills training for further education: see further PARA 613. As to maintained schools see PARA 99 et seq. As to funding of maintained schools see PARA 305 et seq. As to academy arrangements and academies see PARA 345 et seq. As to financing of academies see PARAS 352, 353. As to free schools, university technical colleges and studio schools see PARA 368. As to special educational needs and disabilities see PARA 943 et seq. As to further education generally see PARA 555 et seq.

10 The Elementary School Teachers (Superannuation) Act 1898 refers to the Education Department and the minister: see eg s 1; and PARA 1084. The Education Act 1918 removes the requirement for the approval of the Board of Education for the appointment of trustees in relation to educational charities: see s 47; and PARA 1375. The Physical Training and Recreation Act 1937 refers to the Board of Education: see PARA 502.

11 See the Interpretation Act 1978 s 5, Sch 1.

12 As to the office of Secretary of State see CONSTITUTIONAL AND ADMINISTRATIVE LAW vol 20 (2014) PARA 153.

13 As to the meaning of 'England' see PARA 7 note 3.

14 See the text to note 9.

15 As to the meaning of 'Wales' see PARA 7 note 3.

16 See PARA 59.

59. Functions exercisable by the Welsh Ministers. Under the arrangements originally made[1] for devolved government in Wales[2], many of the ministerial functions relating to education were transferred, subject to prescribed exceptions and qualifications, to the National Assembly for Wales[3]. Functions transferred in this way included functions under the School Sites Act 1841[4], the Physical Training and Recreation Act 1937[5], the Employment and Training Act 1973[6], the Education Act 1980[7], the Education (Fees and Awards) Act 1983[8], the Further Education Act 1985[9], the Education Act 1986[10], the Education (No 2) Act 1986[11], the Education Reform Act 1988[12], the Further and Higher Education Act 1992[13], the Education Act 1994[14], the Education Act 1996[15], the Education Act 1997[16], the Education (Schools) Act 1997[17], the Teaching and Higher Education Act 1998[18] and the School Standards and Framework Act 1998[19].

Following the re-organisation of devolved government in Wales under the Government of Wales Act 2006, the functions thus transferred to the Assembly[20], or otherwise conferred on the Assembly by subsequent legislation, became exercisable by the Welsh Ministers[21]. Legislation made subsequent to the implementation of the re-organisation of devolved government will make specific reference to functions exercisable by the Welsh Ministers[22]. Under the devolved government arrangements the National Assembly for Wales has legislative competence (by way of Assembly Measures[23]) in relation to a number of matters relating to education and training[24].

Her Majesty may by Order in Council: (1) provide for the transfer to the Welsh Ministers, the First Minister or the Counsel General of any function so far as exercisable by a Minister of the Crown in relation to Wales; (2) direct that any function so far as so exercisable is to be exercisable by the Welsh Ministers, the First Minister or the Counsel General concurrently with the Minister of the Crown; or (3) direct that any function so far as exercisable by a Minister of the Crown in relation to Wales is to be exercisable by the Minister of the Crown only with the agreement of, or after consultation with, the Welsh Ministers, the First Minister or the Counsel General[25].

The growing divergence between the education policies operating in England and in Wales has led increasingly to separate provision for England and Wales being made in legislation; and where this is the case those provisions have generally been set out separately in this title, with often less detail in relation to Welsh provisions.

1   Ie under the Government of Wales Act 1998.
2   As to the meaning of 'Wales' see PARA 7 note 3.
3   See the National Assembly for Wales (Transfer of Functions) Order 1999, SI 1999/672, art 2, Sch 1. As to the National Assembly for Wales see CONSTITUTIONAL AND ADMINISTRATIVE LAW vol 20 (2014) PARA 351 et seq.
4   All functions of a Minister of the Crown under the School Sites Act 1841 (see PARA 1297), so far as exercisable in relation to Wales, were transferred to the National Assembly for Wales: see the National Assembly for Wales (Transfer of Functions) Order 1999, SI 1999/672, art 2, Sch 1.
5   All functions of a Minister of the Crown under the Physical Training and Recreation Act 1937 (see PARA 502), so far as exercisable in relation to Wales, were transferred to the National Assembly for Wales: see the National Assembly for Wales (Transfer of Functions) Order 1999, SI 1999/672, art 2, Sch 1.
6   The functions of a Minister of the Crown under the Employment and Training Act 1973 (see PARA 819), subject to certain exceptions and qualifications, so far as exercisable in relation to Wales, were transferred to the National Assembly for Wales: see the National Assembly for Wales (Transfer of Functions) Order 1999, SI 1999/672, art 2, Sch 1.
7   All functions of a Minister of the Crown under the Education Act 1980 (see PARA 1112), so far as exercisable in relation to Wales, were transferred to the National Assembly for Wales: see the National Assembly for Wales (Transfer of Functions) Order 1999, SI 1999/672, art 2, Sch 1.
8   All functions of a Minister of the Crown under the Education (Fees and Awards) Act 1983 (see PARAS 614, 1095, 1110, 1111), so far as exercisable in relation to Wales, were transferred to the National Assembly for Wales: see the National Assembly for Wales (Transfer of Functions) Order 1999, SI 1999/672, art 2, Sch 1; the National Assembly for Wales (Transfer of Functions) Order 2006, SI 2006/1458, art 2.
9   All functions of a Minister of the Crown under the Further Education Act 1985 (see PARA 54), so far as exercisable in relation to Wales, were transferred to the National Assembly for Wales: see the National Assembly for Wales (Transfer of Functions) Order 1999, SI 1999/672, art 2, Sch 1.
10 All functions of a Minister of the Crown under the Education Act 1986 (see PARA 85), so far as exercisable in relation to Wales, were transferred to the National Assembly for Wales: see the National Assembly for Wales (Transfer of Functions) Order 1999, SI 1999/672, art 2, Sch 1.
11 All functions of a Minister of the Crown under the Education (No 2) Act 1986 (see PARAS 6, 772, 872), so far as exercisable in relation to Wales, were transferred to the National Assembly for Wales: see the National Assembly for Wales (Transfer of Functions) Order 1999, SI 1999/672, art 2, Sch 1.
12 All functions of a Minister of the Crown under the Education Reform Act 1988, except s 197 (see PARA 1330), s 199 (see PARA 650), s 209 (repealed with savings), s 226 (see PARA 73), Sch 8 (see PARA 1330) and Sch 11 (see PARA 631), so far as exercisable in relation to Wales, were transferred to the National Assembly for Wales: see the National Assembly for Wales (Transfer of Functions) Order 1999, SI 1999/672, art 2, Sch 1 (amended by SI 2000/1829).
13 All functions of a Minister of the Crown under the Further and Higher Education Act 1992, except s 62(8) (see PARA 698) and Sch 1 para 7(6), (7) (see PARA 693), so far as exercisable in relation to Wales, were transferred to the National Assembly for Wales: see the National Assembly for Wales (Transfer of Functions) Order 1999, SI 1999/672, art 2, Sch 1.
14 All functions of a Minister of the Crown under the Education Act 1994 (see PARAS 60, 705, 1115–1126, 1285–1286), so far as exercisable in relation to Wales, were transferred to the National Assembly for Wales: see the National Assembly for Wales (Transfer of Functions) Order 1999, SI 1999/672, art 2, Sch 1.
15 All functions of a Minister of the Crown under the Education Act 1996, except (1) ss 333(5), (6), 334(2), 335 (see PARA 1034) and s 336 (see PARA 1035); (2) the regulation-making functions under s 493 (see PARA 333) and s 494 (see PARA 331); (3) functions under s 494(4) (see PARA 331) and s 495 (see PARA 66) so far as they relate to a dispute to which only one party is in Wales, so far as exercisable in relation to Wales, were transferred to the National Assembly for Wales: see the National Assembly for Wales (Transfer of Functions) Order 1999, SI 1999/672, art 2, Sch 1. The functions of the Secretary of State mentioned in head (1) were exercisable only with the agreement of the National Assembly for Wales; the regulation-making functions of the Secretary of State mentioned in head (2) were exercisable only after consultation with the National Assembly for Wales; and the functions of the Secretary

of State mentioned in head (3), so far as they relate to a dispute to which only one party is in Wales, were exercisable only after consultation with the National Assembly for Wales: see Sch 2. The functions of the Secretary of State mentioned in head (1) are now exercisable by the Welsh Ministers with the consent of the Secretary of State: see the Transfer of Tribunal Functions Order 2008, SI 2008/2833, art 9(1), Sch 3. As to the Secretary of State see PARA 58.

16 All the functions so transferred have now been repealed.

17 All functions of a Minister of the Crown under the Education (Schools) Act 1997, so far as exercisable in relation to Wales, were transferred to the National Assembly for Wales: see the National Assembly for Wales (Transfer of Functions) Order 1999, SI 1999/672, art 2, Sch 1.

18 The functions of a Minister of the Crown under (1) the Teaching and Higher Education Act 1998 Pt I (ss 1–21) (mostly repealed) (but see PARAS 1066 et seq, 1075 et seq); (2) s 25 so far as it relates to the power to make discretionary awards under the Education Act 1962 (repealed with savings); (3) the Teaching and Higher Education Act 1998 s 26 (repealed); (4) s 28(1)(e) so far as it relates to s 22 (see PARA 1096) and s 26 (repealed); and (5) Pt IV (ss 35–46) (relevant provisions repealed), so far as exercisable in relation to Wales, were transferred to the National Assembly for Wales: see the National Assembly for Wales (Transfer of Functions) Order 1999, SI 1999/672, art 2, Sch 1.

19 All functions of a Minister of the Crown under the School Standards and Framework Act 1998, except s 81 (see PARA 298) and ss 136, 137 (see PARA 1330), so far as exercisable in relation to Wales, were transferred to the National Assembly for Wales: see the National Assembly for Wales (Transfer of Functions) Order 1999, SI 1999/672, art 2, Sch 1; the National Assembly for Wales (Transfer of Functions) Order 2000, SI 2000/253, Sch 1.

20 See the text to notes 1–19.

21 See the Government of Wales Act 2006 s 162(1), Sch 11 para 30. 'Welsh Ministers' means the First Minister and the Welsh Ministers appointed under the Government of Wales Act 2006 s 48: see s 45(2). Where any function is transferred to the Welsh Ministers this is referred in the specific paragraph or paragraphs dealing with that function in this title. As to the First Minister and the Welsh Ministers see the Government of Wales Act 2006 ss 46–48; and CONSTITUTIONAL AND ADMINISTRATIVE LAW vol 20 (2014) PARAS 374, 375. As to devolved government in Wales generally see CONSTITUTIONAL AND ADMINISTRATIVE LAW. As to the exercise of transferred functions and the bringing of subordinate legislation made by the Welsh Ministers before the National Assembly for Wales see Sch 11 paras 33–35 (in the case of functions transferred to the Assembly by Order in Council under the Government of Wales Act 1998 s 22) or the Government of Wales Act 2006 Sch 3 para 9 (in the case of functions transferred to the Welsh Ministers by Order in Council under s 58: see the text to note 25); and CONSTITUTIONAL AND ADMINISTRATIVE LAW vol 20 (2014) PARA 380.

22 See eg the Apprenticeships, Skills, Children and Learning Act 2009 s 18; and PARA 770.

23 See the Government of Wales Act 2006 s 93; and CONSTITUTIONAL AND ADMINISTRATIVE LAW.

24 The matters are: (1) provision about the categories of school that may be maintained by local authorities; (2) provision about the establishment and discontinuance of schools maintained by local authorities, their change from one category to another and their alteration in other respects; (3) conduct and governance of schools maintained by local authorities, including the allocation of functions, property, rights and liabilities relating to such schools; (4) securing collaboration between persons or bodies with functions relating to schools maintained by local authorities; (5) activities by persons or bodies with functions relating to schools maintained by local authorities with respect to the establishment of bodies to do all or any of the carrying out activities relating to education or training (including involvement with such bodies), or the exercise of education functions on behalf of local authorities; (6) provision about the admission of pupils to schools maintained by local authorities; (7) provision about the curriculum in schools maintained by local authorities; (8) the regulation of (a) schools that are not maintained by local authorities; (b) relevant independent educational institutions; (9) provision about school attendance, the behaviour of pupils at school, school discipline and the exclusion of pupils from school (including the duties of parents in connection with those matters); (10) provision about the making of arrangements for the provision of education for persons of compulsory school age who have been excluded from schools or who for any other reason would not otherwise receive suitable education: (11) provision about entitlement to primary, secondary and further education and to training; (12) provision about the provision of services that are intended to encourage, enable or assist people to participate effectively in education or training, to take advantage of opportunities for employment, or to participate effectively in the life of their communities; (13) provision about food and drink provided on school premises or provided for children at a place where they receive education or childcare; (14) arrangements for persons receiving nursery, primary, secondary or further education or training, and persons described in head (22) below receiving higher education. to travel to and from the places where they receive

education or training; (15) provision for and in connection with securing the provision of facilities for post-16 education or training; (16) provision for and in connection with the establishment and dissolution of (a) institutions concerned with the provision of further education, and (b) bodies that conduct such institutions, including the circumstances in which an educational institution becomes or ceases to be an institution concerned with the provision of further education; (17) provision about (a) the conduct and functions of such institutions and bodies that conduct such institutions, (b) the property, rights and liabilities of such institutions and bodies that conduct such institutions, (c) property held by any person for the purposes of such an institution; (d) the governance and staff of such institutions; (18) provision for and in connection with securing collaboration (a) between bodies that conduct institutions concerned with the provision of further education, or (b) between one or more such bodies and other persons or bodies that have functions relating to education or training in Wales, including, in particular, provision for and in connection with the establishment of bodies for the purpose of discharging functions on behalf of one or more persons or bodies that are party to arrangements for collaboration; (19) the provision of financial resources for and in connection with (a) education or training provided by institutions concerned with the provision of further education, (b) post-16 education or training provided otherwise than by such institutions, (c) the carrying out of research relating to education or training falling within head (a) or (b); (20) the inspection of schools, relevant independent educational institutions, education or training provided by institutions concerned with the provision of further education, pre-16 education or training or post-16 education or training, provided otherwise than by the preceding institutions, the training of teachers and specialist teaching assistants for schools, services of the kinds mentioned in head (12) above; (21) the provision of advice and information in connection with, and the carrying out of studies in relation to pre-16 education or training, post-16 education or training, the training of teachers and specialist teaching assistants for schools, and services of the kinds mentioned in head (12) above; (22) education and training for persons who have a greater difficulty in learning than the majority of persons of the same age as those persons, and persons who have, or have had a physical or mental impairment, or a progressive health condition (such as cancer, multiple sclerosis or HIV infection) where it is at a stage involving no physical or mental impairment; (23) the provision for children or young persons of educational activities or facilities for social or physical training: see the Government of Wales Act 2006 s 94, Sch 5 Pt 1 Field 5 (amended by SI 2007/910; the Further Education and Training Act 2007 s 27; the Education and Skills Act 2008 s 149; SI 2008/1036; SI 2008/3132; SI 2010/1158; and SI 2010/1209); and CONSTITUTIONAL AND ADMINISTRATIVE LAW. As to the education functions of local authorities see PARA 25.

25   See the Government of Wales Act 2006 s 58, Sch 3; and CONSTITUTIONAL AND ADMINISTRATIVE LAW vol 20 (2014) PARA 380.

60.   General duties. The Secretary of State[1] must promote the education of the people of England[2], and the Welsh Ministers[3] must promote the education of the people of Wales[4]. The Secretary of State and the Welsh Ministers must exercise the powers in respect of those bodies in receipt of public funds which:

(1)   carry responsibility for securing that the required provision for primary, secondary[5] or further education[6] is made in schools[7], in institutions within the further education sector[8], in 16 to 19 academies[9], in or in any area of England or, as the case may be, Wales[10]; or

(2)   conduct schools, institutions within the further education sector or 16 to 19 academies in England or, as the case may be, Wales[11],

for the purpose of promoting primary, secondary and further education in England or Wales[12].

The Secretary of State or, as appropriate, the Welsh Ministers must, in the case of the powers to regulate the provision made in schools, institutions within the further education sector and 16 to 19 academies in England and Wales, exercise those powers with a view to, among other things, improving standards, encouraging diversity and increasing opportunities for choice[13].

The Secretary of State or the Welsh Ministers may give financial assistance for a number of purposes including enabling any person to receive any training for teachers or non-teaching staff[14]. The Welsh Ministers amongst their general duties above[15] also have a specific duty with respect to arrangements for teacher training[16].

The role of the Secretary of State and the Welsh Ministers in relation to education includes a wide range of duties and powers. They have functions, for example, in relation to school admissions[17], various powers of intervention[18], the appointment of governors[19] and of members of local authority education committees[20], and the setting of limits on infant class sizes[21]. Their powers also include the power to issue guidance, such as codes of practice, for local authorities and maintained schools[22], and to secure proper performance of a local authority's education functions[23].

The Secretary of State and the Welsh Ministers must publish any guidance given by him or them for the purposes of any provision of the Education Act 1996 in such manner as he or they think fit[24].

1   As to the Secretary of State see PARA 58.

2   See the Education Act 1996 s 10.

3   The functions of the Secretary of State under the Education Act 1996 ss 10, 11 (see the text to notes 5–12) and the Education Act 1994 s 11A (repealed), so far as exercisable in relation to Wales, were transferred to the National Assembly for Wales (see the National Assembly for Wales (Transfer of Functions) Order 1999, SI 1999/672, art 2, Sch 1) and are now vested in the Welsh Ministers (see the Government of Wales Act 2006 s 162(1), Sch 11 para 30). As to the Welsh Ministers see PARA 59. As to the meaning of 'Wales' see PARA 7 note 3.

4   See the Education Act 1996 s 10.

5   As to the meaning of 'primary education' see PARA 20. As to the meaning of 'secondary education' see PARA 21.

6   As to the meaning of 'further education' see PARA 23.

7   As to the meaning of 'school' see PARA 91.

8   As to references to institutions within the further education sector see PARA 555.

9   As to the meaning of '16 to 19 academy' see PARA 346 note 13.

10 See the Education Act 1996 s 11(1)(a) (amended by the Education Act 2011 Sch 13 para 9(1), (3)(a)).

11 See the Education Act 1996 s 11(1)(b) (amended by the Education Act 2011 Sch 13 para 9(1), (3)(b)).

12 See the Education Act 1996 s 11(1).

13 See the Education Act 1996 s 11(2) (amended by the Education Act 2011 Sch 13 para 9(1), (3)(c)).

14 See the Education Act 2002 s 14(2)(ca); and PARA 78.

15 Ie under the Education Act 1996 ss 10, 11: see the text to notes 1–13.

16 See the Education Act 2005 s 84A; and PARA 1055.

17 See the School Standards and Framework Act 1998 ss 84–85; and PARAS 225–226.

18 See the School Standards and Organisation (Wales) Act 2013 Pt 2 (ss 2–37); and PARA 1229 et seq.

19 See eg the Education Act 1996 s 497; and PARA 65.

20 See the Education Act 1996 s 499; and PARA 56.

21 See the School Standards and Framework Act 1998 s 1; and PARA 234.

22 See eg the Education Act 1996 s 313; and PARA 1033.

23 See the Education Act 1996 ss 497A–497B; and PARA 62.

24 Education Act 1996 s 571(1) (amended by the Education Act 1997 s 57(1), Sch 7 para 41(a)). The functions of the Secretary of State under the Education Act 1996 s 571, so far as they relate to the exercise of any function of a local authority under the Education Act 1996 s 507B (see PARA 504), are transferred to the Minister for the Cabinet Office: Transfer of Functions (Youth Leisure-time Activities) Order 2013, SI 2013/1721.

61. Power in relation to companies in England. The Secretary of State[1] may[2], if he considers it expedient to do so for purposes connected with any function[3] of his relating to education[4]:

(1)   form, or participate in forming, companies[5] to carry on any activities
       which he considers likely to secure or facilitate the achievement of those
       purposes[6]; or

(2)   invest in any company[7] which is to carry on such activities[8].

1   As to the Secretary of State see PARA 58.
2   The Education Act 2002 s 13 is without prejudice to any powers of the Secretary of State
    exercisable otherwise than by virtue of s 13: s 13(5).
3   As to the meaning of 'function' see PARA 18 note 5 (definition applied by the Education
    Act 2002 s 212(2), (3)).
4   For this purpose, 'education' includes: (1) vocational training, including the preparation of
    young people for employment in general; and (2) social and physical training, including the
    promotion of the development of young children, but does not include higher education:
    Education Act 2002 s 13(2). As to the meaning of 'young person' see PARA 7 note 6; and as to
    the meaning of 'higher education' see PARA 24 (definitions applied by s 212(2), (3)). As to the
    Secretary of State's general duties in relation to education see PARA 60.
5   For this purpose, 'company' means a company as defined in the Companies Act 2006 s 1(1) (see
    COMPANIES vol 14 (2009) PARA 1): Education Act 2002 s 13(3) (amended by SI 2009/1941).
6   Education Act 2002 s 13(1)(a).
7   The reference to investing in a company includes a reference to becoming a member of the
    company and to investing in it by the acquisition of any assets, securities or rights or otherwise:
    Education Act 2002 s 13(4).
8   Education Act 2002 s 13(1)(b).

**62.   Power to secure proper performance of local authority's education
functions.** If the Secretary of State[1] is satisfied, either on a complaint by any
person[2] interested or otherwise, that a local authority[3] is failing in any respect to
perform any of its education functions[4] to an adequate standard, or at all, the
Secretary of State may[5] exercise the following powers[6].

The Secretary of State may give the authority or an officer of the authority
such directions[7] as he thinks expedient for the purpose of securing that the
function is performed on behalf of the authority by such person as is specified in
the direction[8]. Such directions may require that any contract or other
arrangement made by the authority with that person contains such terms and
conditions as may be so specified[9]. The Secretary of State may also direct that the
function is to be exercised by it or a person nominated by him and that the local
authority must comply with any instructions of the Secretary of State or his
nominee in relation to the exercise of the function[10]. Whether or not the
Secretary of State exercises either of these powers[11] in relation to such a function,
he may give the local authority or an officer of the authority such other
directions as he thinks expedient for the purpose of securing that the function is
performed to an adequate standard[12].

The Secretary of State may also exercise his powers to give directions[13] where:
(1) he has given a previous such direction in relation to a local authority in
respect of any of his education functions[14]; and (2) the Secretary of State is
satisfied that it is likely that, if no further such direction were given on the expiry
or revocation of the previous direction, the local authority would fail in any
respect to perform that function to an adequate standard, or at all[15].

Where the Secretary of State gives such directions[16] to a local authority or to
an officer of such an authority, the specified person[17] is, in the performance of
the function or functions specified in the directions, entitled to exercise the
following powers[18]:

(a)   the specified person has, at all reasonable times, a right of entry to the
       premises[19] of the authority, and a right to inspect, and take copies of,
       any records or other documents[20] kept by the local authority, and any

other documents containing information relating to the authority, which he considers relevant to the performance of the specified function or functions[21]; and

(b)   in exercising the right to inspect records or other documents under head (a) above, the specified person: (i) is entitled at any reasonable time to have access to, and inspect and check the operation of, any computer and any associated apparatus or material which is or has been in use in connection with the records or other documents in question[22]; and (ii) may require the person by whom or on whose behalf the computer is or has been so used, or any person having charge of, or otherwise concerned with the operation of, the computer, apparatus or material, to afford him such assistance[23] as he may reasonably require[24].

The local authority must give the specified person all assistance in connection with the performance of the specified function or functions which it is reasonably able to give[25].

Provision is also made for intervention in Wales[26].

1   As to the Secretary of State see PARA 58. The functions of the Secretary of State under the Education Act 1996 ss 497A, 497AA, 497B, so far as exercisable in relation to Wales, were transferred to the National Assembly for Wales (see the National Assembly for Wales (Transfer of Functions) Order 1999, SI 1999/672, art 2, Sch 1) and were subsequently vested the Welsh Ministers (see the Government of Wales Act 2006 s 162(1), Sch 11 para 30) but see now the Education Act 1996 s 497A(1); and note 4. As to the Welsh Ministers see PARA 59. As to the meaning of 'Wales' see PARA 7 note 3. The functions of the Secretary of State under the Education Act 1996 ss 497A, 497AA, 497B, so far as they relate to the exercise of any function of a local authority under the Education Act 1996 s 507B (see PARA 504), are transferred to the Minister for the Cabinet Office: see the Transfer of Functions (Youth Leisure-time Activities) Order 2013, SI 2013/1721.

2   As to the meaning of 'person' see PARA 7 note 6.

3   As to the meaning of 'local authority' see PARA 25.

4   The Education Act 1996 s 497A applies to the education functions of a local authority in England: s 497A(1) (s 497A added by the School Standards and Framework Act 1998 s 8; the Education Act 1996 s 497A(1) substituted by SI 2010/1158; and the Education Act 1996 s 497A(1) amended by the School Standards and Organisation (Wales) Act 2013 Sch 5 para 2(1), (6)). As to the meaning of 'education functions' see PARA 25. The Education Act 1996 s 497A and ss 497AA, 497B (see note 6 and the text to notes 16–25) apply in relation to an English local authority's functions under the Childcare Act 2006 Pt 1 (ss 1–21), as they apply in relation to the education functions of a local authority in England: see the Childcare Act 2006 ss 15, 29; and CHILDREN AND YOUNG PERSONS vol 10 (2012) PARAS 1077, 1091. As to the meaning of 'England' see PARA 7 note 3. As to the application of the Education Act 1996 ss 497A, 497AA, 497B in relation to the relevant functions of a children's services authority see the Children Act 2004 s 50 (amended by the Apprenticeships, Skills, Children and Learning Act 2009 s 194(1), (6); SI 2010/1158; and the School Standards and Organisation (Wales) Act 2013 Sch 5 para 7(1), (2)).

5   The Education Act 1996 s 497A is subject to s 508I (see PARA 811) and s 509AE (see PARA 467) (complaints about transport arrangements etc): s 497A(8) (s 497A as added (see note 4); s 497A(8) added by the Apprenticeships, Skills, Children and Learning Act 2009 s 59, Sch 2 paras 1, 9).

6   Education Act 1996 s 497A(2) (as added (see note 4); and amended by the Education Act 2002 s 60(1), (3)). Where, in relation to any function to which the Education Act 1996 s 497A applies (see note 4), the Secretary of State (1) is satisfied as mentioned in s 497A(2) (see s 497AA(a) (s 497AA added by the Education Act 2002 s 61)), and (2) has notified the local authority that he is so satisfied and that it is contemplating the giving of directions under the Education Act 1996 s 497A(4) (see the text to notes 7–9) or s 497A(4A) (see the text to note 10) (s 497AA(b) (as so added; and amended by SI 2010/1158)), the local authority must give the Secretary of State, and any person authorised by him for these purposes, all such assistance, in connection with the proposed exercise of the function by the Secretary of State or another person in pursuance of directions, as it is reasonably able to give (s 497AA (as so added; and amended by SI 2010/1158)). As to the service of notices see PARA 76.

7   Any direction under the Education Act 1996 s 497A may either: (1) have effect for an indefinite period until revoked by the Secretary of State; or (2) have effect for a period specified in the direction unless revoked earlier by the Secretary of State: s 497A(6) (as added (see note 4); and amended by the Education Act 2002 s 60(1), (9)). Any direction given under the Education Act 1996 s 497A(4), (4A) (see the text to note 10) or s 497A(4B) (see the text to notes 11–12) is enforceable, on an application made on behalf of the Secretary of State, by a mandatory order: s 497A(7) (as so added; and amended by the Education Act 2002 s 60(1), (10)). As to mandatory orders see JUDICIAL REVIEW vol 61 (2010) PARA 703 et seq.

8   Education Act 1996 s 497A(4) (as added (see note 4); and substituted by the Education Act 2002 s 60(1), (6)). See also note 6. Where the Secretary of State considers it expedient that the person specified in directions under the Education Act 1996 s 497A(4) ought to perform other functions to which s 497A applies, in addition to the function to which s 497A(2) (see the text to notes 1–6) or s 497A(2A) (see the text to notes 13–15) applies, the directions under s 497A(4) may relate to the performance of those other functions as well: see s 497A(5) (as so added; and substituted by the Education Act 2002 s 60(1), (8)). In considering whether it is expedient that that person ought to perform any such additional functions, the Secretary of State may have regard to financial considerations: Education Act 1996 s 497A(5) (as so added and substituted).
      As to the general default powers of the Secretary of State see s 497; and PARA 65.

9   Education Act 1996 s 497A(4) (as added and substituted: see note 8). See also note 6. As to the power of the Secretary of State to direct a local authority in England to enter into a contract or other arrangement for the provision of advisory services see the Education Act 2002 s 62A; and PARA 1221. As to similar powers of the Welsh Ministers see the Schools Standards and Organisation (Wales) Act 2013 Pt 2 (ss 2–37); and PARA 1229 et seq.

10   Education Act 1996 s 497A(4A) (s 497A as added (see note 4); s 497A(4A) added by the Education Act 2002 s 60(1), (7), and amended by SI 2010/1158). See also notes 6, 7.
      So far as is appropriate in consequence of a direction given under the Education Act 1996 s 497A(4A), a reference (however expressed) in an enactment, instrument or other document to a local authority is to be read as a reference to the person by whom the function is exercisable: s 497A(4AA) (s 497A(4AA), (4AB), (4AC) added by the Children and Families Act 2014 s 101(1), (2)). If a direction given under the Education Act 1996 s 497A(4A) expires or is revoked without being replaced, so far as is appropriate in consequence of the expiry or revocation, a reference (however expressed) in an instrument or other document to the person by whom the function was exercisable is to be read as a reference to the local authority to which the direction was given: s 497A(4AB), (4AC) (as so added).
      Where the Secretary of State considers it expedient that he or a person nominated by him in directions under s 497A(4A) ought to perform other functions to which s 497A applies, in addition to the function to which s 497A(2) (see the text to notes 1–6) or s 497A(2A) (see the text to notes 13–15) applies, the directions under s 497A(4A) may relate to the performance of those other functions as well: see s 497A(5) (as so added; and substituted by the Education Act 2002 s 60(1), (8)). In considering whether it is expedient that that person ought to perform any such additional functions, the Secretary of State may have regard to financial considerations: Education Act 1996 s 497A(5) (as so added and substituted).

11   Ie the powers conferred by the Education Act 1996 s 497A(4), (4A): see the text to notes 7–10.

12   Education Act 1996 s 497A(4B) (s 497A as added (see note 4); s 497A(4B) added by the Education Act 2002 s 60(1), (7), and amended by SI 2010/1158). See also note 7.

13   Ie under the Education Act 1996 s 497A(4), (4A) or (4B): see the text to notes 7–12.

14   Education Act 1996 s 497A(2A)(a) (s 497A as added (see note 4); s 497A(2A) added by the Education Act 2002 s 60(1), (4), and amended by SI 2010/1158).

15   Education Act 1996 s 497A(2A)(b) (as added (see note 14); and amended by SI 2010/1158). Where, in relation to any education function, the Secretary of State is satisfied as mentioned in s 497A(2A)(b), and has notified the local authority that he is so satisfied and that he is contemplating the giving of directions under s 497A(4) (see the text to notes 7–9) or s 497A(4A) (see the text to note 10), the local authority must give the Secretary of State, and any person authorised by it for these purposes, all such assistance, in connection with the proposed exercise of the function by the Secretary of State or another person in pursuance of directions, as it is reasonably able to give: see s 497AA (as added (see note 6); and amended by SI 2010/1158).

16   Ie under the Education Act 1996 s 497A(4) or (4A): see the text to notes 7–10.

17   'The specified person' means: (1) in relation to directions under the Education Act 1996 s 497A(4) (see the text to notes 7–9), the person specified in the directions; and (2) in relation to directions under s 497A(4A) (see the text to note 10), the Secretary of State or the person nominated by it: s 497B(1A) (s 497B added by the School Standards and Framework Act 1998 s 8; and the Education Act 1996 s 497B(1A) added by the Education Act 2002 s 62(1), (3)). Any

reference in the Education Act 1996 s 497B to the specified person includes a reference to any person assisting him in the performance of the specified function or functions: s 497B(6) (as so added).

18 Education Act 1996 s 497B(1) (as added (see note 17); and amended by the Education Act 2002 s 62(1), (2); and SI 2010/1158).

19 'Premises', in relation to a school, includes any detached playing fields but, except where otherwise expressly provided, does not include a teacher's dwelling-house: Education Act 1996 s 579(1). As to the meaning of 'school' see PARA 91.

20 For these purposes, 'document' and 'records' each includes information recorded in any form: Education Act 1996 s 497B(7) (as added: see note 17).

21 Education Act 1996 s 497B(2) (s 497B as added (see note 17); s 497B(2), (5) amended by SI 2010/1158). The Education Act 1996 s 497B(2) applies in relation to any school maintained by the local authority as it applies in relation to the authority; and without prejudice to s 497B(2) (as it so applies): (1) the governing body of any such school must give the specified person all assistance in connection with the exercise of his functions which it is reasonably able to give (s 497B(5)(a) (as so added and amended)); and (2) the governing body of any such school and the local authority must secure that all such assistance is also given by persons who work at the school (s 497B(5)(b) (as so added and amended)). As to the governing bodies of maintained schools in England see PARA 150 et seq; and in Wales see PARA 195.

22 Education Act 1996 s 497B(3)(a) (as added: see note 17).

23 This includes, in particular, the making of information available for inspection or copying in a legible form: see the Education Act 1996 s 497B(3)(b) (as added: see note 17).

24 Education Act 1996 s 497B(3)(b) (as added: see note 17).

25 Education Act 1996 s 497B(4) (as added (see note 17); and amended by SI 2010/1158). This provision is expressed to be without prejudice to s 497B(2) (see the text to notes 19–21): see s 497B(4) (as so added).

26 See the Children Act 2004 s 50A (added by School Standards and Organisation (Wales) Act 2013 Sch 5 para 7(1), (3)).

63. Power to require information from local authority in England about planned or actual expenditure.

The Secretary of State[1] may direct[2] a local authority in England[3] to provide information about its planned and actual expenditure in connection with: (1) its education functions[4]; (2) its children's social services functions[5]. The Secretary of State may also direct a local authority in England to provide information about accountable resources[6] held, received or expended by any person[7] in relation to a school maintained by the authority[8].

Information to which a direction under these provisions relates must be provided in accordance with the direction[9]. A direction may (in particular) include provision about: (a) the period to which information is to relate[10]; (b) the form and manner in which information is to be provided[11]; (c) the persons to whom information is to be provided[12]; (d) the publication of information[13]. If a direction requires information to be provided to a person other than the Secretary of State, the direction may also require that person to make the information available for inspection in accordance with the direction[14].

1 As to the Secretary of State see PARA 58.

2 As to directions see PARA 75.

3 As to the meaning of 'local authority in England' see PARA 25 (definition applied by the Apprenticeships, Skills, Children and Learning Act 2009 s 264(2), (3)).

4 Apprenticeships, Skills, Children and Learning Act 2009 s 251(1)(a). For the purposes of s 251, the Secretary of State may by order amend s 252 for one or more of the following purposes: (1) specifying additional functions which are to be treated as education functions (see s 252(1), (5)(za) (added by SI 2010/1158)); (2) removing or changing the description of functions that are education functions (see the Apprenticeships, Skills, Children and Learning Act 2009 s 252(1), (5)(b)). As to the meaning of 'education functions' see PARA 25 (definition applied by s 264(2), (3)).

5 Apprenticeships, Skills, Children and Learning Act 2009 s 251(1)(b). The children's social services functions of a local authority in England are: (1) functions conferred on or exercisable by the authority which are social services functions, so far as those functions relate to children

(s 252(1), (3)(a)); (2) functions conferred on the authority under the Children Act 1989 ss 23C–24D (see CHILDREN AND YOUNG PERSONS vol 10 (2012) PARA 925 et seq), so far as not within head (1) above (Apprenticeships, Skills, Children and Learning Act 2009 s 252(1), (3)(b)); (3) functions conferred on the authority under the Children Act 2004 ss 10–12, 12C, 12D and 17A (see CHILDREN AND YOUNG PERSONS vol 9 (2012) PARAS 203–204, 207) (Apprenticeships, Skills, Children and Learning Act 2009 s 252(1), (3)(c) (amended by SI 2010/1158)). The Secretary of State may by order amend the Apprenticeships, Skills, Children and Learning Act 2009 s 252 for one or more of the following purposes: (a) adding to the functions that are children's social services functions (see s 252(1), (5)(a)); (b) removing or changing the description of functions that are children's social services functions (see s 252(1), (5)(b)). 'Children's services authority in England' has the meaning given by the Children Act 2004 s 65(1) (see CHILDREN AND YOUNG PERSONS vol 9 (2012) PARA 203); and 'social services functions' has the same meaning as in the Local Authority Social Services Act 1970 (see s 1A; and LOCAL GOVERNMENT vol 69 (2009) PARA 588): Apprenticeships, Skills, Children and Learning Act 2009 s 252(1), (6).

6   'Accountable resources', in relation to a school maintained by a local authority, means resources that are not provided by the authority in the exercise of its education functions, but in respect of which an obligation is imposed on the school's governing body by virtue of regulations under the Education Act 2002 s 44 (accounts of maintained schools: see PARA 328): Apprenticeships, Skills, Children and Learning Act 2009 s 252(1), (4) (amended by SI 2010/1158). As to the meaning of 'school' see PARA 91 (definition applied by the Apprenticeships, Skills, Children and Learning Act 2009 s 264(2), (3)).

7   As to the meaning of 'person' see PARA 7 note 6.
8   Apprenticeships, Skills, Children and Learning Act 2009 s 251(2).
9   Apprenticeships, Skills, Children and Learning Act 2009 s 251(3).
10   Apprenticeships, Skills, Children and Learning Act 2009 s 251(4)(a).
11   Apprenticeships, Skills, Children and Learning Act 2009 s 251(4)(b).
12   Apprenticeships, Skills, Children and Learning Act 2009 s 251(4)(c).
13   Apprenticeships, Skills, Children and Learning Act 2009 s 251(4)(d).
14   Apprenticeships, Skills, Children and Learning Act 2009 s 251(5).

64. Power to prevent unreasonable exercise of functions by local authority or governing body in England. If the Secretary of State[1] is satisfied, either on a complaint by any person[2] or otherwise, that any local authority in England[3], or the governing body of any community, foundation or voluntary school in England, of any community or foundation special school[4] in England, or any maintained nursery school[5] in England, has acted or is proposing to act unreasonably[6] with respect to the exercise of any power conferred or the performance of any duty imposed by or under the Education Act 1996, the Secretary of State may[7] give such directions[8] as to the exercise of the power or the performance of the duty as appear to it to be expedient, and may do so despite any enactment[9] which makes the exercise of the power or the performance of the duty contingent upon the opinion of the authority or body[10].

1   As to the Secretary of State see PARA 58. The functions of the Secretary of State under the Education Act 1996 s 496, so far as they relate to the exercise of any function of a local authority under the Education Act 1996 s 507B (see PARA 504), are transferred to the Minister for the Cabinet Office: Transfer of Functions (Youth Leisure-time Activities) Order 2013, SI 2013/1721.

2   As to the meaning of 'person' see PARA 7 note 6.

3   See the Education Act 1996 s 496(2)(a) (amended by the School Standards and Framework Act 1998 s 140(1), Sch 30 para 129(a); SI 2010/1158; and the School Standards and Organisation (Wales) Act 2013 Sch 5 para 2(1), (4)(a)). As to the meaning of 'local authority' see PARA 25. As to the meaning of 'England' see PARA 7 note 3.

4   As to the meanings of references to a community, foundation or voluntary school or a community or foundation special school see PARA 106. As to the treatment of temporary governing bodies for the purposes of the Education Act 1996 s 496 see the Education Act 2002 s 34(7); and PARA 155.

5   See the Education Act 1996 s 496(2)(b) (substituted by the School Standards and Framework Act 1998 s 140(1), Sch 30 para 129(b); and amended by the Education and Inspections

Act 2006 s 168(1) and the School Standards and Organisation (Wales) Act 2013 Sch 5 para 2(1), (4)(b)). As to the meaning of 'maintained nursery school' see PARA 99 note 4.

6 The test for unreasonableness is in essence that set out in *Associated Provincial Picture Houses Ltd v Wednesbury Corpn* [1948] 1 KB 223, [1947] 2 All ER 680, CA, ie that the authority's conduct was such that no reasonable authority would engage in it, and unreasonable conduct is 'conduct which no sensible authority acting with due appreciation of its responsibilities would have decided to adopt': *Secretary of State for Education and Science v Tameside Metropolitan Borough Council* [1977] AC 1014 at 1064, [1976] 3 All ER 665 at 695, HL, per Lord Diplock. See further JUDICIAL REVIEW vol 61 (2010) PARA 617.

7 The Education Act 1996 s 496 is subject to s 508I (see PARA 811) and s 509AE (see PARA 467) (complaints about transport arrangements etc): s 496(5) (added by the Apprenticeships, Skills, Children and Learning Act 2009 s 59, Sch 2 paras 1, 7). Nothing in the Education Act 1996 s 496 or the School Standards and Organisation (Wales) Act 2013 Pt 2 Ch 2 (ss 21–31) (see PARA 1235 et seq) applies in relation to any power conferred on a local authority by the Education Act 1996 s 560(1) (see s 560(6) (amended by the School Standards and Organisation (Wales) Act 2013 Sch 5 para 2(1), (7))).

8 As to directions generally see PARA 75. A direction under the Education Act 1996 s 496 imposes on a local authority a statutory duty which it is bound to comply with, and which can be enforced: *Secretary of State for Education and Science v Tameside Metropolitan Borough Council* [1977] AC 1014, [1976] 3 All ER 665, HL (in this case, decided under previous legislation, it was, however, held that the direction was ultra vires).

9 As to the meaning of 'enactment' see PARA 1 note 13.

10 Education Act 1996 s 496(1). The proper exercise by the Secretary of the functions under ss 496–497 (see PARA 65) should have the effect of avoiding the involvement of the courts in education matters: see *R v Secretary of State for Education and Science, ex p Chance* (26 July 1982, unreported); *R v Brent London Borough Council, ex p F* [1999] ELR 32, [1999] COD 38; *R v Secretary of State for Education, ex p Prior* [1994] ELR 231, [1994] ICR 877.

The powers under the Education Act 1996 s 496 and s 497 (see PARA 65) are applied in relation to: (1) the governing body of an institution which is maintained by a local authority and provides higher education or further education or both (see the Education Reform Act 1988 s 219(3) (repealed)); (2) the proprietors of certain schools who are under a duty to secure that all registered pupils are provided with a programme of careers education (see the Education Act 1997 s 43(4); and PARA 822); (3) the governing bodies of a relevant school or a further education institution and appropriate bodies and their duties and powers conferred under the provisions relating to the requirement for teachers to serve induction periods (see the Teaching and Higher Education Act 1998 s 19(12) (repealed)); (4) the proprietors of independent schools and the duties imposed by or under ballot regulations (see the School Standards and Framework Act 1998 s 105(7); and PARA 264); (5) a local authority or the governing body of a maintained school which has adopted a scheme formulated by a local authority for the purpose mentioned in s 89B (see s 89C(2); and PARA 248); (6) a local authority and the duties imposed by the provisions relating to the education functions of the overview and scrutiny committees (see the Local Government Act 2000 Sch A1 paras 6–8, Sch 1 paras 6–10; and PARA 55); (7) a local authority in England in relation to the powers conferred or duties imposed under the Childcare Act 2006 Pt 1 (ss 1–21) or in Wales under Pt 2 (ss 22–30) (see ss 15, 29; and CHILDREN AND YOUNG PERSONS vol 10 (2012) PARAS 1077, 1091); (8) pupil referral units in England (see the Education (Pupil Referral Units) (Application of Enactments) (England) Regulations 2007, SI 2007/2979, regs 1, 3, Sch 1 para 6). As to pupil referral units see PARA 427 et seq.

65. Power to declare local authority or governing body in default of duty.

If the Secretary of State[1] is satisfied, either on a complaint by any person[2] interested or otherwise, that any local authority in England[3], or the governing body of any community, foundation or voluntary school in England, of any community or foundation special school[4] in England, or any maintained nursery school[5] in England, has failed to discharge any duty imposed on it by or for the purposes of the Education Act 1996, the Secretary of State may[6] make an order[7] declaring the authority or body to be in default in respect of that duty, and giving such directions[8] for the purpose of enforcing the performance of the duty as appear to the Secretary of State to be expedient[9].

1 As to the Secretary of State see PARA 58. The functions of the Secretary of State under the Education Act 1996 s 497, so far as exercisable in relation to Wales, were transferred to the

National Assembly for Wales (see the National Assembly for Wales (Transfer of Functions) Order 1999, SI 1999/672, art 2, Sch 1) and then were vested in the Welsh Ministers (see the Government of Wales Act 2006 s 162(1), Sch 11 para 30), but see now the Education Act 1996 s 497(2); and notes 3, 5. As to the Welsh Ministers see PARA 59. As to the meaning of 'Wales' see PARA 7 note 3. The functions of the Secretary of State under the Education Act 1996 s 497, so far as they relate to the exercise of any function of a local authority under the Education Act 1996 s 507B (see PARA 504), are transferred to the Minister for the Cabinet Office: Transfer of Functions (Youth Leisure-time Activities) Order 2013, SI 2013/1721.

2   As to the meaning of 'person' see PARA 7 note 6.

3   See the Education Act 1996 s 497(2)(a) (amended by the School Standards and Framework Act 1998 s 140(1), Sch 30 para 130(a); SI 2010/1158; and the School Standards and Organisation (Wales) Act 2013 Sch 5 para 2(1), (5)(a)). As to the meaning of 'local authority' see PARA 25. As to the meaning of 'England' see PARA 7 note 3.

4   As to the meanings of references to a community, foundation or voluntary school or a community or foundation special school see PARA 106. As to the treatment of temporary governing bodies for the purposes of the Education Act 1996 s 497 see the Education Act 2002 s 34(7); and PARA 155.

5   See the Education Act 1996 s 497(2)(b) (substituted by the School Standards and Framework Act 1998 s 140(1), Sch 30 para 130(b); and amended by the Education and Inspections Act 2006 s 168(2) ; and the School Standards and Organisation (Wales) Act 2013 Sch 5 para 2(1), (5)(b)). As to the meaning of 'maintained nursery school' see PARA 99 note 4.

6   The Education Act 1996 s 497 is subject to s 508I (see PARA 811) and s 509AE (see PARA 467) (complaints about transport arrangements etc): s 497(6) (added by the Apprenticeships, Skills, Children and Learning Act 2009 s 59, Sch 2 paras 1, 8). Nothing in the Education Act 1996 s 497 applies in relation to any function arising by virtue of s 489 so far as it relates to regulations made under s 484: see s 484(7); and PARA 81.

7   Orders under the Education Act 1996 s 497 are not statutory instruments (see s 568(1), (2)) and as such are not recorded in this title. As to the revocation or variation of such orders see PARA 75.

8   Any such directions are enforceable, on an application made on behalf of the Secretary of State or the Welsh Ministers, by a mandatory order: Education Act 1996 s 497(3). As to directions see PARA 75. As to mandatory orders see JUDICIAL REVIEW vol 61 (2010) PARA 703 et seq.

9   Education Act 1996 s 497(1). As to the application of s 497 for the purposes of other enactments see PARA 64 note 10. The Secretary of State has a power, and not a duty, to issue a direction under the Education Act 1996 s 497 if he is satisfied that the school is in breach of its duty: *R v Secretary of State for Education and Employment and the Governors of Southlands Community Comprehensive School, ex p W* [1998] ELR 413 at 421, [1998] COD 112 at 113 per Harrison J. The proper exercise by the Secretary of State of his functions under the Education Act 1996 s 496 (see PARA 64) and s 497 should have the effect of avoiding the involvement of the courts in education matters: see *R v Secretary of State for Education and Science, ex p Chance* (26 July 1982, unreported); *R v Brent London Borough Council, ex p F* [1999] ELR 32, [1999] COD 38; *R v Secretary of State for Education, ex p Prior* [1994] ELR 231, [1994] ICR 877. The existence of the remedy of complaint to the Secretary of State under the Education Act 1996 s 497 does not exclude the remedy of judicial review where 'the public authority flies in the face of the statute, by doing something which the statute expressly prohibits, or by failing to do something which the statute expressly enjoins, or otherwise so conducts itself, by omission or commission, as to frustrate or hinder policy and the objects of the Act': *Meade v Haringey London Borough Council* [1979] 2 All ER 1016 at 1024, [1979] 1 WLR 637 at 647, CA, per Lord Denning MR. See also *Watt v Kesteven County Council* [1955] 1 QB 408, [1955] 1 All ER 473, CA; *Bradbury v Enfield London Borough Council* [1967] 3 All ER 434, [1967] 1 WLR 1311, CA; *R v Inner London Education Authority, ex p Ali* [1990] COD 317, 2 Admin LR 822, DC. It is arguable that the role of the court in these circumstances is to consider whether the default powers under the Education Act 1996 ss 496–497 are an adequate alternative remedy: *R (on the application of Rhodes) v Kingston upon Hull City Council* [2001] ELR 230. In circumstances where an application is made to the Secretary of State and has failed, a judicial review should be sought against the decision of the Secretary of State rather than against the body which was the subject of the application: *R (on the application of Rhodes) v Kingston upon Hull City Council* above. As to judicial review see JUDICIAL REVIEW vol 61 (2010) PARA 601 et seq.

66. Determination of disputes involving local authorities and governing bodies. Except where the Education Act 1996[1] expressly provides otherwise, any dispute between a local authority[2] and the governing body of a school[3] as to the exercise of any power conferred or the performance of any duty imposed by or under that Act may be referred to the appropriate national authority[4] despite any enactment which makes the exercise of the power or the performance of the duty contingent upon the opinion of the authority or of the governing body[5]. The appropriate national authority must determine any dispute so referred to it[6].

Any dispute between two or more local authorities as to which of them is responsible for the provision of education for any pupil[7] must be determined by the appropriate national authority[8].

1　Nothing in the Education Act 1996 s 495 applies in relation to any function arising by virtue of s 489 so far as it relates to regulations made under s 484 (see s 484(7); and PARA 81); and nothing in the Education Act 1996 s 495 or the School Standards and Organisation (Wales) Act 2013 Pt 2 Ch 2 (ss 21–31) (see PARA 1235 et seq) applies in relation to any power conferred on a local authority by the Education Act 1996 s 560(1) (see s 560(6) (amended by the School Standards and Organisation (Wales) Act 2013 Sch 5 para 2(1), (7)); and CHILDREN AND YOUNG PERSONS vol 10 (2012) PARA 706).

2　As to the meaning of 'local authority' see PARA 25.

3　As to the meaning of 'school' see PARA 91. As to the governing bodies of maintained schools see PARA 150 et seq.

4　Ie the Secretary of State or, in relation to Wales, the Welsh Ministers. The functions of the Secretary of State under the Education Act 1996 s 495 (except in so far as they relate to a dispute to which only one party is in Wales), so far as exercisable in relation to Wales, were transferred to the National Assembly for Wales (see the National Assembly for Wales (Transfer of Functions) Order 1999, SI 1999/672, art 2, Sch 1) and are now vested in the Welsh Ministers (see the Government of Wales Act 2006 s 162(1), Sch 11 para 30). As to the Secretary of State see PARA 58. As to the Welsh Ministers see PARA 59. As to the meaning of 'Wales' see PARA 7 note 3.

5　Education Act 1996 s 495(1) (amended by SI 2010/1158). As to the treatment of temporary governing bodies for the purposes of s 495 see the Education Act 2002 s 34(7); and PARA 155. As to the power of the Secretary of State or the Welsh Ministers to require a medical examination where a question is referred under the Education Act 1996 s 495 see s 506; and PARA 498. As to the application of s 495(1), (2) (see the text to note 6) to pupil referral units in England see the Education (Pupil Referral Units) (Application of Enactments) (England) Regulations 2007, SI 2007/2979, regs 1, 3, Sch 1 para 5. As to pupil referral units see PARA 427 et seq.

6　Education Act 1996 s 495(2).

7　As to the meaning of 'pupil' see PARA 20 note 4.

8　Education Act 1996 s 495(3) (amended by SI 2010/1158). As to the treatment of disputes as to whether a person belongs, or does not belong, to the area of a particular local authority see the Education Act 1996 s 579(4); and PARA 27 note 6. As to disputes between local authorities in the context of special needs and disabilities see PARAS 949, 1028.

67. Power to require information from governing bodies. The appropriate national authority[1] may by regulations[2] make provisions requiring: (1) the governing body of every school[3] which is maintained by a local authority[4] or a special school[5] which is not maintained by such an authority[6]; and (2) the proprietor[7] of every independent school and alternative provision academy which is not an independent school[8] to provide such information about the school as may be prescribed[9]. For these purposes, information about the continuing education of pupils[10] leaving a school, or the employment or training taken up by such pupils on leaving, is to be treated as information about the school[11]. No information provided in accordance with such regulations may name any pupil to whom it relates[12].

Where the appropriate national authority exercises such a power, it must do so with a view to making available information which is likely to assist parents[13] in choosing schools for their children[14], increase public awareness of the quality of education provided by the schools concerned and the educational standards achieved in those schools[15], or assist in assessing the degree of efficiency with which the financial resources of those schools are managed[16]. The appropriate national authority may: (a) publish information provided in accordance with regulations under these provisions in such form and manner as it considers appropriate[17]; (b) make arrangements for such information to be published in such form and manner, and by such persons, as it may specify for these purposes[18]; (c) make regulations requiring local authorities to publish prescribed categories of such information, together with such supplementary information as may be prescribed, in such form and manner as may be prescribed[19]. The appropriate national authority may also make regulations requiring the governing body of any school which is maintained by a local authority[20], the proprietor of any city technology college[21], city college for the technology of the arts[22] or academy[23], or any local authority[24], to provide prescribed persons with prescribed categories of information published under heads (a) to (c) above[25].

Regulations under these provisions may make provision for the designation by the appropriate national authority, in accordance with the regulations, of particular schools or classes of schools for the purposes of the application of particular provisions of the regulations in relation to such schools[26].

The provisions described above are not to be taken as restricting, or otherwise affecting, any other powers that the appropriate national authority may have to make regulations with respect to, or otherwise to require, the provision of information by any person[27].

A local authority in Wales must publish any material which the Welsh Ministers[28] provide to the authority for the purpose[29], being material ('qualifying material') the Welsh Ministers consider likely to: (i) assist parents in choosing schools for their children[30]; (ii) increase public awareness of the quality of education provided at schools or a school and of the educational standards achieved there[31]; or (iii) assist in assessing the degree of efficiency with which the financial resources of schools or a school are managed[32]. A local authority in Wales must provide to such persons as the Welsh Ministers may specify any qualifying material which they provide to the authority for the purpose[33]; and the governing body of any school maintained by a local authority in Wales must provide to such persons as the Welsh Ministers may specify any qualifying material which they provide to the body for the purpose[34]. Any material so published or so provided may not name any individual to whom it relates[35] and must be in such form and manner as may be prescribed[36].

1 Ie the Secretary of State or, in relation to Wales, the Welsh Ministers. The functions of the Secretary of State under the Education Act 1996 s 537, so far as exercisable in relation to Wales, were transferred to the National Assembly for Wales (see the National Assembly for Wales (Transfer of Functions) Order 1999, SI 1999/672, art 2, Sch 1) and are now vested in the Welsh Ministers (see the Government of Wales Act 2006 s 162(1), Sch 11 para 30). As to the Secretary of State see PARA 58. As to the Welsh Ministers see PARA 59. As to the meaning of 'Wales' see PARA 7 note 3.

Nothing in any provision made by or under the Education Act 1996 s 537 requires or authorises the provision of information (1) by the principal regulator of an exempt charity (within the meaning of the Charities Act 2011 s 25: see CHARITIES vol 8 (2015) PARA 320), if the information was received by that principal regulator in its capacity as such; or (2) to the principal regulator of an exempt charity in its capacity as such: Education Act 1996 s 537C(1) (s 537C substituted by SI 2011/1726; and amended by the Charities Act 2011 Sch 7 para 74). Nothing in the above provision prevents the disclosure of information under the Charities Act 2011 s 56 or 57 (see CHARITIES vol 8 (2015) PARA 316): Education Act 1996 s 537C(2) (as so substituted and amended).

2 As to the regulations made see the Education (School Performance Information) (England) Regulations 2007, SI 2007/2324 (amended by SI 2008/364; SI 2008/1727; SI 2009/646; SI 2012/765; SI 2012/1274; SI 2013/1759; SI 2013/3212; SI 2015/902; and SI 2015/1566); the School Information (England) Regulations 2008, SI 2008/3093 (amended by SI 2012/8; SI 2012/979; SI 2012/1124; SI 2013/758; SI 2013/2912; and SI 2015/902); the School Information (Wales) Regulations 2011, SI 2011/1944 (amended by SI 2013/437); and the School Performance Information (Wales) Regulations 2011, SI 2011/1963 (amended by SI 2013/437). As to the application of the appropriate regulations to pupil referral units in England see the Education (Pupil Referral Units) (Application of Enactments) (England) Regulations 2007, SI 2007/2979, regs 1, 3, Sch 1 para 29 (substituted by SI 2012/3158). As to pupil referral units see PARA 427 et seq.

3 The Education Act 1996 s 537 does not apply to nursery schools: s 537(13). As to the meanings of 'nursery school' and 'school' see PARA 91. As to the governing bodies of maintained schools see PARA 150 et seq.

4 As to the meaning of 'local authority' see PARA 25.

5 As to the meaning of 'special school' see PARA 1041.

6 Education Act 1996 s 537(1)(a) (s 537(1) substituted by the School Standards and Framework Act 1998 s 140(1), Sch 30 paras 57, 152(a); and amended by SI 2010/1158).

7 As to the meaning of 'proprietor' see PARA 51 note 4.

8 Education Act 1996 s 537(1)(b) (as substituted (see note 6); and amended by the Education Act 2011 Sch 13 para 9(1), (15)). As to the meaning of 'independent school' see PARA 369. As to the meaning of 'alternative provision academy' see PARA 346 note 14. As from a day to be appointed under the Education and Skills Act 2008 s 173(4), the Education Act 1996 s 537 applies in relation to a relevant part-time educational institution as it applies in relation to an independent school: see s 537AA(1) (s 537AA added by the Education and Skills Act 2008 s 169(1), Sch 1 Pt 1 paras 5, 8). In such application of the Education Act 1996 s 537: (1) references to a pupil at an independent school are to be read as references to a student at a relevant part-time educational institution (s 537AA(2)(a) (as so added)); (2) references to the proprietor of an independent school are to be read as references to the person or body of persons responsible for the management of a relevant part-time educational institution (s 537AA(2)(b) (as so added)). 'Relevant part-time educational institution' means an independent educational institution in England that is not an independent school (s 537AA(3)(a) (as so added)); 'independent educational institution' has the same meaning as in the Education and Skills Act 2008 Pt 4 Ch 1 (see s 92; and PARA 382) (Education Act 1996 s 537AA(3)(b) (as so added)); and 'student' has the same meaning as in the Education and Skills Act 2008 Pt 4 Ch 1 (see s 138; and PARA 383 note 4) (Education Act 1996 s 537AA(3)(c) (as so added)). At the date at which this volume states the law no such day had been appointed. As to the meaning of 'person' see PARA 7 note 6. As to the meaning of 'England' see PARA 7 note 3.

9 Education Act 1996 s 537(1) (as substituted: see note 6). 'Prescribed' means prescribed by the regulations: see s 579(1). Information which is required by virtue of regulations made under the Education Act 1996 s 537 must be provided in such form and manner (s 537(4)(a)), on such occasions (s 537(4)(b)), and to such person or persons (s 537(4)(c)), in addition to or in place of the Secretary of State or the Welsh Ministers, as may be prescribed (s 537(4)). The regulations may provide that, in such circumstances as may be prescribed, the provision of information to a person other than the Secretary of State or, as the case may be, the Welsh Ministers is to be treated, for the purposes of any provision of such regulations or s 537, as compliance with any requirement of such regulations relating to the provision of information to the Secretary of State or Welsh Ministers: s 537(4) (amended by the Education Act 1997 s 57(1), Sch 7 para 37). See *R v Secretary of State for Education and Employment, ex p Governing Body of West Horndon County Primary School and the National Association of Head Teachers* [1997] ELR 350, in which it was held that the Education Act 1996 s 537 gives the Secretary of State a wide discretion as to the form and manner in which information may be published.

10 As to the meaning of 'pupil' see PARA 20 note 4.

11 Education Act 1996 s 537(2).

12 Education Act 1996 s 537(5). As to the provision of information about individual pupils see PARA 68.

13 As to the meaning of 'parent' see PARA 7 note 6.

14 Education Act 1996 s 537(3)(a). As to the meaning of 'child' see PARA 7 note 6.

15 Education Act 1996 s 537(3)(b).

16 Education Act 1996 s 537(3)(c).

17 Education Act 1996 s 537(6)(a).

18 Education Act 1996 s 537(6)(b).

19 Education Act 1996 s 537(6)(c) (amended by SI 2010/1158).

20 Education Act 1996 s 537(7)(a) (amended by the School Standards and Framework Act 1998 s 140(3), Sch 30 para 152(b), Sch 31; and SI 2010/1158). Information provided under the Education Act 1996 s 537(7) must be provided in such form and manner as may be prescribed: s 537(8).

21 As to city technology colleges see PARA 345.

22 As to city colleges for the technology of the arts see PARA 345.

23 Education Act 1996 s 537(7)(b) (amended by the Learning and Skills Act 2000 s 149, Sch 9 paras 1, 60; and the Education Act 2002 s 65(3), Sch 7 Pt 2 para 6(1), (5)). See also note 20. As to the meaning of 'academy' see PARA 346.

24 Education Act 1996 s 537(7)(c) (amended by SI 2010/1158). See also note 20.

25 Education Act 1996 s 537(7).

26 Education Act 1996 s 537(11). This provision is expressed to be without prejudice to the generality of s 569(4) (regulations may make different provision for different cases, etc): see s 537(11).

27 Education Act 1996 s 537(12).

28 The functions under the Education Act 2002 s 196 were originally vested in the National Assembly for Wales and are now exercisable by the Welsh Ministers by virtue of the Government of Wales Act 2006 s 162(1), Sch 11 paras 30, 32.

29 See the Education Act 2002 s 196(1) (amended by SI 2010/1158).

30 Education Act 2002 s 196(4)(a).

31 Education Act 2002 s 196(4)(b).

32 Education Act 2002 s 196(4)(c).

33 Education Act 1996 s 196(2) (amended by SI 2010/1158).

34 Education Act 2002 s 196(3) (amended by SI 2010/1158).

35 Education Act 2002 s 196(5).

36 Education Act 2002 s 196(6). 'Prescribed' means prescribed by regulations made by the Welsh Ministers: see the Education Act 2002 s 212(1). At the date at which this volume states the law no such regulations had been made.

68. Provision of information about individual pupils. Regulations[1] made by the appropriate national authority[2] may make provision requiring: (1) the governing body of every school[3] which is maintained by a local authority[4], or a special school[5] which is not maintained by such an authority[6]; and (2) the proprietor[7] of every independent school or alterative provision academy that is not an independent school[8], to provide to the appropriate national authority or any prescribed person[9] (or both) such individual pupil information[10] as may be prescribed[11]. The appropriate national authority may provide any individual pupil information to any information collator[12], to any prescribed person, or to any person falling within a prescribed category[13]. Any information collator:

(a)   may provide any individual pupil information to the appropriate national authority, to any other information collator, or to the governing body or proprietor of the school attended by the pupil or pupils to whom the information relates[14]; and

(b)   may, at such times as the appropriate national authority may determine, provide such individual pupil information as may be prescribed to any prescribed person, or to any person falling within a prescribed category[15].

Any person holding any individual pupil information, other than the Secretary of State, the Welsh Ministers or an information collator, may provide that information to the Secretary of State, the Welsh Ministers, any information collator, or any prescribed person[16].

No information received under or by virtue of these provisions may be published in any form which includes the name of the pupil or pupils to whom it relates[17].

1   'Regulations' means regulations made by the Secretary of State or, in relation to Wales, the Welsh Ministers: see Education Act 1996 s 579(1). As to the regulations made see note 11. The

functions of the Secretary of State under the Education Act 1996 s 537A, so far as exercisable in relation to Wales, were transferred to the National Assembly for Wales (see the National Assembly for Wales (Transfer of Functions) Order 1999, SI 1999/672, art 2, Sch 1) and are now vested in the Welsh Ministers (see the Government of Wales Act 2006 s 162(1), Sch 11 para 30). As to the Secretary of State see PARA 58. As to the Welsh Ministers see PARA 59. As to the meaning of 'Wales' see PARA 7 note 3.

    Nothing in any provision made by or under the Education Act 1996 s 537A requires or authorises the provision of information (1) by the principal regulator of an exempt charity (within the meaning of the Charities Act 2011 s 25: see CHARITIES vol 8 (2015) PARA 320), if the information was received by that principal regulator in its capacity as such; or (2) to the principal regulator of an exempt charity in its capacity as such: Education Act 1996 s 537C(1) (s 537C substituted by SI 2011/1726; and amended by the Charities Act 2011 Sch 7 para 74). Nothing in the above provision prevents the disclosure of information under the Charities Act 2011 s 56 or 57 (see CHARITIES vol 8 (2015) PARA 316): Education Act 1996 s 537C(2) (as so substituted and amended).

2   Ie the Secretary of State or, in relation to Wales, the Welsh Ministers: see note 1.

3   As to the meaning of 'school' see PARA 91. As to the governing bodies of maintained schools see PARA 150 et seq.

4   As to the meaning of 'local authority' see PARA 25.

5   As to the meaning of 'special school' see PARA 1041.

6   Education Act 1996 s 537A(1)(a) (s 537A added by the Education Act 1997 s 20; and substituted by the School Standards and Framework Act 1998 s 140(1), Sch 30 paras 57, 153; and the Education Act 1996 s 537A(1)(a) amended by SI 2010/1158).

7   As to the meaning of 'proprietor' see PARA 51 note 4.

8   Education Act 1996 s 537A(1)(b) (as added and substituted (see note 6); and amended by SI 2012/976). As to the meaning of 'independent school' see PARA 369. As to the meaning of 'alternative provision academy' see PARA 346 note 14. As from a day to be appointed under the Education and Skills Act 2008 s 173(4), the Education Act 1996 s 537A applies in relation to a relevant part-time educational institution as it applies in relation to an independent school: see s 537AA(1) (s 537AA added by the Education and Skills Act 2008 s 169(1), Sch 1 Pt 1 paras 5, 8). In such application of the Education Act 1996 s 537A: (1) references to a pupil at an independent school are to be read as references to a student at a relevant part-time educational institution (s 537AA(2)(a) (as so added)); (2) references to the proprietor of an independent school are to be read as references to the person or body of persons responsible for the management of a relevant part-time educational institution (s 537AA(2)(b) (as so added)). As to the meanings of 'relevant part-time educational institution', 'independent educational institution' and 'student' see PARA 67 note 8. At the date at which this volume states the law no such day had been appointed. As to the meaning of 'person' see PARA 7 note 6.

9   Ie a person prescribed by the regulations: see Education Act 1996 s 579(1). Where any prescribed person receives information by virtue of s 537A(1), the Secretary of State or Welsh Ministers may require that person to provide any such information to him or them, or to any prescribed person: s 537A(3) (as added and substituted: see note 6). Regulations under s 537A may provide that, in such circumstances as may be prescribed, the provision of information to a person other than the Secretary of State or, as the case may be, the Welsh Ministers is to be treated, for the purposes of any provision of such regulations or s 537A, as compliance with any requirement relating to the provision of information to the Secretary of State or the Welsh Ministers imposed by or by virtue of any such provision: s 537A(8) (as so added and substituted).

10   'Individual pupil information' means information relating to and identifying individual pupils or former pupils at any school within the Education Act 1996 s 537A(1), whether obtained under s 537A(1) or otherwise: s 537A(9) (as added and substituted: see note 6). As to the meaning of 'pupil' see PARA 20 note 4. As to the protection of biometric information of children in schools etc see PARA 69. As to the provision of information about children receiving funded education outside school see s 537B; and PARA 70.

11   Education Act 1996 s 537A(1), (2) (as added and substituted: see note 6). The following regulations have been made: the Education (Individual Performance Information) (Identification of Individual Pupils) Regulations 1998, SI 1998/1834 (revoked, in relation to individual pupil information relating to pupils at schools (other than nursery schools) in England, by SI 1999/903); the Education (Information About Children in Alternative Provision) (England) Regulations 2007, SI 2007/1065 (amended by SI 2010/1941; SI 2012/765; SI 2012/956; SI 2012/979; and SI 2012/1274); the Education (School Performance Information) (England) Regulations 2007, SI 2007/2324 (amended by SI 2008/364; SI 2008/1727; SI 2009/646; SI 2012/765; SI 2012/1274; SI 2013/1759; SI 2013/3212; SI 2015/902; and SI 2015/1566); the

Education (Information About Individual Pupils) (Wales) Regulations 2007, SI 2007/3562 (amended by SI 2011/2325; and SI 2013/3137); the Education (Information About Children in Alternative Provision) (Wales) Regulations 2009, SI 2009/3355; the School Performance Information (Wales) Regulations 2011, SI 2011/1963 (amended by SI 2013/437); and the Education (Information About Individual Pupils) (England) Regulations 2013, SI 2013/2094 (amended by SI 2014/852). As to the application of the appropriate regulations to pupil referral units in England see the Education (Pupil Referral Units) (Application of Enactments) (England) Regulations 2007, SI 2007/2979, regs 1, 3, Sch 1 para 29 (substituted by SI 2012/3158). As to pupil referral units see PARA 427 et seq.

12 'Information collator' means any body which, for the purposes of or in connection with the functions of the Secretary of State or the Welsh Ministers relating to education, is responsible for collating or checking information relating to pupils: Education Act 1996 s 573A(9) (as added and substituted: see note 6). As to the meaning of 'functions' see PARA 18 note 5.

13 Education Act 1996 s 537A(4) (as added and substituted: see note 6). As to the prescribed categories of person see the Education (Individual Pupil Information) (Prescribed Persons) (England) Regulations 2009, SI 2009/1563 (amended by SI 2012/765; SI 2012/956; SI 2012/979; SI 2013/235; and SI 2013/1193); and the Education (Information About Individual Pupils) (Wales) Regulations 2007, SI 2007/3562 (amended by SI 2011/2325; and SI 2013/3137). See also PARAS 48, 94.

14 Education Act 1996 s 537A(5)(a) (as added and substituted: see note 6).

15 Education Act 1996 s 537A(5)(b) (as added and substituted: see note 6).

16 Education Act 1996 s 537A(6) (as added and substituted: see note 6).

17 Education Act 1996 s 537A(7) (as added and substituted: see note 6).

69. Protection of biometric information of children in schools etc. The Protection of Freedoms Act 2012[1] applies in relation to any processing[2] of a child's[3] biometric information[4] by or on behalf of the relevant authority[5] of (1) a school; (2) a 16 to 19 academy; or (3) a further education institution[6].

Before the first processing of a child's biometric information on or after 1 September 2013[7], the relevant authority must notify each parent[8] of the child of its intention to process the child's biometric information, and that the parent may object at any time to the processing of the information[9].

The relevant authority must ensure that a child's biometric information is not processed unless (a) at least one parent of the child consents to the information being processed, and (b) no parent of the child has withdrawn his or her consent, or otherwise objected, to the information being processed[10]. However if, at any time, the child refuses to participate in, or continue to participate in, anything that involves the processing of the child's biometric information, or otherwise objects to the processing of that information, the relevant authority must ensure that the information is not processed, irrespective of any consent given[11] by a parent of the child[12]. In relation to any child whose biometric information may not be processed[13], the relevant authority must ensure that reasonable alternative means are available by which the child may do, or be subject to, anything which the child would have been able to do, or be subject to, had the child's biometric information been processed[14].

1   Ie the Protection of Freedoms Act 2012 s 26: see the text and notes 2–15.
2   'Processing' has the meaning given by the Data Protection Act 1998 s 1(1) (see CONFIDENCE AND INFORMATIONAL PRIVACY vol 19 (2011) PARA 97): Protection of Freedoms Act 2012 s 28(1).
3   'Child' means a person under the age of 18: Protection of Freedoms Act 2012 s 28(1).
4   'Biometric information' means information about a person's physical or behavioural characteristics or features which (1) is capable of being used in order to establish or verify the identity of the person, and (2) is obtained or recorded with the intention that it be used for the purposes of a biometric recognition system: Protection of Freedoms Act 2012 s 28(1), (2). Biometric information may, in particular, include (a) information about the skin pattern and other physical characteristics or features of a person's fingers or palms, (b) information about the features of an iris or any other part of the eye, and (c) information about a person's voice or

handwriting: s 28(1), (3). In s 28(2) 'biometric recognition system' means a system which, by means of equipment operating automatically (i) obtains or records information about a person's physical or behavioural characteristics or features, and (ii) compares the information with stored information that has previously been so obtained or recorded, or otherwise processes the information, for the purpose of establishing or verifying the identity of the person, or otherwise determining whether the person is recognised by the system: s 28(1), (4).

5   'Relevant authority' means (1) in relation to a school, the proprietor of the school; (2) in relation to a 16 to 19 academy, the proprietor of the academy; (3) in relation to a further education institution, the governing body of the institution (within the meaning given by paras (a), (c) and (d) of the definition of 'governing body' in the Further and Higher Education Act 1992 s 90(1): see PARA 560 note 6)); Protection of Freedoms Act 2012 s 28(1). As to the meaning of 'school' see PARA 91 (definition applied by the Protection of Freedoms Act 2012 s 28(1)) but a reference to a school is to be read as if it included a reference to any independent educational institution (within the meaning given by the Education and Skills Act 2008 s 92: see PARA 382): Protection of Freedoms Act 2012 s 28(10). As to the meaning of '16 to 19 academy' see PARA 346 note 13 (definition applied by s 28(1).

6   Protection of Freedoms Act 2012 s 26(1). 'Further education institution' means an institution within the further education sector (within the meaning given by the Further and Higher Education Act 1992 s 91(3)(a)–(c): see PARA 555): Protection of Freedoms Act 2012 s 28(1). See also PARA 94.

7   Ie the date of the coming into force of the Protection of Freedoms Act 2012 s 26(3).

8   'Parent' means a parent of the child and any individual who is not a parent of the child but who has parental responsibility for the child: Protection of Freedoms Act 2012 s 28(1), (5). 'Parental responsibility' is to be read in accordance with the Children Act 1989 (see CHILDREN AND YOUNG PERSONS vol 9 (2012) PARA 151): Protection of Freedoms Act 2012 s 28(1), (6). In a case where the relevant authority is satisfied that, by virtue of s 27(1) (see the text to note 11), there is no person falling within s 28(5) (see above) who must be notified or whose consent is required, 'parent' is to be read as including each individual who has care of the child, but this is subject to s 28(7), (8): s 28(1), (6). In a case to which s 28(6) applies where the child is looked after by a local authority (within the meaning given by the Children Act 1989 s 22(1): see CHILDREN AND YOUNG PERSONS vol 9 (2012) PARA 155 note 20), 'parent' is to be read as meaning the local authority looking after the child: Protection of Freedoms Act 2012 s 28(1), (7). In a case to which s 28(6) applies where the child is not looked after by a local authority (within the meaning given by the Children Act 1989 s 22(1)) but a voluntary organisation has provided accommodation for the child in accordance with s 59(1) (see CHILDREN AND YOUNG PERSONS vol 10 (2012) PARA 984) by (1) placing the child with a foster parent; or (2) maintaining the child in a children's home, 'parent' is to be read as meaning the voluntary organisation that so placed or maintains the child: Protection of Freedoms Act 2012 s 28(1), (8).

9   Protection of Freedoms Act 2012 s 26(2).

10   Protection of Freedoms Act 2012 s 26(3). There is further provision about the requirement to notify parents and the obtaining and withdrawal of consent (including when notification and consent are not required): see the Protection of Freedoms Act 2012 ss 26(4), 27.

11   Ie under the Protection of Freedoms Act 2012 s 26(3).

12   Protection of Freedoms Act 2012 s 26(5).

13   Ie by virtue of the Protection of Freedoms Act 2012 s 26.

14   Protection of Freedoms Act 2012 s 26(6), (7).

70.   Provision of information about children receiving funded education outside school. Regulations[1] made by the appropriate national authority[2] may make provision requiring a person[3] who provides funded education[4] to provide to the relevant person[5] such individual child information[6] as may be prescribed[7].

The appropriate national authority may provide any individual child information to any information collator[8], to any prescribed person[9], or to any person falling within a prescribed category[10]. Any information collator may provide any individual child information to the appropriate national authority[11], to any other information collator[12], or to the person who provides the funded education for the child or children to whom the information relates[13]; and may, at such times as the appropriate national authority may determine, provide such individual child information as may be prescribed to any prescribed person[14] or to any person falling within a prescribed category[15].

Any person holding any individual child information (other than the appropriate national authority or an information collator) may provide that information to the appropriate national authority[16], any information collator[17], or any prescribed person[18].

Regulations under these provisions may provide that, in such circumstances as may be prescribed, the provision of information to a person other than the appropriate national authority is to be treated[19] as compliance with any requirement[20] relating to the provision of information to the appropriate national authority[21].

No information received under or by virtue of these provisions must be published in any form which includes the name of the child or children to whom it relates[22].

1   'Regulations' means regulations made by the Secretary of State or, in relation to Wales, the Welsh Ministers: see Education Act 1996 s 579(1). As to the regulations made see note 7. The functions of the Secretary of State under the Education Act 1996 s 537B, so far as exercisable in relation to Wales, were transferred to the National Assembly for Wales (see the National Assembly for Wales (Transfer of Functions) Order 1999, SI 1999/672, art 2, Sch 1) and are now vested in the Welsh Ministers (see the Government of Wales Act 2006 s 162(1), Sch 11 para 30). As to the Secretary of State see PARA 58. As to the Welsh Ministers see PARA 59. As to the meaning of 'Wales' see PARA 7 note 3.
       Nothing in any provision made by or under the Education Act 1996 s 537B requires or authorises the provision of information (1) by the principal regulator of an exempt charity (within the meaning of the Charities Act 2011 s 25: see CHARITIES vol 8 (2015) PARA 320), if the information was received by that principal regulator in its capacity as such; or (2) to the principal regulator of an exempt charity in its capacity as such: Education Act 1996 s 537C(1) (s 537C substituted by SI 2011/1726; and amended by the Charities Act 2011 Sch 7 para 74). Nothing in the above provision prevents the disclosure of information under the Charities Act 2011 s 56 or 57 (see CHARITIES vol 8 (2015) PARA 316): Education Act 1996 s 537C(2) (as so substituted and amended).
2   Ie the Secretary of State or, in relation to Wales, the Welsh Ministers: see note 1.
3   As to the meaning of 'person' see PARA 7 note 6.
4   'Funded education' means education provided under arrangements made by a local authority in pursuance of the duties imposed by the Education Act 1996 s 19(1) and (4) (duty to make special arrangements for provision of education for children of compulsory school age and young persons who may otherwise not receive suitable education: see PARA 427), other than such education provided at a school: s 537B(9) (s 537B added by the Education and Inspections Act 2006 s 164; and the Education Act 1996 s 537B(9) amended by SI 2010/1158). As to the meaning of 'local authority' see PARA 25. As to the meaning of 'school' see PARA 91.
5   'The relevant person' means one or more of the following: the Secretary of State, the Welsh Ministers and any prescribed person: Education Act 1996 s 537B(2) (as added: see note 4). Where any prescribed person receives information by virtue of s 537B(1), the Secretary of State or the Welsh Ministers may require that person to provide any such information to him or, as the case may be, them (s 537B(3)(a) (as so added)), or to any prescribed person (s 537B(3)(b) (as so added)). 'Prescribed' means prescribed by regulations made by the Secretary of State or, as appropriate, the Welsh Ministers: see the Education Act 1996 s 579(1). As to the regulations made see note 7.
6   'Individual child information' means information relating to and identifying individual children for whom funded education is being or has been provided, whether obtained under the Education Act 1996 s 537B(1) or otherwise; and 'child' means a person under the age of 19: s 537B(9) (as added: see note 4). As to the time at which a person attains a particular age see PARA 7 note 6.
7   Education Act 1996 s 537B(1) (as added: see note 4). As to the regulations made under s 537B see the Education (Information About Children in Alternative Provision) (England) Regulations 2007, SI 2007/1065 (amended by SI 2010/941; SI 2012/765; SI 2012/956; and SI 2012/979); and the Education (Information About Children in Alternative Provision) (Wales) Regulations 2009, SI 2009/3355.

8　Education Act 1996 s 537B(4)(a) (as added: see note 4). 'Information collator' means any body which, for the purposes of or in connection with the functions of the Secretary of State or the Welsh Ministers relating to funded education, is responsible for collating or checking information relating to children for whom such education is provided: s 537B(9) (as so added). As to the meaning of 'functions' see PARA 18 note 5.

9　Education Act 1996 s 537B(4)(b) (as added: see note 4). As to the regulations made see note 7.

10　Education Act 1996 s 537B(4)(c) (as added: see note 4). As to the regulations made see note 7.

11　Education Act 1996 s 537B(5)(a)(i) (as added: see note 4).

12　Education Act 1996 s 537B(5)(a)(ii) (as added: see note 4).

13　Education Act 1996 s 537B(5)(a)(iii) (as added: see note 4).

14　Education Act 1996 s 537B(5)(b)(i) (as added: see note 4). As to the regulations made see note 7.

15　Education Act 1996 s 537B(5)(b)(ii) (as added: see note 4). As to the regulations made see note 7.

16　Education Act 1996 s 537B(6)(a) (as added: see note 4).

17　Education Act 1996 s 537B(6)(b) (as added: see note 4).

18　Education Act 1996 s 537B(6)(c) (as added: see note 4). As to the regulations made see note 7.

19　Ie for the purposes of any provision of such regulations or the Education Act 1996 s 537B(8): s 537B(8) (as added: see note 4).

20　Ie any requirement imposed by or by virtue of any such provision as is mentioned in note 19: see s 537B(8) (as added: see note 4).

21　Education Act 1996 s 537B(8) (as added: see note 4). As to the regulations made see note 7.

22　Education Act 1996 s 537B(7) (as added: see note 4).

71.　Supply of information about school workforce. Regulations[1] made, in relation to England by the Secretary of State[2] or, in relation to Wales, the Welsh Ministers[3] may authorise or require:

(1)　the proprietor of a school[4];

(2)　a local authority[5]; or

(3)　any prescribed person[6],

to supply to the Secretary of State[7], the Welsh Ministers[8], or any prescribed person[9], prescribed information relating to persons who are or have been qualifying workers[10] or qualifying trainees[11], for use by the Secretary of State, the Welsh Ministers, or any prescribed person, for a qualifying purpose[12]. Regulations may also authorise the Secretary of State or the Welsh Ministers to supply to the other or to any prescribed person, for use for a qualifying purpose, prescribed information relating to persons who are or have been qualifying workers or qualifying trainees[13].

Regulations may authorise the Secretary of State[14], the Welsh Ministers[15], or any prescribed person[16] to supply to any prescribed person ('the recipient') any information relating to persons who are or have been qualifying workers or qualifying trainees which has been lawfully held by the recipient, or is information which another person was, or could have been, required, whether by virtue of regulations made under these provisions or otherwise, to supply to the recipient[17].

Regulations may also prohibit any person to whom information is supplied by virtue of the above provisions from further disclosing the information otherwise than in prescribed circumstances[18], in relation to England, provide that the default powers of the Secretary of State[19] are, in relation to the duties imposed those provisions, to have effect with modifications[20], and in relation to Wales, provide that the provisions on intervention in local authorities[21] are to have effect with modifications[22].

The provisions described above do not limit the circumstances in which information is otherwise authorised or required to be supplied[23].

1 As to the regulations made under the Education Act 2005 s 114 see the Education (Supply of Information about the School Workforce) (No 2) (England) Regulations 2007, SI 2007/2260 (amended by SI 2009/2266; SI 2012/765; and SI 2012/956).

2 See the Education Act 2005 s 114(10). As to the Secretary of State see PARA 58. As to the meaning of 'England' see PARA 7 note 3.

3 See the Education Act 2005 s 114(10). The functions under the Education Act 2005 s 114 were originally vested in the National Assembly for Wales and are now exercisable by the Welsh Ministers by virtue of the Government of Wales Act 2006 s 162(1), Sch 11 paras 30, 32. As to the Welsh Ministers see PARA 59. As to the meaning of 'Wales' see PARA 7 note 3.

4 Education Act 2005 s 114(1)(a). As to the meaning of 'proprietor' see PARA 51 note 4; and as to the meaning of 'school' see PARA 91 (definitions applied by s 122(2), (3)).

5 Education Act 2005 s 114(1)(b) (substituted by SI 2010/1158). As to the meaning of 'local authority' see PARA 25 (definition applied by the Education Act 2005 s 122(2), (3)).

6 Education Act 2005 s 114(1)(c). 'Prescribed' means prescribed by regulations: Education Act 2005 s 114(10). A person may not be prescribed for these purposes unless he appears to the person making the regulations to be exercising functions of a public nature: s 114(4)(a). As to the meaning of 'person' see PARA 7 note 6.

7 Education Act 2005 s 114(2)(a).

8 Education Act 2005 s 114(2)(b).

9 Education Act 2005 s 114(2)(c). A person may not be prescribed for these purposes unless he appears to the person making the regulations to be exercising functions of a public nature: s 114(4)(a).

10 'Qualifying worker' means any person who: (1) is employed at, or otherwise engaged to work at, a school (Education Act 2005 s 113(1), (2)(a)); (2) does not fall within head (1) above but provides, or assists in the provision of, education under a contract of employment or for services where the other party to the contract is a local authority, or a person exercising a function relating to the provision of education on behalf of such an authority (s 113(1), (2)(b) (amended by SI 2010/1158)); or (3) provides education at a further education institution or 16 to 19 academy (Education Act 2005 s 113(1), (2)(c) (amended by the Education Act 2011 Sch 13 para 15(1), (3)). 'Contract of employment' has the meaning given by the Employment Rights Act 1996 s 230(2) (see EMPLOYMENT vol 39 (2014) PARA 2); and 'further education institution' means an institution which is: (a) an institution (other than a school) which provides further education; or (b) an institution within the further education sector: Education Act 2005 s 113(1), (4). As to the meaning of 'further education' see PARA 23 (definition applied by s 122(2), (3)). As to the meaning of '16 to 19 academy' see PARA 346 note 13.

11 'Qualifying trainee' means a person (other than a qualifying worker) for whom training as a member of the school workforce is being provided: Education Act 2005 s 113(1), (3). 'Member of the school workforce' has the same meaning as in Pt 3 (ss 74–100) (see PARA 1055): s 113(1), (4).

12 Education Act 2005 s 114(1). Information is supplied to a person for use for a qualifying purpose if it is supplied to him for use for: (1) evaluation, planning, research or statistical purposes (s 114(5)(a)); or (2) any other prescribed purpose (s 114(5)(b)).

13 Education Act 2005 s 114(3). A person may not be prescribed for these purposes unless he appears to the person making the regulations to be exercising such functions or carrying out research which relates to education or training and may be expected to be of public benefit: s 114(4)(b). As to the regulations made see note 1.

14 Education Act 2005 s 114(7)(a).

15 Education Act 2005 s 114(7)(b).

16 Education Act 2005 s 114(7)(c).

17 See the Education Act 2005 s 114(6). As to the regulations made see note 1.

18 Education Act 2005 s 114(8)(a). As to the regulations made see note 1.

19 Ie under the Education Act 1996 s 497: see PARA 65.

20 Education Act 2005 s 114(8)(b) (amended by the School Standards and Organisation (Wales) Act 2013 Sch 5 para 8(1), (3)(a), (b)). The modifications are that any reference to a body to which the Education Act 1996 s 497 applies has effect as if it included a reference to a prescribed person: Education Act 2005 s 114(8)(b) (amended by SI 2010/1158). As to the regulations made see note 1.

21 Ie under the School Standards and Organisation (Wales) Act 2013 Pt 2 Ch 2 (ss 21–31): see PARA 1235 et seq.

22 Education Act 2005 s 114(8)(c) (added by the School Standards and Organisation (Wales) Act 2013 Sch 5 para 8(1), (3)(c)). The modifications are that (1) references to a local authority included a reference to a prescribed person; (2) duties imposed by virtue of the Education Act 2005 s 114 were education functions; (3) the only relevant ground for intervention were

ground 1 in the School Standards and Organisation (Wales) Act 2013 s 21 (see PARA 1236); and (4) ss 24–27 (see PARA 1239) did not apply: Education Act 2005 s 114(8) (c) (as so added).
23 See the Education Act 2005 s 114(9).

72. Provision of student information to the Secretary of State, Welsh Ministers and others. A person[1] in England[2] may, in prescribed[3] circumstances, provide student information[4] of a prescribed description to (1) the Secretary of State[5]; (2) an information collator[6]; (3) a prescribed person[7]; or (4) a person falling within a prescribed category[8].

A person in Wales[9] may, in prescribed[10] circumstances, provide student information of a prescribed description to (a) the Welsh Ministers[11]; (b) an information collator[12]; (c) a prescribed person[13]; or (d) a person falling within a prescribed category[14].

The information[15] is not to be published in any form which identifies the individual to whom it relates[16].

The above provisions[17] do not affect any power to provide or publish information which exists apart from these provisions[18], and are subject to any express restriction on the provision of information imposed by another enactment[19].

1 As to the meaning of 'person' see PARA 7 note 6.
2 As to the meaning of 'England' see PARA 7 note 3.
3 'Prescribed' means prescribed by regulations, and 'regulations' means regulations made by the Secretary of State: Apprenticeships, Skills, Children and Learning Act 2009 s 264(1). As to the Secretary of State see PARA 58. As to the regulations made see the Education (Student Information) (England) Regulations 2015, SI 2015/1567.
4 For these purposes, 'student information' means information (whether obtained under the Apprenticeships, Skills, Children and Learning Act 2009 s 253A or otherwise) relating to an individual who is seeking or has sought to obtain, or has obtained, a regulated qualification or a relevant qualification: s 253A(6) (s 253A added by the Small Business, Enterprise and Employment Act 2015 s 79(1)). As to the meaning of 'regulated qualification' see PARA 826 note 7 (definition applied by the Apprenticeships, Skills, Children and Learning Act 2009 s 253A(6) (as so added)). As to the meaning of 'relevant qualification' see PARA 854 (definition applied by s 253A(6) (as so added)). As from a day to be appointed, in the definition of 'relevant qualification' the reference to the Education Act 1997 s 30(5) is replaced by a reference to the Qualifications Wales Act 2015 s 56: Apprenticeships, Skills, Children and Learning Act 2009 s 253A(6) (as so added; prospectively amended by the Qualifications Wales Act 2015 Sch 4 para 9). At the date at which this volume states the law no such day had been appointed.
5 Apprenticeships, Skills, Children and Learning Act 2009 s 253A(1)(a) (as added: see note 4).
6 Apprenticeships, Skills, Children and Learning Act 2009 s 253A(1)(b) (as added: see note 4). For these purposes, 'information collator' means any body which, for the purposes of or in connection with functions of the Secretary of State or the Welsh Ministers, is responsible for collating or checking information relating to regulated qualifications or relevant qualifications: s 253A(6) (as added: see note 4). As to the Welsh Ministers see PARA 59.
7 Apprenticeships, Skills, Children and Learning Act 2009 s 253A(1)(c) (as added: see note 4).
8 Apprenticeships, Skills, Children and Learning Act 2009 s 253A(1)(d) (as added: see note 4).
9 As to the meaning of 'Wales' see PARA 7 note 3.
10 In the Apprenticeships, Skills, Children and Learning Act 2009 s 253A(2) 'prescribed' means prescribed in regulations made by the Welsh Ministers: s 253A(3) (as added: see note 4). See also note 3.
11 Apprenticeships, Skills, Children and Learning Act 2009 s 253A(2)(a) (as added: see note 4).
12 Apprenticeships, Skills, Children and Learning Act 2009 s 253A(2)(b) (as added: see note 4).
13 Apprenticeships, Skills, Children and Learning Act 2009 s 253A(2)(c) (as added: see note 4).
14 Apprenticeships, Skills, Children and Learning Act 2009 s 253A(2)(d) (as added: see note 4).
15 Ie information received under or by virtue of the Apprenticeships, Skills, Children and Learning Act 2009 s 253A.
16 Apprenticeships, Skills, Children and Learning Act 2009 s 253A(4) (as added: see note 4). This is subject to s 253A(5)(a): see the text to notes 17, 18.
17 Ie the provisions of the Apprenticeships, Skills, Children and Learning Act 2009 s 253A.

18 Apprenticeships, Skills, Children and Learning Act 2009 s 253A(5)(a) (as added: see note 4).
19 Apprenticeships, Skills, Children and Learning Act 2009 s 253A(5)(b) (as added: see note 4). As to the meaning of 'enactment' see PARA 1 note 13.

73. Services for schools in other member states providing education for British children. In relation to any school[1] which:

(1) is situated in a member state[2] other than the United Kingdom[3];

(2) provides education for pupils[4] who are British citizens[5], have attained the age of five years but not the age of 19 years[6] and are residing in that member state[7];

(3) has a curriculum which, in the case of any pupil at the school, is broadly similar to the curriculum which he would follow if he were a pupil at a maintained school[8] in England and Wales[9]; and

(4) has such other characteristics as may be prescribed[10],

the Secretary of State must: (a) on a regular basis provide the persons[11] responsible for the management of the school with such information relating to educational developments in England and Wales as he thinks appropriate[12]; and (b) if those persons so request, make arrangements for inspections to be made of the school by Her Majesty's Chief Inspector of Education, Children's Services and Skills[13]. The Secretary of State must charge the persons at whose request any inspection of a school is so made such fees as will cover the full cost of the inspection[14].

1 As to the meaning of 'school' see PARA 91 (definition applied by the Education Reform Act 1988 s 235(7) (amended by the Education Act 1996 s 582(1), Sch 37 Pt I para 81(1), (4)).

2 As to the meaning of 'member state' see the Interpretation Act 1978 s 5, Sch 1; European Communities Act 1972 s 1(2), Sch 1 Pt II.

3 Education Reform Act 1988 s 226(1)(a). 'United Kingdom' means Great Britain and Northern Ireland: Interpretation Act 1978 s 5, Sch 1. 'Great Britain' means England, Scotland and Wales: Union with Scotland Act 1706, preamble art I; Interpretation Act 1978 s 22(1), Sch 2 para 5(a). Neither the Isle of Man nor the Channel Islands are within the United Kingdom. See further CONSTITUTIONAL AND ADMINISTRATIVE LAW vol 20 (2014) PARA 3. As to the meanings of 'England' and 'Wales' see PARA 7 note 3.

4 As to the meaning of 'pupil' see PARA 20 note 4 (definition applied by the Education Reform Act 1988 s 235(7) (as amended: see note 1)).

5 As to British citizenship see BRITISH NATIONALITY vol 4 (2011) PARA 405 et seq, PARA 421 et seq.

6 As to the time at which a person attains a particular age see PARA 7 note 6.

7 Education Reform Act 1988 s 226(1)(b).

8 'Maintained school' means any community, foundation or voluntary school: Education Reform Act 1988 s 226(4) (amended by the School Standards and Framework Act 1998 s 140(1), Sch 30 paras 16, 19). As to the meaning of references to a community, foundation or voluntary school see PARA 106.

9 Education Reform Act 1988 s 226(1)(c). As to the curriculum in England see PARA 856 et seq; and as to the curriculum in Wales see PARA 870 et seq.

10 Education Reform Act 1988 s 226(1)(d). 'Prescribed' means prescribed by regulations made by the Secretary of State: see the Education Act 1996 s 579(1) (definition applied by the Education Reform Act 1988 s 235(7) (as amended: see note 1)). As to the Secretary of State see PARA 58. At the date at which this volume states the law no such regulations had been made.

11 As to the meaning of 'person' see PARA 7 note 6.

12 Education Reform Act 1988 s 226(2)(a).

13 Education Reform Act 1988 s 226(2)(b) (amended by the Education and Inspections Act 2006 s 157, Sch 14 para 8). As to Her Majesty's Chief Inspector of Education, Children's Services and Skills see PARA 1133.

14 Education Reform Act 1988 s 226(3).

74. Persons not covered by the Education Act 1996. No power or duty conferred or imposed by the Education Act 1996 on the appropriate national authority[1] is to be construed as relating to any person who is employed by or under the Crown in any service or capacity with respect to which the appropriate national authority certifies that, by reason of the arrangements made for the education of children[2] and young persons[3] so employed, the exercise and performance of those powers and duties with respect to such children and young persons is unnecessary[4].

No power or duty conferred or imposed by or under the Education Act 1996 on the appropriate national authority[5] is to be construed as relating to any person who is subject to a detention order[6] and is detained in accommodation that is not relevant youth accommodation[7], but a local authority[8] may make arrangements for such a person to receive the benefit of educational facilities provided by the authority[9].

These provisions are applied for the purposes of the School Standards and Framework Act 1998[10] and, with certain exceptions, for the purposes of the Education Act 2002[11], the Education Act 2005[12], the Education and Inspections Act 2006[13], the Education and Skills Act 2008[14] and the Apprenticeships, Skills, Children and Learning Act 2009[15].

1 See the Education Act 1996 s 561(a). The appropriate national authority means the Secretary of State or, in relation to Wales, the Welsh Ministers. The functions of the Secretary of State under ss 561, 562 (see the text to notes 5–9), so far as exercisable in relation to Wales, were transferred to the National Assembly for Wales (see the National Assembly for Wales (Transfer of Functions) Order 1999, SI 1999/672, art 2, Sch 1) and are now vested in the Welsh Ministers (see the Government of Wales Act 2006 s 162(1), Sch 11 para 30). As to the Secretary of State see PARA 58. As to the Welsh Ministers see PARA 59. As to the meaning of 'Wales' see PARA 7 note 3.
2 As to the meaning of 'child' see PARA 7 note 6.
3 As to the meaning of 'young person' see PARA 7 note 6.
4 Education Act 1996 s 561.
5 See the Education Act 1996 s 562(1)(a).
6 As to when a person is subject to a detention order see PARA 46 note 8.
7 As to the meaning of 'relevant youth accommodation' see PARA 46 note 9.
8 As to the meaning of 'local authority' see PARA 25.
9 Education Act 1996 s 562(1) (s 562(1) amended by the Apprenticeships, Skills, Children and Learning Act 2009 s 49; and SI 2010/1158). At the date at which this volume states the law the amendment to the Education Act 1996 s 562(1) made by the Apprenticeships, Skills, Children and Learning Act 2009 s 49 is in force in relation to England and in relation only to persons who are detained in relevant youth accommodation by virtue of being detained in a relevant young offender institution: see the Apprenticeships, Skills, Children and Learning Act 2009 (Commencement No 2 and Transitional and Saving Provisions) Order 2010, SI 2010/303, art 6, Sch 5. The amendment so made is also in force in relation to Wales and in relation only to persons who are detained in relevant youth accommodation by virtue of being detained in a relevant young offender institution: see the Apprenticeships, Skills, Children and Learning Act 2009 (Commencement No 3) (Wales) Order 2011, SI 2011/829. The amendment so made will come into force in relation to England and Wales for remaining purposes on a day or days to be appointed: see the Apprenticeships, Skills, Children and Learning Act 2009 s 269(3)(f), (4). At the date at which this volume states the law no such day had been appointed. As to the meaning of 'relevant young offender institution' see PARA 38 note 2. As to the meaning of 'England' see PARA 7 note 3. Until a day to be appointed the following provisions have effect in relation to England and Wales for those purposes for which the amendment to s 562(1) made by the Apprenticeships, Skills, Children and Learning Act 2009 s 49 is not yet in force: No power or duty conferred or imposed by or under the Education Act 1996 on the Secretary of State or the Welsh Ministers is to be construed as relating to any person who is detained in pursuance of an order made by a court or of an order of recall made by the Secretary of State, but a local authority may make arrangements for a person who is detained in pursuance of such an order to receive the benefit of educational facilities provided by the authority: Education Act 1996 s 1996 s 562(1) (as originally enacted; amended by SI 2010/1158).
10 See the School Standards and Framework Act 1998 s 142(8).
11 See the Education Act 2002 s 212(2), (3).

12 See the Education Act 2005 s 122(2), (3).
13 See the Education and Inspections Act 2006 s 187(2), (3).
14 See the Education and Skills Act 2008 s 168(2), (3), (5).
15 See the Apprenticeships, Skills, Children and Learning Act 2009 s 264(2)–(4).

75.   Directions and orders. Any order or directions made or given under the Education Act 1996 by the Secretary of State[1] or the Welsh Ministers[2] (other than an order made by the Secretary of State or the Welsh Ministers by statutory instrument[3]), or a local authority[4], may be varied or revoked by a further order or directions made or given by the Secretary of State, the Welsh Ministers or the local authority, as the case may be[5]. This provision applies also to directions given by any person or body under the Further and Higher Education Act 1992[6].

Any power conferred by the Education Act 2005 to give directions includes power, exercisable in the same manner and subject to the same conditions or limitations, to revoke or vary directions previously given[7].

A direction given under the Apprenticeships, Skills, Children and Learning Act 2009 may be amended or revoked by the person or body by whom it is given[8]; and may make different provision for different purposes[9].

1 As to the Secretary of State see PARA 58.
2 As to the Welsh Ministers see PARA 59.
3 Ie other than an order to which the Education Act 1996 s 568(1) applies.
4 Education Act 1996 s 570(1) (amended by the School Standards and Framework Act 1998 s 140(1), (3), Sch 30 para 177(a)(ii), Sch 31; and SI 2010/1158). As to the meaning of 'local authority' see PARA 25.
5 Education Act 1996 s 570(2) (amended by the School Standards and Framework Act 1998 s 140(1), (3), Sch 30 para 177(b), Sch 31; and SI 2010/1158). However, where the power to make or give any such order or directions is only exercisable (1) on the application or with the consent of any person or body of persons (Education Act 1996 s 570(3)(a)); or (2) after consultation with any person or body of persons (s 570(3)(b)); or (3) subject to any other conditions (s 570(3)(c)), no order or directions made or given under that power may be varied or revoked under s 570(2) unless the same conditions are complied with (s 570(3)). As to the meaning of 'person' see PARA 7 note 6.
6 The Education Act 1996 s 570 applies to directions given by any person or body under the Further and Higher Education Act 1992 as it applies to directions given by the Secretary of State, the Welsh Ministers or a local authority under the Education Act 1996: Further and Higher Education Act 1992 s 89(5) (substituted by the Apprenticeships, Skills, Children and Learning Act 2009 s 125, Sch 8 paras 1, 11(1), (4); and amended by SI 2010/1158).
7 Education Act 2005 s 120(4).
8 Apprenticeships, Skills, Children and Learning Act 2009 s 263(a).
9 Apprenticeships, Skills, Children and Learning Act 2009 s 263(b).

76.   Service of notices and documents. Any order, notice or other document required or authorised by the Education Act 1996 to be served on, or given to, any person[1] may be served or given[2] (1) by delivering it to that person[3]; or (2) by leaving it at his usual or last known place of residence[4]; or (3) by sending it in a prepaid letter addressed to him at that place[5]. But such a document may not be served or given in an electronic communication[6] to a person as a parent[7] unless the person consents in writing[8] to the receipt of documents of the kind in question from the sender in an electronic communication sent to a specified number or address[9], and the communication is sent to the number or address in question[10].

1 As to the meaning of 'person' see PARA 7 note 6.
2 Education Act 1996 s 572(1) (s 572(1) numbered as such, (2), (3) added, by SI 2004/2521; Education Act 1996 s 572(1) amended by the Anti-social Behaviour Act 2003 s 23(2)).
3 Education Act 1996 s 572(1)(a) (s 572(1) as so numbered: see note 2).
4 Education Act 1996 s 572(1)(b) (s 572(1) as so numbered: see note 2).

5 Education Act 1996 s 572(1)(c) (s 572(1) as so numbered: see note 2). Where an Act (or subordinate legislation) authorises or requires any document to be served by post (whether the expression 'serve' or the expression 'give' or 'send' or any other expression is used) then, unless the contrary intention appears, the service is deemed to be effected by properly addressing, pre-paying and posting a letter containing the document and, unless the contrary is proved, to have been effected at the time at which the letter would be delivered in the ordinary course of post: see the Interpretation Act 1978 ss 7, 23; and STATUTES AND LEGISLATIVE PROCESS vol 96 (2012) PARA 1219. As to proof of posting and proof of delivery see CIVIL PROCEDURE vol 11 (2009) PARAS 945, 946. A requirement to send a document by post is not confined to sending it by the Post Office postal system: see the Postal Services Act 2000 s 127(4), Sch 8 Pt 1; and POSTAL SERVICES.

6 'Electronic communication' means a communication transmitted (whether from one person to another, from one device to another or from a person to a device or vice versa) by means of an electronic communications network, or by other means but while in an electronic form; and 'communication' includes a communication comprising sounds or images or both and a communication effecting a payment: Electronic Communications Act 2000 s 15 (definition amended by the Communications Act 2003 s 406(1), Sch 17 para 158; and applied by the Education Act 1996 s 572(3) (as added: see note 2)). As to electronic communications networks see TELECOMMUNICATIONS vol 97 (2015) PARA 53.

7 As to the meaning of 'parent' see PARA 7 note 6.

8 'Writing' includes typing, printing, lithography, photography and other modes of representing or reproducing words in a visible form, and expressions referring to writing are construed accordingly: Interpretation Act 1978 s 5, Sch 1.

9 Education Act 1996 s 572(2)(a) (as added: see note 2).

10 Education Act 1996 s 572(2)(b) (as added: see note 2).

77. Academy arrangements and academies. The Secretary of State[1] has certain powers to enter into academy arrangements and has certain related duties[2].

1 As to the Secretary of State see PARA 58.
2 As to academy arrangements and academies generally see PARA 345 et seq.

(ii) Provision of Grants

A. GENERAL GRANT-MAKING POWERS

78. Financial assistance for purposes related to education or children etc. The Secretary of State (in relation to England)[1] or the Welsh Ministers (in relation to Wales)[2] may give, or make arrangements[3] for the giving of, financial assistance to any person[4] for or in connection with any of the following purposes[5]:

(1) the provision, or proposed provision, in the United Kingdom[6] or elsewhere, of education[7] or of educational services[8];

(2) the provision, or proposed provision, in the United Kingdom or elsewhere, of childcare or of services related to childcare[9];

(3) enabling any person to undertake any course of education, or any course of higher education provided by an institution within the further education sector[10];

(4) enabling any person to receive any training for teachers or for non-teaching staff[11];

(5) providing for a person's maintenance while he undertakes such a course[12];

(6) the promotion of learning or research[13];

(7) the promotion of the use of educational buildings or facilities for purposes other than those of education[14];

(8) the provision of any form of training for teachers or for non-teaching staff[15];

(9)   the promotion of the recruitment or retention of teachers or non-teaching staff[16];

(10)   the remuneration of, or provision of other benefits to, teachers or non-teaching staff[17];

(11)   the promotion of the welfare of children[18] and their parents[19];

(12)   the provision of support for parenting, including support for prospective parents[20].

Such assistance may be given in any form[21], and may, in particular, be given by way of grants[22], loans[23], guarantees[24], incurring expenditure on the provision of equipment for the benefit of the person assisted[25], or incurring other expenditure for the benefit of the person assisted[26]. Assistance may be given also on such terms as the Secretary of State or, as the case may be, the Welsh Ministers consider appropriate but subject to a qualification[27], and may, in particular, include provisions as to:

(a)   circumstances in which the assistance is to be repaid, or otherwise made good, to the Secretary of State or the Welsh Ministers, and the manner in which that is to be done[28];

(b)   the giving by the person receiving assistance of financial assistance to other persons on such terms as that person or the Secretary of State or the Welsh Ministers consider appropriate, but subject to a qualification[29];

(c)   circumstances in which any payments made by virtue of terms included by virtue of head (b) above are to be repaid, or otherwise made good, to the person receiving assistance from the Secretary of State or the Welsh Ministers, and the manner in which that is to be done[30];

(d)   the keeping, and making available for inspection, of accounts and other records[31].

The person receiving assistance must comply with the terms on which it is given, and compliance may be enforced by the Secretary of State or, as the case may be, the Welsh Ministers[32].

1   As to the Secretary of State see PARA 58. As to the meaning of 'England' see PARA 7 note 3.
2   The functions under the Education Act 2002 ss 14–18 were originally vested in the National Assembly for Wales and are now exercisable by the Welsh Ministers by virtue of the Government of Wales Act 2006 s 162(1), Sch 11 paras 30, 32. As to the Welsh Ministers see PARA 59. As to the meaning of 'Wales' see PARA 7 note 3.
3   Arrangements under the Education Act 2002 s 14 may provide for assistance to be given, or other functions relating to assistance to be exercised, otherwise than by the Secretary of State or the Welsh Ministers (s 17(1)); and such arrangements which so provide may make provision for the functions concerned to be so exercised either wholly or to such extent as may be specified in the arrangements (s 17(2)(a)), and either generally or in such cases or circumstances as may be so specified (s 17(2)(b)), but must not prevent the functions concerned from being exercised by the Secretary of State or, as the case may be, the Welsh Ministers (s 17(2)). As to the meaning of 'functions' see PARA 18 note 5 (definition applied by s 212(2), (3)).
4   As to the meaning of 'person' see PARA 7 note 6.
5   Education Act 2002 s 14(1). The power given in s 14 superseded a number of specific powers (now repealed) under other Acts: see s 18(1). The power to pay grants under the Education Act 1996 s 484 (education standards grants: see PARA 81) is now exercisable only in relation to Wales: see the Education Act 2002 s 18(2). In exercise of s 14, various grants have been made see eg the pupil premium grant, the primary PE and sport premium, and the universal infant free school meals grant, and the education services grant. In exercise of the power under s 16 (see the text and notes 27–32), guidance has been issued for the conditions on which grants are made.
6   As to the meaning of 'United Kingdom' see PARA 73 note 3.
7   'Education' includes:
     (1)   vocational training, including the preparation of young people for employment in general; and

(2) social and physical training, including the promotion of the development of young children,

and 'educational' must be construed accordingly: Education Act 2002 s 14(3). Higher education is not included in this definition, except for the purposes of s 14(2ZA)(a) (see note 11): s 14(3) (amended by the Education Act 2005 s 98, Sch 14 para 23(1), (3)). As to the meaning of 'young person' see PARA 7 note 6; as to the meaning of 'child' see PARA 7 note 6; and as to the meaning of 'higher education' see PARA 24 (definitions applied by the Education Act 2002 s 212(2), (3)).

8 Education Act 2002 s 14(2)(a). 'Educational services' includes administrative, advisory, organisational, training or information services related to education: s 14(3).

9 Education Act 2002 s 14(2)(b). As to a local authority's duties in respect of childcare provision see PARA 30.

10 Education Act 2002 s 14(2)(c). As to the meaning of references to institutions within the further education sector see PARA 555 (definition applied by s 212(2), (3)).

11 Education Act 2002 s 14(2)(ca) (added by the Education Act 2011 s 15(1), (2)(a)). In the Education Act 2002 s 14(2) 'training for teachers or for non-teaching staff' includes: (1) any training or education, whether or not constituting higher education, with the object of fitting persons to be teachers or non-teaching staff, or better teachers or non-teaching staff (s 14(2ZA)(a) (s 14(2ZA) added by the Education Act 2005 Sch 14 para 23(1), (2); and amended by the Education Act 2011 s 15(1), (2)(b))); and (2) any assessment related to the award of a qualification or status to teachers or non-teaching staff, or prospective teachers or non-teaching staff (Education Act 2002 s 14(2ZA)(b) (as so added)). 'Teacher' does not include a teacher at an institution within the higher education sector: s 14(3). As to the meaning of references to institutions within the higher education sector see PARA 619 (definition applied by s 212(2), (3)). As to the training of teachers generally see PARA 1054 et seq.

12 Education Act 2002 s 14(2)(d).

13 Education Act 2002 s 14(2)(e).

14 Education Act 2002 s 14(2)(f).

15 Education Act 2002 s 14(2)(g).

16 Education Act 2002 s 14(2)(h).

17 Education Act 2002 s 14(2)(i).

18 For this purpose, 'children' means persons under the age of 20: Education Act 2002 s 14(2A) (added by the Education Act 2005 Sch 14 para 23(1), (2)). As to the time at which a person attains a particular age see PARA 7 note 6.

19 Education Act 2002 s 14(2)(j) (added by the Children Act 2004 s 59(1), (2)). As to the meaning of 'parent' see PARA 7 note 6 (definition applied by the Education Act 2002 s 212(2), (3)).

20 Education Act 2002 s 14(2)(k) (added by the Children Act 2004 s 59(1), (2)).

21 Education Act 2002 s 15(1).

22 Education Act 2002 s 15(2)(a).

23 Education Act 2002 s 15(2)(b). Assistance given under s 14 to a local authority may not be given by way of loan: s 15(3). As to the meaning of 'local authority' see PARA 25 (definition applied by s 212(2), (3)).

24 Education Act 2002 s 15(2)(c). Assistance given under s 14 to a local authority may not be given by way of guarantee: s 15(3).

25 Education Act 2002 s 15(2)(d).

26 Education Act 2002 s 15(2)(e).

27 Education Act 2002 s 16(1) (amended by the Education Act 2011 s 15(1), (3)(a)). The power under the Education s 16(1) is subject to s 16(2B): s 16(1) (as so amended).

    In the case of (1) financial assistance given under s 14 to an institution within the higher education sector; and (2) financial assistance required by virtue of s 16(2)(b) (see head (b) in the text) to be given to such an institution, the terms on which the assistance is given may not be framed by reference to criteria for the selection and appointment of staff or the admission of students: s 16(2A), (2B) (added by the Education Act 2011 s 15(1), (3)(c)).

28 Education Act 2002 s 16(2)(a).

29 Education Act 2002 s 16(2)(b) (amended by the Education Act 2011 s 15(1), (3)(b)). The Education s 16(2)(b) is subject to s 16(2B) (see note 27): s 16(2)(b) (as so amended). In relation to financial assistance required by virtue of s 16(2)(b), s 15(2) (see the text to notes 22–26) applies as it applies to financial assistance given under s 14: s 16(4).

30 Education Act 2002 s 16(2)(c).

31 Education Act 2002 s 16(2)(d).

32 Education Act 2002 s 16(3).

79.   Supply of information regarding education maintenance allowances.
Information which:

(1)   is held for the purposes of functions relating to tax or tax credits[1] by the Commissioners for Her Majesty's Revenue and Customs[2], or by a person[3] providing services to the Commissioners for Her Majesty's Revenue and Customs, in connection with the provision of those services[4]; or

(2)   is held for the purposes of functions relating to social security by the Secretary of State[5], or by a person providing services to the Secretary of State, in connection with the provision of those services[6],

may be supplied to the Secretary of State[7], the Welsh Ministers[8], and to any person providing services to any of the foregoing[9], for purposes relating to eligibility for education maintenance allowances[10].

Information received under these provisions[11] may be supplied to the Welsh Ministers[12], to any person exercising functions in relation to financial assistance paid in respect of education or training[13], to any person exercising functions under regulations in relation to allowances paid in respect of education or training[14], or to any person providing services to the Welsh Ministers[15], for use for purposes relating to eligibility for education maintenance allowances[16].

A person may, in making a request for the supply to him of information by virtue of the above provisions[17], supply to any person who holds, or is to be supplied with, the information:

(a)   the name, address and date of birth of any person to whom the request relates ('the student')[18];

(b)   the name, address and date of birth of any parent of the student[19], or any other person whose financial circumstances are relevant to the student's eligibility for an education maintenance allowance[20]; and

(c)   any other information, whether relating to the student, any parent of his or any person whose financial circumstances are relevant to the student's eligibility for an education maintenance allowance, which is required for the purpose of determining the student's eligibility for an education maintenance allowance[21].

The provisions described above do not limit the circumstances in which information may be supplied otherwise[22].

A person who discloses information which he has received by virtue of the above provisions[23] and which relates to a particular person commits an offence[24] unless the information is disclosed:

(i)   in accordance with the provisions[25] governing the disclosure of the information[26];

(ii)   in the course of any duty that that person has in connection with the exercise of functions relating to eligibility for education maintenance allowances[27];

(iii)   in accordance with an enactment or an order of a court[28];

(iv)   for the purpose of instituting, or otherwise for the purposes of, civil or criminal proceedings[29]; or

(v)   with consent given by or on behalf of the person to whom the information relates[30].

It is a defence for a person charged with such an offence to prove that he reasonably believed that his disclosure was lawful[31].

1   As to the meaning of 'functions' see PARA 18 note 5 (definition applied by the Education
    Act 2005 s 122(2), (3)). As to tax credits see INCOME TAXATION vol 58A (2014) PARA 1158 et
    seq. See note 2.
2   Education Act 2005 s 108(1)(a)(i) (s 108(1) amended by virtue of the Commissioners for
    Revenue and Customs Act 2005 s 50(1), (7)). As to the Commissioners for Her Majesty's
    Revenue and Customs see INCOME TAXATION vol 58 (2014) PARA 33. As from a day to be
    appointed the words 'or tax credits' are removed: Education Act 2005 a 108(1)(a) (prospectively
    amended by the Welfare Reform Act 2012 Sch 14 Pt 1). At the date at which this volume states
    the law no such day had been appointed.
3   As to the meaning of 'person' see PARA 7 note 6.
4   Education Act 2005 s 108(1)(a)(ii) (as amended: see note 2).
5   See the Education Act 2005 s 108(1)(b)(i). As to the Secretary of State see PARA 58.
6   See the Education Act 2005 s 108(1)(b)(ii).
7   Education Act 2005 s 108(3)(a).
8   Education Act 2005 s 108(3)(c). The functions under the Education Act 2005 s 108 were
    originally vested in the National Assembly for Wales and are now exercisable by the Welsh
    Ministers by virtue of the Government of Wales Act 2006 s 162(1), Sch 11 paras 30, 32. As to
    the Welsh Ministers see PARA 59. As to the meaning of 'Wales' see PARA 7 note 3.
9   See the Education Act 2005 s 108(3)(f) (amended by the Apprenticeships, Skills, Children and
    Learning Act 2009 s 123(2), Sch 6 para 57(c)).
10 Education Act 2005 s 108(2). 'Education maintenance allowance' means: (1) financial assistance
    under the Education Act 2002 s 14 (see PARA 78) paid to or in respect of a person who is over
    compulsory school age in connection with his undertaking any course of education or training
    (Education Act 2005 s 108(8)(a)); or (2) an allowance under the Education Act 2002 s 181 (see
    PARA 484) (Education Act 2005 s 108(8)(b)). As to the meaning of 'compulsory school age' see
    PARA 19 (definition applied by virtue of s 122(2), (3)).
11 Ie information received by virtue of the Education Act 2005 s 108(2) (see the text to notes 1–10)
    or s 108(4).
12 Education Act 2005 s 108(5)(a).
13 Ie any person by whom functions in relation to education maintenance allowances falling within
    the Education Act 2005 s 108(1)(a) (see head (1) in the text) are exercisable by virtue of the
    Education Act 2002 s 14 or s 17 (see PARA 78): Education Act 2005 s 108(5)(d).
14 Ie any person by whom functions under regulations under the Education Act 2002 s 181 (see
    PARA 484) are exercisable by virtue of s 183 or s 184 (see PARA 485): Education Act 2005
    s 108(5)(e).
15 Education Act 2005 s 108(5)(f).
16 See the Education Act 2005 s 108(4).
17 Ie by virtue of the Education Act 2005 s 108(2) or (4): see the text to notes 1–16.
18 Education Act 2005 s 108(6)(a).
19 Education Act 2005 s 108(6)(b)(i). As to the meaning of 'parent' see PARA 7 note 6 (definition
    applied by s 122(2), (3)).
20 Education Act 2005 s 108(6)(b)(ii).
21 Education Act 2005 s 108(6)(c).
22 Education Act 2005 s 108(7).
23 Ie by virtue of the Education Act 2005 s 108(2) or (4): see the text to notes 1–16.
24 A person guilty of such an offence is liable: (1) on conviction on indictment, to imprisonment for
    a term not exceeding two years, to a fine or to both (Education Act 2005 s 109(3)(a)); (2) on
    summary conviction, to imprisonment for a term not exceeding 12 months, to a fine not
    exceeding the statutory maximum or to both (s 109(3)(b)). In relation to an offence committed
    before the commencement of the Criminal Justice Act 2003 s 154(1) (not yet in force), the
    reference in head (2) to 12 months is to be read as a reference to six months: Education
    Act 2005 s 109(4). As to the statutory maximum see SENTENCING AND DISPOSITION OF
    OFFENDERS vol 92 (2010) PARA 140.
25 Ie in accordance with the Education Act 2005 s 108(4): see the text to notes 11–16.
26 Education Act 2005 s 109(1)(a).
27 Education Act 2005 s 109(1)(b).
28 Education Act 2005 s 109(1)(c).
29 Education Act 2005 s 109(1)(d).
30 Education Act 2005 s 109(1)(e).
31 Education Act 2005 s 109(2). As to the standard of proof on the accused see CRIMINAL
    PROCEDURE vol 28 (2010) PARA 466.

80. Financial assistance for overseas scholarships. There is a Commission known as the Commonwealth Scholarship Commission in the United Kingdom[1], whose functions include selecting the recipients of awards[2] and making arrangements for placing the recipients at appropriate educational establishments in the United Kingdom as well as selecting persons to be put forward as candidates from the United Kingdom for appropriate awards that are to be granted in countries outside the United Kingdom[3].

The Secretary of State may also provide scholarships, among other general forms of overseas development assistance[4], on such terms and conditions, if any, as he may determine[5].

1   See the International Development Act 2002 s 13; and PARA 1113. As to the meaning of 'United Kingdom' see PARA 73 note 3.
2   The persons so selected must be Commonwealth citizens or British protected persons (within the meaning of the British Nationality Act 1981: see BRITISH NATIONALITY vol 4 (2011) PARAS 408–409), except where the Commonwealth Scholarship Commission for special reasons approved by the Secretary of State otherwise determines: see the International Development Act 2002 s 14(4); and PARA 1113. As to the Secretary of State see PARA 58.
3   See International Development Act 2002 s 14; and PARA 1113.
4   For these purposes, 'assistance' means assistance in any form or of any nature, including financial or technical assistance and assistance consisting in a supply of materials: International Development Act 2002 s 5(1). 'Technical assistance' includes assistance that consists in know-how in the form of personnel, training or the provision of the results of research, or is provided in the form of a scholarship: s 5(2). Financial assistance may be provided by way of grant or loan (s 6(1)(a)), in the form of a guarantee (s 6(1)(b)) or by the Secretary of State acquiring securities of a company (s 6(1)(c)). More than one form of financial assistance may be provided in any case: s 6(2). 'Company' includes any body corporate, wherever registered; and 'securities', in relation to a company, means shares (including stock), debentures, bonds and other securities, whether constituting a charge on the assets of the company or not: s 6(3). Section 6 is subject to s 7(3) (Treasury approval required for certain financial assistance: see note 5): s 6(4). As to bodies corporate see COMPANIES vol 14 (2009) PARA 2; CORPORATIONS vol 24 (2010) PARA 301 et seq.
5   See the International Development Act 2002 s 7(1). Assistance, other than financial assistance, may be provided free of charge (s 7(2)(a)), or on such terms as to payment as the Secretary of State may determine (s 7(2)(b)). Financial assistance (other than a grant) may be provided only if the Treasury have approved the terms and conditions on which it is provided: s 7(3). Approval may be given either with respect to a particular case or with respect to a class of cases: s 7(4). As to the Treasury see CONSTITUTIONAL AND ADMINISTRATIVE LAW vol 20 (2014) PARA 262 et seq.

B. SPECIFIC GRANT-MAKING POWERS

81. Power of the Welsh Ministers to pay education standards grants. The Welsh Ministers[1] may pay grants[2], known as 'education standards grants', to local authorities[3] in Wales[4] in respect of eligible expenditure incurred or to be incurred by them[5].

'Eligible expenditure' means expenditure of any class or description for the time being specified in regulations[6], being expenditure for or in connection with educational purposes which it appears to the Welsh Ministers that local authorities should be encouraged to incur in the interests of education in Wales[7].

The regulations must provide that any education standards grant payable in pursuance of the regulations is[8]: (1) only payable in respect of eligible expenditure incurred or to be incurred by a local authority in a financial year[9] to the extent to which that expenditure is approved for that year by the Welsh Ministers for the purposes of the regulations[10]; and (2) payable at such rate as may be specified in the regulations[11]. The regulations may provide for the time and manner of payment of any education standards grant[12]. The regulations may provide for expenditure incurred or to be incurred by any local authority in making payments, whether by way of maintenance, assistance or otherwise, to any body or persons[13] who incur expenditure for or in connection with educational purposes (including another local authority) to be treated, in such circumstances as may be specified in the regulations, as eligible expenditure[14].

1   The functions under the Education Act 1996 s 484 were originally vested in the National Assembly for Wales and are now exercisable by the Welsh Ministers by virtue of the Government of Wales Act 2006 s 162(1), Sch 11 paras 30, 32. As to the Welsh Ministers see PARA 59.

2   As to the conditions for the payment of such grants see PARA 83.

3   As to the meaning of 'local authority' see PARA 25.

4   As to the meaning of 'Wales' see PARA 7 note 3.

5   Education Act 1996 s 484(1) (amended by the School Standards and Framework Act 1998 s 140(1), Sch 30 para 125(a); Education Act 2002 s 215(1), Sch 21 para 49; and SI 2010/1158). The power to pay grants under the Education Act 1996 s 484 is exercisable only in relation to Wales: Education Act 2002 s 18(2). In England, a general grant-making power is used: see PARA 78.

6   Ie regulations made by the Welsh Ministers: see Education Act 1996 s 579(1). As to the regulations made see the Education Standards Grants (Wales) Regulations 2002, SI 2002/438 (amended by SI 2005/761; and SI 2013/1466); the Education (Capital Grants) (Wales) Regulations 2002, SI 2002/679 (amended by SI 2005/761; and SI 2013/1466); and the Education (Assembly Learning Grant Scheme) (Wales) Regulations 2002, SI 2002/1857 (amended by SI 2002/2814; SI 2005/761; and SI 2013/1466).

7   Education Act 1996 s 484(2) (amended by the Education Act 2002 Sch 21 para 49; SI 2010/1158).

8   Education Act 1996 s 484(3) (amended by the School Standards and Framework Act 1998 Sch 30 para 125(b)).

9   'Financial year' means a period of 12 months ending with 31 March: Education Act 1996 s 579(1). As to the meaning of 'month' see PARA 54 note 26.

10   Education Act 1996 s 484(3)(a) (amended by the Education Act 2002 Sch 21 para 49(1), (2); SI 2010/1158).

11   Education Act 1996 s 484(3)(b).

12   Education Act 1996 s 484(4) (amended by the School Standards and Framework Act 1998 Sch 30 para 125(b)).

13   As to the meaning of 'person' see PARA 7 note 6.

14   Education Act 1996 s 484(5) (amended by SI 2010/1158). Nothing in the Education Act 1996 s 29(1) (provision of information by local authorities: see PARA 48) or s 507 (repealed) applies in relation to any function of the Welsh Ministers under s 484 or under s 489 (see PARA 83) so far as it relates to regulations under s 484: s 484(7) (amended by the Education Act 2002 Sch 21 para 49(1), (2)). Nothing in the Education Act 1996 s 495 (see PARA 66) or the School Standards and Organisation (Wales) Act 2013 Pt 2 Ch 2 (ss 21–31) (see PARA 1235 et seq) applies in relation to any function arising by virtue of the Education Act 1996 s 489 so far as it relates to such regulations: s 484(7) (amended by the School Standards and Organisation (Wales) Act 2013 Sch 5 par 2(1), (3)). As to the meaning of 'functions' see PARA 18 note 5.

82. Grants in aid of educational services or research. Regulations[1] must make provision for the payment by the Secretary of State or, in relation to Wales, the Welsh Ministers to persons[2] other than local authorities[3] of grants[4] in respect of expenditure incurred or to be incurred by them[5]: (1) for the purposes of, or in connection with, the provision (or proposed provision) of educational services[6]; or (2) for the purposes of educational research[7].

1   Ie regulations made by the Secretary of State or, in relation to Wales, the Welsh Ministers: see the Education Act 1996 s 579(1). As to the Secretary of State see PARA 58. The functions of the Secretary of State under s 485, so far as exercisable in relation to Wales, were transferred to the National Assembly for Wales (see the National Assembly for Wales (Transfer of Functions) Order 1999, SI 1999/672, art 2, Sch 1) and are now vested in the Welsh Ministers (see the Government of Wales Act 2006 s 162(1), Sch 11 para 30). As to the Welsh Ministers see PARA 59. As to the meaning of 'Wales' see PARA 7 note 3.

2   As to the meaning of 'person' see PARA 7 note 6.

3   As to the meaning of 'local authority' see PARA 25.

4 As to the conditions for the payment of such grants see PARA 83.
5 Education Act 1996 s 485 (amended by SI 2010/1158). As to the regulations made see the
   Education (Grants for Early Excellence Centres) (England) Regulations 1998, SI 1998/1877
   (amended by SI 2002/1397); the Education (Post 16 Partnership Grant) (England)
   Regulations 1999, SI 1999/605; the Education (Grants) (Music, Ballet and Choir Schools)
   (England) Regulations 2001, SI 2001/2743 (amended by SI 2002/2004; and SI 2014/852); and
   the Education (Grant) (Financial Support for Students) Regulations 2001, SI 2001/2894
   (amended by SI 2012/979). By virtue of the Education Act 1996 s 582(3), Sch 39 para 1, the
   following regulations also have effect as if made under s 485: the Education (Schools and
   Further Education) Regulations 1981, SI 1981/1086 (amended by SI 1983/262; SI 1989/351;
   SI 1993/559; SI 1995/2089; SI 1999/3181; and SI 2000/1323); the Education (Grants) (City
   Technology Colleges) Regulations 1987, SI 1987/1138; the Education (Grant)
   Regulations 1990, SI 1990/1989 (amended by SI 1991/1975; SI 1992/1296; SI 1993/559;
   SI 1994/2102; SI 1995/2985; SI 1997/678; SI 1997/2961; and SI 1998/86); the Education
   (Grants) (Voluntary Aided Sixth Form Colleges) Regulations 1992, SI 1992/2181; the Education
   (Grants) (Higher Education Corporations) 1992, SI 1992/3237; the Education (Grants) (Music,
   Ballet and Choir Schools) Regulations 1995, SI 1995/2018 (amended by SI 1996/2036;
   SI 1997/1967; SI 1998/1583; SI 1999/1503; SI 2000/2113; and revoked, in relation to England,
   by SI 2001/2743); and the Education (Grants for Nursery Education) (England)
   Regulations 1996, SI 1996/353.
6 Education Act 1996 s 485(a).
7 Education Act 1996 s 485(b).

83. Conditions as to the payment of grants under specific grant-making powers. Regulations made for the purposes of education standards grants in Wales[1], and grants in aid of educational services or research[2], may provide[3]:

(1)   for the payment of grants under the regulations to be dependent on the
       fulfilment of such conditions as may be determined by or in accordance
       with the regulations[4]; and

(2)   for requiring persons[5] to whom payments have been made under the
       regulations to comply with such requirements as may be so determined[6].

Conditions and requirements determined under head (1) or head (2) above by or in accordance with regulations made for the purposes of education standards grants in Wales[7] may include conditions and requirements obliging the local authority[8] in question to delegate decisions about the spending of: (a) education standards grants[9]; and (b) amounts allocated by the authority to meet eligible expenditure[10] which is approved by the Welsh Ministers[11], to such persons as may be determined by or in accordance with the regulations[12].

The appropriate national authority[13] may by order[14] make such modifications[15] of any trust deed[16] or other instrument relating to or regulating any institution that:

(i)   provides or is concerned in the provision of educational services[17]; or

(ii)   is concerned in educational research[18],

as, after consultation[19] with the persons responsible for the management of the institution, appear to the appropriate national authority to be requisite to enable them to fulfil any condition or meet any requirement imposed by regulations[20] for the purposes of grants in aid of educational services or research[21].

1 Ie regulations made under the Education Act 1996 s 484: see PARA 81. As to the meaning of
   'Wales' see PARA 7 note 3.
2 Ie regulations made under the Education Act 1996 s 485: see PARA 82.
3 See the Education Act 1996 s 489(1).
4 Education Act 1996 s 489(1)(a).
5 As to the meaning of 'person' see PARA 7 note 6.
6 Education Act 1996 s 489(1)(b).
7 Ie regulations made under the Education Act 1996 s 484: see PARA 81.
8 As to the meaning of 'local authority' see PARA 25.

9 Education Act 1996 s 489(2)(a) (amended by the School Standards and Framework Act 1998 s 140(1), Sch 30 para 126; and SI 2010/1158).

10 Ie within the meaning of the Education Act 1996 s 484: see PARA 81.

11 Education Act 1996 s 489(2)(b). As to the Welsh Ministers see PARA 59.

12 Education Act 1996 s 489(2).

13 Ie the Secretary of State or, in relation to Wales, the Welsh Ministers. The functions of the Secretary of State under the Education Act 1996 s 489, so far as exercisable in relation to Wales, were transferred to the National Assembly for Wales (see the National Assembly for Wales (Transfer of Functions) Order 1999, SI 1999/672, art 2, Sch 1) and are now vested in the Welsh Ministers (see the Government of Wales Act 2006 s 162(1), Sch 11 para 30). As to the Secretary of State see PARA 58.

14 Such orders are not statutory instruments (see the Education Act 1996 s 568(1), (2)) and as such are not recorded in this title. As to the revocation or variation of such orders see PARA 75.

15 Any modification made by an order under the Education Act 1996 s 489(3) may be made to have permanent effect or to have effect for such period as may be specified in the order: s 489(4). As to the meaning of 'modifications' see PARA 21 note 15.

16 As to the meaning of 'trust deed' see PARA 108 note 6.

17 Education Act 1996 s 489(3)(a).

18 Education Act 1996 s 489(3)(b).

19 As to the exercise of the duty to consult see JUDICIAL REVIEW vol 61 (2010) PARA 627.

20 Ie regulations under the Education Act 1996 s 485: see PARA 82.

21 Education Act 1996 s 489(3).

84. Transfer of property to grant-aided institutions in Wales. Where, in the case of any institution in Wales[1] which is conducted by a body corporate[2] and has a full-time equivalent enrolment number[3] for courses of higher education[4] which exceeds 55 per cent of its total full-time equivalent enrolment number[5]:

(1) the Welsh Ministers[6] proposes to make to the body conducting the institution grants under regulations[7] made for the purposes of grants in aid of educational services or research[8]; and

(2) any land[9] or other property of a local authority[10] is for the time being used or held, or any subsisting rights or liabilities[11] of such an authority were acquired or incurred, for the purposes of the institution[12],

the Welsh Ministers may by order designate the institution for the purposes of these provisions[13].

On the date on which any such designation of an institution takes effect specified property, rights and liabilities[14] are transferred to, and by virtue of the Education Reform Act 1988 vested in, the body corporate by whom the institution is conducted[15]. The property, rights and liabilities in question are:

(a) all land or other property which, immediately before that date, was property of any local authority used or held for the purposes of the designated institution[16]; and

(b) all rights and liabilities of any such authority subsisting immediately before that date which were acquired or incurred for those purposes[17].

1 As to the meaning of 'Wales' see PARA 7 note 3.

2 Education Reform Act 1988 s 228(1)(a). As to bodies corporate see COMPANIES vol 14 (2009) PARA 2; CORPORATIONS vol 24 (2010) PARA 301 et seq.

3 As to the determination of full-time equivalent enrolment numbers see PARA 651.

4 As to the meaning of references to courses of higher education see PARA 684.

5 Education Reform Act 1988 s 228(1)(b).

6 The functions of the Secretary of State under the Education Reform Act 1988 s 228, so far as exercisable in relation to Wales, were transferred to the National Assembly for Wales (see the National Assembly for Wales (Transfer of Functions) Order 1999, SI 1999/672, art 2, Sch 1) and are now vested in the Welsh Ministers (see the Government of Wales Act 2006 s 162(1), Sch 11 para 30). As to the Welsh Ministers see PARA 59.

7 Ie regulations made under the Education Act 1996 s 485: see PARA 82.

8   Education Reform Act 1988 s 228(2)(a) (amended by the Education Act 1996 s 582(1), Sch 37 para 79).
9   'Land' includes buildings and other structures, land covered with water, and any interest in land: Education Reform Act 1988 s 235(1). References to an interest in land include references to any easement, right or charge in, to or over land: s 235(2)(g).
10 As to the meaning of 'local authority' see PARA 25 (definition applied by the Education Reform Act 1988 s 235(7)).
11 'Liability' includes obligation: Education Reform Act 1988 s 235(1).
12 Education Reform Act 1988 s 228(2)(b) (amended by SI 2010/1158).
13 Education Reform Act 1988 s 228(2). Orders under s 228 being local in nature are not recorded in this title.
14 The Education Reform Act 1988 s 228(3) does not apply to: (1) any liability of any such authority in respect of the principal of, or any interest on, any loan (s 228(5)(a)); or (2) any liability of any such authority in respect of compensation for premature retirement of any person formerly employed by it (s 228(5)(b)). As to the meaning of 'employed' see PARA 301 note 2.
15 Education Reform Act 1988 s 228(3). Section 199 (loan liabilities excepted from transfer under Pt II (ss 120–161): see PARA 650) applies to an institution designated under s 228; and, for the purposes of s 199 as it applies by virtue of s 228, s 199(2) applies as if s 199(2)(a) defined an excepted liability as one which would have been transferred under s 228(3) but for s 228(5)(a) (see note 14): s 228(8). Section 198 (transfers under Pt I (repealed) and Pt II: see PARA 1331) applies to a transfer under s 228; and the provisions of s 228(1)–(5) are subject to Sch 10 (supplementary provisions with respect to transfers: see PARA 1330 et seq) (s 228(6)); and in the application of Sch 10 in relation to a transfer under s 228 references in Sch 10 para 1 to a relevant institution include references to an institution so designated (see s 228(7)). Stamp duty is not chargeable in respect of any transfer effected under or by virtue of s 228 (taken with Sch 10): see s 230(1) (amended by the Further and Higher Education Act 1992 s 93, Sch 8 paras 27, 55, Sch 9; the Education Act 1993 s 307(1), (3), Sch 19 paras 112, 137(a), Sch 21 Pt I; the Education Act 1996 s 582(2), Sch 38 Pt I; and the Statute Law (Repeals) Act 2004). This is subject to the requirement that no instrument (other than a statutory instrument) made or executed under or in pursuance of the Education Reform Act 1988 s 228 may be treated as duly stamped unless it is stamped with the duty to which it would, but for s 230 (and, if applicable, the Finance Act 1982 s 129 (see STAMP TAXES vol 96 (2012) PARA 363)), be liable or it has, in accordance with the Stamp Act 1891 s 12 (see STAMP TAXES vol 96 (2012) PARA 384), been stamped with a particular stamp denoting that it is not chargeable with any duty or that it has been duly stamped: Education Reform Act 1988 s 230(4) (amended by the Education Act 1993 s 307(1), (3), Sch 19 paras 112, 137(b), Sch 21 Pt I).
16 Education Reform Act 1988 s 228(4)(a) (amended by SI 2010/1158).
17 Education Reform Act 1988 s 228(4)(b).

85.   Grants in respect of specific institutions.   The appropriate national authority[1] may make grants to the Royal Academy of Engineering[2] in respect of expenditure incurred or to be incurred by that body for the purposes of any of its activities[3]. In making such a grant the appropriate national authority may impose conditions[4] for the purposes of:

(1)   requiring the repayment of the grant in whole or part if any other condition is not complied with[5];

(2)   where the grant is made in respect of capital expenditure, requiring the payment to the appropriate national authority on the sale of, or of any part of, a grant-aided asset[6] of such sums related to the value of the asset at the time of the sale as it may by notice in writing[7] specify to the recipient of the grant as being in its opinion reasonable having regard to the extent to which the asset has been acquired, provided or improved as a result of the grant[8]; and

(3)   requiring the payment of interest in respect of any period during which a sum due to the appropriate national authority in accordance with any other condition remains unpaid[9],

and may also impose such other conditions as it thinks fit[10].

1   Ie the Secretary of State or, in relation to Wales, the Welsh Ministers. The functions of the Secretary of State under the Education Act 1986, so far as exercisable in relation to Wales, were transferred to the National Assembly for Wales (see the National Assembly for Wales (Transfer of Functions) Order 1999, SI 1999/672, art 2, Sch 1) and are now vested in the Welsh Ministers (see the Government of Wales Act 2006 s 162(1), Sch 11 para 30). As to the Secretary of State see PARA 58. As to the Welsh Ministers see PARA 59. As to the meaning of 'Wales' see PARA 7 note 3.

2   Education Act 1986 s 1(1)(a). The statute refers to the body corporate constituted by Royal Charter and known on 18 July 1986 (ie the date the Education Act 1986 was passed) as the Fellowship of Engineering: see s 1(1)(a). This body is now known as the Royal Academy of Engineering.

3   Education Act 1986 s 1(1) (amended by the Education Act 2002 ss 18(1)(b), 215, Sch 21 para 7, Sch 22 Pt 3).

4   See the Education Act 1986 s 1(2) (amended by SI 1995/2985).

5   Education Act 1986 s 1(3)(a).

6   'Grant-aided asset', in relation to a grant, means an asset acquired, provided or improved as a result of the expenditure in respect of which the grant is made: Education Act 1986 s 1(4).

7   As to the meaning of 'writing' see PARA 76 note 8.

8   Education Act 1986 s 1(3)(b) (amended by SI 1995/2985). A condition imposed under head (2) in the text may require a payment to be made even if the grant has been repaid at the time of the sale: Education Act 1986 s 1(4).

9   Education Act 1986 s 1(3)(c) (amended by SI 1995/2985).

10   Education Act 1986 s 1(2).

(iii) Provision for New Legal Frameworks for Schools

A. POWERS TO FACILITATE INNOVATION

86. Purpose of powers. The Secretary of State[1] and the Welsh Ministers[2] have powers[3] whose purpose is to facilitate the implementation by qualifying bodies[4] of innovative projects that may[5]:

(1)   in the opinion of the Secretary of State, contribute to the raising of the educational standards in England[6]; or

(2)   in the opinion of the Welsh Ministers, contribute to the raising of the educational standards in Wales[7].

In forming an opinion as to whether a project may contribute to the raising of the educational standards in England or Wales, the Secretary of State or the Welsh Ministers must[8]:

(a)   have regard to the need for the curriculum for any school affected by the project to be a balanced and broadly based curriculum which promotes the spiritual, moral, cultural, mental and physical development of children[9] and of society[10]; and

(b)   consider the likely effect of the project on all the pupils[11] or students who may be affected by it[12].

1   As to the Secretary of State see PARA 58.

2   The functions under the Education Act 2002 s 1 were originally vested in the National Assembly for Wales and are now exercisable by the Welsh Ministers by virtue of the Government of Wales Act 2006 s 162(1), Sch 11 paras 30, 32. As to the Welsh Ministers see PARA 59.

3   Ie under the Education Act 2002 Pt 1 Ch 1 (ss 1–5): see PARAS 87–88.

4   'Qualifying body' means: (1) a local authority; (2) an education action forum; (3) a qualifying foundation; (4) the governing body of a maintained school; (5) the head teacher of a maintained school; (6) the proprietor of an academy, a city technology college or a city college for the technology of the arts; (7) the proprietor of any special school that is not maintained by a local authority but is for the time being approved by the Secretary of State or the Welsh Ministers under the Education Act 1996 s 342 (see PARA 1042); or (8) the governing body of an institution within the further education sector: Education Act 2002 s 1(3) (definition substituted by the Education and Inspections Act 2006 s 161, Sch 16 Pt 1 para 1(1), (4)(b); and amended by

SI 2010/1158). As from a day to be appointed by order made under the Education and Skills Act 2008 s 173(4), there is substituted for head (7) the following: (7) the proprietor of a school approved under the Education Act 1996 s 342 (non-maintained special schools): Education Act 2002 s 1(3) (definition (as so substituted and amended) prospectively amended by the Education and Skills Act 2008 s 169(1), Sch 1 Pt 1 paras 13, 14). At the date at which this volume states the law no such day had been appointed. As to the meaning of 'local authority' see PARA 25 (definition applied by the Education Act 2002 s 212(2), (3)). As to education action forums see PARA 344. 'Qualifying foundation' means the foundation, as defined by the School Standards and Framework Act 1998 s 21(3)(a) (see PARA 108 note 6), of any foundation or foundation special school that for the purposes of that section has a foundation established otherwise than under that Act: Education Act 2002 s 1(3) (definition added by the Education and Inspections Act 2006 s 161, Sch 16 Pt 1 para 1(1), (4)(c)). 'Maintained school' means (a) a community, foundation or voluntary school; (b) a community or foundation special school; or (c) a maintained nursery school: Education Act 2002 s 1(3) (definition added by the Education and Inspections Act 2006 s 161, Sch 16 Pt 1 para 1(1), (4)(a)). As to the meaning of references in the Education Act 2002 to a community, foundation or voluntary school or a community or foundation special school see PARA 106. As to the meaning of 'maintained nursery school' see PARA 99 note 4; as to the meaning of 'school' see PARA 91; as to the meaning of 'proprietor' see PARA 51 note 4; as to the meaning of 'academy' see PARA 346; as to the meaning of 'institution within the further education sector' see PARA 555; and as to the meaning of 'special school' see PARA 1041 (definitions applied by s 212(2), (3)). 'Head teacher' includes acting head teacher: Education Act 1996 s 579(1) (definition applied by virtue of the Education Act 2002 s 212(2), (3)). As to city technology colleges and city colleges for the technology of the arts see PARA 345 note 3. As to governing bodies of maintained schools see PARA 150 et seq.

5   Education Act 2002 s 1(1).

6   Education Act 2002 s 1(1)(a) (s 1(1)(a), (b) amended by the Education and Inspections Act 2006 s 161, Sch 16 Pt 1 para 1(1), (2)). As to the meaning of 'England' see PARA 7 note 3.

7   Education Act 2002 s 1(1)(b) (as amended: see note 6). See also note 5.

8   Education Act 2002 s 1(2) (amended by the Education and Inspections Act 2006 s 161, Sch 16 Pt 1 para 1(1), (3)(a)). See also note 5.

9   'Children' means persons under the age of 19: Education Act 2002 s 1(3). As to the time at which a person attains a particular age see PARA 7 note 6.

10 Education Act 2002 s 1(2)(a). See also note 5. The requirement specified in head (a) in the text is a general requirement of the curriculum for a maintained school or maintained nursery school in England or Wales. As to the curriculum in England see PARA 856 et seq; and as to the curriculum in Wales see PARA 870 et seq.

11 As to the meaning of 'pupil' see PARA 20 note 4 (definition applied by the Education Act 2002 s 212(2), (3)).

12 Education Act 2002 s 1(2)(b) (amended by the Education and Inspections Act 2006 s 161, Sch 16 Pt 1 para 1(1), (3)(b)). See also note 5.

87.   Powers to suspend or modify statutory requirements.   On the application of one or more qualifying bodies[1] ('the applicant'), the Secretary of State, in relation to England[2], or the Welsh Ministers, in relation to Wales[3], may[4] by order[5] make provision[6]:

(1)   conferring on the applicant[7] exemption from any requirement imposed by education legislation[8];

(2)   relaxing any such requirement in its application to the applicant[9];

(3)   enabling the applicant to exercise any function[10] conferred by education legislation on any other qualifying body, either concurrently with or in place of that other body[11];

(4)   making such modifications[12] of any provision of education legislation, in its application to the applicant or any other qualifying body, as are in the opinion of the Secretary of State or the Welsh Ministers consequential on any provision made by virtue of any of heads (1) to (3) above[13].

An application for an order[14] must be in such form, and contain such information, as may be required by the Secretary of State or, as the case may be, the Welsh Ministers[15]. Before making an application for an order, the qualifying body must[16]:

(a) in the case of an education action forum[17], consult each local authority[18] by whom any participating school[19] is maintained[20];

(b) in the case of a qualifying foundation, consult the governing body of each foundation or foundation special school to which the application relates and the local authority who maintain the school[21];

(c) in the case of the governing body of a maintained school[22], consult the local authority who maintain the school[23], and where the school is a foundation school with a qualifying foundation, that foundation[24]; and

(d) in any case, consult such persons[25] as appear to the qualifying body to be appropriate, having regard to any guidance given from time to time by the Secretary of State or, as the case may be, the Welsh Ministers[26].

No application for an order may be made by the head teacher[27] of a maintained school without the consent of the governing body of the school[28].

The Secretary of State or the Welsh Ministers may from time to time give guidance as to the matters which he or they will take into account in determining whether to grant applications for orders[29]. Before making an order, the Secretary of State or the Welsh Ministers must, if he or they consider it appropriate to do so, consult the Chief Inspector[30]. The Secretary of State or the Welsh Ministers may with the consent of the applicant include in an order provisions different from those requested in the application[31]. No order which relates to teachers' pay and conditions[32] may be made by the Welsh Ministers without the consent of the Secretary of State[33]. An order has effect during a period specified in the order which[34] must not exceed three years[35].

The Secretary of State or the Welsh Ministers must refuse an application for an order if it appears to him or them that the proposed order would be likely to have a detrimental effect on the education of children[36] with special educational needs[37].

1 As to the meaning of 'qualifying body' see PARA 86 note 4.

2 As to the Secretary of State see PARA 58. As to the meaning of 'England' see PARA 7 note 3.

3 The functions under the Education Act 2002 ss 2–4 were originally vested in the National Assembly for Wales and are now exercisable by the Welsh Ministers by virtue of the Government of Wales Act 2006 s 162(1), Sch 11 paras 30, 32. As to the Welsh Ministers see PARA 59. As to the meaning of 'Wales' see PARA 7 note 3.

4 Ie for the purpose of the Education Act 2002 Pt 1 Ch 1 (ss 1–5). As to such purpose see PARA 86.

5 The power conferred on the Secretary of State and the Welsh Ministers by the Education Act 2002 s 2 includes: (1) power by a further order made under s 2 on an application made for those purposes by one or more qualifying bodies to amend any order previously made thereunder so as to extend: (a) the requirements or functions in relation to which the order applies (s 3(1)(a)(i)); (b) the qualifying bodies to which it applies (s 3(1)(a)(ii)); or (c) subject to s 3(2), the period during which it has effect (s 3(1)(a)(iii)); and (2) power by a further order under s 2, which may be made without any application from a qualifying body, to revoke any order previously made thereunder (s 3(1)(b)). An order made under s 2 by virtue of head (1)(c) above may, on one occasion only, extend the period for which a previous such order has effect by a period of not more than three years from the end of the period originally specified in the previous order: s 3(2). Orders under s 2 being local in nature are not recorded in this title.

6 Education Act 2002 s 2(1).

7 Where the applicant is or includes a qualifying foundation, references in the Education Act 2002 s 2(1)(a)–(d) to the applicant (so far as they would otherwise be read as references to the qualifying foundation) are to be read as references to the governing bodies of all or any of the foundation or foundation special schools in respect of which the applicant is the foundation:

s 2(1A) (added by the Education and Inspections Act 2006 s 161, Sch 16 Pt 1 para 2(1), (2)). As to the meaning of 'qualifying foundation' see PARA 86 note 4.

8   Education Act 2002 s 2(1)(a). 'Education legislation' means: (1) the Education Acts as defined by the Education Act 1996 s 578 (see PARA 1 note 13); (2) the Learning and Skills Act 2000; and (3) any subordinate legislation made under any of those Acts, where 'subordinate legislation' has the same meaning as in the Interpretation Act 1978 (see PARA 26 note 3): Education Act 2002 s 1(3).

9   Education Act 2002 s 2(1)(b). See also note 7.

10 As to the meaning of 'function' see PARA 18 note 5 (definition applied by the Education Act 2002 s 212(2), (3)).

11 Education Act 2002 s 2(1)(c). See also note 7.

12 As to the meaning of 'modifications' see PARA 21 note 15 (definition applied by the Education Act 2002 s 212(2), (3)).

13 Education Act 2002 s 2(1)(d). See also note 7.

14 Ie an application for the purposes of the Education Act 2002 s 2: see the text to notes 1–13.

15 Education Act 2002 s 4(1) (amended by the Education and Inspections Act 2006 s 161, Sch 16 Pt 1 para 3(1), (2)).

16 Education Act 2002 s 4(2) (amended by the Education and Inspections Act 2006 s 161, Sch 16 Pt 1 para 3(1), (4)(a)).

17 As to education action forums see PARA 344.

18 As to the meaning of 'local authority' see PARA 25 (definition applied by the Education Act 2002 s 212(2), (3)).

19 Ie as defined by the School Standards and Framework Act 1998 s 10(6)(b): see PARA 429.

20 Education Act 2002 s 4(2)(a) (amended by SI 2010/1158).

21 Education Act 2002 s 4(2)(aa) (added by the Education and Inspections Act 2006 s 161, Sch 16 Pt 1 para 3(1), (4)(b); and amended by SI 2010/1158).

22 As to the meaning of 'maintained school' see PARA 86 note 4. As to governing bodies of maintained schools see PARA 150 et seq.

23 Education Act 2002 s 4(2)(b)(i) (s 4(2)(b) substituted by the Education and Inspections Act 2006 s 161, Sch 16 Pt 1 para 3(1), (4)(c); and amended by SI 2010/1158).

24 Education Act 2002 s 4(2)(b)(ii) (as substituted: see note 23).

25 As to the meaning of 'person' see PARA 7 note 6.

26 Education Act 2002 s 4(2)(c).

27 As to the meaning of 'head teacher' see PARA 86 note 4.

28 Education Act 2002 s 4(1A) (added by the Education and Inspections Act 2006 s 161, Sch 16 Pt 1 para 3(1), (3)).

29 Education Act 2002 s 2(6). As to the publication of guidance see the Education Act 1996 s 571 (applied by the Education Act 2002 s 212(2), (3)); and PARA 60.

30 Education Act 2002 s 2(3). 'The Chief Inspector' means: (1) in relation to England, Her Majesty's Chief Inspector of Education, Children's Services and Skills; and (2) in relation to Wales, Her Majesty's Chief Inspector of Education and Training in Wales: s 1(3) (definition amended by the Education and Inspections Act 2006 s 157, Sch 14 paras 70, 71). As to Her Majesty's Chief Inspector of Education, Children's Services and Skills see PARA 1133. As to Her Majesty's Chief Inspector of Education and Training in Wales see PARA 1148. As to the exercise of the duty to consult see JUDICIAL REVIEW vol 61 (2010) PARA 627.

31 Education Act 2002 s 4(3).

32 Ie which relates to the Education Act 2002 ss 119–129: see PARA 1076 et seq.

33 Education Act 2002 s 2(4).

34 Ie subject to the Education Act 2002 s 3(2): see note 5.

35 Education Act 2002 s 2(2). When either the Secretary of State or the Welsh Ministers has made an order under s 2 he or they must make a report on the matter: see PARA 88.

36 As to the meaning of 'children' see PARA 86 note 9.

37 Education Act 2002 s 2(5). As to the meaning of 'special educational needs' see PARAS 943, 989 (definitions applied by s 212(2), (3)).

88. Annual report on use of powers. Where the Secretary of State[1] has made any order[2] to suspend or modify statutory requirements in any academic year[3], he must prepare a report on all such orders made by him in that academic year[4] and lay a copy of the report before each House of Parliament[5].

Where the Welsh Ministers[6] have made any such order in any academic year, they must prepare and publish a report on all the orders so made by them in that academic year[7].

1　As to the Secretary of State see PARA 58.
2　Ie under the Education Act 2002 s 2: see PARA 87.
3　'Academic year' means a period beginning with 1 August and ending with the next 31 July: Education Act 2002 s 5(3).
4　Education Act 2002 s 5(1)(a).
5　Education Act 2002 s 5(1)(b). As to the laying of documents before Parliament see STATUTES AND LEGISLATIVE PROCESS vol 96 (2012) PARA 1052.
6　The functions under the Education Act 2002 s 5 were originally vested in the National Assembly for Wales and are now exercisable by the Welsh Ministers by virtue of the Government of Wales Act 2006 s 162(1), Sch 11 paras 30, 32. As to the Welsh Ministers see PARA 59.
7　Education Act 2002 s 5(2).

B. EXEMPTIONS RELATED TO SCHOOL PERFORMANCE

89. Exemptions available to qualifying schools. As from a day to be appointed, the following provisions have effect[1].

Regulations[2] may:

(1)　designate any curriculum provision[3] or pay and conditions provision[4] as attracting exemption as of right[5];

(2)　designate any curriculum provision or pay and conditions provision as attracting discretionary exemption[6];

(3)　designate modifications[7] of any curriculum provision or pay and conditions provision as being available as of right[8]; and

(4)　designate modifications of any curriculum provision or pay and conditions provision as being available on a discretionary basis[9].

On the application of the governing body of a qualifying school[10], the Secretary of State, in relation to England, or the Welsh Ministers, in relation to Wales, may by order:

(a)　provide that any pay and conditions provision which is designated under head (1) or head (2) above and specified in the order is not to apply in relation to school teachers employed at the school[11];

(b)　provide that any pay and conditions provision which is designated under head (3) or head (4) above is to apply in relation to school teachers employed at the school with modifications which are specified in the order and fall within the modifications designated as being available as of right or available on a discretionary basis[12];

(c)　provide that any curriculum provision which is designated under head (1) or head (2) above and specified in the order is not to apply in relation to the school[13];

(d)　provide that any curriculum provision which is designated under head (3) or head (4) above is to apply in relation to the school with modifications which are specified in the order and fall within the modifications designated as being available as of right or available on a discretionary basis[14]; or

(e)　revoke or vary any order previously made under heads (a) to (d) above[15].

Where such an application by a qualifying school relates only to exemption from provisions that are designated under head (1) above as attracting exemption as of right or to modifications that fall within the modifications designated under head (3) above as being available as of right (or only to such exemption and such modifications)[16] and does not relate to the revocation or variation of an order previously made under heads (a) to (e) above[17], the Secretary of State or, as the case may be, the Welsh Ministers must make the order requested[18].

An application for the purposes of heads (a) to (e) above must be in such form, and contain such information, as may be required by the Secretary of State or, as the case may be, the Welsh Ministers[19]. Before making such an application, the governing body must:

(i)   consult the local authority[20];

(ii)   where the application relates to a curriculum provision, consult the parents[21] of registered pupils[22] at the school[23];

(iii)   where the application relates to a pay and conditions provision, consult each school teacher employed at the school[24]; and

(iv)   in any case, consult such other persons as appear to be appropriate, having regard to any guidance given from time to time by the Secretary of State or, as the case may be, the Welsh Ministers[25].

The Secretary of State or the Welsh Ministers may with the consent of the applicant include in an order under heads (a) to (e) above provisions different from those requested in the application[26].

The Secretary of State or the Welsh Ministers may from time to time give guidance as to the matters which he or they will take into account in determining whether to grant applications under heads (a) to (e) above which relate to:

(A)   provisions which are designated under head (2) above as attracting discretionary exemption[27]; or

(B)   modifications which fall within the modifications designated under head (4) above as being available on a discretionary basis[28].

1   The Education Act 2002 ss 6–8, 10 come into force, except in relation to Wales, in accordance with provision made by the Secretary of State by order, and in relation to Wales, in accordance with provision made by the Welsh Ministers by order: see s 216(4). At the date at which this volume states the law no such order had been made. As to the Secretary of State see PARA 58. The functions under s 216(4) and under ss 6–10 were originally vested in the National Assembly for Wales and are now exercisable by the Welsh Ministers by virtue of the Government of Wales Act 2006 s 162(1), Sch 11 paras 30, 32. As to the Welsh Ministers see PARA 59. As to the meaning of 'Wales' see PARA 7 note 3.

2   Ie regulations made under the Education Act 2002 by the Secretary of State (in relation to England) or by the Welsh Ministers (in relation to Wales): see s 212(1). As to the meaning of 'England' see PARA 7 note 3. At the date at which this volume states the law no such regulations had been made. No regulations under s 7(1) which relate to a pay and conditions provision may be made by the Welsh Ministers without the consent of the Secretary of State: s 7(5). 'Pay and conditions provision' means any provision of an order under s 122 (see PARA 1078): s 6(4).

3   'Curriculum provision' means: (1) in relation to a maintained school maintained by a local authority in England, any provision of the National Curriculum for England; and (2) in relation to a maintained school maintained by a local authority in Wales, any provision of the National Curriculum for Wales: Education Act 2002 s 6(4) (definition amended by SI 2010/1158). 'Maintained school' means a community, foundation or voluntary school or a community or foundation special school: Education Act 2002 s 6(4). As to the meaning of 'school' see PARA 91; and as to the meaning of 'local authority' see PARA 25 (definitions applied by s 212(2), (3)). As to the National Curriculum for England see PARA 856 et seq. As to the National Curriculum for Wales see PARA 870 et seq. As to the meanings of references to a community, foundation or voluntary school or a community or foundation special school see PARA 106.

4   Where an order under the Education Act 2002 s 7(2) (see heads (a)–(e) in the text) which relates to a pay and conditions provision is in force in relation to a school: (1) the governing body must determine the remuneration and other conditions of employment of each school teacher employed at the school, to the extent that by virtue of the order the pay and conditions provisions do not apply to him (s 10(1)(a)); (2) the local authority must do anything necessary to give effect to the governing body's determination under head (1) (s 10(1)(b) (amended by SI 2010/1158)); and (3) pending a determination under head (1), the terms on which a school

teacher is employed at the school remain unchanged, irrespective of any new order under the Education Act 2002 s 122 except so far as applying to him despite the effect of the order under s 7(2) (s 10(1)(c)). The Secretary of State may make regulations about the application of s 122(2) (see PARA 1078) where an order under s 7(2) is revoked or the exemption conferred by it is restricted: s 10(2). The local authority, in relation to a school maintained (or proposed to be maintained) by a local authority, means that authority: s 212(1) (definition amended by SI 2010/1158). 'School teacher' has the same meaning as in the Education Act 2002 s 122 (see PARA 1078 note 3) (s 6(4)); and a school teacher is 'employed' at a school if he works at the school under a contract falling within s 122(3)(b), (c) and (d) (see PARA 1078) (s 6(3)). As to the governing bodies of maintained schools see PARA 150 et seq.

5   Education Act 2002 s 7(1)(a).
6   Education Act 2002 s 7(1)(b).
7   As to the meaning of 'modifications' see PARA 21 note 15 (definition applied by the Education Act 2002 s 212(2), (3)).
8   Education Act 2002 s 7(1)(c).
9   Education Act 2002 s 7(1)(d).
10 For these purposes, a maintained school is a 'qualifying school' at any time if it is a school of a prescribed description which satisfies prescribed criteria relating to one or more of the following: (1) the performance of the school (Education Act 2002 s 6(1)(a)); (2) the quality of the leadership in the school (s 6(1)(b)); and (3) the quality of the management of the school (s 6(1)(c)). The criteria prescribed for these purposes may include criteria referring to the opinion of the Chief Inspector, the Secretary of State or the Welsh Ministers: s 6(2). 'Prescribed' means prescribed by regulations: s 212(1). As to the meaning of 'the Chief Inspector' see PARA 87 note 30 (definition applied by s 6(4)).
11 Education Act 2002 s 7(2)(a).
12 Education Act 2002 s 7(2)(b).
13 Education Act 2002 s 7(2)(c).
14 Education Act 2002 s 7(2)(d).
15 Education Act 2002 s 7(2)(e).
16 Education Act 2002 s 7(3)(a).
17 Education Act 2002 s 7(3)(b).
18 Education Act 2002 s 7(3).
19 Education Act 2002 s 8(1).
20 Education Act 2002 s 8(2)(a) (amended by SI 2010/1158).
21 As to the meaning of 'parent' see PARA 7 note 6 (definition applied by the Education Act 2002 s 212(2), (3)).
22 As to the meaning of 'registered pupil' see PARA 437 (definition applied by the Education Act 2002 s 212(2), (3)).
23 Education Act 2002 s 8(2)(b).
24 Education Act 2002 s 8(2)(c).
25 Education Act 2002 s 8(2)(d).
26 Education Act 2002 s 8(3).
27 Education Act 2002 s 7(4)(a).
28 Education Act 2002 s 7(4)(b).

90. Removal of exemptions. As from a day to be appointed, the following provisions have effect[1].

Where the Secretary of State or the Welsh Ministers has made an exemption order[2] in relation to a school[3], and, since the making of the exemption order, the school has ceased to be a qualifying school[4], the Secretary of State or the Welsh Ministers may, without any application by the governing body[5], make an order[6] which revokes the exemption order or varies the exemption order so as to restrict any exemption conferred by it[7].

1   The Education Act 2002 s 9 comes into force, except in relation to Wales, in accordance with provision made by the Secretary of State by order, and in relation to Wales, in accordance with provision made by the Welsh Ministers by order: see s 216(4). At the date at which this volume states the law no such order had been made. As to the Secretary of State see PARA 58. The functions under s 216(4) and under s 9 were originally vested in the National Assembly for

Wales and are now exercisable by the Welsh Ministers by virtue of the Government of Wales Act 2006 s 162(1), Sch 11 paras 30, 32. As to the Welsh Ministers see PARA 59. As to the meaning of 'Wales' see PARA 7 note 3.

2   Ie an order under the Education Act 2002 s 7(2): see PARA 89.

3   Education Act 2002 s 9(a). As to the meaning of 'school' see PARA 91 (definition applied s 212(2), (3)).

4   Education Act 2002 s 9(b). As to the meaning of 'qualifying school' see PARA 89 note 10.

5   As to the governing bodies of maintained schools see PARA 150 et seq.

6   Ie under the Education Act 2002 s 7(2): see PARA 89.

7   Education Act 2002 s 9.

2. NURSERY, PRIMARY AND SECONDARY EDUCATION

(1) GENERAL PROVISIONS RELATING TO SCHOOLS

(i) Definition of 'School' etc

91. Meaning of 'school' etc. 'School' means an educational institution which is outside the further education sector[1] and the higher education sector[2] and is an institution for providing primary education[3], secondary education[4] or both primary and secondary education[5], whether or not the institution also provides further education[6]. However, an institution which provides only early years provision[7], and is not a maintained nursery school[8], is not a school[9]; a 16 to 19 academy[10] is not a school[11]; and an alternative provision academy[12] is a school[13].

Many schools are maintained schools[14], which receive funding from local authorities[15] and which do not charge fees[16]. There are also non-maintained schools, generally known as independent schools, which often have charitable status and which are mainly financed by fees and income from investments[17].

At the date at which this volume states the law both academies and free schools are on the increase. 'Academy' is the term applied to an educational institution to which academy arrangements relate, and no charge is made in respect of admission, attendance and education. Certain independent schools, maintained schools and other schools may potentially become academies[18]. A free school in England is a type of academy, and is a non-profit-making, independent, state-funded school which is free to attend but which is not controlled by a local authority[19].

Children[20] under compulsory school age[21] may attend nursery schools[22], and a primary school is a 'nursery school' if it is used wholly or mainly for the purpose of providing education for children who have attained the age of two but are under compulsory school age[23].

'Primary school' means a school for providing primary education, whether or not it also provides further education[24].

'Middle school' means a school which[25] has been established as, or altered so as to become, a school for providing full-time education suitable to the requirements of pupils[26] who have attained a specified age below ten years and six months[27], and are under a specified age above 12 years[28]. The Secretary of State[29] or, in relation to Wales, the Welsh Ministers[30] may make regulations for determining, or enabling him or them to determine, whether a middle school is to be treated for the purposes of the Education Act 1996 and the other enactments relating to education as a primary school or as a secondary school[31].

'Secondary school' means[32] a school for providing secondary education, whether or not it also provides further education[33]. Certain maintained secondary schools in England may be designated as specialist schools, specialising in technology, languages, sports or arts in addition to providing the full National Curriculum[34].

Education may also be provided by special schools[35] and by pupil referral units[36]. A school is a special school if it is specially organised to make special educational provision for pupils with special educational needs, and it is maintained by a local authority, an academy school[37], or a non-maintained special school[38]. Pupil referral units are schools established and maintained by local authorities which are specially organised to provide education for children of compulsory school age who, by reason of illness, exclusion from school or otherwise, may not otherwise receive suitable education[39].

1   As to the meaning of 'institution outside the further education sector' see PARA 555. As to further education generally see PARA 555 et seq.

2   As to the meaning of 'institution outside the higher education sector' see PARA 619. As to higher education generally see PARA 619 et seq.

3   Education Act 1996 s 4(1)(a) (s 4(1) substituted by the Education Act 1997 s 51). As to the meaning of 'primary education' see PARA 20.

4   Education Act 1996 s 4(1)(b) (as substituted: see note 3). As to the meaning of 'secondary education' see PARA 21.

5   Education Act 1996 s 4(1)(c) (as substituted: see note 3).

6   Education Act 1996 s 4(1) (as substituted (see note 3); and amended by the Education Act 2002 s 215(2), Sch 22 Pt 3; the Childcare Act 2006 s 95(1), (2); and the Education Act 2011 Sch 13 para 9(1)(2)(a)). The Education Act 1996 s 4(1) is subject to s 4(1A)–(1C) (see the text to notes 9–13): s 4(1) (as so substituted and amended). However, nothing in the Education Act 1996 s 4(1) is to be taken to preclude the making of arrangements under s 19(1) (exceptional educational provision: see PARA 427) under which part-time education is to be provided at a school: s 4(2) (amended by the Education Act 1997 s 57, Sch 7 para 10(a)). For the purposes of the Education Act 1996, an educational institution that would fall within s 4(1) but for the fact that it provides part-time rather than full-time education must nevertheless be treated as a school if that part-time education is provided under arrangements made under s 19(1): s 4(2) (amended by the Education Act 1997 Sch 7 para 10(a), (b), Sch 8).

     An institution which would have become a school on the coming into force of the Learning and Skills Act 2000 s 110(1) (by virtue of the Education Act 1996 s 4(1)) is not to be treated as being a school by virtue of s 4(1) unless it has been established as a new school in accordance with the School Standards and Framework Act 1998 s 28(1)(a) or (2)(a) or s 31(1)(a) (all repealed see now the Schools Standards and Organisation (Wales) Act 2013 Pt 3 (ss 38–56); and PARA 139 et seq): Learning and Skills Act 2000 s 110(2), (3). A local authority may not continue to maintain an institution which would have become a school on the coming into force of s 110(1) (by virtue of the Education Act 1996 s 4(1)) in pursuance of the Education Act 1996 s 15A (see PARA 34): Learning and Skills Act 2000 s 110(2), (4) (amended by SI 2010/1158). As to the meaning of 'local authority' see PARA 25 (definition applied by the Learning and Skills Act 2000 s 110(6) (added by SI 2010/1158)). The Learning and Skills Act 2000 s 110(1) added the Education Act 1996 s 2(2A), (2B) (see PARA 21) and came into force in relation to England for certain purposes on 1 September 2000, and for the remaining purposes on 1 April 2001: see the Learning and Skills Act 2000 (Commencement No 1) Order 2000, SI 2000/2114, art 2(3), Schedule Pt III; and the Learning and Skills Act 2000 (Commencement No 3 and Savings and Transitional Provisions) Order 2001, SI 2001/654, art 2(2), Schedule Pt II. The Learning and Skills Act 2000 110 came into force in relation to Wales on 1 April 2001: see the Learning and Skills Act 2000 (Commencement No 3 and Transitional Provisions) (Wales) Order 2001, SI 2001/1274, art 2(1), Schedule Pt I. As to the meanings of 'England' and 'Wales' see PARA 7 note 3.

     An accommodation centre established under the Nationality, Immigration and Asylum Act 2002 is not a school within the meaning of the Education Act 1996 s 4: see the Nationality, Immigration and Asylum Act 2002 s 36(9); and see IMMIGRATION AND ASYLUM vol 57 (2012) PARA 355.

7   Education Act 1996 s 4(1A)(a) (s 4(1A) added by the Childcare Act 2006 s 95(1), (3)). 'Early years provision' has the meaning given by the Childcare Act 2006 s 96(2) (see CHILDREN AND YOUNG PERSONS vol 10 (2012) PARA 1090): see the Education Act 1996 s 4(1A) (as so added).

8   Education Act 1996 s 4(1A)(b) (as added: see note 7). As to the meaning of 'maintained nursery school' see PARA 99 note 4.

9   Education Act 1996 s 4(1A) (as added: see note 7).

10   As to the meaning of '16 to 19 academy' see PARA 346 note 13.

11   Education Act 1996 s 4(1B) (s 4(1B), (1C) added by the Education Act 2011 Sch 13 para 9(1), (2)(b)).

12   As to the meaning of 'alternative provision academy' see PARA 346 note 14.

13   Education Act 1996 s 4(1C) (as added: see note 11).

14   As to maintained schools see PARA 99 et seq.

15   As to the education functions of local authorities see PARA 25.

16   As to funding of maintained schools see PARA 305 et seq.

17   As to independent schools see PARA 369 et seq.

18 As to academy arrangements and academies see PARA 346 et seq.

19 As to free schools see PARA 368.

20 As to the meaning of 'child' see PARA 7 note 6.

21 As to the meaning of 'compulsory school age' see PARA 19.

22 As to nursery education see PARA 95 et seq.

23 Education Act 1996 s 6(1) (amended by the Education Act 1997 Sch 7 para 11; and the Education Act 2002 s 156(1)). As to the time at which a person attains a particular age see PARA 7 note 6.

24 Education Act 1996 s 5(1) (amended by the Education Act 2002 Sch 22 Pt 3). This provision is expressed to be subject to regulations made under the Education Act 1996 s 5(4): see the text to notes 29–31.

25 Ie in pursuance of proposals published under any of the following enactments: (1) in relation to England, the School Standards and Framework Act 1998 s 28 or s 28A (repealed) or Sch 7 para 5 (repealed); the Education Act 2005 s 66 (repealed) or Sch 11 para 7 (repealed); and the Education and Inspections Act 2006 s 7 (see PARA 111), s 10 (see PARA 112), s 11 (see PARA 113) or s 19 (see PARA 133); (2) in relation to Wales, the School Standards and Framework Act 1998 s 28 or Sch 7 para 5; and the School Standards and Organisation (Wales) Act 2013 s 48 (see PARA 142), s 59 (see PARA 145) or s 68 (see PARA 1024): see the Education Act 1996 s 5(3), (3A) (s 5(3) substituted by the Education Act 2005 s 72, Sch 12 para 1(1), (2); the Education Act 1996 s 5(3) further substituted, (3A) added, by the Education and Inspections Act 2006 s 30, Sch 3 para 7; and the Education Act 1996 s 5(3A) amended by the School Standards and Organisation (Wales) Act 2013 Sch 5 para 17(1), (2)). The powers conferred by the enactments mentioned above (so far as relating to the establishment of middle schools) and the powers conferred by the Education Act 1996 s 5(4) (see the text to notes 29–31) are exercisable notwithstanding anything in the Education Act 1996 (and in particular s 1: see PARA 18) but without prejudice to the exercise of any other power conferred by the Act: see s 5(5) (amended by the Education Act 2005 s 72, Sch 12 para 1(1), (3)).

26 As to the meaning of 'pupil' see PARA 20 note 4.

27 Education Act 1996 s 5(3)(a) (as substituted: see note 21).

28 Education Act 1996 s 5(3)(b) (as substituted: see note 21).

29 As to the Secretary of State see PARA 58.

30 The functions of the Secretary of State under the Education Act 1996 s 5, so far as exercisable in relation to Wales, were transferred to the National Assembly for Wales (see the National Assembly for Wales (Transfer of Functions) Order 1999, SI 1999/672, art 2, Sch 1) and are now vested in the Welsh Ministers (see the Government of Wales Act 2006 s 162(1), Sch 11 para 30). As to the Welsh Ministers see PARA 59.

31 Education Act 1996 s 5(4). See also s 5(5); and note 25. As to the regulation made see the Education (Middle School) (England) Regulations 2002, SI 2002/1983; and the Education (Middle Schools) (Wales) Regulations 2012, SI 2012/1797.

32 Ie subject to regulations made under the Education Act 1996 s 5(4): see the text to notes 29–31.

33 Education Act 1996 s 5(2). As to the provision of secondary education by the further education sector see PARA 555 et seq. As to the duty to safeguard pupils receiving secondary education in a further education institution see PARA 595.

34 As to specialist schools see PARA 100. As to the National Curriculum see PARA 859 et seq.

35 As to special schools see PARA 1041 et seq.

36 As to pupil referral units see PARA 427 et seq.

37 As to the meaning of 'academy school' see PARA 346 note 12.

38 See the Education Act 1996 s 337; and PARA 1041.

39 See the Education Act 1996 s 19; and PARA 427.

(ii) Home-school and Learning Agreements

92. Home-school agreements. Until a day to be appointed a 'home-school agreement' is a statement specifying:

(1) the school's aims and values[1];

(2) the school's responsibilities, namely the responsibilities which the school intends to discharge in connection with the education of pupils[2] at the school who are of compulsory school age[3];

(3) the parental responsibilities, namely the responsibilities which the

parents[4] of such pupils are expected to discharge in connection with the education of their children while they are registered pupils[5] at the school[6]; and

(4)   the school's expectations of its pupils, namely the expectations of the school as regards the conduct of such pupils while they are registered pupils there[7].

The governing body[8] of a school which is a maintained school[9], or a city technology college[10], a city college for the technology of the arts[11] or an academy school[12], must adopt a home-school agreement for the school, together with a parental declaration[13] to be used in connection with the agreement[14]. The governing body must also take reasonable steps to secure that the parental declaration is signed by every qualifying parent[15]. This does not, however, require the governing body to seek the signature of a qualifying parent if, having regard to any special circumstances relating to the parent or the pupil in question, it considers that it would be inappropriate to do so[16]. Where the governing body considers that a registered pupil at the school has a sufficient understanding of the home-school agreement as it relates to him, it may invite the pupil to sign the parental declaration as an indication that he acknowledges and accepts the school's expectations of its pupils[17]. The governing body must from time to time review the home-school agreement[18]. Before adopting the home-school agreement or parental declaration, or revising that agreement, the governing body must consult all qualifying parents[19], and such other persons as may be prescribed[20].

In discharging any of the above functions[21] the governing body of a school must have regard to any guidance given from time to time by the Secretary of State or, in relation to Wales, the Welsh Ministers[22]. If the Secretary of State or the Welsh Ministers by order so provides[23], the governing body of a maintained school, a city technology college, a city college for the technology of the arts or an academy school[24] must ensure that any form of words specified in the order, or having such effect as is so specified, is not used in a home-school agreement or, as the case may be, in a parental declaration[25]. Neither the governing body of such a school nor the local authority[26] where it is the admission authority[27] for such a school may:

(a)   invite any person to sign the parental declaration at a time when the child in question has not been admitted to the school[28];

(b)   make it a condition of a child being admitted to the school that the parental declaration is signed in respect of the child[29]; or

(c)   make any decision as to whether or not to admit a child to the school by reference to whether any such declaration is or is not likely to be signed in respect of the child[30].

No person may be excluded[31] from such a school or suffer any other adverse consequences on account of any failure to comply with any invitation to sign the parental declaration[32]. A home-school agreement is not capable of creating any obligation in respect of whose breach any liability arises in contract or in tort[33].

1   School Standards and Framework Act 1998 s 110(2)(a) (ss 110, 111 prospectively repealed by the Deregulation Act 2015 Sch 16 para 2(1)). At the date at which this volume states the law no such day had been appointed. As to the meaning of 'school' see PARA 91 (definition applied by the School Standards and Framework Act 1998 s 142(8)).

2   As to the meaning of 'pupil' see PARA 20 note 4 (definition applied by the School Standards and Framework Act 1998 s 142(8)).

3   School Standards and Framework Act 1998 s 110(2)(b) (prospectively repealed: see note 1). As to the meaning of 'compulsory school age' see PARA 19.

4   As to the meaning of 'parent' see PARA 7 note 6 (definition applied by the School Standards and Framework Act 1998 s 142(8)).

5   As to the meaning of 'registered pupil' see PARA 437 (definition applied by the School Standards and Framework Act 1998 s 142(8)).

6   School Standards and Framework Act 1998 s 110(2)(c) (prospectively repealed: see note 1).

7   School Standards and Framework Act 1998 s 110(2)(d) (prospectively repealed: see note 1).

8   As to the governing bodies of maintained schools see PARA 150 et seq.

9   School Standards and Framework Act 1998 s 110(1)(a) (prospectively repealed: see note 1). As to the meaning of 'maintained school' see PARA 99.

10 As to city technology colleges see PARA 345.

11 As to city colleges for the technology of the arts see PARA 345.

12 School Standards and Framework Act 1998 s 110(1)(b) (amended by the Learning and Skills Act 2000 s 149, Sch 9 paras 1, 85; the Education Act 2002 s 65(3), Sch 7 Pt 2 para 9; and the Education Act 2011 Sch 13 para 10(1), (9); prospectively repealed (see note 1)). As to the meaning of 'academy school' see PARA 346 note 12 (definition applied by the School Standards and Framework Act 1998 s 142(8)).

13 'Parental declaration' means a document to be used by qualifying parents for recording that they take note of the school's aims and values and its responsibilities and that they acknowledge and accept the parental responsibilities and the school's expectations of its pupils: School Standards and Framework Act 1998 s 110(2) (prospectively repealed: see note 1). 'Qualifying parent' means a registered parent of a pupil at the school who is of compulsory school age: s 110(10) (as so prospectively repealed).

14 School Standards and Framework Act 1998 s 110(1) (prospectively repealed: see note 1).

15 School Standards and Framework Act 1998 s 110(3) (prospectively repealed: see note 1). The governing body must discharge its duty under s 110(3), in the case of a pupil attending the school on the relevant date, as soon after that date as is reasonably practicable and, in the case of a pupil admitted to the school after the relevant date, as soon after the date of his admission as is reasonably practicable: s 110(6) (as so prospectively repealed). 'The relevant date' means such date as the Secretary of State or, in relation to Wales, the Welsh Ministers may by order appoint or such later date as he or they may determine in the case of the school in question: s 110(10) (as so prospectively repealed). The appointed relevant date is 1 September 1999: see the School Standards and Framework Act 1998 (Home-School Agreements) (Appointed Day) Order 1998, SI 1998/2877. The functions of the Secretary of State under the School Standards and Framework Act 1998 ss 110, 111 (see the text to notes 21–33) so far as exercisable in relation to Wales, were transferred to the National Assembly for Wales (see the National Assembly for Wales (Transfer of Functions) Order 1999, SI 1999/672, art 2, Sch 1) and are now vested in the Welsh Ministers (see the Government of Wales Act 2006 s 162(1), Sch 11 para 30). As to the Secretary of State see PARA 58. As to the Welsh Ministers see PARA 59. As to the meaning of 'Wales' see PARA 7 note 3.

16 School Standards and Framework Act 1998 s 110(4) (prospectively repealed: see note 1).

17 School Standards and Framework Act 1998 s 110(5) (prospectively repealed: see note 1). Where the governing body decides to exercise its power under s 110(5), it must exercise it, in the case of a pupil attending the school on the relevant date, as soon after that date as is reasonably practicable and, in the case of a pupil admitted to the school after the relevant date, as soon after the date of his admission as is reasonably practicable: s 110(6) (as so prospectively repealed).

18 School Standards and Framework Act 1998 s 110(7) (prospectively repealed: see note 1). Where the home-school agreement is revised by the governing body following such a review, the provisions of s 110(3)–(6) (see the text to notes 15–17), in the case of pupils admitted to the school after the revision takes effect, accordingly apply in relation to the revised agreement: s 110(8) (as so prospectively repealed).

19 School Standards and Framework Act 1998 s 110(9)(a) (prospectively repealed: see note 1). As to the exercise of the duty to consult see JUDICIAL REVIEW vol 61 (2010) PARA 627.

20 School Standards and Framework Act 1998 s 110(9)(b) (prospectively repealed: see note 1). As to the meaning of 'person' see PARA 7 note 6. 'Prescribed' means prescribed by regulations made by the Secretary of State or, in relation to Wales, the Welsh Ministers under the School Standards and Framework Act 1998: see s 142(1). At the date at which this volume states the law, no such regulations had been made.

21 Ie any function under the School Standards and Framework Act 1998 s 110 (see the text to notes 1–20). As to the meaning of 'function' see PARA 18 note 5 (definition applied by s 142(8)).

22 School Standards and Framework Act 1998 s 111(1) (prospectively repealed: see note 1).

23 Such an order may apply to any school specified in the order (School Standards and Framework Act 1998 s 111(3)(a) (prospectively repealed: see note 1)), or to any description of school so

specified (s 111(3)(b) (as so prospectively repealed)). An order under s 111(3)(a) is not to be made by statutory instrument (see s 138(2) (as so prospectively repealed)) and as such is not recorded in this title. At the date at which this volume states the law no order had been made under s 111(3)(b).

24 Ie a school to which the School Standards and Framework Act 1998 s 110(1) applies: see the text to notes 8–14.

25 School Standards and Framework Act 1998 s 111(2) (prospectively repealed: see note 1).

26 As to the meaning of 'local authority' see PARA 25 (definition applied by the School Standards and Framework Act 1998 s 142(8)).

27 As to admission authorities see PARA 227 note 6.

28 School Standards and Framework Act 1998 s 111(4)(a) (amended by SI 2010/1158; prospectively repealed (see note 1)).

29 School Standards and Framework Act 1998 s 111(4)(b) (prospectively repealed: see note 1).

30 School Standards and Framework Act 1998 s 111(4)(c) (prospectively repealed: see note 1).

31 As to the meaning of 'exclude' see PARA 316 note 6.

32 School Standards and Framework Act 1998 s 111(5) (prospectively repealed: see note 1).

33 School Standards and Framework Act 1998 s 111(6) (prospectively repealed: see note 1).

93.   Learning agreements. Regulations[1] may require a learning agreement[2] to be in the prescribed form[3] and to be signed by the student and by or on behalf of such other persons[4] as may be prescribed[5]. Regulations may also:

(1)   provide that a person is not eligible to receive an allowance unless the person providing the relevant education or training holds a learning agreement signed by him[6];

(2)   provide that payment of an allowance is conditional on the person providing the relevant education or training from time to time determining that the student has complied with the learning agreement or has done so to a prescribed extent or in prescribed respects[7];

(3)   enable or require a learning agreement to specify targets relating to the attendance, conduct or attainments of the student[8];

(4)   enable or require the Secretary of State or the Welsh Ministers, in any case where the person providing the relevant education or training determines that targets have been met, to make additional payments of allowance to or in respect of the student[9];

(5)   impose obligations relating to learning agreements on the governing body of a maintained school[10], or the governing body of an institution within the further education sector[11];

(6)   contain provision for determining the person by whom any relevant education or training is to be treated for the purposes of these provisions as being provided[12].

A learning agreement is not capable of creating any obligation in respect of whose breach any liability arises in contract or in tort[13].

1   'Regulations' means regulations made under the Education Act 2002 by the Secretary of State (in relation to England) or by the Welsh Ministers (in relation to Wales): s 212(1). As to the Secretary of State see PARA 58. The functions under the Education Act 2002 in relation to Wales were originally vested in the National Assembly for Wales and are now exercisable by the Welsh Ministers by virtue of the Government of Wales Act 2006 s 162(1), Sch 11 paras 30, 32. As to the Welsh Ministers see PARA 59. As to the meanings of 'England' and 'Wales' see PARA 7 note 3. At the date at which this volume states the law no such regulations had been made.

2   For these purposes, a 'learning agreement' is a document which: (1) specifies conditions which: (a) relate to the attendance or conduct of, or completion of assigned tasks by, a person to whom an allowance is or may become payable ('the student') (Education Act 2002 s 182(1)(a)(i)); and (b) are either prescribed by regulations or, if regulations so provide, determined in accordance with any prescribed requirements by the person providing the relevant education or training (s 182(1)(a)(ii)); (2) contains a declaration by the student relating to compliance with those conditions (s 182(1)(b)); and (3) deals with such other matters as may be prescribed

(s 182(1)(c)). 'Allowance' means an allowance under s 181 (see PARA 484); and 'relevant education or training' means the education or training referred to in s 181: s 182(8).

3   Education Act 2002 s 182(2)(a).
4   As to the meaning of 'person' see PARA 7 note 6.
5   Education Act 2002 s 182(2)(b).
6   Education Act 2002 s 182(3)(a). Section 182(3) is expressed to be without prejudice to the generality of the Education Act 2002 s 181(3)(h) (see PARA 484): s 182(3).
7   Education Act 2002 s 182(3)(b). See also note 6.
8   Education Act 2002 s 182(4)(a).
9   Education Act 2002 s 182(4)(b).
10   Education Act 2002 s 182(5)(a). Section 182(5) is expressed to be without prejudice to the generality of s 181(3)(k) (see PARA 484): s 182(5). For the purposes of ss 181 (see PARA 484) and 182, 'maintained school' means a community, foundation or voluntary school, a community or foundation special school or a pupil referral unit: s 181(4)(a). As to the meanings of references to a community, foundation or voluntary school or a community or foundation special school see PARA 106. As to pupil referral units see PARA 427 et seq. As to the governing bodies of maintained schools see PARA 150 et seq.
11   Education Act 2002 s 182(5)(b). See note 10. For the purposes of ss 181 (see PARA 484) and 182, 'governing body', in relation to an institution within the further education sector, has the meaning given by the Further and Higher Education Act 1992 s 90 (see PARA 560 note 6): Education Act 2002 s 181(4)(b). As to the meaning of references to institutions within the further education sector see PARA 555 (definition applied by s 212(2), (3)).
12   Education Act 2002 s 182(6).
13   Education Act 2002 s 182(7).

(iii) Educational Records

94. Educational records for pupils. Regulations[1] may make provision as to:

(1) the keeping, disclosure and transfer of educational records about persons receiving education at any school[2] maintained by a local authority[3], and any special school[4] not maintained by a local authority[5]; and

(2) the supply of copies of such records to such persons, and in such circumstances, as may be determined by or under the regulations[6].

The regulations may authorise persons who supply copies of such records in pursuance of the regulations to charge such fee as they think fit, not exceeding the cost of supply, in respect of each copy so supplied[7].

1   Ie regulations made by the Secretary of State or, in relation to Wales, the Welsh Ministers: see the Education Act 1996 s 579(1). As to the Secretary of State see PARA 58. The functions of the Secretary of State under the Education Act 1996 s 563, so far as exercisable in relation to Wales, were transferred to the National Assembly for Wales (see the National Assembly for Wales (Transfer of Functions) Order 1999, SI 1999/672, art 2, Sch 1) and are now vested in the Welsh Ministers (see the Government of Wales Act 2006 s 162(1), Sch 11 para 30). As to the Welsh Ministers see PARA 59. As to the meaning of 'Wales' see PARA 7 note 3. As to the regulations made see the Education (Pupil Information) (England) Regulations 2005, SI 2005/1437 (amended by SI 2007/3224; SI 2008/1747; SI 2012/765; SI 2012/979; SI 2013/3212; SI 2014/2103; and SI 2015/902); and the Pupil Information (Wales) Regulations 2011, SI 2011/1942; and the Head Teacher's Report to Parents and Adult Pupils (Wales) Regulations 2011, SI 2011/1943 (amended by SI 2013/437).
2   As to the meaning of 'school' see PARA 91.
3   See the Education Act 1996 s 563(3)(a) (amended by the School Standards and Framework Act 1998 s 140(1), Sch 30 para 172; SI 2010/1158). As to the meaning of 'local authority' see PARA 25. Any function of a local authority in England which is conferred by or under s 563 may be exercised by, or by employees of, such person as may be authorised in that behalf by the local authority whose function it is: Contracting Out (Local Authority Education Functions) (England) Order 2002, SI 2002/928, art 3, Sch 1 para (ccc) (art 3 amended by SI 2010/1172). As to the meaning of 'England' see PARA 7 note 3. As to the meaning of 'person' see PARA 7 note 6.
4   As to the meaning of 'special school' see PARA 1041.
5   See the Education Act 1996 s 563(1)(a), (3)(c) (amended by SI 2010/1158).

6   Education Act 1996 s 563(1)(b). In England a distinction is made between a 'curricular record' and an 'educational record'. 'Curricular record' means a formal record of a pupil's academic achievements, his other skills and abilities and his progress in school: see the Education (Pupil Information) (England) Regulations 2005, SI 2005/1437, reg 2(1). 'Educational record' means any record of information, including a pupil's curricular record, which: (1) is processed by or on behalf of the governing body of, or a teacher at, any school maintained by a local authority, or a special school which is not so maintained; (2) relates to any person who is or has been a pupil at the school; and (3) originated from or was supplied by or on behalf of any of the persons specified in heads (a)–(d) below, other than information which is processed by a teacher solely for the teacher's own use: see the Education (Pupil Information) (England) Regulations 2005, SI 2005/1437, reg 3(1), (2). The persons referred to in head (3) are: (a) an employee of the local authority which maintains the school (or, in the case of England only, the former school attended by the pupil to whom the record relates); (b) in the case of a voluntary aided, foundation or foundation special school, or a special school which is not maintained by a local authority, a teacher or other employee at the school (or, in relation to England only, at the pupil's former school), including an educational psychologist engaged by the governing body under a contract for services; (c) the pupil to whom the record relates; and (d) a parent of that pupil: see the Education (Pupil Information) (England) Regulations 2005, SI 2005/1437, reg 3(3). As to the meaning of 'pupil' see PARA 20 note 4. As to governing bodies of maintained schools see PARA 150 et seq. As to the meaning of 'parent' see PARA 7 note 6.

7   Education Act 1996 s 563(2). Within 15 school days of making a request in writing a parent is entitled to inspect the child's educational record, and is entitled to a copy of it, under the conditions provided for by the regulations: see the Education (Pupil Information) (England) Regulations 2005, SI 2005/1437, reg 5 (amended by SI 2012/979); and the Pupil Information (Wales) Regulations 2011, SI 2011/1942, reg 5. Generally as to information see also PARAS 48, 68, 69, 182.

(2) EARLY YEARS PROVISION AND NURSERY EDUCATION

(i) Meaning of 'Early Years Provision', 'Nursery Education', etc

95.   Meanings of 'childcare', 'young child', 'early years provision' and 'nursery education'.   In England there is a duty on local authorities to secure early years provision free of charge[1]. 'Early years provision' means the provision of childcare for a young child[2]. A child is a 'young child' during the period beginning with his birth, and ending immediately before the 1st September next following the date on which he attains the age of five[3]. 'Childcare' means any form of care for a child and includes education for a child, and any other supervised activity for a child, but does not include education (or any other supervised activity) provided by a school during school hours for a registered pupil who is not a young child, or any form of health care for a child[4].

A local authority in Wales must secure that the provision of nursery education is sufficient for its area[5]. For these purposes[6], 'nursery education' means full-time or part-time education suitable for children[7] who have not attained compulsory school age[8] (whether provided at schools[9] or elsewhere)[10].

1   See PARA 96. A local authority may also establish, maintain and assist nursery schools: see PARA 29.

2   See the Childcare Act 2006 ss 20, 96(2); and CHILDREN AND YOUNG PERSONS vol 10 (2012) PARA 1079.

3   See the Childcare Act 2006 s 19; and CHILDREN AND YOUNG PERSONS vol 10 (2012) PARA 1078.

4   See the Childcare Act 2006 s 18(1)–(3); and CHILDREN AND YOUNG PERSONS vol 10 (2012) PARA 1082.

Childcare also does not include care provided for a child by a parent or step-parent, or a person with parental responsibility for the child, a relative, a person who is a local authority foster parent in relation to the child, a person who is a foster parent with whom the child has been placed by a voluntary organisation or a person who fosters the child privately: see the Childcare Act 2006 s 18(4). Neither does it include care provided for a child if the care is provided in specified establishments as part of the establishment's activities, for example a children's home, a care home, a hospital in which the child is a patient, or a residential family centre, and is so provided by the person carrying on the establishment or a person employed to work at the establishment: see s 18(5), (6), (8) (s 18(5) amended by the Children and Young Persons Act 2008 s 8(2), Sch 1 para 19(1), (2); the Childcare Act 2006 s 18(8) amended by the Children and Young Persons Act 2008 ss 8(2), 42, Sch 1 para 19(1), (3), Sch 4; and by SI 2010/813); and CHILDREN AND YOUNG PERSONS vol 10 (2012) PARA 1082. 'Childcare' does not include care provided for a child who is detained in a young offender institution, a secure training centre, or a secure college: see the Childcare Act 2006 s 18(7) (amended by the Criminal Justice and Courts Act 2015 s 38(3), Sch 9 para 21); and CHILDREN AND YOUNG PERSONS vol 10 (2012) PARA 1082.

5 See PARA 97. A local authority may also establish, maintain and assist nursery schools: see PARA 29.
6 Ie the School Standards and Framework Act 1998 Pt V (ss 117–124).
7 As to the meaning of 'child' see PARA 7 note 6 (definition applied by the School Standards and Framework Act 1998 s 142(8)).
8 As to the meaning of 'compulsory school age' see PARA 19. As to the time at which a person attains a particular age see PARA 7 note 6.
9 As to the meaning of 'school' see PARA 91 (definition applied by the School Standards and Framework Act 1998 s 142(8)).
10 School Standards and Framework Act 1998 s 117.

(ii) Duties of the Local Authority as regards Early Years Provision and Nursery Education

96. Duty to secure early years provision free of charge in England. An English local authority must secure that early years provision[1] of such description as may be prescribed is available free of charge, in accordance with any regulations under for these purposes, for each young child in its area who is under compulsory school age, and is of such description as may be prescribed[2]. Such regulations may in particular include provision about how much early years provision is to be made available in pursuance of the duty imposed and the times at which, and periods over which, early years provision is to be made available in pursuance of that duty[3]. In discharging such a duty, a local authority must have regard to any guidance given from time to time by the Secretary of State[4].

1 As to the meanings of 'early years provision' and 'young child' see PARA 95. As to the meaning of 'compulsory school age' see PARA 19.
2 See the Childcare Act 2006 s 7(1) (s 7 substituted by the Education Act 2011 s 1(1), (2)); and CHILDREN AND YOUNG PERSONS vol 10 (2012) PARA 1083. 'Prescribed' means prescribed by regulations: Childcare Act 2006 s 106 (definition added by SI 2010/1080). As to the regulations made see the Local Authority (Duty to Secure Early Years Provision Free of Charge) Regulations 2014, SI 2014/2147. The regulations provide that a young child is of a prescribed description if the young child (1) has attained the age of two years at the start of the term beginning on or following the relevant date; and is an eligible child on or after the relevant date applicable to the child in question; or (2) has attained the age of three years at the start of the term beginning on or following the relevant date (see reg 3(1)–(3)). The relevant date is (a) in the case of a child who was born in the period 1st January to 31st March, 1st April following the child's birthday; (b) in the case of a child who was born in the period 1st April to 31st August, 1st September following the child's birthday; (c) in the case of a child who was born in the period 1st September to 31st December, 1st January following the child's birthday (see reg 3(4)). As to child care and early years provision in England under the Childcare Act 2006 see CHILDREN AND YOUNG PERSONS vol 10 (2012) PARA 1077 et seq.
   A local authority may also establish, maintain and assist nursery schools: see PARA 29.
3 See the Childcare Act 2006 s 7(2) (as substituted: see note 2); and CHILDREN AND YOUNG PERSONS vol 10 (2012) PARA 1083. An English local authority must secure that the prescribed early years provision is available for each young child for a period of 570 hours in any year and during no fewer than 38 weeks in any year: see the Local Authority (Duty to Secure Early Years Provision Free of Charge) Regulations 2014, SI 2014/2147, reg 4.
4 See the Childcare Act 2006 s 7(3) (as substituted: see note 2); and CHILDREN AND YOUNG PERSONS vol 10 (2012) PARA 1083. As to the Secretary of State see PARA 58.

The Childcare Act 2006 Pt 3 Ch 2 (ss 33–51) makes provision as to the regulation of early years provision: see CHILDREN AND YOUNG PERSONS vol 10 (2012) PARA 1091 et seq. In particular, there is a duty to implement the early years foundation stage (which precedes the four key stages of the curriculum: see PARA 860): see s 40; and CHILDREN AND YOUNG PERSONS vol 10 (2012) PARA 1097. As to the inspection of early years provision see PARA 1252.

97. Duty of local authority in Wales as respects availability of nursery education and establishment of early years development and childcare partnerships.

A local authority in Wales[1] must secure that the provision, whether or not by it, of nursery education[2] for children[3] who have not attained compulsory school age[4], but who have attained such age as may be prescribed[5], is sufficient for its area[6]. In determining for these purposes whether the provision of such education is sufficient for its area, a local authority may have regard to any facilities which it expects to be available outside its area for providing such education[7], and must have regard to any guidance given from time to time by the Welsh Ministers[8].

As from a day to be appointed the following provisions have effect[9].

Where a local authority in Wales, in pursuance of this duty[10], makes arrangements with a person[11], other than the governing body of a maintained school[12], for the provision by that person of nursery education[13] in consideration of financial assistance provided by the authority under the arrangements[14], it must:

(1) in making the arrangements, have regard to any guidance given from time to time by the Welsh Ministers as to provision to be made in such arrangements in respect of the requirements to be met by the provider of the nursery education[15]; and

(2) exercise its functions[16] with a view to securing that the provider meets any requirements imposed on him by the arrangements[17].

Subject to any guidance given under head (1) above, the requirements imposed by the arrangements may, in particular, if any specified conditions are not satisfied, require the repayment of the whole or any part of any financial assistance provided by the local authority under the arrangements[18].

Every local authority in Wales must establish for its area a body to be known as an early years development and childcare partnership[19]. In establishing the partnership and determining its constitution the authority must have regard to any guidance given from time to time by the Welsh Ministers[20].

The functions[21] of the partnership are to work with the authority in reviewing[22] the sufficiency of the provision of nursery education for the authority's area[23], and (until a day to be appointed) in reviewing[24] the sufficiency of childcare provision for the authority's area[25]. The Welsh Ministers may by order confer on early years development and childcare partnerships such additional functions as are specified in the order[26].

1 As to the meaning of 'local authority in Wales' see PARA 25 (definition applied by the School Standards and Framework Act 1998 s 142(8)).

2 As to the meaning of 'nursery education' see PARA 95.

3 As to the meaning of 'child' see PARA 7 note 6 (definition applied by the School Standards and Framework Act 1998 s 142(8)).

4 School Standards and Framework Act 1998 s 118(1)(a) (amended by SI 2010/1158). As to the meaning of 'compulsory school age' see PARA 19.

5 School Standards and Framework Act 1998 s 118(1)(b). 'Prescribed' means prescribed by regulations: s 142(1). As to the regulations made see the Education (Nursery Education and Early Years Development and Childcare Plans) (Wales) Regulations 2003, SI 2003/893 (amended by SI 2005/1813; SI 2006/877). As to the time at which a person attains a particular age see PARA 7 note 6.

6 School Standards and Framework Act 1998 s 118(1) (amended by the Childcare Act 2006 s 103(1), Sch 2 para 30(a)). As to the power of local authorities to establish and maintain nursery schools see the Education Act 1996 s 17; and PARA 29. As to local authority functions in relation to childcare see PARA 30.

7 School Standards and Framework Act 1998 s 118(2)(a) (amended by SI 2010/1158).

8 School Standards and Framework Act 1998 s 118(2)(b) (amended by the Childcare Act 2006 s 103(1), Sch 2 para 30(b)). The functions under School Standards and Framework Act 1998 ss 118, 119 (see the text and notes 19–26) and the Education Act 2002 s 153 (see the text to notes 9–18) in relation to Wales were originally vested in the National Assembly for Wales and are now exercisable by the Welsh Ministers by virtue of the Government of Wales Act 2006 s 162(1), Sch 11 paras 30, 32. As to the Welsh Ministers see PARA 59.

9 The Education Act 2002 s 153 will come into force in relation to Wales in accordance with provision made by the Welsh Ministers by order: see s 216(4). At the date at which this volume states the law no such order had been made.

10 Ie the duty imposed on it by the School Standards and Framework Act 1998 s 118: see the text to notes 1–8.

11 As to the meaning of 'person' see PARA 7 note 6.

12 For these purposes, 'maintained school' means a community, foundation or voluntary school, a community special school or a maintained nursery school: Education Act 2002 s 153(4) (definition amended by the School Standards and Organisation (Wales) Act 2013 Sch 5 para 21(1), (8)). As to the meanings of references to a community, foundation or voluntary school or a community special school see PARA 106. As to the meaning of 'maintained nursery school' see PARA 99 note 4 (definition applied by the Education Act 2002 s 212(2), (3)). As to governing bodies of maintained schools see PARA 150 et seq.

13 'Nursery education' means full-time or part-time education suitable for children who have not attained compulsory school age (whether provided at schools or elsewhere): Education Act 2002 s 153(4).

14 Education Act 2002 s 153(1) (amended by the Childcare Act 2006 s 103(1), Sch 2 para 41(a); SI 2010/1158).

15 Education Act 2002 s 153(2)(a) (amended by the Childcare Act 2006 s 103, Sch 2 para 41(b), Sch 3 Pt 2). As to the publication of guidance see the Education Act 1996 s 571 (applied by the Education Act 2002 s 212(2), (3)); and PARA 60.

16 As to the meaning of 'functions' see PARA 18 note 5 (definition applied by the Education Act 2002 s 212(2), (3)).

17 Education Act 2002 s 153(2)(b).

18 Education Act 2002 s 153(3) (amended by SI 2010/1158).

19 School Standards and Framework Act 1998 s 119(1) (amended by the Education Act 2002 s 150(5); Childcare Act 2006 s 103(1), Sch 2 para 32(1), (2); SI 2010/1158). As to child minding and day care for young children generally see CHILDREN AND YOUNG PERSONS vol 10 (2012) PARA 1075 et seq.

20 School Standards and Framework Act 1998 s 119(2) (amended by the Childcare Act 2006 s 103(1), Sch 2 para 32(1), (3)).
      The local authority may establish a sub-committee of the partnership for any part of its area: School Standards and Framework Act 1998 s 119(3). The authority must make arrangements for the meetings and proceedings of the partnership and any such sub-committee, and for the partnership (and any such sub-committee) to be provided with accommodation and with such services as the authority considers appropriate: s 119(4).

21 As to the meaning of 'functions' see PARA 18 note 5 (definition applied by the School Standards and Framework Act 1998 s 142(8)).

22 Ie for the purposes of the School Standards and Framework Act 1998 s 118: see the text and notes 1–8.

23 School Standards and Framework Act 1998 s 119(5)(a) (amended by the Education Act 2002 s 215(2), Sch 22 Pt 3).

24 Ie for the purposes of the School Standards and Framework Act 1998 s 118A: see PARA 30.

25 School Standards and Framework Act 1998 s 119(5)(ab) (added by the Education Act 2002 s 150(1); prospectively repealed by the Childcare Act 2006 s 103, Sch 2 para 32(1), (4), Sch 3 Pt 2). At the date at which this volume states the law no day had been appointed for the coming into force of this repeal.

26 School Standards and Framework Act 1998 s 119(6) (amended by the Education Act 2002 s 150(5); Childcare Act 2006 s 103(1), Sch 2 para 32(1), (5)). At the date at which this volume states the law, no such order had been made.

(iii) Provision of Teaching Services

98. Arrangements to provide teaching services for day nurseries etc. A local authority[1] may, in accordance with arrangements made by it for that purpose, make available to a day nursery[2] in England or Wales[3] or to a registered early years provider[4] in England the services of any teacher who[5] is employed by it in a nursery school[6] or in a primary school[7] having one or more nursery classes[8] and who has agreed to provide his services for the purposes of the arrangements[9]. Such arrangements in respect of a teacher in a foundation or voluntary school[10] require the concurrence of the governing body of the school[11].

The governing body of a community[12], foundation or voluntary primary school having one or more nursery classes may, in accordance with arrangements made by it for that purpose, make available to a day nursery in England or Wales or to a registered early years provider in England the services of any teacher who is employed by it in the school and who has agreed to provide his services for the purposes of the arrangements[13]. No such arrangements may be made except at the request of the local authority and on terms approved by it[14].

Such arrangements[15] may make provision: (1) for the supply of equipment for use in connection with the teaching services made available under the arrangements[16]; (2) for regulating the respective functions[17] of any teacher whose services are made available under the arrangements, the head teacher[18] of his school and the person in charge of the day nursery or (as the case may be) the registered early years provider[19]; and (3) for any supplementary or incidental matters connected with the arrangements, including (a) in relation to England, any charges to be imposed in connection with the arrangements[20], and (b) in relation to Wales, where the teacher's school and the day nursery are in the areas of different local authorities, financial adjustments between those authorities[21].

A teacher is not to be regarded as ceasing to be a member of the teaching staff of his school and subject to the general directions of his head teacher by reason only of his services being made available in pursuance of arrangements as described above[22].

1   As to the meaning of 'local authority' see PARA 25.
2   'Day nursery' means a day nursery provided under the Children Act 1989 s 18 (see CHILDREN AND YOUNG PERSONS vol 10 (2012) PARA 825): Education Act 1996 ss 515(4), 535(4) (both substituted by the Childcare Act 2006 s 103(1), Sch 2 para 26(1), (4)).
3   As to the meanings of 'England' and 'Wales' see PARA 7 note 3.
4   'Registered early years provider' means a person registered under the Childcare Act 2006 Pt 3 (ss 31–98G) (see CHILDREN AND YOUNG PERSONS vol 10 (2012) PARA 1090 et seq): Education Act 1996 ss 515(4), 535(4) (both as substituted: see note 2). As to the meaning of 'person' see PARA 7 note 6.
5   Education Act 1996 s 515(1) (amended by the Childcare Act 2006 s 103(1), Sch 2 para 25(1), (2); SI 2010/1158).
6   As to the meaning of 'nursery school' see PARA 91.
7   As to the meaning of 'primary school' see PARA 91.
8   Education Act 1996 s 515(1)(a).
9   Education Act 1996 s 515(1)(b).
10   As to the meaning of references to foundation schools and voluntary schools see PARA 106 (definitions applied by the School Standards and Framework Act 1998 s 140(2)).
11   Education Act 1996 s 515(2) (amended by the School Standards and Framework Act 1998 s 140(1), Sch 30 paras 57, 136). As to the governing bodies of maintained schools see PARA 150 et seq. While staff who are appointed to work under a contract of employment at voluntary controlled schools are employed by the local authority (see the Education Act 2002 s 35; and

PARA 268), staff who are appointed to work under a contract of employment at foundation schools and voluntary aided schools are employed by the governing body of the school (see the Education Act 2002 s 36; and PARA 280).

12 As to the meaning of references to community schools see PARA 106 (definition applied by the School Standards and Framework Act 1998 s 140(2)).

13 Education Act 1996 s 535(1) (amended by the School Standards and Framework Act 1998 Sch 30 paras 57, 150; Childcare Act 2006 s 103(1), Sch 2 para 26(1), (2)).

14 Education Act 1996 s 535(2) (amended by SI 2010/1158).

15 Ie under the Education Act 1996 ss 515, 535: see the text to notes 1–14.

16 Education Act 1996 ss 515(3)(a), 535(3)(a).

17 As to the meaning of 'functions' see PARA 18 note 5.

18 As to the meaning of 'head teacher' see PARA 86 note 4.

19 Education Act 1996 ss 515(3)(b), 535(3)(b) (both amended by the Childcare Act 2006 s 103(1), Sch 2 para 26(1), (3)(a)).

20 Education Act 1996 ss 515(3)(c)(i), 535(3)(c)(i) (ss 515(3)(c), 535(3)(c) both amended by the Childcare Act 2006 s 103(1), Sch 2 para 26(1), (3)(b)).

21 Education Act 1996 ss 515(3)(c)(ii), 535(3)(c)(ii) (both as amended (see note 20); and further amended by SI 2010/1158).

22 Education Act 1996 ss 515(5), 535(5).

(3) SCHOOLS

(i) General Provisions relating to Maintained Schools

99. Meaning of 'maintained school'. Unless the context otherwise requires[1], 'maintained school' means a community, foundation or voluntary school or a community or foundation special school[2].

'School maintained by a local authority', in relation to any time on or after 1 September 1999[3], means a community, foundation or voluntary school, a community or foundation special school, a maintained nursery school[4] or a pupil referral unit[5].

1 Ie except in the School Standards and Framework Act 1998 Pt III (ss 84–109): see PARA 225 et seq.

2 School Standards and Framework Act 1998 ss 20(7), 142(1). As to community, foundation and voluntary schools and community and foundation special schools see PARA 106 et seq. As to special schools see PARA 1041 et seq. As to the meaning of 'maintained school' in relation to special educational needs see PARAS 943 note 8, 989 note 10. As to academies see PARA 345 et seq.

3 Ie the appointed day: see the School Standards and Framework Act 1998 (Appointed Day) Order 1998, SI 1998/2083, art 2; and PARA 106 note 3.

4 'Maintained nursery school' means a nursery school which is maintained by a local authority and is not a special school: Education Act 1996 s 579(1) (definition added by the Education Act 2002 s 215(1), Sch 21 para 57(a); and amended by SI 2010/1158); School Standards and Framework Act 1998 s 22(9) (amended by SI 2010/1158). As to nursery education see PARA 95 et seq.

5 School Standards and Framework Act 1998 s 142(1) (definition amended by SI 2010/1158). As to the meaning of 'pupil referral unit' see PARA 427 (definition applied by the School Standards and Framework Act 1998 s 142(8)). In the School Standards and Framework Act 1998, in relation to a school maintained (or proposed to be maintained) by a local authority, 'the local authority' means that authority: s 22(8)(a) (amended by SI 2010/1158). As to the meaning of 'local authority' see PARA 25 (definition applied by the School Standards and Framework Act 1998 s 142(8)).

100. Specialist schools. The Specialist Schools Programme helped schools, in partnership with private sector sponsors and supported by additional government funding, to establish distinctive identities through their chosen specialisms and achieve their targets to raise standards. Any maintained secondary school[1] and any maintained or non-maintained special school in

England could apply for specialist status in one of ten curriculum specialisms: arts, business and enterprise, engineering, humanities, languages, mathematics and computing, music, science, sports, and technology. Special schools could, alternatively, apply for a special educational needs specialism[2].

Changes were announced in 2010 which removed the need for schools to designate or re-designate as specialist, and stating that money currently paid as specialist schools grant would continue to be routed to schools through the mainstream funding[3].

1   As to categories of maintained schools see PARA 106.
2   As to special educational needs and disabilities see PARA 941 et seq. As to special schools see PARA 1041 et seq.
3   See *Specialist schools programme: Michael Gove announces changes* (20 October 2010), available at the date at which this volume states the law on the Government website.

101. Grammar schools. The Secretary of State or, in relation to Wales, the Welsh Ministers may designate a maintained school which has selective admission arrangements as a grammar school[1]. A school has selective admission arrangements if its admission arrangements make provision for all, or substantially all, of its pupils to be selected by reference to general ability, with a view to admitting only pupils with high ability[2]. The Secretary of State or the Welsh Ministers may make provision by regulations for a ballot to be held at the request of the parents to determine whether a school should become, remain or cease to be a grammar school[3].

1   See the School Standards and Framework Act 1998 s 104; and PARA 263.
2   See the School Standards and Framework Act 1998 s 104(2); and PARA 263.
3   See the School Standards and Framework Act 1998 s 105; and PARA 264.

102. Charitable status of maintained schools etc. The following bodies are charities[1]:

(1)   the governing body[2] of any foundation, voluntary or foundation special school[3]; and

(2)   any foundation body[4];

but no governing body of a community or community special school may be a charity[5]. Any body to which head (1) or (2) applies is[6] an exempt charity for the purposes of the Charities Act 2011[7].

Any foundation[8] established otherwise than under the School Standards and Framework Act 1998 which has no property other than the premises[9] of any school or schools falling within head (1) above is a charity, and is a relevant institution[10] for the purposes of the Charities Act 2011[11].

1   School Standards and Framework Act 1998 s 23(1) (amended by the Charities Act 2006 s 75(1), (2), Sch 8 paras 193, 194(1), (2), Sch 9). As to charities see CHARITIES. As to educational trusts see PARA 1371 et seq.
2   As to the governing bodies of maintained schools see PARA 150 et seq.
3   School Standards and Framework Act 1998 s 23(1)(a). As to foundation schools, voluntary schools and foundation special schools see PARA 106.
4   School Standards and Framework Act 1998 s 23(1)(b). A foundation body is one established under s 21 (see PARA 108): see s 23(1)(b).
5   School Standards and Framework Act 1998 s 23(1). As to community and community special schools see PARA 106.
6   Ie as a result of its inclusion in the Charities Act 2011 Sch 3: see CHARITIES vol 8 (2015) PARA 318.
7   See the School Standards and Framework Act 1998 s 23(1A) (added by the Charities Act 2006 s 75(1), Sch 8 paras 193, 194(1), (3); and substituted by the Charities Act 2011 Sch 7 para 75(1)). As to exempt charities see CHARITIES vol 8 (2015) PARA 318 et seq.

8 As to the meaning of 'foundation' see PARA 108 note 6.

9 'Premises' includes a teacher's dwelling-house: School Standards and Framework Act 1998 s 23(4)(b). As to the meaning of 'premises' generally see PARA 62 note 19 (definition applied by s 142(8)).

10 'Institution' has the same meaning as in the Charities Act 2011 (see CHARITIES vol 8 (2015) PARA 1): School Standards and Framework Act 1998 s 23(4)(a) (substituted by the Charities Act 2011 Sch 7 paras 75(1), (3)).

11 Ie an institution which is to be treated for the purposes of the Charities Act 2011 s 31(3) (see CHARITIES vol 8 (2015) PARA 308) as if that provision applied to it: see the School Standards and Framework Act 1998 s 23(3) (amended by the Charities Act 2011 Sch 7 para 75(1), (2)).

103. Communications with schools. In considering whether to issue any guidance or other circular to the governing bodies[1] or head teachers[2] of maintained schools[3] in the exercise of functions[4] relating to education[5], the Secretary of State[6] and the Welsh Ministers[7] must have regard to:

(1) the desirability of providing information about good educational practice, while recognising the professional expertise of teachers[8];

(2) the benefits that are expected to result from the issue of the guidance or other circular[9]; and

(3) the desirability of avoiding the sending of excessive material to governing bodies or head teachers, and the imposition of excessive administrative burdens on governing bodies or head teachers[10].

In pursuance of the above duty[11], the Secretary of State must in respect of each academic year[12]:

(a) prepare a report listing: (i) documents sent by him during the year to all governing bodies of maintained schools in England[13] or to all head teachers of such schools[14]; and (ii) documents (not falling within head (i) above) sent by him during the year to all governing bodies of maintained schools in England of a particular kind or to all head teachers of such schools of a particular kind[15]; and

(b) lay a copy of the report before each House of Parliament, and include within it comparative statistics in respect of each of the two preceding academic years on documents[16] sent out by him[17].

In pursuance of the above duty[18], the Welsh Ministers must in respect of each academic year prepare and publish a report listing:

(A) documents sent by them during the year to all governing bodies of maintained schools in Wales or to all head teachers of such schools[19]; and

(B) documents (not falling within head (A) above) sent by them during the year to all governing bodies of maintained schools in Wales of a particular kind or to all head teachers of such schools of a particular kind[20].

The documents referred to above[21] do not include any document sent by the Secretary of State or the Welsh Ministers otherwise than in the exercise of functions relating to education, or at the request of the person[22] to whom it is sent[23].

Each document issued by the Secretary of State or the Welsh Ministers and falling within head (i) or head (ii), or head (A) or head (B) above must list within it previous relevant documents issued by the Secretary of State or the Welsh Ministers and must state clearly those documents which are superseded by the current document[24]; and each such document must also state clearly the persons for whom any advice and guidance is intended[25].

1 As to the governing bodies of maintained schools see PARA 150 et seq.

2   As to the meaning of 'head teacher' see PARA 86 note 4 (definition applied by the Education Act 2002 s 212(2), (3)).

3   For the purposes of the Education Act 2002 Pt 3 Ch 1 (ss 19–40), 'maintained school' means a community, foundation or voluntary school, a community or foundation special school or a maintained nursery school; and 'maintained nursery school' means a nursery school which is maintained by a local authority and is not a special school: s 39(1) (definition amended by SI 2010/1158). As to the meanings of references to a community, foundation or voluntary school or a community or foundation special school see PARA 106. As to the meaning of 'nursery school' see PARA 91; and as to the meaning of 'special school' see PARA 1041 (definitions applied by the Education Act 2002 s 212(2), (3)). As to the meaning of 'local authority' see PARA 25 (definition applied by s 212(1) (amended by SI 2010/1158)).

4   As to the meaning of 'functions' see PARA 18 note 5 (definition applied by the Education Act 2002 s 212(2), (3)).

5   See generally PARA 60 et seq.

6   As to the Secretary of State see PARA 58.

7   The functions under the Education Act 2002 s 38 in relation to Wales were originally vested in the National Assembly for Wales and are now exercisable by the Welsh Ministers by virtue of the Government of Wales Act 2006 s 162(1), Sch 11 paras 30, 32. As to the Welsh Ministers see PARA 59. As to the meaning of 'Wales' see PARA 7 note 3.

8   Education Act 2002 s 38(1)(a).

9   Education Act 2002 s 38(1)(b).

10 Education Act 2002 s 38(1)(c).

11 Ie the duty in the Education Act 2002 s 38(1): see the text to notes 1–10.

12 'Academic year' means a period beginning with 1 August and ending with the next 31 July: Education Act 2002 s 38(7).

13 As to the meaning of 'England' see PARA 7 note 3.

14 Education Act 2002 s 38(2)(a)(i).

15 Education Act 2002 s 38(2)(a)(ii).

16 Ie falling within the Education Act 2002 s 38(2).

17 Education Act 2002 s 38(2)(b). As to the laying of documents before Parliament see STATUTES AND LEGISLATIVE PROCESS vol 96 (2012) PARA 1052.

18 Ie the duty in the Education Act 2002 s 38(1): see the text to notes 1–10.

19 Education Act 2002 s 38(3)(a).

20 Education Act 2002 s 38(3)(b).

21 Ie referred to in the Education Act 2002 s 38(2), (3): see the text to notes 11–20.

22 As to the meaning of 'person' see PARA 7 note 6.

23 Education Act 2002 s 38(4).

24 Education Act 2002 s 38(5).

25 See the Education Act 2002 s 38(6).

104.   Partnership agreements and statements between local authorities and governing bodies in Wales.   The Welsh Ministers[1] may by regulations[2] require any local authority[3] in Wales to enter into a partnership agreement[4] with the governing body of each school maintained by that authority, or each such school of a prescribed class[5]. Where a local authority fails to reach agreement with the governing body of a school for these purposes, the authority may draw up a statement setting out how it and the governing body are to discharge their respective functions[6] in relation to the school[7].

Regulations may:

(1)   require the parties to a partnership agreement to review the agreement[8]; and

(2)   require a local authority that has drawn up a statement and the governing body to which that statement relates to review the statement[9],

at such intervals, or in such circumstances, as may be prescribed[10]. Following a review of a partnership agreement, the parties may agree: (a) not to change the agreement[11]; (b) to amend the agreement in such a manner that it remains a partnership agreement[12]; or (c) to replace the agreement with a new partnership agreement[13]. However, where they fail to do so, the authority may draw up a statement setting out how it and the governing body are to discharge their respective functions in relation to the school[14].

Following a review of a statement, the local authority and governing body in question may agree to replace the statement with a partnership agreement, but, where they fail to do so, the authority may amend the statement or draw up a new one (provided the amended or replacement statement is one that could have been drawn up under the provisions[15] relating to such statements)[16].

Regulations may make provision for the time by which a local authority or governing body must comply with any requirement imposed upon them by or under any of the preceding provisions[17].

In the discharge of their functions in relation to a school maintained by a local authority in Wales the authority[18], and the governing body and head teacher[19], of the school must have regard to any partnership agreement or statement which for the time being has effect in relation to the school[20].

1　The functions under the Education Act 2002 s 197 in relation to Wales were originally vested in the National Assembly for Wales and are now exercisable by the Welsh Ministers by virtue of the Government of Wales Act 2006 s 162(1), Sch 11 paras 30, 32. As to the Welsh Ministers see PARA 59. As to the meaning of 'Wales' see PARA 7 note 3.
2　As to the regulations made see the Maintained Schools (Partnership Agreements) (Wales) Regulations 2007, SI 2007/3066.
3　As to the meaning of 'local authority' see PARA 25 (definition applied by the Education Act 2002 s 212(1) (amended by SI 2010/1158)).
4　For these purposes, a 'partnership agreement' is an agreement about how a local authority and the governing body of a school are to discharge their respective functions in relation to the school as regards: (1) such matters as may be prescribed (Education Act 2002 s 197(2)(a) (s 197(2) amended by SI 2010/1158)); and (2) such other matters as the authority and the governing body may agree (Education Act 2002 s 197(2)(b)). 'Prescribed' means prescribed by regulations: s 212(1). As to the meaning of 'school' see PARA 91; and as to the meaning of 'functions' see PARA 18 note 5 (definitions applied by s 212(2), (3)). As to the governing bodies of maintained schools see PARA 150 et seq. As to maintained schools see PARA 106 et seq.
5　Education Act 2002 s 197(1) (amended by SI 2010/1158).
6　Ie as regards the matters prescribed under the Education Act 2002 s 197(2)(a): see note 4.
7　Education Act 2002 s 197(3) (amended by SI 2010/1158).
8　Education Act 2002 s 197(4)(a).
9　Education Act 2002 s 197(4)(b) (amended by SI 2010/1158).
10　Education Act 2002 s 197(4).
11　Education Act 2002 s 197(5)(a).
12　Education Act 2002 s 197(5)(b).
13　Education Act 2002 s 197(5)(c).
14　Ie the Education Act 2002 s 197(3) (see the text to notes 6–7) applies as it applies where a local authority and governing body fail to reach agreement for the purposes of s 197(1): see s 197(5) (amended by SI 2010/1158).
15　Ie under the Education Act 2002 s 197(3); see the text to notes 6–7.
16　Education Act 2002 s 197(6) (amended by SI 2010/1158).
17　Education Act 2002 s 197(7) (amended by SI 2010/1158).
18　Education Act 2002 s 197(8)(a) (amended by SI 2010/1158).
19　Education Act 2002 s 197(8)(b). As to the meaning of 'head teacher' see PARA 86 note 4 (definition applied by s 212(2), (3)).
20　Education Act 2002 s 197(8).

105. Plans to facilitate the transition from primary school to secondary school of pupils in Wales. The Welsh Ministers[1] may require:
(1)　the governing body[2] of each secondary school[3] maintained by a local authority[4] in Wales, or of each such secondary school belonging to a class specified in the requirement[5]; and
(2)　the governing body of each of its feeder primary schools[6] maintained by such an authority[7],

jointly to draw up plans to facilitate the transition from primary school to secondary school of pupils[8] at those primary schools who are admitted to the secondary school[9].

Regulations[10] may:

(a)   provide for the Welsh Ministers to determine any disputes as to whether a particular school is a feeder primary school of a particular secondary school for these purposes[11]; and

(b)   make provision about plans under these provisions, including provision which specifies the period within which such plans are to be drawn up and provision about the content, review and amendment of such plans[12].

In carrying out any functions[13] conferred on them by or under these provisions, governing bodies must have regard to any guidance given, from time to time, by the Welsh Ministers[14]. In the discharge of their functions under any enactment, the governing body of a school maintained by a local authority in Wales, and the head teacher[15] of that school, must have regard to any plans drawn up by the governing body under these provisions which for the time being have effect[16].

1   The functions under the Education Act 2002 s 198 in relation to Wales were originally vested in the National Assembly for Wales and are now exercisable by the Welsh Ministers by virtue of the Government of Wales Act 2006 s 162(1), Sch 11 paras 30, 32. As to the Welsh Ministers see PARA 59. As to the meaning of 'Wales' see PARA 7 note 3.

2   As to the governing bodies of maintained schools see PARA 150 et seq.

3   As to the meaning of 'secondary school' see PARA 91 (definition applied by the Education Act 2002 s 212(2), (3)).

4   As to the meaning of 'local authority' see PARA 25 (definition applied by the Education Act 2002 s 212(1) (amended by SI 2010/1158)).

5   Education Act 2002 s 198(1)(a) (amended by SI 2010/1158).

6   In determining whether, for these purposes, a particular school is to be regarded as a feeder primary school, in relation to a particular secondary school, regard is to be had to any guidance given, from time to time, by the Welsh Ministers: Education Act 2002 s 198(2). As to the meaning of 'primary school' see PARA 91 (definition applied by s 212(2), (3)). As to the issue of guidance see s 38; and PARA 103.

7   Education Act 2002 s 198(1)(b).

8   As to the meaning of 'pupil' see PARA 20 note 4 (definition applied by the Education Act 2002 s 212(2), (3)).

9   Education Act 2002 s 198(1).

10   Ie regulations made under the Education Act 2002 by the Welsh Ministers: see s 212(1). As to the regulations made see the Transition from Primary to Secondary School (Wales) Regulations 2006, SI 2006/520.

11   Education Act 2002 s 198(3)(a).

12   Education Act 2002 s 198(3)(b).

13   As to the meaning of 'functions' see PARA 18 note 5 (definition applied by the Education Act 2002 s 212(2), (3)).

14   Education Act 2002 s 198(4).

15   As to the meaning of 'head teacher' see PARA 86 note 4 (definition applied by the Education Act 2002 s 212(2), (3)).

16   Education Act 2002 s 198(5)(b) (amended by SI 2010/1158).

(ii) Categories of Maintained Schools

106. Categorisation of maintained schools. Schools[1] maintained by local authorities[2] on or after 1 September 1999[3] are divided into the following categories[4]:

(1)   community schools[5];

(2)   foundation schools[6];

(3)   voluntary schools, comprising: (a) voluntary aided schools[7]; and (b) voluntary controlled schools[8];

(4)   community special schools[9]; and

(5)   foundation special schools[10].

Provision was made for, and in connection with, the allocation to these categories[11] of schools which immediately before 1 September 1999 were: (i) county schools[12], voluntary schools (which comprised controlled schools, aided schools and special agreement schools)[13] or maintained special schools[14]; or (ii) grant-maintained schools[15] or grant-maintained special schools[16].

As from 1 September 1999, a local authority must: (A) maintain (as a school falling within heads (1) to (5) above) any school within head (i) above which was maintained by the authority immediately before that date[17]; and (B) maintain any school within head (ii) above which immediately before that date was situated within the authority's area[18].

Unless the context otherwise requires, any reference in any Act amended by the School Standards and Framework Act 1998, or in the Education Act 2002, the Education Act 2005, the Education and Inspections Act 2006, the Education and Skills Act 2008, the Apprenticeships, Skills, Children and Learning Act 2009 or in any Act amended by those Acts, or in the Academies Act 2010, to a community, foundation or voluntary school or a community or foundation special school is to such a school within the meaning of the above provisions[19].

In the context of categorisation mention should also be made of academies and free schools[20].

1   For the purposes of the School Standards and Framework Act 1998 s 20, 'school' means a primary, secondary or special school including a nursery school which is a special school, but excluding both a nursery school which is not a special school and a pupil referral unit: s 20(6). As to the meanings of 'school' generally, 'primary school', 'secondary school' and 'nursery school' see PARA 91 (definitions applied by s 142(8)). As to the meaning of 'special school' see PARA 1041; and as to the meaning of 'pupil referral unit' see PARA 427 (definitions applied by s 142(8)). 'Schools' can include certain types of academies (see further PARA 91) and as to academies see PARA 345.

2   As to the meaning of 'school maintained by a local authority' see PARA 99. As to the meaning of 'local authority' see PARA 25 (definition applied by the School Standards and Framework Act 1998 s 142(8)).

3   Ie on or after the appointed day: see the School Standards and Framework Act 1998 s 20(1). For the purposes of the School Standards and Framework Act 1998, 'the appointed day' (except in s 144, Sch 32 Pt I (transitional provisions)) means such day as may be appointed for the purposes of s 20 by an order made by the Secretary of State: s 20(7). The day appointed is 1 September 1999: see the School Standards and Framework Act 1998 (Appointed Day) Order 1998, SI 1998/2083, art 2. As to the Secretary of State see PARA 58.

4   School Standards and Framework Act 1998 s 20(1) (amended by SI 2010/1158). A school maintained by a local authority is a school falling within one of the categories set out in the School Standards and Framework Act 1998 s 20(1) if: (1) it became a school of that category on the appointed day in accordance with Sch 2 (and has not changed its category under the change of category provisions) (s 20(2)(a) (s 20(2)(a)–(c) amended by the Education and Inspections Act 2006 s 30, Sch 3 para 13(1), (2); SI 2010/1158)); or (2) it was established as a school of that category under any enactment (and has not changed its category under the change of category provisions) (School Standards and Framework Act 1998 s 20(2)(b) (as so amended; and further amended by the Education Act 2002 s 215(1), Sch 21 para 95)); or (3) it has become a school of that category in accordance with the change of category provisions (School Standards and Framework Act 1998 s 20(2)(c) (as so amended)). 'The change of category provisions' means: (a) in the case of a school in England, Sch 8 (repealed) or the Education and Inspections Act 2006 ss 18–24 (see PARA 132 et seq), and (b) in the case of a school in Wales, the School Standards and Framework Act 1998 Sch 8 (repealed) or the School Standards and Organisation (Wales) Act 2013 ss 45–55 (see PARA 141 et seq): School Standards and Framework Act 1998 s 20(2A) (added by the Education and Inspections Act 2006 s 30, Sch 3 para 13(1), (3); and

amended by the School Standards and Organisation (Wales) Act 2013 Sch 5 para 19(1), (2)). As to the meanings of 'England' and 'Wales' see PARA 7 note 3.

5   School Standards and Framework Act 1998 s 20(1)(a). As to community schools see PARA 107.

6   School Standards and Framework Act 1998 s 20(1)(b). As to foundation schools see PARA 108.

7   School Standards and Framework Act 1998 s 20(1)(c)(i). Any reference in the School Standards and Framework Act 1998 to the categories set out in s 20(1) or to any such category is to be read, in its application to voluntary schools, as (or as including) a reference to the sub-categories set out in s 20(1)(c)(i) (ie voluntary aided schools) and s 20(1)(c)(ii) (ie voluntary controlled schools: see head (3)(b) in the text) or to any such sub-category: s 20(8). As to voluntary schools see PARA 108.

8   School Standards and Framework Act 1998 s 20(1)(c)(ii). See also note 7.

9   School Standards and Framework Act 1998 s 20(1)(d). As to the meaning of 'special school' see PARA 1041 (definition applied by s 142(8)).

10 School Standards and Framework Act 1998 s 20(1)(e).

11 See the School Standards and Framework Act 1998 Sch 2. The allocation of a school to a particular category was not to be taken as authorising or requiring any change as from 1 September 1999 in the character of the school conducted by its governing body (including, in particular, any religious character of the school): Sch 2 para 11. As to schools having a religious character see PARAS 916–917.

Provision was also made in relation to the transfer of staff on the date of reallocation: see s 73 (amended by SI 2010/1158).

12 Before 1 September 1999, a primary or secondary school which was maintained by a local education authority (as then was) was a county school if: (1) it was established by a local education authority (Education Act 1996 s 31(1)(a) (repealed)); or (2) it was not so established but (a) it had been maintained as a county school since before 1 November 1996; or (b) it was maintained as a county school in pursuance of proposals under s 35(1)(b) (repealed) (proposals to maintain as a county school a school not for the time being a county school); or (c) it was maintained as a county school in pursuance of an order under s 50 (repealed) (division of a county school) (s 31(1)(b) (repealed)). Nothing in s 31 (repealed) applied to a nursery school, a special school or a pupil referral unit within the meaning of s 19 (exceptional provision of education in pupil referral units or elsewhere): s 31(3) (repealed). County schools are now community schools: see the School Standards and Framework Act 1998 Sch 2 para 1.

13 Before 1 September 1999, there were three categories of voluntary school: (1) controlled schools; (2) aided schools; and (3) special agreement schools: Education Act 1996 s 32(1) (repealed). The category of a voluntary school depended on whether or not an order had been made in relation to it: see s 32(2)–(4) (repealed). A primary or secondary school which was maintained by a local education authority was a voluntary school if it was not within s 31(1)(a) (repealed) or (1)(b) (repealed) (see note 12): s 31(2) (repealed). Controlled schools are now voluntary controlled schools; and aided schools and special agreement schools are now voluntary aided schools: see the School Standards and Framework Act 1998 Sch 2 para 1.

14 School Standards and Framework Act 1998 s 20(3)(a). Before 1 September 1999, a special school was a maintained special school if it was maintained by a local education authority (as then was): see the Education Act 1996 s 33(1) (repealed), s 337(3) (as originally enacted). Maintained special schools are now community special schools: see the School Standards and Framework Act 1998 Sch 2 para 1.

15 Before 1 September 1999, a school conducted by a governing body incorporated under the Education Act 1996 Pt III (ss 183–311) (repealed), the Education Act 1993 Pt II (ss 22–155) (repealed) or the Education Reform Act 1988 Pt I Ch IV (ss 52–104) (repealed) for the purpose of conducting the school was known as a grant-maintained school: see the Education Act 1996 s 183(1) (repealed). Under the Education Act 1996, a grant-maintained school had to be either a secondary school or a primary school: s 183(3) (repealed). As to the allocation of grant-maintained schools to the categories of schools introduced by the School Standards and Framework Act 1998 see Sch 2 para 3.

16 School Standards and Framework Act 1998 s 20(3)(b). Before 1 September 1999, a special school was a grant-maintained special school if it was conducted by a governing body incorporated in pursuance of proposals for the purpose made by the funding authority under the Education Act 1996 s 339 (repealed) (establishment of maintained or grant-maintained special schools) or under the Education Act 1993 s 183 (repealed) (establishment of maintained or grant-maintained special schools), or made under the Education Act 1996 s 345 (repealed) (maintained special school becoming grant-maintained special school) or the Education Act 1993 s 186 (repealed) (maintained special school becoming grant-maintained special

school): see the Education Act 1996 s 337(4) (as originally enacted). As to the allocation of grant-maintained special schools to the categories of schools introduced by the School Standards and Framework Act 1998 see Sch 2 para 3.

17 School Standards and Framework Act 1998 s 20(4)(a) (s 20(4) amended by SI 2010/1158).

18 School Standards and Framework Act 1998 s 20(4)(b). However, where a grant-maintained school within s 20(3)(b) (see head (ii) in the text) was, immediately before becoming such a school, maintained by a local authority ('the former maintaining authority') other than the one within whose area it was then situated, and remained outside the area of the former maintaining authority immediately before 1 September 1999, nevertheless, if an order made by the Secretary of State before 1 September 1999 so provided, as from that day the school is to be maintained (as a school falling within one of the categories set out in s 20(1) (see heads (1) to (5) in the text)) by the former maintaining authority rather than the authority in whose area it was situated on that day: s 20(5) (amended by SI 2010/1158). Such an order was not to be made by statutory instrument (see the School Standards and Framework Act 1998 s 138(2)) and as such is not recorded in this title. The Secretary of State could only make an order under s 20(5) where he considered it appropriate to do so on an application made for the purpose by the former maintaining authority (within the meaning of s 20(5)) or the local education authority (as then was) in whose area the school in question was situated immediately before 1 September 1999, and received by him not later than 30 November 1998: see s 144(7), Sch 32 para 8.

19 School Standards and Framework Act 1998 s 140(2); Education Act 2002 s 212(5); Education Act 2005 s 122(5); Education and Inspections Act 2006 s 187(5); Education and Skills Act 2008 s 168(6); Apprenticeships, Skills, Children and Learning Act 2009 s 264(6); Academies Act 2010 s 17(5).

20 As to academies see PARAS 91, 345 et seq and as to free schools see PARAS 91, 368. See also note 1.

107. Community schools. Community schools, formerly known as county schools[1], are wholly maintained by their local authorities[2]. In the case of such a school, the local authority owns the school premises[3], employs the staff[4], and is responsible for admissions arrangements[5].

1 See PARA 106.
2 As to local authorities see PARA 25.
3 As to school premises see PARA 1295 et seq.
4 As to staffing of schools see PARA 268 et seq.
5 As to admissions generally see PARA 224 et seq.

108. Foundation and voluntary schools. In the case of a foundation school, the school premises[1] are owned either by the governing body[2] or by a charitable foundation[3], and the governing body employs the staff[4] and is responsible for admissions[5]. There are three kinds of foundation school:

(1) those having a foundation[6] established otherwise than under the School Standards and Framework Act 1998[7];

(2) those belonging to a group of schools for which a foundation body acts under the provisions relating to foundation schools and types of foundations[8]; and

(3) those not falling within either of heads (1) and (2) above[9].

A voluntary school is maintained by the local authority[10], although the school premises are generally owned by a charitable foundation. In the case of a voluntary aided school, the governing body contributes towards the capital costs of running the school[11], employs the staff, and is responsible for admissions. In the case of a voluntary controlled school, the local authority employs the staff and is responsible for admissions. There are three kinds of voluntary controlled or voluntary aided school:

(a) those having a foundation established otherwise than under the School Standards and Framework Act 1998[12];

(b)   those belonging to a group of schools for which a foundation body acts under the provisions relating to voluntary schools and types of foundations[13]; and

(c)   those not falling within either of heads (a) and (b) above but having been, immediately before 1 September 1999[14], either a voluntary school[15] or a grant-maintained school[16] that was a voluntary school immediately before becoming grant-maintained[17].

The appropriate national authority[18] may by regulations[19] make provision for and in connection with the establishment, membership, functions and winding up of a foundation body[20], and the steps to be taken in connection with schools joining or leaving the group[21]. Such regulations may, in particular, make provision:

(i)   with respect to the transfer of property, rights and liabilities[22] to and from a foundation body when schools join or leave the group but do not[23] change category[24];

(ii)   with respect to the revision or replacement of the instruments of government of schools joining or leaving the group in such circumstances and the reconstitution of their governing bodies[25];

(iii)   authorising a foundation body to appoint foundation governors to every school in the group[26];

(iv)   prescribing a model instrument of government for adoption by a foundation body subject to variations approved by the appropriate national authority[27];

(v)   for conferring functions with respect to the resolution of disputes between schools in the group, or between one or more such schools and a foundation body, on such person or body as may be specified in the regulations[28];

(vi)   in connection with a school leaving the group:

      (A)   for requiring the publication of proposals[29] as to the procedure for changing the category of a school[30];

      (B)   for enabling the appropriate national authority to require the publication[31] of proposals for the school to become a school of a category specified by it[32];

(vii)   for the dissolution of a foundation body by order of the appropriate national authority[33];

(viii)   for enabling the appropriate national authority, in the case of any land held by a foundation body immediately before its dissolution which by virtue of the School Standards and Framework Act 1998 could not be disposed of without its consent or to the disposal of which notice of objection is given by the local authority[34], to determine how that land is to be dealt with on its dissolution[35];

(ix)   for conferring functions on adjudicators[36], including any functions which might otherwise be conferred on the appropriate national authority[37].

The appropriate national authority may, after consulting[38] a foundation body, make an order modifying[39] the instrument of government adopted by that body[40].

1   As to school premises see PARA 1295 et seq.
2   As to the governing bodies of maintained schools see PARA 150 et seq.
3   As to the charitable status of maintained schools see PARA 102.
4   As to staffing of schools see PARA 268 et seq.
5   As to admissions generally see PARA 224 et seq.

6 'Foundation', in relation to a foundation or voluntary school, means: (1) any body of persons (whether incorporated or not but excluding the governing body) which holds land on trust for the purposes of the school (School Standards and Framework Act 1998 s 21(3)(a)(i)); or (2) a foundation body (s 21(3)(a)(ii)). A school 'has' a foundation if such a body of persons exists for holding land on trust for the purposes of the school (s 21(3)(b)(i)), or if the school belongs to a group of schools for which a foundation body acts under s 21 (s 21(3)(b)(ii)). References to land or other property held on trust, or by trustees, for the purposes of a school include references to land or other property which: (a) is held on trust for purposes which (whether the trust deed expressly so provides or not) include the purposes of the school (s 21(3)(c)(i)); and (b) is used for the purposes of the school (s 21(3)(c)(ii)). As to the meaning of 'person' see PARA 7 note 6. As to the meaning of 'land' see PARA 116 note 18; and as to the meaning of 'school' see PARA 91 (definitions applied by s 142(8)). 'Trust deed' includes any instrument (other than an instrument of government) regulating the constitution of the school's governing body or the maintenance, management or conduct of the school: Education Act 1996 s 579(1) (definition substituted by the School Standards and Framework Act 1998 s 140(1), Sch 30 paras 57, 183(a)(iv)); (definition applied by the School Standards and Framework Act 1998 s 142(8)).

'Foundation body' means a body corporate established under s 21 to perform, in relation to three or more schools each of which is either a foundation or a voluntary school, the following functions, namely: (i) to hold property of those schools for the purposes of the schools (s 21(4)(a)(i)); and (ii) to appoint foundation governors for those schools (s 21(4)(a)(ii)). 'The group', in relation to a foundation body, means the group of three or more schools for which the body performs those functions: s 21(4)(b). In relation to a foundation school, a foundation special school or a voluntary school, 'foundation governor' means a person appointed as a foundation governor in accordance with regulations under the Education Act 2002 s 19 (see PARA 150): School Standards and Framework Act 1998 s 142(1) (definition added by the Education Act 2002 s 215(1), Sch 21 para 112). As to the meaning of 'functions' see PARA 18 note 5 (definition applied by the School Standards and Framework Act 1998 s 142(8)). As to bodies corporate see COMPANIES vol 14 (2009) PARA 2; CORPORATIONS vol 24 (2010) PARA 301 et seq.

7 School Standards and Framework Act 1998 s 21(1)(a).
8 School Standards and Framework Act 1998 s 21(1)(b). The provisions referred to in the text are those of s 21: see s 21(1)(b).
9 School Standards and Framework Act 1998 s 21(1)(c).
10 As to local authorities see PARA 25.
11 As to the funding of maintained schools see PARA 305 et seq.
12 School Standards and Framework Act 1998 s 21(2)(a).
13 School Standards and Framework Act 1998 s 21(2)(b). The provisions referred to in the text are those of s 21: see s 21(2)(b).
14 Ie the appointed day: see PARA 106 note 3.
15 As to voluntary schools before 1 September 1999 see PARA 106.
16 As to grant-maintained schools see PARA 106.
17 School Standards and Framework Act 1998 s 21(2)(c).
18 Ie the Secretary of State or, in relation to Wales, the Welsh Ministers. The functions of the Secretary of State under the School Standards and Framework Act 1998 s 21, so far as exercisable in relation to Wales, were transferred to the National Assembly for Wales (see the National Assembly for Wales (Transfer of Functions) Order 1999, SI 1999/672, art 2, Sch 1) and are now vested in the Welsh Ministers (see the Government of Wales Act 2006 s 162(1), Sch 11 para 30). As to the Secretary of State see PARA 58. As to the Welsh Ministers see PARA 59. As to the meaning of 'Wales' see PARA 7 note 3.
19 As to the regulations made under the School Standards and Framework Act 1998 s 21(5), (6) see the Education (Foundation Body) (England) Regulations 2000, SI 2000/2872 (amended by SI 2004/3264; SI 2006/1722; SI 2006/2198; and SI 2012/2404); and the Education (Foundation Body) (Wales) Regulations 2001, SI 2001/2709 (amended by SI 2009/2544). Any regulations made under the School Standards and Framework Act 1998 s 21(5) so far as relating to transfers under them, have effect subject to the Education Reform Act 1988 s 198(2), Sch 10 (see PARA 1331 et seq): see s 198(1) (substituted by the School Standards and Framework Act 1998 s 137, Sch 29 para 2(2)).
20 School Standards and Framework Act 1998 s 21(5)(a).
21 School Standards and Framework Act 1998 s 21(5)(b).
22 'Liability' includes obligation: Education Act 1996 s 579(1) (definition applied by the School Standards and Framework Act 1998 s 142(8)).
23 Ie under the Education and Inspections Act 2006 s 19 (see PARA 133) or in accordance with proposals under the School Standards and Organisation (Wales) Act 2013 s 45 (see PARA 141).

24 School Standards and Framework Act 1998 s 21(6)(a) (amended by the Education and Inspections Act 2006 s 30, Sch 3, para 14(a); and the School Standards and Organisation (Wales) Act 2013 Sch 5 para 19(1), (2)).

25 School Standards and Framework Act 1998 s 21(6)(b). Regulations made in pursuance of s 21(6)(b) may, in connection with the making or variation of instruments of government in preparation for schools joining or leaving the group, modify Sch 12 para 1 (repealed) in its operation in relation to such instruments of government: s 21(7).

26 School Standards and Framework Act 1998 s 21(6)(c).

27 School Standards and Framework Act 1998 s 21(6)(d). As to instruments of government see PARA 184 et seq.

28 School Standards and Framework Act 1998 s 21(6)(e).

29 Ie under the Education and Inspections Act 2006 s 19 (see PARA 133) or under the School Standards and Organisation (Wales) Act 2013 s 48 (procedure for changing category of school: see PARA 142).

30 School Standards and Framework Act 1998 s 21(6)(f)(i) (amended by the Education and Inspections Act 2006 s 30, Sch 3 para 14(b)(i); and the School Standards and Organisation (Wales) Act 2013 Sch 5 para 19(1), (3)(b)).

31 Ie under the Education and Inspections Act 2006 s 19 or under the School Standards and Organisation (Wales) Act 2013 s 48: see note 29.

32 School Standards and Framework Act 1998 s 21(6)(f)(ii) (amended by the Education and Inspections Act 2006 s 30, Sch 3 para 14(b)(ii); and the School Standards and Organisation (Wales) Act 2013 Sch 5 para 19(1), (3)(b)).

33 School Standards and Framework Act 1998 s 21(6)(g).

34 Ie to the disposal of which the School Standards and Framework Act 1998 Sch 22 para A9 (see PARA 1306) would apply.

35 School Standards and Framework Act 1998 s 21(6)(h) (amended by the Education and Inspections Act 2006 s 30, Sch 3, para 14(c)).

36 As to the meaning of 'adjudicator' see PARA 147.

37 School Standards and Framework Act 1998 s 21(6)(i) (amended by the Education and Inspections Act 2006 s 30, Sch 3, para 14(d)).

38 As to the exercise of the duty to consult see JUDICIAL REVIEW vol 61 (2010) PARA 627.

39 As to the meaning of 'modify' see PARA 21 note 15 (definition applied by the School Standards and Framework Act 1998 s 142(8)).

40 School Standards and Framework Act 1998 s 21(8). Any such an order is not to be made by statutory instrument see (s 138(2)) and as such is not recorded in this title. Regulations may make provision for applying to foundation special schools, with or without modifications, any of the provisions of s 21(3)–(8) (see note 6 and the text to notes 18–40) or any provision of Sch 21 (transfers of land on appointed day: see PARA 1340 et seq): s 21(9). As to special schools see PARA 1041 et seq. Any regulations made under s 21(9), so far as relating to transfers under them, have effect subject to the Education Reform Act 1988 Sch 10 (see PARA 1331 et seq): see s 198(1) (as substituted: see note 19). As to the regulations made see the School Organisation (Foundation Special Schools) (Application of Provisions Relating to Foundations) (England) Regulations 2007, SI 2007/1329.

109. Foundation and foundation special schools: requirements as to foundations. The following provisions apply to any foundation[1] or foundation special school[2] having a foundation if any one or more of the following conditions is met[3]:

(1) condition A is that the school was established as a foundation or foundation special school in pursuance of proposals falling to be implemented under the Education and Inspections Act 2006[4];

(2) condition B is that the school acquired its foundation[5], or became a school whose instrument of government provides for the majority of governors to be foundation governors[6], in pursuance of proposals falling to be implemented under regulations[7] under that Act[8];

(3) condition C is that the school changed category from voluntary aided school to foundation school in pursuance of proposals falling to be

implemented under regulations[9] under that Act and has an instrument of government providing for the majority of governors to be foundation governors[10].

No institution[11] may act as the foundation of such a school unless (a) it is a body corporate of a prescribed description[12]; (b) it is[13] a charity[14]; and (c) it has as its purpose[15], or one of its purposes, the advancement of the education of pupils[16] at the school or schools in respect of which it acts as the foundation[17].

The foundation of such a school must, in carrying out its functions[18] in relation to the school, promote community cohesion[19]. Where any members of the foundation are to be local authorities[20] or persons[21] appointed by local authorities, the proportion of voting rights exercisable by such members must not exceed 20 per cent of the total voting rights exercisable by members[22]. Where any of the charity trustees[23] in relation to the foundation are to be appointed by local authorities (i) the proportion of the charity trustees who are appointed by local authorities must not exceed 20 per cent of the total number of charity trustees[24]; and (ii) the voting rights exercisable by the charity trustees who are appointed by local authorities must not exceed 20 per cent of the total voting rights exercisable by charity trustees[25]. Regulations may disqualify persons from acting as charity trustee in relation to a school to which these provisions apply[26].

Regulations[27] may make provision enabling the Secretary of State or the Welsh Ministers in prescribed cases by direction (A) to remove any charity trustee of a school to which these provisions apply, even though the person is not[28] disqualified[29]; (B) to appoint a person to be a charity trustee of such a school (whether in place of a trustee removed by him or them under head (A) or otherwise)[30].

1　In the School Standards and Framework Act 1998 ss 23A, 23B, 'foundation' means a foundation established otherwise than under the School Standards and Framework Act 1998: s 23A(10) (ss 23A, 23B added by the Education and Inspections Act 2006 s 33). As to the meaning of 'foundation' generally see PARA 108 note 6.
2　As to the meaning of 'special school' see PARA 1041 (definition applied by the School Standards and Framework Act 1998 s 142(8)).
3　School Standards and Framework Act 1998 s 23A(1) (as added: see note 1).
4　School Standards and Framework Act 1998 s 23A(2) (as added: see note 1). The relevant provisions of the Education and Inspections Act 2006 are those of Sch 2 (see PARA 118 et seq): see the School Standards and Framework Act 1998 s 23A(2) (as so added).
5　School Standards and Framework Act 1998 s 23A(3)(a) (as added: see note 1).
6　School Standards and Framework Act 1998 s 23A(3)(b) (as added: see note 1). As to the meaning of 'foundation governor' see PARA 108 note 6. As to instruments of government see PARA 184 et seq.
7　Ie regulations under the Education and Inspections Act 2006 s 24: see PARA 136.
8　School Standards and Framework Act 1998 s 23A(3) (as added: see note 1).
9　Ie regulations under the Education and Inspections Act 2006 s 24: see PARA 163.
10　School Standards and Framework Act 1998 s 23A(4) (as added: see note 1).
11　'Institution' has the same meaning as in the Charities Act 2011 (see CHARITIES vol 8 (2015) PARA 1): School Standards and Framework Act 1998 s 23A(10) (as added: (see note 1); and definition amended by the Charities Act 2011 Sch 7 para 76).
12　School Standards and Framework Act 1998 s 23A(5)(a) (as added: see note 1). As to bodies corporate see COMPANIES vol 14 (2009) PARA 2; CORPORATIONS vol 24 (2010) PARA 301 et seq. 'Prescribed' means prescribed by regulations made by the Secretary of State or, as appropriate, the Welsh Ministers: see the School Standards and Framework Act 1998 s 142(1). As to the regulations made under ss 23A, 23B see the School Organisation (Requirements as to Foundations) (England) Regulations 2007, SI 2007/1287 (amended by SI 2009/1924; SI 2010/2582; and SI 2011/577).
　　The functions of the Secretary of State under the School Standards and Framework Act 1998 ss 23A, 23B, so far as exercisable in relation to Wales, were transferred to the National

Assembly for Wales (see the National Assembly for Wales (Transfer of Functions) Order 1999, SI 1999/672, art 2, Sch 1) and are now vested in the Welsh Ministers (see the Government of Wales Act 2006 s 162(1), Sch 11 para 30). As to the Secretary of State see PARA 58. As to the Welsh Ministers see PARA 59. As to the meaning of 'Wales' see PARA 7 note 3.

13 Ie whether by virtue of the School Standards and Framework Act 1998 s 23(3) (see PARA 102) or otherwise.

14 School Standards and Framework Act 1998 s 23A(5)(b) (as added: see note 1).

15 'Purpose' includes object: School Standards and Framework Act 1998 s 23A(10) (as added: see note 1).

16 As to the meaning of 'pupil' see PARA 20 note 4 (definition applied by the School Standards and Framework Act 1998 s 142(8)).

17 School Standards and Framework Act 1998 s 23A(5)(c) (as added: see note 1).

18 As to the meaning of 'functions' see PARA 18 note 5 (definition applied by the School Standards and Framework Act 1998 s 142(8)).

19 School Standards and Framework Act 1998 s 23A(6) (as added: see note 1).

20 As to the meaning of 'local authority' see PARA 25 (definition applied by the School Standards and Framework Act 1998 s 142(8)).

21 As to the meaning of 'person' see PARA 7 note 6.

22 School Standards and Framework Act 1998 s 23A(7) (as added: see note 1).

23 'Charity trustee', in relation to a school to which the School Standards and Framework Act 1998 s 23A applies, means any individual who is for the purposes of the Charities Act 2011 a charity trustee (see CHARITIES vol 8 (2015) PARA 255) in relation to the school's foundation: s 23A(10) (as added (see note 1); and definition amended by the Charities Act 2011 Sch 7 para 76).

24 School Standards and Framework Act 1998 s 23A(8)(a) (as added: see note 1).

25 School Standards and Framework Act 1998 s 23A(8)(b) (as added: see note 1).

26 School Standards and Framework Act 1998 s 23A(9) (as added: see note 1). As to the regulations made see note 12.

27 Such regulations may make provision as to the effect of a direction given by the Secretary of State or the Welsh Ministers under the regulations, and may in particular provide for any such direction to have the same effect as an order of the Charity Commission for England and Wales under the Charities Act 2011 s 76 or ss 79–81 (see CHARITIES vol 8 (2015) PARA 567) for the removal or appointment of a charity trustee: School Standards and Framework Act 1998 s 23B(2) (as added (see note 1); and amended by the Charities Act 2011 Sch 7 para 77). As to the regulations made see note 12. Nothing in the School Standards and Framework Act 1998 s 23B affects the powers of the Charity Commission for England and Wales under any enactment: s 23B(3) (as so added). As to the meaning of 'enactment' see PARA 1 note 13. As to the Charity Commission see CHARITIES vol 8 (2015) PARA 543 et seq.

28 Ie by virtue of the School Standards and Framework Act 1998 s 23A(9): see the text to note 26.

29 School Standards and Framework Act 1998 s 23B(1)(a) (as added: see note 1).

30 School Standards and Framework Act 1998 s 23B(1)(b) (as added: see note 1).

(iii) Establishment, Alteration or Discontinuance of Maintained Schools

A. SCHOOLS IN ENGLAND

(A) In general

110. Restriction on establishment, alteration or discontinuance of schools. No maintained school in England[1] may be established[2] or discontinued[3], and no prescribed alteration[4] may be made to a maintained school[5], except in pursuance of proposals falling to be implemented under the Education and Inspections Act 2006[6].

No alteration relating to a proposal by the governing body of any foundation or foundation special school for the removal of the foundation[7] or for the alteration of the instrument of government in such a way that foundation governors will cease to constitute the majority of governors[8], may be made to a foundation or foundation special school except in pursuance of proposals falling to be implemented under the relevant statutory procedures[9].

1 For these purposes, 'maintained school' means any of the following schools in England: (1) a community, foundation or voluntary school; (2) a community or foundation special school; or (3) a maintained nursery school: Education and Inspections Act 2006 s 32(1). As to the meaning of 'England' see PARA 7 note 3. As to references to a community, foundation or voluntary school or a community or foundation special school see PARA 106. As to the meaning of 'maintained nursery school' see PARA 99 note 4 (definition applied by s 187(2), (3)).

2 For the purposes of the Education Act 1996 any other enactment relating to the duties of a local authority neither (1) references in whatever terms to discontinuing a school (including those to a local authority ceasing to maintain a school); nor (2) references in whatever terms to establishing a new school, are to read as applying by reason only of a change such as is mentioned in s 574(2) being made to an existing school (so that, where such a change is made to an existing school, the school is to be regarded as continuing despite the change and as being the same school before and after it, unless for other reasons it is to be regarded as discontinued): s 574(1) (amended by SI 2010/1158) (definition applied by the Education and Inspections Act 2006 s 187(2), (3)). The changes are (a) education beginning or ceasing to be provided for pupils above or below a particular age, for boys as well as girls or for girls as well as boys; (b) an enlargement or alteration of the school premises; and (c) the transfer of the school to a new site: Education Act 1996 s 574(2).

3 Education and Inspections Act 2006 s 28(1)(a). In Pt 2 (ss 6A–32) any reference to a local authority discontinuing a school, or implementing proposals to discontinue a school (whether published by the authority or the governing body), is a reference to the authority ceasing to maintain the school: ss 15(8), 32(1) (s 15(8) amended by SI 2010/1158). As to the meaning of 'local authority' see PARA 25 (definition applied by the Education and Inspections Act 2006 s 187(2), (3)). As to governing bodies of maintained schools see PARA 150 et seq. As to the meaning of 'maintain' see PARA 306 note 4 (definition applied by s 32(1)).

4 For these purposes, 'prescribed alteration', in relation to a maintained school, means an alteration prescribed under the Education and Inspections Act 2006 s 18 (see PARA 132): s 28(2).

5 Education and Inspections Act 2006 s 28(1)(b).

6 Education and Inspections Act 2006 s 28(1) (amended by SI 2010/1080). The relevant provisions of the Education and Inspections Act 2006 are Pt 2 (ss 6A–32) (see PARA 111 et seq): see s 28(1). Section 28(1) has effect subject to: (1) s 17(5) (see PARA 117) and s 68(4) (see PARA 1217) (which relate to powers of the Secretary of State to require a maintained school to be discontinued) (s 28(3)(a)); (2) the School Standards and Framework Act 1998 s 30(9) (notice by governing body to discontinue foundation or voluntary school: see PARA 116) (Education and Inspections Act 2006 s 28(3)(b)); (3) the Academies Act 2010 s 6(2) (requirement to cease to maintain school in respect of which academy order has effect: see PARA 351) (Education and Inspections Act 2006 s 28(3)(c) (added by the Academies Act 2010 Sch 2 paras 19, 20)).

7 As to the meaning of 'foundation' see PARA 108 note 6.

8 Ie no alteration falling within the Education and Inspections Act 2006 s 25(4)(a) or (b): see PARA 137. As to instruments of government see PARA 184 et seq.

9 Education and Inspections Act 2006 s 28(4). The relevant statutory procedures are those under s 27 (see PARA 138): see s 28(4).

(B) Establishment of New Schools

111. Invitation for proposals for establishment of new schools. If a local authority[1] in England[2] thinks a new school[3] needs to be established[4] in its area, it must seek proposals for the establishment of an academy[5]. The local authority must specify a date by which any such proposals must be submitted to it[6]. After the specified date, the local authority must notify the Secretary of State[7] (1) of the steps they have taken to seek proposals for the establishment of an academy[8]; and (2) of any proposals submitted to them as a result before the specified date, or of the fact that no such proposals have been submitted to them before that date[9]. Such a notification must identify a possible site for the academy[10]; and specify such matters as may be prescribed[11].

A local authority in England may with the consent of the Secretary of State publish a notice inviting proposals from persons[12] other than local authorities for the establishment[13] of any new school being[14]: (a) a foundation, voluntary or foundation special school[15], other than one providing education suitable only to the requirements of persons above compulsory school age[16]; or (b) an academy school[17]. The notice must: (i) identify a possible site for the school[18]; (ii) state whether or not the proposed school is to be a special school[19]; (iii) specify a date, being a date after the prescribed[20] interval, by which proposals must be submitted[21]; (iv) specify such other matters as may be prescribed[22]; and (v) be published in the prescribed manner[23]. Before publishing any such notice, the local authority must consult[24] such persons as appear to it to be appropriate; and in discharging this duty the authority must have regard to any guidance given from time to time by the Secretary of State[25].

Proposals made pursuant to such a notice must contain the prescribed information[26], and be submitted to the local authority before the date specified in the notice[27]. After the date specified in a notice published by a local authority, the authority must publish any proposals submitted pursuant to the notice[28].

Where a local authority has published a notice as above[29], at any time before the date specified in the notice (A) the local authority may withdraw it, with the consent of the Secretary of State[30]; or (B) the Secretary of State may direct the local authority to withdraw it[31].

Provision is made in relation to the consideration, approval and implementation of proposals under these provisions[32].

1   As to the meaning of 'local authority' see PARA 25 (definition applied by the Education and Inspections Act 2006 s 187(2), (3)).
2   As to the meaning of 'England' see PARA 7 note 3.
3   As to the meaning of 'school' see PARA 91 (definition applied by the Education and Inspections Act 2006 s 187(2), (3)). As to new schools see also PARA 155.
4   As to the meaning of 'establish' see PARA 110 note 2 (definition applied by the Education and Inspections Act 2006 s 187(2), (3)).
5   Education and Inspections Act 2006 s 6A(1) (s 6A added by the Education Act 2011 Sch 11 paras 1, 2). As to the meaning of 'academy' see PARA 346 (definition applied by the Education and Inspections Act 2006 s 187(2), (3)). See also PARA 31. See *R (on the application of British Humanist Association) v Richmond upon Thames London Borough Council* [2012] EWHC 3622 (Admin), [2013] 2 All ER 146, [2013] LGR 290 (as to the 'need' to establish a new school under the Education and Inspections Act 2006 s 6A).
6   Education and Inspections Act 2006 s 6A(2) (as added: see note 5).
7   As to the Secretary of State see PARA 58.
8   Education and Inspections Act 2006 s 6A(3)(a) (as added: see note 5).
9   Education and Inspections Act 2006 s 6A(3)(b) (as added: see note 5).
10 Education and Inspections Act 2006 s 6A(4)(a) (as added: see note 5).
11 Education and Inspections Act 2006 s 6A(4)(b) (as added: see note 5). 'Prescribed' means prescribed by regulations made under the Education and Inspections Act 2006 Pt 2 (ss 6A–32) by the Secretary of State: see s 32(1). At the date at which this volume states the law no regulations had been made under s 6A. See also note 20.
12 As to the meaning of 'person' see PARA 7 note 6.
13 Proposals under the Education and Inspections Act 2006 s 7 for the establishment of a new maintained school in England may relate to the establishment of the school as a federated school: see s 12(1) (amended by SI 2010/10890; and the Education Act 2011 Sch 11 paras 1, 9). 'Federated school' has the meaning given by the Education Act 2002 s 24(2) (see PARA 156): Education and Inspections Act 2006 s 12(2). As to the meaning of 'maintained school' see PARA 110 note 1.
14 See the Education and Inspections Act 2006 s 7(1) (amended by SI 2010/1158; and the Education Act 2011 Sch 11 paras 1, 3(a)).
15 As to the meaning of references to a foundation, voluntary or foundation special school see PARA 106.
16 Education and Inspections Act 2006 s 7(2)(a). As to the meaning of 'compulsory school age' see PARA 19.
17 Education and Inspections Act 2006 s 7(2)(b) (amended by the Education Act 2011 Sch 13 para 16(1), (2)). As to the meaning of 'academy school' see PARA 346 note 12 (definition applied by the Education and Inspections Act 2006 s 187(2), (3)).
18 Education and Inspections Act 2006 s 7(3)(a).

19 Education and Inspections Act 2006 s 7(3)(b). As to the meaning of 'special school' see PARA 1041 (definition applied by s 187(2), (3)).
20 As to the regulations made under the Education and Inspections Act 2006 ss 7, 13 see the School Organisation (Establishment and Discontinuance of Schools) Regulations 2013, SI 2013/3109.
21 Education and Inspections Act 2006 s 7(3)(c).
22 Education and Inspections Act 2006 s 7(3)(d). As to the regulations made see note 20.
23 Education and Inspections Act 2006 s 7(3)(e). As to the regulations made see note 20.
24 As to consultation see *R (Elphinstone) v City of Westminster* [2008] EWCA Civ 1069, [2009] LGR 158, [2009] ELR 24. As to the exercise of the duty to consult see JUDICIAL REVIEW vol 61 (2010) PARA 627.
25 Education and Inspections Act 2006 s 9(1) (amended by SI 2010/1158). As to the publication of guidance see the Education Act 1996 s 571 (provision applied by the Education and Inspections Act 2006 s 187(2), (3)); and PARA 60.
26 Education and Inspections Act 2006 s 7(4)(a). As to the regulations made see note 20.
27 Education and Inspections Act 2006 s 7(4)(b) (amended by SI 2010/1158). As from a day to be appointed the following provision has effect: The governing body of a maintained school may make proposals pursuant to a notice under the Education and Inspections Act 2006 s 7 only if the governing body is for the time being designated for these purposes by the Secretary of State, or by a person authorised by the Secretary of State to designate governing bodies for those purposes; but the governing body of a maintained nursery school may not be designated for these purposes: see s 11A(1), (2) (s 11A prospectively added by the Children, Schools and Families Act 2010 s 7). At the date at which this volume states the law no such day had been appointed. As to governing bodies of maintained schools see PARA 150 et seq.
28 Education and Inspections Act 2006 s 7(5)(a) (amended by SI 2010/1158). Regulations may prescribe: (1) the time within which proposals must be published (Education and Inspections Act 2006 s 7(6)(a)); and (2) the manner in which they must be published (s 7(6)(b) (s 7(6) amended by the Education Act 2011 Sch 11 paras 1, 3(d))). Regulations may require the local authority to take prescribed steps for the purpose of promoting public awareness of any proposals published by them under the Education and Inspections Act 2006 s 7: s 9(2) (amended by SI 2010/1158). Regulations may modify the provisions of the Education and Inspections Act 2006 ss 7, 12 (see note 4) and Sch 2 (see PARA 118) in their application to cases where the school is proposed to be established in an area in England other than that of the local authority who published the notice: see s 13(a) (amended by SI 2010/1158). As to the regulations made see note 20.
29 Education and Inspections Act 2006 s 7A(1) (s 7A added by the Education Act 2011 Sch 11 paras 1, 4). The reference in the text is a reference to a notice under the Education and Inspections Act 2006 s 7.
30 Education and Inspections Act 2006 s 7A(2)(a) (as added: see note 29).
31 Education and Inspections Act 2006 s 7A(2)(b) (as added: see note 29).
32 See the Education and Inspections Act 2006 s 7(7), Sch 2; and PARA 118 et seq.

112. Publication of proposals with consent of Secretary of State. A local authority in England[1] may with the consent of the Secretary of State[2] publish its proposals to establish[3] a new community, community special school[4], foundation or foundation special school[5], which (1) is not to be one providing education suitable only to the requirements of persons above compulsory school age[6]; and (2) is to replace one or more maintained schools[7], with exceptions[8].

Any persons[9] ('proposers') may with the consent of the Secretary of State publish their proposals to establish (otherwise than pursuant to a notice[10] by a local authority inviting proposals for the establishment of a new school) a new foundation, voluntary[11] controlled or foundation special school in England other than: (a) one providing education suitable only to the requirements of persons above compulsory school age[12]; or (b) one in relation to which proposals fall to be published under[13] other statutory provisions[14].

Proposals under these provisions must contain such information[15], and be published in such manner[16], as may be prescribed[17]. Before publishing any such proposals, the local authority or proposers (as the case may be) must consult[18] such persons as appear to them to be appropriate; and in discharging this duty the authority or proposers must have regard to any guidance given from time to time by the Secretary of State[19]. Where any proposals are published by proposers, they must submit the proposals in accordance with regulations to the local authority who it is proposed should maintain the school[20].

Provision is made in relation to the consideration, approval and implementation of proposals under these provisions[21].

1   As to the meaning of 'local authority in England' see PARA 25 (definition applied by the Education and Inspections Act 2006 s 187(2), (3)).
2   As to the Secretary of State see PARA 58.
3   Proposals under the Education and Inspections Act 2006 s 10 for the establishment of a new maintained school in England may relate to the establishment of the school as a federated school: see s 12(1) (amended by SI 2010/10890; and the Education Act 2011 Sch 11 paras 1, 9). 'Federated school' has the meaning given by the Education Act 2002 s 24(2) (see PARA 156): Education and Inspections Act 2006 s 12(2). Regulations may modify the provisions of ss 10, 12 and Sch 2 (see PARA 118 et seq) in their application to cases where the school is proposed to be established in an area in England other than that of the local authority who it is proposed should maintain the school: see s 13(b) (amended by SI 2010/1158). As to the meaning of 'establish' see PARA 110 note 2 (definition applied by the Education and Inspections Act 2006 s 187(2), (3)). As to the meaning of 'maintain' see PARA 306 note 4. As to the regulations made see note 17.
4   As to the meaning of references to a community school or a community special school see PARA 106.
5   As to the meaning of references to a foundation school or a foundation special school see PARA 106.
6   Education and Inspections Act 2006 s 10(1)(a) (s 10 amended by SI 2010/1158; and the Education Act 2011 Sch 11 paras 1, 6(1), (2)). As to the meaning of 'compulsory school age' see PARA 19.
7   As to the meaning of 'maintained school' see PARA 110 note 1.
8   Education and Inspections Act 2006 s 10(1)(b) (s 10 as amended: see note 7). The exception referred to in the text is where s 11(A2) applies or in a case within s 11(A3) (see PARA 113): s 10(1)(b) (as so amended).
9   As to the meaning of 'person' see PARA 7 note 6.
10 Ie a notice under the Education and Inspections Act 2006 s 7: see PARA 111.
11 As to the meaning of references to a voluntary school see PARA 106.
12 Education and Inspections Act 2006 s 10(2)(a) (s 10(2) amended by the Education Act 2011 Sch 11 para 1, 6(1), (3)(a)).
13 Ie under the Education and Inspections Act 2006 s 11 by virtue of s 11(2): see PARA 113.
14 Education and Inspections Act 2006 s 10(2)(b) (amended by the Education Act 2011 Sch 11 paras 1, 6(1), (3)(b)).
15 Education and Inspections Act 2006 s 10(3)(a).
16 Education and Inspections Act 2006 s 10(3)(b).
17 Education and Inspections Act 2006 s 10(3). 'Prescribed' means prescribed by regulations made under Pt 2 (ss 6A–32) by the Secretary of State: see s 32(1). As to the regulations made see the School Organisation (Establishment and Discontinuance of Schools) Regulations 2013, SI 2013/3109.
18 As to the exercise of the duty to consult see JUDICIAL REVIEW vol 61 (2010) PARA 627.
19 Education and Inspections Act 2006 s 10(4) (amended by SI 2010/1158). As to the publication of guidance see the Education Act 1996 s 571 (provision applied by the Education and Inspections Act 2006 s 187(2), (3)); and PARA 60.
20 Education and Inspections Act 2006 s 10(5) (amended by SI 2010/1158). As to the regulations made see note 17.
21 See the Education and Inspections Act 2006 s 10(6), Sch 2; and PARA 118 et seq.

113.   Publication of proposals to establish maintained schools: special cases.
Where a local authority in England[1] publishes a notice inviting proposals for establishment of new schools[2], and (1) no proposals are made pursuant to the notice[3]; or (2) proposals are made pursuant to the notice but none of the proposals are approved[4] or result in academy arrangements[5] being entered into[6], the local authority may publish[7] proposals of its own to establish[8] a new community, community special[9], foundation or foundation special school[10],

which is not to be one providing education suitable only to the requirements of persons above compulsory school age[11].

Where a local authority in England proposes to establish a new community, community special, foundation or foundation special school, which (a) is to be a primary school[12]; and (b) is to replace a maintained infant school[13] and a maintained junior school[14], the authority must publish its proposals[15].

Where a local authority in England proposes to establish a new maintained nursery school[16] the authority must publish its proposals[17].

Where any persons[18] ('proposers') propose to establish a new voluntary aided school[19] in England[20], they may publish their proposals[21].

Where any persons propose to establish a new foundation, voluntary controlled or foundation special school[22] in England which:

(i)   is to replace one or more foundation or voluntary schools which have a religious character[23];
(ii)   is to replace an independent school[24] that is not an academy, a city technology college or a city college for the technology of the arts[25]; or
(iii)   in the case of a new foundation special school, is to replace a non-maintained special school[26],

they must publish their proposals[27].

Proposals under these provisions must contain such information[28], and be published in such manner[29], as may be prescribed[30]. Before publishing any proposals, the authority or proposers (as the case may be) must consult[31] such persons as appear to them to be appropriate; and in discharging this duty the authority or proposers must have regard to any guidance given from time to time by the Secretary of State[32]. Where any such proposals are published by proposers, they must submit the proposals in accordance with regulations[33] to the local authority who it is proposed should maintain the school[34].

Provision is made in relation to the consideration, approval and implementation of proposals under these provisions[35].

1   As to the meaning of 'local authority in England' see PARA 25 (definition applied by the Education and Inspections Act 2006 s 187(2), (3)).
2   Ie a notice under the Education and Inspections Act 2006 s 7: see PARA 111.
3   Education and Inspections Act 2006 s 11(A1)(a) (s 11(A1)–(A3) added by the Education Act 2011 Sch 11 para 1, 7(1), (2)).
4   Ie under the Education and Inspections Act 2006 Sch 2: see PARA 118 et seq.
5   As to the meaning of 'academy arrangements' see PARA 346 note 4 (definition applied by the Education and Inspections Act 2006 s 187(2), (3)).
6   Education and Inspections Act 2006 s 11(A1)(b) (as added: see note 3).
7   Ie under the Education and Inspections Act 2006 s 11.
8   Proposals under the Education and Inspections Act 2006 s 11 for the establishment of a new maintained school in England may relate to the establishment of the school as a federated school: see s 12(1) (amended by SI 2010/1080; and the Education Act 2011 Sch 11 paras 1, 9). 'Federated school' has the meaning given by the Education Act 2002 s 24(2) (see PARA 185): Education and Inspections Act 2006 s 12(2). Regulations may modify the provisions of ss 11, 12 and Sch 2 (see PARA 118 et seq) in their application to cases where the school is proposed to be established in an area in England other than that of the local authority who it is proposed should maintain the school: see s 13(b) (amended by SI 2010/1158). As to the meaning of 'establish' see PARA 110 note 2 (definition applied by the Education and Inspections Act 2006 s 187(2), (3)). As to the meaning of 'maintain' see PARA 306 note 4. As to the regulations made see note 30.
9   As to the meaning of references to a community school or a community special school see PARA 106.
10 As to the meaning of references to a foundation school or a foundation special school see PARA 106.
11 Education and Inspections Act 2006 s 11(A2) (as added: see note 3). As to the meaning of 'compulsory school age' see PARA 19.

12 Education and Inspections Act 2006 s 11(A3)(a) (as added: see note 3). As to the meaning of 'primary school' see PARA 91 (definition applied by s 187(2), (3)).

13 'Maintained infant school' means a maintained school that provides primary education suitable to the requirements of children of compulsory school age who have not attained the age of 8: Education and Inspections Act 2006 s 11(9) (substituted by the Education Act 2011 Sch 11 para 1, 7(1), (8)).

14 Education and Inspections Act 2006 s 11(A3)(b) (as added: see note 3). 'Maintained junior school' means a maintained school that provides primary education suitable to the requirements of junior pupils who have attained the age of 7: s 11(9) (as substituted: see note 13).

15 Education and Inspections Act 2006 s 11(A3) (as added: see note 3).

16 Education and Inspections Act 2006 s 11(1)(a). As to the meaning of 'maintained nursery school' see PARA 99 note 4 (definition applied by s 187(2), (3)).

17 Education and Inspections Act 2006 s 11(1) (amended by the Apprenticeships, Skills, Children and Learning Act 2009 ss 126(2), (5), 266, Sch 16 Pt 3; and SI 2010/1158).

18 As to the meaning of 'person' see PARA 7 note 6.

19 As to voluntary aided schools see PARAS 106, 108.

20 As to the meaning of 'England' see PARA 7 note 3.

21 Education and Inspections Act 2006 s 11(1A) (added by the Education Act 2011 Sch 11 paras 1, 7(1), (3)).

22 As to the meaning of references to a foundation or voluntary school or a foundation special school see PARAS 106, 108.

23 Education and Inspections Act 2006 s 11(2)(aa) (added by the Education Act 2011 Sch 11 paras 1, 7(1), (4)(b)). For these purposes, a new foundation or voluntary controlled school replaces a foundation or voluntary school which has a religious character if it is proposed that the new school (1) should have the same religious character; (2) should have a different religious character; or (3) should not have a religious character: Education and Inspections Act 2006 s 11(2A) (added by the Education Act 2011 Sch 11 paras 1, 7(1), (5)). As to religious education generally see PARA 910 et seq.

24 A new foundation, voluntary controlled or foundation special school is not to be regarded for these purposes as replacing an independent school unless (s 11(3) (amended by the Education Act 2011 Sch 11 paras 1, 7(1), (6))): (1) the independent school has been registered under the Education and Skills Act 2008 Pt 4 Ch 1 (ss 92–141) (regulation of independent educational institutions in England: see PARA 382 et seq) for a continuous period of at least two years ending with the date of the publication of the proposals under the Education and Inspections Act 2006 s 11 (s 11(3)(a) (amended by the Education and Skills Act 2008 s 169(1), Sch 1 Pt 1 paras 37, 38(1), (2)); and (2) it is proposed that the independent school should continue in existence but should then close as an independent school immediately before the proposals are implemented (Education and Inspections Act 2006 s 11(3)(b)).

25 Education and Inspections Act 2006 s 11(2)(b). As to the meaning of 'academy' see PARA 346 (definition applied by s 187(2), (3)). As to city technology colleges and city colleges for the technology of the arts see PARA 345.

26 Education and Inspections Act 2006 s 11(2)(c). A new foundation special school is not to be regarded for these purposes as replacing a non-maintained special school unless: (1) the non-maintained special school has been approved under the Education Act 1996 s 342 (approval of non-maintained special schools: see PARA 1042) for a continuous period of at least two years ending with the date of the publication of the proposals (Education and Inspections Act 2006 s 11(4)(a)); and (2) it is proposed that the non-maintained special school should continue in existence but should then close as a non-maintained special school immediately before the proposals are implemented (s 11(4)(b)). 'Non-maintained special school' means a school which is approved under the Education Act 1996 s 342: see Education and Inspections Act 2006 s 11(9) (as substituted: see note 13).

27 Education and Inspections Act 2006 s 11(2) (amended by the Apprenticeships, Skills, Children and Learning Act 2009 ss 126(2), (5), 266, Sch 16 Pt 3). As from a day to be appointed the following provision has effect: The governing body of a maintained school may publish proposals under the Education and Inspections Act 2006 s 11(1A) or (2) only if the governing body is for the time being designated for these purposes by the Secretary of State, or by a person authorised by the Secretary of State to designate governing bodies for those purposes; but the governing body of a maintained nursery school may not be designated for these purposes: see s 11A(1), (2) (s 11A prospectively added by the Children, Schools and Families Act 2010 s 7; and amended by the Education Act 2011 para 1, 8). At the date at which this volume states the law no such day had been appointed. As to governing bodies of maintained schools see PARA 150 et seq. As to the Secretary of State see PARA 58.

28 Education and Inspections Act 2006 s 11(5)(a).

29 Education and Inspections Act 2006 s 11(5)(b).
30 Education and Inspections Act 2006 s 11(5). 'Prescribed' means prescribed by regulations made under Pt 2 (ss 6A–32) by the Secretary of State: see s 32(1). As to the regulations made see the School Organisation (Establishment and Discontinuance of Schools) Regulations 2013, SI 2013/3109.
31 As to the exercise of the duty to consult see JUDICIAL REVIEW vol 61 (2010) PARA 627.
32 Education and Inspections Act 2006 s 11(6). As to the publication of guidance see the Education Act 1996 s 571 (provision applied by the Education and Inspections Act 2006 s 187(2), (3)); and PARA 60.
33 As to the regulations made see note 30.
34 Education and Inspections Act 2006 s 11(7) (amended by SI 2010/1158).
35 See the Education and Inspections Act 2006 s 11(8), Sch 2; and PARA 118 et seq.

114. Local authority in England not to establish school in Wales. No proposals may be published[1] for the establishment[2] of a school[3] in Wales[4] which is proposed to be maintained[5] by a local authority in England[6].

1 Ie under the Education and Inspections Act 2006 Pt 2 (ss 6A–32) or any other enactment: see s 14. As to the meaning of 'enactment' see PARA 26 note 15.
2 As to the meaning of 'establish' see PARA 110 note 2 (definition applied by the Education and Inspections Act 2006 s 187(2), (3)).
3 As to the meaning of 'school' see PARA 91 (definition applied by the Education and Inspections Act 2006 s 187(2), (3)).
4 As to the meaning of 'Wales' see PARA 7 note 3.
5 As to the meaning of 'maintain' see PARA 306 note 4.
6 Education and Inspections Act 2006 s 14 (amended by SI 2010/1158). As to the meaning of 'local authority in England' see PARA 25 (definition applied by the Education and Inspections Act 2006 s 187(2), (3)). See also PARA 140.

(C) Discontinuance of Schools

115. Proposals for discontinuance of schools maintained by local authority. Where a local authority in England[1] propose to discontinue[2] a community, foundation or voluntary school[3], a community or foundation special school[4], or a maintained nursery school[5], the authority must publish its proposals[6].

Where the governing body[7] of a foundation or voluntary school in England[8], or a foundation special school in England[9], proposes to discontinue the school, the governing body must publish its proposals[10].

Proposals under these provisions must contain such information[11], and be published in such manner[12], as may be prescribed[13]. Where any proposals are published by a governing body, it must submit the proposals in accordance with regulations[14] to the local authority[15].

The matters to which the relevant body[16] must have regard in formulating any proposals in relation to a rural primary school[17] include: (1) the likely effect of the discontinuance of the school on the local community[18]; (2) the availability, and likely cost to the local authority, of transport to other schools[19]; (3) any increase in the use of motor vehicles which is likely to result from the discontinuance of the school, and the likely effects of any such increase[20]; and (4) any alternatives to the discontinuance of the school[21]. In considering these matters the relevant body must have regard to any guidance given from time to time by the Secretary of State[22].

Before publishing any proposals which relate to a school which is a rural primary school or a community or foundation special school, the relevant body must consult[23]:

(a) the registered parents of registered pupils at the school[24];
(b) in the case of the rural primary school (i) the local authority (where it is

not the relevant body)[25]; (ii) where the local authority is a county council, any district council for the area in which the school is situated[26]; and (iii) any parish council for the area in which the school is situated[27];

(c)   in the case of a community or foundation special school, any local authority which maintains an EHC plan[28] or statement of special educational needs[29] in respect of a registered pupil at the school[30]; and

(d)   such other persons[31] as appear to the relevant body to be appropriate[32].

Before publishing any other proposals, the relevant body must consult such persons as appear to it to be appropriate[33]. In discharging its duty in relation to consultation[34] the relevant body must have regard to any guidance given from time to time by the Secretary of State[35].

Provision is made in relation to the consideration, approval and implementation of proposals published under these proposals[36].

1   As to the meaning of 'local authority in England' see PARA 25 (definition applied by the Education and Inspections Act 2006 s 187(2), (3)).
2   Education and Inspections Act 2006 s 15(1) (amended by SI 2010/1158). As to the meaning of 'discontinue' see PARA 110 note 3.
3   Education and Inspections Act 2006 s 15(1)(a). As to the meaning of references to a community, foundation or voluntary school see PARA 106.
4   Education and Inspections Act 2006 s 15(1)(b). As to the meaning of references to a community or foundation special school see PARA 106.
5   Education and Inspections Act 2006 s 15(1)(c). As to the meaning of 'maintained nursery school' see PARA 99 note 4 (definition applied by s 187(2), (3)).
6   Education and Inspections Act 2006 s 15(1).
7   As to governing bodies of maintained schools see PARA 150 et seq.
8   Education and Inspections Act 2006 s 15(2)(a). As to the meaning of 'England' see PARA 7 note 3.
9   Education and Inspections Act 2006 s 15(2)(b).
10   Education and Inspections Act 2006 s 15(2).
11   Education and Inspections Act 2006 s 15(3)(a).
12   Education and Inspections Act 2006 s 15(3)(b).
13   Education and Inspections Act 2006 s 15(3). 'Prescribed' means prescribed by regulations made under Pt 2 (ss 7–32) by the Secretary of State: see s 32(1). As to the regulations made see the School Organisation (Establishment and Discontinuance of Schools) Regulations 2013, SI 2013/3109. As to the Secretary of State see PARA 58.
14   As to the regulations made see note 13.
15   Education and Inspections Act 2006 s 15(5) (amended by SI 2010/1158).
16   'The relevant body' means the local authority mentioned in the Education and Inspections Act 2006 s 15(1) (see the text to notes 1–6) or the governing body mentioned in s 15(2) (see the text to notes 7–10) (as the case may be): s 15(7)(a) (amended by SI 2010/1158).
17   'Rural primary school' means a primary school designated as such for these purposes by an order made by the Secretary of State: Education and Inspections Act 2006 s 15(7)(b). Such orders, being of local effect, are not recorded in this work. As to the meaning of 'primary school' see PARA 91 (definition applied by s 187(2), (3)).
18   Education and Inspections Act 2006 s 15(4)(a).
19   Education and Inspections Act 2006 s 15(4)(b) (amended by SI 2010/1158).
20   Education and Inspections Act 2006 s 15(4)(c).
21   Education and Inspections Act 2006 s 15(4)(d).
22   Education and Inspections Act 2006 s 15(4). As to the publication of guidance see the Education Act 1996 s 571 (provision applied by the Education and Inspections Act 2006 s 187(2), (3)); and PARA 60.
23   As to the exercise of the duty to consult see JUDICIAL REVIEW vol 61 (2010) PARA 627.
24   Education and Inspections Act 2006 s 16(1)(a). As to the meanings of 'registered', in relation to parents, and 'registered pupil' see PARA 437; and as to the meaning of 'parent' see PARA 7 note 6 (definitions applied by s 187(2), (3)).
25   Education and Inspections Act 2006 s 16(1)(b)(i) (amended by SI 2010/1158).

26 Education and Inspections Act 2006 s 16(1)(b)(ii) (amended by SI 2010/1158). As to local government areas and authorities in England and Wales see LOCAL GOVERNMENT vol 69 (2009) PARA 22 et seq.

27 Education and Inspections Act 2006 s 16(1)(b)(iii). As to parish councils in England see LOCAL GOVERNMENT vol 69 (2009) PARA 27 et seq.

28 As to the meaning of 'EHC plan' see PARA 958 (definition applied by the Education and Inspections Act 2006s 187(2), (3)). As to EHC plans (ie education, health and care plans) generally see PARA 958 et seq.

29 Ie a statement under the Education Act 1996 s 324: see PARA 1002.

30 Education and Inspections Act 2006 s 16(1)(c) (amended by SI 2010/1158; and the Children and Families Act 2014 Sch 3 para 81).

31 As to the meaning of 'person' see PARA 7 note 6.

32 Education and Inspections Act 2006 s 16(1)(d).

33 Education and Inspections Act 2006 s 16(2).

34 Ie its duty under the Education and Inspections Act 2006 s 16(1) or (2): see the text to notes 23–33.

35 Education and Inspections Act 2006 s 16(3).

36 See the Education and Inspections Act 2006 s 15(6), Sch 2; and PARA 118 et seq.

116. Notice by governing body to discontinue foundation or voluntary school. Under the School Standards and Framework Act 1998, the governing body[1] of a foundation or voluntary school[2] in England[3] may discontinue the school by serving on the Secretary of State[4] and the local authority[5] at least two years' notice of its intention to do so[6]. If discontinuing the school would affect the facilities for full-time education suitable to the requirements of persons over compulsory school age[7] who have not attained the age of 19[8], the governing body must, before serving such a notice, consult[9]: (1) if the school is in England (1) the Secretary of State[10]; and (2) each local authority which has secured the provision of education for any such persons at the school[11]. A notice may not be withdrawn without the consent of the local authority[12].

If, while such a notice is in force in respect of a foundation or voluntary school, the governing body informs the local authority that it is unable or unwilling to carry on the school until the notice expires, the authority may conduct the school for all or part of the unexpired period of the notice as if it were a community school[13], and is entitled to use the school premises free of charge for that purpose[14]. While the school is being so conducted, the authority must keep the school premises in good repair[15]; and any interest in the premises which is held for the purposes of the school is to be deemed, for all purposes relating to the condition, occupation or use of the premises, or the making of alterations to them, to be vested in the authority[16]. The governing body may, however, use the premises, or any part of them, when not required for the purposes of the school to the same extent as if it had continued to carry on the school during the unexpired period of the notice[17].

Where land[18] occupied by a foundation or voluntary school is held by any trustees for the purposes of the school[19], and the termination of the school's occupation of that land would have the result that it was not reasonably practicable for the school to continue to be conducted at its existing site[20], then if the trustees (being entitled to do so) give any notice to the governing body which purports to terminate the school's occupation of the land, any such notice is not effective to terminate its occupation of the land unless the following requirements are complied with in relation to the notice (without prejudice to any other statutory or other requirements falling to be so complied with)[21]. The requirements are: (a) that the period of notice must be reasonable having regard to the length of time that would be required to discontinue the school (if the governing body chose to do so)[22], and in any event must not be less than two years[23]; and (b) that a copy of the notice must be given to the Secretary of State and the local authority at the time when the notice is given to the governing body[24].

If a foundation or voluntary school is discontinued under these provisions, the duty of the local authority to maintain[25] the school as a foundation or voluntary school ceases[26].

1   As to the governing bodies of maintained schools see PARA 150 et seq.

2   As to the meaning of 'school' see PARA 91 (definition applied by the School Standards and Framework Act 1998 s 142(8)). As to foundation schools and voluntary schools see PARA 106.

3   As to the meaning of 'England' see PARA 7 note 3.

4   As to the Secretary of State see PARA 58. As to the Welsh equivalent see the School Standards and Organisation (Wales) Act 2013 s 80; and PARA 140.

5   As to the meaning of 'local authority' see PARA 25 (definition applied by the School Standards and Framework Act 1998 s 142(8)).

6   School Standards and Framework Act 1998 s 30(1) (amended by SI 2010/1158; and the School Standards and Organisation (Wales) Act 2013 Sch 5 para 19(1), (5)(a), (d)). No such notice may be served without the consent of the Secretary of State if expenditure has been incurred on the school premises (otherwise than in connection with repairs): (1) by the Secretary of State (School Standards and Framework Act 1998 s 30(2)(a)); (2) by the Funding Agency for Schools (s 30(2)(b)); (3) by any local authority (s 30(2)(c) (amended by SI 2010/1158)); or (4) by an authority which was a local education authority within the meaning of any enactment repealed by the Education Act 1944 (itself now repealed) or an earlier Act (School Standards and Framework Act 1998 s 30(2)(d)). As to the meaning of 'premises' see PARA 62 note 19. The Funding Agency for Schools was dissolved on 1 November 1999: see s 132(1); and the Funding Agency for Schools Dissolution Order 1999, SI 1999/2767. Where the local authority is given a direction by the Secretary of State under the Education and Inspections Act 2006 s 68(1), it must discontinue the school in question on the date specified in the direction; and nothing in the School Standards and Framework Act 1998 s 30 applies to such discontinuance of the school: see the Education and Inspections Act 2006 s 68(4); and PARA 1217.

7   As to the meaning of 'compulsory school age' see PARA 19.

8   As to the time at which a person attains a particular age see PARA 7 note 6.

9   As to the exercise of the duty to consult see JUDICIAL REVIEW vol 61 (2010) PARA 627.

10 School Standards and Framework Act 1998 s 30(3)(a)(i) (s 30(3) amended by SI 2010/1080; and the School Standards and Framework Act 1998 s 30(3)(a)(i) amended by the Education Act 2011 Sch 16 para 12).

11 School Standards and Framework Act 1998 s 30(3)(a)(ii) (as amended: see note 10).

12 School Standards and Framework Act 1998 s 30(7) (amended by SI 2010/1158).

13 School Standards and Framework Act 1998 s 30(4)(a) (amended by SI 2010/1158). As to community schools see PARA 106.

14 School Standards and Framework Act 1998 s 30(4)(b).

15 School Standards and Framework Act 1998 s 30(5)(a).

16 School Standards and Framework Act 1998 s 30(5)(b).

17 See the School Standards and Framework Act 1998 s 30(6).

18 References to an interest in land include any easement, right or charge in, to or over land: Education Act 1996 s 579(2) (definition applied by the School Standards and Framework Act 1998 s 142(8)). 'Land' includes buildings and other structures, land covered with water, and any interest in land: Education Act 1996 s 579(1) (definition as so applied).

19 School Standards and Framework Act 1998 s 30(10)(a). As to the meaning of references to land held by trustees for the purposes of a school see PARA 108 note 6.

20 School Standards and Framework Act 1998 s 30(10)(b). Where trustees give, at the same (or substantially the same) time, notices purporting to terminate a foundation or voluntary school's occupation of two or more pieces of land held by the trustees for the purposes of the school, then for the purpose of determining whether s 30(10)(b) applies in relation to any of those pieces of land, regard may be had to the combined effect of terminating the school's occupation of both or all of them: s 30(12). If a question arises as to whether the termination of a school's occupation of any land would have the result mentioned in s 30(10)(b) (including a question as to whether s 30(12) applies in any particular circumstances), it must be determined by the Secretary of State: s 30(13).

21 School Standards and Framework Act 1998 s 30(10).

22 School Standards and Framework Act 1998 s 30(11)(a)(i).

23 School Standards and Framework Act 1998 s 30(11)(a)(ii).

24 School Standards and Framework Act 1998 s 30(11)(b) (amended by SI 2010/1158).
25 As to the duty to maintain see the School Standards and Framework Act 1998 s 22; and PARA 305.
26 School Standards and Framework Act 1998 s 30(8) (amended by SI 2010/1158). Nothing in any of the following provisions applies in relation to the discontinuance under the School Standards and Framework Act 1998 s 30 of a foundation or voluntary school: the Education and Inspections Act 2006 s 15 (see PARA 115) and s 28 (see PARA 110) (School Standards and Framework Act 1998 s 30(9)(b) (s 30(9) substituted by the Education and Inspections Act 2006 s 30, Sch 3 para 21; and the School Standards and Framework Act 1998 s 30(9)(a) repealed by the School Standards and Organisation (Wales) Sch 5 para 19(1)(5)(c)).

117. Power of the Secretary of State to direct discontinuance of community or foundation special school. The Secretary of State[1] may, if he considers it expedient to do so in the interests of the health, safety or welfare of pupils[2] at a community or foundation special school[3] in England[4], give a direction[5] to the local authority[6] by whom the school is maintained[7] requiring the school to be discontinued[8] on a date specified in the direction[9]. A direction may require the local authority to notify[10] any persons[11] or class of persons specified in the direction[12].

Before giving a direction, the Secretary of State must consult[13]: (1) the local authority[14]; (2) any other local authority who would in his opinion be affected by the discontinuance of the school[15]; (3) in the case of a foundation special school which has a foundation[16], the person who appoints the foundation governors[17]; and (4) such other persons as the Secretary of State considers appropriate[18].

On giving a direction, the Secretary of State must give notice in writing[19] of the direction to the governing body[20] of the school and its head teacher[21].

Where a local authority is given a direction, it must discontinue the school in question on the date specified in the direction[22].

1 As to the Secretary of State see PARA 58.
2 As to the meaning of 'pupil' see PARA 20 note 4 (definition applied by the Education and Inspections Act 2006 s 187(2), (3)).
3 As to the meaning of references to a community or foundation special school see PARA 106.
4 As to the meaning of 'England' see PARA 7 note 3.
5 As to directions see the Education Act 1996 s 570 (provision applied by the Education and Inspections Act 2006 s 187(2), (3)); and PARA 75.
6 As to the meaning of 'local authority' see PARA 25 (definition applied by the Education and Inspections Act 2006 s 187(2), (3)).
7 As to the meaning of 'maintain' see PARA 306 note 4.
8 As to the meaning of 'discontinue' see PARA 110 note 3.
9 Education and Inspections Act 2006 s 17(1) (amended by SI 2010/1158).
10 As to the service of notices see the Education Act 1996 s 572 (provision applied by the Education and Inspections Act 2006 s 187(2), (3)); and PARA 76.
11 As to the meaning of 'person' see PARA 7 note 6.
12 Education and Inspections Act 2006 s 17(2) (amended by SI 2010/1158).
13 As to the exercise of the duty to consult see JUDICIAL REVIEW vol 61 (2010) PARA 627.
14 Education and Inspections Act 2006 s 17(3)(a) (amended by SI 2010/1158).
15 Education and Inspections Act 2006 s 17(3)(b) (amended by SI 2010/1158).
16 As to the meaning of 'foundation' see PARA 108 note 6.
17 Education and Inspections Act 2006 s 17(3)(c).
18 Education and Inspections Act 2006 s 17(3)(d).
19 As to the meaning of 'writing' see PARA 76 note 8.
20 As to governing bodies of maintained schools see PARA 150 et seq.
21 Education and Inspections Act 2006 s 17(4). As to the meaning of 'head teacher' see PARA 86 note 4 (definition applied by s 187(2), (3)).
22 Education and Inspections Act 2006 s 17(5) (amended by SI 2010/1158). Nothing in the Education and Inspections Act 2006 s 15 (see PARA 115) or s 28 (see PARA 110) applies to any such discontinuance of the school under s 17: s 17(5).

(D) Consideration and Implementation of Proposals for the Establishment or Discontinuance of Schools

118.   Objections and comments. Regulations[1] may make provision:
(1)   for the making of objections or comments in relation to proposals[2] within a prescribed[3] period to the relevant authority[4]; and
(2)   requiring the relevant authority, in any case where proposals are to be considered by the Secretary of State or the adjudicator[5], to forward to the Secretary of State or (as the case may be) the adjudicator objections or comments made in relation to the proposals in accordance with the regulations[6].

1   Ie regulations made under the Education and Inspections Act 2006 Pt 2 (ss 6A–32) by the Secretary of State: see s 32(1). As to the regulations made see the School Organisation (Establishment and Discontinuance of Schools) Regulations 2013, SI 2013/3109. As to the Secretary of State see PARA 58.
2   In the Education and Inspections Act 2006 Sch 2, unless a contrary intention appears, 'proposals' means proposals published under any of s 7 (see PARA 111), s 10 (see PARA 112), s 11 (see PARA 113) or s 15 (see PARA 115): Sch 2 para 1(1), (2).
3   'Prescribed' means prescribed by the regulations: see the Education and Inspections Act 2006 s 32(1).
4   Education and Inspections Act 2006 Sch 2 para 5(a). In Sch 2 'the relevant authority' means: (1) in the case of proposals under s 7 (see PARA 111), the local authority who published the notice under that section (Sch 2 para 2(a) (amended by SI 2010/1158)); and (2) in the case of proposals under the Education and Inspections Act 2006 s 10 (see PARA 112), s 11 (see PARA 113) or s 15 (see PARA 115), the local authority who maintains the school or (in the case of a new school) who it is proposed should maintain the school (Sch 2 para 2(b) (amended by SI 2010/1158)). As to the meaning of 'local authority' see PARA 25 (definition applied by the Education and Inspections Act 2006 s 187(2), (3)). As to the meaning of 'maintain' see PARA 306 note 4.
5   As to the meaning of 'adjudicator' see PARA 147 (definition applied by the Education and Inspections Act 2006 s 32(1)).
6   Education and Inspections Act 2006 Sch 2 para 5(b) (amended by the Education Act 2011 Sch 11 paras 10(1), (4)).

119.   Consideration of proposals. Proposals[1] which require consideration under these provisions[2], other than proposals requiring reference to the adjudicator[3], must be considered in the first instance by the relevant authority[4]. Unless the relevant authority is required[5] to refer the proposals to the adjudicator[6]:
(1)   in a case where the proposals were published following an invitation[7] and two or more sets of proposals were published, the authority may:
     (a)   reject all the proposals[8],
     (b)   approve any of the proposals without modification[9], or
     (c)   approve any of the proposals with such modifications as the authority think desirable, after consulting such persons[10] as may be prescribed[11].
(2)   in any other case, the authority may:
     (a)   reject the proposals[12],
     (b)   approve the proposals without modification[13], or
     (c)   approve the proposals with such modifications as the authority think desirable, after consulting such persons as may be prescribed[14].
Any approval given under these provisions may be expressed to take effect only if an event specified in the approval occurs by a date so specified; and regulations may prescribe the events that may be so specified[15]. When deciding

whether or not to give any approval, the relevant authority must have regard to any guidance given from time to time by the Secretary of State[16].

Where proposals[17] appear to the relevant authority to be related to other proposals[18], the authority must consider the proposals together[19]. In deciding for these purposes whether proposals are related to other proposals, the relevant authority must have regard to any guidance given from time to time by the Secretary of State[20].

The following applies where proposals[21] consist of or include academy proposals[22]. The Secretary of State must decide whether to enter into academy arrangements[23] as a result of any of the academy proposals[24]. The Secretary of State must notify the relevant authority of such a decision[25].

The following applies where the proposals[26] include non-academy proposals[27]. If the Secretary of State decides not to enter into academy arrangements as a result of any of the academy proposals, the non-academy proposals require consideration under the above provisions[28]. In any other case, the Secretary of State may direct that all or any of the non-academy proposals require consideration under the provisions[29].

1   As to the meaning of 'proposals' see PARA 118 note 2.
2   Academy proposals do not require consideration under the Education and Inspections Act 2006 Sch 2 para 8 (see Sch 2 para 7A instead; and see the text to notes 21–29)): Sch 2 para 5A(1) (Sch 2 para 5A added by the Education Act 2011 Sch 11 paras 1, 10(1), (7)). If proposals under the Education and Inspections Act 2006 s 7 (see PARA 111) consist wholly of non-academy proposals, the proposals require consideration under Sch 2 para 8: Sch 2 para 5A(2) (as so added). If proposals under s 7 include both academy proposals and non-academy proposals, the non-academy proposals do not require consideration under Sch 2 para 8 unless and until Sch 2 para 7A(5) or (6) (see the text to notes 28, 29) applies: Sch 2 para 5A(3) (as s added). 'Academy proposals' means proposals under s 7 for the establishment of an academy school; and 'non-academy proposals' means proposals under s 7 for the establishment of a school falling within s 7(2)(a) (see PARA 111): Sch 2 para 3A (added by the Education Act 2011 Sch 11 paras 1, 10(1), (2); and amended by Sch 13 para 16(1), (8)). As to the meaning of 'academy school' see PARA 346 note 12 (definition applied by the Education and Inspections Act 2006 s 187(2), (3)).
       All proposals under s 10 (see PARA 112) or s 11 (see PARA 113) require consideration under Sch 2 para 8: Sch 2 para 6 (amended by the Education Act 2011 Sch 11 para 10(1), (8)). Proposals under the Education and Inspections Act 2006 s 15 (see PARA 115) require consideration under Sch 2 para 8 unless the following provisions apply: Sch 2 para 7(1). Proposals under s 15 fall to be dealt with under Sch 2 para 19 (see PARA 122) (and do not require consideration under Sch 2 para 8) if the proposals were made by the relevant authority and either: (1) no objections were made in relation to the relevant proposals in accordance with regulations under Sch 2 para 5 (see PARA 118) (Sch 2 para 7(2)(a)); or (2) all objections so made were withdrawn in writing within the period prescribed by the regulations as that within which any objections must be made (s 32(1), Sch 2 para 7(2)(b)). As to the meaning of 'relevant authority' see PARA 118 note 4. As to the meaning of 'writing' see PARA 76 note 8.
3   Ie proposals to which the Education and Inspections Act 2006 Sch 2 para 10 applies: see PARA 121. As to the meaning of 'adjudicator' see PARA 147 (definition applied by s 32(1)).
4   Education and Inspections Act 2006 Sch 2 para 8(1).
5   Ie by any of the Education and Inspections Act 2006 Sch 2 paras 10–13 and 15: see PARA 121.
6   See the Education and Inspections Act 2006 Sch 2 para 8(2).
7   Ie proposals published under the Education and Inspections Act 2006 s 7: see PARA 111.
8   Education and Inspections Act 2006 Sch 2 para 8(3)(a).
9   Education and Inspections Act 2006 Sch 2 para 8(3)(b). As to the meaning of 'modification' see PARA 21 note 15 (definition applied by s 187(2), (3)).
10 As to the meaning of 'person' see PARA 7 note 6. As to the exercise of the duty to consult see JUDICIAL REVIEW vol 61 (2010) PARA 627.
11 Education and Inspections Act 2006 Sch 2 para 8(3)(c). 'Prescribed' means prescribed by regulations made under Pt 2 (ss 7–32) by the Secretary of State: see s 32(1). As to the regulations made see the School Organisation (Establishment and Discontinuance of Schools) Regulations 2013, SI 2013/3109. As to the Secretary of State see PARA 58.

12 Education and Inspections Act 2006 Sch 2 para 8(4)(a).

13 Education and Inspections Act 2006 Sch 2 para 8(4)(b).

14 Education and Inspections Act 2006 Sch 2 para 8(4)(c). As to the regulations made see note 11.

15 Education and Inspections Act 2006 Sch 2 para 8(5). As to the regulations made see note 11.

16 Education and Inspections Act 2006 Sch 2 para 8(6). As to the publication of guidance see the Education Act 1996 s 571 (applied by the Education and Inspections Act 2006 s 187(2), (3)); and PARA 60.

17 Ie proposals within the Education and Inspections Act 2006 Sch 2 para 9(2A), which are proposals under s 7 (see PARA 111) that require consideration by the authority under Sch 2 para 8; and proposals under s 10 (see PARA 112), s 11 (see PARA 113) or s 15 (see PARA 115): see Sch 2 para 9(2A) (added by the Education Act 2011 Sch 11 paras 1, 10(1), (11)).

18 Ie other proposals within the Education and Inspections Act 2006 Sch 2 para 9(2A) that have not yet been determined.

19 Education and Inspections Act 2006 Sch 2 para 9(2) (substituted by the Education Act 2011 Sch 11 paras 1, 10(1), (11)).

20 Education and Inspections Act 2006 Sch 2 para 9(3).

21 Ie proposals under the Education and Inspections Act 2006 s 7: see PARA 111.

22 Education and Inspections Act 2006 Sch 2 para 7A(1) (Sch 2 para 7A added by the Education Act 2011 Sch 11 paras 1, 10(1), (9)). See note 2.

23 As to the meaning of 'academy arrangements; see PARA 346 note 4 (definition applied by the Education and Inspections Act 2006 s 187(2), (3)).

24 Education and Inspections Act 2006 Sch 2 para 7A(2) (as added: see note 22).

25 Education and Inspections Act 2006 Sch 2 para 7A(3) (as added: see note 22).

26 See note 21.

27 Education and Inspections Act 2006 Sch 2 para 7A(4) (as added: see note 22). See note 2.

28 Education and Inspections Act 2006 Sch 2 para 7A(5) (as added: see note 22). The reference is to Sch 2 para 8.

29 Education and Inspections Act 2006 Sch 2 para 7A (6) (as added: see note 22). See note 28.

120. Withdrawal of proposals. Nothing in the provisions relating to the consideration of proposals[1]:

(1) prevents the proposers[2] by whom any proposals have been made from withdrawing those proposals by notice[3] in writing[4] to the relevant authority[5], and in a case where the proposals have been referred to the adjudicator, also to the adjudicator[6], at any time before the proposals are determined[7] by the authority or by the adjudicator[8];

(2) prevents the relevant authority from withdrawing any proposals made by the authority itself by notice in writing to the adjudicator at any time before the proposals are determined[9] by the adjudicator[10].

1 Ie nothing in the Education and Inspections Act 2006 Sch 2 para 8(1)–(4) (see PARA 119): see Sch 2 para 16(1), (2). As to the meaning of 'proposals' see PARA 118 note 2.

2 In the Education and Inspections Act 2006 Sch 2, 'proposers', in relation to any proposals, means the persons who made the proposals, but does not include a local authority: Sch 2 para 3 (amended by SI 2010/1158). For these purposes: (1) proposals under the Education and Inspections Act 2006 s 7 (see PARA 111) are to be taken to be made by the person who submitted them to the relevant authority under s 7(4)(b) (Sch 2 para 4(a) (amended by the Education Act 2011 Sch 11 paras 1, 10(1), (3))); and (2) proposals under the Education and Inspections Act 2006 s 10 (see PARA 112), s 11 (see PARA 113) or s 15 (see PARA 115) are to be taken to be made by the persons who published them (Sch 2 para 4(b)). As to the meaning of 'person' see PARA 7 note 6. As to the meaning of 'local authority' see PARA 25 (definition applied by the Education and Inspections Act 2006 s 187(2), (3)). As to the meaning of 'relevant authority' see PARA 118 note 4.

3 As to the service of notices see the Education Act 1996 s 572 (applied by the Education and Inspections Act 2006 s 187(2), (3)); and PARA 76.

4 As to the meaning of 'writing' see PARA 76 note 8.

5 Education and Inspections Act 2006 Sch 2 para 16(1)(a).

6 Education and Inspections Act 2006 Sch 2 para 16(1)(b). As to the meaning of 'adjudicator' see PARA 147. As to cases referred to the adjudicator see PARA 121.

7 Ie under the Education and Inspections Act 2006 Sch 2 para 8: see PARA 119.

8 Education and Inspections Act 2006 Sch 2 para 16(1).

9 Ie under the Education and Inspections Act 2006 Sch 2 para 8: see PARA 119.
10 Education and Inspections Act 2006 Sch 2 para 16(2).

121.   Reference to adjudicator. The relevant authority[1] must refer to the adjudicator[2], within a prescribed[3] time:

(1)   all the proposals[4] published[5] in response to a notice by a local authority[6], and which would otherwise require consideration by the authority[7], and consist of or include proposals which relate to the establishment[8] of a foundation school[9] with a qualifying foundation[10];

(2)   any proposals made with the consent of the Secretary of State[11] or which relate to special cases[12] which are made by the relevant authority[13], or relate to the establishment of a foundation school with a qualifying foundation[14].

Regulations may make provision for the making by the relevant authority to the adjudicator of objections to any proposals which are required to be referred to the adjudicator under head (1) or (2) above[15].

Regulations may make provision requiring the relevant authority in prescribed cases to refer to the adjudicator within a prescribed time proposals requiring consideration[16], together with any comments made on the proposals or, as appropriate, any of them[17], by the authority[18].

The Secretary of State may at any time give a direction[19] to a local authority requiring it to refer to the adjudicator by a specified time[20]:

(a)   any proposals which have been published by the authority[21] and which require consideration[22] but which, at the time when the direction is given, have not been determined by the authority[23]; and

(b)   all subsequent proposals so published by the authority until the direction is revoked[24],

together with any comments made on any of the proposals by the authority[25].

If by the end of such period as may be prescribed the relevant authority has not determined whether to give any approval[26], it must within a prescribed time refer to the adjudicator the proposals[27] together with any comments made on the proposals by the authority[28].

The relevant authority must if so requested within a prescribed time by any relevant person[29] refer to the adjudicator within a prescribed time any proposals published with the consent of the Secretary of State[30], relating to special cases[31] or for the discontinuance of a school[32] which the relevant authority has determined[33], together with any reasons given by the authority for its determination[34].

Where the relevant authority are required under any of the above provisions or under the Learning and Skills Act 2000[35] to refer any proposals ('the relevant proposals') to the adjudicator, the authority must also within a prescribed time[36] refer to the adjudicator: (i) any other proposals[37] which relate to the area of the relevant authority and which[38] fall to be considered with the relevant proposals[39]; and (ii) where the relevant proposals are referred to the adjudicator at the request of a relevant person[40], any other proposals[41] which[42] were determined by the relevant authority with the relevant proposals[43].

Where any proposals are referred to the adjudicator under any of the above provision he must consider the proposals or, in a case where the proposals have previously been determined by the relevant authority, must consider them afresh[44]. The revocation of a direction given by the Secretary of State[45] does not affect the determination by the adjudicator of any proposals referred to him before the revocation[46].

1 As to the meaning of 'relevant authority' see PARA 118 note 4.

2 As to the meaning of 'adjudicator' see PARA 147 (definition applied by the Education and Inspections Act 2006 s 32(1)). The adjudicator also has involvement in other areas eg in the context of the School Admissions Code and the procedure regarding admissions complaints: see PARAS 226, 240.

3 'Prescribed' means prescribed by regulations made under the Education and Inspections Act 2006 Pt 2 (ss 6A–32) by the Secretary of State: see s 32(1). As to the regulations made see the School Organisation (Establishment and Discontinuance of Schools) Regulations 2013, SI 2013/3109. As to the Secretary of State see PARA 58.

4 As to the meaning of 'proposals' see PARA 118 note 2.

5 Ie under the Education and Inspections Act 2006 s 7: see PARA 111.

6 Ie under the Education and Inspections Act 2006 s 7: see PARA 111. As to the meaning of 'local authority' see PARA 25 (definition applied by s 187(2), (3)).

7 Education and Inspections Act 2006 Sch 2 para 10(1)(a)(i) (Sch 2 para 10(1)(a) substituted by the Education Act 2011 Sch 11 paras 1, 10(1), (12)). Such consideration would be under the Education and Inspections Act 2006 Sch 2 para 8: see PARA 119.

8 As to the meaning of 'establish' see PARA 110 note 2 (definition applied by the Education and Inspections Act 2006 s 187(2), (3)).

9 As to the meaning of references to a foundation school see PARA 106.

10 See the Education and Inspections Act 2006 Sch 2 para 10(1)(a)(ii) (Sch 2 para 10(1)(a) as substituted: see note 7). A foundation school has a qualifying foundation if it is to be established otherwise than under the School Standards and Framework Act 1998 and any of the following applies: (1) the relevant authority or any person appointed by the relevant authority is to be a member of the foundation (Education and Inspections Act 2006 Sch 2 para 10(2)(a)); (2) any person appointed by the relevant authority is to be a charity trustee (within the meaning of the Charities Act 2011: see CHARITIES vol 8 (2015) PARA 255) of the foundation (Education and Inspections Act 2006 Sch 2 para 10(2)(b) (amended by the Charities Act 2011 Sch 7 para 110); or (3) any voting rights in the foundation are to be exercisable by the relevant authority or persons appointed by the relevant authority (Education and Inspections Act 2006 Sch 2 para 10(2)(c)). As to the meaning of 'foundation' see PARA 108 note 6. As to the meaning of 'person' see PARA 7 note 6.

11 Ie under the Education and Inspections Act 2006 s 10: see PARA 112.

12 Ie under the Education and Inspections Act 2006 s 11: see PARA 113.

13 Education and Inspections Act 2006 Sch 2 para 10(1)(b)(i).

14 Education and Inspections Act 2006 Sch 2 para 10(1)(b)(ii).

15 Education and Inspections Act 2006 Sch 2 para 10(3). As to the regulations made see note 3.

16 Ie under the Education and Inspections Act 2006 Sch 2 para 8 (see PARA 119) (or in the case of proposals under s 7 (see PARA 111) all the proposals requiring consideration under that paragraph).

17 Ie in the case of proposals under the Education and Inspections Act 2006 s 7 (see PARA 111), any of the proposals.

18 Education and Inspections Act 2006 Sch 2 para 11. As to the regulations made see note 3.

19 As to directions see the Education Act 1996 s 570 (applied by the Education and Inspections Act 2006 s 187(2), (3)); and PARA 75.

20 Education and Inspections Act 2006 Sch 2 para 12(1) (amended by SI 2010/1158).

21 Ie under the Education and Inspections Act 2006 s 7: see PARA 111.

22 Ie under the Education and Inspections Act 2006 Sch 2 para 8: see PARA 119.

23 Education and Inspections Act 2006 Sch 2 para 12(1)(a) (amended by the Education Act 2011 Sch 11 paras 1, 10(1), (13)(a)).

24 Education and Inspections Act 2006 Sch 2 para 12(1)(b).

25 Education and Inspections Act 2006 Sch 2 para 12(1).

26 Ie under the Education and Inspections Act 2006 Sch 2 para 8(3) or (4): see PARA 119.

27 Ie (1) in the case mentioned in the Education and Inspections Act 2006 Sch 2 para 8(3) (see PARA 119), all the proposals published under s 7 (see PARA 111) and which require consideration under Sch 2 para 8 (see PARA 119) (Sch 2 para 13(a) (amended by the Education Act 2011 Sch 11 paras 1, 10(1), (4))); and (2) in the case mentioned in the Education and Inspections Act 2006 Sch 2 para 8(4) (see PARA 119), the proposals concerned (Sch 2 para 13(b)).

28 Education and Inspections Act 2006 Sch 2 para 13. As to the regulations made see note 3.

29 The following are relevant persons: (1) the Diocesan Board of Education for any diocese of the Church of England any part of which is comprised in the area of the relevant authority (Education and Inspections Act 2006 Sch 2 para 14(2)(a)); (2) the bishop of any diocese of the Roman Catholic Church any part of which is comprised in the area of the relevant authority (Sch 2 para 14(2)(b)); (3) in the case of proposals made under s 10 (see PARA 112) or s 11 (see

PARA 113) by a person other than the relevant authority and rejected by the authority under Sch 2 para 8(4)(a) (see PARA 119), the proposers (Sch 2 para 14(2)(c)); (4) in the case of proposals published under s 15 (see PARA 115), the governing body or trustees of any foundation, voluntary or foundation special school which is the subject of the proposals (Sch 2 para 14(2)(d)). As to the Church of England see ECCLESIASTICAL LAW vol 34 (2011) PARA 50 et seq. As to the meaning of references to a voluntary school or a foundation special school see PARA 106. As to governing bodies of maintained schools see PARA 150 et seq. As to the time at which a person attains a particular age see PARA 7 note 6.

30 Ie proposals under the Education and Inspections Act 2006 s 10: see PARA 112.
31 Ie proposals under the Education and Inspections Act 2006 s 11: see PARA 113.
32 Ie proposals under the Education and Inspections Act 2006 s 15: see PARA 115.
33 Ie under the Education and Inspections Act 2006 Sch 2 para 8(4): see PARA 119.
34 Education and Inspections Act 2006 Sch 2 para 14(1). As to the regulations made see note 3.
35 Ie the Learning and Skills Act 2000 Sch 7 (repealed).
36 As to the regulations made see note 3.
37 Ie under the Education and Inspections Act 2006 s 7 (see PARA 111), s 10 (see PARA 112), s 11 (see PARA 113) or s 15 (see PARA 115).
38 Ie by virtue of the Education and Inspections Act 2006 Sch 2 para 9(2): see PARA 119.
39 Education and Inspections Act 2006 Sch 2 para 15(a).
40 Ie by virtue of the Education and Inspections Act 2006 Sch 2 para 14: see the text to notes 29–34.
41 Ie under the Education and Inspections Act 2006 s 10 (see PARA 112), s 11 (see PARA 113) or s 15 (see PARA 115).
42 Ie by virtue of the Education and Inspections Act 2006 Sch 2 para 9(2): see PARA 119.
43 Education and Inspections Act 2006 Sch 2 para 15(b).
44 Education and Inspections Act 2006 Sch 2 para 17(1)(a). The following provisions of Sch 2 para 8 (see PARA 119) apply to the adjudicator in connection with his decision on the proposals as they apply to the relevant authority: (1) Sch 2 para 8(3) or (4) (as the case requires) (Sch 2 para 17(1)(b)(i)), and (2) Sch 2 para 8(5) and (6) (Sch 2 para 17(1)(b)(ii)). Sch 2 para 9 (see PARA 119) also applies to him as it applies to the relevant authority: Sch 2 para 17(1)(c).
45 Ie a direction under the Education and Inspections Act 2006 Sch 2 para 12(1): see the text to notes 19–25.
46 Education and Inspections Act 2006 Sch 2 para 17(2).

122. Determination to implement proposals not requiring consideration. Where any proposals have been made for the discontinuance of a school[1] by the relevant authority[2], and the proposals are not subject to the statutory provisions relating to the consideration of proposals[3], the authority must (subject to the following provisions) determine whether the proposals should be implemented[4]. Any such determination must be made within a prescribed period[5].

The requirement to make a determination as referred to above only applies if, at the time when the proposals fall to be considered, the relevant authority is satisfied that the proposals do not relate to any proposals[6] which fall to be determined by the Secretary of State but have not yet been determined by him[7]. Nor does the requirement to make such a determination apply where the proposals appear to the relevant authority to be related to other proposals not yet determined[8]. In deciding whether proposals are related to other proposals, the relevant authority must have regard to any guidance given from time to time by the Secretary of State[9].

Where, in the case of any proposals falling within these provisions[10]: (1) the authority fails to make a determination within the required period[11]; or (2) the requirement to make a determination does not[12] apply[13], the proposals require consideration by the relevant authority[14] and, in a case falling within head (1) above, must be referred to the adjudicator[15].

1 Ie proposals under the Education and Inspections Act 2006 s 15: see PARA 115.
2 As to the meaning of 'relevant authority' see PARA 118 note 4.
3 Ie the Education and Inspections Act 2006 Sch 2 para 7 does not require the proposals to be considered under Sch 2 para 8: see PARA 119.

4   Education and Inspections Act 2006 Sch 2 para 19(1).
5   Education and Inspections Act 2006 Sch 2 para 19(2). 'Prescribed' means prescribed by regulations made under Pt 2 (ss 6A–32) by the Secretary of State: see s 32(1). As to the regulations made see the School Organisation (Establishment and Discontinuance of Schools) Regulations 2013, SI 2013/3109. As to the Secretary of State see PARA 58.
6   Ie under the Learning and Skills Act 2000 s 113A (repealed).
7   Education and Inspections Act 2006 Sch 2 para 19(3).
8   See the Education and Inspections Act 2006 Sch 2 para 19(4). The proposals in question are: (1) other proposals published under s 15 (see PARA 115) and not yet determined (Sch 2 para 19(4)(a)); (2) proposals published under s 7 (see PARA 111) that require consideration under Sch 2 para 8 (see PARA 119) and are not yet determined (Sch 2 para 19(4)(aa) (added by the Education Act 2011 Sch 11 paras 1, 10(1), (16)(a))); (3) proposals published under Education and Inspections Act 2006 s 10 (see PARA 112) or s 11 (see PARA 113) and not yet determined (Sch 2 para 19(4)(b) (amended by the Education Act 2011 Sch 11 paras 1, 10(1), (16)(b))); or (4) proposals published under the Learning and Skills Act 2000 Sch 7 (repealed) and not yet determined (Education and Inspections Act 2006 Sch 2 para 19(4)(c)).
9   Education and Inspections Act 2006 Sch 2 para 19(5). As to the publication of guidance see the Education Act 1996 s 571 (applied by the Education and Inspections Act 2006 s 187(2), (3)); and PARA 60.
10   Ie falling within the Education and Inspections Act 2006 Sch 2 para 19(1): see the text to notes 1–4.
11   Education and Inspections Act 2006 Sch 2 para 19(6)(a). The required period is that mentioned in Sch 2 para 19(2): see the text to note 5.
12   Ie by virtue of the Education and Inspections Act 2006 Sch 2 para 19(3) or (4): see the text to notes 6–8.
13   Education and Inspections Act 2006 Sch 2 para 19(6)(b).
14   Ie under the Education and Inspections Act 2006 Sch 2 para 8: see PARA 119.
15   Education and Inspections Act 2006 Sch 2 para 19(6). As to the meaning of 'adjudicator' see PARA 147 (definition applied by s 32(1)).

123.   Provision of information. Regulations[1] may require one or more of (1) the proposers (if any)[2]; (2) the relevant authority[3]; and (3) the adjudicator[4], to provide such information relating to the proposals[5] to such persons[6], and at such times, as may be prescribed[7].

1   Ie regulations made under the Education and Inspections Act 2006 Pt 2 (ss 6A–32) by the Secretary of State: see s 32(1). As to the regulations made see the School Organisation (Establishment and Discontinuance of Schools) Regulations 2013, SI 2013/3109. As to the Secretary of State see PARA 58.
2   Education and Inspections Act 2006 Sch 2 para 20(a). As to the meaning of 'the proposers' see PARA 120 note 2.
3   Education and Inspections Act 2006 Sch 2 para 20(b). As to the meaning of 'relevant authority' see PARA 118 note 4.
4   Education and Inspections Act 2006 Sch 2 para 20(c). As to the meaning of 'adjudicator' see PARA 147 (definition applied by s 32(1)).
5   As to the meaning of 'proposals' see PARA 118 note 2.
6   As to the meaning of 'person' see PARA 7 note 6.
7   Education and Inspections Act 2006 Sch 2 para 20. 'Prescribed' means prescribed by the regulations: see s 32(1). See note 1.

124.   Requirement to implement proposals. Where any proposals[1] have been approved[2], or the relevant authority[3] has determined[4] to implement any proposals[5], then (subject to the following provisions) the proposals must be implemented[6] in the form in which they were so approved or determined[7].

The relevant authority may, at the request of the proposers[8] who made the proposals, or, where the proposals were made by the authority itself, on its own initiative modify[9] the proposals after consulting[10] such persons[11] as may be prescribed[12], and where any approval was given subject to the occurrence of a specified event[13], specify a later date by which the event in question must occur[14].

If, after consulting such persons as may be prescribed[15], the relevant authority is satisfied that implementation of the proposals would be unreasonably difficult[16], or that circumstances have so altered since approval was given[17] that implementation of the proposals would be inappropriate[18], the authority may determine that the requirement to implement the proposals[19] is to cease to apply to the proposals[20].

The relevant authority must in prescribed cases refer to the adjudicator by a prescribed time any matter which would otherwise fall to be determined by the authority under the above provisions[21]. If by the end of such period as may be prescribed the relevant authority has failed to take any step required by the above provisions, the authority must refer the matter to the adjudicator by the prescribed time[22]. Where any matter is so referred to the adjudicator, the relevant authority may refer to the adjudicator with the matter its comments on it[23], and the adjudicator must consider the matter afresh[24].

1 As to the meaning of 'proposals' see PARA 118 note 2.
2 Education and Inspections Act 2006 Sch 2 para 21(1)(a). The approval referred to is that under Sch 2 para 8: see PARA 119.
3 As to the meaning of 'relevant authority' see PARA 118 note 4.
4 Ie under the Education and Inspections Act 2006 Sch 2 para 19: see PARA 122.
5 Education and Inspections Act 2006 Sch 2 para 21(1)(b).
6 Ie in accordance with the Education and Inspections Act 2006 Sch 2 Pt 3 (paras 21–27): see this paragraph and PARA 125 et seq.
7 Education and Inspections Act 2006 Sch 2 para 21(1).
8 As to the meaning of 'the proposers' see PARA 120 note 2.
9 As to the meaning of 'modify' see PARA 21 note 15 (definition applied by the Education and Inspections Act 2006 s 187(2), (3)).
10 As to the exercise of the duty to consult see JUDICIAL REVIEW vol 61 (2010) PARA 627.
11 As to the meaning of 'person' see PARA 7 note 6.
12 Education and Inspections Act 2006 Sch 2 para 21(2)(a). 'Prescribed' means prescribed by regulations made under Pt 2 (ss 6A–32) by the Secretary of State: see s 32(1). As to the regulations made see the School Organisation (Establishment and Discontinuance of Schools) Regulations 2013, SI 2013/3109. As to the Secretary of State see PARA 58.
13 Ie given in accordance with the Education and Inspections Act 2006 Sch 2 para 8(5): see PARA 119.
14 Education and Inspections Act 2006 Sch 2 para 21(2)(b). Where: (1) any approval under Sch 2 para 8 was given in accordance with Sch 2 para 8(5) (see PARA 119) (Sch 2 para 22(2)(a)); and (2) the event specified under Sch 2 para 8(5) does not occur by the date in question (whether as specified under that provision or as specified under Sch 2 para 21(2)(b)) (Sch 2 para 22(2)(b)), Sch 2 para 21(1) (see the text to notes 1–7) ceases to apply to the proposals (Sch 2 para 22(2)). Where, by virtue of Sch 2 para 22(2), Sch 2 para 21(1) ceases to apply to any proposals approved by the relevant authority under Sch 2 para 8 and not referred to the adjudicator, those proposals must be considered afresh by the authority under Sch 2 para 8: Sch 2 para 22(3). Where, by virtue of Sch 2 para 22(2), Sch 2 para 21(1) ceases to apply to any proposals approved by the adjudicator under Sch 2 para 8, those proposals must be considered afresh by him under that paragraph (and Sch 2 para 17 (see PARA 121) applies accordingly): Sch 2 para 22(4). As to the meaning of 'adjudicator' see PARA 147 (definition applied by s 32(1)).
15 As to the regulations made see note 12.
16 Education and Inspections Act 2006 Sch 2 para 21(3)(a).
17 Ie under the Education and Inspections Act 2006 Sch 2 para 8: see PARA 119.
18 Education and Inspections Act 2006 Sch 2 para 21(3)(b).
19 Ie the Education and Inspections Act 2006 Sch 2 para 21(1): see the text to notes 1–7.
20 Education and Inspections Act 2006 Sch 2 para 21(3). The relevant authority may only make such a determination where proposals that it should do so have been published, in accordance with regulations, by the authority or proposers who made the proposals referred to in Sch 2 para 21(1) (see the text to notes 1–7); and regulations may provide for any of the provisions of ss 7–12 (see PARA 111 et seq), ss 15 and 16 (see PARA 115) and Sch 2 Pt 1 (paras 1–20) (see PARA 118 et seq) and Pt 2 (see this paragraph and PARA 125 et seq) to have effect in relation to any such further proposals with or without modifications: Sch 2 para 21(4). As to the regulations made see note 12. Where, by virtue of Sch 2 para 21(3), Sch 2 para 21(1) ceases to apply to any

proposals, those proposals are to be treated for the purposes of Sch 2 as if they had been rejected under Sch 2 para 8 (see PARA 119): Sch 2 para 22(1).

21 Education and Inspections Act 2006 Sch 2 para 21(5). As to the regulations made see note 12.
22 Education and Inspections Act 2006 Sch 2 para 21(6). As to the regulations made see note 12.
23 Education and Inspections Act 2006 Sch 2 para 21(7)(a).
24 Education and Inspections Act 2006 Sch 2 para 21(7)(b). Such of the provisions of Sch 2 para 21(2)–(4) (see the text to notes 8–20) as are relevant apply to the adjudicator in connection with his decision on that matter as they apply to the authority: Sch 2 para 21(7)(c).

125. Implementation of proposals relating to community, community special schools or maintained nursery schools. Where proposals[1] fall to be implemented[2] and relate to a community school, a community special school[3] or a maintained nursery school[4] or to a proposed such school[5], the proposals must be implemented by the relevant authority[6].

1 As to the meaning of 'proposals' see PARA 118 note 2.
2 Ie under the Education and Inspections Act 2006 Sch 2 para 21: see PARA 124.
3 As to the meaning of references to a community school and a community special school see PARA 106.
4 As to the meaning of 'maintained nursery school' see PARA 99 note 4 (definition applied by the Education and Inspections Act 2006 s 187(2), (3)).
5 Education and Inspections Act 2006 Sch 2 para 23(1).
6 Education and Inspections Act 2006 Sch 2 para 23(2). As to the meaning of 'relevant authority' see PARA 118 note 4.

126. Implementation of proposals relating to foundation or voluntary controlled schools. Where proposals[1] fall to be implemented[2] and relate to a foundation or voluntary controlled school[3] or a proposed such school[4]:

  (1)   proposals made by the relevant authority[5] must be implemented by the authority[6]; and

  (2)   proposals made by proposers[7] (including, in particular, such proposals so far as relating to the provision of the site for a proposed school) must be implemented by the relevant authority and by the proposers, respectively, to such extent as the proposals provide for each of them to do so[8].

1 As to the meaning of 'proposals' see PARA 118 note 2.
2 Ie under the Education and Inspections Act 2006 Sch 2 para 21: see PARA 124.
3 As to the meaning of references to foundation schools and voluntary schools see PARA 106.
4 Education and Inspections Act 2006 Sch 2 para 24(1).
5 As to the meaning of 'relevant authority' see PARA 118 note 4.
6 Education and Inspections Act 2006 Sch 2 para 24(2). As to the provision of sites and buildings for schools see Sch 2 para 28; and PARA 129.
7 As to the meaning of 'the proposers' see PARA 120 note 2.
8 Education and Inspections Act 2006 Sch 2 para 24(3).

127. Implementation of proposals relating to voluntary aided schools. Where proposals[1] fall to be implemented[2] and relate to a voluntary aided school[3] or a proposed voluntary aided school[4], the proposals must be implemented:

  (1)   so far as relating to the provision of any relevant premises[5] for a proposed school, by the relevant authority[6];

  (2)   in the case of proposals for the discontinuance of a school[7] made by proposers[8], by the proposers and the relevant authority[9]; and

  (3)   otherwise by the proposers or, in the case of proposals made by the relevant authority, by the relevant authority[10].

Nothing in heads (1) to (3) above requires the relevant authority to provide any playing fields where: (a) a new voluntary aided school is to be established[11] in place of one or more existing independent[12], foundation[13] or voluntary schools falling to be discontinued[14] on or before the date of implementation of the proposals[15]; and (b) those playing fields were part of the premises[16] of any of the existing schools (whether it was an independent school or a foundation or voluntary school)[17], and (if it was a foundation or voluntary school) were not provided by the authority[18].

1 As to the meaning of 'proposals' see PARA 118 note 2.
2 Ie under the Education and Inspections Act 2006 Sch 2 para 21: see PARA 124.
3 As to the meaning of references to voluntary schools see PARA 106.
4 Education and Inspections Act 2006 Sch 2 para 25(1).
5 'Relevant premises' means: (1) in the case of proposals published under the Education and Inspections Act 2006 s 7 (see PARA 111), the site specified in the notice under that section or playing fields (Sch 2 para 25(3)(a)); and (2) in any other case, playing fields (Sch 2 para 25(3)(b)).
6 Education and Inspections Act 2006 Sch 2 para 25(2)(a). As to the meaning of 'relevant authority' see PARA 118 note 4. As to grants in respect of certain expenditure relating to a proposed voluntary aided school see Sch 2 para 29; and PARA 130. As to certain other assistance relating thereto see Sch 2 paras 30–31; and PARA 131.
7 Ie proposals under the Education and Inspections Act 2006 s 15: see PARA 115.
8 As to the meaning of 'the proposers' see PARA 120 note 2.
9 Education and Inspections Act 2006 Sch 2 para 25(2)(b).
10 Education and Inspections Act 2006 Sch 2 para 25(2)(c).
11 As to the meaning of 'establish' see PARA 110 note 2 (definition applied by the Education and Inspections Act 2006 s 187(2), (3)).
12 As to independent schools see PARA 369 et seq.
13 As to the meaning of references to a foundation school see PARA 106.
14 As to the meaning of 'discontinue' see PARA 110 note 3.
15 Education and Inspections Act 2006 Sch 2 para 25(4)(a).
16 As to the meaning of 'premises' see PARA 62 note 19 (definition applied by the Education and Inspections Act 2006 s 187(2), (3)).
17 Education and Inspections Act 2006 Sch 2 para 25(4)(b)(i).
18 Education and Inspections Act 2006 Sch 2 para 25(4)(b)(ii).

128. Implementation of proposals relating to foundation special schools. Where proposals[1] fall to be implemented[2] and relate to a foundation special school[3] or a proposed foundation special school[4]:

(1) where the proposals were made by the relevant authority[5], they must be implemented by the authority[6];

(2) proposals made by proposers[7] (including, in particular, proposals so far as relating to the provision of the site for a proposed school) must be implemented by the relevant authority and by the proposers, respectively, to such extent as the proposals provide for each of them to do so[8].

1 As to the meaning of 'proposals' see PARA 118 note 2.
2 Ie under the Education and Inspections Act 2006 Sch 2 para 21: see PARA 124.
3 As to the meaning of references to a foundation special school see PARA 106.
4 Education and Inspections Act 2006 Sch 2 para 26(1).
5 As to the meaning of 'relevant authority' see PARA 118 note 4.
6 Education and Inspections Act 2006 Sch 2 para 26(2). As to the provision of sites and buildings for schools see Sch 2 para 28; and PARA 129.
7 As to the meaning of 'the proposers' see PARA 120 note 2.
8 Education and Inspections Act 2006 Sch 2 para 26(3).

129. Provision of site and buildings for proposed foundation, voluntary controlled or foundation special schools. Where a local authority[1] is required[2] to provide a site[3] for a proposed foundation[4] or voluntary controlled school[5], or[6] to provide a site for a proposed foundation special school[7], the authority must transfer its interest[8] in the site and in any buildings on the site which are to form part of the school's premises: (1) to the school's trustees, to be held by them on trust for the purposes of the school[9]; or (2) if the school has no trustees, to the school's foundation body or (in the absence of such a body) to the governing body, to be held by that body for the relevant purposes[10].

If any doubt or dispute arises as to the persons[11] to whom the authority is required to make the transfer, it must be made to such persons as the adjudicator[12] thinks proper[13]. The authority must pay to the persons to whom the transfer is made their reasonable costs in connection with the transfer[14].

Where a transfer is made under these provisions[15], and the transfer is made to persons who possess, or are or may become entitled to, any sum representing proceeds of the sale of other premises which have been used for the purposes of the school[16], those persons must notify[17] the local authority that this provision[18] applies to them; and they or their successors must pay to the local authority so much of that sum as, having regard to the value of the interest transferred, may be determined to be just, either by agreement between them and the authority[19] or, in default of agreement, by the adjudicator[20].

1   As to the meaning of 'local authority' see PARA 25 (definition applied by the Education and Inspections Act 2006 s 187(2), (3)).

2   Ie by virtue of the Education and Inspections Act 2006 Sch 2 para 24(2) or (3) (see PARA 126): see Sch 2 para 28(1) (amended by SI 2010/1158).

3   'Site' does not include playing fields but otherwise includes any site which is to form part of the premises of the school in question: Education and Inspections Act 2006 Sch 2 para 28(10). As to the meaning of 'premises' see PARA 62 note 19 (definition applied by s 187(2), (3)).

4   As to the meaning of references to a foundation school see PARA 106.

5   Education and Inspections Act 2006 Sch 2 para 28(1)(a). As to the meaning of references to a voluntary school see PARA 106.

6   Ie by virtue of the Education and Inspections Act 2006 Sch 2 para 26(2) or (3): see PARA 128.

7   Education and Inspections Act 2006 Sch 2 para 28(1)(b). As to the meaning of references to a foundation special school see PARA 106.

8   As to the meaning of 'interest in land' see PARA 116 note 18 (definition applied by the Education and Inspections Act 2006 s 187(2), (3)).

9   Education and Inspections Act 2006 Sch 2 para 28(2)(a).

10   Education and Inspections Act 2006 Sch 2 para 28(2)(b). 'The relevant purposes' means: (1) in relation to a transfer to a school's foundation body, the purposes of the schools comprising the group for which that body acts; and (2) in relation to a transfer to a school's governing body, the purposes of the school: Sch 2 para 28(10). As to governing bodies of maintained schools see PARA 150 et seq.

11   As to the meaning of 'person' see PARA 7 note 6.

12   As to the meaning of 'adjudicator' see PARA 147 (definition applied by the Education and Inspections Act 2006 s 32(1)).

13   Education and Inspections Act 2006 Sch 2 para 28(3).

14   Education and Inspections Act 2006 Sch 2 para 28(4).

15   Education and Inspections Act 2006 Sch 2 para 28(5)(a).

16   Education and Inspections Act 2006 Sch 2 para 28(5)(b). In this provision the reference to proceeds of the sale of other premises includes a reference to: (1) consideration for the creation or disposition of any kind of interest in other premises, including rent (Sch 2 para 28(6)(a)); and (2) interest which has accrued in respect of any such consideration (Sch 2 para 28(6)(b)).

17   As to the service of notices see the Education Act 1996 s 572 (provision applied by the Education and Inspections Act 2006 s 187(2), (3)); and PARA 76.

18   Ie the Education and Inspections Act 2006 Sch 2 para 28(5)(b): see the text to note 16.

19   For the purposes of any agreed determination under the Education and Inspections Act 2006 Sch 2 para 28(5) regard must be had to any guidance given from time to time by the Secretary of State: Sch 2 para 28(6). As to the publication of guidance see the Education Act 1996 s 571 (applied by the Education and Inspections Act 2006 s 187(2), (3)); and PARA 60. As to the Secretary of State see PARA 58.

20   Education and Inspections Act 2006 Sch 2 para 28(5) (amended by SI 2010/1158). Any sum paid under this provision is to be treated for the purposes of the School Sites Act 1841 s 14

(which relates to the sale or exchange of land held on trust for the purposes of a school: see PARA 1297) as a sum applied in the purchase of a site for the school: Education and Inspections Act 2006 Sch 2 para 28(7). A determination may be made under Sch 2 para 28(5) in respect of any property subject to a trust which has arisen under the Reverter of Sites Act 1987 s 1 (right of reverter replaced by trust for sale: see CHARITIES vol 8 (2015) PARA 70) if, and only if the determination is made by the adjudicator (Education and Inspections Act 2006 Sch 2 para 28(8)(a)), and he is satisfied that steps have been taken to protect the interests of the beneficiaries under the trust (Sch 2 para 28(8)(b)). Sch 2 para 28(5) is to apply for the purpose of compensating the authority notified under that provision only in relation to such part of the sum mentioned in Sch 2 para 28(5)(b) (see the text to note 16) (if any) as remains after the application of the School Standards and Framework Act 1998 Sch 22 paras A1–A16 (see PARAS 1305–1308) or Sch 22 paras 1–3 (see PARAS 1313–1317) to that sum: Education and Inspections Act 2006 Sch 2 para 28(9).

130. Grants in respect of certain expenditure relating to proposed voluntary aided schools. Where any proposers[1] are required[2] to implement proposals[3] involving the establishment[4] of a new voluntary aided school[5], the School Standards and Framework Act 1998[6] applies in relation to the new school as it applies in relation to an existing voluntary aided school[7].

1　As to the meaning of 'the proposers' see PARA 120 note 2.
2　Ie by virtue of the Education and Inspections Act 2006 Sch 2 para 25(2): see PARA 127.
3　As to the meaning of 'proposals' see PARA 118 note 2.
4　As to the meaning of 'establish' see PARA 110 note 2 (definition applied by the Education and Inspections Act 2006 s 187(2), (3)).
5　Education and Inspections Act 2006 Sch 2 para 29(1). As to the meaning of references to a voluntary school see PARA 106.
6　Ie the School Standards and Framework Act 1998 Sch 3 para 5: see PARA 312.
7　Education and Inspections Act 2006 Sch 2 para 29(2). In the application of the School Standards and Framework Act 1998 Sch 3 para 5 in relation to a new voluntary aided school: (1) the references to the governing body, in relation to any time before the governing body is constituted, are to be read as references to the proposers (Education and Inspections Act 2006 Sch 2 para 29(3)(a)); (2) where requirements are imposed in relation to grant paid by virtue of Sch 2 para 29 to the proposers, the requirements must be complied with by the governing body, when they are constituted, as well as by the proposers (Sch 2 para 29(3)(b)). As to governing bodies of maintained schools see PARA 150 et seq.

131. Assistance for proposers of proposed voluntary aided schools. A local authority[1] may give to persons[2] required[3] to implement proposals[4] involving the establishment[5] of a voluntary aided school[6] such assistance as the authority thinks fit in relation to the carrying out by those persons of any obligation arising by virtue of that requirement[7].

Where such assistance consists of the provision of any premises[8] for use for the purposes of a school, the local authority must transfer its interest in the premises[9] to the trustees of the school to be held on trust for the purposes of the school[10], or if the school has no trustees, to the school's foundation body, to be held by that body for the relevant purposes[11].

If any doubt or dispute arises as to the persons to whom the authority is required to make the transfer it must be made to such persons as the adjudicator[12] thinks proper[13]. The authority must pay to the persons to whom the transfer is made their reasonable costs in connection with the transfer[14].

1　As to the meaning of 'local authority' see PARA 25 (definition applied by the Education and Inspections Act 2006 s 187(2), (3)).
2　As to the meaning of 'person' see PARA 7 note 6.
3　Ie by virtue of the Education and Inspections Act 2006 Sch 2 para 25(2): see PARA 127.
4　As to the meaning of 'proposals' see PARA 118 note 2.
5　As to the meaning of 'establish' see PARA 110 note 2 (definition applied by the Education and Inspections Act 2006 s 187(2), (3)).

6   As to the meaning of references to a voluntary school see PARA 106.
7   Education and Inspections Act 2006 Sch 2 para 30 (amended by SI 2010/1158).
8   As to the meaning of 'premises' see PARA 62 note 19 (definition applied by the Education and Inspections Act 2006 s 187(2), (3)).
9   Education and Inspections Act 2006 Sch 2 para 31(1) (amended by SI 2010/1158). As to the meaning of 'interest in land' see PARA 116 note 18 (definition applied by the Education and Inspections Act 2006 s 187(2), (3)).
10 Education and Inspections Act 2006 Sch 2 para 31(1)(a).
11 Education and Inspections Act 2006 Sch 2 para 31(1)(b). 'The relevant purposes' means, in relation to a transfer to a school's foundation body, the purposes of the schools comprising the group for which that body acts: Sch 2 para 31(4).
12 As to the meaning of 'adjudicator' see PARA 147 (definition applied by the Education and Inspections Act 2006 s 32(1)).
13 Education and Inspections Act 2006 Sch 2 para 31(2).
14 Education and Inspections Act 2006 Sch 2 para 31(3).

(E) Alterations to Schools

132.   Alterations that may be made. Prescribed alterations[1] may generally only be made to a maintained school[2] in pursuance of proposals falling to be implemented under the Education and Inspections Act 2006[3]. Regulations[4] may prescribe alterations to maintained schools that may be implemented in pursuance of published proposals[5]. The prescribed alterations must include any alteration that involves one or more of the following:

(1)   in the case of a school falling within any of the statutory categories[6], any change in the category within which the school falls (other than a change prevented by heads (c) to (f) below)[7];

(2)   the acquisition by a foundation or foundation special school[8] of a foundation[9] established otherwise than under School Standards and Framework Act 1998[10]; and

(3)   in the case of a school whose instrument of government does not provide for a majority of the governing body[11] to be foundation governors, any change in the instrument of government which results in the majority of governors being foundation governors[12].

The prescribed alterations may include other alterations of any nature (other than those prevented by heads (a) to (f) below)[13].

None of the following alterations may be made to a maintained school:

(a)   any change in the religious character of the school[14];

(b)   any change whereby the school would acquire or lose a religious character[15];

(c)   any change of category from foundation or voluntary school to community school[16];

(d)   any change of category from foundation special school to community special school[17];

(e)   any change of category from mainstream school[18] to community or foundation special school or from community or foundation special school to mainstream school[19];

(f)   any change from maintained nursery school[20] to any other kind of maintained school, or from any other kind of maintained school to maintained nursery school[21].

1   As to the meaning of 'prescribed alteration' for these purposes see PARA 110 note 4. See also the Education and Inspections Act 2006 s 18; and the text and notes 4–21.
2   As to the meaning of 'maintained school' see PARA 110 note 1.
3   See the Education and Inspections Act 2006 s 28; and PARA 110.

4   Ie regulations made under the Education and Inspections Act 2006 Pt 2 (ss 6A–32) by the Secretary of State: see s 32(1). As to the regulations made see the School Organisation (Prescribed Alterations to Maintained Schools) (England) Regulations 2013, SI 2013/3110. As to the Secretary of State see PARA 58.

5   Education and Inspections Act 2006 s 18(1). The proposals referred to in the text are those published under s 19 (see PARA 133): see s 18(1).

     As to school organisation proposals in Wales including alteration and change of category see the School Standards and Organisation (Wales) Act 2013; and PARA 140 et seq.

6   Ie the categories set out in the School Standards and Framework Act 1998 s 20(1): see PARA 106.

7   Education and Inspections Act 2006 s 18(2)(a).

8   As to the meaning of references to a foundation school and a foundation special school see PARA 106.

9   'Foundation', in relation to a foundation or voluntary school, has (subject to the Education and Inspections Act 2006 s 25(8) (see PARA 137) and s 27(8) (see PARA 138)), the meaning given by the School Standards and Framework Act 1998 s 21(3) (see PARA 108 note 6): Education and Inspections Act 2006 s 32(1). As to the meaning of references to a voluntary school see PARA 106.

10   Education and Inspections Act 2006 s 18(2)(b).

11   As to governing bodies of maintained schools see PARA 150 et seq. As to instruments of government see PARA 184 et seq.

12   Education and Inspections Act 2006 s 18(2)(c).

13   Education and Inspections Act 2006 s 18(3).

14   Education and Inspections Act 2006 s 18(4)(a). A foundation or voluntary school has a religious character if it is designated by order under the School Standards and Framework Act 1998 s 69(3) (see PARA 914) as a school having such a character: Education and Inspections Act 2006 s 32(2).

15   Education and Inspections Act 2006 s 18(4)(b).

16   Education and Inspections Act 2006 s 18(4)(c). As to the meaning of references to a community school see PARA 106.

17   Education and Inspections Act 2006 s 18(4)(d). As to the meaning of references to a community special school see PARA 106.

18   'Mainstream school' means community, foundation or voluntary school: Education and Inspections Act 2006 s 18(5).

19   Education and Inspections Act 2006 s 18(4)(e).

20   As to the meaning of 'maintained nursery school' see PARA 99 note 4 (definition applied by the Education and Inspections Act 2006 s 187(2), (3)).

21   Education and Inspections Act 2006 s 18(4)(f).

133. Publication of proposals for alteration of school. Where the local authority[1] proposes to make a prescribed alteration[2] to a maintained school[3], and the prescribed alteration is one that[4] is capable of being proposed by a local authority[5], the authority must publish its proposals[6]. A prescribed alteration is capable of being proposed by a local authority if:

(1)   in the case of a community school, a community special school[7] or a maintained nursery school[8], it is an alteration designated by regulations[9] as one capable of being proposed by the local authority[10];

(2)   in the case of a foundation or voluntary school[11], it consists of any one or more of the following: an enlargement[12] of the premises[13]; an increase in the number of pupils[14] in any relevant age group[15]; the establishment[16] or discontinuance[17] of educational provision for pupils with special educational needs[18]; the establishment of educational provision suitable to the requirements of pupils over compulsory school age[19]; and

(3)   in the case of a foundation special school[20], it consists of any one or more of the following: an enlargement of the premises[21]; an increase in the number of pupils for whom the school is organised to make provision[22]; a change in the type of special educational needs for which the school is organised to make provision[23].

Where the governing body[24] of a maintained school proposes to make a prescribed alteration to the school[25], and in the case of a community school, a community special school or a maintained nursery school, the prescribed alteration is designated by regulations[26] as one capable of being proposed by the governing body[27], the governing body must publish its proposals[28].

If at any time the governing body of a voluntary aided school is unable or unwilling to carry out its obligations[29] in respect of the funding of the school, it must publish proposals for the school to become either a voluntary controlled school or a foundation school, as the governing body may determine[30].

Regulations may make provision about the publication and determination of proposals[31]. The provision that may be made includes provision: (a) about the information to be included in, or provided in relation to, the proposals[32]; (b) about consultation on the proposals[33]; (c) about the manner in which proposals are to be published[34]; (d) for the making of objections to or comments on the proposals[35]; (e) requiring the proposals to be considered with related proposals published under the above provisions or any other enactment[36]; (f) for the consideration and determination of the proposals by a prescribed person (who may be the person who published the proposals)[37]; (g) for the referral of proposals to the adjudicator[38] in prescribed cases for consideration and determination by him (instead of by a person prescribed by virtue of head (f))[39]; (h) for the referral of proposals to the adjudicator, at the request of a prescribed person, after their initial determination by a person other than the adjudicator[40]; (i) for the approval of proposals with or without modification[41]; (j) for the making in prescribed cases of a conditional approval[42]; (k) for the withdrawal of proposals[43]; (l) as to the manner in which, and time within which, anything required or authorised by the regulations must be done[44].

The regulations may confer functions on the local authority, on any other local authority affected by the proposals, on the governing body of the school concerned and on the adjudicator[45]. In relation to any proposals for a school to cease to be an establishment which admits pupils of one sex only, the regulations may enable the local authority or the adjudicator to make a transitional exemption order[46], and to vary or revoke any order so made[47]. The regulations may require any person exercising functions under the regulations to have regard to any guidance given from time to time by the Secretary of State[48].

1   As to the meaning of 'local authority' see PARA 25 (definition applied by the Education and Inspections Act 2006 s 187(2), (3)).
2   'Prescribed alteration', in relation to a maintained school, means an alteration prescribed under the Education and Inspections Act 2006 s 18 (see PARA 132): s 19(6). As to the meaning of 'maintained school' see PARA 110 note 1.
3   Education and Inspections Act 2006 s 19(1)(a) (amended by SI 2010/1158).
4   Ie under the Education and Inspections Act 2006 s 19(2): see the text to notes 7–23.
5   Education and Inspections Act 2006 s 19(1)(b) (amended by SI 2010/1158).
6   Education and Inspections Act 2006 s 19(1). As to the implementation of proposals see s 24; and PARA 136.
7   As to the meaning of references to a community school and a community special school see PARA 106.
8   As to the meaning of 'maintained nursery school' see PARA 99 note 4 (definition applied by the Education and Inspections Act 2006 s 187(2), (3)).
9   Ie regulations made under the Education and Inspections Act 2006 s 19(2) by the Secretary of State: see ss 19(2)(a), 32(1). As to the regulations made see the School Organisation (Prescribed Alterations to Maintained Schools) (England) Regulations 2013, SI 2013/3110. As to the Secretary of State see PARA 58.
10 Education and Inspections Act 2006 s 19(2)(a) (amended by SI 2010/1158).
11 As to the meaning of references to a foundation or voluntary school see PARA 106.

12 As to the meaning of 'enlargement' see PARA 110 note 2 (definition applied by the Education and Inspections Act 2006 s 187(2), (3)).
13 Education and Inspections Act 2006 s 19(2)(b)(i). As to the meaning of 'premises' see PARA 62 note 19 (definition applied by s 187(2), (3)).
14 As to the meaning of 'pupil' see PARA 20 note 4 (definition applied by the Education and Inspections Act 2006 s 187(2), (3)).
15 Education and Inspections Act 2006 s 19(2)(b)(ii). 'Relevant age group', in relation to a school, means an age group in which pupils are normally admitted (or, as the case may be, will normally be admitted) to the school: School Standards and Framework Act 1998 s 142(1) (definition applied by the Education and Inspections Act 2006 s 19(6)). As to the meaning of 'school' see PARA 91 (definition applied by the School Standards and Framework Act 1998 s 142(8); Education and Inspections Act 2006 s 187(2), (3)). As to school admissions see PARA 224 et seq.
16 As to the meaning of 'establish' see PARA 110 note 2 (definition applied by the Education and Inspections Act 2006 s 187(2), (3)).
17 As to the meaning of 'discontinue' see PARA 110 note 3.
18 Education and Inspections Act 2006 s 19(2)(b)(iii). As to the meaning of 'special educational needs' see PARAS 943 (definition applied by s 187(2), (3)).
19 Education and Inspections Act 2006 s 19(2)(b)(iv). As to the meaning of 'compulsory school age' see PARA 19.
20 As to the meaning of references to a foundation special school see PARA 106.
21 Education and Inspections Act 2006 s 19(2)(c)(i).
22 Education and Inspections Act 2006 s 19(2)(c)(ii).
23 Education and Inspections Act 2006 s 19(2)(c)(iii).
24 As to governing bodies of maintained schools see PARA 150 et seq.
25 Education and Inspections Act 2006 s 19(3)(a).
26 Ie regulations made under the Education and Inspections Act 2006 s 19(3) by the Secretary of State: see ss 19(3)(b), 32(1). As to the regulations made see note 9.
27 Education and Inspections Act 2006 s 19(3)(b).
28 Education and Inspections Act 2006 s 19(3). Section 19 has effect subject to s 20: s 19(5). The governing body of a school as specified below may not publish proposals under s 19 for a prescribed alteration of a kind as specified below, except with the consent of the trustees of the school (s 20(1)(a)), and the person or persons by whom the foundation governors are appointed (s 20(1)(b)):
    (1) a foundation school which, immediately before the commencement date, was a foundation school having a foundation may not publish, as stated above, a relevant change in the instrument of government (see s 20(1) Table para 1);
    (2) a voluntary school may not publish, as stated above, a change of category from voluntary controlled school or voluntary aided school to foundation school (s 20(1) Table para 2);
    (3) a foundation school which, having been a voluntary school immediately before the commencement date, changed category to foundation school on or after that date may not publish, as stated above, a relevant change in the instrument of government (s 20(1) Table para 3).
    A 'relevant change' in the instrument of government of a school is a change which results in the majority of governors being foundation governors: s 20(2). 'The commencement date' means 25 May 2007 (being the day on which Pt 2 (ss 6A–32) came into force, otherwise than merely for the purpose of enabling orders or regulations to be made): s 20(3). As to the meaning of 'foundation' see PARA 108 note 6. As to the meaning of 'person' see PARA 7 note 6. As to instruments of government see PARA 184 et seq.
29 Ie the School Standards and Framework Act 1998 Sch 3: see PARA 310 et seq.
30 Education and Inspections Act 2006 s 19(4). This provision is subject to s 20: see s 19(5); and note 28.
31 Education and Inspections Act 2006 s 21(1). As to the regulations made see note 9.
32 Education and Inspections Act 2006 s 21(2)(a).
33 Education and Inspections Act 2006 s 21(2)(b).
34 Education and Inspections Act 2006 s 21(2)(c).
35 Education and Inspections Act 2006 s 21(2)(d).
36 Education and Inspections Act 2006 s 21(2)(e). As to the meaning of 'enactment' see PARA 26 note 15.
37 Education and Inspections Act 2006 s 21(2)(f).
38 As to the meaning of 'adjudicator' see PARA 147 (definition applied by the Education and Inspections Act 2006 s 32(1)).

39 Education and Inspections Act 2006 s 21(2)(g). Regulations made by virtue of this provision may enable the Secretary of State by direction to require proposals to be referred to the adjudicator: s 21(4). As to directions see the Education Act 1996 s 570 (applied by the Education and Inspections Act 2006 s 187(2), (3)); and PARA 75. In certain cases regulations under s 21 may not make provision under s 21(2)(g): see s 22; and PARA 134. As to the requirement that the regulations provide for the right of local authorities to require proposals to be referred to the adjudicator in certain cases see s 23; and PARA 135.

40 Education and Inspections Act 2006 s 21(2)(h). In certain cases regulations under s 21 may not make provision under s 21(2)(h): see s 22; and PARA 134. As to the requirement that the regulations provide for the right of certain bodies to require proposals to be referred to the adjudicator in certain cases see s 23; and PARA 135.

41 Education and Inspections Act 2006 s 21(2)(i). As to the meaning of 'modifications' see PARA 21 note 15 (definition applied by s 187(2), (3)).

42 Education and Inspections Act 2006 s 21(2)(j).

43 Education and Inspections Act 2006 s 21(2)(k).

44 Education and Inspections Act 2006 s 21(2)(l).

45 Education and Inspections Act 2006 s 21(3) (amended by SI 2010/1158).

46 Ie for the purposes of the Equality Act 2010 Sch 11 paras 3 and 4 (single-sex schools turning co-educational): see PARA 10.

47 Education and Inspections Act 2006 s 21(5) (amended by the Equality Act 2010 Sch 26 paras 92, 93; and SI 2010/1158).

48 Education and Inspections Act 2006 s 21(6). As to the publication of guidance see the Education Act 1996 s 571 (provision applied by the Education and Inspections Act 2006 s 187(2), (3)); and PARA 60.

134. Right of governing body to determine own foundation proposals. In the case of proposals which are published[1] by the governing body[2] of a community, voluntary controlled or community special school[3] and relate only to:

(1)   a change of category from community or voluntary controlled school to foundation school[4], without the acquisition of a foundation[5] or a relevant change[6] in the instrument of government[7]; or

(2)   a change of category from community special school to foundation special school[8], without the acquisition of a foundation[9],

regulations[10]: (a) must provide for the proposals to be determined by the governing body[11]; and (b) may not make any provision[12] enabling the proposals to be referred to the adjudicator[13].

In the case of:

(i)   proposals which are published[14] by the governing body of a community or voluntary controlled school and relate only to a change of category from community or voluntary controlled school to foundation school, together with the acquisition of a foundation or a relevant change in the instrument of government (or both)[15];

(ii)   proposals which are published[16] by the governing body of a community special school and relate only to a change of category from community special school to foundation special school, together with the acquisition of a foundation or together with both the acquisition of a foundation and a relevant change in the instrument of government[17]; and

(iii)   proposals which are published[18] by the governing body of a foundation or foundation special school and relate only to the acquisition of a foundation or a relevant change in the instrument of government (or both)[19],

regulations[20]: (A) must provide for the proposals to be determined by the governing body unless the local authority[21] exercises the right[22] to require the proposals to be referred to the adjudicator[23]; and (B) may not make any provision[24] enabling a person[25] other than the local authority to require the proposals to be referred to the adjudicator[26].

1 Ie under the Education and Inspections Act 2006 s 19: see PARA 133.
2 As to governing bodies of maintained schools see PARA 150 et seq.
3 As to the meaning of references to a community, voluntary or community special school see PARA 106.
4 As to the meaning of references to a foundation school see PARA 106.
5 As to the meaning of 'foundation' see PARA 108 note 6.
6 A 'relevant change' in the instrument of government of a school is a change which results in the majority of governors being foundation governors: Education and Inspections Act 2006 s 22(2).
7 Education and Inspections Act 2006 s 22(1)(a). As to instruments of government see PARA 184 et seq.
8 As to the meaning of references to a community or a foundation special school see PARA 106.
9 Education and Inspections Act 2006 s 22(1)(b).
10 Ie under the Education and Inspections Act 2006 s 21: see PARA 133.
11 Education and Inspections Act 2006 s 22(3)(a).
12 Ie under the Education and Inspections Act 2006 s 21(2)(g) or (h): see PARA 133.
13 Education and Inspections Act 2006 s 22(3)(b). As to the meaning of 'adjudicator' see PARA 147 (definition applied by s 32(1)).
14 Ie under the Education and Inspections Act 2006 s 19: see PARA 133.
15 Education and Inspections Act 2006 s 22(4)(a).
16 Ie under the Education and Inspections Act 2006 s 19: see PARA 133.
17 Education and Inspections Act 2006 s 22(4)(b).
18 Ie under the Education and Inspections Act 2006 s 19: see PARA 133.
19 Education and Inspections Act 2006 s 22(4)(c).
20 Ie under the Education and Inspections Act 2006 s 21: see PARA 133.
21 As to the meaning of 'local authority' see PARA 25 (definition applied by the Education and Inspections Act 2006 s 187(2), (3)).
22 Ie the right conferred on it by regulations made by virtue of the Education and Inspections Act 2006 s 23(1): see PARA 135.
23 Education and Inspections Act 2006 s 22(5)(a) (amended by SI 2010/1158).
24 Ie under the Education and Inspections Act 2006 s 21(2)(g) or (h): see PARA 133.
25 As to the meaning of 'person' see PARA 7 note 6.
26 Education and Inspections Act 2006 s 22(5)(b) (amended by SI 2010/1158).

135. Rights of interested bodies in relation to proposals. If the proposed alteration under proposals[1] for the alteration of a school would result in a community, voluntary controlled or foundation school or community or foundation special school[2] becoming either or both of the following:

(1) a foundation or foundation special school having a foundation[3] established otherwise than under School Standards and Framework Act 1998[4];

(2) a foundation or foundation special school whose instrument of government provides for the majority of governors to be foundation governors[5],

any regulations[6] which enable any such proposals which are published by the governing body[7] of the school to which they relate to be determined by the governing body must include provision[8] enabling the local authority[9] to require the proposals to be referred to the adjudicator[10].

If regulations[11] provide for any proposals[12] to be determined by a person other than the adjudicator, the regulations must include provision[13] enabling each of the following persons[14] to require the proposals to be referred to the adjudicator after their initial determination by the other person: (a) the Diocesan Board of Education for any diocese of the Church of England any part of which is comprised in the area of the authority[15]; (b) the bishop of any diocese of the Roman Catholic Church any part of which is comprised in the area of the authority[16].

If regulations[17] provide for any proposals published by a local authority in relation to a foundation or voluntary school or a foundation special school to be determined by the local authority, the regulations must include provision[18] enabling each of the following persons to require the proposals to be referred to the adjudicator after their initial determination by the authority[19]: (i) the governing body of the school[20]; and (ii) the trustees of the school[21].

1   'Proposals' means proposals under the Education and Inspections Act 2006 s 19: see PARA 133.
2   As to the meaning of references to a community, voluntary or foundation school or community or foundation special school see PARA 106.
3   As to the meaning of 'foundation' see PARA 108 note 6.
4   Education and Inspections Act 2006 s 23(2)(a).
5   Education and Inspections Act 2006 s 23(2)(b). As to instruments of government see PARA 184 et seq.
6   Ie under the Education and Inspections Act 2006 s 21: see PARA 133.
7   As to governing bodies of maintained schools see PARA 150 et seq.
8   Ie by virtue of the Education and Inspections Act 2006 s 21(2)(g): see PARA 133.
9   As to the meaning of 'local authority' see PARA 25 (definition applied by the Education and Inspections Act 2006 s 187(2), (3)).
10 Education and Inspections Act 2006 s 23(1) (amended by SI 2010/1158). Regulations under the Education and Inspections Act 2006 s 21 (see PARA 133) may restrict the matters to which a local authority may have regard in deciding whether to require proposals to be referred to the adjudicator in accordance with provision included in the regulations by virtue of s 23(1): s 23(3) (amended by SI 2010/1158). As to the meaning of 'adjudicator' see PARA 147 (definition applied by the Education and Inspections Act 2006 s 32(1)).
11 Ie under the Education and Inspections Act 2006 s 21: see PARA 133.
12 Ie other than proposals to which the Education and Inspections Act 2006 s 22(3) or (5) applies: see PARA 134.
13 Ie by virtue of the Education and Inspections Act 2006 s 21(2)(h): see PARA 133.
14 As to the meaning of 'person' in this context see PARA 7 note 6.
15 Education and Inspections Act 2006 s 23(4)(a). As to the Church of England see ECCLESIASTICAL LAW vol 34 (2011) PARA 50 et seq.
16 Education and Inspections Act 2006 s 23(4)(b).
17 Ie under the Education and Inspections Act 2006 s 21: see PARA 133.
18 Ie by virtue of the Education and Inspections Act 2006 s 21(2)(h): see PARA 133.
19 Education and Inspections Act 2006 s 23(5) (amended by SI 2010/1158).
20 Education and Inspections Act 2006 s 23(5)(a).
21 Education and Inspections Act 2006 s 23(5)(b).

136.   Implementation of proposals. Regulations[1] may make provision in connection with the implementation of: (1) proposals for the alteration of a school[2] which have[3] been approved[4]; or (2) such proposals in respect of which approval[5] is not required, and which the person[6] making the proposals has determined to implement[7]. The regulations may, in particular;

(a)   enable a prescribed[8] person to determine in prescribed cases that proposals are not to be implemented or are to be implemented with modifications[9];

(b)   enable prescribed matters relating to the implementation of proposals to be referred to the adjudicator[10] in prescribed cases[11];

(c)   make provision about the manner in which, and time within which, anything required or authorised by the regulations must be done[12];

(d)   make provision corresponding to that made by, or that which may be made by, regulations[13] relating to the implementation of proposals for the establishment or discontinuance of a school[14].

Regulations under these provisions relating to an alteration in the category of a school, to the acquisition by a foundation or foundation special school of a foundation, or to any change in the instrument of government of a school which results in the majority of governors being foundation governors[15], may include provision with respect to: (i) the revision or replacement of the school's instrument of government and the reconstitution of its governing body[16]; (ii) the transfer of property, rights and liabilities[17] (including such a transfer to or from a foundation body or trustees)[18]; (iii) the transfer of staff[19]; and (iv) any transitional matters[20].

The regulations may require any prescribed person, in exercising functions under the regulations, to have regard to any guidance given from time to time by the Secretary of State[21].

A school's change of category in pursuance of proposals for the alteration of a school[22] is not to be taken as authorising any change in the religious character of the school, or the acquisition or loss of religious character[23].

1 Ie regulations made under the Education and Inspections Act 2006 Pt 2 (ss 6A–32) by the Secretary of State: see s 32(1). As to the regulations made see the School Organisation (Prescribed Alterations to Maintained Schools) (England) Regulations 2013, SI 2013/3110. As to the Secretary of State see PARA 58.
2 Ie proposals under the Education and Inspections Act 2006 s 19: see PARA 133.
3 Ie in accordance with regulations under the Education and Inspections Act 2006 s 21: see PARA 133.
4 Education and Inspections Act 2006 s 24(1)(a).
5 Ie in accordance with regulations under the Education and Inspections Act 2006 s 21: see PARA 133.
6 As to the meaning of 'person' see PARA 7 note 6.
7 Education and Inspections Act 2006 s 24(1)(b).
8 'Prescribed' means prescribed by the regulations: see the Education and Inspections Act 2006 s 32(1).
9 Education and Inspections Act 2006 s 24(2)(a). As to the meaning of 'modifications' see PARA 21 note 15 (definition applied by s 187(2), (3)).
10 As to the meaning of 'adjudicator' see PARA 147 (definition applied by the Education and Inspections Act 2006 s 32(1)).
11 Education and Inspections Act 2006 s 24(2)(b).
12 Education and Inspections Act 2006 s 24(2)(c).
13 Ie regulations under any provision of the Education and Inspections Act 2006 Sch 2 paras 21–31: see PARAS 124–131.
14 Education and Inspections Act 2006 s 24(7).
15 Ie relating to an alteration falling within the Education and Inspections Act 2006 s 18(2)(a), (b) or (c): see PARA 132.
16 Education and Inspections Act 2006 s 24(3)(a). As to governing bodies of maintained schools see PARA 150 et seq. As to instruments of government see PARA 184 et seq.
17 As to the meaning of 'liability' see PARA 108 note 22 (definition applied by the Education and Inspections Act 2006 s 187(2), (3)).
18 Education and Inspections Act 2006 s 24(3)(b). Regulations made by virtue of s 24(3)(b) in relation to an alteration falling within s 18(2)(a) (alteration in the category of a school: see PARA 132) may, in particular, make provision with respect to: (1) restricting the disposal by a local authority of land which is used or held for the purposes of a school in relation to which proposals to change category are, or may be, published under s 19 (see PARA 133), as from the date of publication of such proposals (s 24(4)(a)(i)), or such other time as may be prescribed (s 24(4)(a)(ii)); (2) restricting the taking of action by virtue of which any such land would cease to be so used or held to any extent (s 24(4)(b)); (3) the consequences of any contravention of any such restriction as is mentioned in head (1) or (2) above (s 24(4)(c)); and (4) conferring on any prescribed body such functions as may be prescribed with respect to any such contravention (s 24(4)(d)). As to the meaning of 'local authority' see PARA 25; as to the meaning of 'land' see PARA 116 note 18; and as to the meaning of 'functions' see PARA 18 note 5 (definitions applied by s 187(2), (3)).

Regulations made by virtue of s 24(3)(b) in relation to an alteration falling within s 18(2)(a) (alteration in the category of a school: see PARA 132) may also make provision with respect to: (a) the division and apportionment of property, rights and liabilities any part of which fall to be transferred by or under the regulations where the property has been used or held, or the rights or liabilities have been acquired or incurred, for the purposes of more than one school or for the purposes of one or more schools and for other purposes (s 24(5)(a)); (b) excluding from transfer in certain circumstances property, rights and liabilities which would otherwise fall to be transferred under any such transfer (s 24(5)(b)); (c) identifying and defining the property, rights and liabilities which fall to be transferred (s 24(5)(c)); (d) requiring prescribed persons to enter into agreements and execute instruments (s 24(5)(d)); (e) the resolution of disputes relating to a transfer (s 24(5)(e)); (f) the construction of agreements (s 24(5)(f)); (g) the position of third parties affected by a transfer (s 24(5)(g)); (h) the production or delivery of documents, or the provision of information, by a prescribed person to another prescribed person (s 24(5)(h)); and (i) enabling a certificate issued by a prescribed person to be conclusive evidence as to whether or not any property, rights or liabilities were transferred by virtue of the regulations (s 24(5)(i)).

19 Education and Inspections Act 2006 s 24(3)(c).
20 Education and Inspections Act 2006 s 24(3)(d).
21 Education and Inspections Act 2006 s 24(6). As to the publication of guidance see the Education Act 1996 s 571 (applied by the Education and Inspections Act 2006 s 187(2), (3)); and PARA 60.
22 Ie proposals under the Education and Inspections Act 2006 s 19: see PARA 133.
23 Education and Inspections Act 2006 s 24(8). As to the meaning of 'religious character' see PARA 132 note 14.

(F) *Removal of Foundation or Reduction in Foundation Governors*

137.   Proposals for removal of foundation or reduction in foundation governors.   Where any foundation or foundation special school[1] having a foundation[2] meets either or both of the following conditions[3], the governing body[4] of such school may at any time publish proposals for either or both of the following alterations to the school:

(1)   the removal of the foundation[5]; or

(2)   the alteration of the instrument of government in such a way that foundation governors will cease to constitute the majority of governors[6].

The first condition is that the school was established (whether or not as a foundation or foundation special school) in pursuance of proposals falling to be implemented[7] under the Education and Inspections Act 2006[8]. The second condition is that the school acquired its foundation in pursuance of proposals falling to be implemented under regulations made[9] under that Act[10].

A prescribed[11] proportion of the governors of a foundation or foundation special school which meets either or both of the conditions above may in the prescribed manner require the governing body of the school to publish proposals under these provisions for either or both of the alterations mentioned in heads (1) and (2) above[12].

Regulations[13] may make provision about the publication and determination of proposals[14]. The provision that may be made includes provision: (a) about the information to be included in, or provided in relation to, the proposals[15]; (b) about consultation on the proposals[16]; (c) about the manner in which proposals are to be published[17]; (d) for the making of objections to or comments on the proposals[18]; (e) for the withdrawal of proposals in prescribed cases[19]; (f) for the consideration of the proposals by the governing body[20]; (g) enabling the governing body to approve or reject the proposals[21]; (h) enabling the governing body to reject any 'required proposals'[22] only by a decision made with the support of a prescribed proportion of the governors[23]; (i) for the approval of required proposals given in the prescribed manner by a prescribed proportion of the governors to be treated as approval by the governing body[24]; (j) for the approval of proposals either without modifications[25] or in prescribed cases with modifications of a prescribed kind[26]; (k) as to the manner in which, and time within which, anything authorised or required by the regulations must be done[27].

The regulations may in prescribed cases: (i) require the governing body to ensure that matters relating to any transfer of property, rights or liabilities which may[28] be required[29], or any payment which might[30] be required[31], is agreed or determined before the proposals are published[32]; and (ii) enable or require any such matter to be referred to the adjudicator[33] for determination before the proposals are published[34]. The regulations may also require any prescribed person[35], in exercising functions[36] under the regulations, to have regard to any guidance given from time to time by the Secretary of State[37].

1 As to the meaning of references to a foundation school or a foundation special school see PARA 106.

2 In the Education and Inspections Act 2006 s 25, 'foundation' means a foundation established otherwise than under the School Standards and Framework Act 1998: Education and Inspections Act 2006 s 25(8). As to the meaning of 'foundation' generally see PARA 108 note 6.

3 See the Education and Inspections Act 2006 s 25(1).

4 As to governing bodies of maintained schools see PARA 150 et seq.

5 Education and Inspections Act 2006 s 25(4)(a). Except in pursuance of proposals falling to be implemented under s 27 (see PARA 138), no alteration falling within s 25(4)(a) or (b) (see the text to note 6) may be made to a foundation or foundation special school: see s 28(4); and PARA 110.

6 Education and Inspections Act 2006 s 25(4)(b). See also note 5. As to instruments of government see PARA 184 et seq.

7 Ie under the Education and Inspections Act 2006 Sch 2: see PARA 118 et seq.

8 Education and Inspections Act 2006 s 25(2).

9 Ie under the Education and Inspections Act 2006 s 24: see PARA 136.

10 Education and Inspections Act 2006 s 25(3).

11 'Prescribed' means prescribed by regulations made under the Education and Inspections Act 2006 Pt 2 (ss 6A–32) by the Secretary of State: see s 32(1). As to the regulations made see the School Organisation (Removal of Foundation, Reduction in Number of Foundation Governors and Ability of Foundation to Pay Debts) (England) Regulations 2007, SI 2007/3475. As to the Secretary of State see PARA 58.

12 See the Education and Inspections Act 2006 s 25(5). Section 25(5) does not require the governing body of a foundation or foundation special school to publish proposals under s 25: (1) at any time within a prescribed period beginning with the date on which (a) proposals for the establishment of the school were implemented under Sch 2 (see PARAS 126, 128) (s 25(6)(a)(i)), or (b) proposals for the acquisition of a foundation, for a relevant change in the instrument of government or for a change of category to foundation school or foundation special school were implemented under regulations under s 24 (see PARA 136) (s 25(6)(a)(ii)); or (2) at any time within a prescribed period beginning with the date on which previous proposals published under s 25 in pursuance of a requirement under s 25(5) were rejected by the governing body in accordance with regulations under s 26 (see the text to notes 13–37) (s 25(6)(b)). 'Relevant change', in relation to the instrument of government of a school, is to be read in accordance with s 22(2) (see PARA 134 note 6): s 25(7).

13 Ie regulations made under the Education and Inspections Act 2006 Pt 2 (ss 6A–32) by the Secretary of State: see s 32(1). As to the regulations made see note 11.

14 Education and Inspections Act 2006 s 26(1). As to the implementation of proposals see s 27; and PARA 138.

15 Education and Inspections Act 2006 s 26(2)(a).

16 Education and Inspections Act 2006 s 26(2)(b).

17 Education and Inspections Act 2006 s 26(2)(c).

18 Education and Inspections Act 2006 s 26(2)(d).

19 Education and Inspections Act 2006 s 26(2)(e).

20 Education and Inspections Act 2006 s 26(2)(f).

21 Education and Inspections Act 2006 s 26(2)(g).

22 Ie proposals published in pursuance of a requirement under the Education and Inspections Act 2006 s 25(5): see the text to notes 11–12.

23 Education and Inspections Act 2006 s 26(2)(h).

24 Education and Inspections Act 2006 s 26(2)(i).

25 As to the meaning of 'modifications' see PARA 21 note 15 (definition applied by the Education and Inspections Act 2006 s 187(2), (3)).

26 Education and Inspections Act 2006 s 26(2)(j).

27 Education and Inspections Act 2006 s 26(2)(k).

28 Ie by virtue of the Education and Inspections Act 2006 s 27(2)(b): see PARA 138.

29 Education and Inspections Act 2006 s 26(3)(a)(i).

30 Ie by virtue of the Education and Inspections Act 2006 s 27(4) or (5): see PARA 138.

31 Education and Inspections Act 2006 s 26(3)(a)(ii).

32 Education and Inspections Act 2006 s 26(3)(a).

33 As to the meaning of 'adjudicator' see PARA 147 (definition applied by the Education and Inspections Act 2006 s 32(1)).

34 Education and Inspections Act 2006 s 26(3)(b).

35 As to the meaning of 'person' see PARA 7 note 6.

36 As to the meaning of 'functions' see PARA 18 note 5 (definition applied by the Education and Inspections Act 2006 s 187(2), (3)).

37 Education and Inspections Act 2006 s 26(4). As to the publication of guidance see the Education Act 1996 s 571 (applied by the Education and Inspections Act 2006 s 187(2), (3)); and PARA 60.

138. Implementation of proposals. Regulations[1] may make provision in connection with the implementation of proposals for the removal of a foundation[2] or a reduction in the number of foundation governors[3] which have[4] been approved[5]. The regulations may, in particular: (1) make provision for the revision or replacement of the school's instrument of government and the reconstitution of its governing body[6]; (2) make provision for the transfer of property, rights and liabilities[7]; (3) make provision about the manner in which, and time within which, anything required or authorised by the regulations must be done[8].

Where:

(a)   any land[9] forming part of the school premises[10] ('the excluded land') is not transferred to the governing body[11]; and

(b)   the governing body, a local authority[12] or a prescribed person[13] has incurred capital expenditure in relation to the excluded land or in relation to other land the proceeds of the disposal of which were used to acquire or enhance the value of the excluded land[14],

the regulations may authorise or require the foundation to pay any part of the value of the excluded land to the governing body, the local authority or a prescribed person[15].

Where:

(i)   any land forming part of the school premises ('the transferred land') is transferred to the governing body[16]; and

(ii)   the foundation has incurred capital expenditure in relation to the transferred land or in relation to other land the proceeds of the disposal of which were used to acquire or enhance the value of the transferred land[17],

the regulations may authorise or require the governing body to pay any part of the value of the transferred land to the foundation[18].

The regulations may require any prescribed person, in exercising functions under the regulations, to have regard to any guidance given from time to time by the Secretary of State[19].

The implementation of proposals[20] is not to be taken as authorising any change in the religious character of the school or the loss of religious character[21].

1   Ie regulations made under the Education and Inspections Act 2006 Pt 2 (ss 6A–32) by the Secretary of State: see s 32(1). As to the regulations made see the School Organisation (Removal of Foundation, Reduction in Number of Foundation Governors and Ability of Foundation to Pay Debts) (England) Regulations 2007, SI 2007/3475. As to the Secretary of State see PARA 58.

2   In the Education and Inspections Act 2006 s 27, 'foundation' means a foundation established otherwise than under the School Standards and Framework Act 1998: Education and Inspections Act 2006 s 27(8). As to the meaning of 'foundation' generally see PARA 108 note 6.

3 Ie proposals under the Education and Inspections Act 2006 s 25: see PARA 137.

4 Ie in accordance with regulations under the Education and Inspections Act 2006 s 26: see PARA 137.

5 Education and Inspections Act 2006 s 27(1).

6 Education and Inspections Act 2006 s 27(2)(a). As to governing bodies of maintained schools see PARA 150 et seq. As to instruments of government see PARA 184 et seq.

7 Education and Inspections Act 2006 s 27(2)(b). As to the meaning of 'liability' see PARA 108 note 22 (definition applied by s 187(2), (3)). Regulations made by virtue of s 27(2)(b) may make provision about any of the matters mentioned in s 24(5)(a)–(i) (see PARA 137): s 27(3).

8 Education and Inspections Act 2006 s 27(2)(c).

9 As to the meaning of 'land' see PARA 116 note 18 (definition applied by the Education and Inspections Act 2006 s 187(2), (3)).

10 As to the meaning of 'premises' see PARA 62 note 19 (definition applied by the Education and Inspections Act 2006 s 187(2), (3)).

11 Education and Inspections Act 2006 s 27(4)(a).

12 As to the meaning of 'local authority' see PARA 25 (definition applied by the Education and Inspections Act 2006 s 187(2), (3)).

13 'Prescribed' means prescribed by the regulations: see the Education and Inspections Act 2006 s 32(1). As to the meaning of 'person' see PARA 7 note 6.

14 Education and Inspections Act 2006 s 27(4)(b) (amended by SI 2010/1158).

15 Education and Inspections Act 2006 s 27(4) (amended by SI 2010/1158).

16 Education and Inspections Act 2006 s 27(5)(a).

17 Education and Inspections Act 2006 s 27(5)(b).

18 Education and Inspections Act 2006 s 27(5).

19 Education and Inspections Act 2006 s 27(6). As to the publication of guidance see the Education Act 1996 s 571 (applied by the Education and Inspections Act 2006 s 187(2), (3)); and PARA 60.

20 Ie under the Education and Inspections Act 2006 s 25: see PARA 137.

21 Education and Inspections Act 2006 s 27(7). As to the meaning of 'religious character' see PARA 132 note 14.

B. SCHOOLS IN WALES

139. School Organisation Code. The Welsh Ministers[1] must issue, and may from time to time revise, a code on school organisation ('the Code')[2]. The Code is to contain provision about the exercise of the functions of the following persons under the School Standards and Organisation (Wales) Act 2013[3]: (1) the Welsh Ministers; (2) local authorities[4]; (3) governing bodies of maintained schools[5]; (4) other persons in connection with proposals made (or to be made)[6] by them[7]. The Code may impose requirements, and may include guidelines setting out aims, objectives and other matters[8]. The persons referred to above[9] must, when exercising functions[10] (a) act in accordance with any relevant requirements contained in the Code, and (b) have regard to any relevant guidelines contained in it:[11]. This duty[12] also applies to a person exercising a function for the purpose of the discharge of functions[13] by (i) the Welsh Ministers, (ii) a local authority, (iii) the governing body of a maintained school, or (iv) other persons in connection with proposals made (or to be made)[14] by them[15]. The Welsh Ministers must publish the Code for the time being in force on their website[16].

There is a procedure that the Welsh Ministers must follow before issuing the Code[17].

1 As to the Welsh Ministers see PARA 59.

2 See the School Standards and Organisation (Wales) Act 2013 s 38(1).

3 Ie under the School Standards and Organisation (Wales) Act 2013 Pt 3 (ss 38–83).

4 'Local authority' (except in the School Standards and Organisation (Wales) Act 2013 s 54(2)(b)) means a county or county borough council in Wales: s 98(3). As to the meaning of 'Wales' see PARA 7 note 3.

5   For these purposes, 'maintained school' means a school in Wales which is a community, foundation or voluntary school, a community special school or a maintained nursery school: School Standards and Organisation (Wales) Act 2013 s 98(3). As to references to categories of maintained school see PARA 106.

6   See note 3.

7   See the School Standards and Organisation (Wales) Act 2013 s 38(2).

8   See the School Standards and Organisation (Wales) Act 2013 s 38(3).

9   Ie in the School Standards and Organisation (Wales) Act 2013 s 38(2).

10   See note 3.

11   See the School Standards and Organisation (Wales) Act 2013 s 38(4). As to a successful judicial review in the case of the closure of a school and merger with another where there had not been compliance with the School Organisation Code see *R (on the application of McCann) v Bridgend County Borough Council* [2014] EWHC 4335 (Admin), [2015] All ER (D) 15 (Jan).

12   Ie the duty imposed by the School Standards and Organisation (Wales) Act 2013 s 38(4).

13   See note 3.

14   See note 3.

15   See the School Standards and Organisation (Wales) Act 2013 s 38(5).

16   See the School Standards and Organisation (Wales) Act 2013 s 38(6). The Welsh Ministers may make separate provision (by means of separate codes) in relation to different functions under Pt 3 of the persons mentioned in s 38(2): see s 38(7). References in s 38 to 'the Code' or to functions under Pt 3 have effect, in relation to a separate code, as references to that code or to functions under Pt 3 to which it relates: see s 38(8).

17   See the School Standards and Organisation (Wales) Act 2013 s 39. See also the School Organisation Code (Appointed Day) (Wales) Order 2013, SI 2013/1799.

140. Proposals for the establishment, alteration or discontinuance of maintained schools. A new community school, voluntary school or community special school may be established in Wales[1] only in accordance with the School Standards and Organisation (Wales) Act 2013[2]. No new foundation school or foundation special school may be established in Wales[3]. A maintained school[4] may be discontinued only in accordance with the 2013 Act[5]. An alteration which is a regulated alteration[6] in relation to the type of school in question may be made to a maintained school only in accordance with the 2013 Act[7]. No alteration may be made to a maintained school that changes the religious character of the school[8] or causes a school to acquire or lose a religious character[9].

A local authority[10] may make proposals to establish a new community school, or a new maintained nursery school[11]. Any person may make proposals to establish a new voluntary school[12].

A local authority may make proposals (1) to make a regulated alteration to a community school; (2) with the consent of the Welsh Ministers, to make an alteration opening or closing a school's sixth form[13] to a voluntary or foundation school; (3) to make an alteration increasing and reducing capacity[14] to a voluntary or foundation school if that school does not have a religious character; (4) to make a regulated alteration to a maintained nursery school[15]. The governing body of a foundation or voluntary school may make proposals to make a regulated alteration to the school[16].

A local authority may make proposals to discontinue a community, foundation or voluntary school, or a maintained nursery school[17]. The governing body of a foundation or voluntary school may make proposals to discontinue the school[18].

A local authority may make proposals (a) to establish a new community special school; (b) to make a regulated alteration to such a school; or (c) to discontinue such a school[19].

1   As to the meaning of 'Wales' see PARA 7 note 3.

2 See the School Standards and Organisation (Wales) Act 2013 s 40(1). The reference is to the School Standards and Organisation (Wales) Act 2013 Pt 3 (ss 38–83). As to community schools see PARA 107. As to foundation and voluntary schools see PARA 108. As to special schools see PARA 1041.

3 See the School Standards and Organisation (Wales) Act 2013 s 40(2).

4 As to the meaning of 'maintained school' see PARA 139 note 5.

5 See the School Standards and Organisation (Wales) Act 2013 s 40(3). The reference is to the School Standards and Organisation (Wales) Act 2013 Pt 3. As to references to the discontinuance of a maintained school see s 83(3). Section 40(3) has effect subject to s 16(5) (power of Welsh Ministers to direct closure of school: see PARA 1234): s 40(6).

6 The School Standards and Organisation (Wales) Act 2013 Sch 2 describes regulated alterations: s 40(7).

7 See the School Standards and Organisation (Wales) Act 2013 s 40(4).

8 As to references to a school which has a religious character see the School Standards and Organisation (Wales) Act 2013 s 98(5).

9 See the School Standards and Organisation (Wales) Act 2013 s 40(5).

10 As to the meaning of 'local authority' see PARA 139 note 4.

11 See the School Standards and Organisation (Wales) Act 2013 s 41(1). Proposals made under the School Standards and Organisation (Wales) Act 2013 Pt 3 to establish a new school may relate to the establishment of the school as a federated school (within the meaning given by the Education (Wales) Measure 2011 s 21(1): see PARA 198): see the School Standards and Organisation (Wales) Act 2013 s 78.

   No proposals may be made for the establishment of a school in England which is proposed to be maintained by a local authority in Wales: see s 79. See also PARA 114. As to the meaning of 'England' see PARA 7 note 3.

12 See the School Standards and Organisation (Wales) Act 2013 s 41(2). See also note 11. 'Proposer', in relation to proposals made under s 41, s 42, s 43, s 44 or s 45, is the local authority, the governing body or other person who has made the proposals: s 56(1).

13 Ie described in the School Standards and Organisation (Wales) Act 2013 Sch 2 para 6.

14 Ie described in the School Standards and Organisation (Wales) Act 2013 Sch 2 para 10, 11, 12 or 13.

15 See the School Standards and Organisation (Wales) Act 2013 s 42(1). As to the Welsh Ministers see PARA 59.

16 See the School Standards and Organisation (Wales) Act 2013 s 42(2).

17 See the School Standards and Organisation (Wales) Act 2013 s 43(1).

18 See the School Standards and Organisation (Wales) Act 2013 s 43(2). The governing body of a foundation or voluntary school may discontinue the school by giving the Welsh Ministers and the local authority that maintains the school two years' notice of its intention to do so: see s 80.

19 See the School Standards and Organisation (Wales) Act 2013 s 44. As to the meaning of 'community special school' see PARA 106.

   The Welsh Ministers may direct a local authority to discontinue a community special school maintained by it on a specified date, if they consider it expedient to do so in the interests of the health, safety or welfare of pupils at the school: see s 81. For transitional exemption orders for the purposes of the Equality Act 2010 see the School Standards and Organisation (Wales) Act 2013 s 82.

141. Proposals for changes of category. The governing body of a community school may make proposals[1] for the school to become a voluntary aided school or a voluntary controlled school[2]. The governing body of a voluntary aided school may make proposals for the school to become a community school or a voluntary controlled school[3]. The governing body of a voluntary controlled school may make proposals for the school to become a community school or a voluntary aided school[4]. The governing body of a foundation school may make proposals for the school to become a community school, a voluntary aided school or a voluntary controlled school[5]. No proposals may be made for a foundation or voluntary school which has a religious character to become a community school[6].

A maintained school[7] within one of the categories set out in the School Standards and Framework Act 1998[8] may become a school within another of those categories (except a foundation school or foundation special school) only in accordance with the School Standards and Organisation (Wales) Act 2013[9]. A school may not change category to become a voluntary aided school unless the governing body of the school satisfies the Welsh Ministers[10] that it will be able to carry out its obligations in regard to funding of voluntary aided schools[11] for a period of at least five years following the date on which it is proposed that the change of category is to take place[12]. A voluntary or foundation school may not become a community school unless any transfer agreement and transfer of rights and liabilities agreement[13] has been entered into[14].

A school's change of category in accordance with proposals above[15] is not to be taken as authorising or requiring any change in the character of the school (including, in particular, any religious character of the school)[16]. A school's change of category in accordance with the proposals[17] is not to be taken as authorising a school to establish, join or leave a foundation body[18].

1 As to the meaning of 'proposer' see PARA 140 note 12.
2 See the School Standards and Organisation (Wales) Act 2013 s 45(1). As to community schools see PARA 107. As to foundation and voluntary schools see PARA 108.
3 See the School Standards and Organisation (Wales) Act 2013 s 45(2). However see s 45(5).
4 See the School Standards and Organisation (Wales) Act 2013 s 45(3). However see s 45(5).
5 See the School Standards and Organisation (Wales) Act 2013 s 45(4). However see s 45(5).
6 See the School Standards and Organisation (Wales) Act 2013 s 45(5). As to references to a school which has a religious character see s 98(5).
7 As to the meaning of 'maintained school' see PARA 139 note 5.
8 Ie the School Standards and Framework Act 1998 s 20(1): see PARA 106.
9 See the School Standards and Organisation (Wales) Act 2013 s 46(1). The reference is to the School Standards and Organisation (Wales) Act 2013 Pt 3 (ss 38–83). As to references to a school's category see s 83(2).
10 As to the Welsh Ministers see PARA 59.
11 Ie under the School Standards and Framework Act 1998 Sch 3: see PARA 310 et seq.
12 See the School Standards and Organisation (Wales) Act 2013 s 46(2).
13 Ie required by the School Standards and Organisation (Wales) Act 2013 Sch 4 Pt 3.
14 See the School Standards and Organisation (Wales) Act 2013 s 46(3).
15 Ie made under the School Standards and Organisation (Wales) Act 2013 s 45.
16 See the School Standards and Organisation (Wales) Act 2013 s 47(1).
17 See note 15.
18 See the School Standards and Organisation (Wales) Act 2013 s 47(2). As to the meaning of 'foundation body' see PARA 108 note 6 (definition applied by s 98(3)).

142. Publication of proposals; consultation and objections. A proposer[1] must publish proposals made under the School Standards and Organisation (Wales) Act 2013[2] in accordance with the code on school organisation ('the Code')[3]. Before publishing proposals[4], a proposer must consult on its proposals in accordance with the Code[5]. The requirement to consult does not apply to proposals to discontinue a school which is a small[6]. Before the end of seven days beginning with the day on which they were published, the proposer must send copies of the published proposals to (1) the Welsh Ministers, and (2) the local authority[7] (if it is not the proposer) that maintains, or that it is proposed will maintain, the school to which the proposals relate[8]. The proposer must publish a report on the consultation it has carried out in accordance with the Code[9].

Any person may object to proposals[10]. Objections must be sent in writing to the proposer before the end of 28 days beginning with the day on which the proposals were published ('the objection period')[11]. The proposer must publish a summary of all objections[12] (and not withdrawn) and its response to those objections (a) in the case of a local authority that is required to determine its

own proposals[13], before the end of seven days beginning with the day of its
determination[14], and (b) in all other cases, before the end of 28 days beginning
with the end of the objection period[15].

1   As to the meaning of 'proposer' see PARA 140 note 12.
2   Ie under the School Standards and Organisation (Wales) Act 2013 Pt 3 Ch 2 (ss 40–56).
3   See the School Standards and Organisation (Wales) Act 2013 s 48(1).
4   Ie made under the School Standards and Organisation (Wales) Act 2013 Pt 3 Ch 2 (ss 40–56).
5   See the School Standards and Organisation (Wales) Act 2013 s 48(2).
6   See the School Standards and Organisation (Wales) Act 2013 s 48(3). In Pt 3 Ch 2 'small school'
    means a school with fewer than ten registered pupils on the third Tuesday in the January
    immediately preceding the date on which the proposals are made: s 56(1). The Welsh Minsters
    may by order amend the definition of 'small school' in s 56(1) so as to substitute a reference to
    a different date for the reference to the date for the time being specified: s 56(2). As to the Welsh
    Ministers see PARA 59.
7   As to the meaning of 'local authority' see PARA 139 note 4.
8   See the School Standards and Organisation (Wales) Act 2013 s 48(4).
9   See the School Standards and Organisation (Wales) Act 2013 s 48(5).
10 See the School Standards and Organisation (Wales) Act 2013 s 49(1). The reference in the text
    to proposals is to proposals published under s 48.
11 See the School Standards and Organisation (Wales) Act 2013 s 49(2).
12 Ie objections made in accordance with the School Standards and Organisation (Wales) Act 2013
    s 49(2).
13 Ie under the School Standards and Organisation (Wales) Act 2013 s 53: see PARA 143.
14 Ie under the School Standards and Organisation (Wales) Act 2013 s 53(1): see PARA 143.
15 See the School Standards and Organisation (Wales) Act 2013 s 49(2).

143.   Approval and determination of proposals.   Proposals published[1] under
the School Standards and Organisation (Wales) Act 2013 require approval[2] by
the Welsh Ministers[3] if the proposals affect sixth form education[4], or the
proposals have been made by a proposer other than the relevant local authority[5]
and an objection has been made by that authority[6] and has not been withdrawn
in writing before the end of 28 days beginning with the end of the objection
period[7]. Where proposals require approval[8], the proposer must send a copy of
specified documents to the Welsh Ministers before the end of 35 days beginning
with the end of the objection period[9]. Where proposals require such approval[10],
the Welsh Ministers may (1) reject the proposals, (2) approve them without
modification, or (3) approve them with modifications (a) after obtaining the
consent of the proposer to the modifications, and (b) (except where the
governing body or local authority, as the case may be, is the proposer), after
consulting the governing body (if any) of the school to which the proposals relate
and the relevant local authority[11]. An approval may be expressed to take effect
only if an event specified in the approval occurs by a date so specified[12]. The
Welsh Ministers may, at the request of the proposer, specify a later date by which
the event[13] is to occur[14].

Certain proposals[15] require approval by a local authority[16] if (i) they do not
require approval under the provisions described above[17], (ii) they have been
made by a proposer other than the relevant local authority, and (iii) an objection
to the proposals has been made[18] and has not been withdrawn in writing before
the end of 28 days beginning with the end of the objection period[19]. Where
proposals require approval[20], the proposer must send a copy of specified
documents to the relevant local authority before the end of 35 days beginning
with the end of the objection period[21]. Where proposals require such approval[22],
the relevant local authority may (A) reject the proposals, (B) approve them
without modification, or (C) approve them with any of the modifications[23] (aa)
after obtaining the consent of the Welsh Ministers and the proposer to the

modifications, and (bb) (except where the governing body is the proposer) after consulting the governing body (if any) of the school to which the proposals relate[24]. An approval may be expressed to take effect only if an event specified in the approval occurs by a date so specified[25]. The relevant local authority may, at the request of the proposer, specify a later date by which the event[26] is to occur[27]. The relevant local authority must make a determination[28] whether to reject or approve the proposals before the end of 16 weeks beginning with the end of the objection period[29]. Provision is made with respect to related proposals[30].

Where any proposals[31] do not require approval[32], the proposer must determine whether the proposals should be implemented[33].

Where a local authority has determined to approve or reject proposals, or determined to implement its own proposals to which there was an objection, the proposals may be referred to the Welsh Ministers for their approval by certain specified bodies[34].

Proposals approved[35], or proposals which the proposer has determined[36] to implement, must[37] be implemented in the form in which they were approved or determined to be implemented[38].

1   Ie under the School Standards and Organisation (Wales) Act 2013 s 48: see PARA 142.
2   Ie under the School Standards and Organisation (Wales) Act 2013 s 50.
3   As to the Welsh Ministers see PARA 59.
4   Proposals affect sixth form education if they are proposals to establish or discontinue a school providing education suitable only to the requirements of persons above compulsory school age, or they are proposals to make a regulated alteration to a school, the effect of which would be that provision of education suitable to the requirements of persons above compulsory school age at the school increases or decreases: see the School Standards and Organisation (Wales) Act 2013 s 50(2). 'Regulated alteration' means an alteration described in the School Standards and Organisation (Wales) Act 2013 Sch 2: see s 56(1).
5   As to the meaning of 'local authority' see PARA 139 note 4. As to the meaning of 'relevant local authority' for the purposes of s 50 see s 50(10).
6   Ie in accordance with the School Standards and Organisation (Wales) Act 2013 s 49(2): see PARA 142.
7   See the School Standards and Organisation (Wales) Act 2013 s 50(1). 'Objection period' has the meaning given by s 49(2): School Standards and Organisation (Wales) Act 2013 s 56(1). Section 50(1) does not prevent proposals from being withdrawn by notice in writing given by the proposer to the Welsh Ministers at any time before they are approved under s 50: see s 50(8). No approval is required under s 50 for proposals made under s 43 or s 44 (see PARA 140) to discontinue a school which is a small school (see s 56 and PARA 142): see s 50(9). As to the Welsh Ministers see PARA 59.
8   Ie under the School Standards and Organisation (Wales) Act 2013 s 50.
9   See the School Standards and Organisation (Wales) Act 2013 s 50(3), (4).
10 Ie under the School Standards and Organisation (Wales) Act 2013 s 50.
11 See the School Standards and Organisation (Wales) Act 2013 s 50(5).
12 See the School Standards and Organisation (Wales) Act 2013 s 50(6).
13 Ie referred to in the School Standards and Organisation (Wales) Act 2013 s 50(6).
14 See the School Standards and Organisation (Wales) Act 2013 s 50(7).
15 Ie proposals published under the School Standards and Organisation (Wales) Act 2013 s 48: see PARA 142.
16 Ie under the School Standards and Organisation (Wales) Act 2013 s 51.
17 Ie under the School Standards and Organisation (Wales) Act 2013 s 50.
18 Ie in accordance with the School Standards and Organisation (Wales) Act 2013 s 49(2): see PARA 142.
19 See the School Standards and Organisation (Wales) Act 2013 s 51(1). Section 51(1) does not prevent proposals from being withdrawn by notice in writing given by the proposer to the relevant local authority at any time before they are approved under s 51: see s 51(9). No approval is required under s 51 for proposals made under s 43 or s 44 (see PARA 140) to discontinue a school which is a small school (see s 56): see s 51(10).
20 Ie under the School Standards and Organisation (Wales) Act 2013 s 51.
21 See the School Standards and Organisation (Wales) Act 2013 s 51(2), (3).

22 Ie under the School Standards and Organisation (Wales) Act 2013 s 51.
23 Ie specified in the School Standards and Organisation (Wales) Act 2013 s 51(5).
24 See the School Standards and Organisation (Wales) Act 2013 s 51(4).
25 See the School Standards and Organisation (Wales) Act 2013 s 51(6).
26 Ie referred to in the School Standards and Organisation (Wales) Act 2013 s 51(6).
27 See the School Standards and Organisation (Wales) Act 2013 s 51(7).
28 Ie under the School Standards and Organisation (Wales) Act 2013 s 51(4).
29 See the School Standards and Organisation (Wales) Act 2013 s 51(8).
30 See the School Standards and Organisation (Wales) Act 2013 s 52.
31 Ie proposals published under the School Standards and Organisation (Wales) Act 2013 s 48: see PARA 142.
32 Ie approval under the School Standards and Organisation (Wales) Act 2013 s 50 or s 51.
33 See the School Standards and Organisation (Wales) Act 2013 s 53.
34 See the School Standards and Organisation (Wales) Act 2013 s 54.
35 Ie approved under the School Standards and Organisation (Wales) Act 2013 s 50 or s 51.
36 Ie under the School Standards and Organisation (Wales) Act 2013 s 53.
37 Ie subject to the provisions of the School Standards and Organisation (Wales) Act 2013 s 55.
38 See the School Standards and Organisation (Wales) Act 2013 s 55. Such implementation is (1) in the case of proposals made under s 41, 42, 43 or 44 (establishment, alteration or discontinuance of schools: see PARA 140), in accordance with Sch 3; (2) in the case of proposals made under s 45 (change of category: see PARA 141), in accordance with Sch 4 (not yet fully in force): see s 55. See also the Government of Maintained Schools (Change of Category) (Wales) Regulations 2015, SI 2015/1521.

144. Directions to make proposals to remedy excessive or insufficient provision. Where the Welsh Ministers[1] are of the opinion that there is excessive provision, or that there is, or there is likely to be, insufficient provision, for primary or secondary education in maintained schools[2] (1) in the area of a local authority[3], or (2) in a part of such an area[4], the Welsh Ministers may (a) direct the local authority to exercise its powers to make proposals to establish, alter or discontinue schools[5], and (b) direct the governing body of a foundation or voluntary school maintained by the authority to exercise its powers to make proposals to alter its school[6].

Such a direction must (i) require the proposals to be published no later than the date specified in the direction, (ii) require the proposals, in giving effect to the direction, to apply any principles specified in it, and (iii) where the Welsh Ministers are of the opinion that there is, or there is likely to be, insufficient provision, specify the additional number of pupils to be accommodated[7]. A direction under head (a) above may not require the proposals to relate to a named school[8].

There is further provision about proposals made after a direction is made[9].

1 As to the Welsh Ministers see PARA 59.
2 For these purposes, 'maintained school' means a school in Wales which is a community, foundation or voluntary school, a community special school or a maintained nursery school: School Standards and Organisation (Wales) Act 2013 s 98(3). As to the meaning of 'Wales' see PARA 7 note 3. See also PARA 106.
3 'Local authority' means a county or county borough council in Wales: School Standards and Organisation (Wales) Act 2013 s 98(3).
4 See the School Standards and Organisation (Wales) Act 2013 s 57(1).
5 'Powers to make proposals to establish, alter or discontinue schools' means all or any of the powers of a local authority to make proposals under the School Standards and Organisation (Wales) Act 2013 ss 41, 42, 43 or 44 (see PARA 140): s 83(1).
6 See the School Standards and Organisation (Wales) Act 2013 s 57(2). 'Powers to make proposals to alter its school', in relation to the governing body of a foundation or voluntary school, means its powers to make proposals under s 42(2) (see PARA 140): s 83(1).
7 See the School Standards and Organisation (Wales) Act 2013 s 57(3).
8 See the School Standards and Organisation (Wales) Act 2013 s 57(4).
9 See the School Standards and Organisation (Wales) Act 2013 s 58.

145. Proposals by Welsh Ministers to rationalise school places. Where (1) the Welsh Ministers[1] have made a direction[2], and (2) either (a) proposals have been published in accordance with the direction, or (b) the time allowed under the direction for the publication of the proposals has expired[3], the Welsh Ministers may make any proposals that could have been made in accordance with the direction[4]. The proposals must be published in accordance with the School Organisation Code [5] for the time being in force[6]. The Welsh Ministers must send a copy of the proposals (i) to the local authority[7] for the area, and (ii) to the governing body of each school to which the proposals relate[8].

Any person may object to proposals[9]. A local inquiry into proposals must be held in certain circumstances[10]. Provision is also made with respect to the adoption of proposals[11] and the implementation of proposals[12].

1　As to the Welsh Ministers see PARA 59.
2　Ie a direction under the School Standards and Organisation (Wales) Act 2013 s 57(2): see PARA 144.
3　See the School Standards and Organisation (Wales) Act 2013 s 59(1).
4　See the School Standards and Organisation (Wales) Act 2013 s 59(2).
5　Ie the code issued under the School Standards and Organisation (Wales) Act 2013 s 38(1): see PARA 139.
6　See the School Standards and Organisation (Wales) Act 2013 s 59(3).
7　As to the meaning of 'local authority' see PARA 144 note 3.
8　See the School Standards and Organisation (Wales) Act 2013 s 59(4).
9　Ie proposals under the School Standards and Organisation (Wales) Act 2013 s 59.
10　See the School Standards and Organisation (Wales) Act 2013 s 61.
11　See the School Standards and Organisation (Wales) Act 2013 s 62.
12　See the School Standards and Organisation (Wales) Act 2013 s 63.

C. MODIFICATION OF TRUST DEEDS

146. Modification of trust deeds. The appropriate national authority[1] may by order[2] make such modifications[3] of any trust deed[4] or other instrument relating to:

(1)　a school[5] which is or is to become a foundation, voluntary or foundation special school[6]; or

(2)　property held on trust for the purposes of such a school[7],

as appear to it to be necessary or expedient in connection with the operation of any provision of the School Standards and Framework Act 1998, the Learning and Skills Act 2000, the Education Act 2002, the Education and Inspections Act 2006, the Academies Act 2010 or the School Standards and Organisation (Wales) Act 2013 or anything done under or for the purposes of any such provision[8]. Before making such an order the appropriate national authority must consult[9]:

(a)　the governing body of the school in question[10];

(b)　any trustees holding property on trust for the purposes of the school[11];

(c)　in the case of a Church of England, Church in Wales or Roman Catholic Church school[12], the appropriate diocesan authority[13]; and

(d)　such other persons as the appropriate national authority considers appropriate[14].

Any modification made by such an order may be made so as to have permanent effect or to have effect for such period as is specified in the order[15].

1　Ie the Secretary of State or, in relation to Wales, the Welsh Ministers. The functions of the Secretary of State under the School Standards and Framework Act 1998 s 82, so far as exercisable in relation to Wales, were transferred to the National Assembly for Wales (see the

National Assembly for Wales (Transfer of Functions) Order 1999, SI 1999/672, art 2, Sch 1) and are now vested in the Welsh Ministers (see the Government of Wales Act 2006 s 162(1), Sch 11 para 30). As to the Secretary of State see PARA 58. As to the meaning of 'Wales' see PARA 7 note 3. As to the Welsh Ministers see PARA 59.

2   Such orders are not made by statutory instrument (see the School Standards and Framework Act 1998 s 138(2)) and as such are not recorded in this title.

3   As to the meaning of 'modifications' see PARA 21 note 15 (definition applied by the School Standards and Framework Act 1998 s 142(8)).

4   As to the meaning of 'trust deed' see PARA 108 note 6 (definition applied by the School Standards and Framework Act 1998 s 142(8)).

5   As to the meaning of 'school' see PARA 91 (definition applied by the School Standards and Framework Act 1998 s 142(8)).

6   School Standards and Framework Act 1998 s 82(1)(a). As to foundation schools, voluntary schools and foundation special schools see PARA 106.

7   School Standards and Framework Act 1998 s 82(1)(b). As to the meaning of references to property held on trust for the purposes of a school see PARA 108 note 6.

8   School Standards and Framework Act 1998 s 82(1) (amended by the Education Act 2002 s 215(1), Sch 21 para 108; the Education and Inspections Act 2006 s 30, Sch 3 para 28; the Academies Act 2010 Sch 1 para 9; and the School Standards and Organisation (Wales) Act 2013 Sch 5 para 19(1), (8)).

9   As to the exercise of the duty to consult see JUDICIAL REVIEW vol 61 (2010) PARA 627.

10   School Standards and Framework Act 1998 s 82(2)(a). As to the governing bodies of maintained schools see PARA 150 et seq.

11   School Standards and Framework Act 1998 s 82(2)(b).

12   'Church of England school' means a foundation or voluntary school in the Province of Canterbury or York in relation to which the religion or religious denomination specified under the School Standards and Framework Act 1998 s 69(4) (see PARA 914) is 'Church of England' and 'appropriate diocesan authority', in relation to such a school, means the Diocesan Board of Education for the diocese of the Church of England in which the school is situated: s 142(1) (definition amended by SI 2003/2037). 'Church in Wales school' means a foundation or voluntary school in the Province of Wales in relation to which the religion or religious denomination specified under the School Standards and Framework Act 1998 s 69(4) is 'Church in Wales' and 'appropriate diocesan authority', in relation to such a school, means the Diocesan Board of Finance for the diocese of the Church in Wales in which the school is situated or such other person as the Welsh Ministers may by order designate in respect of that diocese: s 142(1) (definition amended by SI 2003/2037); Government of Wales Act 2006 Sch 11 para 32. 'Roman Catholic Church school' means a foundation or voluntary school in relation to which the religion or religious denomination specified under the School Standards and Framework Act 1998 s 69(4) is 'Roman Catholic' and 'appropriate diocesan authority', in relation to such a school, means the bishop of the Roman Catholic diocese in which the school is situated: s 142(1) (definition amended by SI 2003/2037). As to the meaning of 'England' see PARA 7 note 3. As to the meaning of 'person' see PARA 7 note 6. As to the Church of England see ECCLESIASTICAL LAW vol 34 (2011) PARA 50 et seq. As to the Church in Wales see ECCLESIASTICAL LAW vol 34 (2011) PARA 28 et seq.

Any reference in the School Standards and Framework Act 1998 to the religion or religious denomination specified in relation to a school under s 69(4) or s 124B(2) (see PARA 378) must be construed, in a case where more than one religion or religious denomination is so specified, as including a reference to any of those religions or religious denominations: s 142(3) (amended by SI 2003/2037). As a result of the School Standards and Framework Act 1998 s 142(3), s 142(1) (definitions) has the effect that a school may, for example, be both a Church of England school and a Roman Catholic Church school and so have a different appropriate diocesan authority in each of those capacities; and, in the case of a school with two appropriate diocesan authorities, any reference in the School Standards and Framework Act 1998 or the Education and Inspections Act 2006 Pt 4 (ss 59–73: see PARA 1207 et seq) to 'the appropriate diocesan authority' is: (1) in relation to anything required to be done by or in relation to that authority, a reference to both of the authorities concerned; or (2) in relation to anything authorised to be done by or in relation to that authority, a reference to either or both of the authorities concerned (or, in the context or of the Education and Inspections Act 2006 s 64(4) or (6) (see PARA 1212), to both of them acting together): School Standards and Framework Act 1998 s 142(4) (amended by the Education and Inspections Act 2006 s 71, Sch 7 Pt 2 para 15(a); and the School Standards and Organisation (Wales) Act 2013 Sch 5 para 4(1), (6)).

13   School Standards and Framework Act 1998 s 82(2)(c).

14   School Standards and Framework Act 1998 s 82(2)(d).

15 School Standards and Framework Act 1998 s 82(3). Where any scheme in force for the regulation of any endowed charity or charities, established or approved before or after 11 May 1891 (ie the date of the passing of the Army Schools Act 1891 s 1), includes any provision for the benefit of children who are or have been scholars in a public elementary school, an army school is to be deemed a public elementary school within the meaning of those provisions: s 1(1). For these purposes, 'army school' means a school established for the purpose of affording education to children of non-commissioned officers and men of Her Majesty's regular land forces, and conducted under the authority of a Secretary of State: see s 1(2) (amended by SI 1964/488).

(iv) Adjudicators

147. Appointment of adjudicators. The Secretary of State[1] must appoint for England[2] such number of persons to act as adjudicators for the purposes of the School Standards and Framework Act 1998 as he considers appropriate[3]. Any matter which by virtue of that Act or the Education and Inspections Act 2006[4] is required to be referred to 'the adjudicator' must be referred to such person appointed under these provisions as may be determined in accordance with regulations[5]. Accordingly, 'the adjudicator', in relation to any such matter, means that person[6].

When asked to do so by the Secretary of State, an adjudicator must give advice to the Secretary of State on such matters relating to the admission of pupils[7] to relevant schools[8] as the Secretary of State may specify[9]. The adjudicator may, for the purposes of providing such advice to the Secretary of State, request any of the following persons[10] to provide him with such information held by them as the adjudicator may specify: (1) the admission authority[11] of a community, foundation or voluntary school[12]; (2) the proprietor[13] of any other relevant school[14]. A person so requested by the adjudicator to provide information must comply with the request[15].

1 As to the Secretary of State see PARA 58.
2 As to the meaning of 'England' see PARA 7 note 3.
3 School Standards and Framework Act 1998 s 25(1). An adjudicator holds and vacates office in accordance with the terms of his appointment: Sch 5 para 2(1). An adjudicator may at any time resign his office by notice in writing to the Secretary of State (Sch 5 para 2(2)(a)); and is eligible for re-appointment if he ceases to hold office (Sch 5 para 2(2)(b)). An adjudicator may be removed from office by the Secretary of State on the ground of incapacity or misbehaviour: Sch 5 para 2(3). As to remuneration and pensions see Sch 5 para 3. The Secretary of State may provide an adjudicator with such administrative staff as the adjudicator may require (Sch 5 para 4(a)); and provide, or defray the expenses of providing, an adjudicator with such accommodation and other facilities as the adjudicator may require (Sch 5 para 4(b)). For the purposes of the Parliamentary Commissioner Act 1967 s 5 (matters subject to investigation: see CONSTITUTIONAL AND ADMINISTRATIVE LAW vol 20 (2014) PARA 634 et seq) administrative functions exercisable by any person provided by the Secretary of State under the School Standards and Framework Act 1998 Sch 5 para 4 must be taken to be administrative functions of the Department for Education: Sch 5 para 9 (amended by SI 2010/1836). In the School Standards and Framework Act 1998 Sch 5 'adjudicator' means a person appointed under s 25: Sch 5 para 1. As to the meaning of 'writing' see PARA 76 note 8.
   An adjudicator appointed under s 25 is disqualified for membership of the House of Commons: see the House of Commons Disqualification Act 1975 s 1, Sch 1 Pt III; and PARLIAMENT vol 78 (2010) PARA 908.
4 Ie the Education and Inspections Act 2006 Pt 2 (ss 6A–32).
5 School Standards and Framework Act 1998 s 25(2) (amended by the Education and Inspections Act 2006 s 30, Sch 3 para 16). The regulations referred to are those made under the School Standards and Framework Act 1998 Sch 5 (see PARA 148): see s 25(2).
6 School Standards and Framework Act 1998 s 25(3).
7 As to the meaning of 'pupil' see PARA 20 note 4 (definition applied by the School Standards and Framework Act 1998 s 142(8)).

8 'Relevant school' means a school in England falling within any of the Education Act 2005 s 5(2)(a)–(f) (see PARA 1162): School Standards and Framework Act 1998 s 25(3D) (s 25(3A)–(3D) added by the Education and Inspections Act 2006 s 163). As to the meaning of 'school' see PARA 91 (definition applied by the School Standards and Framework Act 1998 s 142(8)).

9 School Standards and Framework Act 1998 s 25(3A) (as added: see note 8).

10 As to the meaning of 'person' see PARA 7 note 6.

11 Ie within the meaning of the School Standards and Framework Act 1998 Pt 3 Ch 1 (ss 84–98A): see PARA 227 note 6.

12 School Standards and Framework Act 1998 s 25(3B)(a) (as added: see note 8). As to community, foundation and voluntary schools see PARA 106.

13 As to the meaning of 'proprietor' see PARA 51 note 4 (definition applied by the School Standards and Framework Act 1998 s 142(8)).

14 School Standards and Framework Act 1998 s 25(3B)(b) (as added: see note 8).

15 School Standards and Framework Act 1998 s 25(3C) (as added: see note 8).

148. Procedure. Regulations[1] may make provision as to the procedure to be followed in connection with the reference[2] of matters to adjudicators[3] and their determination of matters so referred[4]. The regulations may, in particular, make provision:

(1) as to the manner in which matters may be referred to adjudicators[5];

(2) for determining the adjudicators to which individual referrals are to be made[6];

(3) authorising adjudicators to hold local inquiries[7];

(4) as to the procedure to be followed where local inquiries are held by adjudicators (whether by virtue of head (3) above or otherwise)[8];

(5) authorising adjudicators to appoint assessors to sit with them at local inquiries to advise them on matters arising[9];

(6) requiring anything falling to be done under the regulations to be done within such period as may be specified in or determined in accordance with the regulations[10].

Subject to any provision made by the regulations, an adjudicator may regulate his own procedure[11].

When taking any decision an adjudicator must have regard (so far as relevant) to the obligations which, by virtue of legislation relating to discrimination[12], are owed by any local authority[13] or governing body which will be affected by the decision[14].

The Secretary of State may make orders[15] as to the costs of the parties at any local inquiry held by an adjudicator (whether by virtue of head (3) above or otherwise), and as to the parties by whom the costs are to be paid[16]. Any costs payable under any such order are subject to assessment in such manner as the Secretary of State may direct[17].

1 Ie regulations made under the School Standards and Framework Act 1998 by the Secretary of State: see s 142(1). As to the Secretary of State see PARA 58. As to the regulations made see the Education (References to Adjudicator) Regulations 1999, SI 1999/702 (amended by SI 1999/1286; and SI 2004/3052); and the School Organisation Proposals by the Learning and Skills Council for England Regulations 2003, SI 2003/507 (amended by SI 2004/696; and SI 2013/235).

2 Ie under the School Standards and Framework Act 1998 Pt II (ss 20–83) or Pt III (ss 84–109) or under the Education and Inspections Act 2006 Pt 2 (ss 6A–32).

3 As to the meaning of 'adjudicator' see PARA 147. The adjudicator also has involvement in other areas eg in the context of the School Admissions Code and the procedure regarding admissions complaints: see PARAS 226, 240.

4 School Standards and Framework Act 1998 Sch 5 para 5(1) (amended by the Education and Inspections Act 2006 s 30, Sch 3 para 32). See *P v Schools Adjudicator* [2006] EWHC 1934 (QB), [2007] LGR 346, [2006] ELR 557.

5 School Standards and Framework Act 1998 Sch 5 para 5(2)(a).
6 School Standards and Framework Act 1998 Sch 5 para 5(2)(b).
7 School Standards and Framework Act 1998 Sch 5 para 5(2)(c).
8 School Standards and Framework Act 1998 Sch 5 para 5(2)(d).
9 School Standards and Framework Act 1998 Sch 5 para 5(2)(e).
10 School Standards and Framework Act 1998 Sch 5 para 5(2)(f).
11 School Standards and Framework Act 1998 Sch 5 para 5(3).
12 Ie the Equality Act 2010 s 149 (see DISCRIMINATION vol 33 (2013) PARAS 1, 266 et seq), or the Equality Act 2010 Pt 3 (ss 28–31) (see DISCRIMINATION vol 33 (2013) PARA 78 et seq), Pt 6 (ss 84–99) (see PARA 9 et seq): School Standards and Framework Act 1998 Sch 5 para 6 (amended by the Equality Act 2010 Sch 26 paras 44, 45; and SI 2011/1060).
13 As to the meaning of 'local authority' see PARA 25 (definition applied by the School Standards and Framework Act 1998 s 142(8)).
14 School Standards and Framework Act 1998 Sch 5 para 6 (amended by SI 2010/1158). As to governing bodies of maintained schools see PARA 150 et seq.
15 Such orders are not made by statutory instrument (see the School Standards and Framework Act 1998 s 138(2)) and as such are not recorded in this title.
16 School Standards and Framework Act 1998 Sch 5 para 5(4).
17 School Standards and Framework Act 1998 Sch 5 para 5(4).

149. Indemnity. The Secretary of State[1] must indemnify an adjudicator[2] against any reasonable legal costs and expenses reasonably incurred by him in connection with any decision or action taken by him in good faith in pursuance of his functions[3] as an adjudicator[4].

1 As to the Secretary of State see PARA 58.
2 As to the meaning of 'adjudicator' see PARA 147.
3 As to the meaning of 'functions' see PARA 18 note 5 (definition applied by the School Standards and Framework Act 1998 s 142(8)).
4 School Standards and Framework Act 1998 Sch 5 para 7.

(v) Governance of Maintained Schools

A. GOVERNANCE OF MAINTAINED SCHOOLS IN ENGLAND

(A) Constitution of Governing Bodies

150. Governing bodies. Each maintained school[1] in England[2] must have a governing body[3], which is a body corporate[4] constituted in accordance with regulations[5]. Regulations[6] must provide for a governing body to consist of:

(1) persons elected or appointed as parent governors[7];
(2) the head teacher of the school[8];
(3) a person elected as a staff governor[9];
(4) a person appointed as a local authority governor[10];
(5) in the case of a foundation school, a foundation special school[11] or a voluntary school[12], persons appointed as foundation governors or partnership governors[13]; and
(6) such other persons as may be prescribed[14].

Regulations[15] may also make provision as to:

(a) the number of governors, or of governors falling within any category[16];
(b) the person[17] or persons by whom, and the manner in which, governors are to be elected or appointed[18];
(c) eligibility for election or appointment as governors of any category, or for voting in an election of such governors[19];
(d) the term of office of governors[20];
(e) resignation or removal from office of governors[21];

(f) the payment of allowances to governors[22];

(g) meetings and proceedings of governing bodies[23];

(h) the election by the governors of a chairman and vice-chairman of the governing body[24];

(i) the establishment by a governing body of committees[25];

(j) the appointment of persons other than governors to serve on committees of governing bodies[26];

(k) the delegation of functions[27] by governing bodies[28]; and

(l) other matters relating to the constitution or procedure of governing bodies[29].

In discharging any function conferred by such regulations, a local authority or the governing body of a maintained school must have regard to any guidance given from time to time by the Secretary of State[30].

The governing body[31] is to be known as 'The governing body of ...' with the addition of the name of the school as for the time being set out in the school's instrument of government[32].

If the school is discontinued, the governing body is dissolved[33] on the discontinuance date[34], or on such later date as the Secretary of State may specify by order[35] made before the discontinuance date[36].

1 As to the meaning of 'maintained school' see PARA 103 note 3. As to academies see PARA 345 et seq.

2 As to the meaning of 'England' see PARA 7 note 3. As to the governance of schools in Wales see PARA 195 et seq.

3 The governing body of a maintained school is a public authority for the purposes of the Human Rights Act 1998: see *A v Head Teacher and Governors of Lord Grey School* [2006] UKHL 14, [2006] 2 AC 363, sub nom *Ali v Head Teacher and Governors of Lord Grey School* [2006] 2 All ER 457, at [79] per Baroness Hale of Richmond. As to public authorities for the purposes of the Human Rights Act 1998 see JUDICIAL REVIEW vol 61 (2010) PARA 605.

4 As to bodies corporate see COMPANIES vol 14 (2009) PARA 2; CORPORATIONS vol 24 (2010) PARA 301 et seq.

5 Education Act 2002 s 19(1). In relation to maintained schools in England s 19(1) has effect subject to s 24 (federations of schools: see PARA 156); and regulations under s 19 may include provision with respect to the governing bodies of federations: s 19(8) (amended by the Education (Wales) Measure 2011 s 19(1), (2)(a)). As to the meaning of 'federation' see PARA 156 note 4. Regulations made under the Education Act 2002 s 19 do not apply to any temporary governing body: see s 34(8); and PARA 155. 'Regulations' means regulations made under the Education Act 2002 by the Secretary of State: see s 212(1). As to the regulations made under s 19 see notes 6, 15. As to the Secretary of State see PARA 58.

6 As to the regulations made under the Education Act 2002 s 19(2) see the School Governance (Constitution) (England) Regulations 2012, SI 2012/1034 (amended by SI 2014/1257; and SI 2015/883); and PARA 151 et seq. See also the Education (Company Directors Disqualification Act 1986: Amendments to Disqualification Provisions) (England) Regulations 2004, SI 2004/3264; the School Governance (Transition from an Interim Executive Board) (England) Regulations 2010, SI 2010/1918 (amended by SI 2015/883); and the School Governance (Federations) (England) Regulations 2012, SI 2012/1035 (amended by SI 2013/1624; SI 2014/1257; and SI 2015/1554).

7 Education Act 2002 s 19(1A)(a) (s 19(1A) added by the Education Act 2011 s 38(1), (2)).

8 Education Act 2002 s 19(1A)(b) (as added: see note 7). As to the meaning of 'head teacher' see PARA 86 note 4 (definition applied by s 212(2), (3); Interpretation Act 1978 s 11).

9 Education Act 2002 s 19(1A)(c) (as added: see note 7).

10 Education Act 2002 s 19(1A)(d) (as added: see note 7). As to the meaning of 'local authority' see PARA 25 (definition applied by the Education Act 2002 s 212(1)).

11 As to the meaning of references to a foundation school or a foundation special school see PARA 106.

12 As to the meaning of references to a voluntary school see PARA 106.

13 Education Act 2002 s 19(1A)(e) (as added: see note 7).

14 Education Act 2002 s 19(1A)(f) (as added: see note 7). 'Prescribed' means prescribed by the regulations: see s 212(1).

15 As to the regulations made under the Education Act 2002 s 19(3) see the Education (Company Directors Disqualification Act 1986: Amendments to Disqualification Provisions) (England) Regulations 2004, SI 2004/3264; the Education (Disqualification Provisions: Bankruptcy and Mental Health) (England) Regulations 2006, SI 2006/2198; the School Organisation (Removal of Foundation, Reduction in Number of Foundation Governors and Ability of Foundation to Pay Debts) (England) Regulations 2007, SI 2007/3475; the School Staffing (England) Regulations 2009, SI 2009/2680 (amended by SI 2015/883; and SI 2015/887); the School Governance (Transition from an Interim Executive Board) (England) Regulations 2010, SI 2010/1918; the School Governance (Federations) (England) Regulations 2012, SI 2012/1035 (amended by SI 2013/1624; SI 2014/1257; and SI 2015/1554); and the School Governance (Roles, Procedures and Allowances) (England) Regulations 2013, SI 2013/1624 (amended by SI 2013/2688; SI 2014/1257; and SI 2014/1959).

16 Education Act 2002 s 19(3)(a). Regulations made by virtue of s 19(3)(a) must secure that the majority of the governors of a voluntary aided school are persons appointed as foundation governors: s 19(4). As to the constitution of the governing body see generally PARA 151 et seq.

17 As to the meaning of 'person' see PARA 7 note 6.

18 Education Act 2002 s 19(3)(b).

19 Education Act 2002 s 19(3)(c). Regulations made by virtue of the Education Act 2002 s 19(3)(c) in relation to a maintained school in England may include provision for eligibility criteria for the school's local authority governor to be such as may be specified by the school's governing body: s 19(4A) (added by the Education Act 2011 s 38(4)).

20 Education Act 2002 s 19(3)(d).

21 Education Act 2002 s 19(3)(e). Regulations made by virtue of the Education Act 2002 s 19(3)(e) in relation to a maintained school in England may include provision allowing the head teacher of the school to resign from office as a governor (and to withdraw any such resignation): s 19(4B) (added by the Education Act 2011 s 38(1), (4)).

22 Education Act 2002 s 19(3)(f). Nothing in the School Standards and Framework Act 1998 s 50(3) (effect of financial delegation) is to be read as authorising the payment of allowances to governors otherwise than in accordance with regulations under the Education Act 2002 s 19: see the School Standards and Framework Act 1998 s 50(5); and PARA 324.

23 Education Act 2002 s 19(3)(g). See further PARA 181.

24 Education Act 2002 s 19(3)(h). See further PARA 181.

25 Education Act 2002 s 19(3)(i). See further PARA 181.

26 Education Act 2002 s 19(3)(j). See further PARA 181.

27 As to the meaning of 'functions' see PARA 18 note 5 (definition applied by the Education Act 2002 s 212(2), (3)).

28 Education Act 2002 s 19(3)(k). Section 19(3)(k) has effect subject to the provisions of any scheme under the School Standards and Framework Act 1998 s 48 (local authorities' financial schemes: see PARA 321) which relates to the school: Education Act 2002 s 19(5) (amended by SI 2010/1158). As to delegation of functions see further PARA 181.

29 Education Act 2002 s 19(3)(l).

30 Education Act 2002 s 19(7) (amended by SI 2010/1158). As to the publication of guidance see the Education Act 1996 s 571 (applied by the Education Act 2002 s 212(2), (3)); and PARA 60. See eg in particular 'The constitution of governing bodies of maintained schools: Statutory guidance for governing bodies of maintained schools and local authorities in England' (March 2015).

31 Ie the governing body of a maintained school incorporated under the Education Act 2002 s 19(1) (see the text to notes 1–5): Sch 1 para 1.

32 Education Act 2002 Sch 1 para 2(1).

33 Ie by virtue of the Education Act 2002 Sch 1 para 5.

34 Education Act 2002 Sch 1 para 5(1)(a). 'The discontinuance date' means in relation to a school in England, whichever of the following is relevant: (1) the date on which proposals for discontinuing the school are implemented under the Education and Inspections Act 2006 Sch 2 Pt 3 (paras 21–27) (see PARA 124 et seq); (2) the date on which the school is discontinued under the School Standards and Framework Act 1998 s 30 (see PARA 116); (3) the date specified in a direction given under the Education and Inspections Act 2006 s 17(1) (see PARA 117) or s 68(1) (see PARA 1217); or (4) the date on which a local authority is required to cease to maintain the school under the Academies Act 2010 s 6(2) (see PARA 351): Education Act 2002 Sch 1 para 5(2)(a) (substituted by the Education and Inspections Act 2006 s 30, Sch 3 para 48; and amended by the Academies Act 2010 Sch 2 para 15; SI 2010/1080).

The Education Act 2002 Sch 1 para 5(1) does not apply if the school is a federated school in England, and immediately after the discontinuance date, there will be more than one other school remaining in the federation: Sch 1 para 5(1A) (Sch 1 para 5(1A), (1B) added by the

Education Act 2011 s 39). As to the meanings of 'federation' and 'federated school' see PARA 156 note 4 (definitions applied by the Education Act 2002 Sch 1 para 5(1B) (as so added)).

35 Orders made under the Education Act 2002 Sch 1 para 5 are not made by statutory instrument (see s 210(2)) and, as such, are not recorded in this work.

36 See the Education Act 2002 Sch 1 para 5(1)(b). See note 34.

151. Constitution of governing bodies: requirements for all maintained schools.

The governing body[1] of every maintained school[2] must be constituted in accordance with the following provisions[3].

The total membership of the governing body of a maintained school must be no fewer than seven governors[4].

The governing body of a maintained school must include the following:

(1)   at least two parent governors[5];

(2)   the head teacher[6] unless the head teacher resigns the office of governor[7];

(3)   one staff governor[8]; and

(4)   one local authority governor[9].

The governing body may in addition appoint such number of co-opted governors as they consider necessary provided that certain relevant requirements[10] are met in respect of governing bodies of foundation and voluntary schools[11].

The total number of co-opted governors who are also eligible to be elected as staff governors[12], when counted with the staff governor and the head teacher, must not exceed one third of the total membership of the governing body[13].

1   As to the election and appointment of governors see PARA 159 et seq.

2   As to the meaning of 'maintained school' see PARA 103 note 3. As to academies see PARA 345 et seq.

3   School Governance (Constitution) (England) Regulations 2012, SI 2012/1034, reg 13(1).

4   School Governance (Constitution) (England) Regulations 2012, SI 2012/1034, reg 13(2). Any reference to 'a governor' is a reference to a member of a governing body of any school to which the provision applies: reg 5(2).

5   School Governance (Constitution) (England) Regulations 2012, SI 2012/1034, reg 13(3)(a). 'Parent governor' means: (1) a person who is elected in accordance with Sch 1 paras 4–8 (see PARA 159) as a governor by parents of registered pupils at the school and is himself such a parent at the time when he is elected (reg 6(1)(a)); or (2) where the school is a maintained nursery school, a person who is elected as a governor by parents of registered pupils at the school, or parents of children for whom educational or other provision is made on the premises of the school (including any such provision made by the governing body under the Education Act 2002 s 27 (see PARA 174)), and is himself such a parent at the time when he is elected (School Governance (Constitution) (England) Regulations 2012, SI 2012/1034, reg 6(1)(b)); or (3) a person appointed as a parent governor in accordance with Sch 1 paras 9–12 (see PARA 159) (reg 6(1)(c) (amended by SI 2014/1257)). As to the meaning of 'maintained nursery school' see PARA 103 note 3. 'Parent' includes any individual who has or has had parental responsibility for, or cares or has cared for, a child or young person under the age of 19: reg 5(1). As to the meaning of 'registered pupil' see PARA 437.

6   As to the meaning of 'head teacher' see PARA 86 note 4 (definition applied by the Education Act 2002 s 212(2), (3); Interpretation Act 1978 s 11).

7   School Governance (Constitution) (England) Regulations 2012, SI 2012/1034, reg 13(3)(b). Such resignation is in accordance with reg 19.

8   School Governance (Constitution) (England) Regulations 2012, SI 2012/1034, reg 13(3)(c). 'Staff governor' means a person who (1) is elected in accordance with Sch 2 as a governor by persons who are employed by either the governing body or the local authority under a contract of employment providing for those persons to work at the school; and (2) is so employed at the time of election: reg 7. 'The local authority' is a reference to the local authority who maintain the school: reg 5(2)(b).

9   School Governance (Constitution) (England) Regulations 2012, SI 2012/1034, reg 13(3)(d). 'Local authority governor' means a person who (1) is nominated by the local authority; and (2) is appointed by the governing body as a governor having, in the opinion of the governing body,

the skills required to contribute to the effective governance and success of the school and having met any additional eligibility criteria set by the governing body: reg 8 (amended by SI 2014/1257).
10 Ie the requirements of the School Governance (Constitution) (England) Regulations 2012, SI 2012/1034, reg 14: see PARA 152.
11 School Governance (Constitution) (England) Regulations 2012, SI 2012/1034, reg 13(4). As to the meaning of references to foundation and voluntary schools see PARA 106.
12 Ie under the School Governance (Constitution) (England) Regulations 2012, SI 2012/1034, Sch 2.
13 School Governance (Constitution) (England) Regulations 2012, SI 2012/1034, reg 13(5).

152. Constitution of governing bodies: additional requirements for foundation and voluntary schools.

The governing body[1] of a foundation school or a foundation special school[2] which, in either case, does not have a foundation[3], must also include at least two (but no more than one quarter of the total) partnership governors[4].

The governing body of a foundation school or a foundation special school which, in either case, has a foundation but which is not a qualifying foundation school[5], must also include at least two (but no more than 45 per cent of the total) foundation governors[6].

The governing body of a qualifying foundation school must also include such number of foundation governors as to outnumber all the other governors by up to two[7].

The governing body of a voluntary aided school[8] must also include such number of foundation governors as to outnumber all the other governors by two[9].

The governing body of a voluntary controlled school must also include at least two (but no more than one quarter of the total) foundation governors[10].

In calculating the number of governors required in order to comply with this provision, the number is to be rounded up or down to the nearest whole number[11].

1 As to the election and appointment of governors see PARA 159 et seq.
2 As to the meaning of references to a foundation school or a foundation special school see PARA 106.
3 Any reference in the School Governance (Constitution) (England) Regulations 2012, SI 2012/1034, to a foundation or to a school having a foundation is to be read in accordance with the School Standards and Framework Act 1998 s 21 (see PARA 108 note 6): School Governance (Constitution) (England) Regulations 2012, SI 2012/1034, reg 5(2)(c).
4 School Governance (Constitution) (England) Regulations 2012, SI 2012/1034, reg 14(1). As to the meaning of references to 'governor' see PARA 151 note 4. 'Partnership governor' means a person who is appointed as such in accordance with Sch 3: reg 10(1). Where the school has a religious character, 'partnership governor' means a person who is appointed for the purpose of securing that such religious character is preserved and developed: reg 10(2). As to schools having a religious character see PARAS 916–917.
5 'Qualifying foundation school' means a foundation or a foundation special school which has a foundation which meets any one or more of the conditions in the School Standards and Framework Act 1998 s 23A(2), (3), (4) (see PARA 109): School Governance (Constitution) (England) Regulations 2012, SI 2012/1034, reg 5(1).
6 School Governance (Constitution) (England) Regulations 2012, SI 2012/1034, reg 14(2). 'Foundation governor' means a person who (1) is appointed as a governor by any person other than the local authority; (2) is appointed for the purpose of securing that the character of the school including, where the school has a particular religious character such religious character, is preserved and developed; (3) where the school has a foundation, is appointed for the purpose of securing that the school is conducted in accordance with the foundation's governing documents, including, where appropriate, any trust deed relating to the school; (4) would, in the opinion of the person entitled to appoint the foundation governor, be capable of achieving the purposes for which they would be appointed as a foundation governor; and (5) has, in the opinion of the

person entitled to appoint the foundation governor, the skills required to contribute to the effective governance and success of the school: reg 9(a) (amended by SI 2014/1257). 'Ex officio foundation governor' means a person who is a foundation governor by virtue of an office held by the person: School Governance (Constitution) (England) Regulations 2012, SI 2012/1034, reg 9(b). 'Substitute governor' means a foundation governor appointed to act in the place of an ex officio foundation governor who is unwilling or unable to act as a governor or has been removed from office under reg 21(1) (see PARA 164): reg 9(c). As to the meaning of references to 'the local authority' see PARA 151 note 8. As to the meaning of 'trust deed' see PARA 108 note 6 (definition applied by the Education Act 2002 s 212(2), (3); Interpretation Act 1978 s 11).

7 School Governance (Constitution) (England) Regulations 2012, SI 2012/1034,, reg 14(3).
8 As to the meaning of references to a voluntary school see PARA 106.
9 School Governance (Constitution) (England) Regulations 2012, SI 2012/1034, reg 14(4).
10 School Governance (Constitution) (England) Regulations 2012, SI 2012/1034, reg 14(5).
11 School Governance (Constitution) (England) Regulations 2012, SI 2012/1034, reg 14(6).

153. Constitution of governing bodies: surplus governors. Where (1) a maintained school[1] has more governors of a particular category than are provided for by the instrument of government[2] for the school[3]; and (2) the excess is not eliminated by the required number of governors resigning, the number of governors of that category required to eliminate the excess must cease to hold office in accordance with the following provisions[4].

Foundation governors[5] must cease to hold office such that, in the opinion of those who appointed them under the instrument of government, the foundation governors remaining in office are those best placed to contribute to the effective governance and success of the school and serve the purposes for which foundation governors are appointed[6].

Governors who are not foundation governors must cease to hold office such that, in the opinion of the governing body[7], the governors remaining in office are those with the most relevant skills to contribute to the effective governance and success of the school[8].

In determining which governors should cease to hold office[9] (a) the governing body must hold a vote in respect of each category in which there are excess governors[10]; (b) governors must not vote in respect of their own category[11]; and (c) no governor ceases to hold office until the votes on all categories are cast[12].

1 As to the meaning of 'maintained school' see PARA 103 note 3. As to academies see PARA 345 et seq.
2 As to instruments of government see PARA 184 et seq.
3 As to the meaning of 'school' see PARA 91 (definition applied by the Education Act 2002 s 212(2), (3); Interpretation Act 1978 s 11).
4 School Governance (Constitution) (England) Regulations 2012, SI 2012/1034, reg 15(1) (reg 15 substituted by SI 2014/1257). The reference in the text to the following provisions is a reference to the School Governance (Constitution) (England) Regulations 2012, SI 2012/1034, reg 15(2)–(4). Any procedure set out in the instrument of government for the removal of excess foundation governors does not apply in the circumstances set out in reg 15(1): reg 15(5) (as so substituted).
5 As to the meaning of 'foundation governor' see PARA 152 note 6.
6 School Governance (Constitution) (England) Regulations 2012, SI 2012/1034, reg 15(2) (as substituted: see note 4).
7 As to the election and appointment of governors see PARA 159 et seq.
8 School Governance (Constitution) (England) Regulations 2012, SI 2012/1034, reg 15(3) (as substituted: see note 3).
9 Ie in accordance with the School Governance (Constitution) (England) Regulations 2012, SI 2012/1034, reg 15(3).
10 School Governance (Constitution) (England) Regulations 2012, SI 2012/1034, reg 15(4)(a) (as substituted: see note 3).
11 School Governance (Constitution) (England) Regulations 2012, SI 2012/1034, reg 15(4)(b) (as substituted: see note 3).

12 School Governance (Constitution) (England) Regulations 2012, SI 2012/1034, reg 15(4)(c) (as substituted: see note 3).

154.   Powers where there is no properly constituted governing body. Where it appears to the Secretary of State[1] that, by reason of the default of any person[2], there is no properly constituted governing body[3] of any community, foundation or voluntary school or any community or foundation special school[4], he may:

(1)   make such appointments and give such directions[5] as he thinks desirable for the purpose of securing that there is a properly constituted governing body of that school[6]; and

(2)   give directions rendering valid any acts or proceedings which in his opinion are invalid or otherwise defective by reason of the default[7].

1   As to the Secretary of State see PARA 58.
2   As to the meaning of 'person' see PARA 7 note 6.
3   As to governing bodies of maintained schools see PARA 150 et seq.
4   See the Education Act 1996 s 498(2) (substituted by the School Standards and Framework Act 1998 s 140(1), Sch 30 para 131). As to the meaning of references to a community, foundation or voluntary school or a community or foundation special school see PARA 106.
5   As to directions see PARA 75.
6   Education Act 1996 s 498(1)(a).
7   Education Act 1996 s 498(1)(b).

155.   Arrangements for government of new schools. Where proposals for the establishment of a maintained school[1] fall to be implemented under any enactment[2], the local authority[3] must make arrangements providing for the constitution of a temporary governing body for the school[4]. Once constituted[5], the temporary governing body continues in existence until such time as the governing body is constituted for the school under an instrument of government[6]. The local authority must secure that the governing body is so constituted before such date as may be determined in accordance with regulations[7].

The temporary governing body of a school must be treated for the purposes of the Education Acts[8] as if it were the governing body during the period beginning with the school opening date[9] and ending with the time when the governing body is constituted for the school under an instrument of government[10].

Regulations[11] may make provision with respect to:

(1)   the making and termination of arrangements for the constitution of temporary governing bodies[12];

(2)   the constitution, meetings and proceedings of temporary governing bodies, the payment of allowances to temporary governors[13], and the appointment of clerks to such bodies[14];

(3)   the exercise by a temporary governing body before the school opening date of the power to provide community facilities[15];

(4)   the transition from a temporary governing body to a governing body constituted under an instrument of government[16]; and

(5)   such other matters relating to temporary governing bodies as the Secretary of State considers appropriate[17].

1   As to the meaning of 'maintained school' see PARA 103 note 3.
2   As to the meaning of 'enactment' see PARA 1 note 13. As to the implementation of proposals for the establishment of a maintained school see PARA 118 et seq.
3   As to the meaning of 'local authority' see PARA 25 (definition applied by the Education Act 2002 s 212(1)).
4   Education Act 2002 s 34(1) (amended by SI 2010/1158). As to governing bodies of maintained schools see PARA 150 et seq.

Regulations made by the Secretary of State may make provision for:
 (1)   the staffing and conduct of a new school in advance of the school opening date (School Standards and Framework Act 1998 s 72(1)(a));
 (2)   the determination of matters in connection with a new school in advance of that date (s 72(1)(b));
 (3)   the taking of decisions by a temporary governing body, or (where power to do so is delegated to him) by the head teacher, as to expenditure in connection with a new school at a time when it does not have a delegated budget (s 72(1)(c));
 (4)   such other matters relating to new schools as the Secretary of State considers appropriate (s 72(1)(d)).
For these purposes, a 'new school' is a school or proposed school: (a) for which there is a temporary governing body constituted under the Education Act 2002 s 34; or (b) for which there is no such body but for which such a body is required by virtue of s 34(1) to be constituted or may be so constituted in accordance with such anticipatory arrangements as are mentioned in s 34(5)(a) (see head (1) in the text): School Standards and Framework Act 1998 s 72(3)(a), (b) (s 72(3)(a) amended by the Education Act 2002 s 215(1), Sch 21 para 106). As to the meaning of 'school' for these purposes see PARA 91 (definition applied by the School Standards and Framework Act 1998 s142(8)). See also PARA 111. As to the meaning of 'head teacher' see PARA 86 note 4 (definition applied by s 142(8)). As to delegated budgets see PARA 323 et seq. As to the Secretary of State see PARA 58.
   The regulations may, in connection with any matters falling within heads (1)–(4) above, apply any provision of the Education Acts with or without modification: School Standards and Framework Act 1998 s 72(2). As to the meaning of 'the Education Acts' see PARA 1 note 13 (definition applied by the School Standards and Framework Act 1998 s 142(8)). As to the meaning of 'modification' see PARA 21 note 15 (definition applied by s 142(8)).
   As to the regulations made see the New School (Admissions) (England) Regulations 2003, SI 2003/1041; the School Governance (New Schools) (England) Regulations 2007, SI 2007/958 (amended by SI 2007/3464; SI 2009/1924; SI 2010/2582 (amended by SI 2011/577; SI 2012/1033; SI 2012/1034, SI 2012/2404; SI 2013/235; and SI 2015/883); and the School Staffing (England) Regulations 2009, SI 2009/2680 (amended by SI 2015/883; and SI 2015/887).
 5   Ie in accordance with arrangements made under the Education Act 2002 s 34(1): see the text to notes 1–4.
 6   Education Act 2002 s 34(2). The requirement for there to be an instrument of government for a school, imposed by s 20 (see PARA 184), takes effect in relation to a school falling within s 34(1) (see the text to notes 1–4) as from the date determined under s 34(3) (see the text to note 7): s 34(4). As to instruments of government see PARA 184 et seq.
 7   Education Act 2002 s 34(3) (amended by SI 2010/1158). 'Regulations' means regulations made by the Secretary of State under the Education Act 2002: see s 212(1). As to the Secretary of State see PARA 58. As at the date at which this volume states the law, no regulations had been made under s 34(3).
 8   As to the meaning of 'the Education Acts' see PARA 1 note 13 (definition applied by the Education Act 2002 s 212(2), (3)).
 9   'School opening date', in relation to a new maintained school, means the date when the school first admits pupils: Education Act 2002 s 34(9). As to the meaning of 'pupil' see PARA 20 note 4 (definition applied by s 212(2), (3)). As to school admissions see PARA 224 et seq.
 10   Education Act 2002 s 34(7). For the purposes of s 30(3) (see PARA 218) and the Education Act 1996 ss 495–498 (general default powers of the Secretary of State: see PARAS 62, 64–66, 154), the temporary governing body of a school is also to be so treated at any time falling before the school opening date: s 34(7). Despite s 34(7), nothing in any of the following provisions, namely: (1) s 20(1) (see PARA 184) (s 34(8)(a)); (2) subject to any regulations made under s 34(5) (see the text to notes 11–17), Sch 1 (see PARA 150) (s 34(8)(b)); or (3) subject to any regulations made under s 34(5), regulations made under s 19 (see PARA 150), s 20 (see PARA 184) or s 23 (see PARA 167) (s 34(8)(c)), applies to any temporary governing body: s 34(8).
 11   Regulations made under the Education Act 2002 s 34(5) may, in connection with any matters falling within s 34(5): (1) modify any provision made under any of s 19 (see PARA 150), s 20 (see PARA 184) or s 23 (see PARA 167) or by Sch 1 (see PARA 150) (s 34(6)(a)); (2) apply any such provision with or without modifications (s 34(6)(b)); (3) make provision corresponding or similar to any such provision (s 34(6)(c)). As to the meanings of 'modify' and 'modifications' see PARA 21 note 15 (definition applied by s 212(2), (3)).
   As to the regulations made under s 34(5), (6) see the Education (Company Directors Disqualification Act 1986: Amendments to Disqualification Provisions) (England) Regulations 2004, SI 2004/3264; the Education (Disqualification Provisions: Bankruptcy and

Mental Health) (England) Regulations 2006, SI 2006/2198; the School Governance (New Schools) (England) Regulations 2007, SI 2007/958 (amended by SI 2007/3464; SI 2009/1924; and SI 2010/2582 (amended by SI 2011/577); SI 2012/1033; SI 2012/1034; SI 2012/2404; SI 2013/235; and SI 2015/883); the School Staffing (England) Regulations 2009, SI 2009/2680 (amended by SI 2015/883; and SI 2015/887); the School Governance (Federations) (England) Regulations 2012, SI 2012/1035 (amended by SI 2013/1624; SI 2014/1257; and SI 2015/1554); and the School Governance (Roles, Procedures and Allowances) (England) Regulations 2013, SI 2013/1624 (amended by SI 2013/2688; SI 2014/1257; and SI 2014/1959).

12 Education Act 2002 s 34(5)(a). The arrangements mentioned include such arrangements made in anticipation of proposals falling to be implemented as are mentioned in s 34(1) (see the text and notes 1–4): s 34(5)(a).

13 In the case of temporary governors of a new school, nothing in the School Standards and Framework Act 1998 s 50(3) (effect of financial delegation) is to be read as authorising the payment of allowances to governors otherwise than in accordance with regulations under the Education Act 2002 s 34(5): see the School Standards and Framework Act 1998 s 50(5); and PARA 324.

14 Education Act 2002 s 34(5)(b).

15 Education Act 2002 s 34(5)(c). The power to provide community facilities is conferred by s 27: see PARA 174.

16 Education Act 2002 s 34(5)(d).

17 See the Education Act 2002 s 34(5)(e).

156. Federations of schools. In prescribed[1] cases, the governing bodies[2]:

(1) of two or more maintained schools in England[3];

(2) of an existing federation[4] and of one or more maintained schools in England[5]; or

(3) of two or more existing federations[6],

may, after complying with prescribed conditions, and in accordance with prescribed procedure, provide for their respective schools to be federated[7]. Where any schools are so federated[8], they must have a single governing body constituted under a single instrument of government[9], and, in prescribed cases, be treated as a single school for the purposes of such enactments[10] as may be prescribed[11]. Regulations[12] may make provision:

(a) as to the dissolution of governing bodies on the formation of a federation[13];

(b) enabling the governing body of a federation to continue in existence as a body corporate[14] when one or more schools join or leave the federation[15];

(c) as to the circumstances in which and manner in which a federation may be dissolved, or one or more schools may leave a federation[16];

(d) enabling the governing body of a federation that is dissolved to be replaced either by governing bodies for each of the constituent schools or by governing bodies which include the governing body of a new federation[17];

(e) as to the transition from one governing body to another[18];

(f) as to the transfer of property, rights and liabilities[19] between governing bodies, or between local authorities[20] and governing bodies[21]; and

(g) as to such other matters relating to federations, federated schools or the formation or dissolution of federations as the Secretary of State considers appropriate[22].

If such regulations[23] allow the formation of a federation comprising schools within different categories[24], the regulations may make provision modifying any enactment which relates to schools within a particular category, or to the governing bodies of schools within a particular category, in the application of the enactment to schools forming part of such a federation or to the governing bodies of such federations[25].

Regulations[26] may make provision modifying certain provisions of the School Standards and Framework Act 1998 relating to financial delegation[27] or the Education and Inspections Act 2006 relating to schools causing concern[28] in the application of those provisions to federated schools in England or their governing bodies[29].

In any enactment: (i) any reference to the governing body or governors of a school is to be construed, in relation to a federated school, as a reference to the governing body or governors of the federation[30]; and (ii) any reference to the instrument of government of a school is to be construed, in relation to a federated school, as a reference to the instrument of government of the federation[31].

1   'Prescribed' means prescribed by regulations made by the Secretary of State under the Education Act 2002: see s 212(1). As to the Secretary of State see PARA 58. As to the regulations made under s 24 and s 25 (see the text to notes 23–29) see the School Governance (Federations) (England) Regulations 2012, SI 2012/1035 (amended by SI 2013/1624; SI 2014/1257; and SI 2015/1554); and the School and Early Years Finance (England) Regulations 2014, SI 2014/3352.

2   As to governing bodies of maintained schools see PARA 150 et seq.

3   Education Act 2002 s 24(1)(a) (amended by the Education (Wales) Measure 2011 s 19(1), (4)(a)). As to the meaning of 'maintained school' see PARA 103 note 3. As to the meaning of 'England' see PARA 7 note 3.

4   For the purposes of the Education Act 2002 Pt 3 Ch 1 (ss 19–40), 'federation' means a group of schools in England that are federated by virtue of s 24; and 'federated school' means a school forming part of a federation: s 24(2) (amended by the Education (Wales) Measure 2011 s 19(1), (4)(c)).

5   Education Act 2002 s 24(1)(b) (amended by the Education (Wales) Measure 2011 s 19(1), (4)(b)).

6   Education Act 2002 s 24(1)(c).

7   Education Act 2002 s 24(1). The text refers to schools being federated for the purposes of Pt 3 Ch 1 (ss 19–40): see s 24(1).

8   Ie by virtue of the Education Act 2002 s 24.

9   Education Act 2002 s 24(3)(a). As to instruments of government see PARA 184 et seq.

10 Ie other than any enactment contained in the School Standards and Framework Act 1998 Pt 2 Ch 2 (s 30) (establishment, alteration or discontinuance of schools: see PARA 116) or in Pt 3 (ss 84–109) (school admissions: see PARA 225 et seq): see the Education Act 2002 s 24(3)(b).

11 Education Act 2002 s 24(3)(b). As to the regulations made see note 1.

12 As to the regulations made see note 1.

13 Education Act 2002 s 24(4)(a).

14 As to bodies corporate see COMPANIES vol 14 (2009) PARA 2; CORPORATIONS vol 24 (2010) PARA 301 et seq.

15 Education Act 2002 s 24(4)(b).

16 Education Act 2002 s 24(4)(c).

17 Education Act 2002 s 24(4)(d).

18 Education Act 2002 s 24(4)(e).

19 As to the meaning of 'liability' see PARA 108 note 22 (definition applied by the Education Act 2002 s 212(2), (3)).

20 As to the meaning of 'local authority' see PARA 25 (definition applied by the Education Act 2002 s 212(1)).

21 Education Act 2002 s 24(4)(f) (amended by SI 2010/1158). Regulations made by virtue of the Education Act 2002 s 24(4)(f) in relation to the transfer of property, rights and liabilities may: (1) provide for prescribed matters to be determined by the Secretary of State (s 24(5)(a) (amended by the Education (Wales) Measure 2011 s 19(1), (4)(e))); (2) apply with modifications any provision of the Education Reform Act 1988 Sch 10 (supplementary provisions with respect to transfers: see PARA 1332 et seq) (Education Act 2002 s 24(5)(b)); or (3) make provision

equivalent to that made by any provision of the Education Reform Act 1988 Sch 10 (Education Act 2002 s 24(5)(c)). As to the meaning of 'modifications' see PARA 21 note 15 (definition applied by s 212(2), (3)).

22 Education Act 2002 s 24(4)(g) (amended by the Education (Wales) Measure 2011 s 19(1), (4)(d)).

23 Ie regulations made by virtue of the Education Act 2002 s 24.

24 In the Education Act 2002 s 25(3), references to categories of maintained schools are references to the categories set out in the School Standards and Framework Act 1998 s 20(1) (see PARA 106): Education Act 2002 s 25(4).

25 Education Act 2002 s 25(3).

26 As to the regulations made see note 1.

27 Ie any provision contained in the School Standards and Framework Act 1998 ss 49–51, and Sch 15 (see PARA 323 et seq): Education Act 2002 s 25(1)(b).

28 Ie any provision contained in the Education and Inspections Act 2006 Pt 4 (ss 59–73) (schools causing concern: see PARA 1207 et seq): Education Act 2002 s 25(1)(za) (added by the Education and Inspections Act 2006 s 71, Sch 7 Pt 2 para 19(a)).

29 See the Education Act 2002 s 25(1) (amended by the Education (Wales) Measure 2011 s 19(1), (5)). The modifications that may be made by virtue of the Education Act 2002 s 25(1) include, in particular, modifications: (1) enabling powers conferred by the provisions referred to in s 25(1) to be exercised in relation to all the schools in a federation even though the circumstances by reference to which the powers are exercisable exist only in relation to one or more of those schools (s 25(2)(a)); and (2) requiring the apportionment of any costs or expenses incurred by the governing body of a federation (s 25(2)(b)).

30 Education Act 2002 s 24(6)(a).

31 Education Act 2002 s 24(6)(b).

157. Collaboration between schools. Regulations[1] may:

(1) enable the governing bodies[2] of two or more maintained schools in England[3] to arrange for any of their functions[4] to be discharged jointly or by a joint committee of theirs[5];

(2) provide for the appointment by two or more governing bodies of a joint committee of those governing bodies for the purposes of discharging any functions in pursuance of any such arrangements[6]; and

(3) provide that any enactment relating to those functions or the governing bodies by whom they are to be discharged is to have effect subject to all necessary modifications[7] in its application in relation to those functions and the governing bodies by whom they are to be discharged[8].

1 Ie regulations made under the Education Act 2002 by the Secretary of State: see s 212(1). As to the Secretary of State see PARA 58. As to the regulations made under s 26 see the School Governance (Collaboration) (England) Regulations 2003, SI 2003/1962 (amended by SI 2007/957; SI 2013/1624; and SI 2015/883); and the School Staffing (England) Regulations 2009, SI 2009/2680 (amended by SI 2015/883; and SI 2015/887).

2 As to governing bodies of maintained schools see PARA 150 et seq.

3 As to the meaning of 'maintained school' see PARA 103 note 3. As to the meaning of 'England' see PARA 7 note 3.

4 As to the meaning of 'functions' see PARA 18 note 5 (definition applied by the Education Act 2002 s 212(2), (3)).

5 Education Act 2002 s 26(a) (amended by the Education (Wales) Measure 2011 s 9(3)(a)). As to collaboration between maintained schools and further education bodies see PARA 569.

6 Education Act 2002 s 26(b).

7 As to the meaning of 'modifications' see PARA 21 note 15 (definition applied by the Education Act 2002 s 212(2), (3)).

8 Education Act 2002 s 26(c).

158. Governing bodies consisting of interim executive members. In a case where a maintained school is eligible for intervention, the local authority has power, with the consent of the Secretary of State, to require the governing body to be constituted so as to consist of interim executive members[1]. The Secretary of State has similar powers[2].

1 See the Education and Inspections Act 2006 s 65; and PARA 1213.
2 See the Education and Inspections Act 2006 s 69; and PARA 1218.

(B) The Governors and Clerk

159. Election and appointment of parent governors. The appropriate authority[1] must make all the necessary arrangements for the election of parent governors[2]. This power does not include power to impose any requirements as to the minimum number of votes required to be cast for a candidate to be elected[3]. Any election which is contested must be held by ballot[4]. The arrangements made must provide for every person who is entitled to vote to have an opportunity to do so by post[5], and may provide for every person who is entitled to vote to have an opportunity to do so by electronic means[6].

Where a vacancy for a parent governor arises, the appropriate authority must take such steps as are reasonably practicable to secure that every person who is known to them to be a parent[7] of a registered pupil[8] at the school, and where the school is a maintained nursery school, a parent of a child[9] for whom educational or other provision[10] is made on the premises[11] of the school, is (1) informed of the vacancy and that it is required to be filled by election[12]; (2) informed that he is entitled to stand as a candidate and vote in the election[13]; and (3) given the opportunity to do so[14].

The number of parent governors required[15] must be made up by parent governors appointed by the governing body, if one or more vacancies for parent governors arises and either: (a) the number of parents standing for election is less than the number of vacancies[16]; (b) at least 50 per cent of the registered pupils at the school are boarders[17] and the appropriate authority thinks it would not be reasonably practical for there to be an election of parent governors[18]; or (c) in the case of a school which is a community special or foundation special school established in a hospital, it would, in the opinion of the appropriate authority, be impractical for there to be an election of parent governors[19]. The governing body must appoint as a parent governor: (i) a parent of a registered pupil at the school[20]; (ii) a parent of a former registered pupil at the school[21], or (iii) a parent of a child under or of compulsory school age[22]. However, where the school is a community special school or a foundation special school, the governing body must appoint: (A) a parent of a registered pupil at the school[23]; (B) a parent of a former registered pupil at the school[24]; (C) a parent of a child under or of compulsory school age with special educational needs[25] for which the school is approved[26]; or (D) a parent with experience of educating a child with special educational needs[27].

1 'Appropriate authority' means: (1) in relation to a community school, a community special school, a maintained nursery school or a voluntary controlled school, the local authority (School Governance (Constitution) (England) Regulations 2012, SI 2012/1034, reg 6, Sch 1 para 1(a)); and (2) in relation to a voluntary aided school, foundation school or foundation special school, the governing body (Sch 1 para 1(b)). Where a local authority is the appropriate authority in relation to a school, that authority may delegate to the head teacher of the school any of its functions under Sch 1: Sch 1 para 2. The local authority may be the appropriate authority in relation to a school within head (2) above if the governing body and the local authority so agree: Sch 1 para 3. As to the meaning of references to a community, foundation or voluntary school or a community or foundation special school see PARA 106. As to the meaning of 'maintained nursery school' see PARA 103 note 3. As to the meaning of references to 'the local authority' see

PARA 151 note 8. As to the meaning of 'head teacher' see PARA 86 note 4; and as to the meaning of 'functions' see PARA 18 note 5 (definitions applied by the Education Act 2002 s 212(2), (3); Interpretation Act 1978 s 11). As to academies and conversion into academies see PARAS 345, 350 et seq.

2 School Governance (Constitution) (England) Regulations 2012, SI 2012/1034, Sch 1 para 4. As to the meaning of 'parent governor' see PARA 151 note 5. The governing body may only appoint as a parent governor a person who has, in the opinion of the governing body, the skills required to contribute to the effective governance and success of the school: Sch 1 para 12 (added by SI 2014/1257). Generally see the Governors' Handbook which may be found on the Department for Education website.

3 School Governance (Constitution) (England) Regulations 2012, SI 2012/1034, Sch 1 para 5.

4 School Governance (Constitution) (England) Regulations 2012, SI 2012/1034, Sch 1 para 6.

5 School Governance (Constitution) (England) Regulations 2012, SI 2012/1034, Sch 1 para 7(1). For these purposes, 'post' includes delivery by hand: Sch 1 para 7(2). As to the service of documents by post generally see PARA 76 note 5.

6 School Governance (Constitution) (England) Regulations 2012, SI 2012/1034, Sch 1 para 7(3).

7 As to the meaning of 'parent' see PARA 151 note 5.

8 As to the meaning of 'registered pupil' see PARA 437 (definition applied by the Education Act 2002 s 212(2), (3); Interpretation Act 1978 s 11).

9 As to the meaning of 'child' see PARA 7 note 6 (definition applied by the Education Act 2002 s 212(2), (3); Interpretation Act 1978 s 11).

10 Ie including any such provision made by the governing body under the Education Act 2002 s 27: see PARA 174.

11 As to the meaning of 'premises' see PARA 62 note 19 (definition applied by the Education Act 2002 s 212(2), (3); Interpretation Act 1978 s 11).

12 School Governance (Constitution) (England) Regulations 2012, SI 2012/1034, Sch 1 para 8(a).

13 School Governance (Constitution) (England) Regulations 2012, SI 2012/1034, Sch 1 para 8(b).

14 School Governance (Constitution) (England) Regulations 2012, SI 2012/1034, Sch 1 para 8(c).

15 As to the constitution of governing bodies see PARA 151 et seq.

16 School Governance (Constitution) (England) Regulations 2012, SI 2012/1034, Sch 1 para 9(a).

17 As to the meaning of 'boarder' see PARA 31 note 19 (definition applied by the Education Act 2002 s 212(2), (3); Interpretation Act 1978 s 11).

18 School Governance (Constitution) (England) Regulations 2012, SI 2012/1034, Sch 1 para 9(b).

19 School Governance (Constitution) (England) Regulations 2012, SI 2012/1034, Sch 1 para 9(c).

20 School Governance (Constitution) (England) Regulations 2012, SI 2012/1034, Sch 1 para 10(1)(a).

21 School Governance (Constitution) (England) Regulations 2012, SI 2012/1034, Sch 1 para 10(1)(b). The governing body may only appoint a person referred to in head (ii) or (iii) in the text if it is not reasonably practicable to appoint a person referred to in the head which immediately precedes it: see Sch 1 para 10(2).

22 School Governance (Constitution) (England) Regulations 2012, SI 2012/1034, Sch 1 para 10(1)(c). See also note 21. As to the meaning of 'compulsory school age' see PARA 19.

23 School Governance (Constitution) (England) Regulations 2012, SI 2012/1034, Sch 1 para 11(1)(a).

24 School Governance (Constitution) (England) Regulations 2012, SI 2012/1034, Sch 1 para 11(1)(b). The governing body may only appoint a person referred to in head (B), (C) or (D) in the text if it is not reasonably practicable to appoint a person referred to in the head which immediately precedes it: Sch 1 para 11(2).

25 As to the meaning of 'special educational needs' see PARAS 943 (definition applied by the Education Act 2002 s 212(2), (3); Interpretation Act 1978 s 11).

26 School Governance (Constitution) (England) Regulations 2012, SI 2012/1034, Sch 1 para 11(1)(c). See also note 24.

27 School Governance (Constitution) (England) Regulations 2012, SI 2012/1034, Sch 1 para 11(1)(d). See also note 25.

160. Election of staff governors. The appropriate authority[1] must make all the necessary arrangements for the election of staff governors[2]. This power does not include power to impose any requirements as to the minimum number of votes required to be cast for a candidate to be elected[3]. Any election which is contested must be held by ballot[4].

Where the local authority[5] is the appropriate authority in relation to a school, that authority may delegate to the head teacher[6] of the school any of its functions under these provisions[7].

1 'Appropriate authority' has the same meaning as in the School Governance (Constitution) (England) Regulations 2012, SI 2012/1034, Sch 1 (see PARA 159 note 1): reg 7, Sch 2 para 1.
2 School Governance (Constitution) (England) Regulations 2012, SI 2012/1034, Sch 2 para 3. As to the meaning of 'staff governor' see PARA 151 note 8. As to the constitution of governing bodies see PARA 151 et seq.
3 School Governance (Constitution) (England) Regulations 2012, SI 2012/1034, Sch 2 para 4.
4 School Governance (Constitution) (England) Regulations 2012, SI 2012/1034, Sch 2 para 5.
5 As to the meaning of references to 'the local authority' see PARA 151 note 8.
6 As to the meaning of 'head teacher' see PARA 86 note 4 (definition applied by the Education Act 2002 s 212(2), (3); Interpretation Act 1978 s 11).
7 See the School Governance (Constitution) (England) Regulations 2012, SI 2012/1034, Sch 2 para 2.

161. Appointment of partnership governors. Where a partnership governor[1] is required in relation to a school which is designated[2] as having a religious character, the governing body must seek nominations from: (1) in the case of a Church of England school[3] or a Roman Catholic Church school[4], the appropriate diocesan authority[5]; and (2) in any other case, the appropriate religious body[6].

Where a partnership governor is required in relation to a school which does not have a religious character, the governing body must seek nominations from parents[7] of registered pupils[8] at the school, and from such other persons[9] in the community served by the school as it considers appropriate[10].

No person is eligible to be nominated for appointment as a partnership governor unless that person has, in the opinion of the person nominating them, the skills required to contribute to the effective governance and success of the school[11]. No person is eligible to be appointed as a partnership governor unless that person has, in the opinion of the governing body, the skills required to contribute to the effective governance and success of the school[12]. No governor may nominate a person for appointment as a partnership governor[13]. The governing body must appoint such number of partnership governors as is required by the instrument of government[14] from among eligible nominees[15]. If the number of eligible nominees is less than the number of vacancies, the number of partnership governors required may be made up by persons selected by the governing body[16].

The governing body must make all necessary arrangements for and determine all other matters relating to the nomination and appointment of partnership governors[17].

1 As to the meaning of 'partnership governor' see PARA 152 note 4.
2 Ie under the School Standards and Framework Act 1998 s 69(3): see PARA 914.
3 As to the meaning of 'Church of England school' see PARA 146 note 12.
4 As to the meaning of 'Roman Catholic Church school' see PARA 146 note 12.
5 School Governance (Constitution) (England) Regulations 2012, SI 2012/1034, reg 17, Sch 3 para 1(a). As to the meaning of 'appropriate diocesan authority' see PARA 146 note 12; definition applied by reg 26, Sch 3 para 8.
6 School Governance (Constitution) (England) Regulations 2012, SI 2012/1034, Sch 3 para 1(b). 'Appropriate religious body', in relation to a school designated under the School Standards and Framework Act 1998 s 69(3) (see PARA 914) as having a religious character that is not a Church of England school or a Roman Catholic Church school, means the body or person, if any, that represents the specified religion or religious denomination that is prescribed under s 88F(3)(e) (see PARA 237): School Governance (Constitution) (England) Regulations 2012, SI 2012/1034, reg 26, Sch 3 para 8. As to the Secretary of State see PARA 58.

7   As to the meaning of 'parent' see PARA 151 note 5.
8   As to the meaning of 'registered pupil' see PARA 437 (definition applied by the Education Act 2002 s 212(2), (3); Interpretation Act 1978 s 11).
9   As to the meaning of 'person' see PARA 7 note 6.
10 School Governance (Constitution) (England) Regulations 2012, SI 2012/1034, Sch 3 para 2.
11 School Governance (Constitution) (England) Regulations 2012, SI 2012/1034, Sch 3 para 4(1) (Sch 3 para 4 substituted by SI 2014/1257).
12 School Governance (Constitution) (England) Regulations 2012, SI 2012/1034, Sch 3 para 4(2) (as substituted: see note 13).
13 School Governance (Constitution) (England) Regulations 2012, SI 2012/1034, Sch 3 para 5. This is expressed to be subject to Sch 3 para 6(2): see the text to note 18.
14 As to instruments of government see PARA 184 et seq.
15 School Governance (Constitution) (England) Regulations 2012, SI 2012/1034, Sch 3 para 6(1).
16 School Governance (Constitution) (England) Regulations 2012, SI 2012/1034, Sch 3 para 6(2). Where the governing body makes an appointment under Sch 3 para 6(2), having rejected any person nominated under Sch 3 paras 1 or 2 (see the text to notes 1–12), it must give written reasons for its decision to (1) the local authority (Sch 3 para 7(a)); (2) the person or body who nominated the person rejected (Sch 3 para 7(b)); and (3) the person rejected (Sch 3 para 7(c)). As to the meaning of 'written' see PARA 76 note 8. As to the meaning of references to 'the local authority' see PARA 151 note 8.
17 School Governance (Constitution) (England) Regulations 2012, SI 2012/1034, Sch 3 para 3.

162.   Qualifications and disqualifications.   A person is disqualified from holding or from continuing to hold office as a governor[1] of a school at any time when the person is a registered pupil[2] at the school[3]. A person is disqualified from being elected or appointed as a governor unless the person is aged 18[4] or over[5]. Save as otherwise provided in the School Governance (Constitution) (England) Regulations 2012[6], the fact that a person is qualified to be elected or appointed as a governor of a particular category at a school does not disqualify him from election or appointment or from continuing as a governor of any other category at that school[7].

Any person who is disqualified from holding office as a governor of a school[8] is likewise disqualified from holding or continuing to hold office as an associate member[9] of the governing body unless the disqualification is in accordance with the above provisions[10].

A person is disqualified from election or appointment as a parent governor[11] of a school if the person is an elected member of the local authority[12]; or is paid to work at the school for more than 500 hours in any 12 consecutive months[13].

A person is disqualified from appointment as a local authority governor[14] if the person is eligible to be a staff governor[15] of the school[16].

A person is disqualified from nomination or appointment as a partnership governor[17] of a school if the person is a parent of a registered pupil at the school[18]; eligible to be a staff governor of the school[19]; an elected member of the local authority[20]; or employed by the local authority in connection with its education functions[21].

Upon ceasing to work at the school, a staff governor of a school is disqualified from continuing to hold office as such a governor[22].

A governor[23] who, without the consent of the governing body, has failed to attend its meetings for a continuous period of six months[24] beginning with the date of the first such meeting the governor fails to attend, is, on the expiry of that period, disqualified from continuing to hold office as a governor of that school[25]. A foundation governor[26], authority governor, co-opted governor[27] or partnership governor who has been disqualified as a governor of a school[28] is not qualified for election, nomination or appointment as a governor of any category at that school for 12 months starting on the date on which they are so disqualified[29].

A person is disqualified from holding or continuing to hold office as a governor of a school:

(1)　if the person's estate has been sequestrated and the sequestration has not been discharged, annulled or reduced[30]; or the person is the subject of a bankruptcy restrictions order, an interim bankruptcy restrictions order, a debt relief restrictions order or an interim debt relief restrictions order[31];

(2)　at any time when the person is subject to a directors disqualification order[32] or a disqualification undertaking[33], or an order[34] relating to a failure to pay under a county court administration order[35];

(3)　if he has been removed from the office of trustee for a charity by an order made by the Charity Commission or Commissioners or the High Court on the grounds of any misconduct or mismanagement in the administration of the charity for which he was responsible or to which he was privy, or to which he contributed or which he facilitated by his conduct[36]; or, in Scotland he has been removed[37] from being concerned in the management or control of any body[38];

(4)　at any time when he is (a) included in the list[39] of those considered by the Secretary of State[40] as unsuitable to work with children[41]; (b) subject to a direction of the Secretary of State under the Education Act 2002[42] (or any other disqualification, prohibition or restriction which takes effect as if contained in such a direction)[43]; (c) subject to a direction of the Secretary of State under the Education and Skills Act 2008[44]; (d) barred[45] from regulated activity relating to children[46]; (e) disqualified[47] from working with children[48]; (f) disqualified from registration[49] for child minding or providing day care[50]; or (g) disqualified from registration[51] for childcare[52];

(5)　if (a) within the period of five years ending with the date immediately preceding the date on which his appointment or election as governor would otherwise have taken effect or, as the case may be, on which he would otherwise have become a governor by virtue of an office, or (b) since his appointment or election as governor or, as the case may be, since he became a governor by virtue of an office, he has been convicted, whether in the United Kingdom[53] or elsewhere[54], of any offence and a sentence of imprisonment (whether suspended or not) has been imposed on him for a period of not less than three months without the option of a fine[55];

(6)　if within the period of 20 years ending with the date immediately preceding the date on which his appointment or election as governor would otherwise have taken effect or, as the case may be, on which he would otherwise have become a governor by virtue of an office, he has been convicted of any offence and a sentence of imprisonment has been imposed on him for a period of not less than two and a half years[56];

(7)　if he has at any time been convicted as aforesaid of any offence and a sentence of imprisonment has been imposed on the person for a period of not less than five years[57];

(8)　if (a) within the period of five years ending with the date immediately preceding the date on which his appointment or election as governor would otherwise have taken effect or, as the case may be, on which he would otherwise have become a governor by virtue of an office[58], or (b) since his appointment or election as governor or, as the case may be, since he became a governor by virtue of an office, he has been convicted[59] of an offence and has been sentenced to a fine[60];

(9)   at any time when the person refuses a request by the clerk to the governing body[61] to make an application[62] for a criminal records certificate[63].

Where a person is, or is proposed to become, a governor and is disqualified[64] from holding, or from continuing to hold, office as a governor, he must give notice of that fact to the clerk to the governing body[65].

1   As to the constitution of governing bodies see PARA 151 et seq. As to the meaning of references to 'governor' see PARA 151 note 4.
2   As to the meaning of 'registered pupil' see PARA 437 (definition applied by the Education Act 2002 s 212(2), (3); Interpretation Act 1978 s 11).
3   School Governance (Constitution) (England) Regulations 2012, SI 2012/1034, reg 17, Sch 4 para 1.
4   As to the time at which a person attains a particular age see PARA 7 note 6.
5   School Governance (Constitution) (England) Regulations 2012, SI 2012/1034, Sch 4 para 2.
6   Ie the School Governance (Constitution) (England) Regulations 2012, SI 2012/1034.
7   School Governance (Constitution) (England) Regulations 2012, SI 2012/1034, Sch 4 para 3.
8   Ie under the School Governance (Constitution) (England) Regulations 2012, SI 2012/1034, Sch 4.
9   'Associate member' means a person who is appointed by the governing body as a member of any committee established by it but who is not a governor: School Governance (Constitution) (England) Regulations 2012, SI 2012/1034, reg 12.
10   School Governance (Constitution) (England) Regulations 2012, SI 2012/1034, Sch 4 para 4. The reference in the text is to Sch 4 paras 1, 2: see the text to notes 1–5.
11   As to the meaning of 'parent governor' see PARA 151 note 5. See note 13.
12   School Governance (Constitution) (England) Regulations 2012, SI 2012/1034, Sch 4 para 5(1)(a). As to the meaning of references to 'local authority' see PARA 151 note 8. See note 13.
13   School Governance (Constitution) (England) Regulations 2012, SI 2012/1034, Sch 4 para 5(1)(b). A person is not disqualified from continuing to hold office as a parent governor because he ceases to be a parent of a registered pupil at the school or to fulfil any of the requirements set out in Sch 1 paras 10, 11 (as the case may be) (see PARA 159): Sch 4 para 5(2).
14   As to the meaning of 'local authority governor' see PARA 151 note 9.
15   As to the meaning of 'staff governor' see PARA 151 note 8.
16   School Governance (Constitution) (England) Regulations 2012, SI 2012/1034, Sch 4 para 6.
17   As to the meaning of 'partnership governor' see PARA 152 note 4.
18   School Governance (Constitution) (England) Regulations 2012, SI 2012/1034, Sch 4 para 7(1)(a).
19   School Governance (Constitution) (England) Regulations 2012, SI 2012/1034, Sch 4 para 7(1)(b).
20   School Governance (Constitution) (England) Regulations 2012, SI 2012/1034, Sch 4 para 7(1)(c).
21   School Governance (Constitution) (England) Regulations 2012, SI 2012/1034, Sch 4 para 7(1)(d). The disqualification criterion in Sch 4 para 7(1)(d) does not apply in the case of a person who is employed by a local authority in England under a contract of employment providing for the person to work wholly at a school or schools maintained by the local authority: Sch 4 para 7(2). As to the meaning of 'England' see PARA 7 note 3.
22   School Governance (Constitution) (England) Regulations 2012, SI 2012/1034, Sch 4 para 8.
23   School Governance (Constitution) (England) Regulations 2012, SI 2012/1034, Sch 4 para 9 applies to every governor, other than governors who are governors by virtue of the office that they hold: Sch 4 para 9(1).
24   As to the meaning of 'month' see PARA 54 note 26.
25   School Governance (Constitution) (England) Regulations 2012, SI 2012/1034, Sch 4 para 9(2).
26   As to the meaning of 'foundation governor' see PARA 152 note 6.
27   'Co-opted governor' means a person who is appointed as a governor by the governing body and who, in the opinion of the governing body, has the skills required to contribute to the effective governance and success of the school: School Governance (Constitution) (England) Regulations 2012, SI 2012/1034, reg 11.

28 Ie under the School Governance (Constitution) (England) Regulations 2012, SI 2012/1034, Sch 4 para 9(2).

29 School Governance (Constitution) (England) Regulations 2012, SI 2012/1034, Sch 4 para 9(3).

30 School Governance (Constitution) (England) Regulations 2012, SI 2012/1034, Sch 4 para 10(a). As to sequestration see CIVIL PROCEDURE vol 12 (2009) PARAS 1249, 1269, 1380–1385.

31 School Governance (Constitution) (England) Regulations 2012, SI 2012/1034, Sch 4 para 10(b). As to interim orders see BANKRUPTCY AND INDIVIDUAL INSOLVENCY vol 5 (2013) PARA 45 et seq.

32 Ie a disqualification order under the Company Directors Disqualification Act 1986 (see COMPANIES vol 15 (2009) PARA 1578) or the Companies (Northern Ireland) Order 1989, SI 1989/2404 (NI 18), Pt 2: see the School Governance (Constitution) (England) Regulations 2012, SI 2012/1034, Sch 4 para 11(a), (b).

33 Ie under the Company Directors Disqualification Act 1986 (see COMPANIES vol 15 (2009) PARA 1579) or the Company Directors Disqualification (Northern Ireland) Order 2002, SI 2002/3150 (NI 4): see the School Governance (Constitution) (England) Regulations 2012, SI 2012/1034, Sch 4 para 11(a), (c).

34 Ie an order made under the Insolvency Act 1986 s 429(2)(b): see BANKRUPTCY AND INDIVIDUAL INSOLVENCY vol 5 (2013) PARA 914.

35 School Governance (Constitution) (England) Regulations 2012, SI 2012/1034, Sch 4 para 11(d).

36 School Governance (Constitution) (England) Regulations 2012, SI 2012/10347, Sch 4 para 12(a). As to such orders see CHARITIES vol 8 (2015) PARA 294 et seq. As to the Charity Commission see CHARITIES vol 8 (2015) PARA 543 et seq.

37 Ie under the Charities and Trustee Investment (Scotland) Act 2005 s 34.

38 School Governance (Constitution) (England) Regulations 2012, SI 2012/1034, Sch 4 para 12(b).

39 Ie the list kept under the Protection of Children Act 1999 s 1 (repealed).

40 As to the Secretary of State see PARA 58.

41 School Governance (Constitution) (England) Regulations 2012, SI 2012/1034, Sch 4 para 13(a).

42 Ie under the Education Act 2002 s 142: see PARA 420.

43 School Governance (Constitution) (England) Regulations 2012, SI 2012/1034, Sch 4 para 13(b).

44 School Governance (Constitution) (England) Regulations 2012, SI 2012/1034, Sch 4 para 13(ba) (added by SI 2014/1257). The reference is to the Educations and Skills Act 2008 s 128: see PARA 409.

45 Ie in accordance with the Safeguarding Vulnerable Groups Act 2006 s 3(2): see CHILDREN AND YOUNG PERSONS vol 9 (2012) PARA 682.

46 School Governance (Constitution) (England) Regulations 2012, SI 2012/1034, Sch 4 para 13(c).

47 Ie under the Criminal Justice and Court Services Act 2000 s 28, 29 or 29A: see SENTENCING AND DISPOSITION OF OFFENDERS vol 92 (2010) PARA 316.

48 School Governance (Constitution) (England) Regulations 2012, SI 2012/1034, Sch 4 para 13(d).

49 Ie under the Children and Families (Wales) Measure 2010 Pt 2 (ss 19–56): see SENTENCING AND DISPOSITION OF OFFENDERS.

50 School Governance (Constitution) (England) Regulations 2012, SI 2012/1034, Sch 4 para 13(e).

51 Ie under the Childcare Act 2006 Pt 3 (ss 32–98): see CHILDREN AND YOUNG PERSONS vol 10 (2012) PARA 1090 et seq.

52 School Governance (Constitution) (England) Regulations 2012, SI 2012/1034, Sch 4 para 13(f).

53 As to the meaning of 'United Kingdom' see PARA 73 note 3.

54 School Governance (Constitution) (England) Regulations 2012, SI 2012/1034, Sch 4 para 14(1), (2). This provision is expressed to be subject to Sch 4 para 14(6).

55 For the purposes of the School Governance (Constitution) (England) Regulations 2012, SI 2012/1034, Sch 4 para 14(2)–(4), any conviction by or before a court outside the United Kingdom of an offence which, if the facts giving rise to the offence had taken place in any part of the United Kingdom, would not have constituted an offence under the law in force in that part of the United Kingdom must be disregarded: Sch 4 para 14(5).

56 School Governance (Constitution) (England) Regulations 2012, SI 2012/1034, Sch 4 para 14(1), (3). See note 55.

57 School Governance (Constitution) (England) Regulations 2012, SI 2012/1034, Sch 4 para 14(1), (4). See note 55.

58 School Governance (Constitution) (England) Regulations 2012, SI 2012/1034, Sch 4 para 14(1), (6)(a).

59 Ie under the Education Act 1996 s 547 (nuisance or disturbance on school premises) (see PARA 1351) or under the Further and Higher Education Act 1992 s 85A (nuisance or disturbance on educational premises) (see PARA 1352).

60 School Governance (Constitution) (England) Regulations 2012, SI 2012/1034, Sch 4 para 14(1), (6)(b).

61 As to the clerk to the governing body see PARA 167.
62 Ie under the Police Act 1997 s 113B: see SENTENCING AND DISPOSITION OF OFFENDERS vol 92 (2010) PARA 713.
63 School Governance (Constitution) (England) Regulations 2012, SI 2012/1043, Sch 4 para 15.
64 Ie by virtue of the School Governance (Constitution) (England) Regulations 2012, SI 2012/1043, Sch 4 paras 10–14: see heads (1)–(8) in the text.
65 School Governance (Constitution) (England) Regulations 2012, SI 2012/1043, Sch 4 para 16.

163. Tenure of office. A governor[1] is to hold office for a fixed period of four years from the date of his election or appointment[2]. However: (1) this does not apply to any staff governor[3] who is the head teacher[4] of the school, or to any ex officio foundation governor[5], who may hold office for as long as he holds the position from which his governorship derives[6]; (2) nor does it apply to any additional governor, additional foundation governor or interim executive member appointed under the Education and Inspections Act 2006[7] whose term of office will be determined by the person[8] who appointed him, up to a maximum of four years[9]; and (3) the instrument of government[10] may, in relation to a particular category of governor, specify a term of office not being a period of less than one year or more than four years or set out that the term of office for any governor within that category may be determined by those appointing the governor, not being a period of less than one year or more than four years[11].

A substitute governor[12] holds office until the earlier of the following: (a) the expiry of four years from the date when his appointment takes effect[13]; (b) the date when the original governor[14] (not having been removed from office)[15] gives written[16] notice to the clerk to the governing body[17] to the effect that he is able and willing to act as a foundation governor[18]; or (c) the date when a person other than the original governor takes office in the post by virtue of which the ex officio foundation governorship exists[19].

The above provisions do not prevent a governor from: (i) being elected or appointed for a further term, save as otherwise[20] provided[21]; (ii) resigning[22] his office[23]; (iii) being removed[24] from office[25]; or (iv) being disqualified[26] from holding or continuing to hold office[27].

An associate member[28] may hold office for a period of four years, or such shorter period (not being less than one year) as may be determined by the governing body at the date of the appointment[29]. These provisions do not prevent an associate member from being reappointed at the expiry of the associate member's term of office[30].

1 As to the meaning of references to 'governor' see PARA 151 note 4.
2 School Governance (Constitution) (England) Regulations 2012, SI 2012/1034, reg 18(1) (amended by SI 2015/883). This provision is expressed to be subject to the School Governance (Constitution) (England) Regulations 2012, SI 2012/1034, reg 18(1A)–(5): see the text to notes 3–19. As to the election and appointment of governors see PARA 159 et seq. As to the constitution of governing bodies see PARA 151 et seq.
3 As to the meaning of 'staff governor' see PARA 151 note 8.
4 As to the meaning of 'head teacher' see PARA 86 note 4 (definition applied by the Education Act 2002 s 212(2), (3); Interpretation Act 1978 s 11).
5 As to the meaning of 'ex officio foundation governor' see PARA 152 note 6.
6 School Governance (Constitution) (England) Regulations 2012, SI 2012/1034, reg 18(2). However note that a governor who is elected or appointed on or after 1 September 2015 may hold office for a period of less than four years, where the instrument of government so allows: see reg 18(1A) (added by SI 2015/883).
7 Ie under the Education and Inspections Act 2006 Pt 4 (ss 59–73). As to the appointment of additional governors and additional foundation governors see ss 64, 67 (PARAS 1212, 1216) and interim executive members see ss 65, 69 (PARAS 1213, 1218).

8   As to the meaning of 'person' see PARA 7 note 6.
9   School Governance (Constitution) (England) Regulations 2012, SI 2012/1034, reg 18(3).
10 As to instruments of government see PARA 184 et seq.
11 School Governance (Constitution) (England) Regulations 2012, SI 2012/1034, reg 18(4) (substituted by SI 2015/883).
12 As to the meaning of 'substitute governor' see PARA 152 note 6.
13 School Governance (Constitution) (England) Regulations 2012, SI 2012/1034, reg 18(5)(a).
14 'The original governor' means the ex officio foundation governor in whose place the substitute governor is appointed to act: School Governance (Constitution) (England) Regulations 2012, SI 2012/1034, reg 18(9).
15 Ie under the School Governance (Constitution) (England) Regulations 2012, SI 2012/1034, reg 21): see PARA 164.
16 As to the meaning of 'written' see PARA 76 note 8.
17 As to the clerk to the governing body see PARA 167.
18 School Governance (Constitution) (England) Regulations 2012, SI 2012/1034, reg 18(5)(b). As to the meaning of 'foundation governor' see PARA 152 note 6.
19 School Governance (Constitution) (England) Regulations 2012, SI 2012/1034, reg 18(5)(c).
20 Ie in the School Governance (Constitution) (England) Regulations 2012, SI 2012/1034.
21 School Governance (Constitution) (England) Regulations 2012, SI 2012/1034, reg 18(6)(a).
22 Ie in accordance with the School Governance (Constitution) (England) Regulations 2012, SI 2012/1034, reg 19(1): see reg 18(6)(b). A governor may at any time resign his office by giving written notice to the clerk to the governing body: reg 19(1). The head teacher's resignation may be withdrawn at any time by the head teacher giving written notice to the clerk to the governing body: reg 19(2).
23 School Governance (Constitution) (England) Regulations 2012, SI 2012/1034, reg 18(6)(b).
24 Ie under the School Governance (Constitution) (England) Regulations 2012, SI 2012/1034, regs 20–25: see PARA 164.
25 School Governance (Constitution) (England) Regulations 2012, SI 2012/1034, reg 18(6)(c).
26 Ie by virtue of any provision of the School Governance (Constitution) (England) Regulations 2012, SI 2012/1034. As to qualifications and disqualifications see PARA 162.
27 School Governance (Constitution) (England) Regulations 2012, SI 2012/1034, reg 18(6)(d).
28 As to the meaning of 'associate member' see PARA 162 note 9.
29 School Governance (Constitution) (England) Regulations 2012, SI 2012/1034, reg 18(7).
30 School Governance (Constitution) (England) Regulations 2012, SI 2012/1034, reg 18(8).

164.   Removal of governors.   Any foundation governor[1] other than an ex officio foundation governor[2] may be removed from office[3] by the person[4] who appointed[5] the foundation governor[6]. Such person must give written[7] notice of the removal from office to the clerk to the governing body[8] and to the foundation governor who is being removed[9].

The governing body may, in accordance with the appropriate procedure[10], remove any ex officio foundation governor at the request of the person named in the instrument of government[11] as the person entitled to make such a request[12]. A person requesting the removal of an ex officio foundation governor must give written reasons for the request to the clerk to the governing body and the governor in question[13].

Any local authority governor[14] may be removed from office by the local authority[15] who nominated[16] the local authority governor[17]. The local authority must give written notice of the removal from office to the clerk to the governing body and to the local authority governor who is being removed[18].

Any co-opted governor or partnership governor may be removed from office by the governing body in accordance with the appropriate procedure[19]. A partnership governor may also be removed from office by the governing body at the request of the nominating body[20]. A nominating body requesting the removal of a partnership governor must give written reasons for the request to the clerk to the governing body and the governor in question[21].

Any parent governor appointed by the governing body[22] may be removed by the governing body in accordance with the appropriate procedure[23].

1   As to the meaning of 'foundation governor' see PARA 152 note 6.
2   As to the meaning of 'ex officio foundation governor' see PARA 152 note 6.
3   As to tenure of office see PARA 163.
4   As to the meaning of 'person' see PARA 7 note 6.
5   As to the election and appointment of governors see PARA 159 et seq. As to the constitution of governing bodies see PARA 151 et seq.
6   School Governance (Constitution) (England) Regulations 2012, SI 2012/1034, reg 20(1).
7   As to the meaning of 'written' see PARA 76 note 8.
8   As to the clerk to the governing body see PARA 167.
9   School Governance (Constitution) (England) Regulations 2012, SI 2012/1034, reg 20(2).
10   Ie the procedure set out in the School Governance (Constitution) (England) Regulations 2012, SI 2012/1034, reg 25: see reg 21(1). Regulation 25 applies in relation to the removal of a governor from office in accordance with reg 21(1), reg 23 (see the text to notes 19–21) or reg 24 (see the text to notes 22–23): reg 25(1). A resolution to remove a governor from office which is passed at a meeting of the governing body will not have effect unless:
    (1)   in relation to the removal of a governor under reg 21(1) (see also the text to notes 11, 12) and reg 23(2) (see the text to note 20), the governing body has considered the reasons for removal and the governor whom it is proposed to remove has been given an opportunity to make a statement in response (reg 25(2)(a));
    (2)   in relation to the removal of a governor ('P') who is a co-opted governor or partnership governor under reg 23(1) or a parent governor under reg 24, the governor proposing P's removal has at that meeting given reasons for doing so and P has been given an opportunity to make a statement in response (reg 25(2)(b);
    (3)   it is confirmed by a resolution passed at a second meeting of the governing body held not less than 14 days after the first meeting (reg 25(2)(c)); and
    (4)   the matter of the governor's removal from office is specified as an item on the agenda for each of those meetings (reg 25(2)(d)).
    As to the meaning of 'co-opted governor' see PARA 162 note 27. As to the meaning of 'partnership governor' see PARA 152 note 4. As to the meaning of 'parent governor' see PARA 151 note 5.
11   As to instruments of government see PARA 184 et seq.
12   School Governance (Constitution) (England) Regulations 2012, SI 2012/1034, reg 21(1).
13   School Governance (Constitution) (England) Regulations 2012, SI 2012/1034, reg 21(2).
14   As to the meaning of 'local authority governor' see PARA 151 note 9.
15   As to the meaning of 'local authority' see PARA 151 note 8.
16   Ie under the School Governance (Constitution) (England) Regulations 2012, SI 2012/1034, reg 8(a): see PARA 151 note 9.
17   School Governance (Constitution) (England) Regulations 2012, SI 2012/1034, reg 22(1).
18   School Governance (Constitution) (England) Regulations 2012, SI 2012/1034, reg 22(2).
19   School Governance (Constitution) (England) Regulations 2012, SI 2012/1034, reg 23(1). The appropriate procedure is that set out in reg 25(2)(b): see note 10.
20   School Governance (Constitution) (England) Regulations 2012, SI 2012/1034, reg 23(2). This is in accordance with reg 25(2)(a): see note 10. 'Nominating body' means any person who nominated the governor in question: reg 5(1).
21   School Governance (Constitution) (England) Regulations 2012, SI 2012/1034, reg 23(3).
22   Ie appointed under the School Governance (Constitution) (England) Regulations 2012, SI 2012/1034, Sch 1 paras 9–11: see PARA 159.
23   School Governance (Constitution) (England) Regulations 2012, SI 2012/1034, reg 24. The appropriate procedure is that set out in reg 25: see note 10.

165.   Governors' allowances. The governing body of a maintained school[1] which has a delegated budget[2] may determine to pay to a member of that governing body or any associate member[3] payments by way of allowance[4] in respect of expenditure necessarily incurred for the purpose of enabling the governor[5] or associate member to perform any duty being either travel payments for private vehicles[6] or payments at a rate determined by the governing body and made on provision of a receipt[7] for the relevant amount[8].

Where a maintained school does not have a delegated budget, the local authority[9] may pay to a governor of the school[10] or to an associate member of the governing body[11], payments by way of allowance in respect of expenditure necessarily incurred by that person for the purposes of enabling him to perform any duty, being either travel payments for private vehicles[12] or payments at a rate determined by the authority and made on provision of a receipt for the relevant amount[13].

Payments for travel expenses incurred through the use of private cars, pedal cycles and motorcycles must be at a rate not exceeding Her Majesty's Revenue and Customs' authorised mileage rate, as published from time to time[14].

1   'Governing body' includes a temporary governing body constituted under the Education Act 2002 s 34 (see PARA 155): School Governance (Roles, Procedures and Allowances) (England) Regulations 2013, SI 2013/1624, reg 27(a). As to the meaning of 'maintained school' see PARA 103 note 3. As to governing bodies of maintained schools see PARA 150 et seq.
2   As to delegated budgets see PARA 323 et seq.
3   As to the meaning of 'associate member' see PARA 162 note 9 (definition applied by the School Governance (Roles, Procedures and Allowances) (England) Regulations 2013, SI 2013/1624, reg 2). As to the different categories of governor see PARA 151 et seq.
4   School Governance (Roles, Procedures and Allowances) (England) Regulations 2013, SI 2013/1624, reg 28(1).
5   'Governor' includes a member of a temporary governing body: School Governance (Roles, Procedures and Allowances) (England) Regulations 2013, SI 2013/1624, reg 27(b). As to temporary governing bodies see PARA 155.
6   Ie under the School Governance (Roles, Procedures and Allowances) (England) Regulations 2013, SI 2013/1624, reg 30: see the text to note 14.
7   A reference to 'receipt' includes other evidence establishing the amount of the expenditure: School Governance (Roles, Procedures and Allowances) (England) Regulations 2013, SI 2013/1624, reg 2.
8   School Governance (Roles, Procedures and Allowances) (England) Regulations 2013, SI 2013/1624, reg 28(2).
9   As to the meaning of 'local authority' see PARA 25.
10 Ie in accordance with the provisions of a scheme made by it for the purposes of the Education Act 1996 s 519 (travelling and subsistence allowances for governors of schools and further or higher education institutions): see PARA 52.
11 School Governance (Roles, Procedures and Allowances) (England) Regulations 2013, SI 2013/1624, reg 29(1).
12 Ie under the School Governance (Roles, Procedures and Allowances) (England) Regulations 2013, SI 2013/1624, reg 30: see the text to note 14.
13 School Governance (Roles, Procedures and Allowances) (England) Regulations 2013, SI 2013/1624, reg 29(2).
14 School Governance (Roles, Procedures and Allowances) (England) Regulations 2013, SI 2013/1624, reg 30.

166.   Training and support of governors.   The local authority in England[1] must[2]:

(1)   to the extent that it is not otherwise required to secure the provision of such information, secure that every governor[3] is provided, free of charge, with such information as it considers appropriate in connection with the discharge of his functions[4] as governor[5]; and

(2)   secure that there is made available to every governor, free of charge, such training as it considers necessary for the effective discharge of those functions[6].

1   As to the meaning of 'England' see PARA 7 note 3.
2   Education Act 2002 s 22 (amended by SI 2010/1158; and the Education (Wales) Measure 2011 s 22(8)). As to the meaning of 'local authority' see PARA 25 (definition applied by the Education Act 2002 s 212(1)). As to academies and conversion into academies see PARAS 345, 350 et seq.
3   As to the appointment of governors see PARA 150 et seq.

4   As to the meaning of 'functions' see PARA 18 note 5 (definition applied by the Education Act 2002 s 212(2), (3)). As to the general powers and duties of governing bodies see PARA 168 et seq.

5   Education Act 2002 s 22(a).

6   Education Act 2002 s 22(b).

167.   Appointment etc of clerk. Regulations[1] may make provision:

(1)   requiring the appointment of a clerk to the governing body of a maintained school[2] and authorising or requiring the appointment of clerks to committees of the governing body[3];

(2)   prescribing[4] the body by whom any such appointment is to be made and any restrictions or other requirements relating to any such appointment[5];

(3)   as to the dismissal of any such clerk and the procedure to be followed in connection with his dismissal[6];

(4)   authorising the governing body or a committee of the governing body, where the clerk fails to attend a meeting, to appoint one of its members to act as clerk for the purposes of the meeting[7].

1   Ie regulations made under the Education Act 2002 by the Secretary of State: see s 212(1). As to the Secretary of State see PARA 58. As to the regulations made see the School Governance (Collaboration) (England) Regulations 2003, SI 2003/1962 (amended by SI 2007/957; SI 2013/1624; and SI 2015/883); and the School Governance (Roles, Procedures and Allowances) (England) Regulations 2013, SI 2013/1624 (amended by SI 2013/2688; SI 2014/1257; and SI 2014/1959).

2   As to the meaning of 'maintained school' see PARA 103 note 3. As to governing bodies of maintained schools see PARA 150 et seq.

3   Education Act 2002 s 23(a). As to the establishment by governing bodies of committees see PARA 181. As to meetings and proceedings see PARA 181.

4   'Prescribed' means prescribed by the regulations: see the Education Act 2002 s 212(1).

5   Education Act 2002 s 23(b).

6   Education Act 2002 s 23(c).

7   Education Act 2002 s 23(d).

(C) General Powers and Duties of Governing Bodies

168.   General responsibility of governing body for conduct of school. The conduct of a maintained school[1] is under the direction of the school's governing body[2]. The governing body must conduct the school with a view to promoting high standards of educational achievement at the school[3].

Regulations[4] may: (1) set out terms of reference for governing bodies of maintained schools[5]; (2) define the respective roles and responsibilities of the local authority[6], the governing body and the head teacher[7] of such schools, whether generally or with respect to particular matters, in relation to the conduct of such schools[8]; and (3) confer functions[9] on governing bodies and head teachers of such schools[10].

The governing body of a maintained school must, in discharging its functions, comply with the instrument of government[11] and any trust deed[12] relating to the school[13]. The governing body of a maintained school must, in discharging its functions relating to the conduct of the school: (a) promote the well-being[14] of pupils at the school[15]; (b) promote community cohesion[16]; (c) have regard to any relevant children and young people's plan[17]; and (d) have regard to any views expressed by parents[18] of registered pupils[19].

The governing body of a maintained school must designate a member of the staff at the school as having responsibility for promoting the educational achievement of registered pupils at the school who are being looked after by a local authority[20].

1 As to the meaning of 'maintained school' see PARA 103 note 3. As to academies see PARA 345 et seq.
2 Education Act 2002 s 21(1). This provision is expressed to be subject to any other statutory provision: see s 21(1). In Pt 3 Ch 1 (ss 19–40), 'statutory provision' means a provision contained in an Act or in subordinate legislation within the meaning of the Interpretation Act 1978 (see PARA 26 note 3): Education Act 2002 s 39(1). As to governing bodies of maintained schools see PARA 150 et seq. As to the application of s 21, with modifications, to pupil referral units see the Education (Pupil Referral Units) (Application of Enactments) (England) Regulations 2007, SI 2007/2979, regs 1(3), 3, Sch 1 Pt 1 para 12. As to pupil referral units see PARA 427 et seq.
3 Education Act 2002 s 21(2).
4 Ie regulations made under the Education Act 2002 by the Secretary of State: see s 212(1). As to the Secretary of State see PARA 58. As to the regulations made see the Education (School Teachers' Appraisal) (England) Regulations 2012, SI 2012/115 (amended by SI 2012/431; and SI 2012/2055); and the School Governance (Roles, Procedures and Allowances) (England) Regulations 2013, SI 2013/1624 (amended by SI 2013/2688; SI 2014/1257; and SI 2014/1959).
5 Education Act 2002 s 21(3)(a).
6 As to the meaning of 'local authority' see PARA 25 (definition applied by the Education Act 2002 s 212(1)).
7 As to the meaning of 'head teacher' see PARA 86 note 4 (definition applied by the Education Act 2002 s 212(2), (3)).
8 Education Act 2002 s 21(3)(b) (amended by SI 2010/1158).
9 As to the meaning of 'functions' see PARA 18 note 5 (definition applied by the Education Act 2002 s 212(2), (3)).
10 Education Act 2002 s 21(3)(c).
11 Education Act 2002 s 21(4)(a). As to instruments of government see PARA 184 et seq.
12 As to the meaning of 'trust deed' see PARA 108 note 6 (definition applied by the Education Act 2002 s 212(2), (3)).
13 Education Act 2002 s 21(4)(b). This provision is expressed to be subject to any other statutory provision: see s 21(4)(b).
14 'Well-being', in relation to a pupils at a school in England, means their well-being so far as relating to the matters mentioned in the Children Act 2004 s 10(2) (see CHILDREN AND YOUNG PERSONS vol 9 (2012) PARA 203): Education Act 2002 s 21(8)(a) (s 21(5)–(9) added by the Education and Inspections Act 2006 s 38(1)). As to the meaning of 'pupil' see PARA 20 note 4. (definition applied by the Education Act 2002 s 212(2), (3)). As to the meaning of 'England' see PARA 7 note 3.
15 Education Act 2002 s 21(5)(a) (as added: see note 14).
16 See the Education Act 2002 s 21(5)(b) (as added: see note 14).
17 See the Education Act 2002 s 21(6) (as added: see note 14). 'Relevant children and young people's plan' means, in relation to a school in England, any plan published by the relevant children's trust board under the Children Act 2004 s 17 (children and young people's plans: England: see CHILDREN AND YOUNG PERSONS vol 9 (2012) PARA 207): Education Act 2002 s 21(9)(a) (as added (see note 14); and substituted by the Apprenticeships, Skills, Children and Learning Act 2009 s 194(9)(a)). 'The relevant children's trust board' means the children's trust board established by arrangements made under the Children Act 2004 s 10 (see CHILDREN AND YOUNG PERSONS vol 9 (2012) PARA 203) by the local authority: Education Act 2002 s 21(10) (added by the Apprenticeships, Skills, Children and Learning Act 2009, s 194(9)(b); and amended by SI 2010/1158).
18 As to the meaning of 'parent' see PARA 7 note 6 (definition applied by the Education Act 2002 s 212(2), (3)).
19 See the Education Act 2002 s 21(7) (as added: see note 14). As to the meaning of 'registered pupil' see PARA 437 (definition applied by s 212(2), (3)).
20 See the Children and Young Persons Act 2008 s 20. See also CHILDREN AND YOUNG PERSONS vol 10 (2012) PARA 868.

169. Powers of governing body. The governing body of a maintained school[1] may do anything which appears to it to be necessary or expedient for the purposes of, or in connection with, the conduct of the school[2] or the provision[3] of community facilities or services[4]. The governing body may also provide advice or assistance to the governing body of any other maintained school, whether or not maintained by the same local authority[5], or to any local authority[6]. The governing body of a maintained school (other than the governing body of a maintained nursery school)[7] may provide advice and assistance to the proprietor[8] of an academy[9].

These powers[10] include, in particular, the power to:

(1)   borrow such sums as the governing body thinks fit and, in connection with such borrowing, grant any mortgage, charge or other security over any land[11] or other property of the governing body[12];

(2)   acquire and dispose of land and other property[13];

(3)   enter into contracts[14];

(4)   invest any sums not immediately required for the purposes of carrying on any activities it has power to carry on[15];

(5)   accept gifts of money, land or other property and apply it, or hold and administer it on trust, for any of those purposes[16]; and

(6)   do anything incidental to the conduct of the school, the provision of advice or assistance[17], or the provision[18] of community facilities or services[19].

The governing body of a maintained school may be a member of the foundation[20] of another maintained school in England[21].

Regulations[22] may make further provision as to the general powers of the governing body[23], and as to other matters relating to it as a body corporate[24].

The governing body of a maintained school[25] may require registered pupils[26] to attend at any place outside the school premises[27] for the purposes of receiving any instruction or training included in the secular curriculum for the school[28], or for the purpose of receiving educational provision which is intended to improve the behaviour of the pupil[29].

1   Ie the governing body of a maintained school incorporated under the Education Act 2002 s 19(1) (see PARA 150): Sch 1 para 1. As to the meaning of 'maintained school' see PARA 103 note 3. As to governing bodies of maintained schools see PARA 150 et seq. As to academies see PARA 345 et seq.

2   As to the general responsibility of the governing body for the conduct of a school see PARA 168.

3   Ie under the Education Act 2002 s 27: see PARA 174.

4   Education Act 2002 Sch 1 para 3(1). The provisions of Sch 1 para 3(1)–(3) (see the text to notes 1–19) have effect subject to: (1) any provisions of the school's instrument of government (Sch 1 para 3(8)(a)); and (2) any provisions of a scheme under the School Standards and Framework Act 1998 s 48 (see PARA 321) which relates to the school (Education Act 2002 Sch 1 para 3(8)(b)). As to instruments of government see PARA 184 et seq. As to the application of the Education Act 2002 Sch 1 para 3(1)–(6), (8) to pupil referral units (as to which see PARA 427 et seq) see the Education (Pupil Referral Units) (Application of Enactments) (England) Regulations 2007, SI 2007/2979, Sch 1 Pt 1 para 20 (substituted by SI 2012/3158).

5   Education Act 2002 Sch 1 para 3(2)(a) (amended by SI 2010/1158). As to the meaning of 'local authority' see PARA 25 (definition applied by the Education Act 2002 s 212(1)).

6   Education Act 2002 Sch 1 para 3(2)(b) (amended by SI 2010/1158).

7   As to the meaning of 'maintained nursery school' see PARA 103 note 3 (definition applied by the Education Act 2002 s 212(2), (3)).

8   As to the meaning of 'proprietor' see PARA 51 note 4 (definition applied by the Education Act 2002 s 212(2), (3)).

9   Education Act 2002 Sch 1 para 3(2A) (added by the Children, Schools and Families Act 2010 s 6(1), (2)). As to the meaning of 'academy' see PARA 346 (definition applied by the Education Act 2002 s 212(2), (3)).

10   Ie the powers conferred by the Education Act 2002 Sch 1 para 3(1), (2), (2A) (see the text to notes 1–9): see Sch 1 para 3(3) (amended by the Children, Schools and Families Act 2010 s 6(1), (3)(a)).

11 As to the meaning of 'land' see PARA 116 note 18 (definition applied by the Education Act 2002 s 212(2), (3)).

12 Education Act 2002 Sch 1 para 3(3)(a). The power to borrow money and grant security mentioned in Sch 1 para 3(2)(a) may only be exercised with the written consent of the Secretary of State or, if an order under Sch 1 para 3(5) so provides, of the local authority: see Sch 1 para 3(4) (amended by SI 2010/1158). Any such consent may be given for particular borrowing or for borrowing of a particular class: Education Act 2002 Sch 1 para 3(4). The Secretary of State may by order make provision for his function of giving consent under Sch 1 para 3(4) to be instead exercisable in the case of all maintained schools, or in the case of any class of such schools specified in the order, by the local authorities by whom those schools are maintained: Sch 1 para 3(5) (amended by SI 2010/1158). In exercising that function those authorities must comply with any directions contained in an order made by the Secretary of State: Education Act 2002 Sch 1 para 3(6). As to the meaning of 'written' see PARA 76 note 8. As to the Secretary of State see PARA 58. At the date at which this volume states the law no order had been made under Sch 1 para 3(5). The power to make an order under Sch 1 para 3(6) is not exercisable by statutory instrument (see s 210(2)) and such orders are not recorded in this work.

13 Education Act 2002 Sch 1 para 3(3)(b). As to the acquisition and disposal of land see PARA 1298 et seq.

14 Education Act 2002 Sch 1 para 3(3)(c). Where the school is a foundation, voluntary aided or foundation special school, the power to enter into contracts mentioned in Sch 1 para 3(3)(c) includes power to enter into contracts for the employment of teachers and other staff; but no such contracts may be entered into by the governing body of a community, voluntary controlled or community special school or of a maintained nursery school: Sch 1 para 3(7). As to the meaning of references to a community, foundation or voluntary school or a community or foundation special school see PARA 106. As to the employment of teachers, and staffing generally, see PARA 268 et seq.

15 Education Act 2002 Sch 1 para 3(3)(d).

16 Education Act 2002 Sch 1 para 3(3)(e).

17 Ie under the Education Act 2002 Sch 1 para 3(2) or (2A): see the text to notes 5–9.

18 Ie under the Education Act 2002 s 27: see PARA 174.

19 Education Act 2002 Sch 1 para 3(3)(f) (amended by the Children, Schools and Families Act 2010 s 6(1), (3)(b)).

20 'Foundation' has the meaning given by the School Standards and Framework Act 1998 s 21(3) (see PARA 108 note 6), except that it does not include a foundation established under that Act: Education Act 2002 Sch 1 para 3(2B) (added by the Children, Schools and Families Act 2010 s 6(1), (2)).

21 Education Act 2002 Sch 1 para 3(2B) (as added: see note 20). As to the meaning of 'England' see PARA 7 note 3.

22 Ie regulations made under the Education Act 2002 by the Secretary of State: see s 212(1). At the date at which this volume states the law no regulations have been made under Sch 1 para 4.

23 Education Act 2002 Sch 1 para 4(a).

24 Education Act 2002 Sch 1 para 4(b). As to governing bodies as bodies corporate see PARA 150.

25 For these purposes 'maintained school' does not include a maintained nursery school: Education Act 2002 ss 29(4), 29A(2) (s 29A added by the Education and Skills Act 2008 s 154).

26 As to the meaning of 'registered pupil' see PARA 437 (definition applied by the Education Act 2002 s 212(2), (3)).

27 As to the meaning of 'premises' see PARA 62 note 19 (definition applied by the Education Act 2002 s 212(2), (3)).

28 Education Act 2002 s 29(3) (amended by the Education Act 2005 s 115). As to the application of the Education Act 2002 s 29(3), with modifications, in relation to pupil referral units see the Education (Pupil Referral Units) (Application of Enactments) (England) Regulations 2007, SI 2007/2979, regs 1(3), 3, Sch 1 Pt 1 para 14. As to pupil referral units see PARA 427 et seq.

29 See the Education Act 2002 s 29A(1) (as added: see note 25). Regulations must make provision: (1) requiring prescribed persons to be given prescribed information relating to the imposition of any requirement under s 29A(1) (s 29A(3)(a) (as so added)); and (2) requiring the governing body of the school to keep under review the imposition of any such requirement (s 29A(3)(b) (as so added)). Regulations may also make provision: (a) requiring a governing body exercising functions under s 29A(1) or under the regulations to have regard to any guidance given from time to time by the Secretary of State (s 29A(4)(a) (as so added)); (b) prohibiting a governing body from exercising the power conferred by s 29A(1) in such a way that any pupil is required to receive educational provision outside the school premises for a greater number of days in a school year than is specified in the regulations (s 29A(4)(b) (as so added)); (c) requiring the governing body to request prescribed persons to participate in any review of the imposition of a

requirement under s 29A(1) (s 29A(4)(c) (as so added)); (d) about the time within which the first review must be held and the intervals at which subsequent reviews must be held (s 29A(4)(d) (as so added)); and (e) in relation to any other matter relating to the exercise of the power conferred by s 29A(1) (s 29A(4)(e) (as so added)). 'Prescribed' means prescribed by the regulations: see s 212(1). As to the publication of guidance see the Education Act 1996 s 571 (applied by the Education Act 2002 s 212(2), (3)); and PARA 60. As to the regulations made see the Education (Educational Provision for Improving Behaviour) Regulations 2010, SI 2010/1156 (amended by SI 2012/2532).

170. Power of governing body to provide higher education. The governing body of a maintained school[1] has the power to arrange the provision to pupils[2] at the school, whether by teachers at the school or other persons[3], of: (1) courses in preparation for professional examinations at a higher level[4]; or (2) courses[5] providing education at a higher level (whether or not in preparation for an examination)[6]. A governing body may exercise this power in relation to a particular pupil only if it is satisfied that the provision to that pupil of the course in question will not to any significant extent interfere with the other education with which he is being provided at the school[7].

This power has effect notwithstanding the fact that nothing in the Education Act 1996[8] confers any functions with respect to higher education[9].

1   As to the meaning of 'maintained school' see PARA 103 note 3. As to governing bodies of maintained schools see PARA 150 et seq.
2   As to the meaning of 'pupil' see PARA 20 note 4 (definition applied by the Education Act 2002 s 212(2), (3)).
3   As to the meaning of 'person' see PARA 7 note 6.
4   Ie courses falling within the Education Reform Act 1988 Sch 6 para 1(g): see PARA 684.
5   Ie courses falling within the Education Reform Act 1988 Sch 6 para 1(h): see PARA 684.
6   Education Act 2002 s 28A(1) (s 28A added by the Education Act 2005 s 105).
7   Education Act 2002 s 28A(2) (as added: see note 6).
8   See the Education Act 1996 s 1(4): see PARA 18.
9   Education Act 2002 s 28A(5) (as added: see note 6).

171. Power of governing body to provide further education. The governing body of any maintained school[1] is responsible for determining whether or not to provide part-time education suitable to the requirements of persons of any age over compulsory school age[2].

1   As to the meaning of 'maintained school' see PARA 99. As to governing bodies of maintained schools see PARA 150 et seq. The governing body of a community or foundation special school may not determine to provide, or to cease to provide, education under the School Standards and Framework Act 1998 s 80 without the consent of the local authority: see s 80(1); and PARA 588.
2   See the School Standards and Framework Act 1998 s 80(1); and PARA 588.

172. Collaboration arrangements: maintained schools and further education bodies. Regulations[1] may enable:
(1)   the governing body of a maintained school[2], whether alone or together with other such governing bodies, to make collaboration arrangements[3] with one or more further education bodies[4];
(2)   a further education body, whether alone or together with other further education bodies, to make collaboration arrangements with the governing body of a maintained school or the governing bodies of two or more such schools[5];
(3)   a further education body to make collaboration arrangements with one or more further education bodies[6].
Regulations[7] may make provision as to:
(a)   the establishment by the collaborating bodies of a joint committee of

those bodies for the purposes of discharging any functions in pursuance of collaboration arrangements made by them ('a joint committee')[8];

(b)　the appointment of persons to serve on a joint committee (including provision as to the restrictions or other requirements relating to any such appointments) and their removal from office[9];

(c)　the appointment of a clerk to a joint committee (including provision as to the restrictions or other requirements relating to any such appointment) and his removal from office[10];

(d)　the appointment by a joint committee of one of its number to act as clerk for the purposes of a meeting where the clerk fails to attend[11];

(e)　rights of persons to attend meetings of a joint committee[12];

(f)　restrictions on persons taking part in proceedings of a joint committee[13];

(g)　other matters relating to the constitution or procedure of a joint committee[14];

(h)　the functions of collaborating bodies which may or may not be discharged jointly, or by a joint committee, in pursuance of collaboration arrangements[15];

(i)　the manner in which such functions are to be discharged jointly, or by a joint committee, in pursuance of collaboration arrangements[16];

(j)　any other matters which are relevant to the discharge of functions by the collaborating bodies jointly, or as the case may be, by a joint committee in pursuance of such arrangements[17].

Regulations[18] may also provide that any enactment[19] relating to the functions of the collaborating bodies which are to be discharged in pursuance of collaboration arrangements[20], or the governing bodies, or as the case may be the further education bodies, by whom those functions are to be discharged[21], is to have effect subject to all necessary modifications[22] in its application in relation to those functions and the bodies by whom they are to be discharged[23].

1　Ie regulations made by the Secretary of State: see the Education and Inspections Act 2006 s 166(6) (amended by the Education (Wales) Measure 2011 s 9(4)(c)). As to the Secretary of State see PARA 58. As to the regulations made see the Collaboration Arrangements (Maintained Schools and Further Education Bodies) (England) Regulations 2007, SI 2007/1321 (amended by SI 2015/883).

2　For these purposes, 'maintained school' means a school in England which is a community, foundation or voluntary school, a community or foundation special school or a maintained nursery school: Education and Inspections Act 2006 s 166(6) (amended by the Education (Wales) Measure 2011 s 9(4)(b)). As to the meaning of 'England' see PARA 7 note 3. As to the meaning of references to a community, foundation or voluntary school or a community or foundation special school see PARA 106. As to the meaning of 'maintained nursery school' see PARA 99 note 4 (definition applied by the Education and Inspections Act 2006s 187(2), (3)).

3　'Collaboration arrangements' are arrangements for any of the functions of any of the bodies who make the arrangements ('the collaborating bodies') to be discharged jointly or by a joint committee of those bodies: Education and Inspections Act 2006 s 166(2). As to the meaning of 'functions' see PARA 18 note 5 (definition applied by s 187(2), (3)). The directions that may be given to a governing body under the Further and Higher Education Act 1992 s 56A include a direction requiring a governing body to make collaboration arrangements (within the meaning of the Education and Inspections Act 2006 s 166) with such bodies and on such terms as may be specified in the direction: see the Further and Higher Education Act 1992 s 56A(7)(a); and PARA 1281.

4　Education and Inspections Act 2006 s 166(1)(a). 'Further education body' means: (1) a further education corporation (as defined by the Further and Higher Education Act 1992 s 17(1): see PARA 555) in England; (2) a sixth form college corporation (as defined in s 90 of that Act: see PARA 577 note 7); or (3) the governing body of a designated institution (as defined by s 28(4) of that Act: see PARA 572) in England which is a body incorporated by virtue of the Learning and

Skills Act 2000 s 143(4) (see PARA 575): Education and Inspections Act 2006 s 166(6) (definition amended by SI 2010/1080; and the Education (Wales) Measure 2011 s 9(4)(a)).
5 Education and Inspections Act 2006 s 166(1)(b).
6 Education and Inspections Act 2006 s 166(1)(c).
7 As to the regulations made see note 1.
8 Education and Inspections Act 2006 s 166(3)(a).
9 Education and Inspections Act 2006 s 166(3)(b).
10 Education and Inspections Act 2006 s 166(3)(c).
11 Education and Inspections Act 2006 s 166(3)(d).
12 Education and Inspections Act 2006 s 166(3)(e).
13 Education and Inspections Act 2006 s 166(3)(f).
14 Education and Inspections Act 2006 s 166(3)(g).
15 Education and Inspections Act 2006 s 166(4)(a).
16 Education and Inspections Act 2006 s 166(4)(b).
17 Education and Inspections Act 2006 s 166(4)(c).
18 As to the regulations made see note 1.
19 As to the meaning of 'enactment' see PARA 26 note 15.
20 Education and Inspections Act 2006 s 166(5)(a).
21 Education and Inspections Act 2006 s 166(5)(b).
22 As to the meaning of 'modifications' see PARA 21 note 15 (definition applied by the Education Act 2006 s 187(2), (3)).
23 Education and Inspections Act 2006 s 166(5).

173.   Power of governing body to form or invest in companies to provide services etc.   The governing body of a maintained school[1] may form, or participate in forming, companies[2] to:
(1)   provide services or facilities[3] for any schools[4];
(2)   exercise relevant local authority functions[5]; or
(3)   make, or facilitate the making of, arrangements under which facilities or services are provided for any schools by other persons[6].
The governing body of a maintained school may, with a view to securing or facilitating:
(a)   the provision by a company of services or facilities for any schools[7];
(b)   the exercise by a company of relevant local authority functions[8]; or
(c)   the making by any person of arrangements of the kind referred to in head (3) above[9],
invest[10] in the company which is to provide the services or facilities or exercise the functions or by which the arrangements are to be made or facilitated[11]. The governing body of a maintained school may form, or participate in forming, companies to purchase services or facilities for that school and other participating schools[12]. The governing body of a maintained school may, with a view to securing or facilitating the purchase by a company of services or facilities for that school and other participating schools, become a member of the company[13].
The above provisions are without prejudice to any powers of the governing body of a maintained school which are exercisable otherwise[14].
The governing body of a maintained school may not exercise any of the above powers[15] except with the consent of the local authority[16], and at a time when the school has a delegated budget[17]. A governing body may not exercise any of those powers in relation to a company unless the company satisfies any applicable requirements of regulations under heads (i) and (ii) below[18], and may not[19] remain a member of a company at any time when the company fails to satisfy any such requirements[20].
Regulations[21]:
(i)   must provide that, except in such cases as may be prescribed[22], the

company is to be prohibited by its constitution from admitting to its membership any person who is not of a prescribed description[23];

(ii) may impose requirements with respect to the constitution of the company, and any other matter connected with the company's affairs[24];

(iii) must provide that where one or more governing bodies have invested in a company[25], a local authority must be designated as the supervising authority for the company[26];

(iv) must specify the persons by whom and the manner in which the power of designation is, or is in specified circumstances, exercisable[27];

(v) must make provision about the duties of a local authority who are for the time being designated as the supervising authority for a company[28].

Regulations[29] may also: (A) require that, where a local authority is for the time being designated as the supervising authority for a company, the company must provide prescribed information relating to its financial affairs to it at such times and in such manner as may be prescribed[30]; (B) provide that in prescribed circumstances a local authority who is for the time being so designated may direct any participating governing body[31] to cease to be a member of the company or to take any other prescribed action in relation to the company[32]; and (C) prescribe the procedure for making such a direction[33].

1   For these purposes, 'maintained school' means a community, foundation or voluntary school, a community or foundation special school or a maintained nursery school: Education Act 2002 s 11(9). As to the meaning of references to a community, foundation or voluntary school or a community or foundation special school see PARA 106. As to the meaning of 'maintained nursery school' see PARA 99 note 4 (definition applied by s 212(2), (3)). As to governing bodies of maintained schools see PARA 150 et seq.

2   'Company' means a company registered under the Companies Act 2006 as a company limited by shares or a company limited by guarantee: Education Act 2002 s 11(9) (definition amended by SI 2009/1941). As to companies limited by guarantee see COMPANIES vol 14 (2009) PARAS 79, 102. As to companies limited by shares see COMPANIES vol 14 (2009) PARA 102. As to the powers of the Secretary of State in relation to companies see PARA 61. As to the Secretary of State see PARA 58.

3   'Facilities' includes the provision of (or of the use of) premises, goods, materials, vehicles, plant or apparatus: Education Act 2002 s 11(9). As to the meaning of 'premises' see PARA 62 note 19 (definition applied by s 212(2), (3)).

4   Education Act 2002 s 11(1)(a). As to the meaning of 'school' see PARA 91 (definition applied by s 212(2), (3)). The governing body of a maintained school may provide staff to any company in relation to which it has exercised a power conferred by any of s 11(1)–(4): s 11(5). The provisions of s 11(1)–(4) have effect subject to s 12 (see the text to notes 15–33): s 11(6). In exercising the power conferred by s 11(5), the governing body of a maintained school must have regard to any guidance given from time to time by the Secretary of State: s 11(7). As to the publication of guidance see the Education Act 1996 s 571 (applied by the Education Act 2002 s 212(2), (3)); and PARA 60.

5   Education Act 2002 s 11(1)(b) (amended by SI 2010/1158). See also note 4. 'Relevant local authority functions', in relation to a company, means the education functions of any local authority that are or may become exercisable by the company in accordance with an authorisation given or direction made by virtue of any enactment: Education Act 2002 s 11(9) (definition amended by SI 2010/1158). As to the meanings of 'local authority' and 'education functions' see PARA 25 (definition applied by the Education Act 2002 s 212(1)–(3)). As to the meaning of 'enactment' see PARA 1 note 13.

6   Education Act 2002 s 11(1)(c). See also note 4. As to the meaning of 'person' see PARA 7 note 6.

7   Education Act 2002 s 11(2)(a).

8   Education Act 2002 s 11(2)(b) (amended by SI 2010/1158).

9   Education Act 2002 s 11(2)(c).

10 References to investing in a company include references to becoming a member of the company and to investing in it by the acquisition of any assets, securities or rights or otherwise: Education Act 2002 s 11(10).

11 Education Act 2002 s 11(2). See also note 4.

12 Education Act 2002 s 11(3). See also note 4. 'Participating school', in relation to a company, means a school whose governing body is, or is to be, a member of the company: s 11(9).

13 Education Act 2002 s 11(4). See also note 4.

14 Education Act 2002 s 11(8).

15 Ie powers conferred by any of the Education Act 2002 s 11(1)–(4): see the text to notes 1–13.

16 Education Act 2002 s 12(1)(a) (amended by SI 2010/1158). Regulations may restrict the circumstances in which a local authority may refuse to give any consent applied for under the Education Act 2002 s 12(1): s 12(8) (amended by SI 2010/1158). 'Regulations' means regulations made under the Education Act 2002 by the Secretary of State: see s 212(1). As to the regulations made see note 21.

17 Education Act 2002 s 12(1)(b). The delegated budget referred to is one within the meaning of the School Standards and Framework Act 1998 Pt II (ss 20–83) (see PARA 323): see the Education Act 2002 s 12(1)(b).

18 Education Act 2002 s 12(2)(a).

19 Ie by virtue of the Education Act 2002 s 11: see the text to notes 1–14.

20 Education Act 2002 s 12(2)(b).

21 As to the regulations made under the Education Act 2002 s 12 see the School Companies Regulations 2002, SI 2002/2978 (amended by SI 2003/2049; SI 2004/3264; SI 2006/2198; SI 2012/979; SI 2012/2404; and SI 2014/2923); the School Companies (Private Finance Initiative Companies) Regulations 2002, SI 2002/3177 (amended by SI 2004/3264; SI 2006/2198; SI 2009/1924; SI 2012/979; and SI 2012/2404); the Education (Company Directors Disqualification Act 1986: Amendments to Disqualification Provisions) (England) Regulations 2004, SI 2004/3264; and the Education (Disqualification Provisions: Bankruptcy and Mental Health) (England) Regulations 2006, SI 2006/2198.

22 'Prescribed' means prescribed by the regulations: see the Education Act 2002 s 212(1).

23 Education Act 2002 s 12(3)(a).

24 Education Act 2002 s 12(3)(b). Without prejudice to the generality of s 12(3)(b), regulations under that provision may require that the company be prohibited by its constitution from borrowing money, except with the consent of a prescribed person: s 12(4).

25 Ie by virtue of the Education Act 2002 s 11: see the text to notes 1–14.

26 Education Act 2002 s 12(5)(a) (amended by SI 2010/1158).

27 Education Act 2002 s 12(5)(b).

28 Education Act 2002 s 12(5)(c) (amended by SI 2010/1158).

29 As to the regulations made see note 21.

30 Education Act 2002 s 12(6)(a) (amended by SI 2010/1158).

31 'Participating governing body', in relation to a company, means any governing body of a maintained school who is a member of the company: Education Act 2002 s 12(7).

32 Education Act 2002 s 12(6)(b) (amended by SI 2010/1158).

33 Education Act 2002 s 12(6)(c).

174. Power of governing body to provide community facilities etc. The governing body of a maintained school[1] has the power[2] to provide any facilities or services whose provision furthers any charitable purpose[3] for the benefit of pupils[4] at the school or their families[5], or people who live or work in the locality in which the school is situated[6]. This power includes, in particular, power for a governing body to: (1) incur expenditure[7]; (2) enter into arrangements or agreements with any person[8]; (3) co-operate with, or facilitate or co-ordinate the activities of, any person[9]; and (4) provide staff, goods, services and accommodation to any person[10]. A governing body may charge for any services or facilities so provided[11].

However, the above power does not enable a governing body to do anything which it is unable to do by virtue of any prohibition, restriction or limitation on its powers which is contained in the school's instrument of government[12], or any local authority's financial scheme[13] which relates to the school[14]; and regulations[15] may make provision preventing governing bodies from doing[16] anything which is specified, or is of a description specified, in the regulations[17].

A governing body must exercise the power only if, and to the extent that, it is satisfied that anything which it proposes to do will not to a significant extent interfere with the performance of any duty imposed on it either in relation to its general responsibility to conduct the school with a view to promoting high standards of educational achievement[18], or by any other provision of the Education Acts[19]. In exercising the power, the governing body of a maintained school must have regard to any relevant children and young people's plan[20].

1   As to the meaning of 'maintained school' see PARA 103 note 3. As to governing bodies of maintained schools see PARA 150 et seq. As to academies see PARA 345 et seq.

2   The Education Act 2002 s 27 has effect subject to s 28 (see the text to notes 12–20): s 27(4). Parent councils have the purpose of advising the governing body in the exercise of its powers under s 27: see s 23A; and PARA 178. As to the application of s 27, with modifications, to pupil referral units see the Education (Pupil Referral Units) (Application of Enactments) (England) Regulations 2007, SI 2007/2979, regs 1(3), 3, Sch 1 Pt 1 para 13. As to pupil referral units see PARA 427 et seq.

3   As to charitable purposes see CHARITIES vol 8 (2015) PARA 1 et seq.

4   As to the meaning of 'pupil' see PARA 20 note 4 (definition applied by the Education Act 2002 s 212(2), (3)).

5   Education Act 2002 s 27(1)(a). As from a day to be appointed the following provision has effect: At least once in every school year the governing body of a maintained school in England must consider whether, and if so how, it should exercise the power under s 27(1): s 27(1A) (prospectively added by the Children, Schools and Families Act 2010 s 4(1)). At the date at which this volume states the law no such day had been appointed. As to the meaning of 'school year' see PARA 19 note 12 (definition applied by the Education Act 2002 s 212(2), (3)).

6   Education Act 2002 s 27(1)(b). See also note 5.

7   Education Act 2002 s 27(2)(a).

8   Education Act 2002 s 27(2)(b). As to the meaning of 'person' see PARA 7 note 6.

9   Education Act 2002 s 27(2)(c).

10   Education Act 2002 s 27(2)(d). Regulations under ss 35(4), 36(4) may make provision with respect to staff employed, or engaged otherwise than under a contract of employment, wholly or partly for the purposes of the provision of facilities and services under s 27, or any other activities which are not school activities but are carried on on the school premises under the management or control of the governing body: see ss 35(5)(c), 36(5)(c); and PARAS 268, 280. As to the meaning of 'premises' see PARA 62 note 19 (definition applied by s 212(2), (3)).

11   Education Act 2002 s 27(3). This provision is expressed to be subject to the provisions of the Education Act 1996 Pt VI Ch III (ss 449–462) (charges in connection with education at maintained schools: see PARA 334 et seq): see the Education Act 2002 s 27(3).

12   Education Act 2002 s 28(1)(a). As to instruments of government see PARA 184 et seq.

13   Ie any scheme under the School Standards and Framework Act 1998 s 48: see PARA 321.

14   Education Act 2002 s 28(1)(b) (amended by SI 2010/1158).

15   'Regulations' means regulations made under the Education Act 2002 by the Secretary of State: see s 212(1). As to the Secretary of State see PARA 58. At the date at which this volume states the law no such regulations had been made.

16   Ie by virtue of the Education Act 2002 s 27(1): see the text to notes 1–6.

17   Education Act 2002 s 28(2).

18   Ie the duty imposed by the Education Act 2002 s 21(2): see PARA 168.

19   Education Act 2002 s 28(3). As to the meaning of 'the Education Acts' see PARA 1 note 13 (definition applied by s 212(2), (3)).

20   Education Act 2002 s 28(4A) (s 28(4A), (4B) added by the Education and Inspections Act 2006 s 38(2)). 'Relevant children and young people's plan' has the meaning given by the Education Act 2002 s 21(9) (see PARA 168 note 17): s 28(4B) (as so added).

175. Duty of governing body in relation to complaints procedures. The governing body of a maintained school[1] must:

(1)   establish procedures for dealing with all complaints relating to the school or to the provision of facilities or services[2], other than complaints falling to be dealt with in accordance with any procedures required to be established in relation to the school by virtue of any other[3] statutory provision[4]; and

(2)   publicise the procedures so established[5].

In establishing or publicising such procedures, the governing body must have regard to any guidance given from time to time by the Secretary of State[6].

1   As to the meaning of 'maintained school' see PARA 103 note 3. As to governing bodies of maintained schools see PARA 150 et seq. As to academies see PARA 345 et seq. As from a day to be appointed this provision is amended so as to specify that it relates only to maintained schools in England and that the power to issue guidance resides with the Secretary of State: see the Education Act 2002 s 29(1), (2) (prospectively amended by the Apprenticeships, Skills, Children and Learning Act 2009 s 260(1)–(3)): at the date at which this volume states the law no such day had been appointed.

2   Ie under the Education Act 2002 s 27: see PARA 174.

3   Ie other than the Education Act 2002 s 29.

4   Education Act 2002 s 29(1)(a). As to the meaning of 'statutory provision' see PARA 168 note 2. If internal school complaints are not resolved there is a possibility of a complaint of maladministration lying to the appropriate body.

5   Education Act 2002 s 29(1)(b).

6   See the Education Act 2002 s 29(2) (prospectively amended: see note 1). As to the Secretary of State see PARA 58. As to the publication of guidance see the Education Act 1996 s 571 (applied by the Education Act 2002 s 212(2), (3)); and PARA 60. As to the application of s 29(1), (2), with modifications, in relation to pupil referral units see the Education (Pupil Referral Units) (Application of Enactments) (England) Regulations 2007, SI 2007/2979, regs 1(3), 3, Sch 1 Pt 1 para 14. As to pupil referral units see PARA 427 et seq.

176. Duty of governing body in relation to health and safety. The governing body[1] and head teacher[2] of a community or voluntary controlled school[3], a community special school[4], or a maintained nursery school[5], must comply with any direction[6] given to it by the local authority[7] concerning the health and safety of persons on the school's premises[8] or taking part in any school activities elsewhere[9].

1   As to governing bodies of maintained schools see PARA 150 et seq. As to academies see PARA 345 et seq.

2   As to the meaning of 'head teacher' see PARA 86 note 4 (definition applied by the Education Act 2002 s 212(2), (3)).

3   Education Act 2002 s 29(5)(a). As to the meaning of references to a community or voluntary school see PARA 106.

4   Education Act 2002 s 29(5)(b). As to the meaning of references to a community special school see PARA 106.

5   Education Act 2002 s 29(5)(c). As to the meaning of 'maintained nursery school' see PARA 103 note 3.

6   As to directions see the Education Act 1996 s 570 (applied by the Education Act 2002 s 212(2), (3)); and PARA 75.

7   As to the meaning of 'local authority' see PARA 25 (definition applied by the Education Act 2002 s 212(1)).

8   As to the meaning of 'premises' see PARA 62 note 19 (definition applied by the Education Act 2002 s 212(2), (3)).

9   Education Act 2002 s 29(5) (amended by SI 2010/1158). As to health and safety on school premises see also PARA 1353. As to the application of the Education Act 2002 s 29(5), with modifications, in relation to pupil referral units see the Education (Pupil Referral Units) (Application of Enactments) (England) Regulations 2007, SI 2007/2979, regs 1(3), 3, Sch 1 Pt 1 para 15. As to pupil referral units see PARA 427 et seq.

177. Duty of governing body in relation to the welfare of children. The governing body[1] of a maintained school[2] must make arrangements for ensuring that its functions[3] relating to the conduct of the school are exercised with a view to safeguarding and promoting the welfare of children[4] who are pupils[5] at the school[6]. The governing body must, in considering what arrangements are required to be made by it, have regard to any guidance given from time to time by the Secretary of State[7].

1 As to governing bodies of maintained schools see PARA 150 et seq.
2 For these purposes, 'maintained school' means a community, foundation or voluntary school, a community or foundation special school or a maintained nursery school: Education Act 2002 s 175(5). As to the meaning of references to a community, foundation or voluntary school or a community or foundation special school see PARA 106. As to the meaning of 'maintained nursery school' see PARA 99 note 4 (definition applied by s 212(2), (3)). As to academies see PARA 345 et seq.
3 As to the meaning of 'functions' see PARA 18 note 5 (definition applied by the Education Act 2002 s 212(2), (3)).
4 'Child' means a person under the age of 18: Education Act 2002 s 175(5). As to the time at which a person attains a particular age see PARA 7 note 6.
5 As to the meaning of 'pupil' see PARA 20 note 4 (definition applied by the Education Act 2002 s 212(2), (3)).
6 Education Act 2002 s 175(2). As to the application of the Education Act 2002 s 175(2), (4) to pupil referral units (as to which see PARA 427 et seq) see the Education (Pupil Referral Units) (Application of Enactments) (England) Regulations 2007, SI 2007/2979, Sch 1 Pt 1 para 19A (added by SI 2012/3158).
7 Education Act 2002 s 175(4). As to the Secretary of State see PARA 58. As to the publication of guidance see the Education Act 1996 s 571 (applied by the Education Act 2002 s 212(2), (3)); and PARA 60. See note 6.

178. Parent councils. The governing body[1] of any qualifying school[2] must establish in accordance with regulations[3] a body to be known as a parent council[4]. The purpose of a parent council is to advise the governing body on matters relating to the conduct of the school and the exercise by the governing body of its powers[5] to provide community facilities[6].

Regulations[7] may make provision as to: (1) the person[8] or persons by whom, and the manner in which, members of a parent council are to be elected or appointed[9]; (2) eligibility for election or appointment[10]; (3) the duration of membership[11]; and (4) meetings and proceedings of a parent council[12]. Regulations[13]: (a) must require the majority of members of a parent council to be parent members[14]; (b) may enable a person who is not the parent of a registered pupil to be a member of a parent council if appointed in accordance with the regulations by the parent members[15]; (c) may confer functions[16] relating to parent councils on the governing bodies of qualifying schools[17].

The governing body of a qualifying school must, in exercising its functions under these provisions with respect to the school's parent council, have regard to any guidance given from time to time by the Secretary of State[18].

1 As to governing bodies of maintained schools see PARA 150 et seq. As to academies see PARA 345 et seq.
2 A school is a 'qualifying school' if it is a foundation or foundation special school in England, it has a foundation established otherwise than under the School Standards and Framework Act 1998, and the instrument of government for the school provides that the majority of governors are to be foundation governors: Education Act 2002 s 23A(1) (s 23A added by the Education and Inspections Act 2006 s 34). As to the meaning of references to a foundation or foundation special school see PARA 106. As to the meaning of 'England' see PARA 7 note 3. The reference in the Education Act 2002 s 23A(1) to a foundation is to be read in accordance with the School Standards and Framework Act 1998 s 21 (see PARA 108 note 6): Education Act 2002 s 23A(8) (as so added). As to instruments of government see PARA 184 et seq.
3 Ie regulations made by under the Education Act 2002 by the Secretary of State: see s 212(1). As to the Secretary of State see PARA 58. As to the regulations made under s 23A see the School Governance (Parent Council) (England) Regulations 2007, SI 2007/1330.
4 Education Act 2002 s 23A(2) (as added: see note 2).
5 Ie under the Education Act 2002 s 27: see PARA 174.
6 Education Act 2002 s 23A(3) (as added: see note 2).
7 As to the regulations made see note 3.
8 As to the meaning of 'person' see PARA 7 note 6.
9 Education Act 2002 s 23A(4)(a) (as added: see note 2).

10 Education Act 2002 s 23A(4)(b) (as added: see note 2).

11 Education Act 2002 s 23A(4)(c) (as added: see note 2).

12 Education Act 2002 s 23A(4)(d) (as added: see note 2).

13 As to the regulations made see note 3.

14 Education Act 2002 s 23A(5)(a) (as added: see note 2). 'Parent member', in relation to a parent council, means a member of the council who is the parent of a registered pupil at the school: s 23A(9) (as so added). As to the meaning of 'parent' see PARA 7 note 6; and as to the meaning of 'registered pupil' see PARA 437 (definitions applied by s 212(2), (3)).

15 Education Act 2002 s 23A(5)(b) (as added: see note 2).

16 As to the meaning of 'functions' see PARA 18 note 5 (definition applied by the Education Act 2002 s 212(2), (3)).

17 Education Act 2002 s 23A(6) (as added: see note 2).

18 Education Act 2002 s 23A(7) (as added: see note 2). As to the publication of guidance see the Education Act 1996 s 571 (applied by the Education Act 2002 s 212(2), (3)); and PARA 60.

179. Consultation with pupils. As from a day to be appointed[1] the governing body of a maintained school[2] must invite the views of pupils about prescribed[3] matters[4]. In exercising any of its functions relating to the conduct of the school, the governing body of a maintained school must consider any relevant views of registered pupils at the school about matters so prescribed (whether expressed by virtue of such an invitation or otherwise) and, in doing so, must have regard to the age and understanding of the pupils who expressed them[5]. In discharging these duties, the governing body of a maintained school must have regard to any guidance given from time to time by the Secretary of State[6].

Nothing in these provisions[7] affects any power or duty relating to consulting pupils which a governing body of a maintained school has otherwise than under them[8].

1 The Education Act 2002 s 29B (see the text and notes 2–8) is added by the Education and Skills Act 2008 s 157 as from a day to be appointed: see s 173(3)(b), (4). At the date at which this volume states the law no such day had been appointed.

2 As to governing bodies of maintained schools see PARA 150 et seq.

3 'Prescribed' means prescribed by regulations made under the Education Act 2002 by the Secretary of State: see ss 29B(6)(a), 212(1) (s 29B prospectively added: see note 1). The following are the matters that may be prescribed under s 29B(1): (1) the exercise, or proposed exercise, of a function of the governing body of a maintained school relating to the conduct of the school (s 29B(4)(a) (as so prospectively added)); (2) the exercise, or proposed exercise, of such a function in a particular way (s 29B(4)(b) (as so prospectively added)). At the date at which this volume states the law no such regulations had been made.

4 Education Act 2002 s 29B(1) (prospectively added: see note 1). For these purposes, a governing body invites the views of pupils about a matter if it invites the views of: (1) all registered pupils at the school (s 29B(3)(a) (as so prospectively added)); (2) such of those pupils as appear to the governing body to be affected by the matter (s 29B(3)(b) (as so prospectively added)); or (3) pupils appearing to the governing body to be representative of pupils within head (1) or (2) (s 29B(3)(c) (as so prospectively added)). As to the meaning of 'registered pupil' see PARA 437 (definition applied by s 212(2), (3)).

5 Education Act 2002 s 29B(2) (prospectively added: see note 1).

6 Education Act 2002 s 29B(5)(a) (prospectively added: see note 1).

7 Ie nothing in the Education Act 2002 s 29B.

8 Education Act 2002 s 29B(7) (prospectively added: see note 1).

180. Control of school premises by governing body. As from a day to be appointed[1] regulations[2] may make provision relating to the control by the governing body of a maintained school[3] of the occupation and use of school premises[4].

1 The Education Act 2002 s 31 (see the text and notes 2–4) comes into force in relation to England by order made under s 216(4) as from a day to be appointed. At the date at which this volume states the law, no such day had been appointed. As to the provision in regard to Wales

see PARA 213. Until such a day is appointed, in relation to the control of school premises, see the School Standards and Framework Act 1998 Sch 13; and PARA 1355 et seq.

2   'Regulations' means regulations made under the Education Act 2002 by the Secretary of State: see s 212(1). As to the Secretary of State see PARA 58. At the date at which this volume states the law no such regulations had been made.

3   As to the meaning of 'maintained school' see PARA 103 note 3. As to governing bodies of maintained schools see PARA 150 et seq. As to academies see PARA 345 et seq.

4   Education Act 2002 s 31. As to the meaning of 'premises' see PARA 62 note 19 (definition applied by s 212(2), (3)). As to land and premises generally see also PARA 1295 et seq.

(D) Meetings and Proceedings

181.   Meetings and proceedings. Regulations[1] make provision as to the meetings and proceedings of governing bodies[2], and in particular in relation to:

(1)   the election of the chair and vice-chair[3];

(2)   the delegation of functions to the chair or vice-chair in cases of urgency[4];

(3)   the appointment and removal of a clerk to the governing body[5] and his functions[6];

(4)   the right of persons to attend meetings of the governing body[7];

(5)   convening meetings of the governing body[8];

(6)   proceedings of the governing body[9];

(7)   minutes and papers of the governing body[10].

(8)   restrictions on persons taking part in proceedings[11] and the suspension of governors for all or some meetings[12];

(9)   the delegation of functions[13] by the governing body and restrictions on such delegation[14];

(10) reporting to the governing body following the exercise of delegated functions[15];

(11) the establishment of committees by the governing body and the appointment of persons other than governors to serve on them[16].

1   Ie regulations made under the Education Act 2002 s 19(3)(g)–(k): see PARA 150. The regulations made are the School Governance (Roles, Procedures and Allowances) (England) Regulations 2013, SI 2013/1624 (amended by SI 2013/2688; SI 2014/1257; and SI 2014/1959). As to the application of these regulations, with modifications, in relation to the procedure of governing bodies of federations see the School Governance (Federations) (England) Regulations 2012, SI 2012/1035, reg 24, Sch 6 (respectively amended and substituted by SI 2013/1624); and in relation to pupil referral units the Education (Pupil Referral Units) (Management Committees etc) (England) Regulations 2007, SI 2007/2978, reg 21, Sch 3 (both substituted by SI 2013/1624). As to federations of schools see PARA 156. As to pupil referral units see PARA 427 et seq.

2   As to governing bodies of maintained schools see PARA 150 et seq. As to academies see PARA 345 et seq.

3   See the School Governance (Roles, Procedures and Allowances) (England) Regulations 2013, SI 2013/1624, reg 7. As to the removal of the chair or vice-chair from office see reg 9.

4   See the School Governance (Roles, Procedures and Allowances) (England) Regulations 2013, SI 2013/1624, reg 8. See also *R v Birmingham City Council, ex p McKenna* (1991) 156 LG Rev 486, (1991) Times, 16 May (decided under previous legislation).

5   See the School Governance (Roles, Procedures and Allowances) (England) Regulations 2013, SI 2013/1624, reg 10. As to the appointment of the clerk see PARA 167.

6   See the School Governance (Roles, Procedures and Allowances) (England) Regulations 2013, SI 2013/1624, reg 11.

7   See the School Governance (Roles, Procedures and Allowances) (England) Regulations 2013, SI 2013/1624, reg 12. As regards the withdrawal of a governor from a meeting over the matter of a pecuniary interest see *Noble v Inner London Education Authority* (1983) 82 LGR 291, CA; *Bostock v Kay* (1989) 87 LGR 583, 153 JP 549, CA; *R v Governors of Small Heath School,*

    ex p Birmingham City Council [1990] COD 23, (1990) Independent, 3 August, CA; *R v Governors of Bacon's School, ex p Inner London Education Authority* [1990] COD 414, DC (all cases decided under previous legislation).

8   See the School Governance (Roles, Procedures and Allowances) (England) Regulations 2013, SI 2013/1624, reg 13 (amended by SI 2013/2688; and SI 2014/1257).

9   See the School Governance (Roles, Procedures and Allowances) (England) Regulations 2013, SI 2013/1624, reg 14 (amended by SI 2014/1257).

10 See the School Governance (Roles, Procedures and Allowances) (England) Regulations 2013, SI 2013/1624, reg 15.

11 See the School Governance (Roles, Procedures and Allowances) (England) Regulations 2013, SI 2013/1624, reg 16, Sch 1 (respectively substituted and amended by SI 2014/1257).

12 See the School Governance (Roles, Procedures and Allowances) (England) Regulations 2013, SI 2013/1624, reg 17.

13 See the School Governance (Roles, Procedures and Allowances) (England) Regulations 2013, SI 2013/1624, reg 18.

14 See the School Governance (Roles, Procedures and Allowances) (England) Regulations 2013, SI 2013/1624, reg 19.

15 See the School Governance (Roles, Procedures and Allowances) (England) Regulations 2013, SI 2013/1624, reg 20.

16 See the School Governance (Roles, Procedures and Allowances) (England) Regulations 2013, SI 2013/1624, Pt 5 (regs 21–26). See also *R v Secretary of State for Education, ex p Prior* [1994] ELR 231, [1994] ICR 877 (decided under previous legislation).

182. Documentary evidence. In any legal proceedings, a document purporting to be an extract from the minutes of the proceedings of the governing body of a maintained school[1], and to be signed by the chairman of the governing body or by its clerk[2], is to be received in evidence and treated, without further proof, as the document which it purports to be and as having been signed by the person by whom it purports to have been signed, unless the contrary is proved[3].

1   As to governing bodies of maintained schools see PARA 150 et seq.

2   As to the clerk to the governing body see PARA 167.

3   Education Act 1996 s 566(1)(b) (amended by the School Standards and Framework Act 1998 s 140(1), Sch 30 paras 57, 173). In any legal proceedings, any such extract as is mentioned in the Education Act 1996 s 566(1)(b) is evidence of the matters stated in it: see s 566(2). As to evidence in civil proceedings see CIVIL PROCEDURE vol 11 (2009) PARA 749 et seq. As to educational records see PARA 94.

183. Seal of governing body. The application of the seal[1] of the governing body[2] must be authenticated by the signature of:

(1)   the chairman of the governing body[3]; or

(2)   some other member authorised either generally or specially by the governing body to act for that purpose[4],

together with the signature of any other member[5].

    Every document purporting to be an instrument made or issued by or on behalf of the governing body and to be duly executed under the seal of the governing body[6], or to be signed or executed by a person authorised by the governing body to act in that behalf[7], is to be received in evidence and to be treated, without further proof, as being so made or issued unless the contrary is shown[8].

1   As to governing bodies as bodies corporate see PARA 150. As to the corporate seal see CORPORATIONS vol 24 (2010) PARA 323 et seq.

2   Ie the governing body of a maintained school incorporated under the Education Act 2002 s 19(1) (see PARA 150): see Sch 1 para 1. As to the meaning of 'maintained school' see PARA 102 note 3. As to governing bodies of maintained schools see PARA 150 et seq.

3   Education Act 2002 Sch 1 para 2(2)(a).

4   Education Act 2002 Sch 1 para 2(2)(b).

5   Education Act 2002 Sch 1 para 2(2).

6   Education Act 2002 Sch 1 para 2(3)(a).
7   Education Act 2002 Sch 1 para 2(3)(b).
8   Education Act 2002 Sch 1 para 2(3). As to evidence in civil proceedings see CIVIL PROCEDURE
    vol 11 (2009) PARA 749 et seq.

(E) Instruments of Government

184. Instruments of government. For every maintained school[1] there must be an instrument ('the instrument of government')[2] which determines the constitution of the governing body[3] and other matters relating to the school[4]. Regulations[5] must make provision with respect to the making of instruments of government, the matters to be dealt with in such instruments, the form of such instruments, and the review and variation of such instruments[6].

The governing body of a maintained school must not conduct the school under a name other than the one for the time being set out in the school's instrument of government[7].

1   As to the meaning of 'maintained school' see PARA 103 note 3. As to academies see PARA 345 et
    seq.
2   As to the form and content of instruments of government see PARA 185; and as to the procedure
    for making instruments of government see PARA 186.
3   As to the constitution of governing bodies of schools see PARA 150 et seq.
4   Education Act 2002 s 20(1). In relation to maintained schools in England, s 20(1) has effect
    subject to s 24 (federations of schools: see PARA 156): s 20(4) (amended by the Education
    (Wales) Measure 2011 s 19(1), (3)(a)). As to the meaning of 'England' see PARA 7 note 3. The
    Education Act 2002 s 20(1) does not apply to any temporary governing body: see s 34(8); and
    PARA 155.
5   Ie regulations made under the Education Act 2002 by the Secretary of State: see s 212(1).
    Regulations under s 20(2) may require any person responsible for the making, review or
    variation of an instrument of government to have regard to any guidance given from time to
    time by the Secretary of State: s 20(3). Regulations under s 20(2) may also include provision
    with respect to instruments of government for federations: s 20(4). As to the Secretary of State
    see PARA 58. As to the meaning of 'person' see PARA 7 note 6. As to the publication of guidance
    see the Education Act 1996 s 571 (applied by the Education Act 2002 s 212(2), (3)); and PARA
    60. As to the meaning of 'federation' see PARA 156 note 4. As to the regulations made under
    s 20(2)–(4) see the School Governance (Constitution) (England) Regulations 2012,
    SI 2012/1034; the School Governance (Federations) (England) Regulations 2012, SI 2012/1035
    (amended by SI 2013/1624; SI 2014/1257; and SI 2015/1554); and PARA 185 et seq.
6   Education Act 2002 s 20(2).
7   Education Act 2002 s 20(5).

185. Contents and form of instrument of government. The instrument of government[1] for a maintained school[2] must set out:

(1)   the name of the school[3];
(2)   the category of school[4] to which the school belongs, and whether the school has a foundation[5], and whether the school is a qualifying foundation school[6];
(3)   the name of the governing body[7] of the school[8];
(4)   the manner in which the governing body is to be constituted[9], specifying the number of governors in each category of governor[10], and the total membership of the governing body[11];
(5)   where the term of office for a category of governor is to be less than four years, the length of that term of office[12];
(6)   whether the term of office for any governor of a particular category may be determined by those appointing that governor[13];
(7)   where the school has foundation governors[14] (a) the name of any person[15] who is entitled to appoint such governors and, if there is more

than one such person, the basis upon which such appointments are made[16]; (b) details of any foundation governorship to be held ex officio[17]; and (c) the name of any person who is entitled to request the removal of any ex officio foundation governor and to appoint any substitute governor[18];

(8)   where the school is a foundation or a voluntary school[19] designated[20] as having a religious character, a description of the religious ethos of the school[21]; and

(9)   the date when the instrument of government takes effect[22].

Where the school has a foundation, the instrument of government must (subject to any statutory provision[23]) comply with the foundation's governing documents, including any trust deed[24] relating to the school[25].

In respect of the matters to be dealt with in the instrument of government and the form of such instruments, governing bodies must have regard to any guidance given from time to time by the Secretary of State[26].

1   As to instruments of government see PARA 184.
2   As to the meaning of 'maintained school' see PARA 103 note 3. As to academies see PARA 345 et seq.
3   School Governance (Constitution) (England) Regulations 2012, SI 2012/1034, reg 28(1)(a). As to the application of reg 28 with modifications, in relation to the governing body of a federation and its members see the School Governance (Federations) (England) Regulations 2012, SI 2012/1035, Sch 5 para 4. As to federations of schools see PARA 156.
4   As to categories of maintained schools see PARA 106.
5   School Governance (Constitution) (England) Regulations 2012, SI 2012/1034, reg 28(1)(b)(i). As to the meaning of 'foundation' and references to a school having a foundation see PARA 108 note 6 (definition applied by the School Governance (Constitution) (England) Regulations 2012, SI 2012/1034, reg 5(2)(c)).
6   School Governance (Constitution) (England) Regulations 2012, SI 2012/1034, reg 28(1)(b)(ii). As to the meaning of 'qualifying foundation school' see PARA 152 note 5.
7   As to governing bodies generally see PARA 150.
8   School Governance (Constitution) (England) Regulations 2012, SI 2012/1034, reg 28(1)(c).
9   Ie in accordance with the School Governance (Constitution) (England) Regulations 2012, SI 2012/1034, Pt 3 (regs 13–15): see PARA 151 et seq. The manner in which the governing body is to be constituted, as set out in accordance with reg 28(1)(d), must accord with the provisions of the 2012 Regulations as they apply to a school of the category to which the school belongs and, where appropriate, the nature of the school as specified in accordance with reg 28(1)(b) (see head (2) in the text): reg 28(2).
10   School Governance (Constitution) (England) Regulations 2012, SI 2012/1034, reg 28(1)(d)(i). As to the meaning of 'governor' see PARA 151 note 4.
11   School Governance (Constitution) (England) Regulations 2012, SI 2012/1034, reg 28(1)(d)(ii).
12   School Governance (Constitution) (England) Regulations 2012, SI 2012/1034, reg 28(1)(e). As to tenure of office see PARA 163.
13   School Governance (Constitution) (England) Regulations 2012, SI 2012/1034, reg 28(1(ea) (added by SI 2015/883).
14   As to the meaning of 'foundation governor' see PARA 152 note 6.
15   As to the meaning of 'person' see PARA 7 note 6.
16   School Governance (Constitution) (England) Regulations 2012, SI 2012/1034, reg 28(1)(f)(i).
17   School Governance (Constitution) (England) Regulations 2012, SI 2012/1034, reg 28(1)(f)(ii). As to the meaning of 'ex officio foundation governor' see PARA 152 note 6.
18   School Governance (Constitution) (England) Regulations 2012, SI 2012/1034, reg 28(1)(f)(iii).
19   As to the meaning of references to a foundation or voluntary school see PARA 106.
20   Ie under the School Standards and Framework Act 1998 s 69(3): see PARA 914.
21   School Governance (Constitution) (England) Regulations 2012, SI 2012/1034, reg 28(1)(g).
22   School Governance (Constitution) (England) Regulations 2012, SI 2012/1034, reg 28(1)(h).
23   As to the meaning of 'statutory provision' see PARA 168 note 2.
24   As to the meaning of 'trust deed' see PARA 108 note 6 (definition applied by the Education Act 2002 s 212(2), (3); Interpretation Act 1978 s 11).
25   School Governance (Constitution) (England) Regulations 2012, SI 2012/1034, reg 28(3).

26 See the School Governance (Constitution) (England) Regulations 2012, SI 2012/1034, reg 27. As to the Secretary of State see PARA 58. As to the publication of guidance see the Education Act 1996 s 571 (applied by the Education Act 2002 s 212(2), (3)); and PARA 60.

186. Duty to make instrument of government and procedure for making it. The governing body[1] must prepare a draft of the instrument of government[2] and submit it to the local authority[3] which will make it in accordance with the following provisions[4]. Where the school has foundation governors[5], the governing body must not submit the draft to the local authority unless it has been approved by the foundation governors[6], the trustees of any foundation[7] relating to the school[8], in the case of a Church of England school or Roman Catholic Church school[9], the appropriate diocesan authority[10], and in the case of any other school designated[11] as having a religious character, the appropriate religious body[12].

On receiving the draft, the local authority must consider whether it complies with all applicable statutory provisions[13], and if:

(1) it is content that the draft so complies[14]; or

(2) there is agreement between it, the governing body and (if the school has foundation governors) the persons mentioned above[15] that the draft should be revised to any extent, and the revised draft complies with all the applicable statutory provisions[16],

it must make the instrument of government in the form of the draft or (as the case may be) in the form of the revised draft[17]. If neither of heads (1) and (2) above applies in the case of a school which does not have foundation governors, the local authority must:

(a) inform the governing body of the reasons why it is not content with the draft instrument of government[18]; and

(b) give the governing body a reasonable opportunity to reach agreement with it on revising the draft[19],

it must make the instrument of government in the form of a revised draft agreed between it and the governing body or (in the absence of such agreement) in such form as the authority thinks fit having regard, in particular, to the category of school[20] to which the school belongs and, where the school has a foundation, to its relationship[21] with its foundation[22].

In respect of the making of instruments of government, the matters to be dealt with in such instruments, and the form of such instruments, governing bodies and local authorities must have regard to any guidance given from time to time by the Secretary of State[23].

1 As to governing bodies generally see PARA 150.
2 As to instruments of government see PARA 184.
3 Ie the local authority that maintains the school: see the School Governance (Constitution) (England) Regulations 2012, SI 2012/1034, reg 5(2)(b). As to the meaning of 'local authority' see PARA 25 (definition applied by the Education Act 2002 s 212(1).
4 School Governance (Constitution) (England) Regulations 2012, SI 2012/1034, reg 29(1). As to the application of reg 29 with modifications, in relation to the governing body of a federation and its members see the School Governance (Federations) (England) Regulations 2012, SI 2012/1035, Sch 5 para 5. As to federations of schools see PARA 156.
5 As to the meaning of 'foundation governor' see PARA 152 note 6.
6 School Governance (Constitution) (England) Regulations 2012, SI 2012/1034, reg 29(2)(a).
7 As to the meaning of 'foundation' and references to a school having a foundation see PARA 108 note 6 (definition applied by the School Governance (Constitution) (England) Regulations 2012, SI 2012/1034, reg 5(2)(c)).
8 School Governance (Constitution) (England) Regulations 2012, SI 2012/1034, reg 29(2)(b).

9   'Church of England school' and 'Roman Catholic Church school' are not defined in the School Governance (Constitution) (England) Regulations 2012, SI 2012/1034, or the Education Act 2002; as to the definitions in the School Standards and Framework Act 1998 see PARA 146 note 12.

10   School Governance (Constitution) (England) Regulations 2012, SI 2012/1034, reg 29(2)(c). As to the meaning of 'appropriate diocesan authority' see PARA 146 note 12 (definition applied by reg 26).

11   Ie under the School Standards and Framework Act 1998 s 69(3): see PARA 914.

12   School Governance (Constitution) (England) Regulations 2012, SI 2012/1034, reg 29(2)(d). As to the meaning of 'appropriate religious body' see PARA 161 note 8.

13   As to the meaning of 'statutory provision' see PARA 168 note 2.

14   School Governance (Constitution) (England) Regulations 2012, SI 2012/1034, reg 29(3)(a).

15   Ie the persons mentioned in the School Governance (Constitution) (England) Regulations 2012, SI 2012/1034, reg 29(2): see the text to notes 5–12.

16   School Governance (Constitution) (England) Regulations 2012, SI 2012/1034, reg 29(3)(b).

17   School Governance (Constitution) (England) Regulations 2012, SI 2012/1034, reg 29(3).

18   School Governance (Constitution) (England) Regulations 2012, SI 2012/1034, reg 29(4)(a).

19   School Governance (Constitution) (England) Regulations 2012, SI 2012/1034, reg 29(4)(b).

20   As to categories of maintained schools see PARA 106.

21   Ie as specified in accordance with the School Governance (Constitution) (England) Regulations 2012, SI 2012/1034, reg 28(1)(b): see PARA 185.

22   School Governance (Constitution) (England) Regulations 2012, SI 2012/1034, reg 29(4).

23   See the School Governance (Constitution) (England) Regulations 2012, SI 2012/1034, reg 27. As to the Secretary of State see PARA 58. As to the publication of guidance see the Education Act 1996 s 571 (applied by the Education Act 2002 s 212(2), (3)); and PARA 60.

187. Review of instruments of government. The governing body[1] or the local authority[2] may review the instrument of government[3] at any time after it is made[4]. Where, on any review, the governing body or the local authority decides that the instrument of government should be varied, the governing body or (as the case may be) the local authority must notify the other of its proposed variation together with its reasons for proposing such a variation[5]. Where the governing body has received such notification, it must inform the local authority as to whether or not it is content with the proposed variation and, if not content, its reasons[6].

If:

(1)   whichever of the governing body and the local authority is the recipient of a notification agrees with the proposed variation[7]; or

(2)   there is agreement between the local authority, the governing body and (if the school has foundation governors) the specified persons[8] that some other variation should be made instead[9],

the instrument of government must be varied accordingly by the local authority[10]. If neither head (1) nor (2) above applies in the case of a school which does not have foundation governors, the local authority must:

(a)   inform the governing body of the reasons why it is not content with the governing body's proposed variation, or as the case may be[11], why it wishes to proceed with its own variation[12]; and

(b)   give the governing body a reasonable opportunity to reach agreement with it with regard to the variation[13],

and the instrument of government must be varied by the authority either in the manner agreed between it and the governing body or (in the absence of such agreement) in such manner as the authority thinks fit, having regard, in particular, to the category of school[14] to which the school belongs and, where appropriate, to the nature[15] of the school[16].

Where the instrument of government is varied under these provisions the instrument must set out the date on which the variation takes effect[17].

In respect of the review and variation of instruments of government, governing bodies and local authorities must have regard to any guidance given from time to time by the Secretary of State[18].

1   As to governing bodies generally see PARA 150.
2   Ie the local authority that maintains the school: see the School Governance (Constitution) (England) Regulations 2012, SI 2012/1034, reg 5(2)(b). As to the meaning of 'local authority' see PARA 25 (definition applied by the Education Act 2002 s 212(1)).
3   As to instruments of government see PARA 184. As to the application of the School Governance (Constitution) (England) Regulations 2012, SI 2012/1034, reg 31 with modifications, in relation to the governing body of a federation and its members see the School Governance (Federations) (England) Regulations 2012, SI 2012/1035, Sch 5 para 6. As to federations of schools see PARA 156.
4   School Governance (Constitution) (England) Regulations 2012, SI 2012/1034, reg 30(1). As to the making of instruments of government see PARA 186.
5   School Governance (Constitution) (England) Regulations 2012, SI 2012/1034, reg 30(2). See also note 6.
6   School Governance (Constitution) (England) Regulations 2012, SI 2012/1034, reg 30(3). Where the school has foundation governors, the governing body must not give the local authority any notification under reg 30(2) (see the text to note 5) (reg 30(4)(a)) or inform the authority under reg 30(3) that it is content with the authority's proposed variation (reg 30(4)(b)), unless the persons listed in reg 29(2) (see PARA 186) have approved the proposed variation (reg 30(4)). As to the meaning of 'foundation governor' see PARA 152 note 6.
7   School Governance (Constitution) (England) Regulations 2012, SI 2012/1034, reg 30(5)(a).
8   Ie the other persons listed in the School Governance (Constitution) (England) Regulations 2012, SI 2012/1034, reg 29(2): see PARA 186.
9   School Governance (Constitution) (England) Regulations 2012, SI 2012/1034, reg 30(5)(b).
10 School Governance (Constitution) (England) Regulations 2012, SI 2012/1034, reg 30(5).
11 School Governance (Constitution) (England) Regulations 2012, SI 2012/1034, reg 30(6)(a)(i).
12 School Governance (Constitution) (England) Regulations 2012, SI 2012/1034, reg 30(6)(a)(ii).
13 School Governance (Constitution) (England) Regulations 2012, SI 2012/1034, reg 30(6)(b).
14 As to categories of maintained schools see PARA 106.
15 Ie as specified in accordance with the School Governance (Constitution) (England) Regulations 2012, SI 2012/1034, reg 28(1)(b): see PARA 185.
16 School Governance (Constitution) (England) Regulations 2012, SI 2012/1034, reg 30(6). The requirement under reg 29(3) (see PARA 186) for the local authority to consider compliance with all applicable statutory provisions, applies in relation to a proposed variation of an instrument of government as it applies in relation to a draft of such an instrument: reg 30(7). As to the meaning of 'statutory provision' see PARA 168 note 2.
17 School Governance (Constitution) (England) Regulations 2012, SI 2012/1034, reg 30(8).
18 School Governance (Constitution) (England) Regulations 2012, SI 2012/1034, reg 27. As to the Secretary of State see PARA 58. As to the publication of guidance see the Education Act 1996 s 571 (applied by the Education Act 2002 s 212(2), (3)); and PARA 60.

188. Copies of instruments of government and other information. The local authority[1] must ensure that the persons[2] specified below are provided (free of charge) with: (1) the school's instrument of government as varied if relevant[3]; (2) where any variation is made to the school's instrument of government[4], a copy of the instrument of government incorporating all variations (other than variations which have ceased to have effect)[5]. The persons who are to be provided with the information are:

(a)   every governor[6] and associate member[7] of the governing body[8] of the school[9];
(b)   the head teacher[10];
(c)   where the school has a foundation[11], the trustees of the foundation[12];
(d)   in the case of a Church of England school or a Roman Catholic Church school[13], the appropriate diocesan authority[14]; and
(e)   in the case of any other school designated[15] as having a religious character, the appropriate religious body[16].

1   Ie the local authority that maintains the school: see the School Governance (Constitution) (England) Regulations 2012, SI 2012/1034, reg 5(2)(b). As to the meaning of 'local authority' see PARA 25 (definition applied by the Education Act 2002 s 212(1)).
2   As to the meaning of 'person' see PARA 7 note 6.
3   School Governance (Constitution) (England) Regulations 2012, SI 2012/1034, reg 31(1)(a). As to instruments of government see PARA 184. As to the application of reg 31 with modifications, in relation to the governing body of a federation and its members see the School Governance (Federations) (England) Regulations 2012, SI 2012/1035, Sch 5 para 7. As to federations of schools see PARA 156.
4   As to variation of an instrument of government see PARA 187.
5   School Governance (Constitution) (England) Regulations 2012, SI 2012/1034, reg 31(1)(b).
6   As to the meaning of 'governor' see PARA 151 note 4.
7   As to the meaning of 'associate member' see PARA 162 note 9.
8   As to governing bodies generally see PARA 150. As to the constitution of governing bodies see PARA 151 et seq.
9   School Governance (Constitution) (England) Regulations 2012, SI 2012/1034, reg 31(2)(a).
10 School Governance (Constitution) (England) Regulations 2012, SI 2012/1034, reg 31(2)(b). As to the meaning of 'head teacher' see PARA 86 note 4 (definition applied by the Education Act 2002 s 212(2), (3); Interpretation Act 1978 s 11).
11 As to the meaning of 'foundation' and of references to a school having a foundation see PARA 108 note 6 (definition applied by the School Governance (Constitution) (England) Regulations 2012, SI 2012/1034, reg 5(2)(c)).
12 School Governance (Constitution) (England) Regulations 2012, SI 2012/1034, reg 31(2)(c).
13 'Church of England school' and 'Roman Catholic Church school' are not defined in the School Governance (Constitution) (England) Regulations 2012, SI 2012/1034, or the Education Act 2002; as to the definitions in the School Standards and Framework Act 1998 see PARA 146 note 12.
14 School Governance (Constitution) (England) Regulations 2012, SI 2012/1034, reg 31(2)(d). As to the meaning of 'appropriate diocesan authority' see PARA 146 note 12 (definition applied by reg 26).
15 Ie under the School Standards and Framework Act 1998 s 69(3): see PARA 914.
16 School Governance (Constitution) (England) Regulations 2012, SI 2012/1034, reg 31(2)(e). As to the meaning of 'appropriate religious body' see PARA 161 note 8.

(F) Reports

189. Reports on discharge of functions. The governing body of a maintained school[1] must provide the local authority[2] with such reports in connection with the discharge of its functions[3] as the authority may require (either on a regular basis or from time to time) for the purposes of the exercise of any of its education functions[4].

The head teacher[5] of a maintained school must provide the governing body or, as the case may be, the local authority with such reports in connection with the discharge of his functions as may be required (either on a regular basis or from time to time)[6] by the governing body for the purposes of the exercise of any of their functions[7], or by the authority for the purposes of the exercise of any of its education functions[8]. Where such a requirement is imposed on the head teacher by the local authority, the authority must notify the governing body of that requirement[9] and the head teacher must give the governing body a copy of any report made by him in complying with it[10].

1   As to the meaning of 'maintained school' see PARA 103 note 3. As to governing bodies of maintained schools see PARA 150 et seq.
2   As to the meaning of 'local authority' see PARA 25 (definition applied by the Education Act 2002 s 212(1)).
3   As to the meaning of 'functions' see PARA 18 note 5 (definition applied by the Education Act 2002 s 212(2), (3)).
4   Education Act 2002 s 30(3) (amended by the Education Act 2005 s 103(1)(b); SI 2010/1158). As to the meaning of 'education functions' see PARA 25 (definition applied by the Education Act 2002 s 212(2), (3)).

5   As to the meaning of 'head teacher' see PARA 86 note 4 (definition applied by the Education
    Act 2002 s 212(2), (3)).
6   Education Act 2002 s 30(4) (amended by the Education Act 2005 s 103(1)(b); and
    SI 2010/1158).
7   Education Act 2002 s 30(4)(a) (added by SI 2010/1158).
8   Education Act 2002 s 30(4)(b) (added by SI 2010/1158).
9   Education Act 2002 s 30(5)(a).
10 Education Act 2002 s 30(5)(b).

(G) Information

190.   Provision of information to the Secretary of State. The governing body[1]
or temporary governing body[2] of a community, foundation or voluntary school
or a community or foundation special school[3] must make such reports and
returns, and give such information, to the Secretary of State[4] as he may require
for the purpose of the exercise of his functions[5] in relation to education[6].

1   As to governing bodies of maintained schools see PARA 150 et seq.
2   As to temporary governing bodies see PARA 155.
3   As to the meaning of references to a community, foundation or voluntary school or a
    community or foundation special school see PARA 106 (definition applied by the School
    Standards and Framework Act 1998 s 140(2)).
4   As to the Secretary of State see PARA 58.
5   As to the meaning of 'functions' see PARA 18 note 5.
6   Education Act 1996 s 538 (amended by the School Standards and Framework Act 1998
    s 140(1), Sch 30 paras 57, 154). As to the Secretary of State's functions in relation to education
    see PARA 58 et seq. As to the application of the Education Act 1996 s 538, with modifications,
    to pupil referral units see the Education (Pupil Referral Units) (Application of Enactments)
    (England) Regulations 2007, SI 2007/2979, Sch 1 Pt 1 para 7. As to pupil referral units see PARA
    427 et seq. As to the power of the Secretary of State to direct participation in international
    surveys see the Education Act 1996 s 538A; and PARA 193.

**191.   Distribution of information about schools providing secondary
education.** Where the governing body[1] of any school[2] providing primary
education[3] receives a request which:

(1)   is made by the governing body of any school providing secondary
       education[4]; and
(2)   relates to the distribution of information about the school providing
       secondary education to parents[5] of pupils[6] at the school providing
       primary education without charge to those parents[7],

the governing body of that school must secure that the request is treated no less
favourably (whether as to services provided or as to the terms on which they are
provided) than any such request made by the governing body of any other school
providing secondary education[8].

1   As to governing bodies of maintained schools see PARA 150 et seq.
2   For these purposes, 'school' means: (1) any community, foundation or voluntary school; or (2)
    any community or foundation special school, which is not established in a hospital: Education
    Act 1996 s 540(2) (substituted by the School Standards and Framework Act 1998 s 140(1),
    Sch 30 paras 57, 156). As to the meaning of references to a community, foundation or voluntary
    school or a community or foundation special school see PARA 106 (definition applied by the
    School Standards and Framework Act 1998 s 140(2)).
3   As to the meaning of 'primary education' see PARA 20.
4   Education Act 1996 s 540(1)(a). As to the meaning of 'secondary education' see PARA 21. As to
    the power of the Secretary of State to direct participation in international surveys see s 538A;
    and PARA 193.
5   As to the meaning of 'parent' see PARA 7 note 6.
6   As to the meaning of 'pupil' see PARA 20 note 4.

7   Education Act 1996 s 540(1)(b).

8   Education Act 1996 s 540(1).

192.   Distribution of information about further education institutions. The Secretary of State[1] may by regulations[2] require:

(1)   the governing body[3] of any school[4] providing secondary education[5]; and

(2)   the proprietor[6] of any city technology college[7], city college for the technology of the arts[8] or academy[9],

to provide such persons[10] as may be prescribed[11] with certain information[12] relating to institutions within the further education sector[13] and which is made available to governing bodies and proprietors for distribution[14]. Information so provided must be provided in such form and manner as may be prescribed[15].

1   As to the Secretary of State see PARA 58.

2   Ie regulations made by the Secretary of State: Education Act 1996 s 579(1). At the date at which this volume states the law no such regulations had been made.

3   As to governing bodies of maintained schools see PARA 150 et seq.

4   For these purposes, 'school' means: (1) any community, foundation or voluntary school; or (2) any community or foundation special school, which is not established in a hospital: Education Act 1996 s 541(4) (substituted by the School Standards and Framework Act 1998 s 140(1), Sch 30 paras 57, 157). As to the meaning of references to a community, foundation or voluntary school or a community or foundation special school see PARA 106 (definition applied by the School Standards and Framework Act 1998 s 140(2)).

5   Education Act 1996 s 541(1)(a). As to the meaning of 'secondary education' see PARA 21. As to the power of the Secretary of State to direct participation in international surveys see s 538A; and PARA 193.

6   As to the meaning of 'proprietor' see PARA 51 note 4.

7   As to city technology colleges see PARA 345.

8   As to city colleges for the technology of the arts see PARA 345.

9   Education Act 1996 s 541(1)(b) (amended by the Learning and Skills Act 2000 s 149, Sch 9 paras 1, 61; and the Education Act 2002 s 65(3), Sch 7 Pt 2 para 6(1), (6)). As to the meaning of 'academy' see PARA 346.

10   As to the meaning of 'person' see PARA 7 note 6.

11   Ie prescribed by regulations: see the Education Act 1996 s 579(1). At the date at which this volume states the law no regulations had been made for this purpose.

12   Education Act 1996 s 541(1). The information to be provided is such categories of information falling within s 541(2) (see the text to notes 13–14) as may be prescribed: see s 541(1). At the date at which this volume states the law no regulations had been made for this purpose.

13   Education Act 1996 s 541(2)(a). The information concerned is that which is published under the Further and Higher Education Act 1992 s 50 (see PARA 606): see the Education Act 1996 s 541(2)(a). As to further education see PARA 555 et seq.

14   Education Act 1996 s 541(2)(b).

15   Education Act 1996 s 541(3). At the date at which this volume states the law no regulations had been made for this purpose.

193.   Power to direct participation in international surveys. The Secretary of State[1] may direct the governing body[2] of a community, foundation or voluntary school[3] in England[4] to secure that the school participates in such international education surveys as may be specified in the direction[5].

1   As to the Secretary of State see PARA 58.

2   As to governing bodies of maintained schools see PARA 150 et seq.

3   As to the meaning of references to a community, foundation or voluntary school see PARA 106.

4   As to the meaning of 'England' see PARA 7 note 3.

5   Education Act 1996 s 538A (added by the Education Act 2011 s 20).

(H) Ex Officio Trustees

194. Governors of foundation or voluntary school as ex officio trustees. Where any provision of a trust deed[1] or other instrument made before 1 July 1981 would otherwise have the effect that the persons who are for the time being governors of a foundation or voluntary school[2] were by virtue of their office trustees of any property held for the purposes of, or in connection with, the school[3], that provision instead has effect as if the only governors of the school were: (1) the foundation governors[4]; (2) those appointed by the local authority[5]; and (3) any co-opted governor nominated by a minor authority[6].

1   As to the meaning of 'trust deed' see PARA 108 note 6 (definition applied by the School Standards and Framework Act 1998 s 142(8)).
2   As to foundation and voluntary schools see PARA 106.
3   As to the meaning of 'land or other property held on trust, or by trustees, for the purposes of a school' see PARA 108 note 6.
4   School Standards and Framework Act 1998 s 83(1)(a). As to the meaning of 'foundation governor' see PARA 108 note 6.
5   School Standards and Framework Act 1998 s 83(1)(b) (amended by SI 2010/1158). As to the meaning of 'local authority' see PARA 25 (definition applied by the School Standards and Framework Act 1998 s 142(8)).
6   School Standards and Framework Act 1998 s 83(1)(c). Section 83(1) is without prejudice to any power to amend any such provision as is mentioned in s 83(1): s 83(2). For the purposes of the School Standards and Framework Act 1998, a maintained school serves an area for which there are one or more minor authorities if the area served by the school is:
    (1)   a parish or, in Wales, a community (s 141(1)(a));
    (2)   an area in England which is not within a parish and is not situated in: (a) a county for which there is no council; or (b) a county in which there are no district councils (s 141(1)(b)); or
    (3)   an area comprising two or more areas each of which falls within head (1) or head (2) (s 141(1)(c)).
    Where the area served by the school is a parish, the parish council (if there is one) or the parish meeting (if there is no parish council) is the minor authority in relation to the school: s 141(2). Where the area served by the school is a community, the community council is the minor authority in relation to the school: s 141(3). Where the area served by the school is an area falling within head (2) above, any district council for the whole or part of the area is a minor authority in relation to the school: s 141(4). Where the area served by the school is an area falling within head (3) above, each of the relevant authorities is a minor authority in relation to the school: s 141(5). 'The relevant authorities' means the bodies which, if the two or more constituent areas referred to in head (3) above were taken separately, would be minor authorities in relation to the school: s 141(6). References in s 141 to the area served by a school are references to the area appearing to the local authority to be served by the school: s 141(7) (amended by SI 2010/1158). As to the meaning of 'maintained school' see PARA 99. As to the meanings of 'England' and 'Wales' see PARA 7 note 3. As to parish councils in England see LOCAL GOVERNMENT vol 69 (2009) PARA 27 et seq. As to community councils in Wales see LOCAL GOVERNMENT vol 69 (2009) PARA 41 et seq. As to local government areas and authorities in England and Wales see LOCAL GOVERNMENT vol 69 (2009) PARA 22 et seq.

B. GOVERNANCE OF MAINTAINED SCHOOLS IN WALES

(A) Constitution of Governing Bodies

195. Governing bodies. Each maintained school in Wales[1] must have a governing body[2], which is a body corporate[3] constituted in accordance with regulations[4]. Regulations[5] must provide for a governing body of a maintained school in Wales to consist of:
   (1)   persons elected or appointed as parent governors[6];
   (2)   persons elected or appointed as staff governors[7];
   (3)   persons appointed as local authority governors[8];

(4)   except in the case of a voluntary aided school[9], persons appointed as community governors[10];

(5)   in the case of a foundation school[11] or a voluntary school, persons appointed as foundation governors or partnership governors[12]; and

(6)   such other persons as may be prescribed[13].

Regulations[14] may also make provision as to:

(a)   the number of governors, or of governors falling within any category[15];

(b)   the person[16] or persons by whom, and the manner in which, governors are to be elected or appointed[17];

(c)   eligibility for election or appointment as governors of any category, or for voting in an election of such governors[18];

(d)   the term of office of governors[19];

(e)   resignation or removal from office of governors[20];

(f)   the payment of allowances to governors[21];

(g)   meetings and proceedings of governing bodies[22];

(h)   the election by the governors of a chairman and vice-chairman of the governing body[23];

(i)   the establishment by a governing body of committees[24];

(j)   the appointment of persons other than governors to serve on committees of governing bodies[25];

(k)   the delegation of functions[26] by governing bodies[27]; and

(l)   other matters relating to the constitution or procedure of governing bodies[28].

In discharging any function conferred by such regulations, a local authority[29] or the governing body of a maintained school must have regard to any guidance given from time to time by the Welsh Ministers[30].

The governing body[31] is to be known as 'The governing body of ...' with the addition of the name of the school as for the time being set out in the school's instrument of government[32].

If the school is discontinued, the governing body is dissolved[33] on the discontinuance date[34], or on such later date as the Welsh Ministers may specify by order[35] made before the discontinuance date[36].

1   As to the meaning of 'maintained school' see PARA 103 note 3. As to the meaning of 'Wales' see PARA 7 note 3. As to the governance of schools in England see PARA 150 et seq.

2   The governing body of a maintained school is a public authority for the purposes of the Human Rights Act 1998: see *A v Head Teacher and Governors of Lord Grey School* [2006] UKHL 14, [2006] 2 AC 363, sub nom *Ali v Head Teacher and Governors of Lord Grey School* [2006] 2 All ER 457, at [79] per Baroness Hale of Richmond. As to public authorities for the purposes of the Human Rights Act 1998 see JUDICIAL REVIEW vol 61 (2010) PARA 605.

3   As to bodies corporate see COMPANIES vol 14 (2009) PARA 2; CORPORATIONS vol 24 (2010) PARA 301 et seq.

4   Education Act 2002 s 19(1). In relation to maintained schools in Wales, s 19(1) has effect subject to the Education (Wales) Measure 2011 Pt 2 Ch 1 (ss 10–21) (federations of schools: see PARA 198); and regulations under the Education Act 2002 s 19 may include provision with respect to the governing bodies of federations (within the meaning of the Education (Wales) Measure 2011 s 21(1) (see PARA 198): Education Act 2002 s 19(9) (added by the Education (Wales) Measure 2011 s 19(1),(2)(b)). Regulations made under the Education Act 2002 s 19 do not apply to any temporary governing body: see s 34(8); and PARA 197. 'Regulations' means regulations made under the Education Act 2002 by the Welsh Ministers: see s 212(1). The functions under s 19 and Sch 1 were originally vested in the National Assembly for Wales and are now exercisable by the Welsh Ministers by virtue of the Government of Wales Act 2006 s 162(1), Sch 11 paras 30, 32. As to the Welsh Ministers see PARA 59. As to the regulations made under the Education Act 2002 s 19 see notes 5, 13, 14.

5   As to the regulations made under the Education Act 2002 s 19(2) see the Government of Maintained Schools (Wales) Regulations 2005, SI 2005/2914 and below (and see also PARAS

200, 214, 217). As to the constitution of governing bodies of community schools see regs 7, 13 (respectively substituted and amended by SI 2010/1142). As to the constitution of governing bodies of maintained nursery schools see the Government of Maintained Schools (Wales) Regulations 2005, SI 2005/2914, reg 14 (amended by SI 2010/1142). As to the constitution of governing bodies of community special schools see the Government of Maintained Schools (Wales) Regulations 2005, SI 2005/2914, regs 12, 15 (amended by SI 2010/1142). As to the constitution of governing bodies of foundation schools see the Government of Maintained Schools (Wales) Regulations 2005, SI 2005/2914, regs 10, 16 (both amended by SI 2010/1142). As to the constitution of governing bodies of foundation special schools see the Government of Maintained Schools (Wales) Regulations 2005, SI 2005/2914, reg 17 (amended by SI 2011/1142). As to the constitution of governing bodies of voluntary controlled schools see the Government of Maintained Schools (Wales) Regulations 2005, SI 2005/2914, reg 18 (amended by SI 2011/1142). As to the constitution of governing bodies of voluntary aided schools see the Government of Maintained Schools (Wales) Regulations 2005, SI 2005/2914, reg 19 (amended by SI 2010/1142). As to additional governors for maintained primary schools and nursery schools see the Government of Maintained Schools (Wales) Regulations 2005, SI 2005/2914, reg 20. As to the notification of vacancies and appointments see reg 21 (amended by SI 2010/1142). As to joint appointments see the Government of Maintained Schools (Wales) Regulations 2005, SI 2005/2914, reg 22. As to adjustments in numbers of governors see reg 23.

See also the School Councils (Wales) Regulations 2005, SI 2005/3200; the School Governance (Transition from an Interim Executive Board) (Wales) Regulations 2012, SI 2012/1643; the Government of Maintained Schools (Training Requirements for Governors) (Wales) Regulations 2013, SI 2013/2124 (amended by SI 2014/2225); and the Federation of Maintained Schools (Wales) Regulations 2014, SI 2014/1132.

6   Education Act 2002 s 19(2)(a) (s 19(2) amended by the Education Act 2011 s 38(1), (3)).

7   Education Act 2002 s 19(2)(b).

8   Education Act 2002 s 19(2)(c) (amended by SI 2010/1158). As to the meaning of 'local authority' see PARA 25 (definition applied by the Education Act 2002 s 212(1) (amended by SI 2010/1158)).

9   As to the meaning of references to a voluntary school see PARA 106.

10 Education Act 2002 s 19(2)(d).

11 As to the meaning of references to a foundation school see PARA 106.

12 Education Act 2002 s 19(2)(e) (amended by the School Standards and Organisation (Wales) Act 2013 Sch 5 para 21(1), (2)).

13 Education Act 2002 s 19(2)(f). 'Prescribed' means prescribed by regulations: see s 212(1). The head teacher of a school must ensure that the school council (see PARA 203 note 10) has the opportunity to nominate up to two pupils from years 11 to 13 (inclusive) from its membership to be associate pupil governors on the school's governing body (School Councils (Wales) Regulations 2005, SI 2005/3200, reg 7(1)); and the governing body must accept any pupil so nominated, and appoint him as an associate pupil governor on the governing body, provided the pupil is not disqualified from membership in accordance with the Government of Maintained Schools (Wales) Regulations 2005, SI 2005/2914, Sch 5 (see PARA 200) (School Councils (Wales) Regulations 2005, SI 2005/3200, reg 7(2)). Regulation 7 does not apply to community special schools or to foundation special schools: reg 5. As to the meaning of references to a community or foundation special school see PARA 106. As to the meaning of 'head teacher' see PARA 86 note 4; and as to the meaning of 'pupil' see PARA 20 note 4 (definitions applied by the Education Act 2002 s 212(2), (3); Interpretation Act 1978 s 11). The maximum number of associate pupil governors on any governing body is two: Government of Maintained Schools (Wales) Regulations 2005, SI 2005/2914, reg 12A(2) (reg 12A added by SI 2005/3200). For the purposes of the Government of Maintained Schools (Wales) Regulations 2005, SI 2005/2914, 'associate pupil governor' means a registered pupil nominated by the school council to be a member of the governing body and appointed as such by the governing body in accordance with the School Councils (Wales) Regulations 2005, SI 2005/3200, reg 7: Government of Maintained Schools (Wales) Regulations 2005, SI 2005/2914, reg 12A(1) (as so added). Any associate pupil governor is in addition to the numbers of governors set out in regs 13–20: reg 20A (added by SI 2005/3200). As to the meaning of 'registered pupil' see PARA 437 (definition applied by the Education Act 2002 s 212(2), (3); Interpretation Act 1978 s 11).

14 As to the regulations made under the Education Act 2002 s 19(3) see the Government of Maintained Schools (Wales) Regulations 2005, SI 2005/2914; and note 5; and PARAS 200, 214, 217. See also the School Councils (Wales) Regulations 2005, SI 2005/3200; the Governor Allowance (Wales) Regulations 2005, SI 2005/2915; the Staffing of Maintained Schools (Wales) Regulations 2006, SI 2006/873 (amended by SI 2007/944; SI 2009/2544; SI 2009/2708; and SI 2014/1609); the Collaboration Between Education Bodies (Wales) Regulations 2012,

SI 2012/2655; the School Governance (Transition from an Interim Executive Board) (Wales) Regulations 2012, SI 2012/1643; the Government of Maintained Schools (Training Requirements for Governors) (Wales) Regulations 2013, SI 2013/2124 (amended by SI 2014/2225); and the Federation of Maintained Schools (Wales) Regulations 2014, SI 2014/1132.

15 Education Act 2002 s 19(3)(a). Regulations made by virtue of s 19(3)(a) must also secure that the majority of the governors of a voluntary aided school are persons appointed as foundation governors: s 19(4).

16 As to the meaning of 'person' see PARA 7 note 6.

17 Education Act 2002 s 19(3)(b).

18 Education Act 2002 s 19(3)(c).

19 Education Act 2002 s 19(3)(d).

20 Education Act 2002 s 19(3)(e).

21 Education Act 2002 s 19(3)(f). Nothing in the School Standards and Framework Act 1998 s 50(3) (effect of financial delegation) is to be read as authorising the payment of allowances to governors otherwise than in accordance with regulations under the Education Act 2002 s 19: see the School Standards and Framework Act 1998 s 50(5); and PARA 324.

22 Education Act 2002 s 19(3)(g).

23 Education Act 2002 s 19(3)(h).

24 Education Act 2002 s 19(3)(i).

25 Education Act 2002 s 19(3)(j).

26 As to the meaning of 'functions' see PARA 18 note 5 (definition applied by the Education Act 2002 s 212(2), (3); Interpretation Act 1978 s 11).

27 Education Act 2002 s 19(3)(k). Section 19(3)(k) has effect subject to the provisions of any scheme under the School Standards and Framework Act 1998 s 48 (local authorities' financial schemes: see PARA 321) which relates to the school: Education Act 2002 s 19(5).

28 Education Act 2002 s 19(3)(l).

29 As to the meaning of 'local authority' see PARA 25 (definition applied by the Education Act 2002 s 212(1)).

30 Education Act 2002 s 19(7) (amended by SI 2010/1158). As to the publication of guidance see the Education Act 1996 s 571 (applied by the Education Act 2002 s 212(2), (3)); and PARA 60.

31 Ie the governing body of a maintained school incorporated under the Education Act 2002 s 19(1) (see the text to notes 1–4): Sch 1 para 1.

32 Education Act 2002 Sch 1 para 2(1). As to instruments of government see PARA 217 et seq.

33 Ie by virtue of the Education Act 2002 Sch 1 para 5.

34 Education Act 2002 Sch 1 para 5(1)(a). 'The discontinuance date' means in relation to a school in Wales, whichever of the following is relevant: (1) the date on which proposals for discontinuing the school are implemented under the School Standards and Organisation (Wales) Act 2013 Pt 3 (ss 38–56) (see PARA 139 et seq); (2) the date on which the school is discontinued under s 80 (see PARA 140); or (3) the date specified in a direction given under s 16(2) or s 81(1) (see PARA 140): Education Act 2002 Sch 1 para 5(2)(b) (substituted by the Education and Inspections Act 2006 s 30, Sch 3 para 48; and amended by the School Standards and Organisation (Wales) Act 2013 Sch 5 para 21(1), (11)).

35 Orders made under the Education Act 2002 Sch 1 para 5 are not made by statutory instrument (see s 210(2)) and, as such, are not recorded in this work.

36 See the Education Act 2002 Sch 1 para 5(1)(b).

196. Powers where there is no properly constituted governing body. Where it appears to the Welsh Ministers[1] that, by reason of the default of any person[2], there is no properly constituted governing body[3] of any community, foundation or voluntary school or any community or foundation special school[4], they may make such appointments and give such directions[5] as they think desirable for the purpose of securing that there is a properly constituted governing body of that school[6]. The Welsh Ministers may also give directions rendering valid any acts or proceedings which in their opinion are invalid or otherwise defective by reason of the default[7].

1 The functions of the Secretary of State under the Education Act 1996 s 498, so far as exercisable in relation to Wales, were transferred to the National Assembly for Wales (see the National Assembly for Wales (Transfer of Functions) Order 1999, SI 1999/672, art 2, Sch 1) and are now

vested in the Welsh Ministers (see the Government of Wales Act 2006 s 162(1), Sch 11 para 30). As to the Welsh Ministers see PARA 59. As to the meaning of 'Wales' see PARA 7 note 3.

2 As to the meaning of 'person' see PARA 7 note 6.
3 As to governing bodies of maintained schools in Wales see PARA 195.
4 As to the meaning of references to a community, foundation or voluntary school or a community or foundation special school see PARA 106.
5 As to directions see PARA 75.
6 Education Act 1996 s 498(1)(a), (2) (s 498(2) substituted by the School Standards and Framework Act 1998 s 140(1), Sch 30 para 131).
7 Education Act 1996 s 498(1)(b).

197. Arrangements for government of new schools. Where proposals for the establishment of a maintained school[1] fall to be implemented under any enactment[2], the local authority[3] must make arrangements providing for the constitution of a temporary governing body for the school[4]. Once constituted[5], the temporary governing body continues in existence until such time as the governing body is constituted for the school under an instrument of government[6]. The local authority must secure that the governing body is so constituted before such date as may be determined in accordance with regulations[7].

The temporary governing body of a school must be treated for the purposes of the Education Acts[8] as if it were the governing body during the period beginning with the school opening date[9] and ending with the time when the governing body is constituted for the school under an instrument of government[10].

Regulations[11] may make provision with respect to:

(1) the making and termination of arrangements for the constitution of temporary governing bodies[12];

(2) the constitution, meetings and proceedings of temporary governing bodies, the payment of allowances to temporary governors[13], and the appointment of clerks to such bodies[14];

(3) the exercise by a temporary governing body before the school opening date of the power[15] to provide community facilities[16];

(4) the transition from a temporary governing body to a governing body constituted under an instrument of government[17]; and

(5) such other matters relating to temporary governing bodies as the Welsh Ministers consider appropriate[18].

1 As to the meaning of 'maintained school' see PARA 103 note 3.
2 As to the meaning of 'enactment' see PARA 1 note 13.
3 As to the meaning of 'local authority' see PARA 25 (definition applied by the Education Act 2002 s 212(1)).
4 Education Act 2002 s 34(1) (amended by SI 2010/1158). As to governing bodies of maintained schools in Wales see PARA 195.
     Regulations made by the Welsh Ministers may make provision for:
     (1) the staffing and conduct of a new school in advance of the school opening date (School Standards and Framework Act 1998 s 72(1)(a));
     (2) the determination of matters in connection with a new school in advance of that date (s 72(1)(b));
     (3) the taking of decisions by a temporary governing body, or (where power to do so is delegated to him) by the head teacher, as to expenditure in connection with a new school at a time when it does not have a delegated budget (s 72(1)(c));
     (4) such other matters relating to new schools as the Welsh Ministers consider appropriate (s 72(1)(d)).
     As to the meaning of 'new school' for these purposes see PARA 155 note 4. As to the meaning of 'school' for these purposes see PARA 91 (definition applied by s 142(8)). See also PARA 111. As to the meaning of 'head teacher' see PARA 86 note 4 (definition applied by s 142(8)). As to delegated budgets see PARA 323 et seq.

The functions of the Secretary of State under s 72, so far as exercisable in relation to Wales, were transferred to the National Assembly for Wales (see the National Assembly for Wales (Transfer of Functions) Order 1999, SI 1999/672, art 2, Sch 1) and are now vested in the Welsh Ministers (see the Government of Wales Act 2006 s 162(1), Sch 11 para 30). As to the Secretary of State see PARA 58. As to the Welsh Ministers see PARA 59. As to the meaning of 'Wales' see PARA 7 note 3.

The regulations may, in connection with any matters falling within heads (1)–(4) above, apply any provision of the Education Acts with or without modification: School Standards and Framework Act 1998 s 72(2). As to the meaning of 'the Education Acts' see PARA 1 note 13 (definition applied by the School Standards and Framework Act 1998 s 142(8)). As to the meaning of 'modification' see PARA 21 note 15 (definition applied by s 142(8)).

As to the regulations made see the Education (New Schools) (Wales) Regulations 1999, SI 1999/2243 (amended by SI 2005/2914; and partially revoked by SI 2005/2912; and SI 2006/873); the New Maintained Schools (Wales) Regulations 2005, SI 2005/2912; the New School (Admissions) (Wales) Regulations 2006, SI 2006/175; and the Staffing of Maintained Schools (Wales) Regulations 2006, SI 2006/873 (amended by SI 2007/944; SI 2009/2544; and SI 2009/2708).

5   Ie in accordance with arrangements made under the Education Act 2002 s 34(1): see the text to notes 1–4.

6   Education Act 2002 s 34(2). The requirement for there to be an instrument of government for a school, imposed by s 20 (see PARA 217), takes effect in relation to a school falling within s 34(1) (see the text to notes 1–4) as from the date determined under s 34(3) (see the text to note 7): s 34(4). As to instruments of government see PARA 217 et seq.

7   Education Act 2002 s 34(3) (amended by SI 2010/1158). 'Regulations' means regulations made under the Education Act 2002 by the Welsh Ministers: s 212(1). At the date at which this volume states the law no such regulations had been made. The functions under s 34 were originally vested in the National Assembly for Wales and are now exercisable by the Welsh Ministers by virtue of the Government of Wales Act 2006 s 162(1), Sch 11 paras 30, 32.

8   As to the meaning of 'the Education Acts' see PARA 1 note 13 (definition applied by the Education Act 2002 s 212(2), (3)).

9   'School opening date', in relation to a new maintained school, means the date when the school first admits pupils: Education Act 2002 s 34(9). As to the meaning of 'pupil' see PARA 20 note 4 (definition applied by s 212(2), (3)).

10 Education Act 2002 s 34(7). For the purposes of s 30(3) (see PARA 218) and the Education Act 1996 ss 495–498 (general default powers: see PARAS 62 et seq, 196) and the School Standards and Organisation (Wales) Act 2013 Pt 2 Ch 1 (ss 2–20) (intervention in conduct of maintained schools in Wales: see PARA 1229 et seq), the temporary governing body of a school is also so treated at any time falling before the school opening date: Education Act 2002 s 34(7) (amended by the School Standards and Organisation (Wales) Act 2013 Sch 5 par 6(1), (2)). Despite the Education Act 2002 s 34(7), nothing in any of the following provisions, namely: (1) s 20(1) (see PARA 217); (2) (subject to any regulations made under s 34(5): see the text to notes 11–18) Sch 1 (see PARA 195); or (3) (subject to any regulations made under s 34(5)) regulations made under s 19 (see PARA 195), s 20 (see PARA 217) or s 23 (see PARA 202), applies to any temporary governing body: s 34(8).

11 Regulations made under the Education Act 2002 s 34(5) may, in connection with any matters falling within s 34(5): (1) modify any provision made under any of s 19 (see PARA 195), s 20 (see PARA 217) or s 23 (see PARA 202) or by Sch 1 (see PARA 195) (s 34(6)(a)); (2) apply any such provision with or without modifications (s 34(6)(b)); (3) make provision corresponding or similar to any such provision (s 34(6)(c)). As to the meanings of 'modify' and 'modifications' see PARA 21 note 15 (definition applied by s 212(2), (3)). As to the regulations made under s 34(5), (6) in relation to Wales see the New Maintained Schools (Wales) Regulations 2005, SI 2005/2912; the Governor Allowance (Wales) Regulations 2005, SI 2005/2915; the Staffing of Maintained Schools (Wales) Regulations 2006, SI 2006/873 (amended by SI 2007/944; SI 2009/2544; SI 2009/2708; and SI 2014/1609); and the Federation of Maintained Schools (Wales) Regulations 2014, SI 2014/1132. As to the application of the Staffing of Maintained Schools (Wales) Regulations 2006, SI 2006/873, with modifications, in relation to pupil referral units in Wales see the Education (Pupil Referral Units) (Application of Enactments) (Wales) Regulations 2007, SI 2007/1069, Sch 1 para 14 (amended by SI 2014/1609). As to pupil referral units see PARA 427 et seq.

12 Education Act 2002 s 34(5)(a). The arrangements mentioned in the text include such arrangements made in anticipation of proposals falling to be implemented as mentioned in s 34(1) (see the text to notes 1–4): s 34(5)(a).

13 In the case of temporary governors of a new school, nothing in the School Standards and Framework Act 1998 s 50(3) (effect of financial delegation) is to be read as authorising the payment of allowances to governors otherwise than in accordance with regulations under the Education Act 2002 s 34(5): see the School Standards and Framework Act 1998 s 50(5); and PARA 324.

14 Education Act 2002 s 34(5)(b).

15 Ie the power conferred by the Education Act 2002 s 27: see PARA 208.

16 Education Act 2002 s 34(5)(c).

17 Education Act 2002 s 34(5)(d).

18 Education Act 2002 s 34(5)(e).

198. Federations of schools. A local authority[1] may make proposals[2] for the federation[3] of two or more maintained schools[4], an existing federation and one or more maintained schools, or two or more existing federations[5]. A local authority must publish such proposals and, in accordance with regulations[6], consult the governing bodies of the schools or federations to be federated, the staff of the schools, one or more bodies, if any, appearing to the authority to represent the interests of the staff of the schools, and, in so far as is practicable, registered pupils at the schools and their parents, on the published proposals[7].

A local authority must, in accordance with regulations, determine whether to confirm proposals, with or without modification or subject to the occurrence of an event, or withdraw them[8]. A local authority may make proposals for a federation that includes a maintained school that it does not maintain only if the local authority that maintains the school gives its consent[9]. A local authority may make proposals for a federation that includes a foundation or voluntary school only if the following persons give their consent (1) in the case of a Church in Wales school or a Roman Catholic Church school, the appropriate diocesan authority; and (2) in the case of any other foundation or voluntary school, the person or persons by whom the foundation governors are appointed[10]. Regulations may make further provision about proposals[11] and may, among other things, make provision about (a) obtaining consent from prescribed persons to the making, publication or confirmation of proposals; (b) the information to be included in, or provided in relation to, the proposals; (c) the publication of proposals; (d) consultation on the proposals; (e) the making of objections to or comments on the proposals; (f) withdrawal or modification of the proposals; (g) confirmation of the proposals by the local authority[12].

1 'Local authority' means a local authority in Wales: Education (Wales) Measure 2011 s 21(1). As to the meaning of 'Wales' see PARA 7 note 3. As to local authorities generally see PARA 25 et seq.

2 As to the implementation of proposals under the Education (Wales) Measure 2011 s 11 see s 12.

3 'Federation' means a group of schools in Wales that are federated by virtue of the Education (Wales) Measure 2011 Pt 2 Ch 1 (ss 10–21) or were federated by virtue of the Education Act 2002 s 24 (see PARA 156) before the coming into force of the Education (Wales) Measure 2011 Pt 2 Ch 1, and 'federated school' means a school forming part of a federation: s 21(1). The Education Act 2002 ss 24, 25 (see PARA 156) are replaced in relation to Wales by the Education (Wales) Measure 2011 Pt 2 Ch 1 (see s 19(4), (5)). As to equivalent provision made in relation to the federation of schools in Wales and regulations in relation to federations see now the Education (Wales) Measure 2011 ss 10, 11, 12. 13, 14 (s 13 amended by the School Standards and Organisation (Wales) Act 2013 Sch 5 para 29(1), (3)) and the Federation of Maintained Schools (Wales) Regulations 2014, SI 2014/1132. See also the Education (Wales) Measure 2011 s 15, 17, 18 (s 18 amended by the School Standards and Organisation (Wales) Act 2013 Sch 5 para 13(1), (3)).

4 For these purposes, 'maintained school' means a school in Wales which is a community, foundation or voluntary school, a community special school or a maintained nursery school: Education (Wales) Measure 2011 s 21(1) (definition amended by the School Standards and Organisation (Wales) Act 2013 Sch 5 para 29(1), (5)). As to references to categories of maintained schools generally see PARA 106.

5 See the Education (Wales) Measure 2011 s 11(1).

6 As to regulations see note 4.

7 See the Education (Wales) Measure 2011 s 11(2), (3). Section 11(2), (3) does not apply in relation to a proposal for a federation consisting only of small schools and, in relation to a proposal for a federation consisting only of small schools, the local authority must, in accordance with regulations, consult the governing bodies of the schools concerned: s 11(4), (5). A 'small school' means a maintained school that, on the date that the proposal is made, is a small maintained school as defined in an order under s 15: s 11(6).

8 See the Education (Wales) Measure 2011 s 11(7).

9 See the Education (Wales) Measure 2011 s 11(8).

10 See the Education (Wales) Measure 2011 s 11(9).

11 Ie proposals under the Education (Wales) Measure 2011 s 11.

12 See the Education (Wales) Measure 2011 s 11(10).

199.   Collaboration between schools. An education body[1] must consider from time to time whether the exercise of its powers of collaboration[2] would further the collaboration objective[3] in the exercise of its other functions, and, if an education body concludes that it would do so, it must seek to exercise, or cause to be exercised, the power[4].

An education body has, for the purpose of discharging or facilitating the discharge of its duty[5], the powers (1) to provide financial assistance, whether by way of grant or loan, to any person; (2) to enter into arrangements or agreements with any person; (3) to co-operate with, or facilitate or co-ordinate the activities of, that person; (4) to exercise on behalf of any person any functions of that person, whether alone or jointly; (5) to make arrangements for any of the education body's functions to be carried out with one or more other education bodies, or by one or more other education bodies; (6) to make arrangements for any of the education body's functions to be carried out by joint committees of two or more education bodies; (7) to provide staff, goods, services or accommodation to any person; and (8) to share and use information for the purpose of exercising any powers of collaboration[6]. These powers are without prejudice to any other powers of an education body, and subject to provision made by way of regulations about the power to collaborate[7].

1 'Education body' means (1) a local authority in Wales; (2) the governing body of a maintained school in Wales; (3) a further education corporation, as defined by the Further and Higher Education Act 1992 s 17(1) (see PARA 555), in Wales; and (4) the governing body of a designated institution, as defined by s 28(4) (see PARA 573), in Wales, which is a body incorporated by virtue of the Learning and Skills Act 2000 s 143(5) (see PARA 575), and is exclusively or mainly providing full-time education for persons who are above compulsory school age but who have not attained the age of 19: Education (Wales) Measure 2011 s 1. For these purposes, 'maintained school' means a community, foundation or voluntary school, a community special school, a maintained nursery school or a pupil referral unit: Education (Wales) Measure 2011 s 8 (amended by the School Standards and Organisation (Wales) Act 2013 Sch 5 para 29(1), (2)). As to the meaning of 'Wales' see PARA 7 note 3. As to references to categories of maintained schools generally see PARA 106. The Education Act 2002 s 26 (see PARA 157) is replaced in relation to Wales by the Education (Wales) Measure 2011 Pt 1 (ss 1–9) (see s 9(3)(a)).

2 'Powers of collaboration' mean (1) the powers in the Education (Wales) Measure 2011 s 5 (see the text to notes 5–7); and (2) in the case of a local authority (a) its power to authorise a person, or the person's employees, to exercise a function on the authority's behalf under an order made under the Deregulation and Contracting Out Act 1994 s 70 (see LOCAL GOVERNMENT vol 69 (2009) PARA 407); (b) its power under the Local Government Act 1972 s 101(1)(b), (5) (see LOCAL GOVERNMENT vol 69 (2009) PARAS 370, 380); (c) a power of the executive of the authority, or a committee or specified member of the executive, to make arrangements for the discharge of their functions under regulations made under the Local Government Act 2000 s 19(1) (see LOCAL GOVERNMENT vol 69 (2009) PARA 361); and (d) a power of the authority to

make arrangements for the discharge of its functions under regulations made under the Local Government Act 2000 s 19(2) (see LOCAL GOVERNMENT vol 69 (2009) PARA 361): Education (Wales) Measure 2011 s 4.

3 The 'collaboration objective' is the effective and efficient use of public resources by an education body in respect of the provision of education and training suitable to the requirements of persons who have not attained the age of 19: Education (Wales) Measure 2011 s 2.

4 See the Education (Wales) Measure 2011 s 3(1), (2). The duty in the Education (Wales) Measure 2011 s 3(1) applies to the bodies mentioned in s 1(c), (d) (see note 1 heads (3), (4)) in so far as it relates to the provision of secondary and further education suitable to the requirements of persons who have not attained the age of 19: see s 3(3). Further, the duty in s 3(1) is without prejudice to the duties in the Learning and Skills Act 2000 s 33K (see PARA 900), the Education Act 2002 s 116J (see PARA 892) and the Local Government (Wales) Measure 2009 s 12 (see LOCAL GOVERNMENT vol 69 (2009) PARA 715): see the Education (Wales) Measure 2011 s 3(4).

5 Ie its duty under the Education (Wales) Measure 2011 s 3, the Learning and Skills Act 2000 s 33K (see PARA 900), the Education Act 2002 s 116J (see PARA 892), or the duty of another education body under those provisions.

6 See the Education (Wales) Measure 2011 s 5(1), (2).

7 See the Education (Wales) Measure 2011 s 5(3). As to the power of the Welsh Ministers to make provision by way of regulations about the power to collaborate see the Education (Wales) Measure 2011 s 6. As to regulations made see the Collaboration Between Education Bodies (Wales) Regulations 2012, SI 2012/2655; and the Federation of Maintained Schools (Wales) Regulations 2014, SI 2014/1132. In exercising its functions, an education body must have regard to guidance given from time to time by the Education (Wales) Measure 2011 s 7.

(B) The Governors and Clerk

200. Election and appointment etc of governors. The appropriate authority[1] must make all the necessary arrangements for the election of parent governors[2].

There are also provisions for the election of teacher governors and staff governors[3], the appointment of partnership governors[4], the appointment of sponsor governors[5], qualifications and disqualifications[6], tenure of office[7], removal of governors[8], and governors' allowances[9].

1 'Appropriate authority' means: (1) in relation to a community school, a community special school, a maintained nursery school or a voluntary controlled school, the local authority (Government of Maintained Schools (Wales) Regulations 2005, SI 2005/2914, Sch 1 para 1(a) (amended by SI 2010/1142)); (2) in relation to a voluntary aided school, foundation school or foundation special school, the governing body (Government of Maintained Schools (Wales) Regulations 2005, SI 2005/2914, Sch 1 para 1(b)). Where a local authority is the appropriate authority in relation to a school, that authority may delegate to the head teacher of the school any of its functions under Sch 1: Sch 1 para 2 (amended by SI 2010/1142). The local authority is the appropriate authority in relation to a school within head (2) above if the governing body and the local authority so agree: Government of Maintained Schools (Wales) Regulations 2005, SI 2005/2914, Sch 1 para 3 (amended by SI 2010/1142). As to the meaning of references to a community, foundation or voluntary school or a community or foundation special school see PARA 106. As to the meaning of 'maintained nursery school' see PARA 103 note 3. Any reference to the local authority is a reference to the local authority that maintains the school: Government of Maintained Schools (Wales) Regulations 2005, SI 2005/2914, reg 3(2)(c). As to the meaning of 'local authority' see PARA 25 (definition applied by the Education Act 2002 s 212(1); Interpretation Act 1978 s 11). As to governing bodies see PARA 195. As to the meaning of 'head teacher' see PARA 86 note 4; and as to the meaning of 'functions' see PARA 18 note 5 (definitions applied by the Education Act 2002 s 212(2), (3); Interpretation Act 1978 s 11).

2 See generally the Government of Maintained Schools (Wales) Regulations 2005, SI 2005/2914, reg 4, Sch 1 (both amended by SI 2010/1142).

3 See the Government of Maintained Schools (Wales) Regulations 2005, SI 2005/2914, regs 5, 6, Sch 2 (amended by SI 2010/1142).

4 See the Government of Maintained Schools (Wales) Regulations 2005, SI 2005/2914, reg 10, Sch 3 (both amended by SI 2010/1142).

5 See the Government of Maintained Schools (Wales) Regulations 2005, SI 2005/2914, reg 11, Sch 4.

6   See the Government of Maintained Schools (Wales) Regulations 2005, SI 2005/2914, reg 24,
    Sch 5 (amended by SI 2005/3200; SI 2009/2544; SI 2010/638; SI 2010/2582; and
    SI 2013/2124).
7   See the Government of Maintained Schools (Wales) Regulations 2005, SI 2005/2914, regs 25,
    26, 49 (reg 25 amended by SI 2005/3200).
8   See the Government of Maintained Schools (Wales) Regulations 2005, SI 2005/2914, regs 27–30
    (reg 27 amended by SI 2010/1142; and the Government of Maintained Schools (Wales)
    Regulations 2005, SI 2005/2914, reg 29 substituted by SI 2005/3200).
9   Government of Maintained Schools (Wales) Regulations 2005, SI 2005/2914, regs 4–7 (regs 5, 6
    amended by SI 2010/1142).

201.   Training and support of governors. Similar provision is made for Wales[1]
as for England[2] in regard to information and training for governors of
maintained schools[3].

1   As to the meaning of 'Wales' see PARA 7 note 3.
2   As to the meaning of 'England' see PARA 7 note 3. See the Education Act 2002 s 22; and PARA
    166.
3   See the Education (Wales) Measure 2011 s 22(1)–(7). The Education Act 2002 s 22 now applies
    in relation to England only (see PARA 166) as a result of the Education (Wales) Measure 2011
    s 22(8). See also the Government of Maintained Schools (Training Requirements for Governors)
    (Wales) Regulations 2013, SI 2013/2124 (amended by SI 2014/2225), made under the Education
    (Wales) Measure 2011 s 22(3), (4).

202.   Appointment etc of clerk. Regulations[1] may make provision:
   (1)   requiring the appointment of a clerk to the governing body of a
         maintained school[2] and authorising or requiring the appointment of
         clerks to committees of the governing body[3];
   (2)   prescribing[4] the body by whom any such appointment is to be made and
         any restrictions or other requirements relating to any such
         appointment[5];
   (3)   as to the dismissal of any such clerk and the procedure to be followed in
         connection with his dismissal[6];
   (4)   authorising the governing body or a committee of the governing body,
         where the clerk fails to attend a meeting, to appoint one of its members
         to act as clerk for the purposes of the meeting[7].
A local authority in Wales must inform, from time to time, each body that is
required to appoint a clerk to the governing body of a maintained school in the
local authority's area under the above provisions[8] that the body may request the
authority to provide a person for appointment as a clerk[9]. Regulations may
require a local authority in Wales to provide a person for appointment if a
request is made[10].
   A local authority in Wales must secure that there is made available to every
person appointed as a clerk such training as the authority considers necessary to
enable the body that appointed the clerk[11] to comply with the relevant
requirements[12]. A local authority in Wales may charge a fee for any training
provided, and may charge different fees in different cases[13].

1   Ie regulations made under the Education Act 2002 by the Welsh Ministers: see s 212(1). As to
    the regulations made see the Government of Maintained Schools (Wales) Regulations 2005,
    SI 2005/2914, regs 42, 43 (reg 42 amended by SI 2010/1142). See also the Government of
    Maintained Schools (Training Requirements for Governors) (Wales) Regulations 2013,
    SI 2013/2124 (amended by SI 2014/2225); and the Government of Maintained Schools (Clerk to
    a Governing Body) (Wales) Regulations 2013, SI 2013/2127. The functions under the Education
    Act 2002 s 23 in relation to Wales were originally vested in the National Assembly for Wales
    and are now exercisable by the Welsh Ministers by virtue of the Government of Wales Act 2006
    s 162(1), Sch 11 paras 30, 32. As to the Welsh Ministers see PARA 59. As to the meaning of
    'Wales' see PARA 7 note 3.

2 As to the meaning of 'maintained school' see PARA 103 note 3. As to governing bodies of maintained schools in Wales see PARA 195 et seq.

3 Education Act 2002 s 23(a). As to the establishment by governing bodies of committees see PARA 214.

4 'Prescribed' means prescribed by the regulations: see the Education Act 2002 s 212(1).

5 Education Act 2002 s 23(b).

6 Education Act 2002 s 23(c).

7 Education Act 2002 s 23(d).

8 Ie under the Education Act 2002 s 23.

9 See the Education (Wales) Measure 2011 s 23(1).

10 See the Education (Wales) Measure 2011 s 23(2). The regulations may, among other things, (1) confer power on a local authority to charge a fee for the provision of a person, including a power to charge different fees in different cases; (2) prescribe the person by whom the fee must be paid; and (3) provide for exceptions and exemptions: see s 23(3). Regulations may also require the body to ensure that a person appointed as clerk has completed prescribed training to a prescribed standard: see s 24(1), (2). The regulations may (a) prohibit the appointment of a person who has not completed the training to the required standard; (b) provide for a person appointed as a clerk who has not completed the training to complete the training to the required standard within a prescribed period; (c) provide for termination of the appointment of a clerk who does not complete the training to the required standard within that period; (d) prescribe training and standards by reference to a document published, as specified in the regulations, by the Welsh Ministers; and (e) provide for exceptions and exemptions: see s 24(3). As to the regulations so made see the Government of Maintained Schools (Clerk to a Governing Body) (Wales) Regulations 2013, SI 2013/2127.

11 Ie under the Education Act 2002 s 23.

12 See the Education (Wales) Measure 2011 s 25(1). The reference to the relevant requirements is a reference to the requirements of s 24 (see note 10).

13 See the Education (Wales) Measure 2011 s 25(2).

(C) General Powers and Duties of Governing Bodies

203. General responsibility of governing body for conduct of school. The conduct of a maintained school[1] is under the direction of the school's governing body[2]. The governing body must conduct the school with a view to promoting high standards of educational achievement at the school[3].

Regulations[4] may: (1) set out terms of reference for governing bodies of maintained schools[5]; (2) define the respective roles and responsibilities of the local authority[6], the governing body and the head teacher[7] of such schools, whether generally or with respect to particular matters, in relation to the conduct such schools[8]; and (3) confer functions[9] on governing bodies and head teachers of such schools[10].

The governing body of a maintained school must, in discharging its functions, comply with the instrument of government[11] and any trust deed[12] relating to the school[13]. The governing body of a maintained school must, in discharging its functions relating to the conduct of the school promote the well-being of pupils at the school[14], and have regard to any relevant children and young people's plan[15].

The governing body of a maintained school must designate a member of the staff at the school as having responsibility for promoting the educational achievement of registered pupils at the school who are being looked after by a local authority[16].

1 As to the meaning of 'maintained school' see PARA 103 note 3.

2 Education Act 2002 s 21(1). This provision is expressed to be subject to any other statutory provision: see s 21(1). As to the meaning of 'statutory provision' see PARA 168 note 2. As to governing bodies of maintained schools in Wales see PARA 195.

3 Education Act 2002 s 21(2).

4   Ie regulations made under the Education Act 2002 by the Welsh Ministers: see s 212(1). As to the regulations made under s 21(3) in relation to Wales see the Education (Review of Staffing Structure) (Wales) Regulations 2005, SI 2005/1910 (amended by SI 2009/2708); the Government of Maintained Schools (Wales) Regulations 2005, SI 2005/2914 (amended by SI 2005/3200; SI 2006/873; SI 2007/944; SI 2009/2544; and SI 2014/1609) (see PARA 214); the School Councils (Wales) Regulations 2005, SI 2005/3200 (see also note 10); and the Education (School Development Plans) (Wales) Regulations 2014, SI 2014/2677. By virtue of the Interpretation Act 1978 s 17(2)(b), the School Government (Terms of Reference) (Wales) Regulations 2000, SI 2000/3027 (amended by SI 2002/1396; SI 2005/2913; and SI 2011/2940) also have effect as if made under the Education Act 2002 s 21(3).

     The functions under the Education Act 2002 s 21 in relation to Wales were originally vested in the National Assembly for Wales and are now exercisable by the Welsh Ministers by virtue of the Government of Wales Act 2006 s 162(1), Sch 11 paras 30, 32. As to the Welsh Ministers see PARA 59. As to the meaning of 'Wales' see PARA 7 note 3.

5   Education Act 2002 s 21(3)(a).

6   As to the meaning of 'local authority' see PARA 25 (definition applied by the Education Act 2002 s 212(1)).

7   As to the meaning of 'head teacher' see PARA 86 note 4 (definition applied by the Education Act 2002 s 212(2), (3)).

8   Education Act 2002 s 21(3)(b) (amended by SI 2010/1158).

9   As to the meaning of 'functions' see PARA 18 note 5 (definition applied by the Education Act 2002 s 212(2), (3)).

10   Education Act 2002 s 21(3)(c). As to school councils see the School Councils (Wales) Regulations 2005, SI 2005/3200, reg 3. As to membership of school councils see reg 4; and as to elections to school councils see reg 6. Certain provisions relating to school councils do not apply to community special schools or foundation special schools: see reg 5. 'School' means a maintained school other than a maintained nursery school or an infant school; and 'infant school' means a maintained school that does not admit pupils who are eight years of age or older: reg 2. As to the meaning of 'maintained nursery school' see PARA 103 note 3. As to the meaning of references to a community or foundation special school see PARA 106. As to the time at which a person attains a particular age see PARA 7 note 6. As to the nomination by a school council of associate pupil governors on the school's governing body see the School Councils (Wales) Regulations 2005, SI 2005/3200, reg 7; and PARA 195 note 13.

11   Education Act 2002 s 21(4)(a). As to instruments of government see PARA 217.

12   As to the meaning of 'trust deed' see PARA 108 note 6 (definition applied by the Education Act 2002 s 212(2), (3)).

13   Education Act 2002 s 21(4)(b). This provision is expressed to be subject to any other statutory provision: see s 21(4)(b).

14   Education Act 2002 s 21(5)(a) (s 21(5)–(9) added by the Education and Inspections Act 2006 s 38(1)). 'Well-being', in relation to pupils at a school in Wales, means their well-being so far as relating to the matters mentioned in the Children Act 2004 s 25(2) (see CHILDREN AND YOUNG PERSONS vol 9 (2012) PARA 209): Education Act 2002 s 21(8)(b) (as so added).

15   Education Act 2002 s 21(6) (as added: see note 14). 'Relevant children and young people's plan' means, in relation to a school in Wales (1) any plan published by the local authority under the Children Act 2004 s 26 (children and young people's plans: Wales: see CHILDREN AND YOUNG PERSONS vol 9 (2012) PARA 209); or (2) in a case where the local authority are not required by regulations under that section to prepare and publish a plan, any plan which is published by the authority and sets out its strategy for discharging its functions in relation to children and relevant young persons within the meaning of that section: Education Act 2002 s 21(9)(b) (as so added; and amended by SI 2010/1158).

16   See the Children and Young Persons Act 2008 s 20.

204. Powers of governing body. The governing body of a maintained school[1] may do anything which appears to it to be necessary or expedient for the purposes of, or in connection with, the conduct of the school[2] or the provision[3] of community facilities or services[4]. The governing body may also provide advice or assistance to the governing body of any other maintained school, whether or not maintained by the same local authority[5], or to any local authority[6].

The above powers include, in particular, the power to:

(1)   borrow such sums as the governing body thinks fit and, in connection

with such borrowing, grant any mortgage, charge or other security over any land[7] or other property of the governing body[8];

(2) acquire and dispose of land and other property[9];

(3) enter into contracts[10];

(4) invest any sums not immediately required for the purposes of carrying on any activities it has power to carry on[11];

(5) accept gifts of money, land or other property and apply it, or hold and administer it on trust, for any of those purposes[12]; and

(6) do anything incidental to the conduct of the school, the provision of advice or assistance, or the provision of community facilities or services[13].

Regulations[14] may make further provision as to the general powers of the governing body[15], and as to other matters relating to it as a body corporate[16].

The governing body of a maintained school[17] may require registered pupils[18] to attend at any place outside the school premises[19] for the purposes of receiving any instruction or training included in the secular curriculum for the school[20].

1   Ie the governing body of a maintained school incorporated under the Education Act 2002 s 19(1) (see PARA 195): Sch 1 para 1. As to the meaning of 'maintained school' see PARA 103 note 3. As to governing bodies of maintained schools in Wales see PARA 195.

2   As to the general responsibility of the governing body for the conduct of a school see PARA 203.

3   Ie under the Education Act 2002 s 27: see PARA 174.

4   Education Act 2002 Sch 1 para 3(1). The provisions of Sch 1 para 3(1)–(3) (see the text to notes 1–13) have effect subject to: (1) any provisions of the school's instrument of government (Sch 1 para 3(8)(a)); and (2) any provisions of a scheme under the School Standards and Framework Act 1998 s 48 (see PARA 321) which relates to the school (Education Act 2002 Sch 1 para 3(8)(b)). As to instruments of government see PARA 217. As to the application of the Education Act 2002 Sch 1 para 3(1)–(6), (8) to pupil referral units (see PARA 427 et seq) see the Education (Pupil Referral Units) (Application of Enactments) (England) Regulations 2007, SI 2007/2979, Sch 1 Pt 1 para 20 (substituted by SI 2012/3158).

5   Education Act 2002 Sch 1 para 3(2)(a) (amended by SI 2010/1158). See also note 4. As to the meaning of 'local authority' see PARA 25 (definition applied by the Education Act 2002 s 212(1)).

6   Education Act 2002 Sch 1 para 3(2)(b) (amended by SI 2010/1158). See also note 4.

7   As to the meaning of 'land' see PARA 116 note 18 (definition applied by the Education Act 2002 s 212(2), (3)).

8   Education Act 2002 Sch 1 para 3(3)(a). See also note 4. The power to borrow money and grant security mentioned in Sch 1 para 3(3)(a) may only be exercised with the written consent of the Welsh Ministers or, if an order under Sch 1 para 3(5) so provides, of the local authority: Sch 1 para 3(4) (amended by SI 2010/1158). Any such consent may be given for particular borrowing or for borrowing of a particular class: Education Act 2002 Sch 1 para 3(4). The Welsh Ministers may by order make provision for their function of giving consent under Sch 1 para 3(4) to be instead exercisable in the case of all maintained schools, or in the case of any class of such schools specified in the order, by the local authorities by whom those schools are maintained: Sch 1 para 3(5) (amended by SI 2010/1158). In exercising that function those authorities must comply with any directions contained in an order made by the Welsh Ministers: Education Act 2002 Sch 1 para 3(6). At the date at which this volume states the law, no order had been made under Sch 1 para 3(5). The power to make an order under Sch 1 para 3(6) is not exercisable by statutory instrument (see s 210(2)) and such orders are not recorded in this work. As to the meaning of 'written' see PARA 76 note 8.

The functions under the Education Act 2002 Sch 1 in relation to Wales were originally vested in the National Assembly for Wales and are now exercisable by the Welsh Ministers by virtue of the Government of Wales Act 2006 s 162(1), Sch 11 paras 30, 32. As to the Welsh Ministers see PARA 59. As to the meaning of 'Wales' see PARA 7 note 3.

9   Education Act 2002 Sch 1 para 3(3)(b). See also note 4. As to the acquisition and disposal of land see PARA 1298 et seq.

10 Education Act 2002 Sch 1 para 3(3)(c). See also note 4. Where the school is a foundation, voluntary aided or foundation special school, the power to enter into contracts mentioned in Sch 1 para 3(3)(c) includes power to enter into contracts for the employment of teachers and

other staff; but no such contracts may be entered into by the governing body of a community, voluntary controlled or community special school or of a maintained nursery school: Sch 1 para 3(7). As to the meaning of references to a community, foundation or voluntary school or a community or foundation special school see PARA 106. As to the meaning of 'maintained nursery school' see PARA 103 note 3. As to the employment of teachers, and staffing generally see PARA 268 et seq.

11 Education Act 2002 Sch 1 para 3(3)(d). See also note 4.
12 Education Act 2002 Sch 1 para 3(3)(e). See also note 4.
13 Education Act 2002 Sch 1 para 3(3)(f). See also note 4.
14 Ie regulations' made under the Education Act 2002 by the Welsh Ministers: see s 212(1). At the date at which this volume states the law no such regulations had been made.
15 Education Act 2002 Sch 1 para 4(a).
16 Education Act 2002 Sch 1 para 4(b). As to governing bodies as bodies corporate see PARA 195.
17 For this purpose, 'maintained school' does not include a maintained nursery school: Education Act 2002 s 29(4).
18 As to the meaning of 'registered pupil' see PARA 437 (definition applied by the Education Act 2002 s 212(2), (3)).
19 As to the meaning of 'premises' see PARA 62 note 19 (definition applied by the Education Act 2002 s 212(2), (3)).
20 Education Act 2002 s 29(3) (amended by the Education Act 2005 s 115). As to the curriculum in Wales see PARA 870 et seq.

205. Power of governing body to provide higher education.

The governing body of a maintained school[1] has the power to arrange the provision to pupils[2] at the school, whether by teachers at the school or other persons[3], of: (1) courses in preparation for professional examinations at a higher level[4]; or (2) courses providing education at a higher level[5] (whether or not in preparation for an examination)[6]. A governing body may exercise this power in relation to a particular pupil only if it is satisfied that the provision to that pupil of the course in question will not to any significant extent interfere with the other education with which he is being provided at the school[7].

The Welsh Ministers[8] may give, or make arrangements for the giving of, financial assistance to any person in connection with the provision of courses mentioned in heads (1) and (2) above by the governing body of a maintained school in Wales[9].

These provisions have effect notwithstanding the fact that nothing in the Education Act 1996 confers any functions with respect to higher education[10].

1 As to the meaning of 'maintained school' see PARA 103 note 3. As to governing bodies of maintained schools in Wales see PARA 195.
2 As to the meaning of 'pupil' see PARA 20 note 4 (definition applied by the Education Act 2002 s 212(2), (3)).
3 As to the meaning of 'person' see PARA 7 note 6.
4 Ie courses falling within the Education Reform Act 1988 Sch 6 para 1(g): see PARA 684.
5 Ie courses falling within the Education Reform Act 1988 Sch 6 para 1(h): see PARA 684.
6 Education Act 2002 s 28A(1) (s 28A added by the Education Act 2005 s 105).
7 Education Act 2002 s 28A(2) (as added: see note 6).
8 The functions under the Education Act 2002 s 28A were originally vested in the National Assembly for Wales and are now exercisable by the Welsh Ministers by virtue of the Government of Wales Act 2006 s 162(1), Sch 11 paras 30, 32. As to the Welsh Ministers see PARA 59.
9 Education Act 2002 s 28A(3) (as added: see note 6). Section 15 (forms of assistance under s 14) and s 16 (terms on which assistance under s 14 is given) (see PARA 78) apply to financial assistance given under s 28A(3) as they apply to financial assistance given under s 14: s 28A(4) (as so added). As to the meaning of 'Wales' see PARA 7 note 3.
10 Education Act 2002 s 28A(5) (as added: see note 6). As to the Education Act 1996 and higher education see s 1(4); and PARA 18.

206. Power of governing body to provide further education. The governing body of any maintained school[1] is responsible for determining whether or not to provide part-time education suitable to the requirements of persons of any age over compulsory school age[2].

1   As to the meaning of 'maintained school' see PARA 99. As to governing bodies of maintained schools in Wales see PARA 195. The governing body of a community or foundation special school may not determine to provide, or to cease to provide, education under the School Standards and Framework Act 1998 s 80 without the consent of the local authority: see s 80(1); and PARA 588.
2   See the School Standards and Framework Act 1998 s 80(1); and PARA 588.

207. Power of governing body to form or invest in companies to provide services etc. As from a day to be appointed, the following provisions have effect[1].

The governing body of a maintained school[2] may form, or participate in forming, companies[3] to:

(1)   provide services or facilities[4] for any schools[5];
(2)   exercise relevant local authority functions[6]; or
(3)   make, or facilitate the making of, arrangements under which facilities or services are provided for any schools by other persons[7].

The governing body of a maintained school may, with a view to securing or facilitating:

(a)   the provision by a company of services or facilities for any schools[8];
(b)   the exercise by a company of relevant local authority functions[9]; or
(c)   the making by any person of arrangements of the kind referred to in head (3) above[10],

invest[11] in the company which is to provide the services or facilities or exercise the functions or by which the arrangements are to be made or facilitated[12]. The governing body of a maintained school may form, or participate in forming, companies to purchase services or facilities for that school and other participating schools[13]. The governing body of a maintained school may, with a view to securing or facilitating the purchase by a company of services or facilities for that school and other participating schools, become a member of the company[14].

The above provisions are without prejudice to any powers of the governing body of a maintained school which are exercisable otherwise[15].

The governing body of a maintained school may not exercise any of the above powers[16] except with the consent of the local authority[17], and at a time when the school has a delegated budget[18]. A governing body may not exercise any of those powers in relation to a company unless the company satisfies any applicable requirements of regulations under heads (i) and (ii) below[19], and may not[20] remain a member of a company at any time when the company fails to satisfy any such requirements[21].

Regulations[22]:

(i)   must provide that, except in such cases as may be prescribed[23], the company is to be prohibited by its constitution from admitting to its membership any person who is not of a prescribed description[24];
(ii)   may impose requirements with respect to the constitution of the company, and any other matter connected with the company's affairs[25];
(iii)   must provide that where one or more governing bodies have invested in a company[26], a local authority must be designated as the supervising authority for the company[27];

(iv)　must specify the persons by whom and the manner in which the power of designation is, or is in specified circumstances, exercisable[28];

(v)　must make provision about the duties of a local authority who are for the time being designated as the supervising authority for a company[29].

Regulations[30] may also: (A) require that, where a local authority is for the time being designated as the supervising authority for a company, the company must provide prescribed information relating to its financial affairs to it at such times and in such manner as may be prescribed[31]; (B) provide that in prescribed circumstances a local authority who is for the time being so designated may direct any participating governing body[32] to cease to be a member of the company or to take any other prescribed action in relation to the company[33]; and (C) prescribe the procedure for making such a direction[34].

1　The Education Act 2002 ss 11–12 come into force in relation to Wales as from a day to be appointed: see s 216(4). At the date at which this volume states the law no such day had been appointed. As to the meaning of 'Wales' see PARA 7 note 3.

2　For these purposes, 'maintained school' means a community, foundation or voluntary school, a community or foundation special school or a maintained nursery school: Education Act 2002 s 11(9). As to the meaning of references to a community, foundation or voluntary school or a community or foundation special school see PARA 106. As to the meaning of 'maintained nursery school' see PARA 103 note 3. As to governing bodies of maintained schools in Wales see PARA 195.

3　'Company' means a company registered under the Companies Act 2006 as a company limited by shares or a company limited by guarantee: Education Act 2002 s 11(9) (definition amended by SI 2009/1941). As to companies limited by guarantee see COMPANIES vol 14 (2009) PARAS 79, 102. As to companies limited by shares see COMPANIES vol 14 (2009) PARA 102.

4　'Facilities' includes the provision of (or of the use of) premises, goods, materials, vehicles, plant or apparatus: Education Act 2002 s 11(9). As to the meaning of 'premises' see PARA 62 note 20 (definition applied by s 212(2), (3)).

5　Education Act 2002 s 11(1)(a). As to the meaning of 'school' see PARA 91 (definition applied by s 212(2), (3)). The governing body of a maintained school may provide staff to any company in relation to which it has exercised a power conferred by any of s 11(1)–(4): s 11(5). The provisions of s 11(1)–(4) have effect subject to s 12 (see the text to notes 16–34): s 11(6). In exercising the power conferred by s 11(5), the governing body of a maintained school must have regard to any guidance given from time to time by the Welsh Ministers: s 11(7). As to the publication of guidance see the Education Act 1996 s 571 (applied by the Education Act 2002 s 212(2), (3)); and PARA 60. The functions under the Education Act 2002 ss 11, 12 in relation to Wales were originally vested in the National Assembly for Wales and are now exercisable by the Welsh Ministers by virtue of the Government of Wales Act 2006 s 162(1), Sch 11 paras 30, 32. As to the Welsh Ministers see PARA 59.

6　Education Act 2002 s 11(1)(b). See also note 5. 'Relevant local authority functions', in relation to a company, means the education functions of any local authority that are or may become exercisable by the company in accordance with an authorisation given or direction made by virtue of any enactment: s 11(9) (definition amended by SI 2010/1158). As to the meanings of 'local authority' and 'education functions' see PARA 25 (definitions applied by the Education Act 2002 s 212(1)–(3)). As to the meaning of 'enactment' see PARA 1 note 13.

7　Education Act 2002 s 11(1)(c). See also note 5. As to the meaning of 'person' see PARA 7 note 6.

8　Education Act 2002 s 11(2)(a).

9　Education Act 2002 s 11(2)(b) (amended by SI 2010/1158).

10　Education Act 2002 s 11(2)(c).

11　References to investing in a company include references to becoming a member of the company and to investing in it by the acquisition of any assets, securities or rights or otherwise: Education Act 2002 s 11(10).

12　Education Act 2002 s 11(2). See also note 5.

13　Education Act 2002 s 11(3). See also note 5. 'Participating school', in relation to a company, means a school whose governing body is, or is to be, a member of the company: s 11(9).

14　Education Act 2002 s 11(4). See also note 5.

15　Education Act 2002 s 11(8).

16　Ie powers conferred by any of the Education Act 2002 s 11(1)–(4): see the text to notes 2–14.

17 Education Act 2002 s 12(1)(a) (amended by SI 2010/1158). Regulations may restrict the circumstances in which a local authority may refuse to give any consent applied for under the Education Act 2002 s 12(1): s 12(8) (amended by SI 2010/1158). 'Regulations' means regulations made under the Education Act 2002 by the Welsh Ministers: see s 212(1). At the date at which this volume states the law no such regulations had been made in relation to Wales.

18 Education Act 2002 s 12(1)(b). The delegated budget referred to is one within the meaning of the School Standards and Framework Act 1998 Pt II (ss 20–83) (see PARA 323): see the Education Act 2002 s 12(1)(b).

19 Education Act 2002 s 12(2)(a).

20 Ie by virtue of the Education Act 2002 s 11: see the text to notes 2–15.

21 Education Act 2002 s 12(2)(b).

22 At the date at which this volume states the law no such regulations had been made in relation to Wales.

23 'Prescribed' means prescribed by the regulations: see the Education Act 2002 s 212(1).

24 Education Act 2002 s 12(3)(a).

25 Education Act 2002 s 12(3)(b). Without prejudice to the generality of s 12(3)(b), regulations under that provision may require that the company be prohibited by its constitution from borrowing money, except with the consent of a prescribed person: s 12(4).

26 Ie by virtue of the Education Act 2002 s 11: see the text to notes 2–15.

27 Education Act 2002 s 12(5)(a) (amended by SI 2010/1158).

28 Education Act 2002 s 12(5)(b).

29 Education Act 2002 s 12(5)(c) (amended by SI 2010/1158).

30 At the date at which this volume states the law no such regulations had been made in relation to Wales.

31 Education Act 2002 s 12(6)(a) (amended by SI 2010/1158).

32 'Participating governing body', in relation to a company, means any governing body of a maintained school who is a member of the company: Education Act 2002 s 12(7).

33 Education Act 2002 s 12(6)(b) (amended by SI 2010/1158).

34 Education Act 2002 s 12(6)(c).

208. Power of governing body to provide community facilities etc. The governing body of a maintained school[1] has the power[2] to provide any facilities or services whose provision furthers any charitable purpose[3] for the benefit of pupils[4] at the school or their families[5], or people who live or work in the locality in which the school is situated[6]. This power includes, in particular, power for a governing body to: (1) incur expenditure[7]; (2) enter into arrangements or agreements with any person[8]; (3) co-operate with, or facilitate or co-ordinate the activities of, any person[9]; and (4) provide staff, goods, services and accommodation to any person[10]. A governing body may charge for any services or facilities so provided[11].

However, the above power does not enable a governing body to do anything which it is unable to do by virtue of any prohibition, restriction or limitation on its powers which is contained in the school's instrument of government[12], or any local authority's financial scheme[13] which relates to the school[14]; and regulations[15] may make provision preventing governing bodies from doing[16] anything which is specified, or is of a description specified, in the regulations[17].

Before exercising the power, the governing body of a maintained school in Wales: (a) must consult[18] the local authority[19], the staff of the school[20], and the parents[21] of registered pupils[22] of the school[23]; (b) where the proposed exercise of the power would affect registered pupils of the school and the governing body considers it appropriate in view of their age and understanding to consult all or some of them, must consult the registered pupils or such of them as the governing body considers it appropriate to consult[24]; and (c) must consult such other persons as the governing body considers appropriate[25]. In exercising the power or carrying out such consultation, the governing body of a maintained school in Wales must have regard to any guidance given from time to time by the Welsh Ministers [26]and to any advice given to it from time to time by the local authority[27].

A governing body must exercise the power only if, and to the extent that, it is satisfied that anything which it proposes to do will not to a significant extent interfere with the performance of any duty imposed on it either in relation to its general responsibility to conduct the school with a view to promoting high standards of educational achievement[28], or by any other provision of the Education Acts[29]. In exercising the power, the governing body of a maintained school must have regard to any relevant children and young people's plan[30].

1 As to the meaning of 'maintained school' see PARA 103 note 3. As to governing bodies of maintained schools in Wales see PARA 195. As to the meaning of 'Wales' see PARA 7 note 3.

2 The Education Act 2002 s 27 has effect subject to s 28 (see the text to notes 12–30): s 27(4).

3 As to charitable purposes see CHARITIES vol 8 (2015) PARA 2.

4 As to the meaning of 'pupil' see PARA 20 note 4 (definition applied by the Education Act 2002 s 212(2), (3)).

5 Education Act 2002 s 27(1)(a).

6 Education Act 2002 s 27(1)(b).

7 Education Act 2002 s 27(2)(a). Expenditure incurred by the governing body of a maintained school in Wales in the exercise of the power conferred by s 27 is, as against third parties, to be treated as part of the expenses of maintaining the school under the School Standards and Framework Act 1998 s 22 (see PARA 305 et seq), but if met by the local authority may be recovered by it from the governing body: s 51A(1) (s 51A added by the Education Act 2002 s 40, Sch 3 para 4; and amended by the Children, Schools and Families Act 2010 s 4(4); and SI 2010/1158). Except as provided by regulations under the School Standards and Framework Act 1998 s 50(3)(b) (see PARA 324), no expenditure incurred by the governing body of a maintained school in the exercise of the power referred to in s 51A(1) is to be met from the school's budget share for any funding period: s 51A(2) (as so added; and amended by the Education Act 2005 s 117, Sch 18 para 9; and the Children, Schools and Families Act 2010 s 4(4)). The School Standards and Framework Act 1998 s 51A(2) applies at a time when the school does not have a delegated budget by virtue of any suspension under Sch 15 (see PARA 325 et seq) or the School Standards and Organisation (Wales) Act 2013 s 8 (see PARA 1233), as well as a time when it does have a delegated budget: School Standards and Framework Act 1998 s 51A(3) (as so added; and amended by the School Standards and Organisation (Wales) Act 2013 Sch 5 para 4(1), (3)). As to the meaning of 'delegated budget' see PARA 323. As to the requirement for maintained schools to have budget shares see PARA 315. As to the meaning of 'local authority' see PARA 25 (definition applied by the School Standards and Framework Act 1998 s 142(8); and the Education Act 2002 s 212(1)).

8 Education Act 2002 s 27(2)(b). As to the meaning of 'person' see PARA 7 note 6.

9 Education Act 2002 s 27(2)(c).

10 Education Act 2002 s 27(2)(d). Regulations under ss 35(4), 36(4) may make provision with respect to staff employed, or engaged otherwise than under a contract of employment, wholly or partly for the purposes of the provision of facilities and services under s 27, or any other activities which are not school activities but are carried on on the school premises under the management or control of the governing body: see ss 35(5)(c), 36(5)(c); and PARAS 268, 280. As to the meaning of 'premises' see PARA 62 note 20 (definition applied by s 212(2), (3)).

11 Education Act 2002 s 27(3). This provision is expressed to be subject to the provisions of the Education Act 1996 Pt VI Ch III (ss 449–462) (charges in connection with education at maintained schools: see PARA 334 et seq): see the Education Act 2002 s 27(3).

12 Education Act 2002 s 28(1)(a). As to instruments of government see PARA 217.

13 Ie any scheme under the School Standards and Framework Act 1998 s 48: see PARA 321.

14 Education Act 2002 s 28(1)(b) (amended by SI 2010/1158).

15 'Regulations' means regulations made under the Education Act 2002 by the Welsh Ministers: see s 212(1). At the date at which this volume states the law no such regulations had been made. The functions under the Education Act 2002 s 28 in relation to Wales were originally vested in the National Assembly for Wales and are now exercisable by the Welsh Ministers by virtue of the Government of Wales Act 2006 s 162(1), Sch 11 paras 30, 32. As to the Welsh Ministers see PARA 59.

16 Ie by virtue of the Education Act 2002 s 27(1): see the text to notes 1–6.

17 Education Act 2002 s 28(2).

18 As to the exercise of the duty to consult see JUDICIAL REVIEW vol 61 (2010) PARA 627.

19 Education Act 2002 s 28(4)(a)(i) (amended by SI 2010/1158; and the Education Act 2002 s 28(4) amended by the Children and Families Act 2014 s 88(1), (2)).

20 Education Act 2002 s 28(4)(a)(ii).

21 As to the meaning of 'parent' see PARA 7 note 6 (definition applied by the Education Act 2002 s 212(2), (3)).

22 As to the meaning of 'registered pupil' see PARA 437 (definition applied by the Education Act 2002 s 212(2), (3)).

23 Education Act 2002 s 28(4)(a)(iii).

24 Education Act 2002 s 28(4)(b).

25 Education Act 2002 s 28(4)(c).

26 See the Education Act 2002 s 28(5)(a) (s 28(5) amended by the Children and Families Act 2014 s 88(1), (4)). As to the publication of guidance see the Education Act 1996 s 571 (applied by the Education Act 2002 s 212(2), (3)); and PARA 60.

27 Education Act 2002 s 28(5)(b) (amended by SI 2010/1158).

28 Ie the duty imposed by the Education Act 2002 s 21(2): see PARA 203.

29 Education Act 2002 s 28(3). As to the meaning of 'the Education Acts' see PARA 1 note 13 (definition applied by s 212(2), (3)).

30 Education Act 2002 s 28(4A) (s 28(4A)–(4C) added by the Education and Inspections Act 2006 s 38(2); and the Education Act 2002 s 28(4C) repealed by the Children and Families Act 2014 s 88(1), (3)). 'Relevant children and young people's plan' has the meaning given by the Education Act 2002 s 21(9) (see PARA 203 note 15): s 28(4B) (as so added).

209. Duty of governing body in relation to complaints procedures. As from a day to be appointed[1] the Welsh Ministers[2] may make regulations establishing procedures in relation to complaints[3] which relate to a maintained school in Wales[4], or to the provision of facilities or services[5] by the governing body of such a school, other than a complaint which falls to be dealt with in accordance with any procedures required to be established in relation to the school by virtue of any other[6] statutory provision[7]. Where the Welsh Ministers establish procedures by such regulations, the governing body of a maintained school in Wales must adopt the procedures[8], and publicise them in the way specified in the regulations[9]. In adopting or publicising the procedures, the governing body must have regard to any guidance given from time to time by the Welsh Ministers[10].

1 The Education Act 2002 s 29(2A)–(2D) (see the text and notes 2–9) are added, as from a day to be appointed, by the Apprenticeships, Skills, Children and Learning Act 2009 s 260(1), (4). At the date at which this volume states the law no such day had been appointed.

2 As to the Welsh Ministers see PARA 59.

3 Education Act 2002 s 29(2A) (prospectively added: see note 1). At the date at which this volume states the law no such regulations had been made.

4 As to the meaning of 'maintained school' see PARA 103 note 3. As to governing bodies of maintained schools in Wales see PARA 195. As to the meaning of 'Wales' see PARA 7 note 3.

5 Ie under the Education Act 2002 s 27: see PARA 208.

6 Ie other than the Education Act 2002 s 29.

7 Education Act 2002 s 29(2B) (prospectively added: see note 1). As to the meaning of 'statutory provision' see PARA 168 note 2.

8 Education Act 2002 s 29(2C)(a) (prospectively added: see note 1).

9 Education Act 2002 s 29(2C)(b) (prospectively added: see note 1).

10 Education Act 2002 s 29(2D) (prospectively added: see note 1).

210. Duty of governing body in relation to health and safety. The governing body[1] and head teacher[2] of a community or voluntary controlled school[3], a community special school[4], or a maintained nursery school[5], must comply with any direction[6] given to it by the local authority[7] concerning the health and safety of persons on the school's premises[8] or taking part in any school activities elsewhere[9].

1   As to governing bodies of maintained schools in Wales see PARA 195. As to the meaning of 'Wales' see PARA 7 note 3.

2   As to the meaning of 'head teacher' see PARA 86 note 4 (definition applied by the Education Act 2002 s 212(2), (3)).

3   Education Act 2002 s 29(5)(a). As to the meaning of references to a community or voluntary school see PARA 106.

4   Education Act 2002 s 29(5)(b). As to the meaning of references to a community special school see PARA 106.

5   Education Act 2002 s 29(5)(c). As to the meaning of 'maintained nursery school' see PARA 103 note 3.

6   As to directions see the Education Act 1996 s 570 (applied by the Education Act 2002 s 212(2), (3)); and PARA 75.

7   As to the meaning of 'local authority' see PARA 25 (definition applied by the Education Act 2002 s 212(1)).

8   As to the meaning of 'premises' see PARA 62 note 19 (definition applied by the Education Act 2002 s 212(2), (3)).

9   Education Act 2002 s 29(5) (amended by SI 2010/1158). As to health and safety on school premises see also PARA 1353.

211.   Duty of governing body in relation to the welfare of children.   The governing body[1] of a maintained school[2] must make arrangements for ensuring that its functions[3] relating to the conduct of the school are exercised with a view to safeguarding and promoting the welfare of children[4] who are pupils[5] at the school[6]. The governing body must, in considering what arrangements are required to be made by it, have regard to any guidance[7] given from time to time by the Welsh Ministers[8].

1   As to governing bodies of maintained schools in Wales see PARA 195. As to the meaning of 'Wales' see PARA 7 note 3.

2   For these purposes, 'maintained school' means a community, foundation or voluntary school, a community or foundation special school or a maintained nursery school: Education Act 2002 s 175(5). As to the meaning of references to a community, foundation or voluntary school or a community or foundation special school see PARA 106. As to the meaning of 'maintained nursery school' see PARA 99 note 4 (definition applied by s 212(2), (3)).

3   As to the meaning of 'functions' see PARA 18 note 5 (definition applied by the Education Act 2002 s 212(2), (3)).

4   'Child' means a person under the age of 18: Education Act 2002 s 175(5). As to the time at which a person attains a particular age see PARA 7 note 6.

5   As to the meaning of 'pupil' see PARA 20 note 4 (definition applied by the Education Act 2002 s 212(2), (3)).

6   Education Act 2002 s 175(2). As to the application of the Education Act 2002 s 175(2), (4) to pupil referral units (see PARA 427 et seq) see the Education (Pupil Referral Units) (Application of Enactments) (England) Regulations 2007, SI 2007/2979, Sch 1 Pt 1 para 19A (added by SI 2012/3158).

7   As to the publication of guidance see the Education Act 1996 s 571 (applied by the Education Act 2002 s 212(2), (3)); and PARA 60.

8   Education Act 2002 s 175(4). See note 6. The functions under the Education Act 2002 s 175 in relation to Wales were originally vested in the National Assembly for Wales and are now exercisable by the Welsh Ministers by virtue of the Government of Wales Act 2006 s 162(1), Sch 11 paras 30, 32. As to the Welsh Ministers see PARA 59.

212.   Consultation with pupils.   As from a day to be appointed[1] the governing body of a maintained school must invite the views of pupils about prescribed[2] matters[3]. In exercising any of its functions relating to the conduct of the school, the governing body of a maintained school must consider any relevant views of registered pupils at the school about matters so prescribed (whether expressed by virtue of such an invitation or otherwise) and, in doing so, must have regard to the age and understanding of the pupils who expressed them[4]. In discharging these duties, the governing body of a maintained school must have regard to any guidance given from time to time by the Welsh Ministers[5].

Nothing in these provisions[6] affects any power or duty relating to consulting pupils which a governing body of a maintained school has otherwise than under them[7].

1 The Education Act 2002 ss 29B, 210A (see the text and notes 2–7) are added by the Education and Skills Act 2008 s 157 ss 157, 169(1), Sch 1 Pt 2 para 79. At the date at which this volume states the law no such day or days had been appointed.
2 'Prescribed' means prescribed by regulations made under the Education Act 2002 by the Welsh Ministers: see ss 29B(6)(b), 212(1) (s 29B prospectively added: see note 1). The following are the matters that may be prescribed under s 29B(1): (1) the exercise, or proposed exercise, of a function of the governing body of a maintained school relating to the conduct of the school (s 29B(4)(a) (as so prospectively added)); (2) the exercise, or proposed exercise, of such a function in a particular way (s 29B(4)(b) (as so prospectively added)). The power of the Welsh Ministers to make regulations under s 29B includes power (a) to make different provisions for different cases or areas (s 210A(3)(a) (as so prospectively added)); (b) to make provision generally or only in relation to specific cases (s 210A(3)(b) (as so prospectively added)); and (c) to make such incidental, supplemental, saving or transitional provisions as the Welsh Ministers think fit (s 210A(3)(c) (as so prospectively added)). Nothing in the Education Act 2002 is to be regarded as affecting the generality of s 210A(3): s 210A(4) (as so prospectively added). At the date at which this volume states the law no such regulations had been made. As to the Welsh Ministers see PARA 59.
3 Education Act 2002 s 29B(1) (prospectively added: see note 1). For these purposes, a governing body invites the views of pupils about a matter if it invites the views of: (1) all registered pupils at the school (s 29B(3)(a) (as so prospectively added)); (2) such of those pupils as appear to the governing body to be affected by the matter (s 29B(3)(b) (as so prospectively added)); or (3) pupils appearing to the governing body to be representative of pupils within head (1) or (2) above (s 29B(3)(c) (as so prospectively added)). As to the meaning of 'registered pupil' see PARA 437 (definition applied by s 212(2), (3)). As to governing bodies of maintained schools see PARA 195.
4 Education Act 2002 s 29B(2) (prospectively added: see note 1).
5 Education Act 2002 s 29B(5)(b) (prospectively added: see note 1).
6 Ie nothing in the Education Act 2002 s 29B: see the text to notes 1–5.
7 Education Act 2002 s 29B(7) (prospectively added: see note 1).

213. Control of school premises by governing body. Regulations[1] may make provision relating to the control by the governing body of a maintained school[2] of the occupation and use of school premises[3].

1 Ie regulations made under the Education Act 2002 by the Welsh Ministers: see s 212(1). As to the regulations made see the Control of School Premises (Wales) Regulations 2008, SI 2008/136 (amended by SI 2008/555). The functions under the Education Act 2002 s 31 in relation to Wales were originally vested in the National Assembly for Wales and are now exercisable by the Welsh Ministers by virtue of the Government of Wales Act 2006 s 162(1), Sch 11 paras 30, 32. As to the Welsh Ministers see PARA 59. As to the meaning of 'Wales' see PARA 7 note 3.
2 As to the meaning of 'maintained school' see PARA 103 note 3. As to governing bodies of maintained schools in Wales see PARA 195.
3 Education Act 2002 s 31. As to the meaning of 'premises' see PARA 62 note 19 (definition applied by s 212(2), (3)).

(D) Meetings and Proceedings

214. Meetings and proceedings. Regulations[1] make provision as to the meetings and proceedings of governing bodies[2], in particular in relation to:
(1) the election of the chair and vice-chair[3];
(2) the delegation of functions to the chair or vice-chair in cases of urgency[4];
(3) the right of persons to attend meetings of the governing body[5];
(4) convening meetings of the governing body[6];

(5)   proceedings of the governing body[7];

(6)   minutes and papers of the governing body[8].

(7)   restrictions on persons taking part in proceedings[9];

(8)   the delegation of functions[10] by the governing body and restrictions on such delegation[11];

(9)   reporting to the governing body following the exercise of delegated functions[12];

(10)   the establishment of committees by the governing bodies and the appointment of persons other than governors to serve on them[13].

1   Ie regulations made under the Education Act 2002 s 19(3): see PARA 195. As to the regulations made see the Government of Maintained Schools (Wales) Regulations 2005, SI 2005/2914; and see the text to notes 2–13. As to provision about training for the chair of a governing body, see the Government of Maintained Schools (Training Requirements for Governors) (Wales) Regulations 2013, SI 2013/2124 (amended by SI 2014/1132).

2   As to governing bodies of maintained schools in Wales see PARA 195.

3   See the Government of Maintained Schools (Wales) Regulations 2005, SI 2005/2914, reg 39. As to the removal of the chair or vice-chair from office see reg 41.

4   See the Government of Maintained Schools (Wales) Regulations 2005, SI 2005/2914, reg 40. See also *R v Birmingham City Council, ex p McKenna* (1991) 156 LG Rev 486, (1991) Times, 16 May (decided under previous legislation).

5   See the Government of Maintained Schools (Wales) Regulations 2005, SI 2005/2914, regs 44, 44A (reg 44 amended, and reg 44A added, by SI 2005/3200). As regards the withdrawal of a governor from a meeting over the matter of a pecuniary interest see *Noble v Inner London Education Authority* (1983) 82 LGR 291, CA; *Bostock v Kay* (1989) 87 LGR 583, 153 JP 549, CA; *R v Governors of Small Heath School, ex p Birmingham City Council* [1990] COD 23, (1990) Independent, 3 August, CA; *R v Governors of Bacon's School, ex p Inner London Education Authority* [1990] COD 414, DC (all cases decided under previous legislation).

6   See the Government of Maintained Schools (Wales) Regulations 2005, SI 2005/2914, reg 45 (amended by SI 2010/1142).

7   See the Government of Maintained Schools (Wales) Regulations 2005, SI 2005/2914, reg 46 (amended by SI 2005/3200).

8   See the Government of Maintained Schools (Wales) Regulations 2005, SI 2005/2914, regs 47–48 (reg 47 amended by SI 2010/1142).

9   See the Government of Maintained Schools (Wales) Regulations 2005, SI 2005/2914, reg 63, Sch 7 (reg 63 amended by SI 2006/873; and the Government of Maintained Schools (Wales) Regulations 2005, SI 2005/2914, Sch 7 amended by SI 2010/638). The Government of Maintained Schools (Wales) Regulations 2005, SI 2005/2914, Sch 7 includes provision in relation to conflicts of interest.

10   See the Government of Maintained Schools (Wales) Regulations 2005, SI 2005/2914, reg 50 (amended by SI 2006/873; and SI 2007/944).

11   See the Government of Maintained Schools (Wales) Regulations 2005, SI 2005/2914, reg 51 (amended by SI 2006/873; SI 2007/944; and SI 2010/1142).

12   See the Government of Maintained Schools (Wales) Regulations 2005, SI 2005/2914, reg 52.

13   See the Government of Maintained Schools (Wales) Regulations 2005, SI 2005/2914, Pt 9 (regs 53–62) (regs 54–58, 60 amended by SI 2005/3200; the Government of Maintained Schools (Wales) Regulations 2005, SI 2005/2914, reg 55 further amended, reg 59 amended, by SI 2006/873; the Government of Maintained Schools (Wales) Regulations 2005, SI 2005/2914, reg 55 further amended by SI 2010/1142; and SI 2014/1609; and the Government of Maintained Schools (Wales) Regulations 2005, SI 2005/2914, reg 61 amended by SI 2010/1142). See also *R v Secretary of State for Education, ex p Prior* [1994] ELR 231, [1994] ICR 877 (decided under previous legislation).

215. Documentary evidence. In any legal proceedings, a document purporting to be an extract from the minutes of the proceedings of the governing body of a maintained school[1], and to be signed by the chairman of the governing body or by its clerk[2], is to be received in evidence and treated, without further proof, as the document which it purports to be and as having been signed by the person by whom it purports to have been signed, unless the contrary is proved[3].

1 As to governing bodies of maintained schools in Wales see PARA 195. As to the meaning of 'Wales' see PARA 7 note 3.
2 As to the clerk to the governing body see PARA 202.
3 Education Act 1996 s 566(1)(b) (amended by the School Standards and Framework Act 1998 s 140(1), Sch 30 paras 57, 173). In any legal proceedings, any such extract as is mentioned in the Education Act 1996 s 566(1)(b) is evidence of the matters stated in it: see s 566(2). As to evidence in civil proceedings see CIVIL PROCEDURE vol 11 (2009) PARA 749 et seq.

216. Seal of governing body. The application of the seal[1] of the governing body[2] must be authenticated by the signature of:

(1) the chairman of the governing body[3]; or
(2) some other member authorised either generally or specially by the governing body to act for that purpose[4],

together with the signature of any other member[5].

Every document purporting to be an instrument made or issued by or on behalf of the governing body and to be duly executed under the seal of the governing body[6], or to be signed or executed by a person authorised by the governing body to act in that behalf[7], is to be received in evidence and to be treated, without further proof, as being so made or issued unless the contrary is shown[8].

1 As to governing bodies as bodies corporate see PARA 195. As to the corporate seal see CORPORATIONS vol 24 (2010) PARA 323 et seq.
2 Ie the governing body of a maintained school incorporated under the Education Act 2002 s 19(1) (see PARA 195): see Sch 1 para 1. As to the meaning of 'maintained school' see PARA 102 note 3. As to governing bodies of maintained schools in Wales see PARA 195. As to the meaning of 'Wales' see PARA 7 note 3.
3 Education Act 2002 Sch 1 para 2(2)(a).
4 Education Act 2002 Sch 1 para 2(2)(b).
5 Education Act 2002 Sch 1 para 2(2).
6 Education Act 2002 Sch 1 para 2(3)(a).
7 Education Act 2002 Sch 1 para 2(3)(b).
8 Education Act 2002 Sch 1 para 2(3). As to evidence in civil proceedings see CIVIL PROCEDURE vol 11 (2009) PARA 749 et seq.

(E) Instruments of Government

217. Instruments of government. For every maintained school[1] there must be an instrument ('the instrument of government')[2] which determines the constitution of the governing body[3] and other matters relating to the school[4]. Regulations[5] must make provision with respect to the making of instruments of government, the matters to be dealt with in such instruments, the form of such instruments, and the review and variation of such instruments[6].

The governing body of a maintained school must not conduct the school under a name other than the one for the time being set out in the school's instrument of government[7].

1 As to the meaning of 'maintained school' see PARA 103 note 3.
2 As to the form and content of instruments of government, the procedure for making instruments of government, and their review see note 5.
3 As to the constitution of governing bodies of schools see PARA 195.
4 Education Act 2002 s 20(1). In relation to maintained school in Wales s 20(1) has effect subject to the Education (Wales) Measure 2011 Pt 2 Ch 1 (ss 10–21) (see PARA 198) and regulations under the Education Act 2002 s 20(2) may include provision with respect to instruments of government for federations (within the meaning of the Education (Wales) Measure 2011 s 21(1) (see PARA 198): Education Act 2002 s 20(4A) (added by the Education (Wales) Measure 2011 s 19(1)(3)(b)). The Education Act 2002 s 20(1) does not apply to any temporary governing body: see s 34(8); and PARA 197. As to the meaning of 'Wales' see PARA 7 note 3.

5   Ie regulations made under the Education Act 2002 by the Welsh Ministers: see s 212(1). The functions under the Education Act 2002 s 20 in relation to Wales were originally vested in the National Assembly for Wales and are now exercisable by the Welsh Ministers by virtue of the Government of Wales Act 2006 s 162(1), Sch 11 paras 30, 32. As to the Welsh Ministers see PARA 59.

       Regulations under the Education Act 2002 s 20(2) may require any person responsible for the making, review or variation of an instrument of government to have regard to any guidance given from time to time by the Welsh Ministers: s 20(3). Regulations under s 20(2) may also include provision with respect to instruments of government for federations: s 20(4). As to the meaning of 'person' see PARA 7 note 6. As to the publication of guidance see the Education Act 1996 s 571 (applied by the Education Act 2002 s 212(2), (3)); and PARA 60. As to the meaning of 'federation' see PARA 156 note 4. As to the regulations made under s 20(2)–(4A) see the Government of Maintained Schools (Wales) Regulations 2005, SI 2005/2914 (see further below); and the Federation of Maintained Schools (Wales) Regulations 2014, SI 2014/1132.

       As to contents and form of instruments of government see the Government of Maintained Schools (Wales) Regulations 2005, SI 2005/2914, reg 33 (amended by SI 2005/3200). As to procedure for making instruments of government see the Government of Maintained Schools (Wales) Regulations 2005, SI 2005/2914, reg 34 (amended by SI 2010/1142). As to review of instruments of government see the Government of Maintained Schools (Wales) Regulations 2005, SI 2005/2914, reg 35 (amended by SI 2010/1142). As to the duty to have regard to guidance see the Government of Maintained Schools (Wales) Regulations 2005, SI 2005/2914, reg 32 (amended by SI 2010/1142). As to copies of instruments of government and other information see the Government of Maintained Schools (Wales) Regulations 2005, SI 2005/2914, reg 36 (amended by SI 2010/1142).

6   Education Act 2002 s 20(2).
7   Education Act 2002 s 20(5).

(F) Reports

218. Governors' reports and other information relating to maintained schools. Once in every school year[1] the governing body of a maintained school[2] in Wales[3] must prepare a report (a 'governors' report') dealing with such matters, and otherwise complying with such requirements, as may be specified in regulations[4]. Such regulations may:

(1)   impose requirements on the governing body of a maintained school[5] with respect to the giving of copies of a governors' report to such persons[6] as may be prescribed[7], and making such copies available for inspection at the school[8];

(2)   make provision for: (a) enabling the governing body to determine the language or languages in which a governors' report is to be produced and the form or forms in which it is to be produced[9]; (b) requiring it to comply with any direction given by the local authority[10] with respect to any additional language to be used or with respect to any additional form in which the report is to be produced[11];

(3)   enable the governors' report to be combined with any other document whose preparation by the governing body is required by or under any enactment[12].

The governing body of a maintained school in Wales must include in a governors' report information about the action taken to promote healthy eating and drinking by pupils[13] of the school[14].

The governing body of a maintained school must provide the local authority with such reports in connection with the discharge of its functions[15] as the authority may require (either on a regular basis or from time to time) for the purposes of the exercise of any of its education functions[16].

The head teacher[17] of a maintained school must provide the governing body or, as the case may be, the local authority with such reports in connection with the discharge of his functions as may be required (either on a regular basis or from time to time) by the governing body for the purposes of the exercise of any of its functions[18], or by the authority for the purposes of the exercise of any of its education functions[19]. Where such a requirement is imposed on the head teacher by the local authority, the authority must notify the governing body of that requirement[20], and the head teacher must give the governing body a copy of any report made by him in complying with it[21].

1 As to the meaning of 'school year' see PARA 19 note 12 (definition applied by the Education Act 2002 s 212(2), (3)).

2 As to the meaning of 'maintained school' see PARA 103 note 3. As to governing bodies of maintained schools in Wales see PARA 195.

3 As to the meaning of 'Wales' see PARA 7 note 3.

4 Education Act 2002 s 30(1) (amended by the Education Act 2005 s 103(1)(a)). 'Regulations' means regulations made under the Education Act 2002 by the Welsh Ministers: see s 212(1). As to regulations made see the School Governors' Annual Reports (Wales) Regulations 2011, SI 2011/1939 (amended by SI 2013/437; and SI 2013/1561). As to special needs information which must be included in the governors' report see PARA 1027; and as to information to be included in the report concerning a statement of action following a school inspection see PARA 1197.

The Welsh Ministers may by order repeal the Education Act 2002 s 30(1), (2) (see the text to notes 5–12) (Education Act 2005 s 103(3)(a)(i)) and make such amendments of any other enactment as appear to them to be necessary or expedient in consequence of any such repeal (s 103(3)(b)). At the date at which this volume states the law no such order had been made. The functions under the Education Act 2002 s 30 and the Education Act 2005 s 103 were originally vested in the National Assembly for Wales and are now exercisable by the Welsh Ministers by virtue of the Government of Wales Act 2006 s 162(1), Sch 11 paras 30, 32. As to the Welsh Ministers see PARA 59.

5 Education Act 2002 s 30(2)(a) (amended by the Education Act 2005 s 103(1)(a)). See also note 4.

6 As to the meaning of 'person' see PARA 7 note 6.

7 Education Act 2002 s 30(2)(a)(i). See also note 4. 'Prescribed' means prescribed by regulations: s 212(1).

8 Education Act 2002 s 30(2)(a)(ii). See also note 4.

9 Education Act 2002 s 30(2)(b)(i). See also note 4.

10 As to directions see the Education Act 1996 s 570 (applied by the Education Act 2002 s 212(2), (3)); and PARA 75. As to the meaning of 'local authority' see PARA 25 (definition applied by s 212(1)).

11 Education Act 2002 s 30(2)(b)(ii) (amended by SI 2010/1158). See also note 4.

12 Education Act 2002 s 30(2)(c). See also note 4.

13 As to the meaning of 'pupil' see PARA 20 note 4 (definition applied by the Education Act 2002 s 212(2), (3)).

14 Education Act 2002 s 30(2A) (added by the Healthy Eating on Schools (Wales) Measure 2009 s 2).

15 As to the meaning of 'functions' see PARA 18 note 5 (definition applied by the Education Act 2002 s 212(2), (3)).

16 Education Act 2002 s 30(3) (amended by the Education Act 2005 s 103(1)(b); and SI 2010/1158). As to the meaning of 'education functions' see PARA 25 (definition applied by the Education Act 2002 s 212(1)).

17 As to the meaning of 'head teacher' see PARA 86 note 4 (definition applied by the Education Act 2002 s 212(2), (3)).

18 Education Act 2002 s 30(4)(a) (s 30(4) amended by the Education Act 2005 s 103(1)(b); and SI 2010/1158).

19 Education Act 2002 s 30(4)(b) (as amended: see note 18).

20 Education Act 2002 s 30(5)(a).

21 Education Act 2002 s 30(5)(b).

219. Duty of governing body of maintained schools to hold meetings following petition by parents.

The governing body of a maintained school[1] must hold a meeting ('the meeting') if it receives a petition from parents[2] of registered pupils[3] at the school requesting a meeting and it is satisfied that each of the following four conditions is satisfied[4].

The first condition is that the petition contains the signatures of the required minimum number of parents[5] of registered pupils at the school[6]. The second condition is that the meeting requested is for the purpose of discussing a matter relating to the school[7]. The third condition is that, should a meeting be held, there would be no more than three meetings held[8] during the school year in which the petition is received[9]. The fourth condition is that there are enough school days left in the school year for the following requirement[10] to be complied with[11].

The requirement referred to above is that the meeting must be held before the end of a 25 day period[12]. For these purposes, the 25 day period (1) begins on the first day after the day on which the petition is received[13]; and (2) does not include any day which is not a school day[14]. If another meeting required to be held[15] as a result of a different petition ('the other meeting') is held on a day during the 25 day period[16], but before the day on which the meeting is held, the 25 day period begins on the first day after the day on which the other meeting is held[17]. The meeting is to be open to (a) all parents of registered pupils at the school; (b) the head teacher[18]; and (c) other persons invited by the governing body[19]. The governing body must, as soon as it reasonably can after receiving a petition that requires a meeting to be held, notify the parents of all registered pupils at the school in writing of the date of the meeting and the matter to be discussed[20].

In exercising its functions[21], the governing body of a maintained school must have regard to guidance given by the Welsh Ministers[22].

1   As to the meaning of 'maintained school' see PARA 139 note 5. As to governing bodies of maintained schools in Wales see PARA 195.
2   As to the meaning of 'parent' see PARA 7 note 6 (definition applied by the School Standards and Organisation (Wales) Act 2013 s 98(1), (2)).
3   As to the meaning of 'registered pupil' see PARA 437 (definition applied by the School Standards and Organisation (Wales) Act 2013 s 98(1), (2)).
4   See the School Standards and Organisation (Wales) Act 2013 s 94(1).
5   The required minimum number of parents is the lower of the following (1) the parents of 10% of registered pupils, or (2) the parents of 30 registered pupils: see the School Standards and Organisation (Wales) Act 2013 s 94(3). For the purpose of s 94(3), the number of registered pupils is to be calculated by reference to the number of registered pupils on the day the petition is received: see s 94(4).
6   See the School Standards and Organisation (Wales) Act 2013 s 94(2).
7   See the School Standards and Organisation (Wales) Act 2013 s 94(5).
8   Ie held under the School Standards and Organisation (Wales) Act 2013 s 94.
9   See the School Standards and Organisation (Wales) Act 2013 s 94(6). As to the meaning of 'school year' see PARA 19 note 12 (definition applied by the School Standards and Organisation (Wales) Act 2013 s 98(1), (2)).
10 Ie the requirement in the School Standards and Organisation (Wales) Act 2013 s 94(8): see the text to note 12.
11 See the School Standards and Organisation (Wales) Act 2013 s 94(7). As to the meaning of 'school day' see PARA 229 note 6 (definition applied by the School Standards and Organisation (Wales) Act 2013 s 98(1), (2)).
12 See the School Standards and Organisation (Wales) Act 2013 s 94(8).
13 Ie subject to the School Standards and Organisation (Wales) Act 2013 s 94(10): see the text to notes 15–17.
14 See the School Standards and Organisation (Wales) Act 2013 s 94(9).
15 See note 8.
16 Ie in the School Standards and Organisation (Wales) Act 2013 s 94(9): see the text to notes 13, 14.
17 See the School Standards and Organisation (Wales) Act 2013 s 94(10).

18　As to the meaning of 'head teacher' see PARA 86 note 4 (definition applied by the School Standards and Organisation (Wales) Act 2013 s 98(1), (2)).

19　See the School Standards and Organisation (Wales) Act 2013 s 94(11).

20　See the School Standards and Organisation (Wales) Act 2013 s 94(12).

21　Ie under the School Standards and Organisation (Wales) Act 2013 s 94.

22　See the School Standards and Organisation (Wales) Act 2013 s 94(13). As to the Welsh Ministers see PARA 59. As to the publication of guidance see the Education Act 1996 s 571 (applied by the School Standards and Organisation (Wales) Act 2013 s 98(1), (2)); and PARA 60.

(G) Information

220. Provision of information to the Welsh Ministers. The governing body[1] or temporary governing body[2] of a community, foundation or voluntary school or a community or foundation special school[3] must make such reports and returns, and give such information, to the Welsh Ministers[4] as they may require for the purpose of the exercise of their functions[5] in relation to education[6].

1　As to governing bodies of maintained schools in Wales see PARA 195. As to the meaning of 'Wales' see PARA 7 note 3.

2　As to temporary governing bodies in relation to Wales see PARA 197.

3　As to the meaning of references to a community, foundation or voluntary school or a community or foundation special school see PARA 106 (definition applied by the School Standards and Framework Act 1998 s 140(2)).

4　The functions of the Secretary of State under the Education Act 1996 s 538, so far as exercisable in relation to Wales, were transferred to the National Assembly for Wales (see the National Assembly for Wales (Transfer of Functions) Order 1999, SI 1999/672, art 2, Sch 1) and are now vested in the Welsh Ministers (see the Government of Wales Act 2006 s 162(1), Sch 11 para 30). As to the Welsh Ministers see PARA 59.

5　As to the meaning of 'functions' see PARA 18 note 5.

6　Education Act 1996 s 538 (amended by the School Standards and Framework Act 1998 s 140(1), Sch 30 paras 57, 154). As to the general duties and functions of the Welsh Ministers in relation to education see PARA 60 et seq.

221. Distribution of information about schools providing secondary education. Where the governing body[1] of any school[2] providing primary education[3] receives a request which:

(1)　is made by the governing body of any school providing secondary education[4]; and

(2)　relates to the distribution of information about the school providing secondary education to parents[5] of pupils[6] at the school providing primary education without charge to those parents[7],

the governing body of that school must secure that the request is treated no less favourably (whether as to services provided or as to the terms on which they are provided) than any such request made by the governing body of any other school providing secondary education[8].

1　As to governing bodies of maintained schools in Wales see PARA 195. As to the meaning of 'Wales' see PARA 7 note 3.

2　For these purposes, 'school' means: (1) any community, foundation or voluntary school; or (2) any community or foundation special school, which is not established in a hospital: Education Act 1996 s 540(2) (substituted by the School Standards and Framework Act 1998 s 140(1), Sch 30 paras 57, 156). As to the meaning of references to a community, foundation or voluntary school or a community or foundation special school see PARA 106 (definition applied by the School Standards and Framework Act 1998 s 140(2)).

3　As to the meaning of 'primary education' see PARA 20.

4　Education Act 1996 s 540(1)(a). As to the meaning of 'secondary education' see PARA 21.

5　As to the meaning of 'parent' see PARA 7 note 6.

6　As to the meaning of 'pupil' see PARA 20 note 4.

7   Education Act 1996 s 540(1)(b).
8   Education Act 1996 s 540(1).

222.   Distribution of information about further education institutions.   The Welsh Ministers[1] may by regulations[2] require:

(1)   the governing body[3] of any school[4] providing secondary education[5]; and

(2)   the proprietor[6] of any city technology college[7], city college for the technology of the arts[8] or academy[9],

to provide such persons[10] as may be prescribed[11] with certain information[12] relating to institutions within the further education sector[13] and which is made available to governing bodies and proprietors for distribution[14]. Information so provided must be provided in such form and manner as may be prescribed[15].

1   The functions of the Secretary of State under the Education Act 1996 s 541, so far as exercisable in relation to Wales, were transferred to the National Assembly for Wales (see the National Assembly for Wales (Transfer of Functions) Order 1999, SI 1999/672, art 2, Sch 1) and are now vested in the Welsh Ministers (see the Government of Wales Act 2006 s 162(1), Sch 11 para 30). As to the Welsh Ministers see PARA 59. As to the meaning of 'Wales' see PARA 7 note 3.

2   Ie regulations made by the Welsh Ministers: see the Education Act 1996 s 579(1). At the date at which this volume states the law, no regulations had been made under s 541 but, by virtue of s 582(3), Sch 39 paras 1, 2, the Education (Distribution by Schools of Information about Further Education Institutions) (Wales) Regulations 1994, SI 1994/1321, have effect as if so made.

3   As to governing bodies of maintained schools in Wales see PARA 195.

4   For these purposes, 'school' means: (1) any community, foundation or voluntary school; or (2) any community or foundation special school, which is not established in a hospital: Education Act 1996 s 541(4) (substituted by the School Standards and Framework Act 1998 s 140(1), Sch 30 paras 57, 157). As to the meaning of references to a community, foundation or voluntary school or a community or foundation special school see PARA 106 (definition applied by the School Standards and Framework Act 1998 s 140(2)).

5   Education Act 1996 s 541(1)(a). As to the meaning of 'secondary education' see PARA 21.

6   As to the meaning of 'proprietor' see PARA 51 note 4.

7   As to city technology colleges see PARA 345.

8   As to city colleges for the technology of the arts see PARA 345.

9   Education Act 1996 s 541(1)(b) (amended by the Learning and Skills Act 2000 s 149, Sch 9 paras 1, 61; Education Act 2002 s 65(3), Sch 7 Pt 2 para 6(1), (6)). As to the meaning of 'academy' see PARA 346.

10   As to the meaning of 'person' see PARA 7 note 6.

11   Ie prescribed by regulations: see the Education Act 1996 s 579(1). As to the regulations made see note 2.

12   Education Act 1996 s 541(1). The information to be provided is such categories of information falling within s 541(2) (see the text to notes 13–14) as may be prescribed: see s 541(1). As to the regulations made see note 2.

13   Education Act 1996 s 541(2)(a). The information concerned is that which is published under the Further and Higher Education Act 1992 s 50 (see PARA 606): see the Education Act 1996 s 541(2)(a). As to further education see PARA 555 et seq.

14   Education Act 1996 s 541(2)(b).

15   Education Act 1996 s 541(3). As to the regulations made see note 2.

(H) Ex Officio Trustees

223.   Governors of foundation or voluntary school as ex officio trustees. Where any provision of a trust deed[1] or other instrument made before 1 July 1981 would otherwise have the effect that the persons who are for the time being governors of a foundation or voluntary school[2] were by virtue of their office trustees of any property held for the purposes of, or in connection with, the school[3], that provision instead has effect as if the only governors of the school were: (1) the foundation governors[4]; (2) those appointed by the local authority[5]; and (3) any co-opted governor nominated by a minor authority[6].

1 As to the meaning of 'trust deed' see PARA 108 note 6 (definition applied by the School Standards and Framework Act 1998 s 142(8)).
2 As to foundation and voluntary schools see PARA 106.
3 As to the meaning of 'land or other property held on trust, or by trustees, for the purposes of a school' see PARA 108 note 6.
4 School Standards and Framework Act 1998 s 83(1)(a). As to the meaning of 'foundation governor' see PARA 108 note 6.
5 School Standards and Framework Act 1998 s 83(1)(b) (amended by SI 2010/1158). As to the meaning of 'local authority' see PARA 25 (definition applied by the School Standards and Framework Act 1998 s 142(8)).
6 School Standards and Framework Act 1998 s 83(1)(c). Section 83(1) is without prejudice to any power to amend any such provision as is mentioned in s 83(1): s 83(2). As to minor authorities see PARA 194 note 6.

(vi) Admission to Schools

A. TIME FOR ADMISSION OF PUPILS

224. Time for admission. A local authority[1] is required to secure that sufficient schools[2] for providing primary education[3] and secondary education[4] are available for its area[5]. However, this requirement must not be construed as imposing any obligation on the proprietor[6] of a school to admit children[7] as pupils[8] otherwise than at the beginning of a school term[9]. Where, however, a child was prevented from entering a school at the beginning of a term:

(1) by his being ill or by other circumstances beyond his parent's[10] control[11]; or

(2) by his parent's having been then resident at a place from which the school was not accessible with reasonable facility[12],

the school's proprietor is not entitled[13] to refuse to admit the child as a pupil during the currency of the term[14]. In cases where heads (1) and (2) above do not apply, the governing body of a school maintained by a local authority[15] must comply with any general directions[16] given by the authority as to the time of admission of children as pupils[17].

Despite the duty of the parent of a child of compulsory school age[18] to cause him to receive full-time education[19], a parent is not under a duty to cause a child to receive full-time education during an period during which, having regard to the provisions described above[20], it is not practicable for the parent to arrange for the child to be admitted as a pupil at a school[21].

1 As to the meaning of 'local authority' see PARA 25.
2 As to the meaning of 'school' see PARA 91.
3 As to the meaning of 'primary education' see PARA 20.
4 As to the meaning of 'secondary education' see PARA 21.
5 See the Education Act 1996 s 14; and PARA 31.
6 As to the meaning of 'proprietor' see PARA 51 note 4.
7 As to the meaning of 'child' see PARA 7 note 6.
8 As to the meaning of 'pupil' see PARA 20 note 4.
9 Education Act 1996 s 433(1) (amended by SI 2010/1158). Any function of a local authority in England which is conferred by or under the Education Act 1996 s 433 may be exercised by, or by employees of, such person as may be authorised in that behalf by the local authority whose function it is: Contracting Out (Local Authority Education Functions) (England) Order 2002, SI 2002/928, art 3, Sch 1 para (cc) (art 3 amended by SI 2010/1172). As to the meaning of 'England' see PARA 7 note 3. As to the meaning of 'person' see PARA 7 note 6.
10 As to the meaning of 'parent' see PARA 7 note 6.
11 Education Act 1996 s 433(2)(a).
12 Education Act 1996 s 433(2)(b).
13 Ie by virtue of the Education Act 1996 s 433(1): see the text to notes 1–9.

14 Education Act 1996 s 433(2).
15 As to the governing bodies of maintained schools in England see PARA 150 et seq; and in Wales see PARA 195.
16 As to directions see the Education Act 1996 s 570; and PARA 75.
17 Education Act 1996 s 433(3) (amended by SI 2010/1158).
18 As to the meaning of 'compulsory school age' see PARA 19.
19 Ie the duty under the Education Act 1996 s 7: see PARA 435.
20 Ie the Education Act 1996 s 433(1), (2): see the text to notes 1–14.
21 Education Act 1996 s 433(5).

B. CODES AND ADVICE

225. Code for school admissions. The appropriate national authority[1] must issue, and may from time to time revise, a code for school admissions[2] containing such provision as it thinks appropriate in respect of the discharge by:

(1)   local authorities[3];
(2)   the governing bodies of maintained schools[4];
(3)   admission forums[5];
(4)   appeal panels[6]; and
(5)   adjudicators[7],

of their respective functions[8] in relation to admission arrangements[9]. The code may impose requirements, and may include guidelines setting out aims, objectives and other matters, in relation to the discharge of their functions in relation to admission arrangements[10] by local authorities and governing bodies of maintained schools[11]. The appropriate national authority must publish the code as for the time being in force[12].

It is the duty of each of the bodies and persons mentioned in heads (1) to (5) above when exercising such functions[13] in relation to admission arrangements[14], and any other person when exercising any function for the purposes of the discharge by a local authority or the governing body of a maintained school of such functions[15], to act in accordance with any relevant provisions of the code[16].

1   Ie the Secretary of State or, in relation to Wales, the Welsh Ministers. The functions of the Secretary of State under the School Standards and Framework Act 1998 s 84, so far as exercisable in relation to Wales, were transferred to the National Assembly for Wales (see the National Assembly for Wales (Transfer of Functions) Order 1999, SI 1999/672, art 2, Sch 1) and are now vested in the Welsh Ministers (see the Government of Wales Act 2006 s 162(1), Sch 11 para 30). As to the Secretary of State see PARA 58. As to the Welsh Ministers see PARA 59. As to the meaning of 'Wales' see PARA 7 note 3.
2   As to the making, revision and approval of such codes see PARA 226.
3   School Standards and Framework Act 1998 s 84(1)(a) (amended by SI 2010/1158). As to the meaning of 'local authority' see PARA 25 (definition applied by the School Standards and Framework Act 1998 s 142(8)).
4   School Standards and Framework Act 1998 s 84(1)(b). In Pt III Ch I (ss 84–98A), 'maintained school' means a community, foundation or voluntary school: s 84(6). As to the governing bodies of maintained schools in England see PARA 150 et seq; and in Wales see PARA 195. As to community, foundation and voluntary schools see PARA 106.
5   School Standards and Framework Act 1998 s 84(1)(ba) (added by the Education and Inspections Act 2006 s 40(1), (2)(b)). As to the meaning of 'admission forum' see PARA 227 note 3.
6   School Standards and Framework Act 1998 s 84(1)(c). For the purposes of Pt III Ch I (ss 84–98A), 'appeal panel' means a panel constituted in accordance with regulations under s 94(5) (see PARA 251) or s 95(3) (see PARA 252) for the purpose of hearing an appeal under Pt III Ch I: s 84(6) (definition amended by the Education Act 2002 s 51, Sch 4 para 2).
7   School Standards and Framework Act 1998 s 84(1)(d). As to the meaning of 'adjudicator' see PARA 147.
8   Ie under the School Standards and Framework Act 1998 Pt III Ch I (ss 84–98A). As to the meaning of 'functions' see PARA 18 note 5 (definition applied by s 142(8)).

9   School Standards and Framework Act 1998 s 84(1) (amended by the Education and Inspections Act 2006 s 40(1), (2)(a)). The appropriate national authority may under the School Standards and Framework Act 1998 s 84(1) make separate provision (by means of separate codes) in relation to different functions under Pt III Ch I (ss 84–98A) of the bodies and persons mentioned in s 84(1) (s 84(5)(a) (s 84(5) amended by the Education and Inspections Act 2006 ss 40(1), (5), 184, Sch 18 Pt 6)); make different provision for England and for Wales (whether or not by means of separate codes) (School Standards and Framework Act 1998 s 84(5)(b) (as so amended)); and references in s 84 to 'the code' or to functions under the Pt III Ch I have effect, in relation to any such separate code, as references to that code or to functions under Pt III Ch I to which it relates (as the case may be) (s 84(5) (as so amended)). As to the meaning of 'person' see PARA 7 note 6.
10   Ie functions under the School Standards and Framework Act 1998 Pt III Ch I (ss 84–98A).
11   School Standards and Framework Act 1998 s 84(2) (amended by the Education and Inspections Act 2006 s 40(1), (3); and SI 2010/1158).
12   School Standards and Framework Act 1998 s 84(4).
13   Ie functions under the School Standards and Framework Act 1998 Pt III Ch I (ss 84–98A).
14   School Standards and Framework Act 1998 s 84(3)(a).
15   School Standards and Framework Act 1998 s 84(3)(b) (amended by SI 2010/1158).
16   School Standards and Framework Act 1998 s 84(3) (amended by the Education and Inspections Act 2006 s 40(1), (4)).

226.   Making and approval of code for school admissions.   Where the appropriate national authority[1] proposes to issue or revise a code for school admissions[2], it must prepare a draft of the code or revised code[3]. The appropriate national authority must consult[4] such persons[5] about the draft as it thinks fit and must consider any representations made by them[6]. Where the appropriate national authority determines to proceed with the draft, either in its original form or with such modifications[7] as it thinks fit, it must take the appropriate procedural steps[8].

1   Ie the Secretary of State or, in relation to Wales, the Welsh Ministers. The functions of the Secretary of State under the School Standards and Framework Act 1998 s 85, so far as exercisable in relation to Wales, were transferred to the National Assembly for Wales (see the National Assembly for Wales (Transfer of Functions) Order 1999, SI 1999/672, art 2, Sch 1) and are now vested in the Welsh Ministers (see the Government of Wales Act 2006 s 162(1), Sch 11 para 30). As to the Secretary of State see PARA 58. As to the Welsh Ministers see PARA 59. As to the meaning of 'Wales' see PARA 7 note 3.
2   Ie a code under the School Standards and Framework Act 1998 s 84: see PARA 225.
3   School Standards and Framework Act 1998 s 85(1) (amended by the Education and Inspections Act 2006 ss 40(1), (8)(a), 184, Sch 18 Pt 6).
4   In relation to a code for school admissions issued under the School Standards and Framework Act 1998 s 84(1) after 26 November 2008 (ie the day of the passing of the Education and Skills Act 2008), the requirement to consult which is imposed by the School Standards and Framework Act 1998 s 85(2) may be satisfied by consultation undertaken before that date, even though the code takes account (to any extent) of any provision made by the Education and Skills Act 2008: s 153(2). Similar provision was made in relation to a code issued under the School Standards and Framework Act 1998 s 84(1) after 8 November 2006: see the Education and Inspections Act 2006 s 40(9). As to the exercise of the duty to consult see JUDICIAL REVIEW vol 61 (2010) PARA 627.
5   As to the meaning of 'person' see PARA 7 note 6.
6   School Standards and Framework Act 1998 s 85(2).
7   As to the meaning of 'modifications' see PARA 21 note 15 (definition applied by the School Standards and Framework Act 1998 s 142(8)).
8   In the case of a code issued or revised by the Secretary of State he must lay a copy of the draft before each House of Parliament: see the School Standards and Framework Act 1998 s 85(3). If, within the 40-day period, either House of Parliament resolves not to approve the draft, the Secretary of State must take no further steps in relation to the proposed code (s 85(4)), but this does not prevent a new draft of a proposed code from being laid before Parliament (s 85(6)). If no such resolution is made within the 40-day period, the Secretary of State may issue the code (or revised code) in the form of the draft, and it will come into force on such date as the Secretary of State may by order appoint: s 85(5). For these purposes, '40-day period', in relation

to the draft of a proposed code, means: (1) if the draft is laid before one House on a day later than the day on which it is laid before the other House, the period of 40 days beginning with the later of the two days (s 85(7)(a)); and (2) in any other case, the period of 40 days beginning with the day on which the draft is laid before each House (s 85(7)(b)). In either case, no account is taken of any period during which Parliament is dissolved or prorogued or during which both Houses are adjourned for more than four days: s 85(7). References to a proposed code include a proposed revised code: s 85(8). As to the laying of documents before Parliament see STATUTES AND LEGISLATIVE PROCESS vol 96 (2012) PARA 1052. As to the adjournment, prorogation and dissolution of Parliament see PARLIAMENT vol 78 (2010) PARA 1016 et seq.

In the case of a draft code issued or revised by the Welsh Ministers, the references in s 85(4)–(7) to a House of Parliament are to be construed as references to the National Assembly for Wales: see the Government of Wales Act 2006 Sch 11 para 33. In the case of a code issued or revised by the Welsh Ministers, the School Standards and Framework Act 1998 s 85(7) (as modified by the Government of Wales Act 2006 Sch 11 para 33) has effect as if the reference to any period during which Parliament is dissolved or prorogued or during which both Houses are adjourned for more than four days were to any period during which the National Assembly for Wales is dissolved or is in recess for more than four days: School Standards and Framework Act 1998 s 85(7A) (added by SI 2007/1388). As to the National Assembly for Wales see CONSTITUTIONAL AND ADMINISTRATIVE LAW vol 20 (2014) PARA 351 et seq.

As to the orders made under the School Standards and Framework Act 1998 s 85(5) see the School Standards and Framework Act 1998 (Commencement No 6 and Saving and Transitional Provisions) Order 1999, SI 1999/1016; the Education (Code of Practice on Local Authority-School Relations) (Appointed Day) (Wales) Order 1999, SI 1999/2022 (amended by SI 2010/1142); the Education (School Admission Appeals: The National Assembly for Wales Code of Practice) (Appointed Day) Order 1999, SI 1999/2893; the Local Authority–School Relations Code of Practice Order 2001, SI 2001/435 (amended by SI 2010/1142); the School Admissions Code (Appointed Day) (England) Order 2007, SI 2007/566; the School Admission Appeals Code (Appointed Day) (England) Order 2008, SI 2008/53; the School Admissions Code (Appointed Day) (England) Order 2009, SI 2009/210; the School Admission Appeals Code (Appointed Day) (England) Order 2009, SI 2009/211; the School Admissions Code (Appointed Day) (Wales) Order 2009, SI 2009/1844; the School Admission Appeals Code (Appointed Day) (Wales) Order 2009, SI 2009/1845; the School Admissions Code (Appointed Day) (England) Order 2010, SI 2010/302; the School Admissions Code and School Admission Appeals Code (Appointed Day) Order 2012, SI 2012/216; the School Admissions Code (Appointed Day) (Wales) Order 2013, SI 2013/1659; the School Admission Appeals Code (Appointed Day) (Wales) Order 2013, SI 2013/3141; and the School Admissions Code (Appointed Day) Order 2014, SI 2014/3321.

The 'School Admissions Code: Statutory guidance for admission authorities, governing bodies, local authorities, schools adjudicators and admission appeal panels' (December 2014) (covering, in relation to England, such matters as determining admission arrangements, applications and offers, ensuring fairness and resolving issues, and with appendices containing relevant legislation and sample admission arrangements, and with an admissions timeline and a glossary), is not reproduced. As to the School Admissions Appeals Code see also PARA 251. As to a case involving the Admissions Code and the 2012 version of the above guidance see *R (on the application of Governing Body of the London Oratory School) v Schools Adjudicator* [2015] EWHC 1012 (Admin), [2015] All ER (D) 113 (Apr). As to the adjudicator see PARA 240.

In relation to Wales, see the 'School admissions code' (July 2013) which at the date at which this volume states the law is to be found on the Welsh Government website.

227. Admission forums in Wales. A local authority in Wales[1] must in accordance with regulations[2] establish for its area a body, to be known as an 'admission forum'[3], for the purpose of:

(1)   advising the authority on such matters connected with the exercise of the authority's functions relating to admission arrangements[4] as may be prescribed[5]; and

(2)   advising the admission authorities[6] for maintained schools in the area for which the forum is established on: (a) such matters connected with the determination of admission arrangements[7]; and (b) such other matters connected with the admission of pupils[8], as may be prescribed[9];

The authority may establish sub-committees of the forum[10]. The bodies mentioned in heads (1) and (2) above must have regard, in carrying out their functions, to any relevant advice given to them by an admission forum under those provisions[11].

Regulations[12] may make provision: (i) as to the constitution, meetings and proceedings of an admission forum and of any sub-committee[13]; (ii) as to the manner in which advice is to be given by a forum[14]; and (iii) as to the establishment by local authorities of joint admission forums[15].

The local authority must make arrangements for the forum, and any sub-committee thereof, to be provided with accommodation and with such services as the authority considers appropriate[16].

1 As to the meaning of 'local authority' see PARA 25 (definition applied by the School Standards and Framework Act 1998 s 142(8)). As to the meaning of 'Wales' see PARA 7 note 3.

2 Ie originally regulations made by the Secretary of State or, in relation to Wales, the Welsh Ministers under the School Standards and Framework Act 1998: see s 142(1). However note now the amendments to s 85A by the Education Act 2011 which make the provision only applicable to Wales. The functions of the Secretary of State under the School Standards and Framework Act 1998 s 85A, so far as exercisable in relation to Wales, were originally transferred to the National Assembly for Wales (see the National Assembly for Wales (Transfer of Functions) Order 1999, SI 1999/672, art 2, Sch 1) and are now vested in the Welsh Ministers (see the Government of Wales Act 2006 s 162(1), Sch 11 para 30). As to the Secretary of State see PARA 58. As to the Welsh Ministers see PARA 59. As to the regulations made under the School Standards and Framework Act 1998 s 85A see the Education (Admission Forums) (Wales) Regulations 2003, SI 2003/2962.

3 In the School Standards and Framework Act 1998 Pt III Ch I (ss 84–98A) 'admission forum' means a forum established under s 85A, including a joint admission forum established in pursuance of regulations under s 85A(3)(c) (see the text to note 15): s 84(6) (definition added by the Education and Inspections Act 2006 s 40(1), (6)).

4 Ie functions under the School Standards and Framework Act 1998 Pt III Ch I (ss 84–98A). As to the meaning of 'functions' see PARA 18 note 5 (definition applied by s 142(8)). In Pt III Ch I 'admission arrangements', in relation to a school, means the arrangements for the admission of pupils to the school, including the school's admission policy: ss 84(6), 88(2) (s 88(2) amended by the Education Act 2011 s 64(1), (2)(c)). As to the meaning of 'school' see PARA 91; and as to the meaning of 'pupil' see PARA 20 note 4 (definitions applied by the School Standards and Framework Act 1998 s 142(8)). As to admission arrangements generally see PARA 231 et seq.

5 School Standards and Framework Act 1998 s 85A(1)(a) (s 85A added by the Education Act 2002 s 46; the School Standards and Framework Act 1998 s 85A(1)(a) amended by the Education and Inspections Act 2006 ss 41(1), (2)(a), 184, Sch 18 Pt 6; and the Education Act 2011 s 34(1), (2)(a)(iii)). 'Prescribed' means prescribed by regulations: School Standards and Framework Act 1998 s 142(1).

6 In the School Standards and Framework Act 1998 Pt III Ch I (ss 84–98A) 'the admission authority': (1) in relation to a community or voluntary controlled school, means the local authority (ss 84(6), 88(1)(a)(i) (amended by SI 2010/1158)), or where with the governing body's agreement the authority has delegated to it responsibility for determining the admission arrangements for the school, the governing body (School Standards and Framework Act 1998 ss 84(6), 88(1)(a)(ii) (amended by the Education Act 2011 s 64(1), (2)(a)); and (2) in relation to a foundation or voluntary aided school, means the governing body (School Standards and Framework Act 1998 ss 84(6), 88(1)(b)); and in relation to an academy school, means the proprietor of the academy school (ss 84(6), 88(1)(c) (added by the Education Act 2011 s 64(1), (2)(b) and amended by Sch 13 para 10(1), (3)). As to the meaning of 'proprietor' see PARA 51 note 4 (definition applied by s 142(8)).Where the admission authority for a community or voluntary controlled school is the local authority, it is the duty of the governing body to implement any decision relating to the admission of pupils to the school which is taken by or on behalf of the admission authority: s 88(1A) (s 88(1A), (1B) added by the Education and Inspections Act 2006 s 43(1); and the School Standards and Framework Act 1998 s 88(1A) amended by SI 2010/1158). The School Standards and Framework Act 1998 s 88(1A) does not affect:

    (a)   any right of appeal which the governing body may have by virtue of arrangements made in pursuance of s 95(2) (appeals in relation to children to whom s 87(2) applies, other than looked after children in England: see PARA 252) (s 88(1B)(a) (as so added));

(b)   any right to refer the matter to the adjudicator which the governing body may have by
       virtue of s 95A(3) (references to the adjudicator in relation to looked after children in
       England to whom s 87(2) applies: see PARA 252) (s 88(1B)(b) (as so added)); or
(c)   the application of s 101(2A) (see PARA 260) or s 109(2) (see PARA 267) (s 88(1B)(c) (as
       so added)).
As to community, foundation and voluntary schools and community and foundation special
schools see PARA 106. As to the governing bodies of maintained schools in in Wales see PARA
195. As to the meaning of 'academy school' see PARA 346 note 12 (definition applied by
s 142(8), (9)). See also note 2.
    The governing body of any community, foundation or voluntary school maintained by the
local authority so far as acting in connection with the admission of pupils to the school or
otherwise performing any of its functions under Pt III Ch I is subject to investigation by a local
commissioner under the Local Government Act 1974 Pt III (ss 23–34): see s 25(5)(d); and LOCAL
GOVERNMENT vol 69 (2009) PARA 853.

7   School Standards and Framework Act 1998 s 85A(1)(b)(i) (as added: see note 5).
8   School Standards and Framework Act 1998 s 85A(1)(b)(ii) (as added: see note 5).
9   School Standards and Framework Act 1998 s 85A(1)(b) (as added: see note 5).
10   School Standards and Framework Act 1998 s 85A(2) (as added: see note 5).
11   School Standards and Framework Act 1998 s 85A(4) (as added: see note 5).
12   As to the regulations made see note 2.
13   School Standards and Framework Act 1998 s 85A(3)(a) (as added: see note 5).
14   School Standards and Framework Act 1998 s 85A(3)(b) (as added (see note 5); and amended by
     the Education and Inspections Act 2006 ss 41(1), (4)(a), 184, Sch 18 Pt 6).
15   School Standards and Framework Act 1998 s 85A(3)(c) (as added (see note 5); and amended by
     SI 2010/1158; and the School Standards and Framework Act 1998 s 85A(3) amended by the
     Education Act 2011 s 34(1), (2)(c)).
16   School Standards and Framework Act 1998 s 85A(5) (as added (see note 5); and amended by
     SI 2010/1158).

C. PARENTAL PREFERENCES

228.   Parental preferences.   A local authority is entitled to apply its admissions
policy (provided that it is lawful and not unreasonable) in determining priority
for admissions, for example in respect of over-subscribed schools[1]. However, a
local authority[2] must make arrangements for enabling the parent[3] of a child[4] in
the area of the authority[5]: (1) to express a preference as to the school[6] at which
he wishes education to be provided for his child in the exercise of the authority's
functions[7]; and (2) to give reasons for his preference[8].
    The admission authority for a maintained school[9] must, subject to the
restrictions described below[10] and those relating to children excluded from two
or more schools[11], comply with any preference expressed in accordance with
such arrangements[12]. However, this duty does not apply:

(a)   if compliance with the preference would prejudice[13] the provision of
       efficient education or the efficient use of resources[14]; or
(b)   if the arrangements for admission to the preferred school are wholly
       based on selection by reference to ability or aptitude[15] and are so based
       with a view to admitting only pupils with high ability or with
       aptitude[16], and compliance with the preference would be incompatible
       with selection under those arrangements[17].

If a mandatory provision of the code for school admissions applies, it must be
complied with[18].

1   See *Cumings v Birkenhead Corpn* [1972] Ch 12, [1971] 2 All ER 881, CA; *R v Greenwich
    London Borough Council, ex p Governors of John Ball Primary School* [1990] Fam Law 469,
    sub nom *R v Shadow Education Committee of Greenwich London Borough Council,
    ex p Governors of John Ball Primary School* (1989) 88 LGR 589, CA; *R v Governors of Bishop
    Challoner Roman Catholic Comprehensive Girls' School, ex p Choudhury* [1992] 2 AC 182,
    sub nom *Choudhury v Governors of Bishop Challoner Roman Catholic Comprehensive School*

[1992] 3 All ER 277, HL; *R v Bradford Metropolitan Borough Council, ex p Sikander Ali* [1994] ELR 299; *R v Governors of the Hasmonean High School, ex p N and E* [1994] ELR 343, CA; *R v Lancashire County Council, ex p M* [1994] ELR 478; *R v Lancashire County Council, ex p F* [1995] ELR 33, sub nom *R v Lancashire County Council, ex p Foster* [1995] 1 FCR 212; *R v Rotherham Metropolitan Borough Council, ex p T* [2000] LGR 338, sub nom *R v Rotherham Metropolitan Borough Council, ex p LT* [2000] ELR 76, CA; *R v Stockton-on-Tees Borough Council, ex p W* [2000] ELR 93, CA; *R v South Gloucestershire Education Appeals Committee, ex p Bryant* [2001] ELR 53, CA; *R (on the application of L) v Independent Appeal Panel of St Edward's College* [2001] EWHC 108 (Admin), [2001] ELR 542.

2   As to the meaning of 'local authority' see PARA 25 (definition applied by the School Standards and Framework Act 1998 s 142(8)).

3   As to the meaning of 'parent' see PARA 7 note 6 (definition applied by the School Standards and Framework Act 1998 s 142(8)).

4   In the School Standards and Framework Act 1998 Pt III Ch 1 (ss 84–98A) 'child' includes a person who has not attained the age of 19, except in s 96 (see PARA 253) and s 97 (see PARA 254) in so far as those sections apply in relation to Wales: s 84(6) (definition substituted by the Apprenticeships, Skills, Children and Learning Act 2009 s 43(1), (2)). As to the meaning of 'child' generally see PARA 7 note 6 (definition applied by the School Standards and Framework Act 1998 s 142(8)). As to the time at which a person attains a particular age see PARA 7 note 6. As to preferences related to sixth form education see PARA 230. See also note 6.

5   School Standards and Framework Act 1998 s 86(1) (amended by SI 2010/1158). Arrangements made under the School Standards and Framework Act 1998 s 86(1) may allow the parent of a child to express preferences for more than one school; but nothing in s 86 requires the admission authority for a maintained school for which a child's parent has expressed a preference to offer the child admission to the school if, in accordance with a scheme adopted or made by virtue of s 89B (see PARA 248), the child is offered admission to a different school for which the parent has also expressed a preference: s 86(2A) (added by the Education Act 2002 s 51, Sch 4 para 3(1), (3)). As to the meaning of 'school' see PARA 91 (definition applied by the School Standards and Framework Act 1998 s 142(8)). As to the meaning of 'the admission authority' see PARA 227 note 6. As to the meaning of 'maintained school' see PARA 225 note 4. As to admission arrangements see PARA 231 et seq.

    Any function of a local authority in England which is conferred by or under s 86 may be exercised by, or by employees of, such person as may be authorised in that behalf by the local authority whose function it is: Contracting Out (Local Authority Education Functions) (England) Order 2002, SI 2002/928, art 3, Sch 2 para (v) (art 3 amended by SI 2010/1172). As to the meaning of 'England' see PARA 7 note 3. As to the meaning of 'person' see PARA 7 note 6.

6   The School Standards and Framework Act 1998 s 86(1) does not apply in relation to: (1) sixth form education (s 86(1ZA)(a) (s 86(1ZA) added by the Education and Skills Act 2008 s 169, Sch 1 Pt 2 paras 53, 54(1), (2))); or (2) any other education to be provided for a child who has ceased to be of compulsory school age, or will have ceased to be of compulsory school age before the education is provided for him (School Standards and Framework Act 1998 s 86(1ZA)(b) (as so added)). In Pt III Ch 1 (ss 84–98A), 'sixth form education' means secondary education suitable to the requirements of pupils who are over compulsory school age; and references, in relation to a child who has been admitted to a school, to his entering the school's sixth form are to his being transferred to a class at the school in which sixth form education is provided from a class in which such education is not so provided: s 98A(1), (2) (s 98A added by the Education and Skills Act 2008 s 153). As to the meaning of 'compulsory school age' see PARA 19; as to the meaning of 'secondary education' see PARA 21; and as to the meaning of 'pupil' see PARA 20 note 4 (definitions applied by the School Standards and Framework Act 1998 s 142(8)). As to preferences related to sixth form education see PARA 230.

    The School Standards and Framework Act 1998 s 86 does not apply in relation to pupil referral units in England or Wales: see the Education (Pupil Referral Units) (Application of Enactments) (Wales) Regulations 2007, SI 2007/1069, regs 1, 4, Sch 2 para 1; and the Education (Pupil Referral Units) (Application of Enactments) (England) Regulations 2007, SI 2007/2979, regs 1, 4, Sch 2 para 1. As to pupil referral units see PARA 427 et seq. As to the application of the School Standards and Framework Act 1998 s 86 to new schools in England see the New School (Admissions) (England) Regulations 2003, SI 2003/1041. As to the meanings of 'England' and 'Wales' see PARA 7 note 3.

7   School Standards and Framework Act 1998 s 86(1)(a). As to the meaning of 'functions' see PARA 18 note 5 (definition applied by s 142(8)). A local authority has to give consideration to the

religious convictions of parents when formulating its admissions policy: *R (on the application of K) v Newham London Borough Council* [2002] EWHC 405 (Admin), [2002] ELR 390, (2002) Times, 28 February.

8   School Standards and Framework Act 1998 s 86(1)(b). See *R v Rotherham Metropolitan Borough Council, ex p Clark* (1997) 96 LGR 214, [1998] 1 FCR 509, [1998] ELR 152, CA; *R v Sheffield City Council, ex p H* [1999] ELR 511, sub nom *R v Sheffield City Council, ex p Hague* [1999] All ER (D) 859, CA (both decided under previous legislation). A local authority in England must provide advice and assistance to parents of children in the area of the authority in connection with the preferences expressed or to be expressed by them in accordance with the arrangements made under the School Standards and Framework Act 1998 s 86(1): s 86(1A) (added by the Education and Inspections Act 2006 s 42; and amended by SI 2010/1158).

9   Where the arrangements for the admission of pupils to a maintained school provide for applications for admission to be made to (or to a person acting on behalf of) the governing body of the school, a parent who makes such an application is regarded for the purposes of the School Standards and Framework Act 1998 s 86 as having expressed a preference for that school in accordance with arrangements made under s 86(1) (see the text to notes 1–8): s 86(7). As to the governing bodies of maintained schools in England see PARA 150 et seq; and in Wales see PARA 195.

10   Ie subject to the School Standards and Framework Act 1998 s 86(3): see the text to notes 13–17.

11   Ie subject to the School Standards and Framework Act 1998 s 87: see PARA 229.

12   School Standards and Framework Act 1998 s 86(2) (amended by the Education and Inspections Act 2006 s 43(2); and the Education and Skills Act 2008 s 169, Sch 1 Pt 2 paras 53, 54(1), (3)). The duty imposed by the School Standards and Framework Act 1998 s 86(2) in relation to a preference expressed in accordance with arrangements made under s 86(1) (see the text to notes 1–8) also applies in relation to: (1) any application for the admission to a maintained school of a child who is not in the area of the authority maintaining the school (s 86(8)(a)); and (2) any application made by a parent as mentioned in the Education Act 1996 s 438(4) (choice of school: see PARA 441) or s 440(2) (application for a particular school to be named in a school attendance order: see PARA 443) (School Standards and Framework Act 1998 s 86(8)(b)). References in s 86(3) to a preference and a preferred school are to be construed accordingly: s 86(8) (amended by the Education and Skills Act 2008 s 169, Sch 1 Pt 2 paras 53, 54(1), (8)).

A failure to uphold a parent's preference did not constitute a breach of the Convention for the Protection of Human Rights and Fundamental Freedoms (Rome, 4 November 1950; TS 71 (1953); Cmd 8969) arts 6, 8 (as to which see PARA 3): *R v Richmond upon Thames London Borough Council, ex p C* [2001] LGR 146, sub nom *R v Richmond upon Thames London Borough Council, ex p JC* [2001] ELR 21, CA. In *R v Cleveland County Council, ex p Commission for Racial Equality* [1993] 1 FCR 597, 91 LGR 139, [1994] ELR 44, CA, it was held that the duty imposed by the School Standards and Framework Act 1998 s 86(2) was a mandatory duty for the purposes of the Race Relations Act 1976 s 41 (repealed) (acts done under statutory authority). See now the Equality Act 2010 Sch 22; and DISCRIMINATION vol 33 (2013) PARA 188.

The effect of the School Standards and Framework Act 1998 s 86(8)(a) (see head (1) above) is that children who live outside the area of the local authority must not, for the purposes of the duty in s 86(2), be discriminated against merely by reason of that fact: *R v Greenwich London Borough Council, ex p Governors of John Ball Primary School* [1990] Fam Law 469, sub nom *R v Shadow Education Committee of Greenwich London Borough Council, ex p Governors of John Ball Primary School* (1989) 88 LGR 589, CA; *R v Kingston-upon-Thames Royal London Borough Council, ex p Kingwell* [1992] 1 FLR 182, [1992] Fam Law 193; *R v Bromley London Borough Council, ex p C* [1992] 1 FLR 174, 156 LG Rev 282; *R v Essex County Council, ex p Jacobs* [1997] ELR 190; *R v Wiltshire County Council, ex p Razazan* [1997] ELR 370, CA; *R v Rotherham Metropolitan Borough Council, ex p T* [2000] LGR 338, sub nom *R v Rotherham Metropolitan Borough Council, ex p LT* [2000] ELR 76, CA. The offer of a school place relied upon by a parent and causing a detriment can give rise to a legitimate expectation, which would be a factor to be taken into account in determining whether it would be unreasonable to withdraw the place: see *R v Beatrix Potter School, ex p K* [1997] ELR 468 (school place offered in error later withdrawn). See also *R v Birmingham City Council, ex p L* [2000] ELR 543.

13   For these purposes, prejudice of the kind referred to in the text may arise by reason of measures required to be taken in order to ensure compliance with the duty imposed by the School Standards and Framework Act 1998 s 1(6) (duty of local authority and governing body to comply with limit on infant class sizes: see PARA 234): s 86(4) (amended by SI 2010/1158).

No prejudice must be taken to arise for the purposes of s 86(3)(a) from the admission to a maintained school in a school year of a number of pupils in a relevant age group which does not exceed the number determined under s 88C (see PARA 237) or s 89 (see PARA 247) as the number of pupils in that age group that it is intended to admit to the school in that year; but this provision does not apply if the conditions set out in s 86(5A) are met in relation to the school and the school year: s 86(5) (s 86(5) substituted, (5A), (5B) added, by the Education Act 2002 s 47(1); and then School Standards and Framework Act 1998 s 86(5) amended by the Education and Skills Act 2008 s 169, Sch 1 Pt 2 paras 53, 54(1), (5)). Those conditions are: (1) that the school is one at which boarding accommodation is provided for pupils (School Standards and Framework Act 1998 s 86(5A)(a) (as so added)); and (2) that the determination under s 88C or s 89 by the admission authority of the admission arrangements which are to apply for that year includes the determinations mentioned in s 88D(2)(a) (see PARA 237) or s 89A(2)(a), (b) (see PARA 247) (s 86(5A)(b) (as so added); and amended by the Education and Skills Act 2008 s 169, Sch 1 Pt 2 paras 53, 54(1), (6)). Where the conditions set out in the School Standards and Framework Act 1998 s 86(5A) are met in relation to a maintained school and a school year, no prejudice will be taken to arise for the purposes of s 86(3)(a) from either of the following: (a) the admission to the school in that year as boarders of a number of pupils in a relevant age group which does not exceed the number determined under s 88C or s 89 as the number of pupils in that age group that it is intended to admit to the school in that year as boarders (s 86(5B)(a) (s 86(5B) (as so added); and s 86(5B)(a), (b) amended by the Education and Skills Act 2008 s 169, Sch 1 Pt 2 paras 53, 54(1), (7))); (b) the admission to the school in that year otherwise than as boarders of a number of pupils in a relevant age group which does not exceed the number determined under the School Standards and Framework Act 1998 s 88C or s 89 as the number of pupils in that age group that it is intended to admit to the school in that year otherwise than as boarders (s 86(5B)(b) (as so added and amended)). As to the meaning of 'school year' see PARA 19 note 12; and as to the meaning of 'boarder' see PARA 31 note 19 (definitions applied by s 142(8)).

14 School Standards and Framework Act 1998 s 86(3)(a) (amended by the Education Act 2002 Sch 4 para 3(4)(a)). As to the restriction mentioned in the School Standards and Framework Act 1998 s 86(3)(a) see further *R v South Glamorgan Appeals Committee, ex p Evans* (10 May 1984, unreported); *R v Comr for Local Administration, ex p Croydon London Borough Council* [1989] 1 All ER 1033, 87 LGR 221; *R v Governors of Bishop Challoner Roman Catholic Comprehensive Girls' School, ex p Choudhury* [1992] 2 AC 182, sub nom *Choudhury v Governors of Bishop Challoner Roman Catholic Comprehensive School* [1992] 3 All ER 277, HL; *R v Governors of the Hasmonean High School, ex p N and E* [1994] ELR 343, CA; *R v Lancashire County Council, ex p M* [1994] ELR 478; *W (A Minor) v Education Appeal Committee of Lancashire County Council* [1994] 3 FCR 1, [1994] ELR 530, CA; *R v Appeal Committee of Brighouse School, ex p G and B* [1997] ELR 39; *R v Education Appeal Committee of Leicestershire County Council, ex p Tarmohamed* [1997] ELR 48; *R v Beatrix Potter School, ex p K* [1997] ELR 468; *R v Education Committee of Blackpool Borough Council, ex p Taylor* [1999] ELR 237; *R v Sheffield City Council, ex p M* [2000] ELR 85; *R v South Gloucestershire Appeals Committee, ex p C* [2000] ELR 220.

15 School Standards and Framework Act 1998 s 86(3)(c)(i). Where admission arrangements for a school provide for all pupils selected under the arrangements to be selected by reference to ability or aptitude, those arrangements must be taken for the purposes of s 86 to be wholly based on selection by reference to ability or aptitude, whether or not they also provide for the use of additional criteria in circumstances where the number of children in a relevant age group who are assessed to be of the requisite ability or aptitude is greater than the number of pupils which it is intended to admit to the school in that age group: s 86(9) (amended by the Education Act 2002 Sch 4 para 3(1), (8); and the Education and Skills Act 2008 s 169, Sch 1 Pt 2 paras 53, 54(1), (9), Sch 2). As to the meaning of 'admission arrangements' see PARA 227 note 4. As to the selection of pupils see PARA 258 et seq.

16 School Standards and Framework Act 1998 s 86(3)(c)(ii).

17 School Standards and Framework Act 1998 s 86(3)(c). See *R v Wirral Metropolitan Borough Council, ex p Pickard* (11 December 1991, unreported); *R v Kingston-upon-Thames Royal London Borough Council, ex p Emsden* [1993] 1 FLR 179, 91 LGR 96.

18 See PARA 225.

229. Children permanently excluded from two or more schools. The duty of an admission authority[1] for a maintained school[2] to comply with preferences as to school[3] or sixth form education[4], does not apply in the case of a child[5] who has been permanently excluded[6] from two or more schools during the period of two years beginning with the date on which the latest of those exclusions took effect[7]. This applies to a child whatever the length of the period or periods elapsing between those exclusions and regardless of whether it has applied to him on a previous occasion[8].

A child who has been permanently excluded from a school in England will not be treated for these purposes[9] as having been so excluded if any of the following applies:

(1)   the child was reinstated as a pupil[10] at the school following a direction[11] from the responsible body[12];

(2)   the child would have been reinstated as a pupil at the school following such a direction from the responsible body[13], if it had been practical for the responsible body to give such a direction[14];

(3)   the review panel has quashed a decision of the responsible body[15] not to reinstate the child as a pupil at the school[16];

(4)   the child was so excluded at a time when the child had not attained compulsory school age[17].

A child who has been permanently excluded from a school in Wales will not be treated for these purposes[18] as having been so excluded:

(a)   if he was reinstated as a pupil at the school following the giving of a direction to that effect[19] by the relevant authority[20];

(b)   if, on a review of his exclusion[21] or on an appeal[22], the relevant authority decided: (i) that it would not be practical to give a direction requiring his reinstatement as a pupil at the school[23]; but (ii) that it would otherwise have been appropriate to give such a direction[24]; or

(c)   he was so excluded at a time when he had not attained compulsory school age[25].

1   As to the meaning of 'the admission authority' see PARA 227 note 6.

2   As to the meaning of 'maintained school' see PARA 225 note 4.

3   Ie the duty under the School Standards and Framework Act 1998 s 86(2): see PARA 228.

4   Ie the duty under the School Standards and Framework Act 1998 s 86B(1): see PARA 230.

5   School Standards and Framework Act 1998 s 87(1) (amended by the Education and Skills Act 2008 s 169, Sch 1 Pt 2 paras 53, 55). As to the meaning of 'child' see PARA 228 note 4. As to the application of the School Standards and Framework Act 1998 s 87 to new schools in England and Wales see the New School (Admissions) (England) Regulations 2003, SI 2003/1041; and the New School (Admissions) (Wales) Regulations 2006, SI 2006/175. As to the meanings of 'England' and 'Wales' see PARA 7 note 3. Any function of a local authority in England which is conferred by or under the School Standards and Framework Act 1998 s 87 may be exercised by, or by employees of, such person as may be authorised in that behalf by the local authority whose function it is: Contracting Out (Local Authority Education Functions) (England) Order 2002, SI 2002/928, art 3, Sch 2 para (w) (art 3 amended by SI 2010/1172). As to the meaning of 'person' see PARA 7 note 6.

6   For these purposes, the permanent exclusion of a child from a school is regarded as having taken effect on the school day as from which the head teacher decided that the child should be permanently excluded: School Standards and Framework Act 1998 s 87(6). As to the meaning of 'exclusion' see PARA 316 note 6. 'School day', in relation to a school, means any day on which at that school there is a school session: Education Act 1996 s 579(1) (definition applied by the School Standards and Framework Act 1998 s 142(8)). As to the meaning of 'school' generally see PARA 91. In s 87, 'school' means: (1) in relation to any time before or after 1 September 1999 (ie the appointed day: see PARA 106 note 3), a school maintained by a local authority (s 87(5)(a) (amended by SI 2010/1158)); or (2) in relation to any time before 1 September 1999, a grant-maintained or grant-maintained special school within the meaning of the Education Act 1996 (School Standards and Framework Act 1998 s 87(5)(b)). As to the meaning of 'school maintained by a local authority' see PARA 99. As to grant-maintained schools and grant-maintained special schools see PARA 106. As to the meaning of 'local authority' see PARA 25; and as to the meaning of 'head teacher' see PARA 86 note 4 (definitions applied by s 142(8)).

7   School Standards and Framework Act 1998 s 87(2). Nothing in s 87 applies to a child unless at
    least one of the two or more exclusions mentioned in s 87(2) took effect on or after 1 September
    1997: s 87(7).
        Because, as a consequence and part of regulating the right to educational access, s 87 only
    removes the obligation to comply with parental preference and the child would still be educated,
    that provision is not incompatible with the Convention for the Protection of Human Rights and
    Fundamental Freedoms (Rome, 4 November 1950; TS 71 (1953); Cmd 8969), First Protocol
    (Paris, 20 March 1952; TS 46 (1954); Cmd 9221) art 2 (as to which see PARA 3): *R (on the
    application of B) v Head Teacher of Alperton Community School, R (on the application of T) v
    Head Teacher of Wembley High School, R (on the application of C) v Governing Body of
    Cardinal Newman High School* [2001] EWHC Admin 229, [2001] ELR 359, [2002] LGR 132;
    affd without comment on this point sub nom *R (on the application of S) v Brent London
    Borough Council, R (on the application of T) v Head Teacher of Wembley High School, R (on
    the application of P) v Oxfordshire County Council Exclusion Appeals Panel* [2002] EWCA Civ
    693, [2002] ELR 556, [2002] All ER (D) 277 (May).
8   School Standards and Framework Act 1998 s 87(3).
9   Ie for the purposes of the School Standards and Framework Act 1998 s 87.
10 As to the meaning of 'pupil' see PARA 20 note 4 (definition applied by the School Standards and
    Framework Act 1998 s 142(8)).
11 Ie (1) in accordance with regulations under the Education Act 2002 s 51A(3)(b) (see PARA 517);
    or (2) following a recommendation from the review panel that the responsible body reconsiders
    the matter under s 51A(4)(b) (see PARA 517): see the School Standards and Framework Act 1998
    s 87(3A)(a)(i), (ii) (s 87(3A), (3B) added by the Education Act 2011 Sch 1 paras 8, 9). 'The
    responsible body' has the same meaning as in the Education Act 2002 s 51A (see PARA 517):
    School Standards and Framework Act 1998 s 87(3B) (as so added).
12 School Standards and Framework Act 1998 s 87(3A)(a) (as added: see note 11).
13 Ie a direction as described in the School Standards and Framework Act 1998 s 87(3A)(a)(i) or
    (ii): see note 11.
14 School Standards and Framework Act 1998 s 87(3A)(b) (as added: see note 11).
15 Ie a decision under the Education Act 2002 s 51A(4)(c): see PARA 517.
16 School Standards and Framework Act 1998 s 87(3A)(c) (as added: see note 11).
17 School Standards and Framework Act 1998 s 87(3A)(d) (as added: see note 11). As to the
    meaning of 'compulsory school age' see PARA 19.
18 See note 9.
19 Ie in accordance with regulations under the Education Act 2002 s 52(3)(b) or (c): see PARA 517.
20 School Standards and Framework Act 1998 s 87(4)(a) (s 87(4) substituted, (4A) added, by the
    Education Act 2002 s 51, Sch 4 para 4; and the School Standards and Framework Act 1998
    s 87(4) amended by the Education Act 2011 Sch 1 paras 8, 10). 'The relevant authority' means:
    (1) the responsible body as defined by the Education Act 2002 s 52(5) (see PARA 517) (School
    Standards and Framework Act 1998 s 87(4A)(a) (as so added)); or (2) a panel constituted in
    accordance with regulations under the Education Act 2002 s 52(3)(c) (see PARA 517) (School
    Standards and Framework Act 1998 s 87(4A)(b) (as so added)).
21 Ie carried out in accordance with regulations under the Education Act 2002 s 52(3)(b): see PARA
    517.
22 Ie made pursuant to regulations under the Education Act 2002 s 52(3)(c): see PARA 517.
23 School Standards and Framework Act 1998 s 87(4)(b)(i) (as substituted: see note 12).
24 School Standards and Framework Act 1998 s 87(4)(b)(ii) (as substituted: see note 12).
25 School Standards and Framework Act 1998 s 87(4)(c) (as substituted: see note 12).

D. PREFERENCES RELATING TO SIXTH FORM EDUCATION

230. Local authority arrangements. A local authority[1] must make
arrangements for enabling[2]:

(1)   a child[3] in the authority's area to express a preference as to the school[4]
      at which he wishes sixth form education[5] to be provided for him in the
      exercise of the authority's functions[6];

(2)   a parent[7] of such a child to express a preference as to the school at
      which he wishes sixth form education to be so provided for his child[8];

(3)   a relevant child[9] to express a preference as to the school at which he

wishes education other than sixth form education to be provided for him in the exercise of the authority's functions[10]; and

(4)   a parent of such a child to express a preference as to the school at which he wishes such education to be so provided for his child[11];

and, in each case, for enabling the person expressing the preference to give reasons for his preference[12]. The arrangements made must allow: (a) a person who is to be able to express a preference under any of heads (1) to (4) above to express preferences for more than one school[13]; (b) preferences to be expressed, in relation to a child, by both the child and a parent of his[14].

Where the arrangements for the admission of pupils[15] to a maintained school[16] provide for applications for admission to be made to (or to a person[17] acting on behalf of) the governing body of the school[18], and a child (whether or not in the area of the authority maintaining the school) or his parent makes such an application[19], that person must be regarded for these purposes[20] as having expressed a preference for that school in accordance with such arrangements[21].

Subject to the provisions relating to children permanently excluded from two or more schools[22], the admission authority[23] for a maintained school must comply with any preference expressed in accordance with arrangements made under the above provisions[24]. However, this duty does not apply if: (i) compliance with the preference would prejudice the provision of efficient education or the efficient use of resources[25]; (ii) in a case where a preference is expressed in relation to sixth form education if the relevant selection arrangements[26] for the preferred school are wholly based on selection by reference to ability or aptitude[27], and compliance with the preference would be incompatible with selection under those arrangements[28].

1   As to the meaning of 'local authority' see PARA 25 (definition applied by the School Standards and Framework Act 1998 s 142(8)).

2   School Standards and Framework Act 1998 s 86A(1) (ss 86A, 86B added by the Education and Skills Act 2008 s 150; and the School Standards and Framework Act 1998 s 86A(1), (2) amended by SI 2010/1158).

3   As to the meaning of 'child' see PARA 228 note 4.

4   As to the meaning of 'school' see PARA 91 (definition applied by the School Standards and Framework Act 1998 s 142(8)).

5   As to the meaning of 'sixth form education' see PARA 228 note 6.

6   School Standards and Framework Act 1998 s 86A(1)(a) (as added: see note 2). As to the meaning of 'functions' see PARA 18 note 5 (definition applied by the School Standards and Framework Act 1998 s 142(8)).

7   As to the meaning of 'parent' see PARA 7 note 6 (definition applied by the School Standards and Framework Act 1998 s 142(8)).

8   School Standards and Framework Act 1998 s 86A(1)(b) (as added: see note 2).

9   'Relevant child', in relation to a local authority and any education, means a child in the authority's area who (1) has ceased to be of compulsory school age (School Standards and Framework Act 1998 s 86A(2)(a) (as added and amended: see note 2)); or (2) will have ceased to be of compulsory school age before the education in question is provided for him (s 86A(2)(b) (as so added and amended)). As to the meaning of 'compulsory school age' see PARA 19.

10   School Standards and Framework Act 1998 s 86A(1)(c) (as added: see note 2).

11   School Standards and Framework Act 1998 s 86A(1)(d) (as added: see note 2).

12   School Standards and Framework Act 1998 s 86A(1) (as added: see note 2).

13   School Standards and Framework Act 1998 s 86A(3)(a) (as added: see note 2).

14   School Standards and Framework Act 1998 s 86A(3)(b) (as added: see note 2).

15   As to the meaning of 'pupil' see PARA 20 note 4 (definition applied by the School Standards and Framework Act 1998 s 142(8)).

16   As to the meaning of 'maintained school' see PARA 225 note 4.

17   As to the meaning of 'person' see PARA 7 note 6.

18 School Standards and Framework Act 1998 s 86A(4)(a) (as added: see note 2). As to the governing bodies of maintained schools in England see PARA 150 et seq; and in Wales see PARA 195.

19 School Standards and Framework Act 1998 s 86A(4)(b) (as added: see note 2).

20 Ie for the purposes of the School Standards and Framework Act 1998 Pt III Ch 1 (ss 84–98A).

21 School Standards and Framework Act 1998 s 86A(4) (as added: see note 2).

22 Ie subject to the School Standards and Framework Act 1998 s 87: see PARA 229.

23 As to the meaning of 'the admission authority' see PARA 227 note 6.

24 School Standards and Framework Act 1998 s 86B(1) (as added: see note 2).

25 School Standards and Framework Act 1998 s 86B(2) (as added: see note 2). Section 86(5)–(5B) (see PARA 228) applies for the purpose of determining whether any prejudice should be taken to arise for the purposes of s 86B(2), but with the substitution of references to that subsection for references to s 86(3)(a): s 86B(3) (as so added).

26 'The relevant selection arrangements', in relation to a school, means: (1) the arrangements for admission to the school for sixth form education (School Standards and Framework Act 1998 s 86B(6)(a) (as added: see note 2)); or (2) those arrangements and the arrangements for entry to the sixth form of children who have been admitted to the school (s 86B(6)(b) (as so added)).

27 School Standards and Framework Act 1998 s 86B(4)(a) (as added: see note 2). Where the relevant selection arrangements for a school provide for all pupils selected under the arrangements to be selected by reference to ability or aptitude, those arrangements must be taken for the purposes of s 86B(4)(a) to be wholly based on selection by reference to ability or aptitude whether or not they also provide for the use of additional criteria in circumstances where the number of children in a relevant age group who are assessed to be of the requisite ability or aptitude is greater than the number of pupils which it is intended to admit to the school in that age group: s 86B(5) (as so added).

28 School Standards and Framework Act 1998 s 86B(4)(b) (as added: see note 2).

E. ADMISSION ARRANGEMENTS

(A) Admission Arrangements Generally

231. Publication of information about admissions. Regulations[1] may:

(1) require the publication by a local authority[2] of such information relating to admissions as may be prescribed[3];

(2) require the publication by the governing body[4] of a foundation or voluntary aided school[5] of such information relating to admissions as may be prescribed[6];

(3) require or allow the publication by the governing body of any school maintained by a local authority[7], or by the local authority on behalf of the governing body, of such information relating to the school as may be prescribed[8]; and

(4) make provision as to the time by which, and the manner in which, information required to be published by virtue of these provisions is to be published[9].

The general power of the Secretary of State or the Welsh Ministers to make regulations requiring information about schools from governing bodies and proprietors of independent schools must be exercised with a view to, inter alia, assisting parents in choosing schools for their children[10].

1 Ie regulations made by the Secretary of State or, in relation to Wales, the Welsh Ministers under the School Standards and Framework Act 1998: see s 142(1). The functions of the Secretary of State under the School Standards and Framework Act 1998 s 92, so far as exercisable in relation to Wales, were transferred to the National Assembly for Wales (see the National Assembly for Wales (Transfer of Functions) Order 1999, SI 1999/672, art 2, Sch 1) and are now vested in the Welsh Ministers (see the Government of Wales Act 2006 s 162(1), Sch 11 para 30). As to the Secretary of State see PARA 58. As to the Welsh Ministers see PARA 59. As to the meanings of 'England' and 'Wales' see PARA 7 note 3.

As to the regulations made under the School Standards and Framework Act 1998 s 92 see the Education (Special Educational Needs) (Information) (Wales) Regulations 1999, SI 1999/1442; the Education (Special Educational Needs) (Information) (England) Regulations 1999, SI 1999/2506 (amended by SI 2002/2469; and SI 2013/235); the School Information (England) Regulations 2008, SI 2008/3093 (amended by SI 2012/8; SI 2012/979; SI 2012/1124; SI 2013/758; and SI 2013/2912); the School Information (Wales) Regulations 2011, SI 2011/1944 (amended by SI 2013/437); and the School Admissions (Admission Arrangements and Co-ordination of Admission Arrangements) (England) Regulations 2012, SI 2012/8 (amended by SI 2014/2886). As to the School Admissions Code see also PARA 226.

As to the application of the School Standards and Framework Act 1998 s 92 to new schools in England see the New School (Admissions) (England) Regulations 2003, SI 2003/1041; and in Wales see the New School (Admissions) (Wales) Regulations 2006, SI 2006/175.

2   As to the meaning of 'local authority' see PARA 25 (definition applied by the School Standards and Framework Act 1998 s 142(8)). Any function of a local authority in England which is conferred by or under the School Standards and Framework Act 1998 s 92 may be exercised by, or by employees of, such person as may be authorised in that behalf by the local authority whose function it is: Contracting Out (Local Authority Education Functions) (England) Order 2002, SI 2002/928, art 3, Sch 2 para (y) (art 3 amended by SI 2010/1172). As to the meaning of 'person' see PARA 7 note 6.

3   School Standards and Framework Act 1998 s 92(a) (s 92 substituted by the Education Act 2002 s 51, Sch 4 para 7; and the School Standards and Framework Act 1998 s 92(a), (c) amended by SI 2010/1158). 'Prescribed' means prescribed by the regulations: see the School Standards and Framework Act 1998 s 142(1).

4   As to the governing bodies of maintained schools in England see PARA 150 et seq; and in Wales see PARA 195.

5   As to foundation and voluntary aided schools see PARA 106.

6   School Standards and Framework Act 1998 s 92(b) (as substituted: see note 3).

7   As to the meaning of 'school maintained by a local authority' see PARA 99.

8   School Standards and Framework Act 1998 s 92(c) (as substituted and amended: see note 3).

9   School Standards and Framework Act 1998 s 92(d) (as substituted: see note 3).

10   See the Education Act 1996 s 537; and PARA 67.

232. Admission conditions relating to home-school agreements. The governing body of a school which is a maintained school[1], a city technology college[2], a city college for the technology of the arts[3] or an academy school[4] must adopt a home-school agreement[5] for the school, together with a parental declaration[6] to be used in connection with the agreement[7]. Neither the governing body of such a school nor the local authority[8] where it is the admission authority[9] may: (1) invite any person to sign the parental declaration at a time when the child[10] in question has not been admitted to the school[11]; (2) make it a condition of a child being admitted to the school that the parental declaration is signed in respect of the child[12]; or (3) make any decision as to whether or not to admit a child to the school by reference to whether any such declaration is or is not likely to be signed in respect of the child[13].

1   School Standards and Framework Act 1998 s 110(1)(a). As to the meaning of 'maintained school' see PARA 99. As to the governing bodies of maintained schools in England see PARA 150 et seq; and in Wales see PARA 195.

2   As to city technology colleges see PARA 345.

3   As to city colleges for the technology of the arts see PARA 345.

4   School Standards and Framework Act 1998 s 110(1)(b) (amended by the Learning and Skills Act 2000 s 149, Sch 9 paras 1, 85; the Education Act 2002 s 65(3), Sch 7 Pt 2 para 9; and the Education Act 2011 Sch 13 para 10(1), (9)). As to the meaning of 'academy school' see PARA 346 note 12 (definition applied by the School Standards and Framework Act 1998 s 142(8)).

5   As to the meaning of 'home-school agreement' see PARA 92.

6   As to the meaning of 'parental declaration' see PARA 92 note 13.

7   School Standards and Framework Act 1998 s 110(1). As to home-school agreements see further PARA 92.

8   As to the meaning of 'local authority' see PARA 25 (definition applied by the School Standards and Framework Act 1998 s 142(8)).

9   School Standards and Framework Act 1998 s 111(4) (amended by SI 2010/1158). As to the meaning of 'the admission authority' see PARA 227 note 6 (definition applied by the School Standards and Framework Act 1998 s 111(4)).

10 As to the meaning of 'child' see PARA 7 note 6 (definition applied by the School Standards and Framework Act 1998 s 142(8)).

11 School Standards and Framework Act 1998 s 111(4)(a).

12 School Standards and Framework Act 1998 s 111(4)(b).

13 School Standards and Framework Act 1998 s 111(4)(c).

233. Discrimination in relation to admissions. It is unlawful to discriminate against, or to victimise, a person in relation to his admission to a school, or to harass a person who has applied for admission as a pupil[1].

1   See the Equality Act 2010 s 85; and PARA 9.

234. Duty to set limit on infant class sizes. The appropriate national authority[1] must by regulations[2]: (1) impose a limit on class[3] sizes for infant classes[4] at maintained schools[5]; and (2) specify the school years in relation to which any such limit is to have effect[6]. Any limit so imposed must specify the maximum number of pupils that a class to which the limit applies may contain while an ordinary teaching session is conducted by a single school teacher[7]. Such regulations must be so framed that the maximum number specified is 30[8].

The regulations may provide for any limit imposed to take effect either at the same time in the case of each of the age groups into which the pupils in infant classes fall[9], or at different times[10] in the case of different such age groups[11]. The regulations may also provide that, in any circumstances specified in the regulations, any such limit either is not to apply or is to operate in such manner as is so specified[12].

Where any limit imposed applies to an infant class at a maintained school, the local authority[13] and the governing body[14] must exercise their functions[15] with a view to securing that that limit is complied with in relation to that class[16].

1   Ie the Secretary of State or, in relation to Wales, the Welsh Ministers. The functions of the Secretary of State under the School Standards and Framework Act 1998 s 1, so far as exercisable in relation to Wales, were transferred to the National Assembly for Wales (see the National Assembly for Wales (Transfer of Functions) Order 1999, SI 1999/672, art 2, Sch 1) and are now vested in the Welsh Ministers (see the Government of Wales Act 2006 s 162(1), Sch 11 para 30). As to the Secretary of State see PARA 58. As to the Welsh Ministers see PARA 59. As to the meaning of 'Wales' see PARA 7 note 3.

2   As to the regulations made under the School Standards and Framework Act 1998 s 1 see the School Admissions (Infant Class Sizes) (England) Regulations 2012, SI 2012/10 (amended by SI 2014/852; and SI 2014/2103); and the School Admissions (Infant Class Sizes) (Wales) Regulations 2013, SI 2013/1141 (amended by SI 2014/852). See eg *R (on the application of DD) v Independent Appeal Panel of the London Borough of Islington* [2013] EWHC 2262 (Admin), [2013] All ER (D) 361 (Jul).

3   'Class' means a group in which pupils are taught in an ordinary teaching session; and 'ordinary teaching session' does not include a school assembly or other school activity usually conducted with large groups of pupils: School Standards and Framework Act 1998 s 4. As to the meaning of 'pupil' see PARA 20 note 4 (definition applied by s 142(8)).

4   'Infant class' means a class containing pupils the majority of whom will attain the age of five, six or seven during the course of the school year: School Standards and Framework Act 1998 s 4. As to the meaning of 'school year' see PARA 19 note 12 (definition applied by s 142(1)). As to the time at which a person attains a particular age see PARA 7 note 6.

5   School Standards and Framework Act 1998 s 1(1)(a). As to the meaning of 'maintained school' see PARA 99. As to the application of s 1 to new schools in England see the New School

(Admissions) (England) Regulations 2003, SI 2003/1041; and in Wales see the New School (Admissions) (Wales) Regulations 2006, SI 2006/175. As to the meaning of 'England' see PARA 7 note 3.

6   School Standards and Framework Act 1998 s 1(1)(b). See eg *R (on the application of the London Borough of Lambeth) v Independent Appeal Panel of the London Borough of Lambeth* [2014] EWHC 3151 (Admin), [2014] All ER (D) 108 (Oct).

7   School Standards and Framework Act 1998 s 1(2) (amended by the Education Act 2002 Sch 21 para 87). 'School teacher' means a person who is a school teacher for the purposes of the Education Act 2002 s 122 (determination of school teachers' pay and conditions: see PARA 1001 note 3): School Standards and Framework Act 1998 s 4 (definition added by the Education Act 2002 Sch 21 para 88).

8   School Standards and Framework Act 1998 s 1(3)(a). The limit specified by s 1(3)(a) had effect in relation to the 2001–2002 school year and any subsequent year: see s 1(3)(b). Section 1(3) may by order be amended by substituting for '30' such other number as is specified in the order, or by substituting for the reference to the 2001–2002 school year a reference to such other school year as is so specified: s 1(5).

9   School Standards and Framework Act 1998 s 1(4)(a)(i).

10   Ie which may be earlier than the beginning of the school year mentioned in the School Standards and Framework Act 1998 s 1(3): see note 8.

11   School Standards and Framework Act 1998 s 1(4)(a)(ii).

12   School Standards and Framework Act 1998 s 1(4)(b). As to excepted pupils see the New School (Admissions) (England) Regulations 2003, SI 2003/1041, reg 5, Schedule (amended by SI 2014/852; and SI 2014/2103) which add new categories of excepted pupils and change the circumstances in which pupils cease to be excepted. 'Excepted pupils' are certain types of children (including those with special educational needs) who cannot be provided with education at the school in an infant class in which the limit is not exceeded without measures being taken which would prejudice efficient education or the efficient use of resources. See also the School Admissions Code 2014 para 2.15. As to the Code generally see PARA 226 note 8.

13   As to the meaning of 'local authority' see PARA 25 (definition applied by the School Standards and Framework Act 1998 s 142(8)).

14   As to the governing bodies of maintained schools in England see PARA 150 et seq; and in Wales see PARA 195.

15   As to the meaning of 'functions' see PARA 18 note 5 (definition applied by the School Standards and Framework Act 1998 s 142(8)).

16   School Standards and Framework Act 1998 s 1(6) (amended by SI 2010/1158).

(B) Admission Arrangements in England

235. Prohibition on interviews. No admission arrangements[1] for a maintained school[2] in England[3] may require or authorise any interview with an applicant for admission to the school or his parents[4], where the interview is to be taken into account (to any extent) in determining whether the applicant is to be admitted to the school[5]. If the maintained school is one at which boarding accommodation is provided for pupils[6], this prohibition does not apply in relation to any interview intended to assess the suitability of an applicant for a boarding place[7]; and where the admission arrangements for a maintained school in England make provision for a permitted form of selection by aptitude[8], this prohibition does not prevent the arrangements from requiring or authorising any audition or other oral or practical test to be carried out in relation to an applicant solely for the purpose of ascertaining the applicant's aptitude in accordance with the arrangements[9].

1   As to the meaning of 'admission arrangements' see PARA 227 note 4. As to admission arrangements in general see PARA 231 et seq.

2   As to the meaning of 'maintained school' see PARA 225 note 4.

3   As to the meaning of 'England' see PARA 7 note 3.

4   As to the meaning of 'parent' see PARA 7 note 6 (definition applied by the School Standards and Framework Act 1998 s 142(8)). As to parental preferences in relation to choice of school see PARAS 228–230.

5   School Standards and Framework Act 1998 s 88A(1) (s 88A added by the Education and
     Inspections Act 2006 s 44; and the School Standards and Framework Act 1998 s 88A(1), (3)
     amended by the Education and Skills Act 2008 s 151(1), (3)). See also the School Admissions
     Code 2014 para 1.9. As to oversubscription criteria see paras 1.6–1.10. As to the Code generally
     see PARA 226 note 8.
6   As to the meaning of 'pupil' see PARA 20 note 4 (definition applied by the School Standards and
     Framework Act 1998 s 142(8)).
7   School Standards and Framework Act 1998 s 88A(2) (as added: see note 5).
8   'Permitted form of selection by aptitude' is to be read in accordance with the School Standards
     and Framework Act 1998 s 99(4) (see PARA 258): s 88A(4) (as added: see note 5).
9   School Standards and Framework Act 1998 s 88A(3) (as added and amended: see note 5).

**236.   Admission arrangements relating to children looked after by local
authority.** Regulations[1] may require the admission authorities[2] for maintained
schools[3] in England[4] to include in their admission arrangements[5] such provision
relating to the admission of children who are looked after by a local authority[6] in
England as may be prescribed[7]. Such regulations may in particular include
provision for securing that[8] such children are to be offered admission in
preference to other children[9].

1   Ie regulations made by the Secretary of State under the School Standards and Framework
     Act 1998: see s 142(1). As to the Secretary of State see PARA 58. As to the regulations made see
     the School Admissions (Admission Arrangements and Co-ordination of Admission
     Arrangements) (England) Regulations 2012, SI 2012/8 (amended by SI 2014/2886). See also
     PARA 226.
2   As to the meaning of 'the admission authority' see PARA 227 note 6.
3   As to the meaning of 'maintained school' see PARA 225 note 4.
4   As to the meaning of 'England' see PARA 7 note 3.
5   As to the meaning of 'admission arrangements' see PARA 227 note 4.
6   In the School Standards and Framework Act 1998 Pt III Ch 1 (ss 84–98A), references to a child
     who is looked after by a local authority are to be read in accordance with the Children Act 1989
     s 22(1) (see CHILDREN AND YOUNG PERSONS vol 10 (2012) PARA 843): School Standards and
     Framework Act 1998 s 84(7) (added by the Education and Inspections Act 2006 s 50(2)). As to
     the meaning of 'child' see PARA 228 note 4. See also the School Admissions Code 2014 para 1.7
     which makes reference to 'looked after children' and 'all previously looked after children'. As to
     the Code see generally PARA 226 note 8.
7   School Standards and Framework Act 1998 s 88B(1) (s 88B added by the Education and Skills
     Act 2008 s 151(1), (4)). 'Prescribed' means prescribed by the regulations: see the School
     Standards and Framework Act 1998 s 142(1).
8   Ie subject to the School Standards and Framework Act 1998 s 86(3) (see PARA 228),
     s 86B(2), (4) (see PARA 230) and s 87 (see PARA 229).
9   School Standards and Framework Act 1998 s 88B(2) (as added: see note 7).

237.   Procedure for determining admission arrangements. The admission
authority[1] for a maintained school[2] in England[3] must, before the beginning of
each school year[4], determine[5] the admission arrangements[6] which are to apply
for that year[7]. The admission authority must, before determining the admission
arrangements that are to apply for a year, carry out such consultation[8] about the
proposed arrangements as may be prescribed[9] by regulations[10]. The regulations
may in particular make provision: (1) specifying persons[11] who must be
consulted, or who must be consulted about prescribed provisions of proposed
arrangements[12]; (2) specifying provisions of proposed arrangements about which
any such consultation is to be carried out[13]; (3) specifying matters to which any
such consultation is, or is not, to relate[14]; (4) as to the manner in which, and the
time by which, any such consultation is to be carried out[15].

When the admission authority has determined the admission arrangements
that are to apply for a year, it must notify the appropriate bodies[16] of those
admission arrangements[17]. A determination of the admission arrangements

which are to apply for a school year must include a determination of the number of pupils[18] in each relevant age group[19] that it is intended to admit to the school in that year[20]. A determination may also, if the school is one at which boarding accommodation is provided for pupils, include a determination of the number of pupils[21] in each relevant age group that it is intended to admit to the school in that year as boarders[22], and a determination of the number of pupils[23] in each relevant age group that it is intended to admit to the school in that year otherwise than as boarders[24].

It should be noted that admission authorities may give priority in their oversubscription criteria[25] to children eligible for the early years pupil premium[26], the pupil premium[27] and also children eligible for the service premium[28]; admission authorities should clearly define in the arrangements the categories of eligible premium recipients to be prioritised[29].

1   As to the meaning of 'the admission authority' see PARA 227 note 6.
2   As to the meaning of 'maintained school' see PARA 225 note 4.
3   As to the meaning of 'England' see PARA 7 note 3.
4   As to the meaning of 'school year' see PARA 19 note 12 (definition applied by the School Standards and Framework Act 1998 s 142(8)).
5   Ie in accordance with the School Standards and Framework Act 1998 s 88C.
6   As to the meaning of 'admission arrangements' see PARA 227 note 4.
7   School Standards and Framework Act 1998 s 88C(1) (ss 88C, 88D, 88F all added by the Education and Skills Act 2008 s 151(1), (4)). As to the variation of admission arrangements see PARA 238.
8   As to the exercise of the duty to consult see JUDICIAL REVIEW vol 61 (2010) PARA 627.
9   'Prescribed' means prescribed by regulations made by the Secretary of State under the School Standards and Framework Act 1998: see s 142(1). As to the Secretary of State see PARA 58. As to the regulations made under ss 88C, 88D (see the text to notes 18–24) and s 88F (see notes 16, 17) see the School Admissions (Admission Arrangements and Co-ordination of Admission Arrangements) (England) Regulations 2012, SI 2012/8 (amended by SI 2014/2886). See also PARA 226.
10 School Standards and Framework Act 1998 ss 88C(2), 142(1) (s 88C as added: see note 7).
11 As to the meaning of 'person' see PARA 7 note 6.
12 School Standards and Framework Act 1998 s 88C(3)(a) (as added: see note 7).
13 School Standards and Framework Act 1998 s 88C(3)(b) (as added: see note 7).
14 School Standards and Framework Act 1998 s 88C(3)(c) (as added: see note 7).
15 School Standards and Framework Act 1998 s 88C(3)(d) (as added: see note 7).
16 In the School Standards and Framework Act 1998 ss 88C and 88E (see PARA 238), the 'appropriate bodies', in relation to an admission authority, means: (1) whichever of the governing body and the local authority are not the admission authority (s 88F(3)(a) (as so added; and amended by SI 2010/1158)); (2) the admission authorities for all other maintained schools in the relevant area or for such class of schools as may be prescribed (School Standards and Framework Act 1998 s 88F(3)(b) (as so added)); (3) the governing bodies for all community and voluntary controlled schools in the relevant area (so far as not falling within head (1) or (2)) (s 88F(3)(c) (as so added)); (4) the admission authorities for maintained schools in England of any prescribed description (s 88F(3)(d) (as so added)); (5) in the case of a foundation or voluntary school which has a religious character for the purposes of Pt II (ss 20–83) (see PARA 914), such body or person representing the religion or religious denomination in question as may be prescribed (s 88F(3)(e) (as so added)); and (6) such other persons as may be prescribed (s 88F(3)(g) (as so added)). 'The relevant area' means (a) the area of the local authority in which the school in question is situated (s 88F(4)(a) (as so added; and amended by SI 2010/1158)); or (b) if regulations so provide, such other area in England (whether more or less extensive than the area of the local authority) as may be determined by or in accordance with the regulations (School Standards and Framework Act 1998 s 88F(4)(b) (as so added; and amended by SI 2010/1158)). As to the regulations made see note 9. As to the governing bodies of maintained schools in England see PARA 150 et seq. As to the meaning of 'local authority' see PARA 25 (definition applied by the School Standards and Framework Act 1998 s 142(8)). As to community, foundation and voluntary schools see PARA 106. As to the meaning of 'admission forum' see PARA 227 note 3.

17 School Standards and Framework Act 1998 s 88C(4) (as added: see note 7). Regulations may make provision (1) as to the manner in which, and the time by which, any such notification is to be given (s 88C(5)(a) (as so added)); (2) specifying cases in which s 88C(4) does not apply (s 88C(5)(b) (as so added)). Regulations may also make provision: (a) requiring an admission authority which has made a determination of a prescribed description under s 88C to publish such information relating to the determination (including information as to the authority's reasons for making the determination) as may be prescribed (s 88F(1)(a) (as so added)); (b) as to such other matters connected with the procedure for determining admission arrangements under ss 88C, 88D (see the text to notes 18–24) as the Secretary of State considers appropriate (see s 88F(1)(b) (as so added)). The power under head (a) to require an admission authority to publish information includes power to require it to publish it: (i) by giving a notice containing the information to prescribed persons (s 88F(2)(a) (as so added)); or (ii) in any other prescribed manner (s 88F(2)(b) (as so added)). As to the regulations made see note 9. As to the reference of objections about admission arrangements to the adjudicator see PARA 240.

18 References in the School Standards and Framework Act 1998 s 88D to the determination of any number include references to the determination of zero as that number: s 88D(3) (as added: see note 7).

19 As to the meaning of 'relevant age group' see PARA 133 note 15.

20 See the School Standards and Framework Act 1998 s 88D(1) (as added: see note 7). Regulations may make provision about the making of any determination required by s 88D(1), and may in particular require the admission authority for a maintained school to have regard, in making any such determination, to: (1) any prescribed method of calculation (s 88D(3)(a) (as so added)); and (2) any other prescribed matter (s 88D(3)(b) (as so added)). As to the regulations made see note 9.

21 See note 18.

22 School Standards and Framework Act 1998 s 88D(2)(a) (as added: see note 7). As to the meaning of 'boarder' see PARA 31 note 19 (definition applied by s 142(8)).

23 See note 18.

24 School Standards and Framework Act 1998 s 88D(2)(b) (as added: see note 7).

25 As to oversubscription criteria generally see the School Admissions Code 2014 paras 1.6–1.10. As to the Code generally see PARA 226 note 8.

26 The early years pupil premium is additional funding paid to support disadvantaged children receiving government-funded early education, under the Childcare Act 2006 s 7: see ss 7, 7A; and CHILDREN AND YOUNG PERSONS vol 10 (2012) PARA 1083.

27 The pupil premium is additional funding paid annually to schools under the Education Act 2002 s 14 or the purposes of supporting the attainment of disadvantaged children: see PARA 78.

28 The service premium is additional funding paid annually to schools under the Education Act 2002 s 14 for the purposes of supporting the pastoral needs of the children of Armed Services personnel. As to s 14 generally see PARA 78.

29 See the School Admissions Code 2014 para 1.39A. See note 25.

238. Variation of admission arrangements. Where an admission authority[1] has determined[2] the admission arrangements[3] which are to apply for a particular school year[4], but at any time before the end of that year considers that the arrangements should be varied in view of a major change in circumstances occurring since they were so determined[5], the authority must refer[6] its proposed variations to the adjudicator [7]and notify the appropriate bodies [8]of the proposed variations[9].

On such a reference, the adjudicator must consider whether the admission arrangements should have effect with the proposed variations until the end of the school year in question[10]. If the adjudicator determines that the arrangements should so have effect[11], or that they should so have effect subject to such modification[12] of those variations as the adjudicator may determine[13], the arrangements are to have effect accordingly as from the date of the adjudicator's determination[14]. Where the adjudicator makes a determination, the admission authority must notify the appropriate bodies of the variations subject to which the arrangements are to have effect[15].

1 As to the meaning of 'the admission authority' see PARA 227 note 6.

2   Ie in accordance with the School Standards and Framework Act 1998 s 88C: see PARA 237.

3   As to the meaning of 'admission arrangements' see PARA 227 note 4.

4   School Standards and Framework Act 1998 s 88E(1)(a) (ss 88E, 88F added by the Education and Skills Act 2008 s 151(1), (4)). As to the meaning of 'school year' see PARA 19 note 12 (definition applied by the School Standards and Framework Act 1998 s 142(8)).

5   School Standards and Framework Act 1998 s 88E(1)(b) (as added: see note 4). Regulations may make provision: (1) specifying matters which are, or are not, to constitute major changes in circumstances for the purposes of s 88E(1)(b) (s 88E(9)(a) (as so added)); (2) authorising an admission authority, where it has in accordance with s 88C (see PARA 237) determined the admission arrangements which are to apply for a particular school year, to vary those arrangements to such extent or in such circumstances as may be prescribed (s 88E(9)(b) (as so added)); (3) for the application of any of the requirements of, or imposed under, s 88E(2)–(8) (see the text to notes 6–15) to variations proposed to be made by virtue of head (2), or to any prescribed description of such variations, as if they were variations proposed to be made under s 88E(1) (s 88E(9)(c) (as so added)). 'Regulations' means regulations made under the School Standards and Framework Act 1998 by the Secretary of State; and 'prescribed' means prescribed by such regulations: see s 142(1). As to the Secretary of State see PARA 58. As to the regulations made under ss 88E, 88F (see note 7) see the School Admissions (Admission Arrangements and Co-ordination of Admission Arrangements) (England) Regulations 2012, SI 2012/8 (amended by SI 2014/2886). See also PARA 226.

6   Where the local authority is the admission authority for a community or voluntary controlled school, it must consult the governing body before making any reference under the School Standards and Framework Act 1998 s 88E(2)(a): s 88E(4) (as so added; and amended by SI 2010/1158). As to the meaning of 'local authority' see PARA 25 (definition applied by the School Standards and Framework Act 1998 s 142(8)). As to community or voluntary controlled schools see PARA 106. As to the governing bodies of maintained schools in England see PARA 150 et seq. As to the exercise of the duty to consult see JUDICIAL REVIEW vol 61 (2010) PARA 627.

7   School Standards and Framework Act 1998 s 88E(2)(a) (as added: see note 4). As to the meaning of 'adjudicator' see PARA 147. Section 88E(2)(a) does not apply in a case where the authority's proposed variations fall within any description of variations prescribed for these purposes: s 88E(3) (as so added). Regulations may make provision as to such other matters connected with the procedure for varying admission arrangements as the Secretary of State considers appropriate: see s 88F(2)(b) (as so added). As to the regulations made see note 5.

8   As to the meaning of 'appropriate bodies' see PARA 237 note 16.

9   School Standards and Framework Act 1998 s 88E(2)(b) (as added: see note 4).

10   School Standards and Framework Act 1998 s 88E(5) (as added: see note 4).

11   School Standards and Framework Act 1998 s 88E(6)(a) (as added: see note 4).

12   As to the meaning of 'modification' see PARA 21 note 15 (definition applied by the School Standards and Framework Act 1998 s 142(8)).

13   School Standards and Framework Act 1998 s 88E(6)(b) (as added: see note 4).

14   School Standards and Framework Act 1998 s 88E(6) (as added: see note 4).

15   School Standards and Framework Act 1998 s 88E(7) (as added: see note 4). Regulations may make provision: (1) as to the manner in which, and the time by which, any such notification is to be given (s 88E(8)(a) (as so added)); (2) specifying cases in which s 88E(7) does not apply (s 88E(8)(b) (as so added)). As to the regulations made see note 5.

239. Power to restrict alteration of admission arrangements following establishment or expansion. In relation to a maintained school[1] in England[2] where:

(1)   proposals for the establishment of, or the making of a prescribed alteration[3] to, the school have[4] been published[5];

(2)   in the case of proposals for the making of a prescribed alteration to the school, the proposals are for an increase in the number of pupils[6] that may be admitted to the school or for an enlargement of the premises[7];

(3)   the proposals fall to be implemented (with or without modifications)[8]; and

(4)   prescribed[9] conditions are satisfied[10],

regulations[11] may provide that:

(a)   the admission arrangements for the initial period[12] and each of a prescribed number of school years[13] following that period are to be the arrangements which fall to be implemented in accordance with the proposals (or in accordance with the proposals as modified)[14]; and

(b)   those arrangements may not be varied by the admission authority for the school except (i) to comply with any duty imposed on them[15] in relation to children looked after by a local authority[16], or (ii) in accordance with regulations[17] prescribing circumstances in which an admission authority may refer to the adjudicator[18] proposals to vary admission arrangements[19].

Regulations may make provision as to the determination by the adjudicator of any such reference made to him[20].

1   As to the meaning of 'maintained school' see PARA 225 note 4.
2   As to the meaning of 'England' see PARA 7 note 3.
3   'Prescribed alteration' means an alteration prescribed for the purposes of the Education and Inspections Act 2006 s 18 (see PARA 132): School Standards and Framework Act 1998 s 88G(7) (s 88G added by the Education and Skills Act 2008 s 151(1), (4)).
4   Ie under the Education and Inspections Act 2006 Pt 2 (ss 6A–32) (see PARA 111 et seq) or under the Learning and Skills Act 2000 s 113A or Sch 7 (repealed).
5   School Standards and Framework Act 1998 s 88G(1)(a) (as added: see note 3).
6   As to the meaning of 'pupil' see PARA 20 note 4 (definition applied by the School Standards and Framework Act 1998 s 142(8)).
7   School Standards and Framework Act 1998 s 88G(1)(b) (as added: see note 3). As to the meaning of 'premises' see PARA 62 note 20 (definition applied by s 142(8)).
8   School Standards and Framework Act 1998 s 88G(1)(c) (as added: see note 3). As to the meaning of 'modifications' see PARA 21 note 15 (definition applied by s 142(8)).
9   'Prescribed' means prescribed by regulations made by the Secretary of State under the School Standards and Framework Act 1998: see s 142(1). As to the Secretary of State see PARA 58. As to the regulations made under s 88G see the School Admissions (Admission Arrangements and Co-ordination of Admission Arrangements) (England) Regulations 2012, SI 2012/8 (amended by SI 2014/2886). See also PARA 226.
10 School Standards and Framework Act 1998 s 88G(1)(d) (as added: see note 3).
11 Regulations under the School Standards and Framework Act 1998 s 88G(2) may: (1) exclude or modify any provision of s 88C, 88E or 88F (see PARAS 237, 238) in its application to cases to which the regulations apply (s 88G(3) (as added: see note 3)); (2) provide that in cases to which the regulations apply the admission arrangements which fall to be implemented in accordance with the proposals (or in accordance with the proposals as modified) are to be treated for the purposes of s 86(5)–(5B) (see PARA 228) as having been determined by the admission authority under s 88C (see PARA 237) (s 88G(4) (as so added)). As to the regulations made see note 9. As to the meaning of 'admission arrangements' see PARA 227 note 4.
12 'Initial period' means: (1) in relation to a maintained school which is being established, the period beginning with the day on which the school opens and ending with the beginning of the first school term to begin after the following July; (2) in relation to a maintained school which is increasing the number of pupils that may be admitted to the school or enlarging its premises, the period beginning with the first day on which additional pupils may be admitted or (as the case may be) the enlarged premises are in use and ending with the beginning of the first school term to begin after the following July: School Standards and Framework Act 1998 s 88G(7) (as added: see note 3).
13 As to the meaning of 'school year' see PARA 19 note 12 (definition applied by the School Standards and Framework Act 1998 s 142(8)).
14 School Standards and Framework Act 1998 s 88G(2)(a) (as added: see note 3).
15 Ie by regulations under the School Standards and Framework Act 1998 s 88B: see PARA 236.
16 School Standards and Framework Act 1998 s 88G(2)(b)(i) (as added: see note 3).
17 See the School Standards and Framework Act 1998 s 88G(2)(b)(ii) (as added: see note 3).
18 As to the meaning of 'adjudicator' see PARA 147.
19 See the School Standards and Framework Act 1998 s 88G(5) (as added: see note 3).
20 See the School Standards and Framework Act 1998 s 88G(6) (as added: see note 3). As to the regulations made see note 9.

240. Reference of objections to adjudicator. Where admission arrangements[1] have been determined by an admission authority[2] for a maintained school[3] in England[4], or where admission arrangements for an academy school[5] have been determined by the proprietor of an academy school under academy arrangements[6], and a body or person[7] wishes to make an objection about the admission arrangements[8], and the objection does not fall within any description of objections prescribed for these purposes[9], that body or person may refer the objection to the adjudicator[10].

On any such reference the adjudicator must decide whether, and (if so) to what extent, the objection should be upheld[11].

Regulations[12] may make provision:

(1) as to any conditions which must be satisfied before an objection can be referred[13] to the adjudicator[14], or the adjudicator is required to determine an objection referred[15] to him[16];

(2) as to circumstances in which the adjudicator is not required to determine an objection[17];

(3) prescribing the steps which may be taken by an admission authority where an objection has been referred to the adjudicator but has not yet been determined[18];

(4) prohibiting or restricting the reference, within such period following a decision by the adjudicator as may be prescribed, of any objection raising the same (or substantially the same) issues in relation to the admission arrangements of the school in question[19].

1   As to the meaning of 'admission arrangements' see PARA 227 note 4.
2   Ie under the School Standards and Framework Act 1998 s 88C: see PARA 237. As to the meaning of 'the admission authority' see PARA 227 note 6.
3   As to the meaning of 'maintained school' see PARA 225 note 4.
4   School Standards and Framework Act 1998 s 88H(1 (s 88H added by the Education and Skills Act 2008 s 151(1), (4)). As to the meaning of 'England' see PARA 7 note 3.
5   As to the meaning of 'academy school' see PARA 346 note 12 (definition applied by the School Standards and Framework Act 1998 s 142(8)).
6   School Standards and Framework Act 1998 s 88H(1A) (added by the Education Act 2011 s 64(1), (3); and amended by Sch 13 para 10(1), (4)(a)). As to the meaning of 'proprietor' see PARA 51 note 4; and as to the meaning of 'academy arrangements' see PARA 346 note 4 (definitions applied by the School Standards and Framework Act 1998 s 142(8)).
7   As to the meaning of 'person' see PARA 7 note 6.
8   School Standards and Framework Act 1998 s 88H(2)(a) (as added (see note 4); and amended by the Education Act 2011 s 36(1), (2)(a)).
9   School Standards and Framework Act 1998 s 88H(2)(b) (as added: see note 4). 'Prescribed' means prescribed by regulations made by the Secretary of State under the School Standards and Framework Act 1998: see s 142(1). As to the Secretary of State see PARA 58. As to the regulations made under s 88H see the School Admissions (Admission Arrangements and Co-ordination of Admission Arrangements) (England) Regulations 2012, SI 2012/8 (amended by SI 2014/2886). See also PARA 226.
10   School Standards and Framework Act 1998 s 88H(2) (as added (see note 4); and amended by the Education Act 2011 s 36(1), (2)(b)). As to the meaning of 'adjudicator' see PARA 147.
11   School Standards and Framework Act 1998 s 88H(4) (as added (see note 4); and amended by the Education Act 2011 s 36(1), (4)). As to such decisions of the adjudicator see further the School Standards and Framework Act 1998 s 88K; and PARA 242.
12   As to the regulations made see note 9.
13   Ie under the School Standards and Framework Act 1998 s 88H(2): see the text to notes 7–8.
14   School Standards and Framework Act 1998 s 88H(5)(a)(i) (as added (see note 4); and amended by the Education Act 2011 s 36(1), (5)(c)).
15   See note 13.
16   School Standards and Framework Act 1998 s 88H(5)(a)(ii) (as added (see note 4); and amended by the Education Act 2011 s 36(1), (5)(b)).
17   School Standards and Framework Act 1998 s 88H(5)(b) (as added: see note 4).

18 School Standards and Framework Act 1998 s 88H(5)(c) (as added (see note 4); and amended by the Education Act 2011 s 36(1), (5)(c)).

19 School Standards and Framework Act 1998 s 88H(5)(d) (as added (see note 4); and amended by the Education Act 2011 s 36(1), (5)(d)). As to the time limit for objections see the School Admissions (Admission Arrangements and Co-ordination of Admission Arrangements) (England) Regulations 2012, SI 2012/8, reg 23 (substituted SI 2014/2886). See note 9. See also generally the School Admissions Code 2014; and PARA 226 note 8.

241. Other functions of adjudicator relating to admission arrangements. The following provisions apply where admission arrangements[1] have been determined[2] (1) by an admission authority[3] for a maintained school[4] in England[5]; or (2) by an admission authority for an academy school[6].

Where it appears to the Secretary of State[7] that the admission arrangements do not, or may not, conform with the requirements relating to admission arrangements[8], the Secretary of State may refer the admission arrangements to the adjudicator[9].

Where the Secretary of State so refers the admission arrangements to the adjudicator[10], the adjudicator must consider the admission arrangements[11], and decide whether they conform with those requirements and, if not, in what respect they do not[12].

Where it appears to the adjudicator that the admission arrangements do not, or may not, conform with the requirements relating to admission arrangements (and the above provisions[13] do not apply) the adjudicator may consider the admission arrangements[14], and if the adjudicator so considers the arrangements he must decide whether they conform with those requirements and, if not, in what respect they do not[15].

Regulations[16] may make provision prescribing the steps which may be taken by an admission authority where the adjudicator is considering[17] the authority's admission arrangements[18] but has not yet made a decision[19] in the case[20].

1 As to the meaning of 'admission arrangements' see PARA 227 note 4.
2 Ie under the School Standards and Framework Act 1998 s 88C: see PARA 237.
3 As to the meaning of 'the admission authority' see PARA 227 note 6.
4 As to the meaning of 'maintained school' see PARA 225 note 4.
5 School Standards and Framework Act 1998 s 88I(1)(a) (ss 88I, 88K added by the Education and Skills Act 2008 s 151(1), (4); and the School Standards and Framework Act 1998 s 88I(1)(a) designated as such by the Education Act 2011 s 64(1), (4)(a)). As to the meaning of 'England' see PARA 7 note 3.
6 School Standards and Framework Act 1998 s 88I(1)(b) (s 88I as added (see note 5); and s 88I(1)(b) added by the Education Act 2011 s 64(1), (4)(b)). As to the meaning of 'academy school' see PARA 346 note 12 (definition applied by the School Standards and Framework Act 1998 s 142(8)).
7 As to the Secretary of State see PARA 58.
8 In the School Standards and Framework Act 1998 ss 88I, 88K 'the requirements relating to admission arrangements' means (1) in relation to a maintained school the requirements imposed by or under the Pt III (ss 84–109) as to the content of admission arrangements for maintained schools in England; and (2) in relation to an academy school, the requirements imposed by or under academy arrangements as to the content of its admission arrangements: s 88K(5) (as added (see note 5); and amended by the Education Act 2011 s 64(1), (5)(b), Sch 10 para 4(1), (2)(d), Sch 13 para 10(1)(6)(b)). As to the meaning of 'academy arrangements' see PARA 346 note 4 (definition applied by the School Standards and Framework Act 1998 s 142(8)).
9 School Standards and Framework Act 1998 s 88I(2) (as added: see note 5). As to the meaning of 'adjudicator' see PARA 147.
10 School Standards and Framework Act 1998 s 88I(3)(a) (as added (see note 5); and s 88(1)(b) repealed by the Education Act 2011 s 34(1), (3)).
11 School Standards and Framework Act 1998 s 88I(4)(a) (as added: see note 5).

12 School Standards and Framework Act 1998 s 88I(4)(b) (as added: see note 5). As to such decisions of the adjudicator see further s 88K; and PARA 242.

13 Ie the School Standards and Framework Act 1998 s 88I(4): see the text to notes 11–12.

14 School Standards and Framework Act 1998 s 88I(5)(a) (as added: see note 5).

15 School Standards and Framework Act 1998 s 88I(5)(b) (as added: see note 5). As to such decisions of the adjudicator see further s 88K; and PARA 242.

16 Ie regulations made by the Secretary of State under the School Standards and Framework Act 1998: see s 142(1). As to the regulations made under s 88I see the School Admissions (Admission Arrangements and Co-ordination of Admission Arrangements) (England) Regulations 2012, SI 2012/8 (amended by SI 2014/2886). See also PARA 226.

17 Ie under the School Standards and Framework Act 1998 s 88I(4)(a) (see the text to note 11) or (5)(a) (see the text to note 14).

18 School Standards and Framework Act 1998 s 88I(6)(a) (as added: see note 5).

19 Ie under the School Standards and Framework Act 1998 s 88I(4)(b) (see the text to note 12) or (5)(b) (see the text to note 15) (as the case may be).

20 School Standards and Framework Act 1998 s 88I(6)(b) (as added: see note 5).

242. Other matters relating to adjudicator's decisions. Any decision of the adjudicator[1]:

(1)   on whether to uphold an objection to admission arrangements[2]; or

(2)   on whether admission arrangements conform with the requirements relating to admission arrangements[3],

is binding on the admission authority[4] in question[5], and any other person[6] or body[7]. In the case of a decision mentioned in head (1) or (2) above, the adjudicator must publish a report containing certain specified information[8].

Regulations[9] may make provision: (a) requiring an admission authority for a maintained school[10] in England[11] or an academy school[12] to provide information which falls within a prescribed[13] description[14], and is requested[15] by the adjudicator[16]; (b) as to the manner in which a report[17] is to be published[18]; (c) requiring such matters to be notified to such persons, and in such manner, as may be prescribed[19]; (d) prescribing circumstances in which an admission authority may revise the admission arrangements for its school in the light of any decision by the adjudicator relating to the admission arrangements for another school, and the procedure to be followed in such a case[20].

1   As to the meaning of 'adjudicator' see PARA 147.

2   School Standards and Framework Act 1998 s 88K(1)(a) (s 88K added by the Education and Skills Act 2008 s 151(1), (4)). The decision referred to in the text is any under the School Standards and Framework Act 1998 s 88H(4) (see PARA 240): see s 88K(1)(a) (as so added). As to the meaning of 'admission arrangements' see PARA 227 note 4.

3   School Standards and Framework Act 1998 s 88K(1)(b) (as added: see note 2). The decisions referred to in the text are any under s 88I(4)(b) or (5)(b) (see PARA 241): see s 88K(1)(b) (as so added; and s 88K(1)(c) repealed by the Education Act 2011 Sch 10 para 4(1), (2)(a)(ii)). As to the meaning of 'the requirements relating to admission arrangements' see PARA 241 note 8.

4   As to the meaning of 'the admission authority' see PARA 227 note 6.

5   School Standards and Framework Act 1998 s 88K(2)(a) (as added: see note 2).

6   As to the meaning of 'person' see PARA 7 note 6.

7   School Standards and Framework Act 1998 s 88K(2)(b) (as added (see note 2); and substituted by the Education Act 2011 s 36(7)).

8   See the School Standards and Framework Act 1998 s 88K(3) (as added (see note 2); and substituted by the Education Act 2011 Sch 10 para 4(1), (2)(b)). The report must contain the following:

(1)   the adjudicator's decision on the objection or (as the case may be) on whether the admission arrangements conform with the requirements relating to admission arrangements (School Standards and Framework Act 1998 s 88K(3)(a) (as so added and substituted)); and

(2)   the reasons for that decision (s 88K(3)(b) (as so added and substituted)).

9   Ie regulations made by the Secretary of State under the School Standards and Framework Act 1998: see s 142(1). As to the Secretary of State see PARA 58. As to the regulations made

under s 88K see the School Admissions (Admission Arrangements and Co-ordination of Admission Arrangements) (England) Regulations 2012, SI 2012/8 (amended by SI 2014/2886). See also PARA 226.

10 As to the meaning of 'maintained school' see PARA 225 note 4.

11 As to the meaning of 'England' see PARA 7 note 3.

12 As to the meaning of 'academy school' see PARA 346 note 12 (definition applied by the School Standards and Framework Act 1998 s 142(8)).

13 'Prescribed' means prescribed by the regulations: see the School Standards and Framework Act 1998 s 142(1).

14 School Standards and Framework Act 1998 s 88K(4)(a)(i) (as added (see note 2); and s 88K(4)(a) and s 88K(4)(a)(i) amended by the Education Act 2011 Sch 10 para 4(1), (2)(c), Sch 13 para 10(1), (6)(a)).

15 Ie for the purposes of the exercise by the adjudicator of functions under the School Standards and Framework Act 1998 ss 88H–88I (see PARAS 240–241) or s 88K or of enabling the adjudicator to decide whether to exercise the power conferred by s 88I(5) (see PARA 241). As to the meaning of 'functions' see PARA 18 note 5 (definition applied by s 142(8)).

16 School Standards and Framework Act 1998 s 88K(4)(a)(ii) (as added (see note 2); and amended by the Education Act 2011 Sch 10 para 4(1), (2)(c)).

17 Ie a report required to be published under the School Standards and Framework Act 1998 s 88K(3): see the text to note 8.

18 School Standards and Framework Act 1998 s 88K(4)(b) (as added: see note 2).

19 School Standards and Framework Act 1998 s 88K(4)(c) (as added: see note 2).

20 School Standards and Framework Act 1998 s 88K(4)(d) (as added: see note 2).

243. Co-ordination of admission arrangements. Regulations[1] may require a local authority in England[2]:

(1) to formulate, for any academic year[3] in relation to which prescribed conditions are satisfied, a qualifying scheme[4] for co-ordinating the arrangements for the admission of pupils to maintained schools[5] in its area[6]; and

(2) to take prescribed action with a view to securing the adoption of the scheme by the authority and each governing body who are the admission authority[7] for a maintained school in its area[8].

The Secretary of State may make, in relation to the area of a local authority in England and an academic year, a scheme for co-ordinating the arrangements, or assisting in the co-ordination of the arrangements, for the admission of pupils to maintained schools in that area[9]. Such a scheme may not be made in relation to a local authority and an academic year if, before the prescribed date in the year preceding the year in which that academic year commences a scheme formulated by the local authority[10] is adopted[11] in the prescribed manner[12], and the authority provide the Secretary of State with a copy of the scheme and inform the Secretary of State that the scheme has been so adopted[13].

Regulations[14] may provide:

(a) that each local authority in England must secure that, subject to such exceptions as may be prescribed, no decision made by any admission authority for a maintained school in its area to offer or refuse a child[15] admission to the school is to be communicated to the parent[16] of the child except on a single day, designated by the local authority, in each year[17]; or

(b) that, subject to such exceptions as may be prescribed, a decision made by the admission authority for a maintained school in England to offer or refuse a child admission to the school is not to be communicated to the parent of the child except on a prescribed day[18].

Regulations may also provide that where any decision as to whether a child is to be granted or refused admission to a maintained school in England falls to be made in prescribed circumstances, the decision must, if a scheme[19] so provides, be made by the local authority regardless of whether it is the admission authority for the school[20].

1   Ie regulations made by the Secretary of State under the School Standards and Framework Act 1998: see s 142(1). As to the Secretary of State see PARA 58. As to the regulations made under ss 88M, 88N see the School Admissions (Admission Arrangements and Co-ordination of Admission Arrangements) (England) Regulations 2012, SI 2012/8 (amended by SI 2014/2886). See also PARA 226.

2   School Standards and Framework Act 1998 s 88M(1) (ss 88M, 88N added by the Education and Skills Act 2008 s 151(1), (4); and amended by SI 2010/1158). Before proposing a scheme for adoption under the School Standards and Framework Act 1998 s 88M(1) a local authority must comply with such requirements as to consultation as may be prescribed: s 88N(5) (as so added and amended). Regulations under the School Standards and Framework Act 1998 s 88N(5) may in particular require consultations to be undertaken with a view to securing that the arrangements for the admission of pupils to maintained schools in the areas of different local authorities are, so far as is reasonably practicable, compatible with each other: s 88N(6) (as so added and amended). As to the meaning of 'local authority in England' see PARA 25; as to the meaning of 'pupil' see PARA 20 note 4 (definitions applied by s 142(8)). 'Prescribed' means prescribed by regulations: see s 142(1). As to the exercise of the duty to consult see JUDICIAL REVIEW vol 61 (2010) PARA 627. As to the meaning of 'maintained school' see PARA 225 note 4. As to the meaning of 'admission arrangements' see PARA 227 note 4.

3   'Academic year' means a period commencing with 1 August and ending with the next 31 July: School Standards and Framework Act 1998 s 88M(5) (as added: see note 2).

4   'Qualifying scheme' means a scheme that meets prescribed requirements: School Standards and Framework Act 1998 s 88M(5) (as added: see note 2).

5   Nothing in the School Standards and Framework Act 1998 s 88M applies in relation to arrangements for the admission to maintained schools of pupils: (1) who have ceased to be of compulsory school age (s 88M(6)(a)(i) (as added: see note 2)), or will have ceased to be of compulsory school age before education is provided for them at the school (s 88M(6)(a)(ii) (as so added)); or (2) for the purpose of receiving sixth form education (s 88M(6)(b) (as so added)). As to the meaning of 'compulsory school age' see PARA 19. As to the meaning of 'sixth form education' see PARA 228 note 6.

6   School Standards and Framework Act 1998 s 88M(1)(a) (as added: see note 2). Regulations may provide that where a local authority in England or the governing body of a maintained school in England have, in such manner as may be prescribed, adopted a scheme formulated by a local authority for the purpose mentioned in s 88M(1)(a), the Education Act 1996 ss 496 and 497 (see PARAS 64, 65) are to apply as if any obligations imposed on the local authority or governing body under the scheme were duties imposed on them by that Act: School Standards and Framework Act 1998 s 88N(2) (as so added and amended). As to the governing bodies of maintained schools in England see PARA 150 et seq.

7   As to the meaning of 'the admission authority' see PARA 227 note 6.

8   School Standards and Framework Act 1998 s 88M(1)(b) (as added: see note 2).

9   School Standards and Framework Act 1998 s 88M(2) (as added and amended: see note 2). Regulations may make provision about the contents of schemes under s 88M(2), including provision about the duties that may be imposed by such schemes on local authorities in England (s 88N(1)(a) (as so added and amended)), and the admission authorities for maintained schools in England (s 88N(1)(b) (as so added)). Before making a scheme under s 88M(2) in relation to the area of any local authority, the Secretary of State must consult the local authority (s 88N(7)(a) (as so added and amended)), and any governing body which is the admission authority for a school which appears to the Secretary of State to be a school to which the scheme will apply (s 88N(7)(b) (as so added)). A scheme made under s 88M(2) may be varied or revoked by the Secretary of State: s 88N(8) (as so added).

10   Ie in accordance with the School Standards and Framework Act 1998 s 88M(1): see the text to notes 1–8.

11   Ie by the persons mentioned in the School Standards and Framework Act 1998 s 88M(1)(b): see the text to notes 7–8.

12   School Standards and Framework Act 1998 s 88M(3)(a) (as added and amended: see note 2).

13   School Standards and Framework Act 1998 s 88M(3)(b) (as added: see note 2).

14   As to the regulations made see note 1.

15   As to the meaning of 'child' see PARA 228 note 4.

16 As to the meaning of 'parent' see PARA 7 note 6 (definition applied by the School Standards and Framework Act 1998 s 142(8)).

17 School Standards and Framework Act 1998 s 88M(4)(a) (as added and amended: see note 2).

18 School Standards and Framework Act 1998 s 88M(4)(b) (as added: see note 2).

19 Ie a scheme adopted or made by virtue of the School Standards and Framework Act 1998 s 88M: see the text to notes 1–18.

20 School Standards and Framework Act 1998 s 88N(3) (as added and amended: see note 2). Where any decision as to whether a child is to be granted or refused admission to a maintained school is (by virtue of regulations under s 88N(3)) made by the local authority although it is not the admission authority, the governing body of the school must implement the decision: s 88N(4) (as so added and amended).

244. Sharing of information by local authorities. The Secretary of State[1] may by regulations[2] require local authorities in England[3] to provide other local authorities with such information as may be required by them in connection with the exercise of any of their functions[4] relating to admission arrangements[5].

1 As to the Secretary of State see PARA 58.

2 As to the regulations made see the School Admissions (Admission Arrangements and Co-ordination of Admission Arrangements) (England) Regulations 2012, SI 2012/8 (amended by SI 2014/2886). See also PARA 226.

3 As to the meanings of 'local authority' and 'local authority in England' see PARA 25 (definition applied by the School Standards and Framework Act 1998 s 142(8)).

4 Ie their functions under the School Standards and Framework Act 1998 Pt III Ch 1 (ss 84–98A). As to the meaning of 'functions' see PARA 18 note 5 (definition applied by s 142(8)).

5 School Standards and Framework Act 1998 s 88O (added by the Education and Skills Act 2008 s 151(1), (4); and amended by SI 2010/1158).

245. Reports by local authorities to adjudicator. A local authority in England[1] must make such reports to the adjudicator[2] about such matters connected with relevant school admissions[3] as may be required by the code for school admissions[4].

A relevant person[5] must, on request, provide a local authority in England with such information as the authority may reasonably require for the purpose of enabling the authority to fulfil its duties above relating to reports[6].

1 As to the meaning of 'local authority in England' see PARA 25 (definition applied by the School Standards and Framework Act 1998 s 142(8)).

2 As to the meaning of 'adjudicator' see PARA 147. As to when the adjudicator receives a report which states that admission arrangements do not, or may not, conform with the requirements relating to admission arrangements see the School Standards and Framework Act 1998 s 88I(3), (4); and PARA 241. As to the meaning of 'admission arrangements' see PARA 227 note 4.

3 'Relevant school admissions', in relation to a local authority, means: (1) the admission of pupils to relevant schools in the authority's area (School Standards and Framework Act 1998 s 88P(2)(a) (ss 88P, 88Q added by the Education and Skills Act 2008 s 151(1), (4); and amended by SI 2010/1158)); (2) the admission of pupils in the authority's area to other relevant schools (School Standards and Framework Act 1998 s 88P(2)(b) (as so added)); (3) the entry to the sixth form of pupils who have been admitted to relevant schools in the authority's area (s 88P(2)(c) (as so added)); and (4) the entry to the sixth form of pupils in the authority's area who have been admitted to other relevant schools (s 88P(2)(d) (as so added)). 'Relevant school' means a maintained school, an academy school, a city technology college, or a city college for the technology of the arts: s 88P(3) (as so added; and amended by the Education Act 2011 Sch 13 para 10(1), (7)). As to the meaning of 'pupil' see PARA 20 note 4; as to the meaning of 'academy school' see PARA 346 note 12 (definitions applied by the School Standards and Framework Act 1998 s 142(8)). As to the meaning of 'maintained school' see PARA 225 note 4. As to the meaning of references to a child entering the sixth form see PARA 228 note 6. As to city technology colleges and city colleges for the technology of the arts see PARA 345.

4 School Standards and Framework Act 1998 s 88P(1) (as added and amended) see note 3); and amended by the Education Act 2011 s 34(1), (5)(a)). As to the code for school admissions see PARA 225.

5   'Relevant person', in relation to a local authority, means: (1) an admission authority (other than the local authority) for a maintained school in the area of the local authority (School Standards and Framework Act 1998 s 88Q(2)(a) (as added and amended: see note 3)); (2) any member of an appeal panel constituted under the School Standards and Framework Act 1998 s 94 (see PARA 251) by the local authority or the governing body of a foundation or voluntary aided school in the area of the local authority (s 88Q(2)(c) (as so added and amended; and s 88Q(2)(b) repealed by the Education Act 2011 Sch 10 para 1(1), (4))); (3) the proprietor of an academy school, a city technology college, or a city college for the technology of the arts, in the area of the local authority (s 88Q(2)(d) (as so added and amended; and further amended by the Education Act 2011 Sch 13 para 10(1), (8))); (4) any other local authority in England (School Standards and Framework Act 1998 s 88Q(2)(e) (as so added and amended)); (5) such other person as may be prescribed (s 88Q(2)(f) (as so added)). As to the meaning of 'the admission authority' see PARA 227 note 6. As to the meaning of 'admission forum' see PARA 227 note 3. As to the governing bodies of maintained schools in England see PARA 150 et seq. As to foundation and voluntary aided schools see PARA 106. As to the meaning of 'proprietor' see PARA 51 note 4 (definition applied by s 142(8)). As to the meaning of 'person' see PARA 7 note 6.

6   School Standards and Framework Act 1998 s 88Q(1) (as added and amended: see note 3).

(C) Admission Arrangements in Wales

246. Prohibition on interviews. No admission arrangements[1] for a maintained school[2] in Wales[3] may require or authorise any interview with an applicant for admission to the school or his parents[4], where the interview is to be taken into account (to any extent) in determining whether the applicant is to be admitted to the school[5]. If the maintained school is one at which boarding accommodation is provided for pupils[6] this prohibition does not apply in relation to any interview intended to assess the suitability of an applicant for a boarding place[7]. Where the admission arrangements for a maintained school in Wales make provision for a permitted form of selection by aptitude[8], the prohibition does not prevent the arrangements from requiring or authorising any audition or other oral or practical test to be carried out in relation to an applicant solely for the purpose of ascertaining the applicant's aptitude in accordance with the arrangements[9].

1   As to the meaning of 'admission arrangements' see PARA 227 note 4.
2   As to the meaning of 'maintained school' see PARA 225 note 4.
3   As to the meaning of 'Wales' see PARA 7 note 3.
4   As to the meaning of 'parent' see PARA 7 note 6 (definition applied by the School Standards and Framework Act 1998 s 142(8)).
5   School Standards and Framework Act 1998 s 88R(1) (s 88R added by the Education and Skills Act 2008 s 169, Sch 1 Pt 2 paras 53, 56).
6   As to the meaning of 'pupil' see PARA 20 note 4 (definition applied by the School Standards and Framework Act 1998 s 142(8)).
7   School Standards and Framework Act 1998 s 88R(2) (as added: see note 5).
8   'Permitted form of selection by aptitude' is to be read in accordance with the School Standards and Framework Act 1998 s 99(4) (see PARA 258): s 88R(4) (as added: see note 5).
9   School Standards and Framework Act 1998 s 88R(3) (as added: see note 5).

247. Procedure for determining admission arrangements in Wales. The admission authority[1] for a maintained school[2] in Wales[3] must, before the beginning of each school year[4], determine in accordance with the following provisions the admission arrangements[5] which are to apply for that year[6]. Before determining the admission arrangements which are to apply for a particular school year, the admission authority must consult[7] the following about the proposed arrangements[8], namely:

    (1)   whichever of the governing body and the local authority[9] are not the admission authority[10];

(2)   the admission authorities for all other maintained schools in the relevant area[11] or for such class of such schools as may be prescribed[12];

(3)   the governing bodies for all community and voluntary controlled schools[13] in the relevant area (so far as not falling within head (1) or (2))[14];

(4)   the admission authorities for maintained schools of any prescribed description[15]; and

(5)   in the case of a foundation or voluntary school which has a religious character[16], such body or person[17] representing the religion or religious denomination in question as may be prescribed[18].

Once the admission authority has carried out any such consultation, the authority must (a) determine that its proposed arrangements (either in their original form or with such modifications[19] as the authority think fit) are to be the admission arrangements for the school year in question[20]; and (b) (except in such cases as may be prescribed[21]) notify the appropriate bodies[22] of those admission arrangements[23].

Where an admission authority has determined the admission arrangements which are to apply for a particular school year[24], but at any time before the end of that year considers that the arrangements should be varied in view of a major change in circumstances occurring since they were so determined[25], the authority must (except in a case where its proposed variations fall within any description of variations prescribed for these purposes[26]) refer the proposed variations to the Welsh Ministers, and must (in every case) notify the appropriate bodies of the proposed variations[27]. The Welsh Ministers must consider whether the arrangements should have effect with those variations until the end of that year; and if they determine that the arrangements should so have effect or that they should so have effect subject to such modification of those variations as they may determine[28] the arrangements have effect accordingly as from the date of their determination[29] and the admission authority must (except in such cases as may be prescribed[30]) notify the appropriate bodies of the variations subject to which the arrangements are to have effect[31].

Regulations[32] may make provision: (i) specifying matters to which any consultation[33] is, or is not, to relate[34]; (ii) as to the manner in which, and the time by which, any such consultation is to be carried out[35]; (iii) as to the manner in which, and the time by which, any notification[36] is to be given[37]; (iv) specifying matters which are, or are not, to constitute[38] major changes in circumstances[39]; (v) authorising an admission authority, where it has[40] determined the admission arrangements which are to apply for a particular school year, to vary those arrangements to such extent or in such circumstances as may be prescribed[41]; (vi) for the application[42] of certain requirements[43] to variations proposed to be made by virtue of head (v), or to any prescribed description of such variations[44]; (vii) requiring an admission authority which has made a determination of a prescribed description to publish such information relating to the determination (including information as to the authority's reasons for making the determination) as may be prescribed[45]; (viii) as to such other matters connected with the procedure for determining or varying admission arrangements as the Welsh Ministers consider appropriate[46].

A determination by the admission authority for a maintained school in Wales of the admission arrangements which are to apply for a school year must include a determination of the number[47] of pupils in each relevant age group[48] that it is intended to admit to the school in that year[49]. A determination may also, if the school is one at which boarding accommodation is provided for pupils, include a determination of the number of pupils in each relevant age group that it is intended to admit to the school in that year as boarders[50], and a determination of the number of pupils in each relevant age group that it is intended to admit to the school in that year otherwise than as boarders[51].

1 As to the meaning of 'the admission authority' see PARA 227 note 6.
2 As to the meaning of 'maintained school' see PARA 225 note 4.
3 As to the meaning of 'Wales' see PARA 7 note 3.
4 As to the meaning of 'school year' see PARA 19 note 12 (definition applied by the School Standards and Framework Act 1998 s 142(8)).
5 As to the meaning of 'admission arrangements' see PARA 227 note 4.
6 School Standards and Framework Act 1998 s 89(1) (amended by the Education and Skills Act 2008 s 169, Sch 1 Pt 2 paras 53, 57(1), (2)).
7 As to the exercise of the duty to consult see JUDICIAL REVIEW vol 61 (2010) PARA 627. The governing body of any foundation or voluntary school which is a Church of England school or an academy must obtain the advice of the Diocesan Board of Education for the diocese in which the school is situated and must have regard to that advice: see the Diocesan Boards of Education Measure 1991 s 3(1)(cc); and ECCLESIASTICAL LAW vol 34 (2011) PARA 248 et seq. As to foundation and voluntary schools see PARA 106. As to the governing bodies of maintained schools in Wales see PARA 195.
8 The School Standards and Framework Act 1998 s 89(2) does not apply in relation to the proposed admission arrangements for a particular school year if the admission authority is the school's governing body, and prescribed conditions are satisfied in relation to that year: s 89(2A) (added by the Education Act 2002 s 51, Sch 4 para 5(1), (2)). 'Prescribed' means prescribed by regulations made by the Welsh Ministers: see s 90ZA (added by the Education and Skills Act 2008 s 169, Sch 1 Pt 2 paras 53, 63). As to the Welsh Ministers see PARA 59. As to the regulations made see the Education (Determination of Admission Arrangements) (Wales) Regulations 2006, SI 2006/174.
9 As to the meaning of 'local authority' see PARA 25 (definition applied by the School Standards and Framework Act 1998 s 142(8)).
10 School Standards and Framework Act 1998 s 89(2)(a) (s 89(2) substituted by the Education Act 2002 s 51, Sch 4 para 5(1), (2); and the School Standards and Framework Act 1998 s 89(2)(a) amended by SI 2010/1158).
11 'The relevant area' means: (1) the area of the local authority (School Standards and Framework Act 1998 s 89(3)(a) (s 89(3)(a), (b) amended by SI 2010/1158)); or (2) if regulations so provide, such other area (whether more or less extensive than the area of the local authority) as may be determined by or in accordance with the regulations (School Standards and Framework Act 1998 s 89(3)(b) (as so amended)). 'Regulations' means regulations made by the Welsh Ministers: see s 90ZA (added by the Education and Skills Act 2008 s 169, Sch 1 Pt 2 paras 53, 63). As to the regulations made see the Education (Determining School Admission Arrangements for the Initial Year) Regulations 1998, SI 1998/3165.
12 School Standards and Framework Act 1998 s 89(2)(b) (as substituted: see note 10). As to the regulations made under s 89(2) see the Education (Determining School Admission Arrangements for the Initial Year) Regulations 1998, SI 1998/3165; and the Education (Determination of Admission Arrangements) (Wales) Regulations 2006, SI 2006/174.
13 As to community and voluntary controlled schools see PARA 106.
14 School Standards and Framework Act 1998 s 89(2)(c) (as substituted (see note 10); and amended by the Education and Inspections Act 2006 ss 45(a), 184, Sch 18 Pt 6).
15 School Standards and Framework Act 1998 s 89(2)(d) (as substituted: see note 10). As to the regulations made see note 12.
16 Ie for the purposes of the School Standards and Framework Act 1998 Pt 2 (ss 20–83): see PARA 914.
17 As to the meaning of 'person' see PARA 7 note 6.
18 School Standards and Framework Act 1998 s 89(2)(e) (s 89(2) as substituted (see note 10); s 89(2)(e) added by the Education and Inspections Act 2006 s 45(b)). As to the regulations made see note 12.
19 As to the meaning of 'modifications' see PARA 21 note 15 (definition applied by the School Standards and Framework Act 1998 s 142(8)).
20 School Standards and Framework Act 1998 s 89(4)(a).
21 At the date at which this volume states the law no regulations had been made for these purposes.

22 'The appropriate bodies', in relation to an admission authority, means the bodies or persons whom it was required to consult under the School Standards and Framework Act 1998 s 89(2) (see the text to notes 7–18), or would but for s 89(2A) (see note 8) have been required to consult: s 89(10) (substituted by the Education and Inspections Act 2006 s 41(1), (7); and amended by the Education and Skills Act 2008 s 169, Sch 1 Pt 2 paras 53, 57(1), (8), Sch 2).

23 School Standards and Framework Act 1998 s 89(4)(b) (amended by the Education Act 2002 s 51, Sch 4 para 5(1), (3)).

24 School Standards and Framework Act 1998 s 89(5)(a).

25 School Standards and Framework Act 1998 s 89(5)(b).

26 At the date at which this volume states the law no regulations had been made for these purposes.

27 School Standards and Framework Act 1998 s 89(5) (amended by the Education Act 2002 s 51, Sch 4 para 5(1), (3); Education and Skills Act 2008 s 169, Sch 1 Pt 2 paras 53, 57(1), (4)). Where the local authority is the admission authority for a community or voluntary controlled school, it must consult the governing body before making any reference under the School Standards and Framework Act 1998 s 89(5): s 89(9) (substituted by the Education Act 2002 s 51, Sch 4 para 5(1), (6); and amended by SI 2010/1158).

28 School Standards and Framework Act 1998 s 89(6) (amended by the Education and Skills Act 2008 s 169, Sch 1 Pt 2 paras 53, 57(1), (5)(a)–(c)).

29 School Standards and Framework Act 1998 s 89(6)(a) (amended by the Education and Skills Act 2008 s 169, Sch 1 Pt 2 paras 53, 57(1), (5)(d)).

30 At the date at which this volume states the law no regulations had been made for these purposes.

31 School Standards and Framework Act 1998 s 89(6)(b) (amended by the Education Act 2002 s 51, Sch 4 para 5(1), (3)).

32 As to the regulations made under the School Standards and Framework Act 1998 s 89(8) see the Education (Determining School Admission Arrangements for the Initial Year) Regulations 1998, SI 1998/3165; the Education (Relevant Areas for Consultation on Admission Arrangements) Regulations 1999, SI 1999/124; the Education (Determination of Admission Arrangements) (Wales) Regulations 2006, SI 2006/174; and the Education (Admission of Looked After Children) (Wales) Regulations 2009, SI 2009/821.

33 Ie required by the School Standards and Framework Act 1998 s 89(2): see the text to notes 7–18.

34 School Standards and Framework Act 1998 s 89(8)(a).

35 School Standards and Framework Act 1998 s 89(8)(b).

36 Ie required by the School Standards and Framework Act 1998 s 89.

37 School Standards and Framework Act 1998 s 89(8)(c).

38 Ie for the purposes of the School Standards and Framework Act 1998 s 89(5)(b): see the text to note 25.

39 School Standards and Framework Act 1998 s 89(8)(d).

40 Ie in accordance with the School Standards and Framework Act 1998 s 89(4): see the text to notes 19–23.

41 School Standards and Framework Act 1998 s 89(8)(e). In exercise of their powers under the School Standards and Framework Act 1998 s 89(8)(e), the Welsh Ministers have made the School Admissions (Variation of Admission Arrangements) (Wales) Regulations 2013, SI 2013/1140.

42 Ie as if they were variations proposed to be made under the School Standards and Framework Act 1998 s 89(5): see the text to notes 24–27.

43 Ie any of the requirements of the School Standards and Framework Act 1998 s 89(5) and (6): see the text to notes 28–31.

44 School Standards and Framework Act 1998 s 89(8)(f).

45 School Standards and Framework Act 1998 s 89(8)(fa) (added by the Education Act 2002 s 51, Sch 4 para 5(1), (4)). The power under the School Standards and Framework Act 1998 s 89(8)(fa) to require an admission authority to publish information includes power to require it to publish it (1) by giving a notice containing the information to prescribed persons (s 89(8A)(a) (s 89(8A) added by the Education Act 2002 s 51, Sch 4 para 5(1), (5))); or (2) in any other prescribed manner (School Standards and Framework Act 1998 s 89(8A)(b) (as so added)).

46 School Standards and Framework Act 1998 s 89(8)(g) (amended by the Education and Skills Act 2008 s 169, Sch 1 Pt 2 paras 53, 57(1), (7)).

47 References in the School Standards and Framework Act 1998 s 89A to the determination of any number include references to the determination of zero as that number: s 89A(4) (s 89A added by the Education Act 2002 s 47(2)).

48 As to the meaning of 'relevant age group' see PARA 133 note 15.

49 School Standards and Framework Act 1998 s 89A(1) (s 89A as added (see note 47); s 89A(1), (3) amended by the Education and Skills Act 2008 s 169, Sch 1, Pt 2 paras 53, 58).

Regulations may make provision about the making of any determination required by the School Standards and Framework Act 1998 s 89A(1), and may in particular require the admission authority for a maintained school in Wales to have regard, in making any such determination, to (1) any prescribed method of calculation (s 89A(3)(a) (as so added and amended)); and (2) any other prescribed matter (s 89A(3)(b) (as so added)). As to the regulations made see the Education (Determination of Admission Arrangements) (Wales) Regulations 2006, SI 2006/174.

50   School Standards and Framework Act 1998 s 89A(2)(a) (as added: see note 47). As to the meaning of 'boarder' see PARA 31 note 19 (definition applied by s 142(8)).

51   School Standards and Framework Act 1998 s 89A(2)(b) (as added: see note 47).

248.   Co-ordination of admission arrangements. Regulations[1] may require a local authority in Wales[2]:

(1)   to formulate, for any academic year[3] in relation to which prescribed[4] conditions are satisfied, a qualifying scheme[5] for co-ordinating the arrangements for the admission[6] of pupils [7]to maintained schools[8] in its area[9]; and

(2)   to take prescribed action with a view to securing the adoption of the scheme by it and each governing body which is the admission authority[10] for a maintained school in its area[11].

Before proposing such a scheme for adoption, a local authority must comply with such requirements as to consultation as may be prescribed[12].

The Welsh Ministers may make, in relation to the area of a local authority in Wales and an academic year, a scheme for co-ordinating the arrangements, or assisting in the co-ordination of the arrangements, for the admission of pupils to maintained schools in that area[13]. Such a scheme may not be made in relation to a local authority and an academic year if, before the prescribed date in the year preceding the year in which that academic year commences: (a) a scheme formulated by the local authority[14] is adopted in the prescribed manner by the persons[15] mentioned in head (2) above[16]; and (b) the authority provides the Welsh Ministers with a copy of the scheme and informs them that the scheme has been so adopted[17].

The Welsh Ministers may by regulations require local authorities in Wales to provide other local authorities with such information as may be required by such authorities in connection with the exercise of any of their functions[18] relating to admission arrangements[19].

Regulations[20] may provide: (i) that each local authority in Wales must secure that, subject to such exceptions as may be prescribed, no decision made by any admission authority for a maintained school in its area to offer or refuse a child[21] admission to the school is to be communicated to the parent[22] of the child except on a single day, designated by the local authority, in each year[23]; or (ii) that, subject to such exceptions as may be prescribed, a decision made by the admission authority for a maintained school in Wales to offer or refuse a child admission to the school is not to be communicated to the parent of the child except on a prescribed day[24].

Regulations[25] may also provide that where any decision as to whether a child is to be granted or refused admission to a maintained school in Wales falls to be made in prescribed circumstances, the decision must, if a scheme adopted or made[26] so provides, be made by the local authority regardless of whether it is the admission authority for the school[27].

1   Ie regulations made by the Welsh Ministers: see the School Standards and Framework Act 1998 s 90ZA (added by the Education and Skills Act 2008 s 169, Sch 1 Pt 2 paras 53, 63). As to the Welsh Ministers see PARA 59. At the date at which this volume states the law no such regulations had been made.

2 School Standards and Framework Act 1998 s 89B(1) (ss 89B, 89C added by the Education Act 2002 s 48; and the School Standards and Framework Act 1998 s 89B(1) amended by SI 2010/1158). As to the meanings of 'local authority' and 'local authority in Wales' see PARA 25 (definition applied by the School Standards and Framework Act 1998 s 142(8)).

3 'Academic year' means a period commencing with 1 August and ending with the next 31 July: School Standards and Framework Act 1998 s 89B(6) (as added: see note 2).

4 'Prescribed' means prescribed by regulations made by the Welsh Ministers: see the School Standards and Framework Act 1998 s 90ZA (added by the Education and Skills Act 2008 s 169, Sch 1 Pt 2 paras 53, 63).

5 'Qualifying scheme' means a scheme that meets prescribed requirements: School Standards and Framework Act 1998 s 89B(6) (as added: see note 2).

6 As to the meaning of 'admission arrangements' see PARA 227 note 4. As to the procedure for determining admission arrangements see PARA 247.

7 As to the meaning of 'pupil' see PARA 20 note 4 (definition applied by the School Standards and Framework Act 1998 s 142(8)).

8 As to the meaning of 'maintained school' see PARA 225 note 4.

9 School Standards and Framework Act 1998 s 89B(1)(a) (as added: see note 2). Regulations may provide that where a local authority in Wales or the governing body of a maintained school in Wales has, in such manner as may be prescribed, adopted a scheme formulated by a local authority for the purpose mentioned in s 89B(1)(a), (1) the School Standards and Organisation (Wales) Act 2013 Pt 2 Ch 1 (ss 2–20) (intervention in conduct of maintained schools in Wales: see PARA 1229 et seq) is to apply as if any obligations imposed on a governing body under the scheme were duties imposed by the Education Acts; (2) the School Standards and Organisation (Wales) Act 2013 Pt 2 Ch 2 (ss 21–31) (intervention in local authorities: see PARA 1235 et seq) is to apply as if any obligation imposed on a local authority were an education function: School Standards and Framework Act 1998 s 89C(2) (as so added; and amended by the Education and Skills Act 2008 s 169, Sch 1 Pt 2 paras 53, 60(1), (3); SI 2010/1158; and the School Standards and Organisation (Wales) Act 2013 Sch 5 para 54(1), (5)). In connection with the School Standards and Framework Act 1998 s 89C(2) see also PARA 64 note 10. As to the governing bodies of maintained schools in Wales see PARA 195. As to the meaning of 'the Education Acts' see PARA 1 note 13. As to the meaning of 'education functions' see PARA 25 (definition applied by the School Standards and Framework Act 1998 s 142(8)).

10 As to the meaning of 'the admission authority' see PARA 227 note 6.

11 School Standards and Framework Act 1998 s 89B(1)(b) (as added: see note 2).

12 School Standards and Framework Act 1998 s 89C(4) (as added (see note 2); and amended by SI 2010/1158). Regulations under the School Standards and Framework Act 1998 s 89C(4) may, in particular, require consultations to be undertaken with a view to securing that the arrangements for the admission of pupils to maintained schools in the areas of different local authorities are, so far as is reasonably practicable, compatible with each other: s 89C(5) (as so added; and amended by SI 2010/1158). At the date at which this volume states the law no such regulations had been made. As to the exercise of the duty to consult see JUDICIAL REVIEW vol 61 (2010) PARA 627.

13 School Standards and Framework Act 1998 s 89B(2) (as added (see note 2); and amended by the Education and Skills Act 2008 s 169, Sch 1 Pt 2 paras 53, 59(1), (3)(a); and SI 2010/1158). Regulations may make provision about the contents of schemes under the School Standards and Framework Act 1998 s 89B(2), including provision about the duties that may be imposed by such schemes on local authorities in Wales and the admission authorities for maintained schools in Wales: s 89C(1) (as so added; and amended by the Education and Skills Act 2008 s 169, Sch 1 Pt 2 paras 53, 60(1), (2); and SI 2010/1158). Before making a scheme under the School Standards and Framework Act 1998 s 89B(2) in relation to the area of any local authority, the Welsh Ministers must consult the local authority, and any governing body who are the admission authority for a school which appears to the Welsh Ministers to be a school to which the scheme will apply: s 89C(6) (as so added; and amended by the Education and Skills Act 2008 s 169, Sch 1 Pt 2 paras 53, 60(1), (5); and SI 2010/1158). A scheme made under the School Standards and Framework Act 1998 s 89B(2) may be varied or revoked by the Welsh Ministers: s 89C(7) (as so added; and amended by the Education and Skills Act 2008 s 169, Sch 1 Pt 2 paras 53, 60(1), (5)).

14 Ie in accordance with the School Standards and Framework Act 1998 s 89B(1): see the text to notes 1–11.

15 As to the meaning of 'person' see PARA 7 note 6.

16 School Standards and Framework Act 1998 s 89B(3)(a) (as added (see note 2); and amended by SI 2010/1158).

17 School Standards and Framework Act 1998 s 89B(3)(b) (as added (see note 2); and amended by the Education and Skills Act 2008 s 169, Sch 1 Pt 2 paras 53, 59(1), (4)).

18 Ie under the School Standards and Framework Act 1998 Pt III Ch 1 (ss 84–98A).

19 School Standards and Framework Act 1998 s 89B(4) (as added (see note 2); and amended by the Education and Skills Act 2008 s 169, Sch 1 Pt 2 paras 53, 59(1), (5)(a); and SI 2010/1158). At the date at which this volume states the law no such regulations had been made.

20 At the date at which this volume states the law no such regulations had been made.

21 As to the meaning of 'child' see PARA 228 note 4.

22 As to the meaning of 'parent' see PARA 7 note 6 (definition applied by the School Standards and Framework Act 1998 s 142(8)).

23 School Standards and Framework Act 1998 s 89B(5)(a) (as added (see note 2); and amended by the Education and Skills Act 2008 s 169, Sch 1 Pt 2 paras 53, 59(6)(a); and SI 2010/1158). In exercise of their powers under the School Standards and Framework Act 1998 s 89B(5), the Welsh Ministers have made the School Admissions (Common Offer Date) (Wales) Regulations 2013, SI 2013/1144.

24 School Standards and Framework Act 1998 s 89B(5)(b) (as added (see note 2); and amended by the Education and Skills Act 2008 s 169, Sch 1 Pt 2 paras 53, 59(6)(b)). See note 23.

25 At the date at which this volume states the law no such regulations had been made.

26 Ie by virtue of the School Standards and Framework Act 1998 s 89B: see the text to notes 1–11, 13–24.

27 School Standards and Framework Act 1998 s 89C(3) (as added (see note 2); and amended by the Education and Inspections Act 2006 s 43(3)(a); the Education and Skills Act 2008 s 169, Sch 1 Pt 2 paras 53, 60(1), (4); and SI 2010/1158). Where any decision as to whether a child is to be granted or refused admission to a maintained school in Wales is (by virtue of regulations under the School Standards and Framework Act 1998 s 89C(3)) made by the local authority although it is not the admission authority, the governing body of the school must implement the decision: s 89C(3A) (s 89C as so added; s 89C(3A) added by the Education and Inspections Act 2006 s 43(3)(a), and amended by the Education and Skills Act 2008 s 169, Sch 1 Pt 2 paras 53, 60(1), (4); and SI 2010/1158).

249. Reference of objections to the Welsh Ministers. Where admission arrangements[1] have been determined[2] by an admission authority[3] but an appropriate body[4] wishes to make an objection about those arrangements[5], and the objection does not fall within any description of prescribed[6] objections[7], that body may refer the objection to the Welsh Ministers[8]. Also, where admission arrangements have been determined[9] by an admission authority[10] but any parent[11] of a prescribed description wishes to make an objection about those arrangements[12] and the objection falls within any description of prescribed objections[13], that person may refer the objection to the Welsh Ministers[14].

Where any objection is referred to the Welsh Ministers, they must decide whether, and (if so) to what extent, the objection should be upheld[15]; and in doing so they may consider whether it would be appropriate for changes to be made to any aspect of the admission arrangements, whether or not they would be required to do so for the purpose of determining the objection[16]. In the case of any objection referred to them, the Welsh Ministers must publish a report containing their decision on the objection[17], any decision they have made on whether it would be appropriate for changes to be made to the admission arrangements, whether in the light of their decision on the objection or otherwise[18], and their reasons for those decisions[19].

The decisions of the Welsh Ministers[20] are, in relation to the admission arrangements in question, binding on the admission authority and on all persons by whom an objection may be made[21]; and, if the Welsh Ministers have decided that it would be appropriate for changes to be made to the admission arrangements, those arrangements must forthwith be revised by the admission authority in such a way as to give effect to the decision[22].

Regulations[23] may make provision:

(1)   as to any conditions which must be satisfied before an objection can be

referred[24] to the Welsh Ministers[25], or the Welsh Ministers are required to determine an objection referred[26] to them[27];

(2) prescribing the steps which may be taken by an admission authority where an objection has been referred to the Welsh Ministers but has not yet been determined[28];

(3) as to the manner in which a report[29] is to be published[30];

(4) requiring such matters to be notified to such persons, and in such manner, as may be prescribed[31];

(5) prohibiting or restricting the reference, within such period following a decision by the Welsh Ministers as may be prescribed, of any objection raising the same (or substantially the same) issues in relation to the admission arrangements of the school in question[32];

(6) prescribing circumstances in which an admission authority may revise the admission arrangements for its school in the light of any decision by the Welsh Ministers relating to the admission arrangements for another school, and the procedure to be followed in such a case[33].

1 As to the meaning of 'admission arrangements' see PARA 227 note 4.

2 Ie under the School Standards and Framework Act 1998 s 89(4): see PARA 247.

3 School Standards and Framework Act 1998 s 90(1)(a). As to the meaning of 'the admission authority' see PARA 227 note 6.

4 'Appropriate body' means, in relation to the admission arrangements determined by an admission authority any body or person whom the admission authority were required to consult under the School Standards and Framework Act 1998 s 89(2), or would but for s 89(2A) have been required to consult (see PARA 247): s 90(11) (added by the Education and Inspections Act 2006 s 41(1), (8)(b); and amended by the Education and Skills Act 2008 s 169, Sch 1 Pt 2 paras 53, 62(1), (11), Sch 2). As to the meaning of 'person' see PARA 7 note 6.

5 School Standards and Framework Act 1998 s 90(1)(b) (substituted by the Education and Inspections Act 2006 s 41(1), (8)(a)).

6 'Prescribed' means prescribed by regulations made by the Welsh Ministers: see the School Standards and Framework Act 1998 s 90ZA (added by the Education and Skills Act 2008 s 169, Sch 1 Pt 2 paras 53, 63). As to the Welsh Ministers see PARA 59. As to the regulations made under the School Standards and Framework Act 1998 s 90 see the Education (Objections to Admission Arrangements) (Wales) Regulations 2006, SI 2006/176.

7 School Standards and Framework Act 1998 s 90(1)(c).

8 School Standards and Framework Act 1998 s 90(1) (amended by the Education and Skills Act 2008 s 169, Sch 1 Pt 2 paras 53, 62(1), (3)).

9 Ie under the School Standards and Framework Act 1998 s 89(4): see PARA 247.

10 School Standards and Framework Act 1998 s 90(2)(a).

11 As to the meaning of 'parent' see PARA 7 note 6 (definition applied by the School Standards and Framework Act 1998 s 142(8)).

12 School Standards and Framework Act 1998 s 90(2)(b).

13 School Standards and Framework Act 1998 s 90(2)(c).

14 School Standards and Framework Act 1998 s 90(2) (amended by the Education and Skills Act 2008 s 169, Sch 1 Pt 2 paras 53, 62(1), (3)).

15 School Standards and Framework Act 1998 s 90(2A) (added by the Education and Skills Act 2008 s 169, Sch 1 Pt 2 paras 53, 62(1), (4)). As to cases concerning challenges to decisions following the consideration of objections see *R v Schools Adjudicator, ex p Wirral Metropolitan Borough Council* [2000] ELR 620; *R (on the application of Wirral Metropolitan Borough Council) v Chief Schools Adjudicator* [2001] ELR 574, [2000] All ER (D) 2297; *R (on the application of Wandsworth London Borough Council) v Schools Adjudicator* [2003] EWHC 2969 (Admin), [2004] ELR 274, [2003] All ER (D) 125 (Dec); *Governing Body of the London Oratory School v Official Schools Adjudicator* [2004] EWHC 3014 (Admin), [2005] ELR 162, [2004] All ER (D) 302 (Dec); *R (on the application of the Governing Body of Drayton Manor High School) v Office of the Schools Adjudicator* [2008] EWHC 3119 (Admin), [2009] ELR 127, [2008] All ER (D) 270 (Oct); *R (on the application of the Governing Body of the London Oratory School) v Schools Adjudicator* [2015] EWHC 1012 (Admin), [2015] ELR 335, [2015] All ER (D) 113 (Apr).

16 See the School Standards and Framework Act 1998 s 90(5A) (s 90(5A)–(5C) added by the Education and Inspections Act 2006 s 47(1), (2); and the School Standards and Framework Act 1998 s 90(5A) amended by the Education and Skills Act 2008 s 169, Sch 1 Pt 2 paras 53, 62(1), (6)).

17 School Standards and Framework Act 1998 s 90(5B)(a) (as added (see note 16); and amended by the Education and Skills Act 2008 s 169, Sch 1 Pt 2 paras 53, 62(1), (7)).

18 School Standards and Framework Act 1998 s 90(5B)(b) (as added (see note 16); and amended by the Education and Skills Act 2008 s 169, Sch 1 Pt 2 paras 53, 62(1), (7)). Where the Welsh Ministers decide that it would be appropriate for changes to be made to the admission arrangements, their decision may specify the modifications that are to be made to the arrangements: School Standards and Framework Act 1998 s 90(5C) (as so added; and amended by the Education and Skills Act 2008 s 169, Sch 1 Pt 2 paras 53, 62(1), (8)). As to the meaning of 'modifications' see PARA 21 note 15 (definition applied by the School Standards and Framework Act 1998 s 142(8)).

19 School Standards and Framework Act 1998 s 90(5B)(d) (as added (see note 16); and amended by the Education and Skills Act 2008 s 169, Sch 1 Pt 2 paras 53, 62(1), (7)).

20 Ie the decisions mentioned in the School Standards and Framework Act 1998 s 90(5B)(a), (b): see the text to notes 17–18.

21 Ie under the School Standards and Framework Act 1998 s 90(1) or (2): see the text to notes 1–14.

22 School Standards and Framework Act 1998 s 90(8) (substituted by the Education and Inspections Act 2006 s 47(1), (4); and amended by the Education and Skills Act 2008 s 169, Sch 1 Pt 2 paras 53, 62(1), (9)(b)).

23 Ie regulations made by the Welsh Ministers: see the School Standards and Framework Act 1998 s 90ZA (added by the Education and Skills Act 2008 s 169, Sch 1 Pt 2 paras 53, 63). As to the regulations made see note 6.

24 Ie under the School Standards and Framework Act 1998 s 90(1) or (2): see the text to notes 1–14.

25 School Standards and Framework Act 1998 s 90(9)(a)(i) (amended by the Education and Skills Act 2008 s 169, Sch 1 Pt 2 paras 53, 62(1), (10)(a)(i)).

26 Ie under the School Standards and Framework Act 1998 s 90(2): see the text to notes 9–14.

27 School Standards and Framework Act 1998 s 90(9)(a)(ii) (amended by the Education and Skills Act 2008 s 169, Sch 1 Pt 2 paras 53, 62(1), (10)(a)).

28 School Standards and Framework Act 1998 s 90(9)(b) (amended by the Education and Skills Act 2008 s 169, Sch 1 Pt 2 paras 53, 62(1), (10)(b)).

29 Ie a report required to be published under the School Standards and Framework Act 1998 s 90(5B): see the text to notes 17–19.

30 School Standards and Framework Act 1998 s 90(9)(c) (amended by the Education and Inspections Act 2006 s 47(1), (5)(b)).

31 School Standards and Framework Act 1998 s 90(9)(d).

32 School Standards and Framework Act 1998 s 90(9)(e) (amended by the Education and Skills Act 2008 s 169, Sch 1 Pt 2 paras 53, 62(1), (10)(d)).

33 School Standards and Framework Act 1998 s 90(9)(f) (amended by the Education and Skills Act 2008 s 169, Sch 1 Pt 2 paras 53, 62(1), (10)(d)).

(D) Admission to Academies

250. Admission to academies. Admission to academies is dealt with elsewhere in this title[1].

1 See PARA 356.

F. ADMISSION APPEALS

(A) Appeal Arrangements for Parents and Sixth Form Children

251. Appeal arrangements. A local authority[1] must make arrangements for enabling the appropriate person[2] to appeal against[3]:

(1) in a case where the local authority is the admission authority[4], any decision made by or on behalf of the authority refusing a child admission to a school[5];

(2)   any other decision made by or on behalf of the authority as to the school at which education is to be provided for a child in the exercise of the authority's functions[6], other than a decision leading to or embodied in a direction[7] for admission[8]; and

(3)   in a case where the governing body[9] of a community or voluntary controlled school maintained by the authority[10] is the admission authority, any decision made by or on behalf of the governing body refusing a child admission to the school[11].

A local authority must also make arrangements for enabling the appropriate person in relation to a child who has been admitted to a community or voluntary controlled school maintained by the authority to appeal against any decision made by or on behalf of the governing body refusing permission for the child to enter the school's sixth form[12].

The governing body of a foundation or voluntary aided school[13] must make arrangements for enabling:

(a)   the appropriate person to appeal against any decision made by or on behalf of the governing body refusing a child admission to the school[14];

(b)   the appropriate person in relation to a child who has been admitted to the school to appeal against any decision made by or on behalf of the governing body refusing permission for the child to enter the school's sixth form[15].

Joint arrangements may be made under head (a) or (b) above by the governing bodies of two or more foundation or voluntary aided schools maintained by the same local authority[16]. A local authority and the governing body or bodies of one or more foundation or voluntary aided schools maintained by the authority may make joint arrangements consisting of such of the arrangements made by the authority[17] as the authority may determine[18], and arrangements made[19] by the governing body or bodies[20].

An appeal pursuant to any arrangements made under these provisions is to an appeal panel[21] constituted in accordance with regulations[22]. Regulations[23] may make provision about the making of appeals pursuant to such arrangements, including provision:

(i)   as to the procedure on such appeals[24];

(ii)   in cases where separate appeals are made by a parent and a child against a decision about sixth form education for the child, for the appeals to be joined, or otherwise for securing that no more than one appeal against the decision is proceeded with[25];

(iii)   for the payment by the local authority of allowances to members of an appeal panel[26]; and

(iv)   as to the grounds on which an appeal panel may, in the case of an appeal against a decision made on the ground that prejudice to the provision of efficient education or the efficient use of educational resources would arise[27], determine that a place is to be offered to the child concerned[28].

The decision of an appeal panel on an appeal pursuant to arrangements under these provisions is binding on[29] (A) the local authority or the governing body by whom or on whose behalf the decision under appeal was made[30]; and (B) in the case of a decision made by or on behalf of a local authority, the governing body of a community or voluntary controlled school at which the appeal panel determines that a place should be offered to the child in question[31].

1   As to the meaning of 'local authority' see PARA 25 (definition applied by the School Standards and Framework Act 1998 s 142(8)).

2   'The appropriate person', in relation to a child, means: (1) in the case of a decision about sixth form education for the child any of (a) the child, (b) a parent of his, (c) the child and a parent of his acting jointly (but subject to regulations made under the School Standards and Framework Act 1998 s 94(5A) (see the text to notes 23–28) (s 94(2B)(a) (s 94(2B) added by the Education and Skills Act 2008 s 152(1), (6)); (2) in any other case, a parent of the child (School Standards and Framework Act 1998 s 94(2B)(b) (as so added)). As to the meaning of 'child' see PARA 228 note 4. As to the meaning of 'parent' see PARA 7 note 6 (definition applied by s 142(8)).

3   School Standards and Framework Act 1998 s 94(1) (amended by the Education and Skills Act 2008 s 152(1), (2)(a); and SI 2010/1158).

4   As to the meaning of 'the admission authority' see PARA 227 note 6.

5   School Standards and Framework Act 1998 s 94(1)(za) (added by the Education and Skills Act 2008 s 152(1), (2)(b); and amended by SI 2010/1158). As to the meaning of 'school' see PARA 91 (definition applied by the School Standards and Framework Act 1998 s 142(8)).

6   As to the meaning of 'functions' see PARA 18 note 5 (definition applied by the School Standards and Framework Act 1998 s 142(8)). As to the general education duties and functions of local authorities see PARA 25 et seq.

7   Ie a direction under the School Standards and Framework Act 1998 s 96 (see PARA 253) or s 97A (see PARA 255).

8   School Standards and Framework Act 1998 s 94(1)(a) (amended by the Education and Inspections Act 2006 s 51(1); and the Education and Skills Act 2008 s 152(1), (2)(c)).

9   As to the governing bodies of maintained schools in England see PARA 150 et seq; and in Wales see PARA 195. As to the meanings of 'England' and 'Wales' see PARA 7 note 3.

10   As to schools maintained by a local authority, and as to community and voluntary controlled schools see PARA 106.

11   School Standards and Framework Act 1998 s 94(1)(b) (amended by the Education and Inspections Act 2006 s 43(4); and the Education and Skills Act 2008 s 152(1), (2)(d)).

12   School Standards and Framework Act 1998 s 94(1A) (added by the Education Act 2002 s 51, Sch 4 para 8(1), (2); and amended by the Education and Skills Act 2008 s 152(1), (3); and SI 2010/1158). In the School Standards and Framework Act 1998 s 94, any reference to a decision about sixth form education for a child is a reference to a decision: (1) made in relation to a preference expressed in accordance with arrangements made under s 86A(1) (see PARA 230) as to where education should be provided for the child (s 94(6A)(a) (s 94(6A) added by the Education and Skills Act 2008 s 152(1), (8))); or (2) refusing permission for the child to enter the sixth form of the school to which he has been admitted (School Standards and Framework Act 1998 s 94(6A)(b) (as so added)). As to the meanings of 'sixth form education' and of references to a child entering a school's sixth form see PARA 228 note 6.

13   As to foundation and voluntary aided schools see PARA 106.

14   School Standards and Framework Act 1998 s 94(2) (amended by the Education and Skills Act 2008 s 152(1), (4)(a); and the Education and Skills Act 2008 s 152(1), (4)(b)).

15   School Standards and Framework Act 1998 s 94(2A) (added by the Education Act 2002 s 51, Sch 4 para 8(1), (3); and amended by the Education and Skills Act 2008 s 152(1), (5)).

16   School Standards and Framework Act 1998 s 94(3) (amended by the Education Act 2002 s 51, Sch 4 para 8(1), (4); and SI 2010/1158).

17   Ie in pursuance of the School Standards and Framework Act 1998 s 94(1) or (1A): see the text to notes 1–12.

18   School Standards and Framework Act 1998 s 94(4)(a) (amended by the Education Act 2002 s 51, Sch 4 para 8(1), (5); and SI 2010/1158).

19   Ie in pursuance of the School Standards and Framework Act 1998 s 94(2) or (2A): see the text to notes 13–15.

20   School Standards and Framework Act 1998 s 94(4)(b) (amended by the Education Act 2002 s 51, Sch 4 para 8(1), (5)).

21   As to the meaning of 'appeal panel' see PARA 225 note 6.

22   School Standards and Framework Act 1998 s 94(5) (s 94(5) substituted, s 94(5A)–(5C) added by the Education Act 2002 s 50). 'Regulations' means regulations made under the School Standards and Framework Act 1998 by the Secretary of State or, in relation to Wales, the Welsh Ministers: see s 142(1). The functions of the Secretary of State under the School Standards and Framework Act 1998 s 94, so far as exercisable in relation to Wales, were transferred to the National Assembly for Wales (see the National Assembly for Wales (Transfer of Functions) Order 1999, SI 1999/672, art 2, Sch 1) and are now vested in the Welsh Ministers (see the Government of Wales Act 2006 s 162(1), Sch 11 para 30). As to the Secretary of State see PARA 58. As to the Welsh Ministers see PARA 59. As to the regulations made under the School Standards and

Framework Act 1998 s 94 see the Education (Admission Appeals Arrangements) (Wales) Regulations 2005, SI 2005/1398; and the School Admissions (Appeals Arrangements) (England) Regulations 2012, SI 2012/9; and see further below.

The School Admissions (Appeals Arrangements) (England) Regulations 2012, SI 2012/9 revoke and replace the former Education (Admissions Appeals Arrangements) (England) Regulations 2002, SI 2002/2899 which previously set out procedural matters in some detail. Procedural matters are not replicated in the 2012 Regulations as generally they are provided for by the School Admission Appeals Code issued under the School Standards and Framework Act 1998 s 84 (see PARA 225). The 2012 Regulations do have provisions on the constitution of appeal panels (see the School Admissions (Appeals Arrangements) (England) Regulations 2012, SI 2012/9, reg 5, Schedule) and payment of allowances (see reg 6). The 'School Admissions Appeals Code: Statutory guidance on how schools should organise and run their pupil admissions appeals' (February 2012) (covering, in relation to England, such matters as constitution of appeal panels, appeal hearings, reaching decisions on appeals, infant class size appeals, further appeals and complaints about appeals, appeals by governing bodies against local authority decisions to admit twice excluded children, and with appendices containing relevant legislation and further information about the Local Government Ombudsman), is not reproduced but it is to be found at the Department for Education website. In relation to Wales, see the 'School admission appeals code' (December 2013) which at the date at which this volume states the law is to be found on the Welsh Government website.

After an appeal hearing, a complaint could lie to the Local Government Ombudsman (in respect of maintained schools) or the Education Funding Agency (in respect of other schools) or in regard to either to the High Court on judicial review. As to the Local Government Ombudsman see CONSTITUTIONAL AND ADMINISTRATIVE LAW vol 20 (2014) PARA 638. As to the Education Funding Agency see PARA 58 note 9. As to judicial review see JUDICIAL REVIEW.

It should be noted that there are two kinds of admission appeal which can be brought, the ordinary ('two-stage') appeals and infant class size appeals, both of which are addressed in the School Admissions Code referred to above. As to infant class size appeals see eg *R (on the application of Hounslow London Borough Council) v Schools Admissions Appeal Board for Hounslow* [2002] EWCA Civ 900, [2002] 1 WLR 3147, [2002] ELR 602; *R (on the application of the London Borough of Lambeth) v Lambeth Independent Appeals Panel* [2012] EWHC 943 (Admin); *R (on the application of DD) v Independent Appeal Panel of the London Borough of Islington* [2013] EWHC 2262 (Admin), [2013] All ER (D) 361 (Jul). As to the duty to limit infant class sizes see PARA 234.

In regard to Wales the Education (Admission Appeals Arrangements) (Wales) Regulations 2005, SI 2005/1398 contain detailed procedural provisions, not unlike the previous position in regard to England under the (former) Education (Admissions Appeals Arrangements) (England) Regulations 2002, SI 2002/2899 (see above). As to the constitution of appeal panels see the Education (Admission Appeals Arrangements) (Wales) Regulations 2005, SI 2005/1398, reg 3, Sch 1 (both amended by SI 2010/1142). As to the duty to advertise for lay members see the Education (Admission Appeals Arrangements) (Wales) Regulations 2005, SI 2005/1398, reg 4. As to procedure for appeals see reg 5, Sch 2 (substituted by SI 2009/823; and amended by SI 2010/1142). As to relevant considerations in appeals under the School Standards and Framework Act 1998 ss 94, 95 see the Education (Admission Appeals Arrangements) (Wales) Regulations 2005, SI 2005/1398, reg 6 (substituted by SI 2013/2535). As to payment of allowances see the Education (Admission Appeals Arrangements) (Wales) Regulations 2005, SI 2005/1398, reg 7 (substituted by SI 2013/2535). As to indemnity see the Education (Admission Appeals Arrangements) (Wales) Regulations 2005, SI 2005/1398, reg 8 (amended by SI 2010/1142).

As to the application of the Convention for the Protection of Human Rights and Fundamental Freedoms (Rome, 4 November 1950; TS 71 (1953); Cmd 8969) art 6(1) (right to a fair hearing: see PARA 3) to admission appeal panels see *R v Richmond upon Thames London Borough Council, ex p C* [2001] LGR 146, sub nom *R v Richmond upon Thames London Borough Council, ex p JC* [2001] ELR 21, CA (decided before the Human Rights Act 1998 came into force, but the Convention was relied upon in arguments advanced for the claimant).

As to the application of the rules of natural justice to appeal panels see *R v Birmingham City Council Education Appeals Committee, ex p B* [1999] ELR 305. Although decisions of a local authority as to admission arrangements are not in principle immune from challenge on judicial review, it would be quite exceptional for it to be appropriate for an appeal before an appeal panel to be interrupted for such a challenge: *R (on the application of Hounslow London Borough Council) v Schools Admissions Appeal Panel for Hounslow London Borough Council* [2002] EWCA Civ 900 at [60], [2002] 1 WLR 3147, [2002] ELR 602 per May LJ, disapproving dicta of Stanley Burnton J in *R (on the application of South Gloucestershire Local Education*

Authority) v South Gloucestershire Schools Appeal Panel [2001] EWHC 732 (Admin) at [50]–[51], [2002] ELR 309, [2001] All ER (D) 81 (Aug). As to the principles of natural justice see JUDICIAL REVIEW vol 61 (2010) PARA 629 et seq.

As to the consideration of appeals by an appeal panel see *R (on the application of M) v Haringey Independent Appeal Panel* [2010] EWCA Civ 1103, (2010) Times, 5 November, [2010] All ER (D) 102 (Oct). See also *R v Comr for Local Administration, ex p Croydon London Borough Council* [1989] 1 All ER 1033, 87 LGR 221; *W (A Minor) v Education Appeal Committee of Lancashire County Council* [1994] 3 FCR 1, [1994] ELR 530, CA; *R v Richmond-upon-Thames London Borough Council, ex p C* [2001] LGR 146, sub nom *R v Richmond London Borough Council, ex p JC* [2001] ELR 21, CA; *R (on the application of O) v St James' Roman Catholic Primary School Appeal Panel* [2001] ELR 469, [2000] All ER (D) 2108; *R v South Gloucestershire Education Appeals Committee, ex p Bryant* [2001] ELR 53, CA; *R (on the application of Hounslow London Borough Council) v Schools Admissions Appeal Panel for Hounslow London Borough Council* [2002] EWCA Civ 900, [2002] 1 WLR 3147, [2002] ELR 602 (all decided under previous legislation). Should the panel have to adjourn and re-convene before all appeals are heard and the decisions reached, it should have the same members as heard the earlier appeals: *R v Camden London Borough Council, ex p S* (1990) 89 LGR 513. Where there are multiple appeals in relation to a school, the panel should normally hear all of them before deciding: *R v Education Appeal Committee of Leicestershire County Council, ex p Tarmohamed* [1997] ELR 48.

An appeal panel constituted in accordance with regulations under the School Standards and Framework Act 1998 s 94(5) is subject to investigation by a local commissioner under the Local Government Act 1974 Pt III (ss 23–34): see s 25(5)(c); and LOCAL GOVERNMENT vol 69 (2009) PARA 853.

23 As to the regulations made see note 22.

24 School Standards and Framework Act 1998 s 94(5A)(a) (as added: see note 22).

25 School Standards and Framework Act 1998 s 94(5A)(aa) (s 94(5A) as added (see note 22); and s 94(5A)(aa) added by the Education and Skills Act 2008 s 152(1), (7)).

26 School Standards and Framework Act 1998 s 94(5A)(b) (as added (see note 22); and amended by SI 2010/1158). Regulations made by virtue of the School Standards and Framework Act 1998 s 94(5A)(b) may provide for any of the provisions of the Local Government Act 1972 ss 173–174 (repealed) (allowances to members of local authorities and other bodies: see LOCAL GOVERNMENT vol 69 (2009) PARAS 171–172, 174) or (in relation to Wales) the Local Government (Wales) Measure 2011 Pt 8 (ss 141–160) (payments and pensions: see LOCAL GOVERNMENT) to apply with prescribed modifications in relation to members of an appeal panel: School Standards and Framework Act 1998 s 94(5C) (as so added; and amended by the Local Government (Wales) Measure 2011 Sch 3 para 4(1), (2)). 'Prescribed' means prescribed by the regulations: see the School Standards and Framework Act 1998 s 142(1).

27 Ie an appeal to which the School Standards and Framework Act 1998 s 94(5B) applies: see s 94(5A)(c) (as added: see note 22). Section 94(5B) applies to any appeal against a decision made on the ground that prejudice of the kind referred to in s 86(3)(a) would arise as mentioned in s 86(4) (see PARA 228): s 94(5B) (as so added).

28 School Standards and Framework Act 1998 s 94(5A)(c) (as added: see note 22).

29 School Standards and Framework Act 1998 s 94(6) (amended by the Education Act 2002 s 51, Sch 4 para 8(1), (6)).

30 School Standards and Framework Act 1998 s 94(6)(a) (amended by SI 2010/1158).

31 School Standards and Framework Act 1998 s 94(6)(b) (amended by SI 2010/1158).

(B) Appeal Arrangements for Governing Bodies in relation to Decisions to Admit Excluded Children

252. Appeal arrangements in relation to excluded children. Nothing in the provisions relating to arrangements for admission appeals[1] requires any arrangements to be made for enabling the appropriate person[2] to appeal against a decision[3] made by or on behalf of the admission authority[4] for a maintained school[5] refusing a child[6] admission to the school[7], in a case where, at the time when the decision was made, the child was excluded from two or more schools[8].

Where a local authority[9] is the admission authority for a community or voluntary controlled school[10], the authority must make arrangements for enabling the governing body of the school[11] to appeal against any decision made by or on behalf of the authority to admit to the school such a child[12]. However, this does not apply in relation to a decision made by or on behalf of a local authority in England[13] to admit to a school a child who is looked after by such an authority[14]; in such cases alternative provision is made for references to the adjudicator[15].

An appeal by the governing body[16] must be to an appeal panel constituted in accordance with regulations[17]. Regulations may make provision about the making of such appeals, including provision: (1) requiring prescribed information to be given to governing bodies in prescribed circumstances[18]; (2) as to the procedure on such appeals[19]; (3) for the payment by the local authority of allowances to members of an appeal panel[20]; and (4) as to the matters to which an appeal panel is to have regard in considering an appeal[21].

The decision of an appeal panel is binding on the local authority and the governing body[22].

1 Ie nothing in the School Standards and Framework Act 1998 s 94(1) or (2): see PARA 251.
2 As to the meaning of 'appropriate person' see PARA 251 note 2 (definition applied by the School Standards and Framework Act 1998 s 95(1A) (added by the Education and Skills Act 2008 s 169, Sch 1 Pt 2 paras 53, 67(1), (3))).
3 School Standards and Framework Act 1998 s 95(1) (amended by the Education and Skills Act 2008 s 169, Sch 1 Pt 2 paras 53, 67(1), (2)(a)). As to the application of the School Standards and Framework Act 1998 s 95 to new schools in England see the New School (Admissions) (England) Regulations 2003, SI 2003/1041 ; and in Wales see the New School (Admissions) (Wales) Regulations 2006, SI 2006/175.
4 As to the meaning of 'the admission authority' see PARA 227 note 6.
5 School Standards and Framework Act 1998 s 95(1)(a). As to the meaning of 'maintained school' see PARA 225 note 4.
6 As to the meaning of 'child' see PARA 228 note 4.
7 School Standards and Framework Act 1998 s 95(1)(b) (amended by the Education and Skills Act 2008 s 169, Sch 1 Pt 2 paras 53, 67(1), (2)(b)).
8 School Standards and Framework Act 1998 s 95(1). The statutory wording is 'in a case where, at the time when the decision was made, s 87(2) (see PARA 229) applies to the child': see s 95(1).
9 As to the meaning of 'local authority' see PARA 25 (definition applied by the School Standards and Framework Act 1998 s 142(8)).
10 As to community and voluntary schools see PARA 106.
11 As to the governing bodies of maintained schools in England see PARA 150 et seq; and in Wales see PARA 195. As to the meanings of 'England' and 'Wales' see PARA 7 note 3.
12 See the School Standards and Framework Act 1998 s 95(2) (amended by SI 2010/1158).
13 As to the disapplication of the School Standards and Framework Act 1998 s 95(2) in relation to a decision made by, or on behalf of, a local authority in Wales to admit to a school a child who is looked after by a Welsh local authority, see the Education (Admission of Looked After Children) (Wales) Regulations 2009, SI 2009/821, reg 9 (amended by SI 2010/1142).
14 As to the meaning of 'child who is looked after by a local authority' see PARA 236 note 6.
15 See the School Standards and Framework Act 1998 s 95(2A) (added by the Education and Inspections Act 2006 s 48(1); and amended by SI 2010/1158). Where the admission authority for a community or voluntary controlled school in England is a local authority, and a decision is made by or on behalf of the authority to admit to the school a child who, at the time when the decision is made, is looked after by a local authority in England and to whom (at that time) s 87(2) (see PARA 229) applies (s 95A(1) (s 95A added by the Education and Inspections Act 2006 s 48(2); and the School Standards and Framework Act 1998 s 95A(1), (2) amended by SI 2010/1158)), the admission authority must give notice of the decision to the governing body of the school (School Standards and Framework Act 1998 s 95A(2) (as so added and amended)). The governing body of the school may, within the period of seven days beginning with the day on which it is notified of the decision, refer the matter to the adjudicator: s 95A(3) (as so added). Such a reference may only be made on the ground that the admission of the child to the school would seriously prejudice the provision of efficient education or the efficient use of resources: s 95A(4) (as so added). If the adjudicator determines that the admission of the child to the school would have that effect the decision to admit the child to the school ceases to have effect (s 95A(5)(a) (as so added)), but the adjudicator may determine that another maintained school in England is to be required to admit the child (s 95A(5)(b) (as so added)). A determination

under s 95A(5)(b) may only be made with the agreement of the local authority who look after the child: s 95A(6) (as so added). A determination under s 95A(5)(b) may not be made if (1) the child is permanently excluded from the other school (s 95A(7)(a) (as so added)); or (2) the admission of the child to the other school would seriously prejudice the provision of efficient education or the efficient use of resources (s 95A(7)(b) (as so added)). If the adjudicator determines under s 95A(5)(b) that another school is to be required to admit the child the admission authority for the school must admit the child to the school (s 95A(8)(a) (as so added)), and if the admission authority is not the governing body of the school, the admission authority must give notice in writing to the governing body and head teacher of the school of the adjudicator's decision (s 95A(8)(b) (as so added)). Regulations may make provision: (a) requiring the adjudicator to consult prescribed persons or persons of a prescribed description before making any determination in connection with a reference under s 95A (s 95A(9)(a) (as so added)); (b) requiring an admission authority for a maintained school to provide information which falls within a prescribed description (s 95A(9)(b)(i) (as so added)), and is requested by the adjudicator for the purposes of any such determination (s 95A(9)(b)(ii) (as so added)). As to the meaning of 'adjudicator' see PARA 147. As to the meaning of 'writing' see PARA 76 note 8. As to the meaning of 'head teacher' see PARA 86 note 4 (definition applied by the School Standards and Framework Act 1998 s 142(8); Interpretation Act 1978 s 11). As to the meaning of 'person' see PARA 7 note 6. 'Regulations' means regulations made under the School Standards and Framework Act 1998 by the Secretary of State; and 'prescribed' means prescribed by such regulations: see s 142(1). As to the Secretary of State see PARA 58. As to the regulations made see the School Admissions (Adjudicator Determinations Relating to Looked After and Certain Other Children) (England) Regulations 2007, SI 2007/105.

16   Ie pursuant to arrangements made under the School Standards and Framework Act 1998 s 95(2): see the text to notes 9–12.

17   School Standards and Framework Act 1998 s 95(3) (s 95(3) substituted, (3A), (3B) added, by the Education Act 2002 s 51, Sch 4 para 9). As to the regulations made see the Education (Admission Appeals Arrangements) (Wales) Regulations 2005, SI 2005/1398 (amended by SI 2009/823; SI 2009/1500; and SI 2013/2535); the School Admissions (Appeals Arrangements) (England) Regulations 2012, SI 2012/9; and see PARA 251 note 22.

     An appeal panel constituted in accordance with regulations under the School Standards and Framework Act 1998 s 95(3) is subject to investigation by a local commissioner under the Local Government Act 1974 Pt III (ss 23–34): see s 25(5)(c); and LOCAL GOVERNMENT vol 69 (2009) PARA 853.

18   School Standards and Framework Act 1998 s 95(3A)(a) (as added: see note 17).

19   School Standards and Framework Act 1998 s 95(3A)(b) (as added: see note 17).

20   School Standards and Framework Act 1998 s 95(3A)(c) (as added (see note 17); and amended by SI 2010/1158). Regulations made by virtue of the School Standards and Framework Act 1998 s 95(3A)(c) may provide for any of the provisions of the Local Government Act 1972 ss 173–174 (repealed) (allowances to members of local authorities and other bodies: see LOCAL GOVERNMENT vol 69 (2009) PARAS 171–172, 174) or (in relation to Wales) the Local Government (Wales) Measure 2011 Pt 8 (ss 141–160) (payments and pensions: see LOCAL GOVERNMENT) to apply with prescribed modifications in relation to members of an appeal panel: School Standards and Framework Act 1998 s 95(3B) (as so added; and amended by the Local Government (Wales) Measure 2011 Sch 3 para 4(1), (3)). As to the meaning of 'modifications' see PARA 21 note 15 (definition applied by the School Standards and Framework Act 1998 s 142(8); Interpretation Act 1978 s 11).

21   School Standards and Framework Act 1998 s 95(3A)(d) (as added: see note 17).

22   See the School Standards and Framework Act 1998 s 95(4) (amended by SI 2010/1158).

G. POWER TO DIRECT ADMISSION OF CHILD TO SCHOOL

253. Direction to admit child to specified school. The local authority[1] may give a direction to admit a child[2] to the governing body[3] of a school[4] for which it is not the admission authority[5], if, in the case of any child in its area[6], either (or both) of the following conditions is satisfied in relation to each school which is a reasonable distance from his home and provides suitable education[7]. The conditions are: (1) he has been refused admission[8] to the school[9]; or (2) he is permanently excluded[10] from the school[11]. Such a direction must specify a school which is a reasonable distance from the child's home[12] and from which the child is not permanently excluded[13]. A direction must, unless it is given on the determination of the appropriate authority[14], specify a school in the area[15] of the local authority[16]. A direction to admit a child must not:

(a)   specify a school which has in place admission arrangements that make provision for selection by ability[17] unless the child satisfies the selection criteria[18];

(b)   specify a school if his admission would result in prejudice to the provision of efficient education or the efficient use of resources[19] by reason of the duty[20] to comply with the limit on infant class sizes[21].

Where a school is specified in a direction, the governing body must admit the child to the school[22], but this does not affect any power to exclude from a school a pupil[23] who is already a registered pupil[24] there[25].

1   As to the meaning of 'local authority' see PARA 25 (definition applied by the School Standards and Framework Act 1998 s 142(8)). Any function of a local authority in England which is conferred by or under the School Standards and Framework Act 1998 s 96 may be exercised by, or by employees of, such person as may be authorised in that behalf by the local authority whose function it is: Contracting Out (Local Authority Education Functions) (England) Order 2002, SI 2002/928, art 3, Sch 2 para (z) (art 3 amended by SI 2010/1172). As to the meaning of 'England' see PARA 7 note 3. As to the meaning of 'person' see PARA 7 note 6.

2   Ie a direction under the School Standards and Framework Act 1998 s 96. As to the meaning of 'child' see PARA 228 note 4. As to the procedure for giving such directions see PARA 254.

3   As to the governing bodies of maintained schools in England see PARA 150 et seq; and in Wales see PARA 195. As to the meaning of 'Wales' see PARA 7 note 3.

4   In the School Standards and Framework Act 1998 ss 96–97C, 'school' means a maintained school: see the School Standards and Framework Act 1998 s 96(8) (amended by the Education and Inspections Act 2006 s 51(2)(b)). As to the meaning of 'maintained school' see PARA 225 note 4.

5   As to the meaning of 'the admission authority' see PARA 227 note 6.

6   As to when a person is treated as belonging to the area of a local authority see PARA 27 note 6.

7   School Standards and Framework Act 1998 s 96(1) (amended by the Education Act 2002 s 51, Sch 4 para 10; and SI 2010/1158). 'Suitable education', in relation to a child, means efficient full-time education suitable to his age, ability and aptitude and to any special educational needs he may have: School Standards and Framework Act 1998 s 96(7). As to the meaning of 'special educational needs' see PARAS 943, 989 (definition applied by s 142(8)). Discretion only arises under s 96(1) if the local authority is satisfied that the conditions are satisfied in relation to 'each' school, meaning 'every' school rather than 'a' school: *R (on the application of B) v Hertfordshire County Council* [2004] EWHC 2324 (Admin), [2005] ELR 17.

As to the application of the School Standards and Framework Act 1998 s 96 to new schools in England see the New School (Admissions) (England) Regulations 2003, SI 2003/1041; and in Wales see the New School (Admissions) (Wales) Regulations 2006, SI 2006/175.

8   As to admission to schools see PARA 224 et seq.

9   School Standards and Framework Act 1998 s 96(1)(a).

10   As to the meaning of 'excluded' see PARA 316 note 6.

11   School Standards and Framework Act 1998 s 96(1)(b).

12   School Standards and Framework Act 1998 s 96(2)(a).

13   School Standards and Framework Act 1998 s 96(2)(b).

14   Ie under the School Standards and Framework Act 1998 s 97(4): see PARA 254. 'The appropriate authority' means, in relation to a local authority in England, the adjudicator; and, in relation to a local authority in Wales, the Welsh Ministers: s 97(6A) (added by the Education and Inspections Act 2006 s 49(e); and amended by SI 2010/1158) (definition applied by the School Standards and Framework Act 1998 s 96(3) (amended by the Education and Inspections Act 2006 s 51(2)(a)). As to the meaning of 'adjudicator' see PARA 147. The functions under the School Standards and Framework Act 1998 ss 96, 97 in relation to Wales were originally vested in the National Assembly for Wales and are now exercisable by the Welsh Ministers by virtue of the Government of Wales Act 2006 s 162(1), Sch 11 paras 30, 32. As to the Welsh Ministers see PARA 59.

15   Ie the area specified in the School Standards and Framework Act 1998 s 96(1): see the text to notes 1–7.

16   School Standards and Framework Act 1998 s 96(3).

17 Ie arrangements falling within the School Standards and Framework Act 1998 s 99(2)(c): see PARA 258.
18 School Standards and Framework Act 1998 s 96(3A) (added by the Apprenticeships, Skills, Children and Learning Act 2009 s 43(1), (3)).
19 Ie under the School Standards and Framework Act 1998 s 86(3)(a): see PARA 228.
20 Ie under the School Standards and Framework Act 1998 s 86(4): see PARA 228.
21 School Standards and Framework Act 1998 s 96(4). As to the duty to limit infant class sizes see PARA 234.
22 School Standards and Framework Act 1998 s 96(5).
23 As to the meaning of 'pupil' see PARA 20 note 4 (definition applied by the School Standards and Framework Act 1998 s 142(8)).
24 As to the meaning of 'registered pupil' see PARA 437 (definition applied by the School Standards and Framework Act 1998 s 142(8)).
25 School Standards and Framework Act 1998 s 96(6).

254. Procedure for giving direction to admit child to specified school. Before deciding to give a direction to admit a child[1] to a specified school[2], the local authority[3] must consult[4]: (1) the child, in a case in which[5] the local authority are a local authority in England[6] and the child is over compulsory school age[7]; (2) the parent[8] of the child[9]; and (3) the governing body[10] of the school it proposes to specify in the direction[11]. Where the local authority decides to give such a direction specifying any school it must[12], before doing so, serve a notice in writing[13] of its decision on the governing body and head teacher[14] of the school[15]; and it must not give the direction until the period for referring the matter to the appropriate authority[16] has expired and, if it is so referred, the appropriate authority has made its determination[17].

The governing body may, within the period of 15 days beginning with the day on which the notice was served, refer the matter to the appropriate authority and, if it does so, must inform the local authority[18]. On such a reference, the appropriate authority may determine[19] which school is to be required to admit the child, and if it does so[20]:

(a) where the local authority is the admission authority[21] for that school, it must admit the child to the school[22] and give notice in writing to the governing body and head teacher of the school of the appropriate authority's determination[23]; and

(b) in any other case, that school must be specified in the direction[24].

The appropriate authority must not make such a determination in relation to a school if the child's admission to the school would result in prejudice to the provision of efficient education or the efficient use of resources[25] by reason of the duty[26] to comply with the limit on infant class sizes[27].

A direction to admit a child to a specified school must be given by notice in writing and a copy of the notice must be given by the local authority to the head teacher of the school[28].

1 As to the meaning of 'child' see PARA 228 note 4.
2 Ie a direction under the School Standards and Framework Act 1998 s 96: see PARA 253. As to the meaning of 'school' see PARA 253 note 4. As to directions in the case of children looked after by a local authority see PARAS 255, 256.
3 As to the meaning of 'local authority' see PARA 25 (definition applied by the School Standards and Framework Act 1998 s 142(8)). Any function of a local authority in England which is conferred by or under the School Standards and Framework Act 1998 s 97 may be exercised by, or by employees of, such person as may be authorised in that behalf by the local authority whose function it is: Contracting Out (Local Authority Education Functions) (England) Order 2002, SI 2002/928, art 3, Sch 2 para (aa) (art 3 amended by SI 2010/1172). As to the meaning of 'England' see PARA 7 note 3. As to the meaning of 'person' see PARA 7 note 6.
4 School Standards and Framework Act 1998 s 97(1) (amended by SI 2010/1158). As to the exercise of the duty to consult see JUDICIAL REVIEW vol 61 (2010) PARA 627. As to the

application of s 97 to new schools in England see the New School (Admissions) (England) Regulations 2003, SI 2003/1041; and in Wales the New School (Admissions) (Wales) Regulations 2006, SI 2006/175. As to the meaning of 'Wales' see PARA 7 note 3.

5 See the School Standards and Framework Act 1998 s 97(1)(za) (added by SI 2010/1080).

6 School Standards and Framework Act 1998 s 97(1A)(a) (s 97(1A) (added by SI 2010/1080)).

7 School Standards and Framework Act 1998 s 97(1A)(b) (as added: see note 6). As to the meaning of 'compulsory school age' see PARA 19.

8 As to the meaning of 'parent' see PARA 7 note 6 (definition applied by the School Standards and Framework Act 1998 s 142(8); Interpretation Act 1978 s 11).

9 School Standards and Framework Act 1998 s 97(1)(a).

10 As to the governing bodies of maintained schools in England see PARA 150 et seq; and in Wales see PARA 195.

11 School Standards and Framework Act 1998 s 97(1)(b).

12 School Standards and Framework Act 1998 s 97(2) (amended by SI 2010/1158).

13 As to the meaning of 'writing' see PARA 76 note 8.

14 As to the meaning of 'head teacher' see PARA 86 note 4 (definition applied by the School Standards and Framework Act 1998 s 142(8); Interpretation Act 1978 s 11).

15 School Standards and Framework Act 1998 s 97(2)(a).

16 Ie the period under the School Standards and Framework Act 1998 s 97(3): see the text to note 18. As to the meaning of 'appropriate authority' see PARA 253 note 14.

17 School Standards and Framework Act 1998 s 97(2)(b) (amended by the Education and Inspections Act 2006 s 49(a)).

18 School Standards and Framework Act 1998 s 97(3) (amended by the Education and Inspections Act 2006 s 49(b); and SI 2010/1158).

19 Regulations may make provision in relation to England (1) requiring the adjudicator to consult prescribed persons or persons of a prescribed description before making any determination in connection with a reference under the School Standards and Framework Act 1998 s 97 (see s 97C(a) (s 97C added by the Education and Inspections Act 2006 s 51(3))); (2) requiring an admission authority for a school to provide information which falls within a prescribed description and is requested by the adjudicator for the purposes of any such determination (School Standards and Framework Act 1998 s 97C(b) (as so added)). 'Regulations' means regulations made under the School Standards and Framework Act 1998 by the Secretary of State; and 'prescribed' means prescribed by regulations: see s 142(1). As to the Secretary of State see PARA 58. As to the meaning of 'adjudicator' see PARA 147. As to the meaning of 'person' see PARA 7 note 6. As to the regulations made see the School Admissions (Adjudicator Determinations Relating to Looked After and Certain Other Children) (England) Regulations 2007, SI 2007/105.

20 School Standards and Framework Act 1998 s 97(4) (substituted by the Education Act 2002 s 51, Sch 4 para 11(1), (2); and amended by the Education and Inspections Act 2006 s 49(c)).

21 As to the meaning of 'the admission authority' see PARA 227 note 6.

22 School Standards and Framework Act 1998 s 97(4)(a)(i) (as substituted (see note 20); and amended by SI 2010/1158).

23 School Standards and Framework Act 1998 s 97(4)(a)(ii) (as substituted and amended: see note 20).

24 School Standards and Framework Act 1998 s 97(4)(b) (as substituted: see note 20).

25 Ie prejudice of the kind referred to in the School Standards and Framework Act 1998 s 86(3)(a): see PARA 228.

26 Ie under the School Standards and Framework Act 1998 s 86(4): see PARA 228.

27 School Standards and Framework Act 1998 s 97(5) (amended by the Education and Inspections Act 2006 s 49(d)).

28 School Standards and Framework Act 1998 s 97(6) (substituted by the Education Act 2002 Sch 4 para 11(1), (3); and amended by SI 2010/1158).

255. Direction to admit looked after child in England to specified school. A local authority in England[1] may, in relation to a child looked after by it[2], give a direction to the admission authority[3] for any school[4] in England other than a school for which the local authority are the admission authority[5]. A direction must not specify a school from which the child is permanently excluded[6]. Where a school is specified in a direction, the admission authority must admit the child to the school[7]; but this does not affect any power to exclude from a school a pupil[8] who is already a registered pupil[9] there[10].

Before deciding to give a direction, the local authority must consult[11] the admission authority for the school it proposes to specify in the direction[12]. The admission authority for the school must, within the period of seven days beginning with the day on which it is so consulted, inform the local authority whether it is willing to admit the child to the school without being directed to do so by the authority[13]. Where the local authority decides to give a direction specifying a school:

(1)   it must, before doing so, serve a notice in writing[14] of its decision on (a) the admission authority for the school[15]; (b) if the school is a community or voluntary controlled school[16] and the governing body[17] of the school is not the admission authority, the governing body of the school[18]; (c) if the school is maintained by a local authority[19] which is not the authority proposing to give the direction and is not the admission authority, the local authority which maintains the school[20]; and (d) the head teacher[21] of the school[22]; and

(2)   it must not give the direction until the period for referring the matter to the adjudicator[23] has expired and, if it is so referred, until the adjudicator has made such determinations as it appears to him to be appropriate to make in connection with the reference[24].

The admission authority[25] and, in the case of a notice relating to a child permanently excluded from two or more schools[26], the governing body of a community or voluntary controlled school[27] may, within the period of seven days beginning with the day on which the notice was served, refer the matter to the adjudicator and, if it does so, must inform the local authority[28]. Such a reference may only be made on the ground that the admission of the child to the school would seriously prejudice the provision of efficient education or the efficient use of resources[29]. If the adjudicator determines[30] that the admission of the child to the school would have that effect the local authority may not give a direction that the school admit the child[31], but the adjudicator may determine that another school in England is to be required to admit the child[32]. If the adjudicator so determines that another school is to be required to admit the child, then: (i) if the local authority proposing to give the direction is the admission authority for that school it must admit the child to the school[33] and give notice in writing to the governing body and head teacher of the school of the adjudicator's decision[34]; and (ii) in any other case, the local authority must specify that school in its direction[35].

A direction must be given by notice in writing and a copy of the notice must be given by the local authority to the head teacher of the school[36].

1   As to the meaning of 'local authority in England' see PARA 25 (definition applied by the School Standards and Framework Act 1998 s 142(8); Interpretation Act 1978 s 11).
2   As to the meaning of 'child who is looked after by a local authority' see PARA 236 note 6.
3   As to the meaning of 'the admission authority' see PARA 227 note 6.
4   As to the meaning of 'school' see PARA 253 note 4.
5   School Standards and Framework Act 1998 s 97A(1) (ss 97A, 97B added by the Education and Inspections Act 2006 s 50(1)). As to the admission of looked after children in Wales see PARA 256.
6   School Standards and Framework Act 1998 s 97A(2) (as added: see note 5). As to the meaning of 'excluded' see PARA 316 note 6.
7   School Standards and Framework Act 1998 s 97A(3) (as added: see note 5).
8   As to the meaning of 'pupil' see PARA 20 note 4 (definition applied by the School Standards and Framework Act 1998 s 142(8); Interpretation Act 1978 s 11).
9   As to the meaning of 'registered pupil' see PARA 437 (definition applied by the School Standards and Framework Act 1998 s 142(8); Interpretation Act 1978 s 11).
10   School Standards and Framework Act 1998 s 97A(4) (as added: see note 5).

11 As to the exercise of the duty to consult see JUDICIAL REVIEW vol 61 (2010) PARA 627.

12 School Standards and Framework Act 1998 s 97B(1) (as added: see note 5).

13 School Standards and Framework Act 1998 s 97B(2) (as added: see note 5).

14 As to the meaning of 'writing' see PARA 76 note 8.

15 School Standards and Framework Act 1998 s 97B(3)(a)(i) (as added: see note 5).

16 As to community and voluntary controlled schools see PARA 106.

17 As to the governing bodies of maintained schools in England see PARA 150 et seq.

18 School Standards and Framework Act 1998 s 97B(3)(a)(ii) (as added: see note 5).

19 As to the meaning of 'school maintained by a local authority' see PARA 99.

20 School Standards and Framework Act 1998 s 97B(3)(a)(iii) (as added (see note 5); and amended by SI 2010/1158).

21 As to the meaning of 'head teacher' see PARA 86 note 4 (definition applied by the School Standards and Framework Act 1998 s 142(8); Interpretation Act 1978 s 11).

22 School Standards and Framework Act 1998 s 97B(3)(a)(iv) (as added: see note 5).

23 Ie under the School Standards and Framework Act 1998 s 97B(4): see the text to notes 25–28. As to the meaning of 'adjudicator' see PARA 147.

24 School Standards and Framework Act 1998 s 97B(3)(b) (as added: see note 5).

25 Ie on whom a notice is served under the School Standards and Framework Act 1998 s 97B(3)(a)(i) (see the text to notes 14–15): see the School Standards and Framework Act 1998 s 97B(4)(a) (as added: see note 5).

26 Ie a child to whom (at the time of service of the notice) the School Standards and Framework Act 1998 s 87(2) (see PARA 229) applies.

27 Ie on whom a notice is served under the School Standards and Framework Act 1998 s 97B(3)(a)(ii) (see the text to notes 16–18): see the School Standards and Framework Act 1998 s 97B(4)(b) (as added: see note 5).

28 School Standards and Framework Act 1998 s 97B(4) (as added: see note 5).

29 School Standards and Framework Act 1998 s 97B(5) (as added: see note 5).

30 Regulations may make provision in relation to England (1) requiring the adjudicator to consult prescribed persons or persons of a prescribed description before making any determination in connection with a reference under the School Standards and Framework Act 1998 s 97B (see s 97C(a) (s 97C added by the Education and Inspections Act 2006 s 51(3))); (2) requiring an admission authority for a school to provide information which falls within a prescribed description and is requested by the adjudicator for the purposes of any such determination (School Standards and Framework Act 1998 s 97C(b) (as so added)). 'Regulations' means regulations made under the School Standards and Framework Act 1998 by the Secretary of State; and 'prescribed' means prescribed by regulations: see s 142(1). As to the Secretary of State see PARA 58. As to the meaning of 'person' see PARA 7 note 6. As to the regulations made see the School Admissions (Adjudicator Determinations Relating to Looked After and Certain Other Children) (England) Regulations 2007, SI 2007/105.

31 School Standards and Framework Act 1998 s 97B(6)(a) (as added: see note 5).

32 School Standards and Framework Act 1998 s 97B(6)(b) (as added: see note 5). A determination under s 97B(6)(b) may only be made with the agreement of the local authority who look after the child: s 97B(7) (as so added). A determination under s 97B(6)(b) may not be made if (1) the child is permanently excluded from the other school (s 97B(8)(a) (as so added)); or (2) the admission of the child to the other school would seriously prejudice the provision of efficient education or the efficient use of resources (s 97B(8)(b) (as so added)).

33 School Standards and Framework Act 1998 s 97B(9)(a)(i) (as added: see note 5).

34 School Standards and Framework Act 1998 s 97B(9)(a)(ii) (as added: see note 5).

35 School Standards and Framework Act 1998 s 97B(9)(b) (as added: see note 5).

36 School Standards and Framework Act 1998 s 97B(10) (as added: see note 5).

256. Admission of looked after children in Wales. The Welsh Ministers[1] may by regulations[2] make provision about the admission of children looked after by local authorities[3] in Wales[4] ('looked after children') to maintained schools[5] in Wales[6]. Such regulations may include provision requiring the admission authorities[7] for such schools:

    (1)   to include in their admission arrangements[8] such provision relating to the admission of looked after children as may be prescribed[9], which

may in particular include provision for securing that, subject to prescribed exceptions, such children are to be offered admission in preference to other children[10];

(2)   to admit looked after children in prescribed circumstances, subject to prescribed exceptions[11].

The regulations may also provide that any of the statutory provisions relating to admission arrangements[12] do not apply in relation to looked after children[13], or apply in relation to such children with prescribed modifications[14].

1   The functions under the School Standards and Framework Act 1998 s 97D were originally vested in the National Assembly for Wales and are now exercisable by the Welsh Ministers by virtue of the Government of Wales Act 2006 s 162(1), Sch 11 paras 30, 32. As to the Welsh Ministers see PARA 59.

2   Ie regulations made under the School Standards and Framework Act 1998 by the Welsh Ministers: see s 142(1). As to the regulations made see the Education (Admission of Looked After Children) (Wales) Regulations 2009, SI 2009/821.

3   As to the meaning of 'child who is looked after by a local authority' see PARA 236 note 6.

4   As to the meaning of 'Wales' see PARA 7 note 3.

5   As to the meaning of 'maintained school' see PARA 225 note 4.

6   School Standards and Framework Act 1998 s 97D(1) (s 97D added by the Education and Inspections Act 2006 s 52(1)).

7   As to the meaning of 'the admission authority' see PARA 227 note 6.

8   As to the meaning of 'admission arrangements' see PARA 227 note 4.

9   'Prescribed' means prescribed by regulations: School Standards and Framework Act 1998 s 142(1).

10   School Standards and Framework Act 1998 s 97D(2)(a) (as added: see note 6).

11   School Standards and Framework Act 1998 s 97D(2)(b) (as added: see note 6).

12   Ie any of the School Standards and Framework Act 1998 ss 84–97C.

13   School Standards and Framework Act 1998 s 97D(3)(a) (as added: see note 6).

14   School Standards and Framework Act 1998 s 97D(3)(b) (as added: see note 6). As to the meaning of 'modifications' see PARA 21 note 15 (definition applied by s 142(8)).

H. NURSERY AND SPECIAL SCHOOLS

257.   Special arrangements for the admission of pupils. The provisions of Chapter I of Part III of the School Standards and Framework Act 1998[1] ('the admissions provisions') govern arrangements for the admission of children[2] to maintained schools[3]. However, special provision is made in relation to admissions to a school[4] for nursery education or to nursery[5] or special schools[6] and in relation to children under the compulsory school age[7] or children with statements of special educational needs[8].

Children admitted to a school for nursery education and subsequently transferred to a reception class[9] at the school are regarded for the purposes of the admissions provisions as admitted to the school, otherwise than for nursery education, on being so transferred[10].

Nothing in the admissions provisions[11] applies in relation to nursery schools or to children who will be under compulsory school age at the time of their proposed admission[12]. However, where the arrangements for the admission[13] of pupils to a maintained school provide for the admission to the school of children who will be under compulsory school age at the time of their proposed admission, the admissions provisions apply in relation to the admission of such pupils to the school otherwise than for nursery education[14].

The person[15] responsible for admitting, or refusing to admit, children to a maintained school for nursery education is the person who[16] is the admission authority[17] for the school[18]. Regulations[19] may make provision as to the person who is to be responsible for admitting, or refusing to admit, children to maintained nursery schools[20].

Regulations may make provision in connection with the arrangements for the admission of pupils to community or foundation special schools[21], and for the allocation between the local authority[22] and the governing body[23] of such a school of functions[24] in connection with such arrangements[25]. Apart from this provision and certain provisions relating to the publication of information[26] nothing in the admissions provisions applies in relation to special schools[27].

Nothing in the admissions provisions applies in relation to children for whom EHC plans are[28] maintained or statements of special educational needs are[29] maintained[30].

1 Ie the School Standards and Framework Act 1998 Pt III Ch I (ss 84–98A).
2 As to the meaning of 'child' see PARA 228 note 4.
3 See PARA 225 et seq. As to the meaning of 'maintained school' see PARA 225 note 4. Reference should also be made to the early years pupils premium which is additional funding paid to support disadvantaged children receiving government-funded early education, under the Childcare Act 2006 s 7: see ss 7, 7A; and CHILDREN AND YOUNG PERSONS vol 10 (2012) PARA 1083. See the School Admissions Code 2014 paras 1.9, 1.39–1.39B. As to the Code generally see PARA 226 note 8.
4 As to the meaning of 'school' see PARA 91 (definition applied by the School Standards and Framework Act 1998 s 142(8)).
5 As to the meaning of 'nursery school' see PARA 91 (definition applied by the School Standards and Framework Act 1998 s 142(8)).
6 As to the meaning of 'special school' see PARA 1041 (definition applied by the School Standards and Framework Act 1998 s 142(8)).
7 As to the meaning of 'compulsory school age' see PARA 19.
8 See the School Standards and Framework Act 1998 s 98; and see the text to notes 9–30. As to the meaning of 'special educational needs' see PARAS 943, 989 (definition applied by s 142(8)).
9 'Reception class' means a class in which education is provided which is suitable to the requirements of pupils aged five and any pupils under or over that age whom it is expedient to educate with pupils of that age: School Standards and Framework Act 1998 s 142(1). As to the meaning of 'pupil' see PARA 20 note 4 (definition applied by s 142(8)). As to the time at which a person attains a particular age see PARA 7 note 6.
10 School Standards and Framework Act 1998 s 98(1). For the purposes of the School Standards and Framework Act 1998 generally children are to be regarded as admitted to a school for nursery education if: (1) in the case of a school in England, they are admitted for early years provision as defined by the Childcare Act 2006 s 20 (see CHILDREN AND YOUNG PERSONS vol 10 (2012) PARA 1079) and are not, or are not to be, placed on admission in a reception class or any more senior class; and (2) in the case of a school in Wales, if they are, or are to be, placed on admission in a nursery class: School Standards and Framework Act 1998 s 142(5) (substituted by the Childcare Act 2006 s 103(1), Sch 2 para 35). As to the meanings of 'England' and 'Wales' see PARA 7 note 3.

The admission of children to a school for nursery education is to be disregarded: (a) for the purposes of any determination under the School Standards and Framework Act 1998 s 88C (procedure for determining admission arrangements in England: see PARA 237) or s 89 (procedure for determining admission arrangements in Wales: see PARA 247) of the number of pupils in any relevant age group that it is intended to admit to a primary school in a school year; and (b) in determining for the purposes of s 88D (determination of admission numbers in England: see PARA 237) or s 89A (determination of admission numbers in Wales: see PARA 247) what is a relevant age group in relation to a primary school: s 98(2) (substituted by the Education Act 2002 s 51, Sch 4 para 12(1), (2); and amended by the Education and Skills Act 2008 s 169, Sch 1 Pt 2 paras 53, 68(1), (2)). As to the meaning of 'relevant age group' see PARA 133 note 15. As to the meaning of 'primary school' see PARA 91; and as to the meaning of 'school year' see PARA 19 note 12 (definitions applied by the School Standards and Framework Act 1998 s 142(8)).

As to the application of the School Standards and Framework Act 1998 s 98 to new schools in England see the New School (Admissions) (England) Regulations 2003, SI 2003/1041; and in Wales see the New School (Admissions) (Wales) Regulations 2006, SI 2006/175.

11 Ie apart from the School Standards and Framework Act 1998 s 98(4A), (4B): see the text to notes 15–20.

12 School Standards and Framework Act 1998 s 98(3) (amended by the Education Act 2002 Sch 4 para 12(1), (3)).

13 As to the meaning of 'admission arrangements' see PARA 227 note 4.

14 School Standards and Framework Act 1998 s 98(4). As to the admission of children below compulsory school age and deferred entry to school and also the admission of children outside their normal age group see the School Admissions Code 2014 paras 2.16–2.17B. As to the Code generally see PARA 226 note 8.

15 As to the meaning of 'person' see PARA 7 note 6.

16 Ie by virtue of the School Standards and Framework Act 1998 s 88(1): see PARA 247.

17 As to the meaning of 'the admission authority' see PARA 227 note 6.

18 School Standards and Framework Act 1998 s 98(4A) (added by the Education Act 2002 Sch 4 para 12(1), (4)).

19 Ie regulations made under the School Standards and Framework Act 1998 by the Secretary of State or, in relation to Wales, the Welsh Ministers: see s 142(1). The functions of the Secretary of State under the School Standards and Framework Act 1998 s 98, so far as exercisable in relation to Wales, were transferred to the National Assembly for Wales (see the National Assembly for Wales (Transfer of Functions) Order 1999, SI 1999/672, art 2, Sch 1) and are now vested in the Welsh Ministers (see the Government of Wales Act 2006 s 162(1), Sch 11 para 30). As to the Secretary of State see PARA 58. As to the Welsh Ministers see PARA 59. At the date at which this volume states the law no such regulations had been made.

20 School Standards and Framework Act 1998 s 98(4B) (added by the Education Act 2002 Sch 4 para 12(1), (4)). As to the meaning of 'maintained nursery school' see PARA 99 note 4.

21 As to community and foundation special schools see PARA 106.

22 As to the meaning of 'local authority' see PARA 25 (definition applied by the School Standards and Framework Act 1998 s 142(8)).

23 As to the governing bodies of maintained schools in England see PARA 150 et seq; and in Wales see PARA 195.

24 As to the meaning of 'functions' see PARA 18 note 5 (definition applied by the School Standards and Framework Act 1998 s 142(8)).

25 School Standards and Framework Act 1998 s 98(5) (amended by SI 2010/1158). As to the regulations made see the Education (Maintained Special Schools) (Wales) Regulations 1999, SI 1999/1780 (amended by SI 2001/3710; SI 2005/3238; SI 2009/48; SI 2010/1142; and SI 2011/190). At the date at which this volume states the law no such regulations had effect in relation to England. However, as to regulations made under the Education Act 1996 in respect of admission to special schools in England see the Education (Special Educational Needs) (England) (Consolidation) Regulations 2001, SI 2001/3455, reg 12A.

26 Ie the School Standards and Framework Act 1998 s 92(c), (d): see PARA 231.

27 School Standards and Framework Act 1998 s 98(6) (amended by SI 2002/2953; and SI 2006/173).

28 Ie under the Children and Families Act 2014 s 37: see PARA 958. As to EHC plans (ie education, health and care plans) generally see PARA 958 et seq.

29 Ie under the Education Act 1996 s 324: see PARA 1002.

30 School Standards and Framework Act 1998 s 98(7) (amended by the Children and Families Act 2014 Sch 3 paras 67, 68(1), (2)). However, any provision made by, or (as the case may be) by virtue of the School Standards and Framework Act 1998 s 84 (code of practice: see PARA 225) or s 92(c), (d) (publication of information: see PARA 231) or s 98 (apart from s 98(4A), (4B) (see the text to notes 15–20)), applies, or (as the case may be) may be made so as to apply, in relation to such children: s 98(8) (amended by the Education Act 2002 Sch 4 para 12(1), (5); SI 2002/2953; and SI 2006/173). Such children must, in addition, be taken into account for the purposes of (1) the references in the School Standards and Framework Act 1998 s 86(5), (5B), (9) (see PARA 228) to a number of pupils (s 98(9)(a) (s 98(9) (substituted by the Education Act 2002 s 51, Sch 4 para 12(1), (6))); and (2) any determination under the School Standards and Framework Act 1998 s 88C (see PARA 237) or s 89 (see PARA 247) of the number of pupils in a relevant age group that it is intended to admit, or to admit either as boarders or otherwise than as boarders, to a school in a school year (s 98(9)(b) (as so substituted; and amended by the Education and Skills Act 2008 s 169, Sch 1 Pt 2 paras 53, 68(1), (3))). In the School Standards and Framework Act 1998 s 98(8) the reference to any provision made by s 98 includes a reference to s 98(4) (see the text to notes 13–14) only so far as it has effect for the purposes mentioned in s 98(9): s 98(10). As to the meaning of 'boarder' see PARA 31 note 19 (definition applied by s 142(8)).

I. SELECTION OF PUPILS

(A) Partial Selection

258. General restriction on selection by ability or aptitude. No admission arrangements[1] for a community, foundation or voluntary school[2] may make provision for selection by ability[3] unless: (1) they make provision for one of the permitted forms of such selection[4]; or (2) the school is a grammar school[5]. The following are permitted forms of selection by ability[6]: (a) any selection by ability authorised[7] in relation to pre-existing arrangements[8]; (b) any selection by ability authorised[9] in relation to pupil banding[10]; and (c) any selection by ability conducted in connection with the admission of pupils to the school for secondary education[11] suitable to the requirements of pupils who are over compulsory school age[12].

No admission arrangements for a maintained school[13] may make provision for selection by aptitude[14] unless they make provision for a permitted form of such selection[15]. The following are permitted forms of selection by aptitude: (i) any selection by aptitude authorised[16] in relation to pre-existing arrangements[17]; and (ii) any selection by aptitude authorised[18] in relation to aptitude for particular subjects[19].

1 As to the meaning of 'admission arrangements' see PARA 227 note 4 (definition applied by the School Standards and Framework Act 1998 s 99(5)(c); Education and Inspections Act 2006 s 39(3)).
2 As to the meaning of references to a community, foundation or voluntary school see PARA 106.
3 For the purposes of the School Standards and Framework Act 1998 Pt III Ch II (ss 99–109) and the Education and Inspections Act 2006 s 39(1), a school's admission arrangements make provision for selection by ability if they make provision for all or any of the pupils who are to be admitted to the school in any relevant age group to be so admitted by reference to ability: see the School Standards and Framework Act 1998 s 99(5)(a); Education and Inspections Act 2006 s 39(2). 'Ability' means either general ability or ability in any particular subject or subjects: School Standards and Framework Act 1998 s 99(5)(b); Education and Inspections Act 2006 s 39(3). As to the meaning of 'pupil' see PARA 20 note 4 (definition applied by s 187(2), (3)). As to the meaning of 'relevant age group' see PARA 133 note 15 (definition applied by s 39(3)).
4 Education and Inspections Act 2006 s 39(1)(a).
5 Education and Inspections Act 2006 s 39(1)(b). As to the meaning of 'grammar school' see PARA 263 note 4 (definition applied by s 39(3)).
6 School Standards and Framework Act 1998 s 99(2) (amended by the Education and Inspections Act 2006 s 39(4)(b)). As to the application of the School Standards and Framework Act 1998 s 99 to new schools in England see the New School (Admissions) (England) Regulations 2003, SI 2003/1041; and in Wales see the New School (Admissions) (Wales) Regulations 2006, SI 2006/175. As to the meanings of 'England' and 'Wales' see PARA 7 note 3.
7 Ie by the School Standards and Framework Act 1998 s 100: see PARA 259.
8 School Standards and Framework Act 1998 s 99(2)(a).
9 Ie by the School Standards and Framework Act 1998 s 101: see PARA 260.
10 School Standards and Framework Act 1998 s 99(2)(b).
11 As to the meaning of 'secondary education' see PARA 21 (definition applied by the School Standards and Framework Act 1998 s 142(8)).
12 School Standards and Framework Act 1998 s 99(2)(c). As to the meaning of 'compulsory school age' see PARA 19.
13 For the purposes of the School Standards and Framework Act 1998 Pt III Ch II (ss 99–109), 'maintained school' means a community, foundation or voluntary school: s 99(5)(d).
14 For the purposes of the School Standards and Framework Act 1998 Pt III Ch II (ss 99–109) a school's admission arrangements make provision for selection by aptitude if they make provision for all or any of the pupils who are to be admitted to the school in any relevant age group to be so admitted by reference to aptitude: see s 99(5)(a).
15 School Standards and Framework Act 1998 s 99(3).
16 Ie by the School Standards and Framework Act 1998 s 100: see PARA 259.
17 School Standards and Framework Act 1998 s 99(4)(a).

18 Ie by the School Standards and Framework Act 1998 s 102: see PARA 261. See in particular the School Admissions Code 2014 para 1.24 referred to in PARA 261 note 5.

19 School Standards and Framework Act 1998 s 99(4)(b).

259. Permitted selection: pre-existing arrangements. Where at the beginning of the 1997–1998 school year[1] the admission arrangements[2] for a maintained school[3] made provision for selection by ability[4] or by aptitude[5], and they have at all times since that date continued to do so, the admission arrangements for the school may continue to make such provision so long as: (1) the proportion of selective admissions[6] in any relevant age group does not exceed the permitted proportion[7]; and (2) there is no significant change in the basis of selection[8].

1   As to the meaning of 'school year' see PARA 19 note 12 (definition applied by the School Standards and Framework Act 1998 s 142(8)).

2   As to the meaning of 'admission arrangements' see PARA 227 note 4 (definition applied by the School Standards and Framework Act 1998 s 99(5)(c)).

3   In relation to any time before 1 September 1999 (ie the appointed day: see PARA 106 note 3), this reference to a maintained school is a reference to the school as a county, voluntary or grant-maintained school within the meaning of the Education Act 1996: School Standards and Framework Act 1998 s 100(2). Nothing in s 100 applies to a school with selective admission arrangements as defined in s 104(2) (see PARA 263): s 100(4). As to the meaning of 'maintained school' see PARA 258 note 13. As to county, voluntary and grant-maintained schools see PARA 106.

4   As to the meanings of 'ability' and 'make provision for selection by ability' see PARA 258 note 3.

5   As to the meaning of 'make provision for selection by aptitude' see PARA 258 note 14.

6   'The proportion of selective admissions', in relation to a relevant age group, means the proportion of the total number of pupils admitted to the school in that age group (determined in the prescribed manner) which is represented by the number of pupils so admitted by reference to ability or to aptitude (as the case may be): School Standards and Framework Act 1998 s 100(3). As to the meaning of 'relevant age group' see PARA 133 note 15. As to the meaning of 'pupil' see PARA 20 note 4 (definition applied by s 142(8)). 'Prescribed' means prescribed by regulations made under the School Standards and Framework Act 1998 by the Secretary of State or, in relation to Wales, the Welsh Ministers: see s 142(1). As to the regulations made see the Education (Proportion of Selective Admissions) Regulations 1998, SI 1998/2229 (amended by SI 2008/3089) (which apply in relation to Wales); and the School Admissions (Admission Arrangements and Co-ordination of Admission Arrangements) (England) Regulations 2012, SI 2012/8 (amended by SI 2014/2886). See also PARA 226.

     The functions of the Secretary of State under the School Standards and Framework Act 1998 s 100, so far as exercisable in relation to Wales, were transferred to the National Assembly for Wales (see the National Assembly for Wales (Transfer of Functions) Order 1999, SI 1999/672, art 2, Sch 1) and are now vested in the Welsh Ministers (see the Government of Wales Act 2006 s 162(1), Sch 11 para 30). As to the Secretary of State see PARA 58. As to the Welsh Ministers see PARA 59. As to the meanings of 'England' and 'Wales' see PARA 7 note 3.

7   School Standards and Framework Act 1998 s 100(1)(a) (s 100(1)(a), (b) substituted by the Education and Inspections Act 2006 s 53(1), (2)). 'The permitted proportion', in relation to any relevant age group, means the lowest proportion of selective admissions provided for by the school's admission arrangements at any time since the beginning of the 1997–1998 school year: School Standards and Framework Act 1998 s 100(1A) (added by the Education and Inspections Act 2006 s 53(1), (3)).

8   School Standards and Framework Act 1998 s 100(1)(b) (as substituted: see note 7). As to the introduction, variation and abandonment of selection see PARA 262.

260. Permitted selection: pupil banding. The admission arrangements[1] for a maintained school[2] in England or Wales may make provision for selection by ability[3] to the extent that the arrangements are designed to secure[4]: (1) that in any year the pupils[5] admitted to the school in any relevant age group[6] are representative of all levels of ability among applicants for admission to the school in that age group[7]; and (2) that no level of ability is substantially over-represented or substantially under-represented[8]. The admission authority[9] for a maintained school in England may make provision for selection by ability to the extent that the arrangements are designed to secure[10]:

(a)   that in any year the pupils admitted to the school in any relevant age group are representative of all levels of ability among such one of the following groups as the admission arrangements may specify ('the reference group'): (i) children[11] who are applicants for admission in that age group to any of two or more schools (including the school in question) in the area of the local authority[12]; (ii) children in that age group who live in the area of the local authority[13]; or (iii) children in that age group who live in England[14]; and

(b)   that no level of ability is substantially over-represented or substantially under-represented by comparison with its representation in the reference group[15].

However, the above provisions[16] do not apply if the arrangements have the effect that, where an applicant for admission has been allocated to a particular range of ability by means of some process of selection by reference to ability, some further such process is required or authorised to be carried out in relation to him for the purpose of determining whether or not he is to be admitted to the school[17]. Also, if the admission authority for a maintained school in England is the local authority, the authority may only introduce such provision for selection by ability as is mentioned in those provisions[18] with the consent of the governing body of the school[19].

Where the admission arrangements for a school make both such provision for selection by ability as is mentioned in the above provisions[20] and provision for selection by aptitude for particular subjects[21], nothing[22] must be taken to prevent those arrangements[23]: (A) from authorising or requiring a process of selection to be carried out at any stage for the purpose of establishing that an applicant for admission has a relevant aptitude[24]; or (B) from having the effect of giving priority to such an applicant with a relevant aptitude irrespective of his level of ability[25].

1   As to the meaning of 'admission arrangements' see PARA 227 note 4 (definition applied by the School Standards and Framework Act 1998 s 99(5)(c)).

2   As to the meaning of 'maintained school' see PARA 258 note 13. As to the application of the School Standards and Framework Act 1998 s 101 to new schools in England see the New School (Admissions) (England) Regulations 2003, SI 2003/1041; and in Wales see the New School (Admissions) (Wales) Regulations 2006, SI 2006/175. As to the meanings of 'England' and 'Wales' see PARA 7 note 3.

3   As to the meanings of 'ability' and 'make provision for selection by ability' see PARA 258 note 3. As to the introduction, variation and abandonment of selection see PARA 262.

4   School Standards and Framework Act 1998 s 101(1) (amended by the Education and Inspections Act 2006 s 54(1)(a)). This provision is expressed to be subject to the School Standards and Framework Act 1998 s 101(2), (2A) (see the text to notes 16–19): see s 101(1) (as so amended). In the case of a school in Wales, admission arrangements to which s 101(1) applies are not authorised by s 101 unless proposals for the school to have such arrangements have been published, and fallen to be implemented, under any enactment: s 101(4) (amended by the Education Act 2002 s 215(1), Sch 21 para 109; and the Education and Inspections Act 2006 s 54(1)(f)).

5   As to the meaning of 'pupil' see PARA 20 note 4 (definition applied by the School Standards and Framework Act 1998 s 142(8)).

6   As to the meaning of 'relevant age group' see PARA 133 note 15.

7   School Standards and Framework Act 1998 s 101(1)(a).

8   School Standards and Framework Act 1998 s 101(1)(b).

9   As to admission authorities see PARA 227 note 6.

10   School Standards and Framework Act 1998 s 101(1A) (added by the Education and Inspections Act 2006 s 54(1)(b)). This provision is expressed to be subject to the School Standards and Framework Act 1998 s 101(2), (2A) (see the text to notes 16–19): see s 101(1A) (as so added).

11   As to the meaning of 'child' see PARA 7 note 6 (definition applied by the School Standards and Framework Act 1998 s 142(8)).

12   School Standards and Framework Act 1998 s 101(1A)(a)(i) (as added (see note 10); and amended by SI 2010/1158). As to the meaning of 'local authority' see PARA 25 (definition applied by the School Standards and Framework Act 1998 s 142(8)).

13   School Standards and Framework Act 1998 s 101(1A)(a)(ii) (as added (see note 10); and amended by SI 2010/1158).

14   School Standards and Framework Act 1998 s 101(1A)(a)(iii) (as added: see note 10).

15   School Standards and Framework Act 1998 s 101(1A)(b) (as added: see note 10).

16   Ie the School Standards and Framework Act 1998 s 101(1) or (1A): see the text to notes 1–15.

17   School Standards and Framework Act 1998 s 101(2) (amended by the Education and Inspections Act 2006 s 54(1)(c)).

18   Ie the School Standards and Framework Act 1998 s 101(1) or (1A): see the text to notes 1–15.

19   School Standards and Framework Act 1998 s 101(2A) (added by the Education and Inspections Act 2006 s 54(1)(d); and amended by SI 2010/1158). As to the governing bodies of maintained schools in England see PARA 150 et seq.

20   Ie the School Standards and Framework Act 1998 s 101(1) or (1A): see the text to notes 1–15.

21   Ie such provision as is mentioned in the School Standards and Framework Act 1998 s 102(1): see PARA 261.

22   Ie nothing in the School Standards and Framework Act 1998 s 101.

23   School Standards and Framework Act 1998 s 101(5) (amended by the Education and Inspections Act 2006 s 54(1)(g)).

24   School Standards and Framework Act 1998 s 101(5)(a).

25   School Standards and Framework Act 1998 s 101(5)(b).

261.   Permitted selection: aptitude for particular subjects. The admission arrangements[1] for a maintained school[2] may make provision for the selection of pupils[3] for admission to the school by reference to their aptitude[4] for one or more prescribed[5] subjects where: (1) the admission authority[6] for the school is satisfied that the school has a specialism[7] in the subject or subjects in question[8]; and (2) the proportion of selective admissions[9] in any relevant age group does not exceed 10 per cent[10]. However, this does not apply if the admission arrangements make provision for any test[11] to be carried out in relation to an applicant for admission which is either a test of ability[12] or one designed to elicit any aptitude of his other than for the subject or subjects in question[13].

1   As to the meaning of 'admission arrangements' see PARA 227 note 4 (definition applied by the School Standards and Framework Act 1998 s 99(5)(c)).

2   As to the meaning of 'maintained school' see PARA 258 note 13. As to the application of the School Standards and Framework Act 1998 s 102 to new schools in England see the New School (Admissions) (England) Regulations 2003, SI 2003/1041; and in Wales see the New School (Admissions) (Wales) Regulations 2006, SI 2006/175. As to the meanings of 'England' and 'Wales' see PARA 7 note 3.

3   As to the meaning of 'pupil' see PARA 20 note 4 (definition applied by the School Standards and Framework Act 1998 s 142(8)).

4   As to the meaning of 'make provision for selection by aptitude' see PARA 258 note 14. As to the introduction, variation and abandonment of selection see PARA 262.

5   'Prescribed' means prescribed by regulations made under the School Standards and Framework Act 1998 by the Secretary of State or, in relation to Wales, the Welsh Ministers: see s 142(1). The functions of the Secretary of State under s 102, so far as exercisable in relation to Wales, were transferred to the National Assembly for Wales (see the National Assembly for Wales (Transfer of Functions) Order 1999, SI 1999/672, art 2, Sch 1) and are now vested in the Welsh Ministers (see the Government of Wales Act 2006 s 162(1), Sch 11 para 30). As to the Secretary of State see PARA 58. As to the Welsh Ministers see PARA 59.

     In relation to England, the following subjects are prescribed for the purposes of the School Standards and Framework Act 1998 s 102: (1) modern foreign languages, or any such language; (2) the performing arts, or any one or more of the performing arts; (3) the visual arts, or any one or more of the visual arts; (4) physical education or sport, or one or more sports; (5) design and technology; (6) information technology: see the School Admissions (Admission Arrangements and Co-ordination of Admission Arrangements) (England) Regulations 2012, SI 2012/8, regs 1(4), 6(1); and see further below in regard to the School Admissions Code. The subjects in heads (5) and (6) above are prescribed in relation to admission arrangements for the school year 2013–2014 and subsequent school years, only if the admission arrangements for that school made provision for the selection of pupils by reference to their aptitude in those subjects in relation to the school year 2007–2008 and each subsequent year: School Admissions (Admission Arrangements and Co-ordination of Admission Arrangements) (England) Regulations 2012, SI 2012/8, reg 6(2) (amended by SI 2014/2886). In relation to Wales, the following subjects are prescribed for the purposes of the School Standards and Framework Act 1998 s 102: (a) modern foreign languages, or any such language; (b) the performing arts, or any one or more of the performing arts; (c) the visual arts, or any one or more of the visual arts; (d) physical education or sport, or one or more sports; (e) design and technology; (f) information technology: see the Education (Aptitude for Particular Subjects) Regulations 1999, SI 1999/258, regs 1A, 2 (reg 1A added by SI 2008/3089).

It should be noted that the School Admissions Code 2014 para 1.24 states that schools that have arrangements to select by aptitude must not allow for more than 10 per cent of the total admissions intake to be allocated on the basis of such aptitude (even if the school has more than one specialism); the *only* specialist subjects on which a school may select by aptitude are: (i) physical education or sport, or one or more sports; (ii) the performing arts, or any one or more of those arts; (iii) the visual arts, or any one or more of those arts; (iv) modern foreign languages, or any such language; and (v) design and technology and information technology; only schools which selected on either of these specialist subjects in the school year 2007/08 and every subsequent year may continue to do so. As to the Code generally see PARA 226 note 8.

6   As to admission authorities see PARA 227 note 6.
7   As to specialist schools see PARA 100.
8   School Standards and Framework Act 1998 s 102(1)(a).
9   'The proportion of selective admissions', in relation to a relevant age group, means the proportion of the total number of pupils admitted to the school in that age group (determined in the prescribed manner) which is represented by the number of pupils so admitted by reference to aptitude for the subject or subjects in question: School Standards and Framework Act 1998 s 102(4). As to the meaning of 'relevant age group' see PARA 133 note 15. As to the regulations made see the Education (Proportion of Selective Admissions) Regulations 1998, SI 1998/2229 (amended by SI 2008/3089) (which apply in relation to Wales); and the School Admissions (Admission Arrangements and Co-ordination of Admission Arrangements) (England) Regulations 2012, SI 2012/8, reg 5 (amended by SI 2014/2886).
10 School Standards and Framework Act 1998 s 102(1)(b).
11 'Test' includes assessment and examination: School Standards and Framework Act 1998 s 102(5).
12 Where, however, the admission arrangements for a school make both such provision for selection by aptitude as is mentioned in the School Standards and Framework Act 1998 s 102(1) (see the text to notes 1–10) and such provision for selection by ability as is mentioned in s 101(1) or (1A) (see PARA 260), the reference in s 102(2) to a test of ability does not include any such test for which provision may be made under s 101 (see PARA 260): s 102(3) (amended by the Education and Inspections Act 2006 s 54(2)). As to the meanings of 'ability' and 'make provision for selection by ability' see PARA 258 note 3.
13 School Standards and Framework Act 1998 s 102(2).

262.   Permitted selection: introduction, variation or abandonment of selection. In connection with the determination of a maintained school's[1] admission arrangements[2] for a particular school year[3], the statutory provisions relating to the procedure for determining admission arrangements[4] apply, except to the specified extent[5], in relation to the making or abandonment by those arrangements of provision for any permitted form of selection by ability[6] or aptitude[7] as they apply in relation to the making or abandonment by those arrangements of provision for other matters[8].

Any admission arrangements which make provision for selection by ability[9] may be varied if (and only if) the arrangements as varied are designed to secure the specified objectives[10].

1   As to the meaning of 'maintained school' see PARA 258 note 13. As to the application of the School Standards and Framework Act 1998 s 103 to new schools in England see the New School (Admissions) (England) Regulations 2003, SI 2003/1041; and in Wales see the New School (Admissions) (Wales) Regulations 2006, SI 2006/175. As to the meanings of 'England' and 'Wales' see PARA 7 note 3.

2   As to the meaning of 'admission arrangements' see PARA 227 note 4 (definition applied by the School Standards and Framework Act 1998 s 99(5)(c)).

3   As to the meaning of 'school year' see PARA 19 note 12 (definition applied by the School Standards and Framework Act 1998 s 142(8)).

4   Ie the School Standards and Framework Act 1998 ss 88C–88K (see PARA 237 et seq) or, as the case may be, ss 89 and 90 (see PARAS 247, 249).

5   'The specified extent' means the extent to which those admission arrangements would effect an alteration in the provision made by the school's admission arrangements as respects any such form of selection (whether by introducing, varying or abandoning any such form of selection) which constitutes: (1) in relation to England, a prescribed alteration for the purposes of the Education and Inspections Act 2006 s 18 (see PARA 132); and (2) in relation to Wales, a regulated alteration within the meaning of the School Standards and Organisation (Wales) Act 2013 Pt 3 Ch 2 (ss 40–56) (see PARA 140): School Standards and Framework Act 1998 s 103(2) (amended by the Education and Inspections Act 2006 s 54(3)(a); and the School Standards and Organisation (Wales) Act 2013 Sch 5 para 19(1), (10)).

6   As to the meanings of 'ability' and 'make provision for selection by ability' see PARA 258 note 3.

7   As to the meaning of 'make provision for selection by aptitude' see PARA 258 note 14.

8   School Standards and Framework Act 1998 s 103(1) (amended by the Education and Skills Act 2008 s 169, Sch 1 Pt 2 paras 53, 69). See *R (on the application Watford Grammar School for Girls) v Adjudicator for Schools* [2003] EWHC 2480 (Admin), [2004] ELR 40, [2003] All ER (D) 135 (Oct), at [62]–[65] per Collins J (since admission arrangements within the meaning of the School Standards and Framework Act 1998 s 103 are made annually, they may be challenged annually regardless of how long they have been in place).

9   Ie any admission arrangements to which the School Standards and Framework Act 1998 s 101(1) or (1A) (see PARA 260) applies (whether authorised by s 100 (see PARA 259) or s 101).

10 School Standards and Framework Act 1998 s 103(3) (amended by the Education and Inspections Act 2006 s 54(3)(b)). The specified objectives are the objectives mentioned in the School Standards and Framework Act 1998 s 101(1)(a) and (b), s 101(1A)(a)(i) and (b), s 101(1A)(a)(ii) and (b) or s 101(1A)(a)(iii) and (b) (see PARA 260): see s 103(3) (as so amended).

(B)   Grammar Schools

263.   Designation of grammar schools. Where the appropriate national authority[1] is satisfied that a maintained school[2] had selective admission arrangements at the beginning of the 1997–1998 school year, it may by order[3] designate the school as a grammar school[4] for the purposes of the statutory provisions[5] relating to the selection of pupils[6]. A school has 'selective admission arrangements' if its admission arrangements make provision for all, or substantially all, of its pupils to be selected by reference to general ability[7], with a view to admitting only pupils with high ability[8].

Regulations[9] may make provision: (1) for enabling the appropriate national authority to make an order designating as a grammar school[10] a maintained school established in substitution for one or more discontinued schools each of which either has been or could have been[11] so designated[12]; and (2) for any of the provisions relating to the selection of pupils[13], or any regulations made under them, to have effect in relation to any such school with such modifications[14] as may be prescribed[15].

1   Ie the Secretary of State or, in relation to Wales, the Welsh Ministers. The functions of the Secretary of State under the School Standards and Framework Act 1998 s 104, so far as exercisable in relation to Wales, were transferred to the National Assembly for Wales (see the National Assembly for Wales (Transfer of Functions) Order 1999, SI 1999/672, art 2, Sch 1) and are now vested in the Welsh Ministers (see the Government of Wales Act 2006 s 162(1), Sch 11 para 30). As to the Secretary of State see PARA 58. As to the Welsh Ministers see PARA 59. As to the meaning of 'Wales' see PARA 7 note 3.

2   For these purposes, 'maintained school' includes, in relation to any time before 1 September 1999 (ie the appointed day: see PARA 106 note 3): (1) a county or voluntary school within the meaning of the Education Act 1996; or (2) a grant-maintained school, within the meaning of the Education Act 1996: see the School Standards and Framework Act 1998 s 104(6)(a), (b). In the application of s 104(1) to a maintained school on or after 1 September 1999, the reference to the school is to be read, in connection with determining the nature of its admission arrangements at the beginning of the 1997–1998 school year, as a reference to it as a school within head (1) or head (2) above: s 104(6). As to the meaning of 'maintained school' see PARA 258 note 13. As to county, voluntary and grant-maintained schools see PARA 106. As to the meaning of 'admission arrangements' see PARA 227 note 4 (definition applied by s 99(5)(c)). As to the meaning of 'school year' see PARA 19 note 12 (definition applied by s 142(8)).

3   As to the order made see the Education (Grammar School Designation) Order 1998, SI 1998/2219 (amended by SI 1999/2456; and SI 2010/1172).

4   For the purposes of the School Standards and Framework Act 1998 Pt III Ch II (ss 99–109), 'grammar school' means a school for the time being designated under s 104: s 104(7). Where a maintained school is a grammar school, ss 105–109 (see PARAS 264–267) have effect for prescribing procedures for altering the school's admission arrangements so that it no longer has selective admission arrangements (s 104(4)(a)), and its admission arrangements must not be so altered except in accordance with ss 105–109 (s 104(4)(b)).

5   Ie the School Standards and Framework Act 1998 Pt III Ch II (ss 99–109).

6   School Standards and Framework Act 1998 s 104(1). As to the meaning of 'pupil' see PARA 20 note 4 (definition applied by s 142(8)). As to the procedure for deciding whether grammar schools should retain selective admission arrangements see PARA 264.

7   As to the meanings of 'ability' and 'make provision for selection by ability' see PARA 258 note 3.

8   School Standards and Framework Act 1998 s 104(2). For the purpose of deciding whether a school's admission arrangements fall within s 104(2), any such additional criteria as are mentioned in s 86(9) (parental preferences: see PARA 228) must be disregarded: s 104(3).

9   Ie regulations made by the Secretary of State or, in relation to Wales, the Welsh Ministers: see the School Standards and Framework Act 1998 s 142(1). As to the regulations made see the Education (Substituted Grammar Schools) Regulations 1999, SI 1999/2102.

10 Ie for the purposes of the School Standards and Framework Act 1998 Pt III Ch II (ss 99–109).

11 Ie by virtue of the School Standards and Framework Act 1998 s 104(1) (see the text to notes 1–6) or by virtue of the regulations.

12 School Standards and Framework Act 1998 s 104(5)(a).

13 Ie the School Standards and Framework Act 1998 Pt III Ch II (ss 99–109).

14 As to the meaning of 'modifications' see PARA 21 note 15 (definition applied by the School Standards and Framework Act 1998 s 142(8)).

15 School Standards and Framework Act 1998 s 104(5)(b). 'Prescribed' means prescribed by regulations: s 142(1).

264.   Procedure for deciding whether grammar schools should retain selective admission arrangements. The appropriate national authority[1] may by regulations[2] make provision for ballots of parents[3] to be held, at their request, for determining whether the grammar schools[4] to which such ballots relate should retain selective admission arrangements[5]. Ballot regulations[6] may provide for a ballot to relate: (1) to all grammar schools within the area of a prescribed local authority[7] or within such other area as may be prescribed[8]; (2) to a prescribed group of grammar schools[9]; or (3) to any grammar school not falling within head (1) or head (2) above[10]. Ballot regulations may make provision:

(a)   requiring a request for a ballot to be made by means of a petition signed by parents eligible to request the ballot[11];

(b)   prescribing the form of any such petition and other requirements (whether as to the procedure to be followed or otherwise) which are to be complied with in relation to any such petition[12];

(c)   prescribing the body ('the designated body') to which any such petition is to be sent and which, under arrangements made by the appropriate national authority, is to make the arrangements for the holding of ballots[13], and is to discharge such other functions[14] with respect to such petitions and the holding of such ballots as may be prescribed[15];

(d)   requiring prescribed bodies or persons, or bodies or persons falling within any prescribed category: (i) to provide the designated body or any other person with any prescribed information requested by that body or person[16]; or (ii) to publish prescribed information in such manner as may be prescribed[17];

(e)   authorising any such bodies or persons to charge a fee[18] for documents supplied by it in pursuance of regulations made by virtue of head (d)(i) above[19];

(f)   prescribing the terms of the question on which a ballot is to be held and the manner in which such a ballot is to be conducted[20];

(g)   enabling the appropriate national authority, in any prescribed circumstances, to declare a previous ballot void and require the holding of a fresh ballot[21];

(h)   requiring anything falling to be done under the regulations to be done within such period as may be specified in or determined in accordance with the regulations[22];

(i)   for parents of any prescribed description to register with the designated body, in such manner and at such time as may be prescribed, in order to be eligible to request or vote in a ballot[23];

(j)   that for all or any prescribed purposes of the regulations references to parents are to be read as excluding those who are not individuals[24];

(k)   for a parent's eligibility for the purposes of making a request for a ballot[25] or voting in a ballot[26] to be determined by reference to such different times as may be determined in accordance with the regulations[27].

Where a ballot has been held[28] and the result of the ballot was to the effect that the schools or school in question should retain selective admission arrangements[29], no further ballot relating to the schools or school may be held within such period as is specified in ballot regulations[30].

1   Ie the Secretary of State or, in relation to Wales, the Welsh Ministers. The functions of the Secretary of State under the School Standards and Framework Act 1998 s 105, so far as exercisable in relation to Wales, were transferred to the National Assembly for Wales (see the National Assembly for Wales (Transfer of Functions) Order 1999, SI 1999/672, art 2, Sch 1) and are now vested in the Welsh Ministers (see the Government of Wales Act 2006 s 162(1), Sch 11 para 30). As to the Secretary of State see PARA 58. As to the Welsh Ministers see PARA 59. As to the meaning of 'Wales' see PARA 7 note 3.

2   'Regulations' means regulations made under the School Standards and Framework Act 1998 by the Secretary of State or, in relation to Wales, the Welsh Ministers: see s 142(1). As to the regulations made see the Education (Grammar School Ballots) Regulations 1998, SI 1998/2876 (amended by SI 1999/2103; and SI 2012/979); and the Education (Proposals for Grammar Schools to cease to have Selective Admission Arrangements) Regulations 1999, SI 1999/2103.

3   As to the meaning of 'parent' see PARA 7 note 6 (definition applied by the School Standards and Framework Act 1998 s 142(8)).

4   As to the meaning of 'grammar school' see PARA 263 note 4.

5   School Standards and Framework Act 1998 s 105(1). As to the meaning of 'selective admission arrangements' see PARA 263. As to restrictions on the publication of material relating to ballots see PARA 265. As to the implementation of a decision that a school cease to have selective admission arrangements see PARA 266.

6   'Ballot regulations' means regulations made under the School Standards and Framework Act 1998 s 105: s 105(11). Ballot regulations may provide for a request for a ballot under s 105 to be made, in any prescribed circumstances, by means of two or more petitions: s 105(5). Ballot regulations may provide for the Education Act 1996 ss 496, 497 (default powers of the Secretary of State and the Welsh Ministers: see PARAS 64, 65) to apply to proprietors of

independent schools in relation to a duty imposed by or under the regulations: School Standards and Framework Act 1998 s 105(7). 'Prescribed' means prescribed by regulations: s 142(1). As to the meaning of 'proprietor' see PARA 51 note 4; and as to the meaning of 'independent school' see PARA 369 (definitions applied by the School Standards and Framework Act 1998 s 142(8)). In connection with s 105(7) see also PARA 64 note 10.

7   As to the meaning of 'local authority' see PARA 25 (definition applied by the School Standards and Framework Act 1998 s 142(8)). Any function of a local authority in England which is conferred by or under the School Standards and Framework Act 1998 s 105 may be exercised by, or by employees of, such person as may be authorised in that behalf by the local authority whose function it is: Contracting Out (Local Authority Education Functions) (England) Order 2002, SI 2002/928, art 3, Sch 2 para (bb) (art 3 amended by SI 2010/1172). As to the meaning of 'person' see PARA 7 note 6. As to the meaning of 'England' see PARA 7 note 3.

8   School Standards and Framework Act 1998 s 105(2)(a) (amended by SI 2010/1158). In relation to a ballot under the School Standards and Framework Act 1998 s 105(2)(a), ballot regulations must provide that, subject to such exceptions as may be prescribed, the parents eligible to request or vote in the ballot are: (1) registered parents of registered pupils at the following schools, namely: (a) where the ballot relates to all grammar schools within the area of a prescribed local authority, all schools maintained by that authority (s 106(1)(a)(i) (s 106(1) amended by SI 2010/1158)); or (b) where the ballot relates to all grammar schools within a prescribed area, all schools maintained by a local authority which are situated in such area as may be prescribed, together with (if the regulations so provide) all schools maintained by such local authority as may be prescribed (School Standards and Framework Act 1998 s 106(1)(a)(ii) (as so amended)); (2) registered parents of registered pupils at independent schools where such parents are resident and the schools are situated within the area of the prescribed local authority or (as the case may be) the prescribed area (s 106(1)(b) (as so amended)); and (3) parents of children of a prescribed description where such parents are resident within the area of the prescribed local authority or (as the case may be) the prescribed area, and have registered with the designated body in accordance with s 105(4)(a) (see the text to note 23) (s 106(1)(c) (as so amended)). Ballot regulations must provide, in relation to a ballot under s 105(2)(a), that a request for such a ballot must be made by a number of eligible parents equal to at least 20% of all parents falling within head (1) or head (2) above: s 106(3)(a). Ballot regulations must provide for a parent's eligibility for the purposes of determining the number of parents required to make a request by virtue of s 106(3) to be determined by reference to such different times as may be determined in accordance with the regulations: see s 106(4)(c). Ballot regulations may make provision for determining whether parents are resident in an area for the purposes of head (2) or head (3) above: s 106(5). For the purposes of ss 105, 106, in relation to any time falling before 1 September 1999 (ie the appointed day: see PARA 106 note 3), a grant-maintained school or a grant-maintained special school within the meaning of the Education Act 1996 (see PARA 106) is taken: (i) to be a school maintained by a local authority; and (ii) to be maintained by the authority in whose area it is situated: School Standards and Framework Act 1998 s 105(10) (amended by SI 2010/1158). As to the meanings of 'registered parent' and 'registered pupil' see PARA 437 (definitions applied by the School Standards and Framework Act 1998 s 142(8)). As to the meaning of 'school maintained by a local authority' see PARA 99. See also *R v Secretary of State for Education and Employment, ex p RCO* [2000] ELR 307.

9   School Standards and Framework Act 1998 s 105(2)(b). In relation to a ballot under s 105(2)(b), ballot regulations must provide that, subject to such exceptions as may be prescribed, the parents eligible to request or vote in the ballot are registered parents of registered pupils at any school from which a prescribed number of pupils have transferred to the grammar school or schools in question at such age or ages and during such period as may be determined in accordance with the regulations: s 106(2). Such regulations may provide that where, within that period, any such grammar school has been established in substitution for another school, the schools are to be treated as a single school for the purposes of determining eligibility: s 106(2). Ballot regulations must provide, in relation to a ballot under s 105(2)(b), that a request for such a ballot must be made by at least 20% of all parents falling within s 106(2): s 106(3)(b). Ballot regulations may provide for a parent's eligibility for the purposes of determining the number of parents required to make a request by virtue of s 106(3) to be determined by reference to such different times as may be determined in accordance with the regulations: s 106(4)(c).

10   School Standards and Framework Act 1998 s 105(2)(c). In relation to a ballot under s 105(2)(c), ballot regulations must provide that, subject to such exceptions as may be prescribed, the parents eligible to request or vote in the ballot are registered parents of registered pupils at any school from which a prescribed number of pupils have transferred to the grammar school or schools in question at such age or ages and during such period as may be determined in

accordance with the regulations: s 106(2). Such regulations may provide that where, within that period, any such grammar school has been established in substitution for another school, the schools are to be treated as a single school for the purposes of determining eligibility: s 106(2). Ballot regulations must provide, in relation to a ballot under s 105(2)(c), that a request for such a ballot must be made by at least 20% of all parents falling within s 106(2): s 106(3)(b). Ballot regulations may provide for a parent's eligibility for the purposes of determining the number of parents required to make a request by virtue of s 106(3) to be determined by reference to such different times as may be determined in accordance with the regulations: s 106(4)(c).

11 School Standards and Framework Act 1998 s 105(3)(a).
12 School Standards and Framework Act 1998 s 105(3)(b).
13 School Standards and Framework Act 1998 s 105(3)(c)(i).
14 As to the meaning of 'functions' see PARA 18 note 5 (definition applied by the School Standards and Framework Act 1998 s 142(8)).
15 School Standards and Framework Act 1998 s 105(3)(c)(ii). This may include the determination of any question arising as to the validity of any request for a ballot or as to a person's eligibility to request or vote in a ballot: s 105(3)(c)(ii).
16 School Standards and Framework Act 1998 s 105(3)(d)(i). The information required to be provided in pursuance of s 105(3)(d) may include the names and addresses of parents of any prescribed description: s 105(6). The appropriate national authority may make (or arrange for the making of) payments in respect of any expenses incurred by: (1) the governing body of a school maintained by a local authority (s 105(9)(a) (s 105(9)(a), (c) amended by SI 2010/1158)); (2) the proprietor of an independent school (School Standards and Framework Act 1998 s 105(9)(b)); or (3) a local authority (s 105(9)(c) (as so amended)), in complying with any obligations which may be imposed by regulations made under heads (d)(i) and (d)(ii) in the text (s 105(9)). Payments under s 105(9) may be made on such terms as the appropriate national authority may determine: s 105(9). As to the governing bodies of maintained schools in England see PARA 150 et seq; and in Wales see PARA 195.
17 School Standards and Framework Act 1998 s 105(3)(d)(ii). See also note 16.
18 Ie not exceeding the cost of supply: see the School Standards and Framework Act 1998 s 105(3)(e).
19 School Standards and Framework Act 1998 s 105(3)(e).
20 School Standards and Framework Act 1998 s 105(3)(f).
21 School Standards and Framework Act 1998 s 105(3)(g).
22 School Standards and Framework Act 1998 s 105(3)(h).
23 School Standards and Framework Act 1998 s 105(4)(a).
24 School Standards and Framework Act 1998 s 105(4)(b). See *R v Secretary of State for Education and Employment, ex p RCO* [2000] ELR 307.
25 School Standards and Framework Act 1998 s 106(4)(a).
26 School Standards and Framework Act 1998 s 106(4)(b).
27 School Standards and Framework Act 1998 s 106(4).
28 School Standards and Framework Act 1998 s 105(8)(a).
29 School Standards and Framework Act 1998 s 105(8)(b).
30 School Standards and Framework Act 1998 s 105(8).

265.   Restriction on publication of material relating to ballots. Expenditure[1] must not be incurred by any local authority[2] or by the governing body of any school maintained by a local authority[3] for the purpose of:

(1)   publishing any material which, in whole or in part, appears designed to influence eligible parents[4] in deciding whether or not to request a ballot[5], or to influence the outcome of a ballot[6]; or

(2)   assisting any person[7] to publish any such material[8]; or

(3)   influencing, or assisting any person to influence, by any other means, eligible parents in deciding whether or not to request a ballot, or to influence the outcome of a ballot[9].

However, this must not be taken to prevent a local authority or body from incurring expenditure on publishing or otherwise providing to any person (whether or not in pursuance of any duty to do so)[10]: (a) any factual information so far as it is presented fairly[11]; or (b) a fair and reasonable assessment[12] by the authority or body of the likely consequences of the result of a ballot[13] being in favour of the school or schools in question ceasing to have selective admission arrangements[14]; or (c) an accurate statement by the authority or body of its intentions or proposals in the event of such a result[15].

1   For these purposes, any reference to expenditure: (1) in relation to the governing body of a school which has a delegated budget within the meaning of the School Standards and Framework Act 1998 Pt II (ss 20–83) (see PARA 323) (or, in relation to any time before 1 September 1999 (ie the appointed day: see PARA 106 note 3), the Education Act 1996 Pt II (ss 31–182) (repealed)), is a reference to expenditure out of the school's budget share (School Standards and Framework Act 1998 s 107(5)(a)); or (2) in relation to the governing body of a grant-maintained or grant-maintained special school within the meaning of the Education Act 1996 (see PARA 106) (where the School Standards and Framework Act 1998 s 107 applies to such a school by virtue of s 105(10)), is a reference to expenditure out of maintenance grants paid under the Education Act 1996 Pt III Ch VI (ss 211–217) (repealed) (School Standards and Framework Act 1998 s 107(5)(b)). In relation to any time falling before 1 October 1998, a grant-maintained school or a grant-maintained special school within the meaning of the Education Act 1996 is taken: (a) to be a school maintained by a local authority (School Standards and Framework Act 1998 s 105(10)(a) (amended by SI 2010/1158)); and (b) to be maintained by the authority in whose area it is situated (School Standards and Framework Act 1998 s 105(10)(b)). As to the governing bodies of maintained schools in England see PARA 150 et seq; and in Wales see PARA 195. As to a maintained school's budget share see PARA 315. As to the meaning of 'school maintained by a local authority' see PARA 99. As to the meaning of 'local authority' see PARA 25 (definition applied by s 142(8)).

2   See the School Standards and Framework Act 1998 s 107(2)(a) (amended by SI 2010/1158).

3   See the School Standards and Framework Act 1998 s 107(2)(b) (amended by SI 2010/1158).

4   As to the meaning of 'parent' see PARA 7 note 6 (definition applied by the School Standards and Framework Act 1998 s 142(8)). As to eligible parents see PARA 264.

5   Ie under the School Standards and Framework Act 1998 s 105: see PARA 264.

6   School Standards and Framework Act 1998 s 107(1)(a).

7   As to the meaning of 'person' see PARA 7 note 6.

8   School Standards and Framework Act 1998 s 107(1)(b).

9   School Standards and Framework Act 1998 s 107(1)(c).

10 School Standards and Framework Act 1998 s 107(3) (amended by SI 2010/1158).

11 School Standards and Framework Act 1998 s 107(3)(a). In determining for the purposes of s 107(3) whether any information is presented fairly, regard must be had to any guidance given from time to time by the Secretary of State or, in relation to Wales, the Welsh Ministers: see s 107(4)(a). The functions of the Secretary of State under the School Standards and Framework Act 1998 s 107, so far as exercisable in relation to Wales, were transferred to the National Assembly for Wales (see the National Assembly for Wales (Transfer of Functions) Order 1999, SI 1999/672, art 2, Sch 1) and are now vested in the Welsh Ministers (see the Government of Wales Act 2006 s 162(1), Sch 11 para 30). As to the Secretary of State see PARA 58. As to the Welsh Ministers see PARA 59. As to the meaning of 'Wales' see PARA 7 note 3.

12 In determining for these purposes whether an assessment is fair and reasonable, regard must be had to any guidance given from time to time by the Secretary of State or, in relation to Wales, the Welsh Ministers: School Standards and Framework Act 1998 s 107(4)(b).

13 Ie under the School Standards and Framework Act 1998 s 105: see PARA 264.

14 School Standards and Framework Act 1998 s 107(3)(b). As to the meaning of 'selective admission arrangements' see PARA 263.

15 School Standards and Framework Act 1998 s 107(3)(c).

266. Implementation of decision that school should cease to have selective admission arrangements. Where the result of a ballot held[1] to decide whether a grammar school or schools[2] should retain selective admission arrangements[3] shows a simple majority of votes cast by persons eligible to vote[4] in the ballot in favour of the grammar school or schools to which the ballot related ceasing to have selective admission arrangements[5], the admission authority[6] for the grammar school to which the ballot related must secure that its admission arrangements are revised[7] so that, as from the beginning of such school year[8] as may be prescribed[9], the school no longer has selective admission arrangements[10].

1   Ie under the School Standards and Framework Act 1998 s 105: see PARA 264.
2   As to the meaning of 'grammar school' see PARA 263 note 4.
3   As to the meaning of 'selective admission arrangements' see PARA 263.
4   As to the persons eligible to vote see PARA 264.
5   School Standards and Framework Act 1998 s 108(1).
6   As to admission authorities see PARA 227 note 6.
7   Ie in accordance with the School Standards and Framework Act 1998 ss 88C–88K (see PARA 237 et seq) or, as the case may be, ss 89 and 90 (see PARAS 247, 249).
8   As to the meaning of 'school year' see PARA 19 note 12 (definition applied by the School Standards and Framework Act 1998 s 142(8)).
9   'Prescribed' means prescribed by regulations made under the School Standards and Framework Act 1998 by the Secretary of State or, in relation to Wales, the Welsh Ministers: see s 142(1). As to the regulations made see the Education (Grammar School Ballots) Regulations 1998, SI 1998/2876 (amended by SI 1999/2103; and SI 2012/979).
    The functions of the Secretary of State under the School Standards and Framework Act 1998 s 108, so far as exercisable in relation to Wales, were transferred to the National Assembly for Wales (see the National Assembly for Wales (Transfer of Functions) Order 1999, SI 1999/672, art 2, Sch 1) and are now vested in the Welsh Ministers (see the Government of Wales Act 2006 s 162(1), Sch 11 para 30). As to the Secretary of State see PARA 58. As to the Welsh Ministers see PARA 59. As to the meaning of 'Wales' see PARA 7 note 3.
10 School Standards and Framework Act 1998 s 108(2) (amended by the Education and Skills Act 2008 s 169, Sch 1 Pt 2 paras 53, 70). Where the Secretary of State or, in relation to Wales, the Welsh Ministers is satisfied that, in pursuance of the School Standards and Framework Act 1998 s 108(2), a grammar school no longer has selective admission arrangements, he or they must revoke the order made with respect to the school under s 104 (see PARA 263): s 108(3).

267.   Proposals by governing body of grammar school to end selective admission arrangements.   The following provisions have effect for enabling the admission arrangements[1] of a grammar school[2] to be revised[3] so that the school no longer has selective admission arrangements[4] and its admission arrangements instead either: (1) make no provision for selection by ability[5]; or (2) make provision for one or more of the following: (a) any authorised[6] selection by ability[7]; (b) any authorised[8] selection by aptitude[9]; and (c) any selection by ability[10] conducted in connection with the admission of pupils to the school for secondary education suitable to the requirements of pupils who are over compulsory school age[11].

Regulations[12] may provide that: (i) in their application to any proposals for any such revision of the admission arrangements of a grammar school, any of the provisions relating to proposals for the alteration of a school[13] are to have effect with such modifications[14] as may be prescribed[15]; (ii) in any prescribed circumstances following the making of a request for a ballot to be held[16], any such proposals[17] are to be of no effect[18]. Where the appropriate national authority[19] is satisfied that, by reason of the implementation of any such proposals, a grammar school no longer has selective admission arrangements, it may revoke the order made[20] with respect to the school[21].

1   As to the meaning of 'admission arrangements' see PARA 227 note 4 (definition applied by the School Standards and Framework Act 1998 s 99(5)(c)).
2   As to the meaning of 'grammar school' see PARA 263 note 4.
3   Ie revised otherwise than in circumstances where the School Standards and Framework Act 1998 s 108(2) (see PARA 266) applies: s 109(1). Any such revision of the admission arrangements of a grammar school is one of the alterations to a maintained school which are prescribed under the Education and Inspections Act 2006 s 18 (see PARA 132); but any proposals for any such revision of the admission arrangements of a grammar school which is a community school must be published under s 19 of that Act (see PARA 133) by the governing body and not by the local authority: School Standards and Framework Act 1998 s 109(2) (amended by the Education and Inspections Act 2006 s 30, Sch 3 para 29(1), (2)(a); and SI 2010/1158). As to the meaning of 'maintained school' see PARA 258 note 13. As to community schools see PARA 106. As to the governing bodies of maintained schools in England see PARA 150 et seq; and in Wales

see PARA 195. As to the meaning of 'local authority' see PARA 25 (definition applied by the School Standards and Framework Act 1998 s 142(8)).

4   As to the meaning of 'selective admission arrangements' see PARA 263.

5   School Standards and Framework Act 1998 s 109(1)(a). As to the meanings of 'ability' and 'make provision for selection by ability' see PARA 258 note 3.

6   Ie by the School Standards and Framework Act 1998 s 101: see PARA 260.

7   School Standards and Framework Act 1998 s 109(1)(b)(i).

8   Ie by the School Standards and Framework Act 1998 s 102: see PARA 261.

9   School Standards and Framework Act 1998 s 109(1)(b)(ii). As to the meaning of 'make provision for selection by aptitude' see PARA 258 note 14.

10 Ie such as is mentioned in the School Standards and Framework Act 1998 s 99(2)(c): see PARA 258.

11 See the School Standards and Framework Act 1998 s 109(1)(b)(iii).

12 'Regulations' means regulations made under the School Standards and Framework Act 1998 by the Secretary of State or, in relation to Wales, the Welsh Ministers: see s 142(1). As to the regulations made see the Education (Proposals for Grammar Schools to cease to have Selective Admission Arrangements) Regulations 1999, SI 1999/2103.

The functions of the Secretary of State under the School Standards and Framework Act 1998 s 109, so far as exercisable in relation to Wales, were transferred to the National Assembly for Wales (see the National Assembly for Wales (Transfer of Functions) Order 1999, SI 1999/672, art 2, Sch 1) and are now vested in the Welsh Ministers (see the Government of Wales Act 2006 s 162(1), Sch 11 para 30). As to the Secretary of State see PARA 58. As to the Welsh Ministers see PARA 59. As to the meaning of 'Wales' see PARA 7 note 3.

13 Ie the Education and Inspections Act 2006 ss 19–24 or regulations under those sections: see PARA 133 et seq.

14 As to the meaning of 'modifications' see PARA 21 note 15 (definition applied by the School Standards and Framework Act 1998 s 142(8)).

15 School Standards and Framework Act 1998 s 109(3)(a) (amended by the Education and Inspections Act 2006 s 30, Sch 3 para 29(1), (3)(a)). 'Prescribed' means prescribed by regulations: School Standards and Framework Act 1998 s 142(1).

16 Ie under the School Standards and Framework Act 1998 s 105: see PARA 264.

17 Ie under the Education and Inspections Act 2006 s 19: see PARA 133.

18 School Standards and Framework Act 1998 s 109(3)(b) (amended by the Education and Inspections Act 2006 s 30, Sch 3 para 29(1), (3)(b)). Regulations made under the School Standards and Framework Act 1998 s 105 (see PARA 264) may make provision, in relation to cases where any such proposals under the Education and Inspections Act 2006 s 19 (see PARA 133) have fallen to be implemented under regulations under s 24 of that Act (see PARA 136), for requiring the school to which the proposals relate to be disregarded for the purposes of any regulations made under the School Standards and Framework Act 1998 s 105(2): s 109(4) (amended by the Education and Inspections Act 2006 s 30, Sch 3 para 29(1), (4)).

19 Ie the Secretary of State or, in relation to Wales, the Welsh Ministers.

20 Ie under the School Standards and Framework Act 1998 s 104: see PARA 263.

21 School Standards and Framework Act 1998 s 109(5).

(vii) Staffing of Schools

A. STAFFING OF PARTICULAR CATEGORIES OF SCHOOLS IN ENGLAND

(A) Community, Voluntary Controlled, Community Special and Maintained Nursery Schools

(a) Schools having a Delegated Budget

268.   In general. Any teacher[1] or other member of staff[2] who is appointed to work under a contract of employment[3] at a community school[4], a voluntary controlled school[5], a community special school[6] or a maintained nursery school[7] is to be employed by the local authority[8]. The teaching staff of any such school must include a person appointed as head teacher[9], or a person appointed to carry out the functions[10] of the head teacher of the school pending the appointment of a head teacher[11] or in the absence of the head teacher[12].

Regulations[13] may make further provision with respect to the staffing of such schools[14] and may, in particular:

(1)   make provision with respect to the appointment, discipline, suspension and dismissal of teachers and other staff[15];

(2)   make provision with respect to the appointment of teachers and other staff to work at a school otherwise than under a contract of employment[16];

(3)   make provision with respect to staff employed, or engaged otherwise than under a contract of employment, wholly or partly for the purposes of the provision of facilities and services[17] or any other activities which are not school activities but are carried on on the school premises[18] under the management or control of the governing body[19]; and

(4)   confer functions on local authorities, governing bodies and head teachers[20].

If at any time a school does not have a delegated budget[21] such regulations do not apply[22], and alternative provisions[23] apply instead[24]. Until a day to be appointed, in discharging any function conferred by such regulations, a local authority or the governing body or head teacher of a maintained school[25] must have regard to any guidance[26] given from time to time by the Secretary of State[27].

The governing body may, with certain exceptions[28], delegate any of the functions conferred upon it by the regulations[29] to the head teacher[30], one or more governors[31], a committee established by the governing body[32], or one or more governors acting together with the head teacher[33]. Any such delegation of the determination that the head teacher should cease to work at the school[34], or the power to appoint or dismiss the head teacher[35], may be to one or more governors, other than a governor who is the head teacher[36].

The governing body must ensure that:

(a)   any person who interviews an applicant for any post has completed the safer recruitment training[37]; or

(b)   in the case where:

(i)   a selection panel is appointed for that purpose[38] in respect of the appointment of a head teacher or deputy head teacher[39]; or

(ii)   in a case where the governing body delegates[40] the appointment of a member of staff to two or more governors or one or more governors and the head teacher[41],

at least one member of that panel or group has completed the safer recruitment training[42].

1   As to the appointment of teachers (other than head teachers) see PARA 271.
2   As to the appointment of support staff see PARA 272.
3   'Contract of employment' has the meaning given by the Employment Rights Act 1996 (see EMPLOYMENT vol 39 (2014) PARA 2): Education Act 2002 s 212(1).
4   Education Act 2002 s 35(1)(a). As to the meaning of references to a community school see PARA 106.
5   Education Act 2002 s 35(1)(b). As to the meaning of references to a voluntary school see PARA 106.
6   Education Act 2002 s 35(1)(c). As to the meaning of references to a community special school see PARA 106.
7   Education Act 2002 s 35(1)(d). As to the meaning of 'maintained nursery school' see PARA 103 note 3.

8   Education Act 2002 s 35(2). As to the meaning of 'local authority' see PARA 25 (definition
     applied by the Education Act 2002 s 212(1) (amended by SI 2010/1158)).
9   Education Act 2002 s 35(3)(a). As to the meaning of 'head teacher' see PARA 86 note 4
     (definition applied by the Education Act 2002 s 212(2), (3)). As to the appointment of head
     teachers see PARA 270.
10   As to the meaning of 'functions' see PARA 18 note 5 (definition applied by the Education
     Act 2002 s 212(2), (3)).
11   Education Act 2002 s 35(3)(b)(i).
12   Education Act 2002 s 35(3)(b)(ii).
13   Ie regulations made under the Education Act 2002 by the Secretary of State: s 212(1). As to the
     Secretary of State see PARA 58. As to the regulations made under the Education Act 2002 s 35
     see the School Staffing (England) Regulations 2009, SI 2009/2680 (amended by SI 2012/1740;
     SI 2013/1940; SI 2014/798; SI 2015/883; and SI 2015/887); and the text to notes 28–42, and
     PARAS 269–289. As to the application of the School Staffing (England) Regulations 2009,
     SI 2009/2680, with modifications, in relation to the staffing of federations (as to which see PARA
     156) see the School Governance (Federations) (England) Regulations 2012, SI 2012/1035,
     reg 25, Sch 7. As to the application of the School Staffing (England) Regulations 2009,
     SI 2009/2680, regs 3, 4, 6–9, 12–22, 41, 43 to pupil referral units (see PARA 427 et seq) see the
     Education (Pupil Referral Units) (Application of Enactments) (England) Regulations 2007,
     SI 2007/2979, Sch 1 Pt 2 para 28 (substituted by SI 2012/3158).
         In relation to teachers at a voluntary controlled school who are reserved teachers within the
     meaning of the School Standards and Framework Act 1998 s 58 (appointment and dismissal of
     certain teachers at schools with a religious character: see PARA 302), regulations under the
     Education Act 2002 s 35(4) have effect subject to the provisions of the School Standards and
     Framework Act 1998 s 58: Education Act 2002 s 35(6).
14   Education Act 2002 s 35(4).
15   Education Act 2002 s 35(5)(a).
16   Education Act 2002 s 35(5)(b).
17   Ie under the Education Act 2002 s 27 (power of governing body to provide community facilities
     etc): see PARA 174.
18   As to the meaning of 'premises' see PARA 62 note 19 (definition applied by the Education
     Act 2002 s 212(2), (3)).
19   Education Act 2002 s 35(5)(c). As to the governing bodies of maintained schools in England see
     PARA 150 et seq.
20   Education Act 2002 s 35(5)(d) (amended by SI 2010/1158). As to the discharge by an education
     action forum of any function of a governing body under the Education Act 2002 s 35, see the
     School Standards and Framework Act 1998 s 12(4); and PARA 344.
21   Ie by virtue of any suspension under the School Standards and Framework Act 1998 Sch 15 (see
     PARAS 325–327), the Education and Inspections Act 2006 s 66 (see PARA 1214) or the School
     Standards and Organisation (Wales) Act 2013 s 8 (see PARA 1233): see the Education Act 2002
     s 35(7) (amended by the Education Act 2011 s 19(1); and the School Standards and
     Organisation (Wales) Act 2013 Sch 5 para 6(1), (3)).
22   Education Act 2002 s 35(7)(a). As to the application of s 35(7) to pupil referral units see the
     Education (Pupil Referral Units) (Application of Enactments) (England) Regulations 2007,
     SI 2007/2979, Sch 1 Pt 1 para 17A (added by SI 2012/3158).
23   Ie the Education Act 2002 Sch 2 Pt 1 (paras 1–4): see PARA 279.
24   See the Education Act 2002 s 35(7)(b). See note 22.
25   As to the meaning of 'maintained school' see PARA 103 note 3.
26   As to the publication of guidance see the Education Act 1996 s 571 (applied by the Education
     Act 2002 s 212(2), (3)); and PARA 60.
27   See the Education Act 2002 s 35(8)(a) (amended by SI 2010/1158; prospectively repealed by the
     Deregulation Act 2015 Sch 16 para 4(1), (2)). At the date at which this volume states the law no
     such day had been appointed. See also PARA 292.
28   The exceptions relate to the functions conferred by the School Staffing (England)
     Regulations 2009, SI 2009/2680, regs 5–8, 9 (see the text to notes 37–42; and PARAS 274, 275),
     and reg 15(3), (5) (see PARA 270): see reg 4(1)(a) (amended by SI 2012/1740).
29   See the School Staffing (England) Regulations 2009, SI 2009/2680, reg 4(1)(a).
30   School Staffing (England) Regulations 2009, SI 2009/2680, reg 4(2)(a).
31   School Staffing (England) Regulations 2009, SI 2009/2680, reg 4(2)(b). Where the governing
     body has made any such delegation to one or more governors and the function being delegated
     does not directly concern the head teacher, (1) the head teacher may attend and offer advice at
     all relevant proceedings (reg 4(3)(a)); and (2) the governor or governors to whom the delegation
     has been made must consider any such advice (reg 4(3)(b)).

32 School Staffing (England) Regulations 2009, SI 2009/2680, reg 4(2)(ba) (added by SI 2015/883). The School Staffing (England) Regulations 2009, SI 2009/2680, reg 4(2)(ba) does not authorise delegation to a committee that includes an associate member who is a pupil or a member of staff at the school: reg 4(5) (added by SI 2015/883).

33 School Staffing (England) Regulations 2009, SI 2009/2680, reg 4(2)(c).

34 School Staffing (England) Regulations 2009, SI 2009/2680, reg 4(4)(a).

35 School Staffing (England) Regulations 2009, SI 2009/2680, reg 4(4)(b).

36 School Staffing (England) Regulations 2009, SI 2009/2680, reg 4(4).

37 School Staffing (England) Regulations 2009, SI 2009/2680, reg 9(a). 'Safer recruitment training' means training provided for the purpose of ensuring that those who undertake it know how to take proper account of the need to safeguard and promote the welfare of children when recruiting staff: reg 3(1) (definition amended by SI 2014/798). As to the meaning of 'person' see PARA 7 note 6.

38 Ie under the School Staffing (England) Regulations 2009, SI 2009/2680, reg 15: see PARA 270.

39 School Staffing (England) Regulations 2009, SI 2009/2680, reg 9(b)(i).

40 Ie under the School Staffing (England) Regulations 2009, SI 2009/2680, reg 4(1): see the text to notes 28–29.

41 School Staffing (England) Regulations 2009, SI 2009/2680, reg 9(b)(ii).

42 School Staffing (England) Regulations 2009, SI 2009/2680, reg 9(b).

269. Manner of appointment. Where a governing body[1] of a community, voluntary controlled, or community special school[2] or a maintained nursery school[3] approves, identifies, selects or recommends a person for appointment as head teacher, deputy head teacher, other teacher or support staff[4], it must determine whether that person is to be appointed: (1) under a contract of employment with the local authority by which the school is maintained[5]; (2) by the authority otherwise than under a contract of employment[6]; or (3) by the governing body otherwise than under a contract of employment[7].

The governing body must, before a person is appointed[8], check the identity of any such person[9], that the person meets all relevant staff qualification requirements[10], and that the person has a right to work in the United Kingdom[11]. Where it is intended that the person will engage in relevant activity the governing body must obtain an enhanced criminal record certificate[12] in respect of any such person before, or as soon as practicable after, the person's appointment[13].

The governing body must keep a register containing information relating to staff and other persons working at the school[14].

Where a member of the school staff who was appointed before 12 May 2006 moves from a post which did not bring the person regularly into contact with children or young persons to a post which does, the governing body must obtain an enhanced criminal record certificate in respect of the person before, or as soon as practicable after the move[15].

A representative of the local authority may attend and offer advice at all proceedings relating to the selection of any teacher[16], and the governing body must consider any such advice offered by the authority[17].

1 As to the governing bodies of maintained schools in England see PARA 150 et seq. As to the delegation by governing bodies of functions under the School Staffing (England) Regulations 2009, SI 2009/2680 (amended by SI 2015/883; and SI 2015/887) see PARA 268.

2 As to the meaning of references to a community or voluntary school or a community special school see PARA 106.

3 See the School Staffing (England) Regulations 2009, SI 2009/2680, reg 11. As to the meaning of 'maintained nursery school' see PARA 103 note 3.

4 Ie an appointment under the School Staffing (England) Regulations 2009, SI 2009/2680, reg 15(5), 15(7) (see PARA 270), reg 16(3) (see PARA 271) or reg 17(1) (see PARA 272). 'Support staff' means any member of a school's staff other than a teacher: reg 3(1). References to support staff include support staff employed, or engaged otherwise than under a contract of employment, to provide community facilities and services under the Education Act 2002 s 27

(see PARA 174): reg 3(4). 'Teacher' means (1) a person who is a school teacher for the purposes of the Education Act 2002 s 122 (see PARA 1078 note 3); and (2) a person who would fall within head (1) but for the fact that the other party to the contract is not a local authority or a governing body of a foundation, voluntary aided or foundation special school: see the School Staffing (England) Regulations 2009, SI 2009/2680, reg 3(1). As to the meaning of 'contract of employment' see PARA 268 note 3. 'Local authority' means the local authority by which a maintained school is, or a proposed school is to be, maintained: see reg 3(1) (definition amended by SI 2010/1172). As to the meaning of 'local authority' see PARA 25 (definition applied by the Education Act 2002 s 212(1) (amended by SI 2010/1158); Interpretation Act 1978 s 11). As to the meaning of 'maintained school' see PARA 103 note 3. As to the meaning of references to a foundation school or a foundation special school see PARA 106. As to the application of the School Staffing (England) Regulations 2009, SI 2009/2680, regs 3, 4, 6–9, 12–22, 41, 43 to pupil referral units (see PARA 427 et seq) see the Education (Pupil Referral Units) (Application of Enactments) (England) Regulations 2007, SI 2007/2979, Sch 1 Pt 2 para 28 (substituted by SI 2012/3158).

5 See the School Staffing (England) Regulations 2009, SI 2009/2680, reg 12(1)(a).
6 School Staffing (England) Regulations 2009, SI 2009/2680, reg 12(1)(b).
7 School Staffing (England) Regulations 2009, SI 2009/2680, reg 12(1)(c).
8 See the School Staffing (England) Regulations 2009, SI 2009/2680, reg 12(5). Regulation 12(2)–(6) (see the text to notes 9–13) also applies in relation to: (1) any person appointed by a local authority for the purpose of working at a community, voluntary controlled, or community special school or a maintained nursery school in the temporary absence of a member of staff of the school (reg 13(a)); and (2) any person appointed by a local authority to work at a school as a member of the school meals staff (reg 13(b)). As to school meals staff see PARA 278.
9 School Staffing (England) Regulations 2009, SI 2009/2680, reg 12(2)(a).
10 School Staffing (England) Regulations 2009, SI 2009/2680, reg 12(2)(b). A person is to be treated as meeting any staff qualification requirements if the person: (1) fulfils any requirements with respect to qualifications or registration which apply to the person as a result of regulations made under the Education Act 2002 ss 132–135 (see PARAS 1047–1048) and regulations made under the Teaching and Higher Education Act 1998 s 19 (repealed) (School Staffing (England) Regulations 2009, SI 2009/2680, reg 3(3)(a)); (2) meets any conditions with respect to health and physical capacity which apply to the person as a result of regulations made under the Education Act 2002 s 141 (see PARA 1050) (School Staffing (England) Regulations 2009, SI 2009/2680, reg 3(3)(b)); (2) is not barred from regulated activity relating to children in accordance with the Safeguarding Vulnerable Groups Act 2006 s 3(2) (see CHILDREN AND YOUNG PERSONS vol 9 (2012) PARA 682) in any case where it is intended that the person will engage in any activity which is a regulated activity relating to children within the meaning of Sch 4 Pt 1 (School Staffing (England) Regulations 2009, SI 2009/2680, reg 3(3)(c) (reg 3(3)(c), (d) substituted and added by SI 2015/887)); and (4) is not subject to a prohibition order or interim prohibition order or subject to any direction made under the Education Act 2002 s 142 (see PARA 420) or any prohibition, restriction or order having effect as such a direction (School Staffing (England) Regulations 2009, SI 2009/2680, reg 3(3)(d) (as so added)). 'Prohibition order' has the meaning given by the Education Act 2002 s 141B (see PARA 1069); and 'interim prohibition order' means an order by virtue of the Education Act 2002 Sch 11A para 3 (see PARA 1069): School Staffing (England) Regulations 2009, SI 2009/2680, reg 3(1) (definitions added by SI 2013/1940).
11 School Staffing (England) Regulations 2009, SI 2009/2680, reg 12(2)(c). As to the meaning of 'United Kingdom' see PARA 73 note 3.
12 'Enhanced criminal record certificate' means an enhanced criminal record certificate issued under the Police Act 1997 s 113B which includes, in such cases as are from time to time prescribed under s 113BA(1), suitability information relating to children within the meaning of s 113BA(2) (see SENTENCING AND DISPOSITION OF OFFENDERS vol 92 (2010) PARA 713): School Staffing (England) Regulations 2009, SI 2009/2680, reg 3(1) (definition amended by SI 2015/887). For the purposes of the 2009 Regulations an enhanced criminal record certificate is subject to up-date arrangements in the circumstances set out in the Police Act 1997 s 116A(3) (see SENTENCING AND DISPOSITION OF OFFENDERS): School Staffing (England) Regulations 2009, SI 2009/2680, reg 3(6) (added by SI 2015/887). See further PARA 273 note 9.
13 School Staffing (England) Regulations 2009, SI 2009/2680, reg 12(3) (amended by SI 2015/887). 'Relevant activity' means any activity which is a regulated activity relating to children within the meaning of (1) the Safeguarding Vulnerable Groups Act 2006 Sch 4 Pt 1 (see CHILDREN AND YOUNG PERSONS vol 9 (2012) PARA 684); or (2) Sch 4 Pt 1 as it had effect immediately before the coming into force of the Protection of Freedoms Act 2012 s 64: School

Staffing (England) Regulations 2009, SI 2009/2680, reg 3(1) (definition added by SI 2015/887). Where a governing body obtains an enhanced criminal record certificate in respect of any such person and that certificate is subject to up-date arrangements, it must consider whether to request up-date information in relation to the certificate under the Police Act 1997 s 116A(1) (see SENTENCING AND DISPOSITION OF OFFENDERS): School Staffing (England) Regulations 2009, SI 2009/2680, reg 12(3A) (added by SI 2015/887). 'Up-date information' has the meaning given by the Police Act 1997 s 116A(8) (see SENTENCING AND DISPOSITION OF OFFENDERS): School Staffing (England) Regulations 2009, SI 2009/2680, reg 3(1) (definition added by SI 2015/887). See also note 8. In the case of any such person for whom, by reason of having lived outside the United Kingdom, obtaining such a certificate is not sufficient to establish that person's suitability to work in a school, the governing body must, before a person is appointed, make such further checks as the local authority considers appropriate, having regard to any guidance issued by the Secretary of State: School Staffing (England) Regulations 2009, SI 2009/2680, reg 12(4), (5). Regulation 12(3), (4) does not apply to a person who has, during a period which ended not more than three months before the person's appointment, worked in: (a) a school in England in a post (i) which brought the person regularly into contact with children or young persons (reg 12(6)(a)(i)); or (ii) to which the person was appointed on or after 12 May 2006 and which did not bring the person regularly into contact with children or young persons (reg 12(6)(a)(ii)); or (b) an institution within the further education sector in England, or in a 16 to 19 academy, in a post which involved the provision of education which brought the person regularly into contact with children or young persons (reg 12(6)(b) (amended by SI 2012/979)). As to the meaning of 'month' see PARA 54 note 26. As to the meaning of 'England' see PARA 7 note 3. As to the meanings of 'child' and 'young person' see PARA 7 note 6; as to the meaning of 'further education' see PARA 23; and as to the meaning of '16 to 19 academy' see PARA 346 note 13 (definitions applied by the Education Act 2002 s 212(2), (3); Interpretation Act 1978 s 11). As to the publication of guidance see the Education Act 1996 s 571 (applied by the Education Act 2002 s 212(2), (3)); and PARA 60. See eg in particular 'National standards of excellence for headteachers: Departmental advice for headteachers, governing boards and aspiring headteachers' (January 2015). As to the Secretary of State see PARA 58.

14 School Staffing (England) Regulations 2009, SI 2009/2680, reg 12(7). As to the information to be included in the register see Sch 2 (amended by SI 2013/1940; and SI 2015/887). The School Staffing (England) Regulations 2009, SI 2009/2680, reg 12(7) (in so far as it relates to Sch 2 paras 2–4, 4A, 7, 8) also applies in relation to: (1) any person appointed by a local authority for the purpose of working at a community, voluntary controlled, or community special school or a maintained nursery school in the temporary absence of a member of staff of the school (reg 13(a) (reg 13 by SI 2013/1940)); and (2) any person appointed by a local authority to work at a school as a member of the school meals staff (School Staffing (England) Regulations 2009, SI 2009/2680, reg 13(b)).

15 School Staffing (England) Regulations 2009, SI 2009/2680, reg 22.

16 See the School Staffing (England) Regulations 2009, SI 2009/2680, reg 14(1). Where the authority is entitled to offer advice to any individual governing body in relation to the exercise of any function under reg 14, it is also entitled to offer advice to any other collaborating governing bodies in relation to the exercise of any such function: see reg 39(1). The collaborating governing bodies must consider any advice so offered by the authority: reg 39(2). As to the meaning of 'collaborating governing bodies' see PARA 270 note 1. As to the exercise of functions by collaborating governing bodies relating to the appointment of staff see PARAS 270 note 1, 271 note 1, 272 note 1.

17 School Staffing (England) Regulations 2009, SI 2009/2680, reg 14(2).

270. Appointment of head teacher and deputy head teacher. The governing body[1] of a community, voluntary controlled, or community special school[2] or a maintained nursery school[3] must notify the local authority in writing[4] of (1) any vacancy[5] for the head teacher[6]; and (2) any post for a deputy head teacher which it has identified as one to be filled[7].

The governing body must advertise any such vacancy or post in such manner as it considers appropriate unless it has good reason not to[8]. Where the governing body advertises any such vacancy or post, it must appoint a selection panel[9], consisting of at least three of its members, other than a governor who is the head teacher or (as the case may be) a deputy head teacher, to: (a) select for interview such applicants for the post as it thinks fit and, where the post is that of head teacher, notify the local authority in writing of the names of the applicants selected[10]; (b) interview those applicants who attend for that purpose[11]; and (c) where it considers it appropriate, recommend to the governing body for appointment one of the applicants interviewed[12]. If, within a period of seven days beginning with the date when it receives notification under head (a) above, the authority makes written representations to the selection panel that any applicant is not a suitable person for the post, the selection panel must consider those representations[13], and where it decides to recommend for appointment any person about whom representations have been made, notify the governing body and authority in writing of its reasons[14].

Subject to the appropriate checks[15], where the person recommended by the selection panel is approved by the governing body for appointment, the authority must appoint that person, unless the governing body has determined[16] that the person is to be appointed by the governing body otherwise than under a contract of employment[17]. If:

(i)   the selection panel does not recommend a person to the governing body[18];

(ii)   the governing body declines to approve the person recommended by the selection panel[19]; or

(iii)   the local authority declines to appoint the person that the governing body approves[20],

the selection panel may recommend another person for appointment in accordance with these provisions (but this does not prevent it from recommending an existing applicant)[21].

Where the governing body decides for good reason not to advertise and conduct a selection process to fill the vacancy or post in accordance with the above provisions[22], the local authority must, subject to the appropriate checks[23], appoint the person identified by the governing body to fill the vacancy or post, unless the governing body has determined[24] that the person is to be appointed by the governing body otherwise than under a contract of employment[25].

1   Where two or more governing bodies agree to collaborate on the discharge of any function relating to individual members of the school staff, the School Staffing (England) Regulations 2009, SI 2009/2680, apply, subject as follows: see reg 35(1). In relation to the appointment of a head teacher under reg 15:

    (1)   the collaborating governing bodies may delegate the notification to the local authority and the advertisement of any vacancy or post to the head teacher of one or more of the collaborating schools (reg 36(1)(a)), one or more governors from any of the collaborating schools (reg 36(1)(b)), or one or more head teachers acting together with one or more governors from any of the collaborating schools (reg 36(1)(c));

    (2)   the selection panel must consist of at least three governors taken from any of the collaborating governing bodies other than a governor who is the head teacher or (as the case may be) a deputy head teacher of the relevant school (reg 36(1)(b)); and

    (3)   the selection panel must make its recommendation to the governing body of the relevant school (reg 36(1)(c)).

If the governing body does not approve the recommendation the selection panel of the collaborating governing bodies must repeat the selection process unless the relevant school's governing body withdraws from the agreement to collaborate: reg 36(2). 'Collaborating governing bodies' means two or more governing bodies which arrange for any of their functions to be discharged jointly; and 'relevant school' means the school or schools to which any member of staff is, or is to be, appointed: reg 35(2). As to the governing bodies of maintained schools in England see PARA 150 et seq. As to the delegation by governing bodies of functions under the School Staffing (England) Regulations 2009, SI 2009/2680, generally see PARA 268. 'Local authority' means the local authority by which a maintained school is, or a proposed school is to be, maintained: see reg 3(1) (definition amended by SI 2010/1172). As to the meaning of 'local authority' see PARA 25; and as to the meaning of 'head teacher' see PARA 86 note 4 (definitions applied by the Education Act 2002 s 212(1)–(3); Interpretation Act 1978 s 11). As to the application of the School Staffing (England) Regulations 2009, SI 2009/2680, regs 3, 4, 6–9, 12–22, 41, 43 to pupil referral units (see PARA 427 et seq) see the Education (Pupil Referral Units) (Application of Enactments) (England) Regulations 2007, SI 2007/2979, Sch 1 Pt 2 para 28 (substituted by SI 2012/3158).

2 As to the meaning of references to a community or voluntary school or a community special school see PARA 106.
3 See the School Staffing (England) Regulations 2009, SI 2009/2680, reg 11. As to the meaning of 'maintained nursery school' see PARA 103 note 3.
4 As to the meaning of 'writing' see PARA 76 note 8.
5 References to a vacancy in any post include a prospective vacancy in the post: School Staffing (England) Regulations 2009, SI 2009/2680, reg 3(2).
6 School Staffing (England) Regulations 2009, SI 2009/2680, reg 15(1)(a).
7 School Staffing (England) Regulations 2009, SI 2009/2680, reg 15(1)(b).
8 School Staffing (England) Regulations 2009, SI 2009/2680, reg 15(2).
9 As to selection panels and the conduct of interviews see further the School Staffing (England) Regulations 2009, SI 2009/2680, reg 9; and PARA 268.
10 School Staffing (England) Regulations 2009, SI 2009/2680, reg 15(3)(a).
11 School Staffing (England) Regulations 2009, SI 2009/2680, reg 15(3)(b).
12 School Staffing (England) Regulations 2009, SI 2009/2680, reg 15(3)(c). As to the manner of appointment see PARA 269.
13 School Staffing (England) Regulations 2009, SI 2009/2680, reg 15(4)(a).
14 School Staffing (England) Regulations 2009, SI 2009/2680, reg 15(4)(b).
15 Ie subject to the School Staffing (England) Regulations 2009, SI 2009/2680, reg 12(2) and, where appropriate, reg 12(4): see PARA 269.
16 Ie pursuant to the School Staffing (England) Regulations 2009, SI 2009/2680, reg 12(1)(c): see PARA 269.
17 School Staffing (England) Regulations 2009, SI 2009/2680, reg 15(5). As to the meaning of 'contract of employment' see PARA 268 note 3.
18 School Staffing (England) Regulations 2009, SI 2009/2680, reg 15(6)(a).
19 School Staffing (England) Regulations 2009, SI 2009/2680, reg 15(6)(b).
20 School Staffing (England) Regulations 2009, SI 2009/2680, reg 15(6)(c).
21 School Staffing (England) Regulations 2009, SI 2009/2680, reg 15(6).
22 Ie in accordance with the School Staffing (England) Regulations 2009, SI 2009/2680, reg 15(2)–(4): see the text to notes 8–14.
23 Ie subject to the School Staffing (England) Regulations 2009, SI 2009/2680, reg 12(2) and, where appropriate, reg 12(4): see PARA 269.
24 Ie pursuant to the School Staffing (England) Regulations 2009, SI 2009/2680, reg 12(1)(c): see PARA 269.
25 School Staffing (England) Regulations 2009, SI 2009/2680, reg 15(7).

271.   Appointment of other teachers.   Where the governing body[1] of a community, voluntary controlled, or community special school[2] or a maintained nursery school[3] identifies any post[4] of teacher (other than a post of head teacher or deputy head teacher[5]) to be filled for a period of more than four months[6], it must provide the local authority[7] with a specification for the post[8].

Subject to the appropriate checks[9], where a person is selected by the governing body for appointment[10], the local authority must appoint that person, unless the governing body has determined[11] that the person is to be appointed by the governing body otherwise than under a contract of employment[12]. If the authority declines to appoint a person that the governing body selects, the governing body may select another person for appointment in accordance with these provisions (but this does not prevent it from selecting an existing applicant)[13].

1 Where two or more governing bodies agree to collaborate on the discharge of any function relating to individual members of the school staff, the School Staffing (England) Regulations 2009, SI 2009/2680, apply, subject as follows: see reg 35(1). The collaborating governing bodies may delegate the appointment of any teacher (other than the head teacher and

deputy head teacher) to: (1) the head teacher of one or more of the collaborating schools (reg 37(1)(a)); (2) one or more governors from any of the collaborating schools (reg 37(1)(b)); (3) one or more head teachers acting together with one or more governors from any of the collaborating schools (reg 37(1)(c)). Where the collaborating governing bodies have delegated the appointment of a member of staff, other than to the head teacher of the relevant school the head teacher of the relevant school may attend all relevant proceedings and offer advice (reg 37(2)(a)), and the person or persons to whom the delegation has been made must consider any such advice (reg 37(2)(b)). As to the governing bodies of maintained schools in England see PARA 150 et seq. As to the delegation by governing bodies of functions under the School Staffing (England) Regulations 2009, SI 2009/2680, generally see PARA 268. As to the meanings of 'collaborating governing bodies' and 'relevant school' see PARA 270 note 1. As to the meaning of 'teacher' see PARA 269 note 4. As to the meaning of 'head teacher' see PARA 86 note 4 (definition applied by the Education Act 2002 s 212(2), (3); Interpretation Act 1978 s 11).

2 As to the meaning of references to a community or voluntary school or a community special school see PARA 106.
3 See the School Staffing (England) Regulations 2009, SI 2009/2680, reg 11. As to the meaning of 'maintained nursery school' see PARA 103 note 3.
4 As to the meaning of references to a vacancy in any post see PARA 270 note 5.
5 See the School Staffing (England) Regulations 2009, SI 2009/2680, reg 16(1). As to the appointment of head teachers and deputy head teachers see PARA 270.
6 As to the meaning of 'month' see PARA 54 note 26.
7 'Local authority' means the local authority by which a maintained school is, or a proposed school is to be, maintained: see the School Staffing (England) Regulations 2009, SI 2009/2680, reg 3(1) (definition amended by SI 2010/1172). As to the meaning of 'local authority' see PARA 25 (definition applied by the Education Act 2002 s 212(1) (amended by SI 2010/1158); Interpretation Act 1978 s 11). As to the application of the School Staffing (England) Regulations 2009, SI 2009/2680, regs 3, 4, 6–9, 12–22, 41, 43 to pupil referral units (see PARA 427 et seq) see the Education (Pupil Referral Units) (Application of Enactments) (England) Regulations 2007, SI 2007/2979, Sch 1 Pt 2 para 28 (substituted by SI 2012/3158).
8 School Staffing (England) Regulations 2009, SI 2009/2680, reg 16(2).
9 Ie subject to the School Staffing (England) Regulations 2009, SI 2009/2680, reg 12(2) and, where appropriate, reg 12(4): see PARA 269.
10 As to the conduct of interviews see the School Staffing (England) Regulations 2009, SI 2009/2680, reg 9; and PARA 268. As to the manner of appointment see PARA 269.
11 Ie pursuant to the School Staffing (England) Regulations 2009, SI 2009/2680, reg 12(1)(c): see PARA 269.
12 School Staffing (England) Regulations 2009, SI 2009/2680, reg 16(3). As to the meaning of 'contract of employment' see PARA 268 note 3.
13 School Staffing (England) Regulations 2009, SI 2009/2680, reg 16(4).

272. Appointment of support staff. Where the governing body[1] of a community, voluntary controlled, or community special school[2] or a maintained nursery school[3] identifies a support staff post to be filled[4], it may recommend a person to the local authority[5] for appointment[6]. Where the governing body so recommends a person to the authority for appointment it must provide the authority with the name of any person it recommends[7], and a job specification for the post[8].

Subject to the appropriate checks[9], the local authority must appoint[10] the person recommended by the governing body to the post, unless the governing body has determined[11] that the person is to be appointed by the governing body otherwise than under a contract of employment[12].

1 Where two or more governing bodies agree to collaborate on the discharge of any function relating to individual members of the school staff, the School Staffing (England) Regulations 2009, SI 2009/2680, apply, subject as follows: see reg 35(1). The collaborating governing bodies may delegate the appointment of any member of the support staff to: (1) the head teacher of one or more of the collaborating schools (reg 37(1)(a)); (2) one or more governors from any of the collaborating schools (reg 37(1)(b)); (3) one or more head teachers acting together with one or more governors from any of the collaborating schools (reg 37(1)(c)). Where the collaborating governing bodies have delegated the appointment of a member of staff,

other than to the head teacher of the relevant school the head teacher of the relevant school may attend all relevant proceedings and offer advice (reg 37(2)(a)), and the person or persons to whom the delegation has been made must consider any such advice (reg 37(2)(b)). As to the governing bodies of maintained schools in England see PARA 150 et seq. As to the delegation by governing bodies of functions under the School Staffing (England) Regulations 2009, SI 2009/2680, generally see PARA 268. As to the meanings of 'collaborating governing bodies' and 'relevant school' see PARA 270 note 1. As to the meaning of 'support staff' see PARA 269 note 4. As to the meaning of 'head teacher' see PARA 86 note 4 (definition applied by the Education Act 2002 s 212(2), (3); Interpretation Act 1978 s 11).

2   As to the meaning of references to a community or voluntary school or a community special school see PARA 106.

3   See the School Staffing (England) Regulations 2009, SI 2009/2680, reg 11. As to the meaning of 'maintained nursery school' see PARA 103 note 3.

4   As to the meaning of references to a vacancy in any post see PARA 270 note 5.

5   'Local authority' means the local authority by which a maintained school is, or a proposed school is to be, maintained: see the School Staffing (England) Regulations 2009, SI 2009/2680, reg 3(1) (definition amended by SI 2010/1172). As to the meaning of 'local authority' see PARA 25 (definition applied by the Education Act 2002 s 212(1) (amended by SI 2010/1158); Interpretation Act 1978 s 11). As to the application of the School Staffing (England) Regulations 2009, SI 2009/2680, regs 3, 4, 6–9, 12–22, 41, 43 to pupil referral units (see PARA 427 et seq) see the Education (Pupil Referral Units) (Application of Enactments) (England) Regulations 2007, SI 2007/2979, Sch 1 Pt 2 para 28 (substituted by SI 2012/3158).

6   School Staffing (England) Regulations 2009, SI 2009/2680, reg 17(1). This provision is expressed to be subject to reg 21 (see PARA 278): see reg 17(1). As to the conduct of interviews see the School Staffing (England) Regulations 2009, SI 2009/2680, reg 9; and PARA 268.

7   School Staffing (England) Regulations 2009, SI 2009/2680, reg 17(2)(a).

8   School Staffing (England) Regulations 2009, SI 2009/2680, reg 17(2)(b). The job specification must include the governing body's recommendations as to: (1) the duties to be performed (reg 17(2)(b)(i)); (2) the hours of work (where the post is part-time) (reg 17(2)(b)(ii)); (3) the duration of the appointment (reg 17(2)(b)(iii)); (4) the grade (reg 17(2)(b)(iv)); and (5) the remuneration (reg 17(2)(b)(v)). The grade must be on the scale of grades applicable in relation to employment with the local authority and such as the governing body considers appropriate: reg 17(3). Where the authority has discretion with respect to remuneration, it must exercise that discretion in accordance with the governing body's recommendation: reg 17(4). The authority may be regarded as having discretion with respect to remuneration if any provisions regulating the rates of remuneration or allowances payable to persons in the authority's employment (a) do not apply in relation to that appointment (reg 17(5)(a)); or (b) leave to the authority any degree of discretion as to the rate of remuneration (reg 17(5)(b)). If, within a period of seven days after receiving the job specification, the authority makes written representations to the governing body relating to the grade or remuneration to be paid, the governing body must consider those representations (reg 17(6)(a)) and, where it decides not to change the grade or remuneration to be paid, notify the authority in writing of its reasons (reg 17(6)(b)). As to the meanings of 'written' and 'writing' see PARA 76 note 8.

9   Ie subject to the School Staffing (England) Regulations 2009, SI 2009/2680, reg 12(2) and, where appropriate, reg 12(4): see PARA 269.

10   As to the manner of appointment see PARA 269.

11   Ie pursuant to the School Staffing (England) Regulations 2009, SI 2009/2680, reg 12(1)(c): see PARA 269.

12   School Staffing (England) Regulations 2009, SI 2009/2680, reg 17(7). As to the meaning of 'contract of employment' see PARA 268 note 3.

273. Supply staff. The governing body[1] of a community, voluntary controlled, or community special school[2] or a maintained nursery school[3] must ensure that no person supplied by an employment business[4] to a school is allowed to begin work as a teacher[5] or member of support staff[6] at the school unless the local authority[7] or (as the case may be) the governing body has received written[8] notification from the employment business in relation to that person[9]. Before a person offered for supply by an employment business may begin work at the school the governing body must check the person's identity (whether or not the employment business made such a check before the person was offered for supply)[10].

1 As to the governing bodies of maintained schools in England see PARA 150 et seq. As to the delegation by governing bodies of functions under the School Staffing (England) Regulations 2009, SI 2009/2680, see PARA 268.

2 As to the meaning of references to a community or voluntary school or a community special school see PARA 106.

3 See the School Staffing (England) Regulations 2009, SI 2009/2680, reg 11. As to the meaning of 'maintained nursery school' see PARA 103 note 3.

4 'Employment business' has the meaning given by the Employment Agencies Act 1973 s 13(3) (see TRADE AND INDUSTRY vol 97 (2015) PARA 974): School Staffing (England) Regulations 2009, SI 2009/2680, reg 3(1). As to the application of the School Staffing (England) Regulations 2009, SI 2009/2680, regs 3, 4, 6–9, 12–22, 41, 43 to pupil referral units (see PARA 427 et seq) see the Education (Pupil Referral Units) (Application of Enactments) (England) Regulations 2007, SI 2007/2979, Sch 1 Pt 2 para 28 (substituted by SI 2012/3158).

5 As to the meaning of 'teacher' see PARA 269 note 4.

6 As to the meaning of 'support staff' see PARA 269 note 4.

7 'Local authority' means the local authority by which a maintained school is, or a proposed school is to be, maintained: see the School Staffing (England) Regulations 2009, SI 2009/2680, reg 3(1) (definition amended by SI 2010/1172). As to the meaning of 'local authority' see PARA 25 (definition applied by the Education Act 2002 s 212(1) (amended by SI 2010/1158); Interpretation Act 1978 s 11).

8 As to the meaning of 'written' see PARA 76 note 8.

9 School Staffing (England) Regulations 2009, SI 2009/2680, reg 18(1)(a). The notification must state:

  (1) that the employment business has made checks (a) to establish the person's identity, (b) to establish that the person is not barred from regulated activity relating to children in accordance with the Safeguarding Vulnerable Groups Act 2006 s 3(2) (see CHILDREN AND YOUNG PERSONS vol 9 (2012) PARA 682) or subject to any direction made under the Education Act 2002 s 142 (see PARA 469) or any prohibition, restriction or order having effect as such a direction, (c) to establish that the person meets the appropriate requirements with respect to qualifications or registration mentioned in the School Staffing (England) Regulations 2009, SI 2009/2680, reg 3(3)(a) (see PARA 269 note 10), (d) to establish the person's right to work in the United Kingdom, that (e) further checks were made pursuant to reg 12(4) (see PARA 269); and (f) in relation to any person supplied by an employment business on or after 2 September 2013, whether a check was made to establish that the person is not subject to a prohibition order or interim prohibition order (see reg 18(1)(a)(i) (amended by SI 2013/1940; and SI 2015/887), the School Staffing (England) Regulations 2009, SI 2009/2680, Sch 2 paras 5(1)(a)(i), 5A (Sch 2 para 5(1) amended by SI 2015/887; and the School Staffing (England) Regulations 2009, SI 2009/2680, Sch 2 para 5A added by SI 2013/1940));

  (2) where it is intended that the person will engage in relevant activity, that it or another employment business has applied for an enhanced criminal record certificate or has obtained such a certificate in response to an application made by that or another employment business (School Staffing (England) Regulations 2009, SI 2009/2680, reg 18(1)(a)(ii) (amended by SI 2015/887)); and

  (3) whether, if the employment business has obtained such a certificate before the person is due to begin work at the school, it disclosed any matter or information, or any information was provided to the employment business in accordance with the Police Act 1997 s 113B(6) (see SENTENCING AND DISPOSITION OF OFFENDERS vol 92 (2010) PARA 718) (School Staffing (England) Regulations 2009, SI 2009/2680, reg 18(1)(a)(iii));

  (4) whether, if the employment business or another employment business has obtained such a certificate before the person is due to begin work at the school and the certificate is or has been subject to up-date arrangements, the employment business or another employment business has been given negative up-date information in relation to the certificate not more than three months before the person is due to begin work at the school (School Staffing (England) Regulations 2009, SI 2009/2680, reg 18(1)(a)(iv) (added by SI 2015/887)).

As to the meaning of 'relevant activity' (see head (2) above) see PARA 269 note 13. 'Negative up-date information' (see head (4) above) means up-date information of a kind falling within the Police Act 1997 s 116A(8)(b)(i) or (c)(i) (see SENTENCING AND DISPOSITION OF OFFENDERS): School Staffing (England) Regulations 2009, SI 2009/2680, reg 3(1) (definition added by SI 2015/887).

Where the employment business has obtained an enhanced criminal record certificate before the person is due to begin work at the school which disclosed any matter or information or any information was provided to the employment business in accordance with the Police Act 1997 s 113B(6), it must also supply a copy of the certificate: see the School Staffing (England) Regulations 2009, SI 2009/2680, reg 18(1)(b). Where an enhanced criminal record certificate is or has been subject to up-date arrangements and the employment business has been given negative up-date information in relation to the certificate not more than three months before the person is due to begin work at the school, it must also supply a copy of the information: see the School Staffing (England) Regulations 2009, SI 2009/2680, reg 18(1)(c) (added by SI 2015/887). Subject to the School Staffing (England) Regulations 2009, SI 2009/2680, reg 18(3), the certificate referred to in reg 18(1)(a)(ii) (see head (2) above) must have been issued and obtained not more than three months before the person is due to begin work at the school unless that certificate is or has been subject to up-date arrangements and the employment business or another employment business has been given negative up-date information in relation to the certificate not more than three months before the person is due to begin work at the school (see reg 18(2) (amended by SI 2015/887)); but this does not apply in relation to a person who has worked in:

(i)   a school in England in a post (A) which brought the person regularly into contact with children or young persons (School Staffing (England) Regulations 2009, SI 2009/2680, reg 18(3)(a)(i)); or (B) to which the person was appointed on or after 12 May 2006 and which did not bring the person regularly into contact with children or young persons (reg 18(3)(a)(ii)); or

(ii)   an institution within the further education sector in England, or in a 16 to 19 academy, in a post which involved the provision of education which brought the person regularly into contact with children or young persons (reg 18(3)(b) (amended by SI 2012/979)),

during a period which ended not more than three months before the person is due to begin work at the school: School Staffing (England) Regulations 2009, SI 2009/2680, reg 18(3). As to the meanings of 'prohibition order' and 'interim prohibition order' see PARA 269 note 10. As to the meaning of 'enhanced criminal record certificate' see PARA 269 note 12. For the purposes of the School Staffing (England) Regulations 2009 a person applies for an enhanced criminal record certificate if: (aa) the person countersigns an application for the certificate as a registered person, within the meaning of the Police Act 1997 s 120 (see SENTENCING AND DISPOSITION OF OFFENDERS vol 92 (2010) PARA 721), or an application is countersigned on the person's behalf; and (bb) the application is submitted in accordance with Pt 5 of that Act (see SENTENCING AND DISPOSITION OF OFFENDERS vol 92 (2010) PARA 711): School Staffing (England) Regulations 2009, SI 2009/2680, reg 3(5) (amended by SI 2015/887). As to the meaning of 'month' see PARA 54 note 26. As to the meaning of 'United Kingdom' see PARA 73 note 3. As to the meaning of 'England' see PARA 7 note 3. As to the meaning of 'school' see PARA 91; as to the meanings of 'child' and 'young person' see PARA 7 note 6; as to the meaning of 'further education' see PARA 23; and as to the meaning of '16 to 19 academy' see PARA 346 note 13 (definitions applied by the Education Act 2002 s 212(2), (3); Interpretation Act 1978 s 11).

The local authority or (as the case may be) the governing body must, either in the contract or in other arrangements which it makes with any employment business, require it, in respect of any person whom the employment business supplies to the school to provide the notification referred to in the School Staffing (England) Regulations 2009, SI 2009/2680, reg 18(1)(a) (reg 18(5)(a)); if any enhanced criminal record certificate which the employment business obtains contains any matter or information, or if any information was provided to the employment business in accordance with the Police Act 1997 s 113B(6), to provide a copy of the certificate (reg 18(5)(b)); and if any such certificate is or has been subject to up-date arrangements and the employment business has been given negative up-date information in relation to the certificate not more than three months before the person is due to begin work at the school, to provide a copy of the information (reg 18(5)(c) (added by SI 2015/887)).

10   School Staffing (England) Regulations 2009, SI 2009/2680, reg 18(4).

274. Conduct, discipline and capability of staff. The governing body[1] of a community, voluntary controlled, or community special school[2] or a maintained nursery school[3] must establish procedures: (1) for the regulation of the conduct and discipline of staff at the school[4]; and (2) by which staff may seek redress for any grievance relating to their work at the school[5]. Where the implementation of any determination made by the governing body in operation of the procedures requires any action which is not within the functions[6] exercisable[7] by the governing body[8], but is within the power of the local authority[9], the authority must take that action at the request of the governing body[10].

The governing body must also establish procedures for dealing with lack of capability on the part of staff at the school[11].

Where a member of the teaching staff at a school ('School A') applies for a teaching post at another school ('School B'), and where School B is a maintained school[12] or an academy school[13], the governing body of School A must, at the request of the governing body or proprietor (as the case may be) of School B (a) advise in writing[14] whether or not that member of staff has, in the preceding two years, been the subject of the above procedures established by the governing body[15]; and, if so, (b) provide written details of the concerns which gave rise to this, the duration of the proceedings and their outcome[16].

1 As to the governing bodies of maintained schools in England see PARA 150 et seq.
2 As to the meaning of references to a community or voluntary school or a community special school see PARA 106.
3 As to the meaning of 'maintained nursery school' see PARA 103 note 3.
4 School Staffing (England) Regulations 2009, SI 2009/2680, reg 7(1)(a). As to the application of the School Staffing (England) Regulations 2009, SI 2009/2680, regs 3, 4, 6–9, 12–22, 41, 43 to pupil referral units (see PARA 427 et seq) see the Education (Pupil Referral Units) (Application of Enactments) (England) Regulations 2007, SI 2007/2979, Sch 1 Pt 2 para 28 (substituted by SI 2012/3158).
5 School Staffing (England) Regulations 2009, SI 2009/2680, reg 7(1)(b).
6 As to the meaning of 'functions' see PARA 18 note 5 (definition applied by the Education Act 2002 s 212(2), (3); Interpretation Act 1978 s 11).
7 Ie by or under the Education Act 2002. As to the general powers and duties of governing bodies see PARA 168 et seq.
8 School Staffing (England) Regulations 2009, SI 2009/2680, reg 7(2)(a).
9 School Staffing (England) Regulations 2009, SI 2009/2680, reg 7(2)(b). 'Local authority' means the local authority by which a maintained school is, or a proposed school is to be, maintained: see reg 3(1) (definition amended by SI 2010/1172). As to the meaning of 'local authority' see PARA 25 (definition applied by the Education Act 2002 s 212(1) (amended by SI 2010/1158); Interpretation Act 1978 s 11).
10 School Staffing (England) Regulations 2009, SI 2009/2680, reg 7(2).
11 School Staffing (England) Regulations 2009, SI 2009/2680, reg 8. As to the suspension of staff see PARA 276. As to the dismissal of staff see PARA 277. As to the performance of head teachers see PARA 275.
12 As to the meaning of 'maintained school' see PARA 99.
13 School Staffing (England) Regulations 2009, SI 2009/2680, reg 8A(1) (reg 8A added by SI 2012/1740). As to the meaning of 'academy school' see PARA 346 note 12 (definition applied by the Education Act 2002 s 212(1); Interpretation Act 1978 s 11).
14 As to the meaning of 'writing' see PARA 76 note 8.
15 School Staffing (England) Regulations 2009, SI 2009/2680, reg 8A(2)(a) (as added: see note 13). The reference in the text is to the procedures established in accordance with reg 8: see the text to note 11. As to the meaning of 'proprietor' see PARA 51 note 4 (definition applied by the Education Act 2002 s 212(1); Interpretation Act 1978 s 11).
16 School Staffing (England) Regulations 2009, SI 2009/2680, reg 8A(2)(b) (as added: see note 13).

275. Performance of head teacher. The governing body[1] of a community, voluntary controlled, or community special school[2] or a maintained nursery school[3] must ensure that the head teacher[4] at the school (1) complies with the duties imposed upon the head teacher[5]; and (2) benefits from any entitlement conferred upon the head teacher[6], by any order[7] relating to teachers' pay and conditions[8]. In discharging its duty under head (1) above, the governing body must have regard to the desirability of the head teacher being able to achieve a satisfactory balance between the time spent discharging the professional duties of a head teacher and the time spent by the head teacher pursuing personal interests outside work[9].

Where the local authority[10] has any serious concerns about the performance of the head teacher of a school it must make a written[11] report of its concerns to the governing body of the school[12] and, at the same time, send a copy of the report to the head teacher[13]. The governing body must notify the authority in writing of the action it proposes to take in the light of the authority's report[14].

1 As to the governing bodies of maintained schools in England see PARA 150.
2 As to the meaning of references to a community or voluntary school or a community special school see PARA 106.
3 As to the meaning of 'maintained nursery school' see PARA 103 note 3.
4 As to the meaning of 'head teacher' see PARA 86 note 4 (definition applied by the Education Act 2002 s 212(2), (3); Interpretation Act 1978 s 11). As to the appointment of the head teacher see PARA 270.
5 School Staffing (England) Regulations 2009, SI 2009/2680, reg 5(1)(a).
6 School Staffing (England) Regulations 2009, SI 2009/2680, reg 5(1)(b).
7 Ie under the Education Act 2002 s 122: see PARA 1078.
8 School Staffing (England) Regulations 2009, SI 2009/2680, reg 5(1).
9 School Staffing (England) Regulations 2009, SI 2009/2680, reg 5(2).
10 'Local authority' means the local authority by which a maintained school is, or a proposed school is to be, maintained: see the School Staffing (England) Regulations 2009, SI 2009/2680, reg 3(1) (definition amended by SI 2010/1172). As to the meaning of 'local authority' see PARA 25 (definition applied by the Education Act 2002 s 212(1) (amended by SI 2010/1158); Interpretation Act 1978 s 11). As to the application of the School Staffing (England) Regulations 2009, SI 2009/2680, regs 3, 4, 6–9, 12–22, 41, 43 to pupil referral units (see PARA 427 et seq) see the Education (Pupil Referral Units) (Application of Enactments) (England) Regulations 2007, SI 2007/2979, Sch 1 Pt 2 para 28 (substituted by SI 2012/3158).
11 As to the meaning of 'written' see PARA 76 note 8.
12 School Staffing (England) Regulations 2009, SI 2009/2680, reg 6(1)(a).
13 School Staffing (England) Regulations 2009, SI 2009/2680, reg 6(1)(b).
14 School Staffing (England) Regulations 2009, SI 2009/2680, reg 6(2).

276. Suspension of staff. The governing body[1] or the head teacher[2] of a community, voluntary controlled, or community special school[3] or a maintained nursery school[4] may suspend[5] any person employed or engaged otherwise than under a contract of employment[6] to work at the school where, in the opinion of the governing body or (as the case may be) the head teacher, such suspension is required[7]. The governing body or (as the case may be) the head teacher must immediately inform the local authority[8] and the head teacher or (as the case may be) the governing body when a person is so suspended[9].

Only the governing body may end a suspension under these provisions[10]; and on ending such a suspension, the governing body must immediately inform the local authority and the head teacher[11].

1 As to the governing bodies of maintained schools in England see PARA 150 et seq. As to the delegation by governing bodies of functions under the School Staffing (England) Regulations 2009, SI 2009/2680, see PARA 268.
2 As to the meaning of 'head teacher' see PARA 86 note 4 (definition applied by the Education Act 2002 s 212(2), (3); Interpretation Act 1978 s 11).
3 As to the meaning of references to a community or voluntary school or a community special school see PARA 106.
4 See the School Staffing (England) Regulations 2009, SI 2009/2680, reg 11. As to the meaning of 'maintained nursery school' see PARA 103 note 3.
5 'Suspend' means suspend without loss of emoluments: School Staffing (England) Regulations 2009, SI 2009/2680, reg 19(5). As to the application of the School Staffing (England) Regulations 2009, SI 2009/2680, regs 3, 4, 6–9, 12–22, 41, 43 to pupil referral units

(see PARA 427 et seq) see the Education (Pupil Referral Units) (Application of Enactments) (England) Regulations 2007, SI 2007/2979, Sch 1 Pt 2 para 28 (substituted by SI 2012/3158).

6 As to the meaning of 'contract of employment' see PARA 268 note 3.

7 School Staffing (England) Regulations 2009, SI 2009/2680, reg 19(1). This provision is expressed to be subject to reg 21 (see PARA 278): see reg 19(1). As to the dismissal of staff see PARA 277.

8 'Local authority' means the local authority by which a maintained school is, or a proposed school is to be, maintained: see the School Staffing (England) Regulations 2009, SI 2009/2680, reg 3(1) (definition amended by SI 2010/1172). As to the meaning of 'local authority' see PARA 25 (definition applied by the Education Act 2002 s 212(1) (amended by SI 2010/1158); Interpretation Act 1978 s 11).

9 School Staffing (England) Regulations 2009, SI 2009/2680, reg 19(2).

10 School Staffing (England) Regulations 2009, SI 2009/2680, reg 19(3).

11 School Staffing (England) Regulations 2009, SI 2009/2680, reg 19(4).

277. Dismissal of staff. Where the governing body[1] of a community, voluntary controlled, or community special school[2] or a maintained nursery school[3] determines that any person employed or engaged by the local authority[4] to work at the school[5] should cease to work there, it must notify the authority in writing[6] of its determination and the reasons for it[7]. A representative of the authority may attend and offer advice at all proceedings relating to the dismissal of any teacher[8], and the governing body must consider any advice so offered by the authority[9].

If the person concerned is employed or engaged to work solely at the school (and does not resign), the local authority must, before the end of the period of 14 days beginning with the date of the notification, either: (1) terminate the person's contract with the authority, giving such notice as is required under that contract[10]; or (2) terminate such contract without notice if the circumstances are such that it is entitled to do so by reason of the person's conduct[11]. If the person concerned is not employed or engaged by the authority to work solely at the school, the authority must require the person to cease to work at the school[12].

1 Where two or more governing bodies agree to collaborate on the discharge of any function relating to individual members of the school staff, the School Staffing (England) Regulations 2009, SI 2009/2680, apply, subject as follows: see reg 35(1). The collaborating governing bodies may delegate; (1) the determination that a member of staff (other than the head teacher) should cease to work at a relevant school (reg 38(1)(a)); or (2) the power to dismiss a member of staff (other than the head teacher) from a relevant school (reg 38(1)(b)). Any such delegation may be to the head teacher of one or more of the collaborating schools (reg 38(2)(a)), one or more governors from any of the collaborating schools (reg 38(2)(b)), one or more head teachers acting together with one or more governors from any of the collaborating schools (reg 38(2)(c)). The collaborating governing bodies may delegate: (a) the determination that the head teacher should cease to work at a relevant school (reg 38(3)(a)); or (b) the power to dismiss the head teacher from a relevant school (reg 38(3)(b)), to one or more governors (reg 38(3)). As to the governing bodies of maintained schools in England see PARA 150 et seq. As to the delegation by governing bodies of functions under the School Staffing (England) Regulations 2009, SI 2009/2680, generally see PARA 268. As to the meanings of 'collaborating governing bodies' and 'relevant school' see PARA 270 note 1. 'Dismissal' is to be interpreted in accordance with the Employment Rights Act 1996 ss 95 and 136 (see EMPLOYMENT vol 41 (2014) PARAS 762, 864, 866–867): School Staffing (England) Regulations 2009, SI 2009/2680, reg 3(1). As to the meaning of 'head teacher' see PARA 86 note 4 (definition applied by the Education Act 2002 s 212(2), (3); Interpretation Act 1978 s 11). As to the application of the School Staffing (England) Regulations 2009, SI 2009/2680, regs 3, 4, 6–9, 12–22, 41, 43 to pupil referral units (see PARA 427 et seq) see the Education (Pupil Referral Units) (Application of Enactments) (England) Regulations 2007, SI 2007/2979, Sch 1 Pt 2 para 28 (substituted by SI 2012/3158).

2 As to the meaning of references to a community or voluntary school or a community special school see PARA 106.

3 See the School Staffing (England) Regulations 2009, SI 2009/2680, reg 11. As to the meaning of 'maintained nursery school' see PARA 103 note 3.

4   'Local authority' means the local authority by which a maintained school is, or a proposed school is to be, maintained: see the School Staffing (England) Regulations 2009, SI 2009/2680, reg 3(1) (definition amended by SI 2010/1172). As to the meaning of 'local authority' see PARA 25 (definition applied by the Education Act 2002 s 212(1) (amended by SI 2010/1158); Interpretation Act 1978 s 11).

5   As to the employment of school staff by the local authority see PARA 268. As to the appointment of head teachers and deputy head teachers see PARA 270. As to the appointment of teachers see PARA 271. As to the appointment of support staff see PARA 272.

6   As to the meaning of 'writing' see PARA 76 note 8.

7   School Staffing (England) Regulations 2009, SI 2009/2680, reg 20(1). This provision is expressed to be subject to reg 21 (see PARA 278): see reg 20(1).

8   See the School Staffing (England) Regulations 2009, SI 2009/2680, reg 14(1). As to the meaning of 'teacher' see PARA 269 note 4. Where the local authority is entitled to offer advice to any individual governing body in relation to the exercise of any function under reg 14, it is also entitled to offer advice to any other collaborating governing bodies (see note 1) in relation to the exercise of any such function: see reg 39(1). The collaborating governing bodies must consider any advice so offered by the authority: reg 39(2).

9   School Staffing (England) Regulations 2009, SI 2009/2680, reg 14(2).

10   School Staffing (England) Regulations 2009, SI 2009/2680, reg 20(2)(a).

11   School Staffing (England) Regulations 2009, SI 2009/2680, reg 20(2)(b).

12   School Staffing (England) Regulations 2009, SI 2009/2680, reg 20(3).

278.   School meals staff.   The local authority[1] is responsible for the appointment, discipline, suspension and dismissal[2] of school meals staff who work or are to work at a community, voluntary controlled, or community special school[3] or a maintained nursery school[4]. Before exercising any such function[5] the authority must consult the school's governing body[6] to such extent as the authority thinks fit[7].

Where an order is in force[8] imposing on the governing body of a school a duty to provide school lunches[9] or a duty to provide school lunches free of charge[10], the following provisions apply as appropriate[11]. Where the governing body and the local authority have agreed that the authority will provide lunches at the school and the governing body determines that any member of the school meals staff should cease to work at the school the governing body must notify the authority in writing[12] of its determination and the reasons for it[13], and the authority must require the person to cease to work at the school[14]. Where no such agreement has been made alternative provisions apply[15].

1   'Local authority' means the local authority by which a maintained school is, or a proposed school is to be, maintained: see the School Staffing (England) Regulations 2009, SI 2009/2680, reg 3(1) (definition amended by SI 2010/1172). As to the meaning of 'local authority' see PARA 24 (definition applied by the Education Act 2002 s 212(1) (amended by SI 2010/1158); Interpretation Act 1978 s 11). As to the application of the School Staffing (England) Regulations 2009, SI 2009/2680, regs 3, 4, 6–9, 12–22, 41, 43 to pupil referral units (see PARA 427 et seq) see the Education (Pupil Referral Units) (Application of Enactments) (England) Regulations 2007, SI 2007/2979, Sch 1 Pt 2 para 28 (substituted by SI 2012/3158).

2   As to the meaning of 'dismissal' see PARA 277 note 1.

3   As to the meaning of references to a community or voluntary school or a community special school see PARA 106.

4   See the School Staffing (England) Regulations 2009, SI 2009/2680, regs 11, 21(1). Regulation 21(1) is expressed to be subject to reg 21(2)–(5): see the text to notes 5–15. As to the meaning of 'maintained nursery school' see PARA 103 note 3.

5   As to the meaning of 'function' see PARA 18 note 5 (definition applied by the Education Act 2002 s 212(2), (3); Interpretation Act 1978 s 11).

6   As to the governing bodies of maintained schools in England see PARA 150 et seq.

7   School Staffing (England) Regulations 2009, SI 2009/2680, reg 21(2).

8   Ie under the Education Act 1996 s 512A(1): see PARA 487.

9   Ie a duty corresponding to a duty of the local authority mentioned in the Education Act 1996 s 512(3), (4): see PARA 486.

10 Ie a duty corresponding to a duty of the local authority mentioned in the Education Act 1996 s 512ZB(1): see PARA 486.

11 School Staffing (England) Regulations 2009, SI 2009/2680, reg 21(3).

12 As to the meaning of 'writing' see PARA 76 note 8.

13 School Staffing (England) Regulations 2009, SI 2009/2680, reg 21(4)(a).

14 School Staffing (England) Regulations 2009, SI 2009/2680, reg 21(4)(b).

15 Ie where no such agreement has been made, the School Staffing (England) Regulations 2009, SI 2009/2680, reg 7 (see PARA 274), reg 17 (see PARA 272), reg 19 (see PARA 276) and reg 20 (see PARA 277) apply in relation to school meals staff: reg 21(5).

(b) Schools not having a Delegated Budget

279. Staffing of schools on suspension of delegated budget. If at any time a community, voluntary controlled or a community special school[1] or a maintained nursery school[2] does not have a delegated budget[3], the usual provisions relating to the staffing at such schools[4] do not apply[5] and the following provisions apply instead[6].

In such circumstances, the arrangements for the staffing of the school are to be determined by the local authority[7], and the authority may appoint, suspend and dismiss teachers and other staff at the school as it thinks fit[8]. The authority must, in connection with the exercise of these functions[9], consult the governing body to such extent as it thinks fit[10].

1 As to the meaning of references to a community or voluntary school or a community special school see PARA 106.

2 See the Education Act 2002 s 35(1). As to the meaning of 'maintained nursery school' see PARA 103 note 3.

3 Ie by virtue of any suspension under the School Standards and Framework Act 1998 Sch 15 (see PARAS 325–327), the Education and Inspections Act 2006 s 66 (see PARA 1214) or the School Standards and Organisation (Wales) Act 2013 s 8 (see PARA 1233): see the Education Act 2002 s 35(7) (amended by the Education Act 2011 s 19(1); and the School Standards and Organisation (Wales) Act 2013 Sch 5 para 6(1), (3)). In the Education Act 2002 Pt 3 Ch 1 (ss 19–40): (1) references to a school having a delegated budget are references to the governing body of the school being entitled to manage the school's budget share (s 39(2)(a)); and (2) where a school has a delegated budget the governing body is accordingly said to have a right to a delegated budget (s 39(2)(b)). As to the governing bodies of maintained schools in England see PARA 150 et seq. As to the meaning of 'budget share' see PARA 315 (definition applied by the Education Act 2002 s 39(1)).

4 Ie regulations made under the Education Act 2002 s 35(4). As to such regulations see PARAS 268–278.

5 See the Education Act 2002 s 35(7)(a).

6 See the Education Act 2002 s 35(7)(b). Where a proposed community, voluntary controlled, community special or maintained nursery school does not have a delegated budget, the provisions of Sch 2 Pt 1 (paras 1–4) (see the text to notes 7–10) apply with modifications: see the School Staffing (England) Regulations 2009, SI 2009/2680, regs 40, 43. As to the application of the School Staffing (England) Regulations 2009, SI 2009/2680, regs 3, 4, 6–9, 12–22, 41, 43 to pupil referral units (see PARA 427 et seq) see the Education (Pupil Referral Units) (Application of Enactments) (England) Regulations 2007, SI 2007/2979, Sch 1 Pt 2 para 28 (substituted by SI 2012/3158).

7 Education Act 2002 Sch 2 para 1 (amended by SI 2010/1158). As to the meaning of 'local authority' see PARA 25 (definition applied by the Education Act 2002 s 212(1) (amended by SI 2010/1158)). As to the application of the Education Act 2002 Sch 2 paras 1–3 to pupil referral units (see PARA 427 et seq) see the Education (Pupil Referral Units) (Application of Enactments) (England) Regulations 2007, SI 2007/2979, Sch 1 Pt 1 para 20A (added by SI 2012/3158).

8 Education Act 2002 Sch 2 para 2. In relation to teachers at a voluntary controlled school who are reserved teachers within the meaning of the School Standards and Framework Act 1998 s 58 (appointment and dismissal of certain teachers at schools with a religious character: see PARA 302), the Education Act 2002 Sch 2 para 2 has effect subject to the provisions of the School Standards and Framework Act 1998 s 58: Education Act 2002 Sch 2 para 4.

9   As to the meaning of 'functions' see PARA 18 note 5 (definition applied by the Education
    Act 2002 s 212(2), (3)).
10 Education Act 2002 Sch 2 para 3. As to the exercise of the duty to consult see JUDICIAL REVIEW
    vol 61 (2010) PARA 627.

(B) Foundation, Voluntary Aided and Foundation Special Schools

(a) Schools having a Delegated Budget

280.   In general.   Except as provided by regulations[1], any teacher[2] or other
member of staff[3] who is appointed to work under a contract of employment[4] at
a foundation school[5], a voluntary aided school[6] or a foundation special school[7]
is to be employed by the governing body of the school[8]. The teaching staff of any
such school must include a person appointed as head teacher[9] or a person
appointed to carry out the functions[10] of the head teacher of the school pending
the appointment of a head teacher[11] or in the absence of the head teacher[12].
Regulations may make further provision with respect to the staffing of such
schools[13] and may, in particular:
  (1)   make provision with respect to the appointment, discipline, suspension
        and dismissal of teachers and other staff[14];
  (2)   make provision with respect to the appointment of teachers and other
        staff to work at a school otherwise than under a contract of
        employment[15];
  (3)   make provision with respect to staff employed, or engaged otherwise
        than under a contract of employment, wholly or partly for the purposes
        of the provision of facilities and services[16] or any other activities which
        are not school activities but are carried on the school premises[17] under
        the management or control of the governing body[18];
  (4)   enable teachers and other staff to be employed by the local authority[19]
        in prescribed[20] cases[21]; and
  (5)   confer functions on local authorities, governing bodies and head
        teachers[22].
Until a day to be appointed, in discharging any function conferred by such
regulations, a local authority or the governing body or head teacher of a
maintained school[23] must have regard to any guidance given from time to time
by the Secretary of State[24].
  The governing body may, with certain exceptions[25], delegate any of the
functions conferred upon it by the regulations[26] and its power to appoint or
dismiss any member of staff[27] to the head teacher[28], one or more governors[29], a
committee established by the governing body[30], or one or more governors acting
together with the head teacher[31]. Any such delegation of the determination that
the head teacher should cease to work at the school[32], or the power to appoint or
dismiss the head teacher[33], may be to one or more governors, other than a
governor who is the head teacher[34].
  The governing body must ensure that:
  (a)   any person who interviews an applicant for any post has completed the
        safer recruitment training[35]; or
  (b)   in the case where:
        (i)   a selection panel is appointed for that purpose[36] in respect of the
              appointment of a head teacher or deputy head teacher[37]; or
        (ii) the governing body delegates[38] the appointment of a member of
              staff to two or more governors or one or more governors and the
              head teacher[39],

at least one member of that panel or group has completed the safer recruitment training[40].

1   Ie regulations under the Education Act 2002 s 36(4): see the text to note 13. 'Regulations' means regulations made under the Education Act 2002 by the Secretary of State: see s 212(1). As to the Secretary of State see PARA 58. As to the regulations made under s 36 see the School Staffing (England) Regulations 2009, SI 2009/2680; and the text to notes 25–40, and PARA 281 et seq. As to the application of the School Staffing (England) Regulations 2009, SI 2009/2680, with modifications, in relation to the staffing of federations (as to which see PARA 156) see the School Governance (Federations) (England) Regulations 2012, SI 2012/1035, reg 25, Sch 7.
2   As to the appointment of teaching staff see PARAS 282–284.
3   As to the appointment of support staff see PARA 285.
4   As to the meaning of 'contract of employment' see PARA 268 note 3.
5   See the Education Act 2002 s 36(1)(a). As to the meaning of references to a foundation school see PARA 106.
6   See the Education Act 2002 s 36(1)(b). As to the meaning of references to a voluntary school see PARA 106.
7   See the Education Act 2002 s 36(1)(c). As to the meaning of references to a foundation special school see PARA 106.
8   Education Act 2002 s 36(2). As to the governing bodies of maintained schools in England see PARA 150 et seq. As to the discharge by an education action forum of any function of a governing body under s 36 see the School Standards and Framework Act 1998 s 12(4); and PARA 344.
9   Education Act 2002 s 36(3)(a). As to the meaning of 'head teacher' see PARA 86 note 4 (definition applied by s 212(2), (3)). As to the appointment of head teachers see PARA 282.
10 As to the meaning of 'functions' see PARA 18 note 5 (definition applied by the Education Act 2002 s 212(2), (3)).
11 Education Act 2002 s 36(3)(b)(i).
12 Education Act 2002 s 36(3)(b)(ii). As to the appointment of deputy head teachers see PARA 282.
13 Education Act 2002 s 36(4). Regulations under s 36(4) have effect subject to the School Standards and Framework Act 1998 s 58 (appointment and dismissal of certain teachers at schools with a religious character: see PARA 302): Education Act 2002 s 36(6). If at any time a school does not have a delegated budget regulations under s 36(4) have effect subject to the provisions of Sch 2 Pt 2 (paras 5–10); see s 36(7) and PARA 290.
14 Education Act 2002 s 36(5)(a). As to the appointment, discipline, suspension and dismissal of teachers and other staff see PARAS 281–289.
15 Education Act 2002 s 36(5)(b).
16 Ie under the Education Act 2002 s 27 (power of governing body to provide community facilities etc): see PARA 174.
17 As to the meaning of 'premises' see PARA 62 note 19 (definition applied by the Education Act 2002 s 212(2), (3)).
18 Education Act 2002 s 36(5)(c).
19 As to the meaning of 'local authority' see PARA 25 (definition applied by the Education Act 2002 s 212(1) (amended by SI 2010/1158)).
20 Ie prescribed by the regulations: see the Education Act 2002 s 212(1).
21 Education Act 2002 s 36(5)(d) (amended by SI 2010/1158).
22 Education Act 2002 s 36(5)(e) (amended by SI 2010/1158).
23 As to the meaning of 'maintained school' see PARA 103 note 3.
24 Education Act 2002 s 36(8)(a) (amended by SI 2010/1158; prospectively repealed by the Deregulation Act 2015 Sch 16 para 5(1), (2)). At the date at which this volume states the law no day had been appointed for the purpose of this repeal. As to the publication of guidance see the Education Act 1996 s 571 (applied by the Education Act 2002 s 212(2), (3)); and PARA 60. See also PARA 294.
25 The exceptions relate to the functions conferred by the School Staffing (England) Regulations 2009, SI 2009/2680, reg 27(3) and (5) (see PARA 282): see reg 4(1)(a).
26 See the School Staffing (England) Regulations 2009, SI 2009/2680, reg 4(1)(a). As to the application of the School Staffing (England) Regulations 2009, SI 2009/2680, regs 3, 4, 6–9, 12–22, 41, 43 to pupil referral units (see PARA 427 et seq) see the Education (Pupil Referral Units) (Application of Enactments) (England) Regulations 2007, SI 2007/2979, Sch 1 Pt 2 para 28 (substituted by SI 2012/3158).
27 See the School Staffing (England) Regulations 2009, SI 2009/2680, reg 4(1)(b).
28 School Staffing (England) Regulations 2009, SI 2009/2680, reg 4(2)(a).

29 School Staffing (England) Regulations 2009, SI 2009/2680, reg 4(2)(b). Where the governing body has made any such delegation to one or more governors and the function being delegated does not directly concern the head teacher, (1) the head teacher may attend and offer advice at all relevant proceedings (reg 4(3)(a)); and (2) the governor or governors to whom the delegation has been made must consider any such advice (reg 4(3)(b)).

30 School Staffing (England) Regulations 2009, SI 2009/2680, reg 4(2)(ba) (added by SI 2015/883). The School Staffing (England) Regulations 2009, SI 2009/2680, reg 4(2)(ba) does not authorise delegation to a committee that includes an associate member who is a pupil or a member of staff at the school: reg 4(5) (added by SI 2015/883).

31 School Staffing (England) Regulations 2009, SI 2009/2680, reg 4(2)(c).

32 School Staffing (England) Regulations 2009, SI 2009/2680, reg 4(4)(a).

33 School Staffing (England) Regulations 2009, SI 2009/2680, reg 4(4)(b).

34 School Staffing (England) Regulations 2009, SI 2009/2680, reg 4(4).

35 School Staffing (England) Regulations 2009, SI 2009/2680, reg 9(a). As to the meaning of 'safer recruitment training' see PARA 268 note 37.

36 Ie under the School Staffing (England) Regulations 2009, SI 2009/2680, reg 27: see PARA 282.

37 School Staffing (England) Regulations 2009, SI 2009/2680, reg 9(b)(i).

38 Ie under the School Staffing (England) Regulations 2009, SI 2009/2680, reg 4(1): see the text to notes 25–27.

39 School Staffing (England) Regulations 2009, SI 2009/2680, reg 9(b)(ii).

40 School Staffing (England) Regulations 2009, SI 2009/2680, reg 9(b).

281. Manner of appointment. Where the governing body[1] of a foundation, voluntary aided or foundation special school[2] has selected[3] a person for appointment it may appoint that person either under a contract of employment[4] or otherwise than under a contract of employment[5].

The governing body must, before a person is appointed[6], check the identity of any such person[7], that the person meets all relevant staff qualification requirements[8], and that the person has a right to work in the United Kingdom[9]. Where it is intended that the person will engage in relevant activity, the governing body must obtain an enhanced criminal record certificate[10] in respect of any such person, before, or as soon as practicable after, the person's appointment[11].

Where a member of the school staff who was appointed before 12 May 2006 moves from a post which did not bring the person regularly into contact with children or young persons to a post which does, the governing body must obtain an enhanced criminal record certificate in respect of the person before, or as soon as practicable after, the move[12].

The governing body must keep a separate register containing information relating to staff and other persons working at the school[13].

The local authority[14] may offer advice to the governing body in relation to the exercise of the governing body's functions[15] of appointment of any teacher[16], to the extent provided by, and subject to, any relevant agreement[17]. The governing body must consider any advice so offered by the authority[18].

1 As to the governing bodies of maintained schools in England see PARA 150 et seq. As to the delegation by governing bodies of functions under the School Staffing (England) Regulations 2009, SI 2009/2680, see PARA 280.

2 See the School Staffing (England) Regulations 2009, SI 2009/2680, reg 23. As to the meaning of references to a foundation, voluntary or foundation special school see PARA 106.

3 As to selection panels and the conduct of interviews see the School Staffing (England) Regulations 2009, SI 2009/2680, reg 9; and PARA 280.

4 School Staffing (England) Regulations 2009, SI 2009/2680, reg 24(1)(a). As to the meaning of 'contract of employment' see PARA 268 note 3.

5 School Staffing (England) Regulations 2009, SI 2009/2680, reg 24(1)(b).

6 See the School Staffing (England) Regulations 2009, SI 2009/2680, reg 24(5). Regulation 24(2)–(6) (see the text to notes 7–11) also applies in relation to any person

appointed by an authority for the purpose of working at a foundation, voluntary aided and
foundation special school in the temporary absence of a member of staff of the school: see
reg 25 (amended by SI 2013/1940).

7   School Staffing (England) Regulations 2009, SI 2009/2680, reg 24(2)(a).
8   School Staffing (England) Regulations 2009, SI 2009/2680, reg 24(2)(b). As to when a person is
    to be treated as meeting any staff qualification requirements see PARA 269 note 10.
9   School Staffing (England) Regulations 2009, SI 2009/2680, reg 24(2)(c). As to the meaning of
    'United Kingdom' see PARA 73 note 3.
10 As to the meaning of 'enhanced criminal record certificate' see PARA 269 note 12. See also PARA
    273 note 9.
11 School Staffing (England) Regulations 2009, SI 2009/2680, reg 24(3) (amended by
    SI 2015/887). As to the meaning of 'relevant activity' see PARA 269 note 13. Where a governing
    body obtains an enhanced criminal record certificate in respect of any such person and that
    certificate is subject to up-date arrangements, it must consider whether to request up-date
    information in relation to the certificate under the Police Act 1997 s 116A(1) (see SENTENCING
    AND DISPOSITION OF OFFENDERS): School Staffing (England) Regulations 2009, SI 2009/2680,
    reg 24(3A) (added by SI 2015/887). As to the meaning of 'up-date information' see PARA 269
    note 13. See also note 6. In the case of any such person for whom, by reason of having lived
    outside the United Kingdom, obtaining such a certificate is not sufficient to establish the
    person's suitability to work in a school, the governing body must make such further checks as it
    considers appropriate, having regard to any guidance issued by the Secretary of State: School
    Staffing (England) Regulations 2009, SI 2009/2680, reg 24(4). Regulation 24(3), (4) do not
    apply to a person who has worked in:
    (1)   a school in England in a post which brought the person regularly into contact with
           children or young persons (reg 24(6)(a)(i)), or to which the person was appointed on or
           after 12 May 2006 and which did not bring the person regularly into contact with
           children or young persons (reg 24(6)(a)(ii)); or
    (2)   an institution within the further education sector in England, or in a 16 to 19 academy,
           in a post which involved the provision of education which brought the person regularly
           into contact with children or young persons (reg 24(6)(b) (amended by SI 2012/979)),
    during a period which ended not more than three months before the person's appointment
    (School Staffing (England) Regulations 2009, SI 2009/2680, reg 24(6)). As to the meaning of
    'school' see PARA 91; as to the meanings of 'child' and 'young person' see PARA 7 note 6; and as
    to the meaning of 'further education' see PARA 23; and as to the meaning of '16 to 19 academy'
    see PARA 346 note 13 (definitions applied by the Education Act 2002 s 212(2), (3);
    Interpretation Act 1978 s 11). As to the Secretary of State see PARA 58. As to the publication of
    guidance see the Education Act 1996 s 571 (applied by the Education Act 2002 s 212(2), (3));
    and PARA 60. As to the meaning of 'month' see PARA 54 note 26.
12 School Staffing (England) Regulations 2009, SI 2009/2680, reg 33.
13 School Staffing (England) Regulations 2009, SI 2009/2680, reg 24(7). As to the information to
    be included in the register see Sch 2 (amended by SI 2013/1940; and SI 2015/887). School
    Staffing (England) Regulations 2009, SI 2009/2680, reg 24(7) (in so far as it relates to Sch 2
    paras 2–4A, 7 and 8) also applies in relation to any person appointed by an authority for the
    purpose of working at a foundation, voluntary aided or foundation special school in the
    temporary absence of a member of staff of the school: see reg 25 (amended by SI 2013/1940).
14 'Local authority' means the local authority by which a maintained school is, or a proposed
    school is to be, maintained: see the School Staffing (England) Regulations 2009, SI 2009/2680,
    reg 3(1) (definition amended by SI 2010/1172). As to the meaning of 'local authority' see PARA
    25 (definition applied by the Education Act 2002 s 212(1) (amended by SI 2010/1158);
    Interpretation Act 1978 s 11). As to the application of the School Staffing (England)
    Regulations 2009, SI 2009/2680, regs 3, 4, 6–9, 12–22, 41, 43 to pupil referral units (see PARA
    427 et seq) see the Education (Pupil Referral Units) (Application of Enactments) (England)
    Regulations 2007, SI 2007/2979, Sch 1 Pt 2 para 28 (substituted by SI 2012/3158).
15 As to the meaning of 'functions' see PARA 18 note 5 (definition applied by the Education
    Act 2002 s 212(2), (3); Interpretation Act 1978 s 11).
16 As to the meaning of 'teacher' see PARA 269 note 4.
17 School Staffing (England) Regulations 2009, SI 2009/2680, reg 26(1). A 'relevant agreement' is
    an agreement in writing between the local authority and the governing body which entitles the
    authority to offer advice to the governing body in relation to the exercise of any such function to
    the extent provided, and which has not been terminated by the governing body by notice in
    writing to the authority: reg 26(2). As to the meaning of 'writing' see PARA 76 note 8. Where the
    local authority is entitled to offer advice to any individual governing body in relation to the
    exercise of any function under reg 26, it is also entitled to offer advice to any other collaborating

governing bodies in relation to the exercise of any such function: see reg 39(1). The collaborating governing bodies must consider any advice so offered by the authority: reg 39(2). As to the meaning of 'collaborating governing bodies' see PARA 270 note 1.

18　School Staffing (England) Regulations 2009, SI 2009/2680, reg 26(2).

282.　Appointment of head teacher and deputy head teacher. The governing body[1] of a foundation, voluntary aided or foundation special school[2] must notify the local authority in writing[3] of: (1) any vacancy for the head teacher[4]; and (2) any post of deputy head teacher which it has identified as one to be filled[5].

The governing body must advertise any such vacancy or post in such manner as it considers appropriate unless it has good reason not to[6]. Where the governing body advertises any such vacancy or post, it must appoint a selection panel[7], consisting of at least three of its members, other than a governor who is the head teacher or (as the case may be) a deputy head teacher, to: (a) select for interview such applicants for the post as it thinks fit and, where the post is that of head teacher, notify the local authority in writing of the names of the applicants so selected[8]; (b) interview those applicants who attend for that purpose[9]; and (c) where it considers it appropriate to do so, recommend to the governing body for appointment one of the applicants interviewed[10]. If, within a period of seven days beginning with the date when it receives notification under head (a) above, the authority makes written representations to the selection panel that any of the applicants is not a suitable person for the post, the selection panel must consider those representations[11], and, where it decides to recommend for appointment the person about whom the representations have been made, notify the authority in writing of its reasons[12].

Subject to making the appropriate checks[13], the governing body may appoint the person recommended by the selection panel to the vacancy or the post to be filled[14]. If the selection panel does not recommend a person to the governing body[15], or the governing body declines to appoint the person recommended by the selection panel[16], the selection panel may recommend another person for appointment in accordance with these provisions (but this does not prevent it from recommending an existing applicant)[17].

If the governing body decides, for good reason, not to advertise and conduct a selection process to fill the vacancy or post[18], it may, subject to the appropriate checks[19], appoint the person it has identified to the vacancy or post to be filled[20].

These provisions[21] are subject to specific provisions[22] relating to the appointment of head teachers for schools of Roman Catholic religious orders[23].

1　Where two or more governing bodies agree to collaborate on the discharge of any function relating to individual members of the school staff, the School Staffing (England) Regulations 2009, SI 2009/2680, apply, subject as follows: see reg 35(1). In relation to the appointment of a head teacher under reg 27:
　　(1)　the collaborating governing bodies may delegate the notification to the local authority and the advertisement of any vacancy or post to the head teacher of one or more of the collaborating schools (reg 36(1)(a)), one or more governors from any of the collaborating schools (reg 36(1)(b)), or one or more head teachers acting together with one or more governors from any of the collaborating schools (reg 36(1)(c));
　　(2)　the selection panel must consist of at least three governors taken from any of the collaborating governing bodies other than a governor who is the head teacher or (as the case may be) a deputy head teacher of the relevant school (reg 36(1)(b)); and
　　(3)　the selection panel must make its recommendation to the governing body of the relevant school (reg 36(1)(c)).
　　If the governing body does not approve the recommendation the selection panel of the collaborating governing bodies must repeat the selection process unless the relevant school's governing body withdraws from the agreement to collaborate: reg 36(2). As to the meanings of 'collaborating governing bodies' and 'relevant school' see PARA 270 note 1. As to the governing

bodies of maintained schools in England see PARA 150 et seq. As to the delegation by governing bodies of functions under the School Staffing (England) Regulations 2009, SI 2009/2680, see PARA 280. 'Local authority' means the local authority by which a maintained school is, or a proposed school is to be, maintained: see reg 3(1) (definition amended by SI 2010/1172). As to the meaning of 'local authority' see PARA 25 (definition applied by the Education Act 2002 s 212(1) (amended by SI 2010/1158); Interpretation Act 1978 s 11). As to the meaning of references to a vacancy in any post see PARA 270 note 5. As to the meaning of 'head teacher' see PARA 86 note 4 (definition applied by s 212(2), (3); Interpretation Act 1978 s 11). As to the application of the School Staffing (England) Regulations 2009, SI 2009/2680, regs 3, 4, 6–9, 12–22, 41, 43 to pupil referral units (see PARA 427 et seq) see the Education (Pupil Referral Units) (Application of Enactments) (England) Regulations 2007, SI 2007/2979, Sch 1 Pt 2 para 28 (substituted by SI 2012/3158).

2 See the School Staffing (England) Regulations 2009, SI 2009/2680, reg 23. As to the meaning of references to a foundation, voluntary or foundation special school see PARA 106.
3 As to the meaning of 'writing' see PARA 76 note 8.
4 School Staffing (England) Regulations 2009, SI 2009/2680, reg 27(1)(a).
5 School Staffing (England) Regulations 2009, SI 2009/2680, reg 27(1)(b).
6 School Staffing (England) Regulations 2009, SI 2009/2680, reg 27(2).
7 As to selection panels and the conduct of interviews see the School Staffing (England) Regulations 2009, SI 2009/2680, reg 9; and PARA 280.
8 School Staffing (England) Regulations 2009, SI 2009/2680, reg 27(3)(a).
9 School Staffing (England) Regulations 2009, SI 2009/2680, reg 27(3)(b).
10 School Staffing (England) Regulations 2009, SI 2009/2680, reg 27(3)(c).
11 School Staffing (England) Regulations 2009, SI 2009/2680, reg 27(4)(a).
12 School Staffing (England) Regulations 2009, SI 2009/2680, reg 27(4)(b).
13 Ie subject to the School Staffing (England) Regulations 2009, SI 2009/2680, reg 24(2) and, where appropriate, reg 24(4): see PARA 281.
14 School Staffing (England) Regulations 2009, SI 2009/2680, reg 27(5). As to the manner of appointment see PARA 281.
15 School Staffing (England) Regulations 2009, SI 2009/2680, reg 27(6)(a).
16 School Staffing (England) Regulations 2009, SI 2009/2680, reg 27(6)(b).
17 School Staffing (England) Regulations 2009, SI 2009/2680, reg 27(6).
18 Ie in accordance with the School Staffing (England) Regulations 2009, SI 2009/2680, reg 27(2)–(4): see the text to notes 6–12.
19 Ie subject to the School Staffing (England) Regulations 2009, SI 2009/2680, reg 24(2) and, where appropriate, reg 24(4): see PARA 281.
20 School Staffing (England) Regulations 2009, SI 2009/2680, reg 27(7).
21 Ie the School Staffing (England) Regulations 2009, SI 2009/2680, reg 27(2)–(7): see the text to notes 6–20.
22 Ie the School Staffing (England) Regulations 2009, SI 2009/2680, reg 34: see PARA 283.
23 School Staffing (England) Regulations 2009, SI 2009/2680, reg 27(8).

283. Appointment of head teachers for schools of Roman Catholic religious orders. In relation to a voluntary aided school[1] where the trustees under a trust deed[2] relating to the school are also trustees of a Roman Catholic religious order ('the order')[3], the following provisions have effect in relation to the filling of a vacancy[4] in the post of head teacher[5] of the school[6].

The governing body[7] must notify the local authority[8] and the major superior[9] in writing[10] of the vacancy[11]. The governing body must interview[12] such persons who are members of the order as are proposed as candidates for appointment to the post by the major superior[13], and appoint to the post one of the persons so interviewed unless[14] the governing body has good reason for not making any such appointment[15]. If the governing body does not make an appointment[16], the usual provisions as to the appointment of a head teacher[17] have effect in relation to the filling of the vacancy[18].

1 As to voluntary aided schools see PARA 106.
2 As to the meaning of 'trust deed' see PARA 108 note 6 (definition applied by the Education Act 2002 s 212(2), (3); Interpretation Act 1978 s 11).

3 See the School Staffing (England) Regulations 2009, SI 2009/2680, reg 34(1). 'Roman Catholic religious order' means a Roman Catholic religious institute or society of apostolic life: reg 34(6).
4 As to the meaning of references to a vacancy in any post see PARA 270 note 5.
5 As to the meaning of 'head teacher' see PARA 86 note 4 (definition applied by the Education Act 2002 s 212(2), (3); Interpretation Act 1978 s 11). As to the appointment of deputy head teachers see PARA 282. As to the appointment of other teachers see PARA 284.
6 Ie, subject to the School Staffing (England) Regulations 2009, SI 2009/2680, reg 34(5) (see the text to notes 16–18), reg 34(3), (4) (see the text to notes 7–15) has effect in relation to the filling of a vacancy in the post of head teacher of the school, in place of reg 27(2)–(7) (see PARA 282): reg 34(2).
7 As to the governing bodies of maintained schools in England see PARA 150 et seq. As to the delegation by governing bodies of functions under the School Staffing (England) Regulations 2009, SI 2009/2680, see PARA 280.
8 'Local authority' means the local authority by which a maintained school is, or a proposed school is to be, maintained: see the School Staffing (England) Regulations 2009, SI 2009/2680, reg 3(1) (definition amended by SI 2010/1172). As to the meaning of 'local authority' see PARA 25 (definition applied by the Education Act 2002 s 212(1) (amended by SI 2010/1158); Interpretation Act 1978 s 11). As to the application of the School Staffing (England) Regulations 2009, SI 2009/2680, regs 3, 4, 6–9, 12–22, 41, 43 to pupil referral units (see PARA 427 et seq) see the Education (Pupil Referral Units) (Application of Enactments) (England) Regulations 2007, SI 2007/2979, Sch 1 Pt 2 para 28 (substituted by SI 2012/3158).
9 'The major superior' means the major superior of the order: School Staffing (England) Regulations 2009, SI 2009/2680, reg 34(6).
10 As to the meaning of 'writing' see PARA 76 note 8.
11 See the School Staffing (England) Regulations 2009, SI 2009/2680, regs 27(1), 34(2), (3).
12 As to the conduct of interviews see the School Staffing (England) Regulations 2009, SI 2009/2680, reg 9; and PARA 280.
13 School Staffing (England) Regulations 2009, SI 2009/2680, reg 34(4)(a).
14 Ie by virtue of the School Staffing (England) Regulations 2009, SI 2009/2680, reg 24(2) (see PARA 281) or otherwise: see reg 34(4)(b).
15 School Staffing (England) Regulations 2009, SI 2009/2680, reg 34(4)(b).
16 Ie under the School Staffing (England) Regulations 2009, SI 2009/2680, reg 34(4)(b): see the text to notes 14–15.
17 Ie the School Staffing (England) Regulations 2009, SI 2009/2680, reg 27(2)–(7): see PARA 282.
18 School Staffing (England) Regulations 2009, SI 2009/2680, reg 34(5).

284. Appointment of other teachers. Where the governing body[1] of a foundation, voluntary aided or foundation special school[2] identifies any post[3] of teacher (other than head teacher or deputy head teacher) which is to be filled for a period of more than four months[4], it must send a specification for the post to the local authority[5].

1 Where two or more governing bodies agree to collaborate on the discharge of any function relating to individual members of the school staff, the School Staffing (England) Regulations 2009, SI 2009/2680, apply, subject as follows: see reg 35(1). The collaborating governing bodies may delegate the appointment of any teacher (other than the head teacher and deputy head teacher) to: (1) the head teacher of one or more of the collaborating schools (reg 37(1)(a)); (2) one or more governors from any of the collaborating schools (reg 37(1)(b)); (3) one or more head teachers acting together with one or more governors from any of the collaborating schools (reg 37(1)(c)). Where the collaborating governing bodies have delegated the appointment of a member of staff, other than to the head teacher of the relevant school the head teacher of the relevant school may attend all relevant proceedings and offer advice (reg 37(2)(a)), and the person or persons to whom the delegation has been made must consider any such advice (reg 37(2)(b)). As to the governing bodies of maintained schools in England see PARA 150 et seq. As to the delegation by governing bodies of functions under the School Staffing (England) Regulations 2009, SI 2009/2680, generally see PARA 280. As to the meanings of 'collaborating governing bodies' and 'relevant school' see PARA 270 note 1. As to the meaning of 'teacher' see PARA 269 note 4. As to the meaning of 'head teacher' see PARA 86 note 4 (definition applied by the Education Act 2002 s 212(2), (3); Interpretation Act 1978 s 11). As to the appointment of head teachers and deputy head teachers see PARA 282.
2 See the School Staffing (England) Regulations 2009, SI 2009/2680, reg 23. As to the meaning of references to a foundation, voluntary or foundation special school see PARA 106.

3   As to the meaning of references to a vacancy in any post see PARA 270 note 5.

4   As to the meaning of 'month' see PARA 54 note 26.

5   School Staffing (England) Regulations 2009, SI 2009/2680, reg 28. 'Local authority' means the local authority by which a maintained school is, or a proposed school is to be, maintained: see reg 3(1) (definition amended by SI 2010/1172). As to the meaning of 'local authority' see PARA 25 (definition applied by the Education Act 2002 s 212(1) (amended by SI 2010/1158); Interpretation Act 1978 s 11). As to the manner of appointment of staff see PARA 281. As to selection panels and the conduct of interviews see reg 9; and PARA 280. As to the application of the School Staffing (England) Regulations 2009, SI 2009/2680, regs 3, 4, 6–9, 12–22, 41, 43 to pupil referral units (see PARA 427 et seq) see the Education (Pupil Referral Units) (Application of Enactments) (England) Regulations 2007, SI 2007/2979, Sch 1 Pt 2 para 28 (substituted by SI 2012/3158).

285. Appointment of support staff. The governing body[1] of a foundation, voluntary aided or foundation special school[2] is responsible for the appointment of support staff unless the governing body and the local authority[3] agree that the authority will make such appointments[4].

1   Where two or more governing bodies agree to collaborate on the discharge of any function relating to individual members of the school staff, the School Staffing (England) Regulations 2009, SI 2009/2680, apply, subject as follows: see reg 35(1). The collaborating governing bodies may delegate the appointment of any member of the support staff to: (1) the head teacher of one or more of the collaborating schools (reg 37(1)(a)); (2) one or more governors from any of the collaborating schools (reg 37(1)(b)); (3) one or more head teachers acting together with one or more governors from any of the collaborating schools (reg 37(1)(c)). Where the collaborating governing bodies have delegated the appointment of a member of staff, other than to the head teacher of the relevant school the head teacher of the relevant school may attend all relevant proceedings and offer advice (reg 37(2)(a)), and the person or persons to whom the delegation has been made must consider any such advice (reg 37(2)(b)). As to the governing bodies of maintained schools in England see PARA 150 et seq. As to the delegation by governing bodies of functions under the School Staffing (England) Regulations 2009, SI 2009/2680, generally see PARA 280. As to the meanings of 'collaborating governing bodies' and 'relevant school' see PARA 270 note 1. As to the meaning of 'support staff' see PARA 269 note 4. As to the meaning of 'head teacher' see PARA 86 note 4 (definition applied by the Education Act 2002 s 212(2), (3); Interpretation Act 1978 s 11).

2   See the School Staffing (England) Regulations 2009, SI 2009/2680, reg 23. As to the meaning of references to a foundation, voluntary or foundation special school see PARA 106.

3   'Local authority' means the local authority by which a maintained school is, or a proposed school is to be, maintained: see the School Staffing (England) Regulations 2009, SI 2009/2680, reg 3(1) (definition amended by SI 2010/1172). As to the meaning of 'local authority' see PARA 25 (definition applied by the Education Act 2002 s 212(1) (amended by SI 2010/1158); Interpretation Act 1978 s 11). As to the application of the School Staffing (England) Regulations 2009, SI 2009/2680, regs 3, 4, 6–9, 12–22, 41, 43 to pupil referral units (see PARA 427 et seq) see the Education (Pupil Referral Units) (Application of Enactments) (England) Regulations 2007, SI 2007/2979, Sch 1 Pt 2 para 28 (substituted by SI 2012/3158).

4   School Staffing (England) Regulations 2009, SI 2009/2680, reg 29. See *Beattie v Leicester City Council* UKEAT0386/09/SM. As to the manner of appointment of staff see PARA 281. As to selection panels and the conduct of interviews see reg 9; and PARA 280.

286. Supply staff. The governing body[1] of a foundation, voluntary aided or foundation special school[2] must ensure that no person supplied by an employment business[3] to a school is allowed to begin work as a teacher[4] or member of support staff[5] at the school unless the governing body has received written[6] notification from the employment business in relation to that person[7]. Before a person offered for supply by an employment business may begin work at the school the governing body must check the person's identity (whether or not the employment business made such a check before the person was offered for supply)[8].

1   As to the governing bodies of maintained schools in England see PARA 150 et seq. As to the delegation by governing bodies of functions under the School Staffing (England) Regulations 2009, SI 2009/2680, see PARA 280.

2   See the School Staffing (England) Regulations 2009, SI 2009/2680, reg 23. As to the meaning of references to a foundation, voluntary or foundation special school see PARA 106.

3   As to the meaning of 'employment business' see PARA 273 note 4.

4   As to the meaning of 'teacher' see PARA 269 note 4.

5   As to the meaning of 'support staff' see PARA 269 note 4.

6   As to the meaning of 'written' see PARA 76 note 8.

7   School Staffing (England) Regulations 2009, SI 2009/2680, reg 30(1)(a). The notification must state:

    (1)   that the employment business has made checks (a) to establish the person's identity, (b) to establish that the person is not barred from regulated activity relating to children in accordance with the Safeguarding Vulnerable Groups Act 2006 s 3(2) (see CHILDREN AND YOUNG PERSONS vol 9 (2012) PARA 682) or subject to any direction made under the Education Act 2002 s 142 (see PARA 420) or any prohibition, restriction or order having effect as such a direction, (c) to establish that the person meets the appropriate requirements with respect to qualifications or registration mentioned in the School Staffing (England) Regulations 2009, SI 2009/2680, reg 3(3)(a) (see PARA 269 note 10), (d) to establish the person's right to work in the United Kingdom, and (e) further checks were made pursuant to reg 24(4) (see PARA 281) (see reg 30(1)(a)(i), Sch 2 para 5(1)(a)(i) (amended by SI 2015/887));

    (2)   where it is intended that the person will engage in relevant activity, that it or another employment business has applied for an enhanced criminal record certificate or has obtained such a certificate in response to an application made by that or another employment business (School Staffing (England) Regulations 2009, SI 2009/2680, reg 30(1)(a)(ii) (amended by SI 2015/887));

    (3)   whether, if the employment business has obtained such a certificate before the person is due to begin work at the school, it disclosed any matter or information, or any information was provided to the employment business in accordance with the Police Act 1997 s 113B(6) (see SENTENCING AND DISPOSITION OF OFFENDERS vol 92 (2010) PARA 713) (School Staffing (England) Regulations 2009, SI 2009/2680, reg 30(1)(a)(iii)); and

    (4)   whether, if the employment business or another employment business has obtained such a certificate before the person is due to begin work at the school and the certificate is or has been subject to up-date arrangements, the employment business or another employment business has been given negative up-date information in relation to the certificate not more than three months before the person is due to begin work at the school (School Staffing (England) Regulations 2009, SI 2009/2680, reg 30(1)(a)(iv) (added by SI 2015/887).

As to the meaning of 'relevant activity' (see head (2) above) see PARA 269 note 13. As to the meaning of 'negative up-date information' (see head (4) above) see PARA 273 note 9.

    Where the employment business has obtained an enhanced criminal record certificate before the person is due to begin work at the school which disclosed any matter or information, or any information was provided to the employment business in accordance with the Police Act 1997 s 113B(6), it must also supply a copy of the certificate: see the School Staffing (England) Regulations 2009, SI 2009/2680, reg 30(1)(b). Where an enhanced criminal record certificate is or has been subject to up-date arrangements and the employment business has been given negative up-date information in relation to the certificate not more than three months before the person is due to begin work at the school, it must also supply a copy of the information: see reg 30(1)(c) (added by SI 2015/887). Subject to the School Staffing (England) Regulations 2009, SI 2009/2680, reg 30(3), the certificate referred to in reg 30(1)(a)(ii) (see head (2) above) must have been issued and obtained not more than three months before the person is due to begin work at the school unless that certificate is or has been subject to up-date arrangements and the employment business or another employment business has been given negative up-date information in relation to the certificate not more than three months before the person is due to begin work at the school: reg 30(2) (amended by SI 2015/887). The School Staffing (England) Regulations 2009, SI 2009/2680, reg 30(2) does not apply in relation to a person who has worked in:

    (i)   a school in England in a post (A) which brought the person regularly into contact with children or young persons (reg 30(3)(a)(i)); or (B) to which the person was appointed on or after 12 May 2006 and which did not bring the person regularly into contact with children or young persons (reg 30(3)(a)(ii)); or

(ii)   an institution within the further education sector in England, or in a 16 to 19 academy, in a post which involved the provision of education which brought the person regularly into contact with children or young persons (reg 30(3)(b) (amended by SI 2012/979)), during a period which ended not more than three months before the person is due to begin work at the school (School Staffing (England) Regulations 2009, SI 2009/2680, reg 30(3)). The governing body must, either in the contract or in other arrangements which it makes with any employment business, require it, in respect of any person whom the employment business supplies to the school (aa) to provide the notification referred to in reg 30(1)(a) (reg 30(5)(a)); (bb) where the employment business obtains an enhanced criminal record certificate which discloses any matter or information, or if any information is provided to the employment business in accordance with the Police Act 1997 s 113B(6), to provide a copy of the certificate (School Staffing (England) Regulations 2009, SI 2009/2680, reg 30(5)(b)); and (cc) if any such certificate is or has been subject to up-date arrangements and the employment business has been given negative up-date information in relation to the certificate not more than three months before the person is due to begin work at the school, to provide a copy of the information (reg 30(5)(c) (added by SI 2015/887). As to the meaning of 'enhanced criminal record certificate' see PARA 269 note 12. As to when a person is taken to have applied for an enhanced criminal record certificate see PARA 273 note 9. As to the meaning of 'month' see PARA 54 note 26. As to the meaning of 'England' see PARA 7 note 3. As to the meaning of 'United Kingdom' see PARA 73 note 3. As to the meaning of 'school' see PARA 91; as to the meanings of 'child' and 'young person' see PARA 7 note 6; and as to the meaning of 'further education' see PARA 23; and as to the meaning of '16 to 19 academy' see PARA 346 note 13 (definitions applied by the Education Act 2002 s 212(2), (3); by virtue of the Interpretation Act 1978 s 11).

8   School Staffing (England) Regulations 2009, SI 2009/2680, reg 30(4).

287.   Conduct, discipline and capability of staff. The governing body[1] of a foundation, voluntary aided or foundation special school[2] must establish procedures: (1) for the regulation of the conduct and discipline of staff at the school[3]; and (2) by which staff may seek redress for any grievance relating to their work at the school[4]. Where the implementation of any determination made by the governing body in operation of the procedures requires any action which is not within the functions[5] exercisable[6] by the governing body[7], but is within the power of the local authority[8], the authority must take that action at the request of the governing body[9].

The governing body must also establish procedures for dealing with lack of capability on the part of staff at the school[10].

Where a member of the teaching staff at a school ('School A') applies for a teaching post at another school ('School B'), and where School B is a maintained school[11] or an academy school[12], the governing body of School A must, at the request of the governing body or proprietor (as the case may be) of School B (a) advise in writing[13] whether or not that member of staff has, in the preceding two years, been the subject of the above procedures established by the governing body[14]; and, if so, (b) provide written details of the concerns which gave rise to this, the duration of the proceedings and their outcome[15].

1   As to the governing bodies of maintained schools in England see PARA 150 et seq.
2   As to the meaning of references to a foundation, voluntary or foundation special school see PARA 106.
3   School Staffing (England) Regulations 2009, SI 2009/2680, reg 7(1)(a). As to the application of the School Staffing (England) Regulations 2009, SI 2009/2680, regs 3, 4, 6–9, 12–22, 41, 43 to pupil referral units (see PARA 427 et seq) see the Education (Pupil Referral Units) (Application of Enactments) (England) Regulations 2007, SI 2007/2979, Sch 1 Pt 2 para 28 (substituted by SI 2012/3158).
4   School Staffing (England) Regulations 2009, SI 2009/2680, reg 7(1)(b).
5   As to the meaning of 'functions' see PARA 18 note 5 (definition applied by the Education Act 2002 s 212(2), (3); Interpretation Act 1978 s 11).
6   Ie by or under the Education Act 2002. As to the general powers and duties of governing bodies see PARA 168 et seq.
7   School Staffing (England) Regulations 2009, SI 2009/2680, reg 7(2)(a).

8   School Staffing (England) Regulations 2009, SI 2009/2680, reg 7(2)(b). 'Local authority' means the local authority by which a maintained school is, or a proposed school is to be, maintained: see reg 3(1) (definition amended by SI 2010/1172). As to the meaning of 'local authority' see PARA 25 (definition applied by the Education Act 2002 s 212(1) (amended by SI 2010/1158); Interpretation Act 1978 s 11).

9   School Staffing (England) Regulations 2009, SI 2009/2680, reg 7(2).

10 School Staffing (England) Regulations 2009, SI 2009/2680, reg 8. As to the suspension and dismissal of staff see PARA 289. As to the performance of head teachers see PARA 288.

11 As to the meaning of 'maintained school' see PARA 99.

12 School Staffing (England) Regulations 2009, SI 2009/2680, reg 8A(1) (reg 8A added by SI 2012/1740). As to the meaning of 'academy school' see PARA 346 note 7 (definition applied by the Education Act 2002 s 212(1); Interpretation Act 1978 s 11).

13 As to the meaning of 'writing' see PARA 76 note 8.

14 School Staffing (England) Regulations 2009, SI 2009/2680, reg 8A(2)(a) (as added: see note 13). The reference in the text is to the procedures established in accordance with reg 8: see the text to note 11. As to the meaning of 'proprietor' see PARA 51 note 4 (definition applied by the Education Act 2002 s 212(1); Interpretation Act 1978 s 11).

15 School Staffing (England) Regulations 2009, SI 2009/2680, reg 8A(2)(b) (as added: see note 13).

288. Performance of head teacher. The governing body[1] of a foundation, voluntary aided or foundation special school[2] must ensure that the head teacher[3] at the school: (1) complies with the duties imposed upon the head teacher[4]; and (2) benefits from any entitlement conferred upon the head teacher[5] by any order[6] relating to teachers' pay and conditions[7]. In discharging its duty under head (1) above, the governing body must have regard to the desirability of the head teacher being able to achieve a satisfactory balance between the time spent discharging the professional duties of a head teacher and the time spent by the head teacher pursuing personal interests outside work[8].

Where the local authority[9] has any serious concerns about the performance of the head teacher of a school it must make a written[10] report of its concerns to the governing body of the school[11] and, at the same time, send a copy of the report to the head teacher[12]. The governing body must notify the authority in writing of the action it proposes to take in the light of the authority's report[13].

1   As to the governing bodies of maintained schools in England see PARA 150 et seq.

2   As to the meaning of references to a foundation, voluntary or foundation special school see PARA 106.

3   As to the meaning of 'head teacher' see PARA 86 note 4 (definition applied by the Education Act 2002 s 212(2), (3); Interpretation Act 1978 s 11). As to the appointment of the head teacher see PARA 282.

4   School Staffing (England) Regulations 2009, SI 2009/2680, reg 5(1)(a).

5   School Staffing (England) Regulations 2009, SI 2009/2680, reg 5(1)(b).

6   Ie under the Education Act 2002 s 122: see PARA 1078.

7   School Staffing (England) Regulations 2009, SI 2009/2680, reg 5(1).

8   School Staffing (England) Regulations 2009, SI 2009/2680, reg 5(2).

9   'Local authority' means the local authority by which a maintained school is, or a proposed school is to be, maintained: see the School Staffing (England) Regulations 2009, SI 2009/2680, reg 3(1) (definition amended by SI 2010/1172). As to the meaning of 'local authority' see PARA 25 (definition applied by the Education Act 2002 s 212(1) (amended by SI 2010/1158); Interpretation Act 1978 s 11). As to the application of the School Staffing (England) Regulations 2009, SI 2009/2680, regs 3, 4, 6–9, 12–22, 41, 43 to pupil referral units (see PARA 427 et seq) see the Education (Pupil Referral Units) (Application of Enactments) (England) Regulations 2007, SI 2007/2979, Sch 1 Pt 2 para 28 (substituted by SI 2012/3158).

10 As to the meaning of 'written' see PARA 76 note 8.

11 School Staffing (England) Regulations 2009, SI 2009/2680, reg 6(1)(a).

12 School Staffing (England) Regulations 2009, SI 2009/2680, reg 6(1)(b).

13 School Staffing (England) Regulations 2009, SI 2009/2680, reg 6(2).

289. Suspension and dismissal of staff. The governing body[1] or the head teacher[2] of a foundation, voluntary aided or foundation special school[3] may suspend[4] any person employed or engaged otherwise than under a contract of employment[5] to work at the school where, in the opinion of the governing body or (as the case may be) the head teacher, the person's suspension from the school is required[6]. The governing body or (as the case may be) head teacher must immediately inform the head teacher or (as the case may be) the governing body when a person is so suspended[7]. Only the governing body may end such a suspension[8]; and on ending such a suspension, the governing body must inform the head teacher[9].

In the case of support staff[10] employed, or engaged otherwise than under a contract of employment by the local authority[11], the governing body or the head teacher may suspend any such person employed or engaged to work at the school where, in the opinion of the governing body or (as the case may be) the head teacher, such suspension is required[12]. The governing body or (as the case may be) the head teacher must immediately inform the local authority and the head teacher or (as the case may be) the governing body when a person is so suspended[13]. Only the governing body may end such a suspension[14], and on ending such a suspension, the governing body must immediately inform the authority and the head teacher[15]. Separate provision is made in respect of the dismissal of such persons[16].

The local authority may offer advice to the governing body in relation to the exercise of the governing body's functions[17] of dismissal of any teacher[18], to the extent provided by, and subject to, any relevant agreement[19]. The governing body must consider any such advice offered by the authority[20].

1 As to the governing bodies of maintained schools in England see PARA 150 et seq. As to the delegation by governing bodies of functions under the School Staffing (England) Regulations 2009, SI 2009/2680, see PARA 280.

2 As to the meaning of 'head teacher' see PARA 86 note 4 (definition applied by the Education Act 2002 s 212(2), (3); Interpretation Act 1978 s 11).

3 See the School Staffing (England) Regulations 2009, SI 2009/2680, reg 23. As to the meaning of references to a foundation, voluntary or foundation special school see PARA 106.

4 'Suspend' means suspend without loss of emoluments: School Staffing (England) Regulations 2009, SI 2009/2680, regs 19(5), 31(5).

5 As to the meaning of 'contract of employment' see PARA 268 note 3.

6 School Staffing (England) Regulations 2009, SI 2009/2680, reg 31(1).

7 School Staffing (England) Regulations 2009, SI 2009/2680, reg 31(2).

8 School Staffing (England) Regulations 2009, SI 2009/2680, reg 31(3).

9 School Staffing (England) Regulations 2009, SI 2009/2680, reg 31(4).

10 As to the meaning of 'support staff' see PARA 269 note 4.

11 Ie in accordance with the School Staffing (England) Regulations 2009, SI 2009/2680, reg 29: see PARA 285. 'Local authority' means the local authority by which a maintained school is, or a proposed school is to be, maintained: see reg 3(1) (definition amended by SI 2010/1172). As to the meaning of 'local authority' see PARA 25 (definition applied by the Education Act 2002 s 212(1) (amended by SI 2010/1158); Interpretation Act 1978 s 11). As to the application of the School Staffing (England) Regulations 2009, SI 2009/2680, regs 3, 4, 6–9, 12–22, 41, 43 to pupil referral units (see PARA 427 et seq) see the Education (Pupil Referral Units) (Application of Enactments) (England) Regulations 2007, SI 2007/2979, Sch 1 Pt 2 para 28 (substituted by SI 2012/3158).

12 See the School Staffing (England) Regulations 2009, SI 2009/2680, regs 19(1), 32.

13 See the School Staffing (England) Regulations 2009, SI 2009/2680, regs 19(2), 32.

14 See the School Staffing (England) Regulations 2009, SI 2009/2680, regs 19(3), 32.

15 See the School Staffing (England) Regulations 2009, SI 2009/2680, regs 19(4), 32.

16 Ie the School Staffing (England) Regulations 2009, SI 2009/2680, reg 20 (see PARA 277) applies: see reg 32.

17 As to the meaning of 'functions' see PARA 18 note 5 (definition applied by the Education Act 2002 s 212(2), (3); Interpretation Act 1978 s 11).
18 As to the meaning of 'teacher' see PARA 269 note 4. As to the appointment of head teachers see PARA 282; and as to the appointment of other teachers see PARA 284.
19 See the School Staffing (England) Regulations 2009, SI 2009/2680, reg 26(1). As to the meaning of 'relevant agreement' see PARA 281 note 17.
20 School Staffing (England) Regulations 2009, SI 2009/2680, reg 26(3).

(b) Schools not having a Delegated Budget

290. Staffing of school on suspension of delegated budget. If at any time a foundation, voluntary aided or foundation special school[1] does not have a delegated budget[2] the usual provisions relating to the staffing at such schools[3] have effect subject to the following provisions[4].

In such circumstances, the arrangements for the staffing of the school are determined by the local authority[5]. Except with the consent of the authority, the governing body[6] must not[7] appoint any teacher to work at the school[8], or dismiss any teacher at the school[9]. The authority may give the governing body directions[10]: (1) as to the educational qualifications of the teachers to be appointed for giving secular education[11]; or (2) requiring it to dismiss any teacher at the school[12]; but the authority must not give any directions under head (1) above except after consulting the governing body[13]. The authority may also give directions to the governing body as to the number and conditions of service of persons employed at the school for the purposes of the care and maintenance of the school premises[14].

1 See the Education Act 2002 s 36(1). As to the meaning of references to a foundation, voluntary or foundation special school see PARA 106.
2 Ie by virtue of any suspension under the School Standards and Framework Act 1998 Sch 15 (see PARAS 325–327), the Education and Inspections Act 2006 s 66 (see PARA 1214) or the School Standards and Organisation (Wales) Act 2013 s 8 (see PARA 1233). As to the meaning of 'delegated budget' see PARA 279 note 3.
3 Ie regulations made under the Education Act 2002 s 36(4): see PARA 280. As to such regulations see PARAS 281–289.
4 Education Act 2002 s 36(7) (amended by the Education Act 2011 s 19(2); and the School Standards and Organisation (Wales) Act 2013 Sch 5 para 6(1), (4)). Where a proposed foundation, voluntary aided or foundation special school does not have a delegated budget, the provisions of the Education Act 2002 Sch 2 Pt 2 (paras 5–11) (see the text to notes 5–14) apply with modifications: see the School Staffing (England) Regulations 2009, SI 2009/2680, regs 40, 44.
5 Education Act 2002 Sch 2 para 5 (amended by SI 2010/1158). As to the meaning of 'local authority' see PARA 25 (definition applied by the Education Act 2002 s 212(1) (amended by SI 2010/1158)).
6 As to the governing bodies of maintained schools in England see PARA 150 et seq. As to the discharge by an education action forum of any function of a governing body under the Education Act 2002 Sch 2 see the School Standards and Framework Act 1998 s 12; and PARA 344.
7 Education Act 2002 Sch 2 para 6. Schedule 2 para 6 has effect subject to the School Standards and Framework Act 1998 s 58 (see PARA 302): see the Education Act 2002 Sch 2 para 10.
8 Education Act 2002 Sch 2 para 6(a).
9 Education Act 2002 Sch 2 para 6(b).
10 As to directions see the Education Act 1996 s 570 (applied by the Education Act 2002 s 212(2), (3)); and PARA 75.
11 Education Act 2002 Sch 2 para 7(a).
12 Education Act 2002 Sch 2 para 7(b). Where a teacher in a foundation, voluntary aided or foundation special school is dismissed by the governing body of the school in pursuance of a requirement of the local authority under Sch 2 para 7, the Employment Rights Act 1996 Pt X (ss 94–134A) has effect (with modifications) in relation to the dismissal: see the Employment Rights Act 1996 s 134(1); and PARA 300.

13 Education Act 2002 Sch 2 para 7. Schedule 2 para 7 has effect subject to the School Standards and Framework Act 1998 s 58 (see PARA 302): see the Education Act 2002 Sch 2 para 10. As to the exercise of the duty to consult see JUDICIAL REVIEW vol 61 (2010) PARA 627.

14 Education Act 2002 Sch 2 para 8. As to the meaning of 'premises' see PARA 62 note 19 (definition applied by s 212(2), (3)). Schedule 2 para 8 has effect subject to (1) any provision made by an order under the Apprenticeships, Skills, Children and Learning Act 2009 s 231(2)(a) (repealed) or s 233(2)(a) (repealed) (Education Act 2002 Sch 2 para 11(a) (Sch 2 para 11 added by the Apprenticeships, Skills, Children and Learning Act 2009 s 237(7))); (2) any provision made by an order under the Apprenticeships, Skills, Children and Learning Act 2009 s 233(2)(d) (repealed) or s 234(2)(b) or (4)(b) (repealed), where the order provides that it is to have effect for determining the conditions of employment of persons to whom it applies (Education Act 2002 Sch 2 para 11(b) (as so added)).

Where the trust deed relating to the school provides for a person other than the governing body to be entitled to control the occupation and use of the school premises to any extent, then, if and to the extent that (disregarding any transfer of control authorised by regulations under s 31: see PARA 180) the use of those premises is or would be under the control of any such person, the reference in Sch 2 para 8 to the governing body must be read as a reference to that person: Sch 2 para 9. As to the meaning of 'trust deed' see PARA 108 note 6 (definition applied by s 212(2), (3)). As to the meaning of 'person' see PARA 7 note 6.

(C) New Maintained Schools

291. Staffing of new schools. The statutory provisions relating to school staffing[1] apply, with modifications[2], in relation to (1) a proposed community, voluntary controlled or community special school[3] or maintained nursery school[4] which has a delegated budget[5] and without a delegated budget[6]; and (2) a proposed foundation, voluntary aided or foundation special school[7] which has a delegated budget[8] and without a delegated budget[9].

1 Ie the Education Act 2002 Sch 2; and the School Staffing (England) Regulations 2009, SI 2009/2680.
2 See the School Staffing (England) Regulations 2009, SI 2009/2680, reg 40.
3 As to the meaning of references to a community, voluntary or community special school see PARA 106.
4 As to the meaning of 'maintained nursery school' see PARA 103 note 3.
5 In such a case the School Staffing (England) Regulations 2009, SI 2009/2680, regs 4–9 (see PARAS 268, 274, 275) and 12–22 (see PARAS 269–273, 276–278) apply: see reg 41.
6 See the School Staffing (England) Regulations 2009, SI 2009/2680, regs 40, 43; and PARA 279 note 6.
7 As to the meaning of references to a foundation, voluntary school or foundation special school see PARA 106.
8 In such a case the School Staffing (England) Regulations 2009, SI 2009/2680, regs 4–9 (see PARAS 280, 287, 288) and 24–34 (see PARAS 281–286, 289) apply: see reg 42.
9 See the School Staffing (England) Regulations 2009, SI 2009/2680, regs 40, 44; and PARA 290 note 4.

B. STAFFING OF PARTICULAR CATEGORIES OF SCHOOLS IN WALES

(A) Community, Voluntary Controlled and Community Special Schools

292. Staffing of schools having a delegated budget. Any teacher[1] or other member of staff[2] who is appointed to work under a contract of employment[3] at a community school[4], a voluntary controlled school[5], a community special school[6] or a maintained nursery school[7] in Wales[8] is to be employed by the local authority[9]. The teaching staff of any such school must include a person appointed as head teacher[10], or a person appointed to carry out the functions[11] of the head teacher of the school pending the appointment of a head teacher[12] or in the absence of the head teacher[13].

Regulations[14] may make further provision with respect to the staffing of such schools[15] and may, in particular:

(1)   make provision with respect to the appointment, discipline, suspension and dismissal of teachers and other staff[16];

(2)   make provision with respect to the appointment of teachers and other staff to work at a school otherwise than under a contract of employment[17];

(3)   make provision with respect to staff employed, or engaged otherwise than under a contract of employment, wholly or partly for the purposes of the provision of facilities and services[18] or any other activities which are not school activities but are carried on on the school premises[19] under the management or control of the governing body[20]; and

(4)   confer functions on local authorities, governing bodies and head teachers[21].

If at any time a school does not have a delegated budget[22] such regulations do not apply[23], and alternative provisions[24] apply instead[25]. Until a day to be appointed, in discharging any function conferred by such regulations, a local authority or the governing body or head teacher of a maintained school[26] must have regard to any guidance[27] given from time to time by the Welsh Ministers[28].

A governing body and a local authority must exercise their respective functions[29] with a view to ensuring that there is employed, or engaged otherwise than under contracts of employment, a staff suitable and sufficient in numbers for the purpose of securing the provision of education appropriate to the ages, abilities, aptitudes and needs of the pupils[30] having regard to any arrangements for the utilisation of the services of staff employed or engaged otherwise than at the school in question[31].

1   As to the appointment of teachers (other than head teachers) see note 14.

2   As to the appointment of support staff see note 14.

3   As to the meaning of 'contract of employment' see PARA 268 note 3.

4   Education Act 2002 s 35(1)(a). As to the meaning of references to a community school see PARA 106.

5   Education Act 2002 s 35(1)(b). As to the meaning of references to a voluntary school see PARA 106.

6   Education Act 2002 s 35(1)(c). As to the meaning of references to a community special school see PARA 106.

7   Education Act 2002 s 35(1)(d). As to the meaning of 'maintained nursery school' see PARA 103 note 3.

8   As to the meaning of 'Wales' see PARA 7 note 3.

9   Education Act 2002 s 35(2) (amended by SI 2010/1158). As to the meaning of 'local authority' see PARA 25 (definition applied by the Education Act 2002 s 212(1) (amended by SI 2010/1158)).

10 Education Act 2002 s 35(3)(a). As to the meaning of 'head teacher' see PARA 86 note 4 (definition applied by the Education Act 2002 s 212(2), (3)). As to the appointment of head teachers see note 14.

11 As to the meaning of 'functions' see PARA 18 note 5 (definition applied by the Education Act 2002 s 212(2), (3)).

12 Education Act 2002 s 35(3)(b)(i).

13 Education Act 2002 s 35(3)(b)(ii). As to the appointment of deputy head teachers see note 14.

14 Ie regulations made under the Education Act 2002 by the Welsh Ministers: s 212(1). The functions under the Education Act 2002 s 35 in relation to Wales were originally vested in the National Assembly for Wales and are now exercisable by the Welsh Ministers by virtue of the Government of Wales Act 2006 s 162(1), Sch 11 paras 30, 32. As to the Welsh Ministers see PARA 59. As to the regulations made under the Education Act 2002 s 35 see the Staffing of Maintained Schools (Wales) Regulations 2006, SI 2006/873, and see below and also the text to notes 29–31; and PARA 294.

As to manner of appointment see regs 9A, 9B, 13, 14, 18A, 19 (regs 9A, 9B, 18A added by SI 2007/944; the Staffing of Maintained Schools (Wales) Regulations 2006, SI 2006/873, regs 9A, 18A amended by SI 2009/2544; and the Staffing of Maintained Schools (Wales) Regulations 2006, SI 2006/873, reg 13 amended by SI 2010/1142). As to appointment of head teachers and deputy head teachers see the Staffing of Maintained Schools (Wales) Regulations 2006, SI 2006/873, regs 10, 11 (reg 10 amended by SI 2009/3161; SI 2010/1142; and SI 2014/1609). As to appointment of other teachers see the Staffing of Maintained Schools (Wales) Regulations 2006, SI 2006/873, regs 5(2), (3), 12 (amended by SI 2007/944; and SI 2010/1142). As to appointment of support staff see the Staffing of Maintained Schools (Wales) Regulations 2006, SI 2006/873, regs 5(2), 15. As to supply staff see reg 15A (added by SI 2007/944; and amended by SI 2009/2544). As to conduct, discipline and capability of staff see the Staffing of Maintained Schools (Wales) Regulations 2006, SI 2006/873, reg 7 (amended by SI 2014/1609). As to the performance of the head teacher see the Staffing of Maintained Schools (Wales) Regulations 2006, SI 2006/873, regs 5A, 6(1) (reg 5A added by SI 2009/2708). As to independent investigators see the Staffing of Maintained Schools (Wales) Regulations 2006, SI 2006/873, reg 7A (added by SI 2014/1609). As to suspension of staff see the Staffing of Maintained Schools (Wales) Regulations 2006, SI 2006/873, reg 16. As to dismissal of staff see reg 17 (amended by SI 2010/1142). As to school meals staff see the Staffing of Maintained Schools (Wales) Regulations 2006, SI 2006/873, reg 18. As to advisory rights for appropriate diocesan authorities see reg 19.

In relation to teachers at a voluntary controlled school who are reserved teachers within the meaning of the School Standards and Framework Act 1998 s 58 (appointment and dismissal of certain teachers at schools with a religious character: see PARA 302), regulations under the Education Act 2002 s 35(4) have effect subject to the provisions of the School Standards and Framework Act 1998 s 58: Education Act 2002 s 35(6).

15 Education Act 2002 s 35(4).
16 Education Act 2002 s 35(5)(a).
17 Education Act 2002 s 35(5)(b).
18 Ie under the Education Act 2002 s 27 (power of governing body to provide community facilities etc): see PARA 174.
19 As to the meaning of 'premises' see PARA 62 note 19 (definition applied by the Education Act 2002 s 212(2), (3)).
20 Education Act 2002 s 35(5)(c). As to the governing bodies of maintained schools in Wales see PARA 195.
21 Education Act 2002 s 35(5)(d) (amended by SI 2010/1158). As to the discharge by an education action forum of any function of a governing body under the Education Act 2002 s 35, see the School Standards and Framework Act 1998 s 12(4); and PARA 344.
22 Ie by virtue of any suspension under the School Standards and Framework Act 1998 Sch 15 (see PARAS 325–327), the Education and Inspections Act 2006 s 66 (see PARA 1214) or the School Standards and Organisation (Wales) Act 2013 s 8 (see PARA 1233): see the Education Act 2002 s 35(7) (amended by the Education Act 2011 s 19(1); and the School Standards and Organisation (Wales) Act 2013 Sch 5 para 6(1), (3)).
23 Education Act 2002 s 35(7)(a).
24 Ie the Education Act 2002 Sch 2 Pt 1 paras 1–4: see PARA 293.
25 See the Education Act 2002 s 35(7)(b).
26 As to the meaning of 'maintained school' see PARA 103 note 3.
27 As to the publication of guidance see the Education Act 1996 s 571 (applied by the Education Act 2002 s 212(2), (3)); and PARA 60.
28 See the Education Act 2002 s 35(8)(b) (amended by SI 2010/1158; prospectively repealed by the Deregulation Act 2015 Sch 16 para 4(1), (2)). At the date at which this volume states the law no day had been appointed for the purpose of this repeal. See also PARA 268.
29 Ie under the Staffing of Maintained Schools (Wales) Regulations 2006, SI 2006/873, and any other enactment.
30 As to the meaning of 'pupil' see PARA 20 note 4 (definition applied by the Education Act 2002 s 212(2), (3); Interpretation Act 1978 s 11).
31 Staffing of Maintained Schools (Wales) Regulations 2006, SI 2006/873, reg 4(1) (amended by SI 2007/944; SI 2010/1142). As to the application of the Staffing of Maintained Schools (Wales) Regulations 2006, SI 2006/873, reg 4(1), with modifications, in relation to pupil referral units in Wales see the Education (Pupil Referral Units) (Application of Enactments) (Wales) Regulations 2007, SI 2007/1069, reg 3, Sch 1 Pt 2 para 14 (amended by SI 2014/1609). As to pupil referral units see PARA 427 et seq.

293. Staffing of schools on suspension of delegated budget. If at any time a community, voluntary controlled or a community special school[1] or a maintained nursery school[2] does not have a delegated budget[3], the usual provisions relating to the staffing at such schools[4] do not apply[5] and the following provisions apply instead[6].

In such circumstances, the arrangements for the staffing of the school are to be determined by the local authority[7], and the authority may appoint, suspend and dismiss teachers and other staff at the school as it thinks fit[8]. The authority must, in connection with the exercise of these functions[9], consult the governing body[10] to such extent as it thinks fit[11].

1 As to the meaning of references to a community or voluntary school or a community special school see PARA 106.
2 See the Education Act 2002 s 35(1). As to the meaning of 'maintained nursery school' see PARA 103 note 3.
3 Ie by virtue of any suspension under the School Standards and Framework Act 1998 Sch 15 (see PARAS 325–327), the Education and Inspections Act 2006 s 66 (see PARA 1214) or the School Standards and Organisation (Wales) Act 2013 s 8 (see PARA 1233): see the Education Act 2002 s 35(7) (amended by the Education Act 2011 s 19(1); and the School Standards and Organisation (Wales) Act 2013 Sch 5 para 6(1), (3)). As to the meaning of references to a school having a delegated budget see PARA 279 note 3.
4 Ie regulations made under the Education Act 2002 s 35(4). As to such regulations see PARA 292.
5 See the Education Act 2002 s 35(7)(a).
6 See the Education Act 2002 s 35(7)(b). Where a proposed community, voluntary controlled, community special or maintained nursery school does not have a delegated budget, the provisions of Sch 2 Pt 1 (paras 1–4) (see the text to notes 7–11) apply with modifications: see the Staffing of Maintained Schools (Wales) Regulations 2006, SI 2006/873, regs 35, 38.
7 Education Act 2002 Sch 2 para 1 (amended by SI 2010/1158). As to the meaning of 'local authority' see PARA 25 (definition applied by the Education Act 2002 s 212(1) (amended by SI 2010/1158)). As to the application of the Education Act 2002 Sch 2 paras 1–3 to pupil referral units (see PARA 427 et seq) see the Education (Pupil Referral Units) (Application of Enactments) (England) Regulations 2007, SI 2007/2979, Sch 1 Pt 1 para 20A (added by SI 2012/3158).
8 Education Act 2002 Sch 2 para 2. In relation to teachers at a voluntary controlled school who are reserved teachers within the meaning of the School Standards and Framework Act 1998 s 58 (appointment and dismissal of certain teachers at schools with a religious character: see PARA 302), the Education Act 2002 Sch 2 para 2 has effect subject to the provisions of the School Standards and Framework Act 1998 s 58: Education Act 2002 Sch 2 para 4.
9 As to the meaning of 'functions' see PARA 18 note 5 (definition applied by the Education Act 2002 s 212(2), (3)).
10 As to the governing bodies of maintained schools in Wales see PARA 195.
11 Education Act 2002 Sch 2 para 3. As to the exercise of the duty to consult see JUDICIAL REVIEW vol 61 (2010) PARA 627.

(B) Foundation, Voluntary Aided and Foundation Special Schools

294. Staffing of schools having a delegated budget. Except as provided by regulations[1], any teacher[2] or other member of staff[3] who is appointed to work under a contract of employment[4] at a foundation school[5], a voluntary aided school[6] or a foundation special school[7] in Wales is to be employed by the governing body of the school[8]. The teaching staff of any such school must include a person appointed as head teacher[9] or a person appointed to carry out the functions[10] of the head teacher of the school pending the appointment of a head teacher[11] or in the absence of the head teacher[12]. Regulations may make further provision with respect to the staffing of such schools[13] and may, in particular:

(1)   make provision with respect to the appointment, discipline, suspension and dismissal of teachers and other staff[14];

(2)   make provision with respect to the appointment of teachers and other staff to work at a school otherwise than under a contract of employment[15];

(3)   make provision with respect to staff employed, or engaged otherwise than under a contract of employment, wholly or partly for the purposes of the provision of facilities and services[16] or any other activities which are not school activities but are carried on the school premises[17] under the management or control of the governing body[18];

(4)   enable teachers and other staff to be employed by the local authority[19] in prescribed[20] cases[21]; and

(5)   confer functions on local authorities, governing bodies and head teachers[22].

In discharging any function conferred by such regulations, a local authority or the governing body or head teacher of a maintained school[23] must have regard to any guidance given from time to time by the Welsh Ministers[24].

A governing body and a local authority must exercise their respective functions[25] with a view to ensuring that there is employed, or engaged otherwise than under contracts of employment, a staff suitable and sufficient in numbers for the purpose of securing the provision of education appropriate to the ages, abilities, aptitudes and needs of the pupils[26] having regard to any arrangements for the utilisation of the services of staff employed or engaged otherwise than at the school in question[27].

1   Ie regulations under the Education Act 2002 s 36(4): see the text to note 13. 'Regulations' means -regulations made under the Education Act 2002 by the Welsh Ministers: see s 212(1). The functions under the Education Act 2002 s 36 in relation to Wales were originally vested in the National Assembly for Wales and are now exercisable by the Welsh Ministers by virtue of the Government of Wales Act 2006 s 162(1), Sch 11 paras 30, 32. As to the Welsh Ministers see PARA 59. As to the meaning of 'Wales' see PARA 7 note 3.

     As to the regulations made under the Education Act 2002 s 36 see the Staffing of Maintained Schools (Wales) Regulations 2006, SI 2006/873; and see below and also the text to notes 25–27.

     As to manner of appointment see regs 20A, 21, 23, 26A (regs 20A, 26A added by SI 2007/944; and amended by SI 2009/2544; and the Staffing of Maintained Schools (Wales) Regulations 2006, SI 2006/873, reg 21 amended by SI 2007/944; and SI 2010/1142). As to the appointment of head teachers and deputy head teachers see the Staffing of Maintained Schools (Wales) Regulations 2006, SI 2006/873, regs 24, 34 (reg 24 amended by SI 2009/3161; and SI 2014/1609; and the Staffing of Maintained Schools (Wales) Regulations 2006, SI 2006/873, reg 34 amended by SI 2007/944; SI 20093161; and SI 2010/1142). As to appointment of head teachers for schools of Roman Catholic religious orders see the Staffing of Maintained Schools (Wales) Regulations 2006, SI 2006/873, reg 33 (amended by SI 2007/944). As to appointment of other teachers see the Staffing of Maintained Schools (Wales) Regulations 2006, SI 2006/873, regs 5(3), 26 (amended by SI 2007/944; and SI 2010/1142). As appointment of support staff see the Staffing of Maintained Schools (Wales) Regulations 2006, SI 2006/873, regs 20, 27. As to supply staff see regs 20, 24A (added by SI 2007/944; and amended by SI 2009/2544). As to conduct, discipline and capability of staff see the Staffing of Maintained Schools (Wales) Regulations 2006, SI 2006/873, reg 7 (amended by SI 2014/1609). As to performance of the head teacher see the Staffing of Maintained Schools (Wales) Regulations 2006, SI 2006/873, regs 5A, 6 (reg 5A added by SI 2009/2708). As to suspension and dismissal of staff see the Staffing of Maintained Schools (Wales) Regulations 2006, SI 2006/873, regs 28–32 (reg 30 amended by SI 2010/1142).

2   As to the appointment of teaching staff see note 1.

3   As to the appointment of support staff see note 1.

4   As to the meaning of 'contract of employment' see PARA 268 note 3.

5   See the Education Act 2002 s 36(1)(a). As to the meaning of references to a foundation school see PARA 106.

6   See the Education Act 2002 s 36(1)(b). As to the meaning of references to a voluntary school see PARA 106.

7   See the Education Act 2002 s 36(1)(c). As to the meaning of references to a foundation special school see PARA 106.

8   Education Act 2002 s 36(2). As to the governing bodies of maintained schools in Wales see PARA 195. As to the discharge by an education action forum of any function of a governing body under s 36 see the School Standards and Framework Act 1998 s 12(4); and PARA 344.

9   Education Act 2002 s 36(3)(a). As to the meaning of 'head teacher' see PARA 86 note 4 (definition applied by s 212(2), (3)). As to the appointment of head teachers see note 1.

10   As to the meaning of 'functions' see PARA 18 note 5 (definition applied by the Education Act 2002 s 212(2), (3)).

11   Education Act 2002 s 36(3)(b)(i).

12   Education Act 2002 s 36(3)(b)(ii). As to the appointment of deputy head teachers see note 1.

13   Education Act 2002 s 36(4). Regulations under s 36(4) have effect subject to the School Standards and Framework Act 1998 s 58 (appointment and dismissal of certain teachers at schools with a religious character: see PARA 302): Education Act 2002 s 36(6). If at any time a school does not have a delegated budget regulations under s 36(4) have effect subject to the provisions of Sch 2 Pt 2 (paras 5–10): see s 36(7); and PARA 295.

14   Education Act 2002 s 36(5)(a). As to the discipline, suspension and dismissal of teachers and other staff see note 1.

15   Education Act 2002 s 36(5)(b).

16   Ie under the Education Act 2002 s 27 (power of governing body to provide community facilities etc): see PARA 174.

17   As to the meaning of 'premises' see PARA 62 note 19 (definition applied by the Education Act 2002 s 212(2), (3)).

18   Education Act 2002 s 36(5)(c).

19   As to the meaning of 'local authority' see PARA 25 (definition applied by the Education Act 2002 s 212(1) (amended by SI 2010/1158)).

20   Ie prescribed by the regulations: see the Education Act 2002 s 212(1).

21   Education Act 2002 s 36(5)(d) (amended by SI 2010/1158).

22   Education Act 2002 s 36(5)(e) (amended by SI 2010/1158).

23   As to the meaning of 'maintained school' see PARA 103 note 3.

24   Education Act 2002 s 36(8)(b) (amended by SI 2010/1158). As to the publication of guidance see the Education Act 1996 s 571 (applied by the Education Act 2002 s 212(2), (3)); and PARA 60.

25   Ie under the Staffing of Maintained Schools (Wales) Regulations 2006, SI 2006/873, and any other enactment.

26   As to the meaning of 'pupil' see PARA 20 note 4 (definition applied by the Education Act 2002 s 212(2), (3); Interpretation Act 1978 s 11).

27   Staffing of Maintained Schools (Wales) Regulations 2006, SI 2006/873, reg 4(1) (amended by SI 2007/944; and SI 2010/1142).

295. Staffing of school on suspension of delegated budget. If at any time a foundation, voluntary aided or foundation special school[1] does not have a delegated budget[2] the usual provisions relating to the staffing at such schools[3] have effect subject to the following provisions[4].

In such circumstances, the arrangements for the staffing of the school are determined by the local authority[5]. Except with the consent of the authority, the governing body[6] must not[7] appoint any teacher to work at the school[8], or dismiss any teacher at the school[9]. The authority may give the governing body directions[10]: (1) as to the educational qualifications of the teachers to be appointed for giving secular education[11]; or (2) requiring it to dismiss any teacher at the school[12]; but the authority must not give any directions under head (1) above except after consulting the governing body[13]. The authority may also give directions to the governing body as to the number and conditions of service of persons employed at the school for the purposes of the care and maintenance of the school premises[14].

1   See the Education Act 2002 s 36(1). As to the meaning of references to a foundation, voluntary or foundation special school see PARA 106.

2 Ie by virtue of any suspension under the School Standards and Framework Act 1998 Sch 15 (see PARAS 325–327), the Education and Inspections Act 2006 s 66 (see PARA 1214) or the School Standards and Organisation (Wales) Act 2013 s 8 (see PARA 1233). As to the meaning of 'delegated budget' see PARA 294.

3 Ie regulations made under the Education Act 2002 s 36(4): see PARA 280. As to such regulations see PARA 294.

4 Education Act 2002 s 36(7) (amended by the Education Act 2011 s 19(2); and the School Standards and Organisation (Wales) Act 2013 Sch 5 para 6(1), (4)). Where a proposed school which will be a foundation, voluntary aided or foundation special school does not have a delegated budget, the Education Act 2002 Sch 2 Pt 2 (paras 5–11) (see the text to notes 5–14) applies with modifications: see the Staffing of Maintained Schools (Wales) Regulations 2006, SI 2006/873, regs 35, 39.

5 Education Act 2002 Sch 2 para 5 (amended by SI 2010/1158). As to the meaning of 'local authority' see PARA 25 (definition applied by the Education Act 2002 s 212(1) (amended by SI 2010/1158)).

6 As to the governing bodies of maintained schools in Wales see PARA 195. As to the discharge by an education action forum of any function of a governing body under the Education Act 2002 Sch 2 see the School Standards and Framework Act 1998 s 12; and PARA 344.

7 Education Act 2002 Sch 2 para 6. Schedule 2 para 6 has effect subject to the School Standards and Framework Act 1998 s 58 (see PARA 302): see the Education Act 2002 Sch 2 para 10.

8 Education Act 2002 Sch 2 para 6(a).

9 Education Act 2002 Sch 2 para 6(b).

10 As to directions see the Education Act 1996 s 570 (applied by the Education Act 2002 s 212(2), (3)); and PARA 75.

11 Education Act 2002 Sch 2 para 7(a).

12 Education Act 2002 Sch 2 para 7(b). Where a teacher in a foundation, voluntary aided or foundation special school is dismissed by the governing body of the school in pursuance of a requirement of the local authority under Sch 2 para 7, the Employment Rights Act 1996 Pt X (ss 94–134A) has effect (with modifications) in relation to the dismissal: see the Employment Rights Act 1996 s 134(1); and PARA 300.

13 Education Act 2002 Sch 2 para 7. Schedule 2 para 7 has effect subject to the School Standards and Framework Act 1998 s 58 (see PARA 302): see the Education Act 2002 Sch 2 para 10. As to the exercise of the duty to consult see JUDICIAL REVIEW vol 61 (2010) PARA 627.

14 Education Act 2002 Sch 2 para 8 (and see also Sch 2 para 11 (added by the Apprenticeships, Skills, Children and Learning Act 2009 s 237(7)). As to the meaning of 'premises' see PARA 62 note 19 (definition applied by the Education Act 2002 s 212(2), (3)). Where the trust deed relating to the school provides for a person other than the governing body to be entitled to control the occupation and use of the school premises to any extent, then, if and to the extent that (disregarding any transfer of control authorised by regulations under s 31: see PARA 180) the use of those premises is or would be under the control of any such person, the reference in Sch 2 para 8 to the governing body must be read as a reference to that person: Sch 2 para 9. As to the meaning of 'trust deed' see PARA 108 note 6 (definition applied by s 212(2), (3)). As to the meaning of 'person' see PARA 7 note 6.

(C) New Maintained Schools

296. Staffing of new schools. The statutory provisions relating to school staffing[1] apply, with modifications[2], in relation to (1) a proposed community, voluntary controlled or community special school[3] or maintained nursery school[4] in Wales[5] which has a delegated budget[6] and without a delegated budget[7]; and (2) a proposed foundation, voluntary aided or foundation special school[8] in Wales which has a delegated budget[9] and without a delegated budget[10].

1 Ie the Education Act 2002 Sch 2 or the Staffing of Maintained Schools (Wales) Regulations 2006, SI 2006/873.

2 See the Staffing of Maintained Schools (Wales) Regulations 2006, SI 2006/873, reg 35.

3 As to the meaning of references to a community, voluntary or community special school see PARA 106.

4 As to the meaning of 'maintained nursery school' see PARA 103 note 3.

5   See the Staffing of Maintained Schools (Wales) Regulations 2006, SI 2006/873, reg 1(2). As to the meaning of 'Wales' see PARA 7 note 3.

6   Where a proposed school which will be a community, voluntary controlled, community special or maintained nursery school has a delegated budget, the Staffing of Maintained Schools (Wales) Regulations 2006, SI 2006/873, regs 4–7, 10–19 (see PARA 292) apply: reg 36. As to the meaning of 'delegated budget' see PARA 279 note 3.

7   Where a proposed school which will be a community, voluntary controlled, community special or maintained nursery school does not have a delegated budget, the Education Act 2002 Sch 2 Pt 1 (paras 1–4) (see PARA 293) applies: Staffing of Maintained Schools (Wales) Regulations 2006, SI 2006/873, reg 38.

8   As to the meaning of references to a foundation, voluntary school or foundation special school see PARA 106.

9   Where a proposed school which will be a foundation, voluntary aided or foundation special school has a delegated budget, the Staffing of Maintained Schools (Wales) Regulations 2006, SI 2006/873, regs 4–7, 21–34 (see PARA 294) apply: reg 37.

10   Where a proposed school which will be a foundation, voluntary aided or foundation special school does not have a delegated budget, the Education Act 2002 Sch 2 Pt 2 (paras 5–10) (see PARA 295) applies: Staffing of Maintained Schools (Wales) Regulations 2006, SI 2006/873, reg 39.

C. STAFFING OF ACADEMIES

297. Staffing of academies. Staffing of academies is dealt with elsewhere in this title[1].

1   See PARA 358.

D. APPLICATION OF EMPLOYMENT LAW

298. Application of employment law during financial delegation. The Secretary of State[1] may by order[2] make such modifications[3] in any enactment relating to employment[4], and in particular in any enactment:

(1)   conferring powers or imposing duties on employers[5];

(2)   conferring rights on employees[6]; or

(3)   otherwise regulating the relations between employers and employees[7],

as he considers necessary or expedient in consequence of the provisions of the Education Act 2002[8] relating to the staffing of schools[9].

Before making any such order the Secretary of State must consult[10] such associations of local authorities[11], such bodies representing the interests of governors of foundation or voluntary schools[12], and such organisations representing staff in maintained schools[13], as appear to him to be concerned[14].

1   As to the Secretary of State see PARA 58.

2   As to the orders made see the Education (Modification of Enactments Relating to Employment) (England) Order 2003, SI 2003/1964 (amended by SI 2004/2325); and the Education (Modification of Enactments Relating to Employment) (Wales) Order 2006, SI 2006/1073. In *Green v Governing Body of Victoria Road Primary School* [2004] EWCA Civ 11, [2004] 2 All ER 763, [2004] ICR 684, it was held that, by virtue of the Education (Modification of Enactments Relating to Employment) Order 1999, SI 1999/2256, arts 3(1)(a), 6 (revoked), the governing body of a school was to be treated as the appropriate respondent in an unfair dismissal claim brought in an employment tribunal (held under legislation now replaced but with no material difference between the provisions). See also *Butt v Bradford Metropolitan District Council* (2010) UKEAT/0210/10/ZT, [2010] All ER (D) 92 (Oct); *Jones v Neath Port Talbot County Borough Council* [2011] EWCA Civ 92, [2011] LGR 630, [2011] ICR 1415. In *Murphy v Slough Borough Council* [2005] EWCA Civ 122, [2005] ICR 721, [2005] IRLR 382, it was held that if a complaint is made under the Disability Discrimination Act 1995 (now the Equality Act 2010) regarding the exercise of an employment power retained by the local authority, then the authority should be named as a respondent.

3	As to the meaning of 'modifications' see PARA 21 note 15 (definition applied by the School Standards and Framework Act 1998 s 142(8)).

4	'Employment' means employment under a contract of employment, and 'employed' must be construed accordingly: School Standards and Framework Act 1998 s 142(1). 'Contract of employment' has the same meaning as in the Employment Rights Act 1996 (see EMPLOYMENT vol 39 (2014) PARA 2): School Standards and Framework Act 1998 s 142(1).

5	School Standards and Framework Act 1998 s 81(1)(a). 'Employer' has the same meaning as in the Employment Rights Act 1996 (see EMPLOYMENT vol 39 (2014) PARA 2): School Standards and Framework Act 1998 s 142(1).

6	School Standards and Framework Act 1998 s 81(1)(b). 'Employee' has the same meaning as in the Employment Rights Act 1996 (see EMPLOYMENT vol 39 (2014) PARA 2): School Standards and Framework Act 1998 s 142(1).

7	School Standards and Framework Act 1998 s 81(1)(c).

8	Ie the Education Act 2002 s 35 (see PARA 268), s 36 (see PARA 280) and s 37 (see PARA 299), or of regulations made under those sections.

9	School Standards and Framework Act 1998 s 81(1) (amended by the Education Act 2002 s 215(1), Sch 21 para 107).

10	As to the exercise of the duty to consult see JUDICIAL REVIEW vol 61 (2010) PARA 627.

11	School Standards and Framework Act 1998 s 81(2)(a). As to the meaning of 'local authority' see PARA 25 (definition applied by s 142(8)).

12	School Standards and Framework Act 1998 s 81(2)(b). As to the meaning of references to a foundation or voluntary school see PARA 106. As to the governing bodies of maintained schools in England see PARA 150 et seq; and in Wales see PARA 195.

13	School Standards and Framework Act 1998 s 81(2)(c). As to the meaning of 'maintained school' see PARA 99.

14	School Standards and Framework Act 1998 s 81(2).

299. Payments in respect of dismissal etc. It is for the governing body of a maintained school[1] to determine: (1) whether any payment should be made by the local authority[2] in respect of the dismissal[3], or for the purpose of securing the resignation, of any member of the staff of the school[4]; and (2) the amount of any such payment[5]. The local authority: (a) must take such steps as may be required for giving effect to any such determination of the governing body[6]; and (b) must not make, or agree to make, a payment[7] except in accordance with such a determination[8].

Costs incurred by the local authority in respect of any premature retirement of a member of the staff of a maintained school must be met from the school's budget share[9] for one or more funding periods[10] except in so far as the authority agrees with the governing body in writing[11], whether before or after the retirement occurs, that they will not be so met[12]. Costs incurred by the local authority in respect of the dismissal, or for the purpose of securing the resignation, of any member of the staff of a maintained school must not be met from the school's budget share for any financial year[13] except in so far as the authority has good reason for deducting those costs, or any part of those costs, from that share[14]. However, where a local authority incurs costs: (i) in respect of any premature retirement of any member of the staff of a maintained school who is employed for community purposes[15]; or (ii) in respect of the dismissal, or for the purpose of securing the resignation, of any member of the staff of a maintained school who is employed for those purposes[16], it must recover those costs from the governing body except in so far as the authority agrees with the governing body in writing, whether before or after the retirement, dismissal or resignation occurs, that they will not be so recoverable[17].

1	As to the governing bodies of maintained schools in England see PARA 150 et seq; and in Wales see PARA 195. As to the meaning of 'maintained school' see PARA 103 note 3.

2	As to the meaning of 'local authority' see PARA 25 (definition applied by the Education Act 2002 s 212(1) (amended by SI 2010/1158)).

3　As to the dismissal of persons employed or engaged to work at schools see PARAS 277, 289, 292, 294.

4　Education Act 2002 s 37(1)(a) (amended by SI 2010/1158). The Education Act 2002 s 37(1) does not apply in relation to a payment which the local authority is required to make (s 37(2) (amended by SI 2010/1158)): (1) by virtue of any contract other than one made in contemplation of the impending dismissal or resignation of the member of staff concerned (Education Act 2002 s 37(2)(a)); or (2) under any statutory provision (s 37(2)(b)). As to the meaning of 'statutory provision' see PARA 168 note 2. The provisions of s 37(1)–(6) do not apply to a maintained school at any time when the school does not have a delegated budget by virtue of any suspension under the School Standards and Framework Act 1998 Sch 15 (see PARAS 325–327) or the School Standards and Organisation (Wales) Act 2013 s 8 (see PARA 1233): Education Act 2002 s 37(11) (amended by the School Standards and Organisation (Wales) Act 2013 Sch 5 para 6(1), (5)). As to the meaning of references to 'school having a delegated budget' see PARA 279 note 3.

　　As to the discharge by an education action forum of any function of a governing body under the Education Act 2002 s 37 see the School Standards and Framework Act 1998 s 12(4); and PARA 344.

　　As to the application of the Education Act 2002 s 37(1)–(7B), (9), (11), (12) to pupil referral units (see PARA 427 et seq) see the Education (Pupil Referral Units) (Application of Enactments) (England) Regulations 2007, SI 2007/2979, Sch 1 Pt 1 para 17B (added by SI 2012/3158).

5　Education Act 2002 s 37(1)(b).

6　Education Act 2002 s 37(3)(a) (s 37(3) amended by SI 2010/1158).

7　Ie a payment in relation to which the Education Act 2002 s 37(1) applies: see the text to notes 1–5.

8　Education Act 2002 s 37(3)(b) (as amended: see note 6).

9　As to the meaning of 'budget share' see PARA 315.

10　As to the meaning of 'funding period' see PARA 315 note 3 (definition applied by the Education Act 2002 s 37(12) (substituted by the Education Act 2005 s 117, Sch 18 para 14(1), (4))).

11　As to the meaning of 'writing' see PARA 76 note 8.

12　Education Act 2002 s 37(4) (amended by the Education Act 2005 Sch 18 para 14(1), (2); SI 2010/1158). This provision is expressed to be subject to the Education Act 2002 s 37(7) (see the text and notes 15–17): see s 37(4).

13　As to the meaning of 'financial year' see PARA 81 note 9 (definition applied by the Education Act 2002 s 212(2), (3)).

14　Education Act 2002 s 37(5) (amended by the Education Act 2005 Sch 18 para 14(1), (3); SI 2010/1158). This provision is expressed to be subject to the Education Act 2002 s 37(7) (see the text and notes 15–17): see s 37(5). The fact that the authority has a policy precluding dismissal of its employees by reason of redundancy is not to be regarded as a good reason for the purposes of s 37(5); and for these purposes the reference to dismissal by reason of redundancy must be read in accordance with the Employment Rights Act 1996 s 139 (see EMPLOYMENT vol 41 (2014) PARA 870): Education Act 2002 s 37(6).

15　Education Act 2002 s 37(7)(a). 'Community purposes' means the purposes of the provision of facilities or services under s 27 (see PARAS 174, 208): s 37(12) (as substituted: see note 10).

16　Education Act 2002 s 37(7)(b).

17　Education Act 2002 s 37(7) (amended by SI 2010/1158). Any amount payable by virtue of the Education Act 2002 s 37 by the governing body of a maintained school in England to the local authority may be met by the governing body out of the school's budget share for any funding period if and to the extent that it is satisfied that meeting the amount out of the school's budget share will not to a significant extent interfere with the performance of any duty imposed on the governing body by s 21(2) (see PARA 168) or by any other provision of the Education Acts: s 37(7A), (7B) (added by the Education Act 2011 s 47(1), 2)). As to the meaning of 'the Education Acts' see PARA 1 note 13 (definition applied by the Education Act 2002 s 212(2), (3). Any amount payable by virtue of the Education Act 2002 s 37(7) by the governing body of a maintained school in Wales to the local authority must not be met by the governing body out of the school's budget share for any funding period: s 37(8) (amended by the Education Act 2005 Sch 18 para 14(1), (3); SI 2010/1158; and the Education Act 2011 s 47(1), (3)). Where a person is employed partly for community purposes and partly for other purposes, any payment or costs in respect of that person is to be apportioned between the two purposes; and the Education Act 2002 s 37(1)–(8) apply separately to each part of the payment or costs: s 37(9). Regulations made under the Education Act 2002 by the Secretary of State (in relation to England) or by the Welsh Ministers (in relation to Wales) may make provision with respect to the recovery from governing bodies of amounts payable by virtue of s 37(7): see ss 37(10), 212(1). At the date at which this volume states the law, no such regulations had been made. As to the Secretary of

State see PARA 58. The functions under the Education Act 2002 s 37 in relation to Wales were originally vested in the National Assembly for Wales and are now exercisable by the Welsh Ministers by virtue of the Government of Wales Act 2006 s 162(1), Sch 11 paras 30, 32. As to the Welsh Ministers see PARA 59. As to the meanings of 'England' and 'Wales' see PARA 7 note 3.

300. Unfair dismissal of teachers at foundation, voluntary aided or foundation special schools. Where a teacher in a foundation, voluntary aided or foundation special school[1] is dismissed by the governing body[2] in pursuance of a requirement of the local authority[3], Part X of the Employment Rights Act 1996[4] has effect in relation to the dismissal[5] as if: (1) the local authority had at all times been the teacher's employer[6]; (2) the local authority had dismissed him[7]; and (3) the reason or principal reason for which it dismissed him had been the reason or principal reason for which it required his dismissal[8].

1 As to foundation, voluntary aided and foundation special schools see PARA 106.
2 As to the governing bodies of maintained schools in England see PARA 150 et seq; and in Wales see PARA 195.
3 Ie under the Education Act 2002 Sch 2 para 7 (see, in relation to England, PARA 290; and, in relation to Wales, PARA 295). As to the meaning of 'local authority' see PARA 25 (definition applied by the Employment Rights Act 1996 s 134(3) (added by SI 2010/1158)).
4 Ie the Employment Rights Act 1996 Pt X (ss 94–134A): see EMPLOYMENT vol 41 (2014) PARA 757 et seq.
5 Employment Rights Act 1996 s 134(1) (amended by the School Standards and Framework Act 1998 s 140(1), Sch 30 para 55; the Education Act 2002 Sch 21 para 30; and SI 2010/1158). For the purpose of a complaint under the Employment Rights Act 1996 s 111 (see EMPLOYMENT vol 41 (2014) PARA 804) as it has effect by virtue of s 134(1), modifications are made to s 117(4)(a) (provisions relating to the disapplication of an additional award of compensation: see EMPLOYMENT vol 41 (2014) PARA 818) and s 123(5) (determination of loss sustained by a complainant attributable to action taken by an employer: see EMPLOYMENT vol 41 (2014) PARA 757): see s 134(2) (amended by SI 2010/1158).
6 Employment Rights Act 1996 s 134(1)(a) (amended by SI 2010/1158). As to the meaning of 'employer' see the Employment Rights Act 1996 s 230(4); and EMPLOYMENT vol 39 (2014) PARA 2.
7 Employment Rights Act 1996 s 134(1)(b) (amended by SI 2010/1158).
8 Employment Rights Act 1996 s 134(1)(c).

301. Avoidance of certain terms in a contract made with an employee. In so far as contract made after 20 November 1987: (1) for purposes connected with a local authority's education functions[1], between the authority and a person employed[2] by the authority[3]; or (2) between a governing body[4] of a foundation, voluntary aided or foundation special school[5] and a person employed by the governing body[6], other than a contract made in contemplation of the employee's[7] pending dismissal by reason of redundancy[8], provides that the employee is not to be dismissed by reason of redundancy or that, if he is so dismissed, he is to be paid a sum in excess of the sum which the employer[9] is liable to pay him under the Employment Rights Act 1996[10], that contract is void and of no effect[11].

1 As to the meanings of 'local authority' and 'education functions' see PARA 24 (definitions applied by the Education Reform Act 1988 s 235(7)).
2 'Employed' means employed under a contract of employment: Education Reform Act 1988 s 235(1). 'Contract of employment' has the same meaning as in the Employment Rights Act 1996 (see EMPLOYMENT vol 39 (2014) PARA 2): Education Reform Act 1988 s 235(1) (definition amended by the Employment Rights Act 1996 s 240, Sch 1 para 37(1), (5)(a)).
3 Education Reform Act 1988 s 221(1)(a) (s 221(1) substituted SI 2010/1158).
4 'Governing body', in relation to an institution, includes a body corporate established for the purpose of conducting that institution: Education Reform Act 1988 s 221(3). As to the governing bodies of maintained schools in England see PARA 150 et seq; and in Wales see PARA 195.
5 As to foundation, voluntary and foundation special schools see PARA 106.

6   Education Reform Act 1988 s 221(1)(b) (as substituted: see note 3).

7   'Employee' has the same meaning as in the Employment Rights Act 1996 (see EMPLOYMENT vol 39 (2014) PARA 2): Education Reform Act 1988 s 235(1) (definition amended by the Employment Rights Act 1996 s 240, Sch 1 para 37).

8   Education Reform Act 1988 s 221(1) (as substituted: see note 3). References to dismissal by reason of redundancy must be read in accordance with the Employment Rights Act 1996 s 139 (see EMPLOYMENT vol 41 (2014) PARA 870): Education Reform Act 1988 s 235(2)(f) (amended by the Employment Rights Act 1996 s 240, Sch 1 para 37(1), (5)(b)).

9   'Employer' has the same meaning as in the Employment Rights Act 1996 (see EMPLOYMENT vol 39 (2014) PARA 2): Education Reform Act 1988 s 235(1) (definition amended by the Employment Rights Act 1996 s 240, Sch 1 para 37).

10 Ie under the Employment Rights Act 1996 s 135 (right to redundancy payment): see EMPLOYMENT vol 41 (2014) PARA 836.

11 Education Reform Act 1988 s 221(2) (amended by the Employment Rights Act 1996 s 240, Sch 1 para 37(1), (4)). As to void contracts see CONTRACT vol 22 (2012) PARAS 424 et seq, 450, 459 et seq.

E. APPOINTMENT AND DISMISSAL OF TEACHERS OF RELIGIOUS EDUCATION

302. Appointment and dismissal of certain teachers at schools with a religious character. In relation to a foundation or voluntary controlled school which has a religious character[1], where the number of teachers at the school is more than two, the teachers must include persons[2]: (1) who are selected for their fitness and competence to give religious education as is required by arrangements[3] for religious education in accordance with the school's trust deed[4] or with the tenets of the school's specified religion or religious denomination[5]; and (2) who are specifically appointed to do so[6]. The number of reserved teachers[7] in such a school must not exceed one-fifth of the total number of teachers, including the head teacher[8]. Where the appropriate body[9] proposes to appoint a person to be a reserved teacher in such a school, that body must consult the foundation governors[10], and must not so appoint that person unless the foundation governors are satisfied as to his fitness and competence to give such religious education as is mentioned in head (1) above[11]. If the foundation governors of such a school consider that a reserved teacher has failed to give such religious education efficiently and suitably, they may[12]: (a) in the case of a teacher who is an employee[13], require the appropriate body to dismiss him from employment[14] as a reserved teacher at the school[15]; and (b) in the case of a teacher who is engaged otherwise than under a contract of employment[16], require the governing body to terminate his engagement[17].

In relation to a voluntary aided school[18], if a teacher appointed to give religious education fails to give such education efficiently and suitably, he may be dismissed on that ground by the governing body without the consent of the local authority[19]. However, this does not apply: (i) where the school has a delegated budget[20]; or (ii) to religious education in accordance with an agreed syllabus[21].

1   The School Standards and Framework Act 1998 s 58(2)–(6) (see the text to notes 2–17) applies to a foundation or voluntary controlled school which has a religious character: s 58(1)(a). References in Pt II Ch V (ss 58–63) to a school which has, or does not have, a religious character are to be construed in accordance with s 69(3) (see PARA 914): s 58(1). As to foundation and voluntary controlled schools see PARA 106.

2   School Standards and Framework Act 1998 s 58(2) (amended by the Education Act 2002 s 40, Sch 3 para 6(1), (2)).

3   Ie under the School Standards and Framework Act 1998 Sch 19 para 3(3): see PARA 916.

4   As to the meaning of 'trust deed' see PARA 108 note 6 (definition applied by the School Standards and Framework Act 1998 s 142(8)).

5   School Standards and Framework Act 1998 s 58(2)(a). As to the meaning of 'specified religion or religious denomination' see PARA 146 note 12.

6   School Standards and Framework Act 1998 s 58(2)(b).
7   'Reserved teacher', in relation to a foundation or voluntary controlled school, means a person
    employed or engaged at the school in pursuance of the School Standards and Framework
    Act 1998 s 58(2) (see the text to notes 1–6): s 58(9) (definition amended by the Education
    Act 2002 Sch 3 para 6(1), (6)). As to the meaning of 'employed' see PARA 298 note 4.
8   School Standards and Framework Act 1998 s 58(3) (amended by the Education Act 2002 Sch 3
    para 6(1), (3)). For this purpose, where the total number of teachers is not a multiple of five, it
    must be treated as if it were the next higher multiple of five: School Standards and Framework
    Act 1998 s 58(3) (as so amended). As to the meaning of 'head teacher' see PARA 86 note 4
    (definition applied by s 142(8)).
9   'The appropriate body' means: (1) in relation to a foundation school, the governing body; and
    (2) in relation to a voluntary controlled school, the local authority: School Standards and
    Framework Act 1998 s 58(9) (amended by SI 2010/1158). As to the governing bodies of
    maintained schools in England see PARA 150 et seq; and in Wales see PARA 195. As to the
    meaning of 'local authority' see PARA 25 (definition applied by the School Standards and
    Framework Act 1998 s 142(8)).
10 School Standards and Framework Act 1998 s 58(5)(a). As to the meaning of 'foundation
    governor' see PARA 108 note 6. As to the exercise of the duty to consult see JUDICIAL REVIEW
    vol 61 (2010) PARA 627.
11 School Standards and Framework Act 1998 s 58(5)(b).
12 School Standards and Framework Act 1998 s 58(6).
13 As to the meaning of 'employee' see PARA 298 note 6.
14 As to the meaning of 'employment' see PARA 298 note 4.
15 School Standards and Framework Act 1998 s 58(6)(a) (s 58(6)(a), (b) substituted by the
    Education Act 2002 Sch 3 para 6(1), (5)).
16 As to the meaning of 'contract of employment' see PARA 298 note 4.
17 School Standards and Framework Act 1998 s 58(6)(b) (as substituted: see note 15).
18 The School Standards and Framework Act 1998 s 58(7) (see the text to note 19) applies (subject
    to s 58(8)) (see the text to notes 20–21) to a voluntary aided school which has a religious
    character: s 58(1)(b). As to voluntary aided schools see PARA 106.
19 School Standards and Framework Act 1998 s 58(7) (amended by SI 2010/1158).
20 School Standards and Framework Act 1998 s 58(8)(a). As to the meaning of 'school having a
    delegated budget' see PARA 323.
21 School Standards and Framework Act 1998 s 58(8)(b). As to the meaning of 'agreed syllabus'
    see PARA 910 note 2 (definition applied by s 142(8)).

F. RELIGIOUS OPINIONS OF STAFF

303.   Religious opinions of staff at community, secular foundation or voluntary, or special school.   In relation to: (1) a community school or a community or foundation special school[1]; or (2) a foundation or voluntary school which does not have a religious character[2], no person may be disqualified by reason of his religious opinions, or of his attending or omitting to attend religious worship, from being a teacher at the school[3], or from being employed[4] or engaged for the purposes of the school otherwise than as a teacher[5]. No teacher at the school may be required to give religious education[6]; and no teacher at the school is to receive any less remuneration or be deprived of or disqualified for, any promotion or other advantage: (a) by reason of the fact that he does or does not give religious education[7]; or (b) by reason of his religious opinions or of his attending or omitting to attend religious worship[8].

1   School Standards and Framework Act 1998 s 59(1)(a). As to community schools and
    community and foundation special schools see PARA 106.
2   School Standards and Framework Act 1998 s 59(1)(b). References in Pt II Ch V (ss 58–63) to a
    school which has, or does not have, a religious character are to be construed in accordance with
    s 69(3) (see PARA 914): see s 58(1). As to foundation and voluntary controlled schools see PARA
    106. As to the application of s 59 to staff at foundation or voluntary schools which have a
    religious character see s 60; and PARA 304.
3   School Standards and Framework Act 1998 s 59(2)(a).
4   As to the meaning of 'employed' see PARA 298 note 4.

5   School Standards and Framework Act 1998 s 59(2) (amended by the Education Act 2002 s 40, Sch 3 para 7).

6   School Standards and Framework Act 1998 s 59(3).

7   School Standards and Framework Act 1998 s 59(4)(a).

8   School Standards and Framework Act 1998 s 59(4)(b).

304. Staff at foundation or voluntary school with religious character. The following provisions apply to a foundation and voluntary school[1] which has a religious character[2].

If the school is a foundation or voluntary controlled school, no person may be disqualified by reason of his religious opinions, or of his attending or omitting to attend religious worship, from being a teacher at the school, or from being employed or engaged for the purposes of the school otherwise than as a teacher[3]. No teacher at the school may be required to give religious education[4]; and no teacher at the school is to receive any less remuneration or be deprived of or disqualified for, any promotion or other advantage by reason of the fact that he does or does not give religious education, or by reason of his religious opinions or of his attending or omitting to attend religious worship[5]. These provisions[6] do not apply to a reserved teacher[7] at such a school, and instead heads (1) and (2) below apply in relation to such a teacher as they apply in relation to a teacher at a voluntary aided school[8]. In connection with the appointment of a person to be head teacher[9] of the school, whether foundation or voluntary controlled, regard may be had to that person's ability and fitness to preserve and develop the religious character of the school[10].

If the school is a voluntary aided school:

(1)   preference may be given, in connection with the appointment, remuneration or promotion of teachers at the school, to persons:

     (a)   whose religious opinions are in accordance with the tenets of the religion or religious denomination specified[11] in relation to the school[12];

     (b)   who attend religious worship in accordance with those tenets[13]; or

     (c)   who give, or are willing to give, religious education at the school in accordance with those tenets[14]; and

(2)   regard may be had, in connection with the termination of the employment[15] or engagement of any teacher at the school, to any conduct on his part which is incompatible with the precepts, or with the upholding of the tenets, of the religion or religious denomination so specified[16].

If the school is a voluntary aided school in Wales[17], no person may be disqualified by reason of his religious opinions, or of his attending or omitting to attend religious worship, from being employed or engaged for the purposes of the school otherwise than as a teacher[18].

1   As to foundation and voluntary schools see PARA 106.

2   School Standards and Framework Act 1998 s 60(1). References in Pt II Ch V (ss 58–63) to a school which has, or does not have, a religious character are to be construed in accordance with s 69(3) (see PARA 914): see s 58(1). As to provision made in relation to the employment of teachers at independent schools having a religious character see PARA 378.

     Where immediately before 1 September 1999 (ie the appointed day: see PARA 106 note 3) a teacher at a school which on that day became a school to which s 60 applied enjoyed, by virtue of the Education Act 1996 ss 304, 305 (both repealed) (religious opinions of staff etc), any rights not conferred on him by the School Standards and Framework Act 1998 s 60 as a teacher at a school to which it applies, he continues to enjoy those rights (in addition to those conferred by s 60) until he ceases to be employed as a teacher at the school: s 60(7). As to the meaning of 'employed' see PARA 298 note 4.

3 School Standards and Framework Act 1998 ss 59(2), 60(2) (s 59(2) amended by the Education Act 2002 s 40, Sch 3 para 7). See further PARA 3 text to notes 20, 21.

4 School Standards and Framework Act 1998 ss 59(3), 60(2).

5 School Standards and Framework Act 1998 ss 59(4), 60(2).

6 Ie the School Standards and Framework Act 1998 s 59(2)–(4) applied by s 60(2): see the text to notes 3–5.

7 'Reserved teacher', in relation to a foundation or voluntary controlled school, means a person employed at the school in pursuance of the School Standards and Framework Act 1998 s 58(2) (see PARA 302): s 60(8).

8 School Standards and Framework Act 1998 s 60(3).

9 As to the meaning of 'head teacher' see PARA 86 note 4 (definition applied by the School Standards and Framework Act 1998 s 142(8)).

10 School Standards and Framework Act 1998 s 60(4).

11 Ie under the School Standards and Framework Act 1998 s 69(4): see PARA 914. As to the meaning of 'specified religion or religious denomination' see PARA 146 note 12.

12 School Standards and Framework Act 1998 s 60(5)(a)(i).

13 School Standards and Framework Act 1998 s 60(5)(a)(ii).

14 School Standards and Framework Act 1998 s 60(5)(a)(iii).

15 As to the meaning of 'employment' see PARA 298 note 4.

16 School Standards and Framework Act 1998 s 60(5)(b) (amended by the Education Act 2002 Sch 3 para 8(1), (2)).

17 As to the meaning of 'Wales' see PARA 7 note 3.

18 School Standards and Framework Act 1998 s 60(6) (amended by the Education Act 2002 Sch 3 para 8(1), (3); and the Education and Inspections Act 2006 s 37(2)(b)).

(viii) Maintenance etc of Maintained Schools

A. IN GENERAL

305. Local authorities' duty to maintain schools. A local authority[1] is under a duty to maintain:

(1) any maintained schools[2] which it is required by virtue of the School Standards and Framework Act 1998[3] to maintain[4];

(2) any maintained schools established by it[5];

(3) any maintained schools established in its area otherwise than by it or any other local authority[6]; and

(4) any maintained nursery school[7] established by it[8].

This provision has effect subject to any statutory provision authorising the discontinuance[9] of a maintained school or maintained nursery school[10].

1 As to the meaning of 'local authority' see PARA 25 (definition applied by the School Standards and Framework Act 1998 s 142(8)).

2 As to the meaning of 'maintained school' see PARA 99. As to academies see PARA 345 et seq.

3 Ie by virtue of the School Standards and Framework Act 1998 s 20(4) or (5): see PARA 106.

4 School Standards and Framework Act 1998 s 22(1)(a). As to provision made in the case of community schools, community special schools and maintained nursery schools see PARA 306. As to provision made in the case of foundation schools, voluntary controlled schools and foundation special schools see PARA 310. As to provision made in the case of voluntary aided schools see PARA 311.

5 School Standards and Framework Act 1998 s 22(1)(b) (amended by the Education Act 2002 s 215, Sch 21 para 96(1), (2)(a), Sch 22 Pt 3). As to the establishment of schools see PARA 116 et seq.

6 School Standards and Framework Act 1998 s 22(1)(c) (amended by the Education Act 2002 Sch 21 para 96(1), (2)(b), Sch 22 Pt 3; and SI 2010/1158).

7 As to the meaning of 'maintained nursery school' see PARA 99 note 4.

8 School Standards and Framework Act 1998 s 22(1)(d).

9 As to the meaning of 'discontinue' see PARA 110 note 2.

10 School Standards and Framework Act 1998 s 22(2) (substituted by the Education and Inspections Act 2006 s 30, Sch 3 para 15). As to the discontinuance of schools see PARA 116 et seq.

B. COMMUNITY, COMMUNITY SPECIAL AND MAINTAINED NURSERY SCHOOLS

306.   Local authorities' duty to defray expenses and provide premises. In the case of a community school, a community special school[1] or a maintained nursery school[2], the duty of the local authority[3] to maintain[4] the school includes the duty of defraying all the expenses of maintaining it, and of making premises[5] available to be used for the purposes of the school[6].

1   As to community and community special schools see PARA 106.
2   As to the meaning of 'maintained nursery school' see PARA 99 note 4.
3   As to the meaning of 'local authority' see PARA 25 (definition applied by the School Standards and Framework Act 1998 s 142(8)).
4   'Maintain', in relation to (1) community, community special or maintained nursery schools (ie schools falling within the School Standards and Framework Act 1998 s 22(3)); (2) foundation, voluntary controlled or foundation special schools (ie schools falling within s 22(4), (6): see PARA 310); and (3) voluntary aided schools (ie schools falling within s 22(5), (6): see PARA 311), is to be read in accordance with those provisions: see s 22(8)(b).
5   As to the meaning of 'premises' see PARA 62 note 19 (definition applied by the School Standards and Framework Act 1998 s 142(8)). As to land and premises generally see PARA 1295 et seq.
6   School Standards and Framework Act 1998 s 22(3) (amended by SI 2010/1158).

C. FOUNDATION, VOLUNTARY AND FOUNDATION SPECIAL SCHOOLS

(A) In general

307.   Default powers of central government. Where it appears to the appropriate national authority[1] that a local authority[2] has defaulted in the discharge of its duties relating to the maintenance[3] of a foundation, voluntary or foundation special school[4], the appropriate national authority may[5]:

(1)   direct that any act done by or on behalf of the school's governing body[6] for the purpose of securing the proper maintenance of the school is taken to have been done by or on behalf of the local authority[7]; and

(2)   reimburse to the governing body any sums which in the opinion of the appropriate national authority it has properly expended for that purpose[8].

The amount of any sum so reimbursed is recoverable by the appropriate national authority as a debt due to it from the local authority; and without prejudice to any other method of recovery the whole or any part of any such sum may be deducted from any sums payable to the local authority by the appropriate national authority in pursuance of any regulations[9] relating to the payment of grants[10].

1   Ie the Secretary of State or, in relation to Wales, the Welsh Ministers. The functions of the Secretary of State under the School Standards and Framework Act 1998 Sch 3, so far as exercisable in relation to Wales, were transferred to the National Assembly for Wales (see the National Assembly for Wales (Transfer of Functions) Order 1999, SI 1999/672, art 2, Sch 1) and are now vested in the Welsh Ministers (see the Government of Wales Act 2006 s 162(1), Sch 11 para 30). As to the Secretary of State see PARA 58. As to the Welsh Ministers see PARA 59. As to the meaning of 'Wales' see PARA 7 note 3.
2   As to the meaning of 'local authority' see PARA 25 (definition applied by the School Standards and Framework Act 1998 s 142(8)).
3   As to the meaning of 'maintain' see PARA 306 note 4.

4   As to foundation, voluntary and foundation special schools see PARA 106. As to a local authority's duties in relation to the maintenance of those schools see PARAS 310–311.

5   School Standards and Framework Act 1998 Sch 3 para 10(1) (amended by SI 2010/1158).

6   As to the governing bodies of maintained schools in England see PARA 150 et seq; and in Wales see PARA 195.

7   School Standards and Framework Act 1998 Sch 3 para 10(1)(a) (amended by SI 2010/1158).

8   School Standards and Framework Act 1998 Sch 3 para 10(1)(b).

9   Ie regulations made under the School Standards and Framework Act 1998 by the Secretary of State or, in relation to Wales, the Welsh Ministers: see s 142(1).

10 School Standards and Framework Act 1998 Sch 3 para 10(2) (amended by SI 2010/1158). As to the regulations made in relation to the payment of grants see the Education (Grants in Respect of Voluntary Aided Schools) Regulations 1999, SI 1999/2020; and PARA 312.

308. Endowments. Where any sums accruing in respect of the income of an endowment are required by virtue of the provisions of a trust deed[1] to be applied towards the maintenance of a foundation, voluntary or foundation special school[2], those sums are not payable to the local authority[3] but must be applied by the governing body of the school[4]: (1) in the case of a voluntary aided school, towards the discharge of its obligations[5]; or (2) in the case of any school, in such manner, if any, as may be determined by a scheme for the administration of the endowment made after 1 April 1945[6].

1   As to the meaning of 'trust deed' see PARA 108 note 6 (definition applied by the School Standards and Framework Act 1998 s 142(8)).

2   As to foundation, voluntary and foundation special schools see PARA 106.

3   As to the meaning of 'local authority' see PARA 25 (definition applied by the School Standards and Framework Act 1998 s 142(8)).

4   School Standards and Framework Act 1998 Sch 3 para 11 (amended by SI 2010/1158). As to the governing bodies of maintained schools in England see PARA 150 et seq; and in Wales see PARA 195.

5   School Standards and Framework Act 1998 Sch 3 para 11(a). The obligations of the governing body referred to are those under Sch 3 para 3 (see PARA 311): see Sch 3 para 11.

6   School Standards and Framework Act 1998 Sch 3 para 11(b).

309. Disapplication of restriction on local authority disposals. The prohibition contained in the Local Government Act 1972[1] on local authorities from making disposals of land[2] below market value without the consent of the Secretary of State[3] or, in relation to Wales, the Welsh Ministers[4] does not apply in the case of a disposal[5] to the governing body of a foundation, voluntary or foundation special school[6] or to persons[7] proposing to establish such a school[8].

1   Ie the Local Government Act 1972 s 123(2): see LOCAL GOVERNMENT vol 69 (2009) PARA 515.

2   Ie under the Local Government Act 1972 s 123: see LOCAL GOVERNMENT vol 69 (2009) PARA 515.

3   As to the Secretary of State see PARA 58.

4   The functions of the Secretary of State under the Local Government Act 1972 s 123, so far as exercisable in relation to Wales, were transferred to the National Assembly for Wales (see the National Assembly for Wales (Transfer of Functions) Order 1999, SI 1999/672, art 2, Sch 1) and are now vested in the Welsh Ministers (see the Government of Wales Act 2006 s 162(1), Sch 11 para 30). As to the Welsh Ministers see PARA 59. As to the meaning of 'Wales' see PARA 7 note 3.

5   For the purposes of the School Standards and Framework Act 1998 references to disposing of land include references to: (1) granting or disposing of any interest in land; (2) entering into a contract to dispose of land or to grant or dispose of any such interest; and (3) granting an option to purchase any land or any such interest: s 142(6). As to the meaning of 'land' see PARA 116 note 18 (definition applied by s 142(8)).

6   As to foundation, voluntary and foundation special schools see PARA 106. As to the governing bodies of maintained schools in England see PARA 150 et seq; and in Wales see PARA 195.

7   As to the meaning of 'person' see PARA 7 note 6.

8   School Standards and Framework Act 1998 Sch 3 para 12. As to the establishment of schools see PARA 111 et seq.

(B) Foundation, Voluntary Controlled and Foundation Special Schools

310. Obligations of local authorities and governing bodies. In the case of a foundation, voluntary controlled or foundation special school[1], the local authority's[2] duty to maintain[3] the school includes the duty of defraying all the expenses of maintaining it[4], and the duty under any enactment of providing new premises[5] for the school[6].

The governing body[7] of a foundation, voluntary controlled or foundation special school is[8] not responsible for any of the expenses of maintaining the school[9]. However, this does not apply to the repayment of the principal of, or interest on, a loan made to the governing body[10].

1   As to foundation, voluntary and foundation special schools see PARA 106.
2   As to the meaning of 'local authority' see PARA 25 (definition applied by the School Standards and Framework Act 1998 s 142(8)).
3   As to the meaning of 'maintain' see PARA 306 note 4.
4   For the purposes of the School Standards and Framework Act 1998, the expenses of maintaining a foundation, voluntary or foundation special school include the payment of rates: s 22(6). As to rates see PARAS 1369–1370.
5   As to the meaning of 'premises' see PARA 62 note 19 (definition applied by the School Standards and Framework Act 1998 s 142(8)).
6   School Standards and Framework Act 1998 s 22(4) (amended by the Education Act 2002 s 215, Sch 21 para 96(1), (3); and SI 2010/1158). As to the duty to provide premises for foundation, voluntary controlled and foundation special schools see PARA 1295 et seq.
7   As to the governing bodies of maintained schools in England see PARA 150 et seq; and in Wales see PARA 195.
8   Ie in accordance with the School Standards and Framework Act 1998 s 22(4): see the text to notes 1–6.
9   School Standards and Framework Act 1998 Sch 3 para 1(1).
10 School Standards and Framework Act 1998 Sch 3 para 1(2).

(C) Voluntary Aided Schools

311. Obligations of local authorities and governing bodies. In the case of a voluntary aided school in England[1], the duty of the local authority[2] to maintain[3] the school includes the duty of defraying all the expenses of maintaining it, except any expenditure that is[4] to be met, by the governing body[5], and the duty under any enactment of providing new premises[6] for the school[7]. In the case of a voluntary aided school, the governing body of the school is responsible for meeting all capital expenditure in relation to school premises[8]. However, this duty does not extend to: (1) capital expenditure[9] in relation to playing fields or any building or other structure erected thereon in connection with the use of playing fields, but does extend to capital expenditure in relation to boundary walls and fences[10]; (2) capital expenditure necessary in consequence of the use of the school premises, in pursuance of a direction or requirement of the local authority, for purposes other than those of the school[11]; or (3) capital expenditure on the provision of any new site which the local authority is[12] to provide[13].

In the case of a voluntary aided school in Wales[14], the local authority's duty to maintain the school includes the duty of defraying all the expenses of maintaining it, except any expenses that are[15] payable by the governing body[16], and the duty under any enactment of providing new premises for the school[17]. In the case of a voluntary aided school, the expenses of discharging any liability[18] incurred by or on behalf of the governing body of the school[19], any former governors of the school[20], or any trustees of the school[21] in connection with the provision of premises or specified equipment[22] for the purposes of the school are payable by the governing body of the school[23]. In addition, any expenses incurred in making to the school buildings[24] of a voluntary aided school such alterations[25] as may be required by the local authority for the purpose of securing that the school premises conform to the prescribed[26] standards[27], or in effecting repairs to the school buildings[28], are payable by the governing body of the school[29]. However, the governing body of a voluntary aided school is not responsible for repairs to the interior of the school buildings[30], or to those buildings necessary in consequence of the use of the school premises in pursuance of a direction or requirement of the local authority for purposes other than those of the school[31].

In England and Wales, a local authority may give to the governing body of a voluntary aided school such assistance as the authority thinks fit in relation to the carrying out by the governing body of these obligations[32]. Where such assistance consists of the provision of any premises for use for the purposes of a school, the local authority must transfer its interest in the premises to the trustees of the school, to be held by them on trust for the purposes of the school[33], or if the school has no trustees, to the school's foundation body[34], to be held by that body for the relevant purposes[35]. If any doubt or dispute arises as to the persons to whom the authority are required to make the transfer, it must be made to such persons as the Secretary of State or, in relation to Wales, the Welsh Ministers thinks proper[36]. The authority must pay to the persons to whom the transfer is made their reasonable costs in connection with the transfer[37].

1   As to voluntary schools see PARA 106. As to the meaning of 'England' see PARA 7 note 3.
2   As to the meaning of 'local authority' see PARA 25 (definition applied by the School Standards and Framework Act 1998 s 142(8)).
3   As to the meaning of 'maintain' see PARA 306 note 4.
4   Ie by virtue of the School Standards and Framework Act 1998 Sch 3 para 3: see the text to notes 8–13.
5   School Standards and Framework Act 1998 s 22(5)(a) (amended by SI 2002/906; and SI 2010/1158). As to the governing bodies of maintained schools in England see PARA 150 et seq. The amendments made to the School Standards and Framework Act 1998 s 22, Sch 3 by the Regulatory Reform (Voluntary Aided Schools Liabilities and Funding) (England) Order 2002, SI 2002/906, apply in relation to England only. As to the School Standards and Framework Act 1998 s 22, Sch 3 para 3 as they apply in relation to Wales see the text to notes 14–31.
6   As to the meaning of 'premises' see PARA 62 note 19 (definition applied by the School Standards and Framework Act 1998 s 142(8)).
7   School Standards and Framework Act 1998 s 22(5)(b) (amended by the Education Act 2002 s 215, Sch 21 para 96(1), (4)). As to the provision of sites for voluntary aided schools see PARA 1296. As to the disposal of a voluntary aided school's land by a local authority in England see PARA 1303.
8   School Standards and Framework Act 1998 Sch 3 para 3(1) (Sch 3 para 3 substituted, in relation to England, by the SI 2002/906). As to land and premises generally see PARA 1295 et seq.
9   The following definition of 'capital expenditure' applies for the purposes of the School Standards and Framework Act 1998 Sch 3 as it applies in relation to England: see Sch 3 para 9A(1) (Sch 3 paras 9A, 9B added by the Education and Inspections Act 2006 s 35(1), (3)). Subject to the School Standards and Framework Act 1998 Sch 3 para 9A(3) and (4) below, references in Sch 3 to capital expenditure, in relation to an appropriate body or the promoters, in the case of a voluntary aided school, are references to: (1) expenditure of the body or, as the case may be, the promoters which falls to be capitalised in accordance with proper accounting practices (Sch 3 para 9A(2)(a) (as so added)); or (2) expenditure which would fall to be so capitalised were it to be incurred by the body or, as the case may be, the promoters (Sch 3 para 9A(2)(b) (as so added)). The Secretary of State may by regulations prescribe classes or descriptions of expenditure which are to be treated for these purposes as being, or as not being, capital expenditure in relation to: (a) any appropriate body, or any prescribed class or description of appropriate body (Sch 3 para 9A(3)(a) (as so added)); (b) any promoters, or any

prescribed class or description of promoters (Sch 3 para 9A(3)(b) (as so added)). The Secretary of State may by direction provide that, in the case of a particular voluntary aided school (i) expenditure of a particular appropriate body which is expenditure of a particular class or description (Sch 3 para 9A(4)(a) (as so added)); (ii) expenditure of particular promoters which is expenditure of a particular class or description (Sch 3 para 9A(4)(b) (as so added)), is to be treated for these purposes as being, or as not being, capital expenditure in relation to that body, or as the case may be, those promoters (Sch 3 para 9A(4) (as so added)). Such directions may be expressed to have effect in specified circumstances or subject to specified conditions (Sch 3 para 9A(5) (as so added). An 'appropriate body', in the case of a voluntary aided school, means the governing body of the school (Sch 3 paras 9A(6)(a), 9B(3) (as so added)), or a relevant body in relation to the school (within the meaning of Sch 3 para 5: see PARA 312 note 7) (Sch 3 paras 9A(6)(b), 9B(3) (as so added)). 'Proper accounting practices', in relation to an appropriate body or the promoters, in the case of a voluntary aided school, means those accounting practices: (A) which, whether by virtue of any enactment or by reference to any generally recognised published code or otherwise, are regarded as proper accounting practices to be followed in the keeping of accounts by the appropriate body, or as the case may be, the promoters (Sch 3 para 9B(1)(a) (as so added)); or (B) which, whether by virtue of any enactment or by reference to any generally recognised published code or otherwise, are regarded as proper accounting practices to be followed in the keeping of accounts by the local authority (Sch 3 para 9B(1)(b) (as so added; and amended by SI 2010/1158)). In the event of conflict between the accounting practices falling within head (A) and those falling within head (B), only those falling within head (A) are to be regarded as proper accounting practices: School Standards and Framework Act 1998 Sch 3 para 9B(2) (as so added). 'Promoters', in relation to a school in England, means persons who are for the purposes of the Education and Inspections Act 2006 Sch 2 (see PARA 118) the proposers in relation to proposals for the establishment of the school: School Standards and Framework Act 1998 Sch 3 para 2A (added by the Education and Inspections Act 2006 s 30, Sch 3 para 31(1), (3)). As to the meaning of 'person' see PARA 7 note 6. As to the Secretary of State see PARA 58. Any expenditure by an appropriate body or any promoters in respect of a new voluntary aided school of an amount less than £2,000 does not constitute capital expenditure: Capital Expenditure in respect of Voluntary Aided Schools (England) Regulations 2007, SI 2007/1322, reg 2.

10   School Standards and Framework Act 1998 Sch 3 para 3(2)(a) (as substituted: see note 8).

11   School Standards and Framework Act 1998 Sch 3 para 3(2)(b) (as substituted (see note 8); and amended by SI 2010/1158).

12   Ie by virtue of the School Standards and Framework Act 1998 Sch 3 para 4: see PARA 1296.

13   School Standards and Framework Act 1998 Sch 3 para 3(2)(c) (as substituted (see note 8); and amended by SI 2010/1158).

14   As to the meaning of 'Wales' see PARA 7 note 3.

15   Ie by virtue of the School Standards and Framework Act 1998 Sch 3 para 3: see the text to notes 18–31.

16   School Standards and Framework Act 1998 s 22(5)(a) (s 22(5) amended by SI 2010/1158). As to the governing bodies of maintained schools in Wales see PARA 195.

17   School Standards and Framework Act 1998 s 22(5)(b) (amended by the Education Act 2002 s 215, Sch 21 para 96(1), (4)).

18   As to the meaning of 'liability' see PARA 108 note 22 (definition applied by the School Standards and Framework Act 1998 s 142(8)).

19   School Standards and Framework Act 1998 Sch 3 para 3(1)(a).

20   School Standards and Framework Act 1998 Sch 3 para 3(1)(b).

21   School Standards and Framework Act 1998 Sch 3 para 3(1)(c).

22   For these purposes, 'specified equipment' means equipment of any description specified by the Welsh Ministers for the purposes of the School Standards and Framework Act 1998 Sch 3 para 3: Sch 3 para 3(1). The functions of the Secretary of State under the School Standards and Framework Act 1998 Sch 3, so far as exercisable in relation to Wales, were transferred to the National Assembly for Wales (see the National Assembly for Wales (Transfer of Functions) Order 1999, SI 1999/672, art 2, Sch 1) and are now vested in the Welsh Ministers (see the Government of Wales Act 2006 s 162(1), Sch 11 para 30). As to the Welsh Ministers see PARA 59.

23   School Standards and Framework Act 1998 Sch 3 para 3(1). Nothing in Sch 3 para 3 imposes on the governing body of a voluntary aided school which was, either before or after 1 September 1999 (ie the appointed day: see PARA 106 note 3), a school of a different description any obligation in respect of a liability incurred at any time before the school became a voluntary aided school, if, at that time, no obligation in respect of that liability was imposed on it, as the

governing body of a school of that description, under the School Standards and Framework Act 1998 or the Education Act 1996, as the case may be: School Standards and Framework Act 1998 Sch 3 para 3(4).

24 As to the meaning of 'school building' see PARA 1296 note 18 (definition applied by the School Standards and Framework Act 1998 s 142(8)).

25 Except where the context otherwise requires, references to the alteration of school premises include making improvements, extensions or additions to the premises: Education Act 1996 s 573(1), (2) (amended by the School Standards and Framework Act 1998 s 140(1), (3), Sch 30 para 178(a), Sch 31) (definition applied by s 142(8)).

26 Ie prescribed under the Education Act 1996 s 542: see PARA 1344.

27 School Standards and Framework Act 1998 Sch 3 para 3(2)(a) (amended by SI 2010/1158).

28 School Standards and Framework Act 1998 Sch 3 para 3(2)(b). This relates to repairs other than those falling within Sch 3 para 3(3) (see the text to notes 30–31): see Sch 3 para 3(2)(b).

29 School Standards and Framework Act 1998 Sch 3 para 3(2).

30 School Standards and Framework Act 1998 Sch 3 para 3(3)(a).

31 School Standards and Framework Act 1998 Sch 3 para 3(3)(b) (amended by SI 2010/1158).

32 School Standards and Framework Act 1998 Sch 3 para 8 (amended by SI 2010/1158).

33 School Standards and Framework Act 1998 Sch 3 para 9(1)(a) (Sch 3 para 9(1) amended by SI 2010/1158). As to the meaning of 'land or other property held on trust, or by trustees, for the purposes of a school' see PARA 108 note 6.

34 As to the meaning of 'foundation body' see PARA 108 note 6.

35 School Standards and Framework Act 1998 Sch 3 para 9(1)(b). For these purposes, 'the relevant purposes' means, in relation to a transfer to a school's foundation body, the purposes of the schools comprising the group for which that body acts: Sch 3 para 9(4). As to the meaning of 'the group' see PARA 108 note 6.

36 School Standards and Framework Act 1998 Sch 3 para 9(2).

37 School Standards and Framework Act 1998 Sch 3 para 9(3).

312. Grants in respect of expenditure on premises or equipment. The Secretary of State[1] may make grants to the governing body[2] of a voluntary aided school[3] in England[4] in respect of capital expenditure[5] incurred or to be incurred by it[6], or to a relevant body[7], in the case of such a school, in respect of capital expenditure incurred or to be incurred by that body on behalf of the governing body[8]. The amount of any such grant in respect of any such expenditure must not exceed 90 per cent of the expenditure or, if the Secretary of State considers that the circumstances are exceptional, must not exceed 100 per cent of the expenditure[9], and in the case of any prescribed[10] class or description of such expenditure, must be such as may be determined in accordance with regulations[11]. The times at which, and the manner in which, payments are made in respect of such grants are such as may be determined from time to time by the Secretary of State[12].

Without prejudice to any other duty of his, the Secretary of State must, in performing functions[13] relating to the exercise of his power[14] to make grants in respect of expenditure on school premises[15], give priority to paying grants in respect of expenditure which is necessary to make such alterations[16] as may be required by the local authority[17] for the purpose of securing that the school premises conform to the required standards for educational premises[18] or as may be required for the purpose of securing that the school premises conform to standards specified by or under any other enactment relating to health and safety[19]. The amount of any such grant paid in the exercise of the power in respect of such expenditure on school premises must be at least 90 per cent of the expenditure[20].

Any body to whom any payment is made in respect of such a grant must comply with such requirements determined by the Secretary of State as he may from time to time impose[21]. Such requirements may be imposed on, or at any time after, the making of any payment by reference to which they are imposed[22], and may at any time be waived, removed or varied by the Secretary of State[23]; but such requirements may be imposed after the making of any such payment only if the Secretary of State is satisfied that in all the circumstances it is reasonable for them to be so imposed[24]. Such requirements may, in particular, if any conditions specified in the requirements are satisfied:

(1)   require the application for purposes connected with the provision of education in appropriate schools[25] of: (a) any premises or equipment in respect of which the grant has been paid[26]; or (b) an amount equal to so much of the value of any such premises or equipment as is determined in accordance with the requirements to be properly attributable to the payment of the grant[27]; and

(2)   in the event that that requirement is not complied with, require the payment to the Secretary of State of the whole or any part of the relevant amount[28].

When deciding whether to make any grant to a body in circumstances where he considers that it would be appropriate to impose requirements[29], the Secretary of State may have regard to whether, if such requirements were imposed, that body would have an enforceable right against some other person[30] to be given by that person such financial assistance as would be necessary to enable it to pay to the Secretary of State the relevant amount[31].

No grant may be paid under the above provisions in respect of any expenses incurred in the provision of any premises which it is the duty of the local authority to provide[32].

The Welsh Ministers[33] may make grants to the governing body[34] of a voluntary aided school in Wales in respect of qualifying expenditure[35] incurred by it[36], or to a relevant body, in the case of such a school, in respect of qualifying expenditure incurred by that body on behalf of the governing body[37]. The amount of any such grant in respect of any such expenditure must not exceed 85 per cent of the expenditure[38], and in the case of any prescribed[39] class or description of such expenditure, must be such as may be determined in accordance with regulations[40]. The times at which, and the manner in which, payments are made in respect of such grants are such as may be determined from time to time by the Welsh Ministers[41]. Without prejudice to any other of their duties, the Welsh Ministers must, in performing functions relating to the exercise of the power to make grants in respect of expenditure on the alterations to school buildings[42] or the repair of school buildings, give priority to paying grants in respect of expenditure which is necessary for the performance by governing bodies of their duties; and the amount of any grant paid in the exercise of that power in respect of such expenditure on the repair of school buildings must be 85 per cent of the expenditure[43].

Any body to whom any payment is made in respect of such a grant must comply with such requirements determined by the Welsh Ministers as they may from time to time impose[44]. Such requirements may be imposed on, or at any time after, the making of any payment by reference to which they are imposed[45], and may at any time be waived, removed or varied by the Welsh Ministers[46]; but such requirements may be imposed after the making of any such payment only if the Welsh Ministers are satisfied that in all the circumstances it is reasonable for them to be so imposed[47]. Such requirements may, in particular, if any conditions specified in the requirements are satisfied:

(i)   require the application for purposes connected with the provision of education in appropriate schools of: (A) any premises or equipment in respect of which the grant has been paid[48]; or (B) an amount equal to so much of the value of any such premises or equipment as is determined in accordance with the requirements to be properly attributable to the payment of the grant[49]; and

(ii) in the event that that requirement is not complied with, require the payment to the Welsh Ministers of the whole or any part of the relevant amount[50].

When deciding whether to make any grant to a body in circumstances where they consider that it would be appropriate to impose requirements[51], the Welsh Ministers may have regard to whether, if such requirements were imposed, that body would have an enforceable right against some other person to be given by that person such financial assistance as would be necessary to enable it to pay to the Welsh Ministers the relevant amount[52].

No grant may be paid by the Welsh Ministers under these provisions in respect of any expenses incurred in the provision of any premises which it is the duty of the local authority to provide[53].

1   As to the Secretary of State see PARA 58.
2   As to the governing bodies of maintained schools in England see PARA 150 et seq.
3   As to voluntary schools see PARA 106.
4   As to the meaning of 'England' see PARA 7 note 3.
5   As to the meaning of 'capital expenditure' see PARA 311 note 9.
6   School Standards and Framework Act 1998 Sch 3 para 5(1)(a) (amended by SI 2002/906). The amendments made to the School Standards and Framework Act 1998 Sch 3 by the Regulatory Reform (Voluntary Aided Schools Liabilities and Funding) (England) Order 2002, SI 2002/906, apply in relation to England only. As to the School Standards and Framework Act 1998 Sch 3 para 5 as it applies in relation to Wales see the text to notes 33–53.
7   'Relevant body', in relation to a voluntary aided school, means the appropriate diocesan authority or the school's trustees: School Standards and Framework Act 1998 Sch 3 para 5(12). As to the meaning of 'appropriate diocesan authority' see PARA 146 note 12.
8   School Standards and Framework Act 1998 Sch 3 para 5(1)(b) (amended by SI 2002/906).
9   School Standards and Framework Act 1998 Sch 3 para 5(3)(a) (substituted by SI 2002/906).
10 'Prescribed' means prescribed by regulations made under the School Standards and Framework Act 1998: see s 142(1). As to the prescribed classes and descriptions of expenditure see the Education (Grants in Respect of Voluntary Aided Schools) Regulations 1999, SI 1999/2020, reg 3 (amended, in relation to England, by SI 2002/1720; and SI 2003/507). The Education (Grants in Respect of Voluntary Aided Schools) Regulations 1999, SI 1999/2020, also provide for the proceeds resulting from the disposal of associated school property (as to the meaning of which see reg 4) to be taken into account in determining the amount of any such grant: see regs 5–6.
11 School Standards and Framework Act 1998 Sch 3 para 5(3)(b).
12 School Standards and Framework Act 1998 Sch 3 para 5(4).
13 As to the meaning of 'functions' see PARA 18 note 5 (definition applied by the School Standards and Framework Act 1998 s 142(8)).
14 Ie under the School Standards and Framework Act 1998 Sch 3 para 5.
15 As to the meaning of 'premises' see PARA 62 note 19 (definition applied by the School Standards and Framework Act 1998 s 142(8)).
16 As to the meaning of 'alteration' see PARA 311 note 25 (definition applied by the School Standards and Framework Act 1998 s 142(8)).
17 As to the meaning of 'local authority' see PARA 25 (definition applied by the School Standards and Framework Act 1998 s 142(8)).
18 Ie the standards prescribed under the Education Act 1996 s 542: see PARA 1344.
19 School Standards and Framework Act 1998 Sch 3 para 5(5) (substituted by SI 2002/906; and amended by SI 2010/1158).
20 School Standards and Framework Act 1998 Sch 3 para 5(5) (as substituted and amended: see note 19).
21 School Standards and Framework Act 1998 Sch 3 para 5(6).
22 School Standards and Framework Act 1998 Sch 3 para 5(7)(a).
23 School Standards and Framework Act 1998 Sch 3 para 5(7)(b).

24 School Standards and Framework Act 1998 Sch 3 para 5(7).

25 'Appropriate schools' means: (1) in relation to a voluntary aided school having a religious character, schools which are either foundation or voluntary schools and whose specified religion or religious denomination under the School Standards and Framework Act 1998 s 69(4) (see PARA 914) is the same as that school's; and (2) in relation to any other voluntary aided school, maintained schools: Sch 3 para 5(12). As to the meaning of 'specified religion or religious denomination' see PARA 146 note 12. As to the meaning of 'maintained school' see PARA 99. As to foundation schools see PARA 106.

26 School Standards and Framework Act 1998 Sch 3 para 5(8)(a)(i).

27 School Standards and Framework Act 1998 Sch 3 para 5(8)(a)(ii).

28 School Standards and Framework Act 1998 Sch 3 para 5(8)(b). The amount is the amount of the payments made in respect of the grant under Sch 3 para 5, or the amount mentioned in Sch 3 para 5(8)(a)(ii) (see head (1)(b) in the text), whichever the Secretary of State determines to be just: Sch 3 para 5(9).

29 Ie falling within the School Standards and Framework Act 1998 Sch 3 para 5(8): see the text to notes 25–28.

30 As to the meaning of 'person' see PARA 7 note 6.

31 School Standards and Framework Act 1998 Sch 3 para 5(10).

32 School Standards and Framework Act 1998 Sch 3 para 5(11) (amended by SI 2010/1158).

33 The functions of the Secretary of State under the School Standards and Framework Act 1998 Sch 3, so far as exercisable in relation to Wales, were transferred to the National Assembly for Wales (see the National Assembly for Wales (Transfer of Functions) Order 1999, SI 1999/672, art 2, Sch 1) and are now vested in the Welsh Ministers (see the Government of Wales Act 2006 s 162(1), Sch 11 para 30). As to the Welsh Ministers see PARA 59. As to the meaning of 'Wales' see PARA 7 note 3.

34 As to the governing bodies of maintained schools in Wales see PARA 195.

35 'Qualifying expenditure' means expenditure in respect of the provision, alteration or repair of premises or equipment for the school: School Standards and Framework Act 1998 Sch 3 para 5(2). 'Repair' does not include repair falling within Sch 3 para 3(3) (see PARA 311): Sch 3 para 5(12).

36 School Standards and Framework Act 1998 Sch 3 para 5(1)(a).

37 School Standards and Framework Act 1998 Sch 3 para 5(1)(b).

38 School Standards and Framework Act 1998 Sch 3 para 5(3)(a).

39 As to the prescribed classes and descriptions of expenditure see the Education (Grants in Respect of Voluntary Aided Schools) Regulations 1999, SI 1999/2020, reg 3 (amended, in relation to Wales, by SI 2004/1576). The Education (Grants in Respect of Voluntary Aided Schools) Regulations 1999, SI 1999/2020, also provide for the proceeds resulting from the disposal of associated school property (as to the meaning of which see reg 4) to be taken into account in determining the amount of any such grant: see regs 5–6.

40 School Standards and Framework Act 1998 Sch 3 para 5(3)(b).

41 School Standards and Framework Act 1998 Sch 3 para 5(4).

42 Ie such as are referred to in the School Standards and Framework Act 1998 Sch 3 para 3(2)(a) (see PARA 311). As to the meaning of 'school building' see PARA 1296 note 18 (definition applied by s 142(8)).

43 School Standards and Framework Act 1998 Sch 3 para 5(5).

44 School Standards and Framework Act 1998 Sch 3 para 5(6).

45 School Standards and Framework Act 1998 Sch 3 para 5(7)(a).

46 School Standards and Framework Act 1998 Sch 3 para 5(7)(b).

47 School Standards and Framework Act 1998 Sch 3 para 5(7).

48 School Standards and Framework Act 1998 Sch 3 para 5(8)(a)(i).

49 School Standards and Framework Act 1998 Sch 3 para 5(8)(a)(ii).

50 School Standards and Framework Act 1998 Sch 3 para 5(8)(b). The amount is the amount of the payments made in respect of the grant under Sch 3 para 5, or the amount mentioned in Sch 3 para 5(8)(a)(ii) (see head (i)(B) in the text), whichever the Welsh Ministers determine to be just: Sch 3 para 5(9).

51 Ie falling within the School Standards and Framework Act 1998 Sch 3 para 5(8): see the text to notes 48–50.

52 School Standards and Framework Act 1998 Sch 3 para 5(10).

53 See the School Standards and Framework Act 1998 Sch 3 para 5(11) (amended by SI 2010/1158).

313. Grants in respect of preliminary expenditure. The Secretary of State[1] may pay grants:

(1) to the governing body[2] of a voluntary aided school[3] in England[4] in respect of preliminary expenditure incurred or to be incurred by it for the purposes of any scheme for the transfer of the school to a new site or the enlargement[5] or alteration[6] of the school premises[7]; or

(2) to a relevant body[8] in the case of such a school, in respect of any preliminary expenditure incurred or to be incurred by it, on behalf of the governing body, for the purposes of any such scheme[9].

Where any persons[10] propose or are considering whether to propose the establishment[11] of a voluntary aided school, the Secretary of State may pay grants to them in respect of any preliminary expenditure incurred or to be incurred by them for the purposes of a scheme for the provision of a site for the school or of any buildings which would be used for the purposes of the school[12]. Such grants[13] must not exceed 90 per cent of the expenditure or, if the Secretary of State considers that the circumstances are exceptional, must not exceed 100 per cent of the expenditure, in respect of which it is paid[14].

Such grants may be paid in respect of schemes for the transfer of the school to a new site or for the enlargement or alteration of the school premises or for the provision of a site for the school or of any buildings whether or not: (a) the details of such a scheme had been formulated at the time when the expenditure was incurred[15]; (b) where such details were not formulated at that time, they are subsequently formulated[16]; (c) the governing body or persons in question had determined to proceed with such a scheme at that time[17]; or (d) where they had not determined to proceed with such a scheme at that time, they subsequently determine to proceed with such a scheme[18].

Expenditure in respect of which such grants are payable includes, in particular, costs incurred in connection with the preparation of plans and specifications for any proposed construction, enlargement or alteration of buildings which are or would be used for the purposes of the school[19], and estimating the sums which would be expended if any such works were carried out[20], but does not include any sums expended in carrying out any such works[21]. Where a grant is paid[22] in the case of any voluntary aided school, or a grant is paid[23] in the case of any school which is established as a voluntary aided school, the grant must, for the purposes of the provision requiring the consent of the Secretary of State if expenditure has been incurred on school premises (otherwise than in connection with repairs) before a notice to discontinue a foundation or voluntary school can be given[24], be treated as expenditure incurred by the Secretary of State, otherwise than in connection with repairs, in respect of the school premises[25].

The Welsh Ministers[26] may pay grants:

(i) to the governing body of a voluntary aided school in Wales in respect of preliminary expenditure incurred by it for the purposes of any scheme for the transfer of the school to a new site or the enlargement or alteration of the school premises[27]; or

(ii) to a relevant body in the case of such a school, in respect of any preliminary expenditure incurred by it, on behalf of the governing body, for the purposes of any such scheme[28].

Where any persons propose or are considering whether to propose the establishment of a voluntary aided school, the Welsh Ministers may pay grants to them in respect of any preliminary expenditure incurred by them for the purposes of a scheme for the provision of a site for the school or of any buildings which would be school buildings[29].

Grants[30] may be paid in respect of a scheme whether or not: (A) the details of such a scheme had been formulated at the time when the expenditure was incurred[31]; (B) where such details were not formulated at that time, they are subsequently formulated[32]; (C) the governing body or persons in question had determined to proceed with such a scheme at that time[33]; or (D) where they had not determined to proceed with such a scheme at that time, they subsequently determine to proceed with such a scheme[34]. Expenditure in respect of which such grants are payable includes, in particular, costs incurred in connection with the preparation of plans and specifications for any proposed construction, enlargement or alteration of buildings which are or would be school buildings[35], and estimating the sums which would be expended if any such works were carried out[36], but does not include any sums expended in carrying out any such works[37].

A grant must not exceed 85 per cent of the expenditure in respect of which it is paid[38]. Where grant is paid[39] in the case of any voluntary aided school[40], or a grant is paid[41] in the case of any school which is established as a voluntary aided school[42], the grant must be treated[43] as expenditure incurred by the Welsh Ministers (otherwise than in connection with repairs) in respect of the school premises[44].

1   As to the Secretary of State see PARA 58.
2   As to the governing bodies of maintained schools in England see PARA 150 et seq.
3   As to voluntary schools see PARA 106.
4   As to the meaning of 'England' see PARA 7 note 3.
5   As to the meaning of 'enlargement' see PARA 110 note 2 (definition applied by the School Standards and Framework Act 1998 s 142(8)).
6   As to the meaning of 'alteration' see PARA 311 note 25 (definition applied by the School Standards and Framework Act 1998 s 142(8)).
7   School Standards and Framework Act 1998 Sch 3 para 6(1)(a) (amended by SI 2002/906). As to the meaning of 'premises' see PARA 62 note 19 (definition applied by the School Standards and Framework Act 1998 s 142(8)). The amendments made to the School Standards and Framework Act 1998 Sch 3 by the Regulatory Reform (Voluntary Aided Schools Liabilities and Funding) (England) Order 2002, SI 2002/906, apply in relation to England only. As to the School Standards and Framework Act 1998 Sch 3 para 6 as it applies in relation to Wales see the text to notes 26–44.
8   'Relevant body', in relation to a voluntary aided school, means the appropriate diocesan authority or the school's trustees: School Standards and Framework Act 1998 Sch 3 para 6(7). As to the meaning of 'appropriate diocesan authority' see PARA 146 note 12.
9   School Standards and Framework Act 1998 Sch 3 para 6(1)(b) (amended by SI 2002/906).
10   As to the meaning of 'person' see PARA 7 note 6.
11   As to the meaning of 'establish' see PARA 110 note 2 (definition applied by the School Standards and Framework Act 1998 s 142(8)).
12   School Standards and Framework Act 1998 Sch 3 para 6(2) (amended by SI 2002/906).
13   Ie grants under the School Standards and Framework Act 1998 Sch 3 para 6(1) (see the text to notes 1–9) or Sch 3 para 6(2) (see the text to notes 10–12).
14   School Standards and Framework Act 1998 Sch 3 para 6(5) (substituted by SI 2002/906).
15   School Standards and Framework Act 1998 Sch 3 para 6(3)(a).
16   School Standards and Framework Act 1998 Sch 3 para 6(3)(b).
17   School Standards and Framework Act 1998 Sch 3 para 6(3)(c).
18   School Standards and Framework Act 1998 Sch 3 para 6(3)(d).
19   School Standards and Framework Act 1998 Sch 3 para 6(4)(a) (amended by SI 2002/906).
20   School Standards and Framework Act 1998 Sch 3 para 6(4)(b).
21   School Standards and Framework Act 1998 Sch 3 para 6(4).
22   Ie under the School Standards and Framework Act 1998 Sch 3 para 6(1): see the text to notes 1–9.

23 Ie under the School Standards and Framework Act 1998 Sch 3 para 6(2): see the text to notes 10–12.
24 Ie for the purposes of the School Standards and Framework Act 1998 s 30(2): see PARA 116.
25 School Standards and Framework Act 1998 Sch 3 para 6(6).
26 The functions of the Secretary of State under the School Standards and Framework Act 1998 Sch 3, so far as exercisable in relation to Wales, were transferred to the National Assembly for Wales (see the National Assembly for Wales (Transfer of Functions) Order 1999, SI 1999/672, art 2, Sch 1) and are now vested in the Welsh Ministers (see the Government of Wales Act 2006 s 162(1), Sch 11 para 30). As to the Welsh Ministers see PARA 59. As to the meaning of 'Wales' see PARA 7 note 3.
27 School Standards and Framework Act 1998 Sch 3 para 6(1)(a). As to the governing bodies of maintained schools in Wales see PARA 195.
28 School Standards and Framework Act 1998 Sch 3 para 6(1)(b).
29 School Standards and Framework Act 1998 Sch 3 para 6(2). As to the meaning of 'school building' see PARA 1296 note 18 (definition applied by s 142(8)).
30 Ie under the School Standards and Framework Act 1998 Sch 3 para 6(1) (see the text to notes 26–28) or 6(2) (see the text to note 29).
31 School Standards and Framework Act 1998 Sch 3 para 6(3)(a).
32 School Standards and Framework Act 1998 Sch 3 para 6(3)(b).
33 School Standards and Framework Act 1998 Sch 3 para 6(3)(c).
34 School Standards and Framework Act 1998 Sch 3 para 6(3)(d).
35 School Standards and Framework Act 1998 Sch 3 para 6(4)(a).
36 School Standards and Framework Act 1998 Sch 3 para 6(4)(b).
37 School Standards and Framework Act 1998 Sch 3 para 6(4).
38 School Standards and Framework Act 1998 Sch 3 para 6(5).
39 Ie under the School Standards and Framework Act 1998 Sch 3 para 6(1): see the text to notes 26–28.
40 School Standards and Framework Act 1998 Sch 3 para 6(6)(a).
41 Ie under the School Standards and Framework Act 1998 Sch 3 para 6(2): see the text to note 29.
42 School Standards and Framework Act 1998 Sch 3 para 6(6)(b).
43 Ie for the purposes of the School Standards and Framework Act 1998 s 30(2): see PARA 116.
44 School Standards and Framework Act 1998 Sch 3 para 6(6).

314. Loans in respect of initial expenses. Where, on the application of the governing body[1] of a voluntary aided school[2] in England[3] and after consulting persons representing the governing body, the Secretary of State[4] is satisfied that the governing body's share of any initial expenditure[5] required in connection with the school premises[6] will involve capital expenditure[7], and having regard to all the circumstances of the case, considers that that capital expenditure ought properly to be met by borrowing[8], he may make a loan to the governing body for the purpose of helping it meet that expenditure[9]. The amount, rate of interest and other terms and conditions applicable to the loan are such as may be specified in an agreement made between the Secretary of State and the governing body with the consent of the Treasury[10]. These provisions[11] apply for the purpose of enabling loans to be made to a relevant body[12] in respect of expenditure incurred by that body on behalf of the governing body as they apply to expenditure incurred by the governing body[13].

Where, on the application of the governing body of a voluntary aided school in Wales[14] and after consulting persons representing the governing body, the Welsh Ministers[15] are satisfied that the governing body's share of any initial expenses[16] required in connection with the school premises will involve capital expenditure[17], and having regard to all the circumstances of the case, consider that that expenditure ought properly to be met by borrowing[18], they may make a loan to the governing body for the purpose of helping it meet that expenditure[19]. The amount, rate of interest and other terms and conditions applicable to the loan is such as may be specified in an agreement made between the Welsh Ministers and the governing body[20]. These provisions[21] apply for the purpose of enabling loans to be made to a relevant body[22] in respect of expenses incurred by that body on behalf of the governing body as they apply to expenses incurred by the governing body[23].

1   As to the governing bodies of maintained schools in England see PARA 150 et seq.

2   As to voluntary schools see PARA 106.

3   As to the meaning of 'England' see PARA 7 note 3.

4   As to the Secretary of State see PARA 58.

5   The governing body's share of any initial expenditure must be taken to be so much of the expenditure as remains to be borne by the governing body after taking into account the amount of any grant under the School Standards and Framework Act 1998 Sch 3 para 5 (see PARA 312) that may be paid or payable in respect of them: Sch 3 para 7(4) (amended by SI 2002/906). For these purposes, 'initial expenditure' is expenditure to be incurred in providing: (1) a site or buildings for a voluntary aided school in connection with the implementation of any proposals for a prescribed alteration to the school published under the School Standards and Framework Act 1998 s 28 (repealed), or the transfer of the school to a new site; or (2) a site or buildings for a new voluntary aided school, being expenditure in respect of which grants may be paid under Sch 3 para 5: Sch 3 para 7(3) (amended by SI 2002/906). As to the meaning of 'alteration' see PARA 311 note 25 (definition applied by the School Standards and Framework Act 1998 s 142(8)). The amendments made to the School Standards and Framework Act 1998 Sch 3 by the Regulatory Reform (Voluntary Aided Schools Liabilities and Funding) (England) Order 2002, SI 2002/906, apply in relation to England only. As to the School Standards and Framework Act 1998 Sch 3 para 7 as it applies in relation to Wales see the text to notes 14–23.

6   As to the meaning of 'premises' see PARA 62 note 19 (definition applied by the School Standards and Framework Act 1998 s 142(8)).

7   School Standards and Framework Act 1998 Sch 3 para 7(1)(a) (amended by SI 2002/906).

8   School Standards and Framework Act 1998 Sch 3 para 7(1)(b) (amended by SI 2002/906).

9   School Standards and Framework Act 1998 Sch 3 para 7(1). Schedule 10 para 3(3) (consent to borrowing) (repealed) does not apply to any borrowing by a governing body under Sch 3 para 7: Sch 3 para 7(6). As to consent to borrowing see now the Education Act 2002 Sch 1 para 3(4); and PARA 204.

10 School Standards and Framework Act 1998 Sch 3 para 7(2). As to the Treasury see CONSTITUTIONAL AND ADMINISTRATIVE LAW vol 20 (2014) PARA 262 et seq.

11 Ie the School Standards and Framework Act 1998 Sch 3 para 7(1)–(4): see the text to notes 1–10.

12 Ie within the meaning of the School Standards and Framework Act 1998 Sch 3 para 5: see PARA 312 note 7.

13 School Standards and Framework Act 1998 Sch 3 para 7(5) (amended by SI 2002/906). In the provisions of the School Standards and Framework Act 1998 Sch 3 para 7(1)–(4) (see the text to notes 1–10), as they apply in relation to a new voluntary aided school, references to the governing body are, in relation to England, to the promoters: see Sch 3 para 7(5)(a) (Sch 3 para 5 amended by the School Standards and Organisation (Wales) Act 2013 Sch 5 para 19(1), (12)(b)(ii)). As to the meaning of 'promoters' see PARA 311 note 9.

14 As to the meaning of 'Wales' see PARA 7 note 3. As to the governing bodies of maintained schools in Wales see PARA 195.

15 The functions of the Secretary of State under the School Standards and Framework Act 1998 Sch 3, so far as exercisable in relation to Wales, were transferred to the National Assembly for Wales (see the National Assembly for Wales (Transfer of Functions) Order 1999, SI 1999/672, art 2, Sch 1) and are now vested in the Welsh Ministers (see the Government of Wales Act 2006 s 162(1), Sch 11 para 30). As to the Welsh Ministers see PARA 59.

16 For these purposes the governing body's share of any initial expenses must be taken to be so much of the expenses as remains to be borne by the governing body after taking into account the amount of any grant under the School Standards and Framework Act 1998 Sch 3 para 5 (see PARA 312) that may be paid or payable in respect of them: Sch 3 para 7(4). 'Initial expenses' are expenses to be incurred in providing (1) a site or school buildings for a voluntary aided school in connection with the implementation of any proposals for a prescribed alteration to the school published under s 28 (repealed), the implementation of proposals under the School Standards and Organisation (Wales) Act 2013 s 42 (see PARA 140), or the transfer of the school to a new site; or (2) a site or school buildings for a new voluntary aided school, being expenses in respect of which grants may be paid under the School Standards and Framework Act 1998 Sch 3 para 5: Sch 3 para 7(3) (amended by the School Standards and Organisation (Wales) Act 2013 Sch 5 para 19(1), (12)(b)).

17 School Standards and Framework Act 1998 Sch 3 para 7(1)(a).

18 School Standards and Framework Act 1998 Sch 3 para 7(1)(b).

19 School Standards and Framework Act 1998 Sch 3 para 7(1). Schedule 10 para 3(3) (consent to borrowing) (repealed) does not apply to any borrowing by a governing body under Sch 3 para 7: Sch 3 para 7(6). As to consent to borrowing see now the Education Act 2002 Sch 1 para 3(4); and PARA 204.

20 School Standards and Framework Act 1998 Sch 3 para 7(2).

21 Ie the School Standards and Framework Act 1998 Sch 3 para 7(1)–(4): see the text to notes 14–20.

22 Ie within the meaning of the School Standards and Framework Act 1998 Sch 3 para 5: see PARA 312 note 7.

23 School Standards and Framework Act 1998 Sch 3 para 7(5). In the provisions of the School Standards and Framework Act 1998 Sch 3 para 7(1)–(4) (see the text to notes 14–20), as they apply in relation to a new voluntary aided school, references to the governing body are, in relation to Wales, to the person who made the proposals under the School Standards and Organisation (Wales) Act 2013 s 41(2) (see PARA 140): see School Standards and Framework Act 1998 Sch 3 para 7(5)(b) (Sch 3 para 7(5) as amended: see note 13).

(ix) Financing of Maintained Schools

315. Maintained schools to have budget shares. For the purposes of the financing of maintained schools[1] by local authorities[2], every such school must have, for each funding period[3], a budget share[4] which is allocated to it by the authority which maintains it[5]. For the purposes of Part II of the School Standards and Framework Act 1998[6]:

(1) a maintained school's 'budget share' for a funding period is such amount as the local authority may determine, in accordance with regulations[7], to allocate to the school out of the authority's individual schools budget for that year[8];

(2) a local authority's 'individual schools budget' for a funding period is the amount remaining after deducting from the authority's schools budget for that period such planned education expenditure by the authority in respect of that period as it may determine should be so deducted in accordance with regulations[9];

(3) a local authority's 'schools budget' for a funding period is the amount[10] appropriated by the authority for meeting all education expenditure by the authority in that period of a class or description prescribed for the purpose, which may include expenditure incurred otherwise than in respect of schools[11]; and

(4) a local authority's 'non-schools education budget' for a relevant period[12] is the amount appropriated by the authority for meeting all education expenditure by the authority in that period of a class or description prescribed for the purpose[13].

1 In the School Standards and Framework Act 1998 Pt II Ch IV (ss 45–53A), 'maintained school' means: (1) a community, foundation or voluntary school; (2) a community or foundation special school; (3) a maintained nursery school; or (4) a pupil referral unit in England: s 45(1A) (added by the Education Act 2002 s 215(1), Sch 21 para 99(1), (2); and amended by the Education Act 2011 s 50(1), (2)). As to community schools, foundation schools, voluntary schools and community and foundation special schools see PARA 106. As to the meaning of 'maintained nursery school' see PARA 99 note 4. As to pupil referral units see PARA 427 et seq. As to academies see PARA 345 et seq.

2 In the School Standards and Framework Act 1998 Pt II Ch IV (ss 45–53A):

(1) references to schools maintained by a local authority do not include pupil referral units in Wales (s 45(3)(a) (amended by the Education Act 2002 s 215(1), Sch 21 para 99(1), (3)(a); SI 2010/1158; and the Education Act 2011 s 50(1), (3)(a));

(2) references to the governing body of a maintained school or of a school maintained by a

local authority must be read, in relation to a pupil referral unit in England, as references to the management committee for the unit (in spite of the Education Act 1996 Sch 1 para 1: see PARA 428) (School Standards and Framework Act 1998 s 45(3)(aa) (s 45(3)(aa), (ab) added by the Education Act 2011 s 50(1), (3)(b)));

(3) references to governors must be read, in relation to a pupil referral unit in England, as references to the members of the management committee for the unit (School Standards and Framework Act 1998 s 45(3)(ab) (as so added));

(4) references, in a context referring to a local authority, to a maintained school or to a school maintained by such an authority must be read as including a new school: (a) which on implementation of proposals under any enactment will be a community, foundation or voluntary school or a community or foundation special school maintained by the authority; and (b) which has a temporary governing body (s 45(3)(b) (amended by the Education Act 2002 Sch 21 para 99(1), (3)(b); and SI 2010/1158)); and

(5) references to the governing body of a maintained school or of a school maintained by a local authority must accordingly be read as including the temporary governing body of a new school falling within head (2) above (s 45(3)(c) (amended by SI 2010/1158)).

As to the meaning of 'local authority' see PARA 25 (definition applied by the School Standards and Framework Act 1998 s 142(8)). As to pupil referral units see PARA 427 et seq. As to the governing bodies of maintained schools in England see PARA 150 et seq; and in Wales see PARA 195. In Pt II Ch IV, 'new school' (without more) has the meaning given by s 72(3) (see PARA 155 note 4): s 45(4). As to the meanings of 'England' and 'Wales' see PARA 7 note 3.

3   For the purposes of the School Standards and Framework Act 1998 Pt II Ch IV (ss 45–53A), 'funding period' means a financial year or such other period as may be prescribed: s 45(1B) (added by the Education Act 2005 Sch 16 para 2(1), (3)). As to the meaning of 'financial year' see PARA 81 note 9 (definition applied by the School Standards and Framework Act 1998 s 142(8)). 'Prescribed' means prescribed by regulations made under the School Standards and Framework Act 1998: see s 142(1). As to the regulations made, in relation to England, see the School and Early Years Finance (England) Regulations 2013, SI 2013/3104.

4   The School Standards and Framework Act 1998 s 45A–47 (see this paragraph and PARAS 316–318) have effect for determining the amount of a school's budget share for a funding period: s 45(2) (amended by the Education Act 2002 s 41(2); the Education Act 2005 s 101, Sch 16 para 2(1), (4); and SI 2003/2316).

5   School Standards and Framework Act 1998 s 45(1) (amended by the Education Act 2005 Sch 16 para 2(1), (2); and SI 2010/1158).

6   Ie the School Standards and Framework Act 1998 Pt II (ss 20–83).

7   As to the provision which may be made by such regulations see further PARA 316. As to the regulations made under the School Standards and Framework Act 1998 s 47(1) see the School Funding (Wales) Regulations 2010, SI 2010/824 (amended by SI 2010/1142); the School and Early Years Finance (England) Regulations 2013, SI 2013/3104; and the School and Early Years Finance (England) Regulations 2014, SI 2014/3352.

8   School Standards and Framework Act 1998 s 47(1) (amended by the Education Act 2005 Sch 16 para 6(1), (2)(a), (b); and SI 2010/1158).

9   School Standards and Framework Act 1998 s 45A(3) (s 45A added by the Education Act 2002 s 41(1); the School Standards and Framework Act 1998 s 45A(3) amended by the Education Act 2005 Sch 16 para 3(1), (6)(a), (b); and SI 2010/1158). Regulations under the School Standards and Framework Act 1998 s 45A(3) may: (1) prescribe classes or descriptions of expenditure which are authorised or required to be deducted from an authority's schools budget (see head (3) in the text) (s 45A(4)(a) (as so added)); (2) provide, in relation to any prescribed class or description of expenditure specified in the regulations, that such expenditure may only be deducted subject to either or both of the following, namely: (a) such limit or limits (however framed) as may be specified by or determined in accordance with the regulations (s 45A(4)(b)(i) (as so added)); and (b) such other conditions as may be so specified or determined (s 45A(4)(b)(ii) (as so added)). Regulations under s 45A(3) may also make provision: (i) enabling any expenditure falling outside any classes or descriptions of expenditure prescribed by virtue of s 45A(4)(a) (see head (1) above) to be deducted from the authority's schools budget if the deduction of such expenditure is authorised, on the application of the authority, by the authority's schools forum or the Secretary of State or, in relation to Wales, the Welsh Ministers (s 45A(4A)(a) (s 45A as so added; and s 45A(4A) added by the Education Act 2005 Sch 16 para 3(1), (7))); and (ii) enabling any limit or condition that would otherwise apply by virtue of the School Standards and Framework Act 1998 s 45A(4)(b)(i) (see head (2)(a) above) or s 45A(4)(b)(ii) (see head (2)(b) above) to be varied or excluded, on the application of the authority, by the authority's schools forum or the Secretary of State or, as the case may be, the

Welsh Ministers (s 45A(4A)(b) (as so added)). For the purposes of Pt II (ss 20–83), the duty imposed on a local authority in England by the Childcare Act 2006 s 7(1) (duty to secure prescribed early years provision free of charge: see CHILDREN AND YOUNG PERSONS vol 10 (2012) PARA 1083) is to be treated as an education function of the authority: School Standards and Framework Act 1998 s 45A(4B) (added by the Apprenticeships, Skills, Children and Learning Act 2009 s 202(1), (2); and amended by SI 2010/1158). As to the meaning of 'education functions' see PARA 25 (definition applied by the School Standards and Framework Act 1998 s 142(8)). As to the schools forums advising on matters relating to the local authority's schools budget see PARA 319. The functions of the Secretary of State under the School Standards and Framework Act 1998 Pt II Ch IV (ss 45–53A), so far as exercisable in relation to Wales, were transferred to the National Assembly for Wales (see the National Assembly for Wales (Transfer of Functions) Order 1999, SI 1999/672, art 2, Sch 1) and are now vested in the Welsh Ministers (see the Government of Wales Act 2006 s 162(1), Sch 11 para 30). As to the Secretary of State see PARA 58. As to the Welsh Ministers see PARA 59.

As to the classes or descriptions of planned expenditure which a local authority may deduct from its schools budget in order to arrive at its individual schools budget for the financial year see the School Funding (Wales) Regulations 2010, SI 2010/824, reg 7, Sch 2; the School and Early Years Finance (England) Regulations 2013, SI 2013/3104, regs 6, 8, Sch 2; and the School and Early Years Finance (England) Regulations 2014, SI 2014/3352, regs 6, 8, Sch 2.

10 The amount referred to in the School Standards and Framework Act 1998 s 45A(2) includes the amount of any grant which is appropriated, for meeting the expenditure mentioned in s 45A(2), in accordance with a condition which: (1) is imposed under the Education Act 2002 s 16 (terms on which assistance under s 14 is given: see PARA 78) or any other enactment (School Standards and Framework Act 1998 s 45A(2A)(a) (s 45A as added (see note 9); s 45A(2A) added by the Education Act 2005 Sch 16 para 3(1), (5))); and (2) requires that the grant be applied as part of the authority's schools budget for the funding period (s 45A(2A)(b)(as so added)).

11 School Standards and Framework Act 1998 s 45A(2) (s 45A as added (see note 9); s 45A(2) amended by the Education Act 2005 Sch 16 para 3(1), (4)(a), (b); and SI 2010/1158). As to the classes or descriptions of local authority expenditure prescribed for the purposes of the School Standards and Framework Act 1998 s 45A(2) and the determination of a local authority's schools budget see the School Funding (Wales) Regulations 2010, SI 2010/824, reg 6; the School and Early Years Finance (England) Regulations 2013, SI 2013/3104, regs 4–11; and the School and Early Years Finance (England) Regulations 2014, SI 2014/3352, regs 4–11.

12 'Relevant period' means a financial year or such other period as may be prescribed: School Standards and Framework Act 1998 s 45A(1A) (s 45A as added (see note 9); s 45A(1A) added by the Education Act 2005 Sch 16 para 3(1), (3)). As to the regulations made see those cited in notes 9, 11.

13 School Standards and Framework Act 1998 s 45A(1) (as added (see note 9); and amended by the Education Act 2005 Sch 16 para 3(1), (2)(a), (b); SI 2010/1158). As to the classes or descriptions of local authority expenditure prescribed for the purposes of the School Standards and Framework Act 1998 s 45A(1) and the determination of a local authority's non-schools education budget see the School Funding (Wales) Regulations 2010, SI 2010/824; School and Early Years Finance (England) Regulations 2013, SI 2013/3104; and the School and Early Years Finance (England) Regulations 2014, SI 2014/3352.

316. Determination of school's budget share. Regulations[1] for the determination of a maintained school's budget share[2] may, in particular, make provision:

(1)   as to the time when schools' budget shares are to be initially determined by local authorities[3];

(2)   specifying factors or criteria which such authorities are to take into account, or requirements as to other matters with which such authorities are to comply, in determining such shares, whether generally or in such cases as are specified in the regulations[4];

(3)   requiring adjustments to be made to such shares by such authorities in respect of pupils[5] permanently excluded[6] from schools maintained[7] by them, or pupils admitted to schools maintained by them who have been permanently excluded from other maintained schools[8];

(4)   as to the treatment of new schools[9], including provision authorising the determination of nil amounts as the budget shares of such schools[10];

(5)   authorising or requiring such authorities to take account of matters arising during the course of a funding period[11] by redetermining budget shares for that funding period, or by making adjustments to such shares for the following funding period, in accordance with the regulations, and requiring them in that connection to disregard such matters as may be specified in the regulations[12];

(6)   requiring consultation to be carried out by such authorities in relation to the factors or criteria which are to be taken into account in determining such shares and as to the time and manner of such consultation[13];

(7)   authorising local authorities in prescribed cases to determine (or redetermine) budget shares, to such extent as may be prescribed, in accordance with arrangements approved by the authority's schools forum[14] or the Secretary of State or, in relation to Wales, the Welsh Ministers in accordance with the regulations (in place of the arrangements provided for by the regulations)[15];

(8)   authorising or requiring local authorities to take account of matters arising after the initial determination of budget shares for a funding period but before the beginning of the funding period, by redetermining budget shares for that period in accordance with the regulations, and requiring them in that connection to disregard such matters as may be specified in the regulations[16]; and

(9)   requiring notice of any initial determination or revised determination to be given in accordance with the regulations to the governing bodies of schools maintained by the authority[17] in question[18].

1   Ie regulations made by the Secretary of State or, in relation to Wales, the Welsh Ministers under the School Standards and Framework Act 1998: see s 142(1). The functions of the Secretary of State under the School Standards and Framework Act 1998 s 47, so far as exercisable in relation to Wales, were transferred to the National Assembly for Wales (see the National Assembly for Wales (Transfer of Functions) Order 1999, SI 1999/672, art 2, Sch 1) and are now vested in the Welsh Ministers (see the Government of Wales Act 2006 s 162(1), Sch 11 para 30). As to the Secretary of State see PARA 58. As to the Welsh Ministers see PARA 59. As to the meaning of 'Wales' see PARA 7 note 3.

       As to the regulations made under the School Standards and Framework Act 1998 s 47 see the School Funding (Wales) Regulations 2010, SI 2010/824; the School and Early Years Finance (England) Regulations 2013, SI 2013/3104; and the School and Early Years Finance (England) Regulations 2014, SI 2014/3352.

2   As to the meaning of 'maintained school' see PARA 315 note 1. As to the meaning of 'budget share' see PARA 315.

3   School Standards and Framework Act 1998 s 47(2)(a) (amended by SI 2010/1158). As to the meaning of 'local authority' see PARA 25 (definition applied by the School Standards and Framework Act 1998 s 142(8)). The time by which regulations made in pursuance of s 47(2)(a) require an initial determination of schools' budget shares for a funding period to be made may be up to 48 months before the beginning of the funding period: s 47(2A) (added by the Education Act 2005 s 101, Sch 16 para 6(1), (4)). As to the meaning of 'funding period' see PARA 315 note 3. As to the meaning of 'month' see PARA 54 note 26.

4   School Standards and Framework Act 1998 s 47(2)(b).

5   As to the meaning of 'pupil' see PARA 20 note 4 (definition applied by the School Standards and Framework Act 1998 s 142(8)).

6   'Exclude', in relation to the exclusion of a child from a school, means exclude on disciplinary grounds; and 'exclusion' must be construed accordingly: School Standards and Framework Act 1998 s 142(1) (definition added by the Education Act 2002 s 215(1), Sch 21 para 112). As to the meaning of 'child' see PARA 7 note 6; and as to the meaning of 'school' see PARA 91 (definitions applied by the School Standards and Framework Act 1998 s 142(8)). As to the

exclusion of pupils see PARA 517 et seq. As to the financial aspects of exclusion see the School Discipline (Pupil Exclusions and Reviews (England) Regulations 2012, SI 2012/1033, regs 7(1)(b), 16(1)(b), 25(1)(b); and PARAS 531, 533, 535; and see also 'Exclusion from maintained schools, academies and pupil referral units in England: Statutory guidance for those with legal responsibilities in relation to exclusion'; and PARA 540 note 13. As to recoupment in regard to excluded pupils see also PARA 331.

7 As to the meaning of 'schools maintained by a local authority' see PARA 315 note 2.

8 School Standards and Framework Act 1998 s 47(2)(c). Regulations made in pursuance of s 47(2)(c) may provide for the adjustments to be made on such basis as may be prescribed, which may involve the deduction from one school's budget share of an amount which is greater or less than that allocated to another school's budget share in respect of the excluded pupil: s 47(3). 'Prescribed' means prescribed by regulations: see s 142(1).

9 As to the meaning of 'new school' see PARA 315 note 2.

10 School Standards and Framework Act 1998 s 47(2)(d).

11 As to the meaning of 'funding period' see PARA 315 note 3.

12 School Standards and Framework Act 1998 s 47(2)(e) (amended by the Education Act 2005 Sch 16 para 6(1), (3)(b)).

13 School Standards and Framework Act 1998 s 47(2)(f).

14 As to schools forums see PARA 319.

15 School Standards and Framework Act 1998 s 47(2)(g) (substituted by the Education Act 2005 Sch 16 para 6(1), (3)(d); and amended by SI 2010/1158).

16 School Standards and Framework Act 1998 s 47(2)(dd) (added by the Education Act 2005 Sch 16 para 6(1), (3)(a); and amended by SI 2010/1158).

17 As to the meaning of 'governing body of a school maintained by a local authority' see PARA 315 note 2. As to the governing bodies of maintained schools in England see PARA 150 et seq; and in Wales see PARA 195.

18 School Standards and Framework Act 1998 s 47(2)(ff) (added by the Education Act 2005 Sch 16 para 6(1), (3)(c)).

317. Determination of local authority's schools budget in England. Regulations[1] may require a local authority[2] in England[3], not later than the prescribed date[4], to make an initial determination of its schools budget[5] for a funding period[6]. Such regulations may: (1) authorise or require local authorities in England to take account of matters arising after the initial determination of their schools budgets for any funding period but before the beginning of the funding period, by redetermining their schools budgets for the period in accordance with the regulations[7]; and (2) require notice of any initial determination or revised determination to be given in accordance with the regulations to the governing bodies of schools maintained by the local authority[8].

1 Ie regulations made by the Secretary of State under the School Standards and Framework Act 1998: see s142(1). As to the regulations made see the School and Early Years Finance (England) Regulations 2013, SI 2013/3104; and the School and Early Years Finance (England) Regulations 2014, SI 2014/3352. As to the Secretary of State see PARA 58.

2 As to the meaning of 'local authority' see PARA 25 (definition applied by the School Standards and Framework Act 1998 s 142(8)).

3 As to the meaning of 'England' see PARA 7 note 3.

4 The date prescribed for the purposes of the School Standards and Framework Act 1998 s 45AA(1) may be a date falling up to 48 months before the beginning of the funding period: s 45AA(2) (s 45AA added by the Education Act 2005 Sch 16 para 4). As to the meaning of 'month' see PARA 54 note 26. As to the meaning of 'funding period' see PARA 315 note 3. 'Prescribed' means prescribed by regulations: School Standards and Framework Act 1998 s 142(1). As to the regulations made see note 1.

5 As to the meaning of a local authority's 'schools budget' see PARA 315.

6 School Standards and Framework Act 1998 s 45AA(1) (as added (see note 4); and amended by SI 2010/1158).

7 School Standards and Framework Act 1998 s 45AA(3)(a) (as added (see note 4); and amended by SI 2010/1158).

8   School Standards and Framework Act 1998 s 45AA(3)(b) (as added (see note 4); and amended by SI 2010/1158). As to the meaning of 'governing body of a school maintained by a local authority' see PARA 315 note 2. As to the governing bodies of maintained schools in England see PARA 150 et seq.

318. Determination of local authority's schools budget in Wales. Regulations[1] may require a local authority in Wales[2], not later than the prescribed date[3], to make an initial determination of its schools budget[4] for a funding period[5]. Such regulations may: (1) authorise or require local authorities in Wales to take account of matters arising after the initial determination of their schools budgets for the funding period but before the beginning of the funding period, by redetermining their schools budgets for the period in accordance with the regulations[6]; and (2) require notice of any initial determination or revised determination to be given in accordance with the regulations to the Welsh Ministers and to the governing bodies of schools maintained by the local authority[7].

If it appears to the Welsh Ministers that, in all the circumstances, the proposed amount of a local authority's schools budget for a funding period[8] is inadequate, the Welsh Ministers may, within the period of 14 days beginning with the schools budget deadline[9] in the funding period preceding that funding period, give the authority a notice[10], which either:

(a)   determines the minimum amount of the authority's schools budget for the period under consideration[11]; or

(b)   specifies the amount which the Welsh Ministers would have determined as the minimum amount of the authority's schools budget for the period under consideration if they had acted under head (a) above and states the Welsh Ministers' intention to determine the minimum amount of the authority's schools budget for the following funding period[12].

If, at the schools budget deadline in any funding period, a local authority in Wales has failed to give the Welsh Ministers a notice[13], the Welsh Ministers may, at any time after that deadline, give the authority a notice under head (a) or head (b) above[14].

The local authority may, within the period of 14 days beginning with the date of a notice given under head (a) above, give the Welsh Ministers notice of its objection to the Welsh Ministers determination, giving reasons for its objection[15]. Where the local authority has given notice of its objection in this way, the notice given under head (a) above ceases to have effect, but the Welsh Ministers may by order prescribe the minimum amount of the authority's schools budget for the period under consideration[16]. However, where a notice under head (a) above has been given to a local authority and no notice of objection has been given during the period specified[17], or where an order has been made[18] by the Welsh Ministers[19], the local authority must determine a schools budget for the period under consideration which is not less than the amount specified in relation to the authority in the notice or order[20].

The Welsh Ministers may by order repeal any of those provisions above as are specified[21], and may make any amendments of other provisions of the School Standards and Framework Act 1998[22] which appear to them to be necessary or expedient in consequence of any such repeal[23].

1   'Regulations' means regulations made by the Welsh Ministers: see the School Standards and Framework Act 1998 s 142(1). As to the regulations made see the School Funding (Wales) Regulations 2010, SI 2010/824 (amended by SI 2010/1142). The functions under the School Standards and Framework Act 1998 ss 45AC, 45B–45D were formerly vested in the National

Assembly for Wales and are now exercisable by the Welsh Ministers by virtue of the Government of Wales Act 2006 s 162(1), Sch 11 paras 30, 32. As to the Welsh Ministers see PARA 59.

2 As to the meaning of 'local authority in Wales' see PARA 25 (definition applied by the School Standards and Framework Act 1998 s 142(8)).

3 'Prescribed' means prescribed by regulations: School Standards and Framework Act 1998 s 142(1). The date prescribed for the purposes of s 45AC(1) may be a date falling up to 48 months before the beginning of the funding period: s 45AC(2) (s 45AC added by the Education Act 2005 s 101, Sch 16 para 4). As to the meaning of 'month' see PARA 54 note 26.

4 As to the meaning of a local authority's 'schools budget' see PARA 315.

5 School Standards and Framework Act 1998 s 45AC(1) (as added (see note 3); and amended by SI 2010/1158). As to the meaning of 'funding period' see PARA 315 note 3.

6 School Standards and Framework Act 1998 s 45AC(3)(a) (as added (see note 3); and amended by SI 2010/1158).

7 School Standards and Framework Act 1998 s 45AC(3)(b) (as added (see note 3); and amended by SI 2010/1158). As to the meaning of 'school maintained by a local authority' see PARA 315 note 2.

8 In the School Standards and Framework Act 1998 s 45B(1), the reference to the proposed amount of a local authority's schools budget for a funding period is a reference to such amount, determined by the authority in accordance with the regulations made under s 45AC(1) (see the text to notes 1–5) and specified in a notice required by those regulations to be given to the Welsh Ministers, as may be prescribed: see s 45B(2)(b) (s 45B added by the Education Act 2002 s 42; and substituted by the Education Act 2005 s 101, Sch 16 para 5; and the School Standards and Framework Act 1998 s 45B(2)(b) amended by SI 2010/1158).

9 In the School Standards and Framework Act 1998 s 45B, 'the schools budget deadline' means the time in the funding period preceding the funding period to which the schools budget relates by which regulations under s 45AC(1) (see the text to notes 1–5) require notice of a revised determination of the schools budget to be given to the Welsh Ministers: s 45B(4)(b) (as added and substituted: see note 8).

10 School Standards and Framework Act 1998 s 45B(1) (as added and substituted (see note 8); and amended by SI 2010/1158).

11 School Standards and Framework Act 1998 s 45B(6) (as added and substituted: see note 8). In s 45B and s 45C (see the text to notes 15–20), 'the period under consideration' means the funding period to which the notice mentioned in s 45B(2)(b) (see note 8) relates or, in a case falling within s 45B(3) (see the text to notes 13–14), the funding period in relation to which such a notice ought to have been given: s 45B(5) (as so added and substituted). A notice under s 45B(6) or s 45B(7) (see head (b) in the text) must include a statement of the reasons for giving the notice (s 45B(8) (as so added and substituted)); and the Welsh Ministers may act under different subsections in relation to different authorities (s 45B(9) (as so added and substituted)).

12 School Standards and Framework Act 1998 s 45B(7) (as added and substituted: see note 8). See also note 11.

13 Ie a notice required as mentioned in the School Standards and Framework Act 1998 s 45B(2)(b): see note 8.

14 School Standards and Framework Act 1998 s 45B(3) (as added and substituted (see note 8); and amended by SI 2010/1158).

15 School Standards and Framework Act 1998 s 45C(1) (s 45C added by the Education Act 2002 s 42; and substituted by the Education Act 2005 s 101, Sch 16 para 5; and the School Standards and Framework Act 1998 s 45C(1), (2), (5) amended by SI 2010/1158).

16 School Standards and Framework Act 1998 s 45C(2) (as added, substituted and amended: see note 15). The amount prescribed under s 45C(2) must not be greater than the amount specified in the notice under s 45B(6) (see head (a) in the text): s 45C(3) (as so added and substituted). An order under s 45C(2) may relate to two or more authorities: s 45C(4) (as so added and substituted). Orders under s 45C(2), being of local effect, are not recorded in this work.

17 School Standards and Framework Act 1998 s 45C(5)(a) (as added, substituted and amended: see note 15). The period mentioned in the text is the period specified in s 45C(1) (see the text to note 15): see s 45C(5)(a) (as so added, substituted and amended).

18 Ie under the School Standards and Framework Act 1998 s 45C(2): see the text to note 16.

19 School Standards and Framework Act 1998 s 45C(5)(b) (as added and substituted: see note 15).

20 School Standards and Framework Act 1998 s 45C(5) (as added, substituted and amended: see note 15).

21 Ie the Welsh Ministers may by order repeal any of the School Standards and Framework Act 1998 s 45B and s 45C (see the text to notes 8–20): see s 45D(a) (s 45D added by the Education Act 2005 s 101, Sch 16 para 5).

22 Ie other provisions of the School Standards and Framework Act 1998 Pt II Ch IV (ss 45–53A).
23 School Standards and Framework Act 1998 s 45D(b) (as added: see note 21).

319.   Schools forums to advise on matters relating to the local authority's schools budget.   Every local authority[1] must, in accordance with regulations[2], establish for its area a body to be known as a schools forum[3]. The purpose of a schools forum is:

(1)   to advise the relevant authority[4] on such matters relating to the authority's schools budget[5] as may be prescribed[6] by regulations[7]; and

(2)   to exercise any other function[8] that may be imposed[9] on the schools forum[10].

In exercising its functions, a schools forum is to have regard to any children and young people's plan[11] prepared by the local children's trust board[12].

Regulations[13] may include provision requiring a relevant authority to have regard to advice given by its schools forum, or requiring a relevant authority to consult its schools forum in relation to prescribed matters or before taking prescribed decisions[14]. Regulations must provide for a schools forum to include (a) members representing governing bodies of schools maintained by the relevant authority[15]; and (b) members representing head teachers of such schools[16]; and regulations may provide for a schools forum to include (c) members representing such other persons[17] as may be prescribed[18], or as the relevant authority may from time to time, in accordance with regulations, determine[19]; and (d) other members[20]. Regulations may also make (i) further provision as to the constitution of a schools forum[21]; (ii) provision as to meetings and proceedings of a schools forum[22]; and (iii) provision with respect to expenses of a schools forum[23].

1   As to the meaning of 'local authority' see PARA 25 (definition applied by the School Standards and Framework Act 1998 s 142(8)). The School Standards and Framework Act 1998 s 47A(1) does not apply in relation to the Common Council of the City of London or the Council of the Isles of Scilly: s 47A(2) (s 47A added by the Education Act 2002 s 43). As to the Common Council of the City of London see LONDON GOVERNMENT vol 71 (2013) PARAS 34–38; and as to the Council of the Isles of Scilly see LOCAL GOVERNMENT vol 69 (2009) PARA 36.

2   Ie regulations made by the Secretary of State or, in relation to Wales, the Welsh Ministers under the School Standards and Framework Act 1998: see s 142(1). As to the regulations made see the Schools Forums (England) Regulations 2012, SI 2012/2261 (amended by SI 2012/2991). See also note 3. The functions of the Secretary of State under the School Standards and Framework Act 1998 s 47A, so far as exercisable in relation to Wales, were transferred to the National Assembly for Wales (see the National Assembly for Wales (Transfer of Functions) Order 1999, SI 1999/672, art 2, Sch 1) and are now vested in the Welsh Ministers (see the Government of Wales Act 2006 s 162(1), Sch 11 para 30). As to the Secretary of State see PARA 58. As to the Welsh Ministers see PARA 59. As to the meaning of 'Wales' see PARA 7 note 3. As to departmental advice for local authorities and members of school forums on the Schools Forums (England) Regulations 2012, SI 2012/2261 see the Department for education website.

3   School Standards and Framework Act 1998 s 47A(1) (s 47A as added (see note 1); s 47A(1) substituted by the Education and Skills Act 2008 s 165(1), (2); and amended by SI 2010/1158). At the date at which this volume states the law, the School Standards and Framework Act 1998 s 47A(1) (as so added and substituted) is in force in relation to England only: see the Education and Skills Act 2008 (Commencement No 1 and Savings) Order 2008, SI 2008/3077, art 5(b). As to the meaning of 'England' see PARA 7 note 3. Until such time as the School Standards and Framework Act 1998 s 47A(1) (as so added and substituted) is brought into force in relation to Wales the following provision applies in relation to Wales: Every local authority must in accordance with regulations establish for its area before such date as may be prescribed a body, to be known as a schools forum, representing the governing bodies and head teachers of schools maintained by the authority and, if the authority so determine, also representing such bodies as the authority may from time to time in accordance with regulations determine: s 47A(1) (as added (see note 1); and amended by SI 2010/1158). 'Prescribed' means prescribed by regulations: see the School Standards and Framework Act 1998 s 142(1). As to the regulations

made see the Schools Forums (Wales) Regulations 2003, SI 2003/2909 (amended by SI 2005/2913; SI 2005/3238; and SI 2006/5). As to the meaning of 'governing body of a school maintained by a local authority' see PARA 315 note 2. As to the meaning of 'head teacher' see PARA 86 note 4 (definition applied by s 142(8)). It should be noted that schools forums are different from admissions forums, which are no longer required in England except in the Isles of Scilly: see the School Standards and Framework Act 1998 s 88M; and PARA 243.

4 'Relevant authority', in relation to a schools forum, means the local authority by whom the forum is established: School Standards and Framework Act 1998 s 47A(9) (s 47A as added (see note 1); s 47A(9) substituted by the Education and Inspections Act 2006 s 57, Sch 5 para 2(1), (4); and amended by SI 2010/1158).

5 As to the meaning of a local authority's 'schools budget' see PARA 315.

6 Ie by regulations under the School Standards and Framework Act 1998 s 45A(3) (see PARA 288) or by regulations under s 47A(3): see s 47A(3)(a) (s 47A as added (see note 1); s 47A(3) substituted by the Education Act 2005 s 101, Sch 16 para 7).

7 School Standards and Framework Act 1998 s 47A(3)(a) (as added and substituted: see note 6). As to the regulations made see notes 2, 3.

8 As to the meaning of 'functions' see PARA 18 note 5 (definition applied by the School Standards and Framework Act 1998 s 142(8)).

9 Ie by or under the School Standards and Framework Act 1998 Pt II Ch IV (ss 45–53A).

10 School Standards and Framework Act 1998 s 47A(3)(b) (as added and substituted (see note 6); and amended by the Education and Inspections Act 2006 s 57, Sch 5 para 2(1), (2)).

11 A 'children and young people's plan' means a plan published by a children's trust board under the Children Act 2004 s 17 (see CHILDREN AND YOUNG PERSONS vol 9 (2012) PARA 190); and 'the local children's trust board', in relation to a schools forum, is the children's trust board established by arrangements made under s 10 of that Act (see CHILDREN AND YOUNG PERSONS vol 9 (2012) PARA 203) by the relevant authority: School Standards and Framework Act 1998 s 47A(10) (s 47A as added (see note 1); s 47A(10) added by the Apprenticeships, Skills, Children and Learning Act 2009 s 194(8)(b); and amended by SI 2010/1158).

12 School Standards and Framework Act 1998 s 47A(3A) (s 47A as added (see note 1); s 47A(3A) added by the Apprenticeships, Skills, Children and Learning Act 2009 s 194(8)(a)).

13 Ie regulations under the School Standards and Framework Act 1998 s 45A(3) (see PARA 315) or under s 47A(3) (see the text to notes 4–10).

14 School Standards and Framework Act 1998 s 47A(4) (as added: see note 1). As to the regulations made see notes 2, 3.

15 School Standards and Framework Act 1998 s 47A(4A)(a) (s 47A as added (see note 1); s 47A(4A), (4B) added by the Education and Skills Act 2008 s 165(1), (3)). At the date at which this volume states the law the School Standards and Framework Act 1998 s 47A(4A), (4B) is in force in relation to England only: see the Education and Skills Act 2008 (Commencement No 1 and Savings) Order 2008, SI 2008/3077, art 5(b). As to the regulations made see note 2.

16 School Standards and Framework Act 1998 s 47A(4A)(b) (as added: see note 15). As to the regulations made see note 2.

17 As to the meaning of 'person' see PARA 7 note 6.

18 School Standards and Framework Act 1998 s 47A(4B)(a)(i) (as added: see note 15). As to the regulations made see note 2.

19 School Standards and Framework Act 1998 s 47A(4B)(a)(ii) (as added: see note 15). As to the regulations made see note 2.

20 School Standards and Framework Act 1998 s 47A(4B)(b) (as added: see note 15). As to the regulations made see note 2.

21 School Standards and Framework Act 1998 s 47A(4B) (as added: see note 15). As to the regulations made see note 2.

22 School Standards and Framework Act 1998 s 47A(5) (as added (see note 1); and amended by the Education and Skills Act 2008 ss 165(1), (4), 169, Sch 2). At the date at which this volume states the law, the School Standards and Framework Act 1998 s 47A(5) (as so added and amended) is in force in relation to England only: see the Education and Inspections Act 2006 (Commencement No 2) Order 2006, SI 2006/3400, art 4(c), (d). Until such time as the School Standards and Framework Act 1998 s 47A(5) (as so added and amended) is brought into force in relation to Wales the following provision applies in relation to Wales: Regulations may make provision as to the constitution, meetings and proceedings of a schools forum: s 47A(5) (as added: see note 1). As to the regulations made see notes 2, 3.

23 School Standards and Framework Act 1998 s 47A(7) (as added: see note 1). Except as provided by regulations, the expenses of a schools forum must be defrayed by the relevant authority: s 47A(8) (as so added). As to the regulations made see notes 2, 3.

320. Budgetary provision in respect of free of charge early years provision in England. Where a local authority in England[1] proposes to allocate an amount of relevant financial assistance[2] to a relevant childcare provider[3] for a funding period[4] out of the authority's individual schools budget[5] for the period[6], the amount to be allocated is to be determined[7] in accordance with regulations[8]. Such regulations may, in particular[9]:

(1)   specify factors or criteria which an authority is to take into account in determining the amount of any relevant financial assistance to be provided by it to a relevant childcare provider[10];

(2)   specify factors or criteria which an authority is to disregard in determining such an amount[11];

(3)   specify requirements as to other matters with which an authority is to comply in determining such an amount[12];

(4)   make provision about consultation to be carried out by an authority in connection with determining such an amount[13];

(5)   authorise an authority, in prescribed[14] circumstances and to a prescribed extent, to determine such an amount in accordance with arrangements approved by the Secretary of State (instead of in accordance with arrangements provided for by the regulations)[15];

(6)   require an authority to provide relevant childcare providers with prescribed information relating to its determination of such an amount[16];

(7)   make provision about the circumstances in which an authority is required to redetermine such an amount[17];

(8)   specify a time by which an authority's determination of such an amount is to take place[18].

1   As to the meaning of 'local authority in England' see PARA 25 (definition applied by the School Standards and Framework Act 1998 s 142(8)).

2   Financial assistance provided by a local authority in England to a childcare provider is 'relevant' financial assistance if it is provided for the purpose of the discharge of the authority's duty under the Childcare Act 2006 s 7 (see CHILDREN AND YOUNG PERSONS vol 10 (2012) PARA 1083), and in respect of the provision of childcare: School Standards and Framework Act 1998 s 47ZA(3) (s 47ZA added by the Apprenticeships, Skills, Children and Learning Act 2009 s 202(1); and the School Standards and Framework Act 1998 s 47ZA(3) amended by SI 2010/1158). 'Childcare' has the meaning given in the Childcare Act 2006 s 18 (see CHILDREN AND YOUNG PERSONS vol 10 (2012) PARA 1082): School Standards and Framework Act 1998 s 47ZA(5)(a) (as so added).

3   'Relevant childcare provider' means a provider of childcare other than the governing body of a maintained school: School Standards and Framework Act 1998 s 47ZA(5)(b) (as added: see note 2). As to the meaning of 'governing body of a maintained school' see PARA 315 note 2. As to the meaning of 'maintained school' see PARA 315 note 1.

4   As to the meaning of 'funding period' see PARA 315 note 3.

5   As to the meaning of a local authority's 'schools budget' see PARA 315.

6   School Standards and Framework Act 1998 s 47ZA(1) (as added (see note 2); and amended by SI 2010/1158).

7   A reference to an authority's determination of the amount of any relevant financial assistance includes a reference to the authority's redetermination of such an amount: School Standards and Framework Act 1998 s 47ZA(5)(c) (as added: see note 2).

8   School Standards and Framework Act 1998 s 47ZA(2) (as added: see note 2). 'Regulations' means regulations made by the Secretary of State under the School Standards and Framework Act 1998: see s 142(1). As to the Secretary of State see PARA 58. As to the regulations made see the School and Early Years Finance (England) Regulations 2014, SI 2014/3352.

9   School Standards and Framework Act 1998 s 47ZA(4) (as added: see note 2).

10 School Standards and Framework Act 1998 s 47ZA(4)(a) (as added: see note 2).

11 School Standards and Framework Act 1998 s 47ZA(4)(b) (as added: see note 2).

12 School Standards and Framework Act 1998 s 47ZA(4)(c) (as added: see note 2).

13 School Standards and Framework Act 1998 s 47ZA(4)(d) (as added: see note 2).
14 'Prescribed' means prescribed by the regulations: see the School Standards and Framework Act 1998 s 142(1).
15 School Standards and Framework Act 1998 s 47ZA(4)(e) (as added: see note 2).
16 School Standards and Framework Act 1998 s 47ZA(4)(f) (as added: see note 2).
17 School Standards and Framework Act 1998 s 47ZA(4)(g) (as added: see note 2).
18 School Standards and Framework Act 1998 s 47ZA(4)(h) (as added: see note 2).

321. Local authorities' financial schemes. Each local authority[1] must maintain a scheme dealing with such matters connected with the financing of the schools maintained by the authority[2] or the exercise by the governing bodies of those schools[3] of the power to provide community facilities etc[4] as are required to be dealt with in the scheme[5] by or by virtue of[6] regulations made by the appropriate national authority[7], or any provision of Part II[8] of the School Standards and Framework Act 1998[9]. Such regulations may, in particular, require a scheme to deal with:

(1) the carrying forward from one funding period to another of surpluses and deficits arising in relation to schools' budget shares[10];

(2) amounts which may be charged against schools' budget shares[11];

(3) amounts received by schools which may be retained by their governing bodies and the purposes for which such amounts may be used[12];

(4) the imposition, by or under the scheme, of conditions which must be complied with by schools in relation to the management of their delegated budgets, including conditions prescribing financial controls and procedures[13];

(5) the imposition, by or under the scheme, of conditions which must be complied with by schools in relation to the exercise by the governing bodies of maintained schools of the power to provide community facilities etc[14], including conditions prescribing financial controls and procedures[15];

(6) terms on which services and facilities are provided by the authority for schools maintained by it[16].

Where there is any inconsistency between a scheme maintained by a local authority[17] and any other rules or regulations made by the authority which relate to the funding or financial management of schools which it maintains, the terms of the scheme must prevail[18].

1 As to the meaning of 'local authority' see PARA 25 (definition applied by the School Standards and Framework Act 1998 s 142(8)). Any function of a local authority in England which is conferred by or under the School Standards and Framework Act 1998 s 48 may be exercised by, or by employees of, such person as may be authorised in that behalf by the local authority whose function it is: Contracting Out (Local Authority Education Functions) (England) Order 2002, SI 2002/928, art 3, Sch 2 para (k) (art 3 amended by SI 2010/1172). As to the meaning of 'person' see PARA 7 note 6. As to the meaning of 'England' see PARA 7 note 3.
2 As to the meaning of 'schools maintained by a local authority' see PARA 315 note 2.
3 As to the meaning of 'governing body of a school maintained by a local authority' see PARA 315 note 2.
4 Ie the power conferred by the Education Act 2002 s 27: see PARAS 174, 208. Expenditure incurred by the governing body of a maintained school in Wales in the exercise of the power conferred by s 27 must, as against third parties, be treated as part of the expenses of maintaining the school under the School Standards and Framework Act 1998 s 22 (see PARA 305 et seq) but if met by the local authority may be recovered by it from the governing body: s 51A(1) (s 51A added by the Education Act 2002 s 40, Sch 3 para 4; and the School Standards and Framework Act 1998 s 51A(1) amended by the Children, Schools and Families Act 2010 s 4(4); and SI 2010/1158). Except as provided by regulations under the School Standards and Framework Act 1998 s 50(3)(b) (see PARA 324), no expenditure incurred by the governing body of a maintained school in Wales in the exercise of the power referred to in s 51A(1) must be met

from the school's budget share for any funding period: s 51A(2) (as so added; and amended by the Education Act 2005 s 117, Sch 18 para 9; and the Children, Schools and Families Act 2010 s 4(4)). The School Standards and Framework Act 1998 s 51A(2) applies at a time when the school does not have a delegated budget by virtue of any suspension under Sch 15 (see PARAS 325–327) or the School Standards and Organisation (Wales) Act 2013 s 8 (see PARA 1233), as well as a time when it does have a delegated budget: School Standards and Framework Act 1998 s 51A(3) (as so added; and amended by the School Standards and Organisation (Wales) Act 2013 Sch 5 para 4(1), (3)). As to the meaning of 'maintained school' see PARA 315 note 1. As to the meaning of 'funding period' see PARA 315 note 3. As to the meaning of 'budget share' see PARA 315. As to the meaning of 'school having a delegated budget' see PARA 323. As to the meaning of 'Wales' see PARA 7 note 3.

5 In the School Standards and Framework Act 1998 Pt II (ss 20–83) any reference to 'the scheme', in relation to a maintained school, is a reference to the scheme for the time being maintained under s 48: s 48(5) (amended by the Education and Inspections Act 2006 s 57, Sch 5 para 3(1), (5)).

6 School Standards and Framework Act 1998 s 48(1) (amended by the Education Act 2002 s 40, Sch 3 para 2(1), (2); the Education and Inspections Act 2006 s 57, Sch 5 para 3(1), (2); and SI 2010/1158).

7 School Standards and Framework Act 1998 s 48(1)(a). 'Appropriate national authority' means the Secretary of State or, in relation to Wales, the Welsh Ministers. The functions of the Secretary of State under the School Standards and Framework Act 1998 s 48, so far as exercisable in relation to Wales, were transferred to the National Assembly for Wales (see the National Assembly for Wales (Transfer of Functions) Order 1999, SI 1999/672, art 2, Sch 1) and are now vested in the Welsh Ministers (see the Government of Wales Act 2006 s 162(1), Sch 11 para 30). As to the Secretary of State see PARA 58. As to the Welsh Ministers see PARA 59. As to the regulations made under the School Standards and Framework Act 1998 s 48(1), (2) (see the text to notes 10–16) see the School Funding (Wales) Regulations 2010, SI 2010/824 (amended by SI 2010/1142); the School and Early Years Finance (England) Regulations 2013, SI 2013/3104; and the School and Early Years Finance (England) Regulations 2014, SI 2014/3352.

8 Ie the School Standards and Framework Act 1998 Pt II (ss 20–83).

9 School Standards and Framework Act 1998 s 48(1)(b).

10 School Standards and Framework Act 1998 s 48(2)(a) (amended by the Education Act 2005 Sch 18 para 7).

11 School Standards and Framework Act 1998 s 48(2)(b).

12 School Standards and Framework Act 1998 s 48(2)(c).

13 School Standards and Framework Act 1998 s 48(2)(d).

14 Ie the power conferred by the Education Act 2002 s 27: see PARAS 174, 208.

15 School Standards and Framework Act 1998 s 48(2)(dd) (added by the Education Act 2002 Sch 3 para 2(1), (3)).

16 School Standards and Framework Act 1998 s 48(2)(e).

17 Ie under the School Standards and Framework Act 1998 s 48(1): see the text to notes 1–9.

18 School Standards and Framework Act 1998 s 48(3) (amended by the Education and Inspections Act 2006 s 57, Sch 5 para 3(1), (3); and SI 2010/1158).

322. Publication and revision of financial schemes. A scheme maintained by a local authority[1] must be published in such manner as may be prescribed[2] (1) on its coming into force as revised under the following provisions[3]; and (2) on such other occasions as may be prescribed[4].

A local authority may revise the whole or part of the scheme maintained by it[5]. In revising the scheme, the local authority must take into account any guidance given by the appropriate national authority[6], whether:

(a) generally[7]; or

(b) in relation to that authority or any class or description of local authorities to which that authority belongs[8],

as to the provisions the appropriate national authority regards as appropriate for inclusion in the scheme[9]. As regards any proposed variation of the scheme, the authority must first consult the governing body[10] and head teacher[11] of every school maintained by the authority[12], and must then submit a copy of its proposals to the authority's schools forum[13] for its approval[14].

The Secretary of State may by a direction revise the whole or any part of a scheme maintained by a local authority in England as from such date as may be specified in the direction[15].

Regulations[16] may make provision preventing schemes as revised from coming into force unless they are approved in accordance with the regulations by the local authority's schools forum or by the appropriate national authority[17]. The regulations may in particular: (i) prescribe circumstances in which proposals which have been submitted to a local authority's schools forum may be submitted to the appropriate national authority[18]; (ii) enable the schools forum or the appropriate national authority to approve proposals with modifications[19]; and (iii) enable the schools forum or the appropriate national authority, in giving approval, to specify the date on which the scheme as revised is to come into force[20].

1 Ie under the School Standards and Framework Act 1998 s 48(1): see PARA 321. As to the meaning of 'local authority' see PARA 25 (definition applied by the School Standards and Framework Act 1998 s 142(8)). Any function of a local authority in England which is conferred by or under Sch 14 may be exercised by, or by employees of, such person as may be authorised in that behalf by the local authority whose function it is: Contracting Out (Local Authority Education Functions) (England) Order 2002, SI 2002/928, art 3, Sch 2 para (k) (art 3 amended by SI 2010/1172). As to the meaning of 'person' see PARA 7 note 6. As to the meaning of 'England' see PARA 7 note 3.

2 'Prescribed' means prescribed by regulations made by the Secretary of State or, in relation to Wales, the Welsh Ministers under the School Standards and Framework Act 1998: see s 142(1). As to the regulations made under Sch 14 see the School Funding (Wales) Regulations 2010, SI 2010/824 (amended by SI 2010/1142); the School and Early Years Finance (England) Regulations 2013, SI 2013/3104; and the School and Early Years Finance (England) Regulations 2014, SI 2014/3352.

The functions of the Secretary of State under the School Standards and Framework Act 1998 Sch 14, so far as exercisable in relation to Wales, were transferred to the National Assembly for Wales (see the National Assembly for Wales (Transfer of Functions) Order 1999, SI 1999/672, art 2, Sch 1) and are now vested in the Welsh Ministers (see the Government of Wales Act 2006 s 162(1), Sch 11 para 30). As to the Secretary of State see PARA 58. As to the Welsh Ministers see PARA 59. As to the meaning of 'Wales' see PARA 7 note 3.

3 School Standards and Framework Act 1998 Sch 14 para 1(7)(a) (Sch 14 para 1(7) substituted by the Education and Inspections Act 2006 s 57, Sch 5 para 5(1), (4)(b); and the School Standards and Framework Act 1998 Sch 14 para 1(7)(a) amended by SI 2010/1158).

4 School Standards and Framework Act 1998 Sch 14 para 1(7)(b) (as substituted: see note 3).

5 School Standards and Framework Act 1998 Sch 14 para 2A(1) (Sch 14 paras 2A, 2B added by the Education and Inspections Act 2006 s 57, Sch 5 para 5(1), (5); and amended by SI 2010/1158).

6 The 'appropriate national authority' means the Secretary of State or, in relation to Wales, the Welsh Ministers.

7 School Standards and Framework Act 1998 Sch 14 para 2A(2)(a) (as added: see note 5).

8 School Standards and Framework Act 1998 Sch 14 para 2A(2)(b) (as added and amended: see note 5).

9 School Standards and Framework Act 1998 Sch 14 para 2A(2) (as added and amended: see note 5).

10 As to the meaning of 'governing body of a school maintained by a local authority' see PARA 315 note 2.

11 As to the meaning of 'head teacher' see PARA 86 note 4 (definition applied by the School Standards and Framework Act 1998 s 142(8)).

12 School Standards and Framework Act 1998 Sch 14 para 2A(3)(a) (as added: see note 5). As to the meaning of 'school maintained by a local authority' see PARA 315 note 2.

13 As to schools forums see PARA 319.

14 School Standards and Framework Act 1998 Sch 14 para 2A(3)(b) (as added: see note 5).

15 School Standards and Framework Act 1998 Sch 14 para 2A(4) (Sch 14 para 2A(4), (5) added by the Education Act 2011 s 46). Before giving such a direction the Secretary of State must consult

the local authority and such other persons as the Secretary of State thinks fit: School Standards and Framework Act 1998 Sch 14 para 2A(5) (as so added).

16 As to the regulations made see note 2.

17 School Standards and Framework Act 1998 Sch 14 para 2B(1) (as added and amended: see note 5).

18 School Standards and Framework Act 1998 Sch 14 para 2B(2)(a) (as added and amended: see note 5).

19 School Standards and Framework Act 1998 Sch 14 para 2B(2)(b) (as added: see note 5). As to the meaning of 'modifications' see PARA 21 note 15 (definition applied by s 142(8)).

20 School Standards and Framework Act 1998 Sch 14 para 2B(2)(c) (as added: see note 5).

323.   Maintained schools to have delegated budgets.   Every maintained school[1] must have a 'delegated budget'[2], which means that the governing body of the school[3] is entitled to manage the school's budget share[4]. Where a school has a delegated budget the governing body is accordingly said to 'have a right to a delegated budget'[5]. A new school[6] must have a delegated budget as from a date determined in accordance with regulations[7].

Subject to:

(1)   the right[8] of a governing body to spend the school's budget share where the school has a delegated budget[9];

(2)   the power[10] of governing body to spend amounts out of the budget share where the delegation of the budget is suspended[11];

(3)   education standards grants[12]; and

(4)   any provisions of the scheme[13],

a local authority may not delegate to the governing body of any maintained school the power to spend any part of the authority's non-schools education budget[14] or schools budget[15].

Any amount made available by a local authority to the governing body of a maintained school[16] remains the property of the authority until spent by the governing body or the head teacher[17], and when spent by the governing body or the head teacher, must be taken to be spent by it or him as the authority's agent[18].

1   As to the meaning of 'maintained school' see PARA 315 note 1. As to academies see PARA 345 et seq.

2   School Standards and Framework Act 1998 s 49(1). As to the effect of financial delegation see PARA 324.

3   As to the meaning of governing bodies of maintained schools see PARA 288 note 2.

4   Schools Standards and Framework Act 1998 s 49(7)(a). As to the meaning of 'budget share' see PARA 315.

5   School Standards and Framework Act 1998 s 49(7)(b).

6   As to the meaning of 'new school' see PARA 315 note 2.

7   School Standards and Framework Act 1998 s 49(2) (s 49(2) substituted, s 49(2A) added, by the Education and Inspections Act 2006 s 57, Sch 5 para 4). Such regulations may: (1) enable the date that would otherwise apply by virtue of the regulations to be varied in accordance with the regulations, on the application of the local authority, by the authority's schools forum or by the appropriate national authority (School Standards and Framework Act 1998 s 49(2A)(a) (as so added; and amended by SI 2010/1158)); and (2) make provision about the respective powers of the schools forum and the appropriate national authority in relation to any application to vary that date (School Standards and Framework Act 1998 s 49(2A)(b) (as so added)). As to schools forums see PARA 319. The 'appropriate national authority' means the Secretary of State or, in relation to Wales, the Welsh Ministers. The functions of the Secretary of State under the School Standards and Framework Act 1998 s 49, so far as exercisable in relation to Wales, were transferred to the National Assembly for Wales (see the National Assembly for Wales (Transfer of Functions) Order 1999, SI 1999/672, art 2, Sch 1) and are now vested in the Welsh Ministers (see the Government of Wales Act 2006 s 162(1), Sch 11 para 30). As to the Secretary of State see PARA 58. As to the Welsh Ministers see PARA 59. As to the meaning of 'Wales' see PARA 7 note 3.

As to the regulations made under the School Standards and Framework Act 1998 s 49(2), (2A) see the School and Early Years Finance (England) Regulations 2013, SI 2013/3104; and the School and Early Years Finance (England) Regulations 2014, SI 2014/3352.

8 Ie the right under the School Standards and Framework Act 1998 s 50: see PARA 324.

9 School Standards and Framework Act 1998 s 49(4)(a).

10 Ie under the School Standards and Framework Act 1998 Sch 15 para 4: see PARA 327.

11 School Standards and Framework Act 1998 s 49(4)(b).

12 School Standards and Framework Act 1998 s 49(4)(c). The education standards grants referred to are those under the Education Act 1996 s 489(2) (see PARA 83): see the School Standards and Framework Act 1998 s 49(4)(c).

13 School Standards and Framework Act 1998 s 49(4)(d). As to the meaning of 'the scheme' see PARA 321 note 5.

14 As to the meaning of a local authority's 'non-schools education budget' see PARA 315.

15 School Standards and Framework Act 1998 s 49(4) (amended by the Education Act 2002 s 215(1), Sch 21 para 100(1), (2); SI 2010/1158). As to the meaning of 'schools budget' see PARA 315.

16 Ie whether under the School Standards and Framework Act 1998 s 50 (see PARA 324) or otherwise: s 49(5) (amended by SI 2010/1158).

17 School Standards and Framework Act 1998 s 49(5)(a). As to the meaning of 'head teacher' see PARA 86 note 4 (definition applied by s 142(8)). See *Coventry City Council v Special Educational Needs and Disability Tribunal* [2007] EWHC 2278 (Admin), [2008] ELR 1, [2007] All ER (D) 60 (Sep).

18 School Standards and Framework Act 1998 s 49(5)(b). Section 49(5)(b) does not apply to any such amount where it is spent by way of repayment of the principal of, or interest on, a loan (s 49(6)(a)), or (in the case of a voluntary aided school) to meet (1) (in relation to Wales) expenses payable by the governing body under Sch 3 para 3(1) or Sch 3 para 3(2) (see PARA 311) or (in relation to England) expenditure payable by the governing body under Sch 3 para 3(1); or (2) the Education Act 2002 Sch 8 para 8 (repealed) or the Schools Standards and Organisation (Wales) Act 2013 s 75(2)(b) (see PARA 1249) or Sch 3 para 4 (proposals relating to voluntary aided schools): see the School Standards and Framework Act 1998 s 49(6)(b) (amended by the Education Act 2002 Sch 21 para 100(1), (3); and, in relation to England, by SI 2002/906; and by the Schools Standards and Organisation (Wales) Act 2013 Sch 5 para 19(1), (7)). As to voluntary aided schools see PARA 106. As to the meaning of 'England' see PARA 7 note 3.

324. Effect of financial delegation. Where a maintained school[1] has a delegated budget[2] in respect of the whole or part of a funding period[3] the local authority[4] must secure that in respect of that period there is available to be spent by the governing body[5]:

(1) where the school has a delegated budget in respect of the whole of that period, a sum equal to the school's budget share[6] for the period[7]; or

(2) where the school has a delegated budget in respect of only part of that period, a sum equal to that portion of the school's budget share for the period which has not been spent[8].

The times at which, and the manner in which, any amounts are made available by the authority to the governing body in respect of any such sum are such as may be provided by or under the scheme[9].

Subject to any provision made by or under the scheme, the governing body may spend any such amounts as it thinks fit for any purposes of the school[10] or (subject also to any prescribed[11] conditions) for such purposes as may be prescribed[12]. However, nothing in this provision[13] must be read as authorising the payment of allowances to governors otherwise than in accordance with the appropriate regulations[14]. The governing body may delegate to the head teacher[15], to such extent as may be permitted by or under the scheme, these powers[16] in relation to any amount such as is mentioned[17] above[18]. The governors of a school will not incur any personal liability in respect of anything done in good faith in the exercise or purported exercise of these powers[19].

1 As to the meaning of 'maintained school' see PARA 315 note 1.

2   As to the meaning of 'school having a delegated budget' see PARA 323.

3   As to the meaning of 'funding period' see PARA 315 note 3.

4   As to the meaning of 'local authority' see PARA 25 (definition applied by the School Standards and Framework Act 1998 s 142(8)). Any function of a local authority in England which is conferred by or under the School Standards and Framework Act 1998 s 50 may be exercised by, or by employees of, such person as may be authorised in that behalf by the local authority whose function it is: Contracting Out (Local Authority Education Functions) (England) Order 2002, SI 2002/928, art 3, Sch 2 para (l) (art 3 amended by SI 2010/1172). As to the meaning of 'person' see PARA 7 note 6. As to the meaning of 'England' see PARA 7 note 3.

5   School Standards and Framework Act 1998 s 50(1) (amended by the Education Act 2005 s 117, Sch 18 para 8(a), (b); and SI 2010/1158). As to the meaning of 'governing body of a school maintained by a local authority' see PARA 315 note 2.

6   As to the meaning of 'budget share' see PARA 315.

7   School Standards and Framework Act 1998 s 50(1)(a) (amended by the Education Act 2005 s 117, Sch 18 para 8(c)).

8   School Standards and Framework Act 1998 s 50(1)(b) (amended by the Education Act 2005 s 117, Sch 18 para 8(c)).

9   School Standards and Framework Act 1998 s 50(2). As to the meaning of 'the scheme' see PARA 321 note 5.

10   School Standards and Framework Act 1998 s 50(3)(a). In the case of a school in Wales, 'purposes of the school' in s 50(3) does not include purposes wholly referable to the provision of:

    (1)   facilities and services under the Education Act 2002 s 27 (power of governing body to provide community facilities etc: see PARA 174) (School Standards and Framework Act 1998 s 50(4)(za) (added by the Education Act 2002 s 40, Sch 3 para 3));

    (2)   part-time education suitable to the requirements of persons of any age over compulsory school age (School Standards and Framework Act 1998 s 50 (4)(a)); or

    (3)   full-time education suitable to the requirements of persons who have attained the age of 19 (s 50(4)(b));

but any such purposes may be prescribed by regulations under s 50(3)(b) (see the text to note 12): s 50(4) (amended by the Children, Schools and Families Act 2010 s 4(3)). As to the meaning of 'Wales' see PARA 7 note 3. As to the meaning of 'compulsory school age' see PARA 19. As to the time at which a person attains a particular age see PARA 7 note 6.

     In the case of a school in England: (a) subject to regulations under head (b) below, the School Standards and Framework Act 1998 s 50(3)(a) has effect as if amounts spent on providing facilities or services under the Education Act 2002 s 27 (power of governing body to provide community facilities etc) were spent for purposes of the school; (b) regulations may impose restrictions as to the matters on which amounts may be spent under s 50(3)(a): s 50(3A) (added by the Children, Schools and Families Act 2010 s 4(2)).

11   'Prescribed' means prescribed by regulations made by the Secretary of State or, in relation to Wales, the Welsh Ministers under the School Standards and Framework Act 1998: see s 142(1). The functions of the Secretary of State under the School Standards and Framework Act 1998 s 50, so far as exercisable in relation to Wales, were transferred to the National Assembly for Wales (see the National Assembly for Wales (Transfer of Functions) Order 1999, SI 1999/672, art 2, Sch 1) and are now vested in the Welsh Ministers (see the Government of Wales Act 2006 s 162(1), Sch 11 para 30). As to the Secretary of State see PARA 58. As to the Welsh Ministers see PARA 59.

12   School Standards and Framework Act 1998 s 50(3)(b). As to the regulations made see the School Budget Shares (Prescribed Purposes) (England) Regulations 2002, SI 2002/378 (amended by SI 2004/444; and SI 2010/190); and the School Budget Shares (Prescribed Purposes and Consequential Amendments) (Wales) Regulations 2008, SI 2008/1866.

13   Ie nothing in the School Standards and Framework Act 1998 s 50(3): see the text to notes 10–12.

14   See the School Standards and Framework Act 1998 s 50(5). The appropriate regulations are those under the Education Act 2002 s 19 (see PARAS 150, 195) (or, in the case of temporary governors of a new school, regulations under s 34(5) of that Act (see PARAS 155, 197)): see the School Standards and Framework Act 1998 s 50(5) (amended by the Education Act 2002 s 215(1), Sch 21 para 101).

15   As to the meaning of 'head teacher' see PARA 86 note 4 (definition applied by the School Standards and Framework Act 1998 s 142(8)).

16   Ie the powers under the School Standards and Framework Act 1998 s 50(3): see the text to notes 10–12.

17   Ie in the School Standards and Framework Act 1998 s 50(3): see the text to notes 10–12.

18 See the School Standards and Framework Act 1998 s 50(6).
19 School Standards and Framework Act 1998 s 50(7). The powers referred to are those in s 50(3) (see the text to notes 10–12) or s 50(6) (see the text to notes 15–18): see s 50(7).

325. Suspension of financial delegation for mismanagement etc. Where it appears to the local authority[1] that the governing body[2] of a school which has a delegated budget[3]:

(1)   has been guilty of a substantial or persistent failure to comply with any delegation requirement or restriction[4];

(2)   is not managing in a satisfactory manner the expenditure or appropriation of the sum[5] equal to the school's budget share for the year or a sum equal to that portion of the school's budget share for the year which has not been spent[6]; or

(3)   is not managing in a satisfactory manner any expenditure, or sums received, in the exercise of the power[7] to provide community facilities[8],

then the authority may suspend the governing body's right to a delegated budget[9] by giving the governing body not less than one month's[10] notice in writing[11] of the suspension, unless by reason of any gross incompetence or mismanagement on the part of the governing body or other emergency it appears to the authority to be necessary to give the governing body a shorter period of notice[12], or to give the governing body a notice suspending its right to such a budget with immediate effect[13]. The notice must specify the grounds for the suspension, giving particulars:

(a)   of any alleged failure on the part of the governing body to comply with any delegation requirement or restriction[14];

(b)   of any alleged mismanagement on its part[15]; and

(c)   if applicable, of the basis upon which a period of notice of less than one month was given[16].

A copy of the notice must be given to the head teacher[17] of the school at the same time as the notice is given to the governing body[18].

1   As to the meaning of 'local authority' see PARA 25 (definition applied by the School Standards and Framework Act 1998 s 142(8)). Any function of a local authority in England which is conferred by or under the School Standards and Framework Act 1998 Sch 15 may be exercised by, or by employees of, such person as may be authorised in that behalf by the local authority whose function it is: Contracting Out (Local Authority Education Functions) (England) Order 2002, SI 2002/928, art 3, Sch 2 para (m) (art 3 amended by SI 2010/1172). As to the meaning of 'England' see PARA 7 note 3. As to the meaning of 'person' see PARA 7 note 6.
2   As to the meaning of 'governing body of a maintained school' see PARA 315 note 2.
3   School Standards and Framework Act 1998 Sch 15 para 1(1) (amended by SI 2010/1158). As to the meaning of 'school having a delegated budget' see PARA 323.
4   School Standards and Framework Act 1998 Sch 15 para 1(1)(a). 'Delegation requirement or restriction' means any requirement or restriction applicable, under or by virtue of the scheme or s 50(3) (see PARA 324), to the management by the governing body of the school's budget share: Sch 15 para 1(7). As to the meaning of 'the scheme' see PARA 321 note 5. As to the meaning of 'budget share' see PARA 315.
5   Ie the sum referred to in the School Standards and Framework Act 1998 s 50(1): see PARA 324.
6   School Standards and Framework Act 1998 Sch 15 para 1(1)(b).
7   Ie the power conferred by the Education Act 2002 s 27: see PARA 174.
8   School Standards and Framework Act 1998 Sch 15 para 1(1)(c) (added by the Education Act 2002 s 40, Sch 3 para 5).
9   As to the meaning of 'right to a delegated budget' see PARA 323.
10 As to the meaning of 'month' see PARA 54 note 26.
11 Any notice given under the School Standards and Framework Act 1998 Sch 15 para 1 must be in writing: Sch 15 para 1(8). As to the meaning of 'writing' see PARA 76 note 8.
12 School Standards and Framework Act 1998 Sch 15 para 1(2)(a).
13 School Standards and Framework Act 1998 Sch 15 para 1(2)(b).

14 School Standards and Framework Act 1998 Sch 15 para 1(3)(a).
15 School Standards and Framework Act 1998 Sch 15 para 1(3)(b).
16 School Standards and Framework Act 1998 Sch 15 para 1(3)(c).
17 As to the meaning of 'head teacher' see PARA 86 note 4 (definition applied by the School Standards and Framework Act 1998 s 142(8)).
18 School Standards and Framework Act 1998 Sch 15 para 1(5).

326. Review of suspension. A local authority[1] which has suspended[2] the right of the governing body of a maintained school[3] to a delegated budget[4]:

(1)   must before the beginning of every funding period[5] review any such suspension which is for the time being in force, unless the suspension took effect less than two months[6] before the beginning of that period[7]; and

(2)   may review at any time any such suspension which is for the time being in force, if it considers it appropriate to do so[8].

For the purposes of any such review, the authority must give the governing body and the head teacher[9] of the school an opportunity to make representations with respect to the suspension[10]. If on the review the authority considers it appropriate to do so, it must revoke the suspension:

(a)   in the case of a review under head (1) above, with effect from the beginning of the funding period next following the review[11]; or

(b)   in the case of a review under head (2) above, with effect from such time before the beginning of the funding period next following the review as it may determine[12].

The authority must give the governing body and the head teacher notice in writing[13] of its decision on the review[14].

1   As to the meaning of 'local authority' see PARA 25 (definition applied by the School Standards and Framework Act 1998 s 142(8)). Any function of a local authority in England which is conferred by or under the School Standards and Framework Act 1998 Sch 15 may be exercised by, or by employees of, such person as may be authorised in that behalf by the local authority whose function it is: Contracting Out (Local Authority Education Functions) (England) Order 2002, SI 2002/928, art 3, Sch 2 para (m) (art 3 amended by SI 2010/1172). As to the meaning of 'England' see PARA 7 note 3. As to the meaning of 'person' see PARA 7 note 6.
2   Ie under the School Standards and Framework Act 1998 Sch 15 para 1: see PARA 325.
3   As to the meaning of 'governing body of a maintained school' see PARA 315 note 2.
4   School Standards and Framework Act 1998 Sch 15 para 2(1) (amended by SI 2010/1158). As to the meaning of 'right to a delegated budget' see PARA 323.
5   As to the meaning of 'funding period' see PARA 315 note 3.
6   As to the meaning of 'month' see PARA 54 note 26.
7   School Standards and Framework Act 1998 Sch 15 para 2(1)(a) (amended by the Education Act 2005 s 117, Sch 18 para 11(1), (2)).
8   School Standards and Framework Act 1998 Sch 15 para 2(1)(b).
9   As to the meaning of 'head teacher' see PARA 86 note 4 (definition applied by the School Standards and Framework Act 1998 s 142(8)).
10 School Standards and Framework Act 1998 Sch 15 para 2(2).
11 School Standards and Framework Act 1998 Sch 15 para 2(3)(a) (amended by the Education Act 2005 s 117, Sch 18 para 11(1), (3)).
12 School Standards and Framework Act 1998 Sch 15 para 2(3)(b) (amended by the Education Act 2005 s 117, Sch 18 para 11(1), (3)).
13 As to the meaning of 'writing' see PARA 76 note 8.
14 School Standards and Framework Act 1998 Sch 15 para 2(4).

327. Effect of suspension of right to delegated budget. During any period when a governing body's[1] right to a delegated budget[2] is suspended[3] the local authority's[4] duty to make available to be spent by the governing body a sum equal to the school's budget share for the year, or to that portion of the school's budget share for the year which has not been spent[5], does not apply in relation to the school[6]. However the authority may permit the governing body to take such decisions as to the spending of sums to be met from the school's budget share[7] as the authority considers appropriate[8]. Where[9] the governing body has consequently decided that a particular sum should be spent, it must, in spending that sum, comply with such reasonable conditions as the authority thinks fit to impose[10]. The governing body may, to such extent as it may specify, delegate its powers in relation to that sum to the head teacher[11].

1   As to the meaning of 'governing body of a maintained school' see PARA 315 note 2.
2   As to the meaning of 'right to a delegated budget' see PARA 323.
3   Ie under the School Standards and Framework Act 1998 Sch 15 para 1: see PARA 325.
4   As to the meaning of 'local authority' see PARA 25 (definition applied by the School Standards and Framework Act 1998 s 142(8)). Any function of a local authority in England which is conferred by or under the School Standards and Framework Act 1998 Sch 15 may be exercised by, or by employees of, such person as may be authorised in that behalf by the local authority whose function it is: Contracting Out (Local Authority Education Functions) (England) Order 2002, SI 2002/928, art 3, Sch 2 para (m) (art 3 amended by SI 2010/1172). As to the meaning of 'England' see PARA 7 note 3. As to the meaning of 'person' see PARA 7 note 6.
5   Ie the duty under the School Standards and Framework Act 1998 s 50(1): see PARA 324.
6   School Standards and Framework Act 1998 Sch 15 para 4(1)(a) (amended by SI 2010/1158).
7   As to the meaning of 'budget share' see PARA 315.
8   School Standards and Framework Act 1998 Sch 15 para 4(1)(b).
9   Ie in accordance with the School Standards and Framework Act 1998 Sch 15 para 4(1)(b): see the text to notes 7–8.
10 School Standards and Framework Act 1998 Sch 15 para 4(2).
11 School Standards and Framework Act 1998 Sch 15 para 4(3). As to the meaning of 'head teacher' see PARA 86 note 4 (definition applied by s 142(8)).

328. Accounts of maintained schools. Regulations[1] may require the governing body of a maintained school[2]:

(1)   to keep prescribed[3] accounts and prescribed records in relation to the accounts[4];

(2)   to prepare prescribed financial statements or reports[5];

(3)   to comply with prescribed conditions with respect to audit[6]; and

(4)   to send copies of the accounts, together with such financial statements or reports as may be prescribed, to the local authority[7].

The regulations may:

(a)   impose on the governing body[8] requirements relating to: (i) resources held by the governing body[9]; and (ii) other resources whose application is controlled by the governing body[10]; and

(b)   provide that for the purposes of the regulations any resources which, although not held by the governing body, appear to the local authority to be available for the purposes of the school or for the purposes of the maintenance of any part of the school premises[11] are to be taken to fall within head (a)(ii) above unless the governing body satisfies the local authority that the governing body does not control the application of those resources[12].

The appropriate national authority[13] may require a local authority to give it copies of accounts or other documents received by the local authority from a governing body in accordance with such regulations[14]. The regulations may also prescribe the form or manner in which, the period by reference to which, and the time within which, anything required by the regulations must be done[15]. The appropriate national authority may:

(A)   publish information provided in accordance with regulations under these provisions in such form and manner as it considers appropriate[16];

(B)   make arrangements for such information to be published in such form and manner, and by such persons, as it may specify for the purpose[17]; and

(C)   make regulations requiring local authorities to publish prescribed categories of such information, together with such supplementary information as may be prescribed, in such form and manner as may be prescribed[18].

1   'Regulations' means regulations made under the Education Act 2002 by the Secretary of State (in relation to England) or the Welsh Ministers (in relation to Wales): s 212(1). The functions of the Secretary of State under s 44, so far as exercisable in relation to Wales, were transferred to the National Assembly for Wales (see the National Assembly for Wales (Transfer of Functions) Order 1999, SI 1999/672, art 2, Sch 1) and are now vested in the Welsh Ministers (see the Government of Wales Act 2006 s 162(1), Sch 11 para 30). As to the Secretary of State see PARA 58. As to the Welsh Ministers see PARA 59. As to the meanings of 'England' and 'Wales' see PARA 7 note 3. At the date at which this volume states the law, s 44 is in force in relation to England only: see the Education Act 2002 (Commencement No 4 and Transitional and Saving Provisions) Order 2003, SI 2003/124, art 4; and the Education Act 2002 (Commencement No 6 and Transitional and Saving Provisions) Order 2003, SI 2003/1667, art 4. As to the regulations made under the Education Act 2002 s 44 see the Consistent Financial Reporting (England) Regulations 2012, SI 2012/674. As to the application of SI 2012/674 to pupil referral units (see PARA 427 et seq) see the Education (Pupil Referral Units) (Application of Enactments) (England) Regulations 2007, SI 2007/2979, Sch 1 Pt 2 para 30 (added by SI 2012/3158).
2   As to the meaning of 'maintained school' see PARA 103 note 3. As to the governing bodies of maintained schools in England see PARA 150 et seq; and in Wales see PARA 195.
3   'Prescribed' means prescribed by regulations: Education Act 2002 s 212(1).
4   Education Act 2002 s 44(1)(a).
5   Education Act 2002 s 44(1)(b).
6   Education Act 2002 s 44(1)(c).
7   Education Act 2002 s 44(1)(d) (amended by SI 2010/1158). As to the meaning of 'local authority' see PARA 25 (definition applied by the Education Act 2002 s 212(1) (amended by SI 2010/1158)).
8   For the purposes of the Education Act 2002 s 44(2), any powers exercisable by the head teacher are to be taken to be exercisable by the governing body: s 44(3). As to the meaning of 'head teacher' see PARA 86 note 4 (definition applied by s 212(2), (3)).
9   Education Act 2002 s 44(2)(a)(i).
10   Education Act 2002 s 44(2)(a)(ii).
11   As to the meaning of 'premises' see PARA 62 note 19 (definition applied by the Education Act 2002 s 212(2), (3)).
12   Education Act 2002 s 44(2)(b) (amended by SI 2010/1158).
13   Ie Secretary of State (in relation to England) or the Welsh Ministers (in relation to Wales): see the Education Act 2002 s 44(4), (6). See also note 1.
14   Education Act 2002 s 44(4) (amended by SI 2010/1158). Any function of a local authority in England which is conferred by or under the Education Act 2002 s 44(4) may be exercised by, or by employees of, such person as may be authorised in that behalf by the local authority whose function it is: see the Contracting Out (Local Authority Education Functions) (England) Order 2002, SI 2002/928, art 3, Sch 3 para (t) (art 3 amended by SI 2010/1172; and the Contracting Out (Local Authority Education Functions) (England) Order 2002, SI 2002/928, Sch 3 para (t) added by SI 2003/2704). As to the meaning of 'person' see PARA 7 note 6.
15   Education Act 2002 s 44(5).
16   Education Act 2002 s 44(6)(a).
17   Education Act 2002 s 44(6)(b).
18   Education Act 2002 s 44(6)(c) (amended by SI 2010/1158).

329.   Financial statements of local authorities.   The Secretary of State[1] may direct a local authority in England[2] to provide information about its planned and actual expenditure in connection with its education and certain other functions[3].

Before the beginning of each financial year[4] a local authority in Wales[5] must prepare a financial statement containing such information relating to its planned education expenditure[6] in that year as may be prescribed[7]. After the end of each financial year a local authority in Wales must prepare a statement containing such information with respect to the following matters as may be prescribed[8]:

(1) the planned education expenditure in that year specified in the financial statement prepared by the authority[9];

(2) education expenditure actually incurred, or treated by the authority as having been incurred, by it in the year[10]; and

(3) any other resources allocated by the authority in the period to schools maintained by it[11] during any part of the period[12].

A statement must be prepared in such form[13], and be published in such manner and at such times[14], as may be prescribed[15]. The authority must furnish the governing body[16] and head teacher[17] of each school maintained by it with a copy of each financial statement prepared by the authority or, if regulations so provide, with a copy of such part or parts of it as may be prescribed[18]. A governing body provided with such a copy must secure that a copy of it is available for inspection, at all reasonable times and free of charge, at the school[19].

1 As to the Secretary of State see PARA 58.

2 As to the meaning of 'England' see PARA 7 note 3.

3 See the Apprenticeships, Skills, Children and Learning Act 2009 s 251; and PARA 63.

4 As to the meaning of 'financial year' see PARA 81 note 9 (definition applied by the School Standards and Framework Act 1998 s 142(8)).

5 As to the meaning of 'local authority in Wales' see PARA 25 (definition applied by the School Standards and Framework Act 1998 s 142(8)).

6 'Education expenditure' has the same meaning as in the School Standards and Framework Act 1998 s 45A (see PARA 315): s 52(7) (added by SI 2010/1158).

7 School Standards and Framework Act 1998 s 52(1) (amended by the Apprenticeships, Skills, Children and Learning Act 2009 s 253(1), (2); and SI 2010/1158). 'Prescribed' means prescribed by regulations made by the Welsh Ministers: see the School Standards and Framework Act 1998 s 142(1). The functions of the Secretary of State under s 52, so far as exercisable in relation to Wales, were transferred to the National Assembly for Wales (see the National Assembly for Wales (Transfer of Functions) Order 1999, SI 1999/672, art 2, Sch 1) and are now vested in the Welsh Ministers (see the Government of Wales Act 2006 s 162(1), Sch 11 para 30). As to the Welsh Ministers see PARA 59. As to the regulations made under the School Standards and Framework Act 1998 s 52 see the Education (Budget Statements) (Wales) Regulations 2002, SI 2002/122 (amended by SI 2005/2913); and the Education (Outturn Statements) (Wales) Regulations 2003, SI 2003/873.

8 School Standards and Framework Act 1998 s 52(2) (amended by the Apprenticeships, Skills, Children and Learning Act 2009 s 253(1), (2); and SI 2010/1158). As to the regulations made see note 7.

9 School Standards and Framework Act 1998 s 52(2)(a) (amended by SI 2010/1158).

10 School Standards and Framework Act 1998 s 52(2)(b) (amended by SI 2010/1158).

11 As to the meaning of 'schools maintained by a local authority' see PARA 315 note 2.

12 School Standards and Framework Act 1998 s 52(2)(c).

13 School Standards and Framework Act 1998 s 52(3)(a).

14 School Standards and Framework Act 1998 s 52(3)(b).

15 School Standards and Framework Act 1998 s 52(3). As to the regulations made see note 7.

16 As to the meaning of 'governing body of a maintained school' see PARA 315 note 2.

17 As to the meaning of 'head teacher' see PARA 86 note 4 (definition applied by the School Standards and Framework Act 1998 s 142(8)).

18 School Standards and Framework Act 1998 s 52(4). As to the regulations made see note 7.

19 School Standards and Framework Act 1998 s 52(5). Section 52(5) does not apply to a temporary governing body of a new school at any time before the school opening date: s 52(6). As to the meaning of 'new school' see PARA 315 note 2. As to temporary governing bodies see PARA 197.

330. Certification of statements in Wales by the Auditor General for Wales. A local authority in Wales[1] must, if directed[2] to do so by the Welsh Ministers[3], require the Auditor General for Wales[4] to make arrangements[5] for certifying such financial statement or statements prepared[6] by the authority[7], or such part or parts of any such statement or statements[8], as may be specified in the directions[9]. The arrangements so made by the Auditor General for Wales must include arrangements for sending to the Welsh Ministers a copy of the statement or statements so certified[10], or a copy of the part or parts so certified[11], as the case may be[12].

1   As to the meaning of 'local authority in Wales' see PARA 25 (definition applied by the School Standards and Framework Act 1998 s 142(8)).
2   Directions given under the School Standards and Framework Act 1998 s 53A(1) may relate to any local authority or to local authorities generally or to any class or description of such authorities: s 53A(3) (s 53A added by the Public Audit (Wales) Act 2004 s 66, Sch 2 paras 39, 41; and the School Standards and Framework Act 1998 s 53A(1), (3) amended by SI 2010/1158).
3   The functions under the School Standards and Framework Act 1998 s 53A were originally vested in the National Assembly for Wales and are now exercisable by the Welsh Ministers by virtue of the Government of Wales Act 2006 s 162(1), Sch 11 paras 30, 32. As to the Welsh Ministers see PARA 59.
4   As to the Auditor General for Wales see LOCAL GOVERNMENT vol 69 (2009) PARA 796 et seq.
5   Ie in accordance with the Government of Wales Act 1998 s 96B(1)(d): see LOCAL GOVERNMENT vol 69 (2009) PARA 796. For the purposes of s 96B(1)(d), any statement under the School Standards and Framework Act 1998 s 52 (see PARA 329) must be treated as a return by the authority: s 53A(1) (as added: see note 2).
6   Ie under the School Standards and Framework Act 1998 s 52: see PARA 329.
7   School Standards and Framework Act 1998 s 53A(1)(a) (as added: see note 2).
8   School Standards and Framework Act 1998 s 53A(1)(b) (as added: see note 2).
9   School Standards and Framework Act 1998 s 53A(1) (as added and amended: see note 2).
10   School Standards and Framework Act 1998 s 53A(2)(a) (as added: see note 2).
11   School Standards and Framework Act 1998 s 53A(2)(b) (as added: see note 2).
12   School Standards and Framework Act 1998 s 53A(2) (as added: see note 2).

(x) Recoupment

331. Excluded pupils. Where a pupil[1] is permanently excluded from any school[2] maintained by a local authority[3] ('the old authority') and, in the funding period[4] in which the exclusion first takes effect[5], he is subsequently provided with education by another local authority ('the new authority'), whether at a school maintained by that authority or otherwise than at school[6], the old authority must pay to the new authority, in connection with the provision of education for that pupil in that funding period, such amount, if any, as is payable in accordance with regulations[7].

Where a pupil is permanently excluded from any school maintained by a local authority and, in the funding period in which the exclusion first takes effect, the following events subsequently occur[8]:

(1)   he is first provided by another local authority ('the intermediate authority') with education in a pupil referral unit[9] or otherwise than at school[10]; and

(2)   at any time afterwards he is provided with education by a local authority other than the intermediate authority ('the last authority'), whether at a school maintained by that authority or otherwise than at school[11],

then, in connection with the provision of the education mentioned in head (2) above, the intermediate authority must pay the last authority such amount, if any, as is payable in accordance with regulations[12].

Any dispute as to whether any local authority is entitled to be paid any amount under these provisions by any other such authority must be determined by the Secretary of State or, where both parties are in Wales, the Welsh Ministers[13].

1 As to the meaning of 'pupil' see PARA 20 note 4.

2 As to the meaning of 'school' see PARA 91. As to exclusion from school see PARA 517 et seq.

3 As to the meaning of 'local authority' see PARA 25.

4 As to the meaning of 'funding period' see PARA 315 note 3 (definition applied by the Education Act 1996 s 494(6) (s 494 substituted by the School Standards and Framework Act 1998 s 140(1), Sch 30 paras 57, 128; and the Education Act 1996 s 494(6) added by the Education Act 2005 s 117, Sch 18 para 5(1), (3))).

5 Regulations may prescribe the time when the permanent exclusion of a pupil is to be regarded as taking effect for these purposes: Education Act 1996 s 494(5) (as substituted: see note 4). 'Regulations' means regulations made by the Secretary of State under the Education Act 1996: see s 579(1). The function of making regulations under s 494, so far as exercisable in relation to Wales, is transferred to the Welsh Ministers: see the Education Act 2002 s 208(2); and the Government of Wales Act 2006 Sch 11 para 32. As to the Secretary of State see PARA 58. As to the Welsh Ministers see PARA 59. As to the meaning of 'Wales' see PARA 7 note 3. As to regulations made under the Education Act 1996 s 494(5) see the School Discipline (Pupil Exclusions and Reviews) (England) Regulations 2012, SI 2012/1033. As to the financial implications see in particular reg 7(5); and PARA 531; and see also 'Exclusion from maintained schools, academies and pupil referral units in England: Statutory guidance for those with legal responsibilities in relation to exclusion'; and PARA 540 note 13. As to the time when the permanent exclusion of a pupil is to be regarded as taking effect for the purposes of the Education Act 1996 s 494 see the Education (Amount to Follow Permanently Excluded Pupil) Regulations 1999, SI 1999/495, reg 4 (amended by SI 2003/3227; SI 2004/402; and SI 2012/1033).

6 Education Act 1996 s 494(1) (as substituted (see note 4); and amended by the Education Act 2005 Sch 18 para 5(1), (2); SI 2010/1158).

7 Education Act 1996 s 494(2) (as substituted (see note 4); and amended by the Education Act 2005 s 117, Sch 18 para 5(1), (2)). As to the amount to be paid and the time within which such payment must be made see the Education (Amount to Follow Permanently Excluded Pupil) Regulations 1999, SI 1999/495, regs 2–3 (reg 2 amended by SI 2001/870; SI 2002/408; SI 2003/3227; SI 2004/402; and SI 2012/1033; and the Education (Amount to Follow Permanently Excluded Pupil) Regulations 1999, SI 1999/495, reg 3 amended by SI 2012/1033).

8 Education Act 1996 s 494(3) (as substituted (see note 4); and amended by the Education Act 2005 s 117, Sch 18 para 5(1), (2); SI 2010/1158).

9 As to pupil referral units see PARA 427 et seq.

10 Education Act 1996 s 494(3)(a) (as substituted (see note 4); and amended by SI 2010/1158).

11 Education Act 1996 s 494(3)(b) (as substituted (see note 4); and amended by SI 2010/1158).

12 See the Education Act 1996 s 494(2), (3) (as substituted: see note 4). As to the amount to be paid and the time within which such payment must be made see the Education (Amount to Follow Permanently Excluded Pupil) Regulations 1999, SI 1999/495, regs 2–3 (as amended: see note 7).

13 Education Act 1996 s 494(4) (as substituted (see note 4); and amended by SI 2010/1158). The functions of the Secretary of State under the Education Act 1996 s 494(4), so far as exercisable in relation to Wales (except in so far as they relate to a dispute to which only one party is in Wales), were transferred to the National Assembly for Wales (see the National Assembly for Wales (Transfer of Functions) Order 1999, SI 1999/672, art 2, Sch 1) and are now vested in the Welsh Ministers (see the Government of Wales Act 2006 s 162(1), Sch 11 para 30). The functions of the Secretary of State under the Education Act 1996 s 494(4), so far as they relate to a dispute to which only one party is in Wales, are exercisable only after consultation with the Welsh Ministers: see the National Assembly for Wales (Transfer of Functions) Order 1999, SI 1999/672, art 5(1), Sch 2; and the Government of Wales Act 2006 s 162(1), Sch 11 para 30.

332. Adjustment between local authorities. Regulations[1] may provide, in relation to cases where any provision[2] for education[3] is made by a local authority[4] ('the providing authority') in respect of a person who belongs to the area of another local authority[5], for requiring or authorising the other authority (the 'home authority') to pay to the providing authority such amount as the authorities may agree[6], or failing agreement, such amount as may be determined by or under the regulations[7]. The regulations may provide for the amounts payable by one authority to another:

(1)   to reflect the whole or any part of the average costs incurred by local authorities in the provision of education, whether in England and Wales as a whole or in any particular area or areas[8]; and

(2)   to be based on figures for average costs determined by such body or bodies representing local authorities, or on such other figures relating to costs so incurred, as the Secretary of State or, as the case may be, the Welsh Ministers considers appropriate[9].

Regulations made for these purposes in relation to Wales by the Welsh Ministers may provide for the amounts so payable, in such cases as may be specified in or determined in accordance with the regulations, to be such amounts as may be determined: (a) where the providing authority and the home authority are both in Wales, by the Welsh Ministers[10]; or (b) where the providing authority is in Wales and the home authority is in England, by the Welsh Ministers with the consent of the Secretary of State[11].

Any dispute between local authorities in Wales as to whether one of them is entitled to be paid any amount by another under the regulations must be determined by the Welsh Ministers[12]. Any dispute between a providing authority in Wales and a home authority in England as to whether the providing authority is entitled to be paid any amount by the home authority under the regulations must be determined by the Welsh Ministers with the consent of the Secretary of State[13].

1   'Regulations' means regulations made under the Education Act 2002 by the Secretary of State (in relation to England) or by the Welsh Ministers (in relation to Wales): s 212(1). As to the Secretary of State see PARA 58. As to the meanings of 'England' and 'Wales' see PARA 7 note 3. The functions under s 207 in relation to Wales were originally vested in the National Assembly for Wales and are now exercisable by the Welsh Ministers by virtue of the Government of Wales Act 2006 s 162(1), Sch 11 paras 30, 32. As to the Welsh Ministers see PARA 59.

At the date at which this volume states the law no regulations had been made under the Education Act 2002 s 207. However, notwithstanding the repeal of the Education Act 1996, s 492, which was effective from 9 January 2004 (see the Education Act 2002 (Commencement No 3) (Wales) Order 2003, SI 2003/2961, art 7, Schedule Pt IV), during the period beginning on that date and ending immediately before the beginning of the day on which regulations made by the Welsh Ministers under the Education Act 2002 s 207 come into force, the Education (Inter-authority Recoupment) Regulations 1994, SI 1994/3251 (amended by SI 2013/492), continue to have effect in relation to Wales as though they were made by the Welsh Ministers under the Education Act 2002 s 207 (subject to a transitional amendment): see the Education Act 2002 (Transitional Provisions and Consequential Amendments) (No 2) (Wales) Regulations 2003, SI 2003/2959, reg 9.

2   In the Education Act 2002 s 207, references to provision for education include provision of any benefits or services for which provision is made by or under the Education Act 2002 or any other enactment relating to education: s 207(7). As to the meaning of 'enactment' see PARA 1 note 13.

3   Ie primary education, secondary education, or education provided under the Education Act 1996 s 562C (detention of persons with special educational needs: appropriate special educational provision: see PARA 549): Education Act 2002 s 207(2) (amended by the Apprenticeships, Skills, Children and Learning Act 2009 s 59, Sch 2 para 14). As to the meaning of 'primary education' see PARA 20; and as to the meaning of 'secondary education' see PARA 21 (definitions applied by the Education Act 2002 s 212(2), (3)).

4   As to the meaning of 'local authority' see PARA 25 (definition applied by the Education Act 2002 s 212(1) (amended by SI 2010/1158)).

5   As to when a person is treated as belonging to the area of a local authority see PARA 27 note 6
    (provision applied by the Education Act 2002 s 212(2), (3)).
6   Education Act 2002 s 207(1)(a) (s 207(1) amended by SI 2010/1158).
7   Education Act 2002 s 207(1)(b) (as amended: see note 6). As to regulations made see the
    Inter-authority Recoupment (England) Regulations 2013, SI 2013/492.
8   Education Act 2002 s 207(3)(a) (amended by SI 2010/1158).
9   Education Act 2002 s 207(3)(b) (amended by SI 2010/1158).
10 Education Act 2002 s 207(4)(a).
11 Education Act 2002 s 207(4)(b).
12 Education Act 2002 s 207(5) (amended by SI 2010/1158).
13 Education Act 2002 s 207(6).

333.   Cross-border provisions. Regulations[1] may make provision requiring or
authorising payments of amounts determined by or under the regulations to be
made by one authority to another where:

(1)   the authority receiving the payment makes, in such cases or
        circumstances as may be specified in the regulations, provision for
        education[2] in respect of a person[3] having such connection with the area
        of the paying authority as may be so specified[4]; and

(2)   one of the authorities is a local authority[5] and the other is an education
        authority in Scotland[6].

Any question concerning the connection of any person with the area of a
particular local authority[7] or education authority must be decided in accordance
with the regulations[8]. The regulations may provide for the amounts payable by
one authority to another:

(a)   to reflect the whole or any part of the average costs incurred by local
        authorities in the provision of education (whether in England[9] and
        Wales as a whole or in any particular area or areas)[10]; and

(b)   to be based on figures for average costs determined by such body or
        bodies representing local authorities, or on such other figures relating to
        costs so incurred, as the Secretary of State considers appropriate[11].

The regulations may also provide for the amounts payable by one authority to
another, in such cases as may be specified by or under the regulations, to be such
amounts as may be determined by the Secretary of State[12].

1   'Regulations' means regulations made by the Secretary of State: Education Act 1996 s 579(1). At
    the date at which this volume states the law no such regulations had been made. As to the
    Secretary of State see PARA 58. The powers to make regulations under s 493 were excepted from
    those functions of the Secretary of State under the Education Act 1996, so far as exercisable in
    relation to Wales, transferred to the National Assembly for Wales: see the National Assembly for
    Wales (Transfer of Functions) Order 1999, SI 1999/672, art 2, Sch 1. As to the meaning of
    'Wales' see PARA 7 note 3. As to the transfer of functions in relation to Wales generally see PARA
    59.
2   'Provision for education' includes provision of any benefits or services for which provision is
    made by or under the Education Act 1996 or any other enactment relating to education:
    s 493(4). As to the meaning of 'enactment' see PARA 1 note 13.
3   As to the meaning of 'person' see PARA 7 note 6.
4   Education Act 1996 s 493(1)(a).
5   As to the meaning of 'local authority' see PARA 25.
6   Education Act 1996 s 493(1)(b) (amended by SI 2010/1158).
7   As to when a person is treated as belonging to the area of a local authority see PARA 27 note 6.
8   Education Act 1996 s 493(3) (amended by SI 2010/1158).
9   As to the meaning of 'England' see PARA 7 note 3.
10 Education Act 2002 s 207(3)(a) (s 207(3) amended by SI 2010/1158; and applied by the
    Education Act 1996 s 493(2) (substituted by the Education Act 2002 s 208(1))).
11 Education Act 2002 s 207(3)(b) (as amended and applied: see note 10).
12 Education Act 1996 s 493(2A) (added by the Education Act 2002 s 208(1)).

(xi) Charges in connection with Education at Maintained Schools

A. PROHIBITION OF CHARGES

334. Prohibition of charges for admission. No charge may be made in respect of admission to a maintained school[1]. However, this does not apply to the admission of any person to any maintained school for the purpose of: (1) part-time education suitable to the requirements of persons of any age over compulsory school age[2]; (2) full-time education suitable to the requirements of persons who have attained the age of 19[3]; or (3) training for members of the school workforce[4].

1   Education Act 1996 s 450(1). For the purposes of Pt VI Ch III (ss 449–462), 'maintained school' means any school maintained by a local authority: s 449 (substituted by the School Standards and Framework Act 1998 s 140(1), Sch 30 paras 57, 119; and amended by SI 2010/1158). As to the meaning of 'school' see PARA 91. As to the meaning of 'local authority' see PARA 25. As to admission to schools see PARA 224 et seq.
     It should be noted that the School Admissions Code 2014 para 1.9 prohibits even refundable deposits. As to the Code generally see PARA 226 note 8. See also PARA 335 note 5.
2   Education Act 1996 s 450(2)(a). As to the meaning of 'compulsory school age' see PARA 19.
3   Education Act 1996 s 450(2)(b). As to the time at which a person attains a particular age see PARA 7 note 6.
4   Education Act 1996 s 450(2)(c) (substituted by the Education Act 2005 s 98, Sch 14 para 17(1), (2)). For this purpose, the reference to training for members of the school workforce is to be read in accordance with the Education Act 2005 s 96(1) and s 100 (see PARA 1059 note 3): Education Act 1996 s 450(3) (added by the Education Act 2005 Sch 14 para 17(1), (3); and amended by the Education Act 2011 Sch 5 paras 10, 12).

335. Prohibition of charges for provision of education. In relation to education provided at any maintained school[1] for a registered pupil[2] at the school[3], no charge may be made in respect of education provided for the pupil during school hours[4]. Regulations[5] may prescribe circumstances in which this prohibition does not apply in relation to tuition in singing or in playing a musical instrument[6]; and regulations may, in relation to England, prescribe circumstances in which the prohibition does not apply in relation to education which is early years provision[7] other than (1) early years provision provided in pursuance of the duty imposed by the Childcare Act 2006[8]; or (2) early years provision for a pupil who is of compulsory school age[9].

Where the education is provided for the pupil outside school hours no charge must be made in respect of it if it is: (a) required as part of a syllabus for a prescribed public examination which is a syllabus for which the pupil is being prepared at the school[10]; (b) provided in pursuance of duties imposed in relation to the implementation of the National Curriculum for England[11] or the National Curriculum for Wales[12], or in relation to[13] securing due provision of religious education[14]; or (c) provided in pursuance of the duty[15] in England to secure that early years provision of a prescribed description is available free of charge[16].

Nothing in the above provisions is to be read as prohibiting the making of a charge in respect of board and lodging provided for a registered pupil at a maintained school on a residential trip[17].

Where a period allowed for any educational activity at a maintained school falls partly during school hours and partly outside school hours, then:

(i)   if 50 per cent or more of the time occupied by that period together with any connected school travelling time[18] falls during school hours, so much of the education provided during that period as is provided outside school hours must be treated for the purposes of the above provisions[19] as provided during school hours[20]; and

(ii) in any other case, so much of the education provided during that period as is provided during school hours is to be treated for those purposes as provided outside school hours[21].

Where any education provided at a maintained school is provided on a residential trip, then: (A) if the number of school sessions taken up by the trip is equal to or greater than 50 per cent of the number of half days[22] spent on the trip, any education provided on the trip which is provided outside school hours is to be treated as provided during school hours[23]; (B) and in any other case, any education provided on the trip which is provided during school hours is to be treated as provided outside school hours[24].

1 As to the meaning of 'maintained school' see PARA 334 note 1.

2 As to the meaning of 'registered pupil' see PARA 437.

3 Education Act 1996 s 451(1) (amended by the School Standards and Framework Act 1998 s 140(1), (3), Sch 30 paras 57, 120(a), Sch 31).

4 See the Education Act 1996 s 451(2). See *R v Hereford and Worcester Local Education Authority, ex p Jones* [1981] 1 WLR 768, 79 LGR 490 (decided in relation to a similarly worded provision of the Education Act 1944 s 61(1) (repealed)). See also note 8.

5 'Regulations' means regulations made by the Secretary of State or, in relation to Wales, the Welsh Ministers: see the Education Act 1996 s 579(1). As to the regulations made see the Charges for Music Tuition (England) Regulations 2007, SI 2007/2239.

   The functions of the Secretary of State under the Education Act 1996 s 451, so far as exercisable in relation to Wales, were transferred to the National Assembly for Wales (see the National Assembly for Wales (Transfer of Functions) Order 1999, SI 1999/672, art 2, Sch 1) and are now vested in the Welsh Ministers (see the Government of Wales Act 2006 s 162(1), Sch 11 para 30). As to the Secretary of State see PARA 58. As to the Welsh Ministers see PARA 59. As to the meaning of 'Wales' see PARA 7 note 3.

6 Education Act 1996 s 451(3) (substituted by the Education and Inspections Act 2006 s 56(1)). At the date at which this volume states the law the Education Act 1996 s 451(3) (as so substituted) is in force in relation to England only: see the Education and Inspections Act 2006 (Commencement No 3 and Transitional Provisions and Savings) Order 2007, SI 2007/1271, art 5. As to the meaning of 'England' see PARA 7 note 3. Until such time as this provision is brought into force in relation to Wales the following provisions apply: The Education Act 1996 s 451(2) does not apply in relation to tuition in playing a musical instrument where the tuition is provided either individually or to a group of not more than four pupils, unless the tuition is: (1) required as part of a syllabus for a prescribed public examination which is a syllabus for which the pupil is being prepared at the school (s 451(3)(a)); or (2) provided in pursuance of a duty imposed by the Education Act 2002 s 109 (see PARA 879) or the School Standards and Framework Act 1998 s 69 (see PARA 914) (see the Education Act 1996 s 451(3)(b) (amended by the School Standards and Framework Act 1998 s 140(1), Sch 30 para 120(b); and the Education Act 2002 s 251(1), Sch 21 para 48(1), (2))). 'Prescribed' means prescribed by regulations: s 579(1).

   For the purposes of Pt VI Ch III (ss 449–462), a pupil is to be regarded as having been prepared at a school for a syllabus for a prescribed public examination if any part of the education provided with a view to preparing him for that examination in that syllabus has been provided for him at that school: s 462(3). In Pt VI Ch III, references to a 'public examination', or a 'prescribed public examination', are references to such an examination as it applies in relation to persons who are entered for a syllabus for that examination with a view to meeting the examination requirements for that syllabus so as to qualify for assessment for the purposes of determining their achievements in that examination on any particular occasion in any year when an assessment takes place: s 462(4). In this context, 'an assessment' means an assessment for the purposes of determining the achievements of persons entered for the examination in question: s 462(5)(a). Such an assessment is to be regarded as taking place on any occasion on which it is determined in relation to each person entered for any syllabus in that examination who has met the examination requirements for that syllabus whether he has passed or failed, and, if grades are assigned for the purposes of the examination, the grade to be assigned in his case: s 462(5)(b). 'Examination requirement', in relation to a syllabus for an examination, means a requirement which a pupil must meet in order to qualify for assessment for the purposes of determining his achievements in that examination in that syllabus: s 462(1).

7   Ie as defined by the Childcare Act 2006 s 20 (see CHILDREN AND YOUNG PERSONS vol 10 (2012) PARA 1079). As to early years provision see ss 7, 7A; and CHILDREN AND YOUNG PERSONS vol 10 (2012) PARA 1083. See also the School Admissions Code 2014 para 1.39A. As to the Code generally see PARA 226 note 8.

8   Education Act 1996 s 451(2A)(a) (s 451(2A) added by the Childcare Act 2006 s 17(1), (2)). The duty referred to is that imposed by the Childcare Act 2006 s 7 (see CHILDREN AND YOUNG PERSONS vol 10 (2012) PARA 1083): see the Education Act 1996 s 451(2A)(a) (as so added).

     The circumstances prescribed for the purposes of s 451(2A) in which s 451(2) (see the text to note 4) does not apply in relation to education which is early years provision are all of the following: (1) that the early years provision is not provided in pursuance of the duty imposed by the Childcare Act 2006 s 7 (duty to secure prescribed early years provision free of charge: see CHILDREN AND YOUNG PERSONS vol 10 (2012) PARA 1083); (2) that the early years provision is for a pupil who is below compulsory school age; and (3) that the early years provision is not otherwise funded by the local authority in accordance with regulations made under the School Standards and Framework Act 1998 s 47 (determination of school's budget share: see PARA 316): see the Education (Charges for Early Years Provision) Regulations 2012, SI 2012/962, reg 2.

9   Education Act 1996 s 451(2A)(b) (as added: see note 8). As to the meaning of 'compulsory school age' see PARA 19. See note 8.

10 Education Act 1996 s 451(4)(a). As to the regulations made see the Education (Prescribed Public Examinations) (England) Regulations 2010, SI 2010/2327.

11 Ie the duty under the Education Act 2002 s 88: see PARA 864.

12 Ie the duty under the Education Act 2002 s 109: see PARA 879.

13 Ie under the School Standards and Framework Act 1998 s 69: see PARA 914.

14 Education Act 1996 s 451(4)(b) (amended by the School Standards and Framework Act 1998 Sch 30 paras 57, 120(c); and the Education Act 2002 Sch 21 para 48(1), (3)).

15 Ie the duty imposed by the Childcare Act 2006 s 7: see CHILDREN AND YOUNG PERSONS vol 10 (2012) PARA 1083.

16 Education Act 1996 s 451(4)(c) (added by the Childcare Act 2006, s 17(1), (3)).

17 Education Act 1996 s 452(6). For the purposes of Pt VI Ch III (ss 449–462), 'residential trip' means any trip which is arranged for registered pupils at a maintained school by or on behalf of the governing body or the local authority, and which requires the pupils taking part to spend one or more nights away from their usual overnight accommodation: s 462(2) (amended by SI 2010/1158). As to the governing bodies of maintained schools in England see PARA 150 et seq; and in Wales see PARA 195. As to the meaning of 'local authority' see PARA 25.

18 'Connected school travelling time' means time spent during school hours by the pupils taking part in the educational activity concerned in getting to or from the place where the activity takes place: Education Act 1996 s 452(2).

19 Ie the Education Act 1996 s 451: see the text to notes 1–16.

20 Education Act 1996 s 452(1)(a).

21 Education Act 1996 s 452(1)(b).

22 'Half day' means any period of 12 hours ending with noon or midnight on any day: Education Act 1996 s 452(4).

23 Education Act 1996 s 452(3)(a). Where 50% or more of a half day is spent on a residential trip, the whole of that half day is to be treated as spent on the trip: s 452(5)(a). A school session on any day on which such a session takes place at the school concerned is to be treated as taken up by a residential trip if the time spent on the trip occupies 50% or more of the time allowed for that session at the school: s 452(5)(b).

24 Education Act 1996 s 452(3)(b).

336. Prohibition of charges in respect of public examinations. No charge may be made in respect of the entry of a registered pupil[1] at a maintained school[2] for a prescribed public examination[3] in any syllabus for that examination for which the pupil has been prepared at the school[4]. Despite that, where:

(1)   the governing body of a maintained school[5] or the local authority[6] has paid or is liable to pay a fee in respect of the entry of a registered pupil at the school for a public examination in any syllabus for that examination[7]; and

(2) the pupil fails without good reason to meet any examination requirement[8] for that syllabus[9],

that body or authority may recover the amount of the fee from the pupil's parent[10].

1 As to the meaning of 'registered pupil' see PARA 437.
2 As to the meaning of 'maintained school' see PARA 334 note 1.
3 As to the meanings of 'prescribed public examination' see PARA 335 note 6.
4 Education Act 1996 s 453(1). As to when a pupil is to be regarded as having been prepared at a school for a syllabus for a prescribed examination see PARA 335 note 6.
5 As to the governing bodies of maintained schools in England see PARA 150 et seq; and in Wales see PARA 195.
6 As to the meaning of 'local authority' see PARA 25. Any function of a local authority in England which is conferred by or under the Education Act 1996 s 453 may be exercised by, or by employees of, such person as may be authorised in that behalf by the local authority whose function it is: Contracting Out (Local Authority Education Functions) (England) Order 2002, SI 2002/928, art 3, Sch 1 para (kk) (art 3 amended by SI 2010/1172). As to the meaning of 'England' see PARA 7 note 3. As to the meaning of 'person' see PARA 7 note 6.
7 Education Act 1996 s 453(2)(a) (amended by SI 2010/1158).
8 As to the meaning of 'examination requirement' see PARA 335 note 6.
9 Education Act 1996 s 453(2)(b). It is for the body or authority which has paid or is liable to pay the fee in question to determine for these purposes any question whether a pupil who has failed to meet an examination requirement had good reason for the failure: s 453(3).
10 Education Act 1996 s 453(2). Any sum payable under s 453(2) by the parent of a registered pupil at a maintained school is recoverable summarily as a civil debt: see s 461. As to the meaning of 'parent' see PARA 7 note 6. As to the summary recovery of civil debts see MAGISTRATES vol 71 (2013) PARA 625.

337. Prohibition of incidental charges. Neither the parent[1] of a registered pupil[2] at a maintained school[3] nor the pupil himself is required to pay for or supply any materials, books, instruments or other equipment[4] for use for the purposes of or in connection with: (1) education provided for the pupil at the school in respect of which no charge[5] may be made[6]; or (2) a syllabus for a prescribed public examination[7] which is a syllabus for which the pupil has been prepared at the school[8]. However, this does not prevent the parent of a pupil from being required to pay for or supply any materials for use for the purposes of the production, in the course of the provision of education for the pupil at the school, of any article incorporating those materials, where the parent has indicated before that requirement is made that he wishes the article to be owned by him or by the pupil[9].

No charge may be made in respect of transport provided for a registered pupil at a maintained school where the transport is either incidental to education provided for the pupil at the school in respect of which no charge[10] may be made[11], or provided for the purpose of enabling him to meet any examination requirement[12] for any syllabus for a prescribed public examination which is a syllabus for which he has been prepared at the school[13].

1 As to the meaning of 'parent' see PARA 7 note 6.
2 As to the meaning of 'registered pupil' see PARA 437.
3 As to the meaning of 'maintained school' see PARA 334 note 1.
4 For the purposes of the Education Act 1996 Pt VI Ch III (ss 449–462), 'equipment' does not include clothing: s 462(1).
5 Ie by virtue of the Education Act 1996 s 451: see PARA 335.
6 Education Act 1996 s 454(1)(a).
7 As to the meaning of 'prescribed public examination' see PARA 335 note 6.
8 Education Act 1996 s 454(1)(b). As to when a pupil is to be regarded as having been prepared at a school for a syllabus for a prescribed examination see PARA 335 note 6.
9 Education Act 1996 s 454(2).

10   Ie by virtue of the Education Act 1996 s 451: see PARA 335.
11   Education Act 1996 s 454(3)(a). For these purposes, transport is incidental to education provided for registered pupils at a school if it is provided for the purpose of carrying such pupils: (1) to or from any part of the school premises in which education is provided for those pupils, from or to any other part of those premises (s 454(4)(a)); or (2) to or from any place outside the school premises in which education is provided for those pupils under arrangements made by or on behalf of the governing body or the local authority, from or to the school premises or any other such place (s 454(4)(b) (amended by SI 2010/1158)). As to the meaning of 'premises' see PARA 62 note 19. As to the meaning of 'local authority' see PARA 25. As to transport arrangements to facilitate attendance see PARA 460 et seq.
12   As to the meaning of 'examination requirement' see PARA 335 note 6.
13   Education Act 1996 s 454(3)(b).

B. PERMITTED CHARGES

338. Permitted charges. A charge may be made in respect of:

(1)   education provided for a registered pupil[1] at a maintained school[2] other than education in respect of which[3] no charge may be made[4];

(2)   the entry of a registered pupil at a maintained school for a public examination[5] in any syllabus for that examination otherwise than in circumstances in which[6] no charge may be made[7];

(3)   travel arrangements provided[8] for a registered pupil at a maintained school in Wales[9], other than arrangements in respect of which[10] no charge may be made[11];

(4)   transport provided for a registered pupil at a maintained school in England[12] other than transport in respect of which[13] no charge may be made[14]; and

(5)   board and lodging provided for a registered pupil at a maintained school on a residential trip[15];

but no such charge may be made unless the education is provided, the pupil is entered for the examination in that syllabus, or the transport is provided, by agreement with the pupil's parent[16].

Any education, examination entry, travel arrangements, or transport in respect of which a charge may be made by virtue of these provisions is known as an 'optional extra'[17].

1   As to the meaning of 'registered pupil' see PARA 437.
2   As to the meaning of 'maintained school' see PARA 334 note 1.
3   Ie by virtue of the Education Act 1996 s 451: see PARA 335.
4   Education Act 1996 s 455(1)(a).
5   As to the meaning of 'public examination' see PARA 335 note 6.
6   Ie by virtue of the Education Act 1996 s 453(1): see PARA 336.
7   Education Act 1996 s 455(1)(b).
8   Ie under the Learner Travel (Wales) Measure 2008 s 6: see PARA 473.
9   As to the meaning of 'Wales' see PARA 7 note 3.
10   Ie by virtue of the Education Act 1996 s 454(3) (see PARA 337) or the Learner Travel (Wales) Measure ss 3 or 4 (see PARAS 470, 472).
11   Education Act 1996 s 455(1)(ba) (added by the Learner Travel (Wales) Measure 2008 s 22(1), (2)(a)).
12   As to the meaning of 'England' see PARA 7 note 3.
13   Ie by virtue of the Education Act 1996 s 454(3) (see PARA 337), s 508B(1) (see PARA 461), s 508F(3) (see PARA 810), or s 508E(2)(d) and Sch 35C para 5(2) (see PARA 463).
14   Education Act 1996 s 455(1)(c) (amended by the Education and Inspections Act 2006 s 85, Sch 10 para 3; and the Learner Travel (Wales) Measure 2008 ss 22(1), (2)(b), 26, Sch 2).
15   Education Act 1996 s 455(1)(d). As to the meaning of 'residential trip' see PARA 335 note 17.
16   See the Education Act 1996 s 455(2) (amended by the Learner Travel (Wales) Measure 2008 ss 22(1), (2), 26, Sch 2). Any sum payable under the Education Act 1996 s 455 by the parent of

a registered pupil at a maintained school is recoverable summarily as a civil debt: see s 461. As to the meaning of 'parent' see PARA 7 note 6. As to the summary recovery of civil debts see MAGISTRATES vol 71 (2013) PARA 625.

17 Education Act 1996 s 455(3) (amended by the Learner Travel (Wales) Measure 2008 s 22(1), (2)(e)). As to the regulation of permitted charges see PARA 339.

339. Regulation of permitted charges. Provision is made in relation to the regulation of permitted charges[1]. The amount of any regulated charge[2] is payable by the parent[3] of the pupil[4] concerned[5]. A regulated charge, except any charge for travel arrangements provided for a registered pupil at a maintained school in Wales[6], must not exceed the cost of the provision of the optional extra[7] or the board and lodging in question[8]. The cost of the provision of an optional extra includes[9] costs, or an appropriate proportion of the costs:

(1) incurred in respect of the provision of any materials, books, instruments or other equipment[10] used for the purposes of or in connection with the provision of the optional extra[11]; or

(2) attributable to the provision of the buildings and accommodation used in connection with the provision of the optional extra[12]; or

(3) attributable to the provision of non-teaching staff for any purpose connected with the provision of the optional extra[13]; or

(4) attributable to the provision of teaching staff engaged under contracts for services for the purpose of providing it[14].

Where the optional extra in question consists of tuition in singing[15] or in playing a musical instrument, the cost of its provision includes costs, or an appropriate proportion of the costs, attributable to the provision of teaching staff employed for the purpose of providing the tuition[16].

Where the optional extra in question consists of education which is early years provision[17], the cost of its provision includes the costs, or an appropriate proportion of the costs, attributable to the provision of teaching staff employed for the purpose of providing the education[18].

Where charging is permitted[19] and the charge would be a regulated charge, the question whether any charge should be made, and the amount of any charge to be made, is to be determined: (a) in a case where the cost of the provision of the optional extra or board and lodging in question is met by or from funds at the disposal of the governing body, by the governing body[20]; and (b) in any other case, by the local authority[21].

1 See the Education Act 1996 s 456(1) (amended by the School Standards and Framework Act 1998 s 140(1), (3), Sch 30 paras 57, 121, Sch 31). The charges referred to in the text are those permitted under the Education Act 1996 s 455 (see PARA 338): see s 456(1) (as so amended). As to departmental advice for governing bodies, school leaders, school staff and local authorities on charges for school activities see the Department for Education website.

2 'Regulated charge' means a charge to which the Education Act 1996 s 456 applies: see s 456(1).

3 As to the meaning of 'parent' see PARA 7 note 6.

4 As to the meaning of 'pupil' see PARA 20 note 4.

5 Education Act 1996 s 456(2).

6 Ie except any charge permitted by virtue of the Education Act 1996 s 455(1)(ba): see PARA 338. As to the meaning of 'Wales' see PARA 7 note 3.

7 As to the meaning of 'optional extra' see PARA 338.

8 Education Act 1996 s 456(3) (amended by the Learner Travel (Wales) Measure 2008 s 22(1), (3)).

9 Ie without prejudice to the generality of the Education Act 1996 s 456(3): see the text to notes 6–8.

10 As to the meaning of 'equipment' see PARA 337 note 4.

11 Education Act 1996 s 456(4)(a).

12 Education Act 1996 s 456(4)(aa) (added by the Education Act 2011 s 48(1), (2)).

13 Education Act 1996 s 456(4)(b).

14 Education Act 1996 s 456(4)(c). Subject to s 456(6), (6A) (see the text to notes 15–18), the cost of the provision of an optional extra is not to be taken to include any costs attributable to the provision of teaching staff other than staff engaged as mentioned in s 456(4)(c): s 456(5) (amended by the Education Act 2011 s 48(1), (3). As to contracts for services see EMPLOYMENT vol 39 (2014) PARA 1.

15 At the date at which this volume states the law the reference to 'singing' applies in relation to England only: see Education and Inspections Act 2006 (Commencement No 3 and Transitional Provisions and Savings) Order 2007, SI 2007/935, art 6(b). This reference is to be brought into force in relation to Wales as from a day to be appointed: see the Education and Inspections Act 2006 s 188(3). At the date at which this volume states the law no such day had been appointed. As to the meaning of 'England' see PARA 7 note 3.

16 Education Act 1996 s 456(6) (amended by the Education and Inspections Act 2006 s 56(2)).

17 Ie as defined by the Childcare Act 2006 s 20: see CHILDREN AND YOUNG PERSONS vol 10 (2012) PARA 1079.

18 Education Act 1996 s 456(6A) (added by the Education Act 2011 s 48(1), (4)).

19 Ie under the Education Act 1996 s 455: see PARA 338.

20 Education Act 1996 s 456(7)(a). As to the governing bodies of maintained schools in England see PARA 150 et seq; and in Wales see PARA 195.

21 Education Act 1996 s 456(7)(b) (amended by SI 2010/1158). The whole or any part of the amount of any charge which the local authority so determines to make is, if the governing body so determines, to be met by or from funds at the disposal of the governing body, and to the extent that it is so met, is not payable by the parent of the pupil concerned: Education Act 1996 s 456(8) (amended by SI 2010/1158). As to the meaning of 'local authority' see PARA 25.

Any function of a local authority in England which is conferred by or under the Education Act 1996 s 456 may be exercised by, or by employees of, such person as may be authorised in that behalf by the local authority whose function it is: Contracting Out (Local Authority Education Functions) (England) Order 2002, SI 2002/928, art 3, Sch 1 para (ll) (art 3 amended by SI 2010/1172). As to the meaning of 'person' see PARA 7 note 6.

340. Charges policies and remissions policies. Every governing body of a maintained school[1] and every local authority[2] must determine and keep under review a policy with respect to the provision of[3], and the classes or descriptions of case in which it proposes to make charges for[4], any optional extra[5] or board and lodging in respect of which charges are[6] permitted[7]. No such body or authority may make such a charge unless it has both: (1) determined a policy ('a charging policy') with respect to the classes or descriptions of case in which it proposes to make charges[8]; and (2) determined a policy ('a remissions policy') setting out any circumstances in which it proposes to remit (in whole or in part) any charge which would otherwise be payable to it in accordance with its charging policy[9]. A remissions policy determined by the governing body of a school must set out any circumstances in which the governing body proposes to meet, in whole or in part, any charge payable to the local authority, in accordance with the authority's charging policy, for an optional extra or board and lodging provided for a registered pupil[10] at the school[11]. A remissions policy must provide for complete remission of any charges otherwise payable in respect of board and lodging provided for a pupil on a residential trip[12] if the education provided on the trip is education in respect of which no charge[13] may be made[14] and the pupil's parent[15] is, in respect of any period wholly or partly comprised in the time spent on the trip, in receipt of specified welfare benefits[16].

A remissions policy must be kept under review by the governing body or local authority by whom it was determined[17].

1   As to the meaning of 'maintained school' see PARA 334 note 1. As to the governing bodies of maintained schools in England see PARA 150 et seq; and in Wales see PARA 195.

2   As to the meaning of 'local authority' see PARA 25.

3   Education Act 1996 s 457(1)(a).

4   Education Act 1996 s 457(1)(b).

5 As to the meaning of 'optional extra' see PARA 338.

6 Ie by the Education Act 1996 s 455: see PARA 338.

7 Education Act 1996 s 457(1) (amended by the School Standards and Framework Act 1998 s 140(1), (3), Sch 30 paras 57, 122(a), Sch 31; and SI 2010/1158). As to charges for board and lodging at boarding schools see PARA 341.

8 See the Education Act 1996 s 457(2)(a).

9 Education Act 1996 s 457(2)(b).

10 As to the meaning of 'registered pupil' see PARA 437.

11 Education Act 1996 s 457(3) (amended by the School Standards and Framework Act 1998 Sch 30 paras 57, 122(b), Sch 31; SI 2010/1158).

12 As to the meaning of 'residential trip' see PARA 335 note 17.

13 Ie by virtue of the Education Act 1996 s 451: see PARA 335.

14 Education Act 1996 s 457(4)(a).

15 As to the meaning of 'parent' see PARA 7 note 6.

16 Education Act 1996 s 457(4)(b) (substituted by the Education Act 2002 s 200). A remissions policy must provide for complete remission of any charges otherwise payable in respect of board and lodging provided for a pupil on a residential trip in these circumstances if the pupil's parent is, in respect of any period wholly or partly comprised in the time spent on the trip, in receipt of universal credit in such circumstances as may be prescribed: Education Act 1996 s 457(4)(b)(ai) (as so substituted; added by the Welfare Reform Act 2012 Sch 2 paras 37, 38). Until a day to be appointed the policy must also provide for remission if the parent is in receipt of income support (Education Act 1996 s 457(4)(b)(i) (as so substituted; prospectively repealed by the Welfare Reform Act 2009 ss 9(3)(b), 58(1), Sch 7 Pt 1 and (along with the Education Act 1996 s 457(4)(b)(ii), (iia)) by the Welfare Reform Act 2012 Sch 14 Pt 1), an income-based jobseeker's allowance payable under the Jobseekers Act 1995 (Education Act 1996 s 457(4)(b)(ii) (as so substituted and prospectively repealed)), or an income-related employment and support allowance (s 457(4)(b)(iia) (as so substituted; added by the Welfare Reform Act 2007 s 28(1), Sch 3 para 16(1), (2); as so prospectively repealed)). The policy must also provide for remission if the parent is in receipt of any other benefit or allowance (or, until a day to be appointed, is entitled to any tax credit under the Tax Credits Act 2002 or element of such a tax credit), prescribed for the purpose, in such circumstances as may be so prescribed: Education Act 1996 s 457(4)(b)(iii) (as so substituted; prospectively amended by the Welfare Reform Act 2012 Sch 14 Pt 1). At the date at which this volume states the law no day had been appointed for the purposes of the amendments referred to as prospective. 'Prescribed' means prescribed by regulations made by the Secretary of State or, in relation to Wales, the Welsh Ministers: see the Education Act 1996 s 579(1). As to the regulations made see the Education (Residential Trips) (Prescribed Tax Credits) (England) Regulations 2003, SI 2003/381 (amended by SI 2005/1014; and SI 2011/730); and the Education (Remission of Charges Relating to Residential Trips) (Wales) Regulations 2003, SI 2003/860 (amended by SI 2011/706; and SI 2013/2731).

As to entitlement to universal credit see WELFARE BENEFITS AND STATE PENSIONS vol 104 (2014) PARA 45 et seq. As to income support see WELFARE BENEFITS AND STATE PENSIONS vol 104 (2014) PARA 292 et seq. As to income-based jobseeker's allowance see WELFARE BENEFITS AND STATE PENSIONS vol 104 (2014) PARA 262 et seq. As to income-related employment and support allowance see WELFARE BENEFITS AND STATE PENSIONS vol 104 (2014) PARAS 252–261. As to tax credits under the Tax Credits Act 2002 see WELFARE BENEFITS AND STATE PENSIONS vol 104 (2014) PARA 335 et seq. The functions of the Secretary of State under the Education Act 1996 s 457, so far as exercisable in relation to Wales, were transferred to the National Assembly for Wales (see the National Assembly for Wales (Transfer of Functions) Order 1999, SI 1999/672, art 2, Sch 1) and are now vested in the Welsh Ministers (see the Government of Wales Act 2006 s 162(1), Sch 11 para 30). As to the Secretary of State see PARA 58. As to the Welsh Ministers see PARA 59. As to the meaning of 'Wales' see PARA 7 note 3.

17 Education Act 1996 s 457(5) (amended by SI 2010/1158).

341. Charges for board and lodging at boarding schools. Where a registered pupil[1] at a maintained school[2] is provided at the school with board and lodging, charges are payable to the local authority[3] in respect of the board and lodging by the parent[4] of the pupil concerned; and such charges must not exceed the cost to the authority of providing the board and lodging[5].

Where the local authority for that pupil's area is of the opinion that education suitable to his age, ability and aptitude and to any special educational needs[6] he may have cannot otherwise be provided for him, then, where the school is maintained by the local authority for his area, that authority must remit the whole of the charges so payable and, in any other case, that authority must pay the whole of the charges so payable to the authority which maintains the school[7].

Where the local authority for the pupil's area is satisfied that payment of the full charges so payable would involve financial hardship to the parent of the pupil concerned, the authority[8]: (1) in the case of charges payable to the authority, must remit so much of those charges as falls[9] to be so remitted[10]; and (2) in the case of charges payable to another local authority in respect of board and lodging, must pay so much of those charges as falls[11] to be so paid[12].

1   As to the meaning of 'registered pupil' see PARA 437.
2   As to the meaning of 'maintained school' see PARA 334 note 1.
3   As to the meaning of 'local authority' see PARA 25. Any function of a local authority in England which is conferred by or under the School Standards and Framework Act 1998 s 458 may be exercised by, or by employees of, such person as may be authorised in that behalf by the local authority whose function it is: Contracting Out (Local Authority Education Functions) (England) Order 2002, SI 2002/928, art 3, Sch 1 para (mm) (art 3 amended by SI 2010/1172). As to the meaning of 'England' see PARA 7 note 3. As to the meaning of 'person' see PARA 7 note 6.
4   As to the meaning of 'parent' see PARA 7 note 6.
5   See the Education Act 1996 s 458(1) (amended by the School Standards and Framework Act 1998 s 140(1), (3), Sch 30 paras 57, 123(a), Sch 31; SI 2010/1158). This provision is expressed to be subject to the Education Act 1996 s 458(2)–(5) (see the text to notes 6–12): see s 458(1). Any sum payable under s 458 by the parent of a registered pupil at a maintained school is recoverable summarily as a civil debt: see s 461. As to the summary recovery of civil debts see MAGISTRATES vol 71 (2013) PARA 625.
6   As to the meaning of 'special educational needs' see PARAS 943, 989.
7   Education Act 1996 s 458(2) (amended by the School Standards and Framework Act 1998, Sch 30 para 123(b), Sch 31; and SI 2010/1158).
8   Education Act 1996 s 458(4) (amended by SI 2010/1158).
9   The amount that falls to be remitted or paid by a local authority by virtue of the Education Act 1996 s 458(4)(a), (b) (see the text to notes 11–12) is such part of the charges in question as the authority considers ought not to be paid by the pupil's parent in order to avoid financial hardship to the parent of the pupil concerned, or the whole of those charges if, in its opinion, such hardship cannot otherwise be avoided: s 458(5) (amended by SI 2010/1158).
10 Education Act 1996 s 458(4)(a).
11 See note 9.
12 Education Act 1996 s 458(4)(b) (amended by the School Standards and Framework Act 1998 Sch 30 paras 57, 123(d), Sch 31; and SI 2010/1158).

342.   Provision of information. Regulations[1] may require, in relation to every maintained school[2], the local authority[3], the governing body[4] or the head teacher[5] to make available either generally or to prescribed[6] persons[7], in such form and manner and at such times as may be prescribed, such relevant information[8] as to the school hours at the school[9], and such information as to the policies[10] which apply in relation to the school[11], as may be prescribed[12].

1   'Regulations' means regulations made by the Secretary of State or, in relation to Wales, the Welsh Ministers: see the Education Act 1996 s 579(1). As to the regulations made see the Education (School Sessions and Charges and Remissions Policies) (Information) (England) Regulations 1999, SI 1999/2255. The Education (School Hours and Policies) (Information) Regulations 1989, SI 1989/398 (revoked, in relation to England, by SI 1999/2255) have effect as if made under the Education Act 1996 s 459, by virtue of s 582(3), Sch 39 Pt I para 1. As to the meanings of 'England' and 'Wales' see PARA 7 note 3.
    The functions of the Secretary of State under the Education Act 1996 s 459, so far as exercisable in relation to Wales, were transferred to the National Assembly for Wales (see the National Assembly for Wales (Transfer of Functions) Order 1999, SI 1999/672, art 2, Sch 1) and are now vested in the Welsh Ministers (see the Government of Wales Act 2006 s 162(1), Sch 11 para 30). As to the Secretary of State see PARA 58. As to the Welsh Ministers see PARA 59.
2   As to the meaning of 'maintained school' see PARA 334 note 1.

3　As to the meaning of 'local authority' see PARA 25.
4　As to the governing bodies of maintained schools in England see PARA 150 et seq; and in Wales see PARA 195.
5　As to the meaning of 'head teacher' see PARA 86 note 4.
6　'Prescribed' means prescribed by regulations: Education Act 1996 s 579(1).
7　As to the meaning of 'person' see PARA 7 note 6.
8　Ie relevant for the purposes of the Education Act 1996 Pt VI Ch III (ss 449–462).
9　Education Act 1996 s 459(a).
10　Ie determined under the Education Act 1996 s 457: see PARA 340.
11　Education Act 1996 s 459(b).
12　Education Act 1996 s 459 (amended by SI 2010/1158).

343.　Unaffected contributions and charges. Nothing in the provisions relating to charges in connection with maintained schools[1] is to be read as prohibiting or in any way restricting or regulating any request or invitation by or on behalf of the governing body of a maintained school[2] or a local authority[3] for voluntary contributions for the benefit of the school or any school activities[4]. Any request or invitation made by or on behalf of such a body or authority for contributions for the benefit of a school or school activities is not to be regarded as a request or invitation for voluntary contributions unless it is clear from the terms in which it is made: (1) that there is no obligation to make any contribution[5]; and (2) that registered pupils[6] at the school will not be treated differently according to whether or not their parents[7] have made any contribution in response to the request or invitation[8].

Further, nothing in those provisions[9] relating to charges in respect of a registered pupil at a maintained school is to be read as relating to: (a) charges made by persons[10] other than the governing body or the local authority[11]; or (b) charges to be paid by persons other than the parent of the pupil or the pupil himself[12].

1　Ie in the Education Act 1996 Pt VI Ch III (ss 449–462): see PARAS 334–342. As to the meaning of 'maintained school' see PARA 334 note 1.
2　As to the governing bodies of maintained schools in England see PARA 150 et seq; and in Wales see PARA 195.
3　As to the meaning of 'local authority' see PARA 25.
4　Education Act 1996 s 460(1) (amended by SI 2010/1158).
5　Education Act 1996 s 460(2)(a).
6　As to the meaning of 'registered pupil' see PARA 437.
7　As to the meaning of 'parent' see PARA 7 note 6.
8　Education Act 1996 s 460(2)(b).
9　Ie in the Education Act 1996 Pt VI Ch III (ss 449–462): see PARAS 334–342.
10　As to the meaning of 'person' see PARA 7 note 6.
11　Education Act 1996 s 460(3)(a) (amended by SI 2010/1158).
12　Education Act 1996 s 460(3)(b).

(xii)　Education Action Zones

344.　Education action zones. Education action zones were introduced by the School Standards and Framework Act 1998 in order to raise educational standards, particularly in the most deprived areas, to provide for a group of schools to work in partnership with the local community, including parents and local businesses, to propose innovative strategies and to set targets for improvement[1].

1　See the School Standards and Framework Act 1998 Pt I Ch III (ss 10–12). Unless the Secretary of State or the Welsh Ministers by order otherwise provide, nothing in the School Standards and Framework Act 1998 Pt I Ch III (ss 10–12) applies in relation to Wales: s 10(8).

As to the establishment of education action zones see s 10 (amended by Education Act 2002 ss 187, 215(2), Sch 15 paras 1, 2, Sch 22). As to the establishment of an education action forum for the zone see the School Standards and Framework Act 1998 s 11 (amended by the Education Act 2002 ss 187, 215(2), Sch 15 paras 1, 3, Sch 22, Pt 3), School Standards and Framework Act 1998 Sch 1 (amended by the Charities Act 2011 s 354(1), Sch 7 Pt 2, para 78), and as to the regulations made under the School Standards and Framework Act 1998 Sch 1 para 4 see the Education Action Forum (Proceedings) Regulations 1998, SI 1998/1964 (amended by SI 2002/2301).

Provision is made as to the constitution of an education action forum (see the School Standards and Framework Act 1998 s 11A (added by the Education Act 2002 s 187, Sch 15, para 4)), and as to its functions (see the School Standards and Framework Act 1998 s 12 (amended by the Education Act 2002 ss 187, 215(1), Sch 15, paras 1, 7, Sch 21 para 90; and by SI 2010/1158). Provision is also made for such a forum to expand an education action zone by adding schools, or remove a participating school from the zone (see the School Standards and Framework Act 1998 ss 11B, 11C (both added by the Education Act 2002 s 187, Sch 15, para 5)). There are also requirements as to information relating to a forum and its zone to be provided to the Secretary of State: see the School Standards and Framework Act 1998 s 11D (added by the Education Act 2002 s 187, Sch 15 para 6).

(4) ACADEMIES

(i) Definition and Types of Academy

345. Academies. The Education Reform Act 1988[1] introduced, and the Education Act 1996 continued to make provision for, the establishment in England of schools known as 'city technology colleges' at which the emphasis of the curriculum was on science and technology, and schools known as 'city colleges for the technology of the arts' at which the emphasis of the curriculum was on technology in its application to the performing and creative arts[2]. The Learning and Skills Act 2000 amended the Education Act 1996 to make provision for schools known as 'city academies' at which the emphasis of the curriculum was on a specified subject area such as modern foreign languages, visual arts, performing arts or media arts, sport, etc[3]. The Education Act 1996 was further amended to make provision for the Secretary of State to enter into agreement with any person for the establishment in England of schools known as 'academies'[4]. As a result of these changes, schools known immediately before 26 July 2002 as city academies became known thereafter as academies; and provision was made for schools known before that date as city technology colleges or city colleges for the technology of the arts to also become known as academies if the proprietor of the school and the Secretary of State so agreed[5].

Academies are publicly funded independent schools. Academies get money direct from the government, not the local authority, and are held accountable through a 'funding agreement'[6] with the Government[7]. They are run by an academy trust which employs the staff and is the admissions authority for the school. They have more flexibility than maintained schools in, for example, setting the curriculum and the length of the school day and terms. Some academies have sponsors such as businesses, universities, other schools, faith groups or voluntary groups[8].

'Traditional' academies are underperforming existing schools which are allocated to an academy sponsor who will take them over. Academy sponsors can be universities, further education colleges, education charities and business sponsors[9]. High performing state schools already in existence can apply to the Department for Education for approval to convert to being an academy ('academy converters')[10].

Schools can also be part of an academy chain or multi-academy trust. All academies in a multi-academy trust are governed by a single trust and a single board of directors, and share staff. The trust can establish a governing body for each of its academies, to which it can delegate some of its functions[11].

Free schools, university technical colleges and studio schools are also publically funded and independent, and are considered elsewhere in this title[12].

1   See the Education Reform Act 1988 s 105 (as originally enacted; repealed).
2   See the Education Act 1996 s 482(3) (as originally enacted; repealed).
3   See the Learning and Skills Act 2000 s 130 (as originally enacted; repealed).
4   See the Education Act 1996 s 482(1)–(5) (as substituted; repealed). As to the Secretary of State see PARA 58.
5   See the Education Act 2002 ss 67, 68 (both repealed).
6   As to academy arrangements and funding agreements see PARA 346.
7   As to academies generally see PARA 346 et seq.
8   See the Department for Education information entitled 'Types of Schools'. As to the curriculum at academies see PARA 359. As to the academy's ability to set terms, holidays and times of session see PARA 360. As to admissions to academies see PARA 356. As to special educational needs and disabilities at academies see PARA 361. As to exclusion from academies see PARA 363. As to staffing for academies see PARA 358. As to funding agreements and finance at academies see PARA 346 et seq. As to sponsorship of academies see PARA 354.
9   See 'Comparison of different types of school: A guide to schools in England' (January 2015) published by the New Schools Network.
10 See 'Comparison of different types of school: A guide to schools in England' (January 2015) published by the New Schools Network. As to the conversion of schools into academies see PARA 350 et seq. In order to convert as a single academy, the school's latest Ofsted rating must be 'outstanding' or 'good with outstanding features', and the school will also need to prove its finances are acceptable. It will also be expected to support at least one other local school when it becomes an academy: see the Department for Education document 'Convert to an academy: a guide for schools'. As to the Office for Standards in Education, Children's Services and Skills (Ofsted) see PARA 1128 et seq.
11 See the Department for Education document 'Convert to an academy: a guide for schools'.
12 See PARA 368.

(ii) Academy Arrangements

346. Academy arrangements and funding agreements. The Secretary of State[1] may enter into academy arrangements with any person[2] ('the other party')[3]. 'Academy arrangements'[4] are arrangements that take the form of: (1) an academy agreement[5]; or (2) arrangements for academy financial assistance[6]. An educational institution to which academy arrangements relate is to be known as an 'academy'[7].

An 'academy agreement' is an agreement between the Secretary of State and the other party under which the other party gives the required undertakings[8], and the Secretary of State agrees to make payments to the other party in consideration of those undertakings[9]. The required undertakings are:

(a)   to establish and maintain an educational institution in England[10] which meets the requirements of any of the following[11]:
   (i)   the provision relating to academy schools[12],
   (ii) the provision relating to 16 to 19 academies[13]; or
   (iii) the provision relating to alternative provision academies[14];
(b)   to carry on, or provide for the carrying on of, the institution[15].

The term usually used to refer to this agreement is 'funding agreement'; and it is the funding agreement which provides the framework within which the academy operates. There are a number of model funding agreements provided by the government to cover the various different types[16] of academies[17].

Academy arrangements must include terms imposed for the purpose of securing that no charge is made in respect of admission to, or attendance at, the institution[18], or (subject to any exceptions specified in the terms) education provided at the institution[19].

'Academy financial assistance' is financial assistance given by the Secretary of his State[20] on terms that require the other party to give the undertakings in heads (a) and (b) above[21].

The governing body of a maintained school[22] in England may: (A) form, or participate in forming, a company[23] to enter into academy arrangements[24]; and (B) do anything which appears to it to be necessary or expedient in connection with a proposal that such academy arrangements be entered into with a company so formed (or proposed to be formed) by it[25]. The governing body of a maintained school in England may be a member of a company which it has formed, or participated in forming, under head (A) above[26], and may be a member of a company which is not within head (A) above but which is party to academy arrangements[27]. However, these provisions[28] are not to be read as limiting any powers that the governing body of a maintained school has otherwise than by virtue of them[29].

1   As to the Secretary of State see PARA 58.
2   As to the meaning of 'person' see PARA 7 note 6.
3   Academies Act 2010 s 1(1). The following provisions apply in relation to references in a provision of an Act or any other instrument or document, in relation to times on and after 29 July 2010 (ie the date on which the Academies Act 2010 s 1 came into force) (see s 15(1), (11)), but not in relation to references in ss 1–8, 15, and subject to any contrary provision made by or under the Academies Act 2010 or any other Act (see s 15(2)):
     (1)   a reference to 'academy arrangements' is to be read as including a reference to an agreement under the Education Act 1996 s 482 (as substituted; repealed) (Academies Act 2010 s 15(3));
     (2)   a reference to an 'academy' is to be read as including a reference to a city technology college and a city college for the technology of the arts (s 15(4));
     (3)   a reference to an agreement under the Education Act 1996 s 482 (as substituted; repealed) is to be read as being or (according to context) including a reference to academy arrangements (Academies Act 2010 s 15(5));
     (4)   if an agreement under the Education Act 1996 s 482 (as substituted; repealed) has effect immediately before 29 July 2010 in relation to a school which is known as an academy, the agreement is to be treated as an academy agreement under the Academies Act 2010 s 1 (see s 15(6), (11));
     (5)   if an agreement under the Education Act 1996 s 482 (as substituted; repealed) has effect immediately before 29 July 2010 in relation to a school which is known as a city technology college or a city college for the technology of the arts (see the Academies Act 2010 s 15(7), (11)):
        (a)   if the proprietor of the school and the Secretary of State agree the agreement under the Education Act 1996 s 482 (as substituted; repealed) is to be treated as an academy agreement under the Academies Act 2010 s 1 (s 15(8)(a)), and the school is accordingly to be known as an academy (s 15(8)(b));
        (b)   in any other case, the continued operation of the agreement under the Education Act 1996 s 482 (as substituted; repealed) is not affected by the repeal of s 482 or the Education Act 2002 s 68 (see the Academies Act 2010 s 15(9)).
     As to the meaning of 'school' see PARA 91; and as to the meaning of 'proprietor' see PARA 51 note 4 (definitions applied by s 17(4)).
4   In the Education Act 1996, 'academy arrangements' has the meaning given by the Academies Act 2010 s 1: Education Act 1996 s 579(1) (definition added by the Academies Act 2010 Sch 2 paras 1, 6).
5   Academies Act 2010 s 1(2)(a).
6   Academies Act 2010 s 1(2)(b). See also note 3.
7   Academies Act 2010 s 1(10) (amended by the Education Act 2011 s 53(1), (6). See also note 3. In the Education Act 1996, 'academy' means an educational institution to which academy arrangements relate: s 579(1) (definition added by the Academies Act 2010 Sch 2 paras 1, 6; and

amended by the Education Act 2011 Sch 13 para 9(1), (17)(a)). For the purposes of the Freedom of Information Act 2000, the proprietor of an academy is a public authority in respect of information held for the purposes of the proprietor's functions under academy arrangements: see s 3, Sch 1 Pt IV para 52A (added by the Academies Act 2010 Sch 2 para 10); and see CONSTITUTIONAL AND ADMINISTRATIVE LAW vol 20 (2014) PARA 425.

8   See the Academies Act 2010 s 1(3)(a). The undertakings are those in s 1(5): see heads (a) and (b) in the text. See also note 3.

9   Academies Act 2010 s 1(3)(b). Payments under an academy agreement may be in respect of capital or current expenditure: s 2(1). So far as payments under an academy agreement relate to current expenditure, the agreement must provide for them to continue (subject to other requirements of the agreement being fulfilled): (1) for at least seven years (s 2(2)(a)); or (2) indefinitely, but terminable by the Secretary of State giving at least seven years' written notice (s 2(2)(b)). As to the meaning of 'written' see PARA 76 note 8. As to the service of notices and documents see the Education Act 1996 s 572 (applied by the Academies Act 2010 s 17(4)); and PARA 76. If an academy agreement makes provision for payments in respect of capital expenditure, the agreement may provide for the repayment to the Secretary of State, in circumstances specified in the agreement, of sums determined in accordance with the agreement: s 2(3). An academy agreement may provide for indemnifying a person, in the event of the Secretary of State terminating the agreement, for expenditure (a) incurred by the person in carrying out the undertakings under the agreement (s 2(4)(a)); or (b) incurred by the person (otherwise than by virtue of s 2(3)) in consequence of the termination of the agreement (s 2(4)(b)).

10   As to the meaning of 'England' see PARA 7 note 3.

11   See the Academies Act 2010 s 1(5)(a) (s 1(5) substituted by the Education Act 2011 s 53(1), (2)).

12   See the Academies Act 2010 s 1(5)(a)(i) (as substituted: see note 11). The reference in the text to the provision relating to academy schools is a reference to s 1A (academy schools).

An educational institution meets the requirements of s 1A if (1) it is an independent school; (2) it has a curriculum satisfying the requirements of the Education Act 2002 s 78 (balanced and broadly based curriculum: see PARA 856); (3) it provides education for pupils of different abilities; (4) it provides education for pupils who are wholly or mainly drawn from the area in which it is situated; and (5) it is not an alternative provision academy (as to which see s 1C and note 14): Academies Act 2010 s 1A(1) (ss 1A–1D added by the Education Act 2011 s 53(7)). An educational institution also meets the requirements of the Academies Act 2010 s 1A if it is an independent school, and it is specially organised to make special educational provision for pupils with special educational needs: s 1A(2) (as so added). An academy which meets the requirements of s 1A is to be known as an 'academy school': s 1A(3) (as so added). As to the meaning of 'independent school' see PARA 369; as to the meaning of 'pupil' see PARA 20 note 4; and as to the meanings of 'special educational needs' and 'special educational provision' see PARAS 943, 989 (definitions applied by the Academies Act 2010 s 17(4)). In the Education Act 1996 'academy school' has the meaning given by the Academies Act 2010 s 1A: Education Act 1996 s 579(1) (definition added by the Education Act 2011 Sch 13 para 9(1), (17)(b)).

13   Academies Act 2010 s 1(5)(a)(ii) (as substituted: see note 11). The reference in the text to the provision relating to 16 to 19 academies is a reference to s 1B (16 to 19 academies).

An educational institution meets the requirements of s 1B if it is principally concerned with providing full-time or part-time education suitable to the requirements of persons over compulsory school age but under 19: s 1B(1) (as added: see note 12). 'Education' includes vocational, social, physical and recreational training: s 1B(2) (as so added). An academy which meets the requirements of s 1B is to be known as a '16 to 19 academy': s 1B(3) (as so added). In the Education Act 1996 '16 to 19 academy' has the meaning given by the Academies Act 2010 s 1B: Education Act 1996 s 579(1) (definition added by the Education Act 2011 Sch 13 para 9(1), (17)(b)).

14   Academies Act 2010 s 1(5)(a)(iii) (as substituted: see note 11). The reference in the text to the provision relating to alternative provision academies is a reference to s 1B (alternative provision academies).

An educational institution meets the requirements of s 1C if (1) it is principally concerned with providing full-time or part-time education for children of compulsory school age who, by reason of illness, exclusion from school or otherwise, may not otherwise receive suitable education for any period; (2) it provides education for children of different abilities; and (3) it provides education for children who are wholly or mainly drawn from the area in which it is situated: s 1C(1) (as added: see note 12). 'Suitable education', in relation to a child, means efficient education suitable to the child's age, ability and aptitude and to any special educational needs the child may have: s 1C(2) (as so added). An academy which meets the requirements of this provision is to be known as an 'alternative provision academy': s 1C(3) (as so added). As to the meaning of 'child' see PARA 7 note 6; and as to the meaning of 'compulsory school age' see PARA 19 (definitions applied by s 17(4)). In the Education Act 1996 'alternative provision academy' has the meaning given by the Academies Act 2010 s 1C: Education Act 1996 s 579(1) (definition added by the Education Act 2011 Sch 13 para 9(1), (17)(b)).

Regulations may provide for a statutory provision relating to maintained schools or a description of maintained school, or to pupil referral units, to apply in relation to alternative provision academies, or a description of alternative provision academy, with or without modifications: Academies Act 2010 s 1D(1) (as added: see note 12). Regulations may provide for a statutory provision relating to academies, academy schools or 16 to 19 academies (a) to apply in relation to alternative provision academies, or a description of alternative provision academy, with or without modifications; (b) not to apply in relation to alternative provision academies or a description of alternative provision academy: s 1D(2) (as so added). Regulations may provide for a statutory provision relating to alternative provision academies or a description of alternative provision academy to apply in relation to a description of alternative provision academy, with modifications, or not to apply in relation to a description of alternative provision academy: s 1D(3) (as so added). 'Statutory provision' means a provision made by or under the Academies Act 2010 or any other Act, whenever passed or made: s 1D(4) (as so added). 'Maintained school' means a community, foundation or voluntary school, or a community or foundation special school: s 17(2). As to the meaning of references to a community, foundation or voluntary school or a community or foundation special school see PARA 106. As to the meaning of 'pupil referral unit' see PARA 427 (definition applied by s 17(4)). As to regulations made under the Academies Act 2010 s 1D(2) see the Education (Pupil Referral Units) (Application of Enactments) (England) (Amendment) Regulations 2012, SI 2012/1201.

15 Academies Act 2010 s 1(5)(b) (as substituted: see note 11).

16 See PARA 345. As to free schools, university technical colleges and studio schools see PARA 368.

17 Model funding agreements for the various types of academies and free schools can be found on the Department for Education website. The model funding agreements contain a clause stating that 'this agreement ... is an academy agreement as defined by Academies Act 2010 s 1'. Where academies are given greater freedom than maintained schools, and where there is no specific statutory obligation in relation to academies or they are exempt from it, it is the funding agreement that specifies, as clauses in the contract, what provision the academy is making in relation to that area, for example, length of the school day or term or content of the curriculum. In those instances, changes can only be made if the funding agreement is changed. There are some statutory obligations, for example in relation to admission and exclusion, which are applied specifically to academies, and they have effect in a similar way as they do to maintained schools. The funding agreement may make further provision, for example specifying which supplementary guidance and Codes of Practice, may also apply to the academy. Any changes to applicable legislation or Code would also take effect in relation to the academy without need for amendment of the funding agreement.

18 Academies Act 2010 s 1(9)(a) (s 1(9)(a), (b) amended by the Education Act 2011 s 53(1), (5)).

Where a registered pupil at an academy school or an alternative provision academy is provided with board and lodging at the academy, and the local authority for the pupil's area is satisfied that education suitable to the pupil's age, ability and aptitude, and to any special educational needs the pupil may have, cannot otherwise be provided for the pupil, the authority must pay the full amount of the charges in respect of the board and lodging to the proprietor of the academy: Academies Act 2010 s 10A(1), (2), (4) (s 10A added by the Education Act 2011 s 61; and the Academies Act 2010 s 10A(1) amended by the Education Act 2011 Sch 13 paras 1, 4)).

Where a registered pupil at an academy school or an alternative provision academy is provided with board and lodging at the academy, and the local authority for the pupil's area is satisfied that payment of the full amount of the charges in respect of the board and lodging would involve financial hardship to the pupil's parent, the authority must pay to the proprietor of the academy so much of the charges in respect of the board and lodging as, in the opinion of the authority, is needed to avoid financial hardship to the pupil's parent: Academies Act 2010 s 10A(1), (3), (5) (s 10A as so added; and s 10A(1) amended by the Education Act 2011 Sch 13 paras 1, 4).

The proprietor of the academy must remit the charges that would otherwise be payable by the pupil's parent, to the extent that it receives a payment from the local authority in respect of those charges under the academies Act 2010 s 10A(4) or (5): s 10A(6). 'Local authority' in relation to a maintained school, means the authority by which the school is maintained: s 17(2). Generally as to the meaning of 'local authority' see PARA 25 (definition applied by s 17(4)).

19 Academies Act 2010 s 1(9)(b) (as amended: see note 18).

20 Ie under the Education Act 2002 s 14: see PARA 78.

21 Academies Act 2010 s 1(4).

22 As to the governing bodies of maintained schools in England see PARA 150 et seq. In the Children, Schools and Families Act 2010 s 5, 'maintained school' means a community, foundation or voluntary school or a community or foundation special school: s 5(5).

23 References in the Children, Schools and Families Act 2010 s 5(1) to a company are to a company registered under the Companies Act 2006 as a company limited by guarantee: s 5(1). As to companies limited by guarantee see COMPANIES vol 14 (2009) PARAS 79, 102.

24 Children, Schools and Families Act 2010 s 5(1)(a) (amended by the Academies Act 2010 Sch 2 para 26(1), (2)(a)). 'Academy arrangements' has the meaning given by the Academies Act 2010 s 1 (see the text to notes 4–6) (definition applied by the Children, Schools and Families Act 2010 s 24(2)).

25 Children, Schools and Families Act 2010 s 5(1)(b) (amended by the Academies Act 2010 Sch 2 para 26(1), (2)(b)). The power conferred by the Children, Schools and Families Act 2010 s 5(1)(b) includes, in particular, power (1) to incur expenditure (s 5(3)(a)); (2) to enter into arrangements or agreements with any person (s 5(3)(b)).

26 Children, Schools and Families Act 2010 s 5(2)(a).

27 Children, Schools and Families Act 2010 s 5(2)(b) (amended by the Academies Act 2010 Sch 2 para 26(1), (3)).

28 Ie the Children, Schools and Families Act 2010 s 5: see the text to notes 20–27.

29 Children, Schools and Families Act 2010 s 5(4).

347. Academy arrangements in relation to additional educational institutions. The following provisions apply if the Secretary of State[1] is deciding whether to enter into academy arrangements[2] in relation to a new educational institution[3], or an existing educational institution that, if the arrangements are entered into, will provide education for pupils[4] of a wider range of ages[5]. The Secretary of State must take into account what the impact of entering into the arrangements would be likely to be on maintained schools, academies, institutions within the further education sector[6] and alternative provision[7] in the area in which the institution is proposed to be, or is, situated[8].

The following provisions apply before a person[9] enters into academy arrangements with the Secretary of State in relation to (1) a new educational institution, other than a new educational institution that is the subject of certain proposals under the Education and Inspections Act 2006[10]; or (2) an existing educational institution that, if the arrangements are entered into, will provide education for pupils of a wider range of ages[11]. The person must carry out a consultation[12] on the question of whether the arrangements should be entered into[13]. The consultation must seek the views of such persons as the person carrying it out thinks appropriate[14].

1 As to the Secretary of State see PARA 58.

2 As to the meaning of 'academy arrangements' see PARA 346.

3 An educational institution is not new for these purposes if (1) it replaces one or more maintained schools, academies or sixth form colleges that have been or are to be discontinued; and (2) it provides education for persons of the same range of ages as the institution it replaces (or, as the case may be, the institutions it replaces, taken together): Academies Act 2010 s 9(3) (s 9 substituted by the Education Act 2011 s 60(1)). As to the meaning of 'maintained school' see PARA 346 note 14. As to the meaning of 'academy' see PARA 346.

4 As to the meaning of 'pupil referral unit' see PARA 20 note 4 (definition applied by the Academies Act 2010 s 17(4)).

5 Academies Act 2010 s 9(1) (as substituted: see note 3).

6 As to the meaning of 'institution within the further education sector' see PARA 555 (definition applied by the Academies Act 2010 s 17(4)).

7 'Alternative provision' means educational provision for which a local authority has made arrangements under the Education Act 1996 s 19 (exceptional provision of education in pupil referral units or elsewhere: see PARA 427): Academies Act 2010 s 9(4) (as substituted: see note 3).

8 Academies Act 2010 s 9(2) (as substituted: see note 3).

9 As to the meaning of 'person' see PARA 7 note 6.

10 Academies Act 2010 s 10(1)(a) (as substituted: see note 3). The reference in the text is to a new institution other than a new educational institution that is the subject of proposals under the Education and Inspections Act 2006 s 7 (proposals to establish new school following invitation from local authority: see PARA 111). The Academies Act 2010 s 9(3) (when educational institution not new: see the text to note 3) applies for the purposes of s 10: s 10(4) (as so substituted).
11 Academies Act 2010 s 10(1)(b) (as substituted: see note 3).
12 As to the exercise of the duty to consult see JUDICIAL REVIEW vol 61 (2010) PARA 627.
13 Academies Act 2010 s 10(2) (as substituted: see note 3).
14 Academies Act 2010 s 10(3) (as substituted: see note 3).

348. Annual reports. For each academic year[1] the Secretary of State[2] must prepare and publish a report containing information on: (1) academy arrangements[3] entered into during the year[4]; and (2) the performance of academies[5] during the year[6]. The report must include information relating to the performance of academies which has been provided to the Secretary of State pursuant to regulations[7] relating to the power of Secretary of State to require information[8], and academy arrangements[9].

The Secretary of State must lay before Parliament a copy of each such report[10].

1 'Academic year' means a period of 12 months beginning on 1 August: Academies Act 2010 s 11(5). As to the meaning of 'month' see PARA 54 note 26. The first report under s 11 must relate to the academic year beginning 1 August 2010: s 11(3).
2 As to the Secretary of State see PARA 58.
3 As to the meaning of 'academy arrangements' see PARA 346.
4 Academies Act 2010 s 11(1)(a).
5 As to the meaning of 'academy' see PARA 346.
6 Academies Act 2010 s 11(1)(b).
7 Ie regulations made under the Education Act 1996 s 537: see PARA 67.
8 See the Academies Act 2010 s 11(2)(a).
9 Academies Act 2010 s 11(2)(b).
10 Academies Act 2010 s 11(4). As to the laying of documents before Parliament see STATUTES AND LEGISLATIVE PROCESS vol 96 (2012) PARA 1052.

349. Charitable and trust corporation status of academy proprietors. A qualifying academy proprietor is a charity[1].

A 'qualifying academy proprietor' is a company which is limited by guarantee[2], whose registered office is situated in England and Wales[3], which in pursuance of academy arrangements[4] is the proprietor[5] of an academy[6], and whose object as expressed in its articles or memorandum of association[7] (or each of whose objects as so expressed) is a charitable purpose[8].

1 Academies Act 2010 s 12(1). A qualifying academy proprietor is an exempt charity under the Charities Act 2011: see Sch 3 para 8; and CHARITIES vol 8 (2015) PARA 318.
  In the definition of 'trust corporation' in the Settled Land Act 1925 s 117(1)(xxx) (see TRUSTS AND POWERS vol 98 (2013) PARA 238); the Trustee Act 1925 s 68(1) para (18) (see TRUSTS AND POWERS vol 98 (2013) PARA 238); the Law of Property Act 1925 s 205(1)(xxviii) (see TRUSTS AND POWERS vol 98 (2013) PARA 238); the Administration of Estates Act 1925 s 55(1)(xxvi) (see WILLS AND INTESTACY vol 103 (2010) PARA 622); the Senior Courts Act 1981 s 128 (see WILLS AND INTESTACY vol 103 (2010) PARA 622), the reference to a corporation appointed by the court in any particular case to be a trustee includes a reference to a qualifying academy proprietor: Academies Act 2010 s 12(1A), (1B) (added by the Education Act 2011 Sch 14 para 20(1), (2)).
2 Academies Act 2010 s 12(2)(a). As to companies limited by guarantee see COMPANIES vol 14 (2009) PARAS 79, 102.
3 Academies Act 2010 s 12(2)(b). As to the registered office of a company see COMPANIES vol 14 (2009) PARA 129. As to the meanings of 'England' and 'Wales' see PARA 7 note 3.
4 As to the meaning of 'academy arrangements' see PARA 346.

5   As to the meaning of 'proprietor' see PARA 51 note 4 (definition applied by the Academies
    Act 2010 s 17(4)).
6   Academies Act 2010 s 12(2)(c). As to the meaning of 'academy' see PARA 346.
7   As to the articles and memorandum of association of a company see COMPANIES vol 14 (2009)
    PARA 228 et seq.
8   Academies Act 2010 s 12(2)(d). As to charitable purposes see CHARITIES vol 8 (2015) PARA 2.

(iii) Conversion of Schools into Academies

350. Applications for academy orders. The governing body of a maintained
school[1] in England may apply to the Secretary of State[2] for an academy order[3] to
be made in respect of the school[4]. In the case of a foundation or voluntary school
that has a foundation[5], the governing body of the school must consult[6] the
foundation before making such an application[7], and may make an application
only with the consent of the trustees of the school[8] and the person[9] or persons by
whom the foundation governors[10] are appointed[11].

The Secretary of State may make an academy order in respect of a maintained
school in England if:

(1)   an application[12] in respect of the school is made for such an order[13]; or
(2)   the school is eligible for intervention[14].

An 'academy order' in respect of a school is an order for the purpose of
enabling the school to be converted into an academy[15].

If, after an application for an academy order has been, the Secretary of State
decides not to make the order in respect of a school, he must inform the
following of the decision and the reasons for it: (a) the governing body and head
teacher of the school[16]; (b) the local authority[17]; and (c) in the case of a
foundation or voluntary school that has a foundation (i) the trustees of the
school[18]; (ii) the person or persons by whom the foundation governors are
appointed[19]; and (iii) in the case of a school which has a religious character, the
appropriate religious body[20].

Before a maintained school in England is converted into an academy, there
must be a consultation on the question of whether the conversion should take
place[21]. The consultation may take place before or after an academy order, or an
application for an academy order, has been made in respect of the school[22].

In the case of a school that is eligible for intervention[23], the consultation may
be carried out by (A) the school's governing body[24]; or (B) a person with whom
the Secretary of State proposes to enter into academy arrangements[25] in respect
of the school or an educational institution that replaces it[26]. In any other case,
the consultation must be carried out by the school's governing body[27]. The
consultation must seek the views of such persons as the person carrying it out
thinks appropriate[28].

1   As to the meaning of 'maintained school' see PARA 346 note 14. As to the governing bodies of
    maintained schools in England see PARA 150 et seq. As to the meaning of 'England' see PARA 7
    note 3.
        In the case of a federated school, references in the Academies Act 2010 s 3 to the governing
    body include references to members of the governing body who together make up a proportion
    of the total number of members that is specified in, or determined in accordance with,
    regulations, and consist of or include members of any prescribed description: s 3(6) (added by
    the Education Act 2011 s 57(2)). As to the meaning of 'federated school' see PARA 156 note 4
    (definition applied by the Academies Act 2010 s 17(2) (definition added by the Education
    Act 2011 s 57(1), (5)). As to regulations made under the Academies Act 2010 s 3(6) see the
    School Governance (Federations) (England) Regulations 2012, SI 2012/1035 (amended by
    SI 2013/1624; SI 2014/1257; and SI 2015/1554).
2   As to the Secretary of State see PARA 58.

3 'Academy order' means an order under the Academies Act 2010 s 4 (see the text to notes 12–20): Education Act 1996 s 579(1) (definition added by the Academies Act 2010 Sch 2 para 6; definition applied by s 17(4)).

4 Academies Act 2010 s 3(1). If, before 29 July 2010 (ie the date on which s 3 came into force) (see s 16(1), (3), (5), (7)):

    (1) the governing body of a maintained school in England made an application to the Secretary of State which, if it had been made on or after that date, would have been an application under s 3 (see s 16(1)), the application is to be treated as an application under s 3 (s 16(2));

    (2) steps were taken by the governing body of a foundation or voluntary school that has a foundation (see s 16(3)(a)), and if s 3 had been in force, those steps would have satisfied the requirement of s 3(3) (consultation of foundation: see the text to notes 6–7) (s 16(3)(b)), the steps are to be treated as satisfying that requirement (s 16(4));

    (3) consent to an application by a governing body was given (see s 16(5)(a)), and if s 3 had been in force, the consent would have satisfied any requirement of s 3(4) (consent of trustees and persons appointing foundation governors: see the text to notes 8–11) (s 16(5)(b)), the consent is to be treated as satisfying that requirement (s 16(6)).

As to the meaning of references to a foundation or voluntary school see PARA 106. As to the meaning of 'foundation' see PARA 108 note 6 (definition applied by s 3(5)).

As to the application of ss 3–5 to pupil referral units see the Education (Pupil Referral Units) (Application of Enactments) (England) Regulations 2007, SI 2007/2979, Sch 1 Pt 1 paras 23B–23D (added by SI 2012/1201). As to pupil referral units see PARA 427 et seq.

5 See the Academies Act 2010 s 3(2).

6 As to the exercise of the duty to consult see JUDICIAL REVIEW vol 61 (2010) PARA 627.

7 See the Academies Act 2010 s 3(3).

8 Academies Act 2010 s 3(4)(a).

9 As to the meaning of 'person' see PARA 7 note 6.

10 As to the meaning of 'foundation governor' see PARA 108 note 6 (definition applied by the Academies Act 2010 s 3(5)).

11 Academies Act 2010 s 3(4)(b).

12 Ie under the Academies Act 2010 s 3: see the text to notes 1–11.

13 Academies Act 2010 s 4(1)(a) (amended by the Education Act 2011 s 57(1), (3)).

14 Academies Act 2010 s 4(1)(b). As to the meaning of 'eligible for intervention' see PARA 1207 note 2 (definition applied by s 4(1)(b)).

Before making an academy order under s 4(1)(b) in respect of a foundation or voluntary school that has a foundation, the Secretary of State must consult (1) the trustees of the school; (2) the person or persons by whom the foundation governors are appointed; and (3) in the case of a school which has a religious character, the appropriate religious body: s 4(1A) (added by the Education Act 2011 s 55(2)). For these purposes 'the appropriate religious body', in relation to a school, means (a) in the case of a Church of England school or a Roman Catholic school, the appropriate diocesan authority; (b) in any other case, such body or person representing the specified religion or religious denomination as is prescribed under the School Standards and Framework Act 1998 s 88F(3)(e) (see PARA 237): Academies Act 2010 s 4(8) (s 4(8)–(11) added by the Education Act 2011 s 55(1), (5)). In the case of a school in relation to which there is more than one religion or religious denomination specified, references to 'the appropriate religious body' are to be read as references to both or all of the bodies concerned: Academies Act 2010 s 4(9) (as so added). In s 4(8), (9), 'specified' means specified in the order under the School Standards and Framework Act 1998 s 69(3) (see PARA 914) relating to the school: Academies Act 2010 s 4(10) (as so added). Expressions used in s 4 and the School Standards and Framework Act 1998 have the same meaning as in the 1998 Act: Academies Act 2010 s 4(11) (as so added).

15 Academies Act 2010 s 4(2). A maintained school is 'converted into' an academy if academy arrangements are entered into in relation to the school or an educational institution that replaces it: s 4(3) (amended by the Education Act 2011 Sch 13 paras 1, 2) As to the meanings of 'academy' and 'academy arrangements' see PARA 346. If an academy order is made in respect of a school, the Secretary of State must give a copy of the order to (1) the governing body and head teacher of the school (s 4(4)(a) (amended by the Education Act 2011 s 55(1), (3)(a)); (2) the local authority (Academies Act 2011 s 4(4)(b)); and (3) in the case of a foundation or voluntary school that has a foundation (a) the trustees of the school; (b) the person or persons by whom the foundation governors are appointed; and (c) in the case of a school which has a religious character, the appropriate religious body (s 4(4)(c) (added by the Education Act 2011 s 55(1), (3)(b)). As to the meaning of 'head teacher' see PARA 86 note 4; and as to the meaning of 'local authority' see PARA 25 (definitions applied by the Academies Act 2010 s 17(4)). Despite

the Education Act 1996 s 568(1) (orders to be made by statutory instrument) (as applied by the Academies Act 2010 s 17(4)) the power of the Secretary of State to make an academy order is not required to be exercised by statutory instrument: s 4(6). An academy order may include incidental, consequential, supplemental and transitional provision: s 4(7). As to the effect of an academy order see PARA 351. As academy orders are not made by statutory instrument they are not recorded in this work.

16 Academies Act 2010 s 4(5)(a) (amended by the Education Act 2011 s 55(1), (4)(a)).
17 Academies Act 2010 s 4(5)(b).
18 Academies Act 2010 s 4(5)(c)(i) (s 4(5)(c) added by the Education Act 2011 s 55(1), (4)(b)).
19 Academies Act 2010 s 4(5)(c)(ii) (as added: see note 18).
20 Academies Act 2010 s 4(5)(c)(iii) (as added: see note 18).
21 Academies Act 2010 s 5(1) (s 5 substituted by the Education Act 2011 s 56).
22 Academies Act 2010 s 5(2) (as substituted: see note 21). In the case of a federated school, references in s 5 to the governing body include references to any of the members of the governing body: s 5(6) (as so substituted).
23 Ie within the meaning of the Education and Inspections Act 2006 Pt 4 (ss 59–73): see note 14.
24 Academies Act 2010 s 5(3)(a) (as substituted: see note 21).
25 As to the meaning of 'academy arrangements' see PARA 346.
26 Academies Act 2010 s 5(3)(b) (as substituted: see note 21).
27 Academies Act 2010 s 5(4) (as substituted: see note 21).
28 Academies Act 2010 s 5(5) (as substituted: see note 21).

351.   Effect of academy orders. If an academy order[1] has effect in respect of a school[2], the local authority[3] must cease to maintain the school on the date ('the conversion date') on which the school, or an educational institution that replaces it, opens as an academy[4] ('the academy')[5]. If the school is a selective school[6] and is to be converted into an academy school[7], the requirement to provide education for pupils of different abilities[8] does not apply in relation to any academy arrangements[9] to be entered into in relation to the school or an educational institution that replaces it[10]. If the academy is an academy school, the relevant independent school standards[11] are to be treated as met in relation to it on the conversion date[12]. If the school is a foundation or voluntary school[13] which is designated[14] as a school having a particular religious character[15], and is to be converted into an academy school[16], the academy is to be treated, on the conversion date, as designated[17] as an independent school[18] having that religious character[19].

If an academy order has effect in respect of a school[20], the order was made following an application[21] for such an order[22], and the school is to be converted into an academy[23], the local authority must determine whether, immediately before the conversion date, the school has a surplus[24] and, if so, the amount of the surplus[25]. The local authority must[26] pay any amount so determined to the proprietor of the academy[27].

If an academy order has effect in respect of a school[28], and the school is to be converted into an academy[29], the Secretary of State may make a scheme (a 'transfer scheme') in relation to property used or held for the purposes of the school by a local authority or the school's governing body[30], and rights and liabilities[31] (including rights and liabilities in relation to staff) of the local authority or the governing body which were acquired or incurred for the purposes of the school[32]. A transfer scheme may provide for the transfer of property, rights and liabilities to a person concerned with the running of the academy[33]; and may:

(1)   create rights, or impose liabilities, in relation to property, rights or liabilities transferred by virtue of the scheme[34];

(2)   provide for anything done by or in relation to the current owner[35] in

connection with any property, rights or liabilities transferred by the scheme to be treated as done, or to be continued, by or in relation to the transferee[36];

(3)   apportion property, rights and liabilities[37];

(4)   make provision about the continuation of legal proceedings[38];

(5)   include incidental, consequential, supplemental and transitional provision[39].

The things that may be transferred by a transfer scheme include: (a) property, rights and liabilities that could not otherwise be transferred[40]; (b) property acquired, and rights and liabilities arising, after the making of the scheme[41]. A transfer made by virtue of a transfer scheme is binding on all persons even if it would otherwise[42] have required the consent or concurrence of any person[43].

1   As to academy orders see PARA 350.

2   Academies Act 2010 s 6(1). As to the meaning of 'school' see PARA 91 (definition applied by s 17(4)). As to the application of ss 6–8 to pupil referral units (see PARA 427 et seq) see the Education (Pupil Referral Units) (Application of Enactments) (England) Regulations 2007, SI 2007/2979, Sch 1 Pt 1 paras 23E, 23F (added by SI 2012/1201).

3   As to the meaning of 'local authority' in relation to a maintained school see PARA 346 note 18. As to the meaning of 'local authority' generally see PARA 25 (definition applied by the Academies Act 2010 s 17(4)). As to the meaning of 'maintained school' see PARA 346 note 14. As to schools maintained by a local authority see PARA 99 et seq.

4   As to the meaning of 'academy' see PARA 346.

5   Academies Act 2010 s 6(2) (amended by the Education Act 2011 Sch 13 paras 1, 3(1), (2)). Nothing in any of the following provisions applies in a case where a local authority ceases to maintain a school as a result of an academy order: (1) the School Standards and Framework Act 1998 s 30 (notice to discontinue school: see PARA 116); (2) the Education and Inspections Act 2006 ss 15–17 (procedure for discontinuance of schools: see PARAS 115–117): Academies Act 2010 s 6(9).

       Section s 6(2) does not prohibit the local authority from providing financial or other assistance in respect of the academy, including by (1) making payments in respect of some (but not all) of the expenses of maintaining the academy; (2) providing premises, goods or services for the academy; or (3) making premises, goods or services available to be used for the purposes of the academy: s 6(2A) (added by the Education Act 2011 s 58).

6   For this purpose a school is a 'selective school' if its admission arrangements make provision for selection of pupils by ability, and: (1) its admission arrangements are permitted to do so by the School Standards and Framework Act 1998 s 100 (permitted selection: pre-existing arrangements) (see PARA 259) (Academies Act 2010 s 6(4)(a)); or (2) the school is designated under the School Standards and Framework Act 1998 s 104 (designation of grammar schools) (see PARA 263) (Academies Act 2010 s 6(4)(b)). The School Standards and Framework Act 1998 s 99(5) (see PARA 258) applies for these purposes as it applies for the purposes of the School Standards and Framework Act 1998 Pt 3 Ch 2 (ss 99–109): Academies Act 2010 s 6(4). As to the meaning of 'pupil' see PARA 20 note 4 (definition applied by s 17(4)).

7   As to the meaning of 'academy school' see PARA 346 note 12.

8   Ie the Academies Act 2010 s 1A(1)(c): see PARA 346.

9   As to the meaning of 'academy arrangements' see PARA 346.

10   Academies Act 2010 s 6(3) (amended by the Education Act 2011 Sch 13 paras 1, 3(1), (3)).

11   'The relevant independent school standards' are the independent school standards (as defined in the Education Act 2002 s 157(2): see PARA 418) that are applicable to the academy on the conversion date: Academies Act 2010 s 6(6).

12   Academies Act 2010 s 6(5) (amended by the Education Act 2011 Sch 13 paras 1, 3(1), (4)).

13   As to the meaning of references to a foundation or voluntary school see PARA 106.

14   Ie by order under the School Standards and Framework Act 1998 s 69(3): see PARA 914.

15   See the Academies Act 2010 s 6(7)(a) (renumbered as such by the Education Act 2011 Sch 13 paras 1, 3(1), (5)).

16   See the Academies Act 2010 s 6(7)(b) (added by the Education Act 2011 Sch 13 paras 1, 3(1), (5)).

17   Ie by order under the School Standards and Framework Act 1998 s 69(3): see PARA 914.

18   As to the meaning of 'independent school' see PARA 369 (definition applied by the Academies Act 2010 s 17(4)).

19 Academies Act 2010 s 6(8).

20 Academies Act 2010 s 7(1)(a).

21 Ie under the Academies Act 2010 s 3: see PARA 350.

22 See the Academies Act 2010 s 7(1)(b).

23 Academies Act 2010 s 7(1)(c). As to when a maintained school is converted into an academy see PARA 350 note 15.

24 Academies Act 2010 s 7(2)(a). For these purposes: (1) a school has a surplus immediately before the conversion date if, at that time, there is an amount made available in respect of the school by a local authority to the school's governing body (under the School Standards and Framework Act 1998 s 50 (see PARA 324) or otherwise) that has not been spent by the governing body or the head teacher (Academies Act 2010 s 7(6)(a) (amended by the Education Act 2010 s 57(1), (4)(a)); (2) the amount of the surplus is that amount (Academies Act 2010 s 7(6)(b)). Section 7(6) is subject to s 7(9) (see below): s 7(6) (amended by the Education Act 2011 s 57(1), (4)(b)). For the purposes of the Academies Act 2010 s 7(6), the amount which, immediately before the conversion date, has been made available in respect of a school to the school's governing body must be calculated taking into account any relevant redetermination for the funding period in which the conversion date falls: s 7(7) (amended by the Education Act 2010 s 57(1), (4)(c)). 'Funding period' has the meaning given by the School Standards and Framework Act 1998 s 45(1B) (see PARA 315 note 3); and 'relevant redetermination' means a redetermination of the school's budget share which is required in accordance with regulations under s 47 of that Act (see PARA 316): Academies Act 2010 s 7(8). As to the governing bodies of maintained schools in England see PARA 150 et seq. As to the meaning of 'head teacher' see PARA 86 note 4 (definition applied by s 17(4)).

   If the school is a federated school, the questions of whether the school has a surplus, and if so, the amount of the surplus, are to be determined in accordance with regulations: Academies Act 2010 s 7(9) (added by the Education Act 2011 s 57(1), (4)(d)). As to the meaning of 'federated school' see PARA 156 note 4 (definition applied by the Academies Act 2010 s 17(2) (definition added by the Education Act 2011 s 57(1), (5)). As to the application of the Academies Act 2010 s 7(1)–(3), (6)–(8) to pupil referral units see Education (Pupil Referral Units) (Application of Enactments) (England) Regulations 2007, SI 2007/2979, Sch 1 Pt 1 para 20EA (added by SI 2012/3158).

25 Academies Act 2010 s 7(2)(b).

26 Ie subject to the provisions of regulations under the Academies Act 2010 s 7(4): see s 7(3). Regulations may make provision in connection with the determination and payment of the amount of a surplus: s 7(4). Such regulations may in particular include provision:

   (1) requiring the local authority to inform the proprietor of the determinations under s 7(2) (see the text to notes 24–25) (s 7(5)(a));

   (2) authorising the proprietor to apply to the Secretary of State for a review of those determinations (s 7(5)(b));

   (3) about the procedure for, and the Secretary of State's powers on, any such review (s 7(5)(c));

   (4) about the effect of any such review on the amount required to be paid by the local authority to the proprietor (including provision requiring repayment of sums by the proprietor or the payment of additional sums by the local authority) (s 7(5)(d));

   (5) about the time limits for doing anything required or permitted to be done under this section or the regulations (s 7(5)(e)).

   As to the meaning of 'proprietor' see PARA 51 note 4 (definition applied by s 17(4)). As to the Secretary of State see PARA 58. As to the regulations made see the Academy Conversions (Transfer of School Surpluses) Regulations 2010, SI 2010/1938.

27 Academies Act 2010 s 7(3).

28 Academies Act 2010 s 8(1)(a).

29 Academies Act 2010 s 8(1)(b).

30 Academies Act 2010 s 8(2)(a) (s 8(2) substituted by the Education Act 2011 s 59(1), (2)).

31 As to the meaning of 'liability' see PARA 108 note 22 (definition applied by the Academies Act 2010 s 17(4)).

32 Academies Act 2010 s 8(2)(b) (as substituted: see note 31). A transfer scheme may not make provision in relation to: (1) land, or rights or liabilities in respect of land (s 8(3)(a) (s 8(3) amended by the Education Act 2011 s 59(1), (3)); or (2) property or rights to which the Academies Act 2010 s 7 applies (see the text to notes 20–27) (s 8(3)(b)). As to the meaning of 'land' see PARA 116 note 18. As to transfers of land in relation to academies see Sch 1; and PARA 1341 et seq.

   Where a school is converting to academy status, there is a responsibility for the employer of the school's staff (usually the local authority or governing body) to follow the process set out in the Transfer of Undertakings (Protection of Employment) Regulations 2006, SI 2006/246 (see EMPLOYMENT vol 39 (2014) PARA 136 et seq): see PARA 358.

33 Academies Act 2010 s 8(4) (amended by the Education Act 2010 s 59(1), (4)).

34 Academies Act 2010 s 8(5)(a) (s 8(5) amended by the Education Act 2010 s 59(1), (3)).

35 'The current owner' means the person by whom the property is held, or in whom the rights or liabilities are vested, immediately before the transfer to be effected by a transfer scheme takes effect: Academies Act 2010 s 8(9) (amended by the Education Act 2010 s 59(1), (3)). As to the meaning of 'person' see PARA 7 note 6.

36 Academies Act 2010 s 8(5)(b). A transfer by virtue of a transfer scheme does not affect the validity of anything done by or in relation to the current owner before the transfer takes effect: s 8(7) (amended by the Education Act 2010 s 59(1), (3)).

37 Academies Act 2010 s 8(5)(c).

38 Academies Act 2010 s 8(5)(d).

39 Academies Act 2010 s 8(8) (amended by the Education Act 2010 s 59(1), (3)).

40 Academies Act 2010 s 8(6)(a) (s 8(6) amended by the Education Act 2010 s 59(1), (3)).

41 Academies Act 2010 s 8(6)(b).

42 Ie apart from the Academies Act 2010 s 8.

43 Academies Act 2010 s 8(10) (amended by the Education Act 2010 s 59(1), (3)).

(iv) Funding of Academies

352. Source of revenue, disbursement and allocation. Academies receive the same funding as maintained schools for every pupil on the register. They also receive extra funding to cover the cost of services that used to be provided by the local authority[1].

Academies are funded from September to August in line with the academic year, unlike maintained schools, which are funded from April to March in line with the financial year[2].

Schools receive a start-up grant with the costs of converting, such as legal fees, stationery and signage, to be paid when the Secretary of State has made an academy order agreeing to the conversion[3].

Most funding for the running of academies comes from the general annual grant. This is paid to academies by the Education Funding Agency (EFA)[4], based on a formula provided by the local authority[5].

Academies are responsible, which means they have full flexibility to allocate funds as is deemed fit, for providing some services previously provided by the local authority, including:

(1)   education welfare service;

(2)   pupil support (for example, school uniform grants);

(3)   music services (for example, instrumental tutors);

(4)   outdoor education including environmental and field studies (not sports);

(5)   therapies and health-related services, that are not funded by the National Health Service;

(6)   visual and performing arts;

(7)   monitoring National Curriculum assessment;

(8)   school improvement such as continuous professional development for staff;

(9)   determination of terms and conditions of service of staff;

(10) early retirement and redundancy costs;

(11) asset management;

(12) producing financial accounts;

(13) internal auditing[6].

Some services remain with the local authority:

(a) home to school transport, including transport for pupils with special educational needs (SEN);

(b) education psychology, SEN statements and assessment;

(c) assigning SEN resources for pupils who require high levels of additional resource;

(d) monitoring of SEN provision and parent partnerships;

(e) prosecuting parents for non-attendance;

(f) provision of pupil referral units for a pupil no longer registered at an academy[7].

Academies receive funding outside their general annual grant including: (i) early years funding; (ii) national non domestic rates; (iii) pupil premium; (iv) PE and sport premium for primary schools; (v) universal infant free school meals; (vi) high needs top-up funding[8]. The academy may also receive capital funding from the EFA for maintenance, and may apply for extra finance for urgent building repairs that they are unable to fund themselves, or if the academy needs to expand to take in more pupils[9].

There may also be additional funding from the academy sponsor.

1 See the Department for Education guidance document 'Academy funding: information for school leaders' (first published March 2014).

2 See the Department for Education guidance 'Academy funding: information for school leaders' (first published March 2014).

3 See the Department for Education guidance 'Academy funding: information for school leaders' (first published March 2014). As to the Secretary of State see PARA 58. As to the conversion of schools into academies see PARA 350 et seq.

4 The Education Funding Agency (EFA) role in relation to academies is to calculate and pay revenue and capital funding to, as well as seek assurance over the use of public funds from, academies of all types, including those that are sponsored, free schools, university technical colleges, and studio schools. It asks academies to do certain tasks so as to ensure they are financially accountable and are meeting the terms of their funding agreements, and responding to any requests made of the Secretary of State as required by the funding agreement (eg approval to enter into a lease; to dispose of land; or to make significant changes to provision, for instance by adding a sixth form): see the guidance document 'EFA academies service statement' (published in March 2014). The EFA also publishes information for academies eg the Academies' Financial Handbook (see PARA 353).

5 See the Department for Education guidance 'Academy funding: information for school leaders' (first published March 2014).

6 See the Department for Education guidance 'Academy funding: information for school leaders' (first published March 2014). As to the welfare of pupils at academies see PARA 362. As to the curriculum and assessment at academies see PARA 359. As to staffing for academies see PARA 358. As to funding agreements and finance at academies see PARA 346 et seq.

7 See the Department for Education guidance 'Academy funding: information for school leaders' (first published March 2014). As to special educational needs and disabilities see PARA 941. As to pupil referral units see PARA 427 et seq.

8 See the Department for Education guidance 'Academies revenue funding allocations' (first published March 2014). As to the pupil premium, the PE and sport premium and universal infant free school meals see PARA 78.

9 See the Department for Education guidance 'Academy funding: information for school leaders' (first published March 2014).

353. Financial assurance. Academy trusts are independent charitable companies[1]. While academies are responsible for their own financial management, they are subject to public standards of accountability, and the Department for Education, rather than the Charity Commission, is the principal regulator of academies and is responsible for overseeing their compliance with the financial accountability framework and with charity law[2]. The Education Funding Agency (EFA)[3] oversees these arrangements[4].

The funding agreement, together with the Academies Financial Handbook, sets out the financial accountability requirements that apply to academies[5].

1   See PARA 349.
2   See the guidance document 'Academies financial assurance' (first published March 2014). As to the Charity Commission see CHARITIES vol 8 (2015) PARA 547.
3   As to the EFA see PARA 58 note 9.
4   See the guidance document 'Academies financial assurance' (first published March 2014).
5   The Academies Financial Handbook is issued by EFA, and sets out the financial management, control and reporting requirements with which academy trusts must comply.

(v) Sponsorship of Academies

354. Sponsors. An academy sponsor is an organisation or person who has received approval from the Department for Education (DfE) to support an underperforming academy or group of academies[1]. Any of the following can apply to become an academy sponsor: (1) schools; (2) further education colleges; (3) sixth-form colleges; (4) universities; (5) businesses and entrepreneurs; (6) educational foundations; (7) charities and philanthropists (8) faith communities[2].

Sponsors work with the academies they support through the academy trust. They are responsible for:

(a)   setting up the academy trust;
(b)   appointing the leadership team;
(c)   selecting the governing body;
(d)   monitoring the academy's performance and taking action where necessary;
(e)   reporting to the Department for Education about the academy's performance;
(f)   involving parents and the wider community in the academy's work through events, mentoring and business links;
(g)   making sure the academy spends its funding cost effectively;
(h)   working with the academy trust, governing body, principal and senior leadership team of the academy[3].

Before applying to be a sponsor, contact should be made with the regional schools commissioner (RSC)[4]. If the application is successful, the RSC will select an appropriate school that needs a sponsor, and the school's governing body must pass a resolution to approve the sponsor, before the Secretary of State gives final approval[5].

1   See the Department for Education guidance document 'Sponsor an Academy' (first published March 2014).
2   See the Department for Education guidance document 'Sponsor an Academy' (first published March 2014). As to schools generally see PARA 91 et seq. As to further education see PARA 555 et seq. As to universities and higher education see PARA 619 et seq. As to charities generally see CHARITIES.
3   See the Department for Education guidance document 'Sponsor an Academy' (first published March 2014). If a sponsor doesn't comply with their responsibilities, the Secretary of State can remove their sponsor status: see the Department for Education guidance document 'Sponsor an Academy' (first published March 2014).
4   As to regional schools commissioners see PARA 366.
5   See the Department for Education guidance document 'Sponsor an Academy' (first published March 2014). As to the Secretary of State see PARA 58.

(vi) Governance of Academies

355. Governance of academies. In terms of their governance, an academy[1] is established as a company limited by guarantee which acts as a trust, with exempt charity status[2]. The trustees are legally accountable for the operation of the academy and oversee the running of the academy sometimes delegating responsibility to a local governing body, with day-to-day management typically conducted by the head teacher and his senior management team. The funding agreement for the academy contains the relevant governance information for each academy[3].

1 As to the meaning of 'academy' see PARA 346. As to academy arrangements and academies generally PARA 546.
2 See further PARA 349.
3 As to funding agreements see PARA 346. Model funding agreements for the various types of academies can be found on the Department for Education website. Governance structures will obviously vary according to the different types of academy and whether, for example, it is a single academy trust or a multi-academy trust (as to which see PARA 345).

(vii) Admission to Academies

356. Admission. Academies are required by their funding agreement[1] to comply with the School Admissions Code[2] and the School Admissions Appeals Code[3] in a similar way to maintained schools[4], though the Secretary of State has the power to vary this requirement where there is demonstrable need[5]. Reference should be made to the statutory provisions on admissions, many of which also make specific reference to academies[6].

The admission authority for academies is the academy trust[7]. The adjudicator[8] deals with complaints about arrangements (ie complaints that arrangements are unlawful, or not in compliance with the Code or the relevant law relating to admissions). The academy trust is responsible for arranging or providing for an appeal against refusal of a place at a school[9].

1 As to the meaning of 'academy' see PARA 346. As to funding agreements see PARA 346. As to the meaning of 'academy agreement' see PARA 346. As to academy arrangements and academies generally PARA 346.
2 As to the School Admissions Code see PARA 226.
3 As to the School Admissions Appeals Code see PARA 251.
4 As to maintained schools generally see PARA 99 et seq.
5 See the 'School Admissions Code: Statutory guidance for admission authorities, governing bodies, local authorities, schools adjudicators and admission appeal panels' (December 2014), available at the date at which this volumes states the law on the Government website. As to the Secretary of State see PARA 58.
6 As to admissions generally see PARA 224 et seq. See eg specifically in regard to academies PARAS 232, 233, 240, 241, 242, 245, 247.
7 As to academy trusts see PARAS 345, 349.
8 As to the adjudicator generally see PARA 147 et seq. As to reference of objections to the adjudicator see PARA 240.
9 See the 'School Admissions Code: Statutory guidance for admission authorities, governing bodies, local authorities, schools adjudicators and admission appeal panels' (December 2014).

(viii) Home-school Agreements for Academies

357. Home-school agreements. The governing body of a city technology college, a city college for the technology of the arts[1], or an academy school[2], must adopt a home-school agreement[3], together with a parental declaration[4] to be used in connection with the agreement[5].

1 As to city technology colleges and city colleges for the technology of the arts see PARA 345.
2 As to the meaning of 'academy' see PARA 346.
3 As to the meaning of 'home-school agreement' see PARA 92.

4   As to the meaning of 'parental declaration' see PARA 92 note 13.
5   See the School Standards and Framework Act 1998 ss 110, 111; and PARA 92.

(ix)   Staffing of Academies

358.   Staffing. Staff at maintained schools are employed by the local authority or the governing body, and there are statutory provisions relating to, for example, the appointment of staff[1], and teachers' pay and conditions[2] which are set out elsewhere in this title. However, in an academy[3], it is the academy trust that employs the staff, and the trust follows the requirements of their funding agreement[4] rather than national legislation. The model funding agreements, for example, contains clauses specifying that the academy trust may, in accordance with any relevant guidance, employ anyone it believes is suitably qualified or is otherwise eligible to teach[5]. It also specifies that the teachers' pay and conditions of service are the responsibility of the academy trust.

Where a maintained school is converting to academy status, there is a responsibility for the employer of the school's staff (usually the local authority or governing body) to follow the process set out in the Transfer of Undertakings (Protection of Employment) Regulations 2006[6]. The academy trust is also responsible for the pension arrangements of the academy's staff, and must arrange for the transfer[7].

Some statutory provisions, for example those relating to teacher misconduct, may also apply to academies as they apply to maintained schools[8]. Provision is also made specifically for staffing at certain academies with a religious character[9].

1   See PARA 268 et seq.
2   See PARA 1076 et seq.
3   As to the meaning of 'academy' see PARA 346. As to academy arrangements and academies generally PARA 346.
4   As to funding agreements see PARA 346.
5   Model funding agreements for the various types of academies can be found on the Department for Education website.
6   See the Department for Education guidance document 'Convert to an academy: guide for schools'. As to the Transfer of Undertakings (Protection of Employment) Regulations 2006, SI 2006/246 see EMPLOYMENT vol 39 (2014) PARA 136 et seq. See also PARA 351 note 32. As to the conversion of schools to academies see PARA 350 et seq.
7   See the Department for Education guidance document 'Convert to an academy: guide for schools'.
8   See PARAS 1067, 1070. See also PARA 1051 in relation to the service of induction period for teachers in England.
9   See PARA 379.

(x)   Curriculum and Assessment at Academies

359.   Curriculum and assessment. Setting the curriculum is one of the areas academies[1] have greater freedom than maintained schools[2]. Academies must teach a balanced and broadly based curriculum[3] including English, mathematics and science[4], but do not have to teach the National Curriculum[5]. Many academies will have particular specialist subject areas.

The funding agreement contains the curriculum framework for an academy, and the model funding agreements contain clauses specifying that the curriculum is the responsibility of the academy trust and detailing requirements relating to the publication of curriculum information and other matters[6].

Academies are required to assess the students in accordance with their funding agreement[7]. Model funding agreements contain clauses requiring the academy trust to ensure that pupils are entered for examinations in line with the requirements on maintained schools[8], and specifying compliance with the relevant guidance and reporting provisions[9].

1   As to the meaning of 'academy' see PARA 346. As to academy arrangements and academies generally PARA 346.
2   As to maintained schools generally see PARA 99 et seq.
3   See eg academies created under the Academies Act 2010 s 1A: see PARA 346. As to curriculums generally see PARA 856 et seq.
4   See the Department for Education information entitled *'The National Curriculum'*.
5   As to the National Curriculum for England see PARA 857. See also PARA 859 et seq.
6   As to funding agreements see PARA 346. Model funding agreements for the various types of academies can be found on the Department for Education website.
7   See 'Comparison of different types of school: A guide to schools in England' (January 2015) published by the New Schools Network.
8   Ie the Education Act 1996 s 402: see PARA 932. As to exams and other external qualifications see PARA 932 et seq.
9   See note 6.

(xi) Terms, Holidays and Times of Session for Academies

360.   Length of school day and term.   Unlike maintained schools which must follow statutory provisions for dates of terms, holidays and times of sessions[1], it is the responsibility of the academy trust to set the length of the school day and year, and there is a clause specifying this in the model funding agreements[2].

1   See PARAS 458–459.
2   As to funding agreements see PARA 346. Model funding agreements for the various types of academies can be found on the Department for Education website. See 'Comparison of different types of school: A guide to schools in England' (January 2015) published by the New Schools Network.

(xii) Special Educational Needs and Disabilities at Academies

361.   Special educational needs and disabilities.   Where a child for whom an EHC plan[1] or statement of special educational needs[2] is maintained attends (or proposes to attend) a city technology college, a city college for the technology of the arts[3] or an academy[4] and certain conditions are met, the Secretary of State may by regulations make provision for securing that arrangements are made for making the special educational provision, and any non-educational provision, specified in the plan or statement[5].

The Children and Families Act 2014 imposes duties directly on academies in respect of pupils with special educational needs, including the admission of pupils with EHC plans[6], and this is stated explicitly in the model funding agreements[7], together with other information relating to special educational needs and disabilities at academies. Academies (including free schools, university technical colleges and studio schools)[8] must also follow the statutory guidance[9].

1   As to the meaning of 'EHC plan' see PARA 958. As to EHC plans (ie education, health and care plans) generally see PARA 958 et seq.
2   Ie a statement under the Education Act 1996 s 324: see PARA 1002.
3   As to city technology colleges and city colleges for the technology of the arts see PARA 345.
4   As to the meaning of 'academy' see PARA 346.
5   See the Education Act 1996 s 483A; and PARA 968. As to the Secretary of State see PARA 58.
6   Many of the provisions of the Children and Families Act 2014 Pt 3 (ss 19–83) (children and young people in England with special educational needs (SEN) or disabilities) (see PARA 943 et

seq) specifically cover academies: see e g PARAS 948, 949, 955, 959, 961, 963, 987, 967, 978. See also PARAS 1001, 1014, 1041, 1042. There is a duty on the proprietors of academy schools to prepare a report containing SEN information: see PARA 969.

7   As to funding agreements see PARA 346. Model funding agreements for the various types of academies can be found on the Department for Education website.

8   See PARA 368.

9   See the *Special Educational Needs and Disability Code of Practice: 0 to 25 years.*

(xiii) Welfare of Pupils at Academies

362.   Welfare of pupils at academies.   There are various statutory provisions regarding the welfare of pupils[1] which are the responsibility of the local authority to provide, and some of these are extended to the pupils at some academies[2], for example legislation relating to the provision of clothing[3].

In other cases, some of the local authority's responsibilities become those of the academy trust, for example to make provision imposing obligations that are equivalent to the local authority's school lunches obligations[4], and clauses to this effect can be found in the model funding agreements[5]. Similarly, both local authorities and academy proprietors have a duty to support pupils at the school with medical conditions[6].

The academy is responsible, which means they have full flexibility to allocate funds as is deemed fit, for providing some services previously provided by the local authority, including the education welfare service, pupil support (for example school uniform grants), music services (for example instrumental tutors) and outdoor education including environmental and field studies[7].

1   As to welfare of pupils see PARA 482 et seq.

2   As to the meaning of 'academy' see PARA 346. As to academy arrangements and academies generally PARA 346.

3   See PARA 482.

4   See PARAS 486, 491.

5   As to funding agreements see PARA 346. Model funding agreements for the various types of academies can be found on the Department for Education website.

6   See PARA 501. See also PARA 361.

7   See the Department for Education guidance document 'Academy funding: information for school leaders' (first published March 2014).

(xiv) Discipline in, and Exclusion from, Academies

363.   Discipline and exclusion of pupils at academies.   Generally law and guidance on such matters as discipline, bullying and behaviour apply to academies[1].

The law and statutory guidance on exclusion of pupils[2] as applied to maintained schools applies to academies in a similar way[3], and the legislation and guidance makes specific references to them[4].

1   See e g PARAS 509, 510, 511, 512, 513, 516. As to the meaning of 'academy' see PARA 346. As to academy arrangements and academies generally see PARA 345 et seq.

2   As to exclusion of pupils see PARA 517 et seq.

3   See e g PARAS 517, 518, 520, 521, 522, 528, 530, 535, 536, 537, 538, 539, 540. As to maintained schools see PARA 99 et seq.

4   See e g the Education Act 2002 s 51A, the School Discipline (Pupil Exclusions and Reviews) (England) Regulations 2012, SI 2012/1033, regs 21–29; and PARA 517. See also the statutory guidance 'Exclusion from maintained schools, academies and pupil referral units in England: A guide for those with legal responsibilities in relation to exclusion' (first published June 2012); available at the date at which this volume states the law on the Government website.

(xv) Duty of Academies to Provide Information

364. Requirement to provide information. In addition to the general requirement relating to independent schools generally[1], the Secretary of State[2] may by regulations require the proprietor[3] of any city technology college, city college for the technology of the arts[4] or academy[5] to provide prescribed categories of information concerning the performance of the college or academy[6].

The Secretary of State may also by regulations require the proprietor of any city technology college, city college for the technology of the arts or academy to provide information with respect to institutions within the further education sector[7].

The proprietor of a city technology college, a city college for the technology of the arts or an academy must provide information about pupils or students at the institution to persons involved in the provision of support services for participation in education or training[8].

The Education (Independent School Standards) Regulations 2014 apply to academies and set out the minimum standards they must meet, including standards as regards the provision of information[9].

The funding agreement also specifies information an academy must provide or publish[10].

1 See PARA 372.
2 As to the Secretary of State see PARA 58.
3 As to the meaning of 'proprietor' see PARA 51 note 4.
4 As to city technology colleges and city colleges for the technology of the arts see PARA 345.
5 As to the meaning of 'academy' see PARA 346.
6 See the Education Act 1996 s 537(6)–(8); and PARA 67.
7 See the Education Act 1996 s 541; and PARA 192.
8 See the Education and Skills Act 2008 s 72; and PARA 804.
9 See PARA 418.
10 As to funding agreements see PARA 346. Model funding agreements for the various types of academies can be found on the Department for Education website.

(xvi) Inspection of Academies

365. Inspection. It is the duty of the Her Majesty's Chief Inspector of Education, Children's Services and Skills[1] to inspect city technology colleges, city colleges for the technology of the arts[2], academy schools[3] and alternative provision academies[4] at prescribed intervals[5].

The Schools Commissioner and regional schools commissioners also monitor the performance of academies and take action where necessary[6].

1 As to Her Majesty's Chief Inspector of Education, Children's Services and Skills see PARA 1133.
2 As to city technology colleges and city colleges for the technology of the arts see PARA 345.
3 As to the meaning of 'academy school' see PARA 346 note 12.
4 As to the meaning of 'alternative provision academy' see PARA 346 note 14.
5 See the Education Act 2005 s 5; and PARA 1162.
6 See PARA 366.

(xvii) Schools Commissioner

366. Schools Commissioner and Regional Schools Commissioners. The Schools Commissioning Group is part of the Department for Education. The Schools Commissioner and regional schools commissioners work with school leaders to promote and monitor academies and free schools.

Regional schools commissioners are responsible for approving and monitoring academies and free schools in their area on behalf of the Secretary of State for Education[1]. Their main responsibilities are to: (1) monitor the performance of the academies in their area; (2) take action when an academy is underperforming; (3) decide on the creation of new academies; (4) make recommendations to ministers about free school applications; (5) encourage organisations to become academy sponsors; (6) approve changes to open academies, including changes to age ranges, mergers between academies and changes to multi-academy trust arrangements[2].

1   As to the Secretary of State see PARA 58.
2   See the Schools Commissioning Group information.

(xviii) Land and Premises in regard to Academies

367.   Land and premises in regard to academies.   The various statutory provisions relating to land and premises[1] affect academies[2], often specifically[3]. The funding agreement contains land clauses dealing with the academy trust's obligations in respect of the academy site, and with protecting the public investment in the land used for the academy[4].

1   See PARA 1295 et seq.
2   As to the meaning of 'academy' see PARA 346. As to academy arrangements and academies generally PARA 346.
3   See eg PARAS 1299, 1301, 1304, 1305–1308, 1311, 1320, 1321, 1324, 1326, 1341–1343, 1350–1352.
4   As to funding agreements see PARA 346. Model funding agreements for the various types of academies can be found on the Department for Education website.

(5) FREE SCHOOLS

368.   Free schools, university technical colleges and studio schools.   A free school[1] in England[2] is a type of academy[3]. Whereas academies discussed previously are usually existing schools which convert to academy status[4], free schools are new schools (including independent schools becoming state schools for the first time), created where it has been demonstrated that there is a clear demand for that type of school in the area[5]. They are all-ability schools (so they can't use academic selection processes), and are funded by the government but run free of the local authority control[6]. This means they can, for example, set their own pay and conditions for staff, and change the length of school terms and the school day, and they do not have to follow the National Curriculum[7]. Like other academies, they are held accountable through the funding agreement[8].

They can be set up by teachers, parents, existing schools, educational charities, universities, community groups. The group must form a company limited by guarantee and choose members and directors to run it, and the companies must use the Department for Education model memorandum and articles of association, meaning that once constituted the company will be an academy trust[9]. An application for funding is submitted to the Department for Education, demonstrating that there is a clear demand for that type of school from the parents in the area. They are run on a not-for-profit basis and are non fee-paying. There are four main categories of free school: mainstream, 16 to 19, special and alternative provision (AP)[10]. As academies, the provisions relating to, for example, finance and funding, admissions, curriculum, inspection, etc which are discussed elsewhere in this title[11] also apply to free schools.

Free schools are also, it seems, subject to the provisions of the Equality Act 2010[12] against discrimination in the provision of education.

Types of free school include university technical colleges and studio schools.

University technical colleges are all-ability and mixed gender state-funded schools, independent of local authorities, for 14–19 year olds. They specialise in subjects that need modern, technical, industry-standard equipment, such as engineering and construction, and teach these disciplines alongside business skills and a broad, general education. They are sponsored by a local university and employers, who design the curriculum and provide work experience. They should provide progression routes into higher education or further learning in work, including apprenticeships[13].

Studio schools are all-ability and mixed sex state-funded schools, independent of local authorities, for pupils aged 14–19 years old. They offer academic and vocational qualifications, but teach them in a practical and project-based way. The schools are set up with the backing of local businesses and employers, and study is combined with work placements with employers who are involved in the school[14].

1　For further information on free schools see the Department for Education website. See e g 'Free schools admissions guidance: Mainstream admissions' (September 2014). Unlike 'academy' the term 'free school' does not appear in the education legislation, though they are accepted to be academies.

2　Like academies, free schools are currently in England only.

3　As to academies see PARA 345 et seq.

4　See PARA 345. As to the conversion of schools into academies see PARA 350 et seq.

5　See 'Comparison of different types of school: A guide to schools in England' (January 2015) published by the New Schools Network. As to independent schools generally see PARA 369 et seq.

6　As to local authorities see PARA 25 et seq.

7　As to the curriculum see PARA 856 et seq.

8　As to the funding agreement see PARA 346. Like other academies, free schools are required by their funding agreement to comply with the School Admissions Code which applies to maintained schools: see the School Admissions Code, December 2014; and PARA 356. As to maintained schools see PARA 99 et seq. As to admissions generally see PARA 224 et seq.

9　See 'Comparison of different types of school: A guide to schools in England' (January 2015) published by the New Schools Network.

10　See the Department for Education guidance document 'Free schools: how to apply: Mainstream, 16 to 19, alternative provision and special free schools' (February 2015).

11　See PARAS 352, 356, 359, 365.

12　Ie the Equality Act 2010 Pt 6 Ch 1 (ss 84–89): see PARA 9.

13　See the Department for Education guidance document 'University technical colleges from 2014: how to apply'.

14　See the Department for Education guidance document 'Studio Schools: How to Apply' (July 2014).

(6)　INDEPENDENT SCHOOLS

(i)　Definition of Independent and Public Schools

369.　Meaning of 'independent school'. 'Independent school' means any school[1] at which full-time education is provided for:

(1)　five or more pupils[2] of compulsory school age[3]; or

(2)　at least one pupil of that age for whom an EHC plan[4] is maintained or for whom a statement of special educational needs is maintained[5], or who is looked after[6] by a local authority[7],

and which is not a school maintained by a local authority[8] non-maintained special school[9].

1   As to the meaning of 'school' see PARA 91.
2   As to the meaning of 'pupil' see PARA 20 note 4.
3   Education Act 1996 s 463(1)(a) (s 463 substituted by the Education Act 2002 s 172). For the purposes of the Education Act 1996 s 463(1)(a), (b) (see the text to notes 4–7), it is immaterial if full-time education is also provided at the school for pupils under or over compulsory school age: s 463(2) (as so substituted). As to the meaning of 'compulsory school age' see PARA 19.
4   As to the meaning of 'EHC plan' see PARA 958. As to EHC plans (ie education, health and care plans) generally see PARA 958 et seq.
5   Ie under the Education Act 1996 s 324: see PARA 1002.
6   Ie within the meaning of the Children Act 1989 s 22: see CHILDREN AND YOUNG PERSONS vol 10 (2012) PARA 843.
7   Education Act 1996 s 463(1)(b) (as substituted (see note 3); and amended by the Children and Families Act 2014 Sch 3 paras 1, 43(a)). See also note 3.
8   As to the meaning of 'local authority' see PARA 25. As to schools maintained by local authorities see PARA 99.
9   Education Act 1996 s 463(1) (as substituted (see note 3); and amended by SI 2010/1158; and the Children and Families Act 2014 Sch 3 paras 1, 43(b)). As to the meaning of 'non-maintained special school' see PARA 1042.

370.   Public schools.   The term 'public school' has no statutory, or generally accepted, definition[1]. The Public Schools Act 1868 applies only to seven ancient schools, namely Eton, Winchester, Westminster, Charterhouse, Harrow, Rugby and Shrewsbury[2]. The provisions outlined here refer only to those schools.

The headmaster of each school to which the Public Schools Act 1868 applies is appointed by and holds his office at the pleasure of the governing body[3]. All other teachers are appointed by and hold their office at the pleasure of the headmaster[4]. No candidate for mastership is entitled to a preference by reason of his having been educated at the school[5].

The chapel of each school to which the Public Schools Act 1868 applies is free from jurisdiction or control of the incumbent of the parish in which the chapel is situated, and is deemed to be a chapel dedicated and allowed by the ecclesiastical law of the realm for the performance of public worship and the administration of the sacraments according to the liturgy of the Church of England[6].

The income of the schools to which the Public Schools Acts apply arises from endowments and from fees paid by pupils, although at each school there are boys on the foundation[7] entitled to education which is wholly or partly gratuitous. The schools are subject to the general law of corporations in respect of their landed property[8]. Eton and Winchester have statutory powers as to land and advowsons[9]. Winchester has statutory power to make a scheme for the aggregation and administration of trusts[10].

Various special provisions as to property, government and other matters are made by the Public Schools Acts in relation to each school to which those Acts apply[11].

1   In their first report in 1968 the Public Schools Commission (chaired by Sir John Newsom) said: 'Everyone uses the term 'public school' and yet there is no generally accepted definition of these schools. Everybody would probably include the nine schools considered by the Clarendon Commission in their Report of 1864 — Eton, Winchester, Westminster, Charterhouse, St. Paul's, Merchant Taylors', Harrow, Rugby and Shrewsbury. Most people would also include those famous schools which became prominent in the 19th century such as Marlborough, Wellington, Cheltenham, Clifton, Oundle, Uppingham and many other notable schools. Some use the term to mean any independent secondary school — a school not receiving grant from public funds. Our terms of reference specifically drew our attention to those independent schools which were (or whose heads were) members of the Headmasters' Conference ('HMC'), the Association of Governing Bodies of Public Schools ('GBA') or the Association of Governing Bodies of Girls' Public Schools ('GBGSA'). There were 288 such schools when we were appointed, including 11 in Scotland'.

2 Eton (The College of the Blessed Mary of Eton) was founded by Henry VI in 1440; Winchester (The Saint Mary College of Winchester) by William of Wykeham in 1382; Westminster (St Peter's College) was founded before 1339 and re-founded by Queen Elizabeth I in 1561; Charterhouse was founded by Thomas Sutton in 1611; Harrow by John Lyon in 1571; Rugby by Lawrence Sheriff in 1567; and Shrewsbury by Edward VI in 1552.

3 Public Schools Act 1868 s 13. As to the meaning of 'governing body' see s 3. The governing body is a body corporate: see s 4A(1) (s 4A added by the Statute Law (Repeals) Act 1998 s 1(2), Sch 2 para 4). If a governing body, in dismissing a head, acts fairly and honestly, the High Court will not interfere: *Hayman v Governors of Rugby School* (1874) LR 18 Eq 28, 43 LJ Ch 834.

4 See the Public Schools Act 1868 s 13. No Roman Catholic may hold office at Eton, Westminster or Winchester: see the Roman Catholic Relief Act 1829 s 16; and ECCLESIASTICAL LAW vol 34 (2011) PARA 574.

5 Public Schools Act 1868 s 13.

6 Public Schools Act 1868 s 31 (amended by the Statute Law Revision Act 1893). This is unaffected by the Extra-Parochial Ministry Measure 1967 s 2(1), under which the bishop of the diocese in which any university or school is situated may license a clergyman to perform specified offices and services there: see s 2(5); and ECCLESIASTICAL LAW vol 34 (2011) PARA 482.

7 As to the meaning of 'boys on the foundation' in relation to each school see the Public Schools Act 1868 s 4. As to qualifications for admission of scholars to Rugby see *Re Rugby School* (1839) 1 Beav 457.

8 See generally CORPORATIONS vol 24 (2010) PARA 449 et seq.

9 See PARA 1329.

10 See PARA 637.

11 See e g the Public Schools Act 1868 s 20 (amended by the Statute Law (Repeals) Act 2004) (miscellaneous provisions as to Westminster School); the Public Schools Act 1868 s 26 (amended by the Statute Law Revision Act 1893; and the Statute Law (Repeals) Act 1973) (power to remove Shrewsbury School to another site); the Public Schools Act 1868 s 29 (change of corporate name of governors of Charterhouse); and s 32 (amended by the Statute Law (Repeals) Act 1973) (power to remove Westminster School to another site).

(ii) General Powers and Duties in relation to Independent Schools

371. Power to arrange provision of education at non-maintained schools. A local authority[1] may make arrangements for the provision of primary[2] and secondary education[3] for pupils[4] at schools[5] not maintained by it or another local authority[6].

1 As to the meaning of 'local authority' see PARA 25. Any function of a local authority in England which is conferred by or under the Education Act 1996 s 18 may be exercised by, or by employees of, such person as may be authorised in that behalf by the local authority whose function it is: Contracting Out (Local Authority Education Functions) (England) Order 2002, SI 2002/928, art 3, Sch 1 para (a) (art 3 amended by SI 2010/1172). As to the meaning of 'England' see PARA 7 note 3. As to the meaning of 'person' see PARA 7 note 6.

2 As to the meaning of 'primary education' see PARA 20.

3 As to the meaning of 'secondary education' see PARA 21.

4 As to the meaning of 'pupil' see PARA 20 note 4.

5 As to the meaning of 'school' see PARA 91.

6 Education Act 1996 s 18 (amended by SI 2010/1158). As to schools maintained by local authorities see PARA 99.

372. Power of Secretary of State and Welsh Ministers to require performance information. The general power of the Secretary of State[1] and the Welsh Ministers[2] to make regulations requiring the provision of information in relation to schools[3] includes power to require such information from the proprietors[4] of independent schools and also alternative provision academies that are not independent schools[5]. Regulations may also require the proprietor of a registered independent educational institution or school[6] to provide information relating to those bodies[7].

1 As to the Secretary of State see PARA 58.

2   As to the Welsh Ministers see PARA 59.
3   Ie the power conferred by the Education Act 1996 s 537: see PARA 67.
4   As to the meaning of 'proprietor' see PARA 51 note 4.
5   See the Education Act 1996 s 537(1)(b); and PARA 67. As to the meaning of 'independent school' see PARA 369. As to the meaning of 'alternative provision academy' see PARA 346 note 14.
6   As to the registration of independent educational institutions and schools see PARAS 384 et seq, 416.
7   See the Education and Skills Act 2008 s 123 (see PARA 393) and the Education Act 2002 s 168 (see PARA 417).

373.   Other general powers of Secretary of State and the Welsh Ministers. Ballot regulations[1] may provide for the general powers of the Secretary of State[2] and the Welsh Ministers[3] to prevent the unreasonable exercise of functions by certain bodies[4], and to take steps where such a body has failed to discharge any duty[5], to apply to proprietors of independent schools[6] in relation to a duty imposed by or under the regulations[7]. The Secretary of State or the Welsh Ministers may arrange for the payment of expenses incurred by the proprietor of an independent school in complying with specified obligations imposed by ballot regulations[8].

1   Ie regulations made under the School Standards and Framework Act 1998 s 105: see PARA 264.
2   As to the Secretary of State see PARA 58.
3   As to the Welsh Ministers see PARA 59.
4   Ie the Education Act 1996 s 496: see PARA 64. Note that ss 496, 497 only apply in regard certain bodies in England.
5   Ie the Education Act 1996 s 497: see PARA 65. See note 4.
6   As to independent schools see PARA 369.
7   See the School Standards and Framework Act 1998 s 105(7); and PARA 264. The Education (Grammar School Ballots) Regulations 1998, SI 1998/2876, reg 21 (amended by SI 2012/979) applies the Education Act 1996 s 497 to the proprietors of independent schools (and also of alternative provision academies that are not independent schools) in respect of certain duties. As to alternative provision academies see PARA 346 note 14.
8   See the School Standards and Framework Act 1998 s 105(9)(b); and PARA 264.

374.   Provision of individual pupil information. Regulations[1] may make provision requiring the proprietor[2] of every independent school[3] (and also of alternative provision academies[4] that are not independent schools) to provide to the relevant person such individual pupil information as may be prescribed[5].

1   Ie regulations made by the Secretary of State or, in relation to Wales, the Welsh Ministers: see the Education Act 1996 s 579(1). As to the Secretary of State see PARA 58. As to the Welsh Ministers see PARA 59. As to the meaning of 'Wales' see PARA 7 note 3.
2   As to the meaning of 'proprietor' see PARA 51 note 4.
3   As to the meaning of 'independent school' see PARA 369.
4   As to the meaning of 'alternative provision academy' see PARA 346 note 14.
5   See the Education Act 1996 s 537A; and PARA 68.

375.   Welfare of children accommodated in independent schools. Where an independent school provides accommodation for any child, it is the duty of the proprietor to safeguard and promote the child's welfare[1].

1   See the Children Act 1989 s 87; and CHILDREN AND YOUNG PERSONS vol 10 (2012) PARA 1152.

376.   Special educational needs in independent schools. The general duty to educate children with special educational needs[1] in mainstream schools[2] in the area of a local authority in Wales does not prevent a child from being educated in an independent school which is not a mainstream school if the cost is met otherwise than by the local authority[3]. In certain circumstances, a local authority in the area of a local authority in Wales may fund special educational provision[4] in a school which is not a maintained school[5].

With the Children and Families Act 2014 separate, different but broadly corresponding provision is now made for children and young persons in England[6] with special educational needs or disabilities[7].

The Secretary of State[8] or, in relation to Wales, the Welsh Ministers[9] may approve, as special schools[10], schools which are not community, foundation special schools or academy schools[11].

A local authority in Wales is under a duty to make arrangements for the avoidance of disagreements between the parents of a child with special educational needs and the proprietor of an independent school named in the child's statement, about the special educational provision made for that child[12]. Until the Children and Families Act 2014 these provisions also applied in England but the 2014 Act also has equivalent general provisions about disagreements[13].

The proprietor or head teacher of an independent school in Wales may request the local authority to make an assessment of the educational needs of a child registered at that school[14]. Again until the Children and Families Act 2014 these provisions also applied in England but the 2014 Act has broadly equivalent provisions about requests for the appropriate assessment[15].

1 As to the meaning of 'special educational needs' in the area of a local authority in Wales see PARA 989. As to the meaning of 'local authority' see PARA 25. As to the meaning of 'Wales' see PARA 7 note 3.

2 Ie the duty under the Education Act 1996 s 316: see PARA 1014. The definition of 'mainstream school' specifically excludes an independent school which is not a city technology college, a city college for the technology of the arts, or an academy: see PARA 1014 note 4. As to special educational provision in such colleges and academies see PARA 1015.

3 See the Education Act 1996 s 316A(1); and PARA 1014.

4 As to the meaning of 'special educational provision' see PARA 989.

5 See the Education Act 1996 s 348; and PARA 1016.

6 As to the meaning of 'England' see PARA 7 note 3.

7 See in particular the Children and Families Act 2014 ss 33, 34, 35; and PARA 954 et seq. As to the 2014 Act see generally PARA 943 et seq, and see PARA 941. As to special educational needs etc in England see PARA 943. As to city colleges and academies see also PARA 1015.

8 As to the Secretary of State see PARA 58.

9 As to the Welsh Ministers see PARA 59.

10 As to the meaning of 'special school' see PARA 1041.

11 See the Education Act 1996 s 342; and PARA 1042. As to the meaning of 'academy school' see PARA 346 note 12.

12 See the Education Act 1996 s 332BA; and PARA 1028.

13 See the Children and Families Act 2014 s 57; and PARA 987.

14 See the Education Act 1996 s 329A; and PARA 1001.

15 See the Children and Families Act 2014 s 36; and PARA 957.

377. Employment of staff. General provision is made in respect of the suitability of persons to work with children and the supervision of such persons[1].

As an employer, a proprietor of an independent school may be vicariously liable for assaults on pupils by staff and may also be liable for engaging unsuitable staff[2].

The requirements as to qualifications of teachers employed in schools do not generally apply to independent schools[3].

1 See the Safeguarding Vulnerable Groups Act 2006; and CHILDREN AND YOUNG PERSONS vol 9 (2012) PARA 678 et seq. See also the Education Act 2002 s 142; and PARA 420.

2   See *Lister v Hesley Hall Ltd* [2001] UKHL 22, [2002] 1 AC 215, [2001] ELR 422 (overruling *Trotman v North Yorkshire County Council* [1998] ELR 625, [1999] LGR 584, CA). See also PARAS 1009–1010. As to vicarious liability generally see TORT vol 97 (2015) PARA 767 et seq.
3   See the Education Act 2002 s 133; and PARA 1048.

378.   Preferment to teachers in independent schools willing to give religious education.   Preference may be given, in connection with the appointment, promotion or remuneration of teachers[1] at an independent school[2] which has a religious character, other than a certain type of academy[3], to persons[4]: (1) whose religious opinions are in accordance with the tenets of the religion or the religious denomination specified[5] in relation to the school[6]; or (2) who attend religious worship in accordance with those tenets[7]; or (3) who give, or are willing to give, religious education at the school in accordance with those tenets[8].

Regard may be had, in connection with the termination of the employment or engagement of any teacher at the school, to any conduct on his part which is incompatible with the precepts, or with the upholding of the tenets, of the religion or religious denomination so specified[9].

1   As to the appointment, promotion or remuneration of teachers generally see PARA 1047 et seq.
2   As to the meaning of 'independent school' see PARA 369 (definition applied by the School Standards and Framework Act 1998 s 142(8)).
3   Ie other than an academy to which the School Standards and Framework Act 1998 s 124AA applies: see PARA 379.
4   School Standards and Framework Act 1998 s 124A(1), (2) (ss 124A, 124B added by SI 2003/2037; and the School Standards and Framework Act 1998 s 124A(1) amended by the Education Act 2011 s 62(1), (2)). The provisions of the School Standards and Framework Act 1998 s 69(3), (5) (see PARA 914), which relates to the designation of foundation or voluntary schools as having a religious character, apply in relation to an independent school other than an alternative provision academy as they apply in relation to a foundation or voluntary school but as if: (1) in s 69(3), the reference to Pt II (ss 20–83) were a reference to Pt 5A (ss 124A–124B); and (2) in s 69(5), the reference to s 69(4) were a reference to s 124A(2): s 124B(1) (as so added; and amended by SI 2012/976). An order made under the School Standards and Framework Act 1998 s 69(3) by virtue of s 124A(1) must specify, in relation to each school designated by the order, the religion or religious denomination (or, as the case may be, each religion or religious denomination) in accordance with whose tenets education is provided at the school or the school is conducted: s 124B(2) (as so added). As to the meaning of references to the religion or the religious denomination in relation to a school see PARA 146 note 12. As to the meaning of 'alternative provision academy' see PARA 346 note 14 (definition applied by s 142(8), (9). Orders made under s 69(3), (5) (as modified by s 124B), being of local effect, are not recorded in this work.
5   Ie specified under the School Standards and Framework Act 1998 s 124B(2): see note 4.
6   School Standards and Framework Act 1998 s 124A(2)(a) (as added: see note 4).
7   School Standards and Framework Act 1998 s 124A(2)(b) (as added: see note 4).
8   School Standards and Framework Act 1998 s 124A(2)(c) (as added: see note 4).
9   School Standards and Framework Act 1998 s 124A(3) (as added: see note 4).

379.   Staff at certain schools with religious character.   The following provisions apply if (1) an academy order has been made in respect of a foundation or voluntary controlled school which is designated[1] as a school having a religious character[2]; (2) the school has been converted[3] into an academy[4]; and (3) the Secretary of State[5] has not made an order[6] in respect of the school[7]. The Secretary of State may by order provide that this provision[8] does not apply to a school specified in the order[9].

Where there are more than two teachers[10] at the academy, the teachers must include persons who (a) are selected for their fitness and competence to give religious education in accordance with the tenets of the religion or the religious denomination specified in relation to the academy in the order[11]; and (b) are specifically appointed to do so[12]. A teacher thus employed or engaged at the academy[13] is a 'reserved teacher', and any other teacher at the academy is a 'non-reserved teacher'[14]. The number of reserved teachers in the academy must not exceed one-fifth of the total number of teachers, including the principal[15]. In connection with the appointment of a person to be the principal of the academy, in a case where the principal is not to be a reserved teacher, regard may be had to that person's ability and fitness to preserve and develop the religious character of the academy[16].

Preference may be given, in connection with the appointment, promotion or remuneration of reserved teachers at the academy, to persons (i) whose religious opinions are in accordance with the tenets of the religion or the religious denomination specified in relation to the academy in the order[17]; or (ii) who attend religious worship in accordance with those tenets[18]; or (iii) who give, or are willing to give, religious education at the academy in accordance with those tenets[19].

Regard may be had, in connection with the termination of employment or engagement of any reserved teacher at the academy, to any conduct on the part of the teacher which is incompatible with the precepts, or with the upholding of the tenets, of the religion or religious denomination specified in the order[20]. No person, other than a reserved teacher, is to be disqualified by reason of their religious opinions, or of their attending or omitting to attend religious worship from being a teacher at the academy, or from being employed or engaged for the purposes of the academy otherwise than as a teacher[21]. A non-reserved teacher must not be required to give religious education[22]. A non-reserved teacher must not receive any less remuneration than any other non-reserved teacher, or be deprived of, or disqualified for, any promotion or other advantage available to other non-reserved teachers (A) for the reason that the teacher gives, or does not give, religious education[23]; or (B) for reasons related to the teacher's religious opinions or to the teacher's attending or omitting to attend religious worship[24].

1   Ie designated by order under the School Standards and Framework Act 1998 s 69(3): see PARA 914. As to foundation or voluntary controlled schools see PARA 106.

2   School Standards and Framework Act 1998 s 124AA(1)(a) (s 124AA added by the Education Act 2011 s 62(1), (3)). As to the meaning of references to the religion or the religious denomination in relation to a school see PARA 146 note 12. As to staffing at academies generally see PARA 358.

3   See the Academies Act 2010 s 4(3); and PARA 350.

4   School Standards and Framework Act 1998 s 124AA(1)(b) (as added: see note 2.) As to the meaning of 'academy' see PARA 346 note 19 (definition applied by the School Standards and Framework Act 1998 s 142(8)).

5   As to the Secretary of State see PARA 58.

6   Ie under the School Standards and Framework Act 1998 s 124AA(2): see the text to notes 8, 9. An order under s 124AA(2) is not to be made by statutory instrument: see s 138(2) (amended by the Education Act 2011 s 62(1), (4)(b)).

7   School Standards and Framework Act 1998 s 124AA(1)(c) (as added: see note 2).

8   Ie the School Standards and Framework Act 1998 s 124AA.

9   School Standards and Framework Act 1998 s 124AA(2) (as added: see note 2).

10 As to the appointment, promotion or remuneration of teachers generally see PARA 1047 et seq.

11 School Standards and Framework Act 1998 s 124AA(3)(a) (as added: see note 2).The reference in the text to the order is a reference to the order under the School Standards and Framework Act 1998 s 69(3) (as applied by the Academies Act 2010 s 6(8)): see PARA 914.

12 School Standards and Framework Act 1998 s 124AA(3)(b) (as added: see note 2).

13 Ie in pursuance of the School Standards and Framework Act 1998 s 124AA.

14 School Standards and Framework Act 1998 s 124AA(3) (as added: see note 2).

15 School Standards and Framework Act 1998 s 124AA(4) (as added: see note 2). For this purpose, where the total number of teachers is not a multiple of five, it is to be treated as if it were the next higher multiple of five: s 124AA(4) (as so added). As to principals of an academy see eg PARA 517 note 5.
16 School Standards and Framework Act 1998 s 124AA(5) (as added: see note 2).
17 School Standards and Framework Act 1998 s 124AA(6)(a) (as added: see note 2). See note 11.
18 School Standards and Framework Act 1998 s 124AA(6)(b) (as added: see note 2).
19 School Standards and Framework Act 1998 s 124AA(6)(c) (as added: see note 2).
20 School Standards and Framework Act 1998 s 124AA(7) (as added: see note 2). See note 11.
21 School Standards and Framework Act 1998 s 124AA(8) (as added: see note 2).
22 School Standards and Framework Act 1998 s 124AA(9) (as added: see note 2).
23 School Standards and Framework Act 1998 s 124AA(10)(a) (as added: see note 2).
24 School Standards and Framework Act 1998 s 124AA(10)(b) (as added: see note 2).

380. Travelling and subsistence allowances for governors representing local authority ('local authority allowances'). A local authority[1] may pay such allowances as may be prescribed[2] to any person appointed to represent the authority on the governing body of an independent school[3], an alternative provision academy[4] that is not an independent school or a non-maintained special school[5].

1 As to the meaning of 'local authority' see PARA 25.
2 'Prescribed' means prescribed by regulations made by the Secretary of State or, in relation to Wales, the Welsh Ministers: see the Education Act 1996 s 579(1). As to the Secretary of State see PARA 58. As to the Welsh Ministers see PARA 59. As to the meaning of 'Wales' see PARA 7 note 3.
3 As to the meaning of 'independent school' see PARA 369.
4 As to the meaning of 'alternative provision academy' see PARA 346 note 14.
5 See the Education Act 1996 s 519(3); and PARA 52. As to the meaning of 'special school' see PARA 1041.

(iii) Fees for Independent Schools

381. Contract between parent and proprietor. In independent schools[1] the relations between the parent and the proprietor of the school are governed by the terms (express or implied) of the contract for the education of the child[2].

Where the contract between the parent and the school proprietor provides that a term's notice must be given of the child's removal from the school, the proprietor can recover a term's fees if the child is removed without due notice[3], and it is no defence to a claim for fees in lieu of notice that the school is closing down[4]. If the pupil is absent for a term owing to illness the parent is not liable for the term's fees in the absence of an express provision in the contract[5]. Where fees are payable in advance and the pupil is absent for a term the proprietor can recover the full fees for the term without making any deduction in respect of board[6]. Where the pupil is excluded from the school as a result of the parent's breach of the contract, the proprietor is entitled to the whole term's fees[7].

Unless the right is expressly or impliedly reserved in the contract, the proprietor may not be able to increase the fees[8]. Notice by the proprietor of an increase in fees may operate as a notice to determine the contract and allow of the parent removing his child without due notice[9].

If, on obtaining a divorce, one parent is granted custody of a child and the other parent gives an undertaking to maintain and educate him, this undertaking is not sufficient of itself to entitle the parent with custody to incur school fees for the child independently of other parent's wishes[10]. The proprietor cannot recover from the parent sums spent on the pupil's behalf without the sanction, express or implied, of the parent[11].

An announcement that a scholarship examination is to be held does not constitute an offer which will result in a contract with the competitor who obtains the highest marks[12].

1 As to independent schools see PARA 369.
2 The terms of the contract are frequently those contained in a school prospectus of which the parent has notice: *Spry v Kent Education Committee* (1924) 40 TLR 559, DC. See also *D'Mello v Loughborough College of Technology* (1970) 114 Sol Jo 665 (college prospectus held to be part of the contract); *Price v Dennis* (1988) [1999] Ed CR 747, CA (broad terms of the prospectus, but not each detail in it, held to be incorporated into the contract; proprietor subject to an implied term of the contract that he would conduct the school in a fit, proper and responsible manner; and the proprietor also subject to a duty to take reasonable steps to retain the confidence of parents who themselves acted reasonably). As to contractual terms see CONTRACT vol 22 (2012) PARA 352 et seq.
3 *Mount v Oldham Corpn* [1973] QB 309, [1973] 1 All ER 26, CA (overruling *Denman v Winstanley* (1887) 4 TLR 127, DC, where it had been held that the appropriate claim was for damages). The court takes judicial notice of the usage of the educational world that, in lieu of giving a term's notice of withdrawal, a term's fees must be paid: see *Mount v Oldham Corpn.*
4 *Tuyn v Creasy* (1956) Times, 7 November, CA. See also *Lennssen v Thornton* (1887) 3 TLR 657, DC; *Eardly v Price* (1806) 2 Bos & PNR 333. In the case of a contract to pay for a course of instruction by instalments, the instalments can be recovered although the student has given notice that he does not intend to continue the course: *International Correspondence Schools Ltd v Ayres* (1912) 106 LT 845.
5 *Simeon v Watson* (1877) 46 LJQB 679; *Boast v Firth* (1868) LR 4 CP 1; c f *Collins v Price* (1828) 5 Bing 132 (where illness after the beginning of the term was held not to excuse from payment of the term's fees).
6 *Jones v Turner* (1891) 7 TLR 421, DC.
7 *Price v Wilkins* (1888) 58 LT 680.
8 *Anon* (1946) 96 L Jo 602.
9 *Pott v Stevens* (1949) 99 L Jo 164.
10 *Roper v S* (1954) Times, 5 May, per Singleton LJ (it would not be right in ordinary justice to make the father pay fees for the son at a school at which he did not wish his son to remain; judgment given for the fees against the mother, but not against the father).
11 *Clements v Williams* (1837) 8 C & P 58 (no general authority to supply clothing to a pupil without the parent's sanction).
12 *Rooke v Dawson* [1895] 1 Ch 480.

(iv) Regulation and Inspection of Independent Schools

A. REGULATION AND INSPECTION IN ENGLAND UNDER THE EDUCATION AND SKILLS ACT 2008

(A) Application of Provisions

382. Regulatory regime under the Education and Skills Act 2008 and meaning of 'independent educational institution'. Part 4 of the Education and Skills Act 2008[1] introduced a new category of independent educational institution to which the regulatory regime for independent schools in England is extended[2]. 'An independent educational institution' means[3], in relation to England[4]:

(1) an independent school[5]; or
(2) an institution other than an independent school which (a) provides part-time education[6] for one or more persons of compulsory school age[7] ('part-time students') whether or not it also provides full-time education for any person[8], and (b) would be an independent school but for the fact that the education provided for the part-time student or students is part-time rather than full-time[9].

1 Ie the Education and Skills Act 2008 Pt 4 Ch 1 (ss 92–141).
2 Prior to the introduction of the Education and Skills Act 2008 Pt 4, the regulatory regime for independent schools as set out in the Education Act 2002 Pt 10 Ch 1 (ss 157–171) also applied

to schools in England; now those provisions of the 2002 Act apply only to Wales (see PARA 416 et seq) and the Education and Skills Act 2008 Pt 4 applies to England. As to savings and transitory provisions following the commencement of the relevant sections of the Education and Skills Act 2008 see the Education and Skills Act 2008 (Commencement No 11 and Saving and Transitory Provisions) Order 2014, SI 2014/3364, arts 3–5.

3   Ie for the purposes of the Education and Skills Act 2008 Pt 4 Ch 1 (ss 92–141): see PARA 383 et seq.

4   References in the Education and Skills Act 2008 Pt 4 Ch 1 (ss 92–141) to an independent educational institution are to an independent educational institution in England: s 93(1). For provision regulating independent schools in Wales, see the Education Act 2002 Pt 10 Ch 1 (ss 156A–171) (see PARA 416 et seq): Education and Skills Act 2008 s 93(2). As to the meanings of 'England' and 'Wales' see PARA 7 note 3. As to the meaning of 'independent school' see PARA 369 (definition applied by s 168(2), (3)(b)). As to the provision made as to continuity of law in relation to independent schools in England see s 139.

Part 4 Ch 1 applies to alternative provision academies that are not independent educational institutions as it applies to independent educational institutions; accordingly, references in ss 92–141, except in ss 95(2), 140(1), to independent educational institutions are to be read as including references to alternative provision academies that are not independent educational institutions: see s 93A(1), (2) (added by SI 2012/976). As to the meaning of 'alternative provision academy' see PARA 346 note 14 (definition applied by the Education and Skills Act 2008 s 168(2), (3)).

5   Education and Skills Act 2008 s 92(1)(a). See also note 4.

6   For these purposes, an institution provides 'part-time' education for a person if it provides education for the person:

  (1)   for at least 12.5 hours a week, for at least 28 weeks, during an academic year at the end of which the person is under the age of 12 (Education and Skills Act 2008 s 92(2)(a)); or

  (2)   for at least 15 hours a week, for at least 28 weeks, during an academic year at the end of which the person is aged 12 or over (s 92(2)(b)),

which does not amount to full-time education (s 92)(2)). 'An academic year' means a period of 12 months ending with 31 August: s 92(4). As to the time at which a person attains a particular age see PARA 7 note 6. Regulations may (a) provide that time spent on a specified activity or on an activity of a specified description is or is not to be treated as time during which education is being provided for the purposes of s 92 (s 92(3)(b)); (b) amend s 92(2)(a) or (b) so as to substitute a different number of weeks for the number of weeks for the time being mentioned there (s 92(3)(c)). See also note 4. 'Regulations' means regulations made under the Education and Skills Act 2008 by the Secretary of State: s 168(1). 'Specified' means specified in regulations under s 92: see s 92(4). As to the Secretary of State see PARA 58. At the date at which this volume states the law no such regulations had been made.

7   As to the meaning of 'compulsory school age' see PARA 19.

8   Education and Skills Act 2008 s 92(1)(b)(i). See also note 4.

9   Education and Skills Act 2008 s 92(1)(b)(ii). See also note 4. Regulations may provide that a specified institution or an institution of a specified description is not an independent educational institution by virtue of s 92(1)(b): s 92(3)(a). At the date at which this volume states the law no such regulations had been made.

383.   Application of provisions to independent colleges for 16 to 18 year olds.

Regulations[1] may provide for any provision of the statutory provisions relating to the regulation and inspection of independent educational institutions[2] in England[3] to apply in relation to an independent post-16 college[4] as it applies in relation to an independent educational institution, subject to such modifications[5] as may be prescribed[6].

1   Regulations' means regulations made under the Education and Skills Act 2008 by the Secretary of State: s 168(1). As to the Secretary of State see PARA 58. At the date at which this volume states the law no such regulations had been made.

2   As to the meaning of 'independent educational institution' see PARA 382. The Education and Skills Act 2008 Pt 4 Ch 1 (ss 92–141) applies to alternative provision academies that are not independent educational institutions as it applies to independent educational institutions; accordingly, references in ss 92–141, except in ss 95(2), 140(1), to independent educational institutions are to be read as including references to alternative provision academies that are not

independent educational institutions: see s 93A(1), (2) (added by SI 2012/976). As to the meaning of 'alternative provision academy' see PARA 346 note 14 (definition applied by the Education and Skills Act 2008 s 168(2), (3)).

3 Ie the provisions of the Education and Skills Act 2008 Pt 4 Ch 1 (ss 92–141). As to the meaning of 'England' see PARA 7 note 3. See note 2.

4 'An independent post-16 college' means an institution in England:

    (1) at which relevant education or training is provided for (a) five or more persons who are not under compulsory school age, including at least one who is over compulsory school age but is under the age of 18 (Education and Skills Act 2008 s 132(2)(a)(i)), or (b) at least one student to whom s 132(4) applies who is over compulsory school age but is under the age of 18 (s 132(2)(a)(ii));

    (2) which is not an independent educational institution, a school maintained by a local authority, a special school not so maintained, or an institution in receipt of funding from the Secretary of State (s 132(2)(b) (amended by SI 2010/1080; SI 2010/1158; the Education Act 2011 Sch 16 paras 40, 44; and the Deregulation Act 2015 Sch 14 Pt 2 paras 60, 64)); and

    (3) which is outside the further education and higher education sectors (Education and Skills Act 2008 s 132(2)(c)).

In s 132(2)(a) (see head (1) above), 'relevant education or training' provided for a person means education or training which (i) is provided for the person for at least 16 hours a week, for at least four weeks, during an academic year (s 132(3)(a)); and (ii) is not education or training provided in connection with facilities for adventure activities (within the meaning of the Activity Centres (Young Persons' Safety) Act 1995 s 1 (licensing of adventure activities: see CHILDREN AND YOUNG PERSONS vol 9 (2012) PARA 662) (Education and Skills Act 2008 s 132(3)(b)). Section 132(4) applies to a person (A) for whom an EHC plan is maintained (s 132(4)(a) (amended by the Children and Families Act 2014 Sch 3 paras 82, 87(a))); or (B) for whom an EHC plan was maintained immediately before the person ceased to be a pupil at his or her last school or (if later) the person ceased to be a student at his or her last post-16 institution (Education and Skills Act 2008 s 132(4)(b)(i) (s 132(4)(b), (b)(i) amended by the Children and Families Act 2014 Sch 3 paras 82, 87(b), (c))), or the institution in England mentioned in the Education and Skills Act 2008 s 132(2) (see above) started providing relevant education or training for the person (s 132(4)(b)(ii) (amended by the Children and Families Act 2014 Sch 3 paras 82, 87(d))). As to the meaning of 'compulsory school age' see PARA 19. As to the time at which a person attains a particular age see PARA 7 note 6. 'Student' means, in relation to an independent school, a pupil within the meaning of the Education Act 1996 s 3 (see PARA 20 note 4); and in relation to an institution within the Education and Skills Act 2008 s 92(1)(b) (see PARA 382), a person for whom the institution provides part-time education within the meaning of that provision or full-time education: s 138(1). As to the meaning of 'independent school' see PARA 369; as to the meaning of 'school' see PARA 91; as to the meaning of 'local authority' see PARA 25; as to the meaning of 'special school' see PARA 1041; as to the meaning of 'further education' see PARA 23; and as to the meaning of 'higher education' see PARA 24 (definitions applied by s 168(2), (3)(b)). As to schools maintained by local authorities see PARA 99. As to the meaning of 'EHC plan' see PARA 958 (definition applied by s 168(2), (3)(b)) and as to EHC plans (ie education, health and care plans) generally see PARA 958 et seq. 'An academic year' means a period of 12 months ending with 31 August: s 132(6). 'Post-16 institution' has the meaning given by the Children and Families Act 2014 s 83(2) (see PARA 943 note 9): Education and Skills Act 2008 s 132(6) (definition added by the Children and Families Act 2014 Sch 3 paras 82, 87(e)). See note 2.

Regulations may: (aa) provide that a specified institution or an institution of a specified description is not an independent post-16 college (Education and Skills Act 2008 s 132(5)(a)); (bb) provide that time spent on a specified activity or on an activity of a specified description is or is not to be treated as time during which education or training is provided for the purposes of s 132 (s 132(5)(b)); (cc) amend s 132(3)(a) (see head (1) above) so as to substitute a different number of hours or weeks for the number of hours or weeks for the time being mentioned there (s 132(5)(c)). 'Specified' means specified in regulations under s 132: s 132(6). At the date at which this volume states the law no such regulations had been made.

5 As to the meaning of 'modifications' see PARA 21 note 15 (definition applied by the Education and Skills Act 2008 s 168(2), (3)(b))

6 Education and Skills Act 2008 s 132(1). See also note 2. 'Prescribed' means prescribed by regulations: s 168(1). Regulations under s 132(1) applying s 120 (see PARA 404), or any of the provisions mentioned in s 124(1) (see PARA 405) or s 125(1) (see PARA 406), in relation to an independent post-16 college must also apply any provision conferring a right of appeal against a decision or order made under that provision: s 133(1). No draft of any regulations under

s 132(1) may be laid before Parliament unless the Secretary of State has first consulted Her Majesty's Chief Inspector of Education, Children's Services and Skills (s 133(2)(a)), and such other persons as the Secretary of State considers appropriate (s 133(2)(b)), about the proposal to make the regulations (s 133(2)). As to the laying of documents before Parliament see STATUTES AND LEGISLATIVE PROCESS vol 96 (2012) PARA 1052. As to the exercise of the duty to consult see JUDICIAL REVIEW vol 61 (2010) PARA 627. As to Her Majesty's Chief Inspector of Education, Children's Services and Skills see PARA 1133. As to the meaning of 'person' see PARA 7 note 6.

(B) Registration

384. The register. The Secretary of State[1] must keep a register of independent educational institutions[2] to be known as 'the register of independent educational institutions in England'[3]. The Secretary of State must publish the register in such manner, and at such times, as he considers appropriate[4].

A person[5] must not conduct an independent educational institution unless it is registered[6]. A person who conducts an independent educational institution in contravention of this prohibition is guilty of an offence[7].

Where Her Majesty's Chief Inspector of Education, Children's Services and Skills[8] has reasonable cause to believe that such an offence is being committed on any premises[9], he may at any reasonable time enter and inspect the premises[10], and inspect and take copies of any records or other documents which he has reasonable cause to believe may be required for the purposes of proceedings in relation to such an offence[11]. It is an offence intentionally to obstruct a person in the exercise of the person's functions[12] in relation to the inspection[13].

1   As to the Secretary of State see PARA 58.
2   Education and Skills Act 2008 s 95(1). On the coming into force of s 95, the register of independent schools in England (see the Education Act 2002 s 158: and PARA 417) became the register of independent educational institutions in England: Education and Skills Act 2008 s 140(1). As to the meaning of 'independent educational institution' see PARA 382.
     The Education and Skills Act 2008 Pt 4 Ch 1 (ss 92–141) applies to alternative provision academies that are not independent educational institutions as it applies to independent educational institutions; accordingly, references in ss 92–141, except in ss 95(2), 140(1), to independent educational institutions are to be read as including references to alternative provision academies that are not independent educational institutions: see s 93A(1), (2) (added by SI 2012/976). As to the meaning of 'alternative provision academy' see PARA 346 note 14 (definition applied by the Education and Skills Act 2008 s 168(2), (3)).
3   Education and Skills Act 2008 s 95(2). See also note 2. As to the meaning of 'England' see PARA 7 note 3.
4   Education and Skills Act 2008 s 95(3). See also note 2.
5   As to the meaning of 'person' see PARA 7 note 6.
6   Education and Skills Act 2008 s 96(1). See also note 2. 'Registered' means entered in the register; and 'the register' means the register of independent educational institutions in England: s 138(1). As to applications for registration see PARA 385.
7   Education and Skills Act 2008 s 96(2). See also note 2. A person guilty of such an offence is liable on summary conviction to imprisonment for a term not exceeding 51 weeks or to a fine not exceeding level 5 on the standard scale (or to both): s 96(3). In relation to an offence committed before the commencement of the Criminal Justice Act 2003 s 281(5) (not yet in force), for '51 weeks' substitute 'six months': Education and Skills Act 2008 s 96(4). As to the standard scale see SENTENCING AND DISPOSITION OF OFFENDERS vol 92 (2010) PARA 142. As to the institution of proceedings for offences see PARA 412. As to offences by bodies corporate see PARA 413. As to offences by unincorporated bodies see PARA 414.
8   As to Her Majesty's Chief Inspector of Education, Children's Services and Skills see PARA 1133.
9   As to the meaning of 'premises' see PARA 62 note 19 (definition applied by the Education and Skills Act 2008 s 168(2), (3)(b)).
10   Education and Skills Act 2008 s 97(1)(a). See also note 2.
11   Education and Skills Act 2008 s 97(1)(b). See also note 2. The Education Act 2005 s 58 (computer records: see PARA 1152 note 7) applies in relation to such inspection of records or other documents: see the Education and Skills Act 2008 s 97(2). Section 97 does not confer power to inspect or take copies of anything of a kind specified in the Police and Criminal

Evidence Act 1984 s 9(2) (legally privileged material etc: see POLICE AND INVESTIGATORY POWERS vol 84A (2013) PARA 453): Education and Skills Act 2008 s 97(3).

12 As to the meaning of 'functions' see PARA 18 note 5 (definition applied by the Education and Skills Act 2008 s 168(2), (3)(b)).

13 Education and Skills Act 2008 s 97(4). See also note 2. A person guilty of such an offence is liable on summary conviction to a fine not exceeding level 4 on the standard scale: s 97(5).

385. Applications for registration. The proprietor[1] of an independent educational institution may apply to the Secretary of State[2] for the institution to be entered on the register[3]. An application to enter an institution in the register must contain the prescribed information[4], and be made in the prescribed manner[5]. The prescribed information must include information as to the following matters relating to the institution[6]:

(1) whether the institution is an independent school[7], or an institution other than an independent school[8];

(2) the age range of students[9];

(3) the maximum number of students[10];

(4) whether the institution is for male or female students or both[11];

(5) whether the institution provides accommodation for students[12];

(6) whether the institution is specially organised to make special educational provision[13] for students with special educational needs[14];

(7) in the case of an institution within head (6) above, the type or types of special educational needs for which the institution is specially organised to make special educational provision[15].

The Secretary of State must notify Her Majesty's Chief Inspector of Education, Children's Services and Skills[16] of an application[17].

1 As to the meaning of 'proprietor' see PARA 415 note 3. In the Education and Skills Act 2008 s 98 the reference to the proprietor of an independent educational institution includes the proprietor of an institution that it is proposed should become an independent educational institution (and accordingly the information required by s 98(3) (see the text to notes 6–15), in the case of such a proprietor, is information about the institution as it is proposed to be): s 138(2). As to the meaning of 'independent educational institution' see PARA 382.

Part 4 Ch 1 (ss 92–141) applies to alternative provision academies that are not independent educational institutions as it applies to independent educational institutions; accordingly, references in ss 92–141, except in ss 95(2), 140(1), to independent educational institutions are to be read as including references to alternative provision academies that are not independent educational institutions: see s 93A(1), (2) (added by SI 2012/976). As to the meaning of 'alternative provision academy' see PARA 346 note 14 (definition applied by the Education and Skills Act 2008 s 168(2), (3)).

2 As to the Secretary of State see PARA 58.

3 Education and Skills Act 2008 s 98(1). See note 1. As to the meaning of 'the register' see PARA 384 note 6. As to the determination of applications for registration see PARA 386.

4 Education and Skills Act 2008 s 98(2)(a). See also notes 1, 3. 'Prescribed' means prescribed by regulations made by the Secretary of State: see s 168(1). As to the regulations made see the Education (Independent Educational Provision in England) (Provision of Information) Regulations 2010, SI 2010/2919 (amended by SI 2012/979).

5 Education and Skills Act 2008 s 98(2)(b). See also notes 1, 3. As to the regulations made see note 4.

6 See note 1.

7 Education and Skills Act 2008 s 98(3)(a)(i). See also notes 1, 3. As to the meaning of 'independent school' see PARA 369 (definition applied by s 168(2), (3)(b)).

8 Ie an institution within the Education and Skills Act 2008 s 92(1)(b) (see PARA 382): see s 98(3)(a)(ii). See also note 3.

9 Education and Skills Act 2008 s 98(3)(b). See also note 3. As to the meaning of 'student' see PARA 383 note 4.

10 Education and Skills Act 2008 s 98(3)(c). See also notes 1, 3.

11 Education and Skills Act 2008 s 98(3)(d). See also notes 1, 3.

12 Education and Skills Act 2008 s 98(3)(e). See also notes 1, 3.

13 As to the meaning of 'special educational provision' see PARA 943 (definition applied by the Education and Skills Act 2008 s 168(2), (3)).
14 Education and Skills Act 2008 s 98(3)(f). See also notes 1, 3. As to the meaning of 'special educational needs' see PARAS 943 (definition applied by s 168(2), (3)).
15 Education and Skills Act 2008 s 98(3)(g). See also notes 1, 3.
16 As to Her Majesty's Chief Inspector of Education, Children's Services and Skills see PARA 1133.
17 Education and Skills Act 2008 s 98(4). See also notes 1, 3.

386. Determination of applications for registration. Where Her Majesty's Chief Inspector of Education, Children's Services and Skills[1] is notified[2] that an institution has applied to be entered on the register[3], he must inspect the institution[4], and make a report to the Secretary of State[5] on the extent to which the independent educational institution standards[6] are likely to be met in relation to the institution once it becomes a registered[7] independent educational institution[8]. The Secretary of State must then decide, taking into account the report of the Chief Inspector[9], and any other evidence relating to the independent educational institution standards[10], whether those standards are likely to be met in relation to the institution once it becomes a registered independent educational institution[11].

The Secretary of State must notify the proprietor[12] of the institution of his decision[13]. If the Secretary of State decides that the independent educational institution standards are likely to be met in relation to the institution once it becomes a registered independent educational institution, he must enter the institution in the register[14]. An entry in the register for an independent educational institution must include: (1) the name and address of the institution[15]; (2) the name of the proprietor of the institution[16]; and (3) the information supplied[17] with the application[18].

1 As to Her Majesty's Chief Inspector of Education, Children's Services and Skills see PARA 1133.
2 Ie under the Education and Skills Act 2008 s 98(4): see PARA 385.
3 As to the meaning of 'the register' see PARA 384 note 6.
4 Education and Skills Act 2008 s 99(1)(a). As to the Chief Inspector's powers of entry and inspection see s 110; and PARA 398. A fee may be payable in respect of an inspection: see s 111; and PARA 399.
5 As to the Secretary of State see PARA 58.
6 As to the meaning of 'independent educational institution standards' see PARA 394.
7 As to the meaning of 'registered' see PARA 384 note 6.
8 Education and Skills Act 2008 s 99(1)(b). As to the meaning of 'independent educational institution' see PARA 382. As to the publication of reports see s 113; and PARA 400.
   The Education and Skills Act 2008 Pt 4 Ch 1 (ss 92–141) applies to alternative provision academies that are not independent educational institutions as it applies to independent educational institutions; accordingly, references in ss 92–141, except in ss 95(2), 140(1), to independent educational institutions are to be read as including references to alternative provision academies that are not independent educational institutions: see s 93A(1), (2) (added by SI 2012/976). As to the meaning of 'alternative provision academy' see PARA 346 note 14 (definition applied by the Education and Skills Act 2008 s 168(2), (3)).
9 Education and Skills Act 2008 s 99(2)(a).
10 Education and Skills Act 2008 s 99(2)(b).
11 Education and Skills Act 2008 s 99(2). As to an appeal against a decision made under s 99(2), see s 125; and PARA 406.
12 As to the service of notices and documents see the Education and Skills Act 2008 s 137; and PARA 415. As to the meaning of 'proprietor' see PARA 415 note 3.
13 See the Education and Skills Act 2008 s 99(3).
14 Education and Skills Act 2008 s 99(4).
15 Education and Skills Act 2008 s 99(5)(a).
16 Education and Skills Act 2008 s 99(5)(b). See also note 12.
17 Ie pursuant to the Education and Skills Act 2008 s 98(3)(a)–(g): see PARA 385.
18 Education and Skills Act 2008 s 99(5)(c).

387. Power to deregister institutions no longer required to register. If the Secretary of State[1]:

(1)   has reasonable cause to believe that a registered[2] institution has ceased to be an independent educational institution[3]; and

(2)   does not have reasonable cause to believe that the institution will become an independent educational institution again within the following 12 months[4],

he may remove the institution from the register[5].

The Secretary of State must notify[6] the proprietor[7] of an institution of any such decision to remove it from the register[8]. The Secretary of State's decision does not have effect during the period in which: (a) an appeal may be brought[9] against the decision[10]; or (b) where such an appeal has been brought, the appeal has not been determined, withdrawn or otherwise disposed of[11].

1   As to the Secretary of State see PARA 58.
2   As to the meaning of 'registered' see PARA 384 note 6.
3   Education and Skills Act 2008 s 100(1)(a). As to the meaning of 'independent educational institution' see PARA 382.
        Part 4 Ch 1 (ss 92–141) applies to alternative provision academies that are not independent educational institutions as it applies to independent educational institutions; accordingly, references in ss 92–141, except in ss 95(2), 140(1), to independent educational institutions are to be read as including references to alternative provision academies that are not independent educational institutions: see s 93A(1), (2) (added by SI 2012/976). As to the meaning of 'alternative provision academy' see PARA 346 note 14 (definition applied by the Education and Skills Act 2008 s 168(2), (3)).
4   Education and Skills Act 2008 s 100(1)(b). See also note 3. As to the meaning of 'month' see PARA 54 note 26.
5   Education and Skills Act 2008 s 100(1). See also note 3. As to the meaning of 'the register' see PARA 384 note 6.
6   As to the service of notices and documents see the Education and Skills Act 2008 s 137; and PARA 415.
7   As to the meaning of 'proprietor' see PARA 415 note 3.
8   Education and Skills Act 2008 s 100(2). See also note 3.
9   Ie under the Education and Skills Act 2008 s 124: see PARA 405.
10   Education and Skills Act 2008 s 100(3)(a). See also note 3.
11   Education and Skills Act 2008 s 100(3)(b). See also note 3.

388. Requirement to apply for approval for material change. For the purposes of the statutory provisions relating to the regulation and inspection of independent educational institutions[1] in England[2], 'a material change' in relation to an independent educational institution[3] means:

(1)   in relation to an institution other than a special institution[4], a change in respect of certain information relating to the institution[5] provided with the application for registration[6];

(2)   in relation to a special institution, a change of proprietor[7], a change of address[8], or a change in respect of any information relating to the institution[9] provided with the application for registration[10].

Where the proprietor of a registered[11] independent educational institution is aware that a material change is to be made in relation to the institution, he must make an application to the Secretary of State[12] for approval of the change[13]. An application for approval must be made in writing[14] and, in the case of approval of a change of proprietor, must be made by the proposed new proprietor[15].

1   As to the meaning of 'independent educational institution' see PARA 382. The Education and Skills Act 2008 Pt 4 Ch 1 (ss 92–141) applies to alternative provision academies that are not independent educational institutions as it applies to independent educational institutions; accordingly, references in ss 92–141, except in ss 95(2), 140(1), to independent educational

institutions are to be read as including references to alternative provision academies that are not independent educational institutions: see s 93A(1), (2) (added by SI 2012/976). As to the meaning of 'alternative provision academy' see PARA 346 note 14 (definition applied by the Education and Skills Act 2008 s 168(2), (3)).

2   Ie the Education and Skills Act 2008 Pt 4 Ch 1 (ss 92–141). As to the meaning of 'England' see PARA 7 note 3. See note 1.

3   See the Education and Skills Act 2008 s 101(1). At the date at which this volume states the law ss 101, 102 are in force for the purposes of making regulations only (see the Education and Skills Act 2008 (Commencement No 3) Order 2009, SI 2009/1513, art 2(2)) and will be brought into force for other purposes on a day to be appointed (see the Education and Skills Act 2008 s 173(4)). At the date at which this volume states the law no such day had been appointed.

4   'A special institution' means an independent educational institution that is specially organised to make special educational provision for students with special educational needs: Education and Skills Act 2008 s 101(4). See also note 3. As to the meanings of 'special educational provision' and 'special educational needs' see PARA 943 (definitions applied by s 168(2), (3)). As to the meaning of 'student' see PARA 383 note 4.

5   Ie a change in respect of any matter referred to in the Education and Skills Act 2008 s 98(3)(e) or (f): see PARA 385.

6   See the Education and Skills Act 2008 s 101(2). See also note 3.

7   Education and Skills Act 2008 s 101(3)(a). See also note 3. As to the meaning of 'proprietor' see PARA 415 note 3.

8   Education and Skills Act 2008 s 101(3)(b). See also note 3.

9   Ie a change in respect of matter referred to in the Education and Skills Act 2008 s 98(3)(a)–(g): see PARA 385.

10 Education and Skills Act 2008 s 101(3)(c). See also note 3.

11 As to the meaning of 'registered' see PARA 384 note 6.

12 As to the Secretary of State see PARA 58.

13 Education and Skills Act 2008 s 102(1). See also note 3. As to inspection of an institution where an application is made see s 103; and PARA 389. As to the determination of applications see s 104; and PARA 390. As to deregistration for making an unapproved material change see s 105; and PARA 391.

14 As to the meaning of 'writing' see PARA 76 note 8.

15 Education and Skills Act 2008 s 102(2). See also note 3.

389. Inspection and report where applications made for approval for material change.

Where an application for approval of a material change[1] is made[2], the Secretary of State[3] may direct Her Majesty's Chief Inspector of Education, Children's Services and Skills[4] to inspect the institution[5]. Where such a direction is given, the Chief Inspector must inspect the institution[6], and make a report to the Secretary of State on the extent to which any relevant standard[7] is likely to continue to be met in relation to the institution if the change is made[8].

1   As to the meaning of 'material change' see PARA 388.

2   Ie under the Education and Skills Act 2008 s 102: see PARA 388.

3   As to the Secretary of State see PARA 58.

4   As to Her Majesty's Chief Inspector of Education, Children's Services and Skills see PARA 1133.

5   Education and Skills Act 2008 s 103(1). At the date at which this volume states the law s 103 is in force for the purposes of making regulations only (see the Education and Skills Act 2008 (Commencement No 3) Order 2009, SI 2009/1513, art 2(2)) and will be brought into force for other purposes on a day to be appointed (see the Education and Skills Act 2008 s 173(4)). At the date at which this volume states the law no such day had been appointed.

6   Education and Skills Act 2008 s 103(2)(a). See also note 5. As to powers of entry and inspection see s 110; and PARA 398. A fee may be payable in respect of an inspection: see s 111; and PARA 399.

7   'Any relevant standard' means any independent educational institution standard: (1) specified by the Secretary of State for the purposes of the inspection (Education and Skills Act 2008 s 103(3)(a)); or (2) considered to be relevant by the Chief Inspector in the circumstances of the case (s 103(3)(b)). See also note 5. As to the meaning of 'independent educational institution standards' see PARA 394.

8   Education and Skills Act 2008 s 103(2)(b). See also note 5. As to the consideration of such a report see s 104; and PARA 390. As to the publication of reports see s 113; and PARA 400.

390. Determination of applications for approval. Where an application for approval of a material change[1] is made[2], the Secretary of State[3] must: (1) approve the change, if satisfied that the independent educational institution standards[4] are likely to continue to be met in relation to the institution if the change is made[5]; (2) in any other case refuse to approve it[6].

In coming to a decision the Secretary of State must take into account any report[7] of Her Majesty's Chief Inspector of Education, Children's Services and Skills[8], and any other evidence relating to the independent educational institution standards[9]. The Secretary of State must notify[10] the proprietor[11] of the institution of his decision[12]. A decision to refuse to approve a material change does not have effect during the period in which: (a) an appeal may be brought[13] against the decision[14]; or (b) where such an appeal has been brought, the appeal has not been determined, withdrawn or otherwise disposed of[15].

1 As to the meaning of 'material change' see PARA 388.
2 Ie under the Education and Skills Act 2008 s 102: see PARA 388.
3 As to the Secretary of State see PARA 58.
4 As to the meaning of 'independent educational institution standards' see PARA 394.
5 Education and Skills Act 2008 s 104(1)(a). At the date at which this volume states the law s 104 is in force for the purposes of making regulations only (see the Education and Skills Act 2008 (Commencement No 3) Order 2009, SI 2009/1513, art 2(2)) and will be brought into force for other purposes on a day to be appointed (see the Education and Skills Act 2008 s 173(4)). At the date at which this volume states the law no such day had been appointed.
    Part 4 Ch 1 (ss 92–141) applies to alternative provision academies that are not independent educational institutions as it applies to independent educational institutions; accordingly, references in ss 92–141, except in ss 95(2), 140(1), to independent educational institutions are to be read as including references to alternative provision academies that are not independent educational institutions: see s 93A(1), (2) (added by SI 2012/976). As to the meaning of 'alternative provision academy' see PARA 346 note 14 (definition applied by the Education and Skills Act 2008 s 168(2), (3)).
6 Education and Skills Act 2008 s 104(1)(b). See also note 5.
7 Ie under the Education and Skills Act 2008 s 103: see PARA 389.
8 Education and Skills Act 2008 s 104(2)(a). See also note 5. As to Her Majesty's Chief Inspector of Education, Children's Services and Skills see PARA 1133.
9 Education and Skills Act 2008 s 104(2)(b). See also note 5.
10 As to the service of notices and documents see the Education and Skills Act 2008 s 137; and PARA 415.
11 As to the meaning of 'proprietor' see PARA 415 note 3.
12 See the Education and Skills Act 2008 s 104(3). See also note 5.
13 Ie under the Education and Skills Act 2008 s 125: see PARA 406.
14 Education and Skills Act 2008 s 104(4)(a). See also note 5.
15 Education and Skills Act 2008 s 104(4)(b). See also note 5.

391. Power to deregister institution that makes unapproved material change. The Secretary of State[1] may remove an independent educational institution[2] from the register[3] if:

(1) there has been a material change[4] in relation to the institution[5];
(2) the change has not[6] been approved[7]; and
(3) either no application has been made[8] for approval of the change[9], or such an application has been made but has been refused[10].

The Secretary of State must notify[11] the proprietor[12] of an institution of any decision to remove it from the register[13]. The Secretary of State's decision does not have effect during the period in which: (a) an appeal may be brought[14] against the decision[15]; or (b) where such an appeal has been brought, the appeal has not been determined, withdrawn or otherwise disposed of[16].

1 As to the Secretary of State see PARA 58.

2   As to the meaning of 'independent educational institution' see PARA 382. The Education and
    Skills Act 2008 Pt 4 Ch 1 (ss 92–141) applies to alternative provision academies that are not
    independent educational institutions as it applies to independent educational institutions;
    accordingly, references in ss 92–141, except in ss 95(2), 140(1), to independent educational
    institutions are to be read as including references to alternative provision academies that are not
    independent educational institutions: see s 93A(1), (2) (added by SI 2012/976). As to the
    meaning of 'alternative provision academy' see PARA 346 note 14 (definition applied by the
    Education and Skills Act 2008 s 168(2), (3)).

3   As to the meaning of 'the register' see PARA 384 note 6.

4   As to the meaning of 'material change' see PARA 388.

5   Education and Skills Act 2008 s 105(1)(a). At the date at which this volume states the law s 105
    is in force for the purposes of making regulations only (see the Education and Skills Act 2008
    (Commencement No 3) Order 2009, SI 2009/1513, art 2(2)) and will be brought into force for
    other purposes on a day to be appointed (see the Education and Skills Act 2008 s 173(4)). At the
    date at which this volume states the law no such day had been appointed.

6   Ie under the Education and Skills Act 2008 Pt 4 Ch 1 (ss 92–141).

7   Education and Skills Act 2008 s 105(1)(b). See also note 5.

8   Ie under the Education and Skills Act 2008 s 102: see PARA 388.

9   Education and Skills Act 2008 s 105(1)(c)(i). See also note 5.

10 Education and Skills Act 2008 s 105(1)(c)(ii). See also note 5. As to the determination of
    applications for a material change see PARA 390.

11 As to the service of notices and documents see the Education and Skills Act 2008 s 137; and
    PARA 415.

12 As to the meaning of 'proprietor' see PARA 415 note 3.

13 Education and Skills Act 2008 s 105(2). See also note 5.

14 Ie under the Education and Skills Act 2008 s 124: see PARA 405.

15 Education and Skills Act 2008 s 105(3)(a). See also note 5.

16 Education and Skills Act 2008 s 105(3)(b). See also note 5.

392.   Unsuitable persons.   The Secretary of State[1] may remove an institution
from the register[2] if satisfied that any person[3] who is subject to a direction, order
or decision of a prescribed[4] description made under any prescribed enactment
having effect in any part of the United Kingdom[5]: (1) carries out work of a
prescribed kind in relation to the institution[6]; or (2) is the proprietor[7] of the
institution[8].

The Secretary of State must notify[9] the proprietor of an institution of any such
decision to remove it from the register[10]. The Secretary of State's decision does
not have effect during the period in which: (a) an appeal may be brought[11]
against the decision[12]; or (b) where such an appeal has been brought, the appeal
has not been determined, withdrawn or otherwise disposed of[13].

1   As to the Secretary of State see PARA 58.

2   As to the meaning of 'the register' see PARA 384 note 6.

3   As to the meaning of 'person' see PARA 7 note 6.

4   'Prescribed' means prescribed by regulations; and 'regulations' means regulations made by the
    Secretary of State: see the Education and Skills Act 2008 s 168(1). As to the regulations made
    see the Education (Independent Educational Provision in England) (Unsuitable Persons)
    Regulations 2009, SI 2009/1633 (amended by SI 2010/2920).

5   See the Education and Skills Act 2008 s 119(2). As to the meaning of 'United Kingdom' see PARA
    73 note 3.

6   Education and Skills Act 2008 s 119(1)(a). The Education and Skills Act 2008 Pt 4 Ch 1
    (ss 92–141) applies to alternative provision academies that are not independent educational
    institutions as it applies to independent educational institutions; accordingly, references in
    ss 92–141, except in ss 95(2), 140(1), to independent educational institutions are to be read as
    including references to alternative provision academies that are not independent educational
    institutions: see s 93A(1), (2) (added by SI 2012/976). As to the meaning of 'alternative
    provision academy' see PARA 346 note 14 (definition applied by the Education and Skills
    Act 2008 s 168(2), (3)).

7   As to the meaning of 'proprietor' see PARA 415 note 3.

8 Education and Skills Act 2008 s 119(1)(b). The reference to the proprietor of the institution is: (1) in a case in which the proprietor is a company, a reference to any director of the company (s 119(5)(a)); (2) in a case in which the proprietor is any other body of persons, whether corporate or unincorporate, a reference to any member of the body (s 119(5)(b)). As to bodies corporate see COMPANIES vol 14 (2009) PARA 2; CORPORATIONS vol 24 (2010) PARA 301 et seq.

9 As to the service of notices and documents see the Education and Skills Act 2008 s 137; and PARA 415.

10 Education and Skills Act 2008 s 119(3).

11 Ie under the Education and Skills Act 2008 s 124: see PARA 405.

12 Education and Skills Act 2008 s 119(4)(a).

13 Education and Skills Act 2008 s 119(4)(b).

393. Provision of information by proprietors. Regulations[1] may make provision for requiring the proprietor[2] of a registered[3] independent educational institution[4] to provide the Secretary of State, on request, with such particulars relating to the institution as may be prescribed[5]. The regulations may in particular;

(1) require the provision of such information as is needed by the local authority[6] in whose area the institution is situated for the purpose of determining whether[7] the institution is a children's home[8];

(2) provide for the Secretary of State to remove from the register[9] any institution in respect of which any requirement imposed by or under the regulations is not complied with[10];

(3) provide that a person who fails to comply with any specified[11] provision of the regulations is guilty of an offence and liable on summary conviction to a fine not exceeding level 5 on the standard scale[12].

1 'Regulations' means regulations made under the Education and Skills Act 2008 by the Secretary of State: s 168(1). As to the Secretary of State see PARA 58. As to the regulations made see the Education (Independent Educational Provision in England) (Provision of Information) Regulations 2010, SI 2010/2919 (amended by SI 2012/979).

2 As to the meaning of 'proprietor' see PARA 415 note 3.

3 As to the meaning of 'registered' see PARA 384 note 6.

4 As to the meaning of 'independent educational institution' see PARA 382. The Education and Skills Act 2008 Pt 4 Ch 1 (ss 92–141) applies to alternative provision academies that are not independent educational institutions as it applies to independent educational institutions; accordingly, references in ss 92–141, except in ss 95(2), 140(1), to independent educational institutions are to be read as including references to alternative provision academies that are not independent educational institutions: see s 93A(1), (2) (added by SI 2012/976). As to the meaning of 'alternative provision academy' see PARA 346 note 14 (definition applied by the Education and Skills Act 2008 s 168(2), (3)).

5 Education and Skills Act 2008 s 123(1). 'Prescribed' means prescribed by regulations: s 168(1).

6 As to the meaning of 'local authority' see PARA 25 (definition applied by the Education and Skills Act 2008 s 168(2), (3)(b)).

7 Ie within the meaning of the Care Standards Act 2000 (see s 1 of that Act): see CHILDREN AND YOUNG PERSONS vol 10 (2012) PARA 992.

8 Education and Skills Act 2008 s 123(2)(a).

9 As to the meaning of 'the register' see PARA 384 note 6.

10 Education and Skills Act 2008 s 123(2)(b). Regulations that include provision by virtue of s 123(2)(b) must include the following provision: see s 123(4). The regulations must require the Secretary of State to notify the proprietor of an institution of any decision to remove the institution from the register by virtue of s 123(2)(b): s 123(5). See also note 2. The regulations must provide that a decision by the Secretary of State to remove an institution from the register by virtue of s 123(2)(b) does not have effect during the period in which (1) an appeal may be brought under s 124 (see PARA 405) against the decision (s 123(6)(a)); or (2) where such an appeal has been brought, the appeal has not been determined, withdrawn or otherwise disposed of (s 123(6)(b)).

11 'Specified' means specified in regulations under the Education and Skills Act 2008 s 123: s 123(3).

12 Education and Skills Act 2008 s 123(2)(c). As to the standard scale see SENTENCING AND DISPOSITION OF OFFENDERS vol 92 (2010) PARA 142.

(C) Standards and Inspection

394. Independent educational institution standards. In the statutory provisions relating to the regulation and inspection of independent educational institutions[1] in England[2], 'independent educational institution standards' means: (1) the standards for the time being prescribed[3] under the following provisions[4]; and (2) in relation to early years provision[5] for children[6] who have attained the age of two[7], the early years foundation stage[8].

The Secretary of State must by regulations prescribe standards for the purposes of the statutory provisions relating to the regulation and inspection of independent educational institutions in England about the following matters:

- (a) the quality of education provided at independent educational institutions[9];
- (b) the spiritual, moral, social and cultural development of students[10] at independent educational institutions[11];
- (c) the welfare, health and safety of students at independent educational institutions[12];
- (d) the suitability of proprietors[13] of and staff at independent educational institutions[14];
- (e) the premises[15] of and accommodation at independent educational institutions[16];
- (f) the provision of information by independent educational institutions[17];
- (g) the manner in which independent educational institutions handle complaints[18];
- (h) the quality of the leadership in and management of independent educational institutions[19].

A standard may be prescribed in relation to: (i) all independent educational institutions[20]; (ii) specified independent educational institutions[21]; or (iii) independent educational institutions of a specified description[22].

1   As to the meaning of 'independent educational institution' see PARA 382. The Education and Skills Act 2008 Pt 4 Ch 1 (ss 92–141) applies to alternative provision academies that are not independent educational institutions as it applies to independent educational institutions; accordingly, references in ss 92–141, except in ss 95(2), 140(1), to independent educational institutions are to be read as including references to alternative provision academies that are not independent educational institutions: see s 93A(1), (2) (added by SI 2012/976). As to the meaning of 'alternative provision academy' see PARA 346 note 14 (definition applied by the Education and Skills Act 2008 s 168(2), (3)).
2   Ie the Education and Skills Act 2008 Pt 4 Ch 1 (ss 92–141). As to the meaning of 'England' see PARA 7 note 3.
3   'Prescribed' means prescribed by regulations; and 'regulations' means regulations made by the Secretary of State under the Education and Skills Act 2008: see s 168(1). As to the Secretary of State see PARA 58. As to regulations made see the Education (Independent School Standards) Regulations 2014, SI 2014/3283.
4   Education and Skills Act 2008 s 94(5)(a).
5   'Early years provision' has the meaning given by the Childcare Act 2006 s 96(2) (see CHILDREN AND YOUNG PERSONS vol 10 (2012) PARA 1090): Education and Skills Act 2008 s 138(1).
6   As to the meaning of 'child' see PARA 7 note 6 (definition applied by the Education and Skills Act 2008 s 168(2), (3)(b)).
7   As to the time at which a person attains a particular age see PARA 7 note 6.
8   Education and Skills Act 2008 s 94(5)(b) (amended by the Small Business, Enterprise and Employment Act 2015 s 75(5)). As to the early years foundation stage see the Childcare Act 2006 s 39: see CHILDREN AND YOUNG PERSONS vol 10 (2012) PARA 1097. The standards do not apply to early years provision for children who have not attained the age of three (separate

requirements as to such provision are imposed by or under the Childcare Act 2006 Pt 3 (ss 32–98) (see CHILDREN AND YOUNG PERSONS vol 10 (2012) PARA 1090 et seq)): Education and Skills Act 2008 s 94(4).

9 Education and Skills Act 2008 s 94(1)(a).
10 As to the meaning of 'student' see PARA 383 note 4.
11 Education and Skills Act 2008 s 94(1)(b).
12 Education and Skills Act 2008 s 94(1)(c).
13 As to the meaning of 'proprietor' see PARA 415 note 3.
14 Education and Skills Act 2008 s 94(1)(d).
15 As to the meaning of 'premises' see PARA 62 note 19 (definition applied by the Education and Skills Act 2008 s 168(2), (3)(b)).
16 Education and Skills Act 2008 s 94(1)(e).
17 Education and Skills Act 2008 s 94(1)(f).
18 Education and Skills Act 2008 s 94(1)(g).
19 Education and Skills Act 2008 s 94(1)(h).
20 Education and Skills Act 2008 s 94(2)(a).
21 Education and Skills Act 2008 s 94(2)(b).
22 Education and Skills Act 2008 s 94(2)(c). 'Specified' means specified in regulations made under s 94: s 94(3).

395. Independent inspectorates. The Secretary of State[1] may: (1) approve a body or bodies to carry out inspections of registered[2] independent educational institutions[3]; (2) withdraw approval previously given under head (1)[4]. A body so approved is known as 'an independent inspectorate'[5].

The Secretary of State may approve a body in relation to specified[6] registered independent educational institutions[7], or registered independent educational institutions of a specified description[8]. The Secretary of State may by regulations specify matters that must be taken into account in deciding to approve or withdraw approval from a body[9].

Her Majesty's Chief Inspector of Education, Children's Services and Skills[10] must, at intervals of no more than a year, prepare and send to the Secretary of State a report about independent inspectorates[11]. In preparing such a report the Chief Inspector must have regard to such matters as the Secretary of State may direct[12]. The Secretary of State may in particular give directions about: (a) matters to be taken into account in preparing a report[13]; and (b) the form and contents of a report[14].

1 As to the Secretary of State see PARA 58.
2 As to the meaning of 'registered' see PARA 384 note 6.
3 Education and Skills Act 2008 s 106(1)(a). As to the meaning of 'independent educational institution' see PARA 382. The Education and Skills Act 2008 ss 106, 107 replace similar provision in the Education Act 2002 s 162A (repealed); by virtue of the Education and Skills Act 2008 s 139 any bodies approved under that section will continue to have effect as if approved under s 106.
   The Education and Skills Act 2008 Pt 4 Ch 1 (ss 92–141) applies to alternative provision academies that are not independent educational institutions as it applies to independent educational institutions; accordingly, references in ss 92–141, except in ss 95(2), 140(1), to independent educational institutions are to be read as including references to alternative provision academies that are not independent educational institutions: see s 93A(1), (2) (added by SI 2012/976). As to the meaning of 'alternative provision academy' see PARA 346 note 14 (definition applied by the Education and Skills Act 2008 s 168(2), (3)).
4 Education and Skills Act 2008 s 106(1)(b). See also note 3.
   It should be noted that information from the Office for Standards in Education, Children's Services and Skills (Ofsted) on approval and withdrawal of approval is to be found on the Department for Education website. As to Ofsted see generally PARA 1128 et seq.
5 Education and Skills Act 2008 s 106(5). See also note 3.
6 'Specified' means specified by the Secretary of State: Education and Skills Act 2008 s 106(2). See also note 3.
7 Education and Skills Act 2008 s 106(2)(a). See also note 3.

8   Education and Skills Act 2008 s 106(2)(b). See also note 3. The power in s 106(2)(b) to specify
     a description of independent educational institution includes power to specify a description by
     reference to membership of a body: s 106(3).
9   Education and Skills Act 2008 s 106(4). See also note 3. As to regulations made under s 106(4)
     see the Independent Inspectorates (Education and Boarding Accommodation) Regulations 2014,
     SI 2014/2158.
10   As to Her Majesty's Chief Inspector of Education, Children's Services and Skills see PARA 1133.
11   Education and Skills Act 2008 s 107(1). See also note 3. As to the publication of reports see
     s 113; and PARA 400.
12   Education and Skills Act 2008 s 107(2). See also note 3. As to directions see the Education
     Act 1996 s 570 (applied by the Education and Skills Act 2008 s 168(2), (3)(b)); and PARA 75.
13   Education and Skills Act 2008 s 107(3)(a). See also note 3.
14   Education and Skills Act 2008 s 107(3)(b). See also note 3.

396. Duty to inspect certain registered institutions at prescribed intervals.

Her Majesty's Chief Inspector of Education, Children's Services and Skills[1] must:
(1) inspect[2] each independent educational institution[3] at such intervals as may be
prescribed[4]; and (2) make a report to the Secretary of State, in relation to each
inspection, on the extent to which any relevant standard[5] is being met, and is
likely to continue to be met, in relation to the institution[6]. However, these
provisions do not require the Chief Inspector to carry out an inspection or make
a report if the Chief Inspector has been notified by the Secretary of State that the
institution is to be inspected instead by an independent inspectorate[7].

1   As to Her Majesty's Chief Inspector of Education, Children's Services and Skills see PARA 1133.
2   As to powers of entry and inspection see the Education and Skills Act 2008 s 110; and PARA
     398. A fee may be payable in respect of an inspection: see s 111; and PARA 399.
3   The Education and Skills Act 2008 s 108 applies to any registered independent educational
     institution that is not an academy, a city technology college, or a city college for the technology
     of the arts: s 108(5). At the date at which this volume states the law s 108 is in force for the
     purposes of making regulations only (see the Education and Skills Act 2008 (Commencement
     No 3) Order 2009, SI 2009/1513, art 2(2)) and will be brought into force for other purposes on
     a day to be appointed (see the Education and Skills Act 2008 s 173(4)). At the date at which this
     volume states the law no such day had been appointed. As to the meaning of 'registered' see
     PARA 384 note 6. As to the meaning of 'independent educational institution' see PARA 382. As to
     the meaning of 'academy' see PARA 346 (definition applied by s 168(2), (3)). As to city
     technology colleges and city colleges for the technology of the arts see PARA 345.
        Part 4 Ch 1 (ss 92–141) applies to alternative provision academies that are not independent
     educational institutions as it applies to independent educational institutions; accordingly,
     references in ss 92–141, except in ss 95(2), 140(1), to independent educational institutions are to
     be read as including references to alternative provision academies that are not independent
     educational institutions: see s 93A(1), (2) (added by SI 2012/976). As to the meaning of
     'alternative provision academy' see PARA 346 note 14 (definition applied by the Education and
     Skills Act 2008 s 168(2), (3)).
4   Education and Skills Act 2008 s 108(1)(a). See also note 3. An interval may be prescribed by
     reference to the time of an inspection carried out (1) by the Chief Inspector in compliance with
     s 108(1) (s 108(4)(a)); or (2) by an independent inspectorate as mentioned in s 108(3) (see the
     text to note 7) (s 108(4)(b)). 'Prescribed' means prescribed by regulations; and 'regulations'
     means regulations made by the Secretary of State under the Education and Skills Act 2008: see
     s 168(1). As to the Secretary of State see PARA 58. At the date at which this volume states the
     law no such regulations had been made. As to the meaning of 'independent inspectorate' see
     PARA 395.
5   'Any relevant standard', in relation to an inspection, means any independent educational
     institution standard that is (1) specified by the Secretary of State for the purposes of the
     inspection (Education and Skills Act 2008 s 108(2)(a)); or (2) considered to be relevant by the
     Chief Inspector in the circumstances of the case (s 108(2)(b)). See also note 3. As to the meaning
     of 'independent educational institution standards' see PARA 394.
6   Education and Skills Act 2008 s 108(1)(b). See also note 3. As to the publication of reports see
     s 113; and PARA 400.
7   Education and Skills Act 2008 s 108(3). See also note 3.

397. Duty to inspect registered institution on direction of Secretary of State.
The Secretary of State[1] may at any time direct[2] Her Majesty's Chief Inspector of Education, Children's Services and Skills[3] to inspect a registered[4] independent educational institution[5] specified in the direction[6]. Where such a direction is made the Chief Inspector must inspect the institution[7], and make a report to the Secretary of State on the extent to which any relevant standard[8] is being met in relation to the institution[9].

The Secretary of State may at any time arrange for an independent inspectorate[10] to inspect a registered independent educational institution in relation to which[11] it is approved[12], and to make a report to the Secretary of State on the extent to which any relevant standard is being met in relation to the institution[13].

1   As to the Secretary of State see PARA 58.
2   As to directions see the Education Act 1996 s 570 (applied by the Education and Skills Act 2008 s 168(2), (3)(b)); and PARA 75.
3   As to Her Majesty's Chief Inspector of Education, Children's Services and Skills see PARA 1133.
      It should be noted that relevant information from the Office for Standards in Education, Children's Services and Skills (Ofsted) is to be found on the Department for Education website. As to Ofsted see generally PARA 1128 et seq.
4   As to the meaning of 'registered' see PARA 384 note 6.
5   As to the meaning of 'independent educational institution' see PARA 382. The Education and Skills Act 2008 Pt 4 Ch 1 (ss 92–141) applies to alternative provision academies that are not independent educational institutions as it applies to independent educational institutions; accordingly, references in ss 92–141, except in ss 95(2), 140(1), to independent educational institutions are to be read as including references to alternative provision academies that are not independent educational institutions: see s 93A(1), (2) (added by SI 2012/976). As to the meaning of 'alternative provision academy' see PARA 346 note 14 (definition applied by the Education and Skills Act 2008 s 168(2), (3)).
6   Education and Skills Act 2008 s 109(1).
7   Education and Skills Act 2008 s 109(2)(a). See also note 5. As to powers of entry and inspection see s 110; and PARA 398. A fee may be payable in respect of an inspection: see s 111; and PARA 399.
8   'Any relevant standard' means any independent educational institution standard that is: (1) specified by the Secretary of State for the purposes of the inspection (Education and Skills Act 2008 s 109(4)(a)); or (2) considered to be relevant by the person carrying out the inspection in the circumstances of the case (s 109(4)(b)). As to the meaning of 'independent educational institution standards' see PARA 394.
9   Education and Skills Act 2008 s 109(2)(b). See also note 5. As to the publication of reports see s 113; and PARA 400.
10 As to the meaning of 'independent inspectorate' see PARA 395.
11 Ie under the Education and Skills Act 2008 s 106: see PARA 395.
12 Education and Skills Act 2008 s 109(3)(a). See also note 5.
13 Education and Skills Act 2008 s 109(3)(b). See also note 5.

398. Powers of entry and inspection. Where any inspection of a registered[1] independent educational institution[2] is carried out[3] by Her Majesty's Chief Inspector of Education, Children's Services and Skills[4], the Chief Inspector has at all reasonable times: (1) a right of entry to the premises[5] of the institution for the purposes of the inspection[6]; and (2) a right to inspect and take copies of any records kept by the institution and any other documents containing information relating to the institution that are required for the purposes of the inspection[7].

It is an offence intentionally to obstruct a person[8] in the exercise of the person's functions[9] in relation to the inspection[10].

1   As to the meaning of 'registered' see PARA 384 note 6.
2   As to the meaning of 'independent educational institution' see PARA 382. The Education and Skills Act 2008 Pt 4 Ch 1 (ss 92–141) applies to alternative provision academies that are not independent educational institutions as it applies to independent educational institutions;

accordingly, references in ss 92–141, except in ss 95(2), 140(1), to independent educational institutions are to be read as including references to alternative provision academies that are not independent educational institutions: see s 93A(1), (2) (added by SI 2012/976). As to the meaning of 'alternative provision academy' see PARA 346 note 14 (definition applied by the Education and Skills Act 2008 s 168(2), (3)).

3   Ie under the Education and Skills Act 2008 Pt 4 Ch 1 (ss 92–141).

4   See the Education and Skills Act 2008 s 110(1). See also note 2. As to Her Majesty's Chief Inspector of Education, Children's Services and Skills see PARA 1133.

5   As to the meaning of 'premises' see PARA 62 note 19 (definition applied by the Education and Skills Act 2008 s 168(2), (3)(b)).

6   Education and Skills Act 2008 s 110(2)(a). See also note 2.

7   Education and Skills Act 2008 s 110(2)(b). See also note 2. The Education Act 2005 s 58 (computer records: see PARA 1152 note 7) applies in relation to the inspection of records or other documents under the Education and Skills Act 2008 s 110(2)(b): s 110(3). Section 110 does not confer power to inspect or take copies of anything of a kind specified in the Police and Criminal Evidence Act 1984 s 9(2) (legally privileged material etc: see POLICE AND INVESTIGATORY POWERS vol 84A (2013) PARA 453): Education and Skills Act 2008 s 110(4).

8   As to the meaning of 'person' see PARA 7 note 6.

9   As to the meaning of 'functions' see PARA 18 note 5 (definition applied by the Education and Skills Act 2008 s 168(2), (3)(b)).

10   Education and Skills Act 2008 s 110(5). See also note 2. A person guilty of such an offence is liable on summary conviction to a fine not exceeding level 4 on the standard scale: s 110(6). As to proceedings for offences see PARA 412. As to offences by bodies corporate see PARA 413. As to offences by unincorporated bodies see PARA 414. As to the standard scale see SENTENCING AND DISPOSITION OF OFFENDERS vol 92 (2010) PARA 142.

399. Fees for inspections. Regulations[1] may require the proprietor[2] of a registered independent educational institution[3] to pay to Her Majesty's Chief Inspector of Education, Children's Services and Skills[4] a fee in respect of an inspection of the institution carried out[5] by the Chief Inspector[6]. The regulations must make provision for determining the amount of any fee[7], and the time at which it must be paid[8]. The regulations may make provision:

(1)   for determining the amount of a fee by reference to circumstances obtaining at a time before the inspection to which it relates takes place[9];

(2)   requiring two or more fees to be paid in respect of an inspection under the provisions[10] relating to inspections at prescribed intervals[11];

(3)   requiring a fee to be paid at a time before the inspection to which it relates takes place[12];

(4)   prescribing circumstances in which the amount of a fee may be varied or a fee may be waived[13];

(5)   conferring a discretion on the Secretary of State[14].

The regulations may[15] make different provision: (a) for inspections of different descriptions of institution[16]; or (b) for inspections carried out for different purposes or in different circumstances[17].

Where the proprietor of an institution fails to pay a fee in accordance with such regulations, the Secretary of State may remove the institution from the register[18]. The Secretary of State must notify[19] the proprietor of an institution of any such decision to remove it from the register[20]. The Secretary of State's decision does not have effect during the period in which (i) an appeal may be brought[21] against the decision[22]; or (ii) where such an appeal has been brought, the appeal has not been determined, withdrawn or otherwise disposed of[23].

1   'Regulations' means regulations made under the Education and Skills Act 2008 by the Secretary of State: s 168(1). As to the Secretary of State see PARA 58. As to the regulations made see the Education (Independent Educational Provision in England) (Inspection Fees) Regulations 2009, SI 2009/1607 (amended by SI 2010/1002). See also the Education (Independent School

Inspection Fees and Publication) (England) Regulations 2008, SI 2008/1801 (amended by SI 2009/1607) which, by virtue of the Education and Skills Act 2008 s 139, have effect as if made under s 111.

2   As to the meaning of 'proprietor' see PARA 415 note 3.

3   The Education and Skills Act 2008 s 111 applies to any independent educational institution that is registered, or is the subject of an application to be registered, other than an academy, a city technology college, or a city college for the technology of the arts: s 111(6) (amended by the Children, Schools and Families Act 2010 s 23). As to the meaning of 'independent educational institution' see PARA 382. As to the meaning of 'registered' see PARA 384 note 6. As to applications for registration see PARA 385. As to the meaning of 'academy' see PARA 346 (definition applied by the Education and Skills Act 2008 s 168(2), (3)(b)). As to city technology colleges and city colleges for the technology of the arts see PARA 345.

Part 4 Ch 1 (ss 92–141) applies to alternative provision academies that are not independent educational institutions as it applies to independent educational institutions; accordingly, references in ss 92–141, except in ss 95(2), 140(1), to independent educational institutions are to be read as including references to alternative provision academies that are not independent educational institutions: see s 93A(1), (2) (added by SI 2012/976). As to the meaning of 'alternative provision academy' see PARA 346 note 14 (definition applied by the Education and Skills Act 2008 s 168(2), (3)).

4   As to Her Majesty's Chief Inspector of Education, Children's Services and Skills see PARA 1133.

5   Ie under the Education and Skills Act 2008 Pt 4 Ch 1 (ss 92–141).

6   Education and Skills Act 2008 s 111(1). See also note 3.

7   Education and Skills Act 2008 s 111(2)(a). See also note 3.

8   Education and Skills Act 2008 s 111(2)(b). See also note 3.

9   Education and Skills Act 2008 s 111(3)(a). See also note 3.

10 Ie under the Education and Skills Act 2008 s 108: see PARA 396.

11 Education and Skills Act 2008 s 111(3)(b). See also note 3.

12 Education and Skills Act 2008 s 111(3)(c). The power in s 111(3)(c): (1) does not include power to make provision requiring a fee in respect of an inspection under s 108 (see PARA 396) to be paid at any time at which an independent inspectorate is approved in relation to the institution (s 111(4)(a)); (2) includes power to make provision as to circumstances in which a fee is not to be refunded (and any requirement to pay a fee is to be unaffected) if the inspection to which it relates does not take place (s 111(4)(b)). As to the meaning of 'independent inspectorate' see PARA 395. See also note 3.

13 Education and Skills Act 2008 s 111(3)(d). See also note 3. The power in s 111(3)(d) to make provision prescribing circumstances in which the amount of a fee may be waived includes power to make such provision in relation to a fee (or any part of a fee) payable by virtue of the Education Act 2002 s 162B(6) (fees payable to Chief Inspector) (repealed): Education and Skills Act 2008 s 140(2).

14 Education and Skills Act 2008 s 111(3)(e). See also note 3.

15 Ie without prejudice to the Education and Skills Act 2008 s 166(6) (general provisions as to orders and regulations).

16 Education and Skills Act 2008 s 111(5)(a). See also note 3.

17 Education and Skills Act 2008 s 111(5)(b). See also note 3.

18 Education and Skills Act 2008 s 112(1). As to the meaning of 'the register' see PARA 384 note 6. See also note 3.

19 As to the service of notices and documents see the Education and Skills Act 2008 s 137; and PARA 415.

20 Education and Skills Act 2008 s 112(2). See also note 3.

21 Ie under the Education and Skills Act 2008 s 124: see PARA 405.

22 Education and Skills Act 2008 s 112(3)(a). See also note 3.

23 Education and Skills Act 2008 s 112(3)(b). See also note 3.

400. Publication of inspection reports. Her Majesty's Chief Inspector of Education, Children's Services and Skills[1] must comply with a direction[2] given by the Secretary of State[3] to publish the report of any inspection carried out[4] by the Chief Inspector[5]. A report so published must be published in the prescribed manner[6].

1   As to Her Majesty's Chief Inspector of Education, Children's Services and Skills see PARA 1133.

2   As to directions see the Education Act 1996 s 570 (applied by the Education and Skills Act 2008 s 168(2), (3)(b)); and PARA 75.

3   As to the Secretary of State see PARA 58.

4   Ie under the Education and Skills Act 2008 Pt 4 Ch 1 (ss 92–141). Part 4 Ch 1 applies to alternative provision academies that are not independent educational institutions as it applies to independent educational institutions; accordingly, references in ss 92–141, except in ss 95(2), 140(1), to independent educational institutions are to be read as including references to alternative provision academies that are not independent educational institutions: see s 93A(1), (2) (added by SI 2012/976). As to the meaning of 'alternative provision academy' see PARA 346 note 14 (definition applied by the Education and Skills Act 2008 s 168(2), (3)).

5   Education and Skills Act 2008 s 113(1). See also note 4.

6   Education and Skills Act 2008 s 113(2). At the date at which this volume states the law s 113(2) is in force for the purposes of making regulations only (see the Education and Skills Act 2008 (Commencement No 3) Order 2009, SI 2009/1513, art 2(2)) and will be brought into force for other purposes on a day to be appointed (see the Education and Skills Act 2008 s 173(4)). At the date at which this volume states the law no such day had been appointed. See also note 4. 'Prescribed' means prescribed by regulations; and 'regulations' means regulations made by the Secretary of State under the Education and Skills Act 2008: see s 168(1). By virtue of s 139, the Education (Independent School Inspection Fees and Publication) (England) Regulations 2008, SI 2008/1801 (amended by SI 2009/1607) have effect as if made under the Education and Skills Act 2008 s 113(2).

401.   Action plans.   If, in relation to a registered[1] independent educational institution[2], the Secretary of State[3] is satisfied, taking into account relevant evidence[4], that one or more of the independent educational institution standards[5] is or are not being met in relation to the institution[6], he may require the proprietor[7] of the registered independent educational institution to submit an action plan[8] to him for approval[9].

Any requirement imposed under these provisions to submit an action plan must be imposed by serving a notice[10] on the proprietor of the institution in question: (1) identifying the standard or standards that the Secretary of State is satisfied is or are not being met in relation to the institution[11]; and (2) specifying a date by which the action plan must be submitted[12]. Where an action plan is submitted in pursuance of such a requirement (whether or not by the date specified in the notice), the Secretary of State may: (a) approve it, with or without modifications[13]; or (b) reject it[14]. Where the Secretary of State rejects an action plan, he may impose a further requirement to submit an action plan[15].

An action plan that has been approved may be varied at any time by the proprietor of the institution in question with the agreement of the Secretary of State[16].

1   As to the meaning of 'registered' see PARA 384 note 6.
2   As to the meaning of 'independent educational institution' see PARA 382. The Education and Skills Act 2008 Pt 4 Ch 1 (ss 92–141) applies to alternative provision academies that are not independent educational institutions as it applies to independent educational institutions; accordingly, references in ss 92–141, except in ss 95(2), 140(1), to independent educational institutions are to be read as including references to alternative provision academies that are not independent educational institutions: see s 93A(1), (2) (added by SI 2012/976). As to the meaning of 'alternative provision academy' see PARA 346 note 14 (definition applied by the Education and Skills Act 2008 s 168(2), (3)).
3   As to the Secretary of State see PARA 58.

4   'Relevant evidence' means: (1) the report of an inspection carried out by Her Majesty's Chief Inspector of Education, Children's Services and Skills or an independent inspectorate (Education and Skills Act 2008 s 114(2)(a)); or (2) any other evidence in respect of the institution (s 114(2)(b)). See also note 2. As to Her Majesty's Chief Inspector of Education, Children's Services and Skills see PARA 1133. As to the meaning of 'independent inspectorate' see PARA 395.
5   As to the meaning of 'independent educational institution standards' see PARA 394.

6   See the Education and Skills Act 2008 s 114(1). See also note 2.
7   As to the meaning of 'proprietor' see PARA 415 note 3.

8　In the Education and Skills Act 2008 Pt 4 Ch 1 (ss 92–141), 'an action plan' means a plan specifying (1) the steps that will be taken to meet a standard or standards (s 114(4)(a)); and (2) the time by which each step will be taken (s 114(4)(b)). See also note 2.

9　See the Education and Skills Act 2008 s 114(3). See also note 2.

10　As to the service of notices and documents see the Education and Skills Act 2008 s 137; and PARA 415.

11　Education and Skills Act 2008 s 114(5)(a). See also note 2.

12　Education and Skills Act 2008 s 114(5)(b). See also note 2.

13　Education and Skills Act 2008 s 114(6)(a). See also note 2. As to the meaning of 'modifications' see PARA 21 note 15 (definition applied by s 168(2), (3)(b)).

14　Education and Skills Act 2008 s 114(6)(b). See also note 2.

15　Education and Skills Act 2008 s 114(7). See also note 2. As to the power of the Secretary of State to take enforcement action following a requirement to submit an action plan see ss 115, 116; and PARA 402.

16　Education and Skills Act 2008 s 114(8). See also note 2.

402. Power of Secretary of State to take enforcement action. If, in relation to a registered[1] independent educational institution[2], the Secretary of State[3] is satisfied, taking into account relevant evidence[4], that one or more of the independent educational institution standards[5] is or are not being met in relation to the institution[6], he may take enforcement action[7] against the proprietor[8] of the registered independent educational institution if either of the following conditions is met[9].

The first condition is that:

(1)　the Secretary of State has, during the period of three years before the enforcement action is taken, required the proprietor of the institution to submit[10] one or more action plans[11]; and

(2)　any action plan required as mentioned in head (1) above (a) has not been submitted, and the date specified by the Secretary of State[12] has passed[13], (b) was submitted but was rejected[14], or (c) was approved but was subsequently not complied with[15].

The second condition is that:

(i)　at least two years before the enforcement action is taken the Secretary of State required the proprietor of the institution to submit an action plan[16];

(ii)　at least one inspection of the institution has been carried out, by Majesty's Chief Inspector of Education, Children's Services and Skills or an independent inspectorate approved[17] in relation to the institution, since that requirement was imposed[18]; and

(iii)　the Secretary of State has not at any time since that requirement was imposed been satisfied that the institution was meeting all of the independent educational institution standards[19].

Where the Secretary of State is entitled[20] to take enforcement action against the proprietor of an institution, he may: (A) impose a relevant restriction[21] on the proprietor[22]; or (B) remove the institution from the register[23]. The Secretary of State must notify[24] the proprietor of the institution in question of any decision to take such enforcement action[25]. A decision to take enforcement action does not have effect during the period in which (aa) an appeal may be brought[26] against the decision[27]; or (bb) where such an appeal has been brought, the appeal has not been determined, withdrawn or otherwise disposed of[28].

1　As to the meaning of 'registered' see PARA 384 note 6.

2　As to the meaning of 'independent educational institution' see PARA 382. The Education and Skills Act 2008 Pt 4 Ch 1 (ss 92–141) applies to alternative provision academies that are not independent educational institutions as it applies to independent educational institutions;

accordingly, references in ss 92–141, except in ss 95(2), 140(1), to independent educational institutions are to be read as including references to alternative provision academies that are not independent educational institutions: see s 93A(1), (2) (added by SI 2012/976). As to the meaning of 'alternative provision academy' see PARA 346 note 14 (definition applied by the Education and Skills Act 2008 s 168(2), (3)).

3   As to the Secretary of State see PARA 58.

4   'Relevant evidence' means: (1) the report of an inspection carried out by Her Majesty's Chief Inspector of Education, Children's Services and Skills or an independent inspectorate (Education and Skills Act 2008 s 115(2)(a)); or (2) any other evidence in respect of the institution (s 115(2)(b)). See also note 2. As to Her Majesty's Chief Inspector of Education, Children's Services and Skills see PARA 1133. As to the meaning of 'independent inspectorate' see PARA 395.

5   As to the meaning of 'independent educational institution standards' see PARA 394.

6   See the Education and Skills Act 2008 s 115(1). See also note 2.

7   Ie under the Education and Skills Act 2008 s 116: see the text to notes 20–28.

8   As to the meaning of 'proprietor' see PARA 415 note 3.

9   See the Education and Skills Act 2008 s 115(3). See also note 2.

10 Ie under the Education and Skills Act 2008 s 114: see PARA 401.

11 Education and Skills Act 2008 s 115(4)(a). See also note 2. As to the meaning of 'an action plan' see PARA 401 note 8.

12 Ie under the Education and Skills Act 2008 s 114(5)(b): see PARA 401.

13 Education and Skills Act 2008 s 115(4)(b)(i). See also note 2.

14 Education and Skills Act 2008 s 115(4)(b)(ii). See also note 2.

15 Education and Skills Act 2008 s 115(4)(b)(iii). See also note 2.

16 Education and Skills Act 2008 s 115(5)(a). See also note 2.

17 Ie under the Education and Skills Act 2008 s 106: see PARA 395.

18 Education and Skills Act 2008 s 115(5)(b). See also note 2.

19 Education and Skills Act 2008 s 115(5)(c). See also note 2.

20 Ie under the Education and Skills Act 2008 s 115(3): see the text to notes 7–9.

21 As to the meaning of 'relevant restriction' see PARA 403.

22 Education and Skills Act 2008 s 116(1)(a). See also note 2. Failure to comply with a relevant restriction is an offence: see s 118; and PARA 403.

23 Education and Skills Act 2008 s 116(1)(b). See also note 2. As to the meaning of 'the register' see PARA 384 note 6.

24 As to the service of notices and documents see the Education and Skills Act 2008 s 137; and PARA 415.

25 Education and Skills Act 2008 s 116(2). See also note 2.

26 Ie under the Education and Skills Act 2008 s 124 (see PARA 405) or s 125 (see PARA 406).

27 Education and Skills Act 2008 s 116(3)(a). See also note 2.

28 Education and Skills Act 2008 s 116(3)(b). See also note 2.

403. Imposition of a relevant restriction. A 'relevant restriction'[1] imposed on the proprietor[2] of a registered[3] independent educational institution[4] is a requirement that the proprietor take one or more of the following steps by a specified[5] time or by specified times:

(1)   to cease to use any part of the institution's premises[6] for all purposes or specified purposes[7];

(2)   to close any part of the institution's operation[8];

(3)   to cease to admit any new students[9] or new students of specified descriptions[10].

Where the proprietor of an institution is subject to a relevant restriction imposed by the Secretary of State under head (1) above[11], if the proprietor fails to comply with the relevant restriction the proprietor is guilty of an offence[12].

The proprietor may apply to the Secretary of State for the restriction to be varied or revoked[13]. On such an application the Secretary of State must: (a) vary or revoke the restriction as requested in the application, if he is satisfied that it is appropriate to do so because of any change of circumstance[14]; and (b) in any other case, refuse to do so[15]. The Secretary of State must notify[16] the proprietor of his decision[17]. A decision to vary or revoke the restriction has effect as from the date on which the proprietor receives notice of it[18].

1   Ie in the Education and Skills Act 2008 Pt 4 Ch 1 (ss 92–141).
2   As to the meaning of 'proprietor' see PARA 415 note 3.
3   As to the meaning of 'registered' see PARA 384 note 6.
4   As to the meaning of 'independent educational institution' see PARA 382. The Education and Skills Act 2008 Pt 4 Ch 1 (ss 92–141) applies to alternative provision academies that are not independent educational institutions as it applies to independent educational institutions; accordingly, references in ss 92–141, except in ss 95(2), 140(1), to independent educational institutions are to be read as including references to alternative provision academies that are not independent educational institutions: see s 93A(1), (2) (added by SI 2012/976). As to the meaning of 'alternative provision academy' see PARA 346 note 14 (definition applied by the Education and Skills Act 2008 s 168(2), (3)).
5   'Specified' means: (1) in the case of a relevant restriction imposed by the Secretary of State under the Education and Skills Act 2008 s 116(1)(a) (see PARA 402), specified by the Secretary of State (s 117(2)(a)); (2) in the case of a relevant restriction imposed by an order of a justice of the peace under s 120 (see PARA 404), specified in the order (s 117(2)(b)); (3) in the case of a relevant restriction imposed by an order of the tribunal under s 124 (see PARA 405), s 125 (see PARA 406) or s 126 (see PARA 407), specified in the order (s 117(2)(c)). See also note 4. As to the Secretary of State see PARA 58.
6   As to the meaning of 'premises' see PARA 62 note 19 (definition applied by the Education and Skills Act 2008 s 168(2), (3)(b)).
7   Education and Skills Act 2008 s 117(1)(a). See also note 4.
8   Education and Skills Act 2008 s 117(1)(b). See also note 4.
9   As to the meaning of 'student' see PARA 383 note 4.
10 Education and Skills Act 2008 s 117(1)(c). See also note 4.
11 Education and Skills Act 2008 s 118(1). See also note 4.
12 Education and Skills Act 2008 s 118(2). See also note 4. The penalty for such an offence is, on summary conviction, imprisonment for a term not exceeding 51 weeks or a fine not exceeding level 5 on the standard scale (or both): see s 118(2). In relation to an offence committed before the commencement of the Criminal Justice Act 2003 s 281(5) (not yet in force), for '51 weeks' in the Education and Skills Act 2008 s 118(2) substitute 'six months': s 118(3). As to proceedings for offences see PARA 412. As to offences by bodies corporate see PARA 413. As to offences by unincorporated bodies see PARA 414. As to the standard scale see SENTENCING AND DISPOSITION OF OFFENDERS vol 92 (2010) PARA 142.
13 Education and Skills Act 2008 s 118(4). See also note 4.
14 Education and Skills Act 2008 s 118(5)(a). See also note 4.
15 Education and Skills Act 2008 s 118(5)(b). See also note 4. As to appeals against such refusal see s 125; and PARA 406.
16 As to the service of notices and documents see the Education and Skills Act 2008 s 137; and PARA 415.
17 See the Education and Skills Act 2008 s 118(6). See also note 4.
18 Education and Skills Act 2008 s 118(7). See also note 4.

404. Emergencies. The Secretary of State[1] may apply to a justice of the peace[2] for: (1) an order imposing a relevant restriction[3] on the proprietor[4] of a registered[5] independent educational institution[6]; or (2) an order that such an institution be removed from the register[7]. Such an application may be made without notice[8].

If it appears to the justice that a student[9] at the institution in question is suffering or is likely to suffer significant harm[10], the justice may make the order[11]. An order must be in writing[12]. A copy of the order must be served[13] on the proprietor of the institution by the Secretary of State as soon as reasonably practicable after the order is made[14], and has effect from the time the copy is served on the proprietor[15].

Where the proprietor of an institution is subject to a relevant restriction imposed by an order of a justice of the peace under head (1) above[16], if the proprietor fails to comply with the relevant restriction, he is guilty of an offence[17].

The Secretary of State must, as soon as reasonably practicable after an order is made against the proprietor of an institution[18], serve on the proprietor a copy of any written statement in support of the application for the order[19], and notice of the right[20] of appeal[21]. In the case of an order made against the proprietor of a special institution[22], the Secretary of State must, as soon as reasonably practicable after the order is made against the proprietor[23], notify the following that the order has been made: (a) the local authority[24] in whose area the institution is situated[25]; (b) any other local authority that the Secretary of State, after reasonable inquiry, is aware has specified the institution in a statement of special educational needs[26] in respect of a student at the institution[27].

1   As to the Secretary of State see PARA 58.
2   As to justices of the peace see MAGISTRATES vol 71 (2013) PARA 401 et seq.
3   As to the meaning of 'relevant restriction' see PARA 403.
4   As to the meaning of 'proprietor' see PARA 415 note 3.
5   As to the meaning of 'registered' see PARA 384 note 6.
6   Education and Skills Act 2008 s 120(1)(a). As to the meaning of 'independent educational institution' see PARA 382.

     Part 4 Ch 1 (ss 92–141) applies to alternative provision academies that are not independent educational institutions as it applies to independent educational institutions; accordingly, references in ss 92–141, except in ss 95(2), 140(1), to independent educational institutions are to be read as including references to alternative provision academies that are not independent educational institutions: see s 93A(1), (2) (added by SI 2012/976). As to the meaning of 'alternative provision academy' see PARA 346 note 14 (definition applied by the Education and Skills Act 2008 s 168(2), (3)).
7   Education and Skills Act 2008 s 120(1)(b). See also note 6. As to the meaning of 'the register' see PARA 384 note 6.
8   Education and Skills Act 2008 s 120(3). See also note 6. As to the use of a statutory emergency procedure and the applicability of the Human Rights Act 1998 thereto see *Jain v Trent Strategic Health Authority* [2009] UKHL 4, [2009] AC 853, [2009] 1 All ER 957.
9   As to the meaning of 'student' see PARA 383 note 4.
10   'Harm' has the same meaning as in the Children Act 1989 and the question of whether harm is significant is to be determined in accordance with s 31(10) of that Act (see CHILDREN AND YOUNG PERSONS vol 9 (2012) PARA 316): Education and Skills Act 2008 s 120(7). See also note 6.
11   Education and Skills Act 2008 s 120(2). See also note 6. As to appeals against such orders, see s 126; and PARA 407.
12   Education and Skills Act 2008 s 120(4). See also note 6. As to the meaning of 'writing' see PARA 76 note 8.
13   As to the service of notices and documents see the Education and Skills Act 2008 s 137; and PARA 415.
14   Education and Skills Act 2008 s 120(5). See also note 6.
15   Education and Skills Act 2008 s 120(6). See also note 6. Accordingly, in the case of an order under s 120(1)(b) (see head (2) in the text), the Secretary of State must not remove the institution from the register in pursuance of the order before that time: see s 120(6).
16   Education and Skills Act 2008 s 121(1). See also note 6.
17   Education and Skills Act 2008 s 121(2). See also note 6. The penalty for such an offence is, on summary conviction, imprisonment for a term not exceeding 51 weeks or a fine not exceeding level 5 on the standard scale (or both): see s 121(2). In relation to an offence committed before the commencement of the Criminal Justice Act 2003 s 281(5) (not yet in force), for '51 weeks' in the Education and Skills Act 2008 s 121(2) substitute 'six months': s 121(3). As to proceedings for offences see PARA 412. As to offences by bodies corporate see PARA 413. As to offences by unincorporated bodies see PARA 414. As to the standard scale see SENTENCING AND DISPOSITION OF OFFENDERS vol 92 (2010) PARA 142.
18   See the Education and Skills Act 2008 s 122(1). See also note 6.
19   Education and Skills Act 2008 s 122(2)(a). See also note 6.

20 Ie conferred by the Education and Skills Act 2008 s 126: see PARA 407.
21 Education and Skills Act 2008 s 122(2)(b). See also note 6.
22 'A special institution' means an institution that is specially organised to make special
    educational provision for students with special educational needs: Education and Skills
    Act 2008 s 122(4). As to the meanings of 'special educational provision' and 'special educational
    needs' see PARA 943 (definitions applied by s 168(2), (3)).
23 See the Education and Skills Act 2008 s 122(1). See also note 6.
24 As to the meaning of 'local authority' see PARA 25 (definition applied by the Education and
    Skills Act 2008 s 168(2), (3)(b)).
25 Education and Skills Act 2008 s 122(3)(a) (amended SI 2010/1158). See also note 6.
26 As to statements of special educational needs see PARA 1002 et seq. As to their equivalents in
    England, ie EHC plans (ie education, health and care plans), see PARA 958 et seq.
27 Education and Skills Act 2008 s 122(3)(b) (amended SI 2010/1158). See also note 6.

(D) Appeals

405. Appeal by proprietor against decision of Secretary of State to deregister.
The proprietor[1] of a registered[2] independent educational institution[3] may appeal
to the First-tier Tribunal[4] against a decision of the Secretary of State[5] to remove
the institution from the register[6]. Any such appeal must be brought within the
period of 28 days beginning with the day on which notice of the decision is
served[7] on the proprietor[8].

On an appeal the tribunal may: (1) confirm the decision[9]; (2) direct that the
decision is of no effect[10]; or (3) in the case of certain appeals[11], direct that the
decision is of no effect and make an order imposing a relevant restriction[12] on
the proprietor of the institution[13]. Where the tribunal confirms the decision, the
Secretary of State must remove the institution from the register on such date as
the tribunal may specify or, if it does not specify a date, from such date as the
Secretary of State may determine[14].

1   As to the meaning of 'proprietor' see PARA 415 note 3.
2   As to the meaning of 'registered' see PARA 384 note 6.
3   As to the meaning of 'independent educational institution' see PARA 382. The Education and
    Skills Act 2008 Pt 4 Ch 1 (ss 92–141) applies to alternative provision academies that are not
    independent educational institutions as it applies to independent educational institutions;
    accordingly, references in ss 92–141, except in ss 95(2), 140(1), to independent educational
    institutions are to be read as including references to alternative provision academies that are not
    independent educational institutions: see s 93A(1), (2) (added by SI 2012/976). As to the
    meaning of 'alternative provision academy' see PARA 346 note 14 (definition applied by the
    Education and Skills Act 2008 s 168(2), (3)).
4   See the Education and Skills Act 2008 ss 124(5), 138(1). As to the First-tier Tribunal see COURTS
    AND TRIBUNALS vol 24 (2010) PARA 874 et seq.
5   As to the Secretary of State see PARA 58.
6   Education and Skills Act 2008 s 124(1). The decisions in question are any: (1) under s 100 (no
    longer required to register: see PARA 387) (s 124(1)(a)); (2) under s 112 (failure to pay fees: see
    PARA 399) (s 124(1)(c)); (3) under s 116 (failure to meet standards: see PARA 402) (s 124(1)(d));
    (4) under s 119 (unsuitable persons: see PARA 392) (s 124(1)(e)); (5) by virtue of s 123 (failure to
    provide information: see PARA 393) (s 124(1)(f)); or (6) (as from a day to be appointed) under
    s 105 (unapproved material change: see PARA 391) (s 124(1)(b) (not yet in force)). See also
    note 3. As to the meaning of 'the register' see PARA 384 note 6.
7   As to the service of notices and documents see the Education and Skills Act 2008 s 137; and
    PARA 415.
8   Education and Skills Act 2008 s 124(2). See also note 3.
9   Education and Skills Act 2008 s 124(3)(a). See also note 3.
10 Education and Skills Act 2008 s 124(3)(b). See also note 3.
11 Ie appeals under the Education and Skills Act 2008 s 124(1)(b), (d) or (e): see note 6.
12 As to the meaning of 'relevant restriction' see PARA 403.
13 Education and Skills Act 2008 s 124(3)(c). See also note 3. As to the effect of such order see
    s 127; and PARA 408.
14 Education and Skills Act 2008 s 124(4). See also note 3.

406.   Appeal by proprietor against other decisions of Secretary of State. The proprietor[1] of an institution may appeal to the First-tier Tribunal[2] against a decision of the Secretary of State[3] in relation to the institution in respect of: (1) the meeting of standards on registration[4]; (2) the imposition of a relevant restriction[5] on the proprietor[6]; (3) a refusal to vary or revoke a relevant restriction[7]; or (4) (as from a day to be appointed) a refusal to approve a material change[8].

Any such appeal must be brought within the period of 28 days beginning with the day on which notice of the decision is served[9] on the proprietor[10].

The tribunal may:

(a)   on an appeal under head (1) above: confirm the decision[11]; or require the Secretary of State to reconsider the decision, taking into account, amongst other things, the findings of the tribunal on the appeal[12];

(b)   on an appeal under head (2) above: confirm the decision[13]; or itself approve the change[14];

(c)   on an appeal under head (3) above: confirm the decision[15]; direct that the relevant restriction is to cease to have effect[16]; or direct that the relevant restriction is to cease to have effect and make an order imposing a different relevant restriction on the proprietor[17];

(d)   on an appeal under head (4) above: confirm the refusal[18]; or, if the tribunal is satisfied that it is appropriate to do so because of a change of circumstance since the restriction in question was imposed, direct that the relevant restriction is to cease to have effect[19], or direct that the relevant restriction is to cease to have effect and make an order imposing a different relevant restriction[20] on the proprietor[21].

1   As to the meaning of 'proprietor' see PARA 415 note 3.
2   See the Education and Skills Act 2008 ss 124(5), 138(1). As to the First-tier Tribunal see COURTS AND TRIBUNALS vol 24 (2010) PARA 874 et seq.
3   As to the Secretary of State see PARA 58.
4   Ie a decision under the Education and Skills Act 2008 s 99(2) (see PARA 386): see s 125(1)(a).
    Part 4 Ch 1 (ss 92–141) applies to alternative provision academies that are not independent educational institutions as it applies to independent educational institutions; accordingly, references in ss 92–141, except in ss 95(2), 140(1), to independent educational institutions are to be read as including references to alternative provision academies that are not independent educational institutions: see s 93A(1), (2) (added by SI 2012/976). As to the meaning of 'alternative provision academy' see PARA 346 note 14 (definition applied by the Education and Skills Act 2008 s 168(2), (3)).
5   As to the meaning of 'relevant restriction' see PARA 403.
6   Ie a decision under the Education and Skills Act 2008 s 116(1)(a) (see PARA 402): see s 125(1)(c). See also note 4.
7   Ie a decision under the Education and Skills Act 2008 s 118(5)(b) (see PARA 403): see s 125(1)(d). See also note 4.
8   Ie a decision under the Education and Skills Act 2008 s 104(1) (see PARA 390): see s 125(1)(b) (not yet in force). See also note 4. As to the meaning of 'material change' see PARA 388.
9   As to the service of notices and documents see the Education and Skills Act 2008 s 137; and PARA 415.
10 Education and Skills Act 2008 s 125(2). See also note 4.
11 Education and Skills Act 2008 s 125(3)(a). See also note 4.
12 Education and Skills Act 2008 s 125(3)(b). See also note 4. Section 99(3), (4) (see PARA 386) applies in relation to the Secretary of State's decision on reconsideration under s 125(3)(b) as it applies to a decision made under s 99(2): s 125(4).
13 Education and Skills Act 2008 s 125(5)(a). See also note 4.
14 Education and Skills Act 2008 s 125(5)(b). See also note 4.
15 Education and Skills Act 2008 s 125(6)(a). See also note 4.
16 Education and Skills Act 2008 s 125(6)(b). See also note 4.

17 Education and Skills Act 2008 s 125(6)(c). See also note 4. As to the effect of a relevant restriction imposed by the tribunal under s 125, see s 127; and PARA 408.
18 Education and Skills Act 2008 s 125(7)(a). See also note 4.
19 Education and Skills Act 2008 s 125(7)(b)(i). See also note 4.
20 See note 17.
21 Education and Skills Act 2008 s 125(7)(b)(ii). See also note 4.

407. Appeal by proprietor against order of justice of the peace. The proprietor[1] of a registered[2] independent educational institution[3] may appeal to the First-tier Tribunal[4] against the making of an order[5] by a justice of the peace[6]. On such an appeal the tribunal may:

(1) confirm the making of the order[7];

(2) direct that the order is to cease to have effect[8]; or

(3) direct that the order is to cease to have effect and make an order (a) imposing a relevant restriction[9] on the proprietor of the institution[10], or (b) requiring the Secretary of State[11] to remove the institution from the register[12] on such date as the tribunal may specify or, if it does not specify a date, from such date as the Secretary of State may determine[13].

Where an appeal is brought against an order that the institution be removed from the register[14] and the tribunal directs that the order is to cease to have effect[15], the institution must be restored to the register by the Secretary of State[16], and is to be treated as if it had not been removed from the register in pursuance of the order[17].

1 As to the meaning of 'proprietor' see PARA 415 note 3.
2 As to the meaning of 'registered' see PARA 384 note 6.
3 As to the meaning of 'independent educational institution' see PARA 382. The Education and Skills Act 2008 Pt 4 Ch 1 (ss 92–141) applies to alternative provision academies that are not independent educational institutions as it applies to independent educational institutions; accordingly, references in ss 92–141, except in ss 95(2), 140(1), to independent educational institutions are to be read as including references to alternative provision academies that are not independent educational institutions: see s 93A(1), (2) (added by SI 2012/976). As to the meaning of 'alternative provision academy' see PARA 346 note 14 (definition applied by the Education and Skills Act 2008 s 168(2), (3)).
4 See the Education and Skills Act 2008 ss 124(5), 138(1). As to the First-tier Tribunal see COURTS AND TRIBUNALS vol 24 (2010) PARA 874 et seq.
5 Ie under the Education and Skills Act 2008 s 120: see PARA 404.
6 Education and Skills Act 2008 s 126(1).
7 Education and Skills Act 2008 s 126(2)(a).
8 Education and Skills Act 2008 s 126(2)(b).
9 As to the meaning of 'relevant restriction' see PARA 403.
10 Education and Skills Act 2008 s 126(2)(c)(i). As to the effect of such an order see s 127; and PARA 408.
11 As to the Secretary of State see PARA 58.
12 As to the meaning of 'the register' see PARA 384 note 6.
13 Education and Skills Act 2008 s 126(2)(c)(ii).
14 Education and Skills Act 2008 s 126(3)(a).
15 Education and Skills Act 2008 s 126(3)(b).
16 Education and Skills Act 2008 s 126(4)(a).
17 Education and Skills Act 2008 s 126(4)(b).

408. Imposition of relevant restriction by Tribunal. Where the First-tier Tribunal[1] makes an order[2] imposing a relevant restriction[3] on the proprietor[4] of an institution[5], the order in question has effect from the time the proprietor receives notice[6] of it[7]. If the proprietor fails to comply with the relevant restriction, he is guilty of an offence[8].

The proprietor may apply to the tribunal for the relevant restriction to be varied or revoked[9]. On such an application the tribunal must: (1) vary or revoke the relevant restriction as requested in the application, if it is satisfied that it is appropriate to do so because of any change of circumstance[10]; and (2) in any other case, refuse to do so[11].

1   See the Education and Skills Act 2008 ss 124(5), 138(1). As to the First-tier Tribunal see COURTS AND TRIBUNALS vol 24 (2010) PARA 874 et seq.
2   Ie under the Education and Skills Act 2008 s 124 (see PARA 405), s 125 (see PARA 406) or s 126 (see PARA 407).
3   As to the meaning of 'relevant restriction' see PARA 403.
4   As to the meaning of 'proprietor' see PARA 415 note 3.
5   Education and Skills Act 2008 s 127(1). The Education and Skills Act 2008 Pt 4 Ch 1 (ss 92–141) applies to alternative provision academies that are not independent educational institutions as it applies to independent educational institutions; accordingly, references in ss 92–141, except in ss 95(2), 140(1), to independent educational institutions are to be read as including references to alternative provision academies that are not independent educational institutions: see s 93A(1), (2) (added by SI 2012/976). As to the meaning of 'alternative provision academy' see PARA 346 note 14 (definition applied by the Education and Skills Act 2008 s 168(2), (3)).
6   Ie in accordance with tribunal procedure rules or from the Secretary of State: see the Education and Skills Act 2008 s 127(2). As to the tribunal procedure rules see COURTS AND TRIBUNALS vol 24 (2010) PARA 918 et seq. As to the Secretary of State see PARA 58.
7   Education and Skills Act 2008 s 127(2).
8   See the Education and Skills Act 2008 s 127(3). The penalty for such an offence is, on summary conviction, imprisonment for a term not exceeding 51 weeks or a fine not exceeding level 5 on the standard scale (or both): see s 127(3). In relation to an offence committed before the commencement of the Criminal Justice Act 2003 s 281(5) (not yet in force), for '51 weeks' in the Education and Skills Act 2008 s 127(3) substitute 'six months': s 127(4). As to proceedings for offences see PARA 412. As to offences by bodies corporate see PARA 413. As to offences by unincorporated bodies see PARA 414. As to the standard scale see SENTENCING AND DISPOSITION OF OFFENDERS vol 92 (2010) PARA 142.
9   Education and Skills Act 2008 s 127(5).
10   Education and Skills Act 2008 s 127(6)(a).
11   Education and Skills Act 2008 s 127(6)(b).

(E) Prohibition on Participation in Management of Independent Educational Institutions

409. Prohibition on participation in management. The appropriate authority[1] may direct[2] that a person:

(1)   may not take part in the management of an independent educational institution[3];

(2)   may take part in the management of such an institution only in circumstances specified in the direction[4];

(3)   may take part in the management of such an institution only if conditions specified in the direction are satisfied[5].

Such a direction may be given in respect of a person only on one or more prescribed grounds connected with the suitability of persons to take part in the management of an independent educational institution[6]. Regulations may prescribe the procedure for giving a direction (including provision about notification of persons who are subject to directions)[7]. The appropriate authority may vary or revoke a direction in prescribed cases[8].

Where the appropriate authority gives a direction, or varies or revokes any such direction, it must notify (a) the Secretary of State (unless the appropriate authority is the Secretary of State)[9]; and (b) the Welsh Ministers[10] and (if different) the appropriate authority for the purposes of the provisions[11] relating to the prohibition on participation in the management of independent schools in Wales[12].

1　In the Education and Skills Act 2008 ss 128–131 and s 141, 'the appropriate authority' means: (1) the Secretary of State (s 128(6)(a)); or (2) such other public authority as may be prescribed (s 128(6)(b)). As to the Secretary of State see PARA 58. 'Prescribed' means prescribed by regulations; and 'regulations' means regulations made by the Secretary of State under the Education and Skills Act 2008: see s 168(1). At the date at which this volume states the law no such regulations had been made.

2　As to directions see the Education Act 1996 s 570 (applied by the Education and Skills Act 2008 s 168(2), (3)); and PARA 75. If:

　　(1)　immediately before the relevant day a person is subject to a direction under the Education Act 2002 s 142 (see PARA 420) given on grounds prescribed for these purposes (Education and Skills Act 2008 s 141(1)(a)); and

　　(2)　prescribed conditions (which may include conditions relating to decisions taken on or after the relevant day by the Disclosure and Barring Service under the Safeguarding Vulnerable Groups Act 2006 (see CHILDREN AND YOUNG PERSONS vol 9 (2012) PARA 672 et seq) are satisfied in relation to the person (Education and Skills Act 2008 s 141(1)(b) (amended by SI 2012/3006),

　　regulations may provide that, as from a time specified in or determined in accordance with the regulations, such persons are to be treated for prescribed purposes as if the direction given under the Education Act 2002 s 142 were a direction given by the appropriate authority under the Education and Skills Act 2008 s 128: s 141(2). See note 1. The regulations may make provision in connection with the determination of any appeal under the Education Act 2002 s 144(1) (see PARA 420), or application for review under s 144(2) (see PARA 420), which is pending on the relevant day: Education and Skills Act 2008 s 141(3). Regulations made by virtue of s 141(3) may, in particular, provide for an appeal, or application for review, under the Education Act 2002 s 144 to be treated as an appeal under the Education and Skills Act 2008 s 129 (see PARA 411): s 141(4). 'The relevant day' means the day on which s 128 comes into force (ie 8 September 2014): s 141(5). See note 3. As to the meaning of 'person' see PARA 7 note 6. As to regulations made under s 141(1), (2) see the Independent Educational Provision in England (Prohibition on Participation in Management) Regulations 2014, SI 2014/1977.

3　Education and Skills Act 2008 s 128(1)(a). As to the meaning of 'independent educational institution' see PARA 382. The Education and Skills Act 2008 Pt 4 Ch 1 (ss 92–141) applies to alternative provision academies that are not independent educational institutions as it applies to independent educational institutions; accordingly, references in ss 92–141, except in ss 95(2), 140(1), to independent educational institutions are to be read as including references to alternative provision academies that are not independent educational institutions: see s 93A(1), (2) (added by SI 2012/976). As to the meaning of 'alternative provision academy' see PARA 346 note 14 (definition applied by the Education and Skills Act 2008 s 168(2), (3)).

4　Education and Skills Act 2008 s 128(1)(b). See note 3.

5　Education and Skills Act 2008 s 128(1)(c). See note 3.

6　Education and Skills Act 2008 s 128(2). See note 3. As to appeals against directions see s 129; and PARA 411. As to regulations made under s 128(2), (3), (4), (5) see the Independent Educational Provision in England (Prohibition on Participation in Management) Regulations 2014, SI 2014/1977.

7　Education and Skills Act 2008 s 128(3). See note 3. As to regulations see note 6.

8　Education and Skills Act 2008 s 128(4). Regulations may prescribe the grounds on which a person subject to a direction may seek to have it varied or revoked under s 128(4): s 128(5). As to appeals against decisions not to vary or revoke a direction see s 129; and PARA 411. As to regulations see note 6.

9　Education and Skills Act 2008 s 131(1). See note 3.

10　As to the Welsh Ministers see PARA 59.

11　Ie the Education Act 2002 ss 167A–167D: see PARA 420.

12　Education and Skills Act 2008 s 131(2). See note 3. As to the meaning of 'Wales' see PARA 7 note 3.

410. Provision of information in connection with directions prohibiting participation in management. Where the appropriate authority[1] is a public authority other than the Secretary of State[2], the Secretary of State may provide to that authority any information relating to a person[3] which appears to the Secretary of State to be relevant to the exercise of the appropriate authority's functions[4] relating to the prohibition on participation in the management of independent educational institutions[5].

Her Majesty's Chief Inspector of Education, Children's Services and Skills[6] may provide to the appropriate authority any information relating to a person which appears to the Chief Inspector to be relevant to the exercise of those functions by the appropriate authority[7]; and the Welsh Ministers[8] may provide to the appropriate authority any information relating to a person which is held[9] by them[10].

The Disclosure and Barring Service[11] may provide to the appropriate authority any information relating to a person which is held by the Service in connection with its functions and which appears to it to be relevant to the exercise of the appropriate authority's functions relating to the prohibition on participation in the management of independent educational institutions[12].

The appropriate authority may provide to the Disclosure and Barring Service, the Education Workforce Council[13], Her Majesty's Chief Inspector of Education, Children's Services and Skills, the Welsh Ministers or, where the appropriate authority is a public authority other than the Secretary of State, the Secretary of State, any information relating to a person which is held by the appropriate authority in connection with its functions[14].

1   As to the meaning of 'appropriate authority' see PARA 409 note 1.
2   As to the Secretary of State see PARA 58.
3   As to the meaning of 'person' see PARA 7 note 6.
4   Ie the functions under the Education and Skills Act 2008 s 128 (see PARA 409) or by virtue of s 129 (see PARA 411). As to the meaning of 'functions' see PARA 18 note 5 (definition applied by s 168(2), (3)(b)).
5   Education and Skills Act 2008 s 130(1). As to the meaning of 'independent educational institution' see PARA 382. Part 4 Ch 1 (ss 92–141) applies to alternative provision academies that are not independent educational institutions as it applies to independent educational institutions; accordingly, references in ss 92–141, except in ss 95(2), 140(1), to independent educational institutions are to be read as including references to alternative provision academies that are not independent educational institutions: see s 93A(1), (2) (added by SI 2012/976). As to the meaning of 'alternative provision academy' see PARA 346 note 14 (definition applied by the Education and Skills Act 2008 s 168(2), (3)).
6   As to Her Majesty's Chief Inspector of Education, Children's Services and Skills see PARA 1133.
7   See the Education and Skills Act 2008 s 130(3).
8   As to the Welsh Ministers see PARA 59.
9   Ie in connection with their functions under the Education Act 2002 Pt 10 Ch 1 (ss 156A–171).
10 Education and Skills Act 2008 s 130(2).
11 As to the Disclosure and Barring Service see CHILDREN AND YOUNG PERSONS vol 9 (2012) PARA 677A.
12 Education and Skills Act 2008 s 130(4) (amended by SI 2012/3006).
13 As to the Education Workforce Council (formerly the General Teaching Council for Wales) see PARA 1075.
14 Education and Skills Act 2008 s 130(5) (amended by SI 2012/3006; and the Education Act 2011 Sch 2 para 20(a)). The functions referred to in this case are those under s 128 (see PARA 409): see s 130(5).

411. Appeals against directions prohibiting participation in management. A person[1] in respect of whom a direction has been given[2] may appeal to the First-tier Tribunal[3]: (1) against the decision to give the direction[4]; (2) against a decision not to vary or revoke the direction[5].

Regulations[6] may;

(a)   provide that the tribunal may not entertain such an appeal in so far as the appellant's case is inconsistent with the appellant having been convicted of an offence[7];

(b)   prescribe circumstances in which the tribunal must allow such an appeal[8];

(c)   prescribe the powers available to the tribunal on allowing such an appeal[9].

1   As to the meaning of 'person' see PARA 7 note 6.
2   Ie under the Education and Skills Act 2008 s 128: see PARA 409.
3   See the Education and Skills Act 2008 ss 124(5), 138(1). As to the First-tier Tribunal see COURTS AND TRIBUNALS vol 24 (2010) PARA 874 et seq.
4   Education and Skills Act 2008 s 129(1)(a).
5   Education and Skills Act 2008 s 129(1)(b). Part 4 Ch 1 (ss 92–141) applies to alternative provision academies that are not independent educational institutions as it applies to independent educational institutions; accordingly, references in ss 92–141, except in ss 95(2), 140(1), to independent educational institutions are to be read as including references to alternative provision academies that are not independent educational institutions: see s 93A(1), (2) (added by SI 2012/976). As to the meaning of 'alternative provision academy' see PARA 346 note 14 (definition applied by the Education and Skills Act 2008 s 168(2), (3)).
6   'Regulations' means regulations made under the Education and Skills Act 2008 by the Secretary of State: s 168(1). As to the Secretary of State see PARA 58. As to regulations made under s 129(2) see the Independent Educational Provision in England (Prohibition on Participation in Management) Regulations 2014, SI 2014/1977.
7   Education and Skills Act 2008 s 129(2)(a). See note 6.
8   Education and Skills Act 2008 s 129(2)(b). See note 6.
9   Education and Skills Act 2008 s 129(2)(c). See note 6.

(F)   Offences and Service of Notices

412.   Proceedings for offences.   No proceedings for an offence under the statutory provisions relating to the regulation and inspection of independent educational institutions[1] in England[2] may be instituted except by or with the consent of the Secretary of State[3].

1   As to the meaning of 'independent educational institution' see PARA 382. The Education and Skills Act 2008 Pt 4 Ch 1 (ss 92–141) applies to alternative provision academies that are not independent educational institutions as it applies to independent educational institutions; accordingly, references in ss 92–141, except in ss 95(2), 140(1), to independent educational institutions are to be read as including references to alternative provision academies that are not independent educational institutions: see s 93A(1), (2) (added by SI 2012/976). As to the meaning of 'alternative provision academy' see PARA 346 note 14 (definition applied by the Education and Skills Act 2008 s 168(2), (3)).
2   Ie the Education and Skills Act 2008 Pt 4 Ch 1 (ss 92–141). As to the meaning of 'England' see PARA 7 note 3.
3   Education and Skills Act 2008 s 134. See also note 1. As to the Secretary of State see PARA 58.

413.   Offences by bodies corporate.   Where an offence under the statutory provisions relating to the regulation and inspection of independent educational institutions[1] in England[2] committed by a body corporate[3] is proved to have been committed with the consent or connivance of, or to be attributable to any neglect on the part of:
(1)   any director, manager, secretary or other similar officer of the body corporate[4]; or
(2)   any person who was purporting to act in any such capacity[5],
that person (as well as the body corporate) is guilty of the offence and liable to be proceeded against and punished accordingly[6]. Where the affairs of a body corporate are managed by its members, this provision applies in relation to the acts and defaults of a member in connection with the member's functions[7] of management as it applies to a director of a body corporate[8].

1   As to the meaning of 'independent educational institution' see PARA 382. The Education and Skills Act 2008 Pt 4 Ch 1 (ss 92–141) applies to alternative provision academies that are not independent educational institutions as it applies to independent educational institutions;

accordingly, references in ss 92–141, except in ss 95(2), 140(1), to independent educational institutions are to be read as including references to alternative provision academies that are not independent educational institutions: see s 93A(1), (2) (added by SI 2012/976). As to the meaning of 'alternative provision academy' see PARA 346 note 14 (definition applied by the Education and Skills Act 2008 s 168(2), (3)).

2 Ie the Education and Skills Act 2008 Pt 4 Ch 1 (ss 92–141). As to the meaning of 'England' see PARA 7 note 3.

3 As to bodies corporate see COMPANIES vol 14 (2009) PARA 2; CORPORATIONS vol 24 (2010) PARA 301 et seq.

4 Education and Skills Act 2008 s 135(1)(a). See also note 1.

5 Education and Skills Act 2008 s 135(1)(b). See also note 1.

6 Education and Skills Act 2008 s 135(1). See also note 1. As to the institution of proceedings for offences see PARA 412. As to offences by unincorporated bodies see PARA 414.

7 As to the meaning of 'functions' see PARA 18 note 5 (definition applied by the Education and Skills Act 2008 s 168(2), (3)(b)).

8 Education and Skills Act 2008 s 135(2). See also note 1.

414. Offences by unincorporated bodies. Proceedings for an offence[1] alleged to have been committed under the statutory provisions relating to the regulation and inspection of independent educational institutions[2] in England[3] by an unincorporated body are to be brought in the name of that body (and not in that of any of its members) and, for the purposes of any such proceedings, any rules of court relating to the service of documents have effect as if that body were a corporation[4]. A fine imposed on an unincorporated body on its conviction of such an offence is to be paid out of the funds of that body[5].

Where the offence committed by an unincorporated body other than a partnership is proved to have been committed with the consent or connivance of, or to be attributable to any neglect on the part of, any officer of the body or any member of its governing body, that person (as well as the body) is guilty of the offence and liable to be proceeded against and punished accordingly[6]. Where the offence committed by a partnership is proved to have been committed with the consent or connivance of, or to be attributable to any neglect on the part of, a partner, the partner (as well as the partnership) is guilty of the offence and liable to be proceeded against and punished accordingly[7].

1 As to the institution of proceedings for offences see PARA 412. As to offences by bodies corporate see PARA 413.

2 As to the meaning of 'independent educational institution' see PARA 382. The Education and Skills Act 2008 Pt 4 Ch 1 (ss 92–141) applies to alternative provision academies that are not independent educational institutions as it applies to independent educational institutions; accordingly, references in ss 92–141, except in ss 95(2), 140(1), to independent educational institutions are to be read as including references to alternative provision academies that are not independent educational institutions: see s 93A(1), (2) (added by SI 2012/976). As to the meaning of 'alternative provision academy' see PARA 346 note 14 (definition applied by the Education and Skills Act 2008 s 168(2), (3)).

3 Ie the Education and Skills Act 2008 Pt 4 Ch 1 (ss 92–141). As to the meaning of 'England' see PARA 7 note 3.

4 Education and Skills Act 2008 s 136(1). See also note 2. If an unincorporated body is charged with such an offence, the Criminal Justice Act 1925 s 33 (see CRIMINAL PROCEDURE vol 27 (2010) PARA 388) and the Magistrates' Courts Act 1980 Sch 3 (see CRIMINAL PROCEDURE vol 27 (2010) PARA 190) (procedure on charge of an offence against a corporation) apply as they do in relation to a body corporate: Education and Skills Act 2008 s 136(3).

5 Education and Skills Act 2008 s 136(2). See also note 2.

6 Education and Skills Act 2008 s 136(4). See also note 2.

7 Education and Skills Act 2008 s 136(5). See also note 2.

415. Service of notices and other documents. For the purposes of the statutory provisions relating to the regulation and inspection of independent educational institutions[1] in England[2], any notice, order or other document required to be given to or served on the proprietor[3] of a registered[4] independent educational institution may be given to or served on the proprietor by delivering it to the registered address of the institution[5].

1 As to the meaning of 'independent educational institution' see PARA 382. The Education and Skills Act 2008 Pt 4 Ch 1 (ss 92–141) applies to alternative provision academies that are not independent educational institutions as it applies to independent educational institutions; accordingly, references in ss 92–141, except in ss 95(2), 140(1), to independent educational institutions are to be read as including references to alternative provision academies that are not independent educational institutions: see s 93A(1), (2) (added by SI 2012/976). As to the meaning of 'alternative provision academy' see PARA 346 note 14 (definition applied by the Education and Skills Act 2008 s 168(2), (3)).

2 Ie the Education and Skills Act 2008 Pt 4 Ch 1 (ss 92–141). As to the meaning of 'England' see PARA 7 note 3.

3 'Proprietor', in relation to an institution, means the person or body of persons responsible for the management of the institution: Education and Skills Act 2008 s 138(1). As to the meaning of 'person' see PARA 7 note 6.

4 As to the meaning of 'registered' see PARA 384 note 6.

5 Education and Skills Act 2008 s 137. See note 1.

B. REGULATION AND INSPECTION IN WALES UNDER THE EDUCATION ACT 2002

416. Regulatory regime under the Education Act 2002. Chapter 1 of Part 10 of the Education Act 2002[1] makes provision for the regulation of independent schools[2] in Wales[3], and references in that Chapter to an independent school are to an independent school in Wales[4].

1 Ie the Education Act 2002 Pt 10 Ch 1 (ss 156A–171).

2 As to the meaning of 'independent school' see PARA 369 (definition applied by the Education Act 2002 s 212(2), (3)).

3 As to the meaning of 'Wales' see PARA 7 note 3.

4 Education Act 2002 s 156A(1) (s 156A added by the Education and Skills Act 2008 s 169(1), Sch 1 Pt 1 paras 13, 15). As to the meaning of 'Wales' see PARA 7 note 3. For provision regulating independent schools in England see the Education and Skills Act 2008 Pt 4 Ch 1 (ss 92–141): Education Act 2002 s 156A(2) (as so added). As to the application of Pt 10 Ch 1 to alternative provision academies that are not independent schools see s 156AA (added by SI 2012/976). As to the meaning of 'alternative provision academy' see PARA 346 note 14 (definition applied by the Education Act 2002 s 212(2), (3)). As to the meanings of 'England' and 'Wales' see PARA 7 note 3.

417. Registration. There continues[1] to be a register[2] of independent schools in Wales[3], which is kept by the Welsh Ministers[4].

An application to enter an independent school in the register must (1) contain the prescribed[5] information[6]; and (2) be made to the registration authority[7] by the proprietor[8] of the school in the prescribed manner[9]. Where the proprietor makes such an application, the registration authority must notify the Chief Inspector[10], who must then inspect the school and report to the registration authority on the extent to which the independent school standards[11] are met, and are likely to continue to be met, in relation to the school[12].

Where a school has been so inspected, the registration authority must determine whether those standards are met, and are likely to continue to be met, in relation to the school[13], and must notify[14] the proprietor of a school of any determination made in relation to the school[15]. If the registration authority determines that the independent school standards are met, and are likely to continue to be met, in relation to a school, the registration authority must enter the school in the register[16].

A person[17] who conducts an independent school which is not a registered school is guilty of an offence[18]. Where the Chief Inspector has reasonable cause to believe that such an offence is being committed on any premises[19], he may at any reasonable time enter and inspect the premises[20], and inspect and take copies of any records or other documents which he has reasonable cause to believe may be required for the purposes of proceedings in relation to such an offence[21]. It is an offence wilfully to obstruct the Chief Inspector in the exercise of these functions[22].

The registration authority may remove a school from the register if there is a material change in relation to the school, and the change has not[23] been approved[24].

The registration authority may also remove a registered school from the register where it is satisfied that any unsuitable person, in relation to the school carries out work of a prescribed[25] kind[26].

1 The Education Act 2002 Pt 10 Ch 1 (ss 157–171) replaces the regulatory regime for independent schools contained in the Education Act 1996 Pt VII Ch II (ss 464–478) (repealed): see PARA 416.
2 In the Education Act 2002 Pt 10 Ch 1, 'the register' means the register of independent schools in Wales, and 'registered' means entered in the register: Education Act 2002 s 171 (definitions amended by the Education and Skills Act 2008 s 169, Sch 1 Pt 1, paras 13, 24, Sch 2). As to the meaning of 'Wales' see PARA 7 note 3.
3 As to the meaning of 'independent school' see PARAS 369 (definition applied by the Education Act 2002 s 212(2), (3)), 416.
4 Education Act 2002 s 158 (amended by the Education and Skills Act 2008 s 169, Sch 1 Pt 1 paras 13, 17, Sch 2). As to the Welsh Ministers see PARA 59.
5 As to the information to be prescribed see the Education Act 2002 s 160(2). 'Prescribed' means prescribed by regulations: s 212(1). As to the regulations made under s 160 see the Independent Schools (Provision of Information) (Wales) Regulations 2003, SI 2003/3230 (amended by SI 2007/947; SI 2009/2544; SI 2010/2582; SI 2011/577; and SI 2012/3006).
6 Education Act 2002 s 160(1)(a).
7 'Registration authority' means the Welsh Ministers: Education Act 2002 s 171 (definition amended by the Education and Skills Act 2008 s 169(1), Sch 1 Pt 1 paras 13, 24(1), (5)).
8 As to the meaning of 'proprietor' see PARA 51 note 4 (definition applied by the Education Act 2002 s 212(2), (3)).
9 Education Act 2002 s 160(1)(b).
10 'Chief Inspector' means Her Majesty's Chief Inspector of Education and Training in Wales: Education Act 2002 s 171 (definition amended by the Education and Skills Act 2008 s 169, Sch 1 Pt 1 paras 13, 24(1), (2), Sch 2). As to Her Majesty's Chief Inspector of Education and Training in Wales see PARA 1148.
11 As to the meaning of 'independent school standards' see PARA 463.
12 Education Act 2002 s 160(3), (4).
13 See the Education Act 2002 s 161(1).
14 As to the service of notices and documents see the Education Act 2002 s 170; and PARA 422.
15 Education Act 2002 s 161(2).
16 Education Act 2002 s 161(3). An entry in the register for a school must include the name and address of the school, the name of the proprietor of the school, and the information supplied pursuant to s 160(2): see s 161(4).
   Regulations may make provision requiring the proprietor of a registered school to provide the registration authority, when the authority so requests, with such particulars relating to the school as may be prescribed: see s 168. As to the regulations made see the Independent Schools (Provision of Information) (Wales) Regulations 2003, SI 2003/3230 (amended by SI 2007/947; SI 2009/2544; SI 2010/2582; SI 2011/577; and SI 2012/3006).
17 As to the meaning of 'person' see PARA 7 note 6.
18 Education Act 2002 s 159(1). A person guilty of such an offence is liable on summary conviction to a fine not exceeding level 5 on the standard scale (s 159(2)(a)), or imprisonment for a term not exceeding six months, or to both (s 159(2)(b)). As to proceedings for offences see PARA 421. As to offences by bodies corporate see PARA 421. As to offences by unincorporated bodies see PARA 421. As to the standard scale see SENTENCING AND DISPOSITION OF OFFENDERS vol 92 (2010) PARA 142.

19 As to the meaning of 'premises' see PARA 62 note 19 (definition applied by the Education Act 2002 s 212(2), (3)).
20 Education Act 2002 s 159(4)(a).
21 Education Act 2002 s 159(4)(b). The Education Act 2005 s 58 (computer records: see PARA 1152 note 7) applies in relation to the inspection of records or other documents under the Education Act 2002 s 159(4)(b): s 159(5) (amended by the Education Act 2005 s 61, Sch 9 para 29).
22 Education Act 2002 s 159(6). A person guilty of such an offence is liable on summary conviction to a fine not exceeding level 4 on the standard scale: s 159(7). As to the meaning of 'functions' see PARA 18 note 5 (definition applied by 2002 s 212(2), (3)).
23 Ie under the Education Act 2002 s 162 or s 167 (see PARA 419).
24 See the Education Act 2002 s 162. As to what constitutes a 'material change' see the Education Act 2002 s 162(2). The registration authority must serve on the proprietor of a registered school notice of any decision made by the authority under s 162 in relation to the school: s 170(1)(a).
   As to appeals against a refusal to approve a material change see s 166; and PARA 419. As to the service of notices and documents see the Education Act 2002 s 170; and PARA 422. As to savings and transitional provisions following the amendments to the Education Act 2002 by the Education and Skills Act 2008, see the Education and Skills Act 2008 (Commencement No 11 and Saving and Transitory Provisions) Order 2014, SI 2014/3364, art 4.
25 'Prescribed' means prescribed by regulations. As to the regulations made under the Education Act 2002 s 169 see the Education (Independent Schools) (Unsuitable Persons) (Wales) Regulations 2009, SI 2009/2558.
26 See the Education Act 2002 s 169 (amended by the Education and Inspections Act 2006 s 170(1)). At the date at which this volume states the law the Education Act 2002 s 169 (as so amended) is in force in relation to Wales only: see the Education and Inspections Act 2006 (Commencement No 4 and Transitional Provisions) (Wales) Order 2009, SI 2009/2545, art 3(1)(b).

418. Standards and inspection. For the purposes of the provisions of the Education Act 2002 relating to the regulation of independent schools[1], regulations[2] must prescribe standards, known as 'independent school standards'[3], in relation to the following matters:

(1)   the quality of education provided at independent schools[4];
(2)   the spiritual, moral, social and cultural development of pupils at independent schools[5];
(3)   the welfare, health and safety of pupils at independent schools[6];
(4)   the suitability of proprietors[7] of and staff at independent schools[8];
(5)   the premises[9] of and accommodation at independent schools[10];
(6)   the provision of information by independent schools[11];
(7)   the manner in which independent schools handle complaints[12].

The registration authority[13] may at any time: (a) require Her Majesty's Chief Inspector of Education and Training in Wales[14] to inspect any registered[15] school or to secure its inspection by one or more registered inspectors; or (b) arrange for the inspection of any registered school by a body approved by the registration authority for these purposes[16]. Such an inspection must relate to: (i) such of the independent school standards as are, at the time of the inspection, specified by the registration authority for the purposes of these provisions in relation to any category of school into which that school falls[17]; or (ii) if the registration authority so determines, such of the independent school standards as the authority may specify in relation to that school[18]. A person[19] who conducts such an inspection must: (A) make a report to the registration authority on the extent to which the school meets the standard or standards to which the inspection relates[20]; and (B) if the registration authority so requires, arrange for the publication of the report in the prescribed[21] manner[22].

Where the registration authority, taking into account such a report[23], or any other evidence in respect of a registered school, is satisfied that any one or more of the independent school standards is or are not being met in relation to the school, the following provisions apply[24]. If the registration authority considers that there is a risk of serious harm to the welfare of pupils[25] at the school, the authority may determine that the school is to be removed from the register[26] on such date after the appeal period[27] as the authority may determine[28]. Where the registration authority does not make such a determination, it must serve a notice on the proprietor of the school identifying the standard or standards in question and requiring the proprietor to submit an action plan[29] to the authority before the date specified in the notice, or such later date as the authority may specify after service of the notice[30]. Where an action plan is so submitted, the registration authority may reject it, or approve it, with or without modifications[31]; the authority has power to remove the school from the register on such date after the appeal period[32] as the authority may determine, or make an order requiring the proprietor of the school to do one or more of the following (aa) to cease using any part of the school premises for all purposes or purposes specified in the order; (bb) to close any part of the school's operation; (cc) to cease to admit any new pupils, or new pupils of a description specified in the order[33]. If the proprietor of a school fails to comply with an order made by the registration authority he is guilty of an offence[34], and the registration authority may determine that the school is to be removed from the register on such date after the appeal period as the authority may determine[35].

Where the registration authority has made a determination under the above provisions to remove a school from the register on a particular date and no appeal is made[36] against the determination, the authority must remove the school from the register on that date[37].

1   Ie for the purposes of the Education Act 2002 Pt 10 Ch 1 (ss 156A–171). As to the meaning of 'independent school' see PARAS 369 (definition applied by the Education Act 2002 s 212(2), (3)), 416.

2   As to the regulations made under the Education Act 2002 s 157 see the Independent School Standards (Wales) Regulations 2003, SI 2003/3234 (amended by SI 2005/2929; SI 2007/947; and SI 2009/2544).

3   In the Education Act 2002 Pt 10 Ch 1 'independent school standards' means: (1) the standards for the time being prescribed under s 157 (s 157(2) (substituted by the Childcare Act 2006 s 47(2))); and amended by the Education and Skills Act 2008 s 169, Sch 1 Pt 1 paras 13, 16, Sch 2).

4   Education Act 2002 s 157(1)(a).

5   Education Act 2002 s 157(1)(b).

6   Education Act 2002 s 157(1)(c).

7   As to the meaning of 'proprietor' see PARA 51 note 4 (definition applied by the Education Act 2002 s 212(2), (3)).

8   Education Act 2002 s 157(1)(d).

9   As to the meaning of 'premises' see PARA 62 note 19 (definition applied by the Education Act 2002 s 212(2), (3)).

10   Education Act 2002 s 157(1)(e).

11   Education Act 2002 s 157(1)(f).

12   Education Act 2002 s 157(1)(g).

13   As to the meaning of 'registration authority' see PARA 417 note 7.

14   As to Her Majesty's Chief Inspector of Education and Training in Wales see PARA 1148.

15   As to the meaning of 'registered' see PARA 417 note 2.

16   See the Education Act 2002 s 163(1)(a), (b) (ss 163, 164 substituted by the Education Act 2005 s 54, Sch 8 paras 1, 3; the Education Act 2002 s 163(1)(a) amended by the Education and Skills Act 2008 s 169, Sch 1 Pt 1 paras 13, 19(b), (2), Sch 2); the Education Act 2002 s 171 (definition amended by the Education and Skills Act 2008 s 169, Sch 1 Pt 1 paras 13, 24(1), (2), Sch 2). 'Registered inspector' means a person registered under the Education Act 2005 s 25 (registration of inspectors in Wales: see PARA 1156): Education Act 2002 s 163(5) (as so substituted). A registered inspector may have assistance in conducting an inspection under s 163(1)(a), and may

be monitored by the Chief Inspector: see s 164(1)–(4) (as so substituted; amended by the Education and Skills Act 2008, s 169, Sch 1 Pt 1, paras 13, 20, Sch 2).

The person conducting the inspection, any person assisting him pursuant to the Education Act 2002 s 164(2), (3), and any person monitoring the inspection have at all reasonable times a right of entry to the premises of the school, and a right to inspect and take copies of any records kept by the school and any other documents containing information relating to the school which are required for the purposes of the inspection: s 164(5) (as so substituted). The Education Act 2005 s 58 (computer records: see PARA 1152 note 7) applies in relation to the inspection of records or other documents under the Education Act 2002 s 164(5): see s 164(6) (as so substituted). It is an offence wilfully to obstruct a person in the exercise of his functions in relation to the inspection: Education Act 2002 s 164(7) (as substituted: see note 16). A person guilty of such an offence is liable on summary conviction to a fine not exceeding level 4 on the standard scale: s 164(8) (as so substituted). As to the standard scale see SENTENCING AND DISPOSITION OF OFFENDERS vol 92 (2010) PARA 142.

A fee of such amount, and by such time, as may be specified in or determined under regulations, must be paid: see s 164(9) (as so substituted; amended by the Education and Skills Act 2008 s 169, Sch 1 Pt 1, paras 13, 20, Sch 2)). As to failure to comply with the Education Act 2002 s 164(9) and the payment of the fee see s 164(10), (11), (12) (as so substituted; s 164(11), (11) amended by the Education and Skills Act 2008 s 169, Sch 1 Pt 1, paras 13, 20, Sch 2)). At the date at which this volume states the law no regulations had been made under the Education Act 2002 s 164.

17 Education Act 2002 s 163(2)(a) (as substituted: see note 16).
18 Education Act 2002 s 163(2)(b) (as substituted: see note 16).
19 As to the meaning of 'person' see PARA 7 note 6.
20 Education Act 2002 s 163(3)(a) (as substituted: see note 16).
21 'Prescribed' means prescribed by regulations. As to the regulations made see the Independent Schools (Publication of Inspection Reports) (Wales) Regulations 2003, SI 2003/3232.
22 Education Act 2002 s 163(3)(b) (as substituted: see note 16). A report published under s 163(3) is privileged for the purposes of the law of defamation unless the publication is shown to be made with malice, but without prejudice to any privilege subsisting apart from s 163(3): s 163(4) (as so substituted). As to privilege in the law of defamation see DEFAMATION vol 32 (2012) PARA 594 et seq.
23 Ie under the Education Act 2002 s 163.
24 Education Act 2002 s 165(1) (amended by the Education Act 2005 s 54, Sch 8 para 4, and the Education and Skills Act 2008 s 169(1), Sch 1 Pt 1 paras 13, 21, Sch 2).
25 As to the meaning of 'pupil' see PARA 20 note 4 (definition applied by the Education Act 2002 s 212(2), (3)).
26 As to the meaning of 'the register' see PARA 417 note 2.
27 For the purposes of the Education Act 2002 Pt 10 Ch 1, the 'appeal period' in relation to a determination or order is the period within which an appeal against it may be made under s 166 (see PARA 419): ss 165(13), 171.
28 Education Act 2002 s 165(2). The registration authority must serve on the proprietor of a registered school notice of any determination made by the authority under s 165 in relation to the school: s 170(1)(b). As to the service of notices and documents see the Education Act 2002 s 170; and PARA 422. As to the meaning of 'proprietor' see PARA 51 note 4 (definition applied by the Education Act 2002 s 212(2), (3)).
29 An action plan is a plan specifying the steps that will be taken to meet a standard or standards and the time by which each step will be taken: Education Act 2002 s 165(4).
30 Education Act 2002 s 165(3).
31 Education Act 2002 s 165(5). As to the meaning of 'modifications' see PARA 21 note 15 (definition applied by s 212(2), (3)).
32 For the purposes of the Education Act 2002 Pt 10 Ch 1, the 'appeal period' in relation to a determination or order is the period within which an appeal against it may be made under s 166 (see PARA 419): ss 165(13), 171.
33 See the Education Act 2002 s 165(6)–(8). The power to make such orders is not exercisable by statutory instrument (see s 210(2)) and such orders are not recorded in this work.

Where the proprietor of a school in respect of which an order is made applies to the registration authority for the order to be varied or revoked, the authority must vary or revoke the order as requested in the application, if it is satisfied that it is appropriate to do so because of any change of circumstance, and in any other case, refuse to do so: s 165(10). The registration authority must serve on the proprietor of a registered school notice of any decision made by the authority under s 165(10) in relation to the school: s 170(1)(c). The variation or revocation of an order under s 165(10) takes effect as from the date on which the proprietor of the school is notified of it: s 165(11).

34 The penalty for such an offence is, on summary conviction, a term of imprisonment not exceeding six months, or a fine not exceeding level 5 on the standard scale, or both: see s 165(9). As to the standard scale see SENTENCING AND DISPOSITION OF OFFENDERS vol 92 (2010) PARA 142.

35 Education Act 2002 s 165(9).

36 Ie under the Education Act 2002 s 166: see PARA 419.

37 Education Act 2002 s 165(12).

419. Appeals. In relation to the registration[1] and inspection[2] of independent schools in Wales[3], appeals may be made to the First-tier Tribunal[4] against[5]:

(1)   a refusal to approve a material change[6] in relation to the school[7];

(2)   a determination[8] to remove the school from the register[9];

(3)   an order[10] relating to actions following a failure to meet standards[11]; or

(4)   a refusal[12] to vary or revoke such an order[13].

An appeal must be made within the period of 28 days beginning with the day on which notice of the refusal, determination or order is served on the proprietor[14].

Where such an appeal is made under head (1) above to approve a material change in relation to the school, the tribunal may either uphold the refusal to approve, or itself approve the change[15].

Where such an appeal is made under head (2) above against a determination to remove the school from the register, the tribunal may uphold the determination or revoke the determination[16]. Where the tribunal upholds a determination, the registration authority[17] must remove the school from the register on such date as the tribunal may specify or, if it does not specify a date, on such date as the registration authority may determine[18]. Where the tribunal revokes a determination, it may order the proprietor of the school to do one or more of the following by such time as may be specified in the order[19]: (a) to cease using any part of the school premises for all purposes or purposes specified in the order[20]; (b) to close any part of the school's operation[21]; (c) to cease to admit any new pupils, or new pupils of a description specified in the order[22]. If the proprietor of a school fails to comply with such an order of the tribunal he is guilty of an offence[23], and the tribunal may, on the application of the registration authority, authorise the registration authority to remove the school from the register on such date as the tribunal may determine[24].

Where an appeal is made under head (3) above requiring the taking of specified action, the tribunal may uphold the order, vary the order, or strike down the order[25].

Where an appeal is made under head (4) above, the tribunal may uphold the refusal, or if in any case it is satisfied that it is appropriate to do so because of any change of circumstance after the making of the order, vary the order in such manner as it thinks fit, or revoke the order[26].

1   See PARA 417.

2   See PARA 418.

3   See PARA 416.

4   As to the First-tier Tribunal see COURTS AND TRIBUNALS vol 24 (2010) PARA 874 et seq.

5   See the Education Act 2002 s 166(1) (amended by SI 2008/2833).

6   Ie under the Education Act 2002 s 162: see PARA 417.

7   See the Education Act 2002 s 166(1)(a).

8   Ie under the Education Act 2002 s 165: see PARA 418.

9   See the Education Act 2002 s 166(1)(b). Where such an appeal is made: (1) if the appeal is withdrawn or otherwise disposed of before it is determined by the tribunal under s 167 (see the text to notes 15–26), the registration authority may remove the school from the register on such date after the appeal period as it may determine; and (2) in any other case the registration authority may only remove the school pursuant to the determination: see s 166(3). As to the meaning of 'registration authority' see note 17. As to the meaning of 'appeal period' see PARA 418 note 27.

In the case of an appeal against a determination under s 165(2), if at any time the tribunal considers that there is a risk of serious harm occurring to the welfare of pupils before the determination of the appeal, it may by order provide that the school is to be regarded as not registered for the purposes of s 159 (see PARA 417) until the tribunal determines the appeal under s 167 (or revokes the order before so determining the appeal): see s 166(5).

10 Ie under the Education Act 2002 s 165(8): see PARA 418.

11 See the Education Act 2002 s 166(1)(c). Where such an appeal is made, the order does not have effect in relation to any time before the appeal is determined by the tribunal under s 167 (see the text to notes 15–26) or withdrawn or otherwise disposed of: s 166(4).

12 Ie under the Education Act 2002 s 165(10): see PARA 418.

13 See the Education Act 2002 s 166(1)(d).

14 See the Education Act 2002 s 166(2).

15 See the Education Act 2002 s 167(1), (2) (s 161(1) amended by SI 2008/2833).

16 See the Education Act 2002 s 167(3).

17 As to the meaning of 'registration authority' see PARA 417 note 7.

18 See the Education Act 2002 s 167(4).

19 See the Education Act 2002 s 167(5). The tribunal may, on the application of the proprietor of a registered school, vary or revoke any order made by it under s 167(5) in relation to the school where it is satisfied that it is appropriate to do so because of any change of circumstance: s 167(8). As to the meaning of 'registered' see PARA 417 note 2.

20 Education Act 2002 s 167(5)(a).

21 Education Act 2002 s 167(5)(b).

22 Education Act 2002 s 167(5)(c).

23 See the Education Act 2002 s 167(9)(a). The penalty for such an offence is, on summary conviction, a term of imprisonment not exceeding six months, or a fine not exceeding level 5 on the standard scale or both: s 167(9)(a). As to the standard scale see SENTENCING AND DISPOSITION OF OFFENDERS vol 92 (2010) PARA 142.

24 Education Act 2002 s 167(9)(b).

25 See the Education Act 2002 s 167(6).

26 See the Education Act 2002 s 167(7).

420. Prohibition on participation in management of independent schools.
The appropriate authority[1] may direct[2] that a person[3]:

(1)   may not take part in the management of an independent school[4];

(2)   may take part in the management of an independent school only in circumstances specified in the direction[5];

(3)   may take part in the management of an independent school only if conditions specified in the direction are satisfied[6].

A direction may be given in respect of a person only on one or more prescribed[7] grounds connected with the suitability of persons to take part in the management of an independent school[8]. Regulations may prescribe the procedure for giving a direction (including provision about notification of persons who are subject to directions)[9].

The appropriate authority may vary or revoke a direction in prescribed cases[10]; and regulations may prescribe the grounds on which a person subject to a direction may seek to have it varied or revoked[11].

A person in respect of whom a direction has been may appeal to the First-tier Tribunal[12]: (a) against the decision to give the direction[13]; (b) against a decision not to vary or revoke the direction[14]. Regulations[15] may:

(i)   provide that the tribunal may not entertain an appeal in so far as the appellant's case is inconsistent with his having been convicted of an offence[16];

(ii)   prescribe circumstances in which the tribunal must allow an appeal[17];

(iii)   prescribe the powers available to the tribunal on allowing an appeal[18].

1   In the Education Act 2002 ss 167A–167D, 'appropriate authority' means the registration authority or such other public authority as may be prescribed: s 167A(6) (ss 167A-167D added by the Education and Inspections Act 2006 s 169; the Education Act 2002 ss 167C, 167D substituted by the Education and Skills Act 2008 s 169(1), Sch 1 Pt 1, paras 13, 23; the Education Act 2002 s 167A(6) amended by the Education and Skills Act 2008 s 169, Sch 1 Pt 1 paras 13, 22, Sch 2). As to the meaning of 'registration authority' see PARA 417 note 7. 'Prescribed' means prescribed by regulations: see s 212(1). At the date at which this volume states the law no such regulations had been made.

2   As to directions generally see the Education Act 1996 s 570 (applied by the Education Act 2002 s 212(2), (3)); and PARA 75. As to the provision to an appropriate authority of any information relating to a person relevant to the exercise of these functions see s 167C (as added (see note 1); substituted by the Education and Skills Act 2008 s 169(1), Sch 1 Pt 1, paras 13, 23; and amended by the Education Act 2011 s 11(1), Sch 2 para 20(b); and SI 2012/3006). Where the appropriate authority gives a direction under the Education Act 2002 s 167A(1), or varies or revokes any such direction, it must notify the registration authority (unless the appropriate authority is the registration authority) and the Secretary of State and (if different) the appropriate authority for the purposes of the Education and Skills Act 2008 ss 128–131 (prohibition on participation in management of independent educational institutions in England: see PARA 409 et seq): see the Education Act 2002 s 167D (as so added); and substituted by the Education and Skills Act 2008 s 169(1), Sch 1 Pt 1 paras 13, 23).

3   Education Act 2002 s 167A(1) (as added: see note 1). As to the meaning of 'person' see PARA 7 note 6.
     Before the Education Act 2002 ss 167A-167D were brought into force, the Education Act 2002 ss 142–144 (s 142 amended by SI 2010/1158; the Education Act 2002 s 144 amended by SI 2008/2833) made provision for directions to be made prohibiting participation in providing education in or the management of, inter alia, independent schools. Those sections are repealed by the Safeguarding Vulnerable Groups Act 2006 s 63(2), Sch 10, save that the Education Act 2002 ss 142–144 continue to have effect for the purpose of enabling the Secretary of State to make a direction under s 142(1)(a) where: (1) the effect of the direction is to prevent a person from taking part in the management of an independent school; and (2) the direction is made on grounds relating to a person's misconduct pursuant to s 142(4)(c): see the Safeguarding Vulnerable Groups Act 2006 (Commencement No 6, Transitional Provisions and Savings) Order 2009, SI 2009/2611, art 4. As to transitional provisions and savings see art 7 (amended by SI 2010/1101; and SI 2012/3006); and the Education and Inspections Act 2006 s 171 (amended by the Education and Skills Act 2008 s 169(1), Sch 1 Pt 1 paras 37, 40; and by SI 2012/3006). As to the Secretary of State see PARA 58. As to the regulations made under the Education Act 2002 ss 142, 144 see the Education (Prohibition from Teaching or Working with Children) Regulations 2003, SI 2003/1184 (amended by SI 2004/1493; SI 2007/195; and SI 2008/2683). See also *Secretary of State for Children, Schools and Families v Philliskirk* [2008] EWHC 2838 (Admin), [2009] ELR 68, [2008] All ER (D) 329 (Oct).

4   Education Act 2002 s 167A(1)(a) (as added: see note 1). As to the meaning of 'independent school' see PARAS 369 (definition applied by the Education Act 2002 s 212(2), (3)), 416.

5   Education Act 2002 s 167A(1)(b) (as added: see note 1).

6   Education Act 2002 s 167A(1)(c) (as added: see note 1).

7   At the date at which this volume states the law no regulations had been made for these purposes.

8   Education Act 2002 s 167A(2) (as added: see note 1).

9   Education Act 2002 s 167A(3) (as added: see note 1). At the date at which this volume states the law no such regulations had been made.

10 Education Act 2002 s 167A(4) (as added: see note 1). At the date at which this volume states the law no regulations had been made for these purposes.

11 Education Act 2002 s 167A(5) (as added: see note 1). At the date at which this volume states the law no such regulations had been made.

12 Education Act 2002 s 167B(1) (s 167B added by the Education and Inspections Act 2006 s 169; and the Education Act 2002 s 167B(1) amended by SI 2008/2833). As to the First-tier Tribunal see COURTS AND TRIBUNALS vol 24 (2010) PARA 874 et seq.

13 Education Act 2002 s 167B(1)(a) (as added: see note 1).

14 Education Act 2002 s 167B(1)(b) (as added: see note 1).
15 At the date at which this volume states the law no such regulations had been made.
16 Education Act 2002 s 167B(2)(a) (as added: see note 1).
17 Education Act 2002 s 167B(2)(b) (as added: see note 1).
18 Education Act 2002 s 167B(2)(c) (as added: see note 1).

421.   Offences. No proceedings for an offence under the provisions of the Education Act 2002 relating to the regulation of independent schools[1] may be instituted except by or with the consent of the registration authority[2].

Where an offence under such provisions committed by a body corporate[3] is proved to have been committed with the consent or connivance of, or to be attributable to any neglect on the part of:

(1)   any director, manager, secretary or other similar officer of the body corporate[4]; or

(2)   any person who was purporting to act in any such capacity[5],

he (as well as the body corporate) is guilty of the offence and liable to be proceeded against and punished accordingly[6]. Where the affairs of a body corporate are managed by its members, this provision applies in relation to the acts and defaults of a member in connection with his functions of management as it applies to a director of a body corporate[7].

Proceedings for an offence alleged to have been committed[8] by an unincorporated body are to be brought in the name of that body (and not in that of any of its members) and, for the purposes of any such proceedings, any rules of court relating to the service of documents have effect as if that body were a corporation[9]. A fine imposed on an unincorporated body on its conviction of such an offence is to be paid out of the funds of that body[10].

Where such an offence committed by an unincorporated body (other than a partnership) is proved to have been committed with the consent or connivance of, or to be attributable to any neglect on the part of, any officer of the body or any member of its governing body, he as well as the body is guilty of the offence and liable to be proceeded against and punished accordingly[11]. Where such an offence committed by a partnership is proved to have been committed with the consent or connivance of, or to be attributable to any neglect on the part of, a partner, he as well as the partnership is guilty of the offence and liable to be proceeded against and punished accordingly[12].

1   Ie the Education Act 2002 Pt 10 Ch 1 (ss 156A–171). As to the meaning of 'independent school' see PARAS 369 (definition applied by the Education Act 2002 s 212(2), (3)), 416.
2   Education Act 2002 s 168A (ss 168A-168C added by the Education and Inspections Act 2006 s 172(1), (2)). As to the meaning of 'registration authority' see PARA 417 note 7.
3   As to bodies corporate see COMPANIES vol 14 (2009) PARA 2; CORPORATIONS vol 24 (2010) PARA 301 et seq.
4   Education Act 2002 s 168B(1)(a) (as added: see note 2).
5   Education Act 2002 s 168B(1)(b) (as added: see note 2).
6   Education Act 2002 s 168B(1) (as added: see note 2).
7   Education Act 2002 s 168B(2) (as added: see note 2).
8   Ie under the Education Act 2002 Pt 10 Ch 1 (ss 156A–171).
9   Education Act 2002 s 168C(1) (as added: see note 2). If an unincorporated body is charged with such an offence, the Criminal Justice Act 1925 s 33 (see CRIMINAL PROCEDURE vol 27 (2010) PARA 388) and the Magistrates' Courts Act 1980 Sch 3 (procedure on charge of an offence against a corporation: see CRIMINAL PROCEDURE vol 27 (2010) PARA 190) apply as they do in relation to a body corporate: Education Act 2002 s 168C(3) (as so added).
10 Education Act 2002 s 168C(2) (as added: see note 2).
11 Education Act 2002 s 168C(4) (as added: see note 2).
12 Education Act 2002 s 168C(5) (as added: see note 2).

422. Service of notices. For the purposes of the provisions of the Education Act 2002 relating to the regulation of independent schools[1], any notice, order or other document required to be given to or served on the proprietor[2] of a registered[3] school may be given to or served on him by delivering it to the registered address of the school[4].

1   Ie the Education Act 2002 Pt 10 Ch 1 (ss 156A–171). As to the meaning of 'independent school' see PARAS 369 (definition applied by the Education Act 2002 s 212(2), (3)), 416.
2   As to the meaning of 'proprietor' see PARA 51 note 4 (definition applied by the Education Act 2002 s 212(2), (3)).
3   As to the meaning of 'registered' see PARA 417 note 2.
4   Education Act 2002 s 170(2).

(v) Discipline and Bullying at Independent Schools

423. No right to give corporal punishment. As in schools generally, the staff in independent schools have no right to administer corporal punishment[1].

1   See the Education Act 1996 s 548, which does not distinguish between independent and maintained schools; and PARA 545, noting also the case law there which deals with the issue of corporal punishment in schools in the context of a parent's philosophical or religious convictions.

424. Disciplinary penalties. The statutory provisions relating to the enforcement of disciplinary penalties[1], and the power of members of staff to restrain[2] and search pupils[3] all apply to independent schools as to other schools.

1   Ie the Education and Inspections Act 2006 ss 90–92: see PARAS 513–515.
2   Ie the Education and Inspections Act 2006 s 93: see PARA 541.
3   Ie the Education Act 1996 ss 550AA, 550ZA–550ZD: see PARAS 543–544.

425. Exclusion from independent schools. A decision to exclude a pupil from an independent school[1] is not amenable to judicial review[2]; instead a complaint must be founded on contract by reference to the contract existing between the pupil's parents and the school[3]. In general, the courts will be reluctant in exclusion cases founded on contract to grant the remedy of specific performance to force one body of persons into daily contact with another against the will of the parties[4].

1   As to the meaning of 'independent school' see PARA 369. It seems that this is likely to be equally relevant for academies as to which see PARA 345 et seq, in particular PARA 363.
2   See *Gray v Marlborough College* [2006] EWCA Civ 1262, [2006] ELR 516, [2006] All ER (D) 145 (Sep). Judicial review may apply to an exclusion consequential to the termination of an assisted place: *R v Cobham Hall School, ex p S* [1998] ELR 389, [1998] Ed CR 79. However, the significance of this exception is now limited as the assisted places scheme has been repealed and continues to operate only in relation to pupils who were already assisted before the 1997–1998 school year: see the Education (Schools) Act 1997. As to judicial review see JUDICIAL REVIEW vol 61 (2010) PARA 601 et seq. As to exclusions generally see PARA 517 et seq. As to permanent exclusion from a maintained school see PARA 531.
3   *R v Fernhill Manor School, ex p A* [1993] 1 FLR 620, [1994] ELR 67; *Gray v Marlborough College* [2006] EWCA Civ 1262, [2006] ELR 516, [2006] All ER (D) 145 (Sep). See also *Price v Wilkins* (1888) 58 LT 680; *Mount v Oldham Corpn* [1973] QB 309, [1973] 1 All ER 26, CA; *Price v Dennis* (1988) [1999] Ed CR 747, CA. See also, in relation to non-maintained schools, *R v Muntham House School, ex p R* [2000] LGR 255, [2000] ELR 287. It is possible that the pupil has his own right in contract against an independent school under the Contracts (Rights of Third Parties) Act 1999: see CONTRACT.
4   *R v Incorporated Froebel Institute, ex p L* [1999] ELR 488. As to specific performance generally see SPECIFIC PERFORMANCE vol 95 (2013) PARA 301 et seq.

(7) HOME SCHOOLING

426. Elective home education or home schooling. Home schooling is permissible provided that the parent[1] involved complies with the requirement in the Education Act 1996[2] that every child[3] of compulsory school age[4] receives efficient and suitable full-time education[5]. Obviously the school and the local authority[6] should be informed if a parent is taking the child out of school.

It should be noted that local authorities have a statutory duty to make arrangements to enable them to establish as far as it is possible the identities of children in their area who are of compulsory age but are not registered pupils at a school, and are not receiving suitable education otherwise than at a school; there is guidance available which makes it clear that this duty does not apply to children who are being educated at home[7].

The local authority has duties under the provisions on pupil referral units which potentially apply to children educated at home[8]. Local authorities also have general duties to make arrangements for ensuring that their education functions are exercised with a view to safeguarding and promoting the welfare of children[9].

As with free schools[10], by implication from the above, children educated at home should have a 'suitable' curriculum but it seems they are obliged to follow the National Curriculum[11].

The Department for Education has appropriate guidance on 'elective home education' and the legal position, roles and responsibilities of local authorities and parents towards children educated at home and relevant funding information for local authorities[12].

1 As to the meaning of 'parent' see PARA 7 note 3.

2 Ie the Education Act 1996 s 7.

3 As to the meaning of 'child' see PARA 7 note 6.

4 As to the meaning of 'compulsory school age' see PARA 19.

5 See PARAS 19, 435. As to the meaning of 'appropriate full-time education or training' in the context of the Education and Skills Act 2008 see s 4; and PARA 726. See also PARA 439 et seq as to school attendance or alternatives. It should be noted in particular that 'efficient' is not defined as such although there are suggestions in case law. The local authority can make an 'informal inquiry' if a parent is educating a child at home, to ensure that the child is receiving a suitable education, if not the authority has power to serve a school attendance order: see the Education Act 1996 s 437(1); and PARA 440. See also ss 444, 444ZA; and PARAS 447, 448. It is to be noted that a child cannot attend school part-time, the requirement being either full-time education at school or being educated at home whilst of compulsory school age.

6 As to local authorities see PARA 25 et seq.

7 See the Education Act 1996 s 436A; and PARA 439. See also the guidance referred to in note 12.

8 See the Education Act 1996 s 19; and PARA 427.

9 See the Education Act 2002 s 175; and PARA 28. As regard to other functions than education see the Children Act 2004 ss 10, 11; and CHILDREN AND YOUNG PERSONS vol 9 (2012) PARA 203. While these powers allow local authorities to insist on seeing children in order to enquire about their welfare where there are grounds for concern (see also the Children Act 1989 ss 17, 47; and CHILDREN AND YOUNG PERSONS vol 9 (2012) PARAS 623, 625–627; vol 10 (2012) PARAS 814–818, 821) it seems that local authorities do not have a general power to see and question children subject to elective home education in order to establish whether they are receiving a suitable education; see also PARA 435 note 12. They can serve school attendance orders however: see note 5.

10 As to free schools see PARA 368.

11 As to the curriculum see PARA 856 et seq.

12 See the Department for Education website; eg 'Elective home education: Guidelines for local authorities' and 'Elective home education: revised funding information for local authorities'.

(8) PUPIL REFERRAL UNITS

427. Provision of education in pupil referral units. Each local authority[1] is under a duty[2] to make arrangements for the provision of suitable education[3] at school[4] or otherwise than at school for those children[5] of compulsory school age who, by reason of illness, exclusion from school or otherwise, may not for any period receive suitable education unless such arrangements are made for them[6]. Any school established[7] in England and maintained by a local authority which is specially organised to provide education for such children[8], and is not a community or foundation school[9], a community or foundation special school[10], or a maintained nursery school[11], is known as a 'pupil referral unit'[12]. Any school established[13] in Wales[14] and maintained by a local authority which is specially organised to provide education for such children[15], and is not a county school[16] or a special school[17], is known as a 'pupil referral unit'[18].

A local authority may secure the provision of boarding accommodation at any pupil referral unit[19]. A local authority may make arrangements for the provision of suitable education otherwise than at school for those young persons who, by reason of illness, exclusion from school or otherwise, may not for any period receive suitable education unless such arrangements are made for them[20].

In determining what arrangements to make[21] in the case of any child or young person, a local authority must have regard to any guidance given from time to time by the Secretary of State or, in relation to Wales, the Welsh Ministers[22].

Any child for whom education is provided otherwise than at school in pursuance of these provisions, and any young person for whom full-time education is so provided, is to be treated for the purposes of the Education Act 1996 as a pupil[23].

1   As to the meaning of 'local authority' see PARA 25.

2   In relation to England, the education to be provided for a child in pursuance of arrangements made by a local authority under the Education Act 1996 s 19(1) must be (1) full-time education (see note 3); or (2) in the case of a child within s 19(3AA) (see below), education on such part-time basis as the authority considers to be in the child's best interests: s 19(3A) ((s 19(3A), (3B) added by the Education and Inspections Act 2006 s 101(1), (2); and the Education Act 1996 s 19(3A) substituted, s 19(3AA) added, by the Children, Schools and Families Act 2010 s 3(1), (3)). A child is within the Education Act 1996 s 19(3AA) if the local authority considers that, for reasons which relate to the physical or mental health of the child, it would not be in the child's best interests for full-time education to be provided for the child: s 19(3AA) (as so added). Regulations may provide that the education to be provided for a child in pursuance of arrangements made by a local authority in England under s 19(1) must be provided from a day that, in relation to the pupil concerned, is determined in accordance with the regulations: s 19(3B) (as so added; and amended by the Children, Schools and Families Act 2010 s 3(1), (4)). As to the meaning of 'England' see PARA 7 note 3. As to the meaning of 'child' see PARA 7 note 6. 'Prescribed' means prescribed by regulations made by the Secretary of State: see s 579(1). As to the regulations made under the Education Act 1996 s 19(3A), (3B) see the Education (Provision of Full-Time Education for Excluded Pupils) (England) Regulations 2007, SI 2007/1870 (amended by SI 2008/532; SI 2010/1172; SI 2012/1033; and SI 2014/3216). As to regulations made under the Education Act 1996 s 19(3B) see the School Discipline (Pupil Exclusions and Reviews) (England) Regulations 2012, SI 2012/1033. As to the Secretary of State see PARA 58.

3   'Suitable education', in relation to a child or young person, means efficient education suitable to his age, ability and aptitude and to any special educational needs he may have (and until a day to be appointed 'suitable full-time education' is to be read accordingly): Education Act 1996 s 19(6) (substituted by the Education and Inspections Act 2006 s 101(1), (3); prospectively amended by the Children, Schools and Families Act 2010 s 25, Sch 4 Pt 1). At the date at which this volume states the law no such day had been appointed. As to the meaning of 'young person' see PARA 7 note 6. As to the meaning of 'special educational needs' see PARAS 943, 989.

4   As to the meaning of 'school' see PARA 91.

5   In relation to England, the Education Act 1996 s 19(1) does not apply in the case of a child who
     will cease to be of compulsory school age within the next six weeks, and does not have any
     relevant examinations to complete: s 19(1A)(a), (b) (s 19(1A) added by the Children, Schools
     and Families Act 2010 s 3(1), (2)). 'Relevant examinations' means any public examinations or
     other assessments for which the child has been entered: Education Act 1996 s 19(1A) (as so
     added). As to the meaning of 'compulsory school age' see PARA 19. The Education Act 1996 s 19
     does not apply in relation to a child who is a resident of an accommodation centre: see the
     Nationality, Immigration and Asylum Act 2002 s 36(5)(c); and IMMIGRATION AND ASYLUM
     vol 57 (2012) PARA 355.
6   Education Act 1996 s 19(1) (amended by the Education Act 1997 ss 47(1), (2), 57(4), Sch 8; and
     SI 2010/1158). See *R v East Sussex County Council, ex p Tandy* [1998] AC 714, [1998]
     2 All ER 769, HL (the question of what is suitable education is to be determined purely with
     reference to educational considerations; but, if there is more than one way of providing suitable
     education, the authority is entitled to have regard to its resources in choosing between the
     different ways of making such provision); *R (on the application of B) v Newham London
     Borough Council* [2001] EWHC Admin 646, [2001] All ER (D) 490 (Jul) (application for
     judicial review refused because it was not shown that the authority had acted in a manifestly
     unreasonable manner).
         In assessing what is reasonably practicable under the Education Act 1996 s 19, the
     unreasonable objections of parents to their child attending a particular school which it is
     reasonably practical for the child to attend must be disregarded: *R (on the application of G) v
     Westminster City Council* [2004] EWCA Civ 45, [2004] 4 All ER 572, [2004] 1 WLR 1113,
     [2004] ELR 135. See also *R (on the application of O) v Hackney London Borough Council*
     [2006] EWHC 3405 (Admin), [2007] ELR 405, [2006] All ER (D) 36 (Dec). If a school is
     unable to prevent a child being subjected to persistent bullying, it may be reasonable for the
     parents to withdraw that child from the school: *R (on the application of G) v Westminster City
     Council* (above) at [49] per Lord Phillips MR.
7   Ie whether before or after the commencement of the Education Act 1996 (ie 1 November 1996:
     see s 583(2)). As to the meaning of 'establish' see PARA 110 note 2.
8   Education Act 1996 s 19(2B)(a) (s 19(2B) added by SI 2007/1507). As from a day to be
     appointed, the words 'such children' are replaced by the words 'children falling within the
     Education Act 1996 s 19(1)': s 19(2B)(a) (as so added; and prospectively amended by the
     Children, Schools and Families Act 2010 s 25, Sch 3 Pt 1 para 1). At the date at which this
     volume states the law no such day had been appointed.
9   As to the meaning of references to a community or foundation school see PARA 106.
10   As to the meaning of references to a community or foundation special school see PARA 106.
11   Education Act 1996 s 19(2B)(b) (as added: see note 8). As to the meaning of 'maintained nursery
     school' see PARA 99 note 4.
12   Education Act 1996 s 19(2B) (as added (see note 8); and amended by virtue of the
     Apprenticeships, Skills, Children and Learning Act 2009 s 249(1); and amended by
     SI 2010/1158). As to the meaning of 'pupil' see PARA 20 note 4.
13   Ie whether before or after the commencement of the Education Act 1996 (ie 1 November 1996:
     see s 583(2)).
14   The Education Act 1996 s 19(2) does not apply in relation to schools in England: s 19(2A)
     (added by SI 2007/1507). As to the meaning of 'Wales' see PARA 7 note 3.
15   Education Act 1996 s 19(2)(a). As from a day to be appointed this refers to children falling
     within s 19(1): s 19(2)(a) (prospectively amended by the Children, Schools and Families
     Act 2010 s 25, Sch 3 Pt 1 para 1). At the date at which this volume states the law no such day
     had been appointed.
16   As to county schools see PARA 106.
17   Education Act 1996 s 19(2)(b). As to the meaning of 'special school' see PARA 1041.
18   Education Act 1996 s 19(2) (amended by SI 2010/1158). A pupil referral unit as defined in
     s 19(2) is a relevant school for the purposes of the Anti-social Behaviour Act 2003 ss 19–21
     (parenting orders and contracts: see CHILDREN AND YOUNG PERSONS vol 10 (2012) PARA 1269
     et seq): see s 24.
19   See the Education Act 1996 s 19(3) (amended by SI 2010/1158).
20   Education Act 1996 s 19(4) (amended by the Education Act 1997 s 47(1), (3), Sch 8; and
     SI 2010/1158).
21   Ie under the Education Act 1996 s 19(1) (see the text to notes 1–6) or s 19(4) (see the text to
     note 20).
22   Education Act 1996 s 19(4A) (added by the Education Act 1997 s 47(1), (4); and amended by
     SI 2010/1158). The functions of the Secretary of State under the Education Act 1996 s 19, so far
     as exercisable in relation to Wales, were transferred to the National Assembly for Wales (see the

National Assembly for Wales (Transfer of Functions) Order 1999, SI 1999/672, art 2, Sch 1) and are now vested in the Welsh Ministers (see the Government of Wales Act 2006 s 162(1), Sch 11 para 30). As to the Welsh Ministers see PARA 59. As to the publication of guidance see the Education Act 1996 s 571; and PARA 60. As to guidance see also PARA 540.

23   Education Act 1996 s 19(5).

428.   Adaptation and modification of enactments in relation to pupil referral units. References in any enactment to the proprietor[1] or governing body[2] of a school[3] must be read, in relation to a pupil referral unit[4], as references to the local authority[5]. Similarly, references in any enactment to the head teacher[6] of a school must be read, in relation to a pupil referral unit, as references to the teacher in charge of the unit, whether known as the head teacher or not[7]. The provisions of the Education Act 1996 relating to charges[8] apply in relation to pupil referral units as if the references to governing bodies were omitted[9].

Regulations[10] may provide for any enactments relating to schools maintained by local authorities, or schools including such schools[11]: (1) to apply in relation to pupil referral units[12]; (2) to apply in relation to such schools and units with such modifications[13] as may be prescribed[14]; or (3) not to apply in relation to such schools and units[15]. Regulations[16] may also: (a) require a local authority in England[17] to obtain the consent of the Secretary of State, in specified circumstances, to the closure of a pupil referral unit[18]; (b) confer a power on the Secretary of State to give directions[19] to a local authority in England about the exercise of its functions[20] relating to the provision of pupil referral units[21], its functions under any enactment applied[22] to pupil referral units[23], and any other function connected with pupil referral units[24]; (c) require a local authority to comply with such directions[25].

The provisions of the Education Act 1996 applying to sex education[26], political indoctrination[27] and the treatment of political issues[28] apply in relation to pupil referral units as they apply in relation to community schools[29]. A pupil referral unit is an educational institution for the purposes of the provisions of the Environmental Protection Act 1990[30] relating to litter[31].

1   As to the meaning of 'proprietor' see PARA 51 note 4.
2   As to the governing bodies of maintained schools in England see PARA 150 et seq; and in Wales see PARA 195.
3   As to the meaning of 'school' see PARA 91.
4   As to the meaning of 'pupil referral unit' see PARA 427.
5   Education Act 1996 Sch 1 para 1 (amended by SI 2010/1158). As to the meaning of 'local authority' see PARA 25.
6   As to the meaning of 'head teacher' see PARA 86 note 4.
7   Education Act 1996 Sch 1 para 2.
8   Ie the Education Act 1996 Pt VI Ch III (ss 449–462): see PARA 334 et seq.
9   Education Act 1996 Sch 1 para 9(1). Section 458(2) (charges for board and lodging: see PARA 341) has effect in relation to a pupil provided with board and lodging at a pupil referral unit where the local authority for his area is of the opinion that for the time being education suitable to his age, ability and aptitude and to any special educational needs he may have cannot otherwise be provided for him: see Sch 1 para 9(2) (amended by SI 2010/1158). As to the meaning of 'pupil' see PARA 20 note 4.
10   'Regulations' means regulations made by the Secretary of State or, in relation to Wales, the Welsh Ministers: see the Education Act 1996 s 579(1). The functions of the Secretary of State under the Education Act 1996 Sch 1, so far as exercisable in relation to Wales, were transferred to the National Assembly for Wales (see the National Assembly for Wales (Transfer of Functions) Order 1999, SI 1999/672, art 2, Sch 1) and are now vested in the Welsh Ministers (see the Government of Wales Act 2006 s 162(1), Sch 11 para 30). As to the Secretary of State see PARA 58. As to the Welsh Ministers see PARA 59. As to the meaning of 'Wales' see PARA 7 note 3.

As to the regulations made under the Education Act 1996 Sch 1 para 3 see the Education (Review of Staffing Structure) (Wales) Regulations 2005, SI 2005/1910 (amended by SI 2009/2708); the Education (Pupil Referral Units) (Application of Enactments) (Wales) Regulations 2007, SI 2007/1069; the Education (Pupil Referral Units) (Management Committees etc) (England) Regulations 2007, SI 2007/2978 (amended by SI 2010/2582 (amended by SI 2011/577); SI 2012/1825; SI 2012/2404; SI 2012/3158; SI 2013/1624; and SI 2014/2677); the Education (Pupil Referral Units) (Application of Enactments) (England) Regulations 2007, SI 2007/2979 (amended by SI 2012/1201; SI 2012/1825; SI 2013/1624; and SI 2014/1609); the School Information (Wales) Regulations 2011, SI 2011/1944 (amended by SI 2013/437); the School Governance (Roles, Procedures and Allowances) (England) Regulations 2013, SI 2013/1624 (amended by SI 2013/2688; SI 2014/1257; and SI 2014/1959); the Academy Conversions (Transfer of School Surpluses) Regulations 2013, SI 2013/3037; the Education (School Development Plans) (Wales) Regulations 2014, SI 2014/2677; and the Education (Pupil Referral Units) (Management Committees etc) (Wales) Regulations 2014, SI 2014/2709.

11 Education Act 1996 Sch 1 para 3 (amended by SI 2010/1158).

12 Education Act 1996 Sch 1 para 3(a).

13 As to the meaning of 'modifications' see PARA 21 note 15.

14 Education Act 1996 Sch 1 para 3(b). 'Prescribed' means prescribed by regulations: s 579(1).

15 Education Act 1996 Sch 1 para 3(c).

16 As to the regulations made see the Education (Pupil Referral Units) (Closure) (England) Regulations 2010, SI 2010/1071 (amended by SI 2010/1920; and SI 2012/1825).

17 As to the meaning of 'England' see PARA 7 note 3.

18 Education Act 1996 Sch 1 para 3A(a) (Sch 1 para 3A added by the Apprenticeships, Skills, Children and Learning Act 2009 s 249(3); and amended by SI 2010/1158, and SI 2010/1891; and the Education Act 1996 Sch 1 para 3A(a) further amended by the Education Act 2011 s 51(4)(a)).

19 As to directions see the Education Act 1996 s 570; and PARA 75.

20 Ie its functions under the Education Act 1996 s 19: see PARA 427. As to the meaning of 'functions' see PARA 18 note 5.

21 Education Act 1996 Sch 1 para 3A(b)(i) (as added and amended: see note 18).

22 Ie with or without modifications by regulations under the Education Act 1996 Sch 1 para 3: see the text to notes 10–15.

23 Education Act 1996 Sch 1 para 3A(b)(ii) (as added and amended (see note 18); and further amended by the Education Act 2011 s 51(4)(b)).

24 Education Act 1996 Sch 1 para 3A(b)(iii) (as added and amended (see note 18) ; and further amended by the Education Act 2011 s 51(4)(b)).

25 Education Act 1996 Sch 1 para 3A(c) (as added and amended: see note 18).

26 Ie the Education Act 1996 s 403: see PARA 905.

27 Ie the Education Act 1996 s 406: see PARA 908.

28 Ie the Education Act 1996 s 407: see PARA 909.

29 Education Act 1996 Sch 1 para 8 (amended by the Learning and Skills Act 2000 s 149, Sch 9 paras 1, 64).

30 Ie the Environmental Protection Act 1990 Pt IV (ss 86–99): see ENVIRONMENTAL QUALITY AND PUBLIC HEALTH vol 46 (2010) PARA 721 et seq.

31 Education Act 1996 Sch 1 para 10.

429. Registration. A person who is registered[1] as a pupil[2] at a school[3] other than a pupil referral unit[4] does not, by reason only of being registered also as a pupil at such a unit, cease for the purposes of the Education Acts[5] to be treated as a registered pupil[6] at that school[7].

1 In the Education Act 1996 Sch 1, 'registered' means shown in the register kept under s 434 (see PARA 437): Sch 1 para 4(2).

2 As to the meaning of 'pupil' see PARA 20 note 4.

3 As to the meaning of 'school' see PARA 91.

4 As to the meaning of 'pupil referral unit' see PARA 427.

5 As to the meaning of 'the Education Acts' see PARA 1 note 13.

6 As to the meaning of 'registered pupil' see PARA 437.

7 Education Act 1996 Sch 1 para 4(1).

430. Curriculum. In relation to every pupil referral unit[1], the local authority[2], the management committee[3] (where applicable) and the teacher in charge must exercise their functions[4] with a view to securing that the curriculum for the unit satisfies the requirements[5] for securing a balanced and broadly based curriculum[6]. Regulations[7] may make provision for the determination and organisation of the curriculum in relation to every pupil referral unit, including provision as to making, and keeping up to date, a written[8] statement of the policy in relation to that curriculum for the unit[9]. Such regulations may require the local authority, the management committee (where applicable) or the teacher in charge to exercise[10], or such of them as may be prescribed[11] to collaborate with each other in exercising[12], such functions in relation to the curriculum as may be prescribed[13].

Partly until a day to be appointed[14] each local authority in Wales must make arrangements for the consideration and disposal of any complaint to the effect that the authority, or the teacher in charge of any pupil referral unit[15]: (1) has acted or is proposing to act unreasonably with respect to the exercise of any power conferred, or the performance of any duty imposed, on it or him by the provisions described above[16]; or (2) has failed to discharge any such duty[17].

1   As to the meaning of 'pupil referral unit' see PARA 427.
2   As to the meaning of 'local authority' see PARA 25.
3   As to management committees see PARA 434.
4   As to the meaning of 'functions' see PARA 18 note 5.
5   Ie the requirements of the Education Act 2002 s 78(1) (general duties in respect of the curriculum for England: see PARA 856) and s 99(1) (general duties in respect of the curriculum for Wales: see PARA 870).
6   Education Act 1996 Sch 1 para 6(1) (substituted by the School Standards and Framework Act 1998 s 140(1), Sch 30 para 184(a)(i); and amended by SI 2002/2953, SI 2002/3184, SI 2010/1158).
7   'Regulations' means regulations made by the Secretary of State or, in relation to Wales, the Welsh Ministers: see the Education Act 1996 s 579(1). As to the regulations made see the Education (Pupil Referral Units) (Management Committees etc) (England) Regulations 2007, SI 2007/2978 (amended by SI 2010/2582 (amended by SI 2011/577); SI 2012/1825; SI 2012/2404; SI 2012/3158; and SI 2013/1624); and the Education (Pupil Referral Units) (Management Committees etc) (Wales) Regulations 2014, SI 2014/2709. The functions of the Secretary of State under the Education Act 1996 Sch 1, so far as exercisable in relation to Wales, were transferred to the National Assembly for Wales (see the National Assembly for Wales (Transfer of Functions) Order 1999, SI 1999/672, art 2, Sch 1) and are now vested in the Welsh Ministers (see the Government of Wales Act 2006 s 162(1), Sch 11 para 30). As to the Secretary of State see PARA 58. As to the Welsh Ministers see PARA 59. As to the meaning of 'Wales' see PARA 7 note 3.
8   As to the meaning of 'written' see PARA 76 note 8.
9   Education Act 1996 Sch 1 para 6(2) (substituted by the School Standards and Framework Act 1998 s 140(1), Sch 30 para 184(a)(i)).
10   Education Act 1996 Sch 1 para 6(2)(a) (as substituted (see note 9); and amended by SI 2010/1158).
11   'Prescribed' means prescribed by regulations: Education Act 1996 s 579(1).
12   Education Act 1996 Sch 1 para 6(2)(b) (as substituted: see note 9).
13   Education Act 1996 Sch 1 para 6(2) (as substituted: see note 9).
14   The Education Act 1996 Sch 1 para 6(3), (4) is repealed, as from a day to be appointed, by the Apprenticeships, Skills, Children and Learning Act 2009 ss 223(1)(c), 266, Sch 16 Pt 7: see s 269(4). At the date at which this volume states the law this repeal is in force only for the purposes of complaints against schools maintained by specified councils: see the Apprenticeships, Skills, Children and Learning Act 2009 (Commencement No 2 and Transitional and Saving Provisions) Order 2010, SI 2010/303, art 5, Sch 4; Apprenticeships, Skills, Children and Learning Act 2009 (Commencement No 3 and Transitional and Transitory Provisions) and (Commencement No 2 (Amendment)) Order 2010, SI 2010/1151, art 4, Sch 2. At the date at which this volume states the law no day had been appointed for bringing the repeal into force for the remaining purposes.

15 Education Act 1996 Sch 1 para 6(3) (amended by SI 2008/2840; SI 2010/1158; and the Education Act 2011 s 45(20(d)(i)).
16 Education Act 1996 Sch 1 para 6(3)(a) (amended by the School Standards and Framework Act 1998 Sch 30 para 184(a)(ii)). The provisions referred to are those of the Education Act 1996 Sch 1 para 6(1), (2): see the text to notes 1–13.
17 Education Act 1996 Sch 1 para 6(3)(b). The Welsh Ministers must not entertain under the School Standards and Organisation (Wales) Act 2013 Pt 2 Ch 2 (ss 21–31) (intervention in local authorities: see PARA 1235 et seq) any complaint in respect of any local authority in Wales if it is a complaint (Education Act 1996 Sch 1 para 6(4) (amended by the Education Act 2011 s 45(2)(d)(ii); and the School Standards and Organisation (Wales) Act 2013 Sch 5 para 2(1), (8)):
    (1)   for which arrangements are required to be made under the Education Act 1996 Sch 1 para 6(3) (Sch 1 para 6(4)(a)); or
    (2)   that a local authority in Wales has failed to exercise its powers to secure compliance by the teacher in charge of a pupil referral unit in Wales with any such duty as is referred to in Sch 1 para 6(3) (Sch 1 para 6(4)(b) (amended by SI 2010/1158; and the Education Act 2011 s 4(2)(d)(ii))),
unless a complaint in respect of the local authority or, as the case may be, the teacher in charge of the school or unit has been made in respect of the same matter and disposed of in accordance with arrangements under the Education Act 1996 Sch 1 para 6(3): Sch 1 para 6(4) (amended by SI 2010/1158).

431. Discipline. The teacher in charge of a pupil referral unit[1] may exclude a pupil from the unit for a fixed period or permanently[2].

1   As to the meaning of 'pupil referral unit' see PARA 427.
2   See the Education Act 2002 ss 51A, 52(2); and PARA 517. Guidance on exclusions (see PARAS 517, 540) also applies to exclusions from pupil referral units: see PARAS 519, 529, 533.

432. Information. Each local authority[1] must, on such occasions[2], and in such form and manner[3], as may be prescribed[4], make available to registered[5] parents[6] of registered pupils[7] at any pupil referral unit[8] such information about the unit as may be prescribed[9].

1   As to the meaning of 'local authority' see PARA 25.
2   Education Act 1996 Sch 1 para 11(a).
3   Education Act 1996 Sch 1 para 11(b).
4   'Prescribed' means prescribed by regulations; and 'regulations' means regulations made by the Secretary of State or, in relation to Wales, the Welsh Ministers: see the Education Act 1996 s 579(1). At the date at which this volume states the law no such regulations had been made under Sch 1 para 11. The functions of the Secretary of State under the Education Act 1996 Sch 1, so far as exercisable in relation to Wales, were transferred to the National Assembly for Wales (see the National Assembly for Wales (Transfer of Functions) Order 1999, SI 1999/672, art 2, Sch 1) and are now vested in the Welsh Ministers (see the Government of Wales Act 2006 s 162(1), Sch 11 para 30). As to the Secretary of State see PARA 58. As to the Welsh Ministers see PARA 59. As to the meaning of 'Wales' see PARA 7 note 3.
5   As to the meaning of 'registered' see PARA 429 note 1.
6   As to the meaning of 'parent' see PARA 7 note 6.
7   As to the meaning of 'pupil' see PARA 20 note 4.
8   As to the meaning of 'pupil referral unit' see PARA 427.
9   Education Act 1996 Sch 1 para 11 (amended by SI 2010/1158). See also note 4.

433. School attendance orders. Where a pupil referral unit[1] is named in a school attendance order[2]:
    (1)   the local authority[3] must inform the teacher in charge of the unit[4]; and
    (2)   if another local authority is responsible for determining the arrangements for the admission of pupils[5] to the pupil referral unit, that authority must admit the child[6] to the unit[7].
However, head (2) above does not affect any power to exclude from a pupil referral unit a pupil who is already a registered[8] pupil there[9]. A local authority

must, before deciding to specify a particular pupil referral unit in a notice[10] where another local authority is responsible for determining the arrangements for the admission of pupils to the unit, consult that authority[11]; and if it decides to specify the unit in the notice, must serve notice in writing[12] of its decision on that authority[13].

The parent[14] of a child in respect of whom a school attendance order is in force may not request[15] the local authority to amend the order by substituting a pupil referral unit for the school[16] named in the order[17].

1　As to the meaning of 'pupil referral unit' see PARA 427.
2　As to the meaning of 'school attendance order' see PARA 440. The Education Act 1996 s 438(4) (see PARA 441) does not apply in relation to a pupil referral unit: Sch 1 para 14(2).
3　As to the meaning of 'local authority' see PARA 25.
4　Education Act 1996 Sch 1 para 14(1)(a) (amended by SI 2010/1158).
5　As to the meaning of 'pupil' see PARA 20 note 4.
6　As to the meaning of 'child' see PARA 7 note 6.
7　Education Act 1996 Sch 1 para 14(1)(b) (amended by SI 2010/1158).
8　As to the meaning of 'registered' see PARA 429 note 1.
9　Education Act 1996 Sch 1 para 14(1). See also PARA 431 note 2.
10　Ie in a notice under the Education Act 1996 s 438(2): see PARA 441.
11　Education Act 1996 Sch 1 para 14(3)(a) (amended by SI 2010/1158). As to the exercise of the duty to consult see JUDICIAL REVIEW vol 61 (2010) PARA 627.
12　As to the meaning of 'writing' see PARA 76 note 8. As to the service of notices and documents see the Education Act 1996 s 572; and PARA 76.
13　Education Act 1996 Sch 1 para 14(3)(b). The provisions of s 439(7), (8) (see PARA 442) apply where a notice is served on a local authority under Sch 1 para 14(3) as they apply where notice is served under s 439(6): Sch 1 para 14(4) (amended by SI 2010/1158).
14　As to the meaning of 'parent' see PARA 7 note 6.
15　Ie under the Education Act 1996 s 440: see PARA 443.
16　As to the meaning of 'school' see PARA 91.
17　Education Act 1996 Sch 1 para 14(5) (amended by SI 2010/1158). Where a child is a registered pupil at both a pupil referral unit and at a school other than a pupil referral unit, the references in the Education Act 1996 s 444 (see PARA 447) to the school at which he is a registered pupil must be read as references to the pupil referral unit: Sch 1 para 14(6).

434.　Management committees. Regulations[1] may make provision for requiring any local authority[2] which maintains a pupil referral unit[3] to establish a committee to act as the management committee for the unit[4], and for that committee to discharge on behalf of the authority such of its functions[5] in connection with the unit as are delegated by it to the committee in accordance with the regulations[6]. Such regulations may in particular make provision:

(1)　for enabling a local authority to establish a joint committee to act as the management committee for two or more pupil referral units maintained by the authority[7];

(2)　for requiring the approval of the Secretary of State or, in relation to Wales, the Welsh Ministers to be obtained before any such joint committee is established[8];

(3)　as to the composition of a management committee established under the regulations, the appointment and removal of its members and their terms of office, and in particular for requiring such a committee to include persons representing schools[9] situated in the area from which the pupil referral unit or units, in question may be expected to draw pupils[10];

(4)　for requiring or, as the case may be, prohibiting the delegation[11] to a management committee of such functions in connection with pupil referral units as are specified in the regulations[12];

(5)   for authorising a management committee to establish sub-committees[13];

(6)   for enabling, subject to any provisions of the regulations, the determination[14] of a management committee's procedure and that of any sub-committee[15];

(7)   for limiting the personal liability of members of any such committee or sub-committee in respect of their acts or omissions as such members[16];

(8)   about the effect of closure of a pupil referral unit on members of the management committee for the unit or members of any sub-committee[17];

(9)   for applying to any such committee or sub-committee, with or without modification[18], any provision of the Education Acts[19], or any provision made by or under any other enactment and relating to committees or (as the case may be) sub-committees of a local authority[20].

1   'Regulations' means regulations made by the Secretary of State or, in relation to Wales, the Welsh Ministers: see the Education Act 1996 s 579(1). The functions of the Secretary of State under the Education Act 1996 Sch 1, so far as exercisable in relation to Wales, were transferred to the National Assembly for Wales (see the National Assembly for Wales (Transfer of Functions) Order 1999, SI 1999/672, art 2, Sch 1) and are now vested in the Welsh Ministers (see the Government of Wales Act 2006 s 162(1), Sch 11 para 30). As to the Secretary of State see PARA 58. As to the Welsh Ministers see PARA 59. As to the meaning of 'Wales' see PARA 7 note 3.
       As to the regulations made under the Education Act 1996 Sch 1 para 15 see the Education (Pupil Referral Units) (Management Committees etc) (England) Regulations 2007, SI 2007/2978 (amended by SI 2010/2582 (amended by SI 2011/577); SI 2012/1825; SI 2012/2404; SI 2012/3158; and SI 2013/1624); the Education (Pupil Referral Units) (Application of Enactments) (England) Regulations 2007, SI 2007/2979 (amended by SI 2012/1201; SI 2012/1825); the Education (Miscellaneous Amendments relating to Safeguarding Children) (England) Regulations 2009, SI 2009/1924 (amended by SI 2012/1153); and the Education (Pupil Referral Units) (Management Committees etc) (Wales) Regulations 2014, SI 2014/2709.
2   As to the meaning of 'local authority' see PARA 25.
3   As to the meaning of 'pupil referral unit' see PARA 427.
4   Education Act 1996 Sch 1 para 15(1)(a) (Sch 1 para 15 added by the Education Act 1997 s 48; and the Education Act 1996 Sch 1 para 15(1)(a) amended by SI 2010/1158).
5   As to the meaning of 'functions' see PARA 18 note 5.
6   Education Act 1996 Sch 1 para 15(1)(b) (as added: see note 4).
7   Education Act 1996 Sch 1 para 15(2)(a) (as added (see note 4); and amended by SI 2010/1158).
8   Education Act 1996 Sch 1 para 15(2)(b) (as added: see note 4).
9   As to the meaning of 'school' see PARA 91.
10   Education Act 1996 Sch 1 para 15(2)(c) (as added (see note 4); and amended by the School Standards and Framework Act 1998 s 140(1), (3), Sch 30 para 184(c), Sch 31). As to the meaning of 'pupil' see PARA 20 note 4.
11   Ie delegation by a local authority or, in the case of a local authority which is operating executive arrangements, by the executive of that authority or any person on behalf of that executive: Education Act 1996 Sch 1 para 15(2)(d) (Sch 1 para 15 as added (see note 4); Sch 1 para 15(2)(d) substituted by SI 2001/2237, SI 2002/808; and amended by SI 2010/1158). For the purposes of the Education Act 1996 Sch 1 para 15(2), 'executive' and 'executive arrangements' have the same meanings as in the Local Government Act 2000 (see LOCAL GOVERNMENT vol 69 (2009) PARAS 303, 327): Education Act 1996 Sch 1 para 15(3) (Sch 1 para 15 as so added; Sch 1 para 15(3) added by SI 2001/2237; and SI 2002/808).
12   Education Act 1996 Sch 1 para 15(2)(d) (as added and substituted: see note 11).
13   Education Act 1996 Sch 1 para 15(2)(e) (as added: see note 4).
14   Ie by: (1) a local authority; (2) in the case of a local authority which is operating executive arrangements, the executive of that authority or any person acting on behalf of that executive; or (3) a management committee: Education Act 1996 Sch 1 para 15(2)(f) (Sch 1 para 15 as added (see note 4); and Sch 1 para 15(2)(f) amended by SI 2001/2237, SI 2002/808; SI 2010/1158).
15   Education Act 1996 Sch 1 para 15(2)(f) (as added and amended: see note 14).
16   Education Act 1996 Sch 1 para 15(2)(g) (as added: see note 4).

17 Education Act 1996 Sch 1 para 15(2)(ga) (added by the Education Act 2011 Sch 13 para 9(1), (19)).
18 As to the meaning of 'modification' see PARA 21 note 15.
19 Education Act 1996 Sch 1 para 15(2)(h)(i) (as added: see note 4). As to the meaning of 'the Education Acts' see PARA 1 note 13.
20 Education Act 1996 Sch 1 para 15(2)(h)(ii) (as added: see note 4).

(9) REGISTRATION AND SCHOOL ATTENDANCE

(i) Duty of Parent to Secure Child's Education

435. Duty of parents to secure education of children of compulsory school age. The parent[1] of every child[2] of compulsory school age[3] must cause him to receive efficient full-time education[4] suitable to his age, ability and aptitude[5], and to any special educational needs[6] he may have[7], either by regular attendance[8] at school[9] or otherwise[10]. This duty may be enforced against the parents of a child who has failed to attend regularly at school[11] but, since the duty is to ensure that the child receives efficient full-time education and not that the child attends school, parents may comply with it by providing education at home[12].

A parent is not under a duty to cause a child to receive full-time education during any period during which[13] it is not practicable for the parent to arrange for him to be admitted as a pupil at a school[14].

1 As to the meaning of 'parent' see PARA 7 note 6. As to the requirement that children be educated in accordance with the wishes of their parents see the Education Act 1996 s 9; and PARA 7. Where an education supervision order is in force under the Children Act 1989 with respect to a child, the duty of the child's parents under the Education Act 1996 s 7 is superseded by their duty to comply with any directions in force under the education supervision order: see the Children Act 1989 Sch 3 Pt III para 13(1); and PARA 453. As to the duty of local authorities to make arrangements to identify children not receiving education see the Education Act 1996 s 436A; and PARA 439.
2 As to the meaning of 'child' see PARA 7 note 6.
3 As to the meaning of 'compulsory school age' see PARA 19.
4 'Efficient' and 'full-time' are not defined for these purposes. In *Baker v Earl* [1960] Crim LR 363, QBD, a lack of structured lessons or prescribed course of study had failed to satisfy the requirements for efficient full-time education. In *Bevan v Shears* [1911] 2 KB 936 at 939, 75 JP 478 at 479 per Lord Alverstone CJ it was held (in the context of previous legislation) that 'in the absence of anything in the bylaws providing that a child of a given age shall receive instruction in given subjects, in my view it cannot be said that as to a particular child there is a standard of education by which the child must be taught ... Therefore, the justices have to decide whether in their opinion the child is being taught efficiently so far as that particular child is concerned'. Justices have jurisdiction to decide that the education which a child was receiving was efficient, without deciding that it was as efficient as he would have received at a public elementary school: see *Bevan v Shears* above. See also *R v Walton Justices, ex p Dutton* (1911) 75 JP 558, 9 LGR 1231 (admissibility of evidence as to the state of a child's education); *R v West Riding of Yorkshire Justices, ex p Broadbent* [1910] 2 KB 192, sub nom *R v Morris, ex p Broadbent* (1910) 74 JP 271, 8 LGR 777 (decided under previous legislation; efficiency of alternative education). The question of what constitutes efficient education is for the local authority to decide and is a matter of opinion and degree: *R v East Sussex County Council, ex p Tandy* [1998] AC 714, [1998] 2 All ER 769, HL (decided under previous legislation).
   As to 'suitable full-time education' for an excluded pupil: see e g the Education (Provision of Full-Time Education for Excluded Pupils) (England) Regulations 2007, SI 2007/1870; and PARAS 522, 528, 729.
5 Education Act 1996 s 7(a).
6 As to the meaning of 'special educational needs' see PARAS 943, 989.
7 Education Act 1996 s 7(b).
8 'Regular' attendance is not defined for these purposes. See *Hinchley v Rankin* [1961] 1 All ER 692, [1961] 1 WLR 421 (decided under previous legislation; absence at the time when the attendance register closed was a failure in regular attendance); *Spiers v Warrington Corpn*

[1954] 1 QB 61, [1953] 2 All ER 1052, DC (decided under previous legislation; a parent failed in his duty to secure the regular attendance at school of his daughter because she was wearing trousers and the parent knew that the head teacher would not admit her).

9 As to the meaning of 'school' see PARA 91.

10 Education Act 1996 s 7. As to the provisions with regard to the duration of the school day and school year and the granting of leave of absence from school see PARA 459. A local authority may be entitled to inspect the home of a child who receives education otherwise than by regular attendance at school: *R v Surrey Quarter Sessions Appeals Committee, ex p Tweedie* (1963) 61 LGR 464, [1963] Crim LR 639 (decided under previous legislation).

11 See the Education Act 1996 s 444 (failure to secure regular attendance at school of registered pupil); and PARA 447. See also the Anti-social Behaviour Act 2003 s 19 (parenting contracts where a child has failed to attend regularly at school); and PARA 450.

12 The powers of local authorities in relation to school attendance orders apply where a local authority determines that a child of compulsory school age is not receiving suitable education either by regular attendance at school or otherwise, and therefore these powers apply in relation to children receiving home education: see the Education Act 1996 s 437; and PARA 440 et seq. In *Osborne v Martin* (1927) 25 LGR 532, (1927) 91 JP 197, DC, Salter J (at 535, 198) held that a parent is not obliged to avail himself of the free education provided by the state but that if he does so while preferring to provide privately for his child's education, he must take it as a whole. Parents educating children at home are under no obligation to provide local authorities with information about the child's teaching, even where the local authorities have asked for it: *Phillips v Brown* (20 June 1980, unreported). There are, however, instances when local authorities may inspect education being provided at home (*R v Surrey Quarter Sessions Appeals Committee, ex p Tweedie* (1963) 61 LGR 464, [1963] Crim LR 639), and interview and test the child (*R v Gwent County Council, ex p Perry* (1985) 129 Sol Jo 737, [1985] LS Gaz R 3356, CA). It has been held by the European Court of Human Rights that parents may be required to co-operate in the assessment of the child: see *H v United Kingdom* 38 DR 105 (1984), EComHR. See also *R v East Sussex County Council, ex p Tandy* [1998] AC 714, [1998] 2 All ER 769, HL. As to home schooling generally see PARA 426.

13 Ie having regard to it not having been reasonably practicable for the parent to arrange for him to be admitted as a pupil at the beginning of the school term by reason of him being ill or by other reason beyond his parent's control, or by his parent's having been resident at a place from which the school was not accessible with reasonable facility: see the Education Act 1996 s 433(1), (2); and PARA 224. As to the meaning of 'pupil' see PARA 20 note 4.

14 Education Act 1996 s 433(5).

436. Persons not covered by the Education Act 1996. No power or duty conferred or imposed by the Education Act 1996 on parents[1] is to be construed as relating to any person who is employed by or under the Crown in any service or capacity with respect to which the Secretary of State[2] or, in relation to Wales, the Welsh Ministers[3] certifies that, by reason of the arrangements made for the education of children[4] and young persons[5] so employed, the exercise and performance of those powers and duties with respect to such children and young persons is unnecessary[6].

No power or duty conferred or imposed by or under the Education Act 1996 on parents[7] is to be construed as relating to any person who is subject to a detention order[8] and is detained in accommodation that is not relevant youth accommodation[9], but a local authority may make arrangements for such a person to receive the benefit of educational facilities provided by the authority[10].

These provisions are applied for the purposes of the School Standards and Framework Act 1998[11] and, with certain exceptions, for the purposes of the Education Act 2002[12], the Education Act 2005[13], the Education and Inspections Act 2006[14], the Education and Skills Act 2008[15] and the Apprenticeships, Skills, Children and Learning Act 2009[16].

1 See the Education Act 1996 s 561(c). As to the meaning of 'parent' see PARA 7 note 6.

2 As to the Secretary of State see PARA 58.

3 The functions of the Secretary of State under the Education Act 1996 s 561, so far as exercisable in relation to Wales, were transferred to the National Assembly for Wales (see the National

Assembly for Wales (Transfer of Functions) Order 1999, SI 1999/672, art 2, Sch 1) and are now vested in the Welsh Ministers (see the Government of Wales Act 2006 s 162(1), Sch 11 para 30). As to the Welsh Ministers see PARA 59. As to the meaning of 'Wales' see PARA 7 note 3.

4   As to the meaning of 'child' see PARA 7 note 6.
5   As to the meaning of 'young person' see PARA 7 note 6.
6   Education Act 1996 s 561.
7   See the Education Act 1996 s 562(1)(c).
8   As to when a person is subject to a detention order see PARA 46 note 8.
9   As to the meaning of 'relevant youth accommodation' see PARA 46 note 9.
10 Education Act 1996 s 562(1) (amended by the Apprenticeships, Skills, Children and Learning Act 2009 s 49; and SI 2010/1158). At the date at which this volume states the law the amendments to the Education Act 1996 s 562(1) made by the Apprenticeships, Skills, Children and Learning Act 2009 s 49 are in force in relation to England and Wales and in relation only to persons who are detained in relevant youth accommodation (see note 9) by virtue of being detained in a relevant young offender institution: see the Apprenticeships, Skills, Children and Learning Act 2009 (Commencement No 2 and Transitional and Saving Provisions) Order 2010, SI 2010/303, art 6, Sch 5; and the Apprenticeships, Skills, Children and Learning Act 2009 (Commencement No 3) (Wales) Order 2011, SI 2011/829, art 2(a). The amendments so made will come into force in relation to England and Wales for remaining purposes on a day to be appointed: see the Apprenticeships, Skills, Children and Learning Act 2009 s 269(3)(f), (4). At the date at which this volume states the law no such day had been appointed. As to the meaning of 'relevant youth offender institution' see PARA 38 note 2. As to the meaning of 'England' see PARA 7 note 3.

Until a day to be appointed the following provisions have effect in relation to England and Wales for those purposes for which the amendments to the Education Act 1996 s 562(1) made by the Apprenticeships, Skills, Children and Learning Act 2009 s 49 are not yet in force: No power or duty conferred or imposed by or under the Education Act 1996 on parents is to be construed as relating to any person who is detained in pursuance of an order made by a court or of an order of recall made by the Secretary of State, but a local authority may make arrangements for a person who is detained in pursuance of such an order to receive the benefit of educational facilities provided by the authority: Education Act 1996 s 1996 s 562(1) (as originally enacted; and amended by SI 2010/1158).
11 See the School Standards and Framework Act 1998 s 142(8).
12 See the Education Act 2002 s 212(2), (3).
13 See the Education Act 2005 s 122(2), (3). As from a day to be appointed, s 122(3)(c) is omitted by the Deregulation Act 2015 s 66(3). At the date at which this volume states the law no such day had been appointed.
14 See the Education and Inspections Act 2006 s 187(2), (3).
15 See the Education and Skills Act 2008 s 168(2), (3), (5).
16 See the Apprenticeships, Skills, Children and Learning Act 2009 s 264(2)–(4).

(ii)   Registration of Pupils

437.   Registration of pupils. The proprietor[1] of a school[2] must cause to be kept, in accordance with regulations[3], a register containing the prescribed[4] particulars in respect of all persons who are pupils[5] at the school[6]. The prescribed particulars must include details of the name and address of every person known to the proprietor to be a parent[7] of a pupil at the school[8]. 'Registered pupil', in relation to a school, means a person registered as a pupil at the school in such a register, and 'registered', in relation to the parents of pupils at a school or in relation to the names or addresses of such parents or pupils, means shown in that register[9].

The regulations must prescribe the grounds on which names are to be deleted from such a register[10], and the name of a person entered in such a register as a pupil at a school must, when any of the prescribed grounds is applicable, be deleted from the register on that ground[11], and must not be deleted from the register otherwise than on any such ground[12]. The regulations may make provision for:

(1)   enabling such registers to be inspected[13];

(2)   enabling extracts from such registers to be taken, for the purposes of the Education Act 1996, by persons[14] authorised to do so under the regulations[15]; and

(3)   requiring the person by whom any such register is required to be kept to make to the Secretary of State or, in relation to Wales, the Welsh Ministers, and local authorities[16] such periodical or other returns as to the contents of the register as may be prescribed[17].

A person who contravenes or fails to comply with any requirement imposed on him by such regulations is guilty of an offence[18].

1   As to the meaning of 'proprietor' see PARA 51 note 4.

2   As to the meaning of 'school' see PARA 91.

3   'Regulations' means regulations made by the Secretary of State or, in relation to Wales, the Welsh Ministers: see the Education Act 1996 s 579(1). As to the Secretary of State see PARA 58. The functions of the Secretary of State under the Education Act 1996 s 434, so far as exercisable in relation to Wales, were transferred to the National Assembly for Wales (see the National Assembly for Wales (Transfer of Functions) Order 1999, SI 1999/672, art 2, Sch 1) and are now vested in the Welsh Ministers (see the Government of Wales Act 2006 s 162(1), Sch 11 para 30). As to the Welsh Ministers see PARA 59. As to the meaning of 'Wales' see PARA 7 note 3.

    As to the regulations made under the Education Act 1996 s 434 see the Education (Pupil Registration) (England) Regulations 2006, SI 2006/1751 (amended by SI 2011/1625; SI 2012/1033; and SI 2013/756); and the Education (Pupil Registration) (Wales) Regulations 2010, SI 2010/1954.

4   'Prescribed' means prescribed by regulations: Education Act 1996 s 579(1).

5   As to the meaning of 'pupil' see PARA 20 note 4.

6   Education Act 1996 s 434(1).

7   As to the meaning of 'parent' see PARA 7 note 6.

8   Education Act 1996 s 434(2).

9   Education Act 1996 s 434(5).

10 The decision to remove a child from the register does not engage the right to a fair hearing under the Convention for the Protection of Human Rights and Fundamental Freedoms (Rome, 4 November 1950; TS 71 (1953); Cmd 8969) art 6 (see RIGHTS AND FREEDOMS vol 88A (2013) PARA 243 et seq) since removal, if well-founded, only precludes a child from being educated at a particular school, rather than denying the right to an education generally: *R (on the application of M-P) v Barking and Dagenham London Borough Council* [2002] EWHC 2483 (Admin), [2003] ELR 144, [2002] All ER (D) 64 (Aug). See also *A v Head Teacher and Governors of Lord Grey School* [2006] UKHL 14, [2006] 2 AC 363, sub nom *Ali v Head Teacher and Governors of Lord Grey School* [2006] 2 All ER 457.

11 Education Act 1996 s 434(3)(a). See *R v Governing Body of Gateway Primary School, ex p X* [2001] ELR 321. See also the Education (Pupil Registration) (England) Regulations 2006, SI 2006/1751, the Education (Pupil Registration) (Wales) Regulations 2010, SI 2010/1954; and note 3.

    Note that according to the Exclusions Guidance 2012 art 81, where a pupil's name is removed from the school register and a discrimination claim is subsequently made, the court has the power to direct that the pupil should be reinstated. As to the Guidance see generally PARA 540 note 13.

12 Education Act 1996 s 434(3)(b).

13 Education Act 1996 s 434(4)(a).

14 As to the meaning of 'person' see PARA 7 note 6.

15 Education Act 1996 s 434(4)(b).

16 As to the meaning of 'local authority' see PARA 25.

17 Education Act 1996 s 434(4)(c) (amended by the School Standards and Framework Act 1998 s 140(1), (3), Sch 30 paras 57, 111, Sch 31; and SI 2010/1158).

18 See the Education Act 1996 s 434(6). The penalty for such an offence is, on summary conviction, a fine not exceeding level 1 on the standard scale: s 434(6). As to the standard scale see SENTENCING AND DISPOSITION OF OFFENDERS vol 92 (2010) PARA 142.

438. Withdrawal of pupils from a primary school for secondary education. A local authority[1] may make arrangements in respect of a primary school[2] maintained by it, other than one that is for the time being organised for the provision of both primary[3] and secondary education[4], under which any registered pupils[5] who are under the age[6] of 12 but have attained the age of ten years and six months may be required to be withdrawn from the school for the purpose of receiving secondary education[7].

1   As to the meaning of 'local authority' see PARA 25. Any function of a local authority in England which is conferred by or under the Education Act 1996 s 435 may be exercised by, or by employees of, such person as may be authorised in that behalf by the local authority whose function it is: Contracting Out (Local Authority Education Functions) (England) Order 2002, SI 2002/928, art 3, Sch 1 para (dd) (art 3 amended by SI 2010/1172). As to the meaning of 'England' see PARA 7 note 3. As to the meaning of 'person' see PARA 7 note 6.
2   As to the meaning of 'primary school' see PARA 91.
3   As to the meaning of 'primary education' see PARA 20.
4   As to the meaning of 'secondary education' see PARA 21.
5   As to the meaning of 'registered pupil' see PARA 437.
6   As to the time at which a person attains a particular age see PARA 7 note 6.
7   Education Act 1996 s 435 (amended by SI 2010/1158).

(iii) School Attendance

439.   Duty to make arrangements to identify children not receiving education. A local authority[1] must make arrangements to enable it to establish (so far as it is possible to do so) the identities of children[2] in its area who are of compulsory school age[3] but are not registered pupils[4] at a school[5], and are not receiving suitable education[6] otherwise than at a school[7]. In exercising these functions[8] a local authority must have regard to any guidance[9] given from time to time by the Secretary of State[10] or, in relation to Wales, the Welsh Ministers[11].

1   As to the meaning of 'local authority' see PARA 25.
2   As to the meaning of 'child' see PARA 7 note 6.
3   Education Act 1996 s 436A(1) (s 436A added by the Education and Inspections Act 2006 s 4(1); and the Education Act 1996 s 436A(1) amended by SI 2010/1158). As to the meaning of 'compulsory school age' see PARA 19.
4   As to the meaning of 'registered pupil' see PARA 437.
5   Education Act 1996 s 436A(1)(a) (as added: see note 3). As to the meaning of 'school' see PARA 91.
6   In the Education Act 1996 Pt VI Ch II (ss 436A–447), 'suitable education', in relation to a child, means efficient full-time education suitable to his age, ability and aptitude and to any special educational needs he may have: s 436A(3) (as added: see note 3). As to the meaning of 'special educational needs' see PARAS 943, 989. As to what constitutes efficient and full-time education see the cases cited in PARA 435 note 4.
7   Education Act 1996 s 436A(1)(b) (as added: see note 3). As to the duty of parents to secure education for children of compulsory school age see s 7; and PARA 435.
8   As to the meaning of 'functions' see PARA 18 note 5.
9   As to the publication of guidance see the Education Act 1996 s 571; and PARA 60. See in particular 'Children missing education: Statutory guidance for local authorities' (January 2015) and 'School attendance parental responsibility measures: Statutory guidance for local authorities, school leaders, school staff, governing bodies and the police' (January 2015).
10 As to the Secretary of State see PARA 58.
11 Education Act 1996 s 436A(2) (as added (see note 3); and amended by SI 2010/1158). The functions of the Secretary of State under the Education Act 1996 s 436A, so far as exercisable in relation to Wales, were transferred to the National Assembly for Wales (see the National Assembly for Wales (Transfer of Functions) Order 1999, SI 1999/672, art 2, Sch 1) and are now vested in the Welsh Ministers (see the Government of Wales Act 2006 s 162(1), Sch 11 para 30). As to the Welsh Ministers see PARA 59. As to the meaning of 'Wales' see PARA 7 note 3.

440.   School attendance orders. If it appears to a local authority[1] that a child[2] of compulsory school age[3] in its area is not receiving suitable education[4], either by regular attendance at school[5] or otherwise, it must serve a notice[6] in writing[7] on the parent[8] requiring him to satisfy it within the period specified in the notice[9] that the child is receiving such education[10]. If:

(1) a parent on whom such a notice has been served fails to satisfy the local authority, within the period specified in the notice, that the child is receiving suitable education[11]; and

(2) in the opinion of the authority it is expedient that the child should attend school[12],

the authority must serve on the parent an order (called a 'school attendance order') in such form as may be prescribed[13], requiring him to cause the child to become a registered pupil[14] at a school named in the order[15].

A school attendance order, subject to any amendment made by the local authority, continues in force for so long as the child is of compulsory school age, unless[16] it is revoked by the authority[17], or a direction[18] is made in respect of it[19]. Where a maintained school[20] is named in a school attendance order, the local authority must inform the governing body[21] and the head teacher[22]. Where a maintained school is named in a school attendance order, the governing body and the local authority must admit the child to the school[23]; but this does not affect any power to exclude from a school a pupil[24] who is already a registered pupil there[25].

1   As to the meaning of 'local authority' see PARA 25. Any function of a local authority in England which is conferred by or under the Education Act 1996 s 437 may be exercised by, or by employees of, such person as may be authorised in that behalf by the local authority whose function it is: Contracting Out (Local Authority Education Functions) (England) Order 2002, SI 2002/928, art 3, Sch 1 para (ee) (art 3 amended by SI 2010/1172). As to the meaning of 'England' see PARA 7 note 3. As to the meaning of 'person' see PARA 7 note 6.
2   As to the meaning of 'child' see PARA 7 note 6.
3   As to the meaning of 'compulsory school age' see PARA 19.
4   As to the meaning of 'suitable education' see PARA 439 note 6. See also *R v East Sussex County Council, ex p Tandy* [1998] AC 714, [1998] 2 All ER 769, HL.
5   As to the meaning of 'school' see PARA 91.
6   As to the service of notices and documents see the Education Act 1996 s 572; and PARA 76.
7   As to the meaning of 'writing' see PARA 76 note 8.
8   As to the meaning of 'parent' see PARA 7 note 6.
9   That period must not be less than 15 days beginning with the day on which the notice is served: Education Act 1996 s 437(2).
10 Education Act 1996 s 437(1) (amended by SI 2010/1158).
11 Education Act 1996 s 437(3)(a) (amended by SI 2010/1158).
12 Education Act 1996 s 437(3)(b).
13 'Prescribed' means prescribed by regulations; and 'regulations' means regulations made by the Secretary of State or, in relation to Wales, the Welsh Ministers: see the Education Act 1996 s 579(1). As to the Secretary of State see PARA 58. The functions of the Secretary of State under the Education Act 1996 s 437, so far as exercisable in relation to Wales, were transferred to the National Assembly for Wales (see the National Assembly for Wales (Transfer of Functions) Order 1999, SI 1999/672, art 2, Sch 1) and are now vested in the Welsh Ministers (see the Government of Wales Act 2006 s 162(1), Sch 11 para 30). As to the Welsh Ministers see PARA 59. As to the meaning of 'Wales' see PARA 7 note 3. At the date at which this volume states the law no such regulations had been made, but by virtue of the Education Act 1996 s 582(3), Sch 39 para 1, the Education (School Attendance Order) Regulations 1995, SI 1995/2090, have effect as if made under the Education Act 1996 s 437(3).
14 As to the meaning of 'registered pupil' see PARA 437.
15 Education Act 1996 s 437(3). As to the choice of school in respect of school attendance orders see further ss 438, 441; and PARAS 441, 444. As to the amendment of orders see s 440; and PARA 443. As to the revocation of orders see s 442; and PARA 445. As to the offence of failing to comply with an order see s 443; and PARA 446. Where an education supervision order is made under the Children Act 1989 with respect to a child, any school attendance order made under the Education Act 1996 s 437 with respect to the child and in force immediately before the making of the education supervision order, ceases to have effect; and while the education supervision order remains in force s 437 does not apply with respect to the child: see the

16 Education Act 1989 Sch 3 Pt III para 13(2); and PARA 453. The making of a care order under the
Children Act 1989 with respect to a child who is the subject of a school attendance order made
under the Education Act 1996 s 437 discharges the school attendance order: see the Children
Act 1989 s 91(5); and CHILDREN AND YOUNG PERSONS vol 9 (2012) PARA 318.
16 Education Act 1996 s 437(4) (amended by SI 2010/1158).
17 Education Act 1996 s 437(4)(a).
18 Ie under the Education Act 1996 s 443(2) (see PARA 446) or s 447(5) (see PARA 452). See *Enfield
London Borough Council v F* (1986) 85 LGR 526, sub nom *Enfield London Borough Council
v Forsyth* (1986) 151 JP 113 (where the parent had previously been prosecuted for failure to
comply with a school attendance order (see PARA 446), a second prosecution could not be
brought under the same order; service of a new school attendance order was required).
19 Education Act 1996 s 437(4)(b).
20 For the purposes of the Education Act 1996 Pt VI Ch II (ss 436A–447), 'maintained school'
means any community, foundation or voluntary school or any community or foundation special
school not established in a hospital: s 437(8) (definition substituted by the School Standards and
Framework Act 1998 s 140(1), Sch 30 para 113(b)). As to community, foundation and
voluntary schools and community and foundation special schools see PARA 106. As to academies
see PARA 345 et seq.
21 As to the governing bodies of maintained schools in England see PARA 150 et seq; and in Wales
see PARA 195.
22 Education Act 1996 s 437(5) (amended by the School Standards and Framework Act 1998
s 140(1), (3), Sch 30 para 113(a), Sch 31; and SI 2010/1158). As to the meaning of 'head
teacher' see PARA 86 note 4.
23 Education Act 1996 s 437(6) (amended by the School Standards and Framework Act 1998
Sch 30 para 113(a), Sch 31; and SI 2010/1158).
24 As to the meaning of 'pupil' see PARA 20 note 4.
25 Education Act 1996 s 437(7). As to the exclusion of pupils see PARA 517 et seq.

**441. Choice of school in school attendance order for child without an EHC
plan or a statement of special educational needs.** Where a local authority[1] is
required[2] to serve a school attendance order[3] in respect of a child[4] (other than a
child for whom it maintains an EHC plan[5] in the case of a local authority in
England or a statement[6] of special educational needs in the case of a local
authority in Wales[7]), before serving the order the authority must serve[8] on the
parent[9] a notice in writing[10] informing him of its intention to serve the order[11],
specifying the school[12] which the authority intends to name in the order and, if it
thinks fit, one or more other schools which it regards as suitable alternatives[13],
and stating the effect of the provisions[14] described below[15].

If the notice specifies one or more alternative schools and the parent selects
one of them within the period of 15 days beginning with the day on which the
notice is served, the school selected by him must be named in the order[16]. If
within that period the parent applies for the child to be admitted to a school
maintained by a local authority[17] and, where that authority is not the authority
by whom the notice was served, notifies the latter authority of the application[18],
and the child is offered a place at the school as a result of the application[19], that
school must be named in the order[20]. If: (1) within that period, the parent applies
to the local authority by whom the notice was served for education to be
provided at a school which is not a school maintained by a local authority[21]; and
(2) the child is offered a place at the school at the authority's expense[22], that
school must be named in the order[23]. If, within that period: (a) the parent applies
for the child to be admitted to a school which is not maintained by a local
authority, and in respect of which no application is made under head (1) or head
(2) above[24], and notifies the local authority by whom the notice was served of
the application[25]; (b) the child is offered a place at the school as a result of the
application[26]; and (c) the school is suitable[27] to his age, ability and aptitude and
to any special educational needs he may have[28], that school must be named in
the order[29].

1   As to the meaning of 'local authority' see PARA 25. Any function of a local authority in England
     which is conferred by or under the Education Act 1996 s 438 may be exercised by, or by
     employees of, such person as may be authorised in that behalf by the local authority whose
     function it is: Contracting Out (Local Authority Education Functions) (England) Order 2002,
     SI 2002/928, art 3, Sch 1 para (ff) (art 3 amended by SI 2010/1172). As to the meaning of
     'England' see PARA 7 note 3. As to the meaning of 'person' see PARA 7 note 6.
2   Ie by virtue of the Education Act 1996 s 437(3): see PARA 440.
3   As to the meaning of 'school attendance order' see PARA 440.
4   As to the meaning of 'child' see PARA 7 note 6.
5   As to the meaning of 'EHC plan' see PARA 958. As to EHC plans (ie education, health and care
     plans) generally see PARA 958 et seq.
6   Ie a statement of special educational needs under the Education Act 1996 s 324: see PARA 1002.
     As to the meaning of 'special educational needs' see PARA 989.
7   Education Act 1996 s 438(1) (amended by SI 2010/1158; and the Children and Families
     Act 2014 Sch 3 paras 1, 39(1), (2)).
8   As to the service of notices and documents see the Education Act 1996 s 572; and PARA 76.
9   As to the meaning of 'parent' see PARA 7 note 6.
10   As to the meaning of 'writing' see PARA 76 note 8.
11   Education Act 1996 s 438(2)(a).
12   As to the meaning of 'school' see PARA 91.
13   Education Act 1996 s 438(2)(b). As to the specification of a school see further s 439; and PARA
     442.
14   Ie the Education Act 1996 s 438(3)–(6): see the text to notes 16–30.
15   Education Act 1996 s 438(2)(c).
16   Education Act 1996 s 438(3).
17   As to the schools maintained by a local authority see PARA 99.
18   Education Act 1996 s 438(4)(a) (substituted by the School Standards and Framework Act 1998
     s 140(1), Sch 30 para 114(a); and amended by SI 2010/1158).
19   Education Act 1996 s 438(4)(b).
20   Education Act 1996 s 438(4). The duty imposed by the School Standards and Framework
     Act 1998 s 86(2) in relation to a preference expressed in accordance with arrangements made
     for enabling the parent of a child to express a preference as to the school at which he wishes
     education to be provided for his child applies also in relation to any application made by a
     parent as mentioned in the Education Act 1996 s 438(4): see the School Standards and
     Framework Act 1998 s 86(8); and PARA 228.
21   Education Act 1996 s 438(5)(a) (substituted by the School Standards and Framework Act 1998
     Sch 30 para 114(b); and amended by SI 2010/1158).
22   Ie: (1) until a day to be appointed, the child is offered a place at the school under arrangements
     made by the authority under which the fees payable in respect of the education provided at the
     school are to be paid by it under the Education Act 1996 s 517 (see PARA 1016); (2) as from that
     day, the child is offered a place at the school and the authority is required by virtue of
     regulations under s 18(3) (see PARA 40) to pay the fees payable in respect of the education
     provided for him at the school: Education Act 1996 s 438(5)(b) (prospectively substituted by the
     School Standards and Framework Act 1998 Sch 30 para 114(b)). At the date at which this
     volume states the law, no such day had been appointed.
23   Education Act 1996 s 438(5) (substituted by the School Standards and Framework Act 1998
     Sch 30 para 114(b)).
24   Education Act 1996 s 438(6)(a)(i) (amended by the School Standards and Framework Act 1998
     s 140(3), Sch 30 para 114(c), Sch 31; and SI 2010/1158).
25   Education Act 1996 s 438(6)(a)(ii) (amended by SI 2010/1158).
26   Education Act 1996 s 438(6)(b).
27   The question of suitability of education is for the local authority to decide: R v East Sussex
     County Council, ex p Tandy [1998] AC 714, [1998] 2 All ER 769, HL (decided under previous
     legislation). As to the meaning of 'suitable education' see PARA 439 note 6.
28   Education Act 1996 s 438(6)(c).
29   Education Act 1996 s 438(6).

442.   Specification of schools in school attendance notices.   A local authority[1]
must not, if it appears to it that the following provision applies in relation to any
school[2], specify the school in a school attendance notice[3] unless it is responsible
for determining the arrangements for the admission of pupils[4] to the school[5]. The

provision is that, if the child[6] concerned were admitted to the school in accordance with a school attendance order[7] resulting from the notice, the number of pupils at the school in the child's age group would exceed the number determined as the number[8] of pupils in that age group which it is intended to admit to the school in the school year[9] in which he would be admitted[10].

However, this does not prevent a local authority specifying in such a notice any maintained school[11] if[12]:

(1)   there is no maintained school in its area which the authority is not[13] so prevented from specifying, and which is, in the opinion of the authority, a reasonable distance from the home of the child concerned[14]; and

(2)   in the opinion of the authority, the school in question is a reasonable distance from the home of the child concerned[15].

A local authority must not specify in a school attendance notice a school from which the child concerned is permanently excluded[16]. Nor must a local authority specify a school in such a notice if the admission of the child concerned would prejudice[17] the provision of efficient education or the efficient use of resources by reason of measures required to be taken[18] in order to ensure compliance with the duty of local authorities and governing bodies to comply with the limit on infant class sizes[19].

Before deciding to specify a particular maintained school in a school attendance notice a local authority must consult[20] the governing body[21], and if another local authority is responsible for determining the arrangements for the admission of pupils to the school, that authority[22]. Where a local authority decides to specify a particular maintained school in such a notice it must, before serving the notice, serve notice[23] in writing[24] of its decision on[25] the governing body and head teacher[26] of the school[27], and if another local authority is responsible for determining the arrangements for the admission of pupils to the school, that authority[28]. A governing body or local authority on whom such notice is served may, within the period of 15 days beginning with the day on which the notice was received, apply to the appropriate national authority[29] for a direction and, if it does so, must inform the local authority which served the notice[30]. Where the appropriate national authority gives such a direction[31], the school or schools to be specified in the notice must be determined in accordance with the direction[32].

1   As to the meaning of 'local authority' see PARA 25. Any function of a local authority in England which is conferred by or under the Education Act 1996 s 439 may be exercised by, or by employees of, such person as may be authorised in that behalf by the local authority whose function it is: Contracting Out (Local Authority Education Functions) (England) Order 2002, SI 2002/928, art 3, Sch 1 para (gg) (art 3 amended by SI 2010/1172). As to the meaning of 'England' see PARA 7 note 3. As to the meaning of 'person' see PARA 7 note 6.

2   As to the meaning of 'school' see PARA 91.

3   Ie a notice under the Education Act 1996 s 438(2): see PARA 441.

4   As to the meaning of 'pupil' see PARA 20 note 4. As to school admissions see PARA 224 et seq.

5   Education Act 1996 s 439(1) (amended by SI 2010/1158). As to the application of the Education Act 1996 s 439 to new schools in England see the New School (Admissions) (England) Regulations 2003, SI 2003/1041; and in Wales see the New School (Admissions) (Wales) Regulations 2006, SI 2006/175. As to the meaning of 'Wales' see PARA 7 note 3.

6   As to the meaning of 'child' see PARA 7 note 6.

7   As to the meaning of 'school attendance order' see PARA 440.

8   Ie determined in accordance with the School Standards and Framework Act 1998 s 89 (see PARA 247) or (as from a day to be appointed) s 88C (see PARA 237): see the Education Act 1996 s 439(2) (amended by the School Standards and Framework Act 1998 s 140(1), Sch 30

para 115(2); Education Act 2002 s 51, Sch 4 para 14; prospectively amended by the Education and Skills Act 2008 s 169(1), Sch 1 Pt 2 paras 48, 49). At the date at which this volume states the law no such day had been appointed.

9 As to the meaning of 'school year' see PARA 19 note 12.

10 Education Act 1996 s 439(2).

11 As to the meaning of 'maintained school' see PARA 440 note 20.

12 Education Act 1996 s 439(3) (amended by the School Standards and Framework Act 1998 Sch 30 para 115(1), (3), Sch 31; and SI 2010/1158).

13 Ie apart from the Education Act 1996 s 439(3).

14 Education Act 1996 s 439(3)(a) (amended by the School Standards and Framework Act 1998 s 140(1), (3), Sch 30 para 115(3), Sch 31).

15 Education Act 1996 s 439(3)(b).

16 Education Act 1996 s 439(4) (amended by SI 2010/1158). As to the exclusion of pupils see PARA 517 et seq.

17 Ie prejudice of the kind referred to in the School Standards and Framework Act 1998 s 86(3)(a) (parental preferences): see PARA 228.

18 Ie measures as mentioned in the School Standards and Framework Act 1998 s 86(4): see PARA 228.

19 Education Act 1996 s 439(4A) (added by the School Standards and Framework Act 1998 Sch 30 para 115(4)). As to the duty to set a limit on infant class sizes see PARA 234.

20 Education Act 1996 s 439(5) (amended by the School Standards and Framework Act 1998 s 140(1), (3), Sch 30 para 115(3), Sch 31; and SI 2010/1158). As to the exercise of the duty to consult see JUDICIAL REVIEW vol 61 (2010) PARA 627.

21 Education Act 1996 s 439(5)(a) (amended by SI 2010/1158). As to the governing bodies of maintained schools in England see PARA 150 et seq; and in Wales see PARA 195.

22 Education Act 1996 s 439(5)(b) (amended by SI 2010/1158).

23 As to the service of notices and documents see the Education Act 1996 s 572; and PARA 76.

24 As to the meaning of 'writing' see PARA 76 note 8.

25 Education Act 1996 s 439(6) (amended by the School Standards and Framework Act 1998 s 140(1), (3), Sch 30 para 115(3), Sch 31; and SI 2010/1158).

26 As to the meaning of 'head teacher' see PARA 86 note 4.

27 Education Act 1996 s 439(6)(a).

28 Education Act 1996 s 439(6)(b) (amended by SI 2010/1158).

29 Ie the Secretary of State or, in relation to Wales, the Welsh Ministers. As to the Secretary of State see PARA 58. The functions of the Secretary of State under the Education Act 1996 s 439, so far as exercisable in relation to Wales, were transferred to the National Assembly for Wales (see the National Assembly for Wales (Transfer of Functions) Order 1999, SI 1999/672, art 2, Sch 1) and are now vested in the Welsh Ministers (see the Government of Wales Act 2006 s 162(1), Sch 11 para 30). As to the Welsh Ministers see PARA 59.

30 Education Act 1996 s 439(7) (amended by SI 2010/1158).

31 As to directions see the Education Act 1996 s 570; and PARA 75.

32 Education Act 1996 s 439(8).

443. Amendment of order at request of parent: child without EHC plan or statement of special educational needs. The following provisions apply where a school attendance order[1] is in force in respect of a child[2], other than a child for whom the local authority[3] maintains an EHC plan[4] (in the case of a local authority in England) or a statement[5] of special educational needs[6] (in the case of a local authority in Wales)[7].

If at any time:

(1)   the parent[8] applies for the child to be admitted to a school[9] maintained by a local authority[10] which is different from the school named in the order[11];

(2)   the child is offered a place at the school as a result of the application[12]; and

(3)   the parent requests the local authority by whom the order was served to amend it by substituting that school for the one currently named[13],

the authority must comply with the request[14].

If at any time:

(a)   the parent applies to the authority for education to be provided for the child at a school which is not a school maintained by a local authority and which is different from the school named in the order[15];

(b)   the child is offered a place at the school at the authority's expense[16]; and

(c)   the parent requests the authority to amend the order by substituting that school for the one currently named[17],

the authority must comply with the request[18].

If at any time:

(i)   the parent applies for the child to be admitted to a school which is not maintained by a local authority, which is different from the school named in the order and in respect of which no application is made under heads (a) to (c) above[19];

(ii)   as a result of the application, the child is offered a place at the school, being a school which is suitable to his age, ability and aptitude and to any special educational needs he may have[20]; and

(iii)   the parent requests the authority to amend the order by substituting that school for the one currently named[21],

the authority must comply with the request[22].

1   As to the meaning of 'school attendance order' see PARA 440.
2   As to the meaning of 'child' see PARA 7 note 6.
3   As to the meaning of 'local authority' see PARA 25. Any function of a local authority in England which is conferred by or under the Education Act 1996 s 440 may be exercised by, or by employees of, such person as may be authorised in that behalf by the local authority whose function it is: Contracting Out (Local Authority Education Functions) (England) Order 2002, SI 2002/928, art 3, Sch 1 para (hh) (art 3 amended by SI 2010/1172). As to the meaning of 'England' see PARA 7 note 3. As to the meaning of 'person' see PARA 7 note 6.
4   As to the meaning of 'EHC plan' see PARA 958. As to EHC plans (ie education, health and care plans) generally see PARA 958 et seq.
5   Ie under the Education Act 1996 s 324: see PARA 1002.
6   As to the meaning of 'special educational needs' see PARAS 943, 989.
7   Education Act 1996 s 440(1) (amended by SI 2010/1158; and the Children and Families Act 2014 Sch 3 paras 1, 40(1), (2)). As to the meaning of 'Wales' see PARA 7 note 3.
8   As to the meaning of 'parent' see PARA 7 note 6.
9   As to the meaning of 'school' see PARA 91.
10   As to schools maintained by a local authority see PARA 99.
11   Education Act 1996 s 440(2)(a) (amended by the School Standards and Framework Act 1998 s 140(1), (3), Sch 30 para 116(a), Sch 31; and SI 2010/1158).
12   Education Act 1996 s 440(2)(b).
13   Education Act 1996 s 440(2)(c) (amended by SI 2010/1158).
14   Education Act 1996 s 440(2). The duty imposed by the School Standards and Framework Act 1998 s 86(2) in relation to a preference expressed in accordance with arrangements made for enabling the parent of a child to express a preference as to the school at which he wishes education to be provided for his child applies also in relation to any application made by a parent as mentioned in the Education Act 1996 s 440(2): see the School Standards and Framework Act 1998 s 86(8); and PARA 228.
15   Education Act 1996 s 440(3)(a) (substituted by the School Standards and Framework Act 1998 Sch 30 para 116(b); and amended by SI 2010/1158).
16   Ie: (1) until a day to be appointed, the child is offered a place at the school under arrangements made by the authority under which the fees payable in respect of the education provided at the school are to be paid by it under the Education Act 1996 s 517 (see PARA 1016); or (2) as from that day, the child is offered a place at the school and the local authority is required by virtue of regulations under s 18(3) (see PARA 40) to pay the fees payable in respect of the education provided for him at the school: s 440(3)(b) (prospectively substituted by the School Standards and Framework Act 1998 Sch 30 para 116(b); and amended by SI 2010/1158). At the date at which this volume states the law, no such day had been appointed.
17   Education Act 1996 s 440(3)(c).
18   Education Act 1996 s 440(3).

19 Education Act 1996 s 440(4)(a) (amended by the School Standards and Framework Act 1998 Sch 30 para 116(c), Sch 31; and SI 2010/1158).
20 Education Act 1996 s 440(4)(b).
21 Education Act 1996 s 440(4)(c).
22 Education Act 1996 s 440(4).

444. Choice of school in school attendance order for child with EHC plan or statement of special educational needs. Where a local authority[1] is required[2] to serve a school attendance order[3] in respect of a child[4] for whom it maintains an EHC plan[5] (in the case of a local authority in England) or a statement[6] of special educational needs[7] (in the case of a local authority in Wales)[8]:

(1)   where the EHC plan or statement specifies the name of a school[9], that school must be named in the order[10];

(2)   where the EHC plan or statement does not specify the name of a school, the authority must amend the EHC plan or statement so that it specifies the name of a school[11], and that school must then be named in the order[12].

Where a school attendance order is in force in respect of a child for whom the local authority maintains an EHC plan or a statement[13] of special educational needs[14], and the name of the school specified in the plan or statement is changed[15], the local authority must amend the order accordingly[16].

1 As to the meaning of 'local authority' see PARA 25. Any function of a local authority in England which is conferred by or under the Education Act 1996 s 441 may be exercised by, or by employees of, such person as may be authorised in that behalf by the local authority whose function it is: Contracting Out (Local Authority Education Functions) (England) Order 2002, SI 2002/928, art 3, Sch 1 para (ii) (art 3 amended by SI 2010/1172). As to the meaning of 'England' see PARA 7 note 3. As to the meaning of 'person' see PARA 7 note 6.
2 Ie by virtue of the Education Act 1996 s 437(3): see PARA 440.
3 As to the meaning of 'school attendance order' see PARA 440.
4 As to the meaning of 'child' see PARA 7 note 6.
5 As to the meaning of 'EHC plan' see PARA 958. As to EHC plans (ie education, health and care plans) generally see PARA 958 et seq.
6 Ie under the Education Act 1996 s 324: see PARA 1002.
7 As to the meaning of 'special educational needs' see PARAS 943, 989.
8 Education Act 1996 s 441(1) (amended by SI 2010/1158; and the Children and Families Act 2014 Sch 3 paras 1, 41(1), (2)). As to the meaning of 'Wales' see PARA 7 note 3.
9 As to the meaning of 'school' see PARA 91.
10 Education Act 1996 s 441(2) (amended by the Children and Families Act 2014 Sch 3 paras 1, 41(1), (3)).
11 Education Act 1996 s 441(3)(a) (amended by the Special Educational Needs and Disability Act 2001 s 42(1), (6), Sch 8 paras 1, 15(1), (2), Sch 9; and the Children and Families Act 2014 Sch 3 paras 1, 41(1), (4)(a)). An amendment to a statement required to be made under the Education Act 1996 s 441(3)(a) must be treated for the purposes of Sch 27 (see PARAS 1000, 1002 et seq) as if it were an amendment proposed following a periodic review: s 441(3A) (added by the Special Educational Needs and Disability Act 2001 Sch 8 paras 1, 15(1), (3)). An amendment to an EHC plan required to be made under the Education Act 1996 s 441(3)(a) must be treated as if it were an amendment made following a review under the Children and Families Act 2014 s 44 (see PARA 964), and that section and regulations made under it apply accordingly: Education Act 1996 s 441(3B) (added by the Children and Families Act 2014 Sch 3 paras 1, 41(1), (5)).
12 Education Act 1996 s 441(3)(b) (amended by the Children and Families Act 2014 Sch 3 paras 1, 41(1), (4)(b)).
13 Ie under the Education Act 1996 s 324: see PARA 1002.
14 Education Act 1996 s 441(4)(a) (amended by SI 2010/1158; and the Children and Families Act 2014 Sch 3 paras 1, 41(1), (6)(a)).
15 Education Act 1996 s 441(4)(b) (amended by the Children and Families Act 2014 Sch 3 paras 1, 41(1), (6)(b)).
16 Education Act 1996 s 441(4) (amended by SI 2010/1158).

445. Revocation of order at request of parent. Where a school attendance order[1] is in force in respect of a child[2], if at any time the parent[3] applies to the local authority[4] requesting that the order be revoked on the ground that arrangements have been made for the child to receive suitable education[5] otherwise than at school[6], the authority must comply with the request, unless it is of the opinion that no satisfactory arrangements have been made for the education of the child otherwise than at school[7].

If a parent is aggrieved by a refusal of the local authority to comply with such a request, he may refer the question to the appropriate national authority[8]. Where a question is so referred, the appropriate national authority must give such direction[9] determining the question as it thinks fit[10].

1 As to the meaning of 'school attendance order' see PARA 440.
2 Education Act 1996 s 442(1). As to the meaning of 'child' see PARA 7 note 6.
3 As to the meaning of 'parent' see PARA 7 note 6.
4 As to the meaning of 'local authority' see PARA 25. Any function of a local authority in England which is conferred by or under the Education Act 1996 s 442 may be exercised by, or by employees of, such person as may be authorised in that behalf by the local authority whose function it is: Contracting Out (Local Authority Education Functions) (England) Order 2002, SI 2002/928, art 3, Sch 1 para (jj) (art 3 amended by SI 2010/1172). As to the meaning of 'England' see PARA 7 note 3. As to the meaning of 'person' see PARA 7 note 6.
5 As to the meaning of 'suitable education' see PARA 439 note 6.
6 As to the meaning of 'school' see PARA 91.
7 Education Act 1996 s 442(2) (amended by SI 2010/1158).
8 See the Education Act 1996 s 442(3) (amended by SI 2010/1158). As to the power of the appropriate national authority to require a medical examination where a question is referred to it under the Education Act 1996 s 442(3) see PARA 498. 'Appropriate national authority' means the Secretary of State or, in relation to Wales, the Welsh Ministers. As to the Secretary of State see PARA 58. The functions of the Secretary of State under the Education Act 1996 s 442, so far as exercisable in relation to Wales, were transferred to the National Assembly for Wales (see the National Assembly for Wales (Transfer of Functions) Order 1999, SI 1999/672, art 2, Sch 1) and are now vested in the Welsh Ministers (see the Government of Wales Act 2006 s 162(1), Sch 11 para 30). As to the Welsh Ministers see PARA 59. As to the meaning of 'Wales' see PARA 7 note 3.
9 As to directions see the Education Act 1996 s 570; and PARA 75.
10 Education Act 1996 s 442(4). Where the child in question is one for whom the authority maintains an ECH plan (in the case of a local authority in England) or a statement of special educational needs under s 324 (n the case of a local authority in Wales) (see PARA 1002) the provisions of s 442(2)–(4) (see the text to notes 3–8) do not apply if the name of a school or other institution is specified in the EHC plan or the statement, and in any other case a direction under s 442(4) may require the authority to make such amendments in the plan or the statement as the appropriate national authority considers necessary or expedient in consequence of its determination: s 442(5) (amended by the Children and Families Act 2014 Sch 3 paras 1, 42). As to the meaning of 'EHC plan' see PARA 958. As to EHC plans (ie education, health and care plans) generally see PARA 958 et seq.

446. Offence of failing to comply with school attendance order. If a parent[1] on whom a school attendance order[2] is served fails to comply with the requirements of the order, he is guilty of an offence[3], unless he proves that he is causing the child to receive suitable education[4] otherwise than at school[5].

If, in proceedings for such an offence, the parent is acquitted, the court may direct that the school attendance order is to cease to be in force[6]. Such a direction does not affect the duty of the local authority to take further action[7] if at any time the authority is of the opinion that, having regard to any change of circumstances, it is expedient to do so[8].

1 As to the meaning of 'parent' see PARA 7 note 6.
2 As to the meaning of 'school attendance order' see PARA 440.
3 A person guilty of such an offence is liable on summary conviction to a fine not exceeding level 3 on the standard scale: Education Act 1996 s 443(4). As to the standard scale see

SENTENCING AND DISPOSITION OF OFFENDERS vol 92 (2010) PARA 142. Proceedings for an offence under s 443 may not be instituted except by a local authority: s 446 (amended by SI 2010/1158). As to the meaning of 'local authority' see PARA 25. Before instituting proceedings for an offence under the Education Act 1996 s 443, a local authority must consider whether it would be appropriate (instead of or as well as instituting the proceedings) to apply for an education supervision order with respect to the child: see s 447(1); and PARA 452. For the purposes of any proceedings for an offence under s 443 (s 445(1)), in so far as it is material, the child in question must be presumed to have been of compulsory school age at any time unless the parent proves the contrary (s 445(2)). Where a court is obliged by virtue of s 445(2) to presume a child to have been of compulsory school age, s 565(1) (provisions as to evidence: see PARA 19) does not apply: s 445(3). As to the meaning of 'child' see PARA 7 note 6. As to the meaning of 'compulsory school age' see PARA 19. As to documentary evidence in proceedings see s 566; and PARA 50. As to the standard of proof on the accused in criminal proceedings see CRIMINAL PROCEDURE vol 28 (2010) PARA 466 et seq.

4   As to the meaning of 'suitable education' see PARA 439 note 6. See also PARA 435.
5   Education Act 1996 s 443(1). As to the meaning of 'school' see PARA 91. See *Enfield London Borough Council v F* (1986) 85 LGR 526, sub nom *Enfield London Borough Council v Forsyth* (1986) 151 JP 113; *Re B (Infants)* [1962] Ch 201, sub nom *Re Baker (Infants)* [1961] 3 All ER 276, CA; *R v Gwent County Council, ex p Perry* (1985) 129 Sol Jo 737, CA; *Philips v Brown* (20 June 1980, unreported), CA; *Re S (A Minor)* [1978] QB 120, sub nom *Re DJMS (A Minor)* [1977] 3 All ER 582, CA; *Oxfordshire County Council v JL* [2010] EWHC 798 (Admin), [2010] All ER (D) 154 (Apr).
6   Education Act 1996 s 443(2).
7   Ie under the Education Act 1996 s 437: see PARA 440.
8   Education Act 1996 s 443(3) (amended by SI 2010/1158).

447.   Offence of parent failing to secure regular attendance at school of registered pupil. If a child[1] of compulsory school age[2] who is a registered pupil[3] at a school[4] fails to attend regularly at the school, his parent[5] is guilty of an offence[6].

If in the circumstances mentioned above the parent knows that his child is failing to attend regularly at the school and fails to cause him to do so, he is guilty of an offence[7]. It is a defence for a person charged with such an offence to prove that he had a reasonable justification for his failure to cause the child to attend regularly at the school[8].

In proceedings for an offence under these provisions in respect of a child who is not a boarder[9] at the school at which he is a registered pupil[10], the child is not to be taken to have failed to attend regularly at the school:

(1)   by reason of his absence from the school at any time if the parent proves that at that time the child was prevented from attending by reason of sickness or any unavoidable cause[11];

(2)   by reason of his absence from the school with leave[12], or on any day exclusively set apart for religious observance by the religious body to which his parent belongs[13];

(3)   where the child's home is in England[14], if the parent proves that:
       (a)   the local authority has a duty to make travel arrangements in relation to the child[15] for the purpose of facilitating the child's attendance at the school and have failed to discharge that duty[16], or
       (b)   the local authority has a duty to make travel arrangements in relation to the child by virtue of a school travel scheme[17] for the purpose of facilitating the child's attendance at the school and have failed to discharge that duty[18];

(4)   where the child's home is in England[19] and where the school is an independent school[20] which is not a qualifying school[21], if the parent proves that the school is not within walking distance[22] of the child's

home[23], that no suitable arrangements have been made by the local authority for boarding accommodation for him at or near the school[24], and that no suitable arrangements have been made by the local authority for enabling him to become a registered pupil at a qualifying school nearer to his home[25];

(5)   where the child's home is in Wales[26], if the parent proves that the local authority has failed to discharge a duty to make transport arrangements[27] in relation to the child[28];

(6)   in respect of a child who is a boarder at the school at which he is a registered pupil, if he is absent from it without leave during any part of the school term unless the parent proves that at that time the child was prevented from being present by reason of sickness or any unavoidable cause[29].

The reasons described above are the only lawful excuses for non-attendance at school[30].

If it is proved that the child has no fixed abode, heads (3), (4) and (5) above do not apply, but it is a defence for the parent to prove[31]:

(i)   that he is engaged in a trade or business of such a nature as to require him to travel from place to place[32];

(ii)   that the child has attended at a school as a registered pupil as regularly as the nature of that trade or business permits[33]; and

(iii)   if the child has attained the age of six, that he has made at least 200 attendances during the period of 12 months[34] ending with the date on which the proceedings were instituted[35].

Where (A) a child of compulsory school age has been excluded for a fixed period on disciplinary grounds from a school in England[36]; (B) he remains for the time being a registered pupil at the school[37]; (C) the appropriate authority[38] make arrangements for the provision of full-time education for him at the school during the period of exclusion[39]; and (D) notice in writing[40] of the arrangements has been given to the child's parent[41], the exclusion does not affect the application of the above provisions[42] to the child's attendance at the school on any day to which the arrangements relate[43].

Where an education supervision order is in force under the Children Act 1989 with respect to a child, the duty of the child's parents under the above provisions is superseded by their duty to comply with any directions in force under the education supervision order[44].

1   As to the meaning of 'child' see PARA 7 note 6.
2   As to the meaning of 'compulsory school age' see PARA 19.
3   As to the meaning of 'registered pupil' see PARA 437.
4   As to the meaning of 'school' see PARA 91.
5   As to the meaning of 'parent' see PARA 7 note 6.
6   Education Act 1996 s 444(1). A person guilty of such an offence is liable on summary conviction to a fine not exceeding level 3 on the standard scale: s 444(8) (amended by the Criminal Justice and Court Services Act 2000 s 72(1)(b), (2)). As to the standard scale see SENTENCING AND DISPOSITION OF OFFENDERS vol 92 (2010) PARA 142. Proceedings for an offence under the Education Act 1996 s 444 may not be instituted except by a local authority: s 446 (amended by SI 2010/1158). As to the meaning of 'local authority' see PARA 25. Before instituting proceedings for an offence under the Education Act 1996 s 444, a local authority must consider whether it would be appropriate (instead of or as well as instituting the proceedings) to apply for an education supervision order with respect to the child: see s 447(1); and PARA 452. For the purposes of any proceedings for an offence under s 444 (s 445(1)), in so far as it is material, the child in question must be presumed to have been of compulsory school age at any time unless the parent proves the contrary (s 445(2)). Where a court is obliged by virtue of s 445(2) to presume a child to have been of compulsory school age, s 565(1) (provisions as to evidence: see

PARA 19) does not apply: s 445(3). As to documentary evidence in proceedings see s 566; and PARA 50. As to the standard of proof on the accused in criminal proceedings see CRIMINAL PROCEDURE vol 28 (2010) PARA 466.

The offence under s 444(1) is an absolute offence and it is unnecessary that the parents have knowledge of the child's absence or are neglectful in ensuring that the child attends regularly: *Crump v Gilmore* (1969) 68 LGR 56, 113 Sol Jo 998, DC (decided under previous legislation). See also *Hampshire County Council v E* [2007] EWHC 2584 (Admin), [2008] ELR 260, [2007] All ER (D) 208 (Oct), DC, in which the court stated that it was very doubtful whether the terms of the Education Act 1996 s 444(1) admitted of the possibility of a defence of duress of circumstances. The strict liability offence imposed by the Education Act 1996 s 444(1) is not in breach of the right to a fair trial guaranteed by the Convention for the Protection of Human Rights and Fundamental Freedoms (Rome, 4 November 1950; TS 71 (1953); Cmd 8969) art 6 (see RIGHTS AND FREEDOMS vol 88A (2013) PARA 243 et seq), which does not restrict the power of Parliament to create strict liability offences: *Barnfather v Islington London Borough Council* [2003] EWHC 418 (Admin), [2003] 1 WLR 2318, [2003] ELR 263, DC. The record of attendance recorded by the school is not to be treated as conclusive; the court must also consider the parent's explanation for the recorded absences and decide whether there was regular school attendance in the light of all the evidence, including the school's record of attendance: *Bromley London Borough Council v C* [2006] EWHC 1110 (Admin), [2006] ELR 358, [2006] All ER (D) 80 (Mar).

As to penalty notices for parents in respect of a failure to secure the regular attendance of a registered pupil at school see the Education Act 1996 s 444A; and PARA 449. See also the Anti-social Behaviour Act 2003 s 19 (parenting contracts where a child has failed to attend regularly at school); and PARA 450.

7   Education Act 1996 s 444(1A) (added by the Criminal Justice and Court Services Act 2000 s 72(1)(a), (2); and amended by the Education and Inspections Act 2006 ss 109(1), 184, Sch 18, Pt 1). A person guilty of such an offence is liable on summary conviction: (1) to a fine not exceeding level 4 on the standard scale (Education Act 1996 s 444(8A)(a) (s 444(8A), (8B) added by the Criminal Justice and Court Services Act 2000 s 72(1)(c), (2)); or (2) to imprisonment for a term not exceeding three months (or, as from a day to be appointed, 51 weeks) (Education Act 1996 s 444(8A)(b) (as so added; prospectively amended by the Criminal Justice Act 2003 s 280(2), (3), Sch 26 para 49(1), (2))), or both (Education Act 1996 s 444(8A) (as so added)). At the date at which this volume states the law no such day had been appointed. If, on the trial of an offence under the Education Act 1996 s 444(8)(1A), the court finds the defendant not guilty of that offence but is satisfied that he is guilty of an offence under s 444(1) (see the text to notes 1–6), the court may find him guilty of that offence: s 444(8B) (as so added). See also note 6.

As a general proposition, if the offence under the Education Act 1996 s 444(1A) was not made out, the magistrates ought to convict under s 444(1) because it was an absolute offence (see note 6); nonetheless, the interests of justice may dictate to the contrary: *R (on the application of P) v Liverpool City Magistrates' Court* [2006] EWHC 887 (Admin), 170 JP 453, [2006] All ER (D) 211 (Mar). It is not necessarily an abuse of process for a local authority to prosecute a parent under s 444(1A) after it has obtained an education supervision order under the Children Act 1989 Sch 3 (see PARA 453). However, in such circumstances, a parent would be entitled to say that the duty under the Education Act 1996 s 444 no longer applied and that the process under the Children Act 1989 Sch 3 para 18 (persistent failure of parent to comply with a direction given under the order: see PARA 455) should have been used instead: *R (on the application of Graves) v London Borough of Islington* [2003] EWHC 2817 (Admin), [2004] ELR 1, [2003] All ER (D) 119 (Nov). In *Sutton London Borough Council v S* [2004] EWHC 2876 (Admin), [2005] ELR 276, [2004] All ER (D) 358 (Oct), DC, a local authority's appeal against an acquittal under the Education Act 1996 s 444(1A) was dismissed with emphasis being given to the fact that the authority had discretion to appeal and that it should have taken into account the likely distress caused to the particular parents in this instance.

8   Education Act 1996 s 444(1B) (added by the Education and Inspections Act 2006 s 109(2)). The Education Act 1996 s 444(1A) creates an evidential burden on the defence; it does not put a burden upon the defence to show that all reasonable steps had been taken to ensure regular school attendance. 'Reasonable justification' to (fail to) cause a child to attend school should be approached as a perfectly understandable English expression; it is not necessary for every possible avenue to be explored to ensure that a child was receiving regular schooling: *R (on the application of P) v Liverpool City Magistrates' Court* [2006] EWHC 887 (Admin), 170 JP 453, [2006] All ER (D) 211 (Mar).

9   As to the meaning of 'boarder' see PARA 31 note 19.

10 Education Act 1996 s 444(2) (amended by the Education and Inspections Act 2006 s 109(3)).

11 See the Education Act 1996 s 444(2A) (added by the Education and Inspections Act 2006 s 109(1), (4)). The unavoidable cause must affect the child, not the parent: *Jenkins v Howells* [1949] 2 KB 218, [1949] 1 All ER 942, DC (decided under previous legislation; family responsibilities do not constitute an excuse for a child not attending school); *Bath and North East Somerset District Council v Warman* [1999] ELR 81 (a 15-year-old child leaving the family home and failing to inform her mother of her whereabouts did not give rise to an unavoidable cause for the child's absence from school).

12 See the Education Act 1996 s 444(3)(a) (amended by the Education and Inspections Act 2006 s 109(5)(a)). 'Leave', in relation to a school, means leave granted by any person authorised to do so by the governing body or proprietor of the school: Education Act 1996 s 444(9). As to the meaning of 'person' see PARA 7 note 6. As to the governing bodies of maintained schools in England see PARA 150 et seq; and in Wales see PARA 195. As to the meanings of 'England' and 'Wales' see PARA 7 note 3. As to the meaning of 'proprietor' see PARA 51 note 4. 'Leave' means leave granted by the school, not leave which the magistrates consider might be justified. The question for the magistrates to decide is had the school granted leave or not: *Bromley London Borough Council v C* [2006] EWHC 1110 (Admin), [2006] ELR 358, [2006] All ER (D) 80 (Mar), DC.

13 Education Act 1996 s 444(3)(c). 'Exclusively' does not mean that during the whole of the 24 hours, or even during the whole of the school hours, there must be some religious observance going on which is inconsistent with the child being at school: *Marshall v Graham, Bell v Graham* [1907] 2 KB 112, 71 JP 270, DC (decided under previous legislation; Ascension Day is a day exclusively set apart for religious observance by the Church of England).

14 See the Education Act 1996 s 444(3A) (s 444(3A)–(3F) added by the Education and Inspections Act 2006 s 82(1), (2)).

15 Ie under the Education Act 1996 s 508B(1): see PARA 461. The reference to 'travel arrangements' has the same meaning as in s 508B (see PARA 461): s 444(3C)(a) (as added: see note 14).

16 Education Act 1996 s 444(3B)(a) (as added (see note 14); and amended by SI 2010/1158).

17 Ie by virtue of the Education Act 1996 s 508E(2)(c): see PARA 463. The reference to 'travel arrangements' has the same meaning as in Sch 35C para 3 (see PARA 463): s 444(3C)(b) (as added: see note 14).

18 Education Act 1996 s 444(3B)(b) (as added (see note 14); and amended by SI 2010/1158).

19 See the Education Act 1996 s 444(3A) (as added: see note 14).

20 As to the meaning of 'independent school' see PARA 369.

21 For these purposes, 'qualifying school' has the same meaning as it has for the purposes of the Education Act 1996 Sch 35B (meaning of 'eligible child' for the purposes of s 508B) (see PARA 461 note 3): s 444(3E) (as added: see note 14).

22 'Walking distance', in relation to a child who is under the age of eight, means 3.218688 kilometres (two miles) (Education Act 1996 s 444(5)(a)), and in relation to a child who has attained the age of eight, means 4.828032 kilometres (three miles) (s 444(5)(b)), in each case measured by the nearest available route (s 444(5) (amended by the Learner Travel (Wales) Measure 2008 s 20(1), (3))). As to the time at which a person attains a particular age see PARA 7 note 6. For a route to be available it must be one along which a child accompanied as necessary can walk, and walk with reasonable safety, to school: *Essex County Council v Rogers* [1987] AC 66, sub nom *Rogers v Essex County Council* [1986] 3 All ER 321, HL (decided under previous legislation). The parent should, if reasonably practicable, accompany the child along the route where it would be unsafe for the child to go unaccompanied: *Devon County Council v George* [1989] AC 573, sub nom *George v Devon County Council* [1988] 3 All ER 1002, HL (decided under previous legislation).

23 Education Act 1996 s 444(3D)(a) (as added: see note 14).

24 Education Act 1996 s 444(3D)(b) (as added (see note 14); and amended by SI 2010/1158).

25 Education Act 1996 s 444(3D)(c) (as added (see note 14); and amended by SI 2010/1158).

26 See the Education Act 1996 s 444(3F) (as added: see note 14).

27 Ie under the Learner Travel (Wales) Measure 2008 s 3 (see PARA 470) or s 4 (see PARA 472).

28 See the Education Act 1996 s 444(4)(a), (b) (s 444(4) substituted by the Learner Travel (Wales) Measure 2008 s 20(1), (2)).

29 Education Act 1996 s 444(7) (amended by the Education and Inspections Act 2006 s 109(7)). In this provision, 'unavoidable cause' is capable of including want of transport: *R v Havering London Borough Council, ex p K* [1998] ELR 402, [1998] 1 FCR 641 (mother's inability to provide transport was not an unavoidable cause as it affected the child only secondarily).

30 *Spiers v Warrington Corpn* [1954] 1 QB 61, [1953] 2 All ER 1052, DC. See also *Happe v Lay* (1977) 76 LGR 313, 8 Fam Law 54; *Jarman v Mid-Glamorgan Education Authority* [1985] LS Gaz R 1249, (1985) Times, 11 February, DC (all decided under previous legislation).

31 Education Act 1996 s 444(6) (amended by the Education and Inspections Act 2006 ss 82(1), (4), 109(6)).
32 Education Act 1996 s 444(6)(a).
33 Education Act 1996 s 444(6)(b).
34 As to the meaning of 'month' see PARA 54 note 26.
35 Education Act 1996 s 444(6)(c).
36 Education Act 1996 s 444(7A)(a) (s 444(7A), (7B) added by the Education and Inspections Act 2006 s 109(8)). The schools in question are (1) a maintained school (Education Act 1996 s 444(7A)(a)(i) (as so added)); (2) a pupil referral unit (s 444(7A)(a)(ii) (as so added)); (3) an academy school (s 444(7A)(a)(iii) (as so added; and substituted by the Education Act 2011 Sch 13 para 9(1), (7))); (4) an alternative provision academy (Education Act 1996 s 444(7A)(iiia) (added by the Education Act 2011 Sch 13 para 9(1), (7)); (5) a city technology college (Education Act 1996 s 444(7A)(a)(iv) (as so added)); or (6) a city college for the technology of the arts (s 444(7A)(a)(v) (as so added)). As to the meaning of 'maintained school' see PARA 440 note 20. As to pupil referral units see PARA 427 et seq. As to the meaning of 'academy school' see PARA 346 note 12. As to the meaning of 'alternative provision academy' see PARA 346 note 14. As to city technology colleges and city colleges for the technology of the arts see PARA 345. As to the exclusion of pupils from school see PARA 517 et seq.
37 Education Act 1996 s 444(7A)(b) (as added: see note 36).
38 'The appropriate authority' means: (1) in relation to a maintained school, the governing body of the school (Education Act 1996 s 444(7B)(a) (as added: see note 36)); (2) in relation to a pupil referral unit, the local authority (s 444(7B)(b) (as so added; and amended by SI 2010/1158)); and (3) in relation to any school mentioned in the Education Act 1996 s 444(7A)(a)(iii)–(v) (see note 36), the proprietor of the school (s 444(7B)(c) (as so added)).
39 Education Act 1996 s 444(7A)(c) (as added: see note 36).
40 As to the meaning of 'writing' see PARA 76 note 8.
41 Education Act 1996 s 444(7A)(d) (as added: see note 36).
42 Ie the Education Act 1996 s 444(1)–(7): see the text to notes 1–35.
43 Education Act 1996 s 444(7A) (as added: see note 36).
44 See the Children Act 1989 Sch 3 Pt III para 13(1); and PARA 453.

448. Offence of parent failing to secure regular attendance in relation to alternative educational provision. Where, in the case of a child[1] of compulsory school age[2] who is not a registered pupil[3] at any school[4], a local authority[5] has made arrangements[6] for the provision of education for him otherwise than at a school or at his home[7], and notice in writing[8] of the arrangements has been given to the child's parent[9], the provisions governing the offence of a parent failing to secure the regular attendance of a registered pupil at school[10] have effect as if the place at which the education is provided were a school and the child were a registered pupil at that school[11]. In proceedings for an offence under these provisions[12], it is a defence for the parent to prove[13] that the child is receiving suitable education[14] otherwise than by regular attendance at a school or at the place[15] at which the education is provided[16].

Where: (1) a child of compulsory school age has been excluded[17] from a relevant school in Wales[18]; (2) he remains for the time being a registered pupil at the school[19]; (3) he is required[20] by the appropriate authority for the school to attend at a place outside the school premises[21] for the purpose of receiving any instruction or training[22]; and (4) notice in writing of the requirement has been given to the child's parent[23], the provisions governing the offence of a parent failing to secure the regular attendance of a registered pupil at school[24] have effect as if the place at which the child is required to attend were a school and the child were a registered pupil at that school, and not at the school mentioned in head (2) above[25].

Where a child of compulsory school age has been excluded for a fixed period on disciplinary grounds from a relevant school in England[26], the child remains for the time being a registered pupil at the school[27], the appropriate authority for the school has made arrangements[28] for the provision of full-time education for the child otherwise than at the school or at the child's home during the period of exclusion[29], and notice in writing of the arrangements has been given to the child's parent[30], the provisions governing the offence of a parent failing to secure the regular attendance of a registered pupil at school[31] have effect during that period as if the child were not a registered pupil at the school and as if the place at which the education is provided were a school and the child were a registered pupil at that school (so far as that would not otherwise be the case)[32].

Where (a) a child of compulsory school age who is a registered pupil at a relevant school in England is required by the appropriate authority for the school to attend at a place outside the school premises for the purpose of receiving any educational provision[33]; and (b) notice in writing of the requirement has been given to the child's parent[34], the provisions governing the offence of a parent failing to secure the regular attendance of a registered pupil at school[35], have effect as if the place at which the child is required to attend were a school and the child were a registered pupil at that school (in addition to being a registered pupil at the school mentioned in head (a) above)[36].

1   As to the meaning of 'child' see PARA 7 note 6.
2   As to the meaning of 'compulsory school age' see PARA 19.
3   As to the meaning of 'registered pupil' see PARA 437.
4   As to the meaning of 'school' see PARA 91.
5   As to the meaning of 'local authority' see PARA 25.
6   Ie under the Education Act 1996 s 19: see PARA 427.
7   Education Act 1996 s 444ZA(1)(a) (s 444ZA added by the Education Act 2005 s 116; and the Education Act 1996 s 444ZA(1)(a) amended by SI 2010/1158).
8   As to the meaning of 'writing' see PARA 76 note 8.
9   Education Act 1996 s 444ZA(1)(b) (as added: see note 7). As to the meaning of 'parent' see PARA 7 note 6. Section 572, which provides for the methods by which notices may be served under the Education Act 1996 (see PARA 76), does not preclude the notice mentioned in s 444ZA(1)(b) from being given to a child's parent by any other effective method: s 444ZA(5) (as so added). A child is not to be taken to have failed to attend regularly, in a case falling within s 444ZA(1), at the place at which education is provided for him, unless he has failed to attend regularly since the giving of the notice mentioned in s 444ZA(1)(b): s 444ZA(4)(a) (as so added).
10   Ie the Education Act 1996 s 444(1)–(7): see PARA 447. In s 444, 'leave', in relation to a place at which education is provided as mentioned in s 444ZA(1), means leave granted by any person authorised to do so by the local authority: s 444ZA(7)(a) (as added (see note 7); and amended by SI 2010/1158).
11   Education Act 1996 s 444ZA(1) (as added: see note 7). As to certificates of attendance see PARA 451.
12   Ie an offence under the Education Act 1996 s 444 (see PARA 447) in a case falling within s 444ZA(1) (see the text to notes 1–11).
13   As to the standard of proof on the accused in criminal proceedings see CRIMINAL PROCEDURE vol 28 (2010) PARA 466.
14   As to the meaning of 'suitable education' see PARA 439 note 6. See also PARAS 435 note 4, 446.
15   Ie the place mentioned in the Education Act 1996 s 444ZA(1): see the text to notes 1–11.
16   Education Act 1996 s 444ZA(6) (as added: see note 7).
17   In relation to a maintained school or a pupil referral unit, the reference in the Education Act 1996 s 444ZA(2)(a) to exclusion is a reference to exclusion under the Education Act 2002 s 52 (see PARA 517): Education Act 1996 s 444ZA(3)(a) (as added: see note 7). As to the meaning of 'maintained school' see PARA 440 note 20. As to pupil referral units see PARA 427 et seq.
18   Education Act 1996 s 444ZA(2)(a) (as added (see note 7); and amended by the Education and Skills Act 2008 s 155(1), (3)). As to the meaning of 'Wales' see PARA 7 note 3. 'Relevant school' means: (1) a maintained school (Education Act 1996 s 444ZA(8)(a)(i) (as so added)); (2) a pupil referral unit (s 444ZA(8)(a)(ii) (as so added)); (3) an academy school (s 444ZA(8)(a)(iii) (as so added; and substituted by the Education Act 2011 Sch 13 para 9(1), (8)(a))); (4) an alternative provision academy (Education Act 1996 s 444ZA(8)(a)(iiia) (added by the Education Act 2011 Sch 13 para 9(1), (8)(b)); (5) a city technology college (Education Act 1996 s 444ZA(8)(a)(iv)

(as so added)); or (6) a city college for the technology of the arts (s 444ZA(8)(a)(v) (as so added)). As to the meaning of 'academy school' see PARA 346 note 12. As to the meaning of 'alternative provision academy' see PARA 346 note 14. As to city technology colleges and city colleges for the technology of the arts see PARA 345.

19 Education Act 1996 s 444ZA(2)(b) (as added: see note 7).
20 In relation to a maintained school or a pupil referral unit, the requirement referred to in the Education Act 1996 s 444ZA(2)(c) is a requirement imposed under the Education Act 2002 s 29(3) (see PARA 169): Education Act 1996 s 444ZA(3)(b) (as added: see note 7). In s 444 (see PARA 447), 'leave', in relation to a place at which education is provided as mentioned in s 444ZA(2)(c), means leave granted by any person authorised to do so by the appropriate authority for the school: s 444ZA(7)(b) (as so added). 'Appropriate authority' means: (1) in relation to a maintained school, the governing body; (2) in relation to a pupil referral unit, the local authority; and (3) in relation to a school falling within s 444ZA(8)(a)(iii), (iiia), (iv) or (v) (see note 18), the proprietor of the school: s 444ZA(8)(b) (as so added; and amended by SI 2010/1158; and the Education Act 2011 Sch 13 para 9(1), (8)(b)). As to the governing bodies of maintained schools in England see PARA 150 et seq; and in Wales see PARA 195. As to the meaning of 'proprietor' see PARA 51 note 4.
21 As to the meaning of 'premises' see PARA 62 note 19.
22 Education Act 1996 s 444ZA(2)(c) (as added: see note 7).
23 Education Act 1996 s 444ZA(2)(d) (as added: see note 7). Section 572, which provides for the methods by which notices may be served under the Education Act 1996 (see PARA 76), does not preclude the notice mentioned in s 444ZA(2)(d) from being given to a child's parent by any other effective method: see s 444ZA(5) (as so added). A child is not to be taken to have failed to attend regularly, in a case falling within s 444ZA(2), at the place at which he is required to attend, unless he has failed to attend regularly since the giving of the notice mentioned in s 444ZA(2)(d): s 444ZA(4)(b) (as so added).
24 Ie the Education Act 1996 s 444(1)–(7): see PARA 447.
25 Education Act 1996 s 444ZA(2) (as added: see note 7).
26 Education Act 1996 s 444ZA(1A)(a) (s 444ZA as added (see note 7); and s 444ZA(1A)–(1D) added by the Education and Skills Act 2008 s 155(1), (2)). As to the meaning of 'England' see PARA 7 note 3. In relation to a maintained school or a pupil referral unit references in the Education Act 1996 s 444ZA(1A) to exclusion are references to exclusion under the Education Act 2002 s 51A (see PARA 517): Education Act 1996 s 444ZA(1D)(a) (as so added; and amended by the Education Act 2011 Sch 1 paras 5, 6).
27 Education Act 1996 s 444ZA(1A)(b) (as added: see notes 7, 26).
28 Ie under the Education Act 1996 s 19 (see PARA 427) or the Education and Inspections Act 2006 s 100 (see PARA 528).
29 Education Act 1996 s 444ZA(1A)(c) (as added: see notes 7, 26). See PARAS 435 note 4, 446.
30 Education Act 1996 s 444ZA(1A)(d) (as added: see notes 7, 26). A child is not to be taken to have failed to attend regularly in a case falling within s 444ZA(1A), at the place at which education is provided for him unless he has failed to attend regularly since the giving of the notice mentioned in s 444ZA(1A)(d): s 444ZA(4)(a) (amended by the Education and Skills Act 2008, s 155(1), (4)). The Education Act 1996 s 572 (see PARA 76), which provides for the methods by which notices may be served under the Education Act 1996, does not preclude the notice mentioned in s 444ZA(1A)(d) from being given to a child's parent by any other effective method: see s 444ZA(5) (amended by the Education and Skills Act 2008 s 155(1), (5)).
31 Ie the Education Act 1996 s 444(1)–(7): see PARA 447. In s 444 'leave', in relation to a place at which education is provided as mentioned in s 444ZA(1A), means leave granted by any person authorised to do so by the appropriate authority for the school: s 444ZA(7)(aa) (added by the Education and Skills Act 2008 s 155(1), (7)(a)).
32 Education Act 1996 s 444ZA(1A) (as added: see notes 7, 26). In proceedings for an offence under s 444 (see PARA 447) in a case falling within s 444ZA(1A), it is a defence for the parent to prove that the child is receiving suitable education otherwise than by regular attendance at a school or at the place mentioned in s 444ZA(1A): see s 444ZA(6) (amended by the Education and Skills Act 2008 s 155(1), (6)).
33 Education Act 1996 s 444ZA(1B)(a) (as added: see notes 7, 26). In relation to a maintained school or a pupil referral unit the requirement referred to in s 444ZA(1B) is a requirement imposed under the Education Act 2002 s 29(3) or s 29A(1) (see PARA 169): Education Act 1996 s 444ZA(1D)(b) (as so added). In s 444 'leave', in relation to a place at which a child is required to attend as mentioned in s 444ZA(1B)(a), means leave granted by any person authorised to do so by the appropriate authority for the school: s 444ZA(7)(b) (amended by the Education and Skills Act 2008 s 155(1), (7)(b)).

34 Education Act 1996 s 444ZA(1B)(b) (as added: see notes 7, 26). A child is not to be taken to
have failed to attend regularly in a case falling within s 444ZA(1B), at the place at which he is
required to attend, unless he has failed to attend regularly since the giving of the notice
mentioned in s 444ZA(1B)(b): s 444ZA(4)(b) (amended by the Education and Skills Act 2008,
s 155(1), (4)). The Education Act 1996 s 572, which provides for the methods by which notices
may be served under the Education Act 1996, does not preclude the notice mentioned in
s 444ZA(1B)(b) from being given to a child's parent by any other effective method: see
s 444ZA(5) (amended by the Education and Skills Act 2008 s 155(1), (5)).

35 Ie the Education Act 1996 s 444(1)–(7): see PARA 447.

36 Education Act 1996 s 444ZA(1B) (as added: see notes 7, 26). The Education Act 1996
s 444ZA(1B) does not apply if (1) the place at which the child is required to attend is another
relevant school (whether in England or elsewhere) (s 444ZA(1C)(a) (as so added)); and (2) the
child is a registered pupil at that other school (s 444ZA(1C)(b) (as so added)).

449. Penalty notice in respect of failure to secure regular attendance. Where
an authorised officer[1] has reason to believe:

(1)   that a person has committed an offence[2] of failing to secure regular
attendance at school of a registered pupil[3]; and

(2)   that the offence relates to a relevant school[4], or[5] to a place at which
education is provided by a local authority[6], or[7] to a place at which
education is provided for a child is certain circumstances[8], or[9] to a place
at which a child is required to attend in certain further circumstances[10],

he may give the person a penalty notice in respect of the offence[11]. A 'penalty
notice' is a notice offering a person the opportunity of discharging any liability to
conviction for the offence[12] to which the notice relates by payment of a penalty[13]
in accordance with the notice[14].

Where a person is given a penalty notice, proceedings for the offence to which
the notice relates (or an offence[15] arising out of the same circumstances) may not
be instituted before the end of such period as may be prescribed[16]. Where a
person is given a penalty notice, he cannot be convicted of the offence to which
the notice relates (or an offence[17] arising out of the same circumstances) if he
pays a penalty in accordance with the notice[18]. Penalties are payable to local
authorities[19].

Regulations[20] may make:

(a)   provision as to the form and content of penalty notices[21];

(b)   provision as to the monetary amount of any penalty and the time by
which it is to be paid[22];

(c)   provision for determining the local authority to which a penalty is
payable[23];

(d)   provision as to the methods by which penalties may be paid[24];

(e)   provision as to the records which are to be kept in relation to penalty
notices[25];

(f)   provision as to the persons[26] who may be authorised by a local
authority or a head teacher to give penalty notices[27];

(g)   provision limiting the circumstances in which authorised officers of a
prescribed description may give penalty notices[28];

(h)   provision for or in connection with the withdrawal, in prescribed
circumstances, of a penalty notice, including repayment of any amount
paid by way of penalty under a penalty notice which is withdrawn, and
prohibition of the institution or continuation of proceedings for the
offence to which the withdrawn notice relates (and any offence[29] arising
out of the same circumstances)[30];

(i)   provision for a certificate purporting to be signed by or on behalf of a
prescribed person, and stating that payment of any amount paid by way

of penalty was or, as the case may be, was not received on or before a date specified in the certificate, to be received in evidence of the matters so stated[31];

(j)   provision as to the action to be taken if a penalty is not paid in accordance with a penalty notice[32];

(k)   provision for or in connection with the preparation of codes of conduct in relation to the giving of penalty notices[33];

(l)   such other provision in relation to penalties or penalty notices as the Secretary of State thinks necessary or expedient[34].

Local authorities, head teachers and authorised officers must, in carrying out their functions in relation to penalty notices, have regard to any guidance which is published[35] by the Secretary of State from time to time in relation to penalty notices[36].

1   For the purposes of the Education Act 1996 ss 444A–444B, 'authorised officer' means: (1) a constable; (2) an officer of a local authority who is authorised by the authority to give penalty notices; or (3) an authorised staff member: s 444B(4) (s 444A, 444B added by the Anti-social Behaviour Act 2003 s 23(1); and definition in the Education Act 1996 s 444B(4) amended by SI 2010/1158; and SI 2013/1657). 'Penalty notice' has the meaning given by the Education Act 1996 s 444A(2) (see the text to notes 12–14); and 'authorised staff member' means a head teacher of a relevant school, or a member of the staff of a relevant school who is authorised by the head teacher of the school to give penalty notices: s 444B(4) (as so added; and definition amended by SI 2013/1657). 'Relevant school' means: (a) a maintained school; (b) a pupil referral unit; (c) an academy school; (d) an alternative provision academy; (e) a city technology college; or (f) a city college for the technology of the arts: Education 1996 s 444B(4) (as so added; and definition amended by the Education Act 2011 Sch 13 para 9(1), (9)). As to the office of constable see POLICE AND INVESTIGATORY POWERS vol 84 (2013) PARA 1 et seq. As to the meaning of 'local authority' see PARA 25. As to the meaning of 'head teacher' see PARA 86 note 4. As to the meaning of 'maintained school' see PARA 440 note 20. As to pupil referral units see PARA 427 et seq. As to the meaning of 'academy school' see PARA 346 note 12. As to the meaning of 'alternative provision academy' see PARA 346 note 14. As to city technology colleges and city colleges for the technology of the arts see PARA 345. The power to give a penalty notice under the Education Act 1996 s 444A is exercisable by a community support officer: see the Police Reform Act 2002 Sch 4 para 1(2)(aa); and POLICE AND INVESTIGATORY POWERS vol 84 (2013) PARA 367.

The Welsh Ministers have the power by order to amend the Education Act 1996 ss 444A–444B by removing the words 'in England' in each place where they occur: see the Anti-social Behaviour Act 2003 s 23(9); and the Anti-social Behaviour Act 2003 (Amendment to the Education Act 1996) (Wales) Order 2013, SI 2013/1657 (and see also above and notes 4, 6, 19). Where such an order is made certain functions of the Secretary of State, so far as they become exercisable in relation to Wales, are to be treated as transferred to the Welsh Ministers by an Order in Council under the Government of Wales Act 1998 s 22 (transfer of ministerial functions: see CONSTITUTIONAL AND ADMINISTRATIVE LAW vol 20 (2014) PARA 380): Anti-social Behaviour Act 2003 s 23(10). As to the Secretary of State see PARA 58. The functions under the Anti-social Behaviour Act 2003 s 23(9), (10) were originally vested in the National Assembly for Wales and are now exercisable by the Welsh Ministers by virtue of the Government of Wales Act 2006 s 162(1), Sch 11 paras 30, 32. As to the Welsh Ministers see PARA 59. As to the meanings of 'England' and 'Wales' see PARA 7 note 3.

2   Ie under the Education Act 1996 s 444(1): see PARA 447.

3   Education Act 1996 s 444A(1)(a) (as added: see note 1).

4   Education Act 1996 s 444A(1)(b)(i) (s 444A as added (see note 1); s 444A(1)(b) substituted by the Education Act 2005 s 117, Sch 18 para 3); and the Education Act 1996 s 444A(1)(b)(i) amended by SI 2013/1657). See note 1.

5   Ie in a case falling within the Education Act 1996 s 444ZA(1): see PARA 448.

6   Education Act 1996 s 444A(1)(b)(ii) (as added and substituted (see note 4); and amended by SI 2010/1158; and SI 2013/1657). See note 1.

7   Ie in a case falling within the Education Act 1996 s 444ZA(1A): see PARA 448.

8   Education Act 1996 s 444A(1)(b)(iii) (as added and substituted (see note 4); and s 444A(1)(b)(iii) further substituted and s 444A(1)(b)(iv) added by the Education and Skills

    Act 2008 s 169(1), Sch 1 Pt 2 paras 48, 50). The circumstances referred to in the text are those mentioned in the Education Act 1996 s 444ZA(1A): see PARA 448.

9   Ie in a case falling within the Education Act 1996 s 444ZA(1B): see PARA 448.

10 Education Act 1996 s 444A(1)(b)(iv) (s 444A(1)(b) as added and substituted (see note 4); and s 444A(1)(b)(iv) as added (see note 8). The circumstances referred to in the text are those mentioned in s 444ZA(1B): see PARA 448.

11 Education Act 1996 s 444A(1) (as added: see note 1).

12 Ie under the Education Act 1996 s 444(1): see PARA 447.

13 'Penalty' means a penalty under a penalty notice: Education Act 1996 s 444B(4) (as added: see note 1).

14 Education Act 1996 s 444A(2) (as added: see note 1).

15 Ie under the Education Act 1996 s 444(1A): see PARA 447.

16 Education Act 1996 s 444A(3) (as added: see note 1). 'Prescribed' means prescribed by regulations; and 'regulations' means regulations made by the Secretary of State: s 579(1). As to the regulations made under ss 444A–444B see the Education (Penalty Notices) (England) Regulations 2007, SI 2007/1867; and the Education (Penalty Notices) (Wales) Regulations 2013, SI 2013/1983. At the date at which this volume states the law the period prescribed for the purposes of the Education Act 1996 s 444A(3) is 28 days: see the Education (Penalty Notices) (England) Regulations 2007, SI 2007/1867, reg 7 (amended by SI 2013/757).

17 Ie under the Education Act 1996 s 444(1A): see PARA 447.

18 Education Act 1996 s 444A(4) (as added: see note 1).

19 Education Act 1996 s 444A(5) (as added (see note 1); and amended by SI 2010/1158; and SI 2013/1657). See note 1. Sums so received by a local authority may be used by the authority for the purposes of any of its functions which may be specified in regulations but, to the extent that they are not so used, must be paid in accordance with regulations to the Secretary of State: s 444A(6) (as so added; and substituted by the Education and Inspections Act 2006 s 110; and amended by SI 2010/1158). The functions of a local authority specified for these purposes are issuing and enforcing penalty notices, and prosecuting recipients who do not pay; and to the extent that sums received by a local authority are not used for those purposes they must be paid to the Secretary of State: see the Education (Penalty Notices) (England) Regulations 2007, SI 2007/1867, reg 23. As to the meaning of 'functions' see PARA 18 note 5.

20 As to the regulations made see note 16.

21 Education Act 1996 s 444B(1)(a) (as added: see note 1).

22 Education Act 1996 s 444B(1)(b) (as added: see note 1). Without prejudice to the generality of s 444B(1) or s 569(4) (general provisions in relation to regulations), regulations under s 444B(1)(b) may make provision for penalties of different amounts to be payable in different cases or circumstances (including provision for the penalty payable under a penalty notice to differ according to the time by which it is paid): s 444B(2) (as so added). The amount of the penalty to be paid is (1) £60, where the amount is paid within 21 days of receipt of the notice; or (2) £120, where head (1) does not apply but where the amount is paid within 28 days of receipt of the notice: Education (Penalty Notices) (England) Regulations 2007, SI 2007/1867, reg 4 (amended by SI 2012/1046; and SI 2013/757).

23 Education Act 1996 s 444B(1)(c) (as added (see note 1); and amended by SI 2010/1158).

24 Education Act 1996 s 444B(1)(d) (as added: see note 1).

25 Education Act 1996 s 444B(1)(e) (as added: see note 1).

26 As to the meaning of 'person' see PARA 7 note 6.

27 Education Act 1996 s 444B(1)(f) (as added (see note 1); and amended by SI 2010/1158).

28 Education Act 1996 s 444B(1)(g) (as added: see note 1).

29 Ie under the Education Act 1996 s 444(1A): see PARA 447.

30 Education Act 1996 s 444B(1)(h) (as added: see note 1).

31 Education Act 1996 s 444B(1)(i) (as added: see note 1).

32 Education Act 1996 s 444B(1)(j) (as added: see note 1).

33 Education Act 1996 s 444B(1)(k) (as added: see note 1).

34 Education Act 1996 s 444B(1)(l) (as added: see note 1).

35 As to the publication of guidance see the Education Act 1996 s 571; and PARA 60.

36 Education Act 1996 s 444B(3) (as added (see note 1); and amended by SI 2010/1158).

450. Parenting contracts in cases of pupil's failure to attend regularly at school. Where a child of compulsory school age has failed to attend regularly at school or other place where educational provision is made for him, a local authority or the governing body of a school may enter into a parenting contract with a parent of the pupil or child[1]. A 'parenting contract' is a document which contains a statement by the parent that he agrees to comply with such requirements as may be specified in the document for such period as may be so specified, and a statement by the local authority or governing body that it agrees to provide support to the parent for the purpose of complying with those requirements[2].

1   See the Anti-social Behaviour Act 2003 s 19(3); and CHILDREN AND YOUNG PERSONS vol 10 (2012) PARA 1283.
2   See the Anti-social Behaviour Act 2003 s 19(4); and CHILDREN AND YOUNG PERSONS vol 10 (2012) PARA 1283. As to parenting contracts in cases of misbehaviour at school see PARA 516. As to parenting contracts in cases of exclusion from school see PARA 525.

451. Documentary evidence. In any legal proceedings, a document purporting to be a certificate giving particulars of the attendance of a child[1] or young person[2] at a school[3], and to be signed by the head teacher[4] of the school, is to be received in evidence and treated, without further proof, as the document which it purports to be and as having been signed by the person by whom it purports to have been signed, unless the contrary is proved[5].

1   As to the meaning of 'child' see PARA 7 note 6.
2   As to the meaning of 'young person' see PARA 7 note 6.
3   As to the meaning of 'school' see PARA 91.
4   As to the meaning of 'head teacher' see PARA 86 note 4.
5   See the Education Act 1996 s 566(1)(c); and PARA 50. In any legal proceedings, any such extract or certificate as is mentioned in s 566(1)(c) is evidence of the matters stated in it: see s 566(2); and PARA 50. Where a child of compulsory school age is required to attend at: (1) any place at which education is provided for him in the circumstances mentioned in s 444ZA(1) or, as from a day to be appointed, s 444ZA(1A) (see PARA 448); or (2) any place in the circumstances mentioned in s 444ZA(1B) or s 444ZA(2) (see PARA 448), s 566(1)(c) has effect as if the place in question were a school and the person in charge of the provision of education or training at that place were its head teacher (and s 566(2) has effect accordingly): s 566(3) (added by the Education Act 2005 s 117, Sch 18 para 6; and amended by the Education and Skills Act 2008 s 169(1), Sch 1 Pt 2 paras 48, 51). As to the meaning of 'compulsory school age' see PARA 19.

(iv) Education Supervision Orders

452. Education supervision orders. Before instituting proceedings for an offence of failing to comply with a school attendance order[1] or for an offence of failing to secure the regular attendance at school of a registered pupil[2], a local authority[3] must consider whether it would be appropriate (instead of or as well as instituting the proceedings) to apply for an education supervision order[4] with respect to the child[5]. The court:

(1)   by which a person is convicted of an offence[6] of failing to comply with a school attendance order[7]; or

(2)   before which a person is charged with an offence[8] of failing to secure regular attendance at school of a registered pupil[9],

may direct the local authority instituting the proceedings to apply for an education supervision order with respect to the child unless the authority decides[10] that the child's welfare will be satisfactorily safeguarded even though no education supervision order is made[11]. Where, following such a direction, a local authority decides not to apply for an education supervision order, it must inform the court of the reasons for its decision[12].

Where a local authority applies for an education supervision order with respect to a child who is the subject of a school attendance order[13], and the court decides that it is prevented[14] from making the order[15], the court may direct that the school attendance order is to cease to be in force[16].

1   Ie an offence under the Education Act 1996 s 443: see PARA 446. As to the meaning of 'school attendance order' see PARA 440.
2   Ie an offence under the Education Act 1996 s 444: see PARA 447.
3   As to the meaning of 'local authority' see PARA 25.
4   'Education supervision order' means an education supervision order under the Children Act 1989 s 36 (see PARA 453): Education Act 1996 s 447(6).
5   Education Act 1996 s 447(1) (amended by SI 2010/1158). See *R (on the application of Graves) v London Borough of Islington* [2003] EWHC 2817 (Admin), [2004] ELR 1, [2003] All ER (D) 119 (Nov).
6   Ie an offence under the Education Act 1996 s 443: see PARA 446.
7   Education Act 1996 s 447(2)(a).
8   Ie an offence under the Education Act 1996 s 444: see PARA 447.
9   Education Act 1996 s 447(2)(b).
10 A local authority may not make such a decision unless it is the appropriate local authority (Education Act 1996 s 447(2A)(a) (s 447(2A) added by SI 2010/1158)), or it has consulted that authority (Education Act 1996 s 447(2A)(b) (as so added)). As to the meaning of 'the appropriate local authority' see PARA 453 note 10 (definition applied by s 447(6)). As to the exercise of the duty to consult see JUDICIAL REVIEW vol 61 (2010) PARA 627.
11 Education Act 1996 s 447(2) (amended by SI 2010/1158). As to the procedure in relation to such directions see generally now the Family Procedure Rules 2010, SI 2010/2955, Pt 12 (amended by SI 2013/3204).
12 Education Act 1996 s 447(3) (amended by SI 2010/1158). Unless the court has directed otherwise, the information required under the Education Act 1996 s 447(3) must be given to the court before the end of the period of eight weeks beginning with the date on which the direction was given: s 447(4). See note 11.
13 Education Act 1996 s 447(5)(a) (amended by SI 2010/1158).
14 Ie by the Children Act 1989 s 36(3): see PARA 453.
15 See the Education Act 1996 s 447(5)(b).
16 Education Act 1996 s 447(5).

453.   Duration and effect of education supervision orders.   On the application of any local authority[1] the court may make an order (known as an 'education supervision order'[2]), putting the child[3] with respect to whom the application is made under the supervision of a designated[4] local authority[5]. A court may only make an education supervision order if it is satisfied that the child concerned is of compulsory school age[6] and is not being properly educated[7]. For these purposes, a child is being properly educated only if he is receiving efficient full-time education suitable to his age, ability and aptitude and any special educational needs[8] he may have[9].

Where a local authority proposes to make an application for an education supervision order it must, before making the application, consult the appropriate local authority, if different[10]. An education supervision order may not be made with respect to a child who is in the care of a local authority[11].

An education supervision order has effect for a period of one year beginning with the date on which it is made[12]. It may be discharged on the application of the child concerned, his parent[13] or the local authority designated in the order[14]. An education supervision order will not expire if, before it would otherwise have expired, the court, on the application of the authority in whose favour the order was made, has extended the period during which it is in force[15]. In any event, an order ceases to have effect on the child's ceasing to be of compulsory school age, or on the making of a care order with respect to the child[16].

Where an education supervision order is in force with respect to a child, it supersedes or precludes the operation of certain statutory provisions regarding that child[17].

1 'Local authority' means, in relation to England, the council of a county, a metropolitan district, a London Borough or the Common Council of the City of London; and in relation to Wales, the council of a county or a county borough: Children Act 1989 s 105(1) (definition amended by the Local Government (Wales) Act 1994 ss 22(4), 66(8), Sch 10 para 13, Sch 18). In relation to the Isles of Scilly, any reference in the Children Act 1989 to a 'local authority' is to be construed as a reference to the Council of the Isles of Scilly: see the Isles of Scilly (Children Act 1989) Order 2010, SI 2010/1116, art 2. As to local government areas and authorities in England and Wales see LOCAL GOVERNMENT vol 69 (2009) PARA 22 et seq. As to the London boroughs and their councils see LONDON GOVERNMENT vol 71 (2013) PARA 20 et seq. As to the Common Council of the City of London see LONDON GOVERNMENT vol 71 (2013) PARAS 34–38. As to the Council of the Isles of Scilly see LOCAL GOVERNMENT vol 69 (2009) PARA 36. As to the meanings of 'England' and 'Wales' see PARA 7 note 3.

2 See the Children Act 1989 s 36(2).

3 'Child' means a person under the age of 18: see the Children Act 1989 s 105(1); and CHILDREN AND YOUNG PERSONS vol 9 (2012) PARA 3. As to the time at which a person attains a particular age see PARA 7 note 6.

4 The local authority designated in an education supervision order must be: (1) the authority within whose area the child concerned is living or will live; or (2) where the child is a registered pupil at a school, and the authority mentioned in head (1) and the authority within whose area the school is situated agree, the latter authority: Children Act 1989 s 36(7) (amended by SI 2010/1158). As to the meaning of 'registered pupil' see PARA 437; and as to the meaning of 'school' see PARA 91 (definitions applied by the Children Act 1989 s105(1) (amended by the Education Act 1996 s 582(1), Sch 37 para 91)).

5 Children Act 1989 s 36(1) (amended by SI 2010/1158). See further CHILDREN AND YOUNG PERSONS vol 9 (2012) PARA 339. As to the procedure in relation to such applications see generally now the Family Procedure Rules 2010, SI 2010/2955, Pt 12 (amended by SI 2013/3204). As to supervision orders generally see CHILDREN AND YOUNG PERSONS vol 9 (2012) PARA 324 et seq. An application for an education supervision order is usually the appropriate procedure to secure a child's attendance at school, but in a proper case application for a care order may be founded on playing truant: *Re O (A Minor) (Care Proceedings: Education)* [1992] 4 All ER 905, [1992] 1 WLR 912. Such an application is not within the definition of 'specified proceedings' in the Children Act 1989 s 41(6) (see CHILDREN AND YOUNG PERSONS vol 9 (2012) PARA 342), and there is no power for a children's guardian to be appointed in a family proceedings court on such an application: *Essex County Council v B* [1993] 1 FCR 145, [1993] 1 FLR 866. As to children's guardians see CHILDREN AND YOUNG PERSONS vol 9 (2012) PARA 342.

The provisions of the Children Act 1989 s 36 replaced the Children and Young Persons Act 1969 s 1(2)(e) (repealed), under which the court had power to make a care order if satisfied that a child of compulsory school age was not receiving efficient full-time education; the Children Act 1989 contains no provision empowering the court to make a care order on educational grounds as such.

The Secretary of State or, in relation to Wales, the Welsh Ministers may by regulations make provision modifying, or displacing, the provisions of any enactment about education in relation to any child with respect to whom an education supervision order is in force to such extent as appears to the Secretary of State or the Welsh Ministers to be necessary or expedient in consequence of the provision made by the Children Act 1989 with respect to such orders: Sch 3 para 20. At the date at which this volume states the law, no such regulations had been made. As to the Secretary of State see PARA 58. The functions of the Secretary of State under the Children Act 1989 s 36, Sch 3, so far as exercisable in relation to Wales, were transferred to the National Assembly for Wales (see the National Assembly for Wales (Transfer of Functions) Order 1999, SI 1999/672, art 2, Sch 1) and are now vested in the Welsh Ministers (see the Government of Wales Act 2006 s 162(1), Sch 11 para 30). As to the Welsh Ministers see PARA 59.

6 As to the meaning of 'compulsory school age' see PARA 19.

7 Children Act 1989 s 36(3).

8 As to the meaning of 'special educational needs' see PARAS 943, 989 (definition applied by the Children Act 1989 s 105(1) (amended by the Education Act 1996 Sch 37 para 91)).

9 Children Act 1989 s 36(4). Where a child: (1) is the subject of a school attendance order which is in force under the Education Act 1996 s 437 (see PARA 440) and which has not been complied with; or (2) he is not attending regularly within the meaning of s 444 (see PARA 447) (a) a school at which he is a registered pupil, or (b) any place at which education is provided for him in the circumstances mentioned in s 444ZA(1) or, as from a day to be appointed, s 444ZA(1A) (see PARA 448), or (c) any place which he is required to attend in the circumstances mentioned in s 444ZA(2) or s 444ZA(1B) (see PARA 448), then, unless it is proved that he is being properly

educated, it is assumed that he is not: Children Act 1989 s 36(5) (amended by the Education Act 1996 Sch 37 para 85; Education Act 2005 s 117, Sch 18 para 1; and the Education and Skills Act 2008 s 169(1), Sch 1 Pt 2 para 43(a)).

10   Children Act 1989 s 36(8) (amended by the Education Act 1993 s 307(1), (3), Sch 19 para 149, Sch 21 Pt II; and SI 2010/1158). The 'appropriate local authority' in the case of a child who is being provided with accommodation by, or on behalf of, a local authority, is that authority; and in any other case is the local authority within whose area the child concerned lives, or will live: Children Act 1989 s 36(9). As to the exercise of the duty to consult see JUDICIAL REVIEW vol 61 (2010) PARA 627.

11   Children Act 1989 s 36(6). Note that a child who is not being properly educated may be suffering or be likely to suffer 'significant harm' for the purposes of s 31 (see CHILDREN AND YOUNG PERSONS vol 9 (2012) PARA 316) such as might justify the making of a care order under the Children Act 1989: *Re O (A Minor) (Care Proceedings: Education)* [1992] 4 All ER 905, [1992] 1 WLR 912. As to children looked after by a local authority see CHILDREN AND YOUNG PERSONS vol 10 (2012) PARA 843 et seq.

12   Children Act 1989 Sch 3 para 15(1).

13   As to the meaning of 'parent' see PARA 7 note 6 (definition applied by the Children Act 1989 Sch 3 para 21 (amended by the Education Act 1996 Sch 37 para 93(1), (3))).

14   Children Act 1989 Sch 3 para 17(1) (amended by SI 2010/1158). On discharging an education supervision order the court may direct the local authority within whose area the child lives, or will live, to investigate the child's circumstances: Sch 3 para 17(2).

15   Children Act 1989 Sch 3 para 15(2). The period may be extended on more than one occasion, but no one extension may be for more than three years: see Sch 3 para 15(4), (5). An application for extension may not be made earlier than three months before the date on which the order would otherwise expire: Sch 3 para 15(3). As to the meaning of 'month' see PARA 54 note 26.

16   See the Children Act 1989 Sch 3 para 15(6). As to care orders see CHILDREN AND YOUNG PERSONS vol 9 (2012) PARA 312 et seq.

17   Where an education supervision order is in force with respect to a child, the duties of the child's parents under the Education Act 1996 s 7 (see PARA 435) and s 444 (duties to secure education of children and to secure regular attendance of registered pupils: see PARA 447) are superseded by their duty to comply with any directions in force under the education supervision order: Children Act 1989 Sch 3 para 13(1) (amended by the Education Act 1996 s 582(1), Sch 37 para 93(1), (2)(a)). Where an education supervision order is made with respect to a child:

(1)   any school attendance order made under the Education Act 1996 s 437 (see PARA 440) with respect to the child, and in force immediately before the making of the education supervision order, ceases to have effect (Children Act 1989 Sch 3 para 13(2)(a) (amended by the Education Act 1996 Sch 37 para 93(1), (2)(b))); and

(2)   while the education supervision order remains in force, the following provisions do not apply with respect to the child: (a) the Education Act 1996 s 437 (school attendance orders: see PARA 440); (b) s 9 (pupils to be educated in accordance with wishes of their parents: see PARA 7) (Children Act 1989 Sch 3 para 13(2)(b) (amended by the Education Act 1996 Sch 37 para 93(1), (2)(b)));

(3)   a youth rehabilitation order made under the Criminal Justice and Immigration Act 2008 Pt 1 (ss 1–8) (see SENTENCING AND DISPOSITION OF OFFENDERS vol 92 (2010) PARA 202 et seq) with respect to the child, while the education supervision order is in force, may not include an education requirement (within the meaning of that Part) (Children Act 1989 Sch 3 para 13(2)(c) (substituted by the Criminal Justice and Immigration Act 2008 s 6(2), Sch 4 Pt 1 paras 33, 37(1), (2)));

(4)   any education requirement of a kind mentioned in head (3) above, which was in force with respect to the child immediately before the making of the education supervision order, ceases to have effect (Children Act 1989 Sch 3 para 13(2)(d)).

454. Duties of the supervisor. Where an education supervision order[1] is in force with respect to a child[2], it is the duty of a supervisor[3] to advise, assist and befriend, and give directions to, the supervised child and his parents[4] in such a way as will, in the opinion of the supervisor, secure that he is properly educated[5]. Where any such directions given to the supervised child or a parent have not been complied with, it is the supervisor's duty to consider what further steps to take in the exercise of the supervisor's powers under the Children Act 1989[6].

Before giving any such directions the supervisor, so far as is reasonably practicable, must ascertain the wishes and feelings of the child and his parents, including in particular their wishes as to the place at which the child should be educated[7]. When settling the terms of any such directions, the supervisor must give due consideration, having regard to the child's age and understanding, to such wishes and feelings of his as the supervisor has been able to ascertain, and to such wishes and feelings of the child's parents as he has been able to ascertain[8].

1   As to education supervision orders see PARA 453.
2   As to the meaning of 'child' see PARA 453 note 3.
3   'Supervised child' and 'supervisor', in relation to an education supervision order, mean respectively the child who is, or is to be, under supervision and the person under whose supervision he is, or is to be, by virtue of the order: see the Children Act 1989 s 105(1).
4   As to the meaning of 'parent' see PARA 7 note 6 (definition applied by the Children Act 1989 Sch 3 para 21 (amended by the Education Act 1996 Sch 37 para 93(1), (3))).
5   Children Act 1989 Sch 3 para 12(1)(a). Directions may be given under Sch 3 para 12 at any time while the education supervision order is in force: Sch 3 para 12(4). As to the duration of education supervision orders see PARA 453.
6   See the Children Act 1989 Sch 3 para 12(1)(b). An education supervision order may require the child to keep the supervisor informed of any change in his address, and to allow the supervisor to visit him at the place where he is living: Sch 3 para 16(1). A person who is the parent of a child with respect to whom an education supervision order has been made must, if asked by the supervisor, inform him of the child's address (if it is known to him); and, if he is living with the child, he must allow the supervisor reasonable contact with the child: Sch 3 para 16(2).
7   Children Act 1989 Sch 3 para 12(2).
8   Children Act 1989 Sch 3 para 12(3).

455. Failure to comply with direction under an education supervision order.
If a parent[1] of a child[2] with respect to whom an education supervision order[3] is in force persistently fails to comply with a direction[4] given under the order, he is guilty of an offence[5]. It is a defence for any person charged with such an offence to prove[6]: (1) that he took all reasonable steps to ensure that the direction was complied with[7]; (2) that the direction was unreasonable[8]; or (3) that he had complied with a requirement included in a supervision order[9] made with respect to the child, or with directions given under such a requirement, and it was not reasonably practicable to comply both with the direction under the education supervision order and with the requirement or directions under the supervision order[10].

Where a child with respect to whom an education supervision order is in force persistently fails to comply with any direction given under the order, the local authority[11] designated in the order must notify the appropriate local authority[12], if different[13], which must investigate the circumstances of the child[14].

1   As to the meaning of 'parent' see PARA 7 note 6 (definition applied by the Children Act 1989 Sch 3 para 21 (amended by the Education Act 1996 Sch 37 para 93(1), (3))).
2   As to the meaning of 'child' see PARA 453 note 3.
3   As to the meaning of 'education supervision order' see PARA 453. As to the duration and effect of education supervision orders see PARA 453. As to supervision orders generally see CHILDREN AND YOUNG PERSONS vol 9 (2012) PARA 324 et seq.
4   As to directions under an education supervision order see PARA 454.
5   Children Act 1989 Sch 3 para 18(1). The penalty for such an offence is, on summary conviction, a fine not exceeding level 3 on the standard scale: see Sch 3 para 18(3). As to the standard scale see SENTENCING AND DISPOSITION OF OFFENDERS vol 92 (2010) PARA 142.
6   As to the standard of proof on the accused see CRIMINAL PROCEDURE vol 28 (2010) PARA 466.
7   Children Act 1989 Sch 3 para 18(2)(a).
8   Children Act 1989 Sch 3 para 18(2)(b).
9   'A supervision order' means an order under the Children Act 1989 s 31(1)(b) (see CHILDREN AND YOUNG PERSONS vol 9 (2012) PARA 313) and (except where express provision to the contrary is made) includes an interim supervision order made under s 38 (see CHILDREN AND YOUNG PERSONS vol 9 (2012) PARA 331): ss 31(11), 105(1).

10 Children Act 1989 Sch 3 para 18(2)(c). Where an education supervision order and a supervision order, or youth rehabilitation order (within the meaning of the Criminal Justice and Immigration Act 2008 Pt 1 (ss 1–8): see SENTENCING AND DISPOSITION OF OFFENDERS vol 92 (2010) PARA 202), are in force at the same time with respect to the same child (Children Act 1989 Sch 3 para 14(1) (amended by the Criminal Justice and Immigration Act 2008 s 6(2), Sch 4 Pt 1 paras 33, 37(1), (3)(a))), any failure to comply with a direction given by the supervisor under the education supervision order must be disregarded if it would not have been reasonably practicable to comply with it without failing to comply with a direction or instruction given under the other order (Children Act 1989 Sch 3 para 14(2) (amended by the Criminal Justice and Immigration Act 2008 s 6(2), Sch 4 Pt 1 paras 33, 37(1), (3)(b))).

11 As to the meaning of 'local authority' see PARA 453 note 1.

12 As to the meaning of 'appropriate local authority' see PARA 453 note 10 (definition applied by the Children Act 1989 Sch 3 para 19(3)).

13 Children Act 1989 Sch 3 para 19(1) (amended by SI 2010/1158).

14 See the Children Act 1989 Sch 3 para 19(2).

456. Removal of truants and excluded pupils to designated premises or school. Where a local authority[1] designates premises in a police area[2] as premises to which children[3] and young persons[4] of compulsory school age[5] may be removed[6], and notifies the chief officer of police[7] for that area of the designation[8], a police officer of or above the rank of superintendent may direct that the powers[9] conferred on a constable[10] to remove a child or young person to designated premises are exercisable as respects any area falling within the police area and specified in the direction[11], and are so exercisable during a period so specified[12].

If a constable has reasonable cause to believe that a child or young person found by him in a public place[13] in a specified area[14] during a specified period is of compulsory school age[15], and that he is absent from a school[16] without lawful authority[17], the constable may remove the child or young person to designated premises, or to the school from which he is so absent[18].

If a constable has reasonable cause to believe that a child or young person found by him in a public place in a specified area[19] during a specified period and during school hours[20]:

(1)   is of compulsory school age[21];

(2)   has been excluded on disciplinary grounds from a relevant school[22] for a fixed period or permanently[23];

(3)   remains excluded from that school[24];

(4)   has not subsequently been admitted as a pupil to any other school[25]; and

(5)   has no reasonable justification for being in the public place[26],

the constable may remove the child or young person to designated premises[27].

1 'Local authority' means: (1) in relation to England, a county council, a district council whose district does not form part of an area that has a county council, a London borough council or the Common Council of the City of London; and (2) in relation to Wales, a county council or a county borough council: Crime and Disorder Act 1998 s 16(5). As to local government areas and authorities in England and Wales see LOCAL GOVERNMENT vol 69 (2009) PARA 22 et seq. As to the London boroughs and their councils see LONDON GOVERNMENT vol 71 (2013) PARA 20 et seq. As to the Common Council of the City of London see LONDON GOVERNMENT vol 71 (2013) PARAS 34–38. As to the meanings of 'England' and 'Wales' see PARA 7 note 3.

2 'Police area' has the same meaning as in the Police Act 1996 s 1(2) (see POLICE AND INVESTIGATORY POWERS vol 84 (2013) PARA 52): Crime and Disorder Act 1998 s 18(1).

3 'Child' means a person under the age of 14: Crime and Disorder Act 1998 s 117(1). For the purposes of the Crime and Disorder Act 1998, the age of a person is deemed to be that which it appears to the court to be after considering any available evidence: s 117(3). As to the time at which a person attains a particular age see PARA 7 note 6.

4 'Young person' means a person who has attained the age of 14 and is under the age of 18: Crime and Disorder Act 1998 s 117(1).
5 As to the meaning of 'compulsory school age' see PARA 19.
6 Crime and Disorder Act 1998 s 16(1)(a).
7 'Chief officer of police' has the same meaning as in the Police Act 1996 s 101(1) (see POLICE AND INVESTIGATORY POWERS vol 84 (2013) PARA 5): Crime and Disorder Act 1998 s 18(1).
8 Crime and Disorder Act 1998 s 16(1)(b).
9 Ie the powers conferred by the Crime and Disorder Act 1998 s 16(3), (3ZA) (see the text to notes 14–27): see s 16(2) (amended by the Education and Inspections Act 2006 s 108(1), (2)(a)).
10 As to the office of constable see POLICE AND INVESTIGATORY POWERS vol 84 (2013) PARA 1 et seq.
11 Crime and Disorder Act 1998 s 16(2)(a). Section 16(2) has effect in relation to the British Transport Police Force; and for that purpose the reference to any area falling within the police area must be treated as a reference to any area in a place specified in the Railways and Transport Safety Act 2003 s 31(1)(a)–(f) (see RAILWAYS AND TRAMWAYS vol 86 (2013) PARA 287): Crime and Disorder Act 1998 s 16(3A) (added by the Police Reform Act 2002 s 75(1); and substituted by SI 2004/1573). For these purposes, 'British Transport Police' means the force of constables appointed under the British Transport Commission Act 1949 s 53 (now repealed) (see RAILWAYS AND TRAMWAYS vol 86 (2013) PARA 285 et seq): Crime and Disorder Act 1998 s 16(5) (definition added by the Police Reform Act 2002 s 75(2)(a)).
12 Crime and Disorder Act 1998 s 16(2)(b).
13 'Public place' has the same meaning as in the Public Order Act 1986 Pt II (ss 11–16) (see CRIMINAL LAW vol 26 (2010) PARA 532): Crime and Disorder Act 1988 s 16(5) (definition amended by the Policing and Crime Act 2009 s 112(1), Sch 7 Pt 13 para 134(1), (3)).
14 References in the Crime and Disorder Act 1998 s 16(3) to specified areas and specified periods are references to areas and periods specified in an order under s 16(2) (see the text to notes 9–12): see s 16(2) (as amended: see note 9).
15 Crime and Disorder Act 1998 s 16(3)(a).
16 As to the meaning of 'school' see PARA 91 (definition applied by the Crime and Disorder Act 1998 s 16(5)).
17 Crime and Disorder Act 1998 s 16(3)(b). A child's or young person's absence from a school must be taken to be without lawful authority unless the child or young person is prevented from attending by sickness or other unavoidable cause or the absence falls within the Education Act 1996 s 444(3) (leave or day set apart for religious observance: see PARA 447): Crime and Disorder Act 1998 s 16(4) (amended by the Education and Inspections Act 2006 s 109(10)).
18 Crime and Disorder Act 1998 s 16(3).
19 References in the Crime and Disorder Act 1998 s 16(3ZA) to specified areas and specified periods are references to areas and periods specified in an order under s 16(2) (see the text to notes 9–12): see s 16(2) (as amended: see note 9).
20 'School hours' means any time during a school session of the school referred to in the Crime and Disorder Act 1998 s 16(3)(ZA)(b) (see the text to notes 22–23) or during a break between sessions of that school on the same day: s 16(3B) (added by the Education and Inspections Act 2006 s 108(1), (4)). As to the regulation of the school day see PARA 459.
21 Crime and Disorder Act 1998 s 16(3ZA)(a) (s 16(3ZA) added by the Education and Inspections Act 2006 s 108(1), (3)).
22 'Relevant school' has the meaning given by the Education and Inspections Act 2006 s 111 (see PARA 521 note 3): Crime and Disorder Act 1998 s 16(5) (definition added by the Education and Inspections Act 2006 s 108(1), (5)).
23 Crime and Disorder Act 1998 s 16(3ZA)(b) (as added: see note 21). As to the exclusion of pupils see PARA 517 et seq.
24 Crime and Disorder Act 1998 s 16(3ZA)(c) (as added: see note 21).
25 Crime and Disorder Act 1998 s 16(3ZA)(d) (as added: see note 21).
26 Crime and Disorder Act 1998 s 16(3ZA)(e) (as added: see note 21).
27 Crime and Disorder Act 1998 s 16(3ZA) (as added: see note 21).

457. School attendance targets. Regulations[1] may make provision for and in connection with requiring, or enabling the appropriate national authority[2] to require, governing bodies[3] of maintained schools[4] to secure that annual targets are set for reducing the level of absences on the part of relevant day pupils[5] at their schools[6]. Such regulations may, in particular, make provision:

   (1)   for the appropriate national authority to impose such a requirement on

the governing body of a maintained school where the specified condition is for the time being satisfied[7] in relation to the school[8], and the appropriate national authority considers it appropriate to impose the requirement[9];

(2)   for such a requirement to be imposed by the appropriate national authority in such manner, and for such period, as may be specified in or determined in accordance with the regulations[10];

(3)   for the appropriate national authority, where it considers it appropriate to do so, to exempt the governing body of a maintained school, in relation to any school year, from a requirement so imposed[11].

1   'Regulations' means regulations made by the Secretary of State or, in relation to Wales, the Welsh Ministers under the School Standards and Framework Act 1998: see s 142(1). As to the Secretary of State see PARA 58. The functions of the Secretary of State under the School Standards and Framework Act 1998 s 63, so far as exercisable in relation to Wales, were transferred to the National Assembly for Wales (see the National Assembly for Wales (Transfer of Functions) Order 1999, SI 1999/672, art 2, Sch 1) and are now vested in the Welsh Ministers (see the Government of Wales Act 2006 s 162(1), Sch 11 para 30). As to the Welsh Ministers see PARA 59. As to the meaning of 'Wales' see PARA 7 note 3.

     As to the regulations made under the School Standards and Framework Act 1998 s 63 see the Education (School Attendance Targets) (England) Regulations 2007, SI 2007/2261 (amended by SI 2010/2838); and the School Performance and Absence Targets (Wales) Regulations 2011, SI 2011/1945.

2   Ie the Secretary of State or, in relation to Wales, the Welsh Ministers.

3   As to the governing bodies of maintained schools in England see PARA 150 et seq; and in Wales see PARA 195.

4   As to the meaning of 'maintained school' see PARA 99.

5   'Relevant day pupil' means a pupil registered at a maintained school who is of compulsory school age and is not a boarder: School Standards and Framework Act 1998 s 63(4). As to the meaning of 'pupil' see PARA 20 note 4; as to the meaning of 'registered pupil' see PARA 437; and as to the meaning of 'boarder' see PARA 31 note 19 (definitions applied by the s 142(8)). As to the meaning of 'compulsory school age' see PARA 19.

6   School Standards and Framework Act 1998 s 63(1) (amended by the Education Act 2002 ss 53(1), (2), 215, Sch 22 Pt 3). Provision made by regulations under the School Standards and Framework Act 1998 s 63 may relate to absences which are authorised pursuant to regulations under the Education Act 1996 s 434 (see PARA 437), or absences which are not so authorised, or both: School Standards and Framework Act 1998 s 63(3A) (added by the Education Act 2002 s 53(1), (3)).

7   For the purposes of the School Standards and Framework Act 1998 s 63(2)(a)(i), the specified condition is for the time being satisfied in relation to a maintained school if in the previous school year the level of absences on the part of relevant day pupils at the school (as determined in accordance with the regulations) exceeded such level as may for that year be specified in or determined in accordance with the regulations: s 63(3) (amended by the Education Act 2002 s 53(1), (4), Sch 22 Pt 3). As to the meaning of 'school year' see PARA 19 note 12 (definition applied by the School Standards and Framework Act 1998 s 142(8)).

8   School Standards and Framework Act 1998 s 63(2)(a)(i).

9   School Standards and Framework Act 1998 s 63(2)(a)(ii).

10 School Standards and Framework Act 1998 s 63(2)(b).

11 School Standards and Framework Act 1998 s 63(2)(c).

(v) School Terms, Holidays and Times of Session

458. Responsibility for fixing dates of terms and holidays and times of sessions. Until a day to be appointed[1], in the case of a community, voluntary controlled or community special school[2] in England[3] or a maintained nursery school[4] in England, the local authority[5] must determine the dates when the school terms and holidays are to begin and end[6], and the governing body[7] must determine the times of the school sessions[8].

In the case of a foundation, voluntary aided or foundation special school[9] in England the governing body must determine[10] the dates and times when the school terms and holidays are to begin and end[11], and the times of the school sessions[12].

Regulations[13] may make provision:

(1) as to the procedure to be followed where the governing body of a community, voluntary controlled or community special school, a maintained nursery school[14] (until a day to be appointed) or (as from that day) a community, voluntary controlled or community special school in England, proposes to make any change in the times of the school sessions[15];

(2) as to the implementation of any such proposal[16];

(3) for enabling the local authority to determine, for any purposes of the regulations, whether any person is to be treated as a parent of a registered pupil at the school[17].

In relation to Wales there are now separate provisions relating to responsibility for fixing term and holiday dates[18], the Welsh Ministers' powers to direct determination of term dates[19] and responsibility for fixing times of school sessions[20].

1   As from a day to be appointed the Education Act 2002 s 32(1) (see the text and notes 2–8) is repealed by the Deregulation Act 2015 Sch 16 para 3(1), (2). At the date at which this volume states the law no such day had been appointed.

2   As to the meaning of references to community schools, voluntary schools and community special schools see PARA 106.

3   As to the meaning of 'England' see PARA 7 note 3.

4   As to the meaning of 'maintained nursery school' see PARA 103 note 3.

5   As to the meaning of 'local authority' see PARA 25 (definition applied by the Education Act 2002 s 212(1) (amended by SI 2010/1158)).

6   Education Act 2002 s 32(1)(a) (amended by SI 2010/1158; and the Education (Wales) Act 2014 Sch 3 para 1(1), (2)(a)(i); prospectively repealed (see note 1)).

7   As to the governing bodies of maintained schools in England see PARA 150 et seq.

8   Education Act 2002 s 32(1)(b) (amended by the Learner Travel (Wales) Measure 2008 s 21(1), (2)(a); and the Education (Wales) Act 2014 Sch 3 para 1(1), (2)(a)(ii); prospectively repealed (see note 1)). See note 6. 'The times of the school sessions' means the times at which each of the school sessions (or, if there is only one, the school session) is to begin and end on any day: Education Act 2002 s 32(4).

As to the application of s 32 to pupil referral units in Wales see the Education (Pupil Referral Units) (Application of Enactments) (Wales) Regulations 2007, SI 2007/1069, reg 3, Sch 1 Pt 1 para 9; and in England see the Education (Pupil Referral Units) (Application of Enactments) (England) Regulations 2007, SI 2007/2979, regs 1(3), 3, Sch 1 Pt 1 para 17 (amended by SI 2010/1172). As to pupil referral units see PARA 427 et seq.

9   As to the meaning of references to foundation and foundation special schools see PARA 106.

10   Education Act 2002 s 32(2) (amended by the Education (Wales) Act 2014 Sch 3 para 1(1), (2)(b)(i)). As from a day to be appointed, the words 'In the case of' to 'governing body' are substituted by the words 'The governing body of a school in England': Education Act 2002 s 32(2) (prospectively amended by the Deregulation Act 2015 Sch 16 para 3(1), (3)). At the date at which this volume states the law no such day had been appointed.

11   Education Act 2002 s 32(2)(a).

12   Education Act 2002 s 32(2)(b) (amended by the Learner Travel (Wales) Measure 2008 s 21(1), (2)(b); and the Education (Wales) Act 2014 Sch 3 para 1(1), (2)(b)(ii)).

13   'Regulations' means regulations made under the Education Act 2002 by the Secretary of State in relation to England or by the Welsh Ministers in relation to Wales: see s 212(1). As to the Secretary of State see PARA 58. As to the Welsh Ministers see PARA 59. As to the meaning of 'Wales' see PARA 7 note 3. The functions under the Education Act 2002 s 32(3) in relation to Wales were originally vested in the National Assembly for Wales and were later exercisable by the Welsh Ministers by virtue of the Government of Wales Act 2006 s 162(1), Sch 11 paras 30, 32. As to the regulations made see the Changing of School Session Times (Wales) Regulations 2009, SI 2009/572 (amended by SI 2010/1142); and the Changing of School Times

(England) (Revocation) Regulations 2011, SI 2011/1954 (which revoke the Changing of School Session Times (England) Regulations 1999, SI 1999/2733). Note that the provisions of the Education Act 2002 s 32(5)–(10), which previously disapplied s 32(1), (2)(b) in relation to schools in Wales, were repealed by the Education (Wales) Act 2014 Sch 3 para 1(1), (2)(c) and that that Act provided new provisions affecting local authorities in Wales and relevant schools: see the text to notes 18–20.

14 Ie a school within the Education Act 2002 s 32(1): see the text to notes 1–7.

15 Education Act 2002 s 32(3)(a) (prospectively amended by the Deregulation Act 2015 Sch 16 para 3(1), (4)). At the date at which this volume states the law no such day had been appointed.

16 Education Act 2002 s 32(3)(b).

17 Education Act 2002 s 32(3)(c) (amended by SI 2010/1158).

18 See the Education Act 2002 s 32A (added by the Education (Wales) Act 2014 s 42); and the Education (Notification of School Term Dates) (Wales) Regulations 2014, SI 2014/1249.

19 See the Education Act 2002 s 32B (added by the Education (Wales) Act 2014 s 42); and the Education (Consultation on School Term Dates) (Wales) Regulations 2014, SI 2014/1462.

20 See the Education Act 2002 s 32C (added by the Education (Wales) Act 2014 s 42).

459. Regulations as to duration of school day etc. Regulations[1] may make provision with respect to the duration of the school day[2] and school year[3] at, and the granting of leave of absence from[4], any school[5] maintained by a local authority[6], and any special school[7] not maintained by a local authority[8].

1 'Regulations' means regulations made by the Secretary of State or, in relation to Wales, the Welsh Ministers: see the Education Act 1996 s 579(1). As to the Secretary of State see PARA 58. The functions of the Secretary of State under the Education Act 1996 s 551, so far as exercisable in relation to Wales, were transferred to the National Assembly for Wales (see the National Assembly for Wales (Transfer of Functions) Order 1999, SI 1999/672, art 2, Sch 1) and are now vested in the Welsh Ministers (see the Government of Wales Act 2006 s 162(1), Sch 11 para 30). As to the Welsh Ministers see PARA 59. As to the meaning of 'Wales' see PARA 7 note 3.

As to the regulations made see the Education (School Day and School Year) (England) Regulations 1999, SI 1999/3181 (amended by SI 2001/1429; SI 2010/604; and SI 2011/154); the Education (School Day and School Year) (Wales) Regulations 2003, SI 2003/3231 (amended by SI 2006/1262; SI 2008/1739; SI 2011/149; and SI 2012/248); the Education (Pupil Registration) (England) Regulations 2006, SI 2006/1751 (amended SI 2007/603; SI 2011/1625; SI 2012/1033; and SI 2013/756); and the Education (Pupil Registration) (Wales) Regulations 2010, SI 2010/1954. In addition the Education (Pupil Registration) Regulations 1995, SI 1995/2089 (amended by SI 1997/2624; SI 2001/1109; SI 2001/2802; SI 2002/3178; SI 2003/3227; SI 2005/2913; revoked in relation to England by SI 2006/1751) have effect as if made under the Education Act 1996 s 551 by virtue of s 582(3), Sch 39 para 1.

2 As to the meaning of 'school day' see PARA 229 note 6.

3 As to the meaning of 'school year' see PARA 19 note 12. The reference to the duration of the school year at any school to which the Education Act 1996 s 551(1) applies is a reference to the number of school sessions that must be held during any such year: s 551(1A) (added by the Education Act 1997 s 57(1), Sch 7 para 39).

4 See the Education Act 1996 s 551(1). As to holidays taken for more than ten days see *R v Governing Body of Gateway Primary School, ex p X* [2001] ELR 321.

5 As to the meaning of 'school' see PARA 91.

6 Education Act 1996 s 551(2)(a) (amended by SI 2010/1158). As to the meaning of 'local authority' see PARA 25. As to schools maintained by local authorities see PARA 99 et seq.

7 As to the meaning of 'special school' see PARA 1041.

8 Education Act 1996 s 551(2)(c) (amended by SI 2010/1158).

(vi) Transport Arrangements to Facilitate Attendance

A. TRANSPORT ARRANGEMENTS IN ENGLAND

460. Duty of local authority to promote sustainable modes of travel. A local authority[1] in England[2] must: (1) prepare for each academic year[3] a document containing its strategy to promote the use of sustainable modes of travel[4] to meet the school travel needs of its area[5] ('a sustainable modes of travel strategy')[6]; (2)

publish the strategy in such manner and by such time as may be prescribed[7]; and (3) promote the use of sustainable modes of travel to meet the school travel needs of its area[8].

Before preparing a sustainable modes of travel strategy, an authority must in particular assess the school travel needs of its area[9], and assess the facilities and services for sustainable modes of travel to, from and within its area[10]. The Secretary of State must issue, and may from time to time revise, guidance[11] in relation to the discharge by a local authority of its duties under these provisions[12]. In discharging these duties an authority must consult such persons as it considers appropriate[13], and have regard to any such guidance given from time to time by the Secretary of State[14].

1   As to the meaning of 'local authority' see PARA 25.
2   As to the meaning of 'England' see PARA 7 note 3.
3   'Academic year' has the same meaning as in the Education Act 1996 s 509AC (see PARA 464 note 3) in the case of local authorities in England: s 508A(11) (s 508A added by the Education and Inspections Act 2006 s 76; and the Education Act 1996 s 508A(11) amended by SI 2010/1158).
4   'Sustainable modes of travel' are modes of travel which the authority considers may improve either or both of the following: (1) the physical well-being of those who use them (Education Act 1996 s 508A(3)(a) (as added: see note 3)); (2) the environmental well-being of the whole or a part of its area (s 508A(3)(b) (as so added)).
5   The 'school travel needs' of a local authority's area are: (1) the needs of children and persons of sixth form age in the authority's area as regards travel mentioned in the Education Act 1996 s 508A(5) (s 508A(4)(a) (s 508A as added (see note 3); and s 508(4) amended by SI 2010/1158)); and (2) the needs of other children and persons of sixth form age as regards travel mentioned in the Education Act 1996 s 508A(6) (s 508A(4)(b) (as so added)). The needs of children and persons of sixth form age in the authority's area as regards travel referred to in s 508A(4)(a) are their needs as regards travel to and from: (a) schools at which they receive or are to receive education or training (s 508A(5)(a) (as so added)); (b) institutions within the further education sector, or 16 to 19 academies, at which they receive or are to receive education or training (s 508A(5)(b) (as so added; and amended by the Education Act 2011 Sch 13 para 9(1), (10)(a)); or (c) any other places where they receive or are to receive education by virtue of arrangements made in pursuance of the Education Act 1996 s 19(1) (see PARA 427) (s 508A(5)(c) (as so added)). The needs of other children and persons of sixth form age as regards travel referred to in s 508A(4)(b) are their needs as regards travel to and from: (i) schools at which they receive or are to receive education or training (s 508A(6)(a) (as so added)); (ii) institutions within the further education sector, or 16 to 19 academies, at which they receive or are to receive education or training (s 508A(6)(b) (as so added; and amended by the Education Act 2011 Sch 13 para 9(1), (10)(b))); or (iii) any other places where they receive or are to receive education by virtue of arrangements made in pursuance of the Education Act 1996 s 19(1) (s 508A(6)(c) (as so added)), in so far as that travel relates to travel within the authority's area (s 508A(6) (as so added)). As to the meaning of 'child' see PARA 7 note 6. References to persons of sixth form age are to be construed in accordance with s 509AC(1) (see PARA 464 note 5): s 508A(10) (as so added). As to the meaning of 'school' see PARA 91. As to the meaning of 'institution within the further education sector' see PARA 555. As to the meaning of '16 to 19 academy' see PARA 346 note 13.
6   Education Act 1996 s 508A(1)(a) (as added: see note 3). As to the duty of a local authority to have regard to religion and belief in the exercise of its travel functions see s 509AD; and PARA 466.
7   Education Act 1996 s 508A(1)(b) (as added: see note 3). 'Prescribed' means prescribed by regulations; and 'regulations' means regulations made by the Secretary of State: see s 579(1). As to the Secretary of State see PARA 58. At the date at which this volume states the law no such regulations had been made.
8   Education Act 1996 s 508A(1)(c) (as added: see note 3).
9   Education Act 1996 s 508A(2)(a) (as added: see note 3).
10 Education Act 1996 s 508A(2)(b) (as added: see note 3).
11 As to the publication of guidance see the Education Act 1996 s 571; and PARA 60. See in particular 'Home-to-school travel and transport guidance: Statutory guidance for local authorities'.

12 Education Act 1996 s 508A(7) (as added: see note 3). Before issuing or revising such guidance, the Secretary of State must consult such persons as he considers appropriate: s 508A(8) (as so added). As to the meaning of 'person' see PARA 7 note 6. As to the exercise of the duty to consult see JUDICIAL REVIEW vol 61 (2010) PARA 627.
13 Education Act 1996 s 508A(9)(a) (as added: see note 3).
14 Education Act 1996 s 508A(9)(b) (as added: see note 3).

461. Home-to-school travel arrangements for eligible children. A local authority[1] in England[2] must make, in the case of an eligible child[3] in the authority's area, such travel arrangements as it considers necessary in order to secure that suitable home to school travel arrangements[4], for the purpose of facilitating the child's attendance at the relevant educational establishment in relation to him, are made and provided free of charge[5] in relation to the child[6], if:

(1) no travel arrangements relating to travel in either direction between his home and the relevant educational establishment in relation to him, or in both directions, are provided free of charge in relation to him by any person[7] who is not the authority[8]; or

(2) such travel arrangements are provided free of charge in relation to him by any person who is not the authority but those arrangements, taken together with any other such travel arrangements which are so provided, do not provide suitable home to school travel arrangements for the purpose of facilitating his attendance at the relevant educational establishment in relation to him[9].

'Travel arrangements', in relation to an eligible child, are travel arrangements of any description and include arrangements for the provision of transport[10]; and any of the following arrangements only if they are made with the consent of a parent[11] of the child:

(a) arrangements for the provision of one or more persons to escort the child (whether alone or together with other children) when travelling to or from the relevant educational establishment in relation to the child[12];

(b) arrangements for the payment of the whole or any part of a person's reasonable travelling expenses[13];

(c) arrangements for the payment of allowances in respect of the use of particular modes of travel[14].

'Travel arrangements', in relation to an eligible child, include travel arrangements of any description made by any parent of the child only if those arrangements are made by the parent voluntarily[15]; but 'travel arrangements', in relation to an eligible child, do not comprise or include travel arrangements which give rise to additional costs and do not include appropriate protection against those costs[16].

The Secretary of State must issue, and may from time to time revise, guidance[17] in relation to the discharge by a local authority of its functions[18] under the above provisions[19]. In discharging those functions an authority must have regard to any such guidance given from time to time by the Secretary of State[20]. Regulations[21] may require a local authority to publish, at such times and in such manner as may be prescribed[22], such information as may be prescribed with respect to the authority's policy and arrangements relating to the discharge of those functions[23].

1 As to the meaning of 'local authority' see PARA 25.
2 As to the meaning of 'England' see PARA 7 note 3.
3 'Eligible child' means a child who falls within any of the provisions of the Education Act 1996 Sch 35B paras 2–7 or 9–13: s 508B(9), Sch 35B para 1 (s 508B added by the Education and

Inspections Act 2006 s 77(1); and the Education Act 1996 Sch 35B added by the Education and Inspections Act 2006 s 77(2), Sch 8). Those provisions concern situations either where the local authority has not made suitable arrangements to enable a child to become a pupil at a school nearer his home, or where the child is receiving education at a place other than a school by virtue of arrangements made in pursuance of the Education Act 1996 s 19(1) (see PARA 427), and where the child (1) is of compulsory school age and lives within walking distance of his school or other place of education, but cannot reasonably be expected to walk to that school or place having regard to his special educational needs, disability or mobility problems (see Sch 35B paras 2, 3 (as so added; Sch 35B para 2 amended by SI 2010/1158) (see also *A v North Somerset Council* [2009] EWHC 3060 (Admin), [2010] ELR 139, [2009] All ER (D) 323 (Nov)); (2) is of compulsory school age and lives within walking distance of his school or other place of education, but cannot reasonably be expected to walk to that school or place having regard to the nature of the routes which he could reasonably be expected to take (see the Education Act 1996 Sch 35B paras 4, 5 (as so added; Sch 35B para 4 amended by SI 2010/1158)); (3) is of compulsory school age and does not live within walking distance of his school or other place of education or has been excluded and appropriate arrangements have been made (see the Education Act 1996 Sch 35B paras 6–8 (as so added; Sch 35B paras 6, 7 amended by SI 2010/1158; and the Education Act 1996 Sch 35B para 8 amended by the Education and Skills Act 2008 Sch 1 paras 48, 52; and the Education Act 2011 Sch 1 paras 5, 7)); (4) either qualifies for free school lunches and milk or has a parent (with whom he is ordinarily resident) who is awarded working tax credit at the maximum rate, and where the child either (a) has attained the age of 8 but not the age of 11, and does not live within two miles of his school or other place of education (see the Education Act 1996 Sch 35B paras 9, 10, 14 (as so added; Sch 35B para 9 amended by SI 2010/1158)); (b) has attained the age of 11, and lives between two and six miles of his school or other place of education (see the Education Act 1996 Sch 35B paras 11, 13, 14 (as so added)); or (c) has attained the age of 11, lives between two and fifteen miles of his school or other place of education, and has a parent who has expressed a wish, based on the parent's religion or belief, for him to be provided with education at that school (see Sch 35B paras 12, 14 (as so added)).

4   'Home to school travel arrangements', in relation to an eligible child, are travel arrangements relating to travel in both directions between the child's home and the relevant educational establishment in question in relation to that child: Education Act 1996 s 508B(3) (as added: see note 3). References to a 'relevant educational establishment', in relation to an eligible child, are references to: (1) in the case of a child who is an eligible child by virtue of falling within any of Sch 35B paras 2, 4, 6, 9, 11, 12 (see note 3), the qualifying school (within the meaning of that Schedule) at which the child is a registered pupil referred to in the paragraph in question (s 508B(10)(a) (as so added)); and (2) in the case of a child who is an eligible child by virtue of falling within any of Sch 35B paras 3, 5, 7, 10, 13 (see note 3), the place other than a school, where the child is receiving education by virtue of arrangements made in pursuance of s 19(1) (see PARA 427), referred to in the paragraph in question (s 508B(10)(b) (as so added)).

5   Travel arrangements are provided free of charge if there is no charge for anything provided in pursuance of the arrangements: Education Act 1996 s 508B(8) (as added: see note 3).

6   Education Act 1996 s 508B(1) (as added (see note 3); and amended by SI 2010/1158). Regulations may modify the Education Act 1996 s 508B(1), (2) (see the text to notes 7–9) to provide for their application in cases where there is more than one relevant educational establishment in relation to a child: s 508B(11) (as so added). 'Regulations' means regulations made by the Secretary of State: s 579(1). As to the Secretary of State see PARA 58. As to the meaning of 'modify' see PARA 21 note 15. As to the regulations made see the School Travel (Pupils with Dual Registration) (England) Regulations 2007, SI 2007/1367. Where a school travel scheme is in force under the Education Act 1996 Sch 35C (see PARA 463), the local authority by which the scheme is made does not have any functions under s 508B in relation to children in its area: see s 508E(3) (s 508E added by the Education and Inspections Act 2006 s 78(1); and the Education Act 1996 s 508E(3) amended by SI 2010/1158). As to the duty of a local authority to have regard to religion and belief in the exercise of its travel functions see the Education Act 1996 s 509AD; and PARA 466. See *R (on the application of P) v East Sussex County Council* [2014] EWHC 4634 (Admin), [2015] ELR 178 (where there was an unsuccessful challenge to the local authority's policy of only providing transport to eligible children at the beginning and end of the normal school day, the claimant (who had a statement of educational needs: as to which see PARA 1002 et seq and see also PARA 958 et seq) contending on the basis of various provisions (including the Education Act 1996 s 508B and also provisions of the Equality Act 2010) that the authority was obliged to provide transport to school after medical appointments and transport home from after-school clubs).

7   As to the meaning of 'person' see PARA 7 note 6.

8   Education Act 1996 s 508B(2)(a) (as added: see note 3). See also note 6.

9   Education Act 1996 s 508B(2)(b) (as added: see note 3). See also note 6.

10   Education Act 1996 s 508B(4)(a) (as added: see note 3).

11   As to the meaning of 'parent' see PARA 7 note 6.

12   Education Act 1996 s 508B(4)(b)(i) (as added: see note 3).

13   Education Act 1996 s 508B(4)(b)(ii) (as added: see note 3).

14   Education Act 1996 s 508B(4)(b)(iii) (as added: see note 3).

15   Education Act 1996 s 508B(5) (as added: see note 3).

16   Education Act 1996 s 508B(6) (as added: see note 3). For the purposes of s 508B(6): (1) travel arrangements give rise to additional costs only if they give rise to any need to incur expenditure in order for the child to take advantage of anything provided for him in pursuance of the arrangements (s 508B(7)(a) (as so added)); and (2) travel arrangements include appropriate protection against those costs only if they include provision for any expenditure that needs to be incurred for the purpose mentioned in head (1) in the case of the child to be met by the person by whom the arrangements are made (s 508B(7)(b) (as so added)).

17   As to the publication of guidance see the Education Act 1996 s 571; and PARA 60. See in particular 'Home-to-school travel and transport guidance: Statutory guidance for local authorities' (July 2014).

18   As to the meaning of 'functions' see PARA 18 note 5.

19   Education Act 1996 s 508D(1) (s 508D added by the Education and Inspections Act 2006 s 77(1); and the Education Act 1996 s 508D(1) amended by SI 2010/1158). Before issuing or revising such guidance, the Secretary of State must consult such persons as he considers appropriate: Education Act 1996 s 508D(2) (as so added). As to the exercise of the duty to consult see JUDICIAL REVIEW vol 61 (2010) PARA 627.

20   Education Act 1996 s 508D(3) (as added: see note 19).

21   At the date at which this volume states the law no such regulations had been made.

22   'Prescribed' means prescribed by regulations: Education Act 1996 s 579(1).

23   Education Act 1996 s 508D(4) (as added (see note 19); and amended by SI 2010/1158).

462.   Travel arrangements etc for other children. A local authority[1] in England[2] may make such school travel arrangements as it considers necessary, in relation to any child in the authority's area who is not an eligible child[3], for the purpose of facilitating the child's attendance at any relevant educational establishment[4] in relation to the child[5]. 'School travel arrangements', in relation to such a child, are travel arrangements[6] relating to travel in either direction between his home and any relevant educational establishment in relation to the child, or in both directions[7].

A local authority in England may pay, in the case of a child in the authority's area who is not an eligible child and in relation to whom no arrangements are made by the authority under the above provisions[8], the whole or any part, as it thinks fit, of a person's reasonable travelling expenses in relation to that child's travel in either direction between his home and any relevant educational establishment in relation to the child, or in both directions[9].

The Secretary of State[10] must issue, and may from time to time revise, guidance[11] in relation to the discharge by a local authority of its functions[12] under these provisions[13]. In discharging those functions an authority must have regard to any such guidance given from time to time by the Secretary of State[14]. Regulations[15] may require a local authority to publish, at such times and in such manner as may be prescribed[16], such information as may be prescribed with respect to the authority's policy and arrangements relating to the discharge of those functions[17].

1   As to the meaning of 'local authority' see PARA 25.

2   As to the meaning of 'England' see PARA 7 note 3.

3   The Education Act 1996 s 508C applies to a child who is not an eligible child for the purposes of s 508B (see PARA 461 note 3): s 508C(2) (ss 508C, 508D added by the Education and Inspections Act 2006 s 77(1)). As to the meaning of 'child' see PARA 7 note 6.

4   References to a 'relevant educational establishment', in relation to a child who is not an eligible child, are references to: (1) any school at which he is a registered pupil (Education Act 1996 s 508C(6)(a) (as added: see note 3)); (2) any institution within the further education sector, or a 16 to 19 academy, at which he is receiving education (s 508C(6)(b) (as so added; and amended by the Education Act 2011 para 9(1), (11)); or (3) any place other than a school where he is receiving education by virtue of arrangements made in pursuance of the Education Act 1996 s 19(1) (see PARA 427) (s 508C(6)(c) (as so added)). As to the meaning of 'school' see PARA 91. As to the meaning of 'registered pupil' see PARA 437. As to the meaning of 'institution within the further education sector' see PARA 555. As to the meaning of '16 to 19 academy' see PARA 346 note 13.

5   Education Act 1996 s 508C(1) (as added (see note 3); and amended by SI 2010/1158). Where a school travel scheme is in force under the Education Act 1996 Sch 35C (see PARA 463), the local authority by which the scheme is made does not have any functions under s 508C in relation to children in its area: see s 508E(3) (s 508E added by the Education and Inspections Act 2006 s 78(1); and the Education Act 1996 s 508E(3) amended by SI 2010/1158). As to the duty of a local authority to have regard to religion and belief in the exercise of its travel functions see the Education Act 1996 s 509AD; and PARA 466.

6   'Travel arrangements', in relation to such a child, are travel arrangements of any description and include: (1) arrangements for the provision of transport (Education Act 1996 s 508C(4)(a) (as added: see note 3)); and (2) any of the following arrangements only if they are made with the consent of a parent of the child (a) arrangements for the provision of one or more persons to escort the child (whether alone or together with other children) when travelling to or from any relevant educational establishment in relation to the child (s 508C(4)(b)(i) (as so added)); (b) arrangements for the payment of the whole or any part of a person's reasonable travelling expenses (s 508C(4)(b)(ii) (as so added)); (c) arrangements for the payment of allowances in respect of the use of particular modes of travel (s 508C(4)(b)(iii) (as so added)). As to the meaning of 'parent' see PARA 7 note 6. As to the meaning of 'person' see PARA 7 note 6.

7   Education Act 1996 s 508C(3) (as added: see note 3).

8   Ie under the Education Act 1996 s 508C(1): see the text to notes 1–5.

9   Education Act 1996 s 508C(5) (as added (see note 3); and amended by SI 2010/1158).

10 As to the Secretary of State see PARA 58.

11 As to the publication of guidance see the Education Act 1996 s 571; and PARA 60. See in particular 'Home-to-school travel and transport guidance: Statutory guidance for local authorities'.

12 As to the meaning of 'functions' see PARA 18 note 5.

13 Education Act 1996 s 508D(1) (as added (see note 3); and amended by SI 2010/1158). Before issuing or revising such guidance, the Secretary of State must consult such persons as he considers appropriate: Education Act 1996 s 508D(2) (as so added). As to the exercise of the duty to consult see JUDICIAL REVIEW vol 61 (2010) PARA 627.

14 Education Act 1996 s 508D(3) (as added: see note 3).

15 'Regulations' means regulations made by the Secretary of State: Education Act 1996 s 579(1). At the date at which this volume states the law no such regulations had been made.

16 'Prescribed' means prescribed by regulations: Education Act 1996 s 579(1).

17 Education Act 1996 s 508D(4) (as added (see note 3); and amended by SI 2010/1158).

463. School travel schemes. A local authority[1] in England[2] may make a school travel scheme for its area[3]. A school travel scheme must set out (in general terms) what arrangements[4] in connection with the attendance of children[5] in the authority's area receiving education:

(1)   at schools[6],

(2)   at any institution within the further education sector[7]; or

(3)   at any other place by virtue of arrangements made[8] by the authority[9],
the scheme authority[10] considers it appropriate to be made in relation to travel to and from such places[11]. A school travel scheme may include travel arrangements of any description and may, in particular, include: (a) arrangements for the provision of transport[12]; (b) any of the specified arrangements[13] only if made with the relevant parental consent[14]: (c) arrangements to facilitate or promote the use of particular modes of travel[15]. A school travel scheme must require that if any arrangements set out in the scheme involve arrangements to be made by

any person other than the scheme authority and those arrangements are not made by that person or by any other persons[16], or are so made but are not given effect to in compliance with the requirements of the scheme[17], the scheme authority must make suitable alternative arrangements[18]. A school travel scheme must require that the scheme authority must make such travel arrangements as it considers necessary in relation to eligible children in its area[19]; and must set out the policy applicable to charging in relation to anything provided in pursuance of the scheme[20].

A school travel scheme is not to come into force unless approved by the Secretary of State[21]. A school travel scheme which has been approved by the Secretary of State is to come into force in accordance with directions given by the Secretary of State[22]. The scheme authority may, with the consent of the Secretary of State[23], amend or revoke a school travel scheme[24], and any amendment is to come into force in accordance with directions given by the Secretary of State[25]. The Secretary of State must issue, and may from time to time revise, guidance[26] as to the matters which he will take into account in exercising his powers in relation to the approval[27] and amendment[28] of school travel schemes[29].

The scheme authority must make such reports and returns to the Secretary of State[30], and compile and give to the Secretary of State such information[31], as he may require for any of the following purposes[32]: (i) the purpose of monitoring the operation or effect of a school travel scheme approved under these provisions[33]; (ii) the purpose of preparing or publishing an evaluation[34] of the operation and effect of approved school travel schemes[35].

Where a school travel scheme is in force[36], the local authority in England by which the scheme is made must give effect to the scheme[37]. Where a school travel scheme is in force, the local authority by which the scheme is made does not have any functions[38] in relation to the making of travel arrangements for children in its area[39]. The Secretary of State must issue, and may from time to time revise, guidance in relation to the discharge by a local authority in England of any duty to give effect to a school travel scheme[40] or of any functions[41] relating to the making of such a scheme[42]; and in discharging any such duty or exercising any such functions, a local authority must have regard to any such guidance given from time to time by the Secretary of State[43].

Provision was made for the school travel scheme provisions[44] to be piloted in accordance with regulations made by the Secretary of State[45]. The Secretary of State was required to prepare and publish, before 1 January 2012, an evaluation of the operation and effect of approved[46] school travel schemes[47]. The Secretary of State could by order provide for the school travel scheme provisions to cease to have effect in relation to local authorities with effect from such date as may be specified in the order[48]. The earliest date which could be specified was 1 August 2012[49], and the latest date which could be specified was 1 August 2015[50].

1 As to the meaning of 'local authority' see PARA 25.

2 As to the meaning of 'England' see PARA 7 note 3.

3 Education Act 1996 Sch 35C para 1(1) (Sch 35C added by the Education and Inspections Act 2006 s 78(2), Sch 9; and the Education Act 1996 Sch 35C para 1 amended by SI 2010/1158). Before making a school travel scheme, a local authority must consult such persons as the authority considers appropriate: Education Act 1996 Sch 35C para 1(2) (as so added and amended). As to the exercise of the duty to consult see JUDICIAL REVIEW vol 61 (2010) PARA 627. As to the meaning of 'person' see PARA 7 note 6. As to the duty of a local authority to have regard to religion and belief in the exercise of its travel functions see s 509AD; and PARA 466.

4   Those arrangements are to be either or both of the following: (1) arrangements to be made by
    the authority (Education Act 1996 Sch 35C para 2(2)(a) (as added: see note 3)); (2)
    arrangements to be made by any other persons (Sch 35C para 2(2)(b) (as so added)).
5   As to the meaning of 'child' see PARA 7 note 6.
6   Education Act 1996 Sch 35C para 2(1)(a) (as added: see note 3). As to the meaning of 'school'
    see PARA 91.
7   Education Act 1996 Sch 35C para 2(1)(b) (as added: see note 3). As to the meaning of
    'institution within the further education sector' see PARA 555.
8   Ie in pursuance of the Education Act 1996 s 19(1): see PARA 427.
9   Education Act 1996 Sch 35C para 2(1)(c) (as added: see note 3).
10 'Scheme authority', in relation to a school travel scheme, means the local authority by which the
    scheme is made: Education Act 1996 Sch 35C para 14 (as added (see note 3); definition
    amended by SI 2010/1158).
11 Education Act 1996 Sch 35C para 2(1) (as added: see note 3).
12 Education Act 1996 Sch 35C para 2(3)(a) (as added: see note 3).
13 The specified arrangements are: (1) arrangements for the provision of one or more persons to
    escort a child (whether alone or together with other children) when travelling to or from any of
    the places mentioned in any of the Education Act 1996 Sch 35C para 2(1)(a)–(c) (see heads
    (1)–(3) in the text) (Sch 35C para 2(3)(b)(i) (as added: see note 3)); (2) arrangements for the
    payment of the whole or any part of a person's reasonable travelling expenses (Sch 35C
    para 2(3)(b)(ii) (as so added)); (3) arrangements for the payment of allowances in respect of the
    use of particular modes of travel (Sch 35C para 2(3)(b)(iii) (as so added)).
14 See the Education Act 1996 Sch 35C para 2(3)(b) (as added: see note 3). The reference to the
    relevant parental consent is to the consent of a parent of each child in relation to whom the
    arrangements in question are made: Sch 35C para 2(4) (as so added). As to the meaning of
    'parent' see PARA 7 note 6.
15 Education Act 1996 Sch 35C para 2(3)(c) (as added: see note 3).
16 Education Act 1996 Sch 35C para 2(5)(a) (as added: see note 3).
17 Education Act 1996 Sch 35C para 2(5)(b) (as added: see note 3).
18 Education Act 1996 Sch 35C para 2(5) (as added: see note 3).
19 See the Education Act 1996 Sch 35C paras 3, 4 (as added: see note 3). See also the School Travel
    (Pupils with Dual Registration) (England) Regulations 2007, SI 2007/1367.
20 See the Education Act 1996 Sch 35C paras 5–9 (as added: see note 3).
21 Education Act 1996 Sch 35C para 10(1) (as added: see note 3). As to the Secretary of State see
    PARA 58.
22 Education Act 1996 Sch 35C para 10(2) (as added: see note 3). As to directions see s 570; and
    PARA 75. The earliest date on which a school travel scheme might come into force was
    31 August 2007: see Sch 35C para 10(3) (as so added).
23 See the Education Act 1996 Sch 35C para 11(3) (as added: see note 3). The Secretary of State
    may consent to the exercise of the power of amendment on an application by the scheme
    authority specifying the proposed exercise of the power: Sch 35C para 11(4) (as so added). If on
    such an application the Secretary of State consents to the exercise of the power of amendment,
    the scheme authority must exercise the power accordingly: Sch 35C para 11(5) (as so added).
24 Education Act 1996 Sch 35C para 11(1) (as added: see note 3). Before amending a school travel
    scheme, the scheme authority must consult such persons as it considers appropriate: Sch 35C
    para 11(2) (as so added).
25 Education Act 1996 Sch 35C para 11(6) (as added: see note 3).
26 As to the publication of guidance see the Education Act 1996 s 571; and PARA 60. See in
    particular 'Home-to-school travel and transport guidance: Statutory guidance for local
    authorities'.
27 Ie his power under the Education Act 1996 Sch 35C para 10(1): see the text to note 21.
28 Ie his power under the Education Act 1996 Sch 35C para 11(3): see the text to note 23.
29 Education Act 1996 Sch 35C para 13(1) (as added: see note 3).
30 Education Act 1996 Sch 35C para 12(1)(a) (as added: see note 3).
31 Education Act 1996 Sch 35C para 12(1)(b) (as added: see note 3).
32 Education Act 1996 Sch 35C para 12(1) (as added: see note 3). Before issuing or revising such
    guidance, the Secretary of State must consult such persons as he considers appropriate: Sch 35C
    para 13(2) (as so added).
33 Education Act 1996 Sch 35C para 12(2)(a) (as added: see note 3).
34 Ie under the Education and Inspections Act 2006 s 80: see the text to notes 46–50.
35 Education Act 1996 Sch 35C para 12(2)(b) (as added: see note 3).
36 Ie under the Education Act 1996 Sch 35C: see the text to notes 1–35.

37 Education Act 1996 s 508E(2) (s 508E added by the Education and Inspections Act 2006 s 78(1); and the Education Act 1996 s 508E(1) amended by SI 2010/1158). The authority must give effect to the scheme by: (1) making the arrangements which are set out in the scheme as described in the Education Act 1996 Sch 35C para 2(1) (see the text to notes 4–11) as arrangements to be made by the authority (s 508E(2)(a) (as so added)); (2) complying with the requirement of the scheme described in Sch 35C para 2(5) (requirement to make suitable alternative arrangements: see the text to notes 16–18) (s 508E(2)(b) (as so added)); (3) complying with the requirement of the scheme described in Sch 35C para 3 (travel arrangements for eligible children: see the text to note 19) (s 508E(2)(c) (as so added)); and (4) complying with the scheme's policy applicable to charging and any other requirements of the scheme (s 508E(2)(d) (as so added)).

38 Ie under the Education Act 1996 s 508B (see PARA 461) or s 508C (see PARA 462). As to the meaning of 'functions' see PARA 18 note 5.

39 See the Education Act 1996 s 508E(3) (as added (see note 37); and amended by SI 2010/1158).

40 Ie any duty under the Education Act 1996 s 508E(2); see the text to notes 36–37.

41 Ie under the Education Act 1996 Sch 35C: see the text to notes 1–35.

42 Education Act 1996 s 508E(4) (as added (see note 37); and amended by SI 2010/1158). Before issuing or revising such guidance, the Secretary of State must consult such persons as he considers appropriate: Education Act 1996 s 508E(5) (as so added; and amended by SI 2010/1158).

43 Education Act 1996 s 508E(6) (as added (see note 37); and amended by SI 2010/1158).

44 'The school travel scheme provisions' means the Education Act 1996 s 508E and Sch 35C (see the text to notes 1–43): Education and Inspections Act 2006 ss 79(3), 80(6).

45 See the Education and Inspections Act 2006 s 79(1), (2). As to the regulations made see the School Travel (Piloting of Schemes) (England) Regulations 2007, SI 2007/1366.

46 Ie under the Education Act 1996 Sch 35C: see the text to notes 1–35.

47 Education and Inspections Act 2006 s 80(1).

48 Education and Inspections Act 2006 s 80(2) (amended by SI 2010/1158). Power to make such an order includes power to make consequential amendments and repeals in any enactment, including the Education and Inspections Act 2006 and enactments passed or made after the passing of that Act (ie 8 November 2006): s 80(5). As to the meaning of 'enactment' see PARA 26 note 15. At the date at which this volume states the law no such order had been made.

49 Education and Inspections Act 2006 s 80(3).

50 Education and Inspections Act 2006 s 80(4).

464. Provision of transport etc for persons of sixth form age. A local authority[1] in England[2] must prepare for each academic year[3] a transport policy statement complying with the following requirements[4].

The statement must specify the arrangements for the provision of transport or otherwise that the authority considers it necessary to make for facilitating the attendance of persons of sixth form age[5] receiving education or training: (1) at schools[6]; (2) at any institution maintained or assisted by the authority which provides further education[7] or higher education[8], or both[9]; (3) at any institution within the further education sector[10]; (4) at any 16 to 19 academy[11]; or (5) at any establishment not falling within head (2), head (3) or head (4) above at which the authority secures the provision[12] of education or training[13]. The statement must specify the arrangements that the authority considers it necessary to make for the provision of financial assistance in respect of the reasonable travelling expenses of persons of sixth form age receiving education or training at any such establishment as is mentioned in heads (1) to (4) above[14]. The statement must specify the arrangements proposed to be made by the governing bodies[15] of:

(a)   schools maintained by the authority at which education suitable to the requirements of persons over compulsory school age is provided[16]; and

(b)   institutions within the further education sector in the authority's area[17], for the provision of transport for facilitating the attendance of persons of sixth form age receiving education or training at the schools and institutions and for the provision of financial assistance in respect of the travelling expenses of such persons[18]. Those governing bodies must co-operate in giving the local authority any information and other assistance that is reasonably required by the authority for the performance of its functions[19] relating to the provision of transport for persons of sixth form age[20]. The statement must specify any travel concessions[21] which are to be provided[22] to persons of sixth form age receiving education at any establishment in the authority's area as is mentioned in heads (1) to (4) above[23].

The authority must publish the statement, in a manner which it considers appropriate, on or before 31 May in the year in which the academic year in question begins[24]; and it must make, and secure that effect is given to, any arrangements specified[25] in the statement[26].

Nothing in the above provisions prevents a local authority from making, at any time in an academic year[27], arrangements which are not specified in the transport policy statement published by the authority for that year[28], but which it has come to consider necessary for the specified purposes[29]. The Secretary of State may, if he considers it expedient to do so, direct[30] a local authority to make for any academic year:

(i) arrangements for the provision of transport or otherwise for facilitating the attendance of persons of sixth form age receiving education or training at establishments as are mentioned in heads (1) to (4) above[31]; or

(ii) arrangements for providing financial assistance in respect of the reasonable travelling expenses of such persons[32],

which have not been specified in the transport policy statement published by the authority for that academic year[33].

1   As to the meaning of 'local authority' see PARA 25.
2   As to the meaning of 'England' see PARA 7 note 3.
3   For the purposes of the Education Act 1996 ss 509AA–509AB, 'academic year' means any period commencing with 1 August and ending with the next 31 July: s 509AC(5) (s 509AC added by the Education Act 2002 s 199, Sch 19 paras 1, 5). The Secretary of State may by order amend the definition of 'academic year' in the Education Act 1996 s 509AC(5): s 509AC(6) (as so added; and amended by the Education and Inspections Act 2006 s 83(3)(a); Learner Travel (Wales) Measure 2008 ss 25, 26, Sch 1 para 4(1), (4)(b), Sch 2). As to the Secretary of State see PARA 58. At the date at which this volume states the law no such order had been made.
4   Education Act 1996 s 509AA(1) (s 509AA added by the Education Act 2002 Sch 19 paras 1, 3; and the Education Act 1996 s 509AA(1) amended by the Learner Travel (Wales) Measure 2008 s 25, Sch 1 para 4(1), (2)(a); and SI 2010/1158). As to the duty of a local authority to have regard to religion and belief in the exercise of its travel functions see the Education Act 1996 s 509AD; and PARA 466.
5   For the purposes of the Education Act 1996 ss 509AA–509AB, a person receiving education or training at an establishment is of 'sixth form age' if he is over compulsory school age but: (1) is under the age of 19 (s 509AC(1)(a) (as added: see note 3)); or (2) has begun a particular course of education or training at the establishment before attaining the age of 19 and continues to attend that course (s 509AC(1)(b) (as so added)). 'Establishment' means an establishment of any kind, including a school or institution: s 509AC(5) (as so added). As to the meaning of 'compulsory school age' see PARA 19. As to the time at which a person attains a particular age see PARA 7 note 6. As to the meaning of 'school' see PARA 91.
6   Education Act 1996 s 509AA(2)(a) (as added: see note 4).
7   As to the meaning of 'further education' see PARA 23.
8   As to the meaning of 'higher education' see PARA 24.
9   Education Act 1996 s 509AA(2)(b) (as added: see note 4).
10 Education Act 1996 s 509AA(2)(c) (as added: see note 4). As to the meaning of 'institution within the further education sector' see PARA 555.
11 Education Act 1996 s 509AA(2)(ca) (added by the Education Act 2011 Sch 13 para 9(1), (13)(a)). As to the meaning of '16 to 19 academy' see PARA 346 note 13.

12 Ie under the Education Act 1996 s 15ZA(1): see PARA 32.
13 Education Act 1996 s 509AA(2)(d) (as added (see note 4); and amended by the Learner Travel (Wales) Measure 2008 ss 25, 26, Sch 1 para 4(1), (2)(b), Sch 2; SI 2010/1080; and the Education Act 2011 Sch 13 para 9(1), (13)(b)). As to the meaning of 'person' see PARA 7 note 6.
14 Education Act 1996 s 509AA(3) (as added: see note 4).
15 In the Education Act 1996 ss 509AA, 509AB, 'governing body', in relation to an institution within the further education sector, has the same meaning as in the Further and Higher Education Act 1992 (see PARA 560 note 6): Education Act 1996 s 509AC(5) (as added: see note 3). As to the governing bodies of maintained schools in England see PARA 150 et seq.
16 Education Act 1996 s 509AA(4)(a) (as added: see note 4).
17 Education Act 1996 s 509AA(4)(b) (as added: see note 4).
18 Education Act 1996 s 509AA(4) (as added: see note 4).
19 Ie its functions under the Education Act 1996 s 509AA and s 509AB (see PARA 465). As to the meaning of 'functions' see PARA 18 note 5.
20 Education Act 1996 s 509AA(5) (as added (see note 4); and amended by SI 2010/1158).
21 Ie within the meaning of the Transport Act 1985 Pt V (ss 88–112): see ROAD TRAFFIC vol 90 (2011) PARA 1025 et seq.
22 Ie under any scheme established under the Transport Act 1985 s 93: see ROAD TRAFFIC vol 90 (2011) PARA 1025.
23 Education Act 1996 s 509AA(6) (as added: see note 4).
24 Education Act 1996 s 509AA(7)(a) (as added: see note 4). The Secretary of State may by order amend s 509AA(7)(a) to change the time by which the statement must be published: s 509AA(10) (as so added; and amended by the Education and Inspections Act 2006 s 83(1)(c), Learner Travel (Wales) Measure 2008 ss 25, 26, Sch 1 para 4(1), (2)(e), Sch 2; and the Apprenticeships, Skills, Children and Learning Act 2009 s 55(2)). At the date at which this volume states the law no such order had been made.
25 Ie specified under the Education Act 1996 s 509AA(2), (3): see the text to notes 5–14.
26 Education Act 1996 s 509AA(7)(b) (as added: see note 4).
27 Education Act 1996 s 509AA(8) (as added (see note 4); and amended by SI 2010/1158).
28 Education Act 1996 s 509AA(8)(a) (as added: see note 4).
29 Education Act 1996 s 509AA(8)(b) (as added: see note 4). The specified purposes are those mentioned in s 509AA(2), (3) (see the text to notes 5–14): see s 509AA(8)(b) (as so added).
30 As to directions see the Education Act 1996 s 570; and PARA 75.
31 Education Act 1996 s 509AA(9)(a) (as added: see note 4).
32 Education Act 1996 s 509AA(9)(b) (as added: see note 4).
33 Education Act 1996 s 509AA(9) (as added (see note 4); and amended by the Learner Travel (Wales) Measure 2008 25, Sch 1 para 4(1), (2)(c); and SI 2010/1158). The Education Act 1996 s 509AA(9) is subject to s 509AE (complaints about transport arrangements etc for persons of sixth form age in England: see PARA 467): s 509AA(11) (s 509AA as so added; s 509AA(11) added by the Apprenticeships, Skills, Children and Learning Act 2009 s 56(1), (3)).

465. Provision of transport etc for disabled persons and persons with learning difficulties of sixth form age. A statement prepared by a local authority[1] in England[2] specifying arrangements for the provision of transport for persons of sixth form age[3] must state to what extent those arrangements[4] include arrangements for facilitating the attendance at the specified establishments[5] of disabled persons[6] and persons with learning difficulties or disabilities[7]. Such a statement[8] must: (1) specify arrangements for persons receiving full-time education or training at establishments other than schools[9] maintained by the local authority[10] which are no less favourable than the arrangements specified for pupils[11] of the same age attending such schools[12]; and (2) specify arrangements for persons with learning difficulties or disabilities receiving education or training at establishments other than schools maintained by the authority which are no less favourable than the arrangements specified for pupils of the same age with learning difficulties or disabilities attending such schools[13].

In considering what arrangements it is necessary to make[14] the local authority must have regard, amongst other things, to[15]: (a) the needs of those for whom it would not be reasonably practicable to attend a particular establishment to receive education or training if no arrangements were made[16]; (b) the need to secure that persons in its area have reasonable opportunities to choose between different establishments at which education or training is provided[17]; (c) what it is required to do under the duty to secure education and training for persons over compulsory school age[18] in relation to persons of sixth form age[19]; (d) the distances, and journey times, between the homes of persons of sixth form age in its area and establishments[20] at which education or training suitable to their needs is provided[21]; (e) the cost of transport to the establishments in question and of any alternative means of facilitating the attendance of persons receiving education or training there[22]. In considering whether or not it is necessary to make arrangements for those purposes in relation to a particular person, a local authority must have regard (amongst other things) to the nature of the route, or alternative routes, which he could reasonably be expected to take[23].

In preparing a statement of arrangements for the provision of transport for persons of sixth form age[24], a local authority must have regard to any guidance issued by the Secretary of State[25]. In preparing such a statement, a local authority must consult[26]: (i) any other local authority that it considers it appropriate to consult[27]; (ii) the governing bodies[28]; (iii) persons in the local authority's area who will be of sixth form age when the statement has effect, and their parents[29]; and (iv) any other person[30] specified for these purposes by the Secretary of State[31]. In preparing such a statement, a local authority must also consult[32]: (A) where it is a district council for an area in a metropolitan county[33], the integrated transport authority[34] for that county[35]; and (B) where it is a London borough council or the Common Council of the City of London[36], Transport for London[37].

In preparing and publishing a statement of arrangements for the provision of transport for persons of sixth form age[38], a local authority must have regard (among other things) to the need to include in the statement sufficient information about the matters that the statement must specify[39], and publish the statement in time[40], to enable persons who will be of sixth form age when the statement has effect and their parents to take reasonable account of those matters when choosing between different establishments at which education or training is provided[41].

1 As to the meaning of 'local authority' see PARA 25.
2 As to the meaning of 'England' see PARA 7 note 3.
3 Ie a statement prepared under the Education Act 1996 s 509AA: see PARA 464. As to the meaning of 'sixth form age' see PARA 464 note 5.
4 Ie arrangements specified in accordance with the Education Act 1996 s 509AA(2): see PARA 464.
5 Ie such establishments as are mentioned in the Education Act 1996 s 509AA(2): see PARA 555. As to the meaning of 'establishment' see PARA 464 note 5.
6 'Disabled person' has the same meaning as in the Equality Act 2010 (see DISCRIMINATION vol 33 (2013) PARA 50 et seq): Education Act 1996 s 509AC(5) (s 509AC added by the Education Act 2002 s 199, Sch 19 paras 1, 5; and definition amended by the Equality Act 2010 Sch 26 paras 35, 38).

7 Education Act 1996 s 509AB(1) (s 509AB added by the Education Act 2002 Sch 19 paras 1, 4; and the Education Act 1996 s 509AB(1) amended by SI 2010/1158; and the Children and Families Act 2014 Sch 3 paras 1, 48(1), (2)). References in the Education Act 1996 s 509AB to persons with learning difficulties or disabilities are to be construed in accordance with s 15ZA(6), (7) (see PARA 32 note 11): Education Act 1996 s 509AC(4) (as added (see note 6); and amended by SI 2010/1080; and the Children and Families Act 2014 Sch 3 paras 1, 49).
8 Ie a statement prepared under the Education Act 1996 s 509AA: see PARA 464.
9 As to the meaning of 'school' see PARA 91.
10 As to schools maintained by a local authority see PARA 99 et seq.
11 As to the meaning of 'pupil' see PARA 20 note 4.

12 Education Act 1996 s 509AB(2)(a) (as added (see note 7); and amended by SI 2010/1158).

13 Education Act 1996 s 509AB(2)(b) (as added (see note 7); and amended by the Children and Families Act 2014 Sch 3 paras 1, 48(1), (3)).

14 Ie for the purposes mentioned in the Education Act 1996 s 509AA(2), (3): see PARA 464.

15 Education Act 1996 s 509AB(3) (as added (see note 7); and amended by SI 2010/1158).

16 Education Act 1996 s 509AB(3)(a) (as added: see note 7).

17 Education Act 1996 s 509AB(3)(b) (as added: see note 7).

18 Ie the duty under the Education Act 1996 s 15ZA(1): see PARA 32. As to the meaning of 'compulsory school age' see PARA 19.

19 Education Act 1996 s 509AB(3)(ba) (s 509AB as added (see note 7): s 509AB(3)(ba) added by the Apprenticeships, Skills, Children and Learning Act 2009 s 53).

20 Ie establishments such as are mentioned in the Education Act 1996 s 509AA(2): see PARA 464.

21 Education Act 1996 s 509AB(3)(c) (as added (see note 7); and amended by the Education and Skills Act 2008 s 83).

22 Education Act 1996 s 509AB(3)(d) (as added: see note 7).

23 Education Act 1996 s 509AB(3A) (s 509AB as added (see note 7); and s 509AB(3A) added by the Education and Inspections Act 2006 s 85, Sch 10, para 5(a), and amended by SI 2010/1158).

24 Ie a statement under the Education Act 1996 s 509AA: see PARA 464.

25 Education Act 1996 s 509AB(5) (as added (see note 7); and amended by the Learner Travel (Wales) Measure 2008 s 25, Sch 1 para 4(1), (3)(b); SI 2010/1080; and SI 2010/1158). As to the Secretary of State see PARA 58. As to the publication of guidance see the Education Act 1996 s 571; and PARA 60.

26 Education Act 1996 s 509AB(6) (as added (see note 7); and amended by SI 2010/1158). As to the exercise of the duty to consult see JUDICIAL REVIEW vol 61 (2010) PARA 627.

27 Education Act 1996 s 509AB(6)(a) (as added (see note 7); and amended by SI 2010/1158).

28 Education Act 1996 s 509AB(6)(b) (as added: see note 7). The governing bodies concerned are those mentioned in s 509AA(4) (see PARA 464): see s 509AB(6)(b) (as so added).

29 Education Act 1996 s 509AB(6)(ca) (s 509AB as added (see note 7); s 509AB(6)(ca) added by the Apprenticeships, Skills, Children and Learning Act 2009 s 54, and amended by SI 2010/1158). As to the meaning of 'parent' see PARA 7 note 6.

30 As to the meaning of 'person' in this context see PARA 7 note 6.

31 Education Act 1996 s 509AB(6)(d) (as added (see note 7); and amended by the Education and Inspections Act 2006 s 83(2)(b); the Learner Travel (Wales) Measure 2008 ss 25, 26, Sch 1 para 4(1), (3)(c)(ii), Sch 2; and SI 2010/1080).

32 Education Act 1996 s 509AB(7) (as added (see note 7); and amended by SI 2010/1158).

33 As to local government areas and authorities in England see LOCAL GOVERNMENT vol 69 (2009) PARA 22 et seq.

34 As to integrated transport authorities see LOCAL GOVERNMENT vol 69 (2009) PARA 49.

35 Education Act 1996 s 509AB(7)(a) (as added (see note 7); and amended by the Local Transport Act 2008 s 77(5), Sch 4 Pt 4 para 60; and SI 2010/1158).

36 As to the London boroughs and their councils see LONDON GOVERNMENT vol 71 (2013) PARA 20 et seq. As to the Common Council of the City of London see LONDON GOVERNMENT vol 71 (2013) PARAS 34–38.

37 Education Act 1996 s 509AB(7)(b) (as added (see note 7); and amended by SI 2010/1158). As to Transport for London see LONDON GOVERNMENT vol 71 (2013) PARA 163 et seq.

38 Ie a statement under the Education Act 1996 s 509AA: see PARA 464.

39 Education Act 1996 s 509AB(7A)(a) (s 509AB as added (see note 7); and s 509AB(7A) added by the Apprenticeships, Skills, Children and Learning Act 2009 s 55(1)).

40 Education Act 1996 s 509AB(7A)(b) (as added: see note 39).

41 Education Act 1996 s 509AB(7A) (as added (see note 39); and amended by SI 2010/1158).

466. Local authority duty to have regard to religion or belief in exercise of travel functions. A local authority[1] in England[2] must have regard, amongst other things, in exercising any of its travel functions[3] in relation to or in connection with the travel of a person or persons to or from a school[4], institution or other place[5]:

(1)   to any wish of a parent[6] of such a person for him to be provided with education or training at a particular school, institution or other place where that wish is based on the parent's religion or belief[7]; and

(2)   in a case where the person in question (or any of the persons in question) is of sixth form age[8], to any wish of that person to be

provided with education or training at a particular school, institution or other place where that wish is based on the person's religion or belief[9].

1 As to the meaning of 'local authority' see PARA 25.
2 As to the meaning of 'England' see PARA 7 note 3.
3 The 'travel functions' of a local authority in England are its functions under any of the following provisions: the Education Act 1996 s 508A (duty to promote sustainable modes of travel etc: see PARA 460); s 508B (travel arrangements for eligible children: see PARA 461); s 508C (travel arrangements etc for other children: see PARA 462); s 508E and Sch 35C (school travel schemes: see PARA 463); s 508F (local authorities in England: provision of transport etc for adult learners: see PARA 810); s 509AA (transport etc for persons of sixth form age: see PARA 464): s 509AD(2) (s 509AD added by the Education and Inspections Act 2006 s 84; and the Education Act 1996 s 509AD(2) amended by the Apprenticeships, Skills, Children and Learning Act 2009 s 57(1), (3); and SI 2010/1158). At the date at which this volume states the law, the Education Act 1996 s 509AD is in force for all purposes except in relation to travel functions under s 508F: see the Education and Inspections Act 2006 (Commencement No 3 and Transitional Provisions and Savings) Order 2007, SI 2007/935, art 5(p); and the Education and Inspections Act 2006 (Commencement No 5 and Saving Provisions) Order 2007, SI 2007/1801, art 4(e). As to the meaning of 'functions' see PARA 18 note 5.
4 As to the meaning of 'school' see PARA 91.
5 Education Act 1996 s 509AD(1) (as added (see note 3); and amended by SI 2010/1158). See *R (on the application of Diocese of Menevia) v City and County of Swansea Council* [2015] EWHC 1436 (Admin), [2015] All ER (D) 21 (Jun) (the authority proposed to amend its policy so that pupils attending faith schools would be entitled to free public transport only if the relevant distance criteria were met and no alternative school was located within two or three miles of home; an application for judicial review was granted, the court holding that black and minority ethnic origin children suffered a particular disadvantage as a consequence of the amended policy, which was not a proportionate means of achieving a legitimate aim).
6 As to the meaning of 'parent' see PARA 7 note 6.
7 Education Act 1996 s 509AD(1)(a) (s 509AD as added (see note 3); and s 509AD(1)(a), (b) substituted by the Education and Skills Act 2008 s 84). For these purposes: (1) 'religion' means any religion (Education Act 1996 s 509AD(3)(a) (as so added)); (2) 'belief' means any religious or philosophical belief (s 509AD(3)(b) (as so added)), (3) a reference to religion includes a reference to lack of religion (s 509AD(3)(c) (as so added)); and (4) a reference to belief includes a reference to lack of belief (s 509AD(3)(d) (as so added)).
8 Ie within the meaning given in the Education Act 1996 s 509AC(1): see PARA 464 note 5.
9 Education Act 1996 s 509AD(1)(b) (as added and substituted: see note 7).

467. Complaints about transport arrangements etc for persons of sixth form age. A local authority[1] may revise a statement specifying transport arrangements for persons of sixth form age[2] to change the arrangements specified[3] if, as a result of a sixth form transport complaint[4], it has come to consider the change necessary for the purpose of those arrangements[5]. A local authority must revise such a statement to change those specified arrangements if, as a result of a sixth form transport complaint, the Secretary of State[6] has directed[7] it to do so[8]. An authority that revises a statement under these provisions[9] must publish the revised statement and a description of the revision as soon as practicable[10].

The Secretary of State need not consider whether to exercise his power of direction above[11], or any power relating to the prevention of unreasonable exercise of functions[12], or any power to require a local authority to make additional transport arrangements[13], in response to a matter that is, or could have been, the subject of a sixth form transport complaint made to him unless satisfied that the matter has been brought to the notice of the local authority concerned[14], and the authority has had a reasonable opportunity to investigate the matter and respond[15].

1 As to the meaning of 'local authority' see PARA 25.

2   Ie a statement prepared under the Education Act 1996 s 509AA: see PARA 464. 'Sixth form age' is to be construed in accordance with s 509AC(1) (see PARA 464 note 5): s 509AE(5) (s 509AE added by the Apprenticeships, Skills, Children and Learning Act 2009 s 56(1), (2)).

3   Ie under the Education Act 1996 s 509AA(2) or (3): see PARA 464.

4   'Sixth form transport complaint' means a complaint that is: (1) about a local authority's exercise of, or failure to exercise, a function under the Education Act 1996 ss 509AA–509AD (see PARAS 464–466) in relation to persons of sixth form age (s 509AE(5)(a) (as added (see note 2); and amended by SI 2010/1158)); and (2) made by a person who is, or will be, a person of sixth form age when the matter complained of has effect, or by a parent of such a person (Education Act 1996 s 509AE(5)(b) (as so added)). As to the meaning of 'function' see PARA 18 note 5. As to the meaning of 'parent' see PARA 7 note 6.

5   See the Education Act 1996 s 509AE(1) (as added (see note 2); and amended by SI 2010/1158). For the purposes of the Education Act 1996 s 509AA(8), (9) (see PARA 464), s 509AB(1)–(5) (see PARA 465), s 509AC (see PARAS 464, 465) and s 509AD (see PARA 466), the revision of a statement under s 509AE is to be treated as the preparation of a statement under s 509AA (see PARA 464): s 509AE(6) (as so added).

6   As to the Secretary of State see PARA 58.

7   As to directions see the Education Act 1996 s 570; and PARA 75.

8   Education Act 1996 s 509AE(2) (as added (see note 2); and amended by SI 2010/1158).

9   Ie under the Education Act 1996 s 509AE(1) or (2): see the text to notes 1–8.

10   Education Act 1996 s 509AE(3) (as added: see note 2). Where a local authority has published in a single document a statement prepared under s 508G (see PARA 810) and a statement prepared under s 509AA (see PARA 464), the requirement to publish a revised statement under s 509AE(3) is to be treated as a requirement to publish a version of the document that includes the revised statement: s 509AE(7) (as so added; and amended by SI 2010/1158)

11   Ie the power under the Education Act 1996 s 509AE(2): see the text to notes 6–8.

12   Ie any power under the Education Act 1996 ss 496–497A: see PARAS 62, 64–65.

13   Ie any power under the Education Act 1996 s 509AA(9): see PARA 464.

14   Education Act 1996 s 509AE(4)(a) (as added (see note 2); and amended by SI 2010/1158).

15   Education Act 1996 s 509AE(4)(b) (as added (see note 2); and amended by SI 2010/1158).

468. Travel arrangements for children receiving early years education otherwise than at school. A local authority[1] in England may provide a child[2] with assistance as to travel arrangements if it is satisfied that, without such assistance, he would be prevented from attending at any premises[3] which are not a school[4] or part of a school[5], but at which relevant early years education[6] is provided[7], for the purpose of receiving such education there[8]. The assistance which may so be provided for a child consists of either making arrangements, whether for the provision of transport or otherwise, for the purpose of facilitating the child's attendance at the premises concerned[9], or paying the whole or any part of his reasonable travel expenses[10].

When considering whether to provide a child with such assistance in connection with his attendance at any premises, a local authority may have regard, among other things, to whether it would be reasonable to expect alternative arrangements to be made for him to receive relevant early years education at any other premises, whether nearer to his home or otherwise[11]. Where the assistance to be provided for a child consists of making arrangements for the provision of transport, the authority may, if it considers it appropriate to do so, determine that the assistance must not be so provided unless the child's parent[12], or the person[13] providing the relevant early years education concerned[14], agrees to make to the authority such payments in respect of the provision of the transport, not exceeding the cost to the authority of its provision, as it may determine[15].

Regulations made by the Secretary of State[16] may require a local authority to publish, at such times and in such manner as may be prescribed[17], such information as may be prescribed with respect to the authority's policy and arrangements relating to the making of provision under the above provisions[18].

1   As to the meaning of 'local authority' see PARA 25. Any function of a local authority in England which is conferred by or under the Education Act 1996 s 509A may be exercised by, or by employees of, such person as may be authorised in that behalf by the local authority whose function it is: Contracting Out (Local Authority Education Functions) (England) Order 2002, SI 2002/928, art 3, Sch 1 para (pp) (art 3 amended by SI 2010/1172). As to the meaning of 'England' see PARA 7 note 3.
2   As to the meaning of 'child' see PARA 7 note 6.
3   As to the meaning of 'premises' see PARA 62 note 19.
4   As to the meaning of 'school' see PARA 91.
5   Education Act 1996 s 509A(1)(a) (s 509A added by the School Standards and Framework Act 1998 s 124).
6   'Relevant early years education' means early years provision as defined by the Childcare Act 2006 s 20 (see CHILDREN AND YOUNG PERSONS vol 10 (2012) PARA 1079) which is provided under arrangements made by a local authority in England in pursuance of the duty imposed by s 7 of that Act (whether or not the local authority provides the early years provision: see CHILDREN AND YOUNG PERSONS vol 10 (2012) PARA 1083): Education Act 1996 s 509A(5) (s 509A as added (see note 5); s 509A(5) substituted by the Childcare Act 2006 s 103(1), Sch 2 para 23(b); and amended by the Learner Travel (Wales) Measure 2008 ss 25, 26, Sch 1 para 4(1), (5)(c), Sch 2). Reference should also be made to the early years pupils premium which is additional funding paid to support disadvantaged children receiving government-funded early education, under the Childcare Act 2006 s 7: see ss 7, 7A; and CHILDREN AND YOUNG PERSONS vol 10 (2012) PARA 1083.
7   Education Act 1996 s 509A(1)(b) (as added (see note 5); and amended by the Childcare Act 2006 s 103(1), Sch 2 para 23(a)).
8   Education Act 1996 s 509A(1) (as added (see note 5); and amended by the Learner Travel (Wales) Measure 2008 s 25, Sch 1 para 4(1), (5)(a); and SI 2010/1158).
9   Education Act 1996 s 509A(2)(a) (as added: see note 5).
10 Education Act 1996 s 509A(2)(b) (as added: see note 5).
11 Education Act 1996 s 509A(3) (as added (see note 5); and amended by the Childcare Act 2006 s 103(1), Sch 2 para 23(a); and SI 2010/1158).
12 Education Act 1996 s 509A(4)(a) (as added: see note 5). As to the meaning of 'parent' see PARA 7 note 6.
13 As to the meaning of 'person' see PARA 7 note 6.
14 Education Act 1996 s 509A(4)(b) (as added (see note 5); and amended by the Childcare Act 2006 s 103(1), Sch 2 para 23(a)).
15 Education Act 1996 s 509A(4) (as added: see note 5).
16 As to the Secretary of State see PARA 58.
17 'Prescribed' means prescribed by regulations: Education Act 1996 s 579(1).
18 Education Act 1996 s 509A(4A) (s 509A as added (see note 5); and s 509A(4A) added by the Education Act 2002 s 199, Sch 19 paras 1, 6; and amended by the Learner Travel (Wales) Measure 2008 s 25, Sch 1 para 4(1), (5)(b); and SI 2010/1158). At the date at which this volume states the law no such regulations had been made.

B. TRANSPORT ARRANGEMENTS IN WALES

469. Local authority duty to assess learner travel needs. In each academic year[1], a local authority[2] must assess the learner travel needs[3] of its area for the following academic year[4], in relation to (1) learners who have not attained the age of 19[5]; (2) learners who have attained the age of 19 who have begun a course of education or training before attaining that age and continue to attend that course[6]; (3) such other learners as may be prescribed[7]. However, this duty does not require the assessment of learner travel needs for learners to travel during the day between relevant places or between different sites of the same institution[8], or for any purpose other than attendance at a relevant place to receive education or training[9].

In making such an assessment a local authority must have regard in particular to: (a) the needs of learners who are disabled persons[10]; (b) the needs of learners with learning difficulties[11]; (c) the needs of learners who are children looked after, or formerly looked after, by a local authority[12]; (d) the age of learners[13];

and (e) the nature of the routes which learners could reasonably be expected to take to the relevant places where they receive education or training[14].

1   'Academic year' means any period from 1 August to 31 July: Learner Travel (Wales) Measure 2008 s 24(1).

2   'Local authority' means a local authority in Wales; but in any reference to a child looked after by a local authority it means a council of a county or county borough in Wales exercising social services functions within the meaning of the Local Authority Social Services Act 1970 (SOCIAL SERVICES AND COMMUNITY CARE vol 95 (2013) PARA 1): Learner Travel (Wales) Measure 2008 s 24(1) (definition amended by SI 2010/1148). References to a child who is looked after by a local authority have the same meaning as they have in the Children Act 1989 s 22(1) (see CHILDREN AND YOUNG PERSONS vol 10 (2012) PARA 843): Learner Travel (Wales) Measure 2008 s 24(2). As to the meaning of 'Wales' see PARA 7 note 3. As to local government areas and authorities in Wales see LOCAL GOVERNMENT vol 69 (2009) PARA 37 et seq.

3   The 'learner travel needs' of a local authority's area are the needs of learners who are ordinarily resident in the authority's area for suitable travel arrangements each day to and from the relevant places where they receive education or training: Learner Travel (Wales) Measure 2008 s 2(3). 'Learners' means persons who receive education or training: s 1(1), (3). 'Education' does not include higher education: s 24(1). As to the meaning of 'higher education' see PARA 24 (definition applied by s 24(3)). 'Travel arrangements' are travel arrangements of any description and include: (1) the provision of transport; (2) the provision of one or more persons to escort a child when travelling; (3) the payment of the whole or any part of a person's reasonable travelling expenses; (4) the payment of allowances in respect of the use of particular modes of travel: s 1(1), (2). As to the meaning of 'child' see PARA 7 note 6 (definition applied by s 24(3)). The following are 'relevant places': (a) maintained schools; (b) institutions in the further education sector; (c) independent schools named in statements maintained under the Education Act 1996 s 324 (see PARA 1002); (d) non-maintained special schools; (e) pupil referral units; (f) places other than pupil referral units where education is arranged under the Education Act 1996 s 19(1) (see PARA 427); (g) places where education or training funded by the Welsh Ministers under the Learning and Skills Act 2000 s 34(1) (see PARA 792) is provided; (h) institutions where education and training and boarding accommodation have been secured by the Welsh Ministers under the Learning and Skills Act 2000 s 41 (see PARA 791); (i) places where nursery education is provided by a local authority or by any other person who is in receipt of financial assistance given by a local authority under arrangements made by it in pursuance of the duty imposed by the School Standards and Framework Act 1998 s 118 (see PARA 96); (j) places where work experience is undertaken: Learner Travel (Wales) Measure 2008 s 1(1), (4). For these purposes, 'maintained school' means a community, foundation or voluntary school, a community special school or a maintained nursery school: s 24(1) (definition amended by the School Standards and Organisation (Wales) Act 2013 Sch 5 para 25). As to community, foundation and voluntary schools, and community special schools see PARA 106. As to the meaning of 'maintained nursery school' see PARA 99 note 4; as to the meaning of 'institution within the further education sector' see PARA 555; as to the meaning of 'independent school' see PARA 369; as to the meaning of 'special school' see PARA 1041 (definitions applied by s 24(3)). 'Non-maintained special school' means a school approved under the Education Act 1996 s 342: Learner Travel (Wales) Measure 2008 s 24(1). As to pupil referral units see PARA 427 et seq. As to the Welsh Ministers see PARA 59. 'Nursery education' means education suitable for children who have not attained compulsory school age: s 24(1). As to the meaning of 'compulsory school age' see PARA 19. As to the meaning of 'person' see PARA 7 note 6. 'Work experience' means work experience arranged for (i) a registered pupil of a maintained school or a pupil referral unit; or (ii) a student enrolled at an institution within the further education sector, by, or on behalf of, the governing body of the relevant educational institution: s 24(1). As to the meaning of 'registered pupil' see PARA 437 (definition applied by s 24(3)). As to the governing bodies of maintained schools in Wales see PARA 195.

If a person has no ordinary residence, that person is to be treated for the purposes of the Learner Travel (Wales) Measure 2008 as being ordinarily resident at the place at which he or she is for the time being resident: s 19(1). In relation to a child or young person who is either a registered pupil at a school (s 19(2)(a)), or enrolled as a full-time student at an institution in the further education sector (s 19(2)(b)):

(A)   a child or young person whose parents are not living together (s 19(3)(a)), and who usually lives with more than one parent in the periods during which the child or young person receives education or training (s 19(3)(b)), is ordinarily resident at the places where each of his or her parents is ordinarily resident (s 19(5)(a));

(B)   a child or young person who usually lives with a parent and also at a children's home in the periods during which the child or young person receives education or training (s 19(4)) is ordinarily resident at the children's home and the place where his or her parent is ordinarily resident (s 19(5)(b));

but if there are more than two such places, the child or young person is ordinarily resident at the two places nearest the school at which the child or young person is a registered pupil (s 19(6)(a)), or the institution in the further education sector at which the child or young person is enrolled as a full-time student (s 19(6)(b)). For these purposes, 'children's home' has the same meaning as in the Care Standards Act 2000 s 1 (see CHILDREN AND YOUNG PERSONS vol 10 (2012) PARA 992); and 'parent' means a parent within the meaning of the Education Act 1996 s 576(1) (see PARA 7 note 6) who is an individual: Learner Travel (Wales) Measure 2008 s 19(7). As to the meaning of 'young person' see PARA 7 note 6 (definition applied by s 24(3)).

4 Learner Travel (Wales) Measure 2008 s 2(2). In exercising its functions under the Learner Travel (Wales) Measure 2008 a local authority must have regard to guidance given from time to time by the Welsh Ministers: see s 15(1)(a). As to the meaning of 'functions' see PARA 18 note 5 (definition applied by s 24(3)). As to the publication of guidance see the Education Act 1996 s 571 (applied by the Learner Travel (Wales) Measure 2008 s 24(3)); and PARA 60. As to the publication of information about travel assessments see s 16; and PARA 481.

5 Learner Travel (Wales) Measure 2008 s 2(1)(a). As to the time at which a person attains a particular age see PARA 7 note 6.

6 Learner Travel (Wales) Measure 2008 s 2(1)(b).

7 Learner Travel (Wales) Measure 2008 s 2(1)(c). 'Prescribed' means prescribed in regulations; and 'regulations' means regulations made by the Welsh Ministers: see s 24(1). At the date at which this volume states the law no such regulations had been made.

8 See the Learner Travel (Wales) Measure 2008 ss 2(2), 5(a).

9 See the Learner Travel (Wales) Measure 2008 ss 2(2), 5(b).

10 Learner Travel (Wales) Measure 2008 s 2(4)(a). 'Disabled person' has the same meaning as in the Disability Discrimination Act 1995 s 1 (repealed) (see now the Equality Act 2010; and DISCRIMINATION vol 33 (2013) PARA 50 et seq): Learner Travel (Wales) Measure 2008 s 24(1).

11 Learner Travel (Wales) Measure 2008 s 2(4)(b). 'Learning difficulty' in respect of a person means: (1) a significantly greater difficulty in learning than the majority of persons of the same age; or (2) a disability which either prevents or hinders that person from using facilities of a kind provided at relevant places, but a person is not to be taken as having a learning difficulty solely because the language (or form of the language) in which the person is taught or will be taught is different from a language (or form of a language) which has at any time been spoken in the person's home: s 24(1). 'Disability' has the same meaning as in the Disability Discrimination Act 1995 s 1 (repealed) (see now the Equality Act 2010; and DISCRIMINATION vol 33 (2013) PARA 50 et seq): Learner Travel (Wales) Measure 2008 s 24(1).

12 Learner Travel (Wales) Measure 2008 s 2(4)(c).

13 Learner Travel (Wales) Measure 2008 s 2(4)(d).

14 Learner Travel (Wales) Measure 2008 s 2(4)(e).

470. Local authority duty to make transport arrangements. In relation to a child[1] of compulsory school age[2] who is ordinarily resident[3] in a local authority's[4] area[5], to whom the statutory circumstances[6] apply[7], and in respect of whom the statutory condition, or all of such conditions[8], are met[9], the local authority must make suitable transport arrangements[10] to facilitate the attendance of the child each day at the relevant places[11] where the child receives education[12] or training[13]. However, this does not require the making of travel arrangements[14] for learners[15] to travel during the day between relevant places or between different sites of the same institution[16], or for any purpose other than attendance at a relevant place to receive education or training[17].

Transport arrangements made in accordance with these provisions may include (a) the provision of transport[18]; and (b) the payment of the whole, but not part, of a child's transport expenses[19]; but the local authority must not charge a child or a parent[20] who is an individual for any such transport arrangements[21].

A local authority must make such learner travel arrangements under the above provisions as the Welsh Ministers direct[22]; and in making such arrangements a local authority must comply with any directions given by the Welsh Ministers[23].

1 As to the meaning of 'child' see PARA 7 note 6 (definition applied by the Learner Travel (Wales) Measure 2008 s 24(3)).
2 As to the meaning of 'compulsory school age' see PARA 19.
3 As to the meaning of 'ordinarily resident' see PARA 469 note 3.
4 As to the meaning of 'local authority' see PARA 469 note 2. As to the duty of local authorities and governing bodies of maintained schools to ensure that every bus used for the learner transport it provides or otherwise secures is one that has a seat belt fitted to every passenger seat, see PARA 471.
5 See the Learner Travel (Wales) Measure 2008 s 3(1)(a).
6 Ie the circumstances set out in an entry in column 1 of the table set out in the Learner Travel (Wales) Measure 2008 s 3.
7 See the Learner Travel (Wales) Measure 2008 s 3(1)(b). Regulations may prescribe circumstances and conditions for the purposes of s 3(1)(b), (c) (see the text to notes 8–9); and such regulations may amend the table set out in s 3 or s 3(6)–(8) (which make provision as to entries in the table) (including repealing an entry in the table or those subsections): see s 3(9). 'Regulations' means regulations made by the Welsh Ministers: s 24(1). As to the Welsh Ministers see PARA 59. At the date at which this volume states the law no such regulations had been made.
8 Ie the condition, or all of the conditions, set out in the corresponding entry in column 2 of the table set out in the Learner Travel (Wales) Measure 2008 s 3. See also s 3(6)–(8).
9 See the Learner Travel (Wales) Measure 2008 s 3(1)(c). See also note 7.
10 Transport arrangements are not suitable if (1) they cause unreasonable levels of stress for the child (Learner Travel (Wales) Measure 2008 s 3(5)(a)); (2) they take an unreasonable amount of time (s 3(5)(b)); or (3) they are unsafe (s 3(5)(c)).
11 As to the meaning of 'relevant places' see PARA 469 note 3.
12 As to the meaning of 'education' see PARA 469 note 3.
13 Learner Travel (Wales) Measure 2008 s 3(2). In exercising its functions under the Learner Travel (Wales) Measure 2008 a local authority must have regard to guidance given from time to time by the Welsh Ministers: see s 15(1)(a). As to the publication of guidance see the Education Act 1996 s 571 (applied by the Learner Travel (Wales) Measure 2008 s 24(3)); and PARA 60. Where a local authority ('authority A') makes travel arrangements under s 3 for a child who is looked after by a local authority responsible for a different area ('authority B') (s 18(1)), authority A may demand reimbursement from authority B for the full cost or part of the cost of making the travel arrangements (s 18(2)) and authority B must comply with the demand (s 18(3)). As to the meaning of 'child who is looked after by a local authority' see PARA 469 note 2. As to the withdrawal of travel arrangements made under s 3, see s 14; and PARA 480. Learner travel arrangements made under s 3 must not favour certain types of education or training: see s 9; and PARA 474.
14 As to the meaning of 'travel arrangements' see PARA 469 note 3.
15 As to the meaning of 'learner' see PARA 469 note 3.
16 See the Learner Travel (Wales) Measure 2008 ss 3(2), 5(a).
17 See the Learner Travel (Wales) Measure 2008 ss 3(2), 5(b).
18 Learner Travel (Wales) Measure 2008 s 3(4)(a).
19 Learner Travel (Wales) Measure 2008 s 3(4)(b).
20 As to the meaning of 'parent' see PARA 7 note 6 (definition applied by the Learner Travel (Wales) Measure 2008 s 24(3)).
21 Learner Travel (Wales) Measure 2008 s 3(3).
22 See the Learner Travel (Wales) Measure 2008 s 15(2). Directions under s 15 may be given to one or more local authorities or local authorities generally: s 15(4). As to directions generally see the Education Act 1996 s 570 (applied by the Learner Travel (Wales) Measure 2008 s 24(3)); and PARA 75.
23 See the Learner Travel (Wales) Measure 2008 s 15(3). See also note 22.

471. Safety on learner transport. A relevant body[1] must ensure that every bus[2] used for the learner transport[3] which it provides or otherwise secures is one that has a seat belt[4] fitted to every passenger seat[5]. The act of making arrangements to pay the whole or any part of a person's[6] reasonable travelling expenses; or arrangements to pay allowances in respect of the use of transport is not to be considered, by itself, as providing or otherwise securing the provision of learner transport[7].

A person who provides learner transport secured by a relevant body must ensure that every bus used for such transport is one that has a seat belt fitted to every passenger seat[8]. A person who fails to comply with the above duties[9] commits an offence[10]. It is a defence to show that the failure to comply[11] was justified by exceptional circumstances[12].

Regulations[13] may make provision to (1) require a relevant body to ensure that only prescribed descriptions of vehicle are used for the learner transport it provides or otherwise secures; (2) require a person who provides learner transport secured by a relevant body to use only prescribed descriptions of vehicle; and (3) provide for criminal offences and penalties for breaches of the any requirements imposed[14].

Regulations may (a) require prescribed arrangements to be made for recording visual images or sound of events occurring on the learner transport provided or otherwise secured by a relevant body; (b) make provision about the use, storage and retention of visual images or sound recorded on learner transport provided or secured by a relevant body; and (c) provide for criminal offences and penalties for breaches of the above requirements[15].

Regulations may require a relevant body to carry out safety risk assessments of the learner transport it provides or otherwise secures[16].

Regulations may require a relevant body that provides or otherwise secures the provision of learner transport to ensure that drivers of vehicles used for such transport have completed prescribed training[17] to a prescribed standard[18].

Regulations may make provision for the supervision of learners using learner transport provided or otherwise secured by a relevant body[19].

Regulations may appoint a person or body (including the Welsh Ministers) to be an enforcement authority[20]. More than one person or body may be appointed as an enforcement authority[21].

The following provisions apply in relation to (i) a vehicle or any premises owned or controlled by a relevant body; and (ii) a vehicle which is or premises which are used, or proposed to be used, by any person in connection with the provision of learner transport provided or otherwise secured by a relevant body; or an inspector[22] reasonably believes to be so used, or proposed to be so used[23]. An inspector may at any reasonable time detain a vehicle or enter a vehicle or premises[24].

An inspector who detains a vehicle or enters a vehicle or premises[25] may (A) inspect the vehicle or premises; (B) inspect, take copies of and remove from the vehicle or premises any documents or records relating to the provision of learner transport; and (C) inspect any other item and remove it from the vehicle or premises[26]. The power under head (B) above includes power to require any person holding or accountable for documents or records kept on the vehicle or premises to produce them, and, in relation to records which are kept by means of a computer, power to require the records to be produced in a legible form which can be taken away[27], but such power does not include power to require a person to produce any document or record in respect of which a claim to legal professional privilege could be maintained in legal proceedings, or to take copies of such a document or record or to remove it[28]. In connection with inspecting any such documents, an inspector may obtain access to, and inspect and check the operation of, any computer and associated apparatus or material which he considers is or has been in use in connection with the documents; and may require a person[29] to afford him such reasonable assistance as may be required for that purpose[30]. An inspector detaining a vehicle or entering a vehicle or premises may require any person to afford him such facilities and assistance with respect to matters within the person's control as are necessary to enable him to exercise the relevant powers[31]. Any person who without reasonable excuse obstructs an inspector exercising any such power; or fails to comply with any requirement imposed[32], is guilty of an offence[33].

An enforcement authority may at any time require any person specified to provide it with any information, documents, records or other items which relate to the provision of learner transport, and which the enforcement authority consider necessary or expedient to have for the purpose of its functions as the enforcement authority[34]. The persons specified are a relevant body and any person who provides learner transport secured by a relevant body[35]. Any person who without reasonable excuse fails to comply with any requirement imposed[36] is guilty of an offence[37].

Where an offence under the relevant provisions of the Learner Travel (Wales) Measure 2008[38] committed by a body corporate is proved to have been committed with the consent or connivance of, or to be attributable to any neglect on the part of, an officer of the body corporate, regulations may provide for the officer to be liable as well as the body corporate itself[39]. Where an offence under those provisions[40] committed by a partnership is proved to have been committed with the consent or connivance of, or to be attributable to any neglect on the part of, a partner of the partnership, regulations may provide for the partner to be liable as well as the partnership itself[41].

1   'Relevant body' means a local authority or a governing body of a maintained school: Learner Travel (Wales) Measure 2008 s 14N(1), (2) (s 14N added by the Safety on Learner Transport (Wales) Measure 2011 s 14)). As to the meaning of 'local authority' see PARA 469 note 2. As to governing bodies of schools in Wales see PARA 195. As to the meaning of 'maintained school' see PARA 469 note 3.

2   'Bus' means a motor vehicle constructed or adapted to carry more than eight seated passengers in addition to the driver: Learner Travel (Wales) Measure 2008 s 14A(6) (s 14A added by the Safety on Learner Transport (Wales) Measure 2011 s 1).

3   'Learner transport' means transport to facilitate the attendance of a child at any relevant place where he receives education or training, but does not include transport provided for the purpose of travel during the day between relevant places or between different sites of the same institution: Learner Travel (Wales) Measure 2008 s 14N(1), (3) (as added: see note 1). As to the meaning of 'education' see PARA 469 note 3. See also s 14(6) (as so added).

4   'Seat belt' means a belt intended to be worn by a person in a vehicle and designed to prevent or lessen injury to its wearer in the event of an accident to the vehicle: Learner Travel (Wales) Measure 2008 s 14A(6) (as added: see note 2).

5   Learner Travel (Wales) Measure 2008 s 14A(1) (as added: see note 2).

6   As to the meaning of 'person' see PARA 7 note 6.

7   Learner Travel (Wales) Measure 2008 s 14N(4), (5) (as added: see note 1).

8   Learner Travel (Wales) Measure 2008 s 14A(2) (as added: see note 2).

9   Ie under the Learner Travel (Wales) Measure 2008 s 14A(1) or (2).

10   Learner Travel (Wales) Measure 2008 s 14A(3) (as added: see note 2). Such a person is liable on summary conviction to a fine not exceeding level 4 on the standard scale: s 14A(3) (as so added). As to the standard scale see SENTENCING AND DISPOSITION OF OFFENDERS vol 92 (2010) PARA 142.

11   Ie with the Learner Travel (Wales) Measure 2008 s 14A(1) or (2).

12   Learner Travel (Wales) Measure 2008 s 14A(4) (as added: see note 2). Nothing in s 14A is to be interpreted as setting technical standards for a vehicle's construction or equipment which differ from the standards that would or might otherwise apply to that vehicle by virtue of any enactment or directly applicable requirement of European Union law: s 14A(5) (as so added).

13   The Welsh Ministers must consult each local authority and such other persons as they consider appropriate before making any regulations under the Learner Travel (Wales) Measure 2008 ss 14B–14F, 14H or 14L or Sch A1: Learner Travel (Wales) Measure 2008 s 14M (added by the Safety on Learner Transport (Wales) Measure 2011 s 13). As to the Welsh Ministers see PARA 59. At the date at which this volume states the law no such regulations had been made.

14   See the Learner Travel (Wales) Measure 2008 s 14B(1) (s 14B added by the Safety on Learner Transport (Wales) Measure 2011 s 2). Regulations under heads (1) and (2) in the text may

describe vehicles by reference to a vehicle's construction, equipment or other characteristics: Learner Travel (Wales) Measure 2008 s 14B(2) (as so added). As to the power to make regulations imposing civil sanctions for a breach of s 14B see the Learner Travel (Wales) Measure 2008 Sch A1 (added by the Safety on Learner Transport (Wales) Measure 2011 s 14G, Schedule). As to consultation on regulations see the Learner Travel (Wales) Measure 2008 s 14M; and note 13.

15 See the Learner Travel (Wales) Measure 2008 s 14C(1) (s 14C added by the Safety on Learner Transport (Wales) Measure 2011 s 3). Such regulations may, among other things, confer powers or duties on a relevant body or a person who provides learner transport secured by a relevant body: Learner Travel (Wales) Measure 2008 s 14C(2) (as so added). Such regulations may not authorise or require recording to be carried out in a manner that is calculated to ensure that persons who are subject to it are unaware that it is or may be taking place: s 14C(3) (as so added). As to the power to make regulations imposing civil sanctions for a breach of s 14C see the Learner Travel (Wales) Measure 2008 Sch A1 (as added: see note 14). As to consultation on regulations see s 14M; and note 13.

16 Learner Travel (Wales) Measure 2008 s 14D(1) (s 14D added by the Safety on Learner Transport (Wales) Measure 2011 s 4). Such regulations may (1) impose requirements as to the nature of the assessment to be carried out; (2) require the production and publication of reports; (3) prescribe the form and manner of publication; and (4) prescribe the frequency of assessments: Learner Travel (Wales) Measure 2008 s 14D(2) (as so added). As to consultation on regulations see s 14M; and note 13.

17 'Training' means training about safety on learner transport and working with children: Learner Travel (Wales) Measure 2008 s 14E(3) (s 14E added by the Safety on Learner Transport (Wales) Measure 2011 s 5).

18 Learner Travel (Wales) Measure 2008 s 14E(1) (as added: see note 17). Training and standards may be prescribed by reference to a document published, as specified in the regulations, by the Welsh Ministers: s 14E(2) (as so added). As to consultation on regulations see s 14M; and note 13.

19 Learner Travel (Wales) Measure 2008 s 14F(1) (s 14F added by the Safety on Learner Transport (Wales) Measure 2011 s 6). Such regulations may, among other things (1) confer powers or impose duties on a relevant body; and (2) make provision about training for persons supervising learners: Learner Travel (Wales) Measure 2008 s 14F(2) (as so added). As to consultation on regulations see s 14M; and note 13.

20 Learner Travel (Wales) Measure 2008 s 14H(1) (s 14H added by the Safety on Learner Transport (Wales) Measure 2011 s 8). Regulations may confer powers or impose duties on an enforcement authority to enforce provision made by s 14A (see the text to notes 1–12) and by regulations under s 14B (see the text to notes 1–14) and s 14C (see the text to note 15) and Sch A1 and may, among other things (1) confer power on an enforcement authority to authorise a person (an 'inspector') to exercise the powers in s 14I (see the text to notes 22–24) and s 14J (see the text to notes 25–33); (2) make modifications to any enactment applying to the enforcement authority; or (3) provide for any such enactment to apply, with or without modifications, for the purposes of s 14A and regulations under ss 14B and 14C, 14H and Sch A1: s 14H(3) (as so added). References to an enforcement authority are references to a person or body appointed under s 14H and include a person appointed by an enforcement authority: s 14H(4) (as so added). As to consultation on regulations see s 14M; and note 13.

21 Learner Travel (Wales) Measure 2008 s 14H(2) (as added: see note 20).

22 As to enforcement authorities see the text to notes 20, 21.

23 See the Learner Travel (Wales) Measure 2008 s 14I(1), (2) (s 14I added by the Safety on Learner Transport (Wales) Measure 2011 s 9).

24 Learner Travel (Wales) Measure 2008 s 14I(3) (as added: see note 23). Such power does not include the power to enter premises used wholly or mainly as a private dwelling: s 14I(4) (as so added). An inspector exercising any power conferred under s 14I(3) or 14J (see the text to notes 25–33) must, if so required, produce some duly authenticated document showing the inspector's authority to do so: s 14I(4) (a so added).

25 Ie under the Learner Travel (Wales) Measure 2008 s 14I: see the text to notes 22–24.

26 See the Learner Travel (Wales) Measure 2008 s 14J(1) (s 14J added by the Safety on Learner Transport (Wales) Measure 2011 s 10). See note 24.

27 Learner Travel (Wales) Measure 2008 s 14J(2) (as added: see note 26).

28 Learner Travel (Wales) Measure 2008 s 14J(3) (as added: see note 26).

29 Ie within the Learner Travel (Wales) Measure 2008 s 14J(5). A person is within s 14J(5) if he is the person by whom or on whose behalf the computer is or has been used, or a person having charge of, or otherwise concerned with the operation of, the computer, apparatus or material: s 14J(5) (as added: see note 26).

30 Learner Travel (Wales) Measure 2008 s 14J(4) (as added: see note 26).
31 Learner Travel (Wales) Measure 2008 s 14J(6) (as added: see note 26). The powers referred to in the text are those under s 14I (see the text to notes 22–24) or s 14J.
32 Ie imposed under the Learner Travel (Wales) Measure 2008 s 14J.
33 Learner Travel (Wales) Measure 2008 s 14J(7) (as added: see note 26). Such a person is liable on summary conviction to a fine not exceeding level 4 on the standard scale: s 14J(7) (as so added). As to the standard scale see SENTENCING AND DISPOSITION OF OFFENDERS vol 92 (2010) PARA 142.
34 Learner Travel (Wales) Measure 2008 s 14K(1) (s 14K added by the Safety on Learner Transport (Wales) Measure 2011 s 11). Such power includes, in relation to information, documents or records kept by means of a computer, power to require provision of them in a legible form which can be taken away: Learner Travel (Wales) Measure 2008 s 14K(3) (as so added). It does not include power to require the provision of information, documents or records in respect of which a claim to legal professional privilege could be maintained in legal proceedings: s 14K(4) (as so added).
35 Learner Travel (Wales) Measure 2008 s 14K(2) (as added: see note 34).
36 Ie imposed by the Learner Travel (Wales) Measure 2008 s 14K.
37 Learner Travel (Wales) Measure 2008 s 14K(5) (as added: see note 34). Such a person is liable on summary conviction to a fine not exceeding level 4 on the standard scale: s 14K(5) (as so added).
38 Ie the Learner Travel (Wales) Measure 2008 s 14A (see the text to notes 1–12), s 14B (see the text to notes 13, 14) or s 14C (see the text to note 15).
39 Learner Travel (Wales) Measure 2008 s 14L(1) (s 14L added by the Safety on Learner Transport (Wales) Measure 2011 s 12). As to consultation on regulations see the Learner Travel (Wales) Measure 2008 s 14M; and note 13.
40 See note 38.
41 Learner Travel (Wales) Measure 2008 s 14L(2) (as added: see note 39). See note 39.

472. Local authority duty to make other travel arrangements. In relation to a child[1] of compulsory school age[2] who:

(1)   is receiving education[3] or training at a relevant place[4]; and

(2)   is ordinarily resident[5] in a local authority's[6] area[7],

where the local authority considers that travel arrangements[8] are necessary[9] to facilitate the attendance of the child each day at the relevant place where the child receives education or training[10], the local authority must make suitable travel arrangements[11] to facilitate the attendance of the child each day at the relevant places where the child receives education or training[12]. However, this does not require the making of travel arrangements for learners[13] to travel during the day between relevant places or between different sites of the same institution[14], or for any purpose other than attendance at a relevant place to receive education or training[15].

Travel arrangements made in accordance with the above provisions may include the payment of the whole, but not part, of a child's travel expenses[16]; but a local authority must not charge a child or a parent[17] who is an individual for any such travel arrangements[18].

A local authority must make such learner travel arrangements under the above provisions as the Welsh Ministers direct[19]; and in making such arrangements a local authority must comply with any directions given by the Welsh Ministers[20].

1   As to the meaning of 'child' see PARA 7 note 6 (definition applied by the Learner Travel (Wales) Measure 2008 s 24(3)).
2   As to the meaning of 'compulsory school age' see PARA 19.
3   As to the meaning of 'education' see PARA 469 note 3.
4   See the Learner Travel (Wales) Measure 2008 s 4(1)(a). As to the meaning of 'relevant place' see PARA 469 note 3.
5   As to the meaning of 'ordinarily resident' see PARA 469 note 3.
6   As to the meaning of 'local authority' see PARA 469 note 2.
7   See the Learner Travel (Wales) Measure 2008 s 4(1)(b).

8 As to the meaning of 'travel arrangements' see PARA 469 note 3.
9 In considering whether travel arrangements are necessary for these purposes, a local authority: (1) must have regard in particular to the matters specified in the Learner Travel (Wales) Measure 2008 s 4(5) (see note 11) (s 4(7)(a)); (2) may have regard in particular to whether or not the child is attending the nearest suitable relevant place to the child's place of ordinary residence (s 4(7)(b)). Section 4(7)(b) (see head (2) above) applies if: (a) the child is not looked after by a local authority (s 4(8)(a)); and (b) arrangements have been made by the local authority for enabling the child to attend a suitable relevant place nearer to the child's place of ordinary residence (s 4(8)(b)). A relevant place is suitable for a child if the education or training provided there is suitable, having regard to the age, ability and aptitudes of the child and any learning difficulties he or she may have: s 4(9). As to the meaning of 'child who is looked after by a local authority' see PARA 469 note 2. As to the meaning of 'learning difficulty' see PARA 469 note 11.
10 See the Learner Travel (Wales) Measure 2008 s 4(1)(c).
11 In considering whether travel arrangements are suitable for these purposes, a local authority must have regard in particular to: (1) the assessment it carries out in accordance with the Learner Travel (Wales) Measure 2008 s 2(2) (see PARA 469) (s 4(5)(a)); (2) the transport arrangements it is under a duty to make for the child under s 3 (see PARA 470) (s 4(5)(b)); (3) the age of the child (s 4(5)(c)); (4) any disability or learning difficulty of the child (s 4(5)(d)); (5) the nature of the routes which the child could reasonably be expected to take (s 4(5)(e)). Travel arrangements are not suitable if: (a) they cause unreasonable levels of stress for the child (s 4(6)(a)); (b) they take an unreasonable amount of time (s 4(6)(b)); or (c) they are unsafe (s 4(6)(c)). As to the meaning of 'disability' see PARA 469 note 11.
12 Learner Travel (Wales) Measure 2008 s 4(2). In exercising its functions under the Learner Travel (Wales) Measure 2008, a local authority must have regard to guidance given from time to time by the Welsh Ministers: see s 15(1)(a). As to the Welsh Ministers see PARA 59. As to the publication of guidance see the Education Act 1996 s 571 (applied by the Learner Travel (Wales) Measure 2008 s 24(3)); and PARA 60. Where a local authority ('authority A') makes travel arrangements under s 4 for a child who is looked after by a local authority responsible for a different area ('authority B') (s 18(1)), authority A may demand reimbursement from authority B for the full cost or part of the cost of making the travel arrangements (s 18(2)), and authority B must comply with the demand (s 18(3)). As to the withdrawal of travel arrangements made under s 4 see s 14; and PARA 480. As to the provision of information about travel arrangements see PARA 481. Learner travel arrangements made under s 4 must not favour certain types of education or training: see s 9; and PARA 474.
13 As to the meaning of 'learner' see PARA 469 note 3.
14 See the Learner Travel (Wales) Measure 2008 ss 4(2), 5(a).
15 See the Learner Travel (Wales) Measure 2008 ss 4(2), 5(b).
16 Learner Travel (Wales) Measure 2008 s 4(4).
17 As to the meaning of 'parent' see PARA 7 note 6 (definition applied by the Learner Travel (Wales) Measure 2008 s 24(3)).
18 Learner Travel (Wales) Measure 2008 s 4(3).
19 See the Learner Travel (Wales) Measure 2008 s 15(2). Directions under s 15 may be given to one or more local authorities or local authorities generally: s 15(4). As to directions generally see the Education Act 1996 s 570 (applied by the Learner Travel (Wales) Measure 2008 s 24(3)); and PARA 75.
20 See the Learner Travel (Wales) Measure 2008 s 15(3). See also note 19.

473. Power of local authorities to make learner travel arrangements. In relation to a learner[1] who:

(1) is ordinarily resident[2] in the local authority's[3] area[4]; or

(2) receives education[5] or training in the local authority's area[6],

the local authority may make travel arrangements[7] to facilitate the attendance of the learner at a place where that person receives education or training[8]. A local authority may charge[9] for travel arrangements so made for registered pupils[10] of compulsory school age[11]. A local authority may also charge for travel arrangements so made for other learners[12].

A local authority must make such learner travel arrangements under the above provisions as the Welsh Ministers direct[13]; and in making arrangements under the above provisions a local authority must comply with any directions given by the Welsh Ministers[14].

1   As to the meaning of 'learner' see PARA 469 note 3.
2   As to the meaning of 'ordinarily resident' see PARA 469 note 3.
3   As to the meaning of 'local authority' see PARA 469 note 2.
4   See the Learner Travel (Wales) Measure 2008 s 6(1)(a).
5   As to the meaning of 'education' see PARA 469 note 3.
6   See the Learner Travel (Wales) Measure 2008 s 6(1)(b).
7   As to the meaning of 'travel arrangements' see PARA 469 note 3.
8   Learner Travel (Wales) Measure 2008 s 6(2). In exercising its functions under the Learner Travel (Wales) Measure 2008 a local authority must have regard to guidance given from time to time by the Welsh Ministers: see s 15(1)(a). As to the Welsh Ministers see PARA 59. As to the publication of guidance see the Education Act 1996 s 571 (applied by the Learner Travel (Wales) Measure 2008 s 24(3)); and PARA 60. As to the provision of information about travel arrangements see PARA 481. Learner travel arrangements made under s 6 must not favour certain types of education or training: see s 9; and PARA 474.
9   Ie in accordance with the provisions of the Education Act 1996 ss 455, 456: see PARAS 338, 339.
10 As to the meaning of 'registered pupil' see PARA 437 (definition applied by the Learner Travel (Wales) Measure 2008 s 24(3)).
11 Learner Travel (Wales) Measure 2008 s 6(3). As to the meaning of 'compulsory school age' see PARA 19.
12 Learner Travel (Wales) Measure 2008 s 6(4).
13 Learner Travel (Wales) Measure 2008 s 15(2). Directions under s 15 may be given to one or more local authorities or local authorities generally: s 15(4). As to directions generally see the Education Act 1996 s 570 (applied by the Learner Travel (Wales) Measure 2008 s 24(3)); and PARA 75.
14 Learner Travel (Wales) Measure 2008 s 15(3). See also note 13.

474.   Learner travel arrangements not to favour certain types of education or training.   If travel arrangements[1] are made in respect of:

(1)   children[2] of compulsory school age[3] receiving education[4] or training at maintained schools[5];

(2)   learners[6] over compulsory school age receiving full-time education or training at maintained schools[7];

(3)   learners with learning difficulties[8] receiving education or training at maintained schools[9];

(4)   learners who have a disability[10] receiving education or training at maintained schools[11];

(5)   children looked after by a local authority[12] receiving education or training at maintained schools[13],

arrangements must also be made[14] in respect of the learners of the following descriptions:

(a)   in respect of children in head (1) above: children of the same age receiving education or training at other relevant places[15];

(b)   in respect of learners in head (2) above: learners of the same age receiving full-time education or training at other relevant places[16];

(c)   in respect of learners in head (3) above: learners of the same age with learning difficulties receiving education or training at other relevant places[17];

(d)   in respect of learners in head (4) above: learners of the same age who have a disability receiving education or training at other relevant places[18];

(e)   in respect of children in head (5) above: children of the same age who are looked after by a local authority receiving education or training at other relevant places[19];

and those arrangements must be no less favourable than the arrangements made in respect of the persons in heads (1) to (5) as the case may be[20].

1   Ie under the Learner Travel (Wales) Measure 2008 s 3 (see PARA 470), s 4 (see PARA 472), or s 6 (see PARA 473).
2   As to the meaning of 'child' see PARA 7 note 6 (definition applied by the Learner Travel (Wales) Measure 2008 s 24(3)).
3   As to the meaning of 'compulsory school age' see PARA 19.
4   As to the meaning of 'education' see PARA 469 note 3.
5   See the Learner Travel (Wales) Measure 2008 s 9(1), Table, column 1. As to the meaning of 'maintained school' see PARA 469 note 3.
6   As to the meaning of 'learner' see PARA 469 note 3.
7   See the Learner Travel (Wales) Measure 2008 s 9(1), Table, column 1.
8   As to the meaning of 'learning difficulties' see PARA 469 note 11.
9   See the Learner Travel (Wales) Measure 2008 s 9(1), Table, column 1.
10 As to the meaning of 'disability' see PARA 469 note 11.
11 See the Learner Travel (Wales) Measure 2008 s 9(1), Table, column 1.
12 As to the meaning of 'child who is looked after by a local authority'; and as to the meaning of 'local authority' see PARA 469 note 2.
13 See the Learner Travel (Wales) Measure 2008 s 9(1), Table, column 1.
14 Ie in accordance with the Learner Travel (Wales) Measure 2008 s 3 (see PARA 470), s 4 (see PARA 472), or s 6 (see PARA 473).
15 See the Learner Travel (Wales) Measure 2008 s 9(2), Table, column 2. As to the meaning of 'relevant places' see PARA 469 note 3.
16 See the Learner Travel (Wales) Measure 2008 s 9(2), Table, column 2.
17 See the Learner Travel (Wales) Measure 2008 s 9(2), Table, column 2.
18 See the Learner Travel (Wales) Measure 2008 s 9(2), Table, column 2.
19 See the Learner Travel (Wales) Measure 2008 s 9(2), Table, column 2.
20 Learner Travel (Wales) Measure 2008 s 9(3).

475.   Travel arrangements for learners in post-16 education or training.   In relation to learners[1] ordinarily resident[2] in Wales[3]:

(1)   who are over compulsory school age[4] but have not attained the age of 19[5], or have attained the age of 19 and have begun a particular course of education[6] or training before attaining that age and continue to attend that course[7]; and

(2)   who receive education or training at a place in Wales[8], or which is funded by the Welsh Ministers[9] at a place outside Wales[10],

regulations[11] may make provision about travel arrangements[12] for learners to and from the places where they receive education or training[13]. The regulations may in particular: (a) confer powers or impose duties on the Welsh Ministers[14], local authorities[15], and institutions in the further education sector[16]; (b) specify the kinds of place to and from which travel arrangements may or must be made[17]; (c) specify the travel arrangements that may or must be made[18]; (d) specify the matters that must be taken into account in making decisions about travel arrangements[19]; (e) make provision about charges[20]; (f) require any person[21] to give any information or other assistance that is reasonably required by any other person in connection with the performance of the other person's functions[22] under the regulations[23]; (g) make provision about the standards of behaviour required of learners while travelling to and from the places where they receive education or training[24].

1   As to the meaning of 'learner' see PARA 469 note 3.
2   As to the meaning of 'ordinarily resident' see PARA 469 note 3.
3   As to the meaning of 'Wales' see PARA 7 note 3.
4   As to the meaning of 'compulsory school age' see PARA 19.
5   Learner Travel (Wales) Measure 2008 s 7(1)(a)(i). As to the time at which a person attains a particular age see PARA 7 note 6.
6   As to the meaning of 'education' see PARA 469 note 3.
7   Learner Travel (Wales) Measure 2008 s 7(1)(a)(ii).
8   Learner Travel (Wales) Measure 2008 s 7(1)(b)(i).

9   As to the Welsh Ministers see PARA 59.
10   Learner Travel (Wales) Measure 2008 s 7(1)(b)(ii).
11   'Regulations' means regulations made by the Welsh Ministers: Learner Travel (Wales) Measure 2008 s 24(1). At the date at which this volume states the law no such regulations had been made.
12   As to the meaning of 'travel arrangements' see PARA 469 note 3.
13   Learner Travel (Wales) Measure 2008 s 7(2).
14   Learner Travel (Wales) Measure 2008 s 7(3)(a)(i).
15   Learner Travel (Wales) Measure 2008 s 7(3)(a)(ii). As to the meaning of 'local authority' see PARA 469 note 2.
16   Learner Travel (Wales) Measure 2008 s 7(3)(a)(iii). As to the meaning of 'institution within the further education sector' see PARA 555 (definition applied by s 24(3)).
17   Learner Travel (Wales) Measure 2008 s 7(3)(b).
18   Learner Travel (Wales) Measure 2008 s 7(3)(c).
19   Learner Travel (Wales) Measure 2008 s 7(3)(d).
20   Learner Travel (Wales) Measure 2008 s 7(3)(e).
21   As to the meaning of 'person' see PARA 7 note 6.
22   As to the meaning of 'functions' see PARA 18 note 5 (definition applied by the Learner Travel (Wales) Measure 2008 s 24(3)).
23   Learner Travel (Wales) Measure 2008 s 7(3)(f).
24   Learner Travel (Wales) Measure 2008 s 7(3)(g). As to the travel behaviour code see s 12; and PARA 479.

476. Travel arrangements to and from nursery education. Regulations[1] may make provision about travel arrangements[2] for children[3] under compulsory school age[4] to and from the places where they receive nursery education[5]. The regulations may in particular:

(1)   require a local authority[6] to make travel arrangements[7];

(2)   permit a local authority to make travel arrangements[8];

(3)   specify the kinds of place to and from which travel arrangements may or must be made[9];

(4)   specify the travel arrangements that may or must be made[10];

(5)   specify the matters that must be taken into account in making decisions about travel arrangements[11];

(6)   make provision about charges[12];

(7)   require any person[13] to give any information or other assistance that is reasonably required by the local authority in connection with the performance of the authority's functions[14] under the regulations[15].

1   'Regulations' means regulations made by the Welsh Ministers: Learner Travel (Wales) Measure 2008 s 24(1). As to the Welsh Ministers see PARA 59. At the date at which this volume states the law no such regulations had been made.
2   As to the meaning of 'travel arrangements' see PARA 469 note 3.
3   As to the meaning of 'child' see PARA 7 note 6 (definition applied by the Learner Travel (Wales) Measure 2008 s 24(3)).
4   As to the meaning of 'compulsory school age' see PARA 19.
5   Learner Travel (Wales) Measure 2008 s 8(1). As to the meaning of 'nursery education' see PARA 469 note 3.
6   As to the meaning of 'local authority' see PARA 469 note 2.
7   Learner Travel (Wales) Measure 2008 s 8(2)(a).
8   Learner Travel (Wales) Measure 2008 s 8(2)(b).
9   Learner Travel (Wales) Measure 2008 s 8(2)(c).
10   Learner Travel (Wales) Measure 2008 s 8(2)(d).
11   Learner Travel (Wales) Measure 2008 s 8(2)(e).
12   Learner Travel (Wales) Measure 2008 s 8(2)(f).
13   As to the meaning of 'person' see PARA 7 note 6.
14   As to the meaning of 'functions' see PARA 18 note 5 (definition applied by the Learner Travel (Wales) Measure 2008 s 24(3)).
15   Learner Travel (Wales) Measure 2008 s 8(2)(g).

477. Promoting access to education and training through the medium of the Welsh language. Each local authority[1] and the Welsh Ministers[2] must promote access to education[3] and training through the medium of the Welsh language when exercising functions[4] under the Learner Travel (Wales) Measure 2008[5].

1 As to the meaning of 'local authority' see PARA 469 note 2.
2 As to the Welsh Ministers see PARA 59.
3 As to the meaning of 'education' see PARA 469 note 3.
4 As to the meaning of 'functions' see PARA 18 note 5 (definition applied by the Learner Travel (Wales) Measure 2008 s 24(3)).
5 Learner Travel (Wales) Measure 2008 s 10. In exercising its functions under the Learner Travel (Wales) Measure 2008 a local authority must have regard to guidance given from time to time by the Welsh Ministers: see s 15(1)(a). As to the publication of guidance see the Education Act 1996 s 571 (applied by s 24(3)); and PARA 60. For provision relating to the Welsh Language see Welsh Language (Wales) Measure 2011; and CONSTITUTIONAL AND ADMINISTRATIVE LAW vol 20 (2014) PARA 78.

478. Promoting use of sustainable modes of travel. Each local authority[1] and the Welsh Ministers[2] must promote the use of sustainable modes of travel when exercising functions[3] under the Learner Travel (Wales) Measure 2008[4]. 'Sustainable modes of travel' are modes of travel which the authority or the Welsh Ministers (as the case may be) consider may improve either or both of the following: (1) the physical well-being of those who use them[5]; (2) the environmental well-being of the whole or part of the local authority's area, in the case of an authority[6], or the whole or part of Wales[7], in the case of the Welsh Ministers[8].

1 As to the meaning of 'local authority' see PARA 469 note 2.
2 As to the Welsh Ministers see PARA 59.
3 As to the meaning of 'functions' see PARA 18 note 5 (definition applied by the Learner Travel (Wales) Measure 2008 s 24(3)).
4 Learner Travel (Wales) Measure 2008 s 11(1). In exercising its functions under the Learner Travel (Wales) Measure 2008 a local authority must have regard to guidance given from time to time by the Welsh Ministers: see s 15(1)(a). As to the publication of guidance see the Education Act 1996 s 571 (applied by s 24(3)); and PARA 60.
5 Learner Travel (Wales) Measure 2008 s 11(2)(a).
6 Learner Travel (Wales) Measure 2008 s 11(2)(b)(i).
7 As to the meaning of 'Wales' see PARA 7 note 3.
8 Learner Travel (Wales) Measure 2008 s 11(2)(b)(ii).

479. Travel behaviour code. The Welsh Ministers[1] must make a travel behaviour code[2]. A 'travel behaviour code' is a code setting out the standards of behaviour required of learners[3] of specified descriptions while they are travelling to and from the relevant places[4] where they receive education[5] or training (whether or not they take advantage of travel arrangements[6] made by a local authority)[7]. The specified descriptions of learner are: (1) learners who have not attained the age of 19[8]; (2) learners who have attained the age of 19 who have begun a course of education or training before attaining that age and continue to attend that course[9]; (3) such other learners as may be prescribed[10].

The Welsh Ministers must review the travel behaviour code from time to time[11], and must publish the code[12]. Before making or revising a code the Welsh Ministers must consult[13] such persons[14] as they consider appropriate[15].

1 As to the Welsh Ministers see PARA 59.
2 Learner Travel (Wales) Measure 2008 s 12(1).
3 As to the meaning of 'learner' see PARA 469 note 3.
4 As to the meaning of 'relevant places' see PARA 469 note 3.
5 As to the meaning of 'education' see PARA 469 note 3.

6   As to the meaning of 'travel arrangements' see PARA 469 note 3.
7   Learner Travel (Wales) Measure 2008 s 12(2). As to the meaning of 'local authority' see PARA 469 note 2. As to the duty of a local authority to assess learner travel needs see s 2; and PARA 469. As to the enforcement of a travel behaviour code see s 14; and PARA 480. In determining standards of behaviour for a school, the head teacher of a relevant school in Wales must require pupils at the school to comply with the travel behaviour code made by the Welsh Ministers under s 12: see the Education and Inspections Act 2006 s 89(2A); and PARA 510.
8   Learner Travel (Wales) Measure 2008 s 12(3)(a). As to the time at which a person attains a particular age see PARA 7 note 6.
9   Learner Travel (Wales) Measure 2008 s 12(3)(b).
10 Learner Travel (Wales) Measure 2008 s 12(3)(c). 'Prescribed' means prescribed by regulations; and 'regulations' means regulations made by the Welsh Ministers: see s 24(1). At the date at which this volume states the law no such regulations had been made.
11 Learner Travel (Wales) Measure 2008 s 12(4).
12 Learner Travel (Wales) Measure 2008 s 12(5).
13 As to the exercise of the duty to consult see JUDICIAL REVIEW vol 61 (2010) PARA 627.
14 As to the meaning of 'person' see PARA 7 note 6.
15 Learner Travel (Wales) Measure 2008 s 12(6).

480.   Enforcement of travel behaviour code.   The local authority[1] may withdraw travel arrangements[2] made for a learner[3] for whom travel arrangements are made[4] if the authority is satisfied that the learner has failed to comply with the travel behaviour code[5], and the following conditions applicable to the learner are satisfied[6]. All six of the following conditions apply to any learner who is a registered pupil[7] at a relevant school[8]. The first, third and fourth of the following conditions apply to any learner who is not a registered pupil at a relevant school[9]. The conditions are as follows:

(1)   the first condition is that before any decision is taken to withdraw travel arrangements the learner and the parent[10] of the learner are given the opportunity to make representations[11], and those representations are considered by the local authority[12];

(2)   the second condition is that the head teacher of the relevant school at which the learner is a registered pupil is consulted[13] about the decision to withdraw travel arrangements[14], and is given notice[15] of the decision at least 24 hours before the withdrawal takes effect[16];

(3)   the third condition is that the decision to withdraw travel arrangements is reasonable in the circumstances[17];

(4)   the fourth condition is that the local authority gives notice[18] of the withdrawal of travel arrangements to the learner's parent at least 24 hours before the withdrawal takes effect[19];

(5)   the fifth condition is that the period of withdrawal does not exceed ten consecutive school days[20];

(6)   the sixth condition is that the period of withdrawal would not result in the learner having travel arrangements withdrawn for more than 30 school days in the school year[21] in which the withdrawal takes effect[22].

Regulations[23] may: (a) amend or repeal either or both of heads (5) and (6) above[24]; (b) make provision for reviews of decisions[25] to withdraw travel arrangements[26]; (c) make provision for appeals from such decisions[27].

1   As to the meaning of 'local authority' see PARA 469 note 2. In exercising its functions under the Learner Travel (Wales) Measure 2008 a local authority must have regard to guidance given from time to time by the Welsh Ministers: see s 15(1)(a). As to the Welsh Ministers see PARA 59. As to the publication of guidance see the Education Act 1996 s 571 (applied by s 24(3)); and PARA 60.
2   As to the meaning of 'travel arrangements' see PARA 469 note 3.
3   As to the meaning of 'learner' see PARA 469 note 3.

4 Ie under the Learner Travel (Wales) Measure 2008 s 3 (see PARA 470) or s 4 (see PARA 472): see s 14(1).

5 Learner Travel (Wales) Measure 2008 s 14(2)(a). The travel behaviour code is the code made under s 12 (see PARA 479): see s 14(2)(a).

6 Learner Travel (Wales) Measure 2008 s 14(2)(b). A head teacher of a relevant school must give a local authority any information or other assistance that is reasonably required by the local authority for the performance of its functions under s 14: s 17(4). As to the meaning of 'head teacher' see PARA 86 note 4; and as to the meaning of 'functions' see PARA 18 note 5 (definitions applied by s 24(3)). For the purposes of ss 14, 17 (see PARA 481), a 'relevant school' means: (1) a maintained school (s 14(13)(a)); (2) a pupil referral unit (s 14(13)(b)); or (3) a non-maintained special school (s 14(13)(c)). As to the meanings of 'maintained school' and 'non-maintained special school' see PARA 469 note 3. As to pupil referral units see PARA 427 et seq.

7 As to the meaning of 'registered pupil' see PARA 437 (definition applied by the Learner Travel (Wales) Measure 2008 s 24(3)).

8 Learner Travel (Wales) Measure 2008 s 14(3).

9 Learner Travel (Wales) Measure 2008 s 14(4).

10 As to the meaning of 'parent' see PARA 7 note 6 (definition applied by the Learner Travel (Wales) Measure 2008 s 24(3)).

11 Learner Travel (Wales) Measure 2008 s 14(5)(a).

12 Learner Travel (Wales) Measure 2008 s 14(5)(b).

13 As to the exercise of the duty to consult see JUDICIAL REVIEW vol 61 (2010) PARA 627.

14 Learner Travel (Wales) Measure 2008 s 14(6)(a).

15 A notice under the Learner Travel (Wales) Measure 2008 s 14(6) or (8) (see the text to note 19) must be in writing and specify (1) the period for which travel arrangements are to be withdrawn (s 14(12)(a)); and (2) the authority's reasons for withdrawal of the travel arrangements (s 14(12)(b)). As to the meaning of 'writing' see PARA 76 note 8. As to the service of notices and documents see the Education Act 1996 s 572 (applied by the Learner Travel (Wales) Measure 2008 s 24(3)); and PARA 76.

16 Learner Travel (Wales) Measure 2008 s 14(6)(b).

17 Learner Travel (Wales) Measure 2008 s 14(7). In determining whether a decision to withdraw travel arrangements is reasonable for these purposes, the following matters in particular must be taken into account: (1) whether the period of withdrawal is proportionate in the circumstances of the case (s 14(11)(a)); (2) any special circumstances relevant to the withdrawal of travel arrangements which are known to the local authority (or of which the authority ought to be aware) including in particular (a) the learner's age (s 14(11)(b)(i)); (b) any special educational needs the learner may have (s 14(11)(b)(ii)); (c) any disability the learner may have (s 14(11)(b)(iii)); (d) whether the learner would lose an opportunity to take a public examination (s 14(11)(b)(iv)); and (e) whether suitable alternative travel arrangements can reasonably be made by the learner's parent (s 14(11)(b)(v)). As to the meaning of 'special educational needs' see PARA 989 (definition applied by s 24(3)). As to the meaning of 'disability' see PARA 469 note 11.

18 See note 15.

19 Learner Travel (Wales) Measure 2008 s 14(8).

20 Learner Travel (Wales) Measure 2008 s 14(9). As to the meaning of 'school day' see PARA 229 note 6 (definition applied by s 24(3)).

21 As to the meaning of 'school year' see PARA 19 note 12 (definition applied by the Learner Travel (Wales) Measure 2008 s 24(3)).

22 Learner Travel (Wales) Measure 2008 s 14(10).

23 'Regulations' means regulations made by the Welsh Ministers: Learner Travel (Wales) Measure 2008 s 24(1). At the date at which this volume states the law no such regulations had been made.

24 Learner Travel (Wales) Measure 2008 s 14(14)(a).

25 Ie under the Learner Travel (Wales) Measure 2008 s 14(2): see the text to notes 5–6.

26 Learner Travel (Wales) Measure 2008 s 14(14)(b).

27 Learner Travel (Wales) Measure 2008 s 14(14)(c). Regulations under s 14(14)(c) may in particular: (1) specify the categories of person who may appeal (s 14(15)(a)); (2) specify the circumstances in which appeals may be made (s 14(15)(b)); (3) provide for the constitution of appeals panels (s 14(15)(c)); (4) provide for appeal procedures (s 14(15)(d)); (5) make provision about the effect of appeal decisions (s 14(15)(e)); (6) provide for the payment of allowances to members of appeals panels (s 14(15)(f)); (7) require the provision of information about appeals (s 14(15)(g)). As to the meaning of 'person' see PARA 7 note 6.

481. Information and other assistance. Regulations[1] may require a local authority[2] to publish, at such times and in such manner as may be prescribed[3], information: (1) received while carrying out assessments[4] of learner travel needs[5]; (2) about assessments made[6] of learner travel needs[7]; (3) about the travel arrangements[8] made under the Learner Travel (Wales) Measure 2008[9]; (4) about the travel behaviour code made[10] under the Measure[11].

The governing body of a maintained school[12] or an institution in the further education sector[13] in Wales[14] must give a local authority any information or other assistance that is reasonably required by it for the performance of its functions[15] under the Learner Travel (Wales) Measure 2008[16]. A local authority must give another local authority any information or other assistance that is reasonably required by the other authority for the performance of its functions relating to the assessment of learner travel needs[17] and the making of travel arrangements[18]. A local authority must give the head teacher[19] of a relevant school[20] any information or other assistance that is reasonably required by the head teacher about the behaviour of a registered pupil[21] of his or her school while the pupil was taking advantage of travel arrangements made[22] by the local authority[23].

1 'Regulations' means regulations made by the Welsh Ministers: Learner Travel (Wales) Measure 2008 s 24(1). As to the Welsh Ministers see PARA 59. As to the regulations made see the Learner Travel Information (Wales) Regulations 2009, SI 2009/569 (amended by SI 2010/192; and SI 2011/1944).

2 As to the meaning of 'local authority' see PARA 469 note 2.

3 'Prescribed' means prescribed by regulations: Learner Travel (Wales) Measure 2008 s 24(1).

4 Ie under the Learner Travel (Wales) Measure 2008 s 2(2): see PARA 469.

5 Learner Travel (Wales) Measure 2008 s 16(a).

6 Ie under the Learner Travel (Wales) Measure 2008 s 2: see PARA 469.

7 Learner Travel (Wales) Measure 2008 s 16(b).

8 As to the meaning of 'travel arrangements' see PARA 469 note 3.

9 Learner Travel (Wales) Measure 2008 s 16(c).

10 Ie under the Learner Travel (Wales) Measure 2008 s 12: see PARA 479.

11 Learner Travel (Wales) Measure 2008 s 16(d).

12 As to the meaning of 'maintained school' see PARA 469 note 3. As to the governing bodies of maintained schools in Wales see PARA 195.

13 As to the meaning of 'institution within the further education sector' see PARA 555 (definition applied by the Learner Travel (Wales) Measure 2008 s 24(3)).

14 As to the meaning of 'Wales' see PARA 7 note 3.

15 As to the meaning of 'functions' see PARA 18 note 5 (definition applied by the Learner Travel (Wales) Measure 2008 s 24(3)).

16 Learner Travel (Wales) Measure 2008 s 17(1). In exercising their functions under the Learner Travel (Wales) Measure 2008, governing bodies of maintained schools and governing bodies of institutions in the further education sector must have regard to guidance given from time to time by the Welsh Ministers: s 15(1)(b), (c). As to the publication of guidance see the Education Act 1996 s 571 (applied by the Learner Travel (Wales) Measure 2008 s 24(3)); and PARA 60.

17 Ie the functions under the Learner Travel (Wales) Measure 2008 s 2: see PARA 469.

18 Learner Travel (Wales) Measure 2008 s 17(2). The functions relating to the making of travel arrangements are those under ss 3, 4, and 6 (see PARAS 470–473): see s 17(2). In exercising its functions under the Learner Travel (Wales) Measure 2008, a local authority must have regard to guidance given from time to time by the Welsh Ministers: s 15(1)(a).

19 As to the meaning of 'head teacher' see PARA 86 note 4 (definition applied by the Learner Travel (Wales) Measure 2008 s 24(3)).

20 As to the meaning of 'relevant school' see PARA 480 note 6.

21 As to the meaning of 'registered pupil' see PARA 437 (definition applied by the Learner Travel (Wales) Measure 2008 s 24(3)).

22 Ie under the Learner Travel (Wales) Measure 2008.

23 Learner Travel (Wales) Measure 2008 s 17(3).

(10) WELFARE OF PUPILS

(i) Clothing and Financial Support for Participation in Education at School

482. Provision of clothing. A local authority[1] may provide clothing[2] for any pupil[3] who is a boarder[4] at an educational institution maintained by the authority[5], any pupil at a nursery school[6] maintained by the authority[7], and any pupil in a nursery class at a school[8] maintained by the authority[9]. A local authority may also provide clothing for any pupil[10] for whom it is providing board and lodging elsewhere than at an educational institution maintained by it[11], and for whom special educational provision[12] is made in pursuance of arrangements made by it[13]. Where it appears to a local authority that a pupil at a school maintained by it[14], or at a special school[15] (whether maintained by it or not)[16], is unable by reason of the inadequacy or unsuitability of his clothing to take full advantage of the education provided at the school, the authority may provide him with such clothing as in its opinion is necessary for the purpose of ensuring that he is sufficiently and suitably clad while he remains a pupil at the school[17].

A local authority may provide:

(1) for pupils at a school maintained by it, or at an institution maintained by it which provides further education[18] or higher education[19] (or both)[20];

(2) for persons who have not attained the age of 19[21] and who are receiving education at an institution within the further education sector or a 16 to 19 academy[22]; and

(3) for persons who make use of facilities for physical training secured[23] or made available[24] for them by the authority[25],

such articles of clothing as the authority may determine suitable for the physical training provided at that school or institution or under those facilities[26].

A local authority may with the consent of the proprietor[27] of a school not maintained by the authority, other than a special school[28], and on such financial and other terms, if any, as may be determined by agreement between the authority and the proprietor[29], make arrangements, in the case of any pupil at the school who is unable by reason of the inadequacy or unsuitability of his clothing to take full advantage of the education provided at the school, for securing for the pupil the provision of such clothing as is necessary for the purpose of ensuring that he is sufficiently and suitably clad while he remains a pupil at the school[30]. Any such arrangements must be such as to secure, so far as is practicable, that the expense incurred by the authority in connection with the provision of any article under the arrangements does not exceed that which would have been incurred by it in the provision of that article if the pupil had been a pupil at a school maintained by it[31].

Provision of clothing[32] may be made in such a way as to confer either a right of property in the clothing or a right of user only (at the option of the providing authority), except in any circumstances for which the adoption of one or other of those ways of making provision is prescribed[33]. Where a local authority has so provided a person with clothing, then, in such circumstances as may be prescribed[34]:

(a) the authority must require his parent[35] to pay to it in respect of its provision such sum, if any, as in its opinion he is able to pay without financial hardship, not exceeding the cost to the authority of its provision[36];

(b)   the authority may require his parent to pay to it in respect of its provision such sum as is mentioned in head (a) above or any lesser sum[37]; or

(c)   his parent is not to be required to pay any sum in respect of its provision[38].

Any sum which a parent is duly required to pay by virtue of head (a) or (b) above may be recovered summarily as a civil debt[39].

1   As to the meaning of 'local authority' see PARA 25. Any function of a local authority in England which is conferred by or under the Education Act 1996 ss 510–511 may be exercised by, or by employees of, such person as may be authorised in that behalf by the local authority whose function it is: Contracting Out (Local Authority Education Functions) (England) Order 2002, SI 2002/928, art 3, Sch 1 paras (qq), (rr) (art 3 amended by SI 2010/1172). As to the meaning of 'England' see PARA 7 note 3. As to the meaning of 'person' see PARA 7 note 6.
2   Education Act 1996 s 510(1) (amended by SI 2010/1158). 'Clothing' includes footwear: Education Act 1996 s 579(1).
3   As to the meaning of 'pupil' see PARA 20 note 4.
4   As to the meaning of 'boarder' see PARA 31 note 19.
5   Education Act 1996 s 510(1)(a) (amended by the School Standards and Framework Act 1998 s 140(1), (3), Sch 30 para 134(a), Sch 31).
6   As to the meaning of 'nursery school' see PARA 91.
7   Education Act 1996 s 510(1)(b).
8   As to the meaning of 'school' see PARA 91.
9   Education Act 1996 s 510(1)(c) (amended by the School Standards and Framework Act 1998 Sch 30 para 134(a), Sch 31). As to schools maintained by a local authority see PARA 99.
10   Education Act 1996 s 510(2) (amended by SI 2010/1158).
11   Education Act 1996 s 510(2)(a).
12   As to the meaning of 'special educational provision' see PARAS 943, 989.
13   Education Act 1996 s 510(2)(b).
14   Education Act 1996 s 510(3)(a) (amended by the School Standards and Framework Act 1998 Sch 30 para 134(b), Sch 31).
15   As to the meaning of 'special school' see PARA 1041.
16   Education Act 1996 s 510(3)(b).
17   Education Act 1996 s 510(3) (amended by SI 2010/1158).
18   As to the meaning of 'further education' see PARA 23.
19   As to the meaning of 'higher education' see PARA 24.
20   Education Act 1996 s 510(4)(a) (amended by the School Standards and Framework Act 1998 Sch 30 para 134(c), Sch 31).
21   As to the time at which a person attains a particular age see PARA 7 note 6.
22   Education Act 1996 s 510(4)(b) (amended by the Education Act 2011 Sch 13 para 9(1), (14)). As to the meaning of 'institution within the further education sector' see PARA 555. As to the meaning of '16 to 19 academy' see PARA 346 note 13.
23   Ie under the Education Act 1996 s 507A (see PARA 503) or s 507B (see PARA 504) if the authority is in England.
24   Ie under the Education Act 1996 s 508(2) (see PARA 505) if the authority is in Wales. As to the meaning of 'Wales' see PARA 7 note 3.
25   See the Education Act 1996 s 510(4)(c) (amended by the Education and Inspections Act 2006 s 6(2), Sch 1 paras 2, 5).
26   Education Act 1996 s 510(4) (amended by SI 2010/1158).
27   As to the meaning of 'proprietor' see PARA 51 note 4.
28   Education Act 1996 s 510(5)(a) (amended by the School Standards and Framework Act 1998 Sch 30 para 134(d), Sch 31).
29   Education Act 1996 s 510(5)(b).
30   Education Act 1996 s 510(5) (amended by SI 2010/1158).
31   Education Act 1996 s 510(6).
32   Ie under the Education Act 1996 s 510: see the text to notes 1–31.
33   Education Act 1996 s 511(1). 'Prescribed' means prescribed by regulations; and 'regulations' means regulations made by the Secretary of State or, in relation to Wales, the Welsh Ministers:

see s 579(1). As to the Secretary of State see PARA 58. As to the Welsh Ministers see PARA 59. The functions of the Secretary of State under the Education Act 1996 s 511, so far as exercisable in relation to Wales, were transferred to the National Assembly for Wales (see the National Assembly for Wales (Transfer of Functions) Order 1999, SI 1999/672, art 2, Sch 1) and are now vested in the Welsh Ministers (see the Government of Wales Act 2006 s 162(1), Sch 11 para 30). At the date at which this volume states the law, no regulations had been made under the Education Act 1996 s 511, but, by virtue of s 582(3), Sch 39 para 1, the Education (Provision of Clothing) Regulations 1980, SI 1980/545, have effect as if so made.

34 Education Act 1996 s 511(2) (amended by SI 2010/1158). As to the regulations made see note 33.

35 As to the meaning of 'parent' see PARA 7 note 6. Where a person who has attained the age of 18 (other than a registered pupil at a school) is provided with clothing under the Education Act 1996 s 510 (see the text to notes 1–31), any reference in s 511(2) or (3) (see the text to note 39) to his parent must be read as a reference to him: s 511(4). As to the meaning of 'registered pupil' see PARA 437.

36 Education Act 1996 s 511(2)(a).

37 Education Act 1996 s 511(2)(b).

38 Education Act 1996 s 511(2)(c).

39 Education Act 1996 s 511(3). See also note 35. As to the summary recovery of civil debts see MAGISTRATES vol 71 (2013) PARA 625.

483. Payment of school expenses and the grant of scholarships. A local authority[1], for the purpose of enabling persons to take advantage of any educational facilities available to them, may in such circumstances as may be specified in or determined in accordance with regulations[2]: (1) pay such expenses of children[3] attending community, foundation, voluntary or special schools[4] as may be necessary to enable them to take part in any school activities[5]; and (2) grant scholarships, exhibitions, bursaries and other allowances in respect of persons over compulsory school age[6]. Regulations may make provision[7]:

(a) for requiring a local authority to make, in relation to each financial year[8], a determination relating to the extent to which it proposes to exercise its power under head (2) above in that year[9]; and

(b) for authorising an authority to determine not to exercise that power in a financial year generally[10], in such cases as may be prescribed[11], or in such cases as may be determined by the authority[12].

1 As to the meaning of 'local authority' see PARA 25. Any function of a local authority in England which is conferred by or under the Education Act 1996 s 518 may be exercised by, or by employees of, such person as may be authorised in that behalf by the local authority whose function it is: Contracting Out (Local Authority Education Functions) (England) Order 2002, SI 2002/928, art 3, Sch 1 para (ww) (art 3 amended by SI 2010/1172). As to the meaning of 'person' see PARA 7 note 6. As to the meaning of 'England' see PARA 7 note 3.

2 Education Act 1996 s 518(1) (s 518 substituted by the School Standards and Framework Act 1998 s 129; and the Education Act 1996 s 518(1) amended by SI 2010/1158).'Regulations' means regulations made by the Secretary of State or, in relation to Wales, the Welsh Ministers: see the Education Act 1996 s 579(1). As to the Secretary of State see PARA 58. As to the Welsh Ministers see PARA 59. As to the meaning of 'Wales' see PARA 7 note 3. The functions of the Secretary of State under s 518, so far as exercisable in relation to Wales, were transferred to the National Assembly for Wales (see the National Assembly for Wales (Transfer of Functions) Order 1999, SI 1999/672, art 2, Sch 1) and are now vested in the Welsh Ministers (see the Government of Wales Act 2006 s 162(1), Sch 11 para 30). As to the regulations made under the Education Act 1996 s 518 see notes 5, 6.

3 As to the meaning of 'child' see PARA 7 note 6.

4 As to community, foundation and voluntary schools see PARA 106. As to the meaning of 'special school' see PARA 1041.

5 Education Act 1996 s 518(1)(a) (as substituted: see note 2). See *R (on the application of CES (A Minor)) v Oxfordshire County Council* [2004] EWHC 133 (Admin), [2004] ELR 489, sub nom *R (on the application of Southern) v Oxfordshire County Council* [2004] All ER (D) 219 (Jan). As to the regulations made in this respect see the Local Education Authority (Payment of School Expenses) Regulations 1999, SI 1999/1727. See also the Scholarships and Other Benefits

Regulations 1977, SI 1977/1443 (amended by SI 1979/260; SI 1979/542; SI 1989/1278; SI 1998/86; SI 1999/120; SI 1999/229; and SI 1999/1727), which have effect, by virtue of the Education Act 1996 s 582(3), Sch 39 para 1, as if made under s 518.

6 Education Act 1996 s 518(1)(b) (as substituted: see note 2). As to the meaning of 'compulsory school age' see PARA 19. As to the regulations made in this respect see the Local Education Authority (Post-Compulsory Education Awards) Regulations 1999, SI 1999/229 (amended by SI 2000/2057; SI 2007/779; and revoked in relation to Wales by SI 2002/1865); and the Local Education Authority (Post-Compulsory Education Awards) (Wales) Regulations 2002, SI 2002/1856.

7 As to the regulations made see note 6.

8 As to the meaning of 'financial year' see PARA 81 note 9.

9 Education Act 1996 s 518(2)(a) (as substituted (see note 2); and amended by SI 2010/1158).

10 Education Act 1996 s 518(2)(b)(i) (as substituted: see note 2).

11 Education Act 1996 s 518(2)(b)(ii) (as substituted: see note 2). 'Prescribed' means prescribed by regulations: s 579(1).

12 Education Act 1996 s 518(2)(b)(iii) (as substituted: see note 2).

484.   Allowances in respect of education or training. Regulations[1] may make provision authorising or requiring the appropriate national authority[2] to pay an allowance to or in respect of any eligible person who is over compulsory school age[3], in connection with his undertaking education or training of a prescribed[4] description[5]. The relevant education or training must not be higher education[6]. Regulations may, in particular, make provision:

(1)   for determining whether a person is an eligible person in relation to any allowance[7];

(2)   prescribing information that must be supplied by or on behalf of any person before any allowance can be paid or continue to be paid to or in respect of him[8];

(3)   prescribing the period by reference to which any allowance of a periodic nature is to be paid[9];

(4)   prescribing the maximum allowance payable to or in respect of any person in respect of any period[10];

(5)   prescribing the maximum period during which an allowance may be payable to or in respect of any person[11];

(6)   where the amount of an allowance may vary to any extent according to a person's circumstances, for determining, or providing for the determination by the appropriate national authority of, the amount required or authorised to be paid to or in respect of him[12];

(7)   specifying whether any allowance in respect of any person is to be paid to him, to a parent[13] of his or to any other person[14];

(8)   for any allowance in respect of education or training[15] to be made available on such terms and conditions as may be prescribed, or determined under the regulations by the appropriate national authority, including terms and conditions requiring repayments to be made in circumstances so prescribed or determined[16];

(9)   requiring the payment of an allowance to be suspended or terminated in any such circumstances[17];

(10)   for appeals with respect to matters arising under the regulations, including provision for determining, or enabling the determination of, the procedure to be followed in connection with appeals[18];

(11)   imposing obligations on the governing body[19] of any maintained school[20] or institution within the further education sector in relation to cases where the school or institution is providing the education or training of a prescribed description referred to above[21].

1 'Regulations' means regulations made under the Education Act 2002 by the Secretary of State (in relation to England) or by the Welsh Ministers (in relation to Wales): s 212(1). As to the Secretary of State see PARA 58. As to the Welsh Ministers see PARA 59. As to the meanings of 'England' and 'Wales' see PARA 7 note 3. The functions under the Education Act 2002 s 181 in relation to Wales were originally vested in the National Assembly for Wales and are now exercisable by the Welsh Ministers by virtue of the Government of Wales Act 2006 s 162(1), Sch 11 paras 30, 32. At the date at which this volume states the law no regulations are in force under the Education Act 2002 s 181.

2 Appropriate national authority means the Secretary of State, in relation to England, or the Welsh Ministers, in relation to Wales: see the Education Act 2002 s 181(1). As to the transfer of functions exercisable by the Secretary of State or the Welsh Ministers by virtue of regulations made under s 181 see ss 183–185; and PARA 485.

3 As to the meaning of 'compulsory school age' see PARA 19.

4 'Prescribed' means prescribed by regulations: Education Act 2002 s 212(1).

5 Education Act 2002 s 181(1).

6 Education Act 2002 s 181(2). As to the meaning of 'higher education' see PARA 24 (definition applied by s 212(2), (3)).

7 Education Act 2002 s 181(3)(a).

8 Education Act 2002 s 181(3)(b).

9 Education Act 2002 s 181(3)(c).

10 Education Act 2002 s 181(3)(d).

11 Education Act 2002 s 181(3)(e).

12 Education Act 2002 s 181(3)(f).

13 As to the meaning of 'parent' see PARA 7 note 6 (definition applied by the Education Act 2002 s 212(2), (3)).

14 Education Act 2002 s 181(3)(g). As to the meaning of 'person' in this context see PARA 7 note 6.

15 Ie any allowance under the Education Act 2002 s 181.

16 Education Act 2002 s 181(3)(h). As to exceptions where a learning agreement has been made see s 182; and PARA 93.

17 Education Act 2002 s 181(3)(i).

18 Education Act 2002 s 181(3)(j).

19 For these purposes, 'governing body': (1) means, in relation to a pupil referral unit, the local authority who maintains the unit; and (2) in relation to an institution within the further education sector, has the meaning given by the Further and Higher Education Act 1992 s 90 (see PARA 560 note 6): Education Act 2002 s 181(4) (amended by SI 2010/1158). As to pupil referral units see PARA 427 et seq. As to the meaning of 'local authority' see PARA 25 (definition applied by the Education Act 2002 s 212(1) (amended by SI 2010/1158)). As to the meaning of 'institution within the further education sector' see PARA 555 (definition applied by the Education Act 2002 s 212(2), (3)).

20 For these purposes, 'maintained school' means a community, foundation or voluntary school, a community or foundation special school or a pupil referral unit: Education Act 2002 s 181(4). As to the meaning of references to a community, foundation or voluntary school or a community or foundation special school see PARA 106.

21 Education Act 2002 s 181(3)(k). The education or training of a prescribed description referred to is the education or training referred to in s 181(1) (see the text to notes 1–5): see s 181(3)(k).

485. Transfer or delegation of functions in respect of education or training allowances.

If the Secretary of State[1] so determines, any function[2] exercisable by him in relation to allowances paid in respect of education or training[3] is, to such extent as is specified in his determination, to be exercisable instead by a local authority[4]. If the Welsh Ministers[5] so determine, any such function exercisable by them[6] is, to such extent as is specified in the determination, exercisable instead by a local authority[7]. A person or body by whom any function is for the time being exercisable by virtue of the above provisions[8] must comply with any directions[9] given by the appropriate national authority[10], as to the exercise of that function[11]. The appropriate national authority may make arrangements for any person[12] or body specified in the arrangements to exercise on its behalf, to such extent as is so specified, any function exercisable by it in relation to allowances paid in respect of education or training[13], including any such function in relation to appeals[14].

The appropriate national authority may make provision for enabling appeals: (1) to be made with respect to such matters arising out of the exercise[15] by any person or body of any function of the appropriate national authority as it may determine[16]; and (2) to be so made to a person or body appointed for the purpose by the appropriate national authority[17]. The appropriate national authority may pay to any body or person by whom any of its functions is exercisable[18]: (a) such amounts as the appropriate national authority considers appropriate for the purpose of meeting expenditure incurred or to be incurred by that body or person in paying allowances[19], or by way of administrative expenses[20], in, or in connection with, the exercise of that function[21]; (b) in a case where the function is exercisable by virtue of arrangements made by the appropriate national authority[22], such remuneration as it may determine[23].

1   As to the Secretary of State see PARA 58.
2   As to the meaning of 'function' see PARA 18 note 5.
3   Ie exercisable by virtue of regulations made under the Education Act 2002 s 181: see PARA 484.
4   Education Act 2002 s 183(1)(b) (amended by SI 2010/1158). As to the meaning of 'local authority' see PARA 25.
5   The functions under the Education Act 2002 s 183 in relation to Wales were originally vested in the National Assembly for Wales and are now exercisable by the Welsh Ministers by virtue of the Government of Wales Act 2006 s 162(1), Sch 11 paras 30, 32. As to the Welsh Ministers see PARA 59. As to the meaning of 'Wales' see PARA 7 note 3.
6   Ie by virtue of regulations made under the Education Act 2002 s 181: see PARA 484.
7   Education Act 2002 s 183(2)(b) (amended by SI 2010/1158).
8   Ie by virtue of the Education Act 2002 s 183(1) or (2): see the text to notes 1–7.
9   As to directions see the Education Act 1996 s 570 (applied by the Education Act 2002 s 212(2), (3)); and PARA 75.
10 'Appropriate national authority' means the Secretary of State or, in relation to Wales, the Welsh Ministers.
11 See the Education Act 2002 s 183(3) (amended by SI 2010/1080). Where any function is so exercisable by a local authority, the function must be taken to be a function of that authority: (1) for the purposes of the Deregulation and Contracting Out Act 1994 s 70 (see LOCAL GOVERNMENT vol 69 (2009) PARA 407); (2) for the purposes of the Local Government Act 2000 Pt II (ss 10–48) (see LOCAL GOVERNMENT vol 69 (2009) PARA 303 et seq); and (3) subject to the provisions of the Local Government Act 2000 s 13 (see LOCAL GOVERNMENT vol 69 (2009) PARAS 324–326), for the purposes of the Local Government Act 1972 s 101 (see LOCAL GOVERNMENT vol 69 (2009) PARA 370): Education Act 2002 s 183(4), (5) (s 183(4) amended by SI 2010/1158). In relation to any function which, by virtue of the Education Act 2002 s 183(1) or (2) (see the text to notes 1–7) or s 184(1) (see the text to notes 13–15) is exercisable to a specified extent, references in s 183(3), (4) to the exercise of that function are accordingly to its exercise to that extent: see s 185(5).
12 As to the meaning of 'person' see PARA 7 note 6.
13 Ie exercisable by virtue of regulations made under the Education Act 2002 s 181: see PARA 484.
14 Education Act 2002 s 184(1). Any arrangements made under s 184(1) do not prevent the Secretary of State, or as the case may be the Welsh Ministers, from exercising the function in question himself or themselves: s 184(2).
15 Ie by virtue of the Education Act 2002 s 183(1) or (2) (see the text to notes 1–8) or s 184(1) (see the text to notes 13–15). In relation to any function which, by virtue of s 183(1) or (2) or s 184(1) is exercisable to a specified extent, references in s 185 to the exercise of that function are accordingly to its exercise to that extent: see s 185(5).
16 Education Act 2002 s 185(1)(a).
17 Education Act 2002 s 185(1)(b). The Secretary of State or the Welsh Ministers may pay to any person or body appointed by him or it under s 185(1) such remuneration or administrative expenses (or both) as he or they may determine: s 185(4).
18 Ie by virtue of the Education At 2002 s 183(1) or (2) (see the text to notes 1–8) or s 184(1) (see the text to notes 13–15).
19 Education Act 2002 s 185(2)(a)(i). The allowances referred to are any under s 181 (see PARA 484): see s 185(2)(a)(i).
20 Education Act 2002 s 185(2)(a)(ii).

21 Education Act 2002 s 185(2)(a). Any payment under s 185(2)(a) may be made subject to such terms and conditions as the Secretary of State or the Welsh Ministers may determine; and any such conditions may in particular: (1) require the provision of returns or other information before any such payment is made (s 185(3)(a)); (2) relate to the use of the amount paid or require the repayment in specified circumstances of all or part of the amount paid (s 185(3)(b)).

22 Ie exercisable by virtue of the Education Act 2002 s 184(1): see the text to notes 13–15.

23 Education Act 2002 s 185(2).

(ii) School Meals

486. Local authority functions concerning provision of meals etc. A local authority[1] may provide registered pupils[2] at any school[3] maintained by it[4], and other persons who receive education at such a school[5], with milk, meals and other refreshments[6], either on the school premises[7] or at any place other than the school premises where education is being provided[8]. A local authority must exercise this power[9] to provide school lunches[10] for any person[11] if: (1) any prescribed[12] requirements are met[13]; (2) a request for the provision of school lunches has been made by or on behalf of that person to the authority[14]; and (3) either that person is eligible[15] for free lunches[16] or, in the case of a registered pupil at a school maintained by the authority[17], it would not be unreasonable for the authority to provide the lunches[18]. Subject to the duty that lunches provided by a local authority must meet nutritional standards[19], any school lunches so provided by a local authority in England[20] may take such form as the authority thinks fit[21].

A local authority may[22] charge for anything so provided[23] by it[24], and where a local authority exercises this power to charge, the price it charges for an item must[25] not exceed the cost of providing that item[26]. However, where the local authority provides a school lunch[27] to a person who is eligible for free lunches[28], the authority must provide the meal free of charge[29]. Where a local authority exercises its power[30] to provide a person[31] with milk, the authority must provide the milk free of charge if[32] the person is a specified person[33], and a request that the milk be provided free of charge has been made by him or on his behalf to the authority[34]. When a school lunch or milk is provided for a pupil in Wales free of charge by a local authority[35], the local authority must take reasonable steps to ensure that the pupil cannot be identified as a pupil who receives a school lunch or milk free of charge by any person other than an authorised person[36]. A local authority in Wales which provides school meals or milk[37] must encourage the take-up of school meals and milk[38], and take reasonable steps to ensure that every pupil who is entitled to receive school lunches and milk free of charge[39] does receive them[40].

A local authority must provide at any school maintained by it such facilities as it considers appropriate for the consumption of any meals or other refreshment brought to the school by registered pupils[41].

Academy arrangements[42] in relation to an academy school[43] or an alternative provision academy[44] must include provision imposing obligations on the proprietor[45] that are equivalent to the school lunches obligations[46].

1 As to the meaning of 'local authority' see PARA 25. Any function of a local authority in England which is conferred by or under the Education Act 1996 s 512 may be exercised by, or by employees of, such person as may be authorised in that behalf by the local authority whose function it is: Contracting Out (Local Authority Education Functions) (England) Order 2002, SI 2002/928, art 3, Sch 1 para (ss) (art 3 amended by SI 2010/1172). As to the meaning of 'England' see PARA 7 note 3. As to the meaning of 'person' see PARA 7 note 6.

2 As to the meaning of 'registered pupil' see PARA 437.

3   As to the meaning of 'school' see PARA 91.

4   Education Act 1996 s 512(1)(a) (s 512 substituted by the Education Act 2002 s 201(1)).
     References, in relation to a local authority, to a school maintained by the authority are
     references to a community, foundation or voluntary school, a community or foundation special
     school, a maintained nursery school or a pupil referral unit maintained by the authority:
     Education Act 1996 s 512(6) (as so substituted; definition amended by SI 2010/1158). As to
     community, foundation or voluntary schools and community or foundation special schools see
     PARA 106. As to the meaning of 'maintained nursery school' see PARA 99 note 4. As to pupil
     referral units see PARA 427 et seq.

5   Education Act 1996 s 512(1)(b) (as substituted: see note 4).

6   Education Act 1996 s 512(1) (as substituted (see note 4); and amended by SI 2010/1158). A
     local authority in England may provide milk, meals and other refreshments to children who
     receive relevant funded early years education: see the Education Act 1996 s 512(1)(c) (as so
     substituted; and amended by the Childcare Act 2006 s 103(1), Sch 2 para 24(a)). At the date at
     which this volume states the law, the amendment made by the Childcare Act 2006 had not been
     brought into force in Wales; therefore, until a day to be appointed, a local authority in Wales
     may provide milk, meals and other refreshments to children who receive relevant funded nursery
     education: see the Education Act 1996 s 512(1)(c) (as so substituted; and prospectively amended
     in relation to Wales by the Childcare Act 2006 s 103(1), Sch 2 para 24(a)). At the date at which
     this volume states the law, no such day had been appointed. As to the meaning of 'child' see
     PARA 7 note 6. 'Relevant funded early years education', in relation to a local authority in
     England, means early years provision as defined by the Childcare Act 2006 s 20 (see CHILDREN
     AND YOUNG PERSONS vol 10 (2012) PARA 1079) which is provided by a person, other than the
     governing body of a maintained school (within the meaning of the School Standards and
     Framework Act 1998 s 20(7): see PARA 99) or a maintained nursery school, under arrangements
     made by a local authority in pursuance of the duty imposed by the Childcare Act 2006 s 7 (duty
     to secure prescribed early years provision free of charge: see CHILDREN AND YOUNG PERSONS
     vol 10 (2012) PARA 1090); and 'relevant funded early years education', in relation to a local
     authority in Wales, means education provided by a person other than the governing body of a
     maintained school (within the meaning of the School Standards and Framework Act 1998
     s 20(7)) or a maintained nursery school: (1) under arrangements made with that person by the
     authority in pursuance of the duty imposed on the authority by s 118 of that Act (duty of local
     authority to secure sufficient nursery education: see PARA 96); and (2) in consideration of
     financial assistance provided by the authority under those arrangements: Education Act 1996
     s 512(6) (as so substituted; definitions added by the Childcare Act 2006 s 103(1), Sch 2
     para 24(b); and amended by SI 2010/1158). 'Relevant funded nursery education', in relation to
     a local authority, means education provided by a person other than the governing body of a
     maintained school (within the meaning of the School Standards and Framework Act 1998
     s 20(7)) or a maintained nursery school: (a) under arrangements made with that person by the
     authority in pursuance of the duty imposed on the authority by s 118 (duty of local authority to
     secure sufficient nursery education); and (b) in consideration of financial assistance provided by
     the authority under those arrangements: Education Act 1996 s 512(6) (as so substituted;
     definition amended by SI 2010/1158). As to the meaning of 'Wales' see PARA 7 note 3. As to the
     governing bodies of maintained schools in England see PARA 150 et seq; and in Wales see PARA
     195.

        Reference should also be made to the early years pupils premium which is additional funding
     paid to support disadvantaged children receiving government-funded early education, under the
     Childcare Act 2006 s 7: see ss 7, 7A; and CHILDREN AND YOUNG PERSONS vol 10 (2012) PARA
     1083.

7   As to the meaning of 'premises' see PARA 62 note 19.

8   See the Education Act 1996 s 512(2)(a) (as substituted: see note 4). Where a local authority
     provides milk, meals and other refreshments in a case within the Education Act 1996 s 512(1)(c)
     (see note 6), it must be provided at any place where education is being provided: see s 512(2)(b)
     (as so substituted). At the date at which this volume states the law, s 512(2)(b) is in force in
     relation to Wales only (see the Education Act 2002 (Commencement No 1) (Wales) Order 2002,
     SI 2002/3185, art 5, Schedule Pt II) and will be brought into force in relation to England as from
     a day to be appointed under the Education Act 2002 s 216(4).

        The School Standards and Organisation (Wales) Act 2013 ss 88–90 requires local authorities
     in Wales to provide breakfasts for pupils at maintained primary schools at the request of the
     governing bodies of those schools: see PARA 493.

9   Ie the power under the Education Act 1996 s 512(1): see the text to notes 1–6.

10   'School lunch' means:

(1)   in relation to a pupil, food made available for consumption by the pupil as his midday meal on a school day; and

(2)   in relation to a child receiving relevant funded nursery education at an establishment other than a school, means food made available for consumption by the child as his midday meal on a day on which he receives that education,

whether involving a set meal or the selection of items by him or otherwise: Education Act 1996 s 512(6) (as substituted: see note 4), s 512ZB(5) (as added: see note 22). As to the meaning of 'pupil' see PARA 20 note 4. As to the meaning of 'school day' see PARA 229 note 6.

Note that the Department for Education announced that from September 2014 all infant school pupils in state-funded schools are eligible for a free school lunch (see the universal free infant school meals grant; and PARA 78). This also applied to disadvantaged students at sixth form colleges and further education colleges. For more information reference should be made to the Department for Education website.

11 Ie for any person within the Education Act 1996 s 512(1)(a) (see the text to notes 1–4) or s 512(1)(c) (see note 6): see s 512(3) (as substituted (see note 4); and amended by SI 2010/1158). At the date at which this volume states the law, the Education Act 1996 s 512(3), in so far as it refers to a person within s 512(1)(c), is in force in relation to Wales only (see the Education Act 2002 (Commencement No 1) (Wales) Order 2002, SI 2002/3185, art 5, Schedule Pt II) and will be brought into force in that regard in relation to England as from a day to be appointed under the Education Act 2002 s 216(4).

12 'Prescribed' means prescribed by the Secretary of State or, in relation to Wales, the Welsh Ministers by order: see the Education Act 1996 s 512(6) (as substituted: see note 4), s 512ZB(5) (as added: see note 22). As to the Secretary of State see PARA 58. As to the Welsh Ministers see PARA 59. The functions of the Secretary of State under ss 512, 512ZB, so far as exercisable in relation to Wales, were transferred to the National Assembly for Wales (see the National Assembly for Wales (Transfer of Functions) Order 1999, SI 1999/672, art 2, Sch 1) and are now vested in the Welsh Ministers (see the Government of Wales Act 2006 s 162(1), Sch 11 para 30). As to the orders made under the Education Act 1996 s 512(3) see the Education (School Lunches) (Prescribed Requirements) (England) Order 2003, SI 2003/382; and the School Lunches (Prescribed Requirement) (Wales) Order 2005, SI 2005/1208.

13 Education Act 1996 s 512(3)(a) (as substituted: see note 4).

14 Education Act 1996 s 512(3)(b) (as substituted: see note 4).

15 Ie eligible for free lunches within the meaning of the Education Act 1996 s 512ZB(2): see note 28.

16 Education Act 1996 s 512(3)(c)(i) (as substituted: see note 4).

17 Ie a person within the Education Act 1996 s 512(1)(a): see the text to notes 1–4.

18 Education Act 1996 s 512(3)(c)(ii) (as substituted: see note 4). As to the transfer of the functions under s 512(3) to governing bodies see PARA 487.

19 Ie subject to the School Standards and Framework Act 1998 s 114A(2): see PARA 492.

20 Ie pursuant to the Education Act 1996 s 512(3): see the text to notes 9–18.

21 Education Act 1996 s 512(4) (as substituted (see note 4); and amended by SI 2010/1158; and the Healthy Eating in Schools (Wales) Measure 2009 s 8(2)(a)). In addition, subject to the Healthy Eating in Schools (Wales) Measure 2009 s 7(4), any school lunches provided by a local authority in Wales pursuant to the Education Act 1996 s 512(3) may take such form as the authority think fit (s 512(4A) (added by the Healthy Eating in Schools (Wales) Measure 2009 s 8(2)(b); and amended by the School Standards and Organisation (Wales) Act 2013 Sch 5 para 35). As to the transfer of the functions under the Education Act 1996 s 512(4) to governing bodies see PARA 487.

22 Ie subject to the Education Act 1996 s 512ZB (see the text to notes 27–34): see s 512ZA(3) (ss 512ZA, 512ZB added by the Education Act 2002 s 201(1)).

23 Ie provided under the Education Act 1996 s 512(1) (see the text to notes 1–6) or s 512(3) (see the text to notes 9–18).

24 Education Act 1996 s 512ZA(1) (as added (see note 22); and amended by the Education and Inspections Act 2006 s 87(1)(a); and SI 2010/1158).

25 Ie subject to the Education Act 1996 s 512ZB (see the text to notes 27–34): see s 512ZA(3) (as added: see note 22).

26 Education Act 1996 s 512ZA(1A) (s 512ZA as added (see note 22); and the Education Act 1996 s 512ZA(1A) added by the Education Act 2011 s 35(1), (2)(a)).

27 Ie in accordance with the Education Act 1996 s 512(3): see the text to notes 9–18.

28 For this purpose a person is eligible for free lunches if: (1) he is within the Education Act 1996 s 512ZB(4) or s 512ZB(4A) or both (see below) (s 512ZB(2)(a) (as added (see note 22) and amended by the Children and Families Act 2014 s 106(1), (2)(a)); and (2) a request that the

school lunches be provided free of charge has been made by him or on his behalf to the authority (Education Act 1996 s 512ZB(2)(b) (as so added)).

A person ('C') is within s 512ZB(4) if:

(1)   C's parent is (a) in receipt of universal credit (see WELFARE BENEFITS AND STATE PENSIONS vol 104 (2014) PARA 45 et seq) in such circumstances as may be prescribed for these purposes; (b) in receipt of income support (see WELFARE BENEFITS AND STATE PENSIONS vol 104 (2014) PARA 292 et seq); (c) in receipt of an income-based jobseeker's allowance (payable under the Jobseekers Act 1995: see WELFARE BENEFITS AND STATE PENSIONS vol 104 (2014) PARA 262 et seq); (d) in receipt of an income-related employment and support allowance (see WELFARE BENEFITS AND STATE PENSIONS vol 104 (2014) PARAS 252–261); or (e) in receipt of support provided under the Immigration and Asylum Act 1999 Pt 6 (ss 94–127) (see IMMIGRATION AND ASYLUM vol 57 (2012) PARA 341 et seq) (Education Act 1996 s 512ZB(4)(a) (as so added; and amended by the Welfare Reform Act 2007 s 28(1), Sch 3 para 16(1), (3); the Child Poverty Act 2010 s 26(1); and the Welfare Reform Act 2012 Sch 2 paras 37, 39(a))); or

(2)   C meets any conditions prescribed for these purposes and C's parent is, in such circumstances as may be so prescribed (a) in receipt of any benefit or allowance not falling within head (1) above that is so prescribed; or (b) entitled to any tax credit under the Tax Credits Act 2002 (see WELFARE BENEFITS AND STATE PENSIONS vol 104 (2014) PARA 335 et seq) or element of such a tax credit, that is so prescribed (Education Act 1996 s 512ZB(4)(aa) (s 512ZB as so added; s 512ZB(4)(aa) added by the Child Poverty Act 2010 s 26(1)(c))); or

(3)   C is in receipt of (a) universal credit in such circumstances as may be prescribed for these purposes; (b) income support, (c) in receipt of an income-based jobseeker's allowance, or (d) in receipt of an income-related employment and support allowance (Education Act 1996 s 512ZB(4)(b) (as so added; and amended by the Welfare Reform Act 2007 s 28(1), Sch 3 para 16(1), (3); the Child Poverty Act 2010 s 26(1)(d); and the Welfare Reform Act 2012 Sch 2 paras 37, 39(b))); or

(4)   C meets any conditions prescribed for these purposes and is in receipt of any benefit or allowance not falling within head (3) above that is so prescribed, or entitled to any tax credit under the Tax Credits Act 2002 or element of such a tax credit, that is so prescribed (Education Act 1996 s 512ZB(4)(c) (s 512ZB as so added; s 512ZB(4)(c) added by the Child Poverty Act 2010 s 26(1)(e))).

As from a day or days to be appointed heads (1)(b), (3)(a) above are repealed by the Welfare Reform Act 2009 ss 9(3)(b), 58(1), Sch 7 Pt 1; and heads (1)(b), (c), (d), (2)(b), (3)(b), (c), (d), (4)(b) above are repealed by the Welfare Reform Act 2012 Sch 14 Pt 1. At the date at which this volume states the law no such day or days had been appointed. As to the meaning of 'parent' see PARA 7 note 6.

As to the regulations made for the above purposes see the Education (Free School Lunches) (Prescribed Tax Credits) (England) Order 2003, SI 2003/383 (amended by SI 2011/728); the Education (Free School Lunches) (Prescribed Tax Credits) (Wales) Order 2003, SI 2003/879 (amended by SI 2011/710); the Education (Free School Lunches) (State Pension Credit) Order 2005, SI 2005/885; the Education (Free School Lunches) (State Pension Credit) (Wales) Order 2005, SI 2005/3110; the Education (Free School Lunches) (Working Tax Credit) (England) Order 2009, SI 2009/830; the Education (Free School Lunches) (Working Tax Credit) (Wales) Order 2009, SI 2009/1673; the Free School Lunches and Milk (Universal Credit) (England) Order 2013, SI 2013/650; and the Free School Lunches and Milk (Universal Credit) (Wales) Order 2013, SI 2013/2021.

A person is within the Education Act 1996 s 512ZB(4A) if the person (i) is a registered pupil at a maintained school or pupil referral unit in England; and (ii) is in reception, year 1, year 2 or any other prescribed year group at the school (s 512ZB(4A) (s 512ZB(4A)–(4C) added by the Children and Families Act 2014 s 106(1), (2)(b)).

The Secretary of State may by order provide for the following to be treated as persons within the Education Act 1996 s 512ZB(4A): (A) registered pupils, or any description of registered pupils, at a maintained nursery school in England; (B) children, or any description of children, who receive relevant funded early years education, or any description of such education, in England (s 512ZB(4B) (as so added)). As to the meaning of 'relevant funded early years education' see note 6 (definition applied by s 512ZB(5) (amended by the Children and Families Act 2012 s 106(2)(c)).

In s 512ZB(4A), 'maintained school' means (aa) a community, foundation or voluntary school; or (bb) a community or foundation special school; 'reception' means a year group in which the majority of children will, in the school year, attain the age of 5; 'year 1' means a year group in which the majority of children will, in the school year, attain the age of 6; 'year 2' means a year group in which the majority of children will, in the school year, attain the age of 7; and 'year group' means a group of children at a school the majority of whom will, in a particular school year, attain the same age: s 512ZB(4C) (as so added).

29 Education Act 1996 s 512ZB(1) (as added (see note 22); and amended by SI 2010/1158). As to the transfer of the functions under the Education Act 1996 s 512ZB(1) to governing bodies see PARA 487.

30 Ie under the Education Act 1996 s 512(1): see the text to notes 1–6.

31 Ie a person within the Education Act 1996 s 512(1)(a) (see the text to notes 1–4) or s 512(1)(c) (see note 6). At the date at which this volume states the law, the reference in s 512ZB(3) to a person within s 512(1)(c) is in force in relation to Wales only and will be brought into force in relation to England as from a day to be appointed under the Education Act 2002 s 216(4). At the date at which this volume states the law no such day had been appointed.

32 Education Act 1996 s 512ZB(3) (as added (see note 22); and amended by SI 2010/1158). As to the transfer of the functions under the Education Act 1996 s 512ZB(3) to governing bodies see PARA 487.

33 Ie a person within the Education Act 1996 s 512ZB(4) (see note 28): see s 512ZB(3)(a) (as added: see note 22).

34 Education Act 1996 s 512ZB(3)(b) (as added: see note 22).

35 Ie under the Education Act 1996 s 512ZB: see the text to notes 27–34.

36 See the Education Act 1996 s 512ZC(1), (2) (s 521ZC added by the Healthy Eating in Schools (Wales) Measure 2009 s 7); the Education Act 1996 s 512ZC(1)–(6) amended by SI 2010/1158). 'Authorised person' means (1) a parent of the pupil (Education Act 1996 s 512ZC(5)(a) (as so added); and (2) a person mentioned in s 512ZC(4) who is authorised by the local authority to have access to information about a pupil's entitlement to receive school lunches free of charge (s 512ZC(5)(b) (as so added and amended)). The persons mentioned in s 512ZC(4) are (a) a teacher in the school (s 512ZC(4)(a) (as so added)); (b) any person (other than a teacher) who is employed (whether by the local authority or by another person) in the school, or working there on an unpaid basis (s 512ZC(4)(b) (as so added and amended)); and (c) any other person employed by the local authority or governing body (s 512ZC(4)(c) (as so added and amended)). A local authority in Wales must take reasonable steps to ensure that none of the persons mentioned in s 512ZC(4) discloses to any person other than an authorised person the fact that the pupil receives school lunches or milk free of charge: s 512ZC(3) (as so added and amended). When deciding what steps to take in order to comply with its duties under s 512ZC(2) and (3) a local authority in Wales must have regard to any guidance issued by the Welsh Ministers: s 512ZC(6) (as so added and amended). As to the publication of guidance see s 571; and PARA 60.

37 Ie under the Education Act 1996 s 512: see the text to notes 1–8.

38 Healthy Eating in Schools (Wales) Measure 2009 s 6(1)(a).

39 Ie under the Education Act 1996 s 512ZB: see the text to notes 27–34.

40 Healthy Eating in Schools (Wales) Measure 2009 s 6(1)(b).

41 Education Act 1996 s 512(5) (as substituted (see note 4); and amended by SI 2010/1158).

42 As to the meaning of 'academy arrangements' see PARA 346.

43 As to the meaning of 'academy school' see PARA 346 note 12.

44 As to the meaning of 'alternative provision academy' see PARA 346 note 14.

45 As to the meaning of 'proprietor' see PARA 51 note 4.

46 Education Act 1996 s 512B(1) (s 512B added by the Children and Families Act 2014 s 106(3). 'The school lunches obligations' are the obligations imposed in relation to maintained schools and pupil referral units in England by (1) the Education Act 1996 s 512(3) (provision of school lunches on request) (see the text to notes 9–18); and (2) s 512ZB(1) (provision of free school lunches to eligible persons) (see the text to notes 27–29): s 512B(2) (as so added).

Academy arrangements in relation to an academy (other than a 16 to 19 academy) that are entered into before the date on which the Children and Families Act 2014 s 106(3) (see above) comes into force are to be treated as if they included the provision required by the Education Act 1996 s 512B(1), to the extent that they do not otherwise include such provision: s 512B(3) (as so added). As to the meaning of 'academy' see PARA 346. As to the meaning of '16 to 19 academy' see PARA 346 note 13.

487. Transfer of functions in respect of provision of meals to governing bodies. The Secretary of State[1] or, in relation to Wales, the Welsh Ministers[2] may by order make provision for imposing on the governing body[3] of any school[4] to which the order applies a duty or duties corresponding to one or more of the following duties of the local authority[5]: (1) the duty to provide school lunches[6]; (2) the duty to provide school lunches free of charge[7]; and (3) the duty to provide milk free of charge[8]. Such an order may apply to (a) all maintained schools[9]; (b) any specified class of such schools[10]; or (c) all such schools, or to any specified class of such schools maintained by specified local authorities[11].

Where any duty falls to be performed by the governing body of a school by virtue of such an order: (i) the corresponding duty mentioned in heads (1) to (3) above[12] no longer falls to be performed by the local authority in relation to the school[13]; and (ii) if the duty corresponds to the one mentioned in head (2) or head (3) above, the order may provide that, notwithstanding the other provisions of the order, the function of determining whether pupils at the school are eligible for the provision of free school lunches or milk[14] is to be exercisable by the local authority[15], and the power of the governing body to charge[16] does not apply to any school lunches or milk provided by it in pursuance of the order[17].

When a school lunch or milk is provided for a pupil in Wales free of charge by the governing body of a maintained school[18], the governing body must take reasonable steps to ensure that the pupil cannot be identified as a pupil who receives a school lunch or milk free of charge by any person[19] other than an authorised person[20]. The governing body must also take reasonable steps to ensure that no person[21] discloses to any person other than an authorised person the fact that the pupil receives school lunches or milk free of charge[22]. When deciding what steps to take in order to comply with these duties[23] a governing body must have regard to any guidance issued by the Welsh Ministers[24].

A governing body of a maintained school in Wales which provides school meals or milk[25] must encourage the take-up of school meals and milk[26], and take reasonable steps to ensure that every pupil who is entitled to receive school lunches and milk free of charge[27] does receive them[28].

1   As to the Secretary of State see PARA 58.

2   The functions of the Secretary of State under the Education Act 1996 s 512A, so far as exercisable in relation to Wales, were transferred to the National Assembly for Wales (see the National Assembly for Wales (Transfer of Functions) Order 1999, SI 1999/672, art 2, Sch 1) and are now vested in the Welsh Ministers (see the Government of Wales Act 2006 s 162(1), Sch 11 para 30). As to the Welsh Ministers see PARA 59. As to the meaning of 'Wales' see PARA 7 note 3.

3   As to the governing bodies of maintained schools in England see PARA 150 et seq; and in Wales see PARA 195.

4   As to the meaning of 'school' see PARA 91.

5   Education Act 1996 s 512A(1) (s 512A added by the School Standards and Framework Act 1998 s 116; and the Education Act 1996 s 521A(1) amended by SI 2010/1158). As to the meaning of 'local authority' see PARA 25. As to the orders made under the Education Act 1996 s 512A see the Education (Transfer of Functions Concerning School Lunches) (Wales) Order 1999, SI 1999/610 (amended by SI 2003/1717; and the School Standards and Organisation (Wales) Act 2013 Sch 5 para 31(2), (3)); the Education (Transfer of Functions Concerning School Lunches) (Wales) (No 2) Order 1999, SI 1999/1779 (amended by SI 2003/1717; and the School Standards and Organisation (Wales) Act 2013 Sch 5 para 31(2), (3)); and the Education (Transfer of Functions Concerning School Lunches) (England) (No 2) Order 1999, SI 1999/2164 (amended by SI 2003/689; and SI 2013/3111).

     An order under the Education Act 1996 s 512A must not operate to impose any duty on the governing body of a school or relieve a local authority of any duty in relation to school, at any time when a school does not have a delegated budget: s 512A(6) (as so added; and amended by SI 2010/1158; and the School Standards and Organisation (Wales) Act 2013 Sch 5 para 31(1)). 'Delegated budget' has the same meaning as in the School Standards and Framework Act 1998 (see PARA 323): Education Act 1996 s 512A(7) (as so added; definition substituted by the Education Act 2002 Sch 21 para 52). As to the meaning of 'pupil' see PARA 20 note 4. As to the meaning of 'modification' see PARA 21 note 15. 'Specified' means specified in the order: Education Act 1996 s 512A(7) (as so added).

6 Ie the duty to provide school lunches in accordance with the Education Act 1996 s 512(3), (4) (see PARA 486): s 512A(2)(a) (as added (see note 5); and amended by the Education Act 2002 s 201(2)(a)(i)). 'School lunch' has the same meaning as in s 512 (see PARA 486 note 10): s 512A(7) (as so added). See PARA 486 note 10 also in regard to the Department for Education announcement in regard to free school meals.

The School Standards and Organisation (Wales) Act 2013 ss 88–90 requires local authorities in Wales to provide breakfasts for pupils at maintained primary schools at the request of the governing bodies of those schools: see PARA 493.

7 Ie the duty to provide school lunches free of charge in accordance with the Education Act 1996 s 512ZB(1) (see PARA 486): s 512A(2)(b) (as added (see note 5); and amended by the Education Act 2002 s 201(2)(a)(ii)).

8 Ie the duty to provide milk free of charge in accordance with the Education Act 1996 s 512ZB(3) (see PARA 486): s 512A(2)(c) (as added (see note 5); and amended by the Education Act 2002 s 201(2)(a)(iii)).

9 Education Act 1996 s 512A(3)(a) (as added: see note 5). For these purposes, 'maintained school' means a maintained school as defined by the School Standards and Framework Act 1998 s 20(7) (see PARA 99) or a maintained nursery school: Education Act 1996 s 512A(7) (definition substituted by the Education Act 2002 s 215(1), Sch 21 para 52). As to the meaning of 'maintained nursery school' see PARA 99 note 4.

10 Education Act 1996 s 512A(3)(b) (as added: see note 5).

11 Education Act 1996 s 512A(3)(c) (as added (see note 5); and amended by SI 2010/1158).

12 Ie the corresponding duty mentioned in the Education Act 1996 s 512A(2).

13 Education Act 1996 s 512A(4)(a) (as added (see note 5); and amended by SI 2010/1158).

14 Ie whether the pupils fall within the Education Act 1996 s 512ZB(4): see PARA 486.

15 Education Act 1996 s 512A(4)(b)(i) (s 512A as added (see note 5); s 512A(4)(b) substituted by the Education Act 2002 s 112, and amended by SI 2010/1158).

16 Ie the Education Act 1996 s 533(3): see PARA 490.

17 Education Act 1996 s 512A(4)(b)(ii) (as added and substituted: see note 15).

18 Ie by virtue of the Education Act 1996 s 512A (see the text to notes 1–17): see s 512ZC(1) (as added: see note 18).

19 As to the meaning of 'person' see PARA 7 note 6.

20 See the Education Act 1996 s 512ZC(2) (s 512ZC added by the Healthy Eating in Schools (Wales) Measure 2009 s 7). As to the meaning of 'authorised person' see PARA 486 note 36.

21 Ie none of the persons mentioned in the 512ZC(4): see PARA 486 note 36.

22 See the Education Act 1996 s 512ZC(3) (as added: see note 20).

23 Ie the duties under the Education Act 1996 s 512ZC(2) and (3): see the text to notes 18–22.

24 See the Education Act 1996 s 512ZC(6) (as added: see note 20). As to the publication of guidance see s 571; and PARA 60.

25 Ie under the Education Act 1996 s 512: see PARA 486.

26 See the Healthy Eating in Schools (Wales) Measure 2009 s 6(1)(a).

27 Ie under the Education Act 1996 s 512ZB: see PARA 486.

28 See the Healthy Eating in Schools (Wales) Measure 2009 s 6(1)(b).

488. Promoting healthy eating and drinking by pupils in maintained schools in Wales. A local authority[1] in Wales must take action to promote healthy eating and drinking by registered pupils[2] of maintained schools[3] in its area[4]. The governing body[5] of a maintained school in Wales must take action to promote healthy eating and drinking by registered pupils of the school[6]. In discharging these duties a local authority and a governing body must have regard to guidance given from time to time by the Welsh Ministers[7] (1) on what constitutes healthy eating and drinking[8]; (2) on appropriate action to promote healthy eating and drinking[9]; (3) on how principles of sustainable development are to apply in relation to the promotion of healthy eating and drinking[10].

1 'Local authority' means a local authority in Wales within the meaning of the Education Act 1996 s 579(1) (see PARA 25): Healthy Eating in Schools (Wales) Measure 2009 s 11 (definition added by SI 2010/1148). As to the meaning of 'Wales' see PARA 7 note 3.

2 As to the registration of pupils see PARA 437.

3 For these purposes, 'maintained school' means a community, foundation or voluntary school, a community special school, a maintained nursery school or a pupil referral unit in Wales: Healthy Eating in Schools (Wales) Measure 2009 s 11 (definition amended by the School Standards and

Organisation (Wales) Act 2013 Sch 5 para 27). As to community, foundation and voluntary schools, and community special schools, see PARA 106.

4   Healthy Eating in Schools (Wales) Measure 2009 s 1(1).
        The School Standards and Organisation (Wales) Act 2013 ss 88–90 requires local authorities in Wales to provide breakfasts for pupils at maintained primary schools at the request of the governing bodies of those schools: see PARA 493.
5   As to the governing bodies of maintained schools in Wales see PARA 195.
6   Healthy Eating in Schools (Wales) Measure 2009 s 1(2).
7   As to the Welsh Ministers see PARA 59.
8   Healthy Eating in Schools (Wales) Measure 2009 s 1(3)(a).
9   Healthy Eating in Schools (Wales) Measure 2009 s 1(3)(b).
10   Healthy Eating in Schools (Wales) Measure 2009 s 1(3)(c).

489.   Provision of meals etc at schools not maintained by local authorities.   A local authority[1] may, with the consent of the proprietor[2] of a school[3] in its area which is not maintained by it[4], make arrangements for securing the provision of milk, meals and other refreshment for pupils[5] in attendance at the school[6]. Any such arrangements must be on such financial and other terms, if any, as may be determined by agreement between the authority and the proprietor of the school[7], and must be such as to secure, so far as is practicable, that the expense incurred by the authority in connection with the provision of any service or item under the arrangements does not exceed the expense which would have been incurred by it in providing the service or item if the pupil had been a pupil at a school maintained by it[8].

1   As to the meaning of 'local authority' see PARA 25.
2   As to the meaning of 'proprietor' see PARA 51 note 4.
3   As to the meaning of 'school' see PARA 91.
4   As to schools maintained by a local authority see PARA 99.
5   As to the meaning of 'pupil' see PARA 20 note 4.
6   Education Act 1996 s 513(1) (amended by SI 2010/1158). Any function of a local authority in England which is conferred by or under the Education Act 1996 s 513 may be exercised by, or by employees of, such person as may be authorised in that behalf by the local authority whose function it is: Contracting Out (Local Authority Education Functions) (England) Order 2002, SI 2002/928, art 3, Sch 1 para (tt) (both amended by SI 2010/1172). As to the meaning of 'England' see PARA 7 note 3. As to the meaning of 'person' see PARA 7 note 6.
        The School Standards and Organisation (Wales) Act 2013 ss 88–90 requires local authorities in Wales to provide breakfasts for pupils at maintained primary schools at the request of the governing bodies of those schools: see PARA 493.
7   Education Act 1996 s 513(2)(a). An order under s 512A (see PARA 487) may provide for s 513(2) not to apply to local authorities generally, or to any specified local authority, either in relation to all pupils for whom provision is made by the authority under s 513 or in relation to all such pupils who are of such ages as may be specified: s 512A(5) (s 512A added by the School Standards and Framework Act 1998 s 116; and the Education Act 1996 s 512A(5) amended by SI 2010/1158). 'Specified' means specified in the order: Education Act 1996 s 512A(7) (as so added).
8   Education Act 1996 s 513(2)(b). See also note 7.

490.   Functions of governing bodies of maintained schools with respect to provision of school meals.   The governing body[1] of any school[2] maintained by a local authority[3] must[4]: (1) afford the authority such facilities as it requires to enable it to perform its functions[5] as to the provision of milk, meals and refreshments[6]; and (2) allow the authority to make such use of the premises[7] and equipment of the school, and such alterations to the school buildings[8], as the authority considers necessary for that purpose[9]. This does not require the governing body of any such school to incur any expenditure[10].

Where the governing body of a school which has a delegated budget[11] provides pupils or other persons who receive education at the school with milk, meals or other refreshment, it may charge for anything so provided[12]; and where the governing body of a school exercises this power to charge, the price it charges for an item must not exceed the cost of providing that item[13].

1   As to the governing bodies of maintained schools in England see PARA 150 et seq; and in Wales see PARA 195.
2   As to the meaning of 'school' see PARA 91.
3   As to the meaning of 'local authority' see PARA 25. As to schools maintained by a local authority see PARA 99.
4   Education Act 1996 s 533(1) (amended by SI 2010/1158).
5   Ie its functions under the Education Act 1996 s 512: see PARA 486. As to the meaning of 'functions' see PARA 18 note 5.
6   Education Act 1996 s 533(1)(a).
     The School Standards and Organisation (Wales) Act 2013 ss 88–90 requires local authorities in Wales to provide breakfasts for pupils at maintained primary schools at the request of the governing bodies of those schools: see PARA 493.
7   As to the meaning of 'premises' see PARA 62 note 19.
8   As to the meaning of 'school building' see PARA 1296 note 18.
9   Education Act 1996 s 533(1)(b).
10 Education Act 1996 s 533(2) (amended by the School Standards and Framework Act 1998 s 140(1), Sch 30 para 148(a)).
11 Ie within the meaning of the School Standards and Framework Act 1998 Part II (ss 20–83): see PARA 323.
12 Education Act 1996 s 533(3) (amended by the School Standards and Framework Act 1998 s 140(1), Sch 30 para 148(b); and the Education and Inspections Act 2006 s 87(2)(a)).
13 Education Act 1996 s 533(3A) (added by the Education Act 2011 s 35(1), (3)(a); and amended by the School Standards and Organisation (Wales) Act 2013 s 91(1), (3)(a)).

491.   Supply of information regarding free school lunches etc. Information which is held:

(1)   for the purposes of functions relating to tax credits[1] by the Commissioners for Her Majesty's Revenue and Customs[2], or by a person[3] providing services to the Commissioners, in connection with the provision of those services[4]; or

(2)   for the purposes of functions relating to social security[5] by the Secretary of State[6], or by a person providing services to him, in connection with the provision of those services[7],

may be supplied to the Secretary of State or to any person providing services to him[8], or to the Welsh Ministers[9], or to any person providing services to the Welsh Ministers[10], for use for the purpose of determining eligibility for free school lunches[11] and milk[12]. Information so received may be supplied to another person to whom it could[13] have been supplied[14], or to a local authority[15], for use for that purpose[16]. Information to which head (2) above applies may be supplied to a local authority for the purpose of determining eligibility for free school lunches and milk[17]. These provisions do not limit the circumstances in which information may be supplied otherwise[18].

A person who discloses information which he has received by virtue of these provisions[19] and which relates to a particular person commits an offence[20] unless the information is disclosed:

(a)   in the case of information received by the Secretary of State or the Welsh Ministers or a person providing services to him or them[21], to another person to whom it could have been supplied or to a local authority in accordance with[22] the above provisions[23];

(b)   in the course of any duty that the person who discloses information has in connection with the exercise of functions relating to eligibility for free school lunches and milk[24];

(c)   in accordance with an enactment or an order of a court[25]; or

(d)   with consent given by or on behalf of the person to whom the information relates[26].

It is a defence for a person charged with such an offence to prove that he reasonably believed that his disclosure was lawful[27].

1   As to tax credits see INCOME TAXATION vol 58A (2014) PARA 1158 et seq.

2   Education Act 2005 s 110(1)(a) (amended by virtue of the Commissioners for Revenue and Customs Act 2005 s 50). As to the Commissioners for Her Majesty's Revenue and Customs see INCOME TAXATION vol 58 (2014) PARA 33. As from a day to be appointed, the Education Act 2005 s 110(1) is repealed by the Welfare Reform Act 2012 Sch 14 Pt 1. At the date at which this volume states the law no such day had been appointed.

     The School Standards and Organisation (Wales) Act 2013 ss 88–90 requires local authorities in Wales to provide breakfasts for pupils at maintained primary schools at the request of the governing bodies of those schools: see PARA 493.

3   As to the meaning of 'person' see PARA 7 note 6.

4   Education Act 2005 s 110(1)(b). See note 2.

5   See WELFARE BENEFITS AND STATE PENSIONS vol 104 (2014) PARA 1 et seq.

6   Education Act 2005 s 110(2)(a). As to the Secretary of State see PARA 58.

7   Education Act 2005 s 110(2)(b).

8   Education Act 2005 s 110(3)(a).

9   The functions under the Education Act 2005 s 110 in relation to Wales were originally vested in the National Assembly for Wales and are now exercisable by the Welsh Ministers by virtue of the Government of Wales Act 2006 s 162(1), Sch 11 paras 30, 32. As to the Welsh Ministers see PARA 59. As to the meaning of 'Wales' see PARA 7 note 3.

10   Education Act 2005 s 110(3)(b). As from a day to be appointed, the reference in s 110(3) to s 110(1) is removed: s 110(3) (prospectively amended by the Welfare Reform Act 2012 Sch 14 Pt 1). At the date at which this volume states the law no such day had been appointed.

11   As to the meaning of 'school lunch' see PARA 486 note 10 (definition applied by the Education Act 2005 s 110(8)).

12   Education Act 2005 s 110(3). For these purposes, a person is eligible for free school lunches and milk if school lunches and milk are required to be provided for him, on request, free of charge: (1) in accordance with the Education Act 1996 s 512ZB(2), (3) (see PARA 486) (Education Act 2005 s 110(7)(a)); (2) in accordance with regulations under the Education Act 1996 s 342 (non-maintained special schools: see PARA 1042) (Education Act 2005 s 110(7)(b)); or (3) in accordance with academy arrangements (Education Act 2005 s 110(7)(c) (amended by the Academies Act 2010 s 14, Sch 2 paras 16, 18)). As to the meaning of 'academy arrangements' see PARA 346 (definition applied by the Education Act 2005 s 122(2), (3))

13   Ie under the Education Act 2005 s 110(3): see the text to notes 8–12.

14   Education Act 2005 s 110(5)(a).

15   Education Act 2005 s 110(5)(b) (amended by SI 2010/1158). The references in the Education Act 2005 s 110(4) (see the text to note 17), (5)(b) to a local authority include references to any person exercising on behalf of such an authority functions relating to eligibility for free school lunches and milk: s 110(6) (amended by SI 2010/1158). As to the meaning of 'functions' see PARA 18 note 5 (definition applied by the Education Act 2005 s 122(2), (3)).

16   Education Act 2005 s 110(5).

17   Education Act 2005 s 110(4) (amended by SI 2010/1158). See also note 15.

18   Education Act 2005 s 110(9).

19   Ie by virtue of the Education Act 2005 s 110(3)–(5): see the text to notes 8–17.

20   A person guilty of such an offence is liable: (1) on conviction on indictment, to imprisonment for a term not exceeding two years, to a fine or to both (Education Act 2005 s 111(4)(a)); or (2) on summary conviction, to imprisonment for a term not exceeding 12 months, to a fine not exceeding the statutory maximum or to both (s 111(4)(b)). In relation to an offence committed before the commencement of the Criminal Justice Act 2003 s 154(1) (not yet in force) (general limit on magistrates' courts power to impose imprisonment), the reference in head (2) above to 12 months is to be read as a reference to six months: Education Act 2005 s 111(5). At the date at which this volume states the law, no day had been appointed for the commencement of the Criminal Justice Act 2003 s 154(1). As to the statutory maximum see SENTENCING AND DISPOSITION OF OFFENDERS vol 92 (2010) PARA 140.

21   Ie received by virtue of the Education Act 2005 s 110(3): see the text to notes 8–12.

22   Ie in accordance with the Education Act 2005 s 110(5): see the text to notes 13–16.

23   See the Education Act 2005 s 111(1)(a).

24 See the Education Act 2005 s 111(1)(b). For this purpose, 'eligibility for free school lunches and milk' is to be read in accordance with s 110(7) (see note 12): s 111(2).
25 Education Act 2005 s 111(1)(c).
26 Education Act 2005 s 111(1)(d).
27 Education Act 2005 s 111(3). As to the standard of proof on the accused see CRIMINAL PROCEDURE vol 28 (2010) PARA 466.

492. Nutritional standards and other requirements. Regulations[1] may prescribe requirements which, subject to such exceptions as may be provided for by or under the regulations, are to be complied with in connection with: (1) food or drink[2] provided on the premises[3] of any school maintained by a local authority in England[4]; or (2) food or drink provided at a place other than school premises[5] by a local authority in England or the governing body of a school maintained by such an authority to any registered pupil[6] at the school[7]. The regulations may in particular:

(a) specify nutritional standards, or other nutritional requirements, which are to be complied with[8];

(b) require that drinking water is to be available, free of charge, on the premises of any school maintained by a local authority[9];

(c) require that specified descriptions of food or drink are not to be provided[10].

Where a local authority or the governing body of a school maintained by such an authority provide food or drink to anyone on the premises of the school[11], or to any registered pupil at the school at a place other than school premises[12], that authority or, as the case may be, that governing body must secure that any applicable provisions of the regulations are complied with[13].

Where food or drink is provided on the premises of a school maintained by a local authority[14], the provision is by a person[15] other than the authority or the governing body of the school[16], and that person uses or occupies the whole or a part of the premises in circumstances related to a use or occupation agreement[17] made (whether by that person or any other person) with the authority or the governing body[18], that authority or, as the case may be, that governing body must secure that any applicable provisions of the regulations are complied with[19].

The regulations may[20] prescribe: (i) different requirements in relation to different classes or descriptions of school as specified in the regulations[21]; (ii) different requirements in connection with food or drink provided by or to different classes or descriptions of person as specified in the regulations[22]; (iii) requirements which apply during different periods of the day as specified in the regulations[23].

The Welsh Ministers may by regulations[24] prescribe requirements which, subject to such exceptions as may be provided for by or under the regulations, are to be complied with in connection with: (A) food or drink[25] provided on the premises of any maintained school in Wales[26]; or (B) food or drink provided at a place other than school premises[27] by a local authority in Wales or the governing body of a maintained school in Wales to any registered pupil at the school[28].

When a local authority in Wales or the governing body of a maintained school in Wales provides food or drink[29] to anyone on the premises of the school[30], or to any registered pupil at the school at a place other than school premises[31], that authority or, as the case may be, that governing body must secure that any applicable provisions of the regulations are complied with[32]. When food or drink is provided on the premises of a maintained school in Wales[33], the provision is by a person other than the authority or the governing body of the school[34], and that person uses or occupies the whole or a part of the premises in circumstances related to a use or occupation agreement[35] made (whether by that person or any other person) with the authority or the governing body[36], that authority or, as the case may be, that governing body must secure that any applicable provisions of the regulations are complied with[37].

A local authority in Wales must ensure that a supply of drinking water is available, free of charge, on the premises of any maintained school[38]. When deciding how best to discharge this duty a local authority must have regard to any guidance issued[39] by the Welsh Ministers[40].

1 'Regulations' means regulations made under the School Standards and Framework Act 1998 by the Secretary of State or, in relation to Wales, the Welsh Ministers: see s 142(1). As to the Secretary of State see PARA 58. As to the Welsh Ministers see PARA 59. As to the meaning of 'Wales' see PARA 7 note 3. The functions of the Secretary of State under the School Standards and Framework Act 1998 s 114A, so far as exercisable in relation to Wales, were transferred to the National Assembly for Wales (see the National Assembly for Wales (Transfer of Functions) Order 1999, SI 1999/672, art 2, Sch 1) and are now vested in the Welsh Ministers (see the Government of Wales Act 2006 s 162(1), Sch 11 para 30).
    As to the regulations made under the School Standards and Framework Act 1998 s 114A see the Healthy Eating in Schools (Nutritional Standards and Requirements) (Wales) Regulations 2013, SI 2013/1984; the Requirements for School Food Regulations 2014, SI 2014/1603; the Food Information Regulations 2014, SI 2014/1855; and the Products Containing Meat etc (England) Regulations 2014, SI 2014/3001.
2 References in the School Standards and Framework Act 1998 s 114A to food or drink provided by a local authority or the governing body of a school include references to food or drink provided in pursuance of an agreement or other arrangement made by such an authority or body for the provision of food or drink: s 114A(10) (s 114A added by the Education and Inspections Act 2006, s 86(1); and the School Standards and Framework Act 1998 s 114A(10) amended by SI 2010/1158). As to the meaning of 'local authority' see PARA 25 (definition applied by the School Standards and Framework Act 1998 s 142(8)). As to the governing bodies of maintained schools in England see PARA 150 et seq; and in Wales see PARA 195. As to the meaning of 'England' see PARA 7 note 3.
3 As to the meaning of 'premises' see PARA 62 note 19 (definition applied by the School Standards and Framework Act 1998 s 142(8)).
4 School Standards and Framework Act 1998 s 114A(1)(a) (as added (see note 2); and amended by SI 2010/1158; and the Healthy Eating in Schools (Wales) Measure 2009 s 8(1)). Requirements prescribed by virtue of the School Standards and Framework Act 1998 s 114A(1)(a) do not apply to food or drink brought on to the premises of a school maintained by a local authority where the food or drink is brought on to those premises by any person for his own consumption: s 114A(3) (as so added; and amended by SI 2010/1158). As to the meaning of 'school maintained by a local authority' see PARA 99.
5 A 'place other than school premises' means a place other than the premises of any school maintained by a local authority: School Standards and Framework Act 1998 s 114A(9) (as added (see note 2); and amended by SI 2010/1158).
6 As to the meaning of 'registered pupil' see PARA 437 (definition applied by the School Standards and Framework Act 1998 s 142(8)).
7 School Standards and Framework Act 1998 s 114A(1)(b) (as added (see note 2); and amended by SI 2010/1158; and the Healthy Eating in Schools (Wales) Measure 2009 s 8(1)).
8 School Standards and Framework Act 1998 s 114A(2)(a) (as added: see note 2).
9 School Standards and Framework Act 1998 s 114A(2)(b) (as added (see note 2); and amended by SI 2010/1158).
10 School Standards and Framework Act 1998 s 114A(2)(c) (as added: see note 2).
11 School Standards and Framework Act 1998 s 114A(4)(a) (as added: see note 2).
12 School Standards and Framework Act 1998 s 114A(4)(b) (as added: see note 2).
13 School Standards and Framework Act 1998 s 114A(4) (as added (see note 2); and amended by SI 2010/1158). This provision applies whether the food or drink is provided in pursuance of any statutory requirement or otherwise: School Standards and Framework Act 1998 s 114A(5) (as so added).
14 School Standards and Framework Act 1998 s 114A(6)(a) (as added (see note 2); and amended by SI 2010/1158).

15 As to the meaning of 'person' see PARA 7 note 6.

16 School Standards and Framework Act 1998 s 144A(6)(b) (as added: see note 2).

17 A 'use or occupation agreement', in relation to the premises of a school, is an agreement or other arrangement relating to the use or occupation of the whole or any part of the premises: School Standards and Framework Act 1998 s 114A(7) (as added: see note 2).

18 School Standards and Framework Act 1998 s 144A(6)(c) (as added: see note 2).

19 School Standards and Framework Act 1998 s 144A(6) (as added: see note 2).

20 Ie without prejudice to the generality of the School Standards and Framework Act 1998 s 138(7) (general provision as to orders and regulations).

21 School Standards and Framework Act 1998 s 144A(8)(a) (as added: see note 2).

22 School Standards and Framework Act 1998 s 144A(8)(b) (as added: see note 2).

23 School Standards and Framework Act 1998 s 144A(8)(c) (as added: see note 2).

24 Without prejudice to the generality of the Healthy Eating in Schools (Wales) Measure 2009 s 10 (general provision as to orders and regulations), regulations under s 4 may prescribe: (1) different requirements in relation to different classes or descriptions of school as specified in the regulations (s 4(8)(a)); (2) different requirements in connection with food or drink (see note 25) provided by or to different classes or descriptions of person as specified in the regulations (s 4(8)(b)); (3) requirements which apply during different periods of the day as specified in the regulations (s 4(8)(c)). Such regulations may in particular: (a) specify nutritional standards, or other nutritional requirements, which are to be complied with (s 4(2)(a)); (b) require that specified descriptions of food or drink are not to be provided (s 4(2)(b)); (c) specify maximum amounts of fat, saturated fat, salt, and sugar, which the food or drink can contain (s 4(2)(c)). Before making any such regulations the Welsh Ministers must: (a) take steps to ascertain the views of pupils as to the provisions proposed to be made by the regulations (s 4(11)(a)); and (b) consult such other persons as they consider appropriate (s 4(11)(b)). As to the exercise of the duty to consult see JUDICIAL REVIEW vol 61 (2010) PARA 627. As to regulations made under s 4(1)–(4), (8) see the Healthy Eating in Schools (Nutritional Standards and Requirements) (Wales) Regulations 2013, SI 2013/1984; the Fruit Juices and Fruit Nectars (Wales) Regulations 2013, SI 2013/2750; and the Food Information (Wales) Regulations 2014, SI 2014/2303.

25 References in the Healthy Eating in Schools (Wales) Measure 2009 s 4 to food or drink provided by a local authority or the governing body of a school include references to food or drink provided in pursuance of an agreement or other arrangement made by such an authority or body for the provision of food or drink: s 4(10). 'Local authority' means a local authority in Wales within the meaning of the Education Act 1996 s 579(1) (see PARA 25): Healthy Eating in Schools (Wales) Measure 2009 s 11 (definition added by SI 2010/1148).

26 Healthy Eating in Schools (Wales) Measure 2009 s 4(1)(a). Requirements prescribed by virtue of s 4(1)(a) do not apply to food or drink brought on to the premises of a maintained school where the food or drink is brought on to those premises by any person for that person's own consumption: s 4(3). As to the meaning of 'maintained school' see PARA 488 note 3.

The School Standards and Organisation (Wales) Act 2013 ss 88–90 requires local authorities in Wales to provide breakfasts for pupils at maintained primary schools at the request of the governing bodies of those schools: see PARA 493.

27 A 'place other than school premises' means a place other than the premises of any maintained school: Healthy Eating in Schools (Wales) Measure 2009 s 4(9).

28 Healthy Eating in Schools (Wales) Measure 2009 s 4(1)(b).

29 The Healthy Eating in Schools (Wales) Measure 2009 s 4(4) applies whether the food or drink is provided in pursuance of any statutory requirement or otherwise: s 4(5).

30 Healthy Eating in Schools (Wales) Measure 2009 s 4(4)(a).

31 Healthy Eating in Schools (Wales) Measure 2009 s 4(4)(b).

32 Healthy Eating in Schools (Wales) Measure 2009 s 4(4).

33 Healthy Eating in Schools (Wales) Measure 2009 s 4(6)(a).

34 Healthy Eating in Schools (Wales) Measure 2009 s 4(6)(b).

35 A 'use or occupation agreement', in relation to the premises of a school, is an agreement or other arrangement relating to the use or occupation of the whole or any part of the premises: Healthy Eating in Schools (Wales) Measure 2009 s 4(7).

36 Healthy Eating in Schools (Wales) Measure 2009 s 4(6)(c).

37 Healthy Eating in Schools (Wales) Measure 2009 s 4(6).

38 Healthy Eating in Schools (Wales) Measure 2009 s 5(1).

39 Ie under the Healthy Eating in Schools (Wales) Measure 2009 s 5.

40 Healthy Eating in Schools (Wales) Measure 2009 s 5(2).

493. Free breakfasts in primary schools in Wales. A local authority in Wales[1] must provide[2] breakfasts on each school day for pupils[3] at a primary school[4] maintained by the authority, if (1) the governing body[5] of the school has asked the authority in writing for breakfasts to be provided, and (2) 90 days have passed, beginning with the day following the day on which the request was received[6].

The above duty[7] does not apply (or ceases to apply) in relation to a request from a governing body if either of the following provisions applies: (a) the governing body has asked the authority in writing to stop providing breakfasts; (b) it would be unreasonable to provide the breakfasts and the local authority has notified the governing body in writing that as a result (i) it is not going to provide breakfasts; or (ii) it is going to stop providing breakfasts[8]. If the duty[9] applies, the local authority must provide breakfast for each pupil who asks the authority for it; for this purpose, the request may be made by or on behalf of the pupil[10].

Breakfasts provided by a local authority[11] (A) may take any form the authority thinks fit, subject to any regulations made under the Healthy Eating in Schools (Wales) Measure 2009[12]; (B) must be provided free of charge; (C) must be available on the school's premises; (D) must be available before the start of each school day, except in the case of a community special school[13] where breakfasts may be made available before or at the start of each school day[14].

In exercising its functions, a local authority or a governing body of a primary school maintained by a local authority must have regard to any guidance given by the Welsh Ministers[15] about providing breakfasts for pupils[16].

1 As to the meaning of 'local authority' see the School Standards and Organisation (Wales) Act 2013 s 98(3). As to the meaning of 'Wales' see PARA 7 note 3.
2 'Provide' includes arranging provision: see the School Standards and Organisation (Wales) Act 2013 ss 90, 98(3).
3 'Pupil' means a child receiving primary education at the school (whether or not the child is a registered pupil); and 'primary school' means a school that provides primary education (whether or not it also provides other kinds of education): see the School Standards and Organisation (Wales) Act 2013 ss 90, 98(3). As to registered pupils see PARA 437.
4 See note 3.
5 As to governing bodies of schools in Wales see PARA 195.
6 See the School Standards and Organisation (Wales) Act 2013 s 88(1). As to transitional provision generally see s 89.
7 Ie the duty in the School Standards and Organisation (Wales) Act 2013 s 88(1).
8 See the School Standards and Organisation (Wales) Act 2013 s 88(2).
9 Ie the duty under the School Standards and Organisation (Wales) Act 2013 s 88(1).
10 See the School Standards and Organisation (Wales) Act 2013 s 88(3).
11 Ie under the School Standards and Organisation (Wales) Act 2013 s 88.
12 Ie under the Healthy Eating in Schools (Wales) Measure 2009 s 4 (requirements for food and drink provided on school premises): see PARA 492.
13 As to community special schools see PARA 106.
14 See the School Standards and Organisation (Wales) Act 2013 s 88(4).
15 As to the Welsh Ministers see PARA 59.
16 See the School Standards and Organisation (Wales) Act 2013 s 88(5). As to guidance see PARA 60.

(iii) Cleanliness

494. Examination of pupils for cleanliness. A local authority[1] may by directions[2] in writing[3] authorise one of its medical officers[4] to have the persons and clothing[5] of pupils[6] in attendance at schools[7] maintained by it examined whenever in his opinion such examinations are necessary in the interests of cleanliness[8]. Such directions may be given with respect to all such schools[9], or any such schools named in the directions[10]. Such an examination must be made by a person authorised by the authority to make such examinations, and, if the examination is of a girl, it must not be made by a man unless he is a registered medical practitioner[11].

1   As to the meaning of 'local authority' see PARA 25.
2   As to directions see the Education Act 1996 s 570; and PARA 75.
3   As to the meaning of 'writing' see PARA 76 note 8.
4   As to the meaning of 'medical officer' see PARA 50 note 5.
5   As to the meaning of 'clothing' see PARA 482 note 2.
6   As to the meaning of 'pupil' see PARA 20 note 4.
7   As to the meaning of 'school' see PARA 91.
8   Education Act 1996 s 521(1), (4)(a) (s 521(1) amended by SI 2010/1158; and the Education Act 1996 s 521(4)(a) amended by the School Standards and Framework Act 1998 s 140(1), (3), Sch 30 para 141, Sch 31). As to schools maintained by local authorities see PARA 99. As to the medical inspection and treatment of pupils see the Education Act 1996 s 520; and PARA 499.
9   Education Act 1996 s 521(2)(a).
10 Education Act 1996 s 521(2)(b).
11 Education Act 1996 s 521(3). As to the meaning of 'registered medical practitioner' see MEDICAL PROFESSIONS vol 74 (2011) PARA 176. As to the compulsory cleansing of pupils see s 522; and PARA 495. As to the suspension of pupils pending examination see s 524; and PARA 497.

495. Compulsory cleansing of a pupil. If, on an examination of pupils[1] for cleanliness[2], the person or clothing[3] of a pupil is found to be infested with vermin or in a foul condition, any officer of the local authority[4] may serve a notice[5] on the pupil's parent[6] requiring him to cause the pupil's person and clothing to be cleansed[7]. The notice must inform the parent that, unless within the period specified in the notice the pupil's person and clothing are cleansed to the satisfaction of such person as is specified in the notice, the cleansing will be carried out under arrangements made by the authority[8]. The period so specified must not be less than 24 hours from the service of the notice[9].

If, on a report being made to him by the specified person at the end of the specified period, a medical officer[10] of the authority is not satisfied that the pupil's person and clothing have been properly cleansed, he may by order direct[11] that they must be cleansed under arrangements made[12] by the authority[13]. Such an order is sufficient to authorise any officer of the authority to cause the pupil's person and clothing to be cleansed in accordance with arrangements made[14] by the authority[15], and for that purpose to convey the pupil to, and detain him at, any premises[16] provided in accordance with such arrangements[17].

If, after the person or clothing of a pupil has been cleansed[18]: (1) his person or clothing is again infested with vermin, or in a foul condition, at any time while he is in attendance at a school maintained by the local authority[19]; and (2) the condition of his person or clothing is due to neglect on the part of his parent[20], the parent is guilty of an offence[21].

1   As to the meaning of 'pupil' see PARA 20 note 4.
2   Ie an examination under the Education Act 1996 s 521: see PARA 494.
3   As to the meaning of 'clothing' see PARA 482 note 2.
4   As to the meaning of 'local authority' see PARA 25.
5   As to the service of notices and documents see the Education Act 1996 s 572; and PARA 76.
6   As to the meaning of 'parent' see PARA 7 note 6.
7   Education Act 1996 s 522(1) (amended by SI 2010/1158). As to the suspension of pupils pending cleansing see the Education Act 1996 s 524; and PARA 497. As to the powers of local authorities in relation to the cleansing of verminous persons generally see ENVIRONMENTAL QUALITY AND PUBLIC HEALTH vol 46 (2010) PARA 859.

8   Education Act 1996 s 522(2). As to arrangements for the cleansing of pupils see s 523; and PARA 496.

9   Education Act 1996 s 522(3).

10 As to the meaning of 'medical officer' see PARA 50 note 5.

11 As to orders and directions generally see the Education Act 1996 s 570; and PARA 75.

12 Ie under the Education Act 1996 s 523: see PARA 496.

13 Education Act 1996 s 522(4).

14 Ie under the Education Act 1996 s 523: see PARA 496.

15 Education Act 1996 s 522(5)(a).

16 As to the meaning of 'premises' see PARA 62 note 19.

17 Education Act 1996 s 522(5)(b).

18 Ie under the Education Act 1996 s 522: see the text to notes 1–17.

19 Education Act 1996 s 525(1), (3) (amended by the School Standards and Framework Act 1998 s 140(1), (3), Sch 30 para 143, Sch 31; and SI 2010/1158).

20 Education Act 1996 s 525(1)(b).

21 Education Act 1996 s 525(1). A person guilty of such an offence is liable on summary conviction to a fine not exceeding level 1 on the standard scale: s 525(2). As to the standard scale see SENTENCING AND DISPOSITION OF OFFENDERS vol 92 (2010) PARA 142.

496.   Arrangements for cleansing of pupils. A local authority[1] must make arrangements for securing that the person or clothing[2] of any pupil[3] required to be cleansed[4] may be cleansed, whether at the request of a parent[5] or in pursuance of an order made by a medical officer[6], at suitable premises[7], by suitable persons and with suitable appliances[8].

Otherwise than in Wales[9], where the council of a district[10] in the area of the local authority is entitled to the use of any premises or appliances for cleansing the person or clothing of persons infested with vermin[11], the authority may require the council to permit the authority to use those premises or appliances for such purposes upon such terms as may be determined by agreement between the authority and the council[12], or in default of such agreement, by the Secretary of State[13].

A girl may be cleansed under arrangements under these provisions only by a registered medical practitioner[14] or by a woman authorised for the purpose by the authority[15].

1   As to the meaning of 'local authority' see PARA 25.

2   As to the meaning of 'clothing' see PARA 482 note 2.

3   As to the meaning of 'pupil' see PARA 20 note 4.

4   Ie under the Education Act 1996 s 522: see PARA 495.

5   As to the meaning of 'parent' see PARA 7 note 6.

6   Ie under the Education Act 1996 s 522(4): see PARA 495. As to the meaning of 'medical officer' see PARA 50 note 5.

7   As to the meaning of 'premises' see PARA 62 note 19.

8   Education Act 1996 s 523(1) (amended by SI 2010/1158).

9   See the Education Act 1996 s 523(3). As to the meaning of 'Wales' see PARA 7 note 3.

10 As to local government areas and authorities in England see LOCAL GOVERNMENT vol 69 (2009) PARA 22 et seq.

11 As to the powers of local authorities in relation to the cleansing of verminous persons generally see ENVIRONMENTAL QUALITY AND PUBLIC HEALTH vol 46 (2010) PARA 859.

12 Education Act 1996 s 523(2)(a).

13 Education Act 1996 s 523(2)(b). As to the Secretary of State see PARA 58.

14 As to the meaning of 'registered medical practitioner' see MEDICAL PROFESSIONS vol 74 (2011) PARA 176.

15 Education Act 1996 s 523(4).

497.   Suspension of a pupil pending examination or cleansing. Where:

    (1)   a medical officer[1] of a local authority[2] suspects that the person or clothing[3] of a pupil[4] in attendance at a school maintained by the local authority[5] is infested with vermin or in a foul condition[6]; but

(2)   action for the examination or cleansing of the pupil's person and clothing cannot be taken immediately[7],

the medical officer may direct[8] that the pupil is to be suspended from the school until such action has been taken, if he considers it necessary to do so in the interests either of the pupil or of other pupils in attendance at the school[9].

Such a direction is a defence to any proceedings[10] in respect of the failure of the pupil to attend school on any day on which he is excluded in pursuance of the direction, unless it is proved that the giving of the direction was necessitated by the wilful default of the pupil or his parent[11].

1   As to the meaning of 'medical officer' see PARA 50 note 5.
2   As to the meaning of 'local authority' see PARA 25.
3   As to the meaning of 'clothing' see PARA 482 note 2.
4   As to the meaning of 'pupil' see PARA 20 note 4.
5   As to the meaning of 'school' see PARA 91. As to schools maintained by local authorities see PARA 99.
6   Education Act 1996 s 524(1)(a), (3)(a) (s 524(1)(a) amended by SI 2010/1158; and the Education Act 1996 s 524(3)(a) amended by the School Standards and Framework Act 1998 s 140(1), (3), Sch 30 para 142(b), Sch 31).
7   Education Act 1996 s 524(1)(b). As to the examination of pupils for cleanliness see s 521; and PARA 494. As to the compulsory cleansing of pupils see s 522; and PARA 495.
8   As to directions see the Education Act 1996 s 570; and PARA 75.
9   Education Act 1996 s 524(1) (amended by the School Standards and Framework Act 1998 Sch 30 para 142(a)).
10 Ie under the Education Act 1996 Pt VI Ch II (ss 437–447): see PARA 441 et seq.
11 Education Act 1996 s 524(2). As to the offence of neglecting the cleanliness of a pupil see s 525; and PARA 495.

(iv) Medical Arrangements

498.   Power to require medical examination of pupils.   Where a question concerning the revocation of a school attendance order[1] or a dispute between a local authority and the governing body of a school[2], is referred to the appropriate national authority[3] for determination[4], and in its opinion the examination of any pupil[5] by a registered medical practitioner[6] appointed by it for the purpose would assist in determining the question[7], the appropriate national authority may serve a notice[8] on the parent[9] of that pupil requiring the parent to present the pupil for examination by such a practitioner[10]. Any parent who without reasonable excuse fails to comply with any requirements of such a notice served on him is guilty of an offence[11].

1   Ie a question under the Education Act 1996 s 442(3): see PARA 445.
2   Ie a question under the Education Act 1996 s 495: see PARA 66.
3   'Appropriate national authority' means the Secretary of State or, in relation to Wales, the Welsh Ministers. The functions of the Secretary of State under the Education Act 1996 s 506, so far as exercisable in relation to Wales, were transferred to the National Assembly for Wales (see the National Assembly for Wales (Transfer of Functions) Order 1999, SI 1999/672, art 2, Sch 1) and are now vested in the Welsh Ministers (see the Government of Wales Act 2006 s 162(1), Sch 11 para 30). As to the Secretary of State see PARA 58. As to the Welsh Ministers see PARA 59. As to the meaning of 'Wales' see PARA 7 note 3.
4   See the Education Act 1996 s 506(1)(a).
5   As to the meaning of 'pupil' see PARA 20 note 4.
6   As to the meaning of 'registered medical practitioner' see MEDICAL PROFESSIONS vol 74 (2011) PARA 176.
7   Education Act 1996 s 506(1)(b).
8   As to the service of notices and documents see the Education Act 1996 s 572; and PARA 76.
9   As to the meaning of 'parent' see PARA 7 note 6.
10 Education Act 1996 s 506(1). As to the duty to support pupils with medical conditions see PARA 501.

11   Education Act 1996 s 506(2). A person guilty of such an offence is liable on summary conviction to a fine not exceeding level 1 on the standard scale: s 506(3). As to the standard scale see SENTENCING AND DISPOSITION OF OFFENDERS vol 92 (2010) PARA 142.

499.   Medical inspection and treatment of pupils. A local authority[1] must make arrangements for encouraging and assisting pupils[2] to take advantage of the provision for medical and dental inspection and treatment made[3] for them[4]. However, if the parent[5] of a pupil gives notice[6] to the authority that he objects to the pupil availing himself of any of the provision so made, the pupil must not be encouraged or assisted to do so[7].

1   As to the meaning of 'local authority' see PARA 25.
2   As to the meaning of 'pupil' see PARA 20 note 4.

3   Ie in pursuance of the National Health Service Act 2006 s 111 or the National Health Service (Wales) Act 2006 s 67 (dental public health: see HEALTH SERVICES vol 54 (2008) PARA 291), or the National Health Service Act 2006 Sch 1 paras 1, 2(1)(a) or 8 or the National Health Service (Wales) Act 2006 Sch 1 paras 1, 2(1)(a) or 8 (medical inspection of pupils and contraceptive services: see HEALTH SERVICES vol 54 (2008) PARAS 33, 34): Education Act 1996 s 520(1)(a), (b) (s 520(1)(a), (b) substituted by the National Health Service (Consequential Provisions) Act 2006 s 2, Sch 1 paras 181, 184).

4   Education Act 1996 s 520(1) (amended by SI 2010/1158). As to the duty to support pupils with medical conditions see PARA 501. For provision requiring local authorities in Wales to secure reasonable provision for a service providing counselling in respect of health, emotional and social needs for specified school pupils and other children see PARA 500.

5   As to the meaning of 'parent' see PARA 7 note 6.
6   As to the service of notices and documents see the Education Act 1996 s 572; and PARA 76.

7   Education Act 1996 s 520(2).

500.   School-based counselling in Wales. A local authority in Wales[1] must secure reasonable provision for a service providing counselling in respect of health, emotional and social needs (an 'independent counselling service') for (1) registered pupils receiving secondary education at (a) schools maintained by the authority, and (b) other schools in its area; (2) other persons belonging to the authority's area who have attained the age of 11 but not the age of 19; (3) registered pupils undertaking their final academic year of primary education at (i) schools maintained by the authority, and (ii) other schools in its area; (4) such other persons receiving primary education as the Welsh Ministers[2] may specify in regulations[3].

In securing provision of an independent counselling service[4], a local authority must have regard (a) to the principle that the service is to be independent of the governing body[5] or other proprietor of a school at which a person to whom the service is provided is receiving education, and the management of a school at which a person to whom the service is provided is receiving education; (b) to guidance given by the Welsh Ministers[6]. A local authority must secure that an independent counselling service is provided on the site of each school maintained by the authority that provides secondary education (whether or not it also provides other kinds of education)[7]. A local authority may secure the provision of an independent counselling service at other locations[8]. The Welsh Ministers may by regulations require the provision of an independent counselling service at other locations[9].

A local authority must comply with a direction given by the Welsh Ministers to the authority (aa) to compile information about the independent counselling service it secures[10]; (bb) to provide information about that service to the Welsh Ministers[11].

1 As to the meaning of 'local authority' see the School Standards and Organisation (Wales) Act 2013 s 98(3). As to the meaning of 'Wales' see PARA 7 note 3.
2 As to the Welsh Ministers see PARA 59.
3 See the School Standards and Organisation (Wales) Act 2013 s 92(1). As to the duty to support pupils with medical conditions see PARA 501.
4 Ie under the School Standards and Organisation (Wales) Act 2013 s 92.
5 As to governing bodies of schools in Wales see PARA 195.
6 See the School Standards and Organisation (Wales) Act 2013 s 92(2).
7 See the School Standards and Organisation (Wales) Act 2013 s 92(3).
8 See the School Standards and Organisation (Wales) Act 2013 s 92(4).
9 See the School Standards and Organisation (Wales) Act 2013 s 92(5). At the date at which this volume states the law no such regulations had been made.
10 See note 4.
11 See the School Standards and Organisation (Wales) Act 2013 s 93.

501. Duty to support pupils with medical conditions. The appropriate authority for a school[1] must make arrangements for supporting pupils[2] at the school with medical conditions[3].

In meeting the above duty[4] the appropriate authority must have regard to guidance issued by the Secretary of State[5]. The duty[6] does not apply in relation to a pupil who is a young child for the purposes of the Childcare Act 2006[7].

1 Ie the appropriate authority for a school to which the Children and Families Act 2014 s 100 applies. 'The appropriate authority for a school' means (1) in the case of a maintained school, the governing body, (2) in the case of an academy, the proprietor, and (3) in the case of a pupil referral unit, the management committee: s 100(5). For these purposes, 'maintained school' means (a) a community, foundation or voluntary school, within the meaning of the School Standards and Framework Act 1998 (see PARA 106); or (b) a community or foundation special school, within the meaning of the School Standards and Framework Act 1998 (see PARA 106): Children and Families Act 2014 s 100(5). As to governing bodies of schools in England see PARA 150 et seq. As to the meaning of 'academy' see PARA 346 note 7; and as to the meaning of 'proprietor' see PARA 51 note 4 (definitions applied by s 100(6)). As to pupil referral units see PARA 427 et seq. Section 100 applies to the following schools in England (i) a maintained school; (ii) an academy school; (iii) an alternative provision academy; (iv) a pupil referral unit: s 100(4). As to the meaning of 'academy school' see PARA 346 note 12; and as to the meaning of 'alternative provision academy' see PARA 346 note 14 (definitions applied by s 100(6)). As to the meaning of 'England' see PARA 7 note 3.
2 As to the meaning of 'pupil' see PARA 20 note 4 (definition applied by the Children and Families Act 2014 s 100(6)).
3 Children and Families Act 2014 s 100(1).
4 Ie the duty in the Children and Families Act 2014 s 100(1).
5 Children and Families Act 2014 s 100(2). As to the publication of guidance see PARA 60. As to the Secretary of State see PARA 58. See in particular 'Supporting pupils at school with medical conditions: Statutory guidance for governing bodies of maintained schools and proprietors of academies in England' (September 2014).
6 See note 4.
7 Children and Families Act 2014 s 100(3). The reference in the text is to a young child for the purposes of the Childcare Act 2006 Pt 3 (ss 31–98) (regulation of provision of childcare in England): see CHILDREN AND YOUNG PERSONS vol 10 (2012) PARA 1090 et seq.

(v) Recreation and Social and Physical Training

502. Powers of appropriate national authority in relation to physical training and recreation. The appropriate national authority[1] may, in accordance with arrangements approved by the Treasury[2], make grants[3]:

(1)   towards the expenses of a local voluntary organisation[4] in providing, whether as a part of wider activities or not, or in aiding the provision of, facilities for physical training and recreation, including the provision and equipment of gymnasiums, playing fields, swimming baths, bathing

places, holiday camps and camping sites, and other buildings and premises for physical training and recreation[5];

(2)   towards the expenses of a local voluntary organisation in respect of the training and supply of teachers and leaders[6]; and

(3)   to the funds of any national voluntary organisation having such objects as are mentioned above, either in aid of its work as a whole, or in aid of any specified branch of its work[7].

When making a grant, the appropriate national authority may attach such conditions to it, including, in the case of a grant to a voluntary association, conditions for securing the continuity of the undertaking assisted, as the appropriate national authority may think proper[8].

The appropriate national authority may, with the approval of the Treasury, take steps for disseminating knowledge with respect to the value of physical training and recreation[9].

1   The Physical Training and Recreation Act 1937 s 3 refers to the 'Board of Education'. Functions of the Board of Education were transferred to the Minister of Education by the Education Act 1944, s 2(1) (repealed) and thence to the Secretary of State by the Secretary of State for Education and Science Order 1964, SI 1964/490, art 2; the Minister of Housing and Local Government by the Transfer of Functions (Physical Training and Recreation) Order 1969, SI 1969/1497; and the Secretary of State for the Environment Order 1970, SI 1970/1681. 'Appropriate national authority' means the Secretary of State or, in relation to Wales, the Welsh Ministers. The functions of the Secretary of State under the Physical Training and Recreation Act 1937 s 3, so far as exercisable in relation to Wales, were transferred to the National Assembly for Wales (see the National Assembly for Wales (Transfer of Functions) Order 1999, SI 1999/672, art 2, Sch 1) and are now vested in the Welsh Ministers (see the Government of Wales Act 2006 s 162(1), Sch 11 para 30). As to the Secretary of State see PARA 58. As to the Welsh Ministers see PARA 59. As to the meaning of 'Wales' see PARA 7 note 3.

2   As to the Treasury see CONSTITUTIONAL AND ADMINISTRATIVE LAW vol 20 (2014) PARA 262 et seq.

3   Physical Training and Recreation Act 1937 s 3(1) (amended by the Education Act 1944 ss 53(4), 121, Sch 9).

4   'Voluntary organisation' means any person or body of persons, whether corporate or unincorporate, carrying on, or proposing to carry on, an undertaking otherwise than for profit: Physical Training and Recreation Act 1937 s 9. As to the meaning of 'person' see PARA 7 note 6.

5   Physical Training and Recreation Act 1937 s 3(1)(a) (s 3(1)(a), (b) amended by the Local Government Act 1958 s 67, Sch 9 Pt II). The powers of the appropriate national authority under the Physical Training and Recreation Act 1937 s 3(1)(a) do not extend to the making of a grant in aid of the maintenance of such facilities, except that, if the appropriate national authority certifies that the circumstances of a local voluntary organisation are such that special hardship or difficulty would be occasioned if such a grant were not made to it, the appropriate national authority may make such a grant: see s 3(1) (as amended: see note 3).

6   Physical Training and Recreation Act 1937 s 3(1)(b) (as amended: see note 5).

7   Physical Training and Recreation Act 1937 s 3(1)(c).

8   Physical Training and Recreation Act 1937 s 3(2).

9   Physical Training and Recreation Act 1937 s 3(3) (amended by the Education Act 1944 Sch 9 Pt I).

503. Functions of local authorities in England in respect of recreation and training facilities for children under 13. A local authority[1] in England[2] must secure that the facilities for primary[3] and secondary education[4] provided for its area include adequate facilities for recreation and social and physical training for children[5] who have not attained the age of 13[6]. For these purposes a local authority may[7]:

(1)   establish, maintain and manage, or assist the establishment, maintenance and management of:

     (a)   camps, holiday classes, playing fields, play centres[8], and

(b)   other places, including playgrounds, gymnasiums and swimming baths not appropriated to any school[9] or other educational institution[10],

at which facilities for recreation and social and physical training are available for persons receiving primary or secondary education[11];

(2)   organise games, expeditions and other activities for such persons[12]; and

(3)   defray, or contribute towards, the expenses of such games, expeditions and other activities[13].

When making arrangements for the provision of facilities or the organisation of activities in the exercise of these powers[14], a local authority must, in particular, have regard to the expediency of co-operating with any voluntary societies or bodies whose objects include the provision of facilities or the organisation of activities of a similar character[15].

1   As to the meaning of 'local authority' see PARA 25.
2   As to the meaning of 'England' see PARA 7 note 3.
3   As to the meaning of 'primary education' see PARA 20.
4   As to the meaning of 'secondary education' see PARA 21. As to the functions of local authorities in respect of the provision of primary and secondary schools see PARA 31.
5   As to the meaning of 'child' see PARA 7 note 6.
6   Education Act 1996 s 507A(1) (s 507A added by the Education and Inspections Act 2006 s 6(1); and the Education Act 1996 s 507A(1) amended by SI 2010/1158). As to the time at which a person attains a particular age see PARA 7 note 6. As to the provision of clothing for physical training see the Education Act 1996 s 510(4); and PARA 482. It is an offence for any person, without lawful authority, to be present on premises provided under s 507A and to cause or permit nuisance or disturbance to the annoyance of persons lawfully using those premises: see s 547; and PARA 1351. As to the duty not to discriminate in the provision of facilities under s 507A see PARA 16.
7   Education Act 1996 s 507A(2) (as added (see note 6); and amended by SI 2010/1158).
8   Education Act 1996 s 507A(2)(a)(i) (as added: see note 6).
9   As to the meaning of 'school' see PARA 91.
10 Education Act 1996 s 507A(2)(a)(ii) (as added: see note 6).
11 Education Act 1996 s 507A(2)(a) (as added: see note 6).
12 Education Act 1996 s 507A(2)(b) (as added: see note 6).
13 Education Act 1996 s 507A(2)(c) (as added: see note 6).
14 Ie the powers under the Education Act 1996 s 507A(2): see the text to notes 7–13.
15 Education Act 1996 s 507A(3) (as added (see note 6); and amended by SI 2010/1158).

504.   Functions of local authorities in England in respect of leisure time activities for young persons.   A local authority[1] in England[2] must, so far as reasonably practicable, secure for qualifying young persons[3] in the authority's area access to[4]: (1) sufficient educational leisure-time activities which are for the improvement of their well-being, and sufficient facilities for such activities[5]; and (2) sufficient recreational leisure-time activities which are for the improvement of their well-being, and sufficient facilities for such activities[6]. For these purposes a local authority may[7]:

(a)   provide facilities for positive leisure-time activities[8];

(b)   assist others in the provision of such facilities[9];

(c)   make arrangements for facilitating access for qualifying young persons to such facilities[10];

(d)   organise positive leisure-time activities[11];

(e)   assist others in the organisation of such activities[12];

(f)   make arrangements for facilitating access for qualifying young persons to such activities[13];

(g)   enter into agreements or make arrangements with any person in connection with anything done or proposed to be done under any of heads (a) to (f) above[14];

(h)   take any other action which the authority think appropriate[15].

Before taking any action for the purposes of heads (1) or (2) above, a local authority must[16] (i) consider whether it is expedient for the proposed action to be taken by another person[17]; and (ii) where the authority considers that it is so expedient, take all reasonable steps to enter into an agreement or make arrangements with such a person for that purpose[18].

In exercising its functions[19] under these provisions a local authority must[20] (A) take steps to ascertain the views of qualifying young persons in the authority's area about positive leisure-time activities, and facilities for such activities, in the authority's area[21], the need for any additional such activities and facilities[22], and access to such activities and facilities[23]; and (B) secure that the views of qualifying young persons in the authority's area are taken into account[24]. A local authority in England must[25] publicise information about positive leisure-time activities, and facilities for such activities, in the authority's area[26], and keep the information so publicised up to date[27]. A local authority may charge in respect of anything provided by it under these provisions where the provision is to a qualifying young person (whether or not in the authority's area)[28]. In exercising these functions[29] a local authority must have regard to any guidance given from time to time by the Minister for the Cabinet Office[30].

1   As to the meaning of 'local authority' see PARA 25.

2   As to the meaning of 'England' see PARA 7 note 3.

3   'Qualifying young persons', for these purposes, are (1) persons who have attained the age of 13 but not the age of 20 (Education Act 1996 s 507B(2)(a) (s 507B added by the Education and Inspections Act 2006 s 6(1))); and (2) persons who have attained the age of 20 but not the age of 25 and have a learning difficulty or disability (within the meaning of the Education Act 1996 s 15ZA(6)(a) and (7): see PARA 32 note 11) (Education Act 1996 s 507B(2)(b) (as so added; and amended by SI 2010/1080; and the Children and Families Act 2014 Sch 3 paras 1, 45)). As to the time at which a person attains a particular age see PARA 7 note 6.

4   Education Act 1996 s 507B(1) (as added (see note 3); and amended by SI 2010/1158). As to the duty not to discriminate in the provision of facilities under s 507B see PARA 16.

5   Education Act 1996 s 507B(1)(a) (as added: see note 3). For the purposes of s 507B(1)(a): 'sufficient educational leisure-time activities' which are for the improvement of the well-being of qualifying young persons in the authority's area must include sufficient educational leisure-time activities which are for the improvement of their personal and social development (s 507B(3)(a) (as so added)); and 'sufficient facilities for such activities' must include sufficient facilities for educational leisure-time activities which are for the improvement of the personal and social development of qualifying young persons in the authority's area (s 507B(3)(b) (as so added)). 'Sufficient', in relation to activities or facilities, means sufficient having regard to quantity: s 507B(13) (as so added). 'Well-being', in relation to a person, means his well-being so far as relating to (1) physical and mental health and emotional well-being; (2) protection from harm and neglect; (3) education, training and recreation; (4) the contribution made by him to society; (5) social and economic well-being: s 507B(13) (as so added). 'Recreation' includes physical training (and 'recreational' is to be construed accordingly): s 507B(13) (as so added). As to the provision of clothing for physical training see s 510(4); and PARA 482. It is an offence for any person, without lawful authority, to be present on premises provided under s 507B and to cause or permit nuisance or disturbance to the annoyance of persons lawfully using those premises: see s 547; and PARA 1351.

6   Education Act 1996 s 507B(1)(b) (as added: see note 3).

7   Education Act 1996 s 507B(5) (as added (see note 3); and amended by SI 2010/1158).

8   Education Act 1996 s 507B(5)(a) (as added: see note 3). The provision mentioned in s 507B(5)(a) may include establishing, maintaining and managing places at which facilities for positive leisure-time activities are provided: s 507B(6)(a) (as so added). References to 'positive leisure-time activities' are references to any activities falling within s 507B(1)(a) or (b) (see heads (1) and (2) in the text): s 507B(4) (as so added).

9 Education Act 1996 s 507B(5)(b) (as added: see note 3). Such assistance may include the provision of financial assistance: see s 507B(6)(b) (as so added).

10 Education Act 1996 s 507B(5)(c) (as added: see note 3). Such arrangements may include the provision of transport, of financial assistance or of information to any person: see s 507B(6)(c) (as so added). As to the meaning of 'person' see PARA 7 note 6.

11 Education Act 1996 s 507B(5)(d) (as added: see note 3).

12 Education Act 1996 s 507B(5)(e) (as added: see note 3). Such assistance may include the provision of financial assistance: see s 507B(6)(b) (as so added).

13 Education Act 1996 s 507B(5)(f) (as added: see note 3). Such arrangements may include the provision of transport, of financial assistance or of information to any person: see s 507B(6)(c) (as so added).

14 Education Act 1996 s 507B(5)(g) (as added: see note 3).

15 Education Act 1996 s 507B(5)(h) (as added: see note 3).

16 Education Act 1996 s 507B(7) (as added (see note 3); and amended by SI 2010/1158).

17 Education Act 1996 s 507B(7)(a) (as added: see note 3). For these purposes a local authority must consult such persons as the authority thinks appropriate as to whether it is expedient for the proposed action to be taken by another person: s 507B(8) (as so added; and amended by SI 2010/1158). As to the exercise of the duty to consult see JUDICIAL REVIEW vol 61 (2010) PARA 627.

18 Education Act 1996 s 507B(7)(b) (as added: see note 3).

19 As to the meaning of 'functions' see PARA 18 note 5.

20 Education Act 1996 s 507B(9) (as added (see note 3); and amended by SI 2010/1158).

21 Education Act 1996 s 507B(9)(a)(i) (as added: see note 3).

22 Education Act 1996 s 507B(9)(a)(ii) (as added: see note 3).

23 Education Act 1996 s 507B(9)(a)(iii) (as added: see note 3).

24 Education Act 1996 s 507B(9)(b) (as added: see note 3). See *R (on the application of Hunt) v North Somerset Council* [2015] UKSC 51, [2015] 1 WLR 3575.

25 Education Act 1996 s 507B(10) (as added (see note 3); and amended by SI 2010/1158).

26 Education Act 1996 s 507B(10)(a) (as added: see note 3).

27 Education Act 1996 s 507B(10)(b) (as added: see note 3).

28 Education Act 1996 s 507B(11) (as added: see note 3).

29 Ie under the Education Act 1996 s 507B.

30 Education Act 1996 s 507B(12) (as added (see note 3); and amended by SI 2010/1158; and SI 2013/1721). As to the Minister for the Cabinet Office see CONSTITUTIONAL AND ADMINISTRATIVE LAW vol 20 (2014) PARA 151. As to the publication of guidance see the Education Act 1996 s 571; and PARA 60.

505. Functions of local authorities in Wales in respect of facilities for recreation and social and physical training. A local authority[1] in Wales[2]: (1) must secure that the facilities for primary[3] and secondary education[4] provided for its area include adequate facilities for recreation and social and physical training[5]; and (2) may provide facilities for recreation and social and physical training as part of the facilities for further education[6] provided, whether or not by it, for its area[7]. For either purpose, a local authority[8]:

(a) may establish, maintain and manage, or assist the establishment, maintenance and management of:

(i) camps, holiday classes, playing fields, play centres[9], and

(ii) other places, including playgrounds, gymnasiums and swimming baths not appropriated to any school[10] or other educational institution[11],

at which facilities for recreation and social and physical training are available for persons receiving primary, secondary or further education[12];

(b) may organise games, expeditions and other activities for such persons[13]; and

(c) may defray, or contribute towards, the expenses of such games, expeditions and other activities[14].

When making arrangements for the provision of facilities or the organisation of activities in the exercise of these powers[15], a local authority must, in particular, have regard to the expediency of co-operating with any voluntary societies or bodies whose objects include the provision of facilities or the organisation of activities of a similar character[16].

1   As to the meaning of 'local authority' see PARA 25.
2   As to the meaning of 'Wales' see PARA 7 note 3.
3   As to the meaning of 'primary education' see PARA 20.
4   As to the meaning of 'secondary education' see PARA 21.
5   See the Education Act 1996 s 508(1) (amended by the Learning and Skills Act 2000 s 137(1), (2); the Education and Inspections Act 2006 s 6(2), Sch 1 paras 2, 4(a); and SI 2010/1158). As to the provision of clothing for physical training see the Education Act 1996 s 510(4); and PARA 482. It is an offence for any person, without lawful authority, to be present on premises provided under s 508 and to cause or permit nuisance or disturbance to the annoyance of persons lawfully using those premises: see s 547; and PARA 1351. As to the duty not to discriminate in the provision of facilities under s 508 see PARA 16.
6   As to the meaning of 'further education' see PARA 23.
7   See the Education Act 1996 s 508(1A) (added by the Learning and Skills Act 2000 s 137(1), (3); and amended by the Education and Inspections Act 2006 s 6(2), Sch 1 paras 2, 4(a); and SI 2010/1158).
8   Education Act 1996 s 508(2) (amended by the Learning and Skills Act 2000 s 137(1), (4); and SI 2010/1158).
9   Education Act 1996 s 508(2)(a)(i).
10 As to the meaning of 'school' see PARA 91.
11 Education Act 1996 s 508(2)(a)(ii).
12 Education Act 1996 s 508(2)(a).
13 Education Act 1996 s 508(2)(b).
14 Education Act 1996 s 508(2)(c).
15 Ie the powers under the Education Act 1996 s 508(2): see heads (a)–(c) in the text.
16 Education Act 1996 s 508(3) (amended by SI 2010/1158).

(vi) Provision of Board and Lodging

506. Provision of board and lodging otherwise than at school. Where a local authority[1] is satisfied with respect to any pupil[2] that:

(1)   primary[3] or secondary education[4] suitable to his age, ability and aptitude and to any special educational needs[5] he may have can best be provided for him at a particular community, foundation or voluntary or community or foundation special school[6]; but

(2)   such education cannot be so provided unless boarding accommodation is provided for him otherwise than at the school[7],

it may provide such board and lodging for him under such arrangements as it thinks fit[8].

Where a local authority is satisfied with respect to a pupil with special educational needs that provision of board and lodging for him is necessary for enabling him to receive the required special educational provision[9], it may provide such board and lodging for him under such arrangements as it thinks fit[10].

In making any such arrangements[11], a local authority must, so far as practicable, give effect to the wishes of the pupil's parent[12] as to the religion or religious denomination of the person with whom the pupil will reside[13]. Where a local authority has provided a pupil with board and lodging under such arrangements, it must require the pupil's parent to pay it such sums, if any, in respect of the board and lodging as in its opinion he is able to pay without financial hardship[14]. However, no sum is so recoverable if the arrangements were made by the authority on the ground that in its opinion education suitable to the pupil's age, ability and aptitude or special educational needs could not otherwise be provided for him[15].

1   As to the meaning of 'local authority' see PARA 25. Any function of a local authority in England which is conferred by or under the Education Act 1996 s 514 may be exercised by, or by employees of, such person as may be authorised in that behalf by the local authority whose function it is: Contracting Out (Local Authority Education Functions) (England) Order 2002, SI 2002/928, art 3, Sch 1 para (uu) (art 3 amended by SI 2010/1172). As to the meaning of 'England' see PARA 7 note 3. As to the meaning of 'person' see PARA 7 note 6.
2   As to the meaning of 'pupil' see PARA 20 note 4.
3   As to the meaning of 'primary education' see PARA 20.
4   As to the meaning of 'secondary education' see PARA 21.
5   As to the meaning of 'special educational needs' see PARAS 943, 989.
6   Education Act 1996 s 514(1)(a) (amended by the School Standards and Framework Act 1998 s 140(1), Sch 30 para 135). As to community, foundation and voluntary and community and foundation special schools see PARA 106.
7   Education Act 1996 s 514(1)(b).
8   Education Act 1996 s 514(1) (amended by SI 2010/1158).
9   As to the meaning of 'special educational provision' see PARAS 943, 989.
10 Education Act 1996 s 514(2) (amended by SI 2010/1158).
11 Ie under the Education Act 1996 s 514.
12 As to the meaning of 'parent' see PARA 7 note 6.
13 Education Act 1996 s 514(3) (amended by SI 2010/1158).
14 Education Act 1996 s 514(4) (amended by SI 2010/1158). The sums recoverable under the Education Act 1996 s 514(4) must not exceed the cost to the authority of providing the board and lodging: s 514(6). Any sum payable under s 514(4) may be recovered summarily as a civil debt: s 514(7). As to the summary recovery of civil debts see MAGISTRATES vol 71 (2013) PARA 625.
15 Education Act 1996 s 514(5).

507.   Provision of boarding accommodation for persons for whom EHC plans are maintained. A local authority[1] in England[2] may secure the provision of boarding accommodation in connection with the provision of education or training[3] for a person in its area who is over compulsory school age[4] and for whom an ECH plan[5] is maintained[6]. For these purposes it is immaterial who provides, or secures the provision of, the education or training[7]; and a local authority may secure the provision of the boarding accommodation either within or outside its area[8].

1   As to the meaning of 'local authority' see PARA 25.
2   As to the meaning of 'England' see PARA 7 note 3.
3   'Education' and 'training' have the same meanings as in the Education Act 1996 s 15ZA (see PARA 32 notes 3, 4): s 514A(4) (s 514A added by the Apprenticeships, Skills, Children and Learning Act 2009 s 46).
4   As to the meaning of 'compulsory school age' see PARA 19.
5   As to the meaning of 'EHC plan' see PARA 958. As to EHC plans (ie education, health and care plans) generally see PARA 958 et seq.
6   Education Act 1996 s 514A(1) (amended by SI 2010/1158; and the Children and Families Act 2014 Sch 3 paras 1, 50(1), (2)).
7   Education Act 1996 s 514A(3) (as added: see note 3).
8   Education Act 1996 s 514A(2) (as added (see note 3); and amended by SI 2010/1158).

(vii)   Prohibition or Restriction on the Employment of Children

508.   Power of local authorities to prohibit or restrict employment of children. If it appears to a local authority[1] that a child[2] who is a registered pupil[3] at a community, foundation, voluntary or special school[4] is being employed[5] in such a manner as to be prejudicial to his health, or otherwise to render him unfit to obtain the full benefit of the education provided for him, the authority may serve a notice[6] in writing[7] on the employer[8] prohibiting him from employing the child[9], or imposing such restrictions upon his employment of the child as appears to it to be expedient in the interests of the child[10].

A local authority may serve a notice in writing on the parent[11] or employer of a child who is a registered pupil at a community, foundation, voluntary or special school requiring the parent or employer to provide the authority, within such period as may be specified in the notice, with such information as appears to the authority to be necessary for the purpose of enabling it to ascertain whether the child is being employed in such a manner as to render him unfit to obtain the full benefit of the education provided for him[12].

Certain statutory powers of entry apply with respect to the provisions of any notice served under the above provisions[13].

A person[14] who employs a child in contravention of any prohibition or restriction imposed[15] with respect to the employment of a child[16], or fails to comply with the requirements of a notice[17] for the provision of information[18], is guilty of an offence[19].

1   As to the meaning of 'local authority' see PARA 25.
2   For the purposes of any enactment relating to the prohibition or regulation of the employment of children or young persons, any person who is not over compulsory school age is deemed to be a child within the meaning of that enactment: Education Act 1996 s 558. As to the meanings of 'child' and 'young person' see PARA 7 note 6. As to the meaning of 'compulsory school age' see PARA 19. As to the time at which a person attains a particular age see PARA 7 note 6.
3   As to the meaning of 'registered pupil' see PARA 437.
4   As to community, foundation and voluntary schools see PARA 106. As to the meaning of 'special school' see PARA 1041. As to the application of the Education Act 1996 s 559 to pupil referral units in England see the Education (Pupil Referral Units) (Application of Enactments) (England) Regulations 2007, SI 2007/2979; and in Wales see the Education (Pupil Referral Units) (Application of Enactments) (Wales) Regulations 2007, SI 2007/1069. As to the meanings of 'England' and 'Wales' see PARA 7 note 3. As to pupil referral units see PARA 427 et seq.
5   As to work experience in the last two years of compulsory schooling see the Education Act 1996 s 560; and CHILDREN AND YOUNG PERSONS vol 10 (2012) PARA 706.
6   As to the service of notices and documents see the Education Act 1996 s 572; and PARA 76.
7   As to the meaning of 'writing' see PARA 76 note 8.
8   Education Act 1996 s 559(1) (amended by the School Standards and Framework Act 1998 s 140(1), Sch 30 para 171(a); and SI 2010/1158).
9   Education Act 1996 s 559(1)(a).
10   Education Act 1996 s 559(1)(b).
11   As to the meaning of 'parent' see PARA 7 note 6.
12   Education Act 1996 s 559(2) (amended by the School Standards and Framework Act 1998 Sch 30 para 171(b); and SI 2010/1158).
13   The provisions of the Children and Young Persons Act 1933 s 28(1), (3) (powers of entry for the enforcement of the provisions as to the employment of children: see CHILDREN AND YOUNG PERSONS vol 10 (2012) PARA 706) apply with respect to the provisions of any notice served under the Education Act 1996 s 559 as they apply with respect to the provisions of the Children and Young Persons Act 1933 Pt II (ss 18–30): Education Act 1996 s 559(5).
14   As to the meaning of 'person' see PARA 7 note 6.
15   Ie any prohibition or restriction imposed under the Education Act 1996 s 559(1): see the text to notes 1–10.
16   Education Act 1996 s 559(3)(a).
17   Ie a notice served under the Education Act 1996 s 559(2): see the text to notes 11–12.
18   Education Act 1996 s 559(3)(b).
19   Education Act 1996 s 559(3). A person guilty of such an offence is liable to a fine not exceeding level 1 on the standard scale (s 559(4)(a)), or imprisonment for a term not exceeding one month (s 559(4)(b)), or both (s 559(4)). As from a day to be appointed, s 559(4)(b) is amended so as to refer to 51 weeks instead of one month: see s 559(4)(b) (prospectively amended by the Criminal Justice Act 2003 s 280(2), (3), Sch 26 para 49(1), (3)). At the date at which this volume states

the law, no such day had been appointed. As to the standard scale see SENTENCING AND DISPOSITION OF OFFENDERS vol 92 (2010) PARA 142.

(11) DISCIPLINE AND BULLYING

(i) Promotion of Good Behaviour and Prevention of Breakdown of Discipline

509. Responsibility of governing body for discipline. The governing body[1] of a relevant school[2] must ensure that policies designed to promote good behaviour and discipline on the part of its pupils[3] are pursued at the school[4]. In particular, the governing body: (1) must make, and from time to time review, a written[5] statement of general principles to which the head teacher[6] is to have regard in determining any measures[7] in relation to a behaviour policy[8]; and (2) where it considers it desirable that any particular measures should be so determined by the head teacher or that he should have regard to any particular matters must notify him of those measures or matters[9], and may give him such guidance as it considers appropriate[10]. In exercising these functions[11] the governing body must have regard to any guidance[12] given from time to time in relation to England by the Secretary of State[13], and in relation to Wales by the Welsh Ministers[14].

1 As to the governing bodies of maintained schools in England see PARA 150 et seq; and in Wales see PARA 195. In the Education and Inspections Act 2006 ss 88, 89 (see PARA 510), 'governing body', in relation to a school approved by the Secretary of State or the Welsh Ministers under the Education Act 1996 s 342 (see PARA 1042), means the proprietor of the school: Education and Inspections Act 2006 s 88(5). As from a day to be appointed this definition is amended to read: 'governing body', in relation to a school approved under the Education Act 1996 s 342, means the proprietor of the school: s 88(5) (definition prospectively amended by the Education and Skills Act 2008 s 169(1), Sch 1 Pt 1 paras 37, 39(b)). At the date at which this volume states the law no such day had been appointed. As to the meaning of 'proprietor' see PARA 51 note 4 (definition applied by the Education and Inspections Act 2006 s 187(2), (3)). As to the meanings of 'England' and 'Wales' see PARA 7 note 3. As to the Secretary of State see PARA 58. As to the Welsh Ministers see PARA 59.

Generally law and guidance on such matters as discipline, bullying and behaviour seem to apply to academies: see eg PARA 516 and the guidance 'Behaviour and discipline in schools: Advice for headteachers and school staff' (February 2014) which is to be found on the Department for Education website. It should also be noted (as mentioned in the above advice) that proprietors of academies have a duty under the Education (Independent School Standards) (England) Regulations 2010, SI 2010/1997, Sch 1 para 7 (see now the Education (Independent School Standards) Regulations 2014, SI 2014/3283, Schedule para 7; and generally PARAS 394, 546) to ensure that arrangements are made to safeguard and promote the welfare of pupils. As to academies see PARA 345 et seq.

The functions under the Education and Inspections Act 2006 s 88 in relation to Wales were originally vested in the National Assembly for Wales and are now exercisable by the Welsh Ministers by virtue of the Government of Wales Act 2006 s 162(1), Sch 11 paras 30, 32.

2 In the Education and Inspections Act 2006 ss 88, 89 (see PARA 510), 'relevant school' means: (1) a community, foundation or voluntary school; (2) a community or foundation special school; (3) a maintained nursery school; (4) a pupil referral unit; or (5) a school approved by the Secretary of State or the Welsh Ministers under the Education Act 1996 s 342 (approval of non-maintained special schools: see PARA 1042): Education and Inspections Act 2006 s 88(5). As from a day to be appointed head (5) of this definition is amended to read: (5) a school approved under the Education Act 1996 s 342: Education and Inspections Act 2006 s 88(5) (definition prospectively amended by the Education and Skills Act 2008 s 169(1), Sch 1 Pt 1 paras 37, 39(a)). At the date at which this volume states the law no such day had been appointed. As to the meaning of references to a community, foundation or voluntary school or a community or foundation special school see PARA 106. As to the meaning of 'maintained nursery school' see PARA 99 note 4 (definition applied by the Education and Inspections Act 2006 s 187(2), (3)). As to pupil referral units see PARA 427 et seq. As to academies see note 1 and also PARA 345 et seq. See note 4.

3   As to the meaning of 'pupil' see PARA 20 note 4 (definition applied by the Education and Inspections Act 2006 s 187(2), (3)).

4   Education and Inspections Act 2006 s 88(1). As to the application of s 88 in relation to a proposed school in England see the School Governance (New Schools) (England) Regulations 2007, SI 2007/958 (amended by SI 2007/3464; SI 2009/1924; SI 2010/2582 (amended by SI 2011/577); SI 2012/1033; SI 2012/1034, SI 2012/2404; SI 2013/235; and SI 2015/883). As from a day to be appointed, an extra provision is added before the Education and Inspections Act 2006 s 88(1) as follows: 'The governing body of a relevant school in England must ensure that the head teacher determines measures under s 89(1)': s 88(A1) (prospectively added by the Deregulation Act 2015 Sch 16 para 1(1), (2)). Also as from a day to be appointed, in the Education and Inspections Act 2996 s 88(1) the words 'in Wales' are added after the words 'relevant school': s 88(1) (prospectively amended by the Deregulation Act 2015 Sch 16 para 1(1), (3)). At the date at which this volume states the law no such day or days had been appointed.

5   As to the meaning of 'written' see PARA 76 note 8.

6   As to the meaning of 'head teacher' see PARA 86 note 4 (definition applied by the Education and Inspections Act 2006 s 187(2), (3)).

7   Ie under the Education and Inspections Act 2006 s 89(1): see PARA 510.

8   Education and Inspections Act 2006 s 88(2)(a). Before making or revising the statement required by s 88(2)(a) the governing body must consult (in such manner as appears to it to be appropriate) the head teacher (s 88(3)(a)), such other persons who work at the school (whether or not for payment) as it appears to the governing body to be appropriate to consult (s 88(3)(b)), parents of registered pupils at the school (s 88(3)(c)), and registered pupils at the school (s 88(3)(d)). As to the meaning of 'parent' see PARA 7 note 6; and as to the meaning of 'registered pupil' see PARA 437 (definitions applied by s 187(2), (3)). As to the exercise of the duty to consult see JUDICIAL REVIEW vol 61 (2010) PARA 627. As from a day to be appointed, in s 88(2) the words 'of a relevant school in Wales' are added after the words 'governing body': s 88(2) (prospectively amended by the Deregulation Act 2015 Sch 16 para 1(1), (4)). At the date at which this volume states the law no such day had been appointed.

9   Education and Inspections Act 2006 s 88(2)(b)(i).

10   Education and Inspections Act 2006 s 88(2)(b)(ii).

11   Ie under the Education and Inspections Act 2006 s 88(2): see the text to notes 5–10. As to the meaning of 'functions' see PARA 18 note 5 (definition applied by s 187(2), (3)).

12   As to the publication of guidance see the Education Act 1996 s 571 (applied by the Education and Inspections Act 2006 s 187(2), (3)); and PARA 60. See eg 'Behaviour and discipline in schools: Guidance for governing bodies' (July 2013) which applies to maintained schools; and 'Parental responsibility measures for school attendance and behaviour: Statutory guidance for maintained schools, academies, local authorities and the police' (November 2013). In relation to bullying in England see eg 'Preventing and tackling bullying: Advice for headteachers, staff and governing bodies' (October 2014) and there is also advice on 'cyberbullying'. As for mental health and behaviour see eg 'Mental health and behaviour is schools: departmental advice for school staff' (June 2014).

13   Education and Inspections Act 2006 s 88(4)(a). As from a day to be appointed, s 88(4)(a) and the 'and' following it are omitted by the Deregulation Act 2015 Sch 16 para 1(1), (5)(a). At the date at which this volume states the law no such day had been appointed.

14   Education and Inspections Act 2006 s 88(4)(b). As from a day to be appointed, the words 'in relation to Wales' are omitted: s 88(4)(b) (prospectively amended by the Deregulation Act 2015 Sch 16 para 1(1), (5)(b)). At the date at which this volume states the law no such day had been appointed.

510.   Duty of head teacher to determine behaviour policy. The head teacher[1] of a relevant school[2] must determine measures to be taken with a view to:

(1)   promoting, among pupils[3], self-discipline and proper regard for authority[4];

(2)   encouraging good behaviour and respect for others on the part of pupils and, in particular, preventing all forms of bullying among pupils[5];

(3)   securing that the standard of behaviour of pupils is acceptable[6];

(4)   securing that pupils complete any tasks reasonably assigned to them in connection with their education[7]; and

(5)   otherwise regulating the conduct of pupils[8].

The head teacher of a relevant school in England must in determining such measures[9] act in accordance with the current statement made[10] by the governing body[11], and have regard to any notification or guidance given to him[12] by the governing body[13]. The head teacher of a relevant school in Wales must in determining such measures act in accordance with the current statement made[14] by the governing body[15], have regard to any notification or guidance given to him[16] by the governing body[17], and require pupils at the school to comply with the travel behaviour code made[18] by the Welsh Ministers[19].

The measures which the head teacher determines[20] must include the making of rules and provision for disciplinary penalties[21]; and may, to such extent as is reasonable[22], include measures to be taken with a view to regulating the conduct of pupils at a time when they are not on the premises[23] of the school and are not under the lawful control or charge of a member of the staff of the school[24]. The measures determined by the head teacher[25] must be publicised by him in the form of a written[26] document as follows: (a) he must make the measures generally known within the school and to parents[27] of registered pupils[28] at the school[29]; and (b) he must in particular, at least once in every school year[30], take steps to bring them to the attention of all such pupils and parents and all persons who work at the school (whether or not for payment)[31].

The disciplinary authority of the head teacher may extend to acts that take place outside school[32], and there may be circumstances in which a failure to exercise those powers would be a breach of the school's duty of care to another pupil[33].

1 As to the meaning of 'head teacher' see PARA 86 note 4 (definition applied by the Education and Inspections Act 2006 s 187(2), (3)).
2 As to the meaning of 'relevant school' see PARA 509 note 2.
3 As to the meaning of 'pupil' see PARA 20 note 4 (definition applied by the Education and Inspections Act 2006 s 187(2), (3)).
4 Education and Inspections Act 2006 s 89(1)(a).
5 Education and Inspections Act 2006 s 89(1)(b).
6 Education and Inspections Act 2006 s 89(1)(c). In relation to a relevant school in England, the standard of behaviour which is to be regarded as acceptable must be determined by the head teacher, so far as it is not determined by the governing body: s 89(3) (amended by the Learner Travel (Wales) Measure 2008 s 13(1), (4)). In relation to a relevant school in Wales, the standard of behaviour which is to be regarded as acceptable must be determined by the head teacher, so far as it is not determined by the governing body (Education and Inspections Act 2006 s 89(3A)(a) (s 89(3A) added by the Learner Travel (Wales) Measure 2008 s 13(1), (5))), or the Welsh Ministers (Education and Inspections Act 2006 s 89(3A)(b) (as so added)). As to the meanings of 'England' and 'Wales' see PARA 7 note 3. As to the Welsh Ministers see PARA 59. As to the meaning of 'governing body' see PARA 509 note 1. As to the governing bodies of maintained schools in England see PARA 150 et seq; and in Wales see PARA 195. As from a day to be appointed, in the Education and Inspections Act 1996 s 89(3) the words ', so far as it is not determined by the governing body' are omitted: s 89(3) (prospectively amended by the Deregulation Act 2015 Sch 16 para 1(1), (6)(b)). At the date at which this volume states the law no such day had been appointed.
7 Education and Inspections Act 2006 s 89(1)(d).
8 Education and Inspections Act 2006 s 89(1)(e).
9 Education and Inspections Act 2006 s 89(2) (amended by the Learner Travel (Wales) Measure 2008 s 13(1), (2)). There is a good deal of guidance available from the Department of Education as to what should be behaviour, discipline and bullying: see eg 'Behaviour and discipline in schools: Advice for headteachers and school staff' (February 2014) which is to be found on the Department for Education website. Such guidance also applies to academies as to which see PARA 345 et seq. As from a day to be appointed, the Education and Inspections Act 1996 s 89(2) is omitted by the Deregulation Act 2015 Sch 16 para 1(1), (6)(a). At the date at which this volume states the law no such day had been appointed.
10 Ie under the Education and Inspections Act 2006 s 88(2)(a): see PARA 509.
11 Education and Inspections Act 2006 s 89(2)(a).

12 Ie under the Education and Inspections Act 2006 s 88(2)(b): see PARA 509. See note 9. There is a good deal of guidance available from the Department of Education as to what should be behaviour, discipline and bullying: see eg 'Behaviour and discipline in schools: Advice for headteachers and school staff' (February 2014) which is to be found on the Department for Education website. Such guidance also applies to academies, as to which see PARA 345 et seq.

13 Education and Inspections Act 2006 s 89(2)(b).

14 Ie under the Education and Inspections Act 2006 s 88(2)(a): see PARA 509.

15 Education and Inspections Act 2006 s 89(2A)(a) (s 89(2A) added by the Learner Travel (Wales) Measure 2008 s 13(1), (3)).

16 Ie under the Education and Inspections Act 2006 s 88(2)(b): see PARA 509.

17 Education and Inspections Act 2006 s 89(2A)(b) (as added: see note 15).

18 Ie under the Learner Travel (Wales) Measure 2008 s 12: see PARA 479.

19 Education and Inspections Act 2006 s 89(2A)(c) (as added: see note 15).

20 Ie under the Education and Inspections Act 2006 s 89(1): see the text to notes 1–8.

21 Education and Inspections Act 2006 s 89(4). As to the meaning of 'disciplinary penalty' see PARA 513. In relation to a school in England, rules made under the Education and Inspections Act 2006 s 89(4) must identify the items for which a search may be made: s 89(4A) (added by the Education Act 2011 s 2(7)).

22 Ie, and, in the case of the head teacher of a relevant school in Wales, to such extent as is not required by the Education and Inspections Act 2006 s 89(2A)(c) (see the text to notes 18–19): see s 89(5A) (added by the Learner Travel (Wales) Measure 2008 s 13(1), (7)).

23 As to the meaning of 'premises' see PARA 62 note 19 (definition applied by the Education and Inspections Act 2006 s 187(2), (3)).

24 See the Education and Inspections Act 2006 s 89(5), (5A) (s 89(5) amended by the Learner Travel (Wales) Measure 2008 s 13(1), (6); and the Education and Inspections Act 2006 s 89(5A) as added: see note 22). As to the duties of teachers towards pupils see PARAS 1087–1088.

25 Ie under the Education and Inspections Act 2006 s 89(1): see the text to notes 1–8.

26 As to the meaning of 'written' see PARA 76 note 8.

27 As to the meaning of 'parent' see PARA 7 note 6 (definition applied by the Education and Inspections Act 2006 s 187(2), (3)).

28 As to the meaning of 'registered pupil' see PARA 437 (definition applied by the Education and Inspections Act 2006 s 187(2), (3)).

29 Education and Inspections Act 2006 s 89(6)(a).

30 As to the meaning of 'school year' see PARA 19 note 12 (definition applied by the Education and Inspections Act 2006 s 187(2), (3)).

31 Education and Inspections Act 2006 s 89(6)(b).

32 *Cleary v Booth* [1893] 1 QB 465, 57 JP 375, DC; *R v Newport (Salop) Justices, ex p Wright* [1929] 2 KB 416, 27 LGR 518; *R v Solihull Borough Council, ex p W* [1997] ELR 489; *R v Newham London Borough Council, ex p X* [1995] ELR 303, (1994) Times, 15 November (head teacher could use his disciplinary powers against a pupil who had attacked another boy outside school); *Bradford-Smart v West Sussex County Council* [2002] EWCA Civ 07, [2002] LGR 489, [2002] ELR 139; *Webster v Ridgeway Foundation School* [2010] EWHC 157 (QB), [2010] ELR 694, [2010] All ER (D) 52 (Feb). Traditionally, this power has been seen to derive from a delegation of parental authority: see PARA 512. As to the non-delegable duty of care of a local authority see *Woodland v Essex County Council* [2013] UKSC 66, [2014] AC 537, [2014] 1 All ER 482 (if third parties to whom the teaching function has been delegated are negligent the authority is in breach of duty, here in the case of a junior school pupil suffering serious brain damage during a school swimming lesson) (see also PARAS 1087 note 3, 1088 note 2). See generally the Department for Education advice at note 9. See also the Department's Exclusions Guidance as to which see generally PARA 540 note 13.

33 *Bradford-Smart v West Sussex County Council* [2002] EWCA Civ 07, [2002] LGR 489, [2002] ELR 139 (in rare circumstances, a head teacher who fails to exercise his disciplinary authority over a pupil who bullies another pupil outside school may be in breach of his duty of care). The prevention of bullying among pupils is within a teacher's ordinary duty of care: see eg *Scott v Lothian Regional Council* (29 September 1998, unreported). See also *H v Isle of Wight Council* [2001] All ER (D) 315 (Feb); and PARA 1087. See *Woodland v Essex County Council* [2013] UKSC 66, [2014] AC 537, [2014] 1 All ER 482; and note 32. As to health and safety generally see also PARA 1353.

511. Reserve power of local authority in England to prevent a breakdown of discipline. Where:

(1)   in the opinion of the local authority in England[1] the behaviour of

registered pupils[2] at a maintained school[3], or any action taken by such pupils or their parents[4], is such that the education of any registered pupils at the school is (or is likely in the immediate future to become) severely prejudiced[5]; and

(2) the governing body[6] has been informed in writing[7] of the authority's opinion[8],

the local authority in England may take such steps in relation to the school as it considers are required to prevent the breakdown, or continuing breakdown, of discipline at the school[9].

Similarly, where, in the case of a maintained school in England[10]:

(a) a warning notice has been given[11] referring to the safety of pupils[12] or staff at a school being threatened by a breakdown of discipline at the school[13];

(b) the governing body have failed to comply, or secure compliance, with the notice to the local authority's satisfaction within the compliance period[14]; and

(c) the authority have given reasonable notice[15] in writing to the governing body that it proposes to exercise its powers[16] of intervention[17],

the local authority in England may take such steps in relation to the school as it considers are required to prevent the breakdown, or continuing breakdown, of discipline at the school[18].

Steps taken by a local authority under the above provisions may include the giving of any direction[19] to the governing body or head teacher[20].

1 As to the meaning of 'local authority' see PARA 25 (definition applied by the School Standards and Framework Act 1998 s 142(8)). As to the meaning of 'England' see PARA 7 note 6. Any function of a local authority in England which is conferred by or under the School Standards and Framework Act 1998 s 62 may be exercised by, or by employees of, such person as may be authorised in that behalf by the local authority whose function it is: Contracting Out (Local Authority Education Functions) (England) Order 2002, SI 2002/928, art 3, Sch 2 para (q) (both amended by SI 2010/1172). As to the meaning of 'person' see PARA 7 note 6. In the case of academies any reserve power would be the Secretary of State's; see generally PARA 345 et seq. As to the Secretary of State see PARA 58.

2 As to the meaning of 'registered pupil' see PARA 437 (definition applied by the School Standards and Framework Act 1998 s 142(8)).

3 See the School Standards and Framework Act 1998 s 62(2)(a)(i). For these purposes, 'maintained school' includes a maintained nursery school: s 62(5) (added by the Education Act 2002 s 215(1), Sch 21 para 103). As to the meaning of 'maintained school' generally see PARA 99. As to the meaning of 'maintained nursery school' see PARA 99 note 4.

4 School Standards and Framework Act 1998 s 62(2)(a)(ii). As to the meaning of 'parent' see PARA 7 note 6 (definition applied by s 142(8)).

5 School Standards and Framework Act 1998 s 62(2)(a).

6 As to the governing bodies of maintained schools in England see PARA 150 et seq.

7 As to the meaning of 'writing' see PARA 76 note 8.

8 School Standards and Framework Act 1998 s 62(2)(b).

9 See the School Standards and Framework Act 1998 s 62(1) (amended by SI 2010/1158; and the School Standards and Organisation (Wales) Act 2013 Sch 5 para 4(1), (4)(a)).

10 See the School Standards and Framework Act 1998 s 62(2A) (added by the Education and Inspections Act 2006 s 71, Sch 7 Pt 2 para 14(1), (3)).

11 Ie in accordance with the Education and Inspections Act 2006 s 60(2): see PARA 1207.

12 As to the meaning of 'pupil' see PARA 20 note 4 (definition applied by the School Standards and Framework Act 1998 s 142(8)).

13 School Standards and Framework Act 1998 s 62(2A)(a) (as added: see note 10).

14 See the School Standards and Framework Act 1998 s 62(2A)(b) (as added: see note 10).

15 As to the service of notices and documents see the Education Act 1996 s 572 (applied by the School Standards and Framework Act 1998 s 142(8)); and PARA 76.

16 Ie its powers under the School Standards and Framework Act 1998 s 62(1) (see the text to note 18) (whether or not in conjunction with exercising its powers under any one or more of the Education and Inspections Act 2006 ss 63–66: see PARAS 1211–1214).

17 See the School Standards and Framework Act 1998 s 62(2A)(c) (as added: see note 10). A notice under s 62(2A)(c) may be combined with a notice under the Education and Inspections Act 2006 s 60(2) (see PARA 1207): School Standards and Framework Act 1998 s 62(2A) (as so added).

18 See the School Standards and Framework Act 1998 s 62(1) (amended by the Education and Inspections Act 2006 s 71, Sch 7 Pt 2 para 14(1), (2); SI 2010/1158; and the School Standards and Organisation (Wales) Act 2013 Sch 5 para 4(1), (4)(a)).

19 As to directions see the Education Act 1996 s 570 (applied by the School Standards and Framework Act 1998 s 142(8)); and PARA 75.

20 School Standards and Framework Act 1998 s 62(4). As to the meaning of 'head teacher' see PARA 86 note 4 (definition applied by s 142(8)).

(ii) Enforcement of Discipline

512. Detention of pupils at common law. The detention of a child for disciplinary purposes is sanctioned at common law provided its use is not for improper purpose or unreasonable[1]. The traditional basis of the teacher's authority to detain pupils is the in loco parentis principle, whereby the parent, when he places his child in school, delegates to the head teacher all his own authority, so far as it is necessary for the welfare of the child, including disciplinary authority[2]. Detention of a child by his parent is unlawful if it is for such a period or in such circumstances as to take it out of the realm of reasonable parental discipline[3]. At common law, if a detention is imposed without the parent's consent it is possible that the parent may succeed in a claim for false imprisonment[4], but statutory provision is now made in relation to detention and the imposition of disciplinary penalties generally[5].

1 *Fitzgerald v Northcote* (1865) 4 F & F 656.
2 *Cleary v Booth* [1893] 1 QB 465, 57 JP 375, DC; *Ryan v Fildes* [1938] 3 All ER 517. See also *Price v Wilkins* (1888) 58 LT 680, 4 TLR 231; *Fitzgerald v Northcote* (1865) 4 F & F 656; *Goldney v King* (1910) Times, 7 February; *Hutt v Governors of Haileybury College* (1888) 4 TLR 623 at 624 per Field J. See also *Mansell v Griffin* [1908] 1 KB 160, 98 LT 51 (teacher's right to punish a child extends to a responsible assistant teacher). Note also the right of the person holding parental responsibility under the Children Act 1989 s 3(1) to arrange for others to exercise it on his behalf (see s 2(9); and CHILDREN AND YOUNG PERSONS vol 9 (2012) PARA 161), and the authority given to a person who has care of a child to do what is reasonable in all the circumstances of the case for the purpose of safeguarding or promoting the child's welfare (see s 3(5); and CHILDREN AND YOUNG PERSONS vol 9 (2012) PARA 154).
3 *R v Rahman* (1985) 81 Cr App Rep 349 at 354, 129 Sol Jo 431 at 432, CA, per Lord Lane LCJ.
4 See *Price v Wilkins* (1888) 58 LT 680, 4 TLR 231. See also *Terrington v Lancashire County Council* (28 August 1986, unreported) (conflict between parent and teacher had to be balanced with the need to administer punishment; blanket detention of the entire class for ten minutes at the end of school was a reasonable punishment). In the latter case, the judge added (obiter) that if there had been evidence showing that the father had withdrawn his parental authority for his son to be detained for minor indiscipline then the claim for false imprisonment would have succeeded: see *Terrington v Lancashire County Council* above. It is submitted that the local authority might, in such a case, be able to establish that the school's disciplinary arrangements include detention after school; that those arrangements were made known to all parents before their children were admitted to the school; and that it is not open to a parent unilaterally to change those arrangements. The Elementary Education Acts 1870 and 1876 (both repealed) did not authorise the setting of lessons to be prepared at home by children attending a board school. The detention at school after hours of a child for not doing home lessons was therefore unlawful, and rendered the master who detained the child liable to be convicted for an assault: *Hunter v Johnson* (1884) 13 QBD 225.
5 See PARA 513 et seq.

513. Meaning of 'disciplinary penalty'. In the provisions of the Education and Inspections Act 2006 relating to school discipline[1], 'disciplinary penalty' means a penalty imposed on a pupil[2], by any school[3] at which education is provided for him, where his conduct falls below the standard which could reasonably be expected of him (whether because he fails to follow a rule in force at any such school or an instruction given to him by a member of its staff[4] or for any other reason)[5]. In this definition, the reference to conduct, in relation to a pupil, includes: (1) conduct which occurs at a time when the pupil is not on the premises[6] of a school and is not under the lawful control or charge of a member of the staff of a school, but only to the extent that it is reasonable for the school imposing the penalty to regulate the pupil's conduct at such a time[7]; and (2) conduct which consists of a failure by the pupil to comply with a penalty previously imposed on him[8].

1 Ie in the Education and Inspections Act 2006 Pt 7 Ch 1 (ss 88–96).
2 As to the meaning of 'pupil' see PARA 20 note 4 (definition applied by the Education and Inspections Act 2006 s 187(2), (3)).
3 As to the meaning of 'school' see PARA 91 (definition applied by the Education and Inspections Act 2006 s 187(2), (3)).
4 'Member of the staff', in relation to a school, means (1) any teacher who works at the school; and (2) any other person who, with the authority of the head teacher, has lawful control or charge of pupils for whom education is being provided at the school: Education and Inspections Act 2006 s 95. As to the meaning of 'head teacher' see PARA 86 note 4 (definition applied by s 187(2), (3)).
5 Education and Inspections Act 2006 s 90(1). As to the duty of a head teacher to determine the behaviour policy of a school see s 89; and PARA 510.
6 As to the meaning of 'premises' see PARA 62 note 19 (definition applied by the Education and Inspections Act 2006 s 187(2), (3)). There is a good deal of guidance available from the Department of Education as to what should be behaviour, discipline and bullying: see eg 'Behaviour and discipline in schools: Advice for headteachers and school staff' (February 2014) which is to be found on the Department for Education website. Such guidance also applies to academies as to which see PARA 345 et seq.
7 Education and Inspections Act 2006 s 90(2)(a).
8 Education and Inspections Act 2006 s 90(2)(b).

514. Enforcement of disciplinary penalties: general. Where a disciplinary penalty[1] is imposed on a pupil[2] by any school[3] at which education is provided for him, other than a penalty which consists of exclusion[4], the imposition of the disciplinary penalty is lawful if the following three conditions are satisfied[5]:

(1) the first condition is that the imposition of the penalty on the pupil is not in breach of any statutory requirement or prohibition[6], and is reasonable in all the circumstances[7];

(2) the second condition is that the decision to impose the penalty on the pupil was made (a) by any paid member of the staff[8] of the school, except in circumstances where the head teacher[9] has determined that the member of staff is not permitted to impose the penalty on the pupil[10], or (b) by any other member of the staff of the school, in circumstances where the head teacher has authorised the member of the staff to impose the penalty on the pupil and it was reasonable for the head teacher to do so[11];

(3) the third condition is that the decision to impose the penalty was made, and any action taken on behalf of the school to implement the decision was taken on the premises[12] of the school[13], or elsewhere at a time when the pupil was under the lawful control or charge of a member of staff of the school[14].

Nothing in these provisions[15] authorises anything to be done in relation to a pupil which constitutes[16] the giving of corporal punishment[17]. These provisions[18] are not to be construed as restricting what may otherwise[19] lawfully be done[20].

Where, as a disciplinary penalty an item which a pupil has with him or in his possessions[21] is seized[22], and the item is retained for any period or is disposed of[23], a person who seizes, retains or disposes of the item is not liable in any proceedings in respect of the seizure, retention or disposal (as the case may be)[24], or any damage or loss which arises in consequence of it[25], if he proves that the seizure, retention or disposal (as the case may be) was[26] lawful[27]. These provisions[28] are not to be construed as preventing any person relying on any defence on which he is otherwise[29] entitled to rely[30].

1   As to the meaning of 'disciplinary penalty' see PARA 513.
2   As to the meaning of 'pupil' see PARA 20 note 4 (definition applied by the Education and Inspections Act 2006 s 187(2), (3)).
3   As to the meaning of 'school' see PARA 91 (definition applied by the Education and Inspections Act 2006 s 187(2), (3)).
4   Education and Inspections Act 2006 s 91(1). As to the exclusion of pupils see PARA 517 et seq.
5   Education and Inspections Act 2006 s 91(2). Where the disciplinary penalty is detention outside school sessions, s 91 has effect subject to s 92 (see PARA 515): s 91(9).
     There is a good deal of guidance available from the Department of Education as to behaviour and discipline and also eg on screening, searching and confiscation: see the Department for Education website. Such guidance usually also applies to academies as to which see PARA 345 et seq.
6   Education and Inspections Act 2006 s 91(3)(a).
7   Education and Inspections Act 2006 s 91(3)(b). In determining for the purposes of s 91(3)(b) whether the imposition of the penalty is reasonable, the following matters must be taken into account: (1) whether the imposition of the penalty constitutes a proportionate punishment in the circumstances of the case (s 91(6)(a)); and (2) any special circumstances relevant to its imposition on the pupil which are known to the person imposing it (or of which he ought reasonably to be aware) including in particular, the pupil's age (s 91(6)(b)(i)), any special educational needs he may have (s 91(6)(b)(ii)), any disability he may have (s 91(6)(b)(iii)), and any religious requirements affecting him (s 91(6)(b)(iv)). For the purposes of s 91(6)(b)(iii) a pupil has a disability if he has a disability for the purposes of the Equality Act 2010 (see DISCRIMINATION vol 33 (2013) PARA 50 et seq): Education and Inspections Act 2006 s 91(7) (amended by the Equality Act 2010 Sch 26 paras 92, 94). As to the meaning of 'special educational needs' see PARAS 943, 989 (definition applied by the Education and Inspections Act 2006 s 187(2), (3)).
8   'Paid member of the staff', in relation to a school, means any member of the staff who works at the school for payment, whether under a contract of employment or a contract for services; and, for this purpose, it is immaterial whether the contract of employment or contract for services is made with the governing body or proprietor of the school or with any other person: Education and Inspections Act 2006 s 91(12). As to the meaning of 'member of staff' see PARA 513 note 4. As to contracts of employment and contracts for services see EMPLOYMENT vol 39 (2014) PARAS 1, 2. As to the governing bodies of maintained schools in England see PARA 150 et seq; and in Wales see PARA 195. As to the meaning of 'proprietor' see PARA 51 note 4 (definition applied by s 187(2), (3)). As to the meaning of 'person' see PARA 7 note 6.
9   As to the meaning of 'head teacher' see PARA 86 note 4 (definition applied by the Education and Inspections Act 2006 s 187(2), (3)).
10 Education and Inspections Act 2006 s 91(4)(a). A determination or authorisation by the head teacher for the purpose of s 91(4)(a) or (b) (see the text to note 11) may be made: (1) in relation to a particular member of staff or members of staff of a particular description (s 91(8)(a)); (2) in relation to a particular disciplinary penalty or disciplinary penalties of a particular description (s 91(8)(b)); (3) in relation to a particular pupil or pupils of a particular description or generally in relation to pupils (s 91(8)(c)).
11 Education and Inspections Act 2006 s 91(4)(b). See also note 10.
12 As to the meaning of 'premises' see PARA 62 note 19 (definition applied by the Education and Inspections Act 2006 s 187(2), (3)).
13 Education and Inspections Act 2006 s 91(5)(a).
14 Education and Inspections Act 2006 s 91(5)(b).
15 Ie in the Education and Inspections Act 2006 s 91.
16 Ie within the meaning of the Education Act 1996 s 548: see PARA 545 note 3.
17 Education and Inspections Act 2006 s 91(10).
18 Ie the Education and Inspections Act 2006 s 91.

19 Ie apart from the Education and Inspections Act 2006 s 91.
20 See the Education and Inspections Act 2006 s 91(11). As to the common law relating to the detention of pupils see PARA 512.
21 'Possessions', in relation to a pupil, includes any goods over which he appears to have control: Education and Inspections Act 2006 s 95.
22 Education and Inspections Act 2006 s 94(1)(a). Nothing in s 94 applies where an item is seized under the Education Act 1996 s 550ZC (see PARA 544) or s 550AA (see PARA 543): Education and Inspections Act 2006 s 94(3) (amended by the Apprenticeships, Skills, Children and Learning Act 2009 s 242(3)).
23 Education and Inspections Act 2006 s 94(1)(b).
24 Education and Inspections Act 2006 s 94(2)(a).
25 Education and Inspections Act 2006 s 94(2)(b).
26 Ie whether or not by virtue of the Education and Inspections Act 2006 s 91: see the text to notes 1–20.
27 Education and Inspections Act 2006 s 94(2)(c).
28 Ie the Education and Inspections Act 2006 s 94.
29 Ie apart from the Education and Inspections Act 2006 s 94.
30 See the Education and Inspections Act 2006 s 94(4).

515. Enforcement of disciplinary penalties: detention outside school sessions.
In relation to a disciplinary penalty[1] which consists of the detention of a pupil[2] outside school[3] sessions[4], the provisions relating to the lawfulness of the imposition of disciplinary penalties[5] have effect as if they required the following additional conditions[6] to be satisfied[7]. The additional conditions are:

(1) that the pupil has not attained the age of 18[8];

(2) that the head teacher[9] of the school has previously determined, and has made generally known within the school and to parents of registered pupils[10] at the school, that the detention of pupils outside school sessions is one of the measures that may be taken with a view to regulating the conduct of pupils[11];

(3) that the detention is on a permitted day of detention[12]; and

(4) that, in relation to a pupil at a school in Wales, the pupil's parent has been given at least 24 hours' notice[13] in writing[14] that the detention is due to take place[15].

The additional conditions set out in heads (1), (3) and (4) do not apply in the case of a detention during a break between school sessions on the same day[16].

These provisions[17] are not to be construed as restricting what may otherwise[18] lawfully be done[19].

1 As to the meaning of 'disciplinary penalty' see PARA 513.
2 As to the meaning of 'pupil' see PARA 20 note 4 (definition applied by the Education and Inspections Act 2006 s 187(2), (3)).
3 As to the meaning of 'school' see PARA 91 (definition applied by the Education and Inspections Act 2006 s 187(2), (3)).
4 See the Education and Inspections Act 2006 s 92(1).
5 Ie the Education and Inspections Act 2006 s 91(2): see PARA 514.
6 Ie as well as the conditions set out in the Education and Inspections Act 2006 s 91(3)–(5): see PARA 514.
7 See the Education and Inspections Act 2006 s 92(2). If arrangements have to be made for the pupil to travel to school for the purposes of the detention or to travel home after the detention, then in determining for the purposes of the condition in s 91(3) (see PARA 514) whether the imposition of the detention is reasonable, s 91(6) (see PARA 514) is to be read as if it also required the question whether suitable travelling arrangements can reasonably be made by his parent to be taken into account: s 92(5). As to the meaning of 'parent' see PARA 7 note 6 (definition applied by s 187(2), (3)). As to the common law relating to the detention of pupils see PARA 512.
8 Education and Inspections Act 2006 s 92(3)(a). As to the time at which a person attains a particular age see PARA 7 note 6.

9 As to the meaning of 'head teacher' see PARA 86 note 4 (definition applied by the Education and Inspections Act 2006 s 187(2), (3)).

10 As to the meaning of 'registered pupil' see PARA 437 (definition applied by the Education and Inspections Act 2006 s 187(2), (3)).

11 Education and Inspections Act 2006 s 92(3)(b). As to the duty of a head teacher to determine behaviour policy at a school and to publicise the policy see s 89; and PARA 510.

12 Education and Inspections Act 2006 s 92(3)(c). 'Permitted day of detention', in relation to a pupil, means any of the following days:

    (1)   a school day, other than a day on which the pupil has leave to be absent, and for this purpose 'leave' means leave granted by a person authorised to do so by the governing body or proprietor of the school (s 92(8)(a));

    (2)   in relation to England only, Saturday or Sunday during a school term, other than a Saturday or Sunday which falls during, or at a weekend immediately preceding or immediately following, a half-term break (s 92(8)(b));

    (3)   a day (whether or not during a school term) which is set aside wholly or mainly for the performance of duties by members of the staff of the school other than teaching, other than such a day which is excluded by regulations made, in relation to England, by the Secretary of State (s 92(8)(c)(i)), and in relation to Wales, by the Welsh Ministers (s 92(8)(c)(ii)).

At the date at which this volume states the law, s 92(8)(b) is in force in relation to England only (see the Education and Inspections Act 2006 (Commencement No 3 and Transitional Provisions and Savings) Order 2007, SI 2007/935, art 4(a)) and will be brought into force in relation to Wales as from a day to be appointed under the Education and Inspections Act 2006 s 188(3). At the date at which this volume states the law no such day had been appointed. As to the meanings of 'England' and 'Wales' see PARA 7 note 6.

As to the meaning of 'school day' see PARA 229 note 6; and as to the meaning of 'proprietor' see PARA 51 note 4 (definitions applied by the Education and Inspections Act 2006 s 187(2), (3)). As to the governing bodies of maintained schools in England see PARA 150 et seq; and in Wales see PARA 195. As to the meaning of 'member of staff' see PARA 513 note 4. As to the Secretary of State see PARA 58. As to the Welsh Ministers see PARA 59. The functions under the Education and Inspections Act 2006 s 92 in relation to Wales were originally vested in the National Assembly for Wales and are now exercisable by the Welsh Ministers by virtue of the Government of Wales Act 2006 s 162(1), Sch 11 paras 30, 32. As to the regulations made under the Education and Inspections Act 2006 s 92(8), see the Education (Excluded Days of Detention) (England) Regulations 2007, SI 2007/1304.

13 As to the service of notices and documents see the Education Act 1996 s 572 (applied by the Education and Inspections Act 2006 s 187(2), (3)); and PARA 76. The Education Act 1996 s 572 does not preclude a notice under the Education and Inspections Act 2006 s 92(3)(d) from being given to the parent by any effective method: s 92(6).

14 As to the meaning of 'writing' see PARA 76 note 8.

15 Education and Inspections Act 2006 s 92(3)(d) (amended by the Education Act 2011 s 5).

16 Education and Inspections Act 2006 s 92(4).

17 Ie the Education and Inspections Act 2006 s 92.

18 Ie apart from the Education and Inspections Act 2006 s 92.

19 Education and Inspections Act 2006 s 92(7).

516. Parenting contracts in cases of misbehaviour at school.

Where a local authority[1] or the governing body[2] of a relevant school has reason to believe that a child[3] who is a registered pupil[4] at a relevant school has engaged in behaviour connected with the school which (1) has caused, or is likely to cause significant disruption to the education of other pupils[5], or significant detriment to the welfare of the child himself or of other pupils or to the health or safety of any staff; or (2) forms part of a pattern of behaviour which (if continued) will give rise to a risk of future exclusion from the school on disciplinary grounds, a local authority or the governing body of a relevant school may enter into a parenting contract with a parent of the pupil or child[6].

1 As to the meaning of 'local authority' see PARA 25 (definition applied by the Anti-social Behaviour Act 2003 s 24 amended by SI 2010/1158).

2 'Governing body', in relation to a relevant school which is an academy school, alternative provision academy, a city technology college or a city college for the technology of the arts,

means the proprietor of the school, as defined by the Education Act 1996 s 579(1) (see PARA 51 note 4): Anti-social Behaviour Act 2003 s 24 (definition added by the Education and Inspections Act 2006 s 99(1), (4)(b); and amended by the Education Act 2011 Sch 13 para 11(a)). 'Relevant school' means (1) a community, foundation or voluntary school; (2) a community or foundation special school; (3) a maintained nursery school as defined in the School Standards and Framework Act 1998 s 22(9) (see PARA 99 note 4); (4) a pupil referral unit as defined the Education Act 1996 s 19(2) (see PARA 427); (5) an academy school; (6) an alternative provision academy; (7) a city technology college; or (8) a city college for the technology of the arts: Anti-social Behaviour Act 2003 s 24 (definition substituted by the Education and Inspections Act 2006 s 161, Sch 16 Pt 2 para 4; and amended by the Education Act 2011 Sch 13 para 11(b)). As to community, foundation and voluntary schools, and community and foundation special schools, see PARA 106. As to the meanings of 'academy school' and 'alternative provision academy' see PARA 346 notes 12, 14 (definitions applied by the Anti-social Behaviour Act 2003 s 24). As to city technology colleges and city colleges for the technology of the arts see PARA 345.

3 As to the meaning of 'child' see PARA 7 note 6 (definition applied by the Anti-social Behaviour Act 2003 s 24).

4 As to the meaning of 'registered pupil' see PARA 437 (definition applied by the Anti-social Behaviour Act 2003 s 24).

5 As to the meaning of 'pupil' see PARA 20 note 4 (definition applied by the Anti-social Behaviour Act 2003 s 24).

6 See the Anti-social Behaviour Act 2003 s 19(1A), (3) (s 19(1A) added by the Education and Inspections Act 2006 s 97(1), (2); and the Anti-social Behaviour Act 2003 s 19(1A), (3) amended by SI 2010/1158); and CHILDREN AND YOUNG PERSONS vol 10 (2012) PARA 1283 et seq. As to parenting contracts in cases of a pupil's failure to attend regularly at school see PARA 450. As to parenting contracts in cases of exclusion from school see PARA 525.

(iii) Exclusion of Pupils

A. POWER TO EXCLUDE PUPILS

517. Power of head teacher or principal to exclude pupils. The head teacher[1] of a maintained school[2] in England[3] may exclude[4] a pupil from the school for a fixed period or permanently, and this applies with modifications to academies[5]. The teacher in charge of a pupil referral unit[6] in England may also exclude a pupil from the unit for a fixed period or permanently[7].

Regulations[8] must make provision:

(1) requiring prescribed persons[9] to be given prescribed information relating to any exclusion[10];

(2) requiring the responsible body[11], in prescribed cases, to consider whether the pupil should be reinstated[12];

(3) requiring the local authority to make arrangements enabling a prescribed person to apply to a review panel for a review, in any prescribed case, of a decision of the responsible body not to reinstate a pupil[13];

(4) about the constitution of a review panel[14];

(5) about the procedure to be followed on a review under head (3) above[15].

Regulations may also make provision:

(a) for the payment by the local authority of allowances to members of the review panel[16];

(b) requiring a person or body exercising functions in relation to the exclusion of pupils[17] to have regard to any guidance given from time to time by the Secretary of State[18];

(c) requiring local authorities to give prescribed information to the Secretary of State[19];

(d)   in relation to any other matter relating to the exercise of the above powers[20].

1   As to the meaning of 'head teacher' see PARA 86 note 4 (definition applied by the Education and Inspections Act 2002 s 212(2), (3)). In discharging of any function under s 52A(1), a head teacher must have regard to any ministerial guidance: see PARA 540.

2   In the Education Act 2002 s 51A, 'maintained school' has the same meaning as in Pt 3 Ch 1 (ss 19–40) (see PARA 103 note 3): s 51A(10) (s 51A added by the Education Act 2011 s 4(1), (2)). See note 5 in relation to s 52. As to exclusion from independent schools see PARA 425. Section 51A is modified as to its application to academies see note 5.

3   As to the meaning of 'England' see PARA 7 note 3.

4   In the Education Act 2002 s 51A, 'exclude', in relation to the exclusion of a pupil from a school or pupil referral unit, means exclude on disciplinary grounds; and 'exclusion' must be construed accordingly: s 51A(10) (as added: see note 2). As to the meaning of 'pupil' see PARA 20 note 4; and as to the meaning of 'school' see PARA 91 (definitions applied by s 212(2), (3)). As to pupil referral units see PARA 427 et seq.

      When investigating and interviewing a pupil, the Police and Criminal Evidence Act 1984 and its codes (see POLICE AND INVESTIGATORY POWERS vol 84A (2013) PARA 433 et seq) may serve as a touchstone of fair procedure outside the criminal justice process: *R v Governors of Dunraven School, ex p B* [2000] LGR 494, sub nom *R v Head Teacher and Independent Appeal Committee of Dunraven School, ex p B* [2000] ELR 156, CA (decided under previous legislation). However, it is important to stress that such matters are not to be conducted as if they are some kind of formal criminal proceeding: *R (on the application of J) v Birmingham City Council Exclusion Appeals Committee* [2003] EWHC 1747 (Admin) at [13], [2003] ELR 743, [2003] All ER (D) 158 (Jul) per Davis J. See also *R (on the application of C) v Sefton Metropolitan Borough Council Independent Appeals Panel and the Governors of Hillside High School* [2001] ELR 393, sub nom *Cahill v Sefton Metropolitan Borough Council* [2000] All ER (D) 2458 (decided under previous legislation). Adequate investigation is important (*R v Camden London Borough Council and the Governors of Hampstead School, ex p H* [1996] ELR 360, sub nom *R v Camden London Borough Council, ex p H (A Minor)* (1996) Times, 15 August, CA; *R v Roman Catholic Schools, ex p S* [1998] ELR 304; *R v Board of Governors and Appeal Committee of Bryn Elian High School, ex p Whippe* [1999] ELR 380 (all cases decided under previous legislation)) and head teachers should keep notes of interviews conducted with pupils (*R v Head Teacher and Independent Appeal Committee of Dunraven School, ex p B* above). The punishment imposed must be proportionate (see *R v Governors of Bacon's City Technology College, ex p W* [1998] ELR 488; *R (on the application of C) v Sefton Metropolitan Borough Council Independent Appeals Panel and the Governors of Hillside High School* above (both cases decided under previous legislation), and the rationality of the decision to exclude may be considered (see *R v Solihull Borough Council, ex p W* [1997] ELR 489 (decided under previous legislation)). In general, though, the courts will be reluctant to question the reasonableness of the punishment in any particular case: *R v Newham London Borough Council, ex p X* [1995] ELR 303, (1994) Times, 15 November (decided under previous legislation).

      It used to be considered that an unjustifiable exclusion was probably not an actionable tort (see *Hunt v Damon* (1930) 46 TLR 579) but it now seems that the unlawful exclusion of a pupil from school may give rise to a claim for damages for denial of his right to education under the Convention for the Protection of Human Rights and Fundamental Freedoms (Rome, 4 November 1950; TS 71 (1953); Cmd 8969), First Protocol (Paris, 20 March 1952; TS 46 (1954); Cmd 9221) art 2: see *A v Head Teacher and Governors of Lord Grey School* [2004] EWCA Civ 382, [2004] QB 1231, [2004] 4 All ER 628 (revsd as to award of damages but not as to principle of potential claim: *A v Head Teacher and Governors of Lord Grey School* [2006] UKHL 14, [2006] 2 AC 363, sub nom *Ali v Head Teacher and Governors of Lord Grey School* [2006] 2 All ER 457); *A v Essex County Council* [2008] EWCA Civ 364, [2009] LGR 182, [2008] ELR 321 (affd [2010] UKSC 33, [2011] 1 AC 280, [2010] 4 All ER 199); *In the Matter of the Application by 'JR17' for Judicial Review* [2010] UKSC 27, [2010] NI 105, [2010] All ER (D) 186 (Jun); and PARA 3.

5   Education Act 2002 s 51A(1) (as added: see note 2). Section 51A was added to apply to schools in England, while the previous provision, s 52, has been amended to apply to schools in Wales in corresponding terms: see s 52 (amended by SI 2010/1058; the Education Act 2011 s 4(1), (3)); and the Local Government (Wales) Measure 2011 Sch 3 para 6). As to the meaning of 'Wales' see PARA 7 note 3.

      As to the power of principals of academy schools to exclude pupils under the Education Act 2002 s 51A see the School Discipline (Pupil Exclusions and Reviews) (England)

Regulations 2012, SI 2012/1033, Pt 4 (regs 21–29). See in particular reg 21 for the modifications to the Education Act 2002 s 51A necessary for that provision's application to academies. 'Academy' means an academy school or an alternative provision academy: School Discipline (Pupil Exclusions and Reviews) (England) Regulations 2012, SI 2012/1033, reg 2(1). As to the meanings of 'academy school' and 'alternative provision academy' see PARA 346 notes 12, 14 (definitions applied by the Education Act 2002 s 212(2), (3); Interpretation Act 1978 s 11). As to academies generally see PARA 345 et seq. A principal may not exercise the power under the Education Act 2002 s 51A(1) (as modified) so as to exclude a pupil for one or more fixed periods if, as a result, the pupil would be excluded for more than 45 school days in any school year: School Discipline (Pupil Exclusions and Reviews) (England) Regulations 2012, SI 2012/1033, reg 22. 'Principal' means the head teacher of an academy: reg 2(1).

A head teacher may not exercise his power under the Education Act 2002 s 51A(1) (in relation to England) or s 52(1) (in relation to Wales) so as to exclude a pupil from the school for one or more fixed periods if, as a result, the pupil would be excluded for more than 45 school days in any one school year: see the School Discipline (Pupil Exclusions and Reviews) (England) Regulations 2012, SI 2012/1033, reg 4; and the Education (Pupil Exclusions and Appeals) (Maintained Schools) (Wales) Regulations 2003, SI 2003/3227, reg 3. In relation to England, any exclusion for a fixed period consisting of the period between the morning and afternoon school sessions must for these purposes be taken as equivalent to half a school day: see the School Discipline (Pupil Exclusions and Reviews) (England) Regulations 2012, SI 2012/1033, regs 1(2), 2(2). In relation to Wales, any exclusion for a fixed period consisting of the period between the morning and afternoon school sessions must for these purposes be taken as equivalent to one-quarter of a school day: see the Education (Pupil Exclusions and Appeals) (Maintained Schools) (Wales) Regulations 2003, SI 2003/3227, regs 1(2), 2(2). As to the meaning of 'school day' see PARA 229 note 6; and as to the meaning of 'school year' see PARA 19 note 12 (definitions applied by the Education Act 2002 s 212(2), (3); Interpretation Act 1978 s 11). As to exclusions see further PARA 518 et seq.

Where it falls to the head teacher, in exercise of the power of exclusion conferred by the Education Act 2002 s 51A(1) or s 52(1), to establish any fact, any question as to whether that fact is established is to be decided on a balance of probabilities: see the School Discipline (Pupil Exclusions and Reviews) (England) Regulations 2012, SI 2012/1033, reg 10(a); and the Education (Pupil Exclusions and Appeals) (Maintained Schools) (Wales) Regulations 2003, SI 2003/3227, reg 8A(a) (reg 8A added by SI 2004/1805). As to the corresponding provision for academies see the School Discipline (Pupil Exclusions and Reviews) (England) Regulations 2012, SI 2012/1033, reg 28(a). As to the civil standard of proof see CIVIL PROCEDURE vol 11 (2009) PARA 775.

For a consideration of the 2012 guidance on exclusion (see PARA 540 note 13) in the context of the Education Act 2002 s 51A and the School Discipline (Pupil Exclusions and Reviews) (England) Regulations 2012, SI 2012/1033 see *R (on the application of CR) v Independent Appeal Panel of the London Borough of Lambeth* [2014] EWHC 2461 (Admin), [2014] ELR 359.

6   As to the teacher in charge of a pupil referral unit see PARA 428.

7   Education Act 2002 s 51A(2), (10) (as added: see note 2). A teacher in charge of a pupil referral unit may not exercise the power under s 51A(2) in relation to England) or s 52(2) (in relation to Wales) so as to exclude a pupil from the pupil referral unit for one or more fixed periods if, as a result, the pupil would be excluded for more than 45 school days in any one school year: see the School Discipline (Pupil Exclusions and Reviews) (England) Regulations 2012, SI 2012/1033, reg 13; and the Education (Pupil Exclusions and Appeals) (Pupil Referral Units) (Wales) Regulations 2003, SI 2003/3246, reg 4. In relation to England, any exclusion for a fixed period consisting of the period between the morning and afternoon school sessions is to be taken as equivalent to half a school day: see the School Discipline (Pupil Exclusions and Reviews) (England) Regulations 2012, SI 2012/1033, reg 2(2). In relation to Wales, any exclusion for a fixed period consisting of the period between the morning and afternoon school sessions is to be taken as equivalent to a quarter of a school day: see the Education (Pupil Exclusions and Appeals) (Pupil Referral Units) (Wales) Regulations 2003, SI 2003/3246, reg 2(2). Where it falls to the teacher in charge of a pupil referral unit, in exercise of the power conferred by the Education Act 2002 s 51A(2) or s 52(2) to establish any fact, any question as to whether that fact is established must be decided on a balance of probabilities: see the School Discipline (Pupil Exclusions and Reviews) (England) Regulations 2012, SI 2012/1033, reg 19(a); and the Education (Pupil Exclusions and Appeals) (Pupil Referral Units) (Wales) Regulations 2003, SI 2003/3246, reg 9A(a) (reg 9A added by SI 2004/1805). As to exclusions from pupil referral units see further PARA 519 et seq.

8 'Regulations' means regulations made under the Education Act 2002 by the Secretary of State (in relation to England) or by the Welsh Ministers (in relation to Wales): see s 212(1). As to the Secretary of State see PARA 58. As to the Welsh Ministers see PARA 59. The functions under the Education Act 2002 s 52 in relation to Wales were originally vested in the National Assembly for Wales and are now exercisable by the Welsh Ministers by virtue of the Government of Wales Act 2006 s 162(1), Sch 11 paras 30, 32. As to the regulations made under the Education Act 2002 s 52 (which now relates to Wales and previously related to both England and Wales: see note 5), see the Education (Pupil Exclusions and Appeals) (Maintained Schools) (Wales) Regulations 2003, SI 2003/3227 (amended by SI 2004/1805); the Education (Pupil Exclusions and Appeals) (Pupil Referral Units) (Wales) Regulations 2003, SI 2003/3246 (amended by SI 2004/1805); the Education (Provision of Full-Time Education for Excluded Pupils) (England) Regulations 2007, SI 2007/1870 (amended by SI 2008/532; SI 2010/1172; SI 2012/1033; and SI 2014/3216); and the School Governance (Roles, Procedures and Allowances) (England) Regulations 2013, SI 2013/1624 (amended by SI 2013/2688; SI 2014/1257; and SI 2014/1959).

    Regulations may make provision for the Education Act 2002 s 51A and regulations made under it to apply, with prescribed modifications, in relation to academies or a description of academy: s 51A(12) (as so added). As to the regulations under s 51A(3), (5)–(10), (12) (s 51A relates to England: see note 5) see the School Discipline (Pupil Exclusions and Reviews) (England) Regulations 2012, SI 2012/1033. See also PARA 518 et seq.

9 As to the meaning of 'person' see PARA 7 note 6.

10 Education Act 2002 s 51A(3)(a) (as added: see note 2), The reference in the text to any exclusion is to any exclusion under s 51A(1) or (2): see the text to notes 1–7.

11 'The responsible body' means, in relation to exclusion from a maintained school, the governing body of the school, and in relation to exclusion from a pupil referral unit, such person as may be prescribed: s 51A(10) (as added: see note 2). In relation to any time when no responsible body is prescribed in relation to permanent exclusion from a pupil referral unit, s 51A(3) has effect in relation to such an exclusion as if head (2) were omitted, and the decision referred to in head (3) were the decision of the teacher in charge of the unit permanently to exclude the pupil: s 51A(11) (as so added).

    For the purposes of s 51A(10) (in relation to England), the management committee of a pupil referral unit is prescribed as the responsible body (see the School Discipline (Pupil Exclusions and Reviews) (England) Regulations 2012, SI 2012/1033, regs 1(2), 12); and for the purposes of the Education Act 2002 s 52(5) (in relation to Wales, ie the equivalent of s 51A(10)), the local authority which maintains a pupil referral unit is prescribed as the responsible body in relation to a fixed period exclusion from that pupil referral unit (see the Education (Pupil Exclusions and Appeals) (Pupil Referral Units) (Wales) Regulations 2003, SI 2003/3246, regs 1(2), 3 (amended by SI 2010/1142)). As to the governing bodies of maintained schools in England see PARA 150 et seq; and in Wales see PARA 195. As to the management committee of a pupil referral unit see PARA 434. As to the meaning of 'local authority' see PARA 25 (definition applied by the Education Act 2002 s 212(1) (definition added by SI 2010/1158)).

12 Education Act 2002 s 51A(3)(b) (as added: see note 2).

13 Education Act 2002 s 51A(3)(c) (as added: see note 2). As to reviews and review panels see PARA 531 et seq. On an application by virtue s 51A(3)(c), the review panel may (1) uphold the decision of the responsible body; (2) recommend that the responsible body reconsiders the matter; or (3) if it considers that the decision of the responsible body was flawed when considered in the light of the principles applicable on an application for judicial review, quash the decision of the responsible body and direct the responsible body to reconsider the matter: s 51A(4) (as so added). Regulations may provide for the panel to have supplementary powers, and in particular may provide that the panel has the power to make a direction about the effect on an excluded pupil of a recommendation under head (2) above or a direction under head (3) above: s 51A(5) (as so added). In a case where the panel gives a direction under head (3) above to the governing body of a maintained school, the panel may, in prescribed circumstances, order an adjustment of the school's budget share for a funding period: s 51A(6) (as so added). For these purposes 'budget share' and 'funding period' have the same meaning as in the School Standards and Framework Act 1998 Pt 2 (ss 20–83) (see PARA 315): Education Act 2002 s 51A(10) (as so added). Regulations must make provision about how the amount of the adjustment is to be determined and the effect of the adjustment on the budget shares of other maintained schools for the funding period: s 51A(7) (as so added). An exclusion review panel constituted by the authority in accordance with regulations under s 51A is subject to investigation: see the Local Government Act 1974 s 25(5)(e); and LOCAL GOVERNMENT vol 69 (2009) PARA 853.

14 Education Act 2002 s 51A(3)(d) (as added: see note 2).

15 Education Act 2002 s 51A(3)(e) (as added: see note 2).

16 Education Act 2002 s 51A(8)(a) (as added: see note 2). Regulations made by virtue of s 51A(8)(a) may provide for any of the provisions of the Local Government Act 1972 ss 173–174 (allowances to members of local authorities and other bodies) (repealed) to apply with prescribed modifications in relation to members of a review panel: Education Act 2002 s 51A(9) (as so added).

17 Ie functions under the Education Act 2002 s 51A(1) or (2) (see the text to notes 1–7) or under the regulations. As to the meaning of 'functions' see PARA 18 note 5 (definition applied by the Education Act 2002 s 212(2), (3)).

18 Education Act 2002 s 51A(8)(b) (as added: see note 2). As to the publication of guidance see the Education Act 1996 s 571 (applied by the Education Act 2002 s 212(2), (3)); and PARA 60. As to guidance see also PARA 540. Specifically as to Exclusions Guidance see generally PARA 540 note 13. Such guidance may well be the first document a head teacher or principal would consult. As to academies see note 5.

19 Education Act 2002 s 51A(8)(c) (as added: see note 2).

20 Education Act 2002 s 51A(8)(d) (as added: see note 2). The powers referred to are those conferred by s 51A(1) or (2): see the text to notes 1–7.

518. Duty of head teacher of maintained school to inform parents of exclusion etc. Where the head teacher[1] of a maintained school[2] in England[3] decides to exclude[4] a pupil for a fixed period, the head teacher must, without delay:

(1) inform the relevant person[5] of the period of the exclusion and the reasons for it[6]; and

(2) give the relevant person notice in writing stating the following matters:

    (a) the period of the exclusion and the reasons for it[7];

    (b) that the relevant person may make representations about the decision to the governing body[8] and that, where the pupil is not the relevant person, the pupil may also be involved in the process of making representations, and an explanation as to how the pupil may be involved[9];

    (c) the means by which representations may be made[10]; and

    (d) where and to whom representations should be sent[11].

Where the head teacher decides to exclude a pupil permanently[12]; or to exclude a pupil and, as a result of the exclusion, the pupil would be excluded for a total of more than five school days[13] in any term[14]; or lose an opportunity to take a public examination or a National Curriculum test[15], the head teacher must do certain things[16]. The head teacher must, without delay:

(i) inform the relevant person, the governing body and the local authority[17] (and, in the case of a permanent exclusion, if applicable, the home local authority[18]) of the period of the exclusion and the reasons for it[19]; and

(ii) give the relevant person notice in writing stating the following matters:

    (A) the period of the exclusion and the reasons for it[20];

    (B) that the relevant person may make representations about the decision to the governing body and that, where the pupil is not the relevant person, the pupil may also be involved in the process of making representations, and an explanation as to how the pupil may be involved[21];

    (C) the means by which representations may be made[22];

    (D) where and to whom representations should be sent[23]; and

    (E) where a meeting of the governing body is to consider the exclusion, that the relevant person may attend and be represented at the meeting (at their own expense), and may be accompanied by a friend[24].

In each term the head teacher must inform the governing body and the local authority of the following:

(aa)   all exclusions that have occurred in that term to which heads (i) and (ii) above[25] do not apply[26];

(bb)   unless the head teacher has already done so, any such exclusions occurring during previous terms in that school year[27]; and

(cc)   the period of each exclusion and the reasons for it[28].

1   As to the meaning of 'head teacher' see PARA 86 note 4 (definition applied by the Education Act 2002 s 212(2), (3); Interpretation Act 1978 s 11). As to the head teacher's power to exclude pupils see PARA 517.

2   As to the meaning of 'maintained school' see PARA 517 note 2.

3   The School Discipline (Pupil Exclusions and Reviews) (England) Regulations 2012, SI 2012/1033 apply only in relation to exclusions of pupils from maintained schools, pupil referral units, academy schools, alternative provision academies, in England, occurring on or after 1 September 2012: see reg 1(2). As to the meaning of 'pupil' see PARA 20 note 4; as to the meaning of 'academy school' see PARA 346 note 12; and as to the meaning of 'alternative provision academy' see PARA 346 note 14 (definitions applied by the Education Act 2002 s 212(2), (3); Interpretation Act 1978 s 11). As to pupil referral units see PARA 427 et seq. As to the equivalent provision to the School Discipline (Pupil Exclusions and Reviews) (England) Regulations 2012, SI 2012/1033, reg 5, in relation to Wales, see the Education (Pupil Exclusions and Appeals) (Maintained Schools) (Wales) Regulations 2003, SI 2003/3227, reg 4. As to the meanings of 'England' and 'Wales' see PARA 7 note 3.

4   As to the meaning of 'exclude' see PARA 517 note 4.

5   'The relevant person' means, in relation to a pupil under the age of 18, a parent of the pupil, and, in relation to a pupil who has attained that age, the pupil himself: School Discipline (Pupil Exclusions and Reviews) (England) Regulations 2012, SI 2012/1033, reg 2(1). As to the meaning of 'parent' see PARA 7 note 6 (definition applied by the Education Act 2002 s 212(2), (3); Interpretation Act 1978 s 11). As to the meaning of 'compulsory school age' see PARA 19. As to the time at which a person attains a particular age see PARA 7 note 6.

6   School Discipline (Pupil Exclusions and Reviews) (England) Regulations 2012, SI 2012/1033, reg 5(1)(a).

7   School Discipline (Pupil Exclusions and Reviews) (England) Regulations 2012, SI 2012/1033, reg 5(1)(b)(i). As to the meaning of 'writing' see PARA 76 note 8.

8   As to the governing bodies of maintained schools in England see PARA 150 et seq; and in Wales see PARA 195.

9   School Discipline (Pupil Exclusions and Reviews) (England) Regulations 2012, SI 2012/1033, reg 5(1)(b)(ii). Any expense in connection with the representation of the relevant person is to be an expense of the relevant person: reg 5(4).

10   School Discipline (Pupil Exclusions and Reviews) (England) Regulations 2012, SI 2012/1033, reg 5(1)(b)(iii).

11   School Discipline (Pupil Exclusions and Reviews) (England) Regulations 2012, SI 2012/1033, reg 5(1)(b)(iv).

12   School Discipline (Pupil Exclusions and Reviews) (England) Regulations 2012, SI 2012/1033, reg 5(2)(a).

13   As to the meaning of 'school day' see PARA 229 note 6 (definition applied by the Education Act 2002 s 212(2), (3); Interpretation Act 1978 s 11). Reference should be made to the Education (Provision of Full-Time Education for Excluded Pupils) (England) Regulations 2007, SI 2007/1870, regs 3(3), 4(3)(b) (as amended SI 2014/3216); and PARA 522 notes 7, 9.

14   School Discipline (Pupil Exclusions and Reviews) (England) Regulations 2012, SI 2012/1033, reg 5(2)(b)(i). 'Term' means (1) in a school which has three terms or fewer in a school year, one of those terms; or (2) in a school which has more than three terms in a school year, any period which falls between two reference dates; and 'reference date' means 31 December, Easter Monday or 31 July: School Discipline (Pupil Exclusions and Reviews) (England) Regulations 2012, SI 2012/1033, reg 2(1). As to the meaning of 'school year' see PARA 19 note 12 (definition applied by the Education Act 2002 s 212(2), (3); Interpretation Act 1978 s 11).

15   School Discipline (Pupil Exclusions and Reviews) (England) Regulations 2012, SI 2012/1033, reg 5(2)(b)(ii). 'National Curriculum test' means any test specified in, or by virtue of, the Education Act 2002 s 87(3)(c) (see PARA 863): School Discipline (Pupil Exclusions and Reviews) (England) Regulations 2012, SI 2012/1033, reg 2(1).

16   See the School Discipline (Pupil Exclusions and Reviews) (England) Regulations 2012, SI 2012/1033, reg 5(3).

17   As to the meaning of 'local authority' see PARA 25 (definition applied by the Education Act 2002 s 212(1); Interpretation Act 1978 s 11).

18 'Home local authority' means the local authority responsible for the area in which the pupil resides where this differs from the local authority in which the pupil's school is located: School Discipline (Pupil Exclusions and Reviews) (England) Regulations 2012, SI 2012/1033, reg 2(1).
19 School Discipline (Pupil Exclusions and Reviews) (England) Regulations 2012, SI 2012/1033, reg 5(3)(a).
20 School Discipline (Pupil Exclusions and Reviews) (England) Regulations 2012, SI 2012/1033, reg 5(3)(b)(i).
21 School Discipline (Pupil Exclusions and Reviews) (England) Regulations 2012, SI 2012/1033, reg 5(3)(b)(ii).
22 School Discipline (Pupil Exclusions and Reviews) (England) Regulations 2012, SI 2012/1033, reg 5(3)(b)(iii).
23 School Discipline (Pupil Exclusions and Reviews) (England) Regulations 2012, SI 2012/1033, reg 5(3)(b)(iv).
24 School Discipline (Pupil Exclusions and Reviews) (England) Regulations 2012, SI 2012/1033, reg 5(3)(b)(v).
25 Ie the School Discipline (Pupil Exclusions and Reviews) (England) Regulations 2012, SI 2012/1033, reg 5(3).
26 School Discipline (Pupil Exclusions and Reviews) (England) Regulations 2012, SI 2012/1033, reg 5(5)(a).
27 School Discipline (Pupil Exclusions and Reviews) (England) Regulations 2012, SI 2012/1033, reg 5(5)(b).
28 School Discipline (Pupil Exclusions and Reviews) (England) Regulations 2012, SI 2012/1033, reg 5(5)(c).

519. Duty of teacher in charge of pupil referral unit to inform parents of exclusion etc. Where the teacher in charge of a pupil referral unit[1] in England[2] decides to exclude[3] a pupil[4] for a fixed period, the teacher in charge must, without delay:

(1) inform the relevant person[5] of the period of the exclusion and the reasons for it[6]; and

(2) give the relevant person notice in writing stating the following matters:
    (a) the period of the exclusion and the reasons for it[7];
    (b) that the relevant person may make representations about the decision to the management committee[8] and that, where the pupil is not the relevant person, the pupil may also be involved in the process of making representations, and an explanation as to how the pupil may be involved[9];
    (c) the means by which representations may be made[10]; and
    (d) where and to whom representations should be sent[11].

Where the teacher in charge decides to exclude a pupil permanently[12]; or to exclude a pupil and, as a result of the exclusion, the pupil would be excluded for a total of more than five school days[13] in any term[14]; or lose an opportunity to take a public examination or a National Curriculum test[15], the teacher in charge must do certain things[16]. The teacher in charge must, without delay:

(i) inform the relevant person, the management committee and the local authority[17] (and, in the case of a permanent exclusion, if applicable, the home local authority[18]) of the period of the exclusion and the reasons for it[19]; and

(ii) give the relevant person notice in writing stating the following matters:
    (A) the period of the exclusion and the reasons for it[20];
    (B) that the relevant person may make representations about the decision to the management committee and that, where the pupil is not the relevant person, the pupil may also be involved in the process of making representations, and an explanation as to how the pupil may be involved[21];

(C)   the means by which representations may be made[22];

(D)   where and to whom representations should be sent[23]; and

(E)   where a meeting of the management committee is to consider the exclusion, that the relevant person may attend and be represented at the meeting (at their own expense), and may be accompanied by a friend[24].

In each term the teacher in charge must inform the management committee and the local authority of the following:

(aa)   all exclusions that have occurred in that term to which heads (i) and (ii) above[25] do not apply[26];

(bb)   unless the teacher in charge has already done so, any such exclusions occurring during previous terms in that school year[27]; and

(cc)   the period of each exclusion and the reasons for it[28].

1   As to the teacher in charge of a pupil referral unit see PARA 428. As to pupil referral units see PARA 427 et seq.

2   The School Discipline (Pupil Exclusions and Reviews) (England) Regulations 2012, SI 2012/1033 apply only in relation to England: reg 1(2). See also PARA 518 note 3. As to the equivalent provision to reg 14 in relation to Wales see the Education (Pupil Exclusions and Appeals) (Pupil Referral Units) (Wales) Regulations 2003, SI 2003/3246, reg 5. As to the meanings of 'England' and 'Wales' see PARA 7 note 3.

3   As to the meaning of 'exclude' see PARA 517 note 4. See also PARA 431.

4   As to the meaning of 'pupil' see PARA 20 note 4 (definition applied by the Education Act 2002 s 212(2), (3); Interpretation Act 1978 s 11).

5   As to the meaning of 'relevant person' see PARA 518 note 5.

6   School Discipline (Pupil Exclusions and Reviews) (England) Regulations 2012, SI 2012/1033, reg 14(1)(a).

7   School Discipline (Pupil Exclusions and Reviews) (England) Regulations 2012, SI 2012/1033, reg 14(1)(b)(i). As to the meaning of 'writing' see PARA 76 note 8.

8   As to the management committee of a pupil referral unit see PARA 434. See also PARA 517 note 11.

9   School Discipline (Pupil Exclusions and Reviews) (England) Regulations 2012, SI 2012/1033, reg 14(1)(b)(ii). Any expense in connection with the representation of the relevant person is to be an expense of the relevant person: reg 14(4).

10   School Discipline (Pupil Exclusions and Reviews) (England) Regulations 2012, SI 2012/1033, reg 14(1)(b)(iii).

11   School Discipline (Pupil Exclusions and Reviews) (England) Regulations 2012, SI 2012/1033, reg 14(1)(b)(iv).

12   School Discipline (Pupil Exclusions and Reviews) (England) Regulations 2012, SI 2012/1033, reg 14(2)(a).

13   As to the meaning of 'school day' see PARA 229 note 6 (definition applied by the Education Act 2002 s 212(2), (3); Interpretation Act 1978 s 11). Reference should be made to the Education (Provision of Full-Time Education for Excluded Pupils) (England) Regulations 2007, SI 2007/1870, regs 3(3), 4(3)(b) (as amended SI 2014/3216); and PARA 522 notes 7, 9.

14   School Discipline (Pupil Exclusions and Reviews) (England) Regulations 2012, SI 2012/1033, reg 14(2)(b)(i). As to the meaning of 'term' see PARA 518 note 14.

15   School Discipline (Pupil Exclusions and Reviews) (England) Regulations 2012, SI 2012/1033, reg 14(2)(b)(ii). As to the meaning of 'National Curriculum test' see PARA 518 note 15.

16   See the School Discipline (Pupil Exclusions and Reviews) (England) Regulations 2012, SI 2012/1033, reg 14(3).

17   As to the meaning of 'local authority' see PARA 25 (definition applied by the Education Act 2002 s 212(1); Interpretation Act 1978 s 11).

18   As to the meaning of 'home local authority' see PARA 518 note 18.

19   School Discipline (Pupil Exclusions and Reviews) (England) Regulations 2012, SI 2012/1033, reg 14(3)(a).

20   School Discipline (Pupil Exclusions and Reviews) (England) Regulations 2012, SI 2012/1033, reg 14(3)(b)(i).

21   School Discipline (Pupil Exclusions and Reviews) (England) Regulations 2012, SI 2012/1033, reg 14(3)(b)(ii).

22 School Discipline (Pupil Exclusions and Reviews) (England) Regulations 2012, SI 2012/1033, reg 14(3)(b)(iii).

23 School Discipline (Pupil Exclusions and Reviews) (England) Regulations 2012, SI 2012/1033, reg 14(3)(b)(iv).

24 School Discipline (Pupil Exclusions and Reviews) (England) Regulations 2012, SI 2012/1033, reg 14(3)(b)(v).

25 Ie the School Discipline (Pupil Exclusions and Reviews) (England) Regulations 2012, SI 2012/1033, reg 14(3).

26 School Discipline (Pupil Exclusions and Reviews) (England) Regulations 2012, SI 2012/1033, reg 14(5)(a).

27 School Discipline (Pupil Exclusions and Reviews) (England) Regulations 2012, SI 2012/1033, reg 14(5)(b). As to the meaning of 'school year' see PARA 19 note 12 (definition applied by the Education Act 2002 s 212(2), (3); Interpretation Act 1978 s 11).

28 School Discipline (Pupil Exclusions and Reviews) (England) Regulations 2012, SI 2012/1033, reg 14(5)(c).

520. Duty of principal of academy to inform parents of exclusion etc. Where the principal[1] of an academy[2] decides to exclude[3] a pupil[4] for a fixed period, the principal must, without delay:

(1) inform the relevant person[5] of the period of the exclusion and the reasons for it[6]; and

(2) give the relevant person notice in writing stating the following matters:

    (a) the period of the exclusion and the reasons for it[7];

    (b) that the relevant person may make representations about the decision to the proprietor[8] and that, where the pupil is not the relevant person, the pupil may also be involved in the process of making representations, and an explanation as to how the pupil may be involved[9];

    (c) the means by which representations may be made[10]; and

    (d) where and to whom representations should be sent[11].

Where the principal decides to exclude a pupil permanently[12]; or to exclude a pupil and, as a result of the exclusion, the pupil would be excluded for a total of more than five school days[13] in any term[14]; or lose an opportunity to take a public examination or a National Curriculum test[15], the principal must do certain things[16]. The principal must, without delay:

(i) inform the relevant person, the proprietor and the local authority[17] (and, in the case of a permanent exclusion, if applicable, the home local authority[18]) of the period of the exclusion and the reasons for it[19]; and

(ii) give the relevant person notice in writing stating the following matters:

    (A) the period of the exclusion and the reasons for it[20];

    (B) that the relevant person may make representations about the decision to the proprietor and that, where the pupil is not the relevant person, the pupil may also be involved in the process of making representations, and an explanation as to how the pupil may be involved[21];

    (C) the means by which representations may be made[22];

    (D) where and to whom representations should be sent[23]; and

    (E) where a meeting of the proprietor is to consider the exclusion, that the relevant person may attend and be represented at the meeting (at their own expense), and may be accompanied by a friend[24].

In each term the principal must inform the proprietor and the local authority of the following:

(aa)   all exclusions that have occurred in that term to which heads (i) and (ii) above[25] do not apply[26];

(bb)   unless the principal has already done so, any such exclusions occurring during previous terms in that school year[27]; and

(cc)   the period of each exclusion and the reasons for it[28].

1   As to the meaning of 'principal' see PARA 517 note 5.

2   As to the meaning of 'academy' see PARA 517 note 5. As to academies generally see PARA 345 et seq.

3   As to the meaning of 'exclude' see PARA 517 note 4.

4   As to the meaning of 'pupil' see PARA 20 note 4 (definition applied by the Education Act 2002 s 212(2), (3); Interpretation Act 1978 s 11).

5   As to the meaning of 'relevant person' see PARA 518 note 5.

6   School Discipline (Pupil Exclusions and Reviews) (England) Regulations 2012, SI 2012/1033, reg 23(1)(a).

7   School Discipline (Pupil Exclusions and Reviews) (England) Regulations 2012, SI 2012/1033, reg 23(1)(b)(i). As to the meaning of 'writing' see PARA 76 note 8.

8   As to the meaning of 'proprietor' see PARA 51 note 4 (definition applied by the Education Act 2002 s 212(2), (3); Interpretation Act 1978 s 11).

9   School Discipline (Pupil Exclusions and Reviews) (England) Regulations 2012, SI 2012/1033, reg 23(1)(b)(ii). Any expense in connection with the representation of the relevant person is to be an expense of the relevant person: reg 23(4).

10 School Discipline (Pupil Exclusions and Reviews) (England) Regulations 2012, SI 2012/1033, reg 23(1)(b)(iii).

11 School Discipline (Pupil Exclusions and Reviews) (England) Regulations 2012, SI 2012/1033, reg 23(1)(b)(iv).

12 School Discipline (Pupil Exclusions and Reviews) (England) Regulations 2012, SI 2012/1033, reg 23(2)(a).

13 As to the meaning of 'school day' see PARA 229 note 6 (definition applied by the Education Act 2002 s 212(2), (3); Interpretation Act 1978 s 11). Reference should be made to the Education (Provision of Full-Time Education for Excluded Pupils) (England) Regulations 2007, SI 2007/1870, regs 3(3), 4(3)(b) (as amended SI 2014/3216); and PARA 522 notes 7, 9.

14 School Discipline (Pupil Exclusions and Reviews) (England) Regulations 2012, SI 2012/1033, reg 23(2)(b)(i). As to the meaning of 'term' see PARA 518 note 14.

15 School Discipline (Pupil Exclusions and Reviews) (England) Regulations 2012, SI 2012/1033, reg 23(2)(b)(ii). As to the meaning of 'National Curriculum test' see PARA 518 note 15.

16 See the School Discipline (Pupil Exclusions and Reviews) (England) Regulations 2012, SI 2012/1033, reg 23(3).

17 As to the meaning of 'local authority' see PARA 25 (definition applied by the Education Act 2002 s 212(1); Interpretation Act 1978 s 11).

18 As to the meaning of 'home local authority' see PARA 518 note 18.

19 School Discipline (Pupil Exclusions and Reviews) (England) Regulations 2012, SI 2012/1033, reg 23(3)(a).

20 School Discipline (Pupil Exclusions and Reviews) (England) Regulations 2012, SI 2012/1033, reg 23(3)(b)(i).

21 School Discipline (Pupil Exclusions and Reviews) (England) Regulations 2012, SI 2012/1033, reg 23(3)(b)(ii).

22 School Discipline (Pupil Exclusions and Reviews) (England) Regulations 2012, SI 2012/1033, reg 23(3)(b)(iii).

23 School Discipline (Pupil Exclusions and Reviews) (England) Regulations 2012, SI 2012/1033, reg 23(3)(b)(iv).

24 School Discipline (Pupil Exclusions and Reviews) (England) Regulations 2012, SI 2012/1033, reg 23(3)(b)(v).

25 Ie the School Discipline (Pupil Exclusions and Reviews) (England) Regulations 2012, SI 2012/1033, reg 23(3).

26 School Discipline (Pupil Exclusions and Reviews) (England) Regulations 2012, SI 2012/1033, reg 23(5)(a).

27 School Discipline (Pupil Exclusions and Reviews) (England) Regulations 2012, SI 2012/1033, reg 23(5)(b). As to the meaning of 'school year' see PARA 19 note 12 (definition applied by the Education Act 2002 s 212(2), (3); Interpretation Act 1978 s 11).

28 School Discipline (Pupil Exclusions and Reviews) (England) Regulations 2012, SI 2012/1033, reg 23(5)(c).

521. Reintegration interviews following temporary exclusion. Regulations[1] may require the head teacher[2] of a relevant school[3] in prescribed[4] cases to request any parent[5] of a temporarily excluded pupil[6] to attend an interview ('a reintegration interview') at the school with the head teacher of the school or any other person authorised by the head teacher[7]. The regulations may make provision about the time within which any reintegration interview must be held, the procedure for arranging the interview and the notification of any request to the parent[8]. The purpose of a reintegration interview is to assist the reintegration of the pupil after the period of exclusion and to promote the improvement of his behaviour[9].

1   'Regulations' means regulations made, in relation to England, by the Secretary of State, or, in relation to Wales, by the Welsh Ministers: Education and Inspections Act 2006 s 102(4). As to the meanings of 'England' and 'Wales' see PARA 7 note 3. As to the Secretary of State see PARA 58. As to the Welsh Ministers see PARA 59. The functions under the Education and Inspections Act 2006 s 102 in relation to Wales were originally vested in the National Assembly for Wales and are now exercisable by the Welsh Ministers by virtue of the Government of Wales Act 2006 s 162(1), Sch 11 paras 30, 32. As to the regulations made under the Education and Inspections Act 2006 s 102 see the School Discipline (Pupil Exclusions and Reviews) (England) Regulations 2012, SI 2012/1033; and the Education (Reintegration Interview) (Wales) Regulations 2010, SI 2010/2953.
2   As to the meaning of 'head teacher' see PARA 86 note 4 (definition applied by the Education and Inspections Act 2006 s 187(2), (3)).
3   In the Education and Inspections Act 2006 Pt 7 Ch 2 (ss 97–111), 'relevant school' means a maintained school, an academy school, an alternative provision academy, a city technology college, or a city college for the technology of the arts; and a 'maintained school' means a community, foundation or voluntary school, a community or foundation special school, or a pupil referral unit: s 111 (definition of 'relevant school' amended by the Education Act 2011 Sch 13 para 16(1), (5)). As to the meanings of 'academy school' and 'alternative provision academy' see PARA 346 notes 12, 14 (definitions applied by the Education and Inspections Act 2006 s 187(2), (3)). As to city technology colleges and city colleges for the technology of the arts see PARA 345. As to the meaning of references to a community, foundation or voluntary school or a community or foundation special school see PARA 106. As to pupil referral units see PARA 427 et seq.
4   'Prescribed' means prescribed by regulations: Education and Inspections Act 2006 s 102(4).
5   As to the meaning of 'parent' see PARA 7 note 6 (definition applied by the Education and Inspections Act 2006 s 187(2), (3)).
6   'A temporarily excluded pupil' means a pupil who is or has been excluded on disciplinary grounds for a fixed period: Education and Inspections Act 2006 s 102(4). As to the meaning of 'pupil' see PARA 20 note 4 (definition applied by s 187(2), (3)). As to the power of a head teacher (or a principal of an academy) to exclude pupils see PARA 517.
7   Education and Inspections Act 2006 s 102(1).
8   Education and Inspections Act 2006 s 102(3).
9   Education and Inspections Act 2006 s 102(2). In deciding whether to make a parenting order under the Anti-social Behaviour Act 2003 s 20, a court must take into account any failure by a parent without reasonable excuse to attend a reintegration interview under the Education and Inspections Act 2006 s 102 when requested to do so in accordance with regulations under that section: see the Anti-social Behaviour Act 2003 s 21(1A); and PARA 526.

522. Duty of parent in relation to excluded pupil. The head teacher[1] of a relevant school[2] in England[3], on excluding from the school a pupil[4] of compulsory school age[5], must give the parent[6] by the prescribed[7] time a notice[8] in writing[9].

Where a pupil of compulsory school age ('the excluded pupil') is excluded on disciplinary grounds from a relevant school in England, whether for a fixed period or permanently[10], and notice[11] has been given to a parent[12] of the pupil[13], the parent of the excluded pupil must ensure that the pupil is not present in a public place[14] at any time during school hours[15] on a day which: (1) is one of the first five school days to which the exclusion[16] relates or, where that exclusion is for a fixed period of five days or less, any of the days to which the exclusion relates[17]; and (2) is stated in the notice to be a day on which the parent is subject to this obligation[18].

If the excluded pupil is present in a public place at any time during school hours on such a school day[19], the parent commits an offence[20]. It is a defence for a person charged with such an offence to prove[21] that he had a reasonable justification for his failure to comply with the duty imposed[22] on him[23].

1   As to the meaning of 'head teacher' see PARA 86 note 4 (definition applied by the Education and Inspections Act 2006 s 187(2), (3)).
2   As to the meaning of 'relevant school' see PARA 521 note 3.
3   As to the meaning of 'England' see PARA 7 note 3.
4   As to the meaning of 'pupil' see PARA 20 note 4 (definition applied by the Education and Inspections Act 2006 s 187(2), (3)). As to the power of a head teacher (or a principal of an academy) to exclude pupils see PARA 517.
5   As to the meaning of 'compulsory school age' see PARA 19.
6   As to the meaning of 'parent' see PARA 7 note 6 (definition applied by the Education and Inspections Act 2006 s 187(2), (3)).

7   'Prescribed' means prescribed by regulations; and 'regulations' means regulations made by the Secretary of State: Education and Inspections Act 2006 s 104(8). As to the Secretary of State see PARA 58. As to the regulations made see the Education (Provision of Full-Time Education for Excluded Pupils) (England) Regulations 2007, SI 2007/1870 (amended by SI 2008/532; SI 2010/1172; SI 2012/1033; and SI 2014/3216); and the School Discipline (Pupil Exclusions and Reviews) (England) Regulations 2012, SI 2012/1033. As to guidance see also PARA 540. Reference in particular should be made to the Education (Provision of Full-Time Education for Excluded Pupils) (England) Regulations 2007, SI 2007/1870, regs 3(3), 4(3)(b) (as amended SI 2014/3216) (definition of 'relevant day'); and note 9.
8   The Education Act 1996 s 572 (see PARA 76), which provides for the methods by which notices may be served under that Act, does not preclude a notice under the Education and Inspections Act 2006 s 104 from being given to the parent of the excluded pupil by any effective method: s 104(6). Regulations may enable such a notice to be combined with a notice required by virtue of the Education Act 2002 s 52(3)(a) (which relates to the exclusion of pupils from maintained schools: see PARA 517): Education and Inspections Act 2006 s 104(7).
9   Education and Inspections Act 2006 s 104(1). As to the meaning of 'writing' see PARA 76 note 8. The notice must comply with s 104(2) and (3) and contain such other information as may be prescribed: see s 104(1). Where the appropriate authority is or will be obliged under the relevant enactment to make arrangements for the provision of full-time education for the excluded pupil during his exclusion, or intends to do so without being so obliged, the notice must specify the first day on which full-time education is to be provided for the excluded pupil: s 104(2). The notice must specify as days on which the parent is to be subject to s 103(2) (see the text to notes 14–18) each school day beginning with the first school day to which the exclusion relates and ending with the earliest of the following: (1) where a day is specified under s 104(2), the school day preceding that day (s 104(3)(a)), (2) the fifth school day to which the exclusion relates (s 104(3)(b)); and (3) the last school day to which the exclusion relates (s 104(3)(c)). Section 103(7) (see note 17) applies for the purposes of s 104(3) as it applies for the purposes of s 103(2)(a): s 104(4). Where the appropriate authority is a local authority, it must provide the head teacher with such information as will enable the head teacher to give a notice complying with s 104(2): s 104(5) (amended by SI 2010/1158). 'The appropriate authority' means: (a) in the case of a permanent exclusion or an exclusion from a pupil referral unit, a local authority; (b) in the case of an exclusion for a fixed period from a maintained school, the governing body of the school; and (c) in the case of an exclusion for a fixed period from a relevant school which is an academy school, an alternative provision academy, a city technology college or a city college for the technology of the arts, the proprietor of the school: Education and Inspections Act 2006 s 104(8) (definition amended by SI 2010/1158; and the Education Act 2011 Sch 12 para 16(1), (4)). As to the meaning of 'local authority' see PARA 25; as to the meaning of 'school day' see PARA 229 note 6; as to the meanings of 'academy school' and 'alternative provision academy see PARA 346 notes 12, 14; and as to the meaning of 'proprietor' see PARA 51 note 4 (definitions applied by the Education and Inspections Act 2006 s 187(2), (3)). As to pupil referral units see PARA 427 et seq. As to the meaning of 'maintained school' see PARA 521 note 3. As to the governing bodies of maintained schools in England see PARA 150 et seq. As to city technology colleges and city colleges for the technology of the arts see PARA 345. 'The relevant

enactment' means, where the appropriate authority is a local authority, the Education Act 1996 s 19 (see PARA 427); and, in any other case, the Education and Inspections Act 2006 s 100 (see PARA 528): s 104(8) (definition amended by SI 2010/1158).

It should be noted that as a result of the Education (Provision of Full-Time Education for Excluded Pupils) (England) Regulations 2007, SI 2007/1870, regs 3(3), 4(3)(b) (as amended SI 2014/3216) (definition of 'relevant day') (see also note 7) consecutive periods of exclusion are considered as one continuous period for the purposes of making arrangements for the provision of suitable full-time education for a pupil of compulsory school age who is excluded for a fixed period on disciplinary grounds.

10 Education and Inspections Act 2006 s 103(1)(a).

11 Ie notice under the Education and Inspections Act 2006 s 104: see the text to notes 1–9.

12 In the Education and Inspections Act 2006 s 103, 'parent', in relation to a pupil, does not include any person who is not an individual: s 103(8).

13 Education and Inspections Act 2006 s 103(1)(b).

14 'Public place' means any highway, and any place to which at the material time the public or any section of the public have access, on payment or otherwise, as of right or by virtue of express or implied permission: Education and Inspections Act 2006 s 103(8).

15 'School hours' means any time during a school session of the school referred to in the Education and Inspections Act 2006 s 103(1)(a) (see the text to note 10) or during a break between sessions of that school on the same day: s 103(8).

16 Ie the exclusion mentioned in the Education and Inspections Act 2006 s 103(1)(a): see the text to note 10.

17 Education and Inspections Act 2006 s 103(2)(a). Where the excluded pupil is excluded during the course of a school day but before the beginning of any afternoon session on that day, that day is to be treated for the purposes of s 103(2)(a) as the first day to which the exclusion relates: s 103(7).

18 See the Education and Inspections Act 2006 s 103(2)(b).

19 Ie a school day falling within the Education and Inspections Act 2006 s 103(2): see the text to notes 14–18.

20 Education and Inspections Act 2006 s 103(3). A person guilty of such an offence is liable on summary conviction to a fine not exceeding level 3 on the standard scale: s 103(5). Proceedings for such an offence may not be instituted except by a local authority: s 103(6) (amended by SI 2010/1158). As to the standard scale see SENTENCING AND DISPOSITION OF OFFENDERS vol 92 (2010) PARA 142. Where an authorised officer has reason to believe that a person has committed an offence under the Education and Inspections Act 2006 s 103(3) he may give the person a penalty notice: see s 105(1); and PARA 523.

21 As to the standard of proof on the accused see CRIMINAL PROCEDURE vol 28 (2010) PARA 466.

22 Ie by the Education and Inspections Act 2006 s 103(2): see the text to notes 14–18.

23 Education and Inspections Act 2006 s 103(4).

523. Penalty notices in relation to presence of excluded pupil. Where an authorised officer[1] has reason to believe that a person has committed an offence in relation to the presence of an excluded pupil in a public place[2], he may give the person a penalty notice in respect of the offence[3]. A 'penalty notice' is a notice offering the person the opportunity of discharging any liability to conviction for the offence to which the notice relates by payment of a penalty in accordance with the notice[4].

Where a person is given a penalty notice, proceedings for the offence to which the notice relates may not be instituted[5] before the end of such period as may be prescribed[6]; and he cannot be convicted of the offence to which the notice relates if he pays a penalty in accordance with the notice[7].

Regulations[8] may make:

(1) provision as to the form and content of penalty notices[9];

(2) provision as to the monetary amount of any penalty[10] and the time by which it is to be paid[11];

(3) provision for determining the local authority to whom a penalty is payable[12];

(4) provision as to the methods by which penalties may be paid[13];

(5)   provision as to the records which are to be kept in relation to penalty notices[14];

(6)   provision as to the persons who may be authorised by a local authority or a head teacher to give penalty notices[15];

(7)   provision limiting the circumstances in which authorised officers of a prescribed description may give penalty notices[16];

(8)   provision for or in connection with the withdrawal, in prescribed circumstances, of a penalty notice, including repayment of any amount by way of penalty under a penalty notice which is withdrawn[17], and prohibition of the institution or continuation of proceedings for the offence to which the withdrawn notice relates[18];

(9)   provision for a certificate purporting to be signed by or on behalf of a prescribed person[19], and stating that payment of any amount paid by way of penalty was or, as the case may be, was not received on or before a date specified in the certificate[20], to be received in evidence of the matters so stated[21];

(10)   provision as to the action to be taken if a penalty is not paid in accordance with a penalty notice[22];

(11)   provision for or in connection with the preparation of codes of conduct in relation to the giving of penalty notices[23];

(12)   such other provision in relation to penalties or penalty notices as the Secretary of State thinks necessary or expedient[24].

Local authorities, head teachers and authorised officers must, in carrying out their functions in relation to penalty notices, have regard to any guidance which is given by the Secretary of State from time to time in relation to penalty notices[25].

1   'Authorised officer' means a constable, an officer of a local authority in England who is authorised by the authority to give penalty notices, or an authorised staff member: Education and Inspections Act 2006 ss 105(6), 106(4) (definition amended by SI 2010/1158). The power of a constable to give a penalty notice may be exercised by a community support officer or an accredited person: see the Police Reform Act 2002 Sch 4 para 1(2)(ab), Sch 5 para 1(2)(ac); and POLICE AND INVESTIGATORY POWERS vol 84 (2013) PARAS 367, 374. As to the office of constable see POLICE AND INVESTIGATORY POWERS vol 84 (2013) PARA 1 et seq. As to the meaning of 'local authority' see PARA 25 (definition applied by the Education and Inspections Act 2006 s 187(2), (3)). 'Authorised staff member' means a head teacher of a relevant school in England, or a member of the staff of a relevant school in England who is authorised by the head teacher of the school to give penalty notices: s 105(6). As to the meaning of 'head teacher' see PARA 86 note 4 (definition applied by s 187(2), (3)). As to the meaning of 'relevant school' see PARA 521 note 3. As to the meaning of 'England' see PARA 7 note 3.

2   Ie an offence under the Education and Inspections Act 2006 s 103(3): see PARA 522.

3   Education and Inspections Act 2006 s 105(1).

4   Education and Inspections Act 2006 s 105(2). Sums received by a local authority under s 105 may be used by the authority for the purposes of any of its functions which may be specified in regulations but, to the extent that they are not so used, must be paid in accordance with regulations to the Secretary of State: s 105(5) (amended by SI 2010/1158). As to the meaning of 'functions' see PARA 18 note 5 (definition applied by the Education and Inspections Act 2006 s 187(2), (3)). 'Regulations' means regulations made by the Secretary of State: ss 105(6), 106(4). As to the Secretary of State see PARA 58. As to the regulations made under ss 105, 106 see the Education (Penalty Notices) (England) Regulations 2007, SI 2007/1867 (amended by SI 2012/1046; and SI 2013/757).

5   As to the institution of proceedings see the Education and Inspections Act 2006 s 103(6); and PARA 522.

6   Education and Inspections Act 2006 s 105(3). 'Prescribed' means prescribed by regulations: Education Act 1996 s 579(1) (definition applied by s 187(2), (3)). As to the regulations made see note 4.

7   Education and Inspections Act 2006 s 105(4).

8   As to the regulations made see note 4.
9   Education and Inspections Act 2006 s 106(1)(a).
10   'Penalty' means a penalty under a penalty notice: Education and Inspections Act 2006 s 106(4).
11   Education and Inspections Act 2006 s 106(1)(b). Without prejudice to the generality of s 106(1) or s 181(2)(a) (general provisions as to regulations and orders), regulations under s 106(1)(b) may make provision for penalties of different amounts to be payable in different cases (including provision for the penalty payable under a penalty notice to differ according to the time by which it is paid): s 106(2).
12   Education and Inspections Act 2006 s 106(1)(c) (amended by SI 2010/1158).
13   Education and Inspections Act 2006 s 106(1)(d).
14   Education and Inspections Act 2006 s 106(1)(e).
15   Education and Inspections Act 2006 s 106(1)(f) (amended by SI 2010/1158).
16   Education and Inspections Act 2006 s 106(1)(g).
17   Education and Inspections Act 2006 s 106(1)(h)(i).
18   Education and Inspections Act 2006 s 106(1)(h)(ii).
19   Education and Inspections Act 2006 s 106(1)(i)(i).
20   Education and Inspections Act 2006 s 106(1)(i)(ii).
21   Education and Inspections Act 2006 s 106(1)(i). As to the evidential effect of certificates admissible by statute see CIVIL PROCEDURE vol 11 (2009) PARA 897.
22   Education and Inspections Act 2006 s 106(1)(j).
23   Education and Inspections Act 2006 s 106(1)(k).
24   Education and Inspections Act 2006 s 106(1)(l).
25   Education and Inspections Act 2006 s 106(3) (amended by SI 2010/1158). As to the publication of guidance see the Education Act 1996 s 571 (applied by the Education and Inspections Act 2006 s 187(2), (3)); and PARA 60. See in particular the Exclusions Guidance; and PARA 540 note 13.

524. Removal of excluded pupils to designated premises. Provided certain statutory requirements are met, a constable has power to remove to designated premises a child or young person found by him in a public place in a specified area during a specified period and during school hours, and whom he has reasonable cause to believe is of compulsory school age and to have been excluded on disciplinary grounds from a relevant school for a fixed period or permanently and to have no reasonable justification for being in the public place[1].

1   See the Crime and Disorder Act 1998 s 16; and PARA 456.

525. Parenting contracts in cases of exclusion from school. Where a pupil has been excluded on disciplinary grounds from a relevant school for a fixed period or permanently, a local authority or the governing body of a relevant school may enter into a parenting contract with a parent of the pupil or child[1]. A 'parenting contract' is a document which contains a statement by the parent that he agrees to comply with such requirements as may be specified in the document for such period as may be so specified, and a statement by the local authority or governing body that it agrees to provide support to the parent for the purpose of complying with those requirements[2].

1   See the Anti-social Behaviour Act 2003 s 19(1), (3); and CHILDREN AND YOUNG PERSONS vol 10 (2012) PARA 1283 et seq.
2   See the Anti-social Behaviour Act 2003 s 19(4); and CHILDREN AND YOUNG PERSONS vol 10 (2012) PARA 1283 et seq. As to parenting contracts in cases of a pupil's failure to attend regularly at school see PARA 450. As to parenting contracts in cases of misbehaviour at school see PARA 516.

526. Parenting orders in cases of exclusion or potential exclusion from school. Where a pupil has been excluded on disciplinary grounds from a school for a fixed period or permanently, and such conditions as may be prescribed in regulations are satisfied, a relevant body may apply to a magistrates' court for a parenting order in respect of a parent of the pupil[1]. A relevant body may also apply to a magistrates' court for a parenting order in respect of a pupil at a relevant school if it appears to the body that the pupil has engaged in behaviour which would warrant the exclusion of the pupil from the school on disciplinary grounds for a fixed period or permanently, and such conditions as may be prescribed in regulations are satisfied[2].

A 'parenting order' is an order which requires the parent to comply, for a period not exceeding 12 months, with such requirements as are specified in the order, and to attend, for a concurrent period not exceeding three months, such counselling or guidance programme as may be specified in directions given by the responsible officer[3].

1　See the Anti-social Behaviour Act 2003 s 20(1), (2); and CHILDREN AND YOUNG PERSONS vol 10 (2012) PARA 1283 et seq.

2　See the Anti-social Behaviour Act 2003 s 20(2A); and CHILDREN AND YOUNG PERSONS vol 10 (2012) PARA 1283 et seq.

3　See the Anti-social Behaviour Act 2003 s 20(4); and CHILDREN AND YOUNG PERSONS vol 10 (2012) PARA 1283 et seq.

527. Functions of governing body in relation to pupils excluded from a maintained school. Where the governing body[1] of a maintained school[2] in England[3] is informed[4] of: (1) the permanent exclusion[5] of a pupil[6]; (2) the exclusion of a pupil where, as a result of the exclusion, the pupil would be excluded for a total of more than 15 school days[7] in any term[8] or lose an opportunity to take a public examination or a National Curriculum test[9]; or (3) the exclusion of a pupil where the pupil would as a result of the exclusion be excluded for a total of more than five school days in any term[10] and the relevant person[11] makes[12] representations[13], the governing body must[14]:

(a)　consider the interests and circumstances of the excluded pupil, including the circumstances in which the pupil was excluded, and have regard to the interests of other pupils and persons working at the school (including persons working at the school voluntarily)[15];

(b)　consider any representations about the exclusion made to the governing body by or on behalf of the relevant person, the head teacher[16] or by the local authority[17];

(c)　take reasonable steps to arrange a meeting at which the exclusion is to be considered for a time and date when each of the following persons is able to attend: the head teacher[18]; the relevant person (and, where requested by the relevant person, a representative or friend of the relevant person)[19]; and a representative of the local authority[20]; and

(d)　allow each of the persons described in head (c) above to attend the meeting and to make representations about the exclusion[21].

The governing body must decide whether or not the pupil should be reinstated and, where it considers that the pupil should be reinstated, it must decide whether the pupil should be reinstated immediately or by a particular date[22]. If the governing body decides that the pupil should be reinstated, it must without delay direct the head teacher accordingly[23], and inform the relevant person and the local authority[24] (and, if applicable, the home local authority[25]) of its decision and the reasons for it in writing[26]. The head teacher must comply with a direction of the governing body to reinstate the pupil[27]. If the governing body decides not to reinstate the pupil, it must without delay:

(i)   inform the relevant person, the head teacher and the local authority (and, if applicable, the home local authority) of its decision and the reasons for it in writing[28]; and

(ii)   in the case of a pupil who is permanently excluded, give the relevant person notice in writing[29] stating the following:

    (A)   that the exclusion is permanent[30];

    (B)   that the relevant person may apply for the governing body's decision to be reviewed by a review panel[31];

    (C)   where the relevant person applies for a review, that the relevant person may require the local authority to appoint a SEN expert[32] to advise the review panel[33];

    (D)   the role of the SEN expert in relation to a review[34];

    (E)   how an application for a review may be made and what the application must contain[35];

    (F)   where and to whom to send the application and the date by which the application must be received[36];

    (G)   that the relevant person may, at their own expense, appoint someone to make representations for the purpose of the review[37]; and

    (H)   that the relevant person may issue a claim under the Equality Act 2010 where the relevant person believes that unlawful discrimination[38] has occurred, and the time within which such a claim should be made[39].

Where a pupil has been excluded in circumstances where the above provisions[40] do not apply, and the governing body receives any representations made[41] from the relevant person about the exclusion, it must consider those representations[42].

1   As to the governing bodies of maintained schools in England see PARA 150 et seq; and in Wales see PARA 195. Any governing body or equivalent should initially consult the Exclusions Guidance, as to which see PARA 540 note 13.

2   As to the meaning of 'maintained school' see PARA 521 note 3.

3   The School Discipline (Pupil Exclusions and Reviews) (England) Regulations 2012, SI 2012/1033, apply in relation to England only: see reg 1(2). See also PARA 518 note 3.As to the equivalent provision to reg 5 in relation to Wales see the Education (Pupil Exclusions and Appeals) (Maintained Schools) (Wales) Regulations 2003, SI 2003/3227, reg 6 (amended by SI 2004/1805: and SI 2010/1142). A governing body of a maintained school in Wales is under a duty to provide certain information in relation to exclusions: see the Education (Pupil Exclusions and Appeals) (Maintained Schools) (Wales) Regulations 2003, SI 2003/3227, reg 5 (amended by SI 2004/1805; and SI 2010/1142). As to the meanings of 'England' and 'Wales' see PARA 7 note 3.

4   Ie under the School Discipline (Pupil Exclusions and Reviews) (England) Regulations 2012, SI 2012/1033, reg 5(3)(a): see PARA 518.

5   As to the meaning of 'exclusion' see PARA 517 note 3.

6   School Discipline (Pupil Exclusions and Reviews) (England) Regulations 2012, SI 2012/1033, reg 6(1)(a). As to the meaning of 'pupil' see PARA 20 note 4 (definition applied by the Education Act 2002 s 212(2), (3); Interpretation Act 1978 s 11). As to the power of a head teacher (or principal of an academy) to exclude pupils see PARA 517.

7   As to the meaning of 'school day' see PARA 229 note 6 (definition applied by the Education Act 2002 s 212(2), (3); Interpretation Act 1978 s 11).

8   School Discipline (Pupil Exclusions and Reviews) (England) Regulations 2012, SI 2012/1033, reg 6(1)(b)(i). As to the meaning of 'term' see PARA 518 note 14.

9   School Discipline (Pupil Exclusions and Reviews) (England) Regulations 2012, SI 2012/1033, reg 6(1)(b)(ii). As to the meaning of 'National Curriculum test' see PARA 518 note 15.

10   School Discipline (Pupil Exclusions and Reviews) (England) Regulations 2012, SI 2012/1033, reg 6(1)(c)(i).

11   As to the meaning of 'relevant person' see PARA 518 note 5.

12 Ie in pursuance of the School Discipline (Pupil Exclusions and Reviews) (England) Regulations 2012, SI 2012/1033, reg 5(3)(b): see PARA 518.

13 School Discipline (Pupil Exclusions and Reviews) (England) Regulations 2012, SI 2012/1033, reg 6(1)(c)(ii).

14 Subject to the School Discipline (Pupil Exclusions and Reviews) (England) Regulations 2012, SI 2012/1033, reg 6(8), after being informed of the matters in reg 5(3)(a) (see PARA 518), the governing body must take each of the steps referred to in reg 6(2) and (3) (see the text to notes 15–22) within: (1) 15 school days in the case of (a) a permanent exclusion (reg 6(7)(a)(i)); an exclusion for a fixed period which would cause the pupil's total number of days of exclusion to exceed 15 school days in any term (reg 6(7)(a)(ii)); or an exclusion where the pupil would, as a result of the exclusion, lose an opportunity to take a public examination or a National Curriculum test (reg 6(7)(a)(iii)); or (2) 50 school days in the case of an exclusion for a fixed period where (a) the pupil would, as a result of the exclusion, be excluded for a total of more than five school days but not more than 15 school days in any term (reg 6(7)(b)(i)); and (b) the relevant person has made representations under reg 5(3)(b) (see PARA 518) (reg 6(7)(b)(ii)). However, where a pupil has been excluded in circumstances in which he would, as a result of the exclusion, lose an opportunity to take a public examination or a National Curriculum test, the governing body must (so far as it is reasonably practical) take each of the steps referred to in reg 6(2) and (3) before the date on which the pupil is due to take the examination or test: reg 6(8). The governing body is not relieved of the duty to take any step referred to in reg 6(2) or (3) because it has not been taken within the period specified in reg 6(7) or (8): reg 6(10).

15 School Discipline (Pupil Exclusions and Reviews) (England) Regulations 2012, SI 2012/1033, reg 6(3)(a). Where it falls to the governing body, in exercise of functions under reg 6 to establish any fact, any question as to whether that fact is established is to be decided on a balance of probabilities: reg 10(b). As to the civil standard of proof see CIVIL PROCEDURE vol 11 (2009) PARA 775.

16 As to the meaning of 'head teacher' see PARA 86 note 4 (definition applied by the Education Act 2002 s 187(2), (3); Interpretation Act 1978 s 11).

17 School Discipline (Pupil Exclusions and Reviews) (England) Regulations 2012, SI 2012/1033, reg 6(3)(b). As to the meaning of 'local authority' see PARA 25 (definition applied by the Education Act 2002 s 212(2), (3); Interpretation Act 1978 s 11).

18 School Discipline (Pupil Exclusions and Reviews) (England) Regulations 2012, SI 2012/1033, reg 6(3)(c)(i).

19 School Discipline (Pupil Exclusions and Reviews) (England) Regulations 2012, SI 2012/1033, reg 6(3)(c)(ii).

20 School Discipline (Pupil Exclusions and Reviews) (England) Regulations 2012, SI 2012/1033, reg 6(3)(c)(iii). As to the role of the officer of the local authority (the term in the previous legislation) see *R (on the application of S) v Brent London Borough Council, R (on the application of T) v Head Teacher of Wembley High School, R (on the application of P) v Oxfordshire County Council Exclusion Appeals Panel* [2002] EWCA Civ 693, [2002] ELR 556, [2002] All ER (D) 277 (May), at [24] (proceedings before an independent appeal panel (now 'review panel'), but the point applies equally to hearings before the governing body; it is no part of the function of the local authority to press for a particular conclusion in relation to a particular pupil). See also *SA (By his litigation friend MA) v London Borough of Camden Independent Appeal Panel* [2013] EWHC 3152 (Admin), [2013] All ER (D) 288 (Oct). In regard to the previous legislation about attending and making representations see *R v Camden London Borough Council and the Governors of Hampstead School, ex p H* [1996] ELR 360, sub nom *R v Camden London Borough Council, ex p H (A Minor)* (1996) Times, 15 August, CA. As a matter of fairness it might be necessary to hear from the child himself: *R v Governors of St Gregory's RC Aided High School and Appeal Committee, ex p M* [1995] ELR 290, sub nom *R v Governors of St Gregory's RC Aided High School, ex p Roberts* (1995) Times, 27 January; *R v Governors of Bacon's City Technology College, ex p W* [1998] ELR 488. See also *R (on the application of C) v Sefton Metropolitan Borough Council Independent Appeals Panel and the Governors of Hillside High School* [2001] ELR 393, sub nom *Cahill v Sefton Metropolitan Borough Council* [2000] All ER (D) 2458 (also decided under previous legislation; where there was no conflict about whether an event had occurred, there was no need for the governing body to carry out searching inquiries). See also *R (on the application of CR) v Independent Appeal Panel of the London Borough of Lambeth* [2014] EWHC 2461 (Admin), [2014] ELR 359. As to the rules of natural justice as they apply to the governing body see *R v Governing Body of the Rectory School and Richmond London Borough Council, ex p WK (A Minor)* [1997] ELR 484; *R v Board of Governors of Stoke Newington School, ex p M* [1994]

ELR 131 (both cases decided under previous legislation). The applicant should be provided with relevant evidence on which the decision to exclude was based: *R (on the application of K) v Governors of the W School* [2001] ELR 311.

21 School Discipline (Pupil Exclusions and Reviews) (England) Regulations 2012, SI 2012/1033, reg 6(3)(d).

22 School Discipline (Pupil Exclusions and Reviews) (England) Regulations 2012, SI 2012/1033, reg 6(2). As to reinstatement see further the cases cited in PARA 531 note 6.

23 School Discipline (Pupil Exclusions and Reviews) (England) Regulations 2012, SI 2012/1033, reg 6(4)(a).

24 As to the meaning of 'local authority' see PARA 25 (definition applied by the Education Act 2002 s 212(1): Interpretation Act 1978 s 11).

25 As to the meaning of 'home local authority' see PARA 518 note 18.

26 School Discipline (Pupil Exclusions and Reviews) (England) Regulations 2012, SI 2012/1033, reg 6(4)(b). As to the meaning of 'writing' see PARA 76 note 8.

27 School Discipline (Pupil Exclusions and Reviews) (England) Regulations 2012, SI 2012/1033, reg 6(5).

28 School Discipline (Pupil Exclusions and Reviews) (England) Regulations 2012, SI 2012/1033, reg 6(6)(a).

29 The notice in writing referred to in the School Discipline (Pupil Exclusions and Reviews) (England) Regulations 2012, SI 2012/1033, reg 6(6)(b), (1) may be given by (a) delivering it directly to the relevant person; (b) delivering it to the relevant person's last known address; or (c) sending it by first class to the relevant person's last known address; and (2) unless the contrary is shown, it will be taken to have been given (a) where first class post is used, on the second working day after the date of posting; or (b) where the notice is delivered, on the date of delivery: reg 6(11). 'Working day' means a day other than a Saturday, a Sunday, Christmas Day, Good Friday or a day which is a bank holiday within the meaning of the Banking and Financial Dealings Act 1971 (see TIME vol 97 (2015) PARA 321): School Discipline (Pupil Exclusions and Reviews) (England) Regulations 2012, SI 2012/1033, reg 2(1). As to the validity of notices see *R (on the application of P) v Haringey Borough Council* [2008] EWHC 2357 (Admin), [2009] ELR 49, [2008] All ER (D) 81 (Sep).

30 School Discipline (Pupil Exclusions and Reviews) (England) Regulations 2012, SI 2012/1033, reg 6(6)(b)(i).

31 School Discipline (Pupil Exclusions and Reviews) (England) Regulations 2012, SI 2012/1033, reg 6(6)(b)(ii). As to reviews see PARA 531 et seq.

32 'SEN expert' means an individual who (1) has expertise and experience of special educational needs considered by the local authority (or, in relation to an academy, the proprietor) as appropriate to perform the functions specified in the School Discipline (Pupil Exclusions and Reviews) (England) Regulations 2012, SI 2012/1033, Sch 1 para 18 (see PARA 539) ; and (2) is not disqualified from appointment under Sch 1 para 3(7): reg 2(1). As to the meaning of 'academy' see PARA 517 note 5.

33 School Discipline (Pupil Exclusions and Reviews) (England) Regulations 2012, SI 2012/1033, reg 6(6)(b)(iii).

34 School Discipline (Pupil Exclusions and Reviews) (England) Regulations 2012, SI 2012/1033, reg 6(6)(b)(iv).

35 School Discipline (Pupil Exclusions and Reviews) (England) Regulations 2012, SI 2012/1033, reg 6(6)(b)(v).

36 School Discipline (Pupil Exclusions and Reviews) (England) Regulations 2012, SI 2012/1033, reg 6(6)(b)(vi).

37 School Discipline (Pupil Exclusions and Reviews) (England) Regulations 2012, SI 2012/1033, reg 6(6)(b)(vii).

38 As to unlawful discrimination under the Equality Act 2010 see PARA 9 et seq.

39 School Discipline (Pupil Exclusions and Reviews) (England) Regulations 2012, SI 2012/1033, reg 6(6)(b)(viii).

40 Ie the School Discipline (Pupil Exclusions and Reviews) (England) Regulations 2012, SI 2012/1033, reg 6(2)–(6): see the text to notes 22–39.

41 Ie made in pursuance of the School Discipline (Pupil Exclusions and Reviews) (England) Regulations 2012, SI 2012/1033, reg 5(1)(b): see PARA 518.

42 School Discipline (Pupil Exclusions and Reviews) (England) Regulations 2012, SI 2012/1033, reg 6(9).

528. Duty of governing body where pupil excluded for fixed period. Except in prescribed[1] cases, the governing body[2] of a relevant school in England[3] must make arrangements for the provision of suitable full-time education[4] for pupils of compulsory school age[5] who are excluded from the school for a fixed period on disciplinary grounds[6]. Such education must be provided from a day that, in relation to the pupil concerned, is determined in accordance with regulations[7]. The education must not be provided at the school unless it is provided there in pursuance of arrangements which are made jointly with the governing body of at least one other relevant school[8], and make provision for the education of pupils excluded on disciplinary grounds from any of the schools that are parties to the arrangements[9].

In determining what arrangements to make[10] in the case of any pupil, a governing body must have regard to any guidance given from time to time by the Secretary of State[11].

1   'Prescribed' means prescribed by regulations; and 'regulations' means regulations made by the Secretary of State: Education and Inspections Act 2006 s 100(5). As to the Secretary of State see PARA 58. As to the regulations made under s 100, see the Education (Provision of Full-Time Education for Excluded Pupils) (England) Regulations 2007, SI 2007/1870 (amended by SI 2008/532; SI 2010/1172; SI 2012/1033; and SI 2014/3216); and the School Discipline (Pupil Exclusions and Reviews) (England) Regulations 2012, SI 2012/1033.
2   'Governing body', in relation to a relevant school which is an academy school, an alternative provision academy, a city technology college or a city college for the technology of the arts, means proprietor: Education and Inspections Act 2006 s 100(5) (definition amended by the Education Act 2011 Sch 13 para 16(1), (3)). In the Education and Inspections Act 2006 s 100, 'relevant school' does not include a pupil referral unit: s 100(5). As to the meaning of 'relevant school' generally see PARA 521 note 3. As to pupil referral units see PARA 427 et seq. As to the meanings of 'academy school' and 'alternative provision academy' see PARA 346 notes 12, 14; and as to the meaning of 'proprietor' see PARA 51 note 4 (definitions applied by s 187(2), (3)). As to city technology colleges and city colleges for the technology of the arts see PARA 345. As to the governing bodies of maintained schools in England see PARA 150 et seq.
3   As to the meaning of 'England' see PARA 7 note 3.
4   'Suitable full-time education', in relation to a pupil, means efficient full-time education suitable to his age, ability and aptitude and to any special educational needs he may have: Education and Inspections Act 2006 s 100(5). As to the meaning of 'pupil' see PARA 20 note 4; and as to the meaning of 'special educational needs' see PARAS 943 (definition applied by s 187(2), (3)).
5   As to the meaning of 'compulsory school age' see PARA 19.
6   Education and Inspections Act 2006 s 100(1). As to the power of a head teacher (or a principal of an academy) to exclude pupils see PARA 517.
7   Education and Inspections Act 2006 s 100(2). As to the regulations made see note 1.
8   Education and Inspections Act 2006 s 100(3)(a).
9   Education and Inspections Act 2006 s 100(3)(b).
10   Ie under the Education and Inspections Act 2006 s 100(1): see the text to notes 1–6.
11   Education and Inspections Act 2006 s 100(4). As to the publication of guidance see the Education Act 1996 s 571 (applied by the Education and Inspections Act 2006 s 187(2), (3)); and PARA 60. As to guidance see also PARA 540. See in particular the Exclusions Guidance; and PARA 540 note 13.

529.   Functions of management committee in relation to pupils excluded from a pupil referral unit.   Where the management committee[1] of a pupil referral unit[2] in England[3] is informed[4] of: (1) the permanent exclusion[5] of a pupil[6]; (2) the exclusion of a pupil where, as a result of the exclusion, the pupil would be excluded from the pupil referral unit for a total of more than 15 school days[7] in any term[8], or lose an opportunity to take a public examination or a National Curriculum test[9]; or (3) the exclusion of a pupil where the pupil would as a result of the exclusion be excluded for a total of more than five school days in any term[10], and the relevant person[11] makes representations[12] to the management committee[13], the management committee must[14]:

(a)   consider the interests and circumstances of the excluded pupil, including the circumstances in which the pupil was excluded, and have regard to the interests of other pupils and persons working at the unit (including persons working at the unit voluntarily)[15];

(b)   consider any representations about the exclusion made to the management committee by or on behalf of the relevant person, the teacher in charge or the local authority[16];

(c)   take reasonable steps to arrange a meeting at which the exclusion is to be considered for a time and date when each of the following persons is able to attend: the teacher in charge[17]; the relevant person (and, where requested by the relevant person, a representative or friend of the relevant person)[18]; and a representative of the local authority[19]; and

(d)   allow each of the persons described head (c) above to attend the meeting and to make representations about the exclusion[20].

The management committee must decide whether or not the pupil should be reinstated; and where it considers that the pupil should be reinstated, it must decide whether the pupil should be reinstated immediately, or reinstated by a particular date[21]. If the management committee decides that the pupil should be reinstated it must without delay direct the teacher in charge accordingly[22], and inform the relevant person and the local authority[23] of its decision[24]. The teacher in charge must comply with a direction of the management committee to reinstate the pupil[25].

If the management committee decides not to reinstate the pupil, it must without delay:

(i)   inform the relevant person, the teacher in charge and the local authority (and, if applicable, the home local authority[26]) of its decision and the reasons for it in writing[27]; and

(ii)   in the case of a pupil who is permanently excluded, give the relevant person notice in writing[28] stating the following:

(A)   that the exclusion is permanent[29];

(B)   that the relevant person may apply for the management committee's decision to be reviewed by a review panel[30];

(C)   where the relevant person applies for a review, that the relevant person may require the local authority to appoint a SEN expert[31] to advise the review panel[32];

(D)   the role of the SEN expert in relation to a review[33];

(E)   how an application for a review may be made and what the application must contain[34];

(F)   where and to whom to send the application and the date by which the application must be received[35];

(G)   that the relevant person may, at their own expense, appoint someone to make representations for the purpose of the review[36]; and

(H)   that the relevant person may issue a claim under the Equality Act 2010 where the relevant person believes that unlawful discrimination[37] has occurred, and the time within which such a claim should be made[38].

Where a pupil has been excluded in circumstances where the above provisions[39] do not apply[40], and the management committee receives representations[41] from the relevant person about the exclusion[42], it must consider those representations[43].

1 As to the management committee of a pupil referral unit see PARA 434. See also PARA 517 note 11. Any management committee should initially consult the Exclusions Guidance, as to which see PARA 540 note 13.

2 As to pupil referral units see PARA 427 et seq.

3 The School Discipline (Pupil Exclusions and Reviews) (England) Regulations 2012, SI 2012/1033, apply only in relation to England: reg 1(2). See also PARA 518 note 3. In relation to Wales similar obligations to those contained in reg 15 are imposed on local authorities: see the Education (Pupil Exclusions and Appeals) (Pupil Referral Units) (Wales) Regulations 2003, SI 2003/3246, reg 7 (amended by SI 2004/1805; and SI 2010/1142). As to the meanings of 'England' and 'Wales' see PARA 7 note 3.

4 Ie under the School Discipline (Pupil Exclusions and Reviews) (England) Regulations 2012, SI 2012/1033, reg 14(3)(a): see PARA 519.

5 As to the meaning of 'exclusion' see PARA 517 note 4.

6 School Discipline (Pupil Exclusions and Reviews) (England) Regulations 2012, SI 2012/1033, reg 15(1)(a). As to the meaning of 'pupil' see PARA 20 note 4 (definition applied by the Education Act 2002 s 212(2), (3); Interpretation Act 1978 s 11). As to the power of a head teacher to exclude pupils see PARA 517.

7 As to the meaning of 'school day' see PARA 229 note 6 (definition applied by the Education Act 2002 s 212(2), (3); Interpretation Act 1978 s 11). Reference should be made to the Education (Provision of Full-Time Education for Excluded Pupils) (England) Regulations 2007, SI 2007/1870, regs 3(3), 4(3)(b) (as amended SI 2014/3216); and PARA 522 notes 7, 9.

8 School Discipline (Pupil Exclusions and Reviews) (England) Regulations 2012, SI 2012/1033, reg 15(1)(b)(i). As to the meaning of 'term' see PARA 518 note 14.

9 School Discipline (Pupil Exclusions and Reviews) (England) Regulations 2012, SI 2012/1033, reg 15(1)(b)(ii). As to the meaning of 'National Curriculum test' see PARA 518 note 15.

10 School Discipline (Pupil Exclusions and Reviews) (England) Regulations 2012, SI 2012/1033, reg 15(1)(c)(i).

11 As to the meaning of 'relevant person' see PARA 518 note 5.

12 Ie under the School Discipline (Pupil Exclusions and Reviews) (England) Regulations 2012, SI 2012/1033, reg 14(3)(b): see PARA 519.

13 School Discipline (Pupil Exclusions and Reviews) (England) Regulations 2012, SI 2012/1033, reg 15(1)(c)(ii).

14 Subject to School Discipline (Pupil Exclusions and Reviews) (England) Regulations 2012, SI 2012/1033, reg 15(8) (see below), after being informed of the matters in reg 14(3)(a) (see PARA 519), the management committee must take the steps referred to in reg 15(2) and (3) (see the text to notes 15–21) within (1) 15 school days in the case of a permanent exclusion; an exclusion for a fixed period which would cause the pupil's total number of days of exclusion to exceed 15 school days in any term; or an exclusion where the pupil would, as a result of the exclusion, lose an opportunity to take a public examination or a National Curriculum test (reg 15(7)(a)); or 50 school days in the case of an exclusion for a fixed period where the pupil would, as a result of the exclusion, be excluded for a total of more than five school days but not more than 15 school days in any term; and the relevant person has made representations under reg 14(3)(b) (see PARA 519) (reg 15(7)(b)). Where a pupil has been excluded in circumstances in which the pupil would, as a result of the exclusion, lose an opportunity to take a public examination or a National Curriculum test, the management committee must (so far as it is reasonably practicable) take the steps referred to in reg 15(2) and (3) before the date on which the pupil is due to take the examination or test: reg 15(8).

15 School Discipline (Pupil Exclusions and Reviews) (England) Regulations 2012, SI 2012/1033, reg 15(3)(a). Where it falls to the management committee, in exercise of functions under reg 15 to establish any fact, any question as to whether that fact is established is to be decided on a balance of probabilities: see reg 19(b). As to the civil standard of proof see CIVIL PROCEDURE vol 11 (2009) PARA 775.

16 School Discipline (Pupil Exclusions and Reviews) (England) Regulations 2012, SI 2012/1033, reg 15(3)(b). See the cases in PARA 527 note 20.

17 School Discipline (Pupil Exclusions and Reviews) (England) Regulations 2012, SI 2012/1033, reg 15(3)(c)(i).

18 School Discipline (Pupil Exclusions and Reviews) (England) Regulations 2012, SI 2012/1033, reg 15(3)(c)(ii).

19 School Discipline (Pupil Exclusions and Reviews) (England) Regulations 2012, SI 2012/1033, reg 15(3)(c)(iii).

20 School Discipline (Pupil Exclusions and Reviews) (England) Regulations 2012, SI 2012/1033, reg 15(3)(d).

21 School Discipline (Pupil Exclusions and Reviews) (England) Regulations 2012, SI 2012/1033, reg 15(2). The management committee will not be relieved of the duty to take any step referred to reg 15(2) or (3) because it has not been taken within the period specified in reg 15(7) or (8) (see note 14): reg 15(10).

22 School Discipline (Pupil Exclusions and Reviews) (England) Regulations 2012, SI 2012/1033, reg 15(4)(a). As to the teacher in charge see PARA 428.

23 As to the meaning of 'local authority' see PARA 25 (definition applied by the Education Act 2002 s 212(1); Interpretation Act 1978 s 11).

24 School Discipline (Pupil Exclusions and Reviews) (England) Regulations 2012, SI 2012/1033, reg 15(4)(b).

25 School Discipline (Pupil Exclusions and Reviews) (England) Regulations 2012, SI 2012/1033, reg 15(5).

26 As to the meaning of 'home local authority' see PARA 518 note 18.

27 School Discipline (Pupil Exclusions and Reviews) (England) Regulations 2012, SI 2012/1033, reg 15(6)(a).

28 The notice in writing referred to in the School Discipline (Pupil Exclusions and Reviews) (England) Regulations 2012, SI 2012/1033, reg 15(6)(b), (1) may be given by (a) delivering it directly to the relevant person; (b) delivering it to the relevant person's last known address; or (c) sending it by first class post to the relevant person's last known address; and (2) unless the contrary is shown, will be taken to have been given (a) where first class post is used, on the second working day after the date of posting; or (b) where the notice is delivered, on the date of delivery: reg 15(11). As to the meaning of 'writing' see PARA 76 note 8. As to the meaning of 'working day' see PARA 527 note 29. As to the validity of notices see *R (on the application of P) v Haringey Borough Council* [2008] EWHC 2357 (Admin), [2009] ELR 49, [2008] All ER (D) 81 (Sep).

29 School Discipline (Pupil Exclusions and Reviews) (England) Regulations 2012, SI 2012/1033, reg 15(6)(b)(i).

30 School Discipline (Pupil Exclusions and Reviews) (England) Regulations 2012, SI 2012/1033, reg 15(6)(b)(ii). As to reviews see PARA 531 et seq.

31 As to the meaning of 'SEN expert' see PARA 527 note 32.

32 School Discipline (Pupil Exclusions and Reviews) (England) Regulations 2012, SI 2012/1033, reg 15(6)(b)(iii).

33 School Discipline (Pupil Exclusions and Reviews) (England) Regulations 2012, SI 2012/1033, reg 15(6)(b)(iv).

34 School Discipline (Pupil Exclusions and Reviews) (England) Regulations 2012, SI 2012/1033, reg 15(6)(b)(v).

35 School Discipline (Pupil Exclusions and Reviews) (England) Regulations 2012, SI 2012/1033, reg 15(6)(b)(vi).

36 School Discipline (Pupil Exclusions and Reviews) (England) Regulations 2012, SI 2012/1033, reg 15(6)(b)(vii).

37 As to unlawful discrimination under the Equality Act 2010 see PARA 9 et seq.

38 School Discipline (Pupil Exclusions and Reviews) (England) Regulations 2012, SI 2012/1033, reg 15(6)(b)(viii).

39 Ie the School Discipline (Pupil Exclusions and Reviews) (England) Regulations 2012, SI 2012/1033, reg 15(2)–(6): see the text to notes 14–38.

40 School Discipline (Pupil Exclusions and Reviews) (England) Regulations 2012, SI 2012/1033, reg 15(9)(a).

41 Ie made under the School Discipline (Pupil Exclusions and Reviews) (England) Regulations 2012, SI 2012/1033, reg 14(1)(b): see PARA 519.

42 School Discipline (Pupil Exclusions and Reviews) (England) Regulations 2012, SI 2012/1033, reg 15(9)(b).

43 School Discipline (Pupil Exclusions and Reviews) (England) Regulations 2012, SI 2012/1033, reg 15(9).

530. Functions of proprietor in relation to pupils excluded from an academy.
Where the proprietor[1] of an academy[2] in England[3] is informed[4] of: (1) the permanent exclusion[5] of a pupil[6]; (2) the exclusion of a pupil where, as a result of the exclusion, the pupil would be excluded for a total of more than 15 school days[7] in any term[8] or would lose an opportunity to take a public examination or a National Curriculum test[9]; or (3) the exclusion of a pupil where the pupil

would as a result of the exclusion be excluded for a total of more than five school days in any term[10] and the relevant person[11] makes[12] representations[13], the proprietor must[14]:

(a) consider the interests and circumstances of the excluded pupil, including the circumstances in which the pupil was excluded, and have regard to the interests of other pupils and persons working at the academy (including persons working at the academy voluntarily)[15];

(b) consider any representations about the exclusion made to the proprietor by or on behalf of the relevant person or the principal[16];

(c) take reasonable steps to arrange a meeting at which the exclusion is to be considered for a time and date when each of the following persons is able to attend: the principal[17]; the relevant person (and, where requested by the relevant person, a representative or friend of the relevant person)[18]; and, where requested by the relevant person, a representative of the local authority[19] (and, if applicable, the home local authority)[20];

(d) allow each of the first two persons described in head (c) above[21] to attend the meeting and to make representations about the exclusion[22]; and

(e) allow the third person described in head (c) above[23] to attend the meeting as an observer, unless the proprietor gives that person permission to make representations[24].

The proprietor must decide whether or not the pupil should be reinstated; and where it considers that the pupil should be reinstated, whether the pupil should be reinstated immediately or by a particular date[25]. If the proprietor decides that the pupil should be reinstated, it must without delay direct the principal accordingly[26]; and inform the relevant person and the local authority (and, if applicable, the home local authority) of its decision and the reasons for it in writing[27]. The principal must comply with a direction of the proprietor to reinstate the pupil[28]. If the proprietor decides not to reinstate the pupil it must without delay:

(i) inform the relevant person, the principal and the local authority (and, if applicable, the home local authority) of its decision and the reasons for it in writing[29]; and

(ii) in the case of a pupil who is permanently excluded, give the relevant person notice in writing[30] stating the following:

(A) that the exclusion is permanent[31];

(B) that the relevant person may apply for the proprietor's decision to be reviewed by a review panel[32];

(C) where the relevant person applies for a review, that the relevant person may require the proprietor to appoint a SEN expert[33] to advise the review panel[34];

(D) the role of the SEN expert in relation to a review[35];

(E) how an application for a review may be made and what the application must contain[36];

(F) where and to whom to send the application and the date by which the application must be received[37];

(G) that the relevant person may, at their own expense, appoint someone to make representations for the purpose of the review[38]; and

(H) that the relevant person may issue a claim under the Equality

Act 2010 where the relevant person believes that unlawful discrimination[39] has occurred, and the time within which such a claim should be made[40].

Where a pupil has been excluded in circumstances where the above provisions[41] do not apply; and the proprietor receives representations[42] from the relevant person about the exclusion, the proprietor must consider those representations[43].

1 As to the meaning of 'proprietor' see PARA 51 note 4 (definition applied by the Education Act 2002 s 212(2), (3); Interpretation Act 1978 s 11). Any proprietor of an academy should initially consult the Exclusions Guidance, as to which see PARA 540 note 13.

2 As to the meaning of 'academy' see PARA 517 note 5. As to academies generally see PARA 345 et seq.

3 The School Discipline (Pupil Exclusions and Reviews) (England) Regulations 2012, SI 2012/1033, apply only in relation to England: reg 1(2). See also PARA 518 note 3.

4 Ie under the School Discipline (Pupil Exclusions and Reviews) (England) Regulations 2012, SI 2012/1033, reg 23(3)(a): see PARA 520.

5 As to the meaning of 'exclusion' see PARA 517 note 4.

6 School Discipline (Pupil Exclusions and Reviews) (England) Regulations 2012, SI 2012/1033, reg 24(1)(a). As to the meaning of 'pupil' see PARA 20 note 4 (definition applied by the Education Act 2002 s 212(2), (3); Interpretation Act 1978 s 11). As to the power of a principal to exclude pupils see PARA 517.

7 As to the meaning of 'school day' see PARA 229 note 6 (definition applied by the Education Act 2002 s 212(2), (3); Interpretation Act 1978 s 11).

8 School Discipline (Pupil Exclusions and Reviews) (England) Regulations 2012, SI 2012/1033, reg 24(1)(b)(i). As to the meaning of 'term' see PARA 518 note 14.

9 School Discipline (Pupil Exclusions and Reviews) (England) Regulations 2012, SI 2012/1033, reg 24(1)(b)(ii). As to the meaning of 'National Curriculum test' see PARA 518 note 15.

10 School Discipline (Pupil Exclusions and Reviews) (England) Regulations 2012, SI 2012/1033, reg 24(1)(c)(i).

11 As to the meaning of 'relevant person' see PARA 518 note 5.

12 Ie under the School Discipline (Pupil Exclusions and Reviews) (England) Regulations 2012, SI 2012/1033, reg 23(3)(b): see PARA 519.

13 School Discipline (Pupil Exclusions and Reviews) (England) Regulations 2012, SI 2012/1033, reg 24(1)(c)(ii).

14 Subject to the School Discipline (Pupil Exclusions and Reviews) (England) Regulations 2012, SI 2012/1033, reg 24(8), after being informed of the matters in reg 23(3)(a) (see PARA 520), the proprietor must take the steps referred to in reg 24(2) and (3) (see the text to notes 15–25) within (1) 15 school days in the case of (a) a permanent exclusion (reg 24(7)(a)(i)); (b) an exclusion for a fixed period which would cause the pupil's total number of days of exclusion to exceed 15 school days in any term (reg 24(7)(a)(ii)); or (c) an exclusion where the pupil would, as a result of the exclusion, lose an opportunity to take a public examination or a National Curriculum test (reg 24(7)(a)(iii)); or (2) 50 school days in the case of an exclusion for a fixed period where (a) the pupil would, as a result of the exclusion, be excluded for a total of more than five school days but not more than 15 school days in any term (reg 24(7)(b)(i)); and (b) the relevant person has made representations under reg 23(3)(b) (see PARA 520) (reg 24(7)(b)(ii)). However, where a pupil has been excluded in circumstances in which the pupil would, as a result of the exclusion, lose an opportunity to take a public examination or a National Curriculum test, the proprietor must (so far as it is reasonably practicable) take the steps referred to in reg 24(2) and (3) before the date on which the pupil is due to take the examination or test: reg 24(8). The proprietor will not be relieved of the duty to take any step referred to in reg 24(2) or (3) because it has not been taken within the period specified in reg 24(7) or (8): reg 24(10).

15 School Discipline (Pupil Exclusions and Reviews) (England) Regulations 2012, SI 2012/1033, reg 24(3)(a). Where it falls to the proprietor, in exercise of functions under reg 24 to establish any fact, any question as to whether that fact is established is to be decided on a balance of probabilities: reg 28(b). As to the civil standard of proof see CIVIL PROCEDURE vol 11 (2009) PARA 775.

16 School Discipline (Pupil Exclusions and Reviews) (England) Regulations 2012, SI 2012/1033, reg 24(3)(b).

17 School Discipline (Pupil Exclusions and Reviews) (England) Regulations 2012, SI 2012/1033, reg 24(3)(c)(i).

18 School Discipline (Pupil Exclusions and Reviews) (England) Regulations 2012, SI 2012/1033, reg 24(3)(c)(ii).

19 As to the meaning of 'local authority' see PARA 25 (definition applied by the Education Act 2002 s 212(1); Interpretation Act 1978 s 11).

20 School Discipline (Pupil Exclusions and Reviews) (England) Regulations 2012, SI 2012/1033, reg 24(3)(c)(iii). As to the meaning of 'home local authority' see PARA 518 note 18.

21 Ie the persons described in the School Discipline (Pupil Exclusions and Reviews) (England) Regulations 2012, SI 2012/1033, reg 24(3)(c)(i), (ii).

22 School Discipline (Pupil Exclusions and Reviews) (England) Regulations 2012, SI 2012/1033, reg 24(3)(d).

23 Ie the person described in the School Discipline (Pupil Exclusions and Reviews) (England) Regulations 2012, SI 2012/1033, reg 24(3)(c)(iii).

24 School Discipline (Pupil Exclusions and Reviews) (England) Regulations 2012, SI 2012/1033, reg 24(3)(e).

25 School Discipline (Pupil Exclusions and Reviews) (England) Regulations 2012, SI 2012/1033, reg 24(2).

26 School Discipline (Pupil Exclusions and Reviews) (England) Regulations 2012, SI 2012/1033, reg 24(4)(a).

27 School Discipline (Pupil Exclusions and Reviews) (England) Regulations 2012, SI 2012/1033, reg 24(4)(b). As to the meaning of 'writing' see PARA 76 note 8.

28 School Discipline (Pupil Exclusions and Reviews) (England) Regulations 2012, SI 2012/1033, reg 24(5).

29 School Discipline (Pupil Exclusions and Reviews) (England) Regulations 2012, SI 2012/1033, reg 24(6)(a).

30 The notice in writing referred to in the School Discipline (Pupil Exclusions and Reviews) (England) Regulations 2012, SI 2012/1033, reg 24(6)(b), (1) may be given by (a) delivering it directly to the relevant person; (b) delivering it to the relevant person's last known address; or (c) sending it by first class post to the relevant person's last known address; and (2) unless the contrary is shown, will be taken to have been given (a) where first class post is used, on the second working day after the date of posting; or (b) where the notice is delivered, on the date of delivery: reg 24(11). As to the meaning of 'working day' see PARA 527 note 29. As to the validity of notices see *R (on the application of P) v Haringey Borough Council* [2008] EWHC 2357 (Admin), [2009] ELR 49, [2008] All ER (D) 81 (Sep).

31 School Discipline (Pupil Exclusions and Reviews) (England) Regulations 2012, SI 2012/1033, reg 24(6)(b)(i).

32 School Discipline (Pupil Exclusions and Reviews) (England) Regulations 2012, SI 2012/1033, reg 24(6)(b)(ii).

33 As to the meaning of 'SEN expert' see PARA 527 note 32.

34 School Discipline (Pupil Exclusions and Reviews) (England) Regulations 2012, SI 2012/1033, reg 24(6)(b)(iii).

35 School Discipline (Pupil Exclusions and Reviews) (England) Regulations 2012, SI 2012/1033, reg 24(6)(b)(iv).

36 School Discipline (Pupil Exclusions and Reviews) (England) Regulations 2012, SI 2012/1033, reg 24(6)(b)(v).

37 School Discipline (Pupil Exclusions and Reviews) (England) Regulations 2012, SI 2012/1033, reg 24(6)(b)(vi).

38 School Discipline (Pupil Exclusions and Reviews) (England) Regulations 2012, SI 2012/1033, reg 24(6)(b)(vii).

39 As to unlawful discrimination under the Equality Act 2010 see PARA 9 et seq.

40 School Discipline (Pupil Exclusions and Reviews) (England) Regulations 2012, SI 2012/1033, reg 24(6)(b)(viii).

41 Ie the School Discipline (Pupil Exclusions and Reviews) (England) Regulations 2012, SI 2012/1033, reg 24(2)–(6): see the text to notes 25–40.

42 Ie made under School Discipline (Pupil Exclusions and Reviews) (England) Regulations 2012, SI 2012/1033, reg 23(1)(b): see PARA 520.

43 School Discipline (Pupil Exclusions and Reviews) (England) Regulations 2012, SI 2012/1033, reg 24(9).

B. REVIEW OF EXCLUSION

531. Review of permanent exclusion of pupils from maintained schools.
Where the relevant person[1] applies for a review[2], the local authority[3] in England[4] must, at its expense (1) make arrangements for the review of the governing body's[5] decision not to reinstate[6] a pupil[7] who has been permanently excluded[8]; and (2) if requested by the relevant person, appoint, for the purpose of that review, a SEN expert[9] to provide impartial advice on how special educational needs[10] may be relevant to the decision to exclude the pupil permanently[11].

The local authority is not to take the steps above where the relevant person has not applied for a review within the specified[12] time limit[13].

Where the relevant person wishes that a SEN expert be appointed for a review, the request must be made in writing[14] to the local authority with, and at the same time as, the application for a review[15].

In exercising its functions[16], the review panel[17] must consider the interests and circumstances of the excluded pupil, including the circumstances in which the pupil was excluded, and have regard to the interests of other pupils and persons working at the school[18] (including persons working at the school voluntarily)[19].

In addition to the powers of the review panel under the Education Act 2002[20], the panel may:

(a)   direct the governing body to place a note on the pupil's educational record[21];

(b)   order that the local authority is to make an adjustment to the school's budget share[22] for the funding period[23] during which the exclusion occurs in the sum of £4,000 if, following a decision by the panel to quash the governing body's original decision, the governing body (i) reconsiders the exclusion and decides not to reinstate the pupil[24]; or (ii) fails to reconsider the exclusion within the specified[25] time limit[26].

The review panel's decision is binding on the relevant person, the governing body, the head teacher[27] and the local authority[28].

1   As to the meaning of 'relevant person' see PARA 518 note 5.
2   'Review' means review of a decision not to reinstate a pupil: School Discipline (Pupil Exclusions and Reviews) (England) Regulations 2012, SI 2012/1033: reg 2(1).
3   As to the meaning of 'local authority' see PARA 25 (definition applied by the Education Act 2002 s 212(1); Interpretation Act 1978 s 11).
4   The School Discipline (Pupil Exclusions and Reviews) (England) Regulations 2012, SI 2012/1033, apply only in relation to England: reg 1(2). See also PARA 518 note 3. As to the equivalent provision to reg 7 in relation to Wales see the Education (Pupil Exclusions and Appeals) (Maintained Schools) (Wales) Regulations 2003, SI 2003/3227, reg 7 (amended by SI 2010/1142) which involves an 'appeal'. As to the meanings of 'England' and 'Wales' see PARA 7 note 3.
5   As to the governing bodies of maintained schools in England see PARA 150 et seq.
6   'Reinstatement' is not defined in the Education (Pupil Exclusions and Appeals) (Maintained Schools) (Wales) Regulations 2003, SI 2003/3227 or its predecessor. Under the School Standards and Framework Act 1998 s 67 (repealed), 'reinstatement' was held to mean that the termination of the school-pupil relationship is reversed and the responsibilities and obligations of the school towards the pupil resumed: *R (on the application of L) v Governors of J School* [2003] UKHL 9, [2003] 2 AC 633, [2003] 1 All ER 1012, [2003] ELR 309 (decided under previous legislation).

     An independent review panel can no longer reinstate which was not the position with the former independent appeal panels. A parent or other 'relevant person' can firstly challenge an exclusion before the governing body (who can reinstate), then if the pupil is not reinstated, there is scope for a review before an independent review panel. If the review panel quashes or directs or recommends reconsideration the case goes back to the governing body who can reinstate, which the panel cannot do. As to the powers of the independent review panel see the School Discipline (Pupil Exclusions and Reviews) (England) Regulations 2012, SI 2012/1033, Sch 1 para 19(2); and PARA 539.

7   As to the meaning of 'pupil' see PARA 20 note 4 (definition applied by the Education Act 2002 s 212(2), (3); Interpretation Act 1978 s 11).

8   School Discipline (Pupil Exclusions and Reviews) (England) Regulations 2012, SI 2012/1033, reg 7(1)(a). The reference is to permanent exclusion from a maintained school. As to the meaning of 'exclude' or 'exclusion' see PARA 517 note 4. As to the meaning of 'maintained school' see PARA 517 note 2. See eg *P v Governing Body of a Primary School* [2013] UKUT 154 (AAC), [2013] EqLR 666 (allegations of discrimination in a permanent exclusion)

9   As to the meaning of 'SEN expert' see PARA 527 note 32. As to special educational needs generally see PARA 943 et seq.

10   See note 9.

11   School Discipline (Pupil Exclusions and Reviews) (England) Regulations 2012, SI 2012/1033, reg 7(1)(b).

12   Ie specified in the School Discipline (Pupil Exclusions and Reviews) (England) Regulations 2012, SI 2012/1033, Sch 1: see PARA 537.

13   School Discipline (Pupil Exclusions and Reviews) (England) Regulations 2012, SI 2012/1033, reg 7(2).

14   As to the meaning of 'writing' see PARA 76 note 8.

15   School Discipline (Pupil Exclusions and Reviews) (England) Regulations 2012, SI 2012/1033, reg 7(3).

16   Ie under the School Discipline (Pupil Exclusions and Reviews) (England) Regulations 2012, SI 2012/1033.

17   'Review panel' means a review panel constituted in accordance with the School Discipline (Pupil Exclusions and Reviews) (England) Regulations 2012, SI 2012/1033, Sch 1 (see PARA 538): reg 2(1).

18   As to the meaning of 'maintained school' see PARA 521 note 3.

19   School Discipline (Pupil Exclusions and Reviews) (England) Regulations 2012, SI 2012/1033, reg 7(4).

20   Ie under the Education Act 2002 s 51A(4): see PARA 517.

21   School Discipline (Pupil Exclusions and Reviews) (England) Regulations 2012, SI 2012/1033, reg 7(5)(a).

22   As to the meanings of 'budget share' and 'funding period' see PARA 517 note 13.

23   See note 22.

24   School Discipline (Pupil Exclusions and Reviews) (England) Regulations 2012, SI 2012/1033, reg 7(5)(b)(i).

25   Ie specified in the School Discipline (Pupil Exclusions and Reviews) (England) Regulations 2012, SI 2012/1033, reg 8(1); see PARA 532.

26   School Discipline (Pupil Exclusions and Reviews) (England) Regulations 2012, SI 2012/1033, reg 7(5)(b)(ii).

27   As to the meaning of 'head teacher' see PARA 86 note 4 (definition applied by the Education Act 2002 s 212(2), (3); Interpretation Act 1978 s 11).

28   School Discipline (Pupil Exclusions and Reviews) (England) Regulations 2012, SI 2012/1033, reg 7(6). An application for judicial review of the decision of a governing body to exclude a pupil is not disallowed by the existence of the right of appeal (or review): see *R (on the application of A) v Governing Body of K School* [2002] EWHC 395 (Admin), [2002] ELR 631, [2000] All ER (D) 173 (Mar) (decided under previous legislation on appeals rather than reviews) (judicial review may be justified in cases involving permanent exclusion or exclusion resulting in a pupil being unable to sit public examinations). However, see also *R (on the application of DR) v Head Teacher of St George's Catholic School, R (on the application of AM) v Governing Body of Kingsmead School* [2002] EWCA Civ 1822, [2003] LGR 371, [2003] ELR 104, where Simon Brown LJ said (obiter) at [45] that, except in very rare cases where a governing body is plausibly said to have acted quite improperly, or where the court's guidance on some real point of principle is required, the court's proper response to an application for judicial review of a governing body's decision is almost always to leave the pupil to his statutory remedy.

532. Reconsideration of exclusion from maintained school by governing body following a review. Where the review panel[1] (1) recommends that the governing body[2] reconsider a decision not to reinstate a pupil[3] who has been permanently excluded[4]; or (2) quashes the governing body's decision and directs the governing body to reconsider the matter[5], the governing body, within 10 school days[6] after notification[7] of the review panel's decision[8], must reconvene in order to reconsider the exclusion[9].

When the governing body has reconsidered its decision it must inform the relevant person[10], the head teacher[11] and the local authority[12] (and, if applicable, the home local authority[13]) of its reconsidered decision and the reasons for it without delay[14].

1 As to the meaning of 'review panel' see PARA 531 note 17.
2 As to the governing bodies of maintained schools in England see PARA 150 et seq.
3 As to the meaning of 'pupil' see PARA 20 note 4 (definition applied by the Education Act 2002 s 212(2), (3); Interpretation Act 1978 s 11).
4 School Discipline (Pupil Exclusions and Reviews) (England) Regulations 2012, SI 2012/1033, reg 8(1)(a). The reference is to permanent exclusion from a maintained school. As to the meaning of 'exclude' or 'exclusion' see PARA 517 note 4. As to the meaning of 'maintained school' see PARA 517 note 2.
5 School Discipline (Pupil Exclusions and Reviews) (England) Regulations 2012, SI 2012/1033, reg 8(1)(b).
6 As to the meaning of 'school day' see PARA 229 note 6 (definition applied by the Education Act 2002 s 212(2), (3); Interpretation Act 1978 s 11).
7 Ie notification under the School Discipline (Pupil Exclusions and Reviews) (England) Regulations 2012, SI 2012/1033, Sch 1 para 19: see PARA 539. Notification of the review panel's decision is taken to be given (1) where first class post is used, on the second working day after the date of posting; or (2) where the notice is delivered, on the date of delivery: reg 8(3). As to the meaning of 'working day' see PARA 527 note 29.
8 As to the review panel's decision see PARA 531.
9 School Discipline (Pupil Exclusions and Reviews) (England) Regulations 2012, SI 2012/1033, reg 8(1).
10 As to the meaning of 'relevant person' see PARA 518 note 5.
11 As to the meaning of 'head teacher' see PARA 86 note 4 (definition applied by the Education Act 2002 s 212(2), (3); Interpretation Act 1978 s 11).
12 As to the meaning of 'local authority' see PARA 25 (definition applied by the Education Act 2002 s 212(1); Interpretation Act 1978 s 11).
13 As to the meaning of 'home local authority' see PARA 518 note 18.
14 School Discipline (Pupil Exclusions and Reviews) (England) Regulations 2012, SI 2012/1033, reg 8(2).

533. Review of permanent exclusion of pupils from pupil referral units.
Where the relevant person[1] applies for a review[2], the local authority[3] in England[4] must, at its expense (1) make arrangements for the review of the management committee's[5] decision not to reinstate a pupil[6] who has been permanently excluded[7]; and (2) if requested by the relevant person, appoint, for the purpose of that review, a SEN expert[8] to provide impartial advice on how special educational needs[9] may be relevant to the decision to exclude the pupil permanently[10].

The local authority is not to take the above steps where the relevant person has not applied for a review within the specified[11] time limit[12].

Where the relevant person wishes that a SEN expert be appointed for a review, the request must be made in writing[13] to the local authority with, and at the same time as, the application for a review[14].

In exercising its functions[15], the review panel[16] must consider the interests and circumstances of the excluded pupil, including the circumstances in which the pupil was excluded, and have regard to the interests of other pupils and persons working at the unit (including persons working at the unit voluntarily)[17].

In addition to the powers of the review panel under the Education Act 2002[18], the panel may:

(a) direct the management committee to place a note on the pupil's educational record[19];

(b) order[20] that the local authority is to make an adjustment to the unit's budget share[21] for the funding period[22] during which the exclusion occurs in the sum of £4,000 if, following a decision by the panel to quash the management committee's original decision, the management committee (i) reconsiders the exclusion and decides not to reinstate the pupil[23]; or (ii) fails to reconsider the exclusion within the specified[24] time limit[25].

The review panel's decision is binding on the relevant person, the management committee, the teacher in charge[26] and the local authority[27].

1   As to the meaning of 'relevant person' see PARA 518 note 5.

2   As to the meaning of 'review' see PARA 531 note 2.

3   As to the meaning of 'local authority' see PARA 25 (definition applied by the Education Act 2002 s 212(1); Interpretation Act 1978 s 11).

4   The School Discipline (Pupil Exclusions and Reviews) (England) Regulations 2012, SI 2012/1033, apply in relation to England only: see reg 1(2). See also PARA 518 note 3. As to the equivalent provision to reg 16 in relation to Wales see the Education (Pupil Exclusions and Appeals) (Pupil Referral Units) (Wales) Regulations 2003, SI 2003/3246, reg 8 (amended by SI 2010/1142) which involves an 'appeal'. As to the meanings of 'England' and 'Wales' see PARA 7 note 3.

5   As to the management committee of a pupil referral unit see PARA 434. See also PARA 517 note 11.

6   As to the meaning of 'pupil' see PARA 20 note 4 (definition applied by the Education Act 2002 s 212(2), (3); Interpretation Act 1978 s 11).

7   School Discipline (Pupil Exclusions and Reviews) (England) Regulations 2012, SI 2012/1033, reg 16(1)(a). The reference is to permanent exclusion from a pupil referral unit. As to the meaning of 'exclude' or 'exclusion' see PARA 517 note 4. As to pupil referral units see PARA 427 et seq.

8   As to the meaning of 'SEN expert' see PARA 527 note 32. As to special educational needs generally see PARA 943 et seq.

9   See note 8.

10   School Discipline (Pupil Exclusions and Reviews) (England) Regulations 2012, SI 2012/1033, reg 16(1)(b).

11   Ie specified in the School Discipline (Pupil Exclusions and Reviews) (England) Regulations 2012, SI 2012/1033, Sch 1: see PARA 537.

12   School Discipline (Pupil Exclusions and Reviews) (England) Regulations 2012, SI 2012/1033, reg 16(2).

13   As to the meaning of 'writing' see PARA 76 note 8.

14   School Discipline (Pupil Exclusions and Reviews) (England) Regulations 2012, SI 2012/1033, reg 16(3).

15   Ie under the School Discipline (Pupil Exclusions and Reviews) (England) Regulations 2012, SI 2012/1033.

16   As to the meaning of 'review panel' see PARA 531 note 17.

17   School Discipline (Pupil Exclusions and Reviews) (England) Regulations 2012, SI 2012/1033, reg 16(4).

18   Ie under the Education Act 2002 s 51A(4): see PARA 517.

19   School Discipline (Pupil Exclusions and Reviews) (England) Regulations 2012, SI 2012/1033, reg 16(5)(a).

20   Ie after the coming into force of the Education Act 2011 s 50 which makes amendments to the School Standards and Framework Act 1998 s 45: see PARA 315.

21   As to the meanings of 'budget share' and 'funding period' see PARA 517 note 13.

22   See note 21.

23   School Discipline (Pupil Exclusions and Reviews) (England) Regulations 2012, SI 2012/1033, reg 16(5)(b)(i).

24   Ie specified in the School Discipline (Pupil Exclusions and Reviews) (England) Regulations 2012, SI 2012/1033, reg 17(1): see PARA 534.

25   School Discipline (Pupil Exclusions and Reviews) (England) Regulations 2012, SI 2012/1033, reg 16(5)(b)(ii).

26   As to the teacher in charge of a pupil referral unit see PARA 428.

27   School Discipline (Pupil Exclusions and Reviews) (England) Regulations 2012, SI 2012/1033, reg 16(6).

534. Reconsideration of exclusion from pupil referral unit by managing committee following a review. Where the review panel[1] (1) recommends that the management committee[2] reconsiders a decision not to reinstate a pupil[3] who has been permanently excluded[4]; or (2) quashes the management committee's decision and directs the management committee to reconsider the matter[5], the management committee, within 10 school days[6] after notification[7] of the review panel's decision[8], must reconvene in order to reconsider the exclusion[9].

When the management committee has reconsidered its decision it must inform the relevant person[10], the teacher in charge[11] and the local authority[12] (and, if applicable, the home local authority[13]) of its reconsidered decision and the reasons for it without delay[14].

1   As to the meaning of 'review panel' see PARA 531 note 17.
2   As to the management committee of a pupil referral unit see PARA 434. See also PARA 517 note 11.
3   As to the meaning of 'pupil' see PARA 20 note 4 (definition applied by the Education Act 2002 s 212(2), (3); Interpretation Act 1978 s 11).
4   School Discipline (Pupil Exclusions and Reviews) (England) Regulations 2012, SI 2012/1033, reg 17(1)(a). The reference is to permanent exclusion from a pupil referral unit. As to the meaning of 'exclude' or 'exclusion' see PARA 517 note 4. As to pupil referral units see PARA 427 et seq.
5   School Discipline (Pupil Exclusions and Reviews) (England) Regulations 2012, SI 2012/1033, reg 17(1)(b).
6   As to the meaning of 'school day' see PARA 229 note 6 (definition applied by the Education Act 2002 s 212(2), (3); Interpretation Act 1978 s 11).
7   Ie notification under the School Discipline (Pupil Exclusions and Reviews) (England) Regulations 2012, SI 2012/1033, Sch 1 para 19: see PARA 539. Notification of the review panel's decision is taken to be given (1) where first class post is used, on the second working day after the date of posting; or (2) where the notice is delivered, on the date of delivery: reg 17(3). As to the meaning of 'working day' see PARA 527 note 29.
8   As to the review panel's decision see PARA 533.
9   School Discipline (Pupil Exclusions and Reviews) (England) Regulations 2012, SI 2012/1033, reg 17(1).
10   As to the meaning of 'relevant person' see PARA 518 note 5.
11   As to the teacher in charge of a pupil referral unit see PARA 428.
12   As to the meaning of 'local authority' see PARA 25 (definition applied by the Education Act 2002 s 212(1); Interpretation Act 1978 s 11).
13   As to the meaning of 'home local authority' see PARA 518 note 18.

14   School Discipline (Pupil Exclusions and Reviews) (England) Regulations 2012, SI 2012/1033, reg 17(2).

535. Review of permanent exclusion of pupils from academies. Where the relevant person[1] applies for a review[2], the proprietor[3] in England[4] must, at its expense (1) make arrangements for the review of its decision not to reinstate a pupil[5] who has been permanently excluded[6]; and (2) if requested by the relevant person, appoint, for the purpose of that review, a SEN expert[7] to provide impartial advice on how special educational needs[8] may be relevant to the decision to exclude the pupil permanently[9].

The proprietor is not to take the above steps where the relevant person has not applied for a review within the specified[10] time limit[11].

Where the relevant person wishes that a SEN expert be appointed for a review, the request must be made in writing[12] to the proprietor with, and at the same time as, the application for a review[13].

In exercising its functions[14], the review panel[15] must consider the interests and circumstances of the excluded pupil, including the circumstances in which the pupil was excluded, and have regard to the interests of other pupils and persons working at the academy (including persons working at the academy voluntarily)[16].

In addition to the powers of the review panel under the Education Act 2002[17], the panel may:

(a) direct the proprietor to place a note on the pupil's educational record[18];

(b) order that the proprietor is to make a payment to the local authority in the sum of £4,000 if, following a decision by the panel to quash the proprietor's original decision, the proprietor (i) reconsiders the exclusion and decides not to reinstate the pupil[19]; or (ii) fails to reconsider the exclusion within the specified[20] time limit[21].

The review panel's decision is binding on the relevant person, the principal[22] and the proprietor[23].

1   As to the meaning of 'relevant person' see PARA 518 note 5.
2   As to the meaning of 'review' see PARA 531 note 2. As to whether exclusion decisions are amenable to judicial review see PARA 425.
3   As to the meaning of 'proprietor' see PARA 51 note 4 (definition applied by the Education Act 2002 s 212(2), (3); Interpretation Act 1978 s 11). Any proprietor of an academy should initially consult the Exclusions Guidance, as to which see PARA 540 note 13.
4   The School Discipline (Pupil Exclusions and Reviews) (England) Regulations 2012, SI 2012/1033, apply in relation to England only: see reg 1(2). See also PARA 518 note 3. There is no equivalent to reg 25 in Wales. As to the meanings of 'England' and 'Wales' see PARA 7 note 3.
5   As to the meaning of 'pupil' see PARA 20 note 4 (definition applied by the Education Act 2002 s 212(2), (3); Interpretation Act 1978 s 11).
6   School Discipline (Pupil Exclusions and Reviews) (England) Regulations 2012, SI 2012/1033, reg 25(1)(a). The reference is to permanent exclusion from an academy. As to the meaning of 'exclude' or 'exclusion' see PARA 517 note 4. As to the meaning of 'academy' see PARA 517 note 5.
7   As to the meaning of 'SEN expert' see PARA 527 note 32. As to special educational needs generally see PARA 943 et seq.
8   See note 7.
9   School Discipline (Pupil Exclusions and Reviews) (England) Regulations 2012, SI 2012/1033, reg 25(1)(b).
10 Ie specified in the School Discipline (Pupil Exclusions and Reviews) (England) Regulations 2012, SI 2012/1033, Sch 1: see PARA 537.
11 School Discipline (Pupil Exclusions and Reviews) (England) Regulations 2012, SI 2012/1033, reg 25(2).
12 As to the meaning of 'writing' see PARA 76 note 8.
13 School Discipline (Pupil Exclusions and Reviews) (England) Regulations 2012, SI 2012/1033, reg 25(3).
14 Ie under the School Discipline (Pupil Exclusions and Reviews) (England) Regulations 2012, SI 2012/1033.
15 As to the meaning of 'review panel' see PARA 531 note 17.
16 School Discipline (Pupil Exclusions and Reviews) (England) Regulations 2012, SI 2012/1033, reg 25(4).
17 Ie under the Education Act 2002 s 51A(4) (as modified): see PARA 517.
18 School Discipline (Pupil Exclusions and Reviews) (England) Regulations 2012, SI 2012/1033, reg 25(5)(a).
19 School Discipline (Pupil Exclusions and Reviews) (England) Regulations 2012, SI 2012/1033, reg 25(5)(b)(i).
20 Ie specified in the School Discipline (Pupil Exclusions and Reviews) (England) Regulations 2012, SI 2012/1033, reg 26(1): see PARA 536.
21 School Discipline (Pupil Exclusions and Reviews) (England) Regulations 2012, SI 2012/1033, reg 25(5)(b)(ii).
22 As to the meaning of 'principal' see PARA 517 note 5.
23 School Discipline (Pupil Exclusions and Reviews) (England) Regulations 2012, SI 2012/1033, reg 25(6).

536. Reconsideration of exclusion from academy by proprietor following a review. Where the review panel[1] (1) recommends that the proprietor[2] reconsiders a decision not to reinstate a pupil[3] who has been permanently excluded[4]; or (2) quashes the proprietor's decision and directs the proprietor to reconsider the matter[5], the proprietor, within 10 school days[6] after notification[7] of the review panel's decision[8], must reconsider the exclusion[9].

When the proprietor has reconsidered its decision it must inform the relevant person[10], the principal[11] and the local authority[12] (and, if applicable, the home local authority[13]) of its reconsidered decision and the reasons for it without delay[14].

1   As to the meaning of 'review panel' see PARA 531 note 17.
2   As to the meaning of 'proprietor' see PARA 51 note 4 (definition applied by the Education Act 2002 s 212(2), (3); Interpretation Act 1978 s 11).
3   As to the meaning of 'pupil' see PARA 20 note 4 (definition applied by the Education Act 2002 s 212(2), (3); Interpretation Act 1978 s 11).
4   School Discipline (Pupil Exclusions and Reviews) (England) Regulations 2012, SI 2012/1033, reg 26(1)(a). The reference is to permanent exclusion from an academy. As to the meaning of 'exclude' or 'exclusion' see PARA 517 note 4. As to the meaning of 'academy' see PARA 517 note 5.
5   School Discipline (Pupil Exclusions and Reviews) (England) Regulations 2012, SI 2012/1033, reg 26(1)(b).
6   As to the meaning of 'school day' see PARA 229 note 6 (definition applied by the Education Act 2002 s 212(2), (3); Interpretation Act 1978 s 11).
7   Ie notification under the School Discipline (Pupil Exclusions and Reviews) (England) Regulations 2012, SI 2012/1033, Sch 1 para 19: see PARA 539. Notification of the review panel's decision is taken to be given (1) where first class post is used, on the second working day after the date of posting; or (2) where the notice is delivered, on the date of delivery: reg 26(3). As to the meaning of 'working day' see PARA 527 note 29.
8   As to the review panel's decision see PARA 535.
9   School Discipline (Pupil Exclusions and Reviews) (England) Regulations 2012, SI 2012/1033, reg 26(1). Where it falls to the proprietor, in exercise of functions under reg 26 to establish any fact, any question as to whether that fact is established is to be decided on a balance of probabilities: reg 28(b). As to the civil standard of proof see CIVIL PROCEDURE vol 11 (2009) PARA 775.
10 As to the meaning of 'relevant person' see PARA 518 note 5.
11 As to the meaning of 'principal' see PARA 517 note 5.
12 As to the meaning of 'local authority' see PARA 25 (definition applied by the Education Act 2002 s 212(1); Interpretation Act 1978 s 11).
13 As to the meaning of 'home local authority' see PARA 518 note 18.
14 School Discipline (Pupil Exclusions and Reviews) (England) Regulations 2012, SI 2012/1033, reg 26(2).

537. Time limits and notices waiving right to review of exclusion. An application for a review[1], and any request that a SEN expert[2] be appointed for the review, must be made to the arranging authority[3] in England[4] within 15 school days[5] after the day on which the relevant person[6] is given notice in writing[7] of the responsible body's[8] decision under the appropriate provision[9].

However, where the relevant person (1) makes a claim under the Equality Act 2010 alleging that the exclusion amounts to unlawful discrimination[10]; and (2) has not applied for a review within the above time limit[11], then the period within which the relevant person must apply will commence from the date on which the discrimination claim is finally determined[12].

Any notice in writing given by the relevant person to the arranging authority which states that the relevant person does not intend to apply for a review will be final[13].

1   As to the meaning of 'review' see PARA 531 note 2.

2   As to the meaning of 'SEN expert' see PARA 527 note 32. As to special educational needs generally see PARA 943 et seq.

3   'Arranging authority' means (1) where the relevant school is a maintained school or a pupil referral unit, the local authority responsible for maintaining that school or unit; (2) where the relevant school is an academy, the proprietor of that academy; and 'relevant school' means the school from which a pupil is permanently excluded: School Discipline (Pupil Exclusions and Reviews) (England) Regulations 2012, SI 2012/1033, Sch 1 para 1(1). As to the meaning of 'maintained school' see PARA 517 note 2. As to pupil referral units see PARA 427 et seq. As to the meaning of 'pupil' see PARA 20 note 4 (definition applied by the Education Act 2002 s 212(2), (3); Interpretation Act 1978 s 11). As to the meaning of 'local authority' see PARA 25 (definition applied by the Education Act 2002 s 212(1); Interpretation Act 1978 s 11). As to the meaning of 'academy' see PARA 517 note 5. As to the meaning of 'proprietor' see PARA 51 note 4 (definition applied by the Education Act 2002 s 212(2), (3); Interpretation Act 1978 s 11). As to the meaning of 'exclude' or 'exclusion' see PARA 517 note 4.

4   The School Discipline (Pupil Exclusions and Reviews) (England) Regulations 2012, SI 2012/1033, apply in relation to England only: see reg 1(2). See also PARA 518 note 3. As to the equivalent provision to Schedule in relation to Wales see the Education (Pupil Exclusions and Appeals) (Maintained Schools) (Wales) Regulations 2003, SI 2003/3227, Schedule (amended by SI 2010/1142) which involves an 'appeal'. As to the meanings of 'England' and 'Wales' see PARA 7 note 3.

5   As to the meaning of 'school day' see PARA 229 note 6 (definition applied by the Education Act 2002 s 212(2), (3); Interpretation Act 1978 s 11). As to what is meant by 'school days' in the context of the previous legislation see *R (on the application of P) v Haringey Borough Council* [2008] EWHC 2357 (Admin), [2009] ELR 49, [2008] All ER (D) 81 (Sep).

6   As to the meaning of 'relevant person' see PARA 518 note 5.

7   As to the meaning of 'writing' see PARA 76 note 8.

8   'Responsible body' means (1) where the relevant school is a maintained school, the governing body of that school; (2) where the relevant school is a pupil referral unit, the management committee of that unit; (3) where the relevant school is an academy, the proprietor of that academy: School Discipline (Pupil Exclusions and Reviews) (England) Regulations 2012, SI 2012/1033, Sch 1 para 1(1). As to the governing bodies of maintained schools in England see PARA 150 et seq. As to pupil referral units see PARA 427 et seq. As to the management committee of a pupil referral unit see PARA 434. See also PARA 517 note 11.

9   School Discipline (Pupil Exclusions and Reviews) (England) Regulations 2012, SI 2012/1033, Sch 1 para 2(1). The reference to the appropriate provision is a reference to reg 6(6)(b) (see PARA 527), reg 15(6)(b) (see PARA 529) or reg 24(6)(b) (see PARA 530).

10   School Discipline (Pupil Exclusions and Reviews) (England) Regulations 2012, SI 2012/1033, Sch 1 para 2(2)(a). As to unlawful discrimination under the Equality Act 2010 see PARA 9 et seq. See eg *P v Governing Body of a Primary School* [2013] UKUT 154 (AAC), [2013] EqLR 666 (allegations of discrimination in a permanent exclusion); *X v Governing Body of a School (SEN)* [2015] UKUT 7 (AAC), [2015] ELR 133 (fixed-period exclusions and discrimination).

11   School Discipline (Pupil Exclusions and Reviews) (England) Regulations 2012, SI 2012/1033, Sch 1 para 2(2)(b). The time limit is that in Sch 1 para 1(1).

12   School Discipline (Pupil Exclusions and Reviews) (England) Regulations 2012, SI 2012/1033, Sch 1 para 2(2). For these purposes, a discrimination claim is 'finally determined' when all rights of appeal under the Equality Act 2010 have been exhausted: School Discipline (Pupil Exclusions and Reviews) (England) Regulations 2012, SI 2012/1033, Sch 1 para 2(3).

13   School Discipline (Pupil Exclusions and Reviews) (England) Regulations 2012, SI 2012/1033, Sch 1 para 2(4).

538. Constitution of review panels. A review[1] must be conducted by a review panel[2] constituted in accordance with the following provisions[3].

A review panel must consist of three or five members appointed by the arranging authority[4] from the following groups:

(1)   persons who are eligible to be lay members[5];

(2)   head teachers[6], or persons who have held that position during the last five years[7]; and

(3)   persons who are or have been a governor of a maintained school[8]; a member of a pupil referral unit management committee[9]; a director of the proprietor of an academy[10], provided they have served in that

capacity for at least 12 consecutive months within the last five years and have not been a teacher or a head teacher in any school during the last five years[11].

Members must be appointed to a review panel as follows:

(a) for a panel of three members, one from each of the three categories in heads (1) to (3) above[12];

(b) for a panel of five members: a person who is eligible to be a lay member (see below)[13]; two persons falling within head (2) above[14]; and two persons falling within head (3) above[15].

A person is eligible to be a lay member if the person has never worked in a school in a paid capacity (disregarding any service as a governor or as a paid volunteer)[16].

The following persons are disqualified from membership of the review panel for the purpose of that review:

(i) any member (or director) of the arranging authority or, if different, the responsible body[17];

(ii) the head teacher of the relevant school[18] (or any person who has held that position within the last five years)[19];

(iii) any person employed by the responsible body or the arranging authority (if different), other than the head teacher of a school other than the relevant school[20];

(iv) any person who has, or at any time has had, any connection with (i) the responsible body, the arranging authority (if different), the relevant school or the relevant person[21]; or (ii) the excluded pupil or the incident leading to the exclusion[22], of a kind which might reasonably be taken to raise doubts about that person's impartiality[23].

Review panel members must satisfy certain training requirements[24].

Where at any time after a review panel has begun a review any member of the panel becomes unable to continue as a member, the panel may continue with the review so long as the number of the remaining members is not less than three and the requirements of head (a) above are satisfied[25].

A review panel must be chaired by the person appointed as a lay member[26].

After a review panel has begun a review a panel member may not be substituted or replaced with a different panel member for any reason[27].

Where a review panel has begun a review and for any reason it ceases to be constituted in accordance with these provisions[28], the review must cease and a new review panel must be constituted to conduct the review afresh[29].

Review panel members and, if appointed, the SEN expert, must declare any known potential conflict of interest, whether pursuant to head (iv) above or otherwise, to the arranging authority before the review begins[30].

An arranging authority may appoint a clerk to advise the members of a review panel and the parties to a review on the procedure of a review and the law and statutory guidance relating to exclusions[31].

There are also provisions as to allowances for members of review panels[32], and as to indemnity[33].

1   As to the meaning of 'review' see PARA 531 note 2.
2   As to the meaning of 'review panel' see PARA 531 note 17.
3   School Discipline (Pupil Exclusions and Reviews) (England) Regulations 2012, SI 2012/1033, Sch 1 para 3(1). The reference is to the provisions of Sch 1 para 3.
    The School Discipline (Pupil Exclusions and Reviews) (England) Regulations 2012, SI 2012/1033, apply in relation to England only: see reg 1(2). See also PARA 518 note 3. As to the equivalent provision to Schedule in relation to Wales see the Education (Pupil Exclusions

and Appeals) (Maintained Schools) (Wales) Regulations 2003, SI 2003/3227, Schedule (amended by SI 2010/1142) which involves an 'appeal'. As to the meanings of 'England' and 'Wales' see PARA 7 note 3.

    The independence of appeal panels (ie under the previous legislation) was commented upon in *R (on the application of S) v Brent London Borough Council, R (on the application of T) v Head Teacher of Wembley High School, R (on the application of P) v Oxfordshire County Council Exclusion Appeals Panel* [2002] EWCA Civ 693, [2002] ELR 556, [2002] All ER (D) 277 (May); and see also, at first instance in the case of one of the appeals, *R (on the application of B) v Head Teacher of Alperton Community School, R (on the application of T) v Head Teacher of Wembley High School, R (on the application of C) v Governing Body of Cardinal Newman High School* [2001] EWHC 229 (Admin) at [70]–[72], [2002] LGR 132, [2001] ELR 359 per Newman J. As to procedural unfairness see *SA (By his litigation friend MA) v London Borough of Camden Independent Appeal Panel* [2013] EWHC 3152 (Admin), [2013] All ER (D) 288 (Oct).

4 As to the meaning of 'arranging authority' see PARA 537 note 3.

5 School Discipline (Pupil Exclusions and Reviews) (England) Regulations 2012, SI 2012/1033, Sch 1 para 3(2)(a). As to the meaning of 'person' see PARA 7 note 6.

6 'Head teacher' means (1) the head teacher of a maintained school; (2) the teacher in charge of a pupil referral unit or the acting teacher in charge; (3) the principal of an academy or the acting principal: School Discipline (Pupil Exclusions and Reviews) (England) Regulations 2012, SI 2012/1033, Sch 1 para 1(1). As to the meaning of 'head teacher' generally see PARA 86 note 4 (definition applied by the Education Act 2002 s 212(2), (3); Interpretation Act 1978 s 11). As to the meaning of 'maintained school' see PARA 517 note 2. As to the teacher in charge of a pupil referral unit see PARA 428. As to pupil referral units see PARA 427 et seq. As to the meaning of 'principal' see PARA 517 note 5. As to the meaning of 'academy' see PARA 517 note 5.

7 School Discipline (Pupil Exclusions and Reviews) (England) Regulations 2012, SI 2012/1033, Sch 1 para 3(2)(b).

8 School Discipline (Pupil Exclusions and Reviews) (England) Regulations 2012, SI 2012/1033, Sch 1 para 3(2)(c)(i). As to the governing bodies of maintained schools in England see PARA 150 et seq.

9 School Discipline (Pupil Exclusions and Reviews) (England) Regulations 2012, SI 2012/1033, Sch 1 para 3(2)(c)(ii). As to the management committee of a pupil referral unit see PARA 434. See also PARA 517 note 11.

10 School Discipline (Pupil Exclusions and Reviews) (England) Regulations 2012, SI 2012/1033, Sch 1 para 3(2)(c)(iii).

11 School Discipline (Pupil Exclusions and Reviews) (England) Regulations 2012, SI 2012/1033, Sch 1 para 3(2)(c).

12 School Discipline (Pupil Exclusions and Reviews) (England) Regulations 2012, SI 2012/1033, Sch 1 para 3(3)(a).

13 School Discipline (Pupil Exclusions and Reviews) (England) Regulations 2012, SI 2012/1033, Sch 1 para 3(3)(b)(i).

14 School Discipline (Pupil Exclusions and Reviews) (England) Regulations 2012, SI 2012/1033, Sch 1 para 3(3)(b)(ii).

15 School Discipline (Pupil Exclusions and Reviews) (England) Regulations 2012, SI 2012/1033, Sch 1 para 3(3)(b)(iii).

16 School Discipline (Pupil Exclusions and Reviews) (England) Regulations 2012, SI 2012/1033, Sch 1 para 3(4).

17 School Discipline (Pupil Exclusions and Reviews) (England) Regulations 2012, SI 2012/1033, Sch 1 para 3(5)(a). As to the meaning of 'responsible body' see PARA 537 note 8.

18 As to the meaning of 'relevant school' see PARA 537 note 3.

19 School Discipline (Pupil Exclusions and Reviews) (England) Regulations 2012, SI 2012/1033, Sch 1 para 3(5)(b).

20 School Discipline (Pupil Exclusions and Reviews) (England) Regulations 2012, SI 2012/1033, Sch 1 para 3(5)(c).

21 School Discipline (Pupil Exclusions and Reviews) (England) Regulations 2012, SI 2012/1033, Sch 1 para 3(5)(d)(i).

22 School Discipline (Pupil Exclusions and Reviews) (England) Regulations 2012, SI 2012/1033, Sch 1 para 3(5)(d)(ii).

23 School Discipline (Pupil Exclusions and Reviews) (England) Regulations 2012, SI 2012/1033, Sch 1 para 3(5)(d). Subject to Sch 1 para 3(8) (see below), a person is not to be appointed as the SEN expert for the purpose of a review if that person would be disqualified under Sch 1 para 3(5)(d) from appointment as a member of a review panel: Sch 1 para 3(7). As to the meaning of 'SEN expert' see PARA 527 note 32. As to special educational needs generally see

PARA 943 et seq. The following employees of an arranging authority are not, by reason only of that employment, disqualified under Sch 1 para 3(5)(d): (1) a head teacher; or (2) any employee appointed as a SEN expert for the purpose of the review: Sch 1 para 3(8).

24 School Discipline (Pupil Exclusions and Reviews) (England) Regulations 2012, SI 2012/1033, Sch 1 para 3(6). The training requirements are to be found in Sch 1 para 5 (see below).

A person satisfies the training requirements if during the two years before the review the person received sufficient information and instruction to know and understand:

    (1)   the requirements of legislation and statutory guidance governing exclusions (Sch 1 para 5(1)(a));

    (2)   the role of the chair of a review panel (Sch 1 para 5(1)(b));

    (3)   the role of the clerk to a review panel (see the text to notes 31) (Sch 1 para 5(1)(c));

    (4)   the relevant effect of the Equality Act 2010 (see PARA 9 et seq) (School Discipline (Pupil Exclusions and Reviews) (England) Regulations 2012, SI 2012/1033, Sch 1 para 5(1)(d));

    (5)   the effect of the Human Rights Act 1998 s 6 (see RIGHTS AND FREEDOMS vol 88A (2013) PARAS 24–26), and the need to act compatibly with human rights protected by that Act (School Discipline (Pupil Exclusions and Reviews) (England) Regulations 2012, SI 2012/1033, Sch 1 para 5(1)(e)); and

    (6)   the need for the review panel to observe procedural fairness and the rules of natural justice(School Discipline (Pupil Exclusions and Reviews) (England) Regulations 2012, SI 2012/1033, Sch 1 para 5(1)(f)).

An arranging authority that is required to make arrangements for a review must ensure that all review panel members and the clerk to the review panel (see the text to note 31) have received the information and instruction referred to in Sch 1 para 5(1) as necessary during the two years before the review: Sch 1 para 5(2).

25 School Discipline (Pupil Exclusions and Reviews) (England) Regulations 2012, SI 2012/1033, Sch 1 para 3(9).

26 School Discipline (Pupil Exclusions and Reviews) (England) Regulations 2012, SI 2012/1033, Sch 1 para 3(10).

27 School Discipline (Pupil Exclusions and Reviews) (England) Regulations 2012, SI 2012/1033, Sch 1 para 3(11).

28 Ie in accordance with the School Discipline (Pupil Exclusions and Reviews) (England) Regulations 2012, SI 2012/1033, Sch 1 para 3.

29 School Discipline (Pupil Exclusions and Reviews) (England) Regulations 2012, SI 2012/1033, Sch 1 para 3(12).

30 School Discipline (Pupil Exclusions and Reviews) (England) Regulations 2012, SI 2012/1033, Sch 1 para 3(13).

31 School Discipline (Pupil Exclusions and Reviews) (England) Regulations 2012, SI 2012/1033, Sch 1 para 4(1). A person who does not satisfy the training requirements of Sch 1 para 5 (see note 24) must not serve as a clerk to a review panel: Sch 1 para 4(2).

Where a clerk is appointed the clerk must:

    (1)   make reasonable efforts to circulate to all the parties to the review copies of relevant documents at least five school days before the start of the review (Sch 1 para 4(3)(a));

    (2)   make reasonable efforts to inform all the parties to a review that (a) they are entitled to make written representations for the purposes of the review; (b) they may attend the review; and (c) if they elect to attend, that they may make, either in person or through a representative, oral representations at the review (Sch 1 para 4(3)(b)(i)–(iii));

    (3)   provide to all parties details of those attending the review and their respective roles (Sch 1 para 4(3)(c));

    (4)   attend the review and ensure that minutes of the review are produced in accordance with any instructions provided by the review panel (Sch 1 para 4(3)(d));

    (5)   report to the arranging authority or the review panel as required on the discharge of the clerk's functions (Sch 1 para 4(3)(e));

    (6)   perform such other functions as may be determined by the arranging authority or the review panel from time to time (Sch 1 para 4(3)(f)).

For the purpose of head (1) above (ie Sch 1 para 4(3)(a)), 'relevant documents' include: (i) the responsible body's decision; (ii) the relevant person's application for a review; and (iii) documents to which the responsible body was required to have regard when making its decision: Sch 1 para 4(4). Where no clerk is appointed or present the arranging authority must exercise the functions in heads (1)–(4) above (ie Sch 1 para 4(3)(a)–(d): Sch 1 para 4(5). As to the meaning of 'school day' see PARA 229 note 6 (definition applied by the Education Act 2002 s 212(2), (3); Interpretation Act 1978 s 11).

As to the independence of the clerk see *R (on the application of S) v Head Teacher of C High School* [2001] EWHC Admin 513 at [29]–[37], [2002] ELR 73 per Richards J (decided under the previous legislation; dual role as clerk to the panel and legal services manager for the local authority); and as to the role of a legal clerk see *R (on the application of A (A Minor)) v Independent Appeal Panel for G College* [2005] EWHC 558 (Admin) at [13]–[16], [2005] ELR 490, [2005] All ER (D) 240 (Mar) per Bean J.

32 Where the relevant school is a maintained school or a pupil referral unit, for the purpose of the payment of financial loss allowance under the Local Government Act 1972 s 173(4) (see LOCAL GOVERNMENT vol 69 (2009) PARA 172), that provision applies to a member of a review panel as if the reference to the performance of an approved duty were a reference to the member's attendance at a meeting of a review panel: School Discipline (Pupil Exclusions and Reviews) (England) Regulations 2012, SI 2012/1033, Sch 1 para 6(1), (2). The Local Government Act 1972 s 174(1) (see LOCAL GOVERNMENT vol 69 (2009) PARA 174) applies in relation to a review panel as if the reference to payments at rates determined by the body in question were a reference to payments at rates determined by the local authority: School Discipline (Pupil Exclusions and Reviews) (England) Regulations 2012, SI 2012/1033, Sch 1 para 6(3).

33 An arranging authority required to make arrangements for a review, must indemnify the members of a review panel and any SEN expert appointed for a review against any reasonable legal costs and expenses which they reasonably incur in connection with any decision or action taken by them in good faith in pursuance of their functions in relation to the review: School Discipline (Pupil Exclusions and Reviews) (England) Regulations 2012, SI 2012/1033, Sch 1 para 7.

539.   Procedure on a review. The provisions below[1] set out the procedure on a review[2].

An application for a review[3] must be in writing[4] setting out the grounds on which a review is sought[5]; and must be made to the arranging authority[6] within the specified[7] time limit[8].

The review panel[9] must meet to consider a review on the date determined by the arranging authority[10]. The date so determined must not be later than the closing date for reviews[11].

For the purpose of fixing the time[12] of the review, the arranging authority must take reasonable steps to ascertain any times falling on or before the closing date for reviews when the following persons would be unable to attend: (1) a person who wishes, and would be entitled, to appear and make[13] oral representations[14]; (2) any SEN expert[15] appointed for the review[16]. When arranging for the review to take place, the arranging authority must, so far as it is reasonably practicable to do so, ensure that the review is fixed for a time when the above persons[17] are able to attend the review[18].

A review panel must allow the following persons, and any representative they instruct, to attend the review and to make representations: (a) the relevant person[19] (and, if requested by the relevant person, a friend of the relevant person)[20]; (b) the head teacher[21] of the relevant school[22]; and (c) the responsible body[23] and, if different, the arranging authority[24]. A review panel must consider written or oral representations made to it by the above persons[25] when determining a review[26]. Where the relevant school is an academy[27], if requested by the relevant person, a representative of the local authority[28] in which that academy is located (and, if applicable, the home local authority[29]) must be permitted to attend the review as an observer but may only make representations with the consent of the arranging authority[30].

A review panel may from time to time adjourn a review but, before doing so, must consider the effect of any adjournment on:

(i)   each of the parties to the review[31];

(ii)   any victim of the incident leading to the exclusion[32]; and

(iii)   where such person is not the relevant person the pupil[33]; or any parent of the pupil[34].

If the relevant person has requested the appointment of a SEN expert but the SEN expert is not in attendance, the relevant person may ask the review panel to adjourn the review to a later date or time so that the SEN expert, or an alternative SEN expert, may attend[35]. Where a relevant person asks the review panel to adjourn the review[36] as above the review panel must adjourn the review[37]. The review panel must ensure that the relevant person is aware of his right to request[38] an adjournment[39]. A review may be adjourned if the effect of the adjournment is that the review will not have concluded before the closing date for reviews[40].

Reviews must be heard in private except where the arranging authority directs otherwise[41].

Two or more reviews may be combined and dealt with in the same proceedings where the review panel considers that it would be fair and expedient to do so because the issues raised by the reviews are the same or connected[42]; and the parties to each review agree[43].

In the event of a disagreement between the members of a review panel, the review under consideration must be decided by a simple majority of the votes cast and, where the votes are tied, the chair of the review panel[44] is to have a second or casting vote[45].

Where a SEN expert is present the review panel must seek and consider the SEN expert's views on how special educational needs[46] may be relevant to the pupil's exclusion[47].

The SEN expert's functions in relation to the review are limited to advising the review panel, orally or in writing or both, impartially, of the relevance of special educational needs in the context and circumstances of the review but do not include making an assessment as to whether the pupil has special educational needs[48].

Upon conclusion of a review the review panel must without delay give notice of its decision in writing to:

(A)   the relevant person[49];
(B)   the responsible body[50];
(C)   the local authority[51]; and
(D)   if applicable, the home local authority[52].

The notice must include:

(aa)   the review panel's decision, indicating whether the review panel upholds the responsible body's decision[53]; recommends that the responsible body reconsiders its decision[54]; or quashes the responsible body's decision[55];
(bb)   the reasons for the review panel's decision[56];
(cc)   any order under the appropriate regulation[57]; and
(dd)   any information that must be recorded on the pupil's educational record[58].

Any other matters of procedure not provided for[59] are to be determined by the arranging authority[60].

Where it falls to the review panel[61] to establish any fact, any question as to whether that fact is established is to be decided on a balance of probabilities[62]. In reaching its decision the appeal panel must apply basic standards of fairness[63].

1   Ie the School Discipline (Pupil Exclusions and Reviews) (England) Regulations 2012, SI 2012/1033, Sch 1 paras 9–20.
2   School Discipline (Pupil Exclusions and Reviews) (England) Regulations 2012, SI 2012/1033, Sch 1 para 8. As to the meaning of 'review' see PARA 531 note 2.

The School Discipline (Pupil Exclusions and Reviews) (England) Regulations 2012, SI 2012/1033, apply in relation to England only: see reg 1(2). See also PARA 518 note 3. As to the equivalent provision to Schedule in relation to Wales see the Education (Pupil Exclusions and Appeals) (Maintained Schools) (Wales) Regulations 2003, SI 2003/3227, Schedule (amended by SI 2010/1142) which involves an 'appeal'. As to the meanings of 'England' and 'Wales' see PARA 7 note 3.

3 An application for a review is taken to be made (1) where first class post is used, on the second working day after the date of posting; or (2) where the notice is delivered, on the date of delivery: School Discipline (Pupil Exclusions and Reviews) (England) Regulations 2012, SI 2012/1033, Sch 1 para 1(2). As to the meaning of 'working day' see PARA 527 note 29.

4 As to the meaning of 'writing' see PARA 76 note 8.

5 School Discipline (Pupil Exclusions and Reviews) (England) Regulations 2012, SI 2012/1033, Sch 1 para 9(a).

6 As to the meaning of 'arranging authority' see PARA 537 note 3.

7 Ie the specified in the School Discipline (Pupil Exclusions and Reviews) (England) Regulations 2012, SI 2012/1033, Sch 1 para 2(1): see PARA 537.

8 School Discipline (Pupil Exclusions and Reviews) (England) Regulations 2012, SI 2012/1033, Sch 1 para 9(b).

9 As to the meaning of 'review panel' see PARA 531 note 17.

10 School Discipline (Pupil Exclusions and Reviews) (England) Regulations 2012, SI 2012/1033, Sch 1 para 10(1).

11 School Discipline (Pupil Exclusions and Reviews) (England) Regulations 2012, SI 2012/1033, Sch 1 para 10(2). 'Closing date for reviews' means the fifteenth school day after the day on which an application for a review is made: Sch 1 para 1(1). As to the meaning of 'school day' see PARA 229 note 6 (definition applied by the Education Act 2002 s 212(2), (3); Interpretation Act 1978 s 11).

12 Ie in accordance with the School Discipline (Pupil Exclusions and Reviews) (England) Regulations 2012, SI 2012/1033, Sch 1 para 10.

13 Ie in accordance with the School Discipline (Pupil Exclusions and Reviews) (England) Regulations 2012, SI 2012/1033, Sch 1 para 12: see the text to notes 19–30.

14 School Discipline (Pupil Exclusions and Reviews) (England) Regulations 2012, SI 2012/1033, Sch 1 para 11(1)(a).

15 As to the meaning of 'SEN expert' see PARA 527 note 32. As to special educational needs generally see PARA 943 et seq.

16 School Discipline (Pupil Exclusions and Reviews) (England) Regulations 2012, SI 2012/1033, Sch 1 para 11(1)(b).

17 Ie the persons described in the School Discipline (Pupil Exclusions and Reviews) (England) Regulations 2012, SI 2012/1033, Sch 1 para 11(1).

18 School Discipline (Pupil Exclusions and Reviews) (England) Regulations 2012, SI 2012/1033, Sch 1 para 11(2).

19 As to the meaning of 'relevant person' see PARA 518 note 5.

20 School Discipline (Pupil Exclusions and Reviews) (England) Regulations 2012, SI 2012/1033, Sch 1 para 12(1)(a). As to adult witnesses see *R (on the application of S) v Brent London Borough Council, R (on the application of T) v Head Teacher of Wembley High School, R (on the application of P) v Oxfordshire County Council Exclusion Appeals Panel* [2002] EWCA Civ 693 at [28], [2002] ELR 556, [2002] All ER (D) 277 (May). See also *R v Governors of St Gregory's RC Aided High School and Appeal Committee, ex p M* [1995] ELR 290, sub nom *R v Governors of St Gregory's RC Aided High School, ex p Roberts* (1995) Times, 27 January (decided under previous legislation); *R v Governors of Bacon's City Technology College, ex p W* [1998] ELR 488; *R v Independent Appeals Tribunal of Hillingdon Borough Council ex p Governing Body of Mellow Lane School* [2001] ELR 200.

21 As to the meaning of 'head teacher' see PARA 538 note 6.

22 School Discipline (Pupil Exclusions and Reviews) (England) Regulations 2012, SI 2012/1033, Sch 1 para 12(1)(b).

23 As to the meaning of 'responsible body' see PARA 537 note 8.

24 School Discipline (Pupil Exclusions and Reviews) (England) Regulations 2012, SI 2012/1033, Sch 1 para 12(1)(c).

25 Ie by the persons in the School Discipline (Pupil Exclusions and Reviews) (England) Regulations 2012, SI 2012/1033, Sch 1 para 12(1).

26 School Discipline (Pupil Exclusions and Reviews) (England) Regulations 2012, SI 2012/1033, Sch 1 para 12(2).

27 As to the meaning of 'academy' see PARA 517 note 5.

28 As to the meaning of 'local authority' see PARA 25 (definition applied by the Education Act 2002 s 212(1); Interpretation Act 1978 s 11).

29 As to the meaning of 'home local authority' see PARA 518 note 18.

30 School Discipline (Pupil Exclusions and Reviews) (England) Regulations 2012, SI 2012/1033, Sch 1 para 12(3).

31 School Discipline (Pupil Exclusions and Reviews) (England) Regulations 2012, SI 2012/1033, Sch 1 para 13(1)(a).

32 School Discipline (Pupil Exclusions and Reviews) (England) Regulations 2012, SI 2012/1033, Sch 1 para 13(1)(b).

33 School Discipline (Pupil Exclusions and Reviews) (England) Regulations 2012, SI 2012/1033, Sch 1 para 13(1)(c)(i). As to the meaning of 'pupil' see PARA 20 note 4 (definition applied by the Education Act 2002 s 212(2), (3); Interpretation Act 1978 s 11).

34 School Discipline (Pupil Exclusions and Reviews) (England) Regulations 2012, SI 2012/1033, Sch 1 para 13(1)(c)(ii). As to the meaning of 'parent' see PARA 7 note 6 (definition applied by the Education Act 2002 s 212(2), (3)).

35 School Discipline (Pupil Exclusions and Reviews) (England) Regulations 2012, SI 2012/1033, Sch 1 para 13(2).

36 Ie in pursuance of the School Discipline (Pupil Exclusions and Reviews) (England) Regulations 2012, SI 2012/1033, Sch 1 para 13(2).

37 School Discipline (Pupil Exclusions and Reviews) (England) Regulations 2012, SI 2012/1033, Sch 1 para 13(3).

38 See note 36.

39 School Discipline (Pupil Exclusions and Reviews) (England) Regulations 2012, SI 2012/1033, Sch 1 para 13(4).

40 School Discipline (Pupil Exclusions and Reviews) (England) Regulations 2012, SI 2012/1033, Sch 1 para 13(5).

41 School Discipline (Pupil Exclusions and Reviews) (England) Regulations 2012, SI 2012/1033, Sch 1 para 14.

42 School Discipline (Pupil Exclusions and Reviews) (England) Regulations 2012, SI 2012/1033, Sch 1 para 15(a).

43 School Discipline (Pupil Exclusions and Reviews) (England) Regulations 2012, SI 2012/1033, Sch 1 para 15(b).

44 As to the chair of the review panel see PARA 538.

45 School Discipline (Pupil Exclusions and Reviews) (England) Regulations 2012, SI 2012/1033, Sch 1 para 16.

46 As to special educational needs generally see PARA 943 et seq.

47 School Discipline (Pupil Exclusions and Reviews) (England) Regulations 2012, SI 2012/1033, Sch 1 para 17.

48 School Discipline (Pupil Exclusions and Reviews) (England) Regulations 2012, SI 2012/1033, Sch 1 para 18.

49 School Discipline (Pupil Exclusions and Reviews) (England) Regulations 2012, SI 2012/1033, Sch 1 para 19(1)(a).

50 School Discipline (Pupil Exclusions and Reviews) (England) Regulations 2012, SI 2012/1033, Sch 1 para 19(1)(b).

51 School Discipline (Pupil Exclusions and Reviews) (England) Regulations 2012, SI 2012/1033, Sch 1 para 19(1)(c).

52 School Discipline (Pupil Exclusions and Reviews) (England) Regulations 2012, SI 2012/1033, Sch 1 para 19(1)(d).

53 School Discipline (Pupil Exclusions and Reviews) (England) Regulations 2012, SI 2012/1033, Sch 1 para 19(2)(a)(i).

54 School Discipline (Pupil Exclusions and Reviews) (England) Regulations 2012, SI 2012/1033, Sch 1 para 19(2)(a)(ii).

55 School Discipline (Pupil Exclusions and Reviews) (England) Regulations 2012, SI 2012/1033, Sch 1 para 19(2)(a)(iii).

56 School Discipline (Pupil Exclusions and Reviews) (England) Regulations 2012, SI 2012/1033, Sch 1 para 19(2)(b).

57 School Discipline (Pupil Exclusions and Reviews) (England) Regulations 2012, SI 2012/1033, Sch 1 para 19(2)(c). The reference to the appropriate regulation is a reference to reg 7 (see PARA 531), reg 16 (see PARA 533) or reg 25 (see PARA 535).

58 School Discipline (Pupil Exclusions and Reviews) (England) Regulations 2012, SI 2012/1033, Sch 1 para 19(2)(d). See PARAS 94, 437.

59 Ie by the School Discipline (Pupil Exclusions and Reviews) (England) Regulations 2012, SI 2012/1033.

60 School Discipline (Pupil Exclusions and Reviews) (England) Regulations 2012, SI 2012/1033, Sch 1 para 20.

61 Ie in exercise of its functions for the purposes of the School Discipline (Pupil Exclusions and Reviews) (England) Regulations 2012, SI 2012/1033, reg 7 (see PARA 531), reg 16 (see PARA 533) or reg 25 (see PARA 535).

62 See the School Discipline (Pupil Exclusions and Reviews) (England) Regulations 2012, SI 2012/1033, regs 10(c), 19(c), 28(c). This principle is consistent with the line of authority which established that the standard of proof as regards the culpability of the excluded pupil for the act or acts in question is the balance of probabilities, although for grounds of exclusion to be established on the balance of probabilities, it must be distinctly more probable that the child did the act than that he did not: see *R (on the application of K) v Governors of the W School* [2001] ELR 311; *R v Governors of Dunraven School, ex p B* [2000] LGR 494, sub nom *R v Head Teacher and Independent Appeal Committee of Dunraven School, ex p B* [2000] ELR 156, CA (applying the test laid down by Lord Nicholls of Birkenhead in *Re H (Minors) (Sexual Abuse: Standard of Proof)* [1996] AC 563 at 566–567, [1996] 1 All ER 1 at 16–18, HL). See also *R (on the application of S) v Brent London Borough Council, R (on the application of T) v Head Teacher of Wembley High School, R (on the application of P) v Oxfordshire County Council Exclusion Appeals Panel* [2002] EWCA Civ 693, [2002] ELR 556, [2002] All ER (D) 277 (May); *R (on the application of S) v Head Teacher of C School* [2001] EWHC Admin 513, [2002] ELR 73; *R (on the application of O) v Independent Appeal Panel of the London Borough of Tower Hamlets* [2007] EWHC 1455 (Admin), [2007] All ER (D) 16 (Jun). In proceedings before an independent appeal panel (now review panel), a school is not required to prove that a pupil's confession was made voluntarily, notwithstanding the Police and Criminal Evidence Act 1984 s 76 (see CRIMINAL PROCEDURE vol 28 (2010) PARA 662 et seq): *R (on the application of M) v Independent Appeal Panel, Governing Body and Head Teacher of CH School* [2004] EWHC 1831 (Admin) at [12], [2005] ELR 38, [2004] All ER (D) 473 (Jul) per Newman J (distinguishing *R v Headteacher and Independent Approval Committee of Dunraven School, ex p B* above. The proceedings of an appeal panel (now a 'review panel') do not engage the Convention for the Protection of Human Rights and Fundamental Freedoms art 6 (right to a fair and public hearing: see RIGHTS AND FREEDOMS vol 88A (2013) PARA 243 et seq): *R (on the application of LG) v Independent Appeal Panel for Tom Hood School (Secretary of State for Children, Schools and Families, interested party)* [2010] EWCA Civ 142, [2010] ELR 291, [2010] All ER (D) 292 (Feb). See also PARA 3. As to the civil standard of proof see CIVIL PROCEDURE vol 11 (2009) PARA 775. It should be noted that the above cases were decided under the previous legislation so should be looked at with caution.

63 Appeal panels (now review panels) and governing bodies should be prepared to disregard anonymised statements of evidence if their use could lead to injustice: *R v Governors of Bacon's City Technology College, ex p W* [1998] ELR 488 (parents not given copies of witness statements relied upon by the school); *R (on the application of S) v Brent London Borough Council, R (on the application of T) v Head Teacher of Wembley High School, R (on the application of P) v Oxfordshire County Council Exclusion Appeals Panel* [2002] EWCA Civ 693 at [29], [2002] ELR 556, [2002] All ER (D) 277 (May); *R (on the application of T) v Head Teacher of Elliott School* [2002] EWCA Civ 1349, [2003] ELR 160, [2002] All ER (D) 537 (Jul). As to procedural unfairness see *SA (By his litigation friend MA) v London Borough of Camden Independent Appeal Panel* [2013] EWHC 3152 (Admin), [2013] All ER (D) 288 (Oct). There is no general rule that there must be full disclosure of all statements made by a witness whose evidence is being considered by a panel: *R (on the application of M) v Independent Appeal Panel, Governing Body and Head Teacher of CH School* [2004] EWHC 1831 (Admin), [2005] ELR 38, [2004] All ER (D) 473 (Jul) (distinguishing *R v Governors of Dunraven School, ex p B* [2000] LGR 494, sub nom *R v Head Teacher and Independent Appeal Committee of Dunraven School, ex p B* [2000] ELR 156, CA). Those carrying out the investigation should, having decided on the factual issues that need resolving and the inquiries that could reasonably resolve them, conduct a reasonably thorough investigation: *R v Camden London Borough Council and the Governors of the Hampstead School, ex p H* [1996] ELR 360, sub nom *R v Camden London Borough Council, ex p H (A Minor)* (1996) Times, 15 August, CA; *R v Roman Catholic Schools, ex p S* [1998] ELR 304. An appeal panel must take account of all relevant evidence: *R v Board of Governors and Appeal Committee of Bryn Elian High School, ex p Whippe* [1999] ELR 380. See also *R (on the application of S) v Oxfordshire School Exclusion Appeals Panel* [2005] EWHC 53 (Admin), [2005] ELR 533, [2005] All ER (D) 241 (Jan) (when deciding whether the appeal panel (now 'review panel') had reached a decision that was unlawful, irrational or perverse or contrary to the principles of natural justice the court had to look at the whole of the proceedings before the appeal panel); *R (on the application of D) v Independent Appeal Panel of Bromley London Borough Council* [2007] EWCA Civ 1010,

[2008] LGR 267, [2008] ELR 12. As to the principles of natural justice see JUDICIAL REVIEW vol 61 (2010) PARA 629 et seq. Again it should be noted that the above cases were decided under the previous legislation so should be looked at with caution.

C. GUIDANCE ON EXCLUSION

540. Guidance on the exclusion of pupils. In exercising their functions[1] under the provisions relating to the exclusion of pupils[2], the head teacher[3] or the governing body of a maintained school[4], the teacher in charge of a pupil referral unit[5], the management committee in regard to a pupil referral unit[6], the principal[7] of an academy[8], the proprietor[9] of an academy, the local authority[10], the review panel[11], and the SEN expert[12] must have regard to any guidance given from time to time by the Secretary of State[13].

1   As to the meaning of 'functions' see PARA 18 note 5 (definition applied by the Education Act 2002 s 212(2), (3); Interpretation Act 1978 s 11).
2   Ie under the Education Act 2002 s 51A(1), (2) (see PARA 517); or the School Discipline (Pupil Exclusions and Reviews) (England) Regulations 2012, SI 2012/1033. The equivalent provision to the Education Act 2002 s 51A for Wales is s 52 (see PARA 517). As to Wales see also note 8.
3   As to the meaning of 'head teacher' see PARA 86 note 4 (definition applied by the Education Act 2002 s 212(2), (3); Interpretation Act 1978 s 11).
4   As to the meaning of 'maintained school' see PARA 517 note 2. As to the governing bodies of maintained schools in England see PARA 150 et seq.
5   As to the teacher in charge of a pupil referral unit see PARA 428. As to pupil referral units see PARA 427 et seq.
6   As to the management committee of a pupil referral unit see PARA 434.
7   As to the meaning of 'principal' see PARA 517 note 5.
8   As to the meaning of 'academy' see PARA 517 note 5.
9   As to the meaning of 'proprietor' see PARA 51 note 4 (definition applied by the Education Act 2002 s 212(2), (3); Interpretation Act 1978 s 11).
10 As to the meaning of 'local authority' see PARA 25 (definition applied by the Education Act 2002 s 212(1); Interpretation Act 1978 s 11).
11 Ie a review panel constituted in accordance with the School Discipline (Pupil Exclusions and Reviews) (England) Regulations 2012, SI 2012/1033, reg 3, Sch 1: see PARA 538.
12 As to the meaning of 'SEN expert' see PARA 527 note 32. As to special educational needs generally see PARA 943 et seq.
13 See the School Discipline (Pupil Exclusions and Reviews) (England) Regulations 2012, SI 2012/1033, regs 9, 18, 27. As to the Secretary of State see PARA 58. The School Discipline (Pupil Exclusions and Reviews) (England) Regulations 2012, SI 2012/1033, apply in relation to England only: see reg 1(2). See also PARA 518 note 3. As to the equivalent provision to regs 9, 18, 27 in relation to Wales see the Education (Pupil Exclusions and Appeals) (Maintained Schools) (Wales) Regulations 2003, SI 2003/3227, reg 8 (amended by SI 2010/1142); and the Education (Pupil Exclusions and Appeals) (Pupil Referral Units) (Wales) Regulations 2003, SI 2003/3246, reg 9 (amended by SI 2010/1142). As to the meanings of 'England' and 'Wales' see PARA 7 note 3. The functions under the Education (Pupil Exclusions and Appeals) (Maintained Schools) (Wales) Regulations 2003, SI 2003/3227, and the Education (Pupil Exclusions and Appeals) (Pupil Referral Units) (Wales) Regulations 2003, SI 2003/3246, were originally vested in the National Assembly for Wales and are now exercisable by the Welsh Ministers by virtue of the Government of Wales Act 2006 s 162(1), Sch 11 paras 30, 32. As to the Welsh Ministers see PARA 59.
    As to guidance in relation to England see in particular 'Exclusion from maintained schools, academies and pupil referral units in England: A guide for those with legal responsibilities in relation to exclusion' (September 2012). For a consideration of the 2012 guidance in the context of the Education Act 2002 s 51A (as to which see PARA 517) and the School Discipline (Pupil Exclusions and Reviews) (England) Regulations 2012, SI 2012/1033 see *R (on the application of CR) v Independent Appeal Panel of the London Borough of Lambeth* [2014] EWHC 2461 (Admin), [2014] ELR 359. New guidance was issued in January 2015, but then withdrawn; at the date at which this volume states the law it is anticipated that updated guidance will be issued shortly.
    Any guidance given neither fetters an appeal panel's (now 'review panel's') discretion nor detracts from its independence as it is not directory; there is nothing in the statutory scheme

which blocks the application of the longstanding default principle that the common law will supplement procedures to the extent necessary to ensure that they operate fairly: *R (on the application of S) v Brent London Borough Council, R (on the application of T) v Head Teacher of Wembley High School, R (on the application of P) v Oxfordshire County Council Exclusion Appeals Panel* [2002] EWCA Civ 693 at [14]–[15], [2002] ELR 556, [2002] All ER (D) 277 (May). See also eg *SA (By his litigation friend MA) v London Borough of Camden Independent Appeal Panel* [2013] EWHC 3152 (Admin), [2013] All ER (D) 288 (Oct). One consequence is that the content of the guidance has not only to stay within and promote the statutory purposes but, at least since 2 October 2000, has also to be compliant with the Convention for the Protection of Human Rights and Fundamental Freedoms (Rome, 4 November 1950; TS 71 (1953); Cmd 8969): *R (on the application of S) v Brent London Borough Council, R (on the application of T) v Head Teacher of Wembley High School, R (on the application of P) v Oxfordshire County Council Exclusion Appeals Panel* above. Guidance which collapses the constitutional distinction between the adjudicative and the administrative (ie policy-making) functions of the state has been said (obiter) to be highly objectionable: *R (on the application of S) v Brent London Borough Council, R (on the application of T) v Head Teacher of Wembley High School, R (on the application of P) v Oxfordshire County Council Exclusion Appeals Panel* above.

(iv) Restraint and Search of Pupils

541. Power of members of staff to use force. A person who is, in relation to a pupil[1], a member of the staff[2] of any school[3] at which education is provided for the pupil[4], may use such force as is reasonable[5] in the circumstances for the purpose of preventing a pupil from doing (or continuing to do) any of the following[6], namely:

(1) committing any offence[7];

(2) causing personal injury to, or damage to the property of, any person[8] (including the pupil himself)[9]; or

(3) prejudicing the maintenance of good order and discipline at the school or among any pupils receiving education at the school, whether during a teaching session or otherwise[10].

This power may be exercised only where the member of the staff and the pupil are on the premises[11] of the school in question[12], or they are elsewhere and the member of the staff has lawful control or charge of the pupil concerned[13]. It does not authorise anything to be done in relation to a pupil which constitutes the giving[14] of corporal punishment[15]. The power is in addition to any powers otherwise[16] exercisable and is not to be construed as restricting what may otherwise[17] lawfully be done[18].

1   As to the meaning of 'pupil' see PARA 20 note 4 (definition applied by the Education and Inspections Act 2006 s 187(2), (3)).

2   As to the meaning of 'member of staff' see PARA 513 note 4.

3   As to the meaning of 'school' see PARA 91 (definition applied by the Education and Inspections Act 2006 s 187(2), (3)).

4   See the Education and Inspections Act 2006 s 93(2).

5   For a case where a teacher was found to have behaved unreasonably while trying to restrain a pupil, albeit in the context of a claim for compensation by the teacher for injuries sustained, see *R (Criminal Injuries Compensation Appeals Panel) v Shields* [2001] ELR 164 (claim for compensation refused on grounds that teacher lacked training in restraint methods, had failed to call for help, and had a natural advantage over the child). As to a teacher's duties towards pupils, and liability in respect of a breach of such duties, see PARAS 1087–1088.

6   As to the recording and reporting of the use of force by members of staff at school in England see the Education and Inspections Act 2006 s 93A; and PARA 542. As to the powers of members of staff to search pupils for weapons and prohibited items see PARAS 543–544.

7   Education and Inspections Act 2006 s 93(1)(a). 'Offence' includes anything that would be an offence but for the operation of any presumption that a person under a particular age is incapable of committing an offence: s 93(6). As to incapacity to commit offences see CHILDREN AND YOUNG PERSONS vol 10 (2012) PARA 1191 et seq; CRIMINAL LAW vol 25 (2010) PARA 36.

8 As to the meaning of 'person' see PARA 7 note 6.
9 Education and Inspections Act 2006 s 93(1)(b).
10 Education and Inspections Act 2006 s 93(1)(c). As to school discipline generally see PARA 509 et seq. As to the exclusion of pupils see PARA 517 et seq.
11 As to the meaning of 'premises' see PARA 62 note 19 (definition applied by the Education and Inspections Act 2006 s 187(2), (3)).
12 Education and Inspections Act 2006 s 93(3)(a).
13 Education and Inspections Act 2006 s 93(3)(b).
14 Ie within the meaning of the Education Act 1996 s 548: see PARA 545 note 3.
15 Education and Inspections Act 2006 s 93(4).
16 Ie apart from the Education and Inspections Act 2006 s 93.
17 Ie apart from the Education and Inspections Act 2006 s 93.
18 See the Education and Inspections Act 2006 s 93(5).

542. Recording and reporting of use of force by members of staff in England.
As from a day to be appointed the following provisions have effect[1].

The governing body[2] of a school in England[3] must ensure that a procedure is in place for:

(1) recording each significant incident in which a member of the staff[4] uses force on a pupil[5] for whom education is being provided at the school (a 'use of force incident')[6]; and

(2) reporting each use of force incident (except those where the pupil is aged 20 or over[7] or special provision is made[8]) to each parent of the pupil as soon as practicable after the incident[9].

The procedure must require that a record of a use of force incident is made in writing[10] as soon as practicable after the incident[11]. The governing body must take all reasonable steps to ensure that the procedure is complied with[12]; and must[13] have regard to any guidance issued[14] by the Secretary of State[15].

1 The Education and Inspections Act 2006 s 93A is added by the Apprenticeships, Skills, Children and Learning Act 2009 s 246 as from a day to be appointed: see s 269(4). At the date at which this volume states the law no such day had been appointed.
2 'Governing body', in relation to a school which is not a maintained school, means the proprietor of the school; and 'maintained school' means a community, foundation or voluntary school, a community or foundation special school, or a maintained nursery school: Education and Inspections Act 2006 s 93A(7) (as added: see note 1). As to the governing bodies of maintained schools in England see PARA 150 et seq. As to the meaning of 'school' see PARA 91; as to the meaning of 'proprietor' see PARA 51 note 4; and as to the meaning of 'maintained nursery school' see PARA 99 note 4 (definitions applied by the Education and Inspections Act 2006 s 187(2), (3)). As to the meaning of references to a community, foundation or voluntary school or a community or foundation special school see PARA 106.
3 As to the meaning of 'England' see PARA 7 note 3.
4 As to the meaning of 'member of staff' see PARA 513 note 4.
5 As to the meaning of 'pupil' see PARA 20 note 4 (definition applied by the Education and Inspections Act 2006 s 187(2), (3)). As to the power of members of staff to use force see PARA 541.
6 Education and Inspections Act 2006 s 93A(1)(a) (as added: see note 1).
7 As to the time at which a person attains a particular age see PARA 7 note 6.
8 Ie where provision made under the Education and Inspections Act 2006 s 93A(5) applies: see s 93A(1)(b) (as added: see note 1). A procedure under s 93A(1) must include provision to the effect: (1) that a person ('R') who would otherwise be required by the procedure to report an incident to a parent must not report it to that parent if it appears to R that doing so would be likely to result in significant harm to the pupil (s 93A(5)(a) (as so added)); and (2) that if it appears to R that there is no parent of the pupil to whom R could report the incident without that being likely to result in significant harm to the pupil, R must report the incident to the local authority (within the meaning of the Children Act 1989: see PARA 453 note 1) within whose area the pupil is ordinarily resident (s 93A(5)(b) (as so added)). In deciding for the purposes of provision made under s 93A(5) whether reporting an incident to a parent would be likely to result in significant harm to the pupil, R must have regard to any guidance issued by the Secretary of State about the meaning of 'significant harm' for those purposes: s 93A(6) (as so

added). As to the meaning of 'person' see PARA 7 note 6. 'Parent', in relation to a pupil, has the meaning given by the Education Act 1996 s 576 (see PARA 7 note 6) in relation to a child or young person, but includes a local authority which provides accommodation for the pupil under the Children Act 1989 s 20 (see CHILDREN AND YOUNG PERSONS vol 10 (2012) PARAS 840–842): Education and Inspections Act 2006 s 93A(7) (as so added). As to the meanings of 'child' and 'young person' see PARA 7 note 6 (definitions applied by s 187(2), (3)). As to the Secretary of State see PARA 58.

As to the publication of guidance see the Education Act 1996 s 571 (applied by the Education and Inspections Act 2006 s 187(2), (3)); and PARA 60. See in particular 'Use of reasonable force in schools: Advice for headteachers, staff and governing bodies' (July 2013) which is said to apply to all schools including academies (as to which see PARA 345 et seq). It should be noted that there has been a change of emphasis in regard to reporting to parents, the Advice considering that 'it is up to schools to decide whether it is appropriate to report the use of force to parents'.

9   Education and Inspections Act 2006 s 93A(1)(b) (as added: see note 1).
10 As to the meaning of 'writing' see PARA 76 note 8.
11 Education and Inspections Act 2006 s 93A(3) (as added: see note 1).
12 Education and Inspections Act 2006 s 93A(2) (as added: see note 1).
13 Ie in discharging its duty under the Education and Inspections Act 2006 s 93A(1): see the text to notes 2–9.
14 Ie for the purposes of the Education and Inspections Act 2006 s 93A(1): see the text to notes 2–9.
15 Education and Inspections Act 2006 s 93A(4) (as added: see note 1).

543.   Power of members of staff to search pupils for weapons in Wales. A member of the staff[1] of a school in Wales[2] who has reasonable grounds for suspecting that a pupil at the school may have with him or in his possessions[3] (1) an article[4] which has a blade or is sharply pointed[5], or (2) an offensive weapon[6], may search that pupil or his possessions for such articles and weapons[7]. Such a search may be carried out only where the member of the staff and the pupil are on the premises[8] of the school[9], or they are elsewhere and the member of the staff has lawful control or charge of the pupil[10]; and a pupil's possessions may not be searched except in his presence and in the presence of another member of the staff[11].

A person may carry out a search under these provisions only if (a) he is the head teacher of the school[12], or (b) he has been authorised by the head teacher to carry out the search[13]. A person who carries out a search of a pupil may not require the pupil to remove any clothing other than outer clothing[14]; must be of the same sex as the pupil[15]; and may carry out the search only in the presence of another member of the staff who is also of the same sex as the pupil[16].

If, in the course of a search, the person carrying out the search finds anything which he has reasonable grounds for suspecting constitutes falls within head (1) or (2) above[17], or any other thing which he has reasonable grounds for suspecting is evidence in relation to an offence[18], he may seize and retain it[19].

A person who exercises a power under the above provisions may use such force as is reasonable in the circumstances for exercising that power[20]. The powers conferred by those provisions are in addition to any powers otherwise[21] exercisable by the member of the staff in question and are not to be construed as restricting such powers[22].

1   'Member of the staff', in relation to a school, means: (1) any teacher who works at the school; and (2) any other person who, with the authority of the head teacher, has lawful control or charge of pupils for whom education is being provided at the school: Education Act 1996 s 550AA(12) (s 550AA added by the Violent Crime Reduction Act 2006 s 45). As to the meaning of 'school' see PARA 91. As to the meaning of 'head teacher' see PARA 86 note 4. As to the meaning of 'pupil' see PARA 20 note 4.
2   As to the meaning of 'Wales' see PARA 7 note 3.

3 'Possessions', in relation to a pupil of a school, includes any goods over which he has or appears to have control: Education Act 1996 s 550AA(12) (as added: see note 1).

4 Ie an article to which the Criminal Justice Act 1988 s 139 applies: see CRIMINAL LAW vol 26 (2010) PARA 654.

5 See the Education Act 1996 s 550AA(1)(a) (as added: see note 1).

6 See the Education Act 1996 s 550AA(1)(b) (as added: see note 1). An 'offensive weapon' is one within the meaning of the Prevention of Crime Act 1953 (see CRIMINAL LAW vol 26 (2010) PARA 653): see the Education Act 1996 s 550AA(1)(b) (as so added).

7 Education Act 1996 s 550AA(1) (as added (see note 1); and amended by the Apprenticeships, Skills, Children and Learning Act 2009 s 243(1), (2)).

8 As to the meaning of 'premises' see PARA 62 note 19.

9 Education Act 1996 s 550AA(2)(a) (as added: see note 1).

10 Education Act 1996 s 550AA(2)(b) (as added: see note 1).

11 Education Act 1996 s 550AA(6) (as added: see note 1).

12 Education Act 1996 s 550AA(3)(a) (as added: see note 1).

13 Education Act 1996 s 550AA(3)(b) (as added: see note 1). An authorisation for the purposes of s 550AA(3)(b) may be given either in relation to a particular search or generally in relation to searches under s 550AA or to a particular description of such searches: s 550AA(11) (as so added). Nothing in any enactment, instrument or agreement is to be construed as authorising a head teacher of a school in Wales to require a person other than a member of the security staff of the school to carry out a search under s 550AA: s 550AA(4) (as so added; and amended by the Apprenticeships, Skills, Children and Learning Act 2009 s 243(1), (2)). 'Member of the security staff' means a member of the staff whose work at the school consists wholly or mainly of security-related activities: Education Act 1996 s 550AA(12) (as so added).

14 Education Act 1996 s 550AA(5)(a) (as added: see note 1). 'Outer clothing' means (1) any item of clothing that is being worn otherwise than wholly next to the skin or immediately over a garment being worn as underwear; or (2) a hat, shoes, boots, gloves or a scarf: s 550AA(12) (as so added). As to the meaning of 'clothing' see PARA 482 note 2.

15 Education Act 1996 s 550AA(5)(b) (as added: see note 1).

16 Education Act 1996 s 550AA(5)(c) (as added: see note 1).

17 Education Act 1996 s 550AA(7)(a) (as added: see note 1).

18 Education Act 1996 s 550AA(7)(b) (as added: see note 1).

19 Education Act 1996 s 550AA(7) (as added: see note 1). A person who seizes anything under s 550AA(7) must deliver it to a police constable as soon as reasonably practicable: s 550AA(9) (as so added). The Police (Property) Act 1897 (disposal of property in the possession of the police: see POLICE AND INVESTIGATORY POWERS vol 84A (2013) PARA 635 et seq) applies to property which has come into the possession of a police constable under the Education Act 1996 s 550AA as it applies to property which has come into the possession of the police in the circumstances mentioned in the Police (Property) Act 1897: Education Act 1996 s 550AA(10) (as so added). As to the office of constable see POLICE AND INVESTIGATORY POWERS vol 84 (2013) PARA 1 et seq.

20 Education Act 1996 s 550AA(8) (as added: see note 1). For a case in which consideration was given to the reasonableness of a teacher's actions while trying to restrain a pupil, albeit in the context of a claim for compensation by the teacher for injuries sustained, see *R (Criminal Injuries Compensation Appeals Panel) v Shields* [2001] ELR 164. As to a teacher's duties towards pupils, and liability in respect of a breach of such duties, see PARAS 1087–1088.

21 Ie apart from the Education Act 1996 s 550AA.

22 Education Act 1996 s 550AA(13) (as added: see note 1). As to the power of members of staff to use force see PARA 541.

544. Power of members of staff to search pupils for prohibited items in England. Where a member of staff[1] of a school in England[2] has reasonable grounds for suspecting that a pupil at the school may have a prohibited item[3] with him or her or in his or her possessions[4], and is a qualifying person[5], the member of staff may search the pupil or the pupil's possessions for that item[6]. A pupil's possessions may not be searched except in the presence of the pupil[7] and another member of staff unless a certain condition is satisfied[8].

A search may be carried out only where the member of staff and the pupil are on the premises[9] of the school[10], or they are elsewhere and the member of staff has lawful control or charge of the pupil[11]. A person exercising the power of search[12] may use such force as is reasonable in the circumstances for exercising that power[13]. A person carrying out a search may not require the pupil to remove any clothing other than outer clothing[14]; must be of the same sex as the pupil unless a certain condition is satisfied[15]; may carry out the search only in the presence of another member of staff unless that same condition is satisfied[16]; and must ensure that the other member of staff is of the same sex as the pupil if it is reasonably practicable to do so[17].

A person carrying out a search may seize any of the following found in the course of the search[18]:

(1)   anything which that person has reasonable grounds for suspecting is a prohibited item[19];

(2)   any other thing which that person has reasonable grounds for suspecting is evidence in relation to an offence[20];

and may in regard to certain matters[21] use such force as is reasonable in the circumstances[22].

The powers conferred by the above provisions[23] are in addition to any powers otherwise[24] exercisable by the member of staff in question and are not to be construed as restricting such powers[25]. Where a person seizes, retains or disposes of[26] certain items[27], and proves that the seizure, retention or disposal was lawful[28], that person is not liable in any proceedings in respect of the seizure, retention or disposal[29], or any damage or loss which arises in consequence of it[30]. In addition where a person erases data or a file from an electronic device[31] and proves that the erasure was lawful[32], that person is similarly not liable in any proceedings in respect of the erasure[33], or any damage or loss which arises in consequence of it[34].

1   'Member of staff', in relation to a school, means: (1) any teacher who works at the school; and (2) any other person who, with the authority of the head teacher, has lawful control or charge of pupils for whom education is being provided at the school: Education Act 1996 s 550ZA(5) (ss 550ZA–550ZD added by the Apprenticeships, Skills, Children and Learning Act 2009 s 242(1)). As to the meaning of 'school' see PARA 91. As to the meaning of 'head teacher' see PARA 86 note 4. As to the meaning of 'pupil' see PARA 20 note 4.
2   As to the meaning of 'England' see PARA 7 note 3.
3   Each of the following is a 'prohibited item':
    (1)   an article to which the Criminal Justice Act 1988 s 139 applies (knives and blades etc: see CRIMINAL LAW vol 26 (2010) PARA 654) (Education Act 1996 s 550ZA(3)(a) (as added: see note 1));
    (2)   an offensive weapon, within the meaning of the Prevention of Crime Act 1953 (see CRIMINAL LAW vol 26 (2010) PARA 653) (Education Act 1996 s 550ZA(3)(b) (as so added));
    (3)   alcohol, within the meaning of the Licensing Act 2003 s 191 (see LICENSING AND GAMBLING vol 67 (2008) PARA 30) (Education Act 1996 s 550ZA(3)(c) (as so added));
    (4)   a controlled drug, within the meaning of the Misuse of Drugs Act 1971 s 2 (see MEDICAL PRODUCTS AND DRUGS vol 75 (2013) PARA 481), which s 5(1) of that Act (see CRIMINAL LAW vol 26 (2010) PARA 723) makes it unlawful for the pupil to have in his possession (Education Act 1996 s 550ZA(3)(d) (as so added));
    (5)   a stolen article (s 550ZA(3)(e) (as so added));
    (6)   an article that the member of staff reasonably suspects has been, or is likely to be, used to commit an offence, or to cause personal injury to, or damage to the property of, any person (including the pupil) (s 550ZA(3)(ea) (added by the Education Act 2011 s 2(1), (2)(a))
    (7)   an article of a kind specified in regulations (Education 1996 s 550ZA(3)(f) (as so added));
    (8)   any other item which the school rules identify as an item for which a search may be made (s 550ZA(g) (added by the Education Act 2011 s 2(1), (2)(b)).
In head (5) above 'stolen', in relation to an article, has the same meaning as it has by virtue of the Theft Act 1968 s 24 (see CRIMINAL LAW vol 25 (2010) PARA 299) in the provisions of that Act relating to goods which have been stolen: see the Education Act 1996 s 550ZA(4) (as so

added). In head (6) above, 'offence' includes anything that would be an offence but for the operation of any presumption that a person under a particular age is incapable of committing an offence: s 550ZA(4A) (s 550ZA(4A)–(4C) added by the Education Act 2011 s 2(1), (2)(c)). In head (8) above, the 'school rules' means (a) in the case of a maintained school or a non-maintained special school, rules in force at the school that are made under measures determined and publicised by the head teacher under the Education and Inspections Act 2006 s 89 (see PARA 510); (b) in the case of any other school, measures relating to discipline in the school that are determined and publicised in accordance with regulations: Education Act 1996 s 550ZA(4B) (as so added). In head (a) above 'maintained school' means a community, foundation or voluntary school, a community or foundation special school, a maintained nursery school, or a pupil referral unit; and 'non-maintained special school' means a school that is approved under the Education Act 1996 s 342 (see PARAS 1042, 1043): s 550ZA(4C) (as so added). As to community, foundation or voluntary schools, community or foundation special schools see PARA 106. As to the meaning of 'maintained nursery school' see PARA 99 note 4. As to pupil referral units see PARA 427 et seq. 'Regulations' means regulations made by the Secretary of State: s 579(1). As to the Secretary of State see PARA 58. Tobacco and cigarette papers, a firework and a pornographic image are articles each of which is a prohibited item for the purposes of the Education Act 1996 ss 550ZA, 550ZC: Schools (Specification and Disposal of Articles) Regulations 2012, SI 2012/951, reg 3. 'Tobacco' includes the items listed in the Children and Young Persons Act 1933 s 7(5) (see CHILDREN AND YOUNG PERSONS vol 9 (2012) PARA 656); 'firework' means a device within the meaning of the Fireworks Act 2003 s 1 (see EXPLOSIVES vol 47 (2014) PARA 461); 'pornographic image' means an article containing an image of such a nature that it must reasonably be assumed to have been produced solely or principally for the purpose of sexual arousal; and 'image' means (i) a moving or still image, produced by any means, or (ii) data, stored by any means, which is capable of conversion into an image within head (i) above: Schools (Specification and Disposal of Articles) Regulations 2012, SI 2012/951, reg 2. As to the disposal of such articles see reg 4. As to regulations setting out the processes that the principal of an academy school or alternative provision academy must follow where they wish to determine measures that identify items for which a pupil may be searched without the pupil's consent, see the School Behaviour (Determination and Publicising of Measures in Academies) Regulations 2012, SI 2012/619, which were made under the Education Act 1996 s 550ZA(4B)(b) (see head (b) above). As to the meaning of 'academy school' see PARA 346 note 12. As to the meaning of 'alternative provision academy' see PARA 346 note 14.

4   Education Act 1996 s 550ZA(1)(a) (as added: see note 1). 'Possessions', in relation to a pupil, includes any goods over which he or she has or appears to have control: see s 550ZA(5) (as so added).

5   Ie a person who falls within the Education Act 1996 s 550ZB(1): see s 550ZA(1)(b) (as added: see note 1). A person may carry out a search under s 550ZA only if that person (1) is the head teacher of the school (s 550ZB(1)(a) (as so added)); or (2) has been authorised by the head teacher to carry out the search (s 550ZB(1)(b) (as so added)). An authorisation for the purposes of head (2) above may be given in relation to (a) searches under s 550ZA generally (s 550ZB(2)(a) (as so added)); (b) a particular search under that section (s 550ZB(2)(b) (as so added)); (c) a particular description of searches under that section (s 550ZB(2)(c) (as so added)). Nothing in any enactment, instrument or agreement is to be construed as authorising a head teacher of a school in England to require a person other than a member of the security staff of the school to carry out a search under s 550ZA: s 550ZB(3) (as so added). 'Member of the security staff', in relation to a school, means a member of staff whose work at the school consists wholly or mainly of security-related activities: s 550ZB(8) (as so added).

6   See the Education Act 1996 s 550ZB(2) (as added: see note 1).

7   See the Education Act 1996 s 550ZB(7)(a) (as added: see note 1).

8   Education Act 1996 s 550ZB(7)(b) (as added (see note 1); and amended by the Education Act 2011 s 2(1), (3)(d)). The condition referred to in the text is the condition in the Education Act 2011 s 550ZB(7A). The condition is satisfied if (1) the person carrying out the search reasonably believes that there is a risk that serious harm will be caused to a person if the search is not carried out as a matter of urgency; and (2) in the time available it is not reasonably practicable for the search to be carried out in the presence of another member of staff: s 550ZB(7A) (added by the Education Act 2011 s 2(1), (3)(e)).

9   As to the meaning of 'premises' see PARA 62 note 19.

10 Education Act 1996 s 550ZB(4)(a) (as added: see note 1).

11 Education Act 1996 s 550ZB(4)(b) (as added: see note 1).

12 Ie the power in the Education Act 1996 s 550ZA to search for an item within s 550ZA(3)(a)–(f): see note 3 heads (1)–(7).

13   Education Act 1996 s 550ZB(5) (as added (see note 1); and amended by the Education Act 2011 s 2(1), (3)(a)). For a case in which consideration was given to the reasonableness of a teacher's actions while trying to restrain a pupil, albeit in the context of a claim for compensation by the teacher for injuries sustained, see *R (Criminal Injuries Compensation Appeals Panel) v Shields* [2001] ELR 164. As to a teacher's duties towards pupils, and liability in respect of a breach of such duties, see PARAS 1087–1088.

14   Education Act 1996 s 550ZB(6)(a) (as added: see note 1). 'Outer clothing' means (1) any item of clothing that is being worn otherwise than wholly next to the skin or immediately over a garment being worn as underwear; or (2) a hat, shoes, boots, gloves or a scarf: s 550ZB(8) (as so added). As to the meaning of 'clothing' see PARA 482 note 2.

15   Education Act 1996 s 550ZB(6)(b) (as added (see note 1); and amended by the Education Act 2011 s 2(1), (3)(b)(i)). The condition referred to in the text is the condition in the Education Act 1996 s 550ZB(6A). The condition is satisfied if (1) the person carrying out the search reasonably believes that there is a risk that serious harm will be caused to a person if the search is not carried out as a matter of urgency; and (2) in the time available it is not reasonably practicable for the search to be carried out by a person of the same sex as the pupil or in the presence of another member of staff (as the case may be): s 550ZB(6A) (added by the Education Act 2011 s 2(1), (3)(c)).

16   Education Act 1996 s 550ZB(6)(c) (as added (see note 1); and amended by the Education Act 2011 s 2(1), (3)(b)(ii)). The condition referred to in the text is the condition in the Education Act 1996 s 550ZB(6A): see note 15.

17   Education Act 1996 s 550ZB(6)(d) (as added: see note 1).

18   A person who seizes alcohol under the Education Act 1996 s 550ZC(1) may retain or dispose of the alcohol and its container: s 550ZC(3) (as added: see note 1). A person who seizes a controlled drug must deliver it to a police constable as soon as reasonably practicable (s 550ZC(4)(a) (as so added)), but may dispose of it if the person thinks that there is a good reason to do so (s 550ZC(4)(b) (as so added)). A person who seizes a stolen article must deliver it to a police constable as soon as reasonably practicable (s 550ZC(5)(a) (as so added)), but may return it to its owner (or, if returning it to its owner is not practicable, may retain it or dispose of it) if the person thinks that there is a good reason to do so (s 550ZC(5)(b) (as so added)). In determining, for the purposes of s 550ZC(4), (5), whether there is a good reason to dispose of a controlled drug or to return a stolen article to its owner, retain it or dispose of it, the person must have regard to any guidance issued by the Secretary of State: s 550ZC(6) (as so added). As to the office of constable see POLICE AND INVESTIGATORY POWERS vol 84 (2013) PARA 1 et seq.

     A person who seizes an item that is a prohibited item by virtue of the Education Act 1996 s 550ZA(3)(ea) (article used in commission of offence or to cause personal injury or damage to property) (see note 3 head (6)) under s 550ZC(1) must (1) deliver the item to a police constable as soon as reasonably practicable; (2) return the item to its owner; (3) retain the item; or (4) dispose of the item: s 550ZC(6A) (s 550ZC(6A)–(6G) added by the Education Act 2011 s 2(1), (4)(b)). A person who seizes an item that is a prohibited item by virtue of the Education Act 1996 s 550ZA(3)(g) (item for which search may be made under school rules) (see note 3 head (8)) under s 550ZC(1) must return it to its owner, retain it or dispose of it: s 550ZC(6B) (as so added). In deciding what to do with an item under s 550ZC(6A) or (6B), the person who seized it must have regard to guidance issued for these purposes by the Secretary of State: s 550ZC(6C) (as so added). Section 550ZC(6E) and (6F) below apply to an item that (a) has been seized under s 550ZC(1); (b) is a prohibited item by virtue of s 550ZA(3)(ea) or (g); and (c) is an electronic device: s 550ZC(6D) (as so added). The person who seized the item may examine any data or files on the device, if the person thinks there is a good reason to do so: s 550ZC(6E) (as so added). Following an examination under s 550ZC(6E), if the person has decided to return the item to its owner, retain it or dispose of it, the person may erase any data or files from the device if the person thinks there is a good reason to do so: s 550ZC(6F) (as so added). In determining whether there is a good reason for the purposes of s 550ZC(6E) or (6F), the person must have regard to any guidance issued for these purposes by the Secretary of State: s 550ZC(6G) (as so added). As to the publication of guidance see s 571; and PARA 60. See in particular 'Searching, screening and confiscation: Advice for headteachers, school staff and governing bodies' (February 2014). This departmental advice is actually said to be for school leaders, school staff, governing bodies and local authorities. It applies to maintained schools, community schools, foundation schools, voluntary schools, community special schools, foundation special schools, academies and free schools, pupil referral units and non-maintained special schools. The advice covers powers to search without consent, prohibited items schools can search for and powers to confiscate items found during searches.

     Regulations may prescribe what must or may be done by a person who seizes an article of a kind specified in regulations under s 550ZA(3)(f) (see note 3 head (7)) (or an article which the person has reasonable grounds for suspecting to be such an article): s 550ZC(7) (as so added). Regulations under s 550ZC(7) may make provision corresponding to any provision of s 550ZD (see below; and the text to notes 26–30): s 550ZD(5) (as so added).

A person who seizes (i) an article to which the Criminal Justice Act 1988 s 139 applies (knives and blades etc: see CRIMINAL LAW vol 26 (2010) PARA 654) (Education Act 1996 s 550ZC(8)(a) (as so added)); (ii) an offensive weapon (s 550ZC(8)(b) (as so added)); or (iii) anything which that person has reasonable grounds for suspecting is evidence in relation to an offence (s 550ZC(8)(c) (as so added)), must deliver it to a police constable as soon as reasonably practicable: s 550ZC(8) (as so added). Section 550ZC(8)(c) is subject to s 550ZC(3), (4), (5), (6A) and regulations made under s 550ZC(7): s 550ZC(9) (as so added; and amended by the Education Act 2011 s 2(1), (4)(c)).

In the Education Act 1996 s 550ZC(3)–(8), references to alcohol, a controlled drug, a stolen article, an article to which the Criminal Justice Act 1988 s 139 applies and an offensive weapon include references to anything which the person has reasonable grounds for suspecting is alcohol, a controlled drug, a stolen article, an article to which the Criminal Justice Act 1988 s 139 applies or an offensive weapon: s 550ZC(10) (as so added). The Police (Property) Act 1897 (disposal of property in the possession of the police: see POLICE AND INVESTIGATORY POWERS vol 84A (2013) PARA 635 et seq) applies to property which has come into the possession of a police constable under the Education Act 1996 s 550ZC(4)(a), (5)(a), (6A)(a) or (8) as it applies to property which has come into the possession of the police in the circumstances mentioned in the Police (Property) Act 1897: Education Act 1996 s 550ZD(1) (as so added; and amended by the Education Act 2011 s 2(1), (5)(a)).

19 Education Act 1996 s 550ZC(1)(a) (as added: see note 1).
20 Education Act 1996 s 550ZC(1)(b) (as added: see note 1).
21 Ie in order to seize an item within the Education Act 1996 s 550ZA(3)(a)–(f) (see note 3 heads (1)–(7)) or anything within s 550ZC(1)(b) (see head (2) in the text).
22 See the Education Act 1996 s 550ZC(2) (as added (see note 1); and amended by the Education Act 2011 s 2(1), (4)(a)). See also note 13.
23 Ie by the Education Act 1996 ss 550ZA, 550ZB and 550ZC: see the text to notes 1–22.
24 Ie apart from the Education Act 1996 ss 550ZA, 550ZB and 550ZC.
25 Education Act 1996 s 550ZA(6) (as added: see note 1).
26 Ie under the Education Act 1996 s 550ZC: see the text to notes 18–22.
27 Education Act 1996 s 550ZD(2)(a) (as added (see note 1); and amended by the Education Act 2011 s 2(1), (5)(b)). The items referred to in the text are those in the Education Act 1996 s 550ZD(2A). Those items are (1) alcohol or its container; (2) a controlled drug; (3) a stolen article; (4) an item that is a prohibited item by virtue of s 550ZA(3)(ea) or (g) (see note 3 heads (6), (8)): s 550ZD(2A) (s 550ZD(2A), (2B) added by the Education Act 2011 s 2(1), (5)(c)).
28 Education Act 1996 s 550ZD(2)(b) (as added: see note 1).
29 Education Act 1996 s 550ZD(3)(a) (as added: see note 1). See also note 30.
30 Education Act 1996 s 550ZD(3)(b) (as added: see note 1). Section 550ZD(2), (2B), (3) does not prevent any person from relying on any defence on which the person is entitled to rely apart from those provisions: s 550ZD(4) (as so added; and amended by the Education Act 2011 s 2(1), (5)(e)).
31 Ie under the Education Act 1996 s 550ZC(6F) (see note 18): s 550ZB(2B)(a) (as added: see note 27). See note 30.
32 Education Act 1996 s 550ZB(2B)(b) (as added: see note 27). See note 30.
33 Education Act 1996 s 550ZD(3)(a) (as added (see note 1); and amended by the Education Act 2011 s 2(1), (5)(d)). See note 30.
34 Education Act 1996 s 550ZD(3)(b) (as added: see note 1). See note 30.

545. No right to give corporal punishment. Within limits, corporal punishment is neither contrary to the prohibition on torture, inhuman and degrading treatment or punishment contained in the European Convention for the Protection of Fundamental Rights and Freedoms[1], nor unlawful as a battery at common law[2].

However, corporal punishment[3] given by, or on the authority of, a member of staff[4] to a child for whom:

(1)   education is provided at any school[5]; or

(2)   education is provided, otherwise than at school, under any arrangements made by a local authority[6]; or

(3)   specified early years education[7] is provided otherwise than at school[8], cannot be justified in any proceedings on the ground that it was given in pursuance of a right exercisable by the member of staff by virtue of his position as such[9]. This applies to corporal punishment so given to a child at any time, whether at the school or other place at which education is provided for the child, or elsewhere[10].

1   Ie the Convention for the Protection of Human Rights and Fundamental Freedoms (Rome, 4 November 1950; TS 71 (1953); Cmd 8969) art 3: see RIGHTS AND FREEDOMS vol 88A (2013) PARA 158 et seq. See *Tyrer v United Kingdom* (1978) 2 EHRR 1, ECtHR; *Costello-Roberts v United Kingdom* [1994] ELR 1, [1994] 1 FCR 65, ECtHR; *A v United Kingdom (Human Rights: Punishment of Child)* (1998) 27 EHRR 611, [1998] 2 FLR 959, ECtHR; *Warwick v United Kingdom* 60 DR 5 (1986); Application 14229/88 *Y v United Kingdom* (1992) 17 EHRR 238, ECtHR. Corporal punishment may, however, be in conflict with a parent's philosophical convictions for the purposes of the Convention for the Protection of Human Rights and Fundamental Freedoms, First Protocol (Paris, 20 March 1952; TS 46 (1954); Cmd 9221) art 2 (see RIGHTS AND FREEDOMS vol 88A (2013) PARA 548): Application 7511/76 *Campbell and Cosans v United Kingdom* (1982) 4 EHRR 293, ECtHR. See further note 9.

2   At common law, it was implicit that the school had authority to administer punishment within the limits set by the common law: *Mansell v Griffin* [1908] 1 KB 160, 98 LT 51; *Ryan v Fildes* [1938] 3 All ER 517. See also *R v Hopley* (1860) 2 F & F 202; *Mansell v Griffin* [1908] 1 KB 160, 98 LT 51; *Cleary v Booth* [1893] 1 QB 465; *Gray v Hawthorn* 1964 JC 69; *M'Shane v Paton* 1922 JC 26; *Gardner v Bygrave* (1889) 6 TLR 23; *Scorgie v Lawrie* (1883) 10 R (Ct of Sess) 610; *Ryan v Fildes* [1938] 3 All ER 517; *R v Newport (Salop) Justices, ex p Wright* [1929] 2 KB 416, DC; *Re Basingstoke School* (1877) 41 JP Jo 118. As to assault and battery see TORT vol 97 (2015) PARA 528 et seq; and see also CRIMINAL LAW vol 25 (2010) PARA 157 et seq.

3   For these purposes, any reference to giving corporal punishment to a child is a reference to doing anything for the purpose of punishing that child, whether or not there are other reasons for doing it, which, apart from any justification, would constitute battery: Education Act 1996 s 548(3), (4) (s 548 substituted by the School Standards and Framework Act 1998 s 131(1)). However, corporal punishment must not be taken to be given to a child by virtue of anything done for reasons that include averting an immediate danger of personal injury to (Education Act 1996 s 548(5)(a) (as so substituted)), or an immediate danger to the property of any person (s 548(5)(b) (as so substituted)), including the child himself: s 548(5) (as so substituted). 'Child' (except in s 548(8) (see note 7)) means a person under the age of 18: s 548(3), (7) (as so substituted). As to the time at which a person attains a particular age see PARA 7 note 6. As to the meaning of 'person' see PARA 7 note 6.

4   'Member of staff', in relation to the child concerned, means: (1) any person who works as a teacher at the school or other place at which education is provided for the child (Education Act 1996 s 548(6)(a) (as substituted: see note 3)); or (2) any other person who, whether in connection with the provision of education for the child or otherwise, works at that school or place (s 548(6)(b)(i) (as so substituted)), or otherwise provides his services there (whether or not for payment) (s 548(6)(b)(ii) (as so substituted)), and has lawful control or charge of the child (s 548(6)(b)) (as so substituted)). As from a day to be appointed, s 548(6)(a), (b)(i) are amended by the substitution for the word 'school' of the words 'relevant educational institution': s 548(6)(a), (b)(i) (as so substituted; and prospectively amended by the Education and Skills Act 2008 s 169(1), Sch 1 Pt 1 paras 5, 9(1), (4)). At the date at which this volume states the law no such day had been appointed. As to the meaning of 'school' see PARA 91. 'Relevant educational institution' means a school, or an independent educational institution in England other than a school: Education Act 1996 s 548(7A) (s 548 as so substituted; s 548(7A), (7B) added, as from a day to be appointed, by the Education and Skills Act 2008 s 169(1), Sch 1 Pt 1 paras 5, 9(1), (5)). At the date at which this volume states the law no such day had been appointed. 'Independent educational institution' has the same meaning as in the Education and Skills Act 2008 Pt 4 Ch 1 (ss 92–141) (see s 92; and PARA 382): Education Act 1996 s 548(7B) (as so substituted and prospectively added). As to the meaning of 'England' see PARA 7 note 3.

5   Education Act 1996 s 548(1)(a) (as substituted: see note 3). As from a day to be appointed, s 548(1)(a) is amended by the substitution for the word 'school' of the words 'relevant educational institution': s 548(1)(a) (as so substituted; and prospectively amended by the Education and Skills Act 2008 s 169(1), Sch 1 Pt 1 paras 5, 9(1), (2)(a)). At the date at which this volume states the law no such day had been appointed.

6   Education Act 1996 s 548(1)(b) (as substituted (see note 3); and amended by SI 2010/1158). As from a day to be appointed, the Education Act 1996 s 548(1)(b) is amended by the substitution

for the word 'school' of the words 'relevant educational institution': s 548(1)(b) (as so substituted; and prospectively amended by the Education and Skills Act 2008 s 169(1), Sch 1 Pt 1 paras 5, 9(1), (2)(b)). At the date at which this volume states the law no such day had been appointed. As to the meaning of 'local authority' see PARA 25.

7 'Specified early years education' means: (1) in relation to England, early years provision as defined by the Childcare Act 2006 s 20 (see CHILDREN AND YOUNG PERSONS vol 10 (2012) PARA 1079) which is provided under arrangements made by a local authority in England in pursuance of the duty imposed by s 7 of that Act (whether or not the local authority provides the early years provision: see CHILDREN AND YOUNG PERSONS vol 10 (2012) PARA 1090); (2) in relation to Wales, full-time or part-time education suitable for children who have not attained compulsory school age which is provided (a) by a local authority in Wales, or (b) by any other person who is in receipt of financial assistance given by such an authority under arrangements made by it in pursuance of the duty imposed by the School Standards and Framework Act 1998 s 118 (see PARA 96): Education Act 1996 s 548(8) (s 548 as substituted (see note 3); s 548(8) further substituted by the Childcare Act 2006 s 103(1), Sch 2 para 27(1), (3); and amended by SI 2010/1158). At the date at which this volume states the law, the further substitution of the Education Act 1996 s 548(8) applies in relation to England only and will be brought into force in relation to Wales as from a day to be appointed under the Childcare Act 2006 s 109(2). At the date at which this volume states the law no such day had been appointed. As to the meaning of 'Wales' see PARA 7 note 3. As to the meaning of 'compulsory school age' see PARA 19.

Until such day is appointed, the Education Act 1996 s 548(1)(c) refers, in relation to Wales, to 'specified nursery education': see s 548(1)(c) (as substituted: see note 3). 'Specified nursery education' means full-time or part-time education suitable for children who have not attained compulsory school age which is provided: (1) by a local authority; or (2) by any other person who is, or is to be, in receipt of financial assistance given by such an authority and whose provision of nursery education is taken into account by the authority in formulating proposals for the purposes of the School Standards and Framework Act 1998 s 120(2)(a) (repealed): Education Act 1996 s 548(8) (s 548 as so substituted; and s 548(8) amended by the Education Act 2002 s 215(2), Sch 22 Pt 3; and SI 2010/1158).

8 Education Act 1996 s 548(1)(c) (as substituted (see note 3); and amended by the Childcare Act 2006 s 103(1), Sch 2 para 27(1), (2)). As from a day to be appointed, the Education Act 1996 s 548(1)(c) is amended by the substitution for the word 'school' of the words 'relevant educational institution': s 548(1)(c) (as so substituted and amended; and prospectively amended by the Education and Skills Act 2008 s 169(1), Sch 1 Pt 1 paras 5, 9(1), (2)(b)). At the date at which this volume states the law no such day had been appointed.

9 Education Act 1996 s 548(1) (as substituted: see note 3). See also PARA 423. The phrase 'by virtue of his position as such' limits the application of s 548(1) to corporal punishment given by a teacher while discharging his functions as a teacher and it cannot be used to draw a distinction in cases where a parent expressly delegates to the teacher the common law right to administer physical punishment: *R (on the application of Williamson) v Secretary of State for Education and Employment* [2005] UKHL 15, [2005] 2 AC 246, [2005] 2 All ER 1 (prohibition of corporal punishment in independent religious schools). The Education Act 1996 s 548 is a justified infringement on: (1) a parent's (or a teacher's) right to manifest a belief under the Convention for the Protection of Human Rights and Fundamental Freedoms (Rome, 4 November 1950; TS 71 (1953); Cmd 8969) art 9 (see RIGHTS AND FREEDOMS vol 88A (2013) PARA 368 et seq), in the form that the duty of education in the Christian context allows teachers to stand in loco parentis and administer corporal punishment as a means of discipline; and (2) the rights of a parent under the First Protocol (Paris, 20 March 1952; TS 46 (1954); Cmd 9221) art 2 (see RIGHTS AND FREEDOMS vol 88A (2013) PARA 548) to ensure that a child's education should conform with their religious and philosophical convictions, in that the term 'education' is wide enough to include the manner in which discipline is administered in a school: *R (on the application of Williamson) v Secretary of State for Education and Employment* above.

10 Education Act 1996 s 548(2) (as substituted: see note 3). As from a day to be appointed, the Education Act 1996 s 548(2) is amended by the substitution for the word 'school' of the words 'relevant educational institution': s 548(2) (as so substituted; and prospectively amended by the Education and Skills Act 2008 s 169(1), Sch 1 Pt 1 paras 5, 9(1), (3)). At the date at which this volume states the law no such day had been appointed.

(12) COMPLAINTS ABOUT SCHOOLS

546. Making complaints about schools. In most circumstances a complaint should be made to the relevant school before complaining to any other organisation[1]. Every state[2] and private[3] school must have a complaints procedure[4]. A complaint may be taken further if the person complaining is still not satisfied after going through all the steps in the complaints procedure[5].

In regard to a state school in England, a complaint may be made to the Office for Standards in Education, Children's Services and Skills (Ofsted)[6] if there is a problem affecting the whole school, such as a problem with the quality of education or poor management[7].

Complaints about maintained schools may be made to the Department for Education[8].

The Department for Education cannot investigate individual complaints about private, independent or non-maintained schools, but it does have certain powers as a regulator if the school is not meeting standards set by the Department[9]. The Department may consider any reports of failure to meet those standards, and can arrange emergency inspection to look at pupil welfare and health and safety, and make sure that serious failings are dealt with; it can ask school inspectorates to take any minor failings into account when the school is next inspected[10].

In regard to academies, free schools, university technical colleges or studio schools[11] complaints may be made to the Education Funding Agency (EFA)[12] if there is a problem with the school's complaints procedure, or if the school is not following the terms of its funding agreement[13].

Local authorities must make arrangements for appeals against decisions relating to school admissions[14].

A decision to exclude a pupil may be challenged, and a complaint may be made about the alternative education provided[15].

Concerns about a problem relating to special educational needs (SEN) should be raised with the school[16]. An SEN assessment[17] from the local authority may be requested if the school cannot provide all the help the child needs[18].

In the case of examination maladministration[19], complaints should be made in the first place to the relevant awarding body; once that body's appeal process has been exhausted, a complaint may be made to the Office of Qualifications and Examinations Regulation (Ofqual)[20]. Complaints about examination malpractice may be taken straight to Ofqual[21].

Complaints about matters such as child protection, criminal behaviour, data protection, discrimination or employment may be made to the relevant agency or body[22].

If the outcome of a complaint to a Welsh school is unsatisfactory, then the complaint may be taken up with the relevant Welsh body[23].

1   As to guidance concerning complaints about schools in England see in particular 'Complain about a school or childminder', available on the Department for Education website. As to guidance on the procedure see 'School complaints procedure: departmental advice for schools setting up or reviewing complaints procedures' (August 2014). As to a complaints procedure statement see 'Statutory policies for schools: Advice on the policies and documents that governing bodies and proprietors of schools are required to have by law' (September 2014) p 13, which makes reference to the Education Act 2002 s 29 (in regard to maintained schools) (see PARAS 175, 209), the Education (Independent School Standards) (England) Regulations 2010, SI 2010/1997 (now replaced by the Education (Independent School Standards) Regulations 2014, SI 2014/3283) (in regard to academies, free schools and independent schools) (see PARAS 394, 509) and the Education (Non-maintained Special Schools) (England) Regulations 2011, SI 2011/1627 (now replaced by the Non-Maintained Special

Schools (England) Regulations 2015, SI 2015/728) (in regard to non-maintained special schools) (see PARAS 919, 1000, 1042–1044). As to maintained schools see PARA 99 et seq. As to academies see PARA 345 et seq. As to free schools see PARA 368. As to independent schools see PARA 369 et seq. As to non-maintained special schools see PARA 1042.

2 For these purposes state schools include maintained schools, academies and free schools.

3 Ie non-maintained or independent schools.

4 See note 1. See also the Education Act 2002 s 29; and PARAS 175, 209.

5 See note 1.

6 As to the Office for Standards in Education, Children's Services and Skills (Ofsted) see PARA 1128 et seq. As to complaining to Ofsted, and in particular making online complaints, see Ofsted's website. See also 'Complaints to Ofsted about schools: Guidance for parents and carers' (April 2014) which is available on the Department for Education website.

7 See note 1. Teacher misconduct in England may be reported to the National College for Teaching and Leadership, and in Wales may be reported to the Education Workforce Council. As to the National College for Teaching and Leadership see PARA 1066; and as to the Education Workforce Council see PARA 1075.

8 See note 1.

9 Eg for education; pupil welfare and health and safety; school premises; staff suitability; or making information available to parents. As to welfare of pupils generally see PARA 482 et seq. As to health and safety see PARA 1353. As to school premises see PARA 1344 et seq. As to staffing of schools see PARA 268 et seq. As to information etc see eg PARA 940.

10 See note 1. As to inspection and intervention see PARA 1127 et seq.

11 As to university technical colleges and studio schools see PARA 368.

12 As to the Education Funding Agency see PARA 58 note 9.

13 See note 1. As to funding agreements etc see PARA 346.

14 See PARA 251 et seq. As to local authorities see PARA 25 et seq.

15 See note 1. See in particular 'School discipline and exclusions'. In the case of fixed period exclusions, complaint about the alternative education or the failure to make arrangements may be made to the school; in the case of permanent exclusions, complaint may be made to the local authority. As to exclusions generally see PARA 517 et seq. As to guidance on exclusions see PARA 540.

16 See note 1. As to special educational needs and disabilities generally see PARA 941 et seq. A complaint as to special educational needs may be investigated by a local commissioner (or ombudsman): see the Local Government Act 1974 s 26, Sch 5 para 5(2); and LOCAL GOVERNMENT vol 69 (2009) PARA 851. It should be noted that this is an exception to the general ban on investigation as to educational matters in Sch 5 para 5(2).

17 See note 1. See also 'Children with special educational needs (SEN)'. As to assessment of educational, health care needs in England see PARA 957. As to education, health and care (EHC) plans in England see PARA 958 et seq.

18 See note 1. If the response to a request for an assessment is unsatisfactory, an appeal may be made to the First-tier Tribunal (Special Educational Needs and Disability): see the Department for Education website; and note 1. See in particular 'Appeal to the Special Educational Needs and Disability Tribunal'. As to appeals, mediation and dispute resolution in England see PARA 980 et seq.

19 Eg the setting, marking or grading of an examination. As to curriculum, assessment and external qualifications see PARA 824 et seq. As to external qualifications see PARA 932 et seq.

20 See note 1. As to the Office of Qualifications and Examinations Regulation (Ofqual) see PARA 825 et seq.

21 See note 1.

22 Child protection issues (see generally CHILDREN AND YOUNG PERSONS vol 9 (2012) PARA 601 et seq) should be raised with the local authority; criminal behaviour should be reported to the police; data protection issues (see generally CONFIDENCE AND INFORMATIONAL PRIVACY vol 19 (2011) PARA 95 et seq) should be raised with the Information Commissioner's Office; complaints about discrimination (as to which see PARA 9 et seq) should be raised with the Equality Advisory and Support Service; and employment issues (as to which see generally EMPLOYMENT) should be taken to an employment tribunal (see in particular 'Make a claim to an employment tribunal').

23 As to complaints about schools in Wales see 'Complaints procedures for school governing bodies in Wales' (October 2012). Complaints about admissions should be raised with the relevant local authority, but complaints about admission appeals may be taken to the Public Services Ombudsman for Wales. If a pupil is permanently excluded, an appeal may be made to an independent appeal panel constituted by the local authority. There are also special statutory processes for complaints and appeals relating to matters such as the curriculum, religious worship, special educational needs, staff grievance, staff disciplinary and teacher capability.

(13) PERSONS DETAINED IN YOUTH ACCOMMODATION

547. Application of Education Act 1996 to detained persons. In its application in relation to detained persons[1], the Education Act 1996 has effect subject to modifications[2] prescribed by regulations made by the appropriate national authority[3]. This power may not be exercised to modify the application of a provision of the Act if:

(1)   the provision makes special provision in relation to detained persons, or a description of detained persons[4];

(2)   the application of the provision in relation to detained persons, or a description of detained persons, is excluded by provision made by the Act[5]; or

(3)   the provision has effect in relation to detained persons, or a description of detained persons, subject to modifications made by the Act[6].

1   References in the Education Act 1996 Pt X Ch 5A (ss 562A–562J) to a 'detained person' are to a child or young person who is subject to a detention order and detained in relevant youth accommodation (s 562A(3)(a), (b) (ss 562A, 562J added by the Apprenticeships, Skills, Children and Learning Act 2009 s 50)); and, in provisions applying on a person's release, also include references to a person who, immediately before release, was a detained person (Education Act 1996 s 562A(3) (as so added)). As to the meaning of 'child' see PARA 7 note 6. 'Young person' includes a person aged 18: s 562J(1) (as so added). As to the meaning of 'young person' generally see PARA 7 note 6. As to when a person is subject to a detention order see PARA 46 note 8. As to the meaning of 'relevant youth accommodation' see PARA 46 note 9.
    At the date at which this volume states the law, s 562A(3) is in force: see the Apprenticeships, Skills, Children and Learning Act 2009 (Commencement No 2 and Transitional and Saving Provisions) Order 2010, SI 2010/303, art 6, Sch 5; and the Apprenticeships, Skills, Children and Learning Act 2009 (Commencement No 3) (Wales) Order 2011, SI 2011/829. The Education Act 1996 s 562A is to be brought into force for remaining purposes as from a day to be appointed under the Apprenticeships, Skills, Children and Learning Act 2009 s 269(3)(f), (4). At the date at which this volume states the law no such day had been appointed.
2   As to the meaning of 'modifications' see PARA 21 note 15.
3   Education Act 1996 s 562A(1) (as added: see note 1). 'The appropriate national authority' means, in relation to England, the Secretary of State; and in relation to Wales, the Welsh Ministers: s 562J(1). As to the meanings of 'England' and 'Wales' see PARA 7 note 3. As to the Secretary of State see PARA 58. As to the Welsh Ministers see PARA 59. At the date at which this volume states the law no such regulations had been made.
4   Education Act 1996 s 562A(2)(a) (as added: see note 1).
5   Education Act 1996 s 562A(2)(b) (as added: see note 1).
6   Education Act 1996 s 562A(2)(c) (as added: see note 1).

548. Duty to take steps to promote fulfilment of potential. In relation to a detained person[1] who is not a looked after child[2], the home authority[3] must during the period of detention in relevant youth accommodation[4], and on the person's release from detention in relevant youth accommodation[5], take such steps as it considers appropriate to promote the person's fulfilment of his or her learning potential[6]. Those steps must include, where it appears to the home authority appropriate for it to do so, making arrangements for the provision, on the person's release from detention of education[7], or in the case of a person who is over compulsory school age[8], of education or training[9].

Where the host authority[10] makes any determination as to the education or training to be provided for a detained person, the authority must have regard to any information provided[11] by a local authority as to the level of the person's literacy and numeracy skills[12], and any other information provided by the home authority[13] for the purpose of assisting any such determination[14].

1   As to the meaning of 'detained person' see PARA 547 note 1.

2   Education Act 1996 s 562B(1) (ss 562B, 562J added by the Apprenticeships, Skills, Children and Learning Act 2009 s 50). 'Looked after child' means a person who, for the purposes of the Children Act 1989 is a child looked after by a local authority (see CHILDREN AND YOUNG PERSONS vol 10 (2012) PARA 843); and references to the local authority looking after the person are to be read accordingly: Education Act 1996 s 562J(1) (as so added).

At the date at which this volume states the law, of s 562B, only s 562B(1)–(3) is in force, and this in relation to England for certain purposes see the Apprenticeships, Skills, Children and Learning Act 2009 (Commencement No 2 and Transitional and Saving Provisions) Order 2010, SI 2010/303, art 6, Sch 5. The Education Act 1996 s 562B(1)–(3) has also been brought into force in relation to Wales: see the Apprenticeships, Skills, Children and Learning Act 2009 (Commencement No 3) (Wales) Order 2011, SI 2011/829. The Education Act 1996 s 562B is to be brought into force for remaining purposes, as from a day to be appointed under the Apprenticeships, Skills, Children and Learning Act 2009 s 269(3)(f), (4). At the date at which this volume states the law no such day had been appointed. As to the meanings of 'England' and 'Wales' see PARA 7 note 3.

3   'The home authority': (1) in relation to a child or young person who immediately before the beginning of the detention was, or at any time since then has been, a looked after child, means the local authority who are the local authority looking after, or who have most recently been looking after, the person; (2) in relation to any other child or young person, means the local authority in whose area the person is ordinarily resident: Education Act 1996 s 562J(1) (as added (see note 2); definition amended by SI 2010/1158). In determining for these purposes where a child or young person is ordinarily resident, any period when the person is subject to a detention order is to be disregarded: s 562J(3) (as so added). Regulations made by the appropriate national authority may make further provision for determining where a person is ordinarily resident for these purposes: s 562J(4) (as so added). As to the meanings of 'child' and 'young person' see PARA 7 note 6. As to the meaning of 'local authority' see PARA 25. As to when a person is subject to a detention order see PARA 46 note 8. As to the meaning of 'appropriate national authority' see PARA 547 note 3. At the date at which this volume states the law no such regulations had been made.

'Beginning of the detention', in relation to a person detained in relevant youth accommodation, means: (a) the beginning of the period of detention in such accommodation; or (b) where that period is part of a continuous period, comprising periods of detention in relevant youth accommodation and in other accommodation, the beginning of that continuous period: s 562J(1) (as so added). For the purposes of this definition, it is immaterial whether or not a period of detention is pursuant to a single order: s 562J(2) (as so added). As to the meaning of 'relevant youth accommodation' see PARA 46 note 9.

4   Education Act 1996 s 562B(2)(a) (as added: see note 2).

5   Education Act 1996 s 562B(2)(b) (as added: see note 2).

6   Education Act 1996 s 562B(2) (as added: see note 2). As to the duty of an authority to regard to any guidance issued by the appropriate national authority see PARA 554.

7   Education Act 1996 s 562B(3)(a) (as added: see note 2).

8   As to the meaning of 'compulsory school age' see PARA 19.

9   Education Act 1996 s 562B(3)(b) (as added: see note 2).

10 'The host authority', in relation to a child or young person detained in relevant youth accommodation, means the local authority in whose area the child or young person is detained: Education Act 1996 s 562J(1) (as added (see note 2); definition amended by SI 2010/1158).

11 Ie under the Education Act 1996 s 562F: see PARA 551.

12 Education Act 1996 s 562B(4)(a) (as added (see note 2); and amended by SI 2010/1158).

13 Ie under the Education Act 1996 s 562F: see PARA 551.

14 Education Act 1996 s 562B(4)(b) (as added: see note 2).

549. Detained persons with special educational needs in Wales. Where, immediately before the beginning of the detention[1], a local authority in Wales[2] was maintaining a statement of special educational needs[3] for a detained person[4], the authority must keep the statement while the person is detained in relevant youth accommodation[5]. The host authority[6] must use best endeavours to secure that appropriate special educational provision[7] is made for the detained person while the person is detained in relevant youth accommodation[8].

Where special educational provision is secured for a person in circumstances referred to above[9], a local authority in Wales may supply goods and services to[10] the host authority[11] or any other person[12] making the special educational provision in question[13]. Such goods and services may be supplied only for the purpose of assisting the making or securing of that special educational provision[14].

The position in regard to detained persons with special educational needs and disabilities in England is now covered by provisions under the Children and Families Act 2014[15].

1   As to the meaning of 'beginning of the detention' see PARA 548 note 3.
2   As to the meaning of 'local authority' see PARA 25. As to the meaning of 'Wales' see PARA 7 note 3.
3   Ie a statement under the Education Act 1996 s 324: see PARA 1002.
4   Education Act 1996 s 562C(1) (ss 562C, 562D added by the Apprenticeships, Skills, Children and Learning Act 2009 s 50; and the Education Act 1996 s 562C(1) amended by SI 2010/1158; and the Children and Families Act 2014 Sch 3 paras 1, 55(1), (3)).
    At the date at which this volume states the law, of the Education Act 1996 ss 562C, 562D, only s 562C(1), (2) is in force, and this in relation to England for certain purposes: see the Apprenticeships, Skills, Children and Learning Act 2009 (Commencement No 2 and Transitional and Saving Provisions) Order 2010, SI 2010/303, art 6, Sch 5. The Education Act 1996 s 562C(1), (2) has also been brought into force in relation to Wales: see the Apprenticeships, Skills, Children and Learning Act 2009 (Commencement No 3) (Wales) Order 2011, SI 2011/829. The Education Act 1996 s 562C was to be brought into force in relation to England for remaining purposes and s 562D in relation to England for remaining purposes and in relation to Wales as from a day to be appointed under the Apprenticeships, Skills, Children and Learning Act 2009 s 269(3)(f), (4). At the date at which this volume states the law no such day had been appointed. However in relation to England see also the text and note 15. As to the meaning of 'England' see PARA 7 note 3.
5   Education Act 1996 s 562C(2) (as added: see note 4). As to the meaning of 'relevant youth accommodation' see PARA 46 note 9. As to the duty of an authority to regard to any guidance issued by the appropriate national authority see PARA 554.
6   As to the meaning of 'host authority' see PARA 548 note 10.
7   'Appropriate special educational provision' is: (1) the special educational provision that, immediately before the beginning of the detention, was specified in the statement (Education Act 1996 s 562C(4)(a) (as added: see note 4)); (2) educational provision corresponding as closely as practicable to the special educational provision so specified (s 562C(4)(b) (as so added)); or (3) if it appears to the host authority that the special educational provision so specified is no longer appropriate for the person, such special educational provision as reasonably appears to the host authority to be appropriate for the person (s 562C(4)(c) (as so added)).
8   Education Act 1996 s 562C(3) (as added: see note 4).
9   Ie circumstances where the Education Act 1996 s 562C (see the text to notes 1–8) applies: see s 562D(1) (as added: see note 4).
10 Education Act 1996 s 562D(2) (as added (see note 4); and amended by SI 2010/1158; and the Children and Families Act 2014 Sch 3 paras 1, 56).
11 Education Act 1996 s 562D(2)(a) (as added: see note 4).
12 As to the meaning of 'person' see PARA 7 note 6.
13 Education Act 1996 s 562D(2)(b) (as added: see note 4).
14 Education Act 1996 s 562D(3) (as added: see note 4).
15 See in particular the Children and Families Act 2014 ss 70–75; the Special Educational Needs and Disability (Detained Persons) Regulations 2015, SI 2015/62; and PARAS 957, 958, 964, 970–975, 976, 982. Reference should be made to 'Special Educational Needs and Disability Code of Practice: 0 to 25 years': see PARA 978 note 36. See also generally the Special Educational Needs and Disability Regulations 2014, SI 2014/1530; and PARAS 951, 957, 958, 961, 964, 965, 969, 976, 980, 982.

550.   Literacy and numeracy assessments. As from a day to be appointed the following provisions have effect[1].

In relation to a detained person[2] who is detained in particular relevant youth accommodation[3], the host authority[4] must arrange for the level of the detained person's literacy and numeracy skills to be assessed as soon as reasonably practicable after the beginning of the period during which the person is detained[5] in that accommodation[6]. However, this does not apply if the authority is satisfied that it has evidence of the current level of the person's literacy and numeracy skills[7].

1   The Education Act 1996 s 562E is added by the Apprenticeships, Skills, Children and Learning Act 2009 s 50. At the date at which this volume states the law the Education Act 1996 s 562E is only in force for certain purposes in regard to England: see the Apprenticeships, Skills, Children and Learning Act 2009 (Commencement No 2 and Transitional and Saving Provisions) Order 2010, SI 2010/303, art 6, Sch 5. The Education Act 1996 s 562G is to be brought into force in relation to England for remaining purposes and in relation to Wales as from a day to be appointed under the Apprenticeships, Skills, Children and Learning Act 2009 s 269(3)(f), (4). At the date at which this volume states the law no such day had been appointed. As to the meanings of 'England' and 'Wales' see PARA 7 note 3.
2   As to the meaning of 'detained person' see PARA 547 note 1.
3   See the Education Act 1996 s 562E(1) (as added: see note 1). As to the meaning of 'relevant youth accommodation' see PARA 46 note 9.
4   As to the meaning of 'host authority' see PARA 548 note 10.
5   As to the meaning of 'beginning of the detention' see PARA 548 note 3.
6   Education Act 1996 s 562E(2) (as added: see note 1). As to the duty of an authority to regard to any guidance issued by the appropriate national authority see PARA 554.
7   Education Act 1996 s 562E(3) (as added: see note 1). The 'current level' of a detained person's literacy and numeracy skills is the level of those skills at the beginning of the period during which the person is detained in the relevant youth accommodation in question: s 562E(4) (as so added).

551.   Provision of information about detained persons.   Any person[1] who has provided education or training for a detained person[2] (whether before or during the period of detention) may provide information relating to the detained person to the home authority[3] or the host authority[4] for the purposes of, or in connection with, the provision of education or training for the detained person[5].

A local authority must, on a request made by a specified person[6] asking only for information which that person requires for the purposes of, or in connection with, the provision of education or training for the detained person (including education or training to be provided after the detained person's release from detention)[7], as soon as practicable provide to the person making the request such information that it holds relating to a detained person as is requested[8].

The Welsh Ministers[9] must, on a request by the home authority or the host authority, provide a copy of any relevant assessment report[10] for the purposes of the exercise of any function[11] of that authority[12].

If it appears to the host authority that a detained person is to be released from detention in relevant youth accommodation[13], the host authority must provide to the home authority any information it holds which relates to the detained person[14] and may be relevant for the purposes of, or in connection with, the provision of education or training for the detained person after the release[15]. The information must be provided at such time as the host authority thinks reasonable for the purpose of enabling education or training to be provided for the detained person after the release[16].

1   As to the meaning of 'person' see PARA 7 note 6.
2   As to the meaning of 'detained person' see PARA 547 note 1. As to the provision of education and training for detained persons see PARAS 547, 548.
3   Education Act 1996 s 562F(1)(a) (s 562F added by the Apprenticeships, Skills, Children and Learning Act 2009 s 50). As to the meaning of 'home authority' see PARA 548 note 3.
      At the date at which this volume states the law, of the Education Act 1996 s 562F, s 562F(1)–(4), (11) is in force, and this in relation to England only and for certain purposes: see the Apprenticeships, Skills, Children and Learning Act 2009 (Commencement No 2 and

Transitional and Saving Provisions) Order 2010, SI 2010/303, art 6, Sch 5. The Education Act 1996 s 562F(1)–(6), (11) has also been brought into force in relation to Wales: see the Apprenticeships, Skills, Children and Learning Act 2009 (Commencement No 3) (Wales) Order 2011, SI 2011/829. The Education Act 1996 s 562F is to be brought into force for remaining purposes as from a day to be appointed under the Apprenticeships, Skills, Children and Learning Act 2009 s 269(3)(f), (4). At the date at which this volume states the law no such day had been appointed. As to the meanings of 'England' and 'Wales' see PARA 7 note 3.

4   Education Act 1996 s 562F(1)(b) (as added: see note 3). In s 562F any reference to the 'host authority', in relation to a detained person, includes a reference to any local authority in whose area the person is expected to be detained: s 562F(11) (as so added; and amended by SI 2010/1158). As to the meaning of 'host authority' see PARA 548 note 10. As to the meaning of 'local authority' see PARA 25.

5   Education Act 1996 s 562F(1) (as added: see note 3).

6   See the Education Act 1996 s 562F(2), (3)(a) (as added: see note 3). The specified persons are: (1) any other local authority (s 562F(4)(a) (as so added; and amended by SI 2010/1158)); (2) a youth offending team established under the Crime and Disorder Act 1998 s 39 (see CHILDREN AND YOUNG PERSONS vol 10 (2012) PARA 1192) (Education Act 1996 s 562F(4)(b) (as so added)); (3) the person in charge of any place at which the detained person is detained or is expected to be detained (s 562F(4)(c) (as so added)); (4) any person providing or proposing to provide education or training for the detained person (s 562F(4)(d) (as so added)).

7   See the Education Act 1996 s 562F(2), (3)(b) (as added: see note 3).

8   Education Act 1996 s 562F(2) (as added (see note 3); and amended by SI 2010/1158). As to the duty of a local authority to regard to any guidance issued by the appropriate national authority see PARA 554.

9   As to the Welsh Ministers see PARA 59.

10   'Relevant assessment report' means a report of an assessment of a detained person conducted (whether before or during the period of detention) under the Learning and Skills Act 2000 s 140 (see PARA 998) (Education Act 1996 s 562F(6)(a) (as added: see note 3)), and by virtue of arrangements made by the Welsh Ministers (s 562F(6)(b) (as so added)).

11   Ie under the Education Act 1996 s 18A (see PARA 38) or Pt X Ch 5A (ss 562A–562J). As to the meaning of 'function' see PARA 18 note 5.

12   Education Act 1996 s 562F(5) (as added: see note 3).

13   See the Education Act 1996 s 562F(7) (as added: see note 3). As to the meaning of 'relevant youth accommodation' see PARA 46 note 9.

14   Education Act 1996 s 562F(8)(a) (as added: see note 3).

15   Education Act 1996 s 562F(8)(b) (as added: see note 3).

16   Education Act 1996 s 562F(9) (as added: see note 3). Nothing in s 562F(7)–(9) requires the host authority to provide to the home authority information which it appears to the host authority that the home authority already has: s 562F(10) (as so added).

552.   Information to be provided where statement of special educational needs previously maintained.   As from a day to be appointed the following provisions have effect[1].

The following provisions apply in relation to a detained person[2] if, immediately before the beginning of the detention[3], a local authority in Wales[4] was maintaining a statement of special educational needs[5] for the person[6].

Where the home authority[7], where it is a local authority in Wales, becomes aware[8] that the person has become subject to a detention order[9] and is detained in relevant youth accommodation[10], or that the person has been transferred from one place of accommodation to another place of accommodation which is relevant youth accommodation[11]:

(1)   if, immediately before the beginning of the detention, the home authority was maintaining the statement, it must send a copy of the statement to the host authority[12];

(2)   if the home authority is or becomes aware that, immediately before the beginning of the detention, another local authority in Wales was

maintaining a statement for the person[13], it must notify the host authority of that fact[14], and of the identity of that other local authority[15].

Where the person is released from detention in relevant youth accommodation[16], the host authority must notify the following of the person's release: (a) the home authority, where it is a local authority in Wales[17]; and (b) if different, the authority in Wales who, immediately before the beginning of the detention, was maintaining the statement[18]. If the home authority, where it is a local authority in Wales, is not the authority who, immediately before the beginning of the detention, was maintaining the statement, the host authority must also notify the home authority of the fact that immediately before the beginning of the detention a statement was being maintained[19] for the person by a local authority in Wales[20], and of the identity of that authority[21].

Nothing in the above provisions requires any local authority to notify another authority of any matter of which the other authority is already aware, or to send a copy of any statement to another authority who already has a copy of it[22].

The position in regard to detained persons with special educational needs and disabilities in England is now covered by provisions under the Children and Families Act 2014[23].

1   The Education Act 1996 s 562G is added by the Apprenticeships, Skills, Children and Learning Act 2009 s 50. At the date at which this volume states the law the Education Act 1996 s 562G is only in force for certain purposes in regard to England: see the Apprenticeships, Skills, Children and Learning Act 2009 (Commencement No 2 and Transitional and Saving Provisions) Order 2010, SI 2010/303, art 6, Sch 5. The Education Act 1996 s 562G was to be brought into force in relation to England for remaining purposes and in relation to Wales as from a day to be appointed under the Apprenticeships, Skills, Children and Learning Act 2009 s 269(3)(f), (4). At the date at which this volume states the law no such day had been appointed. However in relation to England see also the text and note 23. As to the meanings of 'England' and 'Wales' see PARA 7 note 3.
2   As to the meaning of 'detained person' see PARA 547 note 1.
3   As to the meaning of 'beginning of the detention' see PARA 548 note 3.
4   As to the meaning of 'local authority' see PARA 25.
5   Ie a statement under the Education Act 1996 s 324: see PARA 1002.
6   Education Act 1996 s 562G(1) (as added (see note 1); and amended by the Children and Families Act 2014 Sch 3 paras 1, 57(1), (2)).
7   As to the meaning of 'home authority' see PARA 548 note 3. As to the duty of an authority to regard to any guidance issued by the appropriate national authority see PARA 554.
8   Ie whether by notice under the Crime and Disorder Act 1998 s 39A(2) (detention of child or young person: local authorities to be notified) (see CHILDREN AND YOUNG PERSONS) or otherwise: Education Act 1996 s 562G(2) (as added (see note 1); and amended by SI 2010/1158; and the Children and Families Act 2014 Sch 3 paras 1, 57(1), (3)).
9   Education Act 1996 s 562G(2)(a)(i) (as added: see note 1). As to when a person is subject to a detention order see PARA 46 note 8.
10 Education Act 1996 s 562G(2)(a)(ii) (as added: see note 1). As to the meaning of 'relevant youth accommodation' see PARA 46 note 9.
11 Education Act 1996 s 562G(2)(b) (as added: see note 1).
12 Education Act 1996 s 562G(3) (as added: see note 1). As to the meaning of 'host authority' see PARA 548 note 10.
13 Ie under the Education Act 1996 s 324: see PARA 1002.
14 Education Act 1996 s 562G(4)(a) (as added (see note 1); and amended by SI 2010/1158; and the Education Act 1996 s 562G(4) amended by the Children and Families Act 2014 Sch 3 paras 1, 57(1), (4)).
15 Education Act 1996 s 562G(4)(b) (as added (see note 1); and amended by SI 2010/1158). The local authority in Wales who, immediately before the beginning of the detention, was maintaining the statement must, on a request by the host authority, send a copy of the statement to the host authority: Education Act 1996 s 562G(5) (as so added and amended; and amended by the Children and Families Act 2014 Sch 3 paras 1, 57(1), (5)).
16 Education Act 1996 s 562G(6) (as added: see note 1).

17 Education Act 1996 s 562G(7)(a) (as added (see note 1); and amended by the Children and Families Act 2014 Sch 3 paras 1, 57(1), (6)(a)).
18 Education Act 1996 s 562G(7)(b) (as added (see note 1); and amended by the Children and Families Act 2014 Sch 3 paras 1, 57(1), (6)(b)).
19 Ie under the Education Act 1996 s 324: see PARA 1002.
20 Education Act 1996 s 562G(8)(a) (as added (see note 1); and amended by SI 2010/1158; and the Education Act 1996 s 562G(8) further amended by the Children and Families Act 2014 Sch 3 paras 1, 57(1), (7)).
21 Education Act 1996 s 562G(8)(b) (as added: see note 1).
22 Education Act 1996 s 562G(9) (as added (see note 1); and amended by SI 2010/1158).
23 See in particular the Children and Families Act 2014 ss 70–75; the Special Educational Needs and Disability (Detained Persons) Regulations 2015, SI 2015/62; and PARAS 957, 958, 964, 970–975, 976, 982. Reference should be made to 'Special Educational Needs and Disability Code of Practice: 0 to 25 years': see PARA 978 note 36. See also generally the Special Educational Needs and Disability Regulations 2014, SI 2014/1530; and PARAS 951, 957, 958, 961, 964, 965, 976, 969, 980, 982.

553. Release of detained person appearing to host authority to require assessment as to special educational needs. As from a day to be appointed the following provisions have effect[1].

The following provisions apply in relation to the release from detention in relevant youth accommodation[2] of a detained person[3] in relation to whom, immediately before the beginning of the detention[4], no local authority[5] was maintaining a statement[6] of special educational needs, and for whom the home authority[7] is a local authority in Wales[8].

Where it appears to the host authority[9] that the detained person will, on release, be a child[10], if the host authority is of the opinion that the person has, or may have, special educational needs[11], it must, on the person's release, notify the home authority of its opinion[12].

Where, on release, the detained person will be over compulsory school age[13], or will cease to be of compulsory school age within one year[14], if the host authority is of the opinion that the person has, or may have, a learning difficulty[15], the host authority must, on the person's release, notify the Welsh Ministers[16] of its opinion[17].

The position in regard to detained persons with special educational needs and disabilities in England is now covered by provisions under the Children and Families Act 2014[18].

1 The Education Act 1996 s 562H is added by the Apprenticeships, Skills, Children and Learning Act 2009 s 50. At the date at which this volume states the law the Education Act 1996 s 562H is only in force for certain purposes in regard to England: see the Apprenticeships, Skills, Children and Learning Act 2009 (Commencement No 2 and Transitional and Saving Provisions) Order 2010, SI 2010/303, art 6, Sch 5. The Education Act 1996 s 562H was to be brought into force in relation to England for remaining purposes and in relation to Wales as from a day to be appointed under the Apprenticeships, Skills, Children and Learning Act 2009 s 269(3)(f), (4). At the date at which this volume states the law no such day had been appointed. However in relation to England see also the text and note 18. As to the meanings of 'England' and 'Wales' see PARA 7 note 3.
2 As to the meaning of 'relevant youth accommodation' see PARA 46 note 9.
3 As to the meaning of 'detained person' see PARA 547 note 1.
4 As to the meaning of 'beginning of the detention' see PARA 548 note 3.
5 As to the meaning of 'local authority' see PARA 25.
6 Ie a statement under the Education Act 1996 s 324: see PARA 1002.
7 As to the meaning of 'home authority' see PARA 548 note 3.
8 See the Education Act 1996 s 562H(1) (as added (see note 1); and amended by the Children and Families Act 2014 Sch 3 paras 1, 58(1), (2)). The detained person referred to is one in relation to whom the Education Act 1996 s 562G (see PARA 552) does not apply: see s 562H(1) (as so added and amended).

9 As to the meaning of 'host authority' see PARA 548 note 10. As to the duty of an authority to regard to any guidance issued by the appropriate national authority see PARA 554.

10 Education Act 1996 s 562H(2) (as added: see note 1). 'Child' means a child within the meaning of Pt IV (ss 311A–349) (see PARA 989 note 1): see s 562H(2) (as so added).

11 As to the meaning of 'special educational needs' see PARA 989.

12 Education Act 1996 s 562H(3) (as added: see note 1).

13 Education Act 1996 s 562H(4)(a) (as added (see note 1); and amended by the Children and Families Act 2014 Sch 3 paras 1, 58(1), (3)). As to the meaning of 'compulsory school age' see PARA 19.

14 Education Act 1996 s 562H(4)(b) (as added: see note 1).

15 Education Act 1996 s 562H(6)(a) (as added: see note 1). 'Learning difficulty' means a learning difficulty within the meaning of the Learning and Skills Act 2000 s 41 (assessments relating to learning difficulties: Wales) (see PARA 791 note 6): see the Education Act 1996 s 562H(6)(a) (as so added).

16 As to the Welsh Ministers see PARA 59.

17 Education Act 1996 s 562H(6) (as added (see note 1); and s 562H(6)(b) repealed by the Children and Families Act 2014 Sch 3 paras 1, 58(1), (3)).

18 See in particular the Children and Families Act 2014 ss 70–75; the Special Educational Needs and Disability (Detained Persons) Regulations 2015, SI 2015/62; and PARAS 957, 958, 964, 970–975, 976, 982. Reference should be made to 'Special Educational Needs and Disability Code of Practice: 0 to 25 years': see PARA 978 note 36. See also generally the Special Educational Needs and Disability Regulations 2014, SI 2014/1530; and PARAS 951, 957, 958, 961, 964, 965, 969, 976, 980, 982.

554. Guidance. In performing its functions[1] under the statutory provisions relating to persons detained in youth accommodation[2], a local authority[3] must have regard to any guidance[4] issued by the appropriate national authority[5].

1 As to the meaning of 'functions' see PARA 18 note 5.

2 Ie the Education Act 1996 Pt X Ch 5A (ss 562A–562J).

3 As to the meaning of 'local authority' see PARA 25.

4 As to the publication of guidance see the Education Act 1996 s 571; and PARA 60. In particular in relation to England and children with special needs and disabilities see 'Special Educational Needs and Disability Code of Practice: 0 to 25 years'; and PARA 978 note 36.

5 Education Act 1996 s 562I (added by the Apprenticeships, Skills, Children and Learning Act 2009 s 50). As to the meaning of 'appropriate national authority' see PARA 547 note 3.

At the date at which this volume states the law, the Education Act 1996 s 562I is in force in relation to England for certain purposes: see the Apprenticeships, Skills, Children and Learning Act 2009 (Commencement No 2 and Transitional and Saving Provisions) Order 2010, SI 2010/303, art 6, Sch 5. The Education Act 1996 s 562I has also been brought into force in relation to Wales: see the Apprenticeships, Skills, Children and Learning Act 2009 (Commencement No 3) (Wales) Order 2011, SI 2011/829. The Education Act 1996 s 562I will be brought into force in relation to England for remaining purposes as from a day to be appointed under the Apprenticeships, Skills, Children and Learning Act 2009 s 269(3)(f), (4). At the date at which this volume states the law no such day had been appointed. As to the meanings of 'England' and 'Wales' see PARA 7 note 3.

3. FURTHER EDUCATION

(1) INSTITUTIONS WITHIN THE FURTHER EDUCATION SECTOR

(i) The Institutions

555. Meaning of 'institution within the further education sector'. Further education[1] is provided at a variety of institutions, generally described as 'institutions within the further education sector'. For the purposes of the Education Acts[2], references to 'institutions within the further education sector' are references to institutions conducted by further education corporations[3], designated institutions[4], and sixth form colleges[5]; and references to 'institutions outside the further education sector' are to be read accordingly[6].

Institutions within the further education sector may also provide secondary or higher education[7].

1   As to the meaning of 'further education' see PARA 23 (definition applied by the Further and Higher Education Act 1992 s 90(1) (amended by the Education Act 1996 Sch 37 Pt I para 115(2))).

2   See the Further and Higher Education Act 1992 s 91(1). As to the meaning of 'the Education Acts' see PARA 1 note 13 (definition applied by s 90(1) (amended by the Education Act 1996 Sch 37 Pt I para 115(2))).

3   Further and Higher Education Act 1992 s 91(3)(a). 'Further education corporation' means a body corporate established under s 15 (see PARA 559) or s 16 (see PARA 560), or which has become a further education corporation by virtue of s 33D (see PARA 580) or s 47 (see PARA 556): s 17(1) (amended by the Teaching and Higher Education Act 1998 Sch 3 para 7; and the Apprenticeships, Skills, Children and Learning Act 2009 Sch 8 paras 1, 2). As to bodies corporate see COMPANIES vol 14 (2009) PARA 2; CORPORATIONS vol 24 (2010) PARA 301 et seq.

4   Ie institutions designated for the purposes of the Further and Higher Education Act 1992 Pt 1 (ss 1–61A): see s 91(3)(b). As to the meaning of 'designated institution' see PARA 572.

5   Further and Higher Education Act 1992 s 91(3)(c) (added by the Apprenticeships, Skills, Children and Learning Act 2009 Sch 8 paras 1, 13(1), (2)). References to 'sixth form colleges' are to institutions conducted by sixth form college corporations: Further and Higher Education Act 1992 s 91(3A) (added by the Apprenticeships, Skills, Children and Learning Act 2009 Sch 8 paras 1, 13(1), (3)). As to the meaning of 'sixth form college corporation' see PARA 577 note 7.

6   Further and Higher Education Act 1992 s 91(3). For the purposes of the Education Act 1996 an institution is outside the further education sector if it is not (1) an institution conducted by a further education corporation established under the Further and Higher Education Act 1992 s 15 (see PARA 559) or s 16 (see PARA 560); or (2) a designated institution for the purposes of Pt I of that Act (see PARA 572); or (3) a sixth form college; and references to institutions within that sector must be construed accordingly: Education Act 1996 s 4(3) (amended by SI 2010/1080). As to institutions outside the further education sector providing further education see PARA 587 et seq.

7   See PARAS 567, 572.

556. Transfer of higher education institutions to further education sector. The appropriate national authority[1] may by order[2] provide for the transfer of a higher education corporation[3] to the further education sector[4]. On such date as may be specified in the order the corporation ceases to be a higher education corporation and becomes a further education corporation[5].

An order[6] in respect of any institution designating it as a further education institution may revoke any order[7] in respect of that institution designating it as a higher education institution[8].

1   Ie the Secretary of State or, in relation to Wales, the Welsh Ministers. As to the Secretary of State see PARA 58. As to the Welsh Ministers see PARA 59. As to the meaning of 'Wales' see PARA 7

note 3. The functions of the Secretary of State under the Further and Higher Education Act 1992 s 47, so far as exercisable in relation to Wales, were transferred to the National Assembly for Wales (see the National Assembly for Wales (Transfer of Functions) Order 1999, SI 1999/672, art 2, Sch 1) and are now vested in the Welsh Ministers (see the Government of Wales Act 2006 s 162(1), Sch 11 para 30).

2   Such orders, being of local effect, are not recorded in this work.

3   As to the meaning of 'higher education corporation' see PARA 645.

4   Further and Higher Education Act 1992 s 47(1). Where an order is made under s 47 in respect of a higher education corporation, the provisions of s 20 (see PARA 562) and s 21 (see PARA 563) have effect as if, on the date the order has effect, the corporation were established as a further education corporation; and the order may make provision as to the initial name of the corporation as a further education corporation: s 47(2) (amended by the School Standards and Framework Act 1998 s 140(1), Sch 30 paras 33, 43). As to the meaning of 'further education corporation' see PARA 555 note 3.

5   Further and Higher Education Act 1992 s 47(3).

6   Ie an order under the Further and Higher Education Act 1992 s 28: see PARA 572.

7   Ie an order under the Education Reform Act 1988 s 129: see PARA 671.

8   Further and Higher Education Act 1992 s 47(4).

557. Transfer of further education corporations to higher education sector.

The appropriate national authority[1] may by order[2] provide for the transfer of a further education corporation[3] to the higher education sector if it appears to it that the full-time equivalent enrolment number[4] of the institution conducted by the corporation for courses of higher education[5] exceeds 55 per cent of its total full-time equivalent enrolment number[6]. On such date as may be specified in the order the corporation ceases to be a further education corporation and becomes a higher education corporation[7] and any member of the further education corporation who is not re-appointed by the appropriate national authority[8] ceases to hold office[9].

1   Ie the Secretary of State or, in relation to Wales, the Welsh Ministers. As to the Secretary of State see PARA 58. As to the Welsh Ministers see PARA 59. As to the meaning of 'Wales' see PARA 7 note 3. The functions of the Secretary of State under the Education Reform Act 1988 s 122A, so far as exercisable in relation to Wales, were transferred to the National Assembly for Wales (see the National Assembly for Wales (Transfer of Functions) Order 1999, SI 1999/672, art 2, Sch 1) and are now vested in the Welsh Ministers (see the Government of Wales Act 2006 s 162(1), Sch 11 para 30).

2   Such orders, being of local effect, are not recorded in this work.

3   As to the meaning of 'further education corporation' see PARA 555 note 3.

4   As to the meaning of 'full-time equivalent enrolment number' see PARA 651.

5   As to the meaning of 'courses of higher education' see PARA 684.

6   Education Reform Act 1988 s 122A(1) (s 122A added by the Further and Higher Education Act 1992 s 74(1)). As to the calculation of full-time equivalent enrolment numbers see PARA 651.

7   As to the meaning of 'higher education corporation' see PARA 645.

8   Ie in pursuance of the Education Reform Act 1988 s 122A(2)(b): see note 9.

9   Education Reform Act 1988 s 122A(4) (as added: see note 6). Where an order under s 122A (see the text to notes 1–6) is made in respect of a further education corporation s 124A (constitution and conduct of corporations: see PARA 657) and s 125 (articles of government: see PARA 664) have effect as if: (1) on the date the order has effect, the corporation were established as a higher education corporation (s 122A(2)(a) (as so added)); and (2) the appropriate national authority were the appointing authority in relation to the first members of the higher education corporation (s 122A(2)(b) (as so added)). In determining in pursuance of s 122A(2)(b) the number of members to appoint within each variable category of members, the appropriate national authority must secure that at least half of all the members of the higher education corporation as first constituted are independent members: s 122A(3) (as so added). As to the meaning of references to 'variable category of members' see PARA 660 note 5; and as to the meaning of 'independent members' see PARA 652 note 8 (definitions applied by s 122A(3) (as so added)).

558. Unauthorised use of 'university' in title of institution. An institution within the further education sector[1] in England or Wales [2]must not, when making available (or offering to make available)[3] educational services, do so under a name which includes the word 'university' unless the inclusion of that word in that name is authorised by or by virtue of any Act or Royal Charter[4], or is approved by the Privy Council[5]. A person[6] carrying on such an institution must not, when making available (or offering to make available) educational services through the institution, use with reference either to himself or the institution a name which includes the word 'university', unless the inclusion of that word in that name is so authorised or approved[7].

In approving the inclusion of the word 'university' in any name, the Privy Council must have regard to the need to avoid names which are or may be confusing[8].

1   As to the meaning of 'institution within the further education sector' see PARA 555.
2   As to the meanings of 'England' and 'Wales' see PARA 7 note 3.
3   The provisions of the Teaching and Higher Education Act 1998 s 39(1), (2) (see the text to notes 6–7) apply where the educational services are made available, or (as the case may be) the offer to make such services available is made, in any part of the United Kingdom: s 39(3). As to the meaning of 'United Kingdom' see PARA 73 note 3.
4   Teaching and Higher Education Act 1998 s 39(1)(a). For the purposes of s 39(1) or (2) (see the text to notes 6–7), the inclusion of the word 'university' in any name must not be taken to be authorised by or by virtue of a Royal Charter relating to a university by reason of any provision of the Royal Charter with respect to the affiliation or association of other institutions to the university (s 39(4)(a)), or the accreditation by the university of educational services provided by other institutions (s 39(4)(b)). As to the meaning of 'university' in the context of the reference in s 39(4) to a Royal Charter relating to a university see PARA 621 note 3 (definition applied by s 39(7)). See also PARA 621. As to incorporation by Royal Charter see CORPORATIONS vol 24 (2010) PARA 331 et seq.
5   Teaching and Higher Education Act 1998 s 39(1)(b). The Privy Council's power of approval under s 39(1) or (2) (see the text to notes 6–7) is not exercisable in a case where the inclusion of the word 'university' in the name in question may be authorised by virtue of any other Act or any Royal Charter: s 39(6). See also *R (on the application of Liverpool Hope University College) v Secretary of State for Education and Employment* [2001] EWCA Civ 362, [2001] ELR 552, [2001] All ER (D) 170 (Mar). As to the Privy Council see CONSTITUTIONAL AND ADMINISTRATIVE LAW vol 20 (2014) PARA 268 et seq.
6   As to the meaning of 'person' see PARA 7 note 6.
7   Teaching and Higher Education Act 1998 s 39(2). See also notes 3–5.
8   Teaching and Higher Education Act 1998 s 39(5).

(ii) Further Education Corporations

A. INCORPORATION

559. Initial incorporation of existing institutions. A body corporate had to be established on 30 September 1992[1] for each institution[2] then existing and specified by order[3] made by the Secretary of State, for the purpose of conducting the institution as from the operative date[4].

1   Ie the day appointed under the Further and Higher Education Act 1992 s 94 for the commencement of s 15(4): s 15(7).
2   Ie an institution falling within one of the following provisions: (1) each educational institution maintained by a local education authority for which it appeared to the Secretary of State that on 1 November 1990 its enrolment number calculated in accordance with the Further and Higher Education Act 1992 Sch 3 para 1(1) was not less than 15% of its total enrolment number calculated in accordance with Sch 3 para 1(2) (see s 15(1)(a), (2)); and (2) each county school, controlled school or grant-maintained school for which it appeared to the Secretary of State that on 17 January 1991 not less than 60% of the pupils at the institution were receiving full-time

education suitable to the requirements of persons over compulsory school age who have not attained the age of 19 years (see s 15(1)(b), (3)). As to the Secretary of State see PARA 58. As to county schools, controlled schools and grant-maintained schools see PARA 106. As to the meaning of 'pupil' see PARA 20 note 4 (definition applied by s 90(5) (amended by the Education Act 1996 s 582(1), Sch 37 Pt I para 115(1), (3))). As to the meaning of 'compulsory school age' see PARA 19.

Where an educational institution, being an institution maintained by a local education authority or a grant-maintained school, was established after 1 November 1990 or, as the case may be, 17 January 1991 by a merger of two or more institutions existing on that date, the institution had to be treated as falling within the Further and Higher Education Act 1992 s 15(2) or, as the case may be s 15(3) if it would have done so if the merger had taken place before that date: s 15(6).

3 The name given in the order as the name of the institution was the initial name of the body corporate: Further and Higher Education Act 1992 s 15(5). Orders under s 15, being of local effect, are not recorded in this work.

4 See the Further and Higher Education Act 1992 s 15(1), (4). In the case of a further education corporation established under s 15, the 'operative date' means such date as the Secretary of State may by order appoint in relation to the corporations so established: s 17(2)(a). The operative date for these purposes is 1 April 1993: see the Education (Further Education Corporations) Order 1992, SI 1992/2097. As to the meaning of 'further education corporation' see PARA 555 note 3.

560. Orders incorporating further institutions. The appropriate national authority[1] may by order[2] make provision for the establishment of a body corporate[3] for the purpose of establishing and conducting an educational institution[4], or for the purpose of conducting an existing educational institution[5]. An order may not, however, be made in respect of an existing institution without the consent of the governing body[6].

The appropriate national authority may also by order[7] make provision for the establishment of a body corporate[8] for the purpose of conducting an institution which: (1) is maintained by a local authority[9]; and (2) is principally concerned with the provision of full-time education suitable to the requirements of persons over compulsory school age[10] who have not attained the age of 19 years[11].

Any order under the above provisions must provide for the institution to be conducted by the body corporate as from the operative date[12].

1 Ie the Secretary of State or, in relation to Wales, the Welsh Ministers. As to the Secretary of State see PARA 58. As to the Welsh Ministers see PARA 59. As to the meaning of 'Wales' see PARA 7 note 3. The functions of the Secretary of State under the Further and Higher Education Act 1992 ss 16, 90, so far as exercisable in relation to Wales, were transferred to the National Assembly for Wales (see the National Assembly for Wales (Transfer of Functions) Order 1999, SI 1999/672, art 2, Sch 1) and are now vested in the Welsh Ministers (see the Government of Wales Act 2006 s 162(1), Sch 11 para 30).

2 Such orders, being of local effect, are not recorded in this work.

3 The name given in the order as the name of the institution is to be the initial name of the body corporate: see the Further and Higher Education Act 1992 s 16(4). As to bodies corporate see COMPANIES vol 14 (2009) PARA 2; CORPORATIONS vol 24 (2010) PARA 301 et seq.

4 Further and Higher Education Act 1992 s 16(1)(a). Section 16(1) does not apply to an institution which is maintained by a local authority: s 16(2) (substituted by the Learning and Skills Act 2000 s 111(1); and amended by SI 2010/1158). As to the publication of proposals under the Further and Higher Education Act 1992 s 16(1), (3) see s 16A; and PARA 561.

5 Further and Higher Education Act 1992 s 16(1)(b). See also note 4.

6 Further and Higher Education Act 1992 s 16(1). 'Governing body', in relation to an institution, means: (1) in the case of an institution conducted by a further education corporation, a sixth form college corporation, or a higher education corporation, the corporation; (2) in the case of a university not falling within head (1), the executive governing body which has responsibility for the management and administration of its revenue and property and the conduct of its affairs; (3) in the case of any other institution not falling within head (1) or head (2) for which there is an instrument of government providing for the constitution of a governing body, the governing body so provided for; and (4) in any other case, any board of governors of the

institution or any persons responsible for the management of the institution, whether or not formally constituted as a governing body or board of governors: s 90(1) (definition amended by the Apprenticeships, Skills, Children and Learning Act 2009 s 125, Sch 8 paras 1, 12(1), (2)). As to the meaning of 'further education corporation' see PARA 555 note 3. As to the meaning of 'sixth form college corporation' see PARA 577 note 7. As to the meaning of 'higher education corporation' see PARA 645. As to the meaning of 'person' see PARA 7 note 6. The appropriate national authority may by order provide for any reference in the Education Acts to the governing body of an institution, in relation to an institution which is a designated institution for the purposes of the Further and Higher Education Act 1992 Pt I (ss 15–61A) or Pt II (ss 62–81) and which is conducted by a company, to be read as a reference to the governing body provided for in the instrument of government, or to the company, or to both: s 90(2). As to the order made see the Education (Designated Institutions in Further and Higher Education) (Interpretation) Order 1993, SI 1993/563 (amended by SI 1993/870). As to the meaning of 'the Education Acts' see PARA 1 note 13 (definition applied by the Further and Higher Education Act 1992 s 90(1) (definition amended by the Education Act 1996 s 582(1), Sch 37 Pt I para 115))).

7 Such orders, being of local effect, are not recorded in this work.
8 The name given in the order as the name of the institution is to be the initial name of the body corporate: see the Further and Higher Education Act 1992 s 16(4).
9 Further and Higher Education Act 1992 s 16(3)(a) (s 16(3) substituted by the Learning and Skills Act 2000 s 111(1); and the Further and Higher Education Act 1992 s 16(3)(a) amended by SI 2010/1158). As to the meaning of 'local authority' see PARA 25 (definition applied by the Further and Higher Education Act 1992 s 90(1) (definition amended by SI 2010/1158)). See note 4.
10 As to the meaning of 'compulsory school age' see PARA 19.
11 Further and Higher Education Act 1992 s 16(3)(b) (as substituted: see note 9). As to the time at which a person attains a particular age see PARA 7 note 4. See note 4.
12 See the Further and Higher Education Act 1992 s 16(5). In the case of a further education corporation established under s 16, the 'operative date' means such date as the appropriate national authority may by order appoint in relation to that corporation: see s 17(2)(b). Such orders, being of local effect, are not recorded in this work.

561. Publication of draft proposals for incorporation. The appropriate authority[1] may not make an order for incorporating further institutions[2] unless the authority has published a draft of the proposed order, or of an order in substantially the same form, by such time and in such manner as may be prescribed[3]. A draft proposal or order in respect of an institution which is maintained by a local authority[4] may not be published without the consent of the governing body[5] and the local authority[6].

1 For these purposes, 'appropriate authority' means (1) in relation to a proposal or order in respect of an institution in England, the Secretary of State; (2) in relation to a proposal or order in respect of an institution in Wales, the Welsh Ministers: Further and Higher Education Act 1992 s 16A(3) (s 16A added by the Education Act 2011 Sch 12 paras 1, 2). As to the Secretary of State see PARA 58. As to the Welsh Ministers see PARA 59. As to the meanings of 'England' and 'Wales see PARA 7 note 3.
2 Ie under the Further and Higher Education Act 1992 s 16(1) or s 16(3): see PARA 560.
3 Further and Higher Education Act 1992 s 16A(1) (as added: see note 1). As to regulations made under s 16A(1) see the Further Education Corporations (Publication of Proposals) (England) Regulations 2012, SI 2012/1157.
4 As to the meaning of 'local authority' see PARA 25 (definition applied by the Further and Higher Education Act 1992 s 90(1) (definition amended by SI 2010/1158)).
5 As to the meaning of 'governing body' see PARA 560 note 6.
6 Further and Higher Education Act 1992 s 16A(2) (as added: see note 1).

B. CONSTITUTION AND GOVERNANCE

562. Requirement for instruments of government and articles of government. For every further education corporation[1] established to conduct an educational institution there must be:

(1) an instrument providing for the constitution of the corporation (the 'instrument of government')[2]; and

(2) an instrument in accordance with which the corporation, and the institution, are to be conducted (the 'articles of government')[3].

Instruments of government and articles of government must comply with the statutory requirements[4], and may make any authorised provision[5] and such other provision as may be necessary or desirable[6]. Every document purporting to be an instrument made or issued by or on behalf of a further education corporation and to be duly executed under the seal of the corporation, or to be signed or executed by a person authorised by the corporation to act in that behalf, is to be received in evidence and to be treated, without further proof, as being so made or issued unless the contrary is shown[7].

An instrument[8] must provide for (a) the number of members of the body[9]; (b) the eligibility of persons for membership[10]; (c) the members to include staff and students at the institution, and in the case of a sixth form college corporation, parents of students at the institution aged under 19[11]; and (d) the appointment of members, if the institution is in England[12], or the appointment or election of members, if the institution is in Wales[13].

An instrument must make provision about the procedures of the body and the institution[14]. In particular, an instrument must specify how the body may resolve for its dissolution and the transfer of its property, rights and liabilities[15].

An instrument must make provision for there to be a chief executive of the institution, and a clerk to the body[16]. An instrument must make provision about the respective responsibilities of the body[17], the chief executive and the clerk[18].

An instrument must require the body to publish arrangements for obtaining the views of staff and students on the matters for which the body is responsible[19].

In the case of an institution in Wales, an instrument must require the body to consult persons in the locality of the institution receiving education or training, employers[20] in that locality and bodies representing persons living in that locality as to the education provided at the institution and the planning of its curriculum[21].

An instrument must permit the body to change its name with the approval of, in the case of an institution in England, the Secretary of State[22]; in the case of an institution in Wales, the Welsh Ministers[23].

An instrument must specify how the body may modify or replace the instrument of government and articles of government[24].

An instrument must prohibit the body from making changes to the instrument of government or articles of government that would result in the body ceasing to be a charity[25].

An instrument must provide for (i) a copy of the instrument to be given free of charge to every member of the body[26]; (ii) a copy of the instrument to be given free of charge, or at a charge not exceeding the cost of copying, to anyone else who requests it[27]; and (iii) a copy of it to be available for inspection at the institution on request, during normal office hours, to every member of staff of, and student at, the institution[28].

An instrument must provide for the authentication of the application of the seal of the body[29].

1   As to the meaning of 'further education corporation' see PARA 555 note 3.

2   Further and Higher Education Act 1992 s 20(1)(a).

3   Further and Higher Education Act 1992 s 20(1)(b).

4   Ie the requirements of the Further and Higher Education Act 1992 Sch 4 (see the text to notes 8–29): see s 20(2)(a) (s 20(2) substituted by the Further and Higher Education (Governance and Information) (Wales) Act 2014 s 20(1)).

5   Ie any provision authorised to be made by the Further and Higher Education Act 1992 Sch 4: see the text to notes 8–29.

6   Further and Higher Education Act 1992 s 20(2)(b) (as substituted: see note 4).

7   Further and Higher Education Act 1992 s 20(4).

8   In the Further and Higher Education Act 1992 Sch 4 'instrument' means an instrument of government or articles of association: Sch 4 para 2 (Sch 4 substituted by the Further and Higher Education (Governance and Information) (Wales) Act 2014 Sch 1).

9   Further and Higher Education Act 1992 Sch 4 para 3(1)(a) (as substituted: see note 8). 'Body' means (1) in the case of a further education corporation or a sixth form college corporation, the corporation; and (2) in the case of the governing body of a designated institution, the governing body; and 'institution' means (a) in the case of a further education corporation, the institution which the corporation are established to conduct; (b) in the case of the governing body of a designated institution, the institution; (c) in the case of a sixth form college corporation, the relevant sixth form college: Sch 4 para 2 (as so substituted). Schedule 4 applies in relation to (i) a further education corporation; (ii) the governing body of a designated institution; and (iii) a sixth form college corporation: Sch 4 para 1 (as so substituted). As to the meaning of 'sixth form college corporation' see PARA 577 note 7. As to the meaning of 'designated institution' see PARA 572. As to the meaning of 'governing body' see PARA 560 note 6.

10 Further and Higher Education Act 1992 Sch 4 para 3(1)(b) (as substituted: see note 8).

11 Further and Higher Education Act 1992 Sch 4 para 3(1)(c) (as substituted: see note 8). As to the meaning of 'parent' see PARA 7 note 6. As to the time at which a person attains a particular age see PARA 7 note 6.

12 As to the meaning of 'England' see PARA 7 note 3.

13 Further and Higher Education Act 1992 Sch 4 para 3(1)(d) (as substituted: see note 8). As to the meaning of 'Wales' see PARA 7 note 3. The validity of any proceedings of a further education corporation, or of any committee of the corporation, is not affected by a vacancy amongst the members or by any defect in the appointment or nomination of a member: s 20(3).

    In the case of an institution in Wales the provision made by an instrument must include provision:

    (1)   for the members of the body to include (a) the chief executive; (b) at least two other members of staff at the institution; (c) at least two students at the institution; and (d) one or more representatives of local employers or businesses (Sch 4 para 3(2)(a) (as so substituted));

    (2)   for at least one of the members who are members of staff to be a member of the teaching staff, and at least one to be a member of the non-teaching staff, elected at an election open to all members of staff from those nominated by any member of staff (Sch 4 para 3(2)(b) (as so substituted)); and

    (3)   for the members who are students to be elected at an election open to all the students at the institution from those nominated by any student or (if the body so determines) to be elected at an election open to all the members of an association which represents students at the institution, and is recognised by the body, from those nominated by any member of the association (Sch 4 para 3(2)(c) (as so substituted)).

14 Further and Higher Education Act 1992 Sch 4 para 4(1) (as substituted: see note 8). However, an instrument does not lay down a complete and exhaustive code for the conduct of meetings: *R v City of Bath College Corpn, ex p Bashforth* [1999] ELR 459 at 469 per Dyson J (under previous legislation).

15 Further and Higher Education Act 1992 Sch 4 para 4(2) (as substituted: see note 8). As to dissolution see PARA 571.

16 Further and Higher Education Act 1992 Sch 4 para 5(1) (as substituted: see note 8).

17 The responsibilities of the body must include:

    (1)   in the case of a sixth form college corporation to which the Further and Higher Education Act 1992 s 33J applies (see PARA 583), the preservation and development of the educational character and mission of the institution and the oversight of its activities (Sch 4 para 5(3)(a) (as substituted: see note 8);

    (2)   in the case of any other sixth form college corporation, a further education corporation or a governing body, the determination and periodic review of the educational character and mission of the institution and the oversight of its activities (Sch 4 para 5(3)(b) (as so substituted));

(3) in any case, the effective and efficient use of resources, the solvency of the institution and the body and the safeguarding of their assets (Sch 4 para 5(3)(c) (as so substituted)).

18 Further and Higher Education Act 1992 Sch 4 para 5(2) (as substituted: see note 8).
19 Further and Higher Education Act 1992 Sch 4 para 6 (as substituted: see note 8). The reference in the text to matters for which the body is responsible is a reference to the matters for which the body is responsible under Sch 4 para 5(3)(a) or (b): see note 17 heads (1), (2).
20 As to the meaning of 'employer' see PARA 569 note 9.
21 Further and Higher Education Act 1992 Sch 4 para 7 (as substituted: see note 8).
22 As to the Secretary of State see PARA 58.
23 Further and Higher Education Act 1992 Sch 4 para 8 (as substituted: see note 8). As to the Welsh Ministers see PARA 59.
24 Further and Higher Education Act 1992 Sch 4 para 9 (as substituted: see note 8).
25 Further and Higher Education Act 1992 Sch 4 para 10 (as substituted: see note 8). As to the charitable status of a further education corporation see PARA 566. As to charities generally see CHARITIES.
26 Further and Higher Education Act 1992 Sch 4 para 11(a) (as substituted: see note 8).
27 Further and Higher Education Act 1992 Sch 4 para 11(b) (as substituted: see note 8).
28 Further and Higher Education Act 1992 Sch 4 para 11(c) (as substituted: see note 8).
29 Further and Higher Education Act 1992 Sch 4 para 12 (as substituted: see note 8).

563. Initial instruments of government and articles of government. As from the date on which a further education corporation[1] is established, the instrument of government and articles of government[2] are to be such as are prescribed by regulations[3]. Such regulations[4]:

(1) may provide for all or any of the persons who, on the date on which a corporation is established to conduct the existing institution, are the members of the governing body[5] of the institution to be the initial members of the corporation[6]; and

(2) may make such other provision in relation to existing institutions as appears to the appropriate national authority necessary or desirable to secure continuity in their government[7].

In the case of a further education corporation established to conduct an institution which, on the date the corporation was established, was a maintained school[8], the governing body[9] is, on the operative date[10], dissolved[11].

1 As to the meaning of 'further education corporation' see PARA 555 note 3.
2 As to the requirement for instruments of government and articles of government see PARA 562.
3 Further and Higher Education Act 1992 s 21(1) (amended by the School Standards and Framework Act 1998 s 140(1), (3), Sch 30 paras 33, 35, Sch 31). 'Regulations' means regulations made by the appropriate national authority: see the Further and Higher Education Act 1992 s 61(1). 'Appropriate national authority' means the Secretary of State or, in relation to Wales, the Welsh Ministers. As to the Secretary of State see PARA 58. As to the Welsh Ministers see PARA 59. As to the meaning of 'Wales' see PARA 7 note 3. The functions of the Secretary of State under s 21, so far as exercisable in relation to Wales, were transferred to the National Assembly for Wales (see the National Assembly for Wales (Transfer of Functions) Order 1999, SI 1999/672, art 2, Sch 1) and are now vested in the Welsh Ministers (see the Government of Wales Act 2006 s 162(1), Sch 11 para 30). Regulations made under the Further and Higher Education Act 1992 s 21 are local in nature, and are not recorded in this work.
4 Further and Higher Education Act 1992 s 21(2) (amended by the School Standards and Framework Act 1998 Sch 30 paras 33, 35, Sch 31).
5 As to the meaning of 'governing body' see PARA 560 note 6.
6 Further and Higher Education Act 1992 s 21(2)(a) (as amended: see note 4).
7 Further and Higher Education Act 1992 s 21(2)(b) (as amended: see note 4).
8 As to the meaning of 'maintained school' see PARA 99 (definition applied by the Further and Higher Education Act 1992 s 90(5)).
9 Ie incorporated under the Education Act 2002 s 19: see PARAS 150, 195.
10 As to the meaning of 'operative date' see PARAS 559 note 4, 560 note 12.

11 Further and Higher Education Act 1992 s 21(3) (amended by the School Standards and Framework Act 1998 Sch 30 paras 33, 35; and the Education Act 2002 s 215(2), Sch 21 para 12).

564. Subsequent instruments of government and articles of government. A further education corporation[1] may modify or replace its instrument of government or articles of government[2].

1 As to the meaning of 'further education corporation' see PARA 555 note 3.
2 Further and Higher Education Act 1992 s 22 (substituted by the Further and Higher Education (Governance and Information) (Wales) Act 2014 s 2(3)).

565. Liability of members. Where a member of a further education corporation[1] is found liable in civil legal proceedings in respect of something which he did or omitted to do in the course of carrying out his duties as a member of the corporation[2], a court[3] may make an order extinguishing, reducing or varying the liability[4] if the member applies to the court for such an order[5] and the court considers that the action or omission which gives rise to the member's liability was honest and reasonable[6]. Where a member of such a corporation applies to a court for such an order, the court may make any order which: (1) relates to liability in civil legal proceedings which may come to be incurred by the member in respect of a specified course of action[7]; and (2) is of a kind which the court could have made if the liability had already been incurred[8].

1 Ie a further education corporation established by virtue of the Further and Higher Education Act 1992 s 15 (see PARA 559), s 16 (see PARA 560) or s 47 (see PARA 556): Learning and Skills Act 2000 s 145(3)(a). As to the meaning of 'further education corporation' in the Further and Higher Education Act 1992 see PARA 555 note 3.
2 See the Learning and Skills Act 2000 s 145(1). As to membership of a further education corporation see PARA 562.
3 'A court' means the High Court or the county court: Learning and Skills Act 2000 s 145(5) (amended by the Crime and Courts Act 2013 Sch 9 para 52(1)(b), (2)). However, the Learning and Skills Act 2000 s 145(5) is subject to any order under the Courts and Legal Services Act 1990 s 1 (allocation of business between High Court and county courts: see COURTS AND TRIBUNALS vol 24 (2010) PARA 863): see the Learning and Skills Act 2000 s 145(5). As to the High Court of Justice in England and Wales see COURTS AND TRIBUNALS vol 24 (2010) PARA 695 et seq. As the county courts see COURTS AND TRIBUNALS vol 24 (2010) PARA 758 et seq.
4 Learning and Skills Act 2000 s 145(2).
5 Learning and Skills Act 2000 s 145(2)(a).
6 Learning and Skills Act 2000 s 145(2)(b).
7 Learning and Skills Act 2000 s 145(4)(a).
8 Learning and Skills Act 2000 s 145(4)(b).

566. Charitable status of a further education corporation. A further education corporation[1] is a charity within the meaning of the Charities Act 2011[2] and is an exempt charity[3] for the purposes of that Act[4].

1 As to the meaning of 'further education corporation' see PARA 555 note 3.
2 As to this meaning see CHARITIES vol 8 (2015) PARA 1.
3 Ie in accordance with the Charities Act 2011 Sch 3: see CHARITIES vol 8 (2015) PARA 318.
4 Further and Higher Education Act 1992 s 22A (added by the Teaching and Higher Education Act 1998 s 41(2); and substituted by the Charities Act 2011 Sch 7 para 58).

C. POWERS OF FURTHER EDUCATION CORPORATIONS

567. Principal powers of a further education corporation. A further education corporation[1] has powers (its 'principal powers'[2]) under which it may:
  (1)   provide further and higher education[3];

(2) provide secondary education[4] suitable to the requirements of persons who have attained the age of 14 years[5];

(3) provide education which is secondary education by virtue of the provisions of the Education Act 1996[6] which extend the definition of secondary education to include full-time education received partly at a school[7] and partly at another institution[8];

(4) participate in the provision of secondary education at a school[9]; and

(5) supply goods[10] or services[11] in connection with its provision of education[12].

A further education corporation may not provide education of a kind specified in head (2), (3) or (4) above unless it has consulted[13] such local authorities[14] as it considers appropriate[15].

1 As to the meaning of 'further education corporation' see PARA 555 note 3.
2 See the Further and Higher Education Act 1992 s 18(1) (amended by the School Standards and Framework Act 1998 s 125(1), (3); and the Learning and Skills Act 2000 s 149, Sch 9 paras 1, 21).
3 Further and Higher Education Act 1992 s 18(1)(a). As to the meaning of 'further education' see PARA 23; and as to the meaning of 'higher education' see PARA 24 (definitions applied by the Further and Higher Education Act 1992 s 90(1) (amended by the Education Act 1996 s 582(1), Sch 37 Pt I para 115(1), (2))).
4 As to the meaning of 'secondary education' see PARA 21 (definition applied by the Further and Higher Education Act 1992 s 90(5)).
5 Further and Higher Education Act 1992 s 18(1)(aa) (added by the School Standards and Framework Act 1998 s 113(1); substituted by the Learning and Skills Act 2000 s 142(1)(a); and amended by the Education Act 2002 s 215(1), Sch 21 para 11). As to the time at which a person attains a particular age see PARA 7 note 6.
6 Ie by virtue of the Education Act 1996 s 2(2B): see PARA 21.
7 As to the meaning of 'school' see PARA 91 (definition applied by the Further and Higher Education Act 1992 s 90(5)). 'Schools' can include certain types of academies (see further PARA 91) and as to academies see PARA 345 et seq.
8 Further and Higher Education Act 1992 s 18(1)(ab) (added by the Learning and Skills Act 2000 s 142(1)(a)).
9 Further and Higher Education Act 1992 s 18(1)(ac) (added by the Learning and Skills Act 2000 s 142(1)(a)).
10 For these purposes, goods are supplied in connection with the provision of education by a further education corporation if they result from:
    (1) its provision of education or anything done by it under the Further and Higher Education Act 1992 for the purpose of or in connection with its provision of education (s 18(2)(a));
    (2) the use of its facilities or the expertise of persons employed by it in the fields in which they are so employed (s 18(2)(b)); or
    (3) ideas of a person employed by it, or of one of its students, arising out of its provision of education (s 18(2)(c)).
    As to the meaning of 'employed' see PARA 568 note 9.
11 For these purposes, services are supplied in connection with the provision of education by a further education corporation if:
    (1) they result from its provision of education or anything done by it under the Further and Higher Education Act 1992 for the purpose of or in connection with its provision of education (s 18(3)(a));
    (2) they are provided by making available its facilities or the expertise of persons employed by it in the fields in which they are so employed (s 18(3)(b)); or
    (3) they result from ideas of a person employed by it, or of one of its students, arising out of its provision of education (s 18(3)(c)).
12 Further and Higher Education Act 1992 s 18(1)(b).
13 As to the exercise of the duty to consult see JUDICIAL REVIEW vol 61 (2010) PARA 627.
14 As to the meaning of 'local authority' see PARA 25 (definition applied by the Further and Higher Education Act 1992 s 90(1)).
15 Further and Higher Education Act 1992 s 18(1A) (added by the Learning and Skills Act 2000 s 142(1)(b); and amended by SI 2010/1158).

568. Supplementary powers of a further education corporation. A further education corporation[1] may do anything which appears to it to be necessary or expedient for the purpose of or in connection with the exercise of any of its principal powers[2]. In particular, a further education corporation may conduct an educational institution for the purpose of carrying on activities undertaken in the exercise of its powers to provide further or higher education[3] and, in particular, may assume as from the operative date[4] the conduct of the institution in respect of which the corporation is established[5]. A further education corporation may provide facilities of any description appearing to the corporation to be necessary or desirable for the purposes of or in connection with carrying on any activities undertaken in the exercise of its principal powers (including boarding accommodation and recreational facilities for students and staff and facilities to meet the needs of students having learning difficulties)[6].

A further education corporation may also:

(1)   acquire and dispose of land[7] and other property[8];

(2)   enter into contracts, including in particular: (a) contracts for the employment[9] of teachers and other staff for the purposes of or in connection with carrying on any activities undertaken in the exercise of its principal powers[10]; and (b) contracts with respect to the carrying on by the corporation of any such activities[11];

(3)   form, participate in forming or invest[12] in a company[13];

(4)   form, participate in forming or otherwise become a member of a charitable incorporated organisation[14];

(5)   borrow such sums as the corporation thinks fit for the purposes of carrying on any activities it has power to carry on or meeting any liability[15] transferred to it[16] and, in connection with such borrowing, may grant any mortgage, charge or other security in respect of any land or other property of the corporation[17];

(6)   invest any sums not immediately required for the purposes of carrying on any activities it has power to carry on[18];

(7)   accept gifts of money, land or other property and apply it, or hold and administer it on trust for, any of those purposes[19];

(8)   do anything incidental to the conduct of an educational institution providing further or higher education, including founding scholarships or exhibitions, making grants and giving prizes[20];

(9)   provide advice or assistance to any other person where it appears to the corporation to be appropriate for it to do so for the purpose of or in connection with the provision of education by the other person[21].

1   As to the meaning of 'further education corporation' see PARA 555 note 3.
2   Further and Higher Education Act 1992 s 19(1). As to the principal powers of further education corporations see PARA 567. As to powers and duties see also PARA 594 et seq.
3   As to the meaning of 'further education' see PARA 23; and as to the meaning of 'higher education' see PARA 24 (definitions applied by the Further and Higher Education Act 1992 s 90(1) (amended by the Education Act 1996 s 582(1), Sch 37 Pt I para 115(1), (2))).
4   As to the meaning of 'operative date' see PARAS 559 note 4, 560 note 12.
5   Further and Higher Education Act 1992 s 19(2).
6   Further and Higher Education Act 1992 s 19(3) (s 19(3) amended, 19(6), (7) added, by the Learning and Skills Act 2000 s 149, Sch 9 paras 1, 22). A person has a learning difficulty if: (1) he has a significantly greater difficulty in learning than the majority of persons of his age; or (2) he has a disability which either prevents or hinders him from making use of facilities of a kind generally provided by institutions within the further education sector for persons of his age: Further and Higher Education Act 1992 s 19(6) (as so added). A person is not, however, to be taken to have a learning difficulty solely because the language (or form of language) in which he is or will be taught is different from a language (or form of language) which has at any time

been spoken in his home: Further and Higher Education Act 1992 s 19(7) (as so added). As to the meaning of 'person' see PARA 7 note 6. As to learning difficulties which call for special educational provision see PARAS 943, 989.

7 'Land' includes buildings and other structures, land covered with water and any interest in land; and 'interest in land' includes any easement, right or charge in, to or over land: Further and Higher Education Act 1992 s 90(1). As to easements see REAL PROPERTY AND REGISTRATION vol 87 (2012) PARA 802 et seq. As to charges over land see MORTGAGE vol 77 (2010) PARA 113.

8 Further and Higher Education Act 1992 s 19(4)(a).

9 'Contract of employment' has the same meaning as in the Employment Rights Act 1996 as do 'employee' and 'employer' (see EMPLOYMENT): Further and Higher Education Act 1992 s 90(1) (definitions amended by the Employment Rights Act 1996 s 240, Sch 1 para 52). 'Employed' means employed under a contract of employment: Further and Higher Education Act 1992 s 90(1). References in Pt I (ss 15–61A) to the transfer of any person's rights or liabilities do not include rights or liabilities under a contract of employment, or liabilities of that person in respect of compensation for premature retirement of any person formerly employed by him: see s 61(2). As to the meaning of 'person' see PARA 7 note 6.

10 Further and Higher Education Act 1992 s 19(4)(b)(i).

11 Further and Higher Education Act 1992 s 19(4)(b)(ii).

12 A reference the Further and Higher Education Act 1992 s 19 to investing in a company includes a reference to becoming a member of the company and to investing in it by the acquisition of any assets, securities or rights or otherwise: s 19(8) (added by the Further Education and Training Act 2007 s 21(1), (6)).

13 Further and Higher Education Act 1992 s 19(4)(bb) (added by the Learning and Skills Act 2000 Sch 9 paras 1, 22; and substituted by the Further Education and Training Act 2007 s 21(1), (2)).

14 Further and Higher Education Act 1992 s 19(4)(bc) (added by the Further Education and Training Act 2007 s 21(1), (2)). 'Charitable incorporated organisation' means such an organisation within the meaning of the Charities Act 2011 Pt 11 (ss 204–250) (see CHARITIES vol 8 (2015) PARA 226): see the Further and Higher Education Act 1992 s 19(4)(bc) (as so added; and amended by the Charities Act 2011 s 355).

15 'Liability' includes obligation: Further and Higher Education Act 1992 s 90(1).

16 Ie under the Further and Higher Education Act 1992 s 27 (see PARA 571) or s 33P (see PARA 586).

17 Further and Higher Education Act 1992 s 19(4)(c) (amended by the Education Act 2011 Sch 12 paras 1, 3(1), (2); and the Deregulation Act 2015 Sch 15 para 4(1), (5)(a)).

18 Further and Higher Education Act 1992 s 19(4)(d).

19 Further and Higher Education Act 1992 s 19(4)(e).

20 Further and Higher Education Act 1992 s 19(4)(f).

21 Further and Higher Education Act 1992 s 19(9) (added by the Apprenticeships, Skills, Children and Learning Act 2009 s 256(1), (2)).

569. Collaboration arrangements with maintained schools and further education bodies in England. Regulations[1] may enable:

(1) the governing body of a maintained school[2], whether alone or together with other such governing bodies, to make collaboration arrangements[3] with one or more further education bodies[4];

(2) a further education body, whether alone or together with other further education bodies, to make collaboration arrangements with the governing body of a maintained school or the governing bodies of two or more such schools[5];

(3) a further education body to make collaboration arrangements with one or more further education bodies[6].

Regulations may make provision as to:

(a) the establishment by the collaborating bodies of a joint committee of those bodies for the purposes of discharging any functions in pursuance of collaboration arrangements made by them ('a joint committee')[7];

(b) the appointment of persons to serve on a joint committee (including provision as to the restrictions or other requirements relating to any such appointments) and their removal from office[8];

(c) the appointment of a clerk to a joint committee (including provision as to the restrictions or other requirements relating to any such appointment) and his removal from office[9];

(d) the appointment by a joint committee of one of their number to act as clerk for the purposes of a meeting where the clerk fails to attend[10];

(e) rights of persons to attend meetings of a joint committee[11];

(f) restrictions on persons taking part in proceedings of a joint committee[12];

(g) other matters relating to the constitution or procedure of a joint committee[13].

Regulations may also make provision as to:

(i) the functions of collaborating bodies which may or may not be discharged jointly, or by a joint committee, in pursuance of collaboration arrangements[14];

(ii) the manner in which such functions are to be discharged jointly, or by a joint committee, in pursuance of collaboration arrangements[15];

(iii) any other matters which are relevant to the discharge of functions by the collaborating bodies jointly, or as the case may be, by a joint committee in pursuance of such arrangements[16].

Regulations may provide that any enactment[17] relating to:

(A) the functions of the collaborating bodies which are to be discharged in pursuance of collaboration arrangements[18]; or

(B) the governing bodies, or as the case may be the further education bodies, by whom those functions are to be discharged[19],

is to have effect subject to all necessary modifications[20] in its application in relation to those functions and the bodies by whom they are to be discharged[21].

1 'Regulations' means regulations made by the Secretary of State (in relation to England): Education and Inspections Act 2006 s 166(6) (definition amended by the Education (Wales) Measure 2011 s 9(4)(c)). As to the Secretary of State see PARA 58. As to the meaning of 'England' see PARA 7 note 3. As to the regulations made see the Collaboration Arrangements (Maintained Schools and Further Education Bodies) (England) Regulations 2007, SI 2007/1321.

2 'Maintained school' means a school in England which is community, foundation or voluntary school, a community or foundation special school or a maintained nursery school: Education and Inspections Act 2006 s 166(6) (definition amended by the Education (Wales) Measure 2011 s 9(4)(b)). As to the meaning of references to a community, foundation or voluntary school or a community or foundation special school see PARA 106. As to the meaning of 'maintained nursery school' see PARA 99 note 4 (definition applied by s 187(2), (3)). As to the governing bodies of maintained schools in England see PARA 150 et seq. As to academies see PARA 345 et seq.

3 'Collaboration arrangements' are arrangements for any of the functions of any of the bodies who make the arrangements ('the collaborating bodies') to be discharged jointly or by a joint committee of those bodies: Education and Inspections Act 2006 s 166(2). As to the meaning of 'functions' see PARA 18 note 5 (definition applied by s 187(2), (3)).

4 Education and Inspections Act 2006 s 166(1)(a). 'Further education body' means: (1) a further education corporation (as defined by the Further and Higher Education Act 1992 s 17(1) in England: see PARA 555 note 3); (2) a sixth form college corporation (as defined in the Further and Higher Education Act 1992 s 90: see PARA 577 note 7); or (3) the governing body of a designated institution (as defined by the Further and Higher Education Act 1992 s 28(4): see PARA 572) in England which is a body incorporated by virtue of the Learning and Skills Act 2000 s 143(4) (see PARA 575): Education and Inspections Act 2006 s 166(6) (definition amended by SI 2010/1080; and the Education (Wales) Measure 2011 s 9(4)(a)).

As to collaboration by education bodies in Wales, see now the Education (Wales) Measure 2011 ss 1–9; and PARA 199.

5 Education and Inspections Act 2006 s 166(1)(b).

6 Education and Inspections Act 2006 s 166(1)(c).

7 Education and Inspections Act 2006 s 166(3)(a).

8   Education and Inspections Act 2006 s 166(3)(b).
9   Education and Inspections Act 2006 s 166(3)(c).
10   Education and Inspections Act 2006 s 166(3)(d).
11   Education and Inspections Act 2006 s 166(3)(e).
12   Education and Inspections Act 2006 s 166(3)(f).
13   Education and Inspections Act 2006 s 166(3)(g).
14   Education and Inspections Act 2006 s 166(4)(a).
15   Education and Inspections Act 2006 s 166(4)(b).
16   Education and Inspections Act 2006 s 166(4)(c).
17   As to the meaning of 'enactment' see PARA 26 note 15.
18   Education and Inspections Act 2006 s 166(5)(a).
19   Education and Inspections Act 2006 s 166(5)(b).
20   As to the meaning of 'modifications' see PARA 21 note 15 (definition applied by the Education
     and Inspections Act 2006 s 187(2), (3)).
21   Education and Inspections Act 2006 s 166(5).

570.   Consultation in Wales. As from a day to be appointed the following
provisions have effect[1].

In exercising its functions[2] the governing body[3] of an institution within the
further education sector[4] in Wales must have regard to any guidance given from
time to time by the Welsh Ministers[5] about consultation with persons who are or
are likely to become students of the institution[6], or employers[7], in connection
with the taking of decisions affecting them[8].

1   The Further and Higher Education Act 1992 s 49A is added by the Further Education and
     Training Act 2007 s 2; and repealed in relation to England by the Education Act 2011 Sch 12
     paras 1, 22. At the date at which this volume states the law the Further and Higher Education
     Act 1992 s 49A is not yet in force in relation to Wales. As to the meanings of 'England' and
     'Wales' see PARA 7 note 3.
2   'Functions' include powers and duties: Further and Higher Education Act 1992 s 61(1).
3   As to the meaning of 'governing body' see PARA 560 note 6.
4   As to the meaning of 'institution within the further education sector' see PARA 555.
5   As to the Welsh Ministers see PARA 59.
6   Further and Higher Education Act 1992 s 49A(1)(a) (as added: see note 1). Any guidance under
     s 49A about consultation with persons falling within s 49A(1)(a) must provide for the views of
     such a person to be considered in the light of his age and understanding: s 49A(2) (as so added).
7   Further and Higher Education Act 1992 s 49A(1)(b) (as added: see note 1). As to the meaning of
     'employer' see PARA 569 note 8.
8   Further and Higher Education Act 1992 s 49A(1) (as added (see note 1); and amended, as from
     a day to be appointed, by the Education Act 2011 s 49, Sch 12 para 45). As to the exercise of
     the duty to consult see JUDICIAL REVIEW vol 61 (2010) PARA 627.

D. DISSOLUTION

571.   Dissolution of further education corporations. If a further education
corporation[1] proposes that the corporation should be dissolved[2], the corporation
must publish (1) details of the proposal[3], and (2) such other information as may
be prescribed[4] by regulations made by the appropriate authority[5].

The publication is to be in accordance with regulations made by the
appropriate authority[6]. The corporation must consult on the proposal, and take
account of the views of those consulted, in accordance with regulations made by
the appropriate authority[7].

The provisions below[8] apply if, after complying with the above provision[9], a
further education corporation resolves that the corporation should be dissolved
on a specified date (the 'dissolution date')[10]. The corporation must notify the
appropriate authority[11] of the resolution and the dissolution date as soon as
reasonably practicable[12]. The corporation is dissolved on the dissolution date[13].

At any time before the dissolution date, the corporation may transfer any of its property, rights or liabilities[14] to such person[15] or body, or a person or body of such description, as may be prescribed by regulations made by the appropriate authority[16]. The corporation may do so only with the consent of the person or body concerned[17]. Such a transfer[18] has effect on the dissolution date[19].

If a person or body prescribed, or of a description prescribed as above[20] is not a charity established for charitable purposes which are exclusively educational purposes[21], any property transferred to the person or body must be transferred on trust to be used for charitable purposes which are exclusively educational purposes[22].

1   As to the meaning of 'further education corporation' see PARA 555 note 3.
2   Further and Higher Education Act 1992 s 27(1) (s 27 substituted by the Further and Higher Education (Governance and Information) (Wales) Act 2014 s 3). The Further and Higher Education Act 1992 ss 27, 27A, 27B replace the previous ss 27, 27A–27C which were substituted and added in place of s 27 (as originally enacted) by the Education Act 2011 Sch 12 paras 1, 7.
3   Further and Higher Education Act 1992 s 27(2)(a) (as substituted: see note 2). As to regulations see note 5.
4   'Prescribed' means prescribed by regulations: see the Education Act 1996 s 579(1) (definition applied by the Further and Higher Education Act 1992 s 90(5)). 'Regulations' means regulations made by the Secretary of State or the Welsh Ministers: s 61(1) (definition amended by the Further and Higher Education (Governance and Information)) (Wales) Act 2014 Sch 2 para 1(c)). As to the Secretary of State see PARA 58. As to the Welsh Ministers see PARA 59.
5   Further and Higher Education Act 1992 s 27(2)(b) (as substituted: see note 2). 'Appropriate authority' means (1) in relation to a further education corporation in England, the Secretary of State; and (2) in relation to a further education corporation in Wales, the Welsh Ministers: s 27(5) (as so substituted). As to the meanings of 'England' and 'Wales' see PARA 7 note 3. As to regulations made see the Further Education Corporations (Publication of Proposals) (England) Regulations 2012, SI 2012/1157; and the Dissolution of Further Education Corporations (Publication of Proposals and Prescribed Bodies) (Wales) Regulations 2014, SI 2014/2126.
6   Further and Higher Education Act 1992 s 27(3) (as substituted: see note 2). As to regulations see note 5.
7   Further and Higher Education Act 1992 s 27(4) (as substituted: see note 2). As to regulations see note 5.
8   Ie the Further and Higher Education Act 1992 ss 27A, 27B.
9   Ie the Further and Higher Education Act 1992 s 27.
10 Further and Higher Education Act 1992 s 27A(1) (s 27A added by the Further and Higher Education (Governance and Information) (Wales) Act 2014 s 3). The 'dissolution date' means the date specified in a resolution under the Further and Higher Education Act 1992 s 27A(1): s 27A(2) (as so added). See note 2.
11 As to the meaning of 'appropriate authority' see note 5 (definition applied by the Further and Higher Education Act 1992 s 27A(5) (as added: see note 10). See note 2.
12 Further and Higher Education Act 1992 s 27A(3) (as added: see note 10). See note 2.
13 Further and Higher Education Act 1992 s 27A(4) (as added: see note 10). See note 2.
14 As to the meaning of 'liability' see PARA 568 note 15. As to references to the transfer of rights or liabilities see PARA 568 note 7. As to the disposal of land held by further education corporations see PARA 1328.
15 As to the meaning of 'person' see PARA 7 note 6.
16 Further and Higher Education Act 1992 s 27B(1) (s 27B added by the Further and Higher Education (Governance and Information)) (Wales) Act 2014 s 3). As to the meaning of 'appropriate authority' see note 5 (definition applied by the Further and Higher Education Act 1992 s 27B(6) (as so added)). See note 2. As to regulations made see the Dissolution of Further Education Corporations and Sixth Form College Corporations (Prescribed Bodies) Regulations 2012, SI 2012/1167; and the Dissolution of Further Education Corporations (Publication of Proposals and Prescribed Bodies) (Wales) Regulations 2014, SI 2014/2126.
    Stamp duty is not chargeable in respect of any transfer effected under or by virtue of the Further and Higher Education Act 1992 s 27B: see the Further and Higher Education Act 1992 s 88(1) (amended by the Education Act 2011 Sch 12 paras 1, 38(a)). However, no instrument (other than a statutory instrument) made or executed under or in pursuance of the Further and Higher Education Act 1992 s 27B is to be treated as duly stamped unless it is stamped with the

duty to which it would, but for s 88 (and, if applicable, the Finance Act 1982 s 129 (see STAMP TAXES vol 96 (2012) PARA 363)), be liable or it has, in accordance with the provisions of the Stamp Act 1891 s 12 (see STAMP TAXES vol 96 (2012) PARA 384), been stamped with a particular stamp denoting that it is not chargeable with any duty or that it has been duly stamped: Further and Higher Education Act 1992 s 88(2). A land transaction effected under or by virtue of s 27B is also exempt from charge for the purposes of stamp duty land tax: see s 88A(1) (s 88A added by SI 2003/2867; and amended by the Education Act 2011 Sch 12 para 1, 39(a)). Relief under the Further and Higher Education Act 1992 s 88A must be claimed in a land transaction return or an amendment of such a return: s 88A(2) (as so added). 'Land transaction' has the meaning given by the Finance Act 2003 s 43(1) (see STAMP TAXES vol 96 (2012) PARA 426); and 'land transaction return' has the meaning given by the Finance Act 2003 s 76(1) (see STAMP TAXES vol 96 (2012) PARA 477): Further and Higher Education Act 1992 s 88A(3) (as so added).

17 Further and Higher Education Act 1992 s 27B(2) (as added: see note 16). See note 2.
18 Ie a transfer under the Further and Higher Education Act 1992 s 27B(1).
19 Further and Higher Education Act 1992 s 27B(3) (as added: see note 16). See note 2.
20 Ie prescribed under the Further and Higher Education Act 1992 s 27B(1).
21 Further and Higher Education Act 1992 s 27B(4) (as added: see note 16). See note 2. As to the charitable status of further education corporations see PARA 566.
22 Further and Higher Education Act 1992 s 27B(5) (as added: see note 16). See note 2.

(iii) Designated Institutions

A. DESIGNATION OF INSTITUTIONS

572. Designation. The appropriate national authority[1] may by order[2] designate[3] any educational institution principally concerned with the provision of one or both of the following:

(1) full-time education suitable to the requirements of persons over compulsory school age[4] who have not attained the age of 19 years[5]; and

(2) courses of further or higher education[6],

if the institution is[7] a voluntary aided school[8] (other than one belonging to a group of schools for which a foundation body acts[9]), an institution which is grant-aided or eligible to receive aid by way of grant[10], or an institution established for the purpose of being principally concerned with the provision of one or both of the kinds of education specified in head (1) and head (2) above[11]. An institution in relation to which such a designation has effect is known as a 'designated institution'[12].

The appropriate national authority must not make such an order in respect of a voluntary aided school without the consent of the governing body[13] and the local authority[14].

1 Ie the Secretary of State or, in relation to Wales, the Welsh Ministers. As to the Secretary of State see PARA 58. As to the Welsh Ministers see PARA 59. As to the meaning of 'Wales' see PARA 7 note 3. The functions of the Secretary of State under the Further and Higher Education Act 1992 s 28, so far as exercisable in relation to Wales, were transferred to the National Assembly for Wales (see the National Assembly for Wales (Transfer of Functions) Order 1999, SI 1999/672, art 2, Sch 1) and are now vested in the Welsh Ministers (see the Government of Wales Act 2006 s 162(1), Sch 11 para 30).
2 An order under the Education Reform Act 1988 s 129 (designation of institutions for the purposes of the higher education sector: see PARA 671) in respect of any institution may revoke any order in respect of that institution under the Further and Higher Education Act 1992 s 28: s 74(2). An order under s 28 in respect of any institution may revoke any order in respect of that institution under the Education Reform Act 1988 s 129: Further and Higher Education Act 1992 s 47(4). Orders under s 28, being of local effect, are not recorded in this work.
3 Ie for the purposes of the Further and Higher Education Act 1992 s 28.
4 As to the meaning of 'compulsory school age' see PARA 19.
5 Further and Higher Education Act 1992 s 28(1)(a). As to the time at which a person attains a particular age see PARA 7 note 6. As to 16 to 19 academies see PARA 346 note 13.

6 Further and Higher Education Act 1992 s 28(1)(b). As to the meaning of 'further education' see PARA 23; and as to the meaning of 'higher education' see PARA 24 (definitions applied by s 90(1) (amended by the Education Act 1996 s 582(1), Sch 37 Pt I para 115)). As to academies see PARA 345 et seq.

7 See the Further and Higher Education Act 1992 s 28(1) (amended by the Learning and Skills Act 2000 s 143(1)(a)).

8 For the purposes of the Further and Higher Education Act 1992, references to a 'voluntary aided school' are: (1) in relation to any time before 1 September 1999 (ie the appointed day: see PARA 106), references to a voluntary aided school within the meaning of the Education Act 1996 (see PARA 106); or (2) in relation to any time on or after that date, references to a voluntary aided school within the meaning of the School Standards and Framework Act 1998 (see PARA 106): Further and Higher Education Act 1992 s 90(3A) (added by the School Standards and Framework Act 1998 Sch 30 paras 33, 46). As to the meaning of references to a foundation school see PARA 106 (definition applied by the Further and Higher Education Act 1992 s 90(5)). As to the governing bodies of maintained schools in England see PARA 150 et seq; and in Wales see PARA 195.

9 Ie under the School Standards and Framework Act 1998 s 21 (see PARA 108): see the Further and Higher Education Act 1992 s 28(2)(a) (amended by the School Standards and Framework Act 1998 s 140(1), Sch 30 para 38).

10 Further and Higher Education Act 1992 s 28(2)(c). For these purposes, an institution is grant-aided or eligible to receive aid by way of grant if it is maintained by persons other than local authorities who receive any grants under regulations made under the Education Act 1996 s 485 (see PARA 82) or who are eligible to receive such grants: Further and Higher Education Act 1992 s 28(3) (amended by the Education Act 1996 Sch 37 Pt I para 109; SI 2010/1158). As to the meaning of 'local authority' see PARA 25 (definition applied by the Further and Higher Education Act 1992 s 90(5)). As to the meaning of 'person' see PARA 7 note 6.

11 Further and Higher Education Act 1992 s 28(2)(d) (added by the Learning and Skills Act 2000 ss 143(1), 153, Sch 11).

12 See the Further and Higher Education Act 1992 s 28(4).

13 As to the meaning of 'governing body' see PARA 560 note 6. As to academies see PARA 345 et seq.

14 Further and Higher Education Act 1992 s 28(3A) (added by the Learning and Skills Act 2000 s 112; and amended by SI 2010/1158).

B. CONSTITUTION AND GOVERNANCE

573. Requirement for instruments of government and articles of government. For each designated institution[1], other than (1) an institution conducted by a company[2]; or (2) an institution conducted by an unincorporated association if the order designating the institution provides for its exemption[3], there must be:

(a)   an instrument providing for the constitution of a governing body[4] of the institution (to be known as the 'instrument of government')[5]; and

(b)   an instrument in accordance with which the institution is to be conducted (to be known as the 'articles of government')[6].

The first post-designation instrument and articles of government of a designated institution[7] must each meet one of the following requirements[8]:

(i)   the instrument[9] was in force when the designation took effect and is approved for these purposes by the appropriate national authority[10];

(ii)   the instrument is made in pursuance of a power under a regulatory instrument[11] or (where there is no such power) by the governing body of the institution[12], and (in either case) is approved for these purposes by the appropriate authority[13]; or

(iii)   the instrument is made by the appropriate authority by order[14].

An instrument made by the governing body under head (ii) above or the appropriate authority under head (iii) above may replace wholly or in part an existing regulatory instrument[15].

The governing body of the institution[16] may modify[17] or replace its instrument of government and articles of government[18].

If the institution is in Wales and is an institution to which the special provision below[19] applies, the governing body may do any of the things mentioned above[20] only with the consent of the trustees of the institution[21].

The instrument of government and articles of government (as modified or replaced) must comply with the relevant requirements[22]; and, subject to that, may make such other provision as may be necessary or desirable[23].

Notwithstanding anything in the provisions described above, the instrument of government of a designated institution which, when designated, was (A) a voluntary aided school[24]; or (B) an institution specified, or falling within a class specified, by the appropriate authority by order[25], must provide: (aa) for the governing body of the institution to include persons appointed for the purpose of securing so far as practicable that the established character of the institution[26] at the time of its designation is preserved and developed and, in particular, that the institution is conducted in accordance with any trust deed[27] relating to it[28]; and (bb) for the majority of members of the governing body to be such governors[29].

1 Ie to which the Further and Higher Education Act 1992 s 29 applies: see s 29(1); and the text to notes 2, 3. As to the meaning of 'designated institution' see PARA 572.
2 Further and Higher Education Act 1992 s 29(1)(a) (s 29 substituted and ss 29A–29C added by the Education Act 2011 Sch 12 paras 1, 8). As to designated institutions conducted by companies see PARA 574.
3 Further and Higher Education Act 1992 s 29(1)(b) (as substituted: see note 2).
4 As to the meaning of 'governing body' see PARA 560 note 6.
5 Further and Higher Education Act 1992 s 29(2)(a) (as substituted: see note 2).
6 Further and Higher Education Act 1992 s 29(2)(b) (as substituted: see note 2).
7 Ie to which the Further and Higher Education Act 1992 applies, s 29 applying to a designated institution other than the institutions set out in heads (1) and (2) in the text. The 'first post-designation instrument and articles of government' of a designated institution are the first instrument of government and articles of government that the institution has after the designation takes effect: s 29A(2) (as added: see note 2).
8 See the Further and Higher Education Act 1992 s 29A(1) (as added (see note 2); and amended by the Further and Higher Education (Governance and Information) (Wales) Act 2014 s 4(1)(c)). The reference is to compliance with the Further and Higher Education Act 1992 s 29A(3).
9 In the Further and Higher Education Act 1992 ss 29A, 29B, 'instrument' means an instrument of government or articles of government: s 29(3) (as substituted: see note 2).
10 Further and Higher Education Act 1992 s 29A(3)(a) (as added: see note 2). For these purposes, 'appropriate authority' (1) in relation to an institution in England, means the Secretary of State; (2) in relation to an institution in Wales, means the Welsh Ministers: s 29A(7) (as so added). As to the Secretary of State see PARA 58. As to the Welsh Ministers see PARA 59. As to the meanings of 'England' and 'Wales' see PARA 7 note 3.
11 In the Further and Higher Education Act 1992 ss 29A, 29B, 'regulatory instrument', in relation to an institution, means (1) any instrument of government or articles of government; or (2) any other instrument relating to or regulating the institution: s 29(3) (as substituted: see note 2).
12 Further and Higher Education Act 1992 s 29A(3)(b)(i) (as added: see note 2).
13 Further and Higher Education Act 1992 s 29A(3)(b)(ii) (as added: see note 2).
14 Further and Higher Education Act 1992 s 29A(3)(c) (as added: see note 2). Before making an instrument under s 29A(3)(c), the appropriate authority must, so far as it appears practicable to do so, consult (1) the governing body of the institution; and (2) where there is power under a regulatory instrument to make the instrument, and that power is exercisable by persons other than the governing body of the institution, the persons by whom the power is exercisable: s 29A(5) (as so added).
15 Further and Higher Education Act 1992 s 29A(4) (as added: see note 2).
16 Ie the designated institution to which the Further and Higher Education Act 1992 s 29 applies: see s 29B(1) (as added (see note 2); and substituted, together with s 29C, by the Further and Higher Education (Governance and Information) (Wales) Act 2014 s 4(2)).
17 'Modifications' includes additions, alterations and omissions and 'modify' must be construed accordingly: Further and Higher Education Act 1992 s 61(1).

18 Further and Higher Education Act 1992 s 29B(2) (as added and substituted: see note 16).
19 Ie the Further and Higher Education Act 1992 s 30: see the text and notes 24–29.
20 Ie in the Further and Higher Education Act 1992 s 29B(2).
21 Further and Higher Education Act 1992 s 29B(3) (as added and substituted: see note 16).
22 Further and Higher Education Act 1992 s 29B(4)(a) (as added and substituted: see note 16). The reference in the text to the relevant requirements is a reference to the requirements of Sch 4: see PARA 562.
23 Further and Higher Education Act 1992 s 29B(4)(b) (as added and substituted: see note 16).
24 See the Further and Higher Education Act 1992 s 30(1), (2)(a) (s 30 substituted by the Learning and Skills Act 2000 s 143(2); and the Further and Higher Education Act 1992 s 30(1) amended by the Education Act 2011 Sch 12 paras 1, 9; and the Further and Higher Education (Governance and Information) (Wales) Act 2014 Sch 2 para 1(a)). As to the meaning of references to a voluntary aided school see PARA 572 note 8.
25 See the Further and Higher Education Act 1992 s 30(1), (2)(b) (as substituted: see note 24). The appropriate authority may specify an institution or a class of institutions only if the institution or each member of the class is principally concerned with the provision of the education specified in s 28(1)(a) (see PARA 572): s 30(3) (as so substituted). As to the 'appropriate authority' see also note 10.
26 The reference to the established character of an institution is, in relation to an institution established shortly before or at the same time as being designated, a reference to the character which the institution is intended to have on its establishment: Further and Higher Education Act 1992 s 30(4) (as substituted: see note 24).
27 As to the meaning of 'trust deed' see PARA 108 note 6 (definition applied by the Further and Higher Education Act 1992 s 90(5)).
28 Further and Higher Education Act 1992 s 30(1)(a) (as substituted: see note 24).
29 Further and Higher Education Act 1992 s 30(1)(b) (as substituted: see note 24).

574. Designated institutions in Wales conducted by companies. Where a designated institution[1] in Wales is conducted by a company[2], the articles of association of the company[3] must incorporate:

(1)   provision with respect to the constitution of a governing body[4] of the institution (the 'instrument of government of the institution')[5]; and

(2)   provision with respect to the conduct of the institution (the 'articles of government of the institution')[6].

The appropriate national authority[7] may give to the persons[8] who appear to it to have effective control over the company such directions[9] as it thinks fit for securing that:

(a)   the articles of association of the company[10]; or

(b)   any rules or byelaws made in pursuance of any power conferred by the articles of association of the company[11],

are amended in such manner as may be specified in the direction[12]. Before giving any such directions the appropriate national authority must consult[13] the persons who appear to it to have effective control over the company[14].

No amendment of the articles of association of the company (other than one required under head (a) above) may take effect until it has been submitted to the appropriate national authority for approval and the authority has notified its approval to the company[15].

1 As to the meaning of 'designated institution' see PARA 572.
2 See the Further and Higher Education Act 1992 s 31(1) (amended by the Deregulation Act 2015 Sch 15 par 5(2)). The Further and Higher Education Act 1992 s 31 ceased to have effect in relation to England as a result of the Deregulation Act 2015 Sch 15 para 5(1). As to the meanings of 'England' and 'Wales' see PARA 7 note 3.
3 As to the articles of association of a company see COMPANIES vol 14 (2009) PARA 228 et seq.
4 As to the meaning of 'governing body' see PARA 560 note 6.
5 Further and Higher Education Act 1992 s 31(2)(a).
6 Further and Higher Education Act 1992 s 31(2)(b).

7   Ie the Welsh Ministers. As to the Secretary of State see PARA 58. As to the Welsh Ministers see
    PARA 59. The functions of the Secretary of State under the Further and Higher Education
    Act 1992 s 31, so far as exercisable in relation to Wales, were transferred to the National
    Assembly for Wales (see the National Assembly for Wales (Transfer of Functions) Order 1999,
    SI 1999/672, art 2, Sch 1) and are now vested in the Welsh Ministers (see the Government of
    Wales Act 2006 s 162(1), Sch 11 para 30). See also note 2.
8   As to the meaning of 'person' see PARA 7 note 6.
9   As to directions see the Education Act 1996 s 570 (applied by the Further and Higher Education
    Act 1992 s 89(5) (amended by the Apprenticeships, Skills, Children and Learning Act 2009
    s 125, Sch 8 paras 1, 11(1), (4); and SI 2010/1158)); and PARA 75.
10 Further and Higher Education Act 1992 s 31(3)(a) (amended by SI 2009/1941).
11 Further and Higher Education Act 1992 s 31(3)(b).
12 See the Further and Higher Education Act 1992 s 31(3).
13 As to the exercise of the duty to consult see JUDICIAL REVIEW vol 61 (2010) PARA 627.
14 Further and Higher Education Act 1992 s 31(5).
15 See the Further and Higher Education Act 1992 s 31(4) (amended by SI 2009/1941).

575. Orders incorporating governing bodies. The Secretary of State[1] may
make an order[2] providing for the constitution as a body corporate of the
governing body[3] of an institution in England[4] which is designated[5] under the
Further and Higher Education Act 1992[6]. Likewise, the Welsh Ministers[7] may
make an order providing for the constitution as a body corporate of the
governing body of an institution in Wales which is so designated[8]. Any such
order may:

(1)   make provision similar to that of the Further and Higher Education
       Act 1992[9] relating to the powers of further education corporations[10];
(2)   make provision for the continuity of the body corporate[11];
(3)   make provision expressed to have effect subject to the institution's
       instrument or articles of government[12];
(4)   make provision which confers exempt charitable status for the purposes
       of the Charities Act 2011[13], and which relates to the governing body or
       to an institution administered by or established for the purposes of that
       body[14];
(5)   make provision about the discontinuance of the institution[15];
(6)   make provision about the dissolution of the body corporate, including
       provision about the treatment of property, rights and liabilities[16].

Before making such an order in relation to an institution the Secretary of State
or the Welsh Ministers must consult[17] the governing body of the institution[18],
and the trustees of any trust relating to the institution[19].

1   As to the Secretary of State see PARA 58.
2   Orders made under the Learning and Skills Act 2000 s 143, being of local effect, are not
    recorded in this work.
3   As to the meaning of 'governing body' in the Further and Higher Education Act 1992 see PARA
    560 note 6.
4   As to the meaning of 'England' see PARA 7 note 3.
5   Ie under the Further and Higher Education Act 1992 s 28: see PARA 572.
6   Learning and Skills Act 2000 s 143(4).
7   The functions under the Learning and Skills Act 2000 s 143 in relation to Wales were originally
    vested in the National Assembly for Wales and are now exercisable by the Welsh Ministers by
    virtue of the Government of Wales Act 2006 s 162(1), Sch 11 paras 30, 32. As to the Welsh
    Ministers see PARA 59. As to the meaning of 'Wales' see PARA 7 note 3.
8   Learning and Skills Act 2000 s 143(5).
9   Ie any provision of the Further and Higher Education Act 1992 s 18 (see PARA 567) or s 19 (see
    PARA 568).
10 See the Learning and Skills Act 2000 s 143(6)(a). As to the meaning of 'further education
    corporation' in the Further and Higher Education Act 1992 see PARA 555 note 3.

11 See the Learning and Skills Act 2000 s 143(6)(b). Such provision may include for the continuation of anything done under the Further and Higher Education Act 1992 ss 29–29B (government and conduct of designated institutions: see PARA 573): see the Learning and Skills Act 2000 s 143(6)(b) (amended by the Education Act 2011 Sch 12 para 44(1), (3)).

12 Learning and Skills Act 2000 s 143(6)(c). As to an institution's instrument and articles of government see PARA 574.

13 As to exempt charities for the purposes of the Charities Act 2011 see CHARITIES vol 8 (2015) PARA 318.

14 Learning and Skills Act 2000 s 143(6)(d) (amended by the Charities Act 2011 Sch 7 para 88).

15 Learning and Skills Act 2000 s 143(6)(e).

16 Learning and Skills Act 2000 s 143(6)(f).

17 As to the exercise of the duty to consult see JUDICIAL REVIEW vol 61 (2010) PARA 627.

18 Learning and Skills Act 2000 s 143(7)(a).

19 Learning and Skills Act 2000 s 143(7)(b).

576. Liability. Where a member of a body corporate[1] is found liable in civil legal proceedings in respect of something which he did or omitted to do in the course of carrying out his duties as a member of the body[2], a court[3] may make an order extinguishing, reducing or varying the liability[4] if the member applies to the court for such an order[5] and the court considers that the action or omission which gives rise to the member's liability was honest and reasonable[6]. Where a member of such a body applies to a court for such an order, the court may make any order which: (1) relates to liability in civil legal proceedings which may come to be incurred by the member in respect of a specified course of action[7]; and (2) is of a kind which the court could have made if the liability had already been incurred[8].

1 Ie established by virtue of the Learning and Skills Act 2000 s 143(4) or (5) (see PARA 575): see s 145(3)(b).

2 See the Learning and Skills Act 2000 s 145(1).

3 As to the meaning of 'a court' see PARA 565 note 3.

4 Learning and Skills Act 2000 s 145(2).

5 Learning and Skills Act 2000 s 145(2)(a).

6 Learning and Skills Act 2000 s 145(2)(b).

7 Learning and Skills Act 2000 s 145(4)(a).

8 Learning and Skills Act 2000 s 145(4)(b).

(iv) Sixth Form College Corporations

A. ESTABLISHMENT

577. Initial designation of existing bodies corporate as sixth form college corporations. The Secretary of State[1] may by order[2] designate a body corporate which is:

(1) a further education corporation[3] established in respect of an institution in England[4]; or

(2) a body corporate established by an order[5] in respect of an institution in England[6],

as a sixth form college corporation[7], for the purpose of conducting an educational institution specified in the order[8]. On the date specified in the order:

(a) a body corporate within head (1) above ceases to be a further education corporation and becomes a sixth form college corporation[9];

(b) a body corporate within head (2) above ceases to be subject to the order[10] establishing it and becomes a sixth form college corporation[11];

(c)   in the case of a body corporate within head (2) above, a designation[12] which has effect in relation to the relevant sixth form college[13] ceases to have effect[14].

An order may: (i) make provision for the continuity of the body corporate, including provision for the continuation of the instrument and articles of government[15] of the body and the relevant sixth form college[16]; (ii) make provision as to the initial name of the corporation as a sixth form college corporation[17].

The power to make an order under these provisions[18] is exercisable only once[19], and is not exercisable after the date specified in an order made by the Secretary of State[20].

1   As to the Secretary of State see PARA 58.
2   Such orders, being of local effect, are not recorded in this work.
3   As to the meaning of 'further education corporation' see PARA 555 note 3.
4   Further and Higher Education Act 1992 s 33A(2)(a) (s 33A added by the Apprenticeships, Skills, Children and Learning Act 2009 s 125, Sch 8 paras 1, 3). As to the meaning of 'England' see PARA 7 note 3.
5   Ie under the Learning and Skills Act 2000 s 143(4): see PARA 575.
6   Further and Higher Education Act 1992 s 33A(2)(b) (as added: see note 4).
7   'Sixth form college corporation' means a body corporate: (1) designated as a sixth form college corporation under the Further and Higher Education Act 1992 s 33A or s 33B (see PARA 578); or (2) established under s 33C (see PARA 760): s 90(1) (definition added by the Apprenticeships, Skills, Children and Learning Act 2009 s 125, Sch 8 paras 1, 12(1), (3)). As to bodies corporate see COMPANIES vol 14 (2009) PARA 2; CORPORATIONS vol 24 (2010) PARA 301 et seq.
8   Further and Higher Education Act 1992 s 33A(1) (as added: see note 4).
9   Further and Higher Education Act 1992 s 33A(3)(a) (as added: see note 4).
10   Ie under the Learning and Skills Act 2000 s 143(4): see PARA 575.
11   Further and Higher Education Act 1992 s 33A(3)(b) (as added: see note 4).
12   Ie under the Further and Higher Education Act 1992 s 28: see PARA 572.
13   'Relevant sixth form college', in relation to a sixth form college corporation, means the educational institution specified in the order under the Further and Higher Education Act 1992 designating the corporation as a sixth form college corporation or establishing it as such: s 90(1) (definition added by the Apprenticeships, Skills, Children and Learning Act 2009 s 125, Sch 8 paras 1, 12(1), (3)).
14   Further and Higher Education Act 1992 s 33A(3)(c) (as added: see note 4).
15   As to the instrument and articles of government of further education corporations see PARA 562; and of designated institutions see PARA 573. As to the instrument and articles of government of sixth form college corporations see PARA 583.
16   Further and Higher Education Act 1992 s 33A(4)(a) (as added: see note 4).
17   Further and Higher Education Act 1992 s 33A(4)(b) (as added: see note 4).
18   Ie the power conferred by the Further and Higher Education Act 1992 s 33A(1): see the text to notes 1–8.
19   Further and Higher Education Act 1992 s 33A(5)(a) (as added: see note 4).
20   Further and Higher Education Act 1992 s 33A(5)(b) (as added: see note 4). The power to make an order under s 33A(5)(b) is not exercisable by statutory instrument (see s 89(1), (2) (s 89(1) amended by the Further and Higher Education (Governance and Information) (Wales) Act 2014 Sch 2 para 1(d)(i); and the Further and Higher Education Act 1992 s 89(2) amended by the Apprenticeships, Skills, Children and Learning Act 2009 s 125, Sch 8 paras 1, 11(1), (2)(a))) and such orders are not recorded in this work.

578. Subsequent designation of existing bodies corporate as sixth form college corporations. The Secretary of State[1] may, after the specified date[2], by order[3] designate a body corporate which is:

(1)   a further education corporation[4] established in respect of an institution in England[5]; or

(2)   a body corporate established by an order[6] in respect of an institution in England[7],

as a sixth form college corporation[8], for the purpose of conducting an educational institution specified in the order[9]. Such an order may be made only if an application for the order has been made by the governing body[10] of the institution mentioned in head (1) or (2) above[11], and the institution is one[12] in respect of which it appears to the Secretary of State that on the date on which the application is made at least 80 per cent of its total enrolment number[13] will be persons over compulsory school age[14] but under 19[15].

On the date specified in the order:

(a) a body corporate within head (1) above ceases to be a further education corporation and becomes a sixth form college corporation[16];

(b) a body corporate within head (2) above ceases to be subject to the order[17] establishing it and becomes a sixth form college corporation[18];

(c) in the case of a body corporate within head (2) above, a designation[19] which has effect in relation to the relevant sixth form college ceases to have effect[20].

An order may: (i) make provision for the continuity of the body corporate, including provision for the continuation of the instrument and articles of government[21] of the body and the relevant sixth form college[22]; (ii) make provision as to the initial name of the corporation as a sixth form college corporation[23].

1   As to the Secretary of State see PARA 58.
2   The power conferred by the Further and Higher Education Act 1992 s 33B(1) is exercisable only after the date specified in an order under s 33A(5)(b) (see PARA 577): s 33B(8) (s 33B added by the Apprenticeships, Skills, Children and Learning Act 2009 s 125, Sch 8 paras 1, 3).
3   Such orders, being of local effect, are not recorded in this work.
4   As to the meaning of 'further education corporation' see PARA 555 note 3.
5   Further and Higher Education Act 1992 s 33B(2)(a) (as added: see note 2). As to the meaning of 'England' see PARA 7 note 3.
6   Ie under the Learning and Skills Act 2000 s 143(4): see PARA 575.
7   Further and Higher Education Act 1992 s 33B(2)(b) (as added: see note 2).
8   As to the meaning of 'sixth form college corporation' see PARA 577 note 7.
9   Further and Higher Education Act 1992 s 33B(1) (as added: see note 2).
10 As to the meaning of 'governing body' see PARA 560 note 6.
11 Further and Higher Education Act 1992 s 33B(3)(a) (as added: see note 2).
12 See the Further and Higher Education Act 1992 s 33B(3)(b) (as added: see note 2).
13 The total enrolment number of an institution is to be calculated in accordance with the Further and Higher Education Act 1992 Sch 3 para 1(2): s 33B(5) (as added: see note 2).
14 As to the meaning of 'compulsory school age' see PARA 19.
15 See the Further and Higher Education Act 1992 s 33B(4) (as added: see note 2). As to the time at which a person attains a particular age see PARA 7 note 6.
16 Further and Higher Education Act 1992 s 33B(6)(a) (as added: see note 2).
17 Ie under the Learning and Skills Act 2000 s 143(4): see PARA 575.
18 Further and Higher Education Act 1992 s 33B(6)(b) (as added: see note 2).
19 Ie under the Further and Higher Education Act 1992 s 28: see PARA 572.
20 Further and Higher Education Act 1992 s 33B(6)(c) (as added: see note 2).
21 As to the instrument and articles of government of further education corporations see PARA 740; and of designated institutions see PARA 573. As to the instrument and articles of government of sixth form college corporations see PARA 583.
22 Further and Higher Education Act 1992 s 33B(7)(a) (as added: see note 2). As to the meaning of 'the relevant sixth form college' see PARA 577 note 13.
23 Further and Higher Education Act 1992 s 33B(7)(b) (as added: see note 2).

579.   Establishment of new bodies corporate as sixth form college corporations. The Secretary of State[1] may by order[2] make provision for the establishment of a body corporate[3] as a sixth form college corporation[4], for the purpose of establishing and conducting an educational institution specified in the order[5]. Such an order may be made only if:

(1) a proposal relating to the order has been made by a person[6] or body ('the proposer') and it appears to the Secretary of State that the statutory requirements have been met in relation to the proposal[7]; and

(2) it appears to the Secretary of State that the institution will when established be[8] an institution in England[9], and an institution in relation to which, on the date on which it is proposed to be established, at least 80 per cent of its total enrolment number[10] will be persons over compulsory school age[11] but under 19[12].

The statutory requirements referred to in head (1) above are that: (a) the proposer has published the proposal by the prescribed time and in the prescribed manner[13]; (b) the proposal as published contained prescribed information[14]; (c) the proposer has considered any representations about the proposal made to the proposer within the prescribed period[15].

An order must provide for the institution to be established and conducted by the body corporate as from the date specified in the order[16], and may make provision as to the initial name of the corporation as a sixth form college corporation[17].

1 As to the Secretary of State see PARA 58.
2 Such orders, being of local effect, are not recorded in this work.
3 As to bodies corporate see COMPANIES vol 14 (2009) PARA 2; CORPORATIONS vol 24 (2010) PARA 301 et seq.
4 As to the meaning of 'sixth form college corporation' see PARA 577 note 7.
5 Further and Higher Education Act 1992 s 33C(1) (s 33C added by the Apprenticeships, Skills, Children and Learning Act 2009 s 125, Sch 8 paras 1, 3).
6 As to the meaning of 'person' see PARA 7 note 6.
7 Further and Higher Education Act 1992 s 33C(2)(a) (as added (see note 5); and amended by the Education Act 2011 Sch 12 paras 1, 11(1), (2)).
8 See the Further and Higher Education Act 1992 s 33C(2)(b) (as added: see note 5).
9 See the Further and Higher Education Act 1992 s 33C(4)(a) (as added: see note 5). As to the meaning of 'England' see PARA 7 note 3.
10 The total enrolment number of an institution is to be calculated in accordance with the Further and Higher Education Act 1992 Sch 3 para 1(2): s 33C(5) (as added: see note 5).
11 As to the meaning of 'compulsory school age' see PARA 19.
12 See the Further and Higher Education Act 1992 s 33C(4)(b) (as added: see note 5). As to the time at which a person attains a particular age see PARA 7 note 6.
13 Further and Higher Education Act 1992 s 33C(3)(a) (as added (see note 5); and amended by the Education Act 2011 Sch 12 paras 1, 11(1), (3)). 'Prescribed' means prescribed by regulations; and 'regulations' means regulations made by the Secretary of State: see the Education Act 1996 s 579(1) (definition applied by the Further and Higher Education Act 1992 s 90(5)); and the Further and Higher Education Act 1992 s 61(1). As to the regulations made under s 33C(3) see the Sixth Form College Corporations (Publication of Proposals) (England) Regulations 2012, SI 2012/1158.
14 Further and Higher Education Act 1992 s 33C(3)(b) (as added: see note 5).
15 Further and Higher Education Act 1992 s 33C(3)(c) (as added (see note 5); and amended by the Education Act 2011 Sch 12 paras 1, 11(1), (4)).
16 Further and Higher Education Act 1992 s 33C(6)(a) (as added: see note 5).
17 Further and Higher Education Act 1992 s 33C(6)(b) (as added: see note 5).

580. Conversion of sixth form college corporations into further education corporations. The Secretary of State[1] may by order[2] convert a sixth form college corporation[3] into a further education corporation[4]. Such an order may be made only if an application for the order has been made by the governing body[5] of the relevant sixth form college[6].

On the date specified in the order, the body ceases to be a sixth form college corporation and becomes a further education corporation[7]. The order may: (1) make provision for the continuity of the body corporate[8], including provision for the continuation of the instrument and articles of government[9] of the body and the relevant sixth form college[10]; (2) make provision as to the initial name of the corporation as a further education corporation[11].

1   As to the Secretary of State see PARA 58.

2   Such orders, being of local effect, are not recorded in this work.

3   As to the meaning of 'sixth form college corporation' see PARA 577 note 7.

4   Further and Higher Education Act 1992 s 33D(1) (s 33D added by Apprenticeships, Skills, Children and Learning Act 2009 s 125, Sch 8 paras 1, 3; and amended by the Deregulation Act 2015 Sch 15 para 6). As to the meaning of 'further education corporation' see PARA 555 note 3.

5   As to the meaning of 'governing body' see PARA 560 note 6.

6   Further and Higher Education Act 1992 s 33D(2)(a) (as added: see note 4). As to the meaning of 'the relevant sixth form college' see PARA 577 note 13. An application under s 33D(2)(a) may not be made during the period of two years beginning with the date on which the body's designation or establishment as a sixth form college corporation takes effect: s 33D(3) (as so added). As to the designation of bodies as sixth form college corporations see PARAS 577–578; and as to the establishment of sixth form college corporations see PARA 579.

7   Further and Higher Education Act 1992 s 33D(5) (as added: see note 4).

8   As to bodies corporate see COMPANIES vol 14 (2009) PARA 2; CORPORATIONS vol 24 (2010) PARA 301 et seq.

9   As to the instrument and articles of government of further education corporations see PARA 562; and of designated institutions see PARA 573. As to the instrument and articles of government of sixth form college corporations see PARA 583.

10   Further and Higher Education Act 1992 s 33D(6)(a) (as added: see note 4).

11   Further and Higher Education Act 1992 s 33D(6)(b) (as added: see note 4).

B. POWERS

581. Principal powers of a sixth form college corporation. A sixth form college corporation[1] may do any of the following (amongst the corporation's 'principal powers')[2]:

(1)   provide further and higher education[3];

(2)   provide secondary education[4] suitable to the requirements of persons who have attained the age of 14[5];

(3)   provide education which is secondary education by virtue of the provisions of the Education Act 1996[6] which extend the definition of secondary education to include full-time education received partly at a school[7] and partly at another institution[8];

(4)   participate in the provision of secondary education at a school[9];

(5)   supply goods or services in connection with its provision of education[10].

A sixth form college corporation may not provide education of a kind specified in head (2), (3) or (4) above unless it has consulted[11] such local authorities[12] as it considers appropriate[13].

1   As to the meaning of 'sixth form college corporation' see PARA 577 note 7. As to the designation and establishment of sixth form college corporations see PARAS 577–579.

2   The powers in the Further and Higher Education Act 1992 s 33E(1) and (in the case of a sixth form college corporation to which s 33J applies) s 33J(1A) (see PARA 583) are referred to as the corporation's 'principal powers': see s 33E(2) (s 33E added by the Apprenticeships, Skills, Children and Learning Act 2009 s 125, Sch 8 paras 1, 3; and the Further and Higher Education Act 1992 s 33E(2) amended by the Education Act 2011 Sch 12 paras 1, 12).

3 Further and Higher Education Act 1992 s 33E(1)(a) (as added: see note 2). As to the meaning of 'further education' see PARA 23; and as to the meaning of 'higher education' see PARA 24 (definitions applied by the Further and Higher Education Act 1992 s 90(1) (amended by the Education Act 1996 Sch 37 para 115(2))).

4 As to the meaning of 'secondary education' see PARA 21 (definition applied by the Further and Higher Education Act 1992 s 90(5)).

5 Further and Higher Education Act 1992 s 33E(1)(b) (as added: see note 2). As to the time at which a person attains a particular age see PARA 7 note 6.

6 Ie by virtue of the Education Act 1996 s 2(2B): see PARA 21.

7 As to the meaning of 'school' see PARA 91 (definition applied by the Further and Higher Education Act 1992 s 90(5)).

8 See the Further and Higher Education Act 1992 s 33E(1)(c) (as added: see note 2).

9 Further and Higher Education Act 1992 s 33E(1)(d) (as added: see note 2).

10 Further and Higher Education Act 1992 s 33E(1)(e) (as added: see note 2). For these purposes, goods are supplied in connection with the provision of education by a sixth form college corporation if they result from: (1) its provision of education or anything done by it under the Further and Higher Education Act 1992 for the purpose of or in connection with its provision of education (s 33E(4)(a) (as so added)); (2) the use of its facilities or the expertise of persons employed by it in the fields in which they are so employed (s 33E(4)(b) (as so added)); or (3) ideas of a person employed by it, or one of its students, arising out of its provision of education (s 33E(4)(c) (as so added)). For these purposes, services are supplied in connection with the provision of education by a sixth form college corporation if: (a) they result from its provision of education or anything done by it under the Further and Higher Education Act 1992 for the purpose of or in connection with its provision of education (s 33E(5)(a) (as so added)); (b) they are provided by making available its facilities or the expertise of persons employed by it in the fields in which they are so employed (s 33E(5)(b) (as so added)); or (c) they result from ideas of a person employed by it, or one of its students, arising out of its provision of education (s 33E(5)(c) (as so added)). As to the meaning of 'employed' see PARA 568 note 9.

11 As to the exercise of the duty to consult see JUDICIAL REVIEW vol 61 (2010) PARA 627.

12 As to the meaning of 'local authority' see PARA 25 (definition applied by the Further and Higher Education Act 1992 s 90(1) (amended by SI 2010/1158)).

13 Further and Higher Education Act 1992 s 33E(3) (as added (see note 2); and amended by SI 2010/1158).

582. Supplementary powers of a sixth form college corporation. A sixth form college corporation[1] may do anything (including in particular the things referred to below[2]) which appears to the corporation to be necessary or expedient for the purpose of or in connection with the exercise of any of its principal powers[3].

A sixth form college corporation may conduct an educational establishment for the purpose of carrying on activities undertaken in the exercise of its powers to provide further or higher education[4]; and in particular, a sixth form college corporation may conduct the relevant sixth form college[5] as from the date specified in the order designating or establishing the corporation as a sixth form college corporation[6]. A sixth form college corporation may provide facilities of any description appearing to the corporation to be necessary or desirable for the purposes of or in connection with carrying on any activities undertaken in the exercise of its principal powers[7].

A sixth form college corporation may:

(1) acquire and dispose of land[8] and other property[9];

(2) enter into contracts, including in particular: (a) contracts for the employment[10] of teachers and other staff for the purposes of or in connection with carrying on any activities undertaken in the exercise of its principal powers[11]; and (b) contracts with respect to the carrying on by the corporation of any such activities[12];

(3) form, participate in forming or invest[13] in a company[14];

(4) form, participate in forming or otherwise become a member of a charitable incorporated organisation[15];

(5)   borrow such sums as the corporation think fit for the purposes of carrying on any activities it has power to carry on[16], or meeting any liability transferred[17] to it[18];

(6)   in connection with its borrowing, grant any mortgage, charge or other security in respect of any land or other property of the corporation[19];

(7)   invest any sums not immediately required for the purpose of carrying on any activities it has power to carry on[20];

(8)   accept gifts of money, land or other property and apply it, or hold and administer it on trust for, any of those purposes[21];

(9)   do anything incidental to the conduct of an educational institution providing further or higher education, including founding scholarships or exhibitions, making grants and giving prizes[22];

(10)   provide advice or assistance to any other person[23] where it appears to the corporation to be appropriate for it to do so for the purpose of or in connection with the provision of education by the other person[24].

1   As to the meaning of 'sixth form college corporation' see PARA 577 note 7.
2   Ie in the Further and Higher Education Act 1992 s 33F(2)–(6): see the text to notes 4–22.
3   Further and Higher Education Act 1992 s 33F(1) (s 33F added by the Apprenticeships, Skills, Children and Learning Act 2009 s 125, Sch 8 paras 1, 3). As to the principal powers of a sixth form college corporation see PARA 581 note 2.
4   Further and Higher Education Act 1992 s 33F(2) (as added: see note 3). As to the meaning of 'further education' see PARA 23; and as to the meaning of 'higher education' see PARA 24 (definitions applied by s 90(1) (amended by the Education Act 1996 Sch 37 para 115(2))).
5   As to the meaning of 'the relevant sixth form college' see PARA 577 note 13.
6   Further and Higher Education Act 1992 s 33F(3) (as added: see note 3). As to the designation and establishment of sixth form college corporations see PARAS 577–579.
7   Further and Higher Education Act 1992 s 33F(4) (as added: see note 3). The facilities include: (1) boarding accommodation and recreational facilities for students and staff (s 33F(5)(a) (as so added)); and (2) facilities to meet the needs of students with learning difficulties (s 33F(5)(b) (as so added)). For these purposes a person has a learning difficulty if: (a) the person has a significantly greater difficulty in learning than the majority of persons of the same age (s 33F(8)(a) (as so added)); or (b) the person has a disability which either prevents or hinders the person from making use of facilities of a kind generally provided by institutions within the further education sector for persons of the same age (s 33F(8)(b) (as so added)). However a person is not to be taken to have a learning difficulty solely because the language (or form of language) in which the person is or will be taught is different from a language (or form of language) which has at any time been spoken in the person's home: s 33F(9) (as so added). As to the meaning of 'institution within the further education sector' see PARA 555. As to learning difficulties generally under the Children and Families Act 2014 see also PARA 943.
8   As to the meaning of 'land' see PARA 568 note 7.
9   Further and Higher Education Act 1992 s 33F(6)(a) (as added: see note 3).
10 As to the meaning of 'contract of employment' see PARA 568 note 9.
11 Further and Higher Education Act 1992 s 33F(6)(b)(i) (as added: see note 3).
12 Further and Higher Education Act 1992 s 33F(6)(b)(ii) (as added: see note 3).
13 A reference in the Further and Higher Education Act 1992 s 33F to investing in a company includes a reference to becoming a member of the company and to investing in it by the acquisition of any assets, securities or rights or otherwise: s 33F(10) (as added (see note 3); and amended by the Education Act 2011 Sch 12 paras 1, 13(c)).
14 Further and Higher Education Act 1992 s 33F(6)(c) (as added: see note 3).
15 Further and Higher Education Act 1992 s 33F(6)(d) (as added: see note 3). 'Charitable incorporated organisation' means such an organisation within the meaning of the Charities Act 2011 Pt 11 (ss 204–250) (see CHARITIES vol 8 (2015) PARA 226): see the Further and Higher Education Act 1992 s 33F(6)(d) (as so added; and amended by the Charities Act 2011 Sch 7 para 60).
16 Further and Higher Education Act 1992 s 33F(6)(e)(i) (as added: see note 3).
17 Ie under the Further and Higher Education Act 1992 ss 27–27B or s 33P: see PARAS 571, 586. As to the meaning of 'liability' see PARA 568 note 15. As to the meaning of references to the transfer of rights or liabilities see PARA 568 note 9.

18 Further and Higher Education Act 1992 s 33F(6)(e)(ii) (as added (see note 3); and amended by the Education Act 2011 Sch 12 paras 1, 13(a)).
19 Further and Higher Education Act 1992 s 33F(6)(f) (as added: see note 3).
20 Further and Higher Education Act 1992 s 33F(6)(g) (as added: see note 3).
21 Further and Higher Education Act 1992 s 33F(6)(h) (as added: see note 3).
22 Further and Higher Education Act 1992 s 33F(6)(i) (as added: see note 3).
23 As to the meaning of 'person' see PARA 7 note 6.
24 Further and Higher Education Act 1992 s 33F(11) (as added: see note 3).

C. GOVERNANCE

583.   Constitution of sixth form college corporation and conduct of sixth form college.   For every sixth form college corporation[1] there is to be:

(1)   an instrument providing for the constitution of the corporation (to be known as the 'instrument of government')[2]; and

(2)   an instrument in accordance with which the corporation, and the relevant sixth form college[3], are to be conducted (to be known as 'articles of government')[4].

The first instrument of government and articles of government of a new sixth form college corporation[5] are to be made by the Secretary of State by order[6]. Such an order may not be made unless the Secretary of State has consulted the corporation, and in certain cases[7] the trustees of the relevant sixth form college have given their consent[8].

Instruments of government and articles of government must comply with certain requirements[9], and subject to that may make such other provision as may be necessary or desirable[10]. The validity of any proceedings of a sixth form college corporation, or of any committee of the corporation, is not affected by a vacancy among the members[11], or a defect in the appointment or nomination of a member[12]. A sixth form college corporation is a charity and[13] in an exempt charity for the purposes of the Charities Act 2011[14].

An instrument[15] must provide for (a) the number of members of the body[16]; (b) the eligibility of persons for membership[17]; (c) the members to include staff and students at the institution, and in the case of a sixth form college corporation, parents of students at the institution aged under 19[18]; and (d) the appointment of members, if the institution is in England[19], or the appointment or election of members, if the institution is in Wales[20].

An instrument must make provision about the procedures of the body and the institution[21]. In particular, an instrument must specify how the body may resolve for its dissolution and the transfer of its property, rights and liabilities[22].

An instrument must make provision for there to be a chief executive of the institution, and a clerk to the body[23]. An instrument must make provision about the respective responsibilities of the body[24], the chief executive and the clerk[25].

An instrument must require the body to publish arrangements for obtaining the views of staff and students on the matters for which the body is responsible[26].

In the case of an institution in Wales, an instrument must require the body to consult persons in the locality of the institution receiving education or training, employers[27] in that locality and bodies representing persons living in that locality as to the education provided at the institution and the planning of its curriculum[28].

An instrument must permit the body to change its name with the approval of, in the case of an institution in England, the Secretary of State; in the case of an institution in Wales, the Welsh Ministers[29].

An instrument must specify how the body may modify or replace the instrument of government and articles of government[30].

An instrument must prohibit the body from making changes to the instrument of government or articles of government that would result in the body ceasing to be a charity[31].

An instrument must provide for (i) a copy of the instrument to be given free of charge to every member of the body[32]; (ii) a copy of the instrument to be given free of charge, or at a charge not exceeding the cost of copying, to anyone else who requests it[33]; and (iii) a copy of it to be available for inspection at the institution on request, during normal office hours, to every member of staff of, and student at, the institution[34].

An instrument must provide for the authentication of the application of the seal of the body[35]. A document purporting to be an instrument made or issued by or on behalf of a sixth form college corporation and to be duly executed under the seal of the corporation[36], or signed or executed by a person authorised by the corporation to act in that behalf[37], is to be received in evidence and treated, without further proof, as being made or issued by or on behalf of the corporation unless the contrary is shown[38].

1   As to the meaning of 'sixth form college corporation' see PARA 577 note 7. As to the designation and establishment of sixth form college corporations see PARAS 577–579.
2   Further and Higher Education Act 1992 s 33I(1)(a) (ss 33I, 33J, 33K, 33M added by the Apprenticeships, Skills, Children and Learning Act 2009 s 125, Sch 8 paras 1, 3). As to changes to instruments and articles of government see PARA 584. As to the dissolution of sixth form college corporations see PARA 586.
3   As to the meaning of 'the relevant sixth form college' see PARA 577 note 13.
4   Further and Higher Education Act 1992 s 33I(1)(b) (as added: see note 2).
5   Ie a sixth form college corporation established under the Further and Higher Education Act 1992 s 33C: see PARA 579.
6   Further and Higher Education Act 1992 s 33K(1) (as added (see note 2); and amended by the Education Act 2011 Sch 12 paras 1, 18(a)). As to the Secretary of State see PARA 58.
7   Ie in the case of a sixth form college corporation to which the Further and Higher Education Act 1992 s 33J applies: see note 10.
8   See the Further and Higher Education Act 1992 s 33K(2) (as added (see note 2); and amended by the Education Act 2011 Sch 12 paras 1, 18(b)). As to the exercise of the duty to consult see JUDICIAL REVIEW vol 61 (2010) PARA 627.
9   Ie the requirements of the Further and Higher Education Act 1992 Sch 4 (see the text to notes 15–35): s 33I(2)(a) (as added (see note 2); and amended by the Education Act 2011 Sch 12 paras 1, 16(a); and the Further and Higher Education (Governance and Information) Act 2014 Sch 2 para 1(b)). See also note 10.
10 Further and Higher Education Act 1992 s 33I(2)(b) (as added (see note 2); and substituted by the Education Act 2011 Sch 12 paras 1, 16(b)). The Further and Higher Education Act 1992 s 33I(2) is subject to s 33J: s 33I(3) (as so added). Despite anything in s 33I, the instrument of government of a sixth form college corporation in respect of which the relevant sixth form college is specified, or falls within a class specified, by the Secretary of State by order (see s 33J(1), (2) (as so added)) must provide: (1) for the governing body of the relevant sixth form college to include persons appointed for the purpose of securing so far as practicable that the established character of the sixth form college is preserved and developed and, in particular, that the sixth form college is conducted in accordance with any trust deed relating to it (s 33J(1)(a) (as so added)); and (2) for the majority of members of the governing body of the relevant sixth form college to be such governors (s 33J(1)(b) (as so added)). A sixth form college corporation to which s 33J applies (see s 33J(1), (2) above) may (accordingly) conduct the relevant sixth form college in a way that secures that the established character of the sixth form college is preserved and developed (and, in particular, in a way that is in accordance with any trust deed relating to the college): s 33J(1A) (added by the Education Act 2014 Sch 12 paras 1, 17(1), (2)). The references in the Further and Higher Education Act 1992 s 33J(1)(a), (1A) to the established character of a sixth form college is, in relation to a sixth form college established shortly before or at the same time as the designation or establishment of the sixth form college corporation in respect of which it is the relevant sixth form college, references to the character which the sixth

form college is intended to have on its establishment: s 33J(3) (as so added; and amended by the Education Act 2011 Sch 12 paras 1, 17(1), (3)). Orders under the Further and Higher Education Act 1992 s 33J, being of local effect, are not recorded in this work. As to the meaning of 'governing body' see PARA 560 note 6. As to the meaning of references to 'sixth form colleges' see PARA 555 note 5. As to the meaning of 'trust deed' see PARA 108 note 6 (definition applied by the Further and Higher Education Act 1992 s 90(5)).

11 Further and Higher Education Act 1992 s 33I(4)(a) (as added: see note 2).
12 Further and Higher Education Act 1992 s 33I(4)(b) (as added: see note 2).
13 Ie as a result of its inclusion in the Charities Act 2011 Sch 3.
14 Further and Higher Education Act 1992 s 33M (as added (see note 2); and amended by the Charities Act 2011 Sch 7 para 61; and SI 2011/1396). As to the meaning of charity see CHARITIES vol 8 (2015) PARA 1.
15 Ie instruments of government and articles of government. As to the meaning of 'instrument' in the Further and Higher Education Act 1992 Sch 4 see PARA 562 note 8.
16 Further and Higher Education Act 1992 Sch 4 para 3(1)(a) (Sch 4 substituted by the Further and Higher Education (Governance and Information) (Wales) Act 2014 Sch 1). As to the meanings of 'body' and 'institution' see PARA 562 note 9. As to the application of Sch 4 see PARA 562 note 9.
17 Further and Higher Education Act 1992 Sch 4 para 3(1)(b) (as substituted: see note 16).
18 Further and Higher Education Act 1992 Sch 4 para 3(1)(c) (as substituted: see note 16). As to the meaning of 'parent' see PARA 7 note 6. As to the time at which a person attains a particular age see PARA 7 note 6.
19 As to the meaning of 'England' see PARA 7 note 3.
20 Further and Higher Education Act 1992 Sch 4 para 3(1)(d) (as substituted: see note 16). As to the meaning of 'Wales' see PARA 7 note 3. In the case of an institution in Wales the provision made by an instrument must include provision:
  (1) for the members of the body to include (a) the chief executive; (b) at least two other members of staff at the institution; (c) at least two students at the institution; and (d) one or more representatives of local employers or businesses (Sch 4 para 3(2)(a) (as so substituted));
  (2) for at least one of the members who are members of staff to be a member of the teaching staff, and at least one to be a member of the non-teaching staff, elected at an election open to all members of staff from those nominated by any member of staff (Sch 4 para 3(2)(b) (as so substituted)); and
  (3) for the members who are students to be elected at an election open to all the students at the institution from those nominated by any student or (if the body so determines) to be elected at an election open to all the members of an association which represents students at the institution, and is recognised by the body, from those nominated by any member of the association (Sch 4 para 3(2)(c) (as so substituted)).
21 Further and Higher Education Act 1992 Sch 4 para 4(1) (as substituted: see note 16).
22 Further and Higher Education Act 1992 Sch 4 para 4(2) (as substituted: see note 16). As to dissolution see PARA 586.
23 Further and Higher Education Act 1992 Sch 4 para 5(1) (as substituted: see note 16).
24 As to the responsibilities of the body see PARA 562 note 17.
25 Further and Higher Education Act 1992 Sch 4 para 5(2) (as substituted: see note 16).
26 Further and Higher Education Act 1992 Sch 4 para 6 (as substituted: see note 16). The reference in the text to matters for which the body is responsible is a reference to the matters for which the body is responsible under Sch 4 para 5(3)(a) or (b): see PARA 562 note 17.
27 As to the meaning of 'employer' see PARA 569 note 9.
28 Further and Higher Education Act 1992 Sch 4 para 7 (as substituted: see note 16).
29 Further and Higher Education Act 1992 Sch 4 para 8 (as substituted: see note 16). As to the Welsh Ministers see PARA 59.
30 Further and Higher Education Act 1992 Sch 4 para 9 (as substituted: see note 16).
31 Further and Higher Education Act 1992 Sch 4 para 10 (as substituted: see note 16). As to the charitable status of a further education corporation see PARA 566. As to charities generally see CHARITIES.
32 Further and Higher Education Act 1992 Sch 4 para 11(a) (as substituted: see note 16).
33 Further and Higher Education Act 1992 Sch 4 para 11(b) (as substituted: see note 16).
34 Further and Higher Education Act 1992 Sch 4 para 11(c) (as substituted: see note 16).
35 Further and Higher Education Act 1992 Sch 4 para 12 (as substituted: see note 16).
36 Further and Higher Education Act 1992 s 33I(5)(a) (as added: see note 2).
37 Further and Higher Education Act 1992 s 33I(5)(b) (as added: see note 2).
38 Further and Higher Education Act 1992 s 33I(6) (as added: see note 2).

584. Changes to instruments and articles. A sixth form college corporation[1] may modify[2] or replace its instrument of government or articles of government[3].

A sixth form college corporation[4] may do the things mentioned above[5] only with the consent of the trustees of the relevant sixth form college[6].

1   As to the meaning of 'sixth form college corporation' see PARA 577 note 7. As to the designation and establishment of sixth form college corporations see PARAS 577–579.
2   As to the meaning of 'modify' see PARA 573 note 17.
3   Further and Higher Education Act 1992 s 33L(1) (s 33L added by the Apprenticeships, Skills, Children and Learning Act 2009 s 125, Sch 8 paras 1, 3; and substituted by the Education Act 2011 Sch 12 paras 1, 19). As to instruments of government see PARA 583.
4   Ie a sixth form college corporation to which the Further and Higher Education Act 1992 s 33J applies: see PARA 583 note 10.
5   Ie in the Further and Higher Education Act 1992 s 33L(1).
6   Further and Higher Education Act 1992 s 33L(2) (as added and substituted: see note 3). As to the meaning of 'relevant sixth form college' see PARA 577 note 13.

585. Liability of members. Where a member of a sixth form college corporation[1] is found liable in civil legal proceedings in respect of something which he did or omitted to do in the course of carrying out his duties as a member of the corporation[2], a court[3] may make an order extinguishing, reducing or varying the liability[4] if the member applies to the court for such an order[5] and the court considers that the action or omission which gives rise to the member's liability was honest and reasonable[6]. Where a member of such a corporation applies to a court for such an order, the court may make any order which: (1) relates to liability in civil legal proceedings which may come to be incurred by the member in respect of a specified course of action[7]; and (2) is of a kind which the court could have made if the liability had already been incurred[8].

1   Ie a sixth form college corporation as defined in the Further and Higher Education Act 1992 s 90 (see PARA 577 note 7): Learning and Skills Act 2000 s 145(3)(aa) (added by SI 2010/1080).
2   See the Learning and Skills Act 2000 s 145(1).
3   'A court' means the High Court or the county court: Learning and Skills Act 2000 s 145(5) (amended by the Crime and Courts Act 2013 Sch 9 para 52(1)(b), (2)). However, Learning and Skills Act 2000 s 145(5) is subject to any order under the Courts and Legal Services Act 1990 s 1 (allocation of business between High Court and county courts: see COURTS AND TRIBUNALS vol 24 (2010) PARA 863): see the Learning and Skills Act 2000 s 145(5). As to the High Court of Justice in England and Wales see COURTS AND TRIBUNALS vol 24 (2010) PARA 695 et seq. As to county courts see COURTS AND TRIBUNALS vol 24 (2010) PARA 758 et seq.
4   Learning and Skills Act 2000 s 145(2).
5   Learning and Skills Act 2000 s 145(2)(a).
6   Learning and Skills Act 2000 s 145(2)(b).
7   Learning and Skills Act 2000 s 145(4)(a).
8   Learning and Skills Act 2000 s 145(4)(b).

D. DISSOLUTION

586. Dissolution of sixth form college corporations. If a sixth form college corporation[1] proposes that the corporation should be dissolved[2], the corporation must publish details of the proposal, and such other information as may be prescribed[3], in accordance with regulations[4].

The corporation must consult on the proposal, and take account of the views of those consulted, in accordance with regulations[5].

The provisions below[6] apply if, after complying with the above provision[7], a sixth form college corporation resolves that the corporation should be dissolved on a specified date (the 'dissolution date')[8]. The corporation must notify the

Secretary of State of the resolution and the dissolution date as soon as reasonably practicable[9]. The corporation is dissolved on the dissolution date[10].

At any time before the dissolution date, the corporation may transfer any of its property, rights or liabilities[11] to such person or body[12], or a person or body of such description, as may be prescribed, subject to a qualification[13]. The corporation may do so only with the consent of the person or body concerned[14]. Such a transfer[15] has effect on the dissolution date[16].

If a person or body prescribed, or of a description prescribed as above[17], is not a charity established for charitable purposes which are exclusively educational purposes[18], any property transferred to the person or body must be transferred on trust to be used for charitable purposes which are exclusively educational purposes[19].

1   As to the meaning of 'sixth form college corporation' see PARA 577 note 7. As to the designation and establishment of sixth form college corporations see PARAS 577–579.
2   Further and Higher Education Act 1992 s 33N(1) (ss 33N–33P substituted and added by the Education Act 2011 Sch 12 paras 1, 20). The Further and Higher Education Act 1992 ss 33N–33P replace the previous s 33N which was originally added by the Apprenticeships, Skills, Children and Learning Act 2009 s 125, Sch 8 paras 1, 3.
3   'Prescribed' means prescribed by regulations: see the Education Act 1996 s 579(1) (definition applied by the Further and Higher Education Act 1992 s 90(5). 'Regulations' means regulations made by the Secretary of State: s 61(1). As to the Secretary of State see PARA 58.
4   Further and Higher Education Act 1992 s 33N(2) (as substituted: see note 2). As to regulations made under s 33N(2), (3) see the Sixth Form College Corporations (Publication of Proposals) (England) Regulations 2012, SI 2012/1158.
5   Further and Higher Education Act 1992 s 33N(3) (as substituted: see note 2). As to the exercise of the duty to consult see JUDICIAL REVIEW vol 61 (2010) PARA 627.
6   Ie the Further and Higher Education Act 1992 ss 33O, 33P.
7   Ie the Further and Higher Education Act 1992 s 33N.
8   Further and Higher Education Act 1992 s 33O(1) (as added: see note 2). The 'dissolution date' means the date specified in a resolution under s 33O(1): s 33O(2) (as so added).
9   Further and Higher Education Act 1992 s 33O(3) (as added: see note 2).
10   Further and Higher Education Act 1992 s 33O(4) (as added: see note 2).
11   As to the meaning of 'liability' see PARA 568 note 15. As to references to the transfer of rights and liabilities see PARA 568 note 9.
12   As to the meaning of 'person' see PARA 7 note 6.
13   Further and Higher Education Act 1992 s 33P(1) (as added: see note 2). The qualification referred to in the text is in s 33P(4). In the case of a sixth form college corporation to which s 33J applies (see PARA 583 note 10), any property held by the corporation on trust for the purposes of the relevant sixth form college must be transferred to the trustees of the relevant sixth form college: s 33P(4) (as so added). As the meaning of 'relevant sixth form college' see PARA 577 note 13. As to regulations made under s 33P(1) see the Dissolution of Further Education Corporations and Sixth Form College Corporations (Prescribed Bodies) Regulations 2012, SI 2012/1167.
        Stamp duty is not chargeable in respect of any transfer effected under or by virtue of the Further and Higher Education Act 1992 s 33P: see the Further and Higher Education Act 1992 s 88(1) (amended by the Education Act 2011 Sch 12 paras 1, 38(b)). However, no instrument (other than a statutory instrument) made or executed under or in pursuance of the Further and Higher Education Act 1992 s 33P is to be treated as duly stamped unless it is stamped with the duty to which it would, but for s 88 (and, if applicable, the Finance Act 1982 s 129 (see STAMP TAXES vol 96 (2012) PARA 363)), be liable or it has, in accordance with the provisions of the Stamp Act 1891 s 12 (see STAMP TAXES vol 96 (2012) PARA 384), been stamped with a particular stamp denoting that it is not chargeable with any duty or that it has been duly stamped: Further and Higher Education Act 1992 s 88(2). A land transaction effected under or by virtue of s 33P is also exempt from charge for the purposes of stamp duty land tax: see s 88A(1) (s 88A added by SI 2003/2867; and amended by the Education Act 2011 Sch 12 para 1, 39(b)). Relief under the Further and Higher Education Act 1992 s 88A must be claimed in a land transaction return or an amendment of such a return: s 88A(2) (as so added). As to the meanings of 'land transaction' and 'land transaction return' see PARA 571 note 16.
14   Further and Higher Education Act 1992 s 33P(2) (as added: see note 2).

15 Ie a transfer under the Further and Higher Education Act 1992 s 33P(1)

16 Further and Higher Education Act 1992 s 33P(3) (as added: see note 2).

17 Ie prescribed under the Further and Higher Education Act 1992 s 33P(1).

18 Further and Higher Education Act 1992 s 33P(5) (as added: see note 2). As to charities see generally CHARITIES.

19 Further and Higher Education Act 1992 s 33P(6) (as added: see note 2). Section 33P(6) does not apply to property transferred to the person or body by virtue of s 33P(4) (see note 13): s 33P(7) (as so added).

(2) OTHER INSTITUTIONS PROVIDING FURTHER EDUCATION

587. Provision of further education by other institutions. Further education may be provided by institutions outside the further education sector[1], such as schools[2] and institutions within the higher education sector[3]. An institution not within the further education sector may be maintained by a local authority in the exercise of its further education functions[4].

1 As to the meaning of 'institution outside the further education sector' see PARA 555.
2 See PARA 588.
3 See PARA 665.
4 See PARA 589.

588. Provision of further education by a maintained school. The governing body of any maintained school[1] is responsible for determining whether or not to provide:

(1) part-time education suitable to the requirements of persons of any age over compulsory school age[2]; or

(2) full-time education suitable to the requirements of persons who have attained the age of 19[3].

However, the governing body of a community or foundation special school[4] may not determine to provide, or to cease to provide, such education without the consent of the local authority[5].

It is the duty of the governing body of any such school which provides such education to secure that, except in such circumstances as may be prescribed[6], such education is not provided at any time in a room where pupils[7] are at that time being taught[8].

1 As to the meaning of 'maintained school' see PARA 99. As to the governing bodies of maintained schools in England see PARA 150 et seq; and in Wales see PARA 195. As to academies see PARA 345 et seq.

2 School Standards and Framework Act 1998 s 80(1)(a). As to the meaning of 'compulsory school age' see PARA 19. As to the time at which a person attains a particular age see PARA 7 note 6. Section 80 does not apply to part-time education provided under a partnership arrangement to which the Further and Higher Education Act 1992 s 60A (repealed) (partnership arrangements to secure provision of certain further education in Wales) applied: see the School Standards and Framework Act 1998 s 80(3). Section 80 does not apply to any course of training provided under the Education Act 2005 s 95: see s 95(5); and PARA 1059 note 3. As to the duty under the Equality Act 2010 not to discriminate in the provision of courses under the School Standards and Framework Act 1998 s 80, see PARA 15.

3 School Standards and Framework Act 1998 s 80(1)(b).

4 As to community or foundation special schools see PARA 106.

5 School Standards and Framework Act 1998 s 80(1) (amended by SI 2010/1158). As to the meaning of 'local authority' see PARA 25 (definition applied by the School Standards and Framework Act 1998 s 142(8)). Any function of a local authority in England which is conferred by or under s 80 may be exercised by, or by employees of, such person as may be authorised in that behalf by the local authority whose function it is: Contracting Out (Local Authority

Education Functions) (England) Order 2002, SI 2002/928, art 3, Sch 2 para (u) (both amended by SI 2010/1172). As to the meaning of 'England' see PARA 7 note 3. As to the meaning of 'person' see PARA 7 note 6.

6 'Prescribed' means prescribed by regulations; and 'regulations' means regulations made under the School Standards and Framework Act 1998 by the Secretary of State or, in relation to Wales, the Welsh Ministers: see s 142(1). As to the Secretary of State see PARA 58. As to the Welsh Ministers see PARA 59. As to the meaning of 'Wales' see PARA 7 note 3. The functions of the Secretary of State under s 80, so far as exercisable in relation to Wales, were transferred to the National Assembly for Wales (see the National Assembly for Wales (Transfer of Functions) Order 1999, SI 1999/672, art 2, Sch 1) and are now vested in the Welsh Ministers (see the Government of Wales Act 2006 s 162(1), Sch 11 para 30). As to the regulations made under the School Standards and Framework Act 1998 s 80 see the Education (Further Education in Schools) Regulations 1999, SI 1999/1867.

7 As to the meaning of 'pupil' see PARA 20 note 4 (definition applied by the School Standards and Framework Act 1998 s 142(8)).

8 School Standards and Framework Act 1998 s 80(2).

589. Government of institutions maintained by local education authorities in the exercise of further education functions. A local authority[1] may, in relation to any institution not within the further education sector[2] or the higher education sector[3] which is maintained by it in the exercise of its further or higher education functions[4]:

(1) make such provision as it thinks fit in respect of the government of the institution[5]; and

(2) delegate to the governing body[6] of the institution such functions relating to the management of the finances of the institution, and such other functions relating to the management of the institution (including the appointment and dismissal of staff), as the authority may determine[7].

1 As to the meaning of 'local authority' see PARA 25 (definition applied by the Further and Higher Education Act 1992 s 90(1)).

2 As to the meaning of 'institution outside the further education sector' see PARA 555.

3 As to the meaning of 'institution outside the higher education sector' see PARA 619.

4 See the Further and Higher Education Act 1992 s 85(2), (3) (s 85(2) amended by SI 2010/1158). As to the meaning of 'further education' see PARA 23; and as to the meaning of 'higher education' see PARA 24 (definitions applied by the Further and Higher Education Act 1992 s 90(1)). As to the meaning of 'functions' see PARA 570 note 2.

5 Further and Higher Education Act 1992 s 85(3)(a). The power under s 85(3)(a) includes power to replace any instrument of government or articles of government made under the Education Reform Act 1988 Pt II Ch III (ss 139–155) (repealed) or s 156 (repealed in relation to designated institutions): see the Further and Higher Education Act 1992 s 85(3)(a).

6 As to the meaning of 'governing body' see PARA 560 note 6.

7 Further and Higher Education Act 1992 s 85(3)(b).

590. Institutions ceasing to be maintained by local authority. Where an institution which provides full-time education and is maintained by a local authority[1] in exercise of the authority's further or higher education functions[2] ceases to be maintained by a local authority or (as the case may be) by the authority in question, any provision of any instrument relating to any land[3] or other property held for the purposes of the institution[4] which:

(1) confers on any person[5] an option to acquire an interest in that land[6] or other property[7]; or

(2) provides (in whatever terms) for the determination or forfeiture of any such interest[8],

has effect, if the institution becomes an institution within the further education sector[9] or an institution within the higher education sector[10] or a grant-aided institution[11], as if the event referred to were the institution's ceasing to be a publicly funded institution[12].

1   As to the meaning of 'local authority' see PARA 25 (definition applied by the Education Reform Act 1988 s 235(7) (amended by the Education Act 1996 s 582(1), Sch 37 Pt I para 81)).

2   Education Reform Act 1988 s 157(5)(a) (amended by SI 2010/1158). References in the Education Reform Act 1988 Pt II (ss 120–161) to the further or higher education functions of a local authority are references to the functions of the authority (except in so far as they relate to secondary education) under the Education Act 1996 s 15ZA (see PARA 32), s 15A (see PARA 34), s 15B (see PARA 36), and the Education Reform Act 1988 s 120 (see PARA 678): s 161(1)(b) (substituted by the Learning and Skills Act 2000 s 149, Sch 9 paras 1, 17; and amended by SI 2010/1080; and SI 2010/1158). 'Functions' includes powers and duties: Education Reform Act 1988 s 235(1).

3   As to the meaning of 'land' see PARA 84 note 9.

4   See the Education Reform Act 1988 s 157(4) (amended by the Further and Higher Education Act 1992 s 93, Sch 8 paras 27, 39(a)(i), Sch 9; and SI 2010/1158).

5   As to the meaning of 'person' see PARA 7 note 6.

6   As to the meaning of 'interest in land' see PARA 84 note 9.

7   Education Reform Act 1988 s 157(4)(a).

8   Education Reform Act 1988 s 157(4)(b).

9   As to the meaning of 'institution within the further education sector' see PARA 555.

10   As to references to institutions within the higher education sector see PARA 619.

11   In the Education Reform Act 1988 references to an institution which is or was grant-aided at any time are references to an institution maintained by persons who have received any grants under regulations made under the Education Act 1944 s 100(1)(b) (repealed) or the Education Act 1996 s 485 (see PARA 82) in respect of expenditure incurred or to be incurred for any academic year of that institution current at the time in question: Education Reform Act 1988 s 235(2)(c) (amended by the Education Act 1996 s 582(1), Sch 37 para 81(1), (3)). References to an institution which is eligible to receive aid by way of grant are references to an institution maintained by persons other than local authorities who for the time being satisfy any requirements of regulations so made with respect to the eligibility of such persons to receive grants under those regulations: Education Reform Act 1988 s 235(2)(d) (amended by SI 2010/1158).

12   Education Reform Act 1988 s 157(4) (amended by the Further and Higher Education Act 1992 Sch 8 paras 27, 39(a)(ii), (iii)). 'Publicly funded institution' means an institution which is an institution of any one or more of the following descriptions, that is to say: (1) an institution maintained or assisted by a local authority (Education Reform Act 1988 s 157(6)(a) (amended by SI 2010/1158)); (2) an institution within the further education sector or an institution within the higher education sector (Education Reform Act 1988 s 157(6)(b) (amended by the Further and Higher Education Act 1992 s 93, Sch 8 paras 27, 39(c))); and (3) a grant-aided institution (Education Reform Act 1988 s 157(6)(c)).

(3) RIGHTS AND LIABILITIES OF INSTITUTIONS PROVIDING FURTHER EDUCATION

(i) Property

591. Transfers. Property transfers may be made when a further education corporation[1] is established to conduct an institution[2] or when an institution is designated as a further education institution[3].

1   As to the meaning of 'further education corporation' see PARA 555 note 3.

2   As to the establishment of further education corporations see PARA 559 et seq.

3   As to designated institutions see PARA 572 et seq.

(ii) Trust Deeds

592. Variation of trust deeds. The appropriate national authority[1] may by order[2] make such modifications[3] as it thinks fit in any trust deed[4] or other instrument: (1) relating to or regulating an institution within the further education sector[5]; or (2) relating to any land[6] or other property held by any person[7] for the purposes of such an institution[8]. Before making any such modifications of any trust deed or other instrument, the appropriate national authority must, so far as it appears to it to be practicable to do so, consult[9]:

(a)   the governing body[10] of the institution[11];

(b)   where that deed or instrument, or any other instrument relating to or regulating the institution concerned, confers power on any other persons to modify or replace that deed or instrument, those persons[12]; and

(c)   where the instrument to be modified is a trust deed and the trustees are different from the persons mentioned in heads (a) and (b) above, the trustees[13].

1   Ie the Secretary of State or, in relation to Wales, the Welsh Ministers. As to the Secretary of State see PARA 58. As to the Welsh Ministers see PARA 59. As to the meaning of 'Wales' see PARA 7 note 3. The functions of the Secretary of State under the Further and Higher Education Act 1992 s 46, so far as exercisable in relation to Wales, were transferred to the National Assembly for Wales (see the National Assembly for Wales (Transfer of Functions) Order 1999, SI 1999/672, art 2, Sch 1) and are now vested in the Welsh Ministers (see the Government of Wales Act 2006 s 162(1), Sch 11 para 30).

2   Orders under the Further and Higher Education Act 1992 s 46 are not made by statutory instrument (see s 89(2)) and are not recorded in this work.

3   As to the meaning of 'modifications' see PARA 573 note 17.

4   As to the meaning of 'trust deed' see PARA 108 note 6 (definition applied by the Further and Higher Education Act 1992 s 90(5) (amended by the Education Act 1996 s 582(1), Sch 37 Pt I para 115(1), (3))).

5   Further and Higher Education Act 1992 s 46(1)(a). As to the meaning of 'institution within the further education sector' see PARA 555.

6   As to the meaning of 'land' see PARA 568 note 7.

7   As to the meaning of 'person' see PARA 7 note 6.

8   Further and Higher Education Act 1992 s 46(1)(b).

9   As to the exercise of the duty to consult see JUDICIAL REVIEW vol 61 (2010) PARA 627.

10 As to the meaning of 'governing body' see PARA 560 note 6.

11 Further and Higher Education Act 1992 s 46(2)(a).

12 Further and Higher Education Act 1992 s 46(2)(b).

13 Further and Higher Education Act 1992 s 46(2)(c).

(iii) Employees

593. Avoidance of certain terms in a contract made with an employee. Any contract made between the governing body[1] of an institution within the further education sector[2] and any person employed[3] by it, not being a contract made in contemplation of the employee's[4] pending dismissal by reason of redundancy[5], is void and of no effect in so far as it provides that the employee: (1) is not to be dismissed by reason of redundancy[6]; or (2) if he is so dismissed, is to be paid a sum in excess of the sum which the employer[7] is liable[8] to pay to him[9].

1   As to the meaning of 'governing body' see PARA 560 note 6.

2   As to the meaning of 'institution within the further education sector' see PARA 555.

3   As to the meaning of 'employed' see PARA 568 note 9.

4   As to the meaning of 'employee' see PARA 568 note 9.

5   Further and Higher Education Act 1992 s 49(1). As to dismissal by reason of redundancy see EMPLOYMENT vol 41 (2014) PARA 835 et seq.

6   Further and Higher Education Act 1992 s 49(2)(a).

7   As to the meaning of 'employer' see PARA 568 note 9.

8   Ie under the Employment Rights Act 1996 Pt XI (ss 135–181): see EMPLOYMENT vol 41 (2014) PARA 835 et seq.

9   Further and Higher Education Act 1992 s 49(2)(b) (amended by the Employment Rights Act 1996 s 240, Sch 1 para 52).

(4) POWERS AND DUTIES OF INSTITUTIONS PROVIDING FURTHER EDUCATION

(i) Powers and Duties in relation to the Provision of Education

594. Powers of further education corporations. The principal powers of an institution within the further education sector[1] relating to the provision of education are dealt with elsewhere in this title[2]. An institution within the further education sector also has supplementary powers which enable it to do anything which appears to it to be necessary or expedient for the purpose of or in connection with the exercise of any of its principal powers[3].

1   As to the meaning of 'institution within the further education sector' see PARA 555.
2   See PARAS 567, 581.
3   See PARAS 568, 582.

595. Duty to safeguard pupils receiving secondary education. Where secondary education[1] is provided to persons of compulsory school age[2]:

(1)   by a further education corporation[3];
(2)   by a sixth form college corporation[4]; or
(3)   by a designated institution[5] in pursuance of arrangements made by a local authority[6], or by the governing body[7] of a school[8] on behalf of such an authority[9],

the governing body of the corporation or institution must secure that, except in such circumstances as may be prescribed by regulations[10], no education is provided to a person who has attained the age of 19 years[11] in a room in which any persons of compulsory school age are for the time being receiving secondary education[12].

1   As to the meaning of 'secondary education' see PARA 21 (definition applied by virtue of the Further and Higher Education Act 1992 s 90(5) (amended by the Education Act 1996 s 582(1), Sch 37, para 115(3))).
2   Further and Higher Education Act 1992 s 52A(1) (s 52A added by the School Standards and Framework Act 1998 s 113(2); and the Further and Higher Education Act 1992 s 52A(1) amended by the Learning and Skills Act 2000 s 149, Sch 9 paras 1, 30; and the Education Act 2002 s 215(1), Sch 21 para 19(1), (2)(a)). As to the meaning of 'compulsory school age' see PARA 19.
3   Ie in pursuance of arrangements falling within the Further and Higher Education Act 1992 s 18(1)(aa) or (ab) (see PARA 567): see s 52A(1)(a) (as added (see note 2); and amended by the Education Act 2002 Sch 21 para 19(1), (2)(b)). As to the meaning of 'further education corporation' see PARA 555 note 3.
4   Ie by virtue of the Further and Higher Education Act 1992 s 33E(1)(b) or (c) (see PARA 581): see s 52A(1)(aa) (s 52A as added (see note 2); s 52A(1)(aa) added by the Apprenticeships, Skills, Children and Learning Act 2009 s 125, Sch 8 paras 1, 5). As to the meaning of 'sixth form college corporation' see PARA 577 note 7.
5   As to the meaning of 'designated institution' see PARA 572.
6   Further and Higher Education Act 1992 s 52A(1)(b)(i) (as added (see note 2); and amended by SI 2010/1158). As to the meaning of 'local authority' see PARA 25 (definition applied by the Further and Higher Education Act 1992 s 90(1) (amended by SI 2010/1158)).
7   As to the meaning of 'governing body' see PARA 560 note 6.
8   As to the meaning of 'school' see PARA 91 (definition applied by the Further and Higher Education Act 1992 s 90(5) (amended by the Education Act 1996 s 582(1), Sch 37 Pt I para 115)).
9   Further and Higher Education Act 1992 s 52A(1)(b)(ii) (as added: see note 2).
10   'Regulations' means regulations made by the Secretary of State or, in relation to Wales, the Welsh Ministers: see the Further and Higher Education Act 1992 s 61(1) (amended by the Further and Higher Education (Governance and Information) (Wales) Act 2014 Sch 2 para 1(c)). As to the Secretary of State see PARA 58. As to the Welsh Ministers see PARA 59. As to the

meaning of 'Wales' see PARA 7 note 3. The functions of the Secretary of State under the Further and Higher Education Act 1992 s 52A, so far as exercisable in relation to Wales, were transferred to the National Assembly for Wales (see the National Assembly for Wales (Transfer of Functions) Order 1999, SI 1999/672, art 2, Sch 1) and are now vested in the Welsh Ministers (see the Government of Wales Act 2006 s 162(1), Sch 11 para 30). The prescribed circumstances are that a teacher must be present in the room: see the Education (Secondary Education in Further Education Institutions) Regulations 1999, SI 1999/954, reg 2 (amended by SI 2010/1172).

11 As to the time at which a person attains a particular age see PARA 7 note 6.

12 Further and Higher Education Act 1992 s 52A(2) (as added (see note 2)); and amended by the Education Act 2002 Sch 21 para 19(1), (3)).

596. Duties of governing body in relation to the welfare of children. The governing body[1] of an institution within the further education sector[2] must make arrangements for ensuring that its functions[3] relating to the conduct of the institution are exercised with a view to safeguarding and promoting the welfare of children[4] receiving education or training at the institution[5]. The governing body must, in considering what arrangements are required to be made by it, have regard to any guidance[6] given from time to time (in relation to England[7]) by the Secretary of State[8] or (in relation to Wales[9]) by the Welsh Ministers[10].

1 As to the meaning of 'governing body' see PARA 560 note 6 (definition applied by the Education Act 2002 s 175(5)).

2 As to the meaning of 'institution within the further education sector' see PARA 555.

3 As to the meaning of 'functions' see PARA 18 note 5 (definition applied by the Education Act 2002 s 212(2), (3)).

4 'Child' means a person under the age of 18: Education Act 2002 s 175(5). As to the time at which a person attains a particular age see PARA 7 note 6.

5 Education Act 2002 s 175(3).

6 As to the publication of guidance see the Education Act 1996 s 571 (applied by the Education Act 2002 s 212(2), (3)); and PARA 60.

7 As to the meaning of 'England' see PARA 7 note 3.

8 As to the Secretary of State see PARA 58.

9 As to the meaning of 'Wales' see PARA 7 note 3.

10 See the Education Act 2002 s 175(4). The functions under the Education Act 2002 s 175 in relation to Wales were originally vested in the National Assembly for Wales and are now exercisable by the Welsh Ministers by virtue of the Government of Wales Act 2006 s 162(1), Sch 11 paras 30, 32. As to the Welsh Ministers see PARA 59.

As to the application of the Education Act 2002 s 175(2), (4) (see also PARAS 177, 211) to pupil referral units (see PARA 427 et seq) see the Education (Pupil Referral) (Application of Enactments) (England) Regulations 2007, SI 2007/2979, Sch 1 Pt 1 para 19A (added by SI 2012/3158).

597. Duty to provide for named individuals. A local authority[1] may by notice given to the governing body[2] of an institution in England[3] within the further education sector[4] which provides education suitable to the requirements of persons over compulsory school age[5] but under the age of 19[6]:

(1) require it to provide specified individuals[7] with such education[8] as is appropriate to the individuals' abilities and aptitudes[9];

(2) withdraw such a requirement[10].

Before giving such a notice imposing a requirement on a governing body, a local authority must consult[11] the governing body[12], and such other persons[13] as the authority thinks appropriate[14]. In deciding whether to require a particular institution to provide education to a particular individual a local authority in England must have regard to any guidance given from time to time by the Secretary of State[15].

The governing body of an institution must secure compliance with a requirement that has been imposed by such a notice and has not been withdrawn[16].

Where an institution in Wales[17] within the further education sector provides education suitable to the requirements of persons over compulsory school age who have not attained the age of 19 years[18], the Welsh Ministers[19] may by notice given to the governing body of such an institution[20]:

(a)   require it to provide for such individuals as may be specified in the notice such education[21] as is appropriate to their abilities and aptitudes[22]; or

(b)   withdraw such a requirement[23].

The governing body of such an institution must, for any academic year in respect of which it receives financial support from the Welsh Ministers, secure compliance with any requirement in respect of any individual who has not attained the age of 19 years which is or has been imposed by the Welsh Ministers under such a notice and has not been withdrawn[24].

1   As to the meaning of 'local authority' see PARA 25 (definition applied by the Further and Higher Education Act 1992 s 90(5)).
2   See the Further and Higher Education Act 1992 s 51A(2) (s 51A added by the Apprenticeships, Skills, Children and Learning Act 2009 s 44(1); and the Further and Higher Education Act 1992 s 51A(2) amended by SI 2010/1158). As to the meaning of 'governing body' see PARA 560 note 6.
3   As to the meaning of 'England' see PARA 7 note 3.
4   As to the meaning of 'institution within the further education sector' see PARA 555.
5   As to the meaning of 'compulsory school age' see PARA 19.
6   See the Further and Higher Education Act 1992 s 51A(1) (as added: see note 2). As to the time at which a person attains a particular age see PARA 7 note 6.
7   A local authority may specify an individual in a notice under the Further and Higher Education Act 1992 s 51A(2) only if the individual is in the authority's area, and is over compulsory school age but under the age of 19: s 51A(3) (amended by SI 2010/1158).
8   Ie falling within the Further and Higher Education Act 1992 s 51A(1): see the text to notes 3–6.
9   Further and Higher Education Act 1992 s 51A(2)(a) (as added: see note 2).
10   Further and Higher Education Act 1992 s 51A(2)(b) (as added: see note 2).
11   Further and Higher Education Act 1992 s 51A(4) (as added (see note 2); and amended by SI 2010/1158). As to the exercise of the duty to consult see JUDICIAL REVIEW vol 61 (2010) PARA 627.
12   Further and Higher Education Act 1992 s 51A(4)(a) (as added: see note 2).
13   As to the meaning of 'person' see PARA 7 note 6.
14   Further and Higher Education Act 1992 s 51A(4)(b) (as added: see note 2).
15   See the Further and Higher Education Act 1992 s 51A(6) (as added (see note 2); and amended by SI 2010/1158). As to the Secretary of State see PARA 58.
16   Further and Higher Education Act 1992 s 51A(5) (as added: see note 2).
17   As to the meaning of 'Wales' see PARA 7 note 3.
18   Further and Higher Education Act 1992 s 52(1) (amended by the Learning and Skills Act 2000 ss 149, 153, Sch 9 paras 1, 29, Sch 11; and the Apprenticeships, Skills, Children and Learning Act 2009 s 44(2)(a)).
19   The functions under the Education Act 2002 s 52 in relation to Wales were originally vested in the National Assembly for Wales and are now exercisable by the Welsh Ministers by virtue of the Government of Wales Act 2006 s 162(1), Sch 11 paras 30, 32. As to the Welsh Ministers see PARA 59.
20   Further and Higher Education Act 1992 s 52(2) (amended by SI 2005/3238; and SI 2010/1080).
21   Ie falling within the Further and Higher Education Act 1992 s 52(1): see the text to notes 17–18.
22   Further and Higher Education Act 1992 s 52(2)(a).
23   Further and Higher Education Act 1992 s 52(2)(b).
24   Further and Higher Education Act 1992 s 52(3) (amended by SI 2005/3238; and SI 2010/1080).

598.   Collective worship.   In relation to any institution within the further education sector[1] which is principally concerned with the provision of full-time education suitable to the requirements of persons over compulsory school age[2] who have not attained the age of 19 years[3], the governing body[4] must ensure that at an appropriate time on at least one day in each week during which the institution is open an act of collective worship is held at the institution which persons receiving education at the institution may attend[5].

In an institution of voluntary origin[6] the act of collective worship must be in such forms as to comply with the provisions of any trust deed[7] affecting the institution[8], and must reflect the religious traditions and practices of the institution before it joined the further education sector[9]. In all other institutions, the act of collective worship must be wholly or mainly of a broadly Christian character in that it must reflect the broad traditions of Christian belief but need not be distinctive of any particular Christian denomination[10].

If the governing body of an institution considers it appropriate to do so, it may also provide for acts of worship[11] which reflect the practices of some or all of the other religious traditions represented in Great Britain[12].

1   As to the meaning of 'institution within the further education sector' see PARA 555.
2   As to the meaning of 'compulsory school age' see PARA 19.
3   Further and Higher Education Act 1992 s 44(1) (substituted by the Learning and Skills Act 2000 s 149, Sch 9 paras 1, 27). As to the time at which a person attains a particular age see PARA 7 note 6.
4   As to the meaning of 'governing body' see PARA 560 note 6.
5   Further and Higher Education Act 1992 s 44(2A) (added by the Learning and Skills Act 2000 Sch 9 paras 1, 27).
6   An institution is of voluntary origin for these purposes if:
    (1)   immediately before it joined the further education sector it was a voluntary school (within the meaning of the Education Act 1996: see PARA 106 note 13) (Further and Higher Education Act 1992 s 44(2)(a) (s 44(2) substituted by the Learning and Skills Act 2000 Sch 9 paras 1, 27));
    (2)   immediately before it joined the further education sector it was a foundation or voluntary school (within the meaning of the School Standards and Framework Act 1998: see PARA 106) having a foundation established otherwise than under that Act (Further and Higher Education Act 1992 s 44(2)(b) (as so substituted));
    (3)   it is designated for these purposes by order of the Secretary of State or, in relation to Wales, the Welsh Ministers (s 44(2)(c) (as so substituted)); or
    (4)   it is formed by or for the purpose of merging two institutions both of which were within heads (1)–(3) (s 44(2)(d) (as so substituted)).
    As to the Secretary of State see PARA 58. As to the Welsh Ministers see PARA 59. As to the meaning of 'Wales' see PARA 7 note 3. The functions of the Secretary of State under s 44, so far as exercisable in relation to Wales, were transferred to the National Assembly for Wales (see the National Assembly for Wales (Transfer of Functions) Order 1999, SI 1999/672, art 2, Sch 1) and are now vested in the Welsh Ministers (see the Government of Wales Act 2006 s 162(1), Sch 11 para 30). Orders under the Further and Higher Education Act 1992 s 44(2)(c) are not made by statutory instrument (see s 89(2) (amended by the Learning and Skills Act 2000 s 149, Sch 9 paras 1, 40)) and are not recorded in this work.
7   As to the meaning of 'trust deed' see PARA 108 note 6 (definition applied by the Further and Higher Education Act 1992 s 90(5) (amended by the Education Act 1996 s 582(1), Sch 37 Pt I para 115(1), (3)).
8   Further and Higher Education Act 1992 s 44(3)(a).
9   Further and Higher Education Act 1992 s 44(3)(b) (amended by the Learning and Skills Act 2000 Sch 9 paras 1, 27). In the application of the Further and Higher Education Act 1992 s 44 to an institution which is of voluntary origin by virtue of s 44(2)(d) (see note 6), s 44(3)(b) is to be taken as referring to the religious traditions and practices of the two institutions mentioned in s 44(2)(d): s 44(7) (added by the Learning and Skills Act 2000 Sch 9 paras 1, 27).
10 Further and Higher Education Act 1992 s 44(4) (amended by the Learning and Skills Act 2000 Sch 9 paras 1, 27).
11 Ie in addition to the act of collective worship referred to in the Further and Higher Education Act 1992 s 44(3) (see the text to notes 6–9) or s 44(4) (see the text to note 10).
12 Further and Higher Education Act 1992 s 44(5) (amended by the Learning and Skills Act 2000 Sch 9 paras 1, 27). As to the meaning of 'Great Britain' see PARA 73 note 3.

599. Religious education. In relation to any institution within the further education sector[1] which is principally concerned with the provision of full-time education suitable to the requirements of persons over compulsory school age[2] who have not attained the age of 19 years[3], the governing body[4] must ensure that religious education is provided at the institution for all persons attending the institution who wish to receive it[5]. The governing body is deemed to be fulfilling this duty if religious education is provided at a time or times at which it is convenient for the majority of full-time students to attend[6].

For these purposes, religious education may take the form of a course of lectures or classes or of single lectures or classes provided on a regular basis and may include a course of study leading to an examination or the award of a qualification[7]. The form and content of religious education provided is to be determined from time to time by the governing body of the institution[8]. In the case of an institution of voluntary origin[9], the form and content of religious education must be in accordance with the provisions of any trust deed[10] affecting the institution[11], and must not be contrary to the religious traditions of the institution before it joined the further education sector[12]. In the case of all other institutions, the form and content of religious education must reflect the fact that religious traditions in Great Britain[13] are in the main Christian whilst taking account of the teaching and practices of the other principal religions represented in Great Britain[14].

1   As to the meaning of 'institution within the further education sector' see PARA 555.
2   As to the meaning of 'compulsory school age' see PARA 19.
3   Ie an institution to which the Further and Higher Education Act 1992 s 44(1) (see PARA 598) applies: see s 45(1) (substituted by the Learning and Skills Act 2000 Sch 9 paras 1, 28). As to the time at which a person attains a particular age see PARA 7 note 6.
4   As to the meaning of 'governing body' see PARA 560 note 6.
5   Further and Higher Education Act 1992 s 45(2A) (added by the Learning and Skills Act 2000 Sch 9 paras 1, 28).
6   Further and Higher Education Act 1992 s 45(3) (amended by the Learning and Skills Act 2000 Sch 9 paras 1, 28).
7   Further and Higher Education Act 1992 s 45(4).
8   Further and Higher Education Act 1992 s 45(5) (amended by the Learning and Skills Act 2000 Sch 9 paras 1, 28).
9   An institution is of voluntary origin for these purposes if it is of voluntary origin for the purposes of the Further and Higher Education Act 1992 s 44 (see PARA 598 note 6): s 45(2) (substituted by the Learning and Skills Act 2000 Sch 9 paras 1, 28).
10   As to the meaning of 'trust deed' see PARA 108 note 6 (definition applied by the Further and Higher Education Act 1992 s 90(5) (amended by the Education Act 1996 s 582(1), Sch 37 Pt I para 115(1), (3))).
11   Further and Higher Education Act 1992 s 45(5)(a)(i).
12   Further and Higher Education Act 1992 s 45(5)(a)(ii) (amended by the Learning and Skills Act 2000 Sch 9 paras 1, 28). In the application of the Further and Higher Education Act 1992 s 45 to an institution which is an institution of voluntary origin by virtue of s 44(2)(d) (see PARA 598 note 6), s 45(5)(a)(ii) is to be taken as referring to the religious traditions and practices of the two institutions mentioned in s 44(2)(d): s 45(7) (added by the Learning and Skills Act 2000 Sch 9 paras 1, 28).
13   As to the meaning of 'Great Britain' see PARA 73 note 3.
14   Further and Higher Education Act 1992 s 45(5)(b) (amended by the Learning and Skills Act 2000 Sch 9 paras 1, 28).

600. Provision of transport. In certain circumstances, a local authority must make arrangements for the provision of transport for the purpose of facilitating the attendance of persons receiving education at any institution maintained or assisted by the authority which provides further education or within the further education sector[1].

1　See, in relation to England, the Education Act 1996 s 508F (see PARA 810), s 509AA (see PARA 464); and, in relation to Wales, s 509 (repealed) and the Learner Travel (Wales) Measure 2008 (see PARA 469 et seq).

601. Provision of clothing. A local authority may provide such articles of clothing as it may determine suitable for the physical training provided at an institution maintained by the authority which provides further education or at an institution within the further education sector[1].

1　See the Education Act 1996 s 510(4); and PARA 482.

602. Approval for the use of certain materials and apparatus. The Secretary of State[1] may by regulations[2] require the governing body[3] of a further education institution[4] in England[5] to prevent the use in the institution of specified equipment or specified materials without the approval of the Secretary of State[6]. The Secretary of State may by regulations require the proprietor[7] of a 16 to 19 academy[8] to prevent the use in the academy of specified equipment or specified materials without the approval of the Secretary of State[9]. The Secretary of State may specify equipment or materials in this way only if he thinks the equipment or materials might endanger a person's health or safety[10].

The Welsh Ministers[11] may by regulations[12] require the governing body of a further education institution in Wales to prevent the use in the institution of specified equipment or specified materials without the approval of the Welsh Ministers[13]. The Welsh Ministers may specify equipment or materials in this way only if they think the equipment or materials might endanger a person's health or safety[14].

1　As to the Secretary of State see PARA 58.
2　As to the regulations made see the Education (Hazardous Equipment and Materials) (England) Regulations 2004, SI 2004/571.
3　'Governing body' is not defined in the Education Act 2002. As to the meaning of 'governing body' in the Further and Higher Education Act 1992 see PARA 560 note 6.
4　For the purposes of the Education Act 2002 s 203, 'further education institution' means an institution within the further education sector: s 203(5). As to the meaning of 'institution within the further education sector' see PARA 555.
5　As to the meaning of 'England' see PARA 7 note 3.
6　Education Act 2002 s 203(1).
7　As to the meaning of 'proprietor' see PARA 51 note 4 (definition applied by the Education Act 2002 s 203(5) (amended by the Education Act 2011 Sch 13 para 13(1), (5)(a))).
8　As to the meaning of '16 to 19 academy' see PARA 346 note 13 (definition applied by the Education Act 2002 s 212(2), (3)).
9　Education Act 2002 s 203(1A) (added by the Education Act 2011 Sch 13 para 13(1), (5)(a)).
10　Education Act 2002 s 203(2).
11　The functions under the Education Act 2002 s 203 in relation to Wales were originally vested in the National Assembly for Wales and are now exercisable by the Welsh Ministers by virtue of the Government of Wales Act 2006 s 162(1), Sch 11 paras 30, 32. As to the Welsh Ministers see PARA 59. As to the meaning of 'Wales' see PARA 7 note 3.
12　As to the regulations made see the Education (Schools and Further and Higher Education) Regulations 1989, SI 1989/351 (amended by SI 2001/3708; revoked in relation to England by SI 2008/1701) which, by virtue of the Interpretation Act 1978 s 17(2)(b), have effect in relation to Wales as if made under the Education Act 2002 s 203.
13　Education Act 2002 s 203(3).
14　Education Act 2002 s 203(4).

603. Efficiency studies. The Welsh Ministers[1] in respect of an institution in Wales[2] within the further education sector[3], the Secretary of State[4] in respect of an institution in England[5] within the further education sector (other than a sixth form college[6]), and the Secretary of State in respect of a sixth form college, may arrange for efficiency studies[7] to be promoted or carried out by any person[8] in respect of the institution concerned[9]. A person promoting or carrying out such efficiency studies may require the governing body[10] of the institution concerned:

(1)   to furnish the person, or any person authorised by him, with such information[11]; and

(2)   to make available to him, or any person so authorised, for inspection its accounts and such other documents[12],

as the person may reasonably require for that purpose[13].

1   As to the Welsh Ministers see PARA 59.
2   As to the meaning of 'Wales' see PARA 7 note 3.
3   As to the meaning of 'institution within the further education sector' see PARA 555.
4   As to the Secretary of State see PARA 58.
5   As to the meaning of 'England' see PARA 7 note 3.
6   As to the meaning of references to 'sixth form colleges' see PARA 555 note 5.
7   'Efficiency studies' are studies designed to improve economy, efficiency and effectiveness in the management or operations of an institution: Further and Higher Education Act 1992 s 83(1A) (s 83(1) substituted, (1A), (1B) added, by SI 2010/1080).
8   As to the meaning of 'person' see PARA 7 note 6.
9   See the Further and Higher Education Act 1992 s 83(1), (1B) (s 83(1) as substituted, (1B) as added (see note 8); and s 83(1B) amended by the Education Act 2011 Sch 12 paras 1, 37; and the Deregulation Act 2015 Sch 14 paras 36, 40). As from a day to be appointed, the Further and Higher Education Act 1992 s 83(1B) is further amended by the Higher Education (Wales) Act 2015 Schedule paras 1, 3). At the date at which this volume states the law no such day had been appointed. See generally PARA 721.
10   As to the meaning of 'governing body' see PARA 560 note 6.
11   Further and Higher Education Act 1992 s 83(2)(a).
12   Further and Higher Education Act 1992 s 83(2)(b).
13   See the Further and Higher Education Act 1992 s 83(2) (amended by SI 2010/1080).

(ii) Records and Information

604. Power to make regulations relating to records. Regulations[1] may make provision about the compilation, retention and disclosure of educational records of further education institutions[2]. The regulations may, in particular, impose a function on a local authority[3] or the governing body[4] of a further education institution[5], and make a duty to provide a copy of a record conditional on the payment of a charge which does not exceed the cost of providing the copy[6].

1   'Regulations' means regulations made under the Education Act 2002 by the Secretary of State (in relation to England) or by the Welsh Ministers (in relation to Wales): s 212(1). As to the Secretary of State see PARA 58. As to the Welsh Ministers see PARA 59. As to the meaning of 'Wales' see PARA 7 note 3. The functions under the Education Act 2002 s 202 in relation to Wales were originally vested in the National Assembly for Wales and are now exercisable by the Welsh Ministers by virtue of the Government of Wales Act 2006 s 162(1), Sch 11 paras 30, 32.
      At the date at which this volume states the law, no regulations had been made under the Education Act 2002 s 202. However, the Education (Schools and Further and Higher Education) Regulations 1989, SI 1989/351 (amended by SI 2001/3708; revoked in relation to England by SI 2008/1701), made under the Education Reform Act 1988 s 218(1)(f) (repealed), have effect, by virtue of the Interpretation Act 1978 s 17(2)(b), in relation to Wales, as if made under the Education Act 2002 s 202.
2   Education Act 2002 s 202(1). 'Further education institution' has the same meaning as in the Education Act 2002 s 140 (see PARA 1049 note 1): s 202(4).
3   Education Act 2002 s 202(2)(a) (amended by SI 2010/1158). As to the meaning of 'local authority' see PARA 25 (definition applied by the Education Act 2002 s 212(1) (amended by SI 2010/1158)).
4   'Governing body' is not defined in the Education Act 2002. As to the meaning of 'governing body' in the Further and Higher Education Act 1992 see PARA 560 note 6.
5   Education Act 2002 s 202(2)(b).
6   Education Act 2002 s 202(3).

605.   Duty to give information. Each of the following must give the Secretary of State[1] or the Welsh Ministers[2] such information as the Secretary of State or (as the case may be) the Welsh Ministers may require for the purposes of the exercise of any of the functions[3] of the Secretary of State under Part 4 of the Apprenticeships, Skills, Children and Learning Act 2009[4] or (as the case may be) for the purposes of the exercise of any of the functions of the Welsh Ministers under any enactment[5]:

(1)   a local authority[6];

(2)   the governing body[7] of any institution maintained by a local authority, city technology college, city college for the technology of the arts[8] or academy[9];

(3)   the governing body of any institution within the further education sector[10] or the higher education sector[11]; and

(4)   the governing body of any institution which is receiving or has received certain financial support[12].

1   As to the Secretary of State see PARA 58.
2   The functions under the Further and Higher Education Act 1992 s 54 in relation to Wales were originally vested in the National Assembly for Wales and are now exercisable by the Welsh Ministers by virtue of the Government of Wales Act 2006 s 162(1), Sch 11 paras 30, 32. As to the Welsh Ministers see PARA 59. As to the meaning of 'Wales' see PARA 7 note 3.
3   As to the meaning of 'functions' see PARA 570 note 2.
4   Ie the Apprenticeships, Skills, Children and Learning Act 2009 Pt 4 (s 183–121): see PARA 776 et seq.
5   Further and Higher Education Act 1992 s 54(1) (amended by the Education Act 2002 s 215(1), Sch 21 para 20; SI 2005/3238; the Apprenticeships, Skills, Children and Learning Act 2009 s 123(2), Sch 6 paras 2, 6; and the Deregulation Act 2015 Sch 14 paras 36, 37)).
6   Further and Higher Education Act 1992 s 54(1)(a) (amended by SI 2010/1158). As to the meaning of 'local authority' see PARA 25 (definition applied by the Further and Higher Education Act 1992 s 90(1)).
7   As to the meaning of 'governing body' see PARA 560 note 6.
8   As to city technology colleges and city colleges for the technology of the arts see PARA 345.
9   Further and Higher Education Act 1992 s 54(1)(b) (amended by the School Standards and Framework Act 1998 s 140(3), Sch 31; the Learning and Skills Act 2000 s 149, Sch 9 paras 1, 31; Education Act 2002 s 65(3), Sch 7 Pt 2 para 4; and SI 2010/1158). As to the meaning of 'academy' see PARA 346 (definition applied by the Further and Higher Education Act 1992 s 90(5)).
10 As to the meaning of 'institution within the further education sector' see PARA 555.
11 Further and Higher Education Act 1992 s 54(1)(c). As to references to institutions within the higher education sector see PARA 619.
12 Further and Higher Education Act 1992 s 54(1)(d). The financial support referred to in the text is financial support under s 5 (repealed), which provided for financial support from the Further Education Funding Councils. See now, in relation to Wales, the Learning and Skills Act 2000 s 34 (see PARA 792), and, in relation to England, the Apprenticeships, Skills, Children and Learning Act 2009 s 100 (see PARA 783).

606.   Publication of information by institutions within the further education sector. The appropriate national authority[1] may by regulations[2] require the governing body[3] of any institution within the further education sector[4] to publish such information as may be prescribed[5] about:

(1)   the educational provision made or proposed to be made for its students[6];

(2)   the educational achievements of its students on entry to the institution and the educational achievements of its students while at the institution (including in each case the results of examinations, tests and other assessments)[7];

(3) the financial and other resources of the institution and the effectiveness of the use made of such resources[8]; and

(4) the careers of its students after completing any course or leaving the institution[9].

The information must be published in such form and manner and at such times as may be prescribed[10]. The published information must not name any student to whom it relates[11].

1 Ie the Secretary of State or, in relation to Wales, the Welsh Ministers. As to the Secretary of State see PARA 58. As to the Welsh Ministers see PARA 59. As to the meaning of 'Wales' see PARA 7 note 3. The functions of the Secretary of State under the Further and Higher Education Act 1992 s 50, so far as exercisable in relation to Wales, were transferred to the National Assembly for Wales (see the National Assembly for Wales (Transfer of Functions) Order 1999, SI 1999/672, art 2, Sch 1) and are now vested in the Welsh Ministers (see the Government of Wales Act 2006 s 162(1), Sch 11 para 30).

2 As to the regulations made see the Education (Further Education Institutions Information) (Wales) Regulations 1993, SI 1993/2169 (amended by SI 1994/1321); and the Education (Distribution by Schools of Information about Further Education Institutions) (Wales) Regulations 1994, SI 1994/1321.

3 As to the meaning of 'governing body' see PARA 560 note 6.

4 As to the meaning of 'institution within the further education sector' see PARA 555.

5 'Prescribed' means prescribed by regulations: Further and Higher Education Act 1992 s 50(5).

6 Further and Higher Education Act 1992 s 50(1)(a).

7 Further and Higher Education Act 1992 s 50(1)(b).

8 Further and Higher Education Act 1992 s 50(1)(c).

9 Further and Higher Education Act 1992 s 50(1)(d). For these purposes, a person's career includes any education, training, employment or occupation: s 50(2). The regulations may in particular require the published information to show: (1) the numbers of students not undertaking any career (s 50(2)(a)); and (2) the persons providing students with education, training or employment (s 50(2)(b)). As to the meaning of 'person' see PARA 7 note 6.

10 Further and Higher Education Act 1992 s 50(3).

11 Further and Higher Education Act 1992 s 50(4).

607. Provision of destination information. The Secretary of State[1] may provide destination information[2] to the governing body[3] of an institution in England[4] within the further education sector[5].

The Welsh Ministers may provide destination information to the governing body of an institution in Wales[6] within the further education sector[7].

Information received under the above provisions[8] is not to be published in any form which identifies the individual to whom it relates[9].

The above provisions[10] (1) do not affect any power to provide or publish information which exists apart from these provisions[11]; and (2) are subject to any express restriction on the provision of information imposed by another enactment[12].

1 As to the Secretary of State see PARA 58.

2 For these purposes, 'destination information', in relation to an institution, means information which (1) relates to a former student of the institution; and (2) includes information as to prescribed activities of the former student after leaving the institution: Further and Higher Education Act 1992 s 49B(3) (s 49B added by the Small Business, Enterprise and Employment Act 2015 s 80). Regulations under head (2) above which prescribe activities as to which the Welsh Ministers may provide information are to be made by the Welsh Ministers: Further and Higher Education Act 1992 s 49B(4) (as so added). As to the meaning of 'student' see PARA 67 note 8 (definition applied by the Further and Higher Education Act 1992 s 90(5)). 'Prescribed' means prescribed by regulations: see the Education Act 1996 s 579(1) (definition applied by the Further and Higher Education Act 1992 s 90(5)). 'Regulations' means regulations made by the Secretary of State or the Welsh Ministers: s 61(1) (definition amended by the Further and Higher Education (Governance and Information)) (Wales) Act 2014 Sch 2 para 1(c)). As to the Welsh Ministers see PARA 59. As to the regulations made see the Education (Destination Information)

(Prescribed Activities) (England) Regulations 2015, SI 2015/1564, which prescribe any form of education, employment or training (or any combination of those activities) undertaken by the student.

3　As to the meaning of 'governing body' see PARA 560 note 6.

4　As to the meaning of 'England' see PARA 7 note 3.

5　Further and Higher Education Act 1992 s 49B(1) (as added: see note 2). As to the meaning of 'institution within the further education sector' see PARA 555.

6　As to the meaning of 'Wales' see PARA 7 note 3.

7　Further and Higher Education Act 1992 s 49B(2) (as added: see note 2).

8　Ie under the provisions of the Further and Higher Education Act 1992 s 49B.

9　Further and Higher Education Act 1992 s 49B(5) (as added: see note 2). This is subject to s 49B(6)(a): see the text to notes 10, 11.

10　Ie the provisions of the Further and Higher Education Act 1992 s 49B.

11　Further and Higher Education Act 1992 s 49B(6)(a) (as added: see note 2).

12　Further and Higher Education Act 1992 s 49B(6)(b) (as added: see note 2). As to the meaning of 'enactment' see PARA 1 note 13.

(iii) Discipline and Bullying

608. Power of members of staff in England to search students for prohibited items. Where a member of staff[1] of an institution within the further education sector in England[2], or a 16 to 19 academy, has reasonable grounds for suspecting that a student at the institution may have a prohibited item[3] with him or in his possessions[4], and the member of staff is a qualifying person[5], he may search the student or his possessions for that item[6]. A search may be carried out only where the member of staff and the student are on the premises[7] of the institution[8], or they are elsewhere and the member of staff has lawful control or charge of the student[9]. A student's possessions may not be searched except in the presence of the student[10] and another member of staff, unless a certain condition is satisfied[11].

A person carrying out a search may not require the student to remove any clothing[12] other than outer clothing[13], must be of the same sex as the student, unless a certain condition is satisfied[14], may carry out the search only in the presence of another member of staff, unless the same condition is satisfied[15], and must ensure that the other member of staff is of the same sex as the student if it is reasonably practicable to do so[16]. A person exercising the power of search may use such force as is reasonable in the circumstances for exercising that power[17].

The powers conferred by these provisions[18] are in addition to any powers otherwise[19] exercisable by the member of staff in question and are not to be construed as restricting such powers[20].

1　'Member of staff', in relation to an institution within the further education sector or a 16 to 19 academy, means any person who works at that institution whether or not as its employee: Further and Higher Education Act 1992 s 85AA(6) (ss 85AA, 85AB added by the Apprenticeships, Skills, Children and Learning Act 2009 s 244(1); and the definition in the Further and Higher Education Act 1992 s 85AA(6) amended by the Education Act 2011 Sch 13 para 8(1), (30(b))). As to the meaning of '16 to 19 academy' see PARA 346 note 13 (definition applied by the Further and Higher Education Act 1992 s 90(5)). As to the meaning of 'institution within the further education sector' see PARA 555. As to the meaning of 'employee' see PARA 568 note 9.

2　As to the meaning of 'England' see PARA 7 note 3.

3　Each of the following is a 'prohibited item':

　　(1)　an article to which the Criminal Justice Act 1988 s 139 applies (knives and blades etc: see CRIMINAL LAW vol 26 (2010) PARA 654) (Further and Higher Education Act 1992 s 85AA(3)(a) (as added: see note 1));

　　(2)　an offensive weapon, within the meaning of the Prevention of Crime Act 1953 (see CRIMINAL LAW vol 26 (2010) PARA 653) (Further and Higher Education Act 1992 s 85AA(3)(b) (as so added));

(3)   alcohol, within the meaning of the Licensing Act 2003 s 191 (see LICENSING AND GAMBLING vol 67 (2008) PARA 30) (Further and Higher Education Act 1992 s 85AA(3)(c) (as so added));

(4)   a controlled drug, within the meaning of the Misuse of Drugs Act 1971 s 2 (see MEDICAL PRODUCTS AND DRUGS vol 75 (2013) PARA 481), which s 5(1) of that Act (see CRIMINAL LAW vol 26 (2010) PARA 723) makes it unlawful for the student to have in his possession (see the Further and Higher Education Act 1992 s 85AA(3)(d) (as so added));

(5)   a stolen article (s 85AA(3)(e) (as so added));

(6)   an article that the member of staff reasonably suspects has been, or is likely to be, used to commit an offence, or to cause personal injury to, or damage to the property of, any person (including the student) (s 85AA(3)(ea) (added by the Education Act 2011 s 3(1), (2)));

(7)   an article of a kind specified in regulations (Further and Higher Education Act 1992 s 85AA(3)(f) (as so added)).

In head (5) above 'stolen', in relation to an article, has the same meaning as it has by virtue of the Theft Act 1968 s 24 (see CRIMINAL LAW vol 25 (2010) PARA 299) in the provisions of that Act relating to goods which have been stolen: Further and Higher Education Act 1992 s 85AA(4) (as so added). Further prohibited items are specified in the Further Education Institutions and 16 to 19 Academies (Specification and Disposal of Articles) Regulations 2012, SI 2012/1925, made under the Further and Higher Education Act 1992 s 85AA(3)(f).

4   Further and Higher Education Act 1992 s 85AA(1)(a) (as added (see note 1); and amended by the Education Act 2011 Sch 13 para 8(1), (3)(a)). 'Possessions', in relation to a student, includes any goods over which he has or appears to have control: see s 85AA(6) (as so added).

5   Ie he falls within the Further and Higher Education Act 1992 s 85AB(1): see s 85AA(1)(b) (as added: see note 1). A person may carry out a search under s 85AA only if that person: (1) is the principal of the institution (s 85AB(1)(a) (as so added)); or (2) has been authorised by the principal to carry out the search (s 85AB(1)(b) (as so added)). An authorisation for the purposes of s 85AB(1)(b) may be given in relation to: (a) searches under s 85AA generally (s 85AB(2)(a) (as so added)); (b) a particular search under that section (s 85AB(2)(b) (as so added)); (c) a particular description of searches under that section (s 85AB(2)(c) (as so added)). Nothing in any enactment, instrument or agreement is to be construed as authorising a principal of an institution within the further education sector in England, or a principal of a 16 to 19 academy, to require a person other than a member of the security staff of the institution to carry out a search under s 85AA: s 85AB(3) (as so added; and amended by the Education Act 2011 Sch 13 para 8(1), (4)). 'Member of the security staff', in relation to an institution, means a member of staff whose work at the institution consists wholly or mainly of security-related activities: Further and Higher Education Act 1992 s 85AB(8) (as so added).

6   See the Further and Higher Education Act 1992 s 85AA(2) (as added: see note 1). However, a member of staff may not search a student or his possessions for alcohol if the student is aged 18 or over: see s 85AA(5) (as so added). As to the time at which a person attains a particular age see PARA 7 note 6. As to the power to seize items found during a search see PARA 610.

7   As to the meaning of 'premises' see PARA 62 note 19 (definition applied by the Further and Higher Education Act 1992 s 90(5)).

8   Further and Higher Education Act 1992 s 85AB(4)(a) (as added: see note 1).

9   Further and Higher Education Act 1992 s 85AB(4)(b) (as added: see note 1).

10   Further and Higher Education Act 1992 s 85AB(7)(a) (as added: see note 1).

11   Further and Higher Education Act 1992 s 85AB(7)(b) (as added (see note 1); and amended by the Education Act 2011 s 3(1), (3)(c)). The condition referred to in the text is the condition in the Further and Higher Education Act 1992 s 85AB(7A). The condition is satisfied if (1) the person carrying out the search reasonably believes that there is a risk that serious harm will be caused to a person if the search is not carried out as a matter of urgency (s 85AB(7A)(a) (s 85AB(7A) added by the Education Act 2011 s 3(1), (3)(d)); and (2) in the time available it is not reasonably practicable for the search to be carried out in the presence of another member of staff (Further and Higher Education Act 1992s 85AB(7A)(b) (as so added)).

12   As to the meaning of 'clothing' see PARA 482 note 2 (definition applied by the Further and Higher Education Act 1992 s 90(5)).

13   See the Further and Higher Education Act 1992 s 85AB(6)(a) (as added: see note 1). 'Outer clothing' means: (1) any item of clothing that is being worn otherwise than wholly next to the skin or immediately over a garment being worn as underwear; or (2) a hat, shoes, boots, gloves or a scarf: s 85AB(8) (as so added).

14   See the Further and Higher Education Act 1992 s 85AB(6)(b) (as added (see note 1); and amended by the Education Act 2011 s 3(1), (3)(a)(i)). The condition referred to in the text is the

condition in the Further and Higher Education Act 1992 s 85AB(6A). The condition is satisfied if (1) the person carrying out the search reasonably believes that there is a risk that serious harm will be caused to a person if the search is not carried out as a matter of urgency (s 85AB(6A)(a) (s 85AB(6A) added by the Education Act 2011 s 3(1), (3)(b)); and (2) in the time available it is not reasonably practicable for the search to be carried out by a person of the same sex as the student or in the presence of another member of staff (as the case may be) (Further and Higher Education Act 1992 s 85AB(6A)(b) (as so added)).

15 Further and Higher Education Act 1992 s 85AB(6)(c) (as added (see note 1); and amended by the Education Act 2011 s 3(1), (3)(a)(ii)). As to the condition referred to in the text see note 14.

16 See the Further and Higher Education Act 1992 s 85AB(6)(d) (as added: see note 1).

17 Further and Higher Education Act 1992 s 85AB(5) (as added: see note 1). As to the recording and reporting of the use of force by members of staff in England see PARA 612.

18 Ie by the Further and Higher Education Act 1992 ss 85AA, 85AB.

19 Ie apart from under the Further and Higher Education Act 1992 ss 85AA, 85AB.

20 Further and Higher Education Act 1992 s 85AA(7) (as added: see note 1).

609. Power of members of staff in Wales to search students for weapons. A member of staff[1] of an institution within the further education sector in Wales[2] who has reasonable grounds for suspecting that a student at the institution may have with him or in his possessions[3] (1) an article[4] which has a blade or is sharply pointed[5]; or (2) an offensive weapon[6], may search that student or his possessions for such articles and weapons[7]. Such a search may be carried out only where the member of staff and the student are on the premises[8] of the institution[9], or they are elsewhere and the member of staff has lawful control or charge of the student[10]. A student's possessions may not be searched except in his presence and in the presence of another member of staff[11].

A person may carry out a search only if he is the principal of the institution[12] or he has been authorised by the principal to carry out the search[13]. A person who carries out a search of a student may not require the student to remove any clothing other than outer clothing[14], must be of the same sex as the student[15], and may carry out the search only in the presence of another member of staff who is also of the same sex as the student[16].

If, in the course of a search, the person carrying out the search finds (a) anything which he has reasonable grounds for suspecting falls within head (1) or (2) above[17]; or (b) any other thing which he has reasonable grounds for suspecting is evidence in relation to an offence[18], he may seize and retain it[19]. A person who seizes anything under these powers must deliver it to a police constable[20] as soon as reasonably practicable[21].

A person who exercises a power under these provisions[22] may use such force as is reasonable in the circumstances for exercising that power[23]. The powers conferred by these provisions are in addition to any powers otherwise[24] exercisable by the member of staff in question and are not to be construed as restricting such powers[25].

1 'Member of staff', in relation to an institution within the further education sector, means any person who works at that institution whether or not as its employee: Further and Higher Education Act 1992 s 85B(11) (s 85B added by the Violent Crime Reduction Act 2006 s 46). As to the meaning of 'institution within the further education sector' see PARA 555. As to the meaning of 'employee' see PARA 568 note 9.

2 As to the meaning of 'Wales' see PARA 7 note 3.

3 'Possessions', in relation to a student of an institution within the further education sector, includes any goods over which he has or appears to have control: Further and Higher Education Act 1992 s 85B(11) (as added: see note 1).

4 Ie an article to which the Criminal Justice Act 1988 s 139 applies: see CRIMINAL LAW vol 26 (2010) PARA 654.

5 Further and Higher Education Act 1992 s 85B(1)(a) (as added: see note 1).

6 Further and Higher Education Act 1992 s 85B(1)(b) (as added: see note 1). An 'offensive weapon' is one within the meaning of the Prevention of Crime Act 1953 (see CRIMINAL LAW vol 26 (2010) PARA 653): see the Further and Higher Education Act 1992 s 85B(1)(b) (as so added).

7 Further and Higher Education Act 1992 s 85B(1) (as added (see note 1); and amended by the Apprenticeships, Skills, Children and Learning Act 2009 s 245(1), (3)).

8 As to the meaning of 'premises' see PARA 62 note 19 (definition applied by the Further and Higher Education Act 1992 s 90(5)).

9 Further and Higher Education Act 1992 s 85B(2)(a) (as added: see note 1).

10 Further and Higher Education Act 1992 s 85B(2)(b) (as added: see note 1).

11 Further and Higher Education Act 1992 s 85B(5) (as added: see note 1).

12 Further and Higher Education Act 1992 s 85B(3)(a) (as added: see note 1).

13 Further and Higher Education Act 1992 s 85B(3)(b) (as added: see note 1). An authorisation for the purposes of s 85B(3)(b) may be given either in relation to a particular search or generally in relation to searches under s 85B or to a particular description of such searches: s 85B(10) (as so added).

14 Further and Higher Education Act 1992 s 85B(4)(a) (as added: see note 1). 'Outer clothing' means: (1) any item of clothing that is being worn otherwise than wholly next to the skin or immediately over a garment being worn as underwear; or (2) a hat, shoes, boots, gloves or a scarf: s 85B(11) (as so added). As to the meaning of 'clothing' see PARA 482 note 2 (definition applied by s 90(5)).

15 Further and Higher Education Act 1992 s 85B(4)(b) (as added: see note 1).

16 Further and Higher Education Act 1992 s 85B(4)(c) (as added: see note 1).

17 Further and Higher Education Act 1992 s 85B(6)(a) (as added: see note 1).

18 Further and Higher Education Act 1992 s 85B(6)(b) (as added: see note 1).

19 Further and Higher Education Act 1992 s 85B(6) (as added: see note 1).

20 As to the office of constable see POLICE AND INVESTIGATORY POWERS vol 84 (2013) PARA 1 et seq.

21 Further and Higher Education Act 1992 s 85B(8) (as added: see note 1). The Police (Property) Act 1897 (disposal of property in the possession of the police: see POLICE AND INVESTIGATORY POWERS vol 84A (2013) PARA 635 et seq) applies to property which has come into the possession of a police constable under the Further and Higher Education Act 1992 s 85B as it applies to property which has come into the possession of the police in the circumstances mentioned in that Act: Further and Higher Education Act 1992 s 85B(9) (as so added).

22 Ie under the Further and Higher Education Act 1992 s 85B.

23 Further and Higher Education Act 1992 s 85B(7) (as added: see note 1).

24 Ie apart from the Further and Higher Education Act 1992 s 85B.

25 Further and Higher Education Act 1992 s 85B(12) (as added: see note 1).

610. Power in England to seize items found during search for prohibited items. A member of staff of an institution within the further education sector in England[1] who is carrying out a search for prohibited items[2] may seize any of the following found in the course of the search[3]:

(1) anything which that person has reasonable grounds for suspecting is a prohibited item[4];

(2) any other thing which that person has reasonable grounds for suspecting is evidence in relation to an offence[5];

and may use such force as is reasonable in the circumstances[6].

The powers conferred by these provisions[7] are in addition to any powers otherwise[8] exercisable by the member of staff in question and are not to be construed as restricting such powers[9]. Where a member of staff seizes, retains or disposes of a relevant item[10], and proves that the seizure, retention or disposal was lawful[11], and also where he erases data or a file from an electronic device[12], and proves that the erasure was lawful[13], that person is not liable in any proceedings in respect of the seizure, retention, disposal or erasure[14], or any damage or loss which arises in consequence of it[15].

1   As to the meaning of 'member of staff' see PARA 608 note 1. As to the meaning of 'institution
     within the further education sector' see PARA 555. As to the meaning of 'England' see PARA 7
     note 3.

2   Ie a search under the Further and Higher Education Act 1992 s 85AA: see PARA 608.

3   A person may not seize alcohol from a student where the student is aged 18 or over: see the
     Further and Higher Education Act 1992 s 85AC(1) (ss 85AA, 85AC, 85AD added by the
     Apprenticeships, Skills, Children and Learning Act 2009 s 244(1)). As to the time at which a
     person attains a particular age see PARA 7 note 6. A person who seizes alcohol under s 85AC(1)
     may retain or dispose of the alcohol and its container: Further and Higher Education Act 1992
     s 85AC(3) (as so added). A person who seizes a controlled drug under s 85AC(1): (1) must
     (subject to head (2)) deliver it to a police constable as soon as reasonably practicable
     (s 85AC(4)(a) (as so added)); but (2) may dispose of it if the person thinks that there is a good
     reason to do so (s 85AC(4)(b) (as so added)). A person who seizes a stolen article under
     s 85AC(1): (a) must (subject to head (b) below) deliver it to a police constable as soon as
     reasonably practicable (s 85AC(5)(a) (as so added)); but (b) may return it to its owner (or, if
     returning it to its owner is not practicable, may retain it or dispose of it) if the person thinks that
     there is a good reason to do so (s 85AC(5)(b) (as so added)). In determining, for the purposes of
     s 85AC(4), (5), whether there is a good reason to dispose of a controlled drug or to return a
     stolen article to its owner, retain it or dispose of it, the person must have regard to any guidance
     issued by the Secretary of State: s 85AC(6) (as so added).
         A person who seizes an item that is a prohibited item by virtue of s 85AA(3)(ea) (article used
     in commission of offence or to cause personal injury or damage to property) (see PARA 608
     note 3 head (6)) under s 85AC(1) must: (i) deliver the item to a police constable as soon as
     reasonably practicable (s 85AC(6A)(a) (s 85(6A)–(6E) added by the Education Act 2011
     s 3(1), (4)(a))); (ii) return the item to its owner (Further and Higher Education Act 1992
     s 85AC(6A)(b) (as so added)); (iii) retain the item (s 85AC(6A)(c) (as so added)); or (iv) dispose
     of the item (s 85AC(6A)(d) (as so added)). In deciding what to do with an item under
     s 85AC(6A), the person who seized it must have regard to guidance issued for the purpose of
     s 85AC by the Secretary of State: s 85AC(6A) (as so added). As to the publication of guidance
     see the Education Act 1996 s 571 (applied by the Further and Higher Education Act 1992
     s 90(5)); and PARA 60. As to the Secretary of State see PARA 58.
         Section 85AC(6C), (6D) (see below) apply to an item that (A) has been seized under
     s 85AC(1) (s 85AC(6B)(a) (as so added)); (B) is a prohibited item by virtue of s 85AA(3)(ea)
     (s 85AC(6B)(b) (as so added)); and (C) is an electronic device (s 85AC(6B)(c) (as so added)). The
     person who seized the item may examine any data or files on the device, if the person thinks
     there is a good reason to do so: s 85AC(6C) (as so added). Following an examination under
     s 85AC(6C), if the person has decided to return the item to its owner, retain it or dispose of it,
     the person may erase any data or files from the device if the person thinks there is a good reason
     to do so: s 85AC(6D) (as so added). In determining whether there is a good reason for the
     purposes of s 85AC(6C) or (6D), the person must have regard to any guidance issued for the
     purposes of s 85AC by the Secretary of State: s 85AC(6E) (as so added).
         Regulations may prescribe what must or may be done by a person who seizes an article of a
     kind specified in regulations under s 85AA(3)(f) (see PARA 608 note 3 head (7)) (or an article
     which the person has reasonable grounds for suspecting to be such an article): s 85AC(7) (as so
     added). Regulations under s 85AC(7) may make provision corresponding to any provision of
     s 85AD (see below and the text to notes 10–15): s 85AD(5) (as so added). A person who seizes:
     (aa) an article to which the Criminal Justice Act 1988 s 139 applies (knives and blades etc: see
     CRIMINAL LAW vol 26 (2010) PARA 654) (Further and Higher Education Act 1992 s 85AC(8)(a)
     (as so added)); (bb) an offensive weapon (s 85AC(8)(b) (as so added)); or (cc) anything which
     that person has reasonable grounds for suspecting is evidence in relation to an offence
     (s 85AC(8)(c) (as so added)), must deliver it to a police constable as soon as reasonably
     practicable (s 85AC(8) (as so added)). Section 85AC(8)(c) is subject to s 85AC(3)–(5), (6A) (see
     above) and regulations made under s 85AC(7): s 85AC(9) (as so added; and amended by the
     Education Act 2011 s 3(1), (4)(b))). In the Further and Higher Education Act 1992
     s 85AC(3)–(8), references to alcohol, a controlled drug, a stolen article, an article to which the
     Criminal Justice Act 1988 s 139 applies and an offensive weapon include references to anything
     which a person has reasonable grounds for suspecting is alcohol, a controlled drug, a stolen
     article, an article to which the Criminal Justice Act 1988 s 139 applies or an offensive weapon:
     Further and Higher Education Act 1992 s 85AC(10) (as so added). As to the office of constable
     see POLICE AND INVESTIGATORY POWERS vol 84 (2013) PARA 1 et seq. As to regulations made
     under s 85AC(7) see the Further Education Institutions and 16 to 19 Academies (Specification
     and Disposal of Articles) Regulations 2012, SI 2012/1925.

The Police (Property) Act 1897 (disposal of property in the possession of the police: see POLICE AND INVESTIGATORY POWERS vol 84A (2013) PARA 635 et seq) applies to property which has come into the possession of a police constable under the Further and Higher Education Act 1992 s 85AC(4)(a), (5)(a), (6A)(a) or (8) as it applies to property which has come into the possession of the police in the circumstances mentioned in that Act: s 85AD(1) (as so added; and amended by the Education Act 2011 s 3(1), (5)(a)).

4 Further and Higher Education Act 1992 s 85AC(1)(a) (as added: see note 3). As to the meaning of 'prohibited item' see PARA 608 note 3.

5 Further and Higher Education Act 1992 s 85AC(1)(b) (as added: see note 3).

6 See the Further and Higher Education Act 1992 s 85AC(2) (as added: see note 3). As to the recording and reporting of the use of force by members of staff in England see PARA 612.

7 Ie by the Further and Higher Education Act 1992 s 85AC.

8 Ie apart from the Further and Higher Education Act 1992 s 85AC.

9 See the Further and Higher Education Act 1992 s 85AA(7) (as added: see note 3).

10 See the Further and Higher Education Act 1992 s 85AD(2)(a) (as added (see note 3); and amended by the Education Act 2011 s 3(1), (5)(b)). The reference in the text to a relevant item is a reference to an item within the Further and Higher Education Act 1992 s 85AD(2A) (see below). The items referred to in s 85AD(2)(a) are: (1) alcohol or its container (s 85AD(2A)(a) (s 85AD(2A), (2B) added by the Education Act 2011 s 3(1), (5)(c)); (2) a controlled drug (Further and Higher Education Act 1992 s 85AD(2A)(b) (as so added)); (3) a stolen article (s 85AD(2A)(c) (as so added)); (4) an article that is a prohibited item by virtue of s 85AA(3)(ea) (see PARA 608 note 3 head (6)) (s 85AD(2A)(d) (as so added)).

11 See the Further and Higher Education Act 1992 s 85AD(2)(b) (as added: see note 3). Section 85AD(2), (2B) and (3) (see the text to notes 12–15) does not prevent any person from relying on any defence on which the person is entitled to rely apart from those provisions: s 85AD(4) (as so added; and amended by the Education Act 2011 s 3(1), (5)(e)).

12 See the Further and Higher Education Act 1992 s 85AD(2B)(a) (as added: see note 10). The reference is to erasing data or a file from an electronic device under s 85AC(6D): see note 3.

13 See the Further and Higher Education Act 1992 s 85AD(2B)(b) (as added: see note 10).

14 See the Further and Higher Education Act 1992 s 85AD(3)(a) (as added (see note 3); and amended by the Education Act 2011 s 3(1), (5)(d)).

15 See the Further and Higher Education Act 1992 s 85AD(3)(b) (as added: see note 3).

611. Power of members of staff to use force. A member of the staff[1] of an institution which is within the further education sector or is a 16 to 19 academy may use such force[2] as is reasonable in the circumstances for the purpose of preventing a student at the institution from doing (or continuing to do) any of the following, namely[3]:

(1) committing any offence[4];

(2) causing personal injury to, or damage to the property of, any person[5] (including the student himself)[6]; or

(3) prejudicing the maintenance of good order and discipline at the institution or among any of its students, whether during a teaching session or otherwise[7].

This power may be exercised only where the member of the staff and the student are on the premises[8] of the institution[9], or they are elsewhere and the member of the staff has lawful control or charge of the student[10]. The power does not authorise anything to be done in relation to a student which constitutes the giving of corporal punishment[11]. The power is in addition to any powers otherwise[12] exercisable and is not to be construed as restricting what may otherwise[13] lawfully be done[14].

1 'Member of the staff', in relation to an institution within the further education sector or a 16 to 19 academy, means any person who works at that institution whether or not as its employee: Further and Higher Education Act 1992 s 85C(5) (s 85C added by the Education and Inspections Act 2006 s 165; and the Further and Higher Education Act 1992 s 85C(5) amended by the Education Act 2011 Sch 13 para 8(1), (5)(b)). As to the meaning of 'institution within the

further education sector' see PARA 555. As to the meaning of '16 to 19 academy' see PARA 346 note 13 (definition applied by the Further and Higher Education Act 1992 s 90(5)). As to the meaning of 'employee' see PARA 568 note 9.

At the date at which this volume states the law s 85C is in force in relation to England only (see the Education and Inspections Act 2006 (Commencement No 3 and Transitional Provisions and Savings) Order 2007, SI 2007/935, art 4(b)) and will be brought into force in relation to Wales on a day to be appointed under the Education and Inspections Act 2006 s 188(3). At the date at which this volume states the law no such day had been appointed. As to the meanings of 'England' and 'Wales' see PARA 7 note 3.

2 As to the recording and reporting of the use of force by members of staff in England see PARA 612.

3 Further and Higher Education Act 1992 s 85C(1) (as added (see note 1); and amended by the Education Act 2011 Sch 13 para 8(1), (5)(a)).

4 Further and Higher Education Act 1992 s 85C(1)(a) (as added: see note 1).

5 As to the meaning of 'person' see PARA 7 note 6.

6 Further and Higher Education Act 1992 s 85C(1)(b) (as added: see note 1).

7 Further and Higher Education Act 1992 s 85C(1)(c) (as added: see note 1).

8 As to the meaning of 'premises' see PARA 62 note 19 (definition applied by the Further and Higher Education Act 1992 s 90(5)).

9 Further and Higher Education Act 1992 s 85C(2)(a) (as added: see note 1).

10 Further and Higher Education Act 1992 s 85C(2)(b) (as added: see note 1).

11 Further and Higher Education Act 1992 s 85C(3) (as added: see note 1). 'Corporal punishment' means such punishment within the meaning of the Education Act 1996 s 548 (see PARA 545 note 3): see the Further and Higher Education Act 1992 s 85C(3) (as so added).

12 Ie apart from the Further and Higher Education Act 1992 s 85C.

13 Ie apart from the Further and Higher Education Act 1992 s 85C.

14 See the Further and Higher Education Act 1992 s 85C(4) (as added: see note 1).

612. Recording and reporting the use of force by members of staff in England. As from a day to be appointed the following provisions have effect[1]. The governing body[2] of an institution within the further education sector[3] in England[4] must ensure that a procedure is in place for:

(1) recording each significant incident in which a member of the staff uses force on a student at the institution (a 'use of force incident')[5]; and

(2) reporting each use of force incident (except those where the student is aged 20 or over[6] or in respect of which special provision is made[7]) to each parent of the student as soon as practicable after the incident[8].

In discharging this duty, the governing body must have regard to any guidance issued by the Secretary of State for these purposes[9]. The governing body must take all reasonable steps to ensure that the procedure is complied with[10]; and the procedure must require that a record of a use of force incident is made in writing[11] as soon as practicable after the incident[12].

1 The Further and Higher Education Act 1992 s 85D is added by the Apprenticeships, Skills, Children and Learning Act 2009 s 247 as from a day to be appointed under s 269(4). At the date at which this volume states the law no such day had been appointed.

2 As to the meaning of 'governing body' see PARA 560 note 6.

3 As to the meaning of 'institution within the further education sector' see PARA 555.

4 As to the meaning of 'England' see PARA 7 note 3.

5 Further and Higher Education Act 1992 s 85D(1)(a) (as added: see note 1). As to the power of a member of staff to use force see s 85C; and PARA 611. Powers to use force are also given in relation to the search of students for prohibited items (see s 85AA; and PARA 608) and the seizure of such items (see s 85AC; and PARA 610).

6 As to the time at which a person attains a particular age see PARA 7 note 6.

7 Ie where provision under the Further and Higher Education Act 1992 s 85D(5) applies: see s 85D(1)(b) (as added: see note 1). A procedure under s 85D(1) must include provision to the effect: (1) that a person ('R') who would otherwise be required by the procedure to report an incident to a parent must not report it to that parent if it appears to R that doing so would be likely to result in significant harm to the student (s 85D(5)(a) (as so added)); and (2) that if it appears to R that there is no parent of the student to whom R could report the incident without

that being likely to result in significant harm to the student, R must report the incident to the local authority (within the meaning of the Children Act 1989: see PARA 453 note 1) within whose area the student is ordinarily resident (Further and Higher Education Act 1992 s 85D(5)(b) (as so added)). In deciding for the purposes of provision made under s 85D(5) whether reporting an incident to a parent would be likely to result in significant harm to the student, R must have regard to any guidance issued by the Secretary of State about the meaning of 'significant harm' for those purposes: s 85D(6) (as so added). 'Parent', in relation to a student, has the meaning given by the Education Act 1996 s 576 in relation to a child or young person (see PARA 7 note 6), but includes a local authority which provides accommodation for the student under the Children Act 1989 s 20 (see CHILDREN AND YOUNG PERSONS vol 10 (2012) PARA 839 et seq): Further and Higher Education Act 1992 s 85D(7) (as so added). As to the meaning of 'person' see PARA 7 note 6. As to the Secretary of State see PARA 58.

8   Further and Higher Education Act 1992 s 85D(1)(b) (as added: see note 1).
9   Further and Higher Education Act 1992 s 85D(4) (as added: see note 1).
10   Further and Higher Education Act 1992 s 85D(2) (as added: see note 1).
11   As to the meaning of 'writing' see PARA 76 note 8.
12   Further and Higher Education Act 1992 s 85D(3) (as added: see note 1).

(5) FINANCIAL PROVISION FOR FURTHER EDUCATION

(i) Sources of Funding for Institutions providing Further Education

613. Financial provision for institutions providing further education. Institutions providing further education receive their funding from a variety of sources, including fees[1] and grants[2]. In addition, the Secretary of State (in relation to England)[3] or the Welsh Ministers (in relation to Wales) may secure the provision of financial resources to certain persons providing such education or training[4]. The Skills Funding Agency (SFA) is an executive agency of the Department for Business, Innovation and Skills, which funds further education in England[5].

1   See PARA 614.
2   See PARAS 615–616.
3   See PARA 783 et seq.
4   See PARA 792 et seq.
5   For more information see the SFA's website.

(ii) Charging of Student Fees for Further Education

614. Power to make regulations relating to fees for students. In respect of certain institutions[1], the appropriate national authority[2] may make regulations[3] requiring or authorising the charging of fees[4] which are higher in the case of students not having such connection with the United Kingdom[5] or any part of it as may be specified in the regulations than in the case of students having such a connection[6]. The regulations may provide for exceptions and make different provision for different cases or purposes[7].

1   The Education (Fees and Awards) Act 1983 s 1 applies to the following further education institutions:
    (1)   any institution which provides higher education or further education (or both) and is either: (a) maintained by a local authority; or (b) is substantially dependent for its maintenance on public funds and either is specified in the regulations made under s 1 or is of a class or description so specified (s 1(3)(c), (3A) (s 1(3)(c) substituted, s 1(3A) added, by the Education Reform Act 1988 s 237(1), Sch 12 Pt III para 91; Education (Fees and Awards) Act 1983 s 1(3)(c) amended by SI 2010/1158));
    (2)   any institution within the further education sector (Education (Fees and Awards) Act 1983 s 1(3)(ca) (added by the Further and Higher Education Act 1992 s 93(1), Sch 8 Pt I para 19));

(3)   any training provider, within the meaning of the Education Act 2005 Pt 3 (ss 84A–100) (see PARA 1059 note 3) who is receiving financial assistance from the Secretary of State or the Welsh Ministers under the Education Act 2002 s 14 (see PARAS 78, 615), or from a person who is receiving financial assistance under that provision (Education (Fees and Awards) Act 1983 s 1(3)(e) (added by the Education Act 1994 s 24, Sch 2 para 7; substituted by the Education Act 2005 s 98, Sch 14 para 9; and further substituted by the Education Act 2011 Sch 5 para 5));

(4)   any institution which receives funding from the Secretary of State (whatever proportion that funding represents of the institution's total funding) and which is specified in, or is of a class or description specified in, the regulations (Education (Fees and Awards) Act 1983 s 1(3)(f) (added by the Learning and Skills Act 2000 s 149, Sch 9 paras 1, 11; and amended by SI 2010/1080; the Education Act 2011 Sch 16 para 5; and the Deregulation Act 2015 Sch 14 Pt 2 para 32));

(5)   any institution which receives funding from the Welsh Ministers (whatever proportion that funding represents of the institution's total funding) and which is specified in, or is of a class or description specified in, the regulations (Education (Fees and Awards) Act 1983 s 1(3)(g) (added by the Learning and Skills Act 2000 Sch 9 paras 1, 11; and amended by SI 2005/3238)).

The Education (Fees and Awards) Act 1983 s 1 also applies to certain higher education institutions: see PARA 1111. As to the regulations made under s 1 see note 3. As to the meaning of 'higher education' see PARA 24; as to the meaning of 'further education' see PARA 23; as to the meaning of 'local authority' see PARA 25 (definitions applied by s 1(4) (amended by the Education Reform Act 1988 Sch 12 Pt III para 91; and the Education Act 1996 s 582(1), Sch 37 Pt I para 57). 'Public funds' means assistance from a local authority or grants under the Education Act 1996 s 485 (see PARA 82): see the Education (Fees and Awards) Act 1983 s 1(4) (definition amended by the Education Act 1996 Sch 37 Pt I para 57). As to the meaning of 'institution within the further education sector' see PARA 555. As to the Secretary of State see PARA 58. As to the Welsh Ministers see PARA 59.

2   Ie the Secretary of State or, in relation to Wales, the Welsh Ministers. As to the meaning of 'Wales' see PARA 7 note 3. The functions of the Secretary of State under the Education (Fees and Awards) Act 1983 s 1, so far as exercisable in relation to Wales, were transferred to the National Assembly for Wales (see the National Assembly for Wales (Transfer of Functions) Order 2006, SI 2006/1458, arts 2(a), 3) and are now vested in the Welsh Ministers (see the Government of Wales Act 2006 s 162(1), Sch 11 para 30).

3   As to the regulations made see the Education (Fees and Awards) (England) Regulations 2007, SI 2007/779 (amended by SI 2007/2263; SI 2011/1987; SI 2012/765; SI 2012/956; and SI 2012/1653); and the Education (Fees and Awards) (Wales) Regulations 2007, SI 2007/2310 (amended by SI 2008/1259; SI 2011/1978; and SI 2013/1792). See also *R (on the application of Mitchell) v Coventry University and the Secretary of State for Education and Employment* [2001] EWHC Admin 167, [2001] ELR 594, [2001] All ER (D) 34 (Mar) where it was held that, as the purpose behind the regulations was a reasonable and objective justification for the discrimination which resulted, there was no conflict with the Convention for the Protection of Human Rights and Fundamental Freedoms (Rome, 4 November 1950; TS 71 (1953); Cmd 8969) art 14, or with the First Protocol (Paris, 20 March 1952; TS 46 (1954); Cmd 9221) art 2 (see PARA 3).

4   'Fees' includes charges however described (including charges for board and lodging): Education (Fees and Awards) Act 1983 s 1(4).

5   For these purposes, references to the United Kingdom include references to the Channel Islands and the Isle of Man, but the Education (Fees and Awards) Act 1983 does not extend to Northern Ireland: see s 3(2). As to the meaning of 'United Kingdom' generally see PARA 73 note 3.

6   Education (Fees and Awards) Act 1983 s 1(1).

7   Education (Fees and Awards) Act 1983 s 1(2).

(iii) Grants to Institutions providing Further Education

615.   General grant-making powers. The Secretary of State[1] (in relation to England[2]) or the Welsh Ministers[3] (in relation to Wales) may give, or make arrangements[4] for the giving of, financial assistance[5] for various purposes, including: (1) the provision or proposed provision of education or of educational services[6]; (2) enabling any person to undertake any course of education, or any course of higher education[7] provided by an institution within the further education sector[8]; (3) enabling any person to receive any training for teachers or for non-teaching staff[9]; and (4) providing for a person's maintenance while he undertakes such a course[10].

1 As to the Secretary of State see PARA 58.
2 As to the meaning of 'England' see PARA 7 note 3.
3 As to the Welsh Ministers see PARA 59. The functions under the Education Act 2002 s 14 in relation to Wales were originally vested in the National Assembly for Wales and are now exercisable by the Welsh Ministers by virtue of the Government of Wales Act 2006 s 162(1), Sch 11 paras 30, 32. As to the meaning of 'Wales' see PARA 7 note 3.
4 As to such arrangements see the Education Act 2002 s 17; and PARA 78.
5 See the Education Act 2002 s 14(1). As to the forms of financial assistance under s 14 and terms on which it may be given see ss 15, 16; and PARA 78.
6 Education Act 2002 s 14(2)(a). As to the meaning of 'education' PARA 78 note 7.
7 As to the meaning of 'higher education' see PARA 24 (definition applied by the Education Act 2002 s 212(2), (3)).
8 Education Act 2002 s 14(2)(c). As to the meaning of 'institution within the further education sector' see PARA 555.
9 Education Act 2002 s 14(2)(ca) (added by the Education Act 2011 s 15(1), (2)(a)). As to the meaning of 'training for teachers or for non-teaching staff' and 'teacher' see PARA 78 note 11.
10 Education Act 2002 s 14(2)(d).

616. Grants to institutions providing further education. There are various specific grants that may be paid to educational institutions, which are dealt with elsewhere in this work[1].

1 See PARAS 81–85.

(iv) Recoupment

617. Recoupment. Such information relating to the provision which has been made by a local authority[1] in respect of any pupil[2] at an institution as the authority may require for the purposes of claiming any amount in respect of the pupil from another authority[3] must, where the institution becomes an institution within the further education sector[4], be provided to the authority by the governing body[5] of the institution[6].

1 As to the meaning of 'local authority' see PARA 25 (definition applied by the Further and Higher Education Act 1992 s 90(1)).
2 As to the meaning of 'pupil' see PARA 20 note 4 (definition applied by the Further and Higher Education Act 1992 s 90(5) (amended by the Education Act 1996 s 582(1), Sch 37 Pt I para 115(1), (3))).
3 Ie under regulations made under the Education Act 1996 s 493: see PARA 333.
4 As to the meaning of 'institution within the further education sector' see PARA 555.
5 As to the meaning of 'governing body' see PARA 560 note 6.
6 Further and Higher Education Act 1992 s 54(2) (amended by the Education Act 1996 s 582(1), Sch 37 Pt I para 111; and SI 2010/1158).

(6) COMPLAINTS BY STUDENTS AGAINST PROVIDERS OF FURTHER EDUCATION AND TRAINING

618. Complaints against providers of further education and training. Complaints about further education and training should generally be raised in the first place with the institution concerned, and that institution's complaints procedure should be followed. If the outcome of that process is unsatisfactory, complaints about providers of further education and training in England may be made to the Skills Funding Agency (SFA)[1], and if the SFA response is unsatisfactory the matter may be taken further with the complaints adjudicator. There is a separate procedure for making an appeal about examination results; and if an enquiry about the results does not provide a satisfactory outcome, the matter may be taken up with the Office of Qualifications and Examinations Regulation ('Ofqual')[2]. If the outcome of a complaint to a Welsh institution is unsatisfactory, then the complaint may be taken up with the relevant Welsh body[3].

1 As to the SFA see PARA 613. The SFA can investigate complaints about matters such as the quality or management of education and training, undue delay or non-compliance with published procedures, poor administration by the provider, equality and diversity issues (except where there is a more appropriate mechanism for dealing with the matter through the court, tribunals or other organisations), and health and safety concerns (unless these are matters for the Health and Safety Executive); and although the SFA does not fund higher education courses in further education, it will investigate complaints made by learners following higher education courses in further education colleges: see the SFA guidance entitled 'Procedure for dealing with complaints about Providers of Education and Training' (1 July 2014; updated 26 May 2015).

2 As to Ofqual see PARA 824 et seq.

3 The Welsh Ministers provide funding for further education in Wales: see PARA 792 et seq. As to the Welsh Ministers see PARA 59. As from September 2015, Qualifications Wales is to take over responsibility for quality assurance from the Welsh Ministers; it is anticipated that it will in the longer term also take over responsibility for awarding qualifications: see PARA 853; and see also PARA 855.

4. HIGHER EDUCATION

(1) INSTITUTIONS WITHIN THE HIGHER EDUCATION SECTOR

(i) The Institutions

619. Institutions. Higher education[1] is provided at various institutions, including universities which have been established by charter[2], institutions conducted by higher education corporations[3], designated institutions[4], certain institutions conducted by further education corporations which have been transferred to the higher education sector[5], and certain institutions maintained by local authorities[6].

For the purposes of the Education Acts[7], references to 'institutions within the higher education sector' are references to: (1) universities[8] receiving financial support[9] under the Further and Higher Education Act 1992[10]; (2) institutions conducted by higher education corporations[11]; and (3) designated institutions[12] for the purposes of Part II of the Further and Higher Education Act 1992[13]. References to 'institutions outside the higher education sector' are to be read accordingly[14].

Certain institutions within the higher education sector may also provide further education[15].

1 As to the meaning of 'higher education' see PARA 24 (definition applied by the Further and Higher Education Act 1992 s 90(1)).
2 As to universities established by charter see PARAS 624–644.
3 As to the meaning of 'higher education corporation' see PARA 645.
4 As to designated institutions see PARA 671 et seq.
5 See PARA 620.
6 As to such institutions see PARA 680.
7 As to the meaning of 'the Education Acts' see PARA 1 note 13.
8 As to the meaning of 'university' see PARA 621 note 3. As to universities generally see PARA 621 et seq.
9 Ie under the Further and Higher Education Act 1992 s 65: see PARA 701.
10 Further and Higher Education Act 1992 s 91(1), (5)(a). See also the Education Act 1996 s 4(4)(a).
   As from a day to be appointed, a new provision is added to the Further and Higher Education Act 1992 s 91(5) as follows: '(aa) universities that are regulated institutions': s 91(5)(aa) (prospectively added by the Higher Education (Wales) Act 2015 Schedule paras 1, 4(1), (2)). Also as from a day to be appointed, the following is added: 'For the purposes of the Further and Higher Education Act 1992 s 91(5)(aa), a regulated institution is an institution to which an approved plan, within the meaning given in the Higher Education (Wales) Act 2015 s 7, relates: Further and Higher Education Act 1992 s 91(5A) (prospectively added by the Higher Education (Wales) Act 2015 Schedule paras 1, 4(1), (3)). At the date at which this volume states the law no such day had been appointed. See generally PARA 721.
11 Further and Higher Education Act 1992 s 91(1), (5)(b). See also the Education Act 1996 s 4(4)(b).
12 Ie as defined in the Further and Higher Education Act 1992 s 72(3): see PARA 701 note 5.
13 Further and Higher Education Act 1992 s 91(1), (5)(c). See also the Education Act 1996 s 4(4)(c).
   As from a day to be appointed, a new provision is added to s 4(4): '(d) a university to which an approved plan, within the meaning given in the Higher Education (Wales) Act 2015 s 7, relates: Education Act 1996 s 4(4)(d) (prospectively added by the Higher Education (Wales) Act 2015 Schedule para 5). At the date at which this volume states the law no such day had been appointed. See generally PARA 721.
14 Further and Higher Education Act 1992 s 91(1), (5). See also the Education Act 1996 s 4(4).
15 See e g PARA 665.

620. Orders transferring further education corporations to higher education sector. The appropriate national authority[1] may by order[2] provide for the transfer of a further education corporation[3] to the higher education sector if it appears to the appropriate national authority that the full-time equivalent enrolment number[4] of the institution conducted by the corporation for courses of higher education[5] exceeds 55 per cent of its total full-time equivalent enrolment number[6]. On such date as may be specified in the order the corporation ceases to be a further education corporation and becomes a higher education corporation[7] and any member of the further education corporation who is not re-appointed by the appropriate national authority[8] ceases to hold office[9].

1   Ie the Secretary of State or, in relation to Wales, the Welsh Ministers. As to the Secretary of State see PARA 58. As to the Welsh Ministers see PARA 59. As to the meaning of 'Wales' see PARA 7 note 3. The functions of the Secretary of State under the Education Reform Act 1988 s 122A, so far as exercisable in relation to Wales, were transferred to the National Assembly for Wales (see the National Assembly for Wales (Transfer of Functions) Order 1999, SI 1999/672, art 2, Sch 1) and are now vested in the Welsh Ministers (see the Government of Wales Act 2006 s 162(1), Sch 11 para 30).
2   Such orders, being of local effect, are not recorded in this work.
3   As to further education corporations see PARA 559 et seq.
4   As to the meaning of 'full-time equivalent enrolment number' see PARA 651.
5   As to the meaning of 'courses of higher education' see PARA 684.
6   Education Reform Act 1988 s 122A(1) (s 122A added by the Further and Higher Education Act 1992 s 74(1)). As to the calculation of full-time equivalent enrolment numbers see PARA 651. As to the meaning of 'total full-time equivalent enrolment number' see PARA 647 note 5.
7   As to the meaning of 'higher education corporation' see PARA 645.
8   Ie in pursuance of the Education Reform Act 1988 s 122A(2)(b): see note 9.
9   Education Reform Act 1988 s 122A(4) (as added: see note 6). Where an order under s 122A is made in respect of a further education corporation, s 124A (constitution and conduct of corporations: see PARA 657) and s 125 (articles of government: see PARA 664) have effect as if: (1) on the date the order has effect, the corporation were established as a higher education corporation (s 122A(2)(a) (as so added)); and (2) the appropriate national authority were the appointing authority in relation to the first members of the higher education corporation (s 122A(2)(b) (as so added)). In determining in pursuance of s 122A(2)(b) the number of members to appoint within each variable category of members, the appropriate national authority must secure that at least half of all the members of the higher education corporation as first constituted are independent members: s 122A(3) (as so added). As to the meaning of 'independent members' see PARA 659; and as to the meaning of 'variable category of members' see PARA 660 note 5 (definitions applied by s 122A(3) (as so added)).

(ii) Meaning and Use of the Term 'University'

621. Meaning of 'university'. 'University' is not a term of art, and although the institutions to which it refers are readily identifiable, precise and accurate definition is difficult[1]. It has been described as the whole body of teachers and scholars engaged, at a particular place, in giving and receiving instruction in the higher branches of learning; such persons associated together as a society or corporate body, with definite organisation and acknowledged powers and privileges (especially that of conferring degrees), and forming an institution for the promotion of education in the higher or more important branches of learning; also, the colleges, buildings and other property belonging to such a body[2]. Until the enactment of the Further and Higher Education Act 1992, which made new provision for the powers of higher education institutions to award degrees and to style themselves as universities[3], the essential feature of a university seems to have been that it was incorporated[4] as such by the sovereign power.

Other attributes of a university appear to be the admission of students from all parts of the world, a plurality of masters, the teaching of one at least of the higher faculties, namely theology, law or philosophy (which in some definitions are regarded as identical) and medicine, provision for residence, and the right to confer degrees; but possession of these attributes will not make an institution a university in the absence of any express intention of the sovereign power to make it one[5].

The Privy Council may, in some circumstances, confer the title 'university' on an institution not currently in possession of it[6].

Although it has been said that a university involves the relation of tutor and pupil and that the university is charged with the supervision and upbringing of the pupil under tuition[7], today the relationship between student and university is usually seen rather more as one of consumer and provider.

1   *St David's College, Lampeter v Ministry of Education* [1951] 1 All ER 559.
2   Ie in the Oxford English Dictionary. 'In our modern languages the Roman term ['universitas'] that most nearly answered to our corporation stands for the corporations of one small class, the learned corporations that were founded in the twelfth and thirteenth centuries and others that in later days were fashioned after their likeness. These were in the Middle Ages the corporations by pre-eminence, and if the universities of Oxford and Cambridge cared to assert that they are the oldest of English corporations something might be said in favour of their claim': Pollock and Maitland *History of English Law before the time of Edward I* (2nd Edn) (1898, reissued 1968) 495.
3   See the Further and Higher Education Act 1992 s 76 (see PARA 685), s 77 (see PARA 622). In the Further and Higher Education Act 1992, 'university', except where the context otherwise requires, includes a university college and any college, or institution in the nature of a college, in a university; but where a college or institution would not, apart from this provision, fall to be treated separately it must not be so treated for the purpose of determining whether any institution is in England or in Wales: Further and Higher Education Act 1992 s 90(3) (amended by the Teaching and Higher Education Act 1998 s 44(1), Sch 3 para 8). As to the meanings of 'England' and 'Wales' see PARA 7 note 3. In the Education Reform Act 1988, 'university' includes a university college and any college, or institution in the nature of a college, in a university: s 235(1). 'University' is similarly defined in the Education (No 2) Act 1986 s 43: see s 43(6); and PARA 6 note 1.
4   1 Bl Com (14th Edn) 371.
5   *St David's College, Lampeter v Ministry of Education* [1951] 1 All ER 559.
6   See PARA 622.
7   *Glynn v Keele University* [1971] 2 All ER 89 at 95, [1971] 1 WLR 487 at 494 per Pennycuick VC.

622.   Use of 'university' in title of institution.   Where power is conferred by any enactment or instrument to change the name of any educational institution or any body corporate[1] carrying on such an institution, and the institution is within the higher education sector[2], then, if the said power is exercisable with the consent of the Privy Council[3], it may be exercised with the consent of the Privy Council so as to include the word 'university' in the name of the institution and, if it is carried on by a body corporate, in the name of the body[4]. Any educational institution whose name includes the word 'university' by virtue of the exercise of any such power[5] is treated as a university for all purposes, unless in that name that word is immediately followed by the word 'college' or 'collegiate'[6].

In exercising any such power[7] to consent to a change in any name the Privy Council must have regard to the need to avoid names which are or may be confusing[8].

1   The reference to a power to change the name of an institution or body includes any power (however expressed and whether or not subject to any conditions or restrictions) in the exercise of which the name of the institution or body may be changed; but the power as extended by the

Further and Higher Education Act 1992 s 77(1) has effect subject to any such conditions or restrictions: s 77(2). For the powers to change the name of an institution or body see PARAS 646 note 7, 647 note 10, 658.

2 As to the meaning of 'institution within the higher education sector' see PARA 619.

3 As to the Privy Council see CONSTITUTIONAL AND ADMINISTRATIVE LAW vol 20 (2014) PARA 268 et seq.

4 Further and Higher Education Act 1992 s 77(1). The power contained in s 77(1) is exercisable whether or not the institution would apart from s 77 be a university: s 77(1). As to the meaning of 'university' see PARA 621 note 3. As to the unauthorised use of the word 'university' in the title of an educational institution see PARA 623.

5 Ie any power as extended by the Further and Higher Education Act 1992 s 77(1): see the text to notes 1–4.

6 Further and Higher Education Act 1992 s 77(4) (amended by the Teaching and Higher Education Act 1998 s 40).

7 Ie any power exercisable by virtue of the Further and Higher Education Act 1992 s 77.

8 Further and Higher Education Act 1992 s 77(3). See *London College of Science and Technology Ltd v Islington London Borough Council* [1997] ELR 162.

623. Unauthorised use of 'university' in title of institution. An institution within the higher education sector[1] in England or Wales[2] must not, when making available (or offering to make available)[3] educational services, do so under a name which includes the word 'university' unless the inclusion of that word in that name is[4] authorised by or by virtue of any Act[5] or Royal Charter[6], or is approved[7] by the Privy Council[8]. A person[9] carrying on such an institution must not, when making available (or offering to make available) educational services through the institution, use with reference either to himself or the institution a name which includes the word 'university', unless the inclusion of that word in that name is so authorised or approved[10].

In approving the inclusion of the word 'university' in any name[11] the Privy Council must have regard to the need to avoid names which are or may be confusing[12].

1 As to the meaning of 'institution within the higher education sector' see PARA 619.

2 As to the meanings of 'England' and 'Wales' see PARA 7 note 3.

3 The provisions of the Teaching and Higher Education Act 1998 s 39(1), (2) apply where the educational services are made available, or (as the case may be) the offer to make such services available is made, in any part of the United Kingdom: s 39(3). As to the meaning of 'United Kingdom' see PARA 73 note 3.

4 See the Teaching and Higher Education Act 1998 s 39(1), (7).

5 As to the use of 'university' in the title of an institution see PARA 622. As to the meaning of 'university' generally see PARA 621.

6 Teaching and Higher Education Act 1998 s 39(1)(a). For the purposes of s 39(1) or s 39(2) (see the text to notes 9–10), the inclusion of the word 'university' in any name must not be taken to be authorised by or by virtue of a Royal Charter relating to a university by reason of any provision of the Royal Charter with respect to the affiliation or association of other institutions to the university (s 39(4)(a)), or the accreditation by the university of educational services provided by other institutions (s 39(4)(b)). 'University', in the context of the reference in s 39(4) to a Royal Charter relating to a university, has the meaning given by the Further and Higher Education Act 1992 s 90(3) (see PARA 621 note 3): Teaching and Higher Education Act 1998 s 39(7). As to universities incorporated by charter see PARA 624 et seq.

7 Ie for the purposes of the Teaching and Higher Education Act 1998 s 39.

8 Teaching and Higher Education Act 1998 s 39(1)(b). The Privy Council's power of approval under s 39(1) or s 39(2) (see the text to notes 9–10) is not exercisable in a case where the inclusion of the word 'university' in the name in question may be authorised by virtue of any other Act or any Royal Charter: s 39(6). See also *R (on the application of Liverpool Hope University College) v Secretary of State for Education and Employment* [2001] EWCA Civ 362, [2001] ELR 552, [2001] All ER (D) 170 (Mar). As to the Privy Council see CONSTITUTIONAL AND ADMINISTRATIVE LAW vol 20 (2014) PARA 268 et seq.

9 As to the meaning of 'person' see PARA 7 note 6.

10 Teaching and Higher Education Act 1998 s 39(2). See also notes 6, 8.

11 Ie for the purposes of the Teaching and Higher Education Act 1998 s 39.
12 Teaching and Higher Education Act 1998 s 39(5).

(iii) Universities Established by Charter

A. INCORPORATION AND GOVERNANCE

624. Incorporation. Incorporation of a university was anciently effected by papal grant[1] or charter[2], and later by Royal Charter or Act of Parliament[3]. The practice subsequently adopted in the case of the more recent foundations was to incorporate the university by Royal Charter, to which there was annexed a schedule containing the original statutes of the university, and thereafter to obtain the passing of a local Act of Parliament vesting in the university the property and liabilities of any institution which it replaces and making other necessary provisions[4]. Modern universities are incorporated by way of the establishment of a higher education corporation[5] or the designation of a higher education institution[6].

A copy of any application for a charter for the foundation of any college or university which is referred by the Queen in Council for the report of a committee of the Privy Council must be laid before Parliament, together with a copy of the draft charter, not less than 30 days before the committee reports upon it[7].

1 See CORPORATIONS vol 24 (2010) PARA 331.
2 The charter was sometimes confirmed by Act of Parliament. As to Oxford and Cambridge see the Oxford and Cambridge Act 1571, passed with the intent that the ancient privileges, liberties and franchises of either of those universities 'here before granted, ratified and confirmed' by the Sovereign and her progenitors may be had in greater estimation and be of greater force and strength (see the preamble to the Act). See also 4 Co Inst 227.
3 Cf 1 Bl Com (14th Edn) 472.
4 See PARA 626.
5 See PARAS 646–647.
6 See PARA 671.
7 See the College Charter Act 1871 s 2 (amended by the Statute Law Revision (No 2) Act 1893; and SI 1999/1820).

625. Constitution. The constitution, functions and privileges of universities are governed by the terms of their instruments of foundation, or by Acts of Parliament. In so far as there can be said to be any general law relating to universities or their colleges, it belongs, strictly speaking, either to the law of charities or to that of corporations[1].

A university usually consists of a chancellor, a vice-chancellor[2], a body of graduates and students. Its government is usually provided for by the creation of a council or senate, which acts as the executive, and has an initiative in such legislation as the university is empowered to carry out, sometimes subject to the Queen in Council, sometimes with the further assent of Parliament[3].

1 The chartered corporation is an artificial person whose legal capacities are limited by its charter or by any statutes regulating it; cf the statutory corporation whose powers are limited by the statute which created it: see CORPORATIONS vol 24 (2010) PARA 431 et seq. As an exempt charity, it is unlikely that the existence of a chartered corporation can be challenged in court unless its assets are misapplied: see CHARITIES vol 8 (2015) PARAS 514–542, 589.
    The universities of Oxford, Cambridge, London, Durham, Newcastle and Manchester, and King's College London and Queen Mary and Westfield College in the University of London (see PARA 626), so far as they are charities, are designated as exempt charities within the meaning of the Charities Act 2011: see Sch 3 paras 2, 3; and CHARITIES vol 8 (2015) PARA 318. Similarly, the following, so far as they are charities, are designated as exempt charities within the meaning

of the Charities Act 2011, if Her Majesty declares it by Order in Council to be an exempt charity for the purposes of the Act: (1) a university in England; (2) a university college in England; or (3) an institution which is connected with a university in England or a university college in England (see Sch 3 para 4(1)); but this does not include (a) any college in the university of Oxford; (b) any college or hall in the university of Cambridge or Durham; (c) any students' union (Sch 3 para 4(2)); and see further CHARITIES vol 8 (2015) PARA 318. As to the meaning of 'England' see PARA 7 note 3. As to students' unions see PARA 1115 et seq.

2   The powers of a vice-chancellor to suspend and exclude are so fundamental to the position of a student in the university that he must be considered as acting in a quasi-judicial capacity when he exercises them and he must observe the rules of natural justice; the powers should not be treated as merely matters of internal discipline: *Glynn v Keele University* [1971] 2 All ER 89, [1971] 1 WLR 487. As to the appropriate test to be applied on an application for judicial review of a vice-chancellor's decision involving the question of fitness of practice see *R (on the application of Higham) v University of Plymouth* [2005] EWHC 1492 (Admin), [2005] ELR 547, [2005] All ER (D) 231 (Jul); affd [2005] EWCA Civ 1596, [2005] All ER (D) 398 (Nov) (vice-chancellor confirming a decision of the medical school's professional behaviour committee). As to the principles of natural justice generally see JUDICIAL REVIEW vol 61 (2010) PARA 629 et seq.

3   Local Acts of Parliament and Orders in Council approving statutes of universities are notified in the London Gazette: see e g the issue dated 3 July 1951, at 3629 (University of Oxford and Emmanuel College, Cambridge).

626.   Governance of particular universities.   The executive government of the University of Oxford[1] is for the most part vested in a hebdomadal council possessing an initiative in legislation, which is first submitted to congregation or the resident body of masters of arts, and finally to convocation or the entire body of masters[2].

The legislative body of the University of Cambridge[3] is the senate. The council of the senate offers to the senate proposals for confirmation or rejection[4].

The University of London[5] has a senate consisting of the chancellor and 54 members and five advisory committees.

The constitution of Durham University includes a chancellor, a senate, a council and convocation. The council of the Durham colleges, itself incorporated, provides for the teaching, residence, maintenance and discipline of students in Durham[6].

Universities have been founded by charter[7] as follows: Manchester[8], Birmingham[9], Liverpool[10], Leeds[11], Sheffield[12], Bristol[13], Reading[14], Nottingham[15], Southampton[16], Hull[17], Exeter[18], Leicester[19], Sussex[20], Keele[21], East Anglia[22], Newcastle upon Tyne[23], York[24], Lancaster[25], Kent at Canterbury[26], Essex[27], Warwick[28], The City University[29], Loughborough University of Technology[30], Aston in Birmingham[31], Brunel[32], Surrey[33], Bradford[34], Bath[35], Salford[36], the Open University[37], and Buckingham[38]. Under their respective Royal Charters, the Royal College of Art and Cranfield Institute of Technology grant degrees. These universities have varying constitutions but usually have a large court as the official governing body and a smaller council to perform executive government. Generally, the nominal head is the chancellor, the principal executive is the vice-chancellor, and the senate has the general control and regulation of instruction and education.

The federal University of Wales, also founded by charter[39], has a similar constitution, but differs from the other modern universities in that teaching for initial degrees is entrusted to the five constituent university colleges, namely, University College of Wales at Aberystwyth[40], University College Cardiff[41], University College of North Wales at Bangor[42], University College of Swansea[43], and the University of Wales Institute of Science and Technology at Cardiff[44], together with St David's University College, Lampeter[45], and the University of Wales College of Medicine[46].

1　The University of Oxford, founded in the 12th century, was incorporated by charter in the fourteenth century. The incorporation was confirmed by the Oxford and Cambridge Act 1571.

2　See the Oxford University Act 1854. For other statutes as to the University of Oxford see the Oxford University Act 1857; the Oxford University Act 1860; the Oxford University Act 1862; the Oxford University, Vinerian Foundation, Act 1865; the Universities Tests Act 1871; the Universities of Oxford and Cambridge Act 1877; the Universities of Oxford and Cambridge Act 1923; the Universities and College Estates Acts 1925 and 1964 (see PARA 1329); and the Universities and Colleges (Trusts) Act 1943 (see PARA 637).

3　The University of Cambridge was founded early in the thirteenth century. Its incorporation by charter was confirmed by the Oxford and Cambridge Act 1571.

4　See the Cambridge University Act 1856. For other statutes as to Cambridge University see the Universities Tests Act 1871; the Universities of Oxford and Cambridge Act 1877; the Universities of Oxford and Cambridge Act 1923; the Universities and College Estates Acts 1925 and 1964 (see PARA 1329); and the Universities and Colleges (Trusts) Act 1943 (see PARA 637).

5　Charters dated 28 November 1836 constituted the university and university college. Developed by various other charters in 1850, 1858, 1863, 1867 and 1878, the university was reconstituted by the University of London Act 1898 (repealed).

6　The University of Durham was founded by private Act (2 & 3 Will 4 c xix (1832)), and by charter dated 1 June 1837, and was reconstituted by the University of Durham Act 1908 (repealed). It was reorganised in 1937 and 1963. See also the Universities and College Estates Acts 1925 and 1964 (see PARA 1329); the University of Durham Act 1935 (repealed); and the Universities of Durham and Newcastle upon Tyne Act 1963.

7　For private Acts relating to universities and colleges see the current index to Local and Personal Acts and the annual indexes to Local and Personal Acts.

8　Founded as Owens College in 1851, the Victoria University (see notes 10–11) was created by charter dated 20 April 1880 and the Victoria University of Manchester by charter dated 15 July 1903: see the Victoria University of Manchester Act 1904. The charter of 1903 was revoked and replaced by a supplemental charter dated 12 February 1973.

9　Formed from Mason College, it became the University of Birmingham by charter dated 24 March 1900: see the Birmingham University Act 1900.

10　University College, Liverpool, was founded by charter dated 18 October 1881. Together with the Royal Infirmary Medical School, established in 1844, it became a constituent college of the Victoria University in 1884 (see note 8). It became incorporated as the University of Liverpool by charter dated 15 July 1903 (see the Liverpool University Act 1903), and was reconstituted by a supplemental charter dated 1 August 1961 (amended August 1969).

11　The Yorkshire College of Science, founded in 1874, became a constituent college of the Victoria University in 1887 (see note 8), and was reconstituted as the University of Leeds by charter dated 25 April 1904: see the University of Leeds Act 1904 (repealed). See also the University of Leeds Act 1965.

12　Firth College, founded in 1879, was merged with a medical school and a technical school in 1897 to form a university college which, by charter dated 31 May 1905, became the University of Sheffield: see the University of Sheffield Act 1905.

13　Founded originally as a university college in 1876, the University of Bristol was created by charter dated 21 May 1909: see the Oxford and Cambridge Act 1909. See also the University of Bristol Acts 1960 and 1974.

14　A university extension college, associated with the University of Oxford, was founded at Reading in 1892. It became a university college in 1902, and the University of Reading by charter dated 17 March 1926: see the University of Reading Act 1926.

15　Founded as a university college in 1881, and incorporated in 1903, the University of Nottingham was granted its charter on 20 August 1948: see the University of Nottingham Act 1949.

16　The Hartley Institute, founded at Southampton in 1862, became a university college in 1902 and the University of Southampton was created by charter dated 29 April 1952: see the University of Southampton Act 1953.

17　A university college was incorporated at Hull on 7 October 1927. It became the University of Hull by charter dated 6 September 1954: see the University of Hull Act 1955.

18　The Exeter Technical and University Extension College was founded in 1893. Renamed the Royal Albert Memorial College in 1899, it was reorganised as a university college in 1901. It became the University College of the South West of England in 1922 and the University of Exeter by charter dated 21 December 1955: see the University of Exeter Act 1957.

19 The Leicester, Leicestershire and Rutland College, founded in 1918, changed its name to University College, Leicester in 1927, was incorporated by charter dated 4 December 1950, and became the University of Leicester by charter dated 1 May 1957: see the University of Leicester Act 1958.

20 The University of Sussex was founded at Brighton by charter dated 16 August 1961: see the University of Sussex Act 1962.

21 The University College of North Staffordshire, incorporated by charter dated 11 August 1949, became the University of Keele by charter dated 26 January 1962: see the University of Keele Act 1962.

22 The University of East Anglia was founded at Norwich by charter dated 7 January 1963.

23 A medical school at Newcastle upon Tyne, founded in 1934, became the medical school of the University of Durham in 1852, and joined with a college of physical science, later Armstrong College, founded in 1871, to become King's College in 1937. It was the Newcastle division of the University of Durham, but by charter dated 1 August 1963 became the University of Newcastle upon Tyne: see the Universities of Durham and Newcastle upon Tyne Act 1963.

24 The University of York, which is organised on a collegiate basis, was founded by charter dated 1 October 1963.

25 The University of Lancaster, which is organised on a collegiate basis, was founded by charter dated 14 September 1964.

26 The University of Kent at Canterbury, which is organised on a collegiate basis, was founded by charter dated 4 January 1965.

27 The University of Essex was founded at Colchester and incorporated as a limited company on 21 September 1962. It was granted a charter on 11 January 1965.

28 The University of Warwick was incorporated at Coventry by charter in 1965.

29 The Northampton Polytechnic Institute was founded in the City of London on 1 June 1907. It became a college of advanced technology in 1956, and was incorporated as The City University by charter dated 6 April 1966: see The City University Act 1967.

30 Loughborough Technical Institute was founded in 1909, and became Loughborough College in 1918. Part of it became a college of advanced technology in 1956 and was constituted as Loughborough University of Technology by charter dated 19 April 1966: see the Loughborough University of Technology Act 1966.

31 The Birmingham Municipal Technical School was founded in 1895. In 1927 it became the Central Technical School, in 1951 the College of Technology, and in 1956 the first designated college of advanced technology. It was constituted as the University of Aston in Birmingham by charter dated 22 April 1966: see the University of Aston in Birmingham Act 1967.

32 Acton Technical College was founded in 1928. The section dealing with higher education became Brunel College in 1956, and in 1962 was designated a college of advanced technology. It moved to Uxbridge, and was constituted Brunel University by charter dated 6 July 1966: see the Brunel University Act 1967.

33 The Battersea Polytechnic Institute, founded on 23 June 1891, became a college of advanced technology in 1956, and was reconstituted at Guildford as the University of Surrey by charter dated 9 September 1966: see the University of Surrey Act 1966.

34 The Bradford Mechanics Institute was founded in 1882. It became a college of advanced technology in 1957 and by charter dated 18 October 1966 was constituted as the University of Bradford: see the University of Bradford Act 1967.

35 The Bristol Trade School, founded in 1856, came under the patronage of the Society of Merchant Venturers in 1880, and in 1894 became the Merchant Venturers' Technical College. Control passed to the Bristol education authority in 1949, and it was designated as a college of advanced technology in 1960. It became independent in 1962 and was granted a charter as the Bath University of Technology on 25 October 1966, when it moved to a new site at Claverton Down, Bath: see the Bath University of Technology Act 1967. The charter was amended in March 1971 when the university became the University of Bath.

36 The Royal Technical Institute, later the Royal Technical College, was founded at Salford in 1896, and became a college of advanced technology in 1956. It was reconstituted as the University of Salford by charter dated 4 April 1967: see the University of Salford Act 1968.

37 The Open University, originally the University of the Air (see the Command Paper *University of The Air* (1965–66; Cmnd 2922)), was created by charter dated 30 May 1969, since when it has received grant in aid: see Treasury Minute dated 5 November 1970.

38 The University of Buckingham, founded in 1973, was incorporated by charter in 1983.

39 The original charter of the University of Wales was dated 30 November 1893, and was supplemented by a charter dated 11 December 1967, revoking earlier supplemental charters granted in 1906, 1920, 1931 and 1960.

40 The University College of Aberystwyth was founded in 1872 and was incorporated by charter granted in 1889. It became a constituent part of the University of Wales in 1903.

41 The University College of Cardiff was founded in 1883 and was incorporated by charter granted in 1884. It became a constituent part of the University of Wales in 1903.

42 The University College of Bangor was founded in 1884 and was incorporated by charter granted in 1885. It became a constituent part of the University of Wales in 1903.

43 The University College of Swansea was founded in 1920 and was incorporated by charter granted in 1920, when it became a constituent part of the University of Wales.

44 The University of Wales Institute of Science and Technology was incorporated at Cardiff by charter granted in 1967, when it became a constituent part of the University of Wales: see the University of Wales Institute of Science and Technology Act 1968.

45 St David's College, Lampeter, was founded in 1822, and was granted charters in 1828, 1852, 1865 and 1971. It became a constituent part of the University of Wales in 1971.

46 The University of Wales College of Medicine at Cardiff was incorporated by charter granted in 1931, when it became an independent constituent institution of the University of Wales. It adopted its present name in 1984.

627. Foundation and governance of university colleges and colleges of universities.
University colleges, like universities, are corporate bodies[1], constituted and managed according to the terms of their charters, their founders' statutes or their other instruments of foundation.

Universities may contain colleges which are independent corporations founded in a similar way to universities themselves[2].

The older colleges within the universities of Oxford and Cambridge are governed by statutes which were made by commissioners appointed for that purpose[3]. These relate not merely to the internal organisation and government of the colleges, but to their contributions to various university purposes and in so far as they affect the university may not be altered without the consent of the university[4].

1 As to colleges 'in reputation' and not incorporated see *Adams' Case* (1602) 4 Co Rep 104b at 106b, 107b; cf *Gilford's Case* (1585) 4 Leon 156 at 160.

2 Cf the College Charter Act 1871 s 2, which applies to any institution in the nature of a college or university (s 3), as well as to colleges and universities; and cf the University of London Act 1926 s 7 (repealed), as regards the incorporation of schools and colleges of the university.

3 See the Universities of Oxford and Cambridge Act 1923 ss 1, 6. The powers of the commissioners were to continue in force until the end of the year 1925 and no longer, but the powers of the Oxford University Commissioners were extended until 31 December 1926 (see the Order in Council under the Universities of Oxford and Cambridge Act 1923 continuing the powers of the University of Oxford Commissioners until December 31, 1926, SR & O 1925/607). The powers of the Cambridge University Commissioners were extended until 31 December 1927 (see the Order in Council under the Universities of Oxford and Cambridge Act 1923 continuing the powers of the University of Cambridge Commissioners until December 31, 1927, SR & O 1925/630). Since the cesser of the powers of the commissioners a statute for a college made by the commissioners, and any statute, ordinance or regulation relating to a college made under any authority other than the Universities of Oxford and Cambridge Act 1923, is subject to alteration by the university under that Act, but if and so far as any such statute (not being a statute prescribing the scale or basis of assessment of the contributions to be made by the colleges to university purposes) affects a college, it cannot be altered without the consent of the college: Universities of Oxford and Cambridge Act 1923 s 7(1) (amended by the Statute Law (Repeals) Act 1998). Statutes must be approved by Order in Council and laid before Parliament: see the Universities of Oxford and Cambridge Act 1923 s 7(3), Schedule (both amended by the Statute Law (Repeals) Act 1998) (incorporating the Universities of Oxford and Cambridge Act 1877 s 49).

4 Se the Universities of Oxford and Cambridge Act 1923 s 7(2)(b).

628. Inspection of accounts. The accounts of any university[1] are open to the inspection of the Comptroller and Auditor General[2].

1   As to the meaning of 'university' see PARA 621 note 3.
2   See the Education Reform Act 1988 s 135(1)(a). The power conferred by s 135(1) is exercisable only in, or in relation to accounts or other documents which relate to, any financial year in which expenditure is incurred by the governing body of the university in respect of which financial support has been given under the Further and Higher Education Act 1992 s 65 (see PARA 701): see the Education Reform Act 1988 s 135(2)(a) (s 135(2) amended by the Further and Higher Education Act 1992 Sch 8 paras 27, 36(b)). The powers under the National Audit Act 1983 ss 6, 8 (examinations into the economy, efficiency and effectiveness of certain bodies and access to documents and information: see CONSTITUTIONAL AND ADMINISTRATIVE LAW vol 20 (2014) PARA 489) conferred on the Comptroller and Auditor General by virtue of s 6(3)(c) are correspondingly restricted: see the Education Reform Act 1988 s 135(2)(b) (as so amended). In the Education Reform Act 1988 Pt II (ss 120–161) 'governing body' includes, in relation to any institution, a board of governors of the institution or any persons responsible for the management of the institution (but not formally constituted as such a body or board): s 161(1)(d). 'Financial year' means a period of 12 months ending with 31 March: s 235(1). As to the meaning of 'month' see PARA 54 note 26. As to the Comptroller and Auditor General see CONSTITUTIONAL AND ADMINISTRATIVE LAW vol 20 (2014) PARAS 494–496.

B.   ADMINISTRATION OF INTERNAL LAWS

629. Jurisdiction of visitors. The universities of Oxford and Cambridge, being civil and lay corporations[1] have, it seems, no visitor[2]. The colleges of Oxford and Cambridge, unlike the universities themselves, are eleemosynary corporations[3] and subject to visitation[4]. Other universities are likewise visitable, the Crown usually being the visitor in the case of those incorporated by modern charter[5]. Where the university's charter provides for the appointment of a visitor by the Crown but no visitor has been appointed under the power, the Crown as founder of the university is the visitor[6]. The visitor's power to investigate and right wrongs arising from the application of the statutes or other internal laws of the institution is limited by statute[7]. However, where a visitor has jurisdiction then, subject to the supervisory jurisdiction of the High Court[8], the jurisdiction of the court in the first instance is ousted[9].

1   As to the visitation of corporations see CHARITIES vol 8 (2015) PARA 514 et seq; CORPORATIONS vol 24 (2010) PARA 399.
2   As to the resolution of academic disputes, in the absence of a visitor, at the universities of Oxford and Cambridge see *R v University of Cambridge, ex p Persaud* [2001] EWCA Civ 534, [2001] ELR 480, [2001] All ER (D) 103 (Apr); *R (on the application of Ahmed) v University of Oxford* (7 November 2000, unreported); *R v Cambridge University, ex p Beg* [1999] ELR 404; *R v University of Cambridge, ex p Evans (No 2)* [1999] Ed CR 556; *R v University of Cambridge, ex p Evans* [1998] ELR 515. In certain cases an order of mandamus (now known as a mandatory order: see JUDICIAL REVIEW vol 61 (2010) PARA 703 et seq) has been issued in the domestic matters of these universities: *R v Vice-Chancellor of Cambridge* (1765) 3 Burr 1647; *Dr Walker's Case* (1735) Lee *temp* Hard 212; *R v Cambridge University, Bentley's Case* (1723) 8 Mod Rep 148 (mandamus to restore to a degree); cf *R v Patrick* (1667) 2 Keb 164; *R v Askew* (1768) 4 Burr 2186 at 2189 per Lord Mansfield. But see *R v Cambridge University Chancellor etc* (1794) 6 Term Rep 89 at 104, 107. In *R v Vice-Chancellor of Oxford* (1872) LR 7 QB 471, a decision of the hebdomadal court was reviewed by mandamus. As to a writ of prohibition see *Re Chancellor of Oxford University and Taylor* (1841) 1 QB 952. As to the hebdomadal court of the University of Oxford see PARA 816.
3   See CHARITIES vol 8 (2015) PARA 225; CORPORATIONS vol 24 (2010) PARA 306. See also 1 Bl Com (14th Edn) 470–471.
4   See CHARITIES vol 8 (2015) PARAS 514, 528.
5   As to the constitution of particular universities see PARA 626.
6   *Thomas v University of Bradford* [1987] AC 795, [1987] 1 All ER 834, HL; *Patel v University of Bradford Senate* [1978] 3 All ER 841, [1978] 1 WLR 1488 (affd [1979] 2 All ER 582, [1979] 1 WLR 1066, CA); *A-G v Dedham School* (1857) 23 Beav 350.

7　See PARAS 630, 1090. As to student redress and complaints see PARA 1089 et seq. In particular as to the Office of the Independent Adjudicator for Higher Education see PARA 1091 note 5.

8　Any decision of the university visitor may be amenable to judicial review: *R v Lord President of the Privy Council, ex p Page* [1993] AC 682, sub nom *Page v Hull University Visitor* [1993] 1 All ER 97, HL. See also *R v Visitor of the University of East Anglia, ex p Hanuman* [1999] Ed CR 781, CA; *Jemchi v Visitor of Brunel University* [2002] EWHC 2126 (Admin), [2003] ELR 125, [2002] All ER (D) 27 (Oct) (application for judicial review of visitor's decision on basis, inter alia, that the common law requirement of fairness had required the visitor to hold an oral hearing before changing his mind on a provisional decision); *R (on the application of Ferguson) v Visitor of University of Leicester* [2003] EWCA Civ 1082, [2003] ELR 562. As to judicial review see JUDICIAL REVIEW.

9　*Thomas v University of Bradford* [1987] AC 795, [1987] 1 All ER 834, HL; *R v Lord President of the Privy Council, ex p Page* [1993] AC 682, sub nom *Page v Hull University Visitor* [1993] 1 All ER 97, HL; *M v London Guildhall University* [1998] ELR 149, CA; *Hines v Birkbeck College* [1986] Ch 524, [1985] 3 All ER 156 (affd [1987] Ch 457n, [1987] 3 All ER 1040n, CA); *Hines v Birkbeck College (No 2)* [1992] Ch 33, [1991] 4 All ER 450, CA; *Patel v University of Bradford* [1978] 3 All ER 841, [1978] 1 WLR 1488 (affd [1979] 2 All ER 582, [1979] 1 WLR 1066, CA); *Herring v Templeman* [1973] 2 All ER 581, 71 LGR 295 (affd [1973] 3 All ER 569, 72 LGR 162, CA); *Thorne v University of London* [1966] 2 QB 237, [1966] 2 All ER 338, CA; *R v Dunsheath, ex p Meredith* [1951] 1 KB 127, [1950] 2 All ER 741, DC; *R v Hertford College, Oxford* (1878) 3 QBD 693, CA; *R v Dean and Chapter of Chester* (1850) 15 QB 513; *St John's College, Cambridge v Todington* (1757) 1 Burr 158; *A-G v Talbot* (1747) 3 Atk 662, 1 Ves Sen 78; *Philips v Bury* (1694) Skin 447, 1 Ld Raym 5. But see *R v University College London, ex p Idriss* (24 April 1998, unreported). As to the power of the visitor see *R v HM the Queen in Council, ex p Vijayatunga* [1990] 2 QB 444, sub nom *R v University of London Visitor, ex p Vijayatunga* [1989] 2 All ER 843, CA. The courts' jurisdiction over contractual disputes may not be precluded: see e g *Nottingham University v Fishel* [2000] ELR 385, [2000] ICR 1462 (university sued reader in respect of outside consultancy work generating profits); see also *University of Nottingham v Eyett* [1999] 2 All ER 437, [1999] ELR 141. It may be appropriate for a visitor to appoint a judge as his commissary because, although he cannot delegate his decision-making powers, he has a very wide discretion in adopting an appropriate procedure: *R (on application of Varma) v HRH The Duke of Kent* [2004] EWHC 1705 (Admin), [2004] ELR 616, [2004] ACD 320.

630. Exclusion of visitor's jurisdiction in relation to certain matters. The visitor of a qualifying institution[1] has no jurisdiction[2] in respect of:

(1)　any dispute relating to a member of staff which concerns his appointment or employment or the termination of his appointment or employment[3];

(2)　any other dispute between a member of staff and the qualifying institution in respect of which proceedings could be brought before any court or tribunal[4]; or

(3)　any dispute as to the application of the statutes or other internal laws of the institution in relation to a matter falling within head (1) or head (2) above[5].

The visitor's jurisdiction is also excluded in relation to student complaints[6].

1　'Qualifying institution' has the meaning given by the Higher Education Act 2004 s 11 (see PARA 1090 note 2): s 46(2).

2　As to the jurisdiction of visitors see PARA 629.

3　Higher Education Act 2004 s 46(1)(a).

4　Higher Education Act 2004 s 46(1)(b). In determining whether a dispute falls within s 46(1)(b), it is to be assumed that the visitor does not have jurisdiction to determine the dispute: s 46(3).

5　Higher Education Act 2004 s 46(1)(c).

6　See the Higher Education Act 2004 s 20; and PARA 1090.

631.   The University Commissioners. The University Commissioners were established[1] in order to make such modifications[2] of the statutes[3] of any qualifying institution[4] as they considered necessary or expedient[5] for the purpose of securing that such statutes included:

(1)   provision enabling an appropriate[6] body, or any delegate of such a body, to dismiss[7] any member of the academic staff[8] by reason of redundancy[9];

(2)   provision enabling an appropriate officer, or any delegate of such an officer, acting in accordance with procedures determined by the Commissioners, to dismiss any member of the academic staff for good cause[10];

(3)   provision establishing disciplinary procedures determined by the Commissioners for dealing with any complaints made against any member of the academic staff relating to his appointment or employment[11];

(4)   provision establishing procedures determined by the Commissioners for hearing and determining appeals by any members of the academic staff who are dismissed or under notice of dismissal (whether or not in pursuance of such provision as is mentioned in head (1) or head (2) above) or who were otherwise disciplined[12]; and

(5)   provision establishing procedures determined by the Commissioners for affording to any member of the academic staff opportunities for seeking redress for any grievances relating to his appointment or employment[13].

In exercising their functions, the Commissioners were required to have regard to the need:

(a)   to ensure that academic staff had freedom within the law to question and test received wisdom, and to put forward new ideas and controversial or unpopular opinions, without placing themselves in jeopardy of losing their jobs or privileges they may have at their institutions[14];

(b)   to enable qualifying institutions to provide education, promote learning and engage in research efficiently and economically[15]; and

(c)   to apply the principles of justice and fairness[16].

The Commissioners' powers and duties were due to cease on 29 July 1991[17] unless continued for a longer period specified by order of the Secretary of State[18]. The last of a series of such orders provided that the Commissioners' powers and duties ceased on 1 April 1996[19].

1   As to the appointment, tenure and duration of office, powers, remuneration, staff, expenses and proceedings of the Commissioners see the Education Reform Act 1988 s 202(4), Sch 11. See also, however, the text to notes 17–19.

2   'Modifications' includes additions, alterations and omissions; and 'modify' must be construed accordingly: Education Reform Act 1988 s 235(1).

3   'Statutes', in relation to an institution, includes any regulations, ordinances or other instruments which, in the opinion of the Commissioners, serve as statutes for the purposes of that institution and are designated as such by the Commissioners: Education Reform Act 1988 s 203(8).

4   For the purposes of the Education Reform Act 1988 ss 202–205, 'qualifying institution' means:

    (1)   any university or other institution to which, during the period of three years beginning 1 August 1987, grants in aid were or were to have been made by the Universities Funding Council, or by the Secretary of State acting on the advice of the University Grants Committee (s 202(3)(a));

    (2)   any constituent college, school or hall or other institution of a university falling within head (1) (s 202(3)(b)); and

    (3)   any institution not falling within head (1) which was authorised by charter to grant

degrees and to which, during the period of three years beginning 1 August 1987, grants were or were to have been made by the Secretary of State (s 202(3)(c)).

The University Grants Committee (a non-statutory body) was replaced by the Universities Funding Council established under s 131(1) (repealed), which was itself replaced by the Higher Education Funding Council for England (see the Further and Higher Education Act 1992 s 63; and PARA 691 et seq). As to the meaning of 'university' see PARA 621 note 3. As to the Secretary of State see PARA 58.

5   Education Reform Act 1988 s 204(1). Proposed modifications to the statutes of qualifying institutions were required to be submitted to the Privy Council for approval or remission and reconsideration before the modifications were put into effect (whatever the requirements in this regard contained in the statutes themselves): see ss 203(3), 204(9), 205(1), (3)–(5). Prior to submission to the Privy Council the proposed modifications were required to be sent to the affected bodies and other appropriate bodies and organisations for the purposes of making representations: s 205(1), (2) (amended by the Further and Higher Education Act 1992 s 93(1), Sch 8 paras 27, 45(a)). The Commissioners' powers under the Education Reform Act 1988 s 204 included power to make such incidental, supplementary and transitional provision as they considered necessary or expedient: s 204(8). Incidental, consequential or supplementary provision in connection with the Commissioners' powers or the exercise of those powers could be made by Order in Council: see s 207(1)(a), (b), (2). No such orders were made.

6   'Appropriate', in relation to a body or officer of a qualifying institution, means appearing to the Commissioners to be appropriate having regard to the nature and circumstances of the institution: Education Reform Act 1988 s 203(7).

7   'Dismiss' and 'dismissal' include 'remove' or, as the case may be, 'removal from office' (Education Reform Act 1988 s 203(7)(a)); and, in relation to employment under a contract, must be construed in accordance with the Employment Rights Act 1996 Pt X (ss 94–134A) (see EMPLOYMENT vol 41 (2014) PARA 757 et seq): Education Reform Act 1988 s 203(7)(b) (amended by the Employment Rights Act 1996 s 240, Sch 1 para 37(1), (3)). As to the meaning of 'contract of employment' see PARA 301 note 2.

8   A reference to academic staff includes a reference to persons whose terms of appointment or contracts of employment are, in the opinion of the Commissioners, so similar to those of academic staff as to justify their being treated as academic staff for the purposes of the Education Reform Act 1988 s 203: s 203(4).

9   Education Reform Act 1988 s 203(1)(a). The dismissal of a member of staff was to be taken to be a dismissal by reason of redundancy if it was attributable wholly or mainly to: (1) the fact that the institution had ceased, or intended to cease, to carry on the activity for the purposes of which he was appointed or employed by the institution, or had ceased, or intended to cease, to carry on that activity in the place in which he carried out his work (s 203(5)(a)); or (2) the fact that the requirements of that activity for members of staff to carry out work of a particular kind, or for members of staff to carry out work of a particular kind in that place, had ceased or diminished or were expected to cease or diminish (s 203(5)(b)). No provision such as is mentioned in s 203(1)(a) or (b) (see the text to note 10) which was included in the statutes of a qualifying institution was to enable any member of the academic staff to be dismissed unless the reason for his dismissal could, in the circumstances (including the size and administrative resources of the institution), reasonably be treated as a sufficient reason for dismissing him: s 203(2). Provision as to the persons in relation to whom the proposed modifications were to apply was made by s 204(2)–(6). As to the meaning of 'employed' see PARA 301 note 2.

10   Education Reform Act 1988 s 203(1)(b). 'Good cause', in relation to a member of the academic staff of a qualifying institution, means a reason which is related to his conduct or to his capability or qualifications for performing work of the kind which he was appointed or employed to do: s 203(6). In relation to such a member 'capability' means capability assessed by reference to skill, aptitude, health or any other physical or mental quality (s 203(6)(a)); and 'qualifications' means any degree, diploma or other academic, technical or professional qualification relevant to the office or position held by him (s 203(6)(b)). Provision as to the application of modifications made for the purpose of complying with the requirements of s 203(1)(b) was made by s 204(7), (9). See also note 9.

11   Education Reform Act 1988 s 203(1)(c).

12   Education Reform Act 1988 s 203(1)(d).

13   Education Reform Act 1988 s 203(1)(e).

14   Education Reform Act 1988 s 202(2)(a).

15   Education Reform Act 1988 s 202(2)(b).

16   Education Reform Act 1988 s 202(2)(c).

17 Ie the end of the period of three years beginning with 29 July 1988 (ie the date on which the Education Reform Act 1988 received Royal Assent and on which, by virtue of s 236(1) (repealed), s 202 was brought into force).

18 Education Reform Act 1988 Sch 11 para 3(1), (2)(b).

19 The Education (University Commissioners) Order 1991, SI 1991/1427, extended the Commissioners' powers and duties until 31 December 1992; the Education (University Commissioners) Order 1992, SI 1992/3064, extended the Commissioners' powers and duties until 1 January 1994; the Education (University Commissioners) Order 1993, SI 1993/3056, extended the Commissioners' powers and duties until 1 January 1995; the Education (University Commissioners) Order 1994, SI 1994/3106, extended the Commissioners' powers and duties until 1 April 1995; and the Education (University Commissioners) Order 1995, SI 1995/604, extended the Commissioners' powers and duties until 1 April 1996.

C. ELECTIONS AND FELLOWSHIPS

632. Regulation of elections. Questions relating to college elections generally are determined by the visitor[1] in accordance with the statutes which govern such institutions, but these elections are regulated to a certain extent by Act of Parliament[2].

Neither the court[3] nor the visitor[4] can compel the election of any particular candidate, if the college is by its statutes given absolute discretion in the matter, except where the discretion is exercised corruptly[5].

1 As to the jurisdiction of visitors see PARAS 629–630.
2 See eg the Universities Tests Act 1871 s 3, under which no religious qualification may be imposed: see PARA 644.
3 *R v Hertford College* (1878) 3 QBD 693 at 705, CA, per Lord Coleridge CJ. See also CHARITIES vol 8 (2015) PARA 532.
4 *Ex p Wrangham* (1795) 2 Ves 609 at 625. See also CHARITIES vol 8 (2015) PARA 517.
5 *R v Hertford College* (1878) 3 QBD 693 at 701, CA, per Lord Coleridge CJ.

633. Powers of majority. Elections by the dean, warden, provost, master, president or other head of any college, by whatsoever name it may be incorporated or founded, with the consent of the majority of the fellows or brethren of the corporation who have power to consent, are as valid as if made by all the members of the corporation[1].

Where college statutes direct fellows to be elected by the head of the college and the majority of the fellows, the concurrence of the head is necessary[2].

1 This is the rule at common law: see CORPORATIONS vol 24 (2010) PARA 409.
2 *Case of Catherine Hall* (1802) 5 Russ 85n; *Re Queen's College, Cambridge* (1828) 5 Russ 64. The contrary was formerly held: see *Case of Clare Hall* (1788) 5 Russ 73n; *Case of Gonville and Caius College* (1617) 5 Russ 76n. As to the removal of fellows by visitors see CHARITIES vol 8 (2015) PARA 525.

634. Corrupt elections. Elections of fellows, scholars, officers and other persons as members of colleges, schools, halls or societies, if made corruptly or for any money consideration, direct or indirect, are void[1].

Any fellow, officer or scholar receiving a bribe for resigning his office or place[2] is liable on summary conviction to a fine[3] in addition to any non-pecuniary forfeiture to which he would have been liable[4], and the person giving the bribe is disqualified for the office 'for that tyme or turne'[5].

1 See the Simony Act 1588 s 1 (amended by the Statute Law Revision Act 1948). By the Common Informers Act 1951 s 1, Schedule (repealed) no proceedings for a penalty or forfeiture under the Simony Act 1588 may be brought save where no part of the penalty is payable to a common informer.
2 See the Simony Act 1588 s 2 (amended by the Statute Law Revision Act 1888).

3 Ie a fine not exceeding level 3 on the standard scale. As to the standard scale see SENTENCING
AND DISPOSITION OF OFFENDERS vol 92 (2010) PARA 142.
4 Common Informers Act 1951 s 1(3) (amended by the Criminal Justice Act 1982 ss 37, 38, 46).
5 See the Simony Act 1588 s 2 (as amended: see note 2).

635. Qualification of candidates. The passing of an examination may be a
condition precedent to election to a fellowship, but it does not follow that
superiority in the examination gives an absolute and unqualified title to be
elected, unless there are words to this effect in the college statutes[1].

If there is only one candidate for a close fellowship, he must nonetheless pass
the usual fellowship examination; but in such a case the standard of ability
required of the candidate must be decided on general grounds without reference
to the standard of ability of any particular individuals who do not satisfy the
conditions of the close fellowship[2].

Where by the endowment deed of a college the person to be elected to a
fellowship is directed to be a native of a particular town if any such shall be
found able within the university, a person not having the requisite birth
qualification but being eligible as regards capacity may be elected, if the persons
who are qualified by birth do not attain to the fellowship standard of ability[3].

When the possession of real estate is a necessary qualification for certain
college offices, the modern doctrines of equity are not strictly applied, and an
interest in land which in equity would be considered personal estate may be
sufficient[4].

If a qualification for a fellowship is that a candidate must be 'in sacerdotio
constitutus'[5], an admission to deacon's orders is enough[6].

1 *R v Hertford College* (1878) 3 QBD 693 at 698–699, 701, CA, per Lord Coleridge CJ. As to the
construction of college statutes with respect to fellowship examinations see also *Downing
College Case* (1837) 2 My & Cr 642; *Watson and Freemantle v Warden etc of All Souls'
College, Oxford* (1864) 11 LT 166.
2 *Re Catherine Hall, ex p Inge* (1831) 2 Russ & M 590.
3 *Re St John's College, Cambridge* (1831) 2 Russ & M 603. In open fellowships the principle is
'detur digniori' (let it be given to him who most deserves it), in proprieties, 'detur, sed digno' (let
it be given if deserved): *Re St John's College, Cambridge* at 605.
4 *Case of Queen's College, Cambridge* (1821) Jac 1 at 37–38.
5 Ie in priest's orders.
6 *Re University College, Oxford* (1848) 17 LJ Ch 298. See also *Glasgow College v A-G* (1848) 1
HL Cas 800; *Re St Catherine's Hall, Cambridge* (1849) 1 Mac & G 473.

636. Forfeiture of fellowship. The acceptance of a professorship may, under
college statutes, cause the professor to forfeit his fellowship[1].

Where a condition, for example that a certain portion of the fellowship term
should be spent abroad, is attached to a fellowship, and the fellow, after
receiving the emoluments for some years at home, resigns the fellowship without
going abroad, acceptance by the trustees of the fellow's resignation dispenses, it
seems, with the condition, and consequently the money received by the fellow
need not be refunded; but in such circumstances the trustees might refuse to
accept the resignation and compel the fellow either to comply with the condition
or to refund[2].

Where the question is whether a fellowship has been forfeited under the
college statutes, the expression 'a collegii emolumentis recedere' means absolute
forfeiture, not merely temporary suspension, and the word 'discedere' as applied
to a fellow vacating his fellowship is not confined to a vacancy created by death[3].

1 *Re Trinity College, Cambridge, ex p Edleston* (1854) 3 De GM & G 742.

2   *A-G v Stephens* (1737) 1 Atk 358. It is not certain whether it would be the trustees' duty to refuse to accept the resignation.

3   *Re St Catherine's Hall, Cambridge* (1849) 1 Mac & G 473.

D. INCOME, LAND AND PROPERTY ETC

637.   Unification of trusts. A university or college to which the Universities and Colleges (Trusts) Act 1943 applies[1] may make schemes providing for the aggregation and administration as a single fund of all property, with such exceptions as may be specified, held upon trusts of any particular class or classes which are administered by the university or college or administered by other trustees for purposes connected with the university or college[2]. Such a scheme may provide for the transfer to the college or university of certain property held on any trust to which the scheme relates[3], for valuing the fund and determining the shares of the various trusts therein[4], for distributing the income in accordance with those shares and enabling advances to be made out of the capital[5], for authorising part of the income to be placed to reserve[6], for conferring powers of investment including power to invest in land[7], for the extension of the scheme to trusts subsequently created (unless the trust expressly provides to the contrary or, in the case of trusts not administered by the university or college, the trustees withhold consent)[8], and for incidental, consequential and supplementary matters[9]. Any power to purchase land conferred by a scheme may, subject to certain exceptions, only be exercised with the consent of the Secretary of State[10]. A scheme cannot lawfully affect a variation of the trusts of the fund if the variation adversely affects another person or body who has not acquiesced in the variation[11].

If a college in a university is required by a statute of the university to make contributions for university purposes in respect of income arising from any property held on trust by or on behalf of the college or for purposes connected with it, the amount of the contributions may be charged on the property[12].

1   The Universities and Colleges (Trusts) Act 1943 applies to the Universities of Oxford and Cambridge, to the colleges in those universities, and to the College of St Mary of Winchester, near Winchester; and the expressions 'university' and 'college' are to be construed accordingly: s 1(1). For these purposes, the Cathedral or House of Christ Church in Oxford, Keble College, St Peter's Hall, Somerville College, Lady Margaret Hall, St Hugh's College and St Hilda's College are deemed to be colleges in the University of Oxford, and Selwyn College, Girton College and Newnham College are deemed to be colleges in the University of Cambridge: s 1(2).

2   See the Universities and Colleges (Trusts) Act 1943 s 2(1)(a)–(c). Different schemes may be made in relation to different classes of trusts: s 2(4). Schemes must be submitted to the Queen in Council for approval by Order in Council (s 3(1)), having first been laid before Parliament for 40 days (see s 3(2), (3)). On approval a scheme has effect notwithstanding any instrument (including an Act) relating to any trust to which the scheme applies (s 3(4)), but a scheme may be varied or revoked by a subsequent scheme (s 3(5)). Property may be included in a scheme only with the trustees' consent: s 2(1)(a).

3   See the Universities and Colleges (Trusts) Act 1943 s 2(1)(d) (amended by SI 1955/554).

4   Universities and Colleges (Trusts) Act 1943 s 2(1)(e).

5   See the Universities and Colleges (Trusts) Act 1943 s 2(1)(f).

6   See the Universities and Colleges (Trusts) Act 1943 s 2(1)(g).

7   See the Universities and Colleges (Trusts) Act 1943 s 2(1)(h).

8   See the Universities and Colleges (Trusts) Act 1943 s 2(1)(i).

9   See the Universities and Colleges (Trusts) Act 1943 s 2(1)(k).

10 See the Universities and Colleges (Trusts) Act 1943 s 2(2), (5) (s 2(2) amended by SI 1955/554; and the Universities and Colleges (Trusts) Act 1943 s 2(5) added by the Universities and Colleges Estates Act 1964 s 4(1), Sch 3 Pt I); and the Secretaries of State for Transport, Local

Government and the Regions and for Environment, Food and Rural Affairs Order 2001, SI 2001/2568 (amended by SI 2002/2626). As to the Secretary of State see PARA 58.

11 *Re Freeston's Charity, Sylvester v Master and Fellows of University College, Oxford* [1979] 1 All ER 51, [1978] 1 WLR 741, CA.

12 Universities and Colleges (Trusts) Act 1943 s 4.

638. Rights of patronage. Subject to the general restrictions on the transfer of rights of patronage[1], the Universities of Oxford, Cambridge and Durham, and any of their colleges, may purchase and sell advowsons[2] and annex to them land in lieu of annual rents[3], and they may transfer gratuitously to a bishop, dean and chapter or other ecclesiastical corporation willing to accept it any right of patronage[4].

1 See ECCLESIASTICAL LAW vol 34 (2011) PARA 583.
2 As to advowsons generally see ECCLESIASTICAL LAW vol 34 (2011) PARA 550.
3 See the Universities and College Estates Act 1925 ss 33–35 (s 33 amended by the Statute Law (Repeals) Act 1986); and ECCLESIASTICAL LAW vol 34 (2011) PARA 574. See also the Oxford University Act 1857 s 3.
4 Universities and College Estates Act 1925 s 37. As to the severance of benefices from headships of colleges see s 36; and ECCLESIASTICAL LAW vol 34 (2011) PARA 574.

639. Financial provisions. The income of universities, university colleges and colleges of universities is derived in part from endowments and in part from fees and dues from members[1]. Universities and university colleges also receive grants out of money provided by Parliament through the medium of the Higher Education Funding Council[2]. In addition, universities, university colleges and colleges of universities may receive grants from the Secretary of State or, in relation to Wales, the Welsh Ministers under the power to make grants to persons other than local authorities in respect of expenditure on educational services or educational research[3].

1 As to the power of colleges of the Universities of Oxford and Cambridge to charge certain contributions for university purposes or trust funds see PARA 637. As to fees see also PARAS 715 et seq, 1111.
2 As to the meaning of references to the Higher Education Funding Council see PARA 691 note 1.
3 See the Education Act 1996 s 485; and PARA 82.

640. Rights in respect of land required for future development. Restrictions are placed on a person's right to acquire the freehold or an extended lease under the Leasehold Reform Act 1967[1] where the landlord is a university body[2] and a minister of the Crown certifies that the property will in ten years or less be required for relevant development[3]. Where a tenant of a house and premises acquires the freehold or an extended lease of premises from a university under that Act, statutory provision is made for the instrument effecting the transfer or extending the lease to contain such covenants on the part of the tenant restricting the carrying out of development or clearing of land as are necessary to reserve the land for possible development by the university[4].

1 Ie under the Leasehold Reform Act 1967 Pt I (ss 1–37).
2 Ie any university, university college or college of a university; and for this purpose 'college of a university' includes, in the case of a university organised on a collegiate basis, a constituent college or other society recognised by the university and, in the case of a London University, a college incorporated in the university or a school of the university: Leasehold Reform Act 1967 s 28(5)(c).
3 See the Leasehold Reform Act 1967 s 28; and LANDLORD AND TENANT vol 64 (2012) PARA 1603. 'Relevant development' means development for purposes (other than investment purposes) of the university body: see s 28(6); and LANDLORD AND TENANT vol 64 (2012) PARA 1603.

4   See the Leasehold Reform Act 1967 s 29; and LANDLORD AND TENANT vol 64 (2012) PARA 1572.

E.   RIGHTS AND PRIVILEGES

641.   Privileges of jurisdiction. Oxford and Cambridge universities have special privileges of jurisdiction over their members[1].

1   See further PARAS 642–644.

642.   Privileges regarding publications. The libraries of the universities of Oxford and Cambridge have certain rights under the Copyright Acts[1], and their presses have rights as regards their imprints[2].

1   See COPYRIGHT vol 23 (2013) PARA 606. The same right is enjoyed by their colleges, by the universities of Aberdeen, Edinburgh, Glasgow and St Andrews, and by the colleges of Eton, Westminster and Winchester. The Bodleian Library, Oxford, and the University Library, Cambridge, are among the deposit libraries which may demand from the publisher a copy of any qualifying work published in the United Kingdom: see COPYRIGHT vol 23 (2013) PARA 616.
2   See the Newspapers, Printers, and Reading Rooms Repeal Act 1869 s 1, Sch 2 (re-enacting the Printers and Publishers Act 1839 s 3); and see PUBLISHING vol 85 (2012) PARA 714.

643.   Graduate privileges. The general privileges of graduates of the universities of Oxford, Cambridge and London in respect of offices open, or exemption granted, to them by any Act of Parliament or regulation of a public authority have been extended to graduates of other universities in England and Wales[1].

1   See the Victoria University Act 1888 s 1 (repealed); the University of Wales Act 1902 s 1 (repealed); the University of Liverpool Act 1904 s 1 (repealed); the Leeds University Act 1904 s 1 (repealed); and the Sheffield University Act 1914 s 1 (repealed). As to graduates of other universities see the several local Acts of Parliament regulating those universities, many of which are cited in PARA 626.

644.   Religion. No religious qualification is required for a person taking a degree (other than a degree in divinity[1]) at the Universities of Oxford, Cambridge or Durham, or to enable a person to hold office in any of those universities or such of their colleges as existed before 16 June 1871[2], except where such office is, either by Act of Parliament or by university or college statute in force at that date, restricted to persons in holy orders, or is confined to members of the Church of England by reason of a degree in divinity being a qualification for holding that office[3]. There is no objection, however, to new colleges being created subsequent to 1871 with endowments limited to members of particular religious communities[4].

Where the University of Oxford Commissioners or the University of Cambridge Commissioners[5] by any statute made by them[6] erected or endowed an office, other than a headship or fellowship of a college, and declared that the holder of it must have a theological qualification, the provisions described above regarding religious qualification take effect with reference to that office as if the statute made by the Commissioners had been made before 16 June 1871[7].

The abolition of religious qualifications does not interfere with the lawfully established system of religious instruction, worship and discipline in the universities of Oxford, Cambridge and Durham and their colleges[8]. Colleges subsisting on 16 June 1871 must provide sufficient religious instruction for undergraduates belonging to the Church of England[9], and morning and evening prayer according to the Book of Common Prayer[10]. No one must be required to attend any college or university lecture to which he (or, if he is under full age, his parent or guardian) objects on religious grounds[11].

1   University statutes have modified this restriction: see the Statute passed by Convocation of the University of Oxford on 25 November 1925 (candidates for the degrees of BD and DD need not be ordained clergymen of the Church of England); and Statute 42 of the University of Durham (no religious test required of any student, except for candidates for the licence in theology, which has not been awarded for many years).

2   Ie the date on which the Universities Tests Act 1871 was passed (ie received Royal Assent): see ECCLESIASTICAL LAW.

3   See the Universities Tests Act 1871 s 3. For a case predating the Universities Tests Act 1871 see *Case of Queen's College, Cambridge* (1821) Jac 1.

4   *R v Hertford College* (1878) 3 QBD 693 at 707, CA, per Lord Coleridge CJ.

5   The University of Oxford Commissioners and the University of Cambridge Commissioners were established under the Universities of Oxford and Cambridge Act 1877 s 3 (repealed). By s 7 (repealed) the powers of the Commissioners could not continue beyond the end of 1881. As to the jurisdiction of the Commissioners to alter conditions of eligibility for any emolument or office connected with a college see *Re Pauncefort, Sons of Clergy Corpn v Christ Church, Oxford* (1889) 42 ChD 624.

6   Ie under the Universities of Oxford and Cambridge Act 1877.

7   See the Universities of Oxford and Cambridge Act 1877 s 58.

8   See the Universities Tests Act 1871 s 4.

9   Universities Tests Act 1871 s 5.

10 See the Universities Tests Act 1871 s 6 (amended by the Church of England (Worship and Doctrine) Measure 1974 s 6(3), Sch 2). At the request of the governing body the visitor may permit the use of shortened forms of morning and evening prayer: see the Universities Tests Act 1871 s 6 (as so amended). As to the power of a bishop to license a clergyman to perform offices and services in a college chapel see ECCLESIASTICAL LAW vol 34 (2011) PARA 482.

11 Universities Tests Act 1871 s 7.

(iv) Higher Education Corporations

A. INCORPORATION

645.   Meaning of 'higher education corporation'. References in the Education Reform Act 1988 to a 'higher education corporation' are references to a body corporate established under that Act[1] or which has become a higher education corporation[2] by virtue of that Act[3].

1   Ie established under the Education Reform Act 1988 s 121 (see PARA 646) or s 122 (see PARA 647).

2   Ie by virtue of the Education Reform Act 1988 s 122A: see PARA 620.

3   Education Reform Act 1988 s 123(1) (amended by the Further and Higher Education Act 1992 s 93(1), Sch 8 paras 27, 32(a)).

646.   Incorporation of specified higher education institutions. The Secretary of State[1] was required, before 21 November 1988[2] (or, in one case, 1 February 1989[3]) by order to specify certain institutions[4] maintained by local education authorities, and on that date a number of bodies corporate were established for the purpose of conducting each specified institution as from 1 April 1989[5]. A higher education corporation so established before 6 May 1992[6] was required to be established initially under the name given as the name of that institution in the order specifying that institution[7].

1   As to the Secretary of State see PARA 58.

2   Ie the date appointed for the purposes of the Education Reform Act 1988 s 121 in relation to all institutions falling within s 121(2) other than the Southampton Institute of Higher Education: see s 121(1) (repealed by the Statute Law (Repeals) Act 2004); and the Education Reform Act 1988 (Commencement No 2) Order 1988, SI 1988/1794, art 2.

3 Ie the date appointed for the purposes of the Education Reform Act 1988 s 121 in relation to the Southampton Institute of Higher Education: see s 121(1) (repealed); and the Education Reform Act 1988 (Commencement No 4) Order 1988, SI 1988/2271, art 2.

4 The institutions required to be specified under the Education Reform Act 1988 s 121(1) were those appearing to the Secretary of State to fall within s 121(2): s 121(1) (repealed). An institution fell within s 121(2) if on 1 November 1985 either its full-time equivalent enrolment number for courses of advanced further education exceeded 350 and also exceeded 55% of its total full-time equivalent enrolment number or its full-time equivalent enrolment number for such courses exceeded 2,500: s 121(2) (repealed by the Statute Law (Repeals) Act 2004). Where an institution maintained by a local education authority had been established since 1 November 1985 by a merger of two or more institutions existing on that date, the institution was to be treated as falling within the Education Reform Act 1988 s 121(2) (repealed) if it would have done so if the merger had taken place before that date: s 121(3) (repealed by the Statute Law (Repeals) Act 2004).

5 Ie the transfer date applicable in relation to bodies corporate established under the Education Reform Act 1988 s 121; that is, the date appointed under s 126 (see PARA 649 note 6) in relation to the transfer under s 126 of property, rights and liabilities to the corporation: see s 121(1) (repealed), s 123(2); the Education (Higher Education Corporations) Order 1988, SI 1988/1799, art 4; and the Education (Higher Education Corporations) (No 5) Order 1989, SI 1989/17, art 3.

6 Ie the appointed day: see the Education Reform Act 1988 s 123(3), (4) (s 123(3) substituted, s 123(4) added, by the Further and Higher Education Act 1992 s 93(1), Sch 8 paras 27, 32(b)); the Education Reform Act 1988 s 124A(10) (added by the Further and Higher Education Act 1992 s 71(1)); and the Further and Higher Education Act 1992 (Commencement No 1 and Transitional Provisions) Order 1992, SI 1992/831. As to the constitution and government of higher education corporations established after 6 May 1992 see PARA 657 et seq.

7 Education Reform Act 1988 s 123(3), Sch 7 para 1(1) (s 123(3) as substituted: see note 6). This requirement applies unless an instrument of government for the corporation made under s 124A (see PARA 657) has effect: see s 123(3) (as so substituted). A corporation may change its name with the consent of the Privy Council: Sch 7 para 1(4) (substituted by the Further and Higher Education Act 1992 s 93(1), Sch 8 paras 27, 59(a)). See further PARA 622. The power under the Education Reform Act 1988 Sch 7 para 1(4) is not exercisable by statutory instrument: see s 232(1), (2) (amended by the Education Act 1996 s 582(1), Sch 37 para 80(a)). As to the Privy Council see CONSTITUTIONAL AND ADMINISTRATIVE LAW vol 20 (2014) PARA 268 et seq.

647. Further incorporations. If at any time it appears to the appropriate national authority[1], in the case of any institution maintained by a local authority[2], that its full-time equivalent enrolment number[3] for courses of higher education[4] exceeds 55 per cent of its total full-time equivalent enrolment number[5], the appropriate national authority may by order[6] make provision for the establishment of a body corporate for the purpose of conducting that institution as from the transfer date[7]. A higher education corporation established under these provisions before the appointed day[8] is established initially under the name given in the order establishing the corporation unless an instrument of government for the corporation[9] has effect[10]. A higher education corporation established under these provisions on or after the appointed day must be established initially under the name given as the name of that institution in the order specifying that institution[11].

1 Ie the Secretary of State or, in relation to Wales, the Welsh Ministers. As to the Secretary of State see PARA 58. As to the Welsh Ministers see PARA 59. As to the meaning of 'Wales' see PARA 7 note 3. The functions of the Secretary of State under the Education Reform Act 1988 s 122, so far as exercisable in relation to Wales, were transferred to the National Assembly for Wales (see the National Assembly for Wales (Transfer of Functions) Order 1999, SI 1999/672, art 2, Sch 1) and are now vested in the Welsh Ministers (see the Government of Wales Act 2006 s 162(1), Sch 11 para 30).

2 As to the meaning of 'local authority' see PARA 25 (definition applied by the Education Reform Act 1988 s 235(7) (amended by the Education Act 1996 s 582(1), Sch 37 para 81(4)).

3 As to the determination of full-time equivalent enrolment numbers see PARA 651.

4 As to the meaning of 'courses of higher education' see PARA 684.

5 References in the Education Reform Act 1988 Pt II (ss 120–161) to the 'total full-time equivalent enrolment number' of any institution at any time are references to the aggregate of its full-time equivalent enrolment numbers at that time for courses of all descriptions then offered by that institution (s 161(2)); and for these purposes the full-time equivalent enrolment number at any time of any institution for courses of any description is to be determined in accordance with Sch 9 (see PARA 651) (s 161(3)).

6 Such orders, being of local effect, are not recorded in this work.

7 Education Reform Act 1988 s 122(1), (6). 'Transfer date' means, in relation to a higher education corporation, the date appointed under s 126 (see PARA 649 note 6) in relation to the transfer under that section of property, rights and liabilities to that corporation: s 123(2). As to the meaning of 'liability' see PARA 84 note 11.

8 Ie 6 May 1992: see PARA 646 note 6.

9 Ie made under the Education Reform Act 1988 s 124A: see PARA 657.

10 See the Education Reform Act 1988 s 123(3), Sch 7 para 1(2) (s 123(3) substituted by the Further and Higher Education Act 1992 s 93(1), Sch 8 paras 27, 32(b)). Such a corporation may change its name with the consent of the Privy Council: Education Reform Act 1988 Sch 7 para 1(4) (substituted by the Further and Higher Education Act 1992 s 93(1), Sch 8 paras 27, 59(a)). See further PARA 622. The power under the Education Reform Act 1988 Sch 7 para 1(4) is not exercisable by statutory instrument: see s 232(1), (2) (amended by the Education Act 1996 s 582(1), Sch 37 para 80(a)). As to the Privy Council see CONSTITUTIONAL AND ADMINISTRATIVE LAW vol 20 (2014) PARA 268 et seq.

11 Education Reform Act 1988 s 123(4) (added by the Further and Higher Education Act 1992 s 93(1), Sch 8 paras 27, 32(b)).

648. Transfer of staff. Where a higher education corporation[1] is established[2], the contract of employment[3] between:

(1)   any person who, immediately before the transfer date[4], is employed by the transferor authority[5] to work solely at the institution the corporation is established to conduct[6] or is employed by that authority to work at that institution and is designated[7] by an order made by the appropriate national authority[8]; and

(2)   the transferor authority,

has effect from the transfer date as if originally made between him and the corporation[9].

Without prejudice to this requirement[10]:

(a)   all the transferor authority's rights, powers, duties and liabilities[11] under or in connection with an applicable contract[12] are transferred[13] to the corporation on the transfer date[14]; and

(b)   anything done before that date by or in relation to the transferor authority in respect of that contract or the employee is deemed from that date to have been done by or in relation to the corporation[15].

These requirements[16] are without prejudice to any right of an employee to terminate his contract of employment if a substantial change is made to his detriment in his working conditions, but no such right arises by reason only of the change in employer as described above[17].

1 As to the meaning of 'higher education corporation' see PARA 645.

2 As to the establishment of corporations see the Education Reform Act 1988 s 121 (see PARA 646) and s 122 (see PARA 647).

3 As to the meaning of 'contract of employment' and related expressions see PARA 301 note 2.

4 As to the meaning of 'transfer date' see PARA 647 note 7.

5 References in the Education Reform Act 1988 s 127, in relation to a higher education corporation, to 'the transferor authority' are references to the local authority by whom the institution that corporation is established to conduct is maintained immediately before the transfer date: s 127(6) (amended by SI 2010/1158). As to the meaning of 'local authority' see PARA 25 (definition applied by s 235(7) (amended by the Education Act 1996 s 582(1), Sch 37 para 81(4)).

6 Education Reform Act 1988 s 127(1)(a).

7 Ie designated for the purposes of the Education Reform Act 1988 s 127.
8 Education Reform Act 1988 s 127(1)(b). An order under s 127 may designate a person either individually or as a member of a class or description of employees: s 127(5). Such orders, being of local effect, are not recorded in this work. 'Appropriate national authority' means the Secretary of State or, in relation to Wales, the Welsh Ministers. As to the Secretary of State see PARA 58. As to the Welsh Ministers see PARA 59. As to the meaning of 'Wales' see PARA 7 note 3. The functions of the Secretary of State under the Education Reform Act 1988 s 127, so far as exercisable in relation to Wales, were transferred to the National Assembly for Wales (see the National Assembly for Wales (Transfer of Functions) Order 1999, SI 1999/672, art 2, Sch 1) and are now vested in the Welsh Ministers (see the Government of Wales Act 2006 s 162(1), Sch 11 para 30).
9 Education Reform Act 1988 s 127(2).
10 Ie the requirement of the Education Reform Act 1988 s 127(2): see the text to notes 1–9.
11 As to the meaning of 'liability' see PARA 84 note 11.
12 Ie a contract to which the Education Reform Act 1988 s 127(2) applies: see the text to notes 1–9.
13 Ie by virtue of the Education Reform Act 1988 s 127.
14 Education Reform Act 1988 s 127(3)(a).
15 Education Reform Act 1988 s 127(3)(b).
16 Ie the Education Reform Act 1988 s 127(2), (3): see the text to notes 1–15.
17 Education Reform Act 1988 s 127(4). As to the transfer of employees on transfers of undertakings generally see EMPLOYMENT vol 39 (2014) PARA 136 et seq.

649. Transfer of property, rights and liabilities. Where a higher education corporation[1] is established[2], specified property, rights and liabilities[3] are transferred to, and by virtue of the Education Reform Act 1988 vested in, that corporation[4]. The property, rights and liabilities in question are all land[5] or other property which, immediately before the transfer date[6], was property of any local authority used or held for the purposes of the transferred institution[7], and all rights and liabilities of any such authority subsisting immediately before that date which were acquired or incurred[8] for those purposes[9]. Such transfers of property, rights and liabilities take place on the transfer date[10].

1 As to the meaning of 'higher education corporation' see PARA 645.
2 Ie under the Education Reform Act 1988 s 121 (see PARA 646) or s 122 (see PARA 647).
3 As to the meaning of 'liability' see PARA 84 note 11.
4 See the Education Reform Act 1988 s 126(3). Section 126(3) is subject to s 198 (land and property transfers: see PARA 1330 et seq); and does not apply to: (1) rights and liabilities under any contract of employment (s 126(5)(a)); (2) any liability of a local authority in respect of the principal of, or any interest on, any loan (s 126(5)(b) (amended by SI 2010/1158)); or (3) any liability of any such authority in respect of compensation for premature retirement of any person formerly employed by it (Education Reform Act 1988 s 126(5)(c)). As to the transfer of staff see PARA 648. As to liabilities of a local authority in respect of loans see PARA 650. As to the meanings of 'contract of employment' and 'employed' see PARA 301 note 2. As to the meaning of 'local authority' see PARA 25 (definition applied by s 235(7) (amended by the Education Act 1996 s 582(1), Sch 37 para 81(4))).
   Stamp duty is not chargeable in respect of any transfer effected under or by virtue of the Education Reform Act 1988 s 126 (taken with Sch 10): see s 230(1) (amended by the Education Act 1993 s 307(1), (3), Sch 19 paras 112, 137(a), Sch 21 Pt I; the Education Act 1996 s 582(2), Sch 38 Pt I; the Further and Higher Education Act 1992 s 93, Sch 8 paras 27, 55, Sch 9; and the Statute Law (Repeals) Act 2004). This is subject to the requirement that no instrument (other than a statutory instrument) made or executed under or in pursuance of the Education Reform Act 1988 s 126 may be treated as duly stamped unless it is stamped with the duty to which it would, but for s 230 (and, if applicable, the Finance Act 1982 s 129 (see STAMP TAXES vol 96 (2012) PARA 363)), be liable or it has, in accordance with the Stamp Act 1891 s 12 (see STAMP TAXES vol 96 (2012) PARA 384), been stamped with a particular stamp denoting that it is not chargeable with any duty or that it has been duly stamped: Education Reform Act 1988 s 230(4) (amended by the Education Act 1993 s 307(1), (3), Sch 19 paras 112, 137(b), Sch 21 Pt I).
5 As to the meaning of 'land' see PARA 84 note 9. Where at any time land is used for the purposes of an institution to which the Education Reform Act 1988 s 126(4)(a) applies, any interest of a local authority in that land subsisting at that time must be taken for the purposes of s 126(4)(a)

to be land held for the purposes of that institution (whether or not it is by virtue of that interest that the land is so used): s 138(1)(a), (2) (amended by SI 2010/1158).

6   The transfer date in relation to corporations established under the Education Reform Act 1988 s 121 (see PARA 646) is 1 April 1989; that is, the date appointed under s 126 in relation to the corporations so established: see s 126(1); the Education (Higher Education Corporations) Order 1988, SI 1988/1799, art 4; and the Education (Higher Education Corporations) (No 5) Order 1989, SI 1989/17, art 3. The transfer date applicable in relation to corporations established under the Education Reform Act 1988 s 122 (see PARA 647) is such date as the appropriate national authority may by order appoint in relation to that corporation: see s 126(2). Such orders, being of local effect, are not recorded in this work. 'Appropriate national authority' means the Secretary of State or, in relation to Wales, the Welsh Ministers. As to the Secretary of State see PARA 58. As to the Welsh Ministers see PARA 59. As to the meaning of 'Wales' see PARA 7 note 3. The functions of the Secretary of State under s 126 and the Further and Higher Education Act 1992 s 84 (see note 7), so far as exercisable in relation to Wales, were transferred to the National Assembly for Wales (see the National Assembly for Wales (Transfer of Functions) Order 1999, SI 1999/672, art 2, Sch 1) and are now vested in the Welsh Ministers (see the Government of Wales Act 2006 s 162(1), Sch 11 para 30).

7   Education Reform Act 1988 s 126(4)(a) (amended by SI 2010/1158). 'The transferred institution' means, in relation to any higher education corporation, the institution the corporation is established to conduct: s 126(6). Where (apart from the Further and Higher Education Act 1992 s 84) any land or other property of a local authority would on any date ('the date of transfer') be transferred under the Education Reform Act 1988 Pt II (ss 120–161) to the governing body of an institution within the higher education sector (see the Further and Higher Education Act 1992 s 84(1)(a)), and at any time before that date the authority, the governing body of the institution and the governing body of any other institution which will on that date be an institution within the higher education sector have agreed in writing that the land or property should be transferred on that or a subsequent date to the governing body of that other institution (s 84(1)(b)), then, if the appropriate national authority has approved the agreement at any time before the date of transfer, the Education Reform Act 1988 Pt II has effect as if it required the property to be transferred in accordance with the agreement (see the Further and Higher Education Act 1992 s 84(2)). References to anything done include anything done before 6 March 1992 (ie the date on which the Education Reform Act 1988 was passed (ie received Royal Assent)): see the Further and Higher Education Act 1992 s 84(3). In s 84, 'local authority' includes a non-metropolitan district council for an area for which there is a county council: s 84(4) (added by SI 2010/1158). As to the meaning of 'local authority' generally see PARA 25 (definition applied by the Further and Higher Education Act 1992 s 90(1) (amended by SI 2010/1158)). As to local government areas and authorities in England and Wales see LOCAL GOVERNMENT vol 69 (2009) PARA 22 et seq. As to the meaning of 'land' see PARA 568 note 7. As to the meaning of 'governing body' see PARA 560 note 6. As to the meaning of 'institution within the higher education sector' see PARA 619. As to the meaning of 'writing' see PARA 76 note 8.

8   Any reference in the Education Reform Act 1988 s 126 to liabilities incurred by a local authority are not to be read as including liabilities of such an authority to make payments to or in respect of any person in pursuance of any duty imposed on the authority under any statutory provision: see s 235(5) (amended by the Education Act 1993 s 307(1), (3), Sch 19 paras 112, 139(c), Sch 21 Pt I; and SI 2010/1158). 'Statutory provision' means a provision of an enactment or a statutory instrument: Education Reform Act 1988 s 235(1).

9   Education Reform Act 1988 s 126(4)(b).

10   See the Education Reform Act 1988 s 126(3).

650. Loan liabilities excepted from transfer.

For the purposes of the provisions[1] enabling certain liabilities[2] of local authorities[3] to be excepted from transfer[4] to a higher education corporation on the establishment of that corporation[5], a liability is an 'excepted liability' if it would have been transferred by virtue of the establishment of the corporation but for the statutory exclusion of any such transfer[6]. The amount of any liability of a local authority in respect of the principal of any loan which is an excepted liability in relation to an institution conducted by a higher education corporation[7] is to be treated on and after the date on which that liability would have been transferred ('the operative date') as having been borrowed from that authority by the body of persons[8] to whom the liability would have been transferred ('the default transferee') on such terms as to repayment and the payment of interest as may be agreed[9] or determined by the Secretary of State[10].

There is a duty to arrive, so far as practicable, at such written[11] agreements as may be necessary for determining the amount of any excepted liability and the terms to apply in relation to the liability imposed[12] on the default transferee by reference to that liability[13].

Notwithstanding any terms so agreed or determined, any liability in respect of any sum treated[14] as having been borrowed from a local authority may at any time be discharged by a single payment of a sum equal to the aggregate of the amount of the principal of the loan outstanding at the time of the payment and the amount of any interest accrued before that time[15].

1   Ie for the purposes of the Education Reform Act 1988 s 199.
2   As to the meaning of 'liability' see PARA 84 note 11.
3   As to the meaning of 'local authority' see PARA 25 (definition applied by the Education Reform Act 1988 s 235(7) (amended by the Education Act 1996 s 582(1), Sch 37 para 81(4)).
4   Ie under the Education Reform Act 1988 s 126(3): see PARA 649.
5   As to the meaning of 'higher education corporation' see PARA 645. Higher education corporations may be established under the Education Reform Act 1988 s 121 (see PARA 646) or s 122 (see PARA 647).
6   See the Education Reform Act 1988 s 199(2)(a). The statutory exclusion is that contained in s 126(5)(b) (see PARA 649): see s 199(2)(a).
7   See the Education Reform Act 1988 s 199(1), (2).
8   As to the meaning of 'person' see PARA 7 note 6.
9   The Education Reform Act 1988 s 199 originally referred to agreement made between the Education Assets Board and the authority. The Education Assets Board was renamed the Education Transfer Council by the School Standards and Framework Act 1998 s 136(1) and, by virtue of s 136(2), all statutory references to the Education Assets Board are to be construed as references to the Education Transfer Council. However, the Education Transfer Council was wound up in 2000. See further PARA 1330.
10 Education Reform Act 1988 s 199(1) (amended by the School Standards and Framework Act 1998 s 136(2)). As to the giving of assistance and advice to the Secretary of State for the purpose of determining any matter under s 199 see s 199(8). As to the Secretary of State see PARA 58.
11 As to the meaning of 'written' see PARA 76 note 8.
12 Ie under the Education Reform Act 1988 s 199.
13 See the Education Reform Act 1988 s 199(3). An agreement made under s 199(3) must be delivered to the default transferee: s 199(9). Any such agreement must be treated as made between the authority and the default transferee: s 199(10). The Secretary of State must be notified if it appears that it is unlikely in the case of any matter on which agreement is required to be reached under s 199(3) that such an agreement will be reached: s 199(5). Where the Secretary of State has received such a notification he may, whether before or after the operative date, give a direction determining the matter, and may include in the direction any provision which might have been included in an agreement under s 199(3): s 199(6). The Secretary of State must consult the authority before giving a direction under s 199: s 199(7).
14 Ie by virtue of the Education Reform Act 1988 s 199(1): see the text to notes 1–10.
15 Education Reform Act 1988 s 199(4) (amended by SI 2010/1158).

651. Determination of full-time equivalent enrolment numbers. The full-time equivalent enrolment number at any time of any educational institution for courses of any description is the aggregate of:

(1)   the number of full-time students[1] enrolled at that institution at that time to follow courses of that description[2]; and

(2)   the numbers for each mode of attendance at specified courses[3] arrived at by multiplying by the appropriate multiplier[4] the number of students enrolled at the institution at the time in question to follow such courses by that mode of attendance[5].

For the purpose of determining[6] the full-time equivalent enrolment number at any time of any educational institution for courses of any description, any student enrolled at the institution whose ordinary place of residence then was or is in a country or territory other than a member state[7] must be disregarded[8].

1   A student is a full-time student in relation to a course of any description if all his studies for the purposes of that course are full-time studies: Education Reform Act 1988 Sch 9 para 3(1). The Secretary of State or, in relation to Wales, the Welsh Ministers may by order amend Sch 9 paras 1–3 except so far as they apply for determining an institution's full-time equivalent enrolment number for any courses or (as the case may be) an institution's total full-time equivalent enrolment number on 1 November 1985: Sch 9 para 4. Such orders are not made by statutory instrument (see s 232(1), (2)) and are not recorded in this work. As to the Secretary of State see PARA 58. As to the Welsh Ministers see PARA 59. As to the meaning of 'Wales' see PARA 7 note 3. The functions of the Secretary of State under Sch 9, so far as exercisable in relation to Wales, were transferred to the National Assembly for Wales (see the National Assembly for Wales (Transfer of Functions) Order 1999, SI 1999/672, art 2, Sch 1) and are now vested in the Welsh Ministers (see the Government of Wales Act 2006 s 162(1), Sch 11 para 30).

2   Education Reform Act 1988 Sch 9 para 1(1)(a). See also note 1.

3   Ie the courses specified in note 4.

4   The appropriate multipliers, in relation to a mode of attendance so specified, are:
    (1)   in relation to a mode of attendance by way of a sandwich course, 0.9 (in the case of courses of advanced further education or courses of higher education), or 0.75 (in any other case) (Education Reform Act 1988 Sch 9 paras 1(3), 2, Table);
    (2)   in relation to a mode of attendance by way of block release or day release, 0.4 (in the case of courses of advanced further education or courses of higher education), or 0.3 (in any other case) (Sch 9 paras 1(3), 2, Table);
    (3)   in relation to a mode of attendance which is part-time (other than day release but including some day-time study), 0.4 (in the case of courses of advanced further education or courses of higher education), or 0.125 (in any other case) (Sch 9 paras 1(3), 2, Table);
    (4)   in relation to a mode of attendance which is part-time (evening only study) or by way of open or distance learning, 0.2 (in the case of courses of advanced further education or courses of higher education), or 0.075 (in any other case) (Sch 9 paras 1(3), 2, Table).
    A student's mode of attendance at a course of any description is by way of a sandwich course if in following that course, he engages in periods of full-time study for the purposes of the course alternating with periods of full-time work experience which form part of that course, and his average period of full-time study for the purposes of the course for each academic year included in the course is 19 weeks or more: Sch 9 para 3(2)(a). A student's mode of attendance at a course of any description is by way of block release if the course involves a period of full-time study interrupted by a period of industrial training or employment (whether or not it also includes study on one or two days a week during any other period), and his average period of full-time study for the purposes of the course for each academic year included in the course is less than 19 weeks: Sch 9 para 3(2)(b). As to the meaning of 'employment' and related expressions see PARA 301 note 2. A student's mode of attendance at a course of any description is by way of day release if he is in employment and he is released by his employer to follow that course during any part of the working week: Sch 9 para 3(2)(c). A student's mode of attendance at a course of any description is by way of open or distance learning if he is provided for the purposes of the course with learning material for private study, and his written work for the purposes of the course is subject to a marking and comment service provided for students following the course by private study (whether or not any additional advisory or teaching services are also provided for such students as part of the course): Sch 9 para 3(2)(d). As to the meaning of 'courses of higher education' see PARA 684. See also note 1.

5   Education Reform Act 1988 Sch 9 para 1(1)(b), (2). See also note 1.

6   Ie under the Education Reform Act 1988 Sch 9 paras 1–3.

7   As to the meaning of 'member state' see the Interpretation Act 1978 s 5, Sch 1; and the European Communities Act 1972 s 1(2), Sch 1 Pt II.

8   Education Reform Act 1988 Sch 9 para 5.

B. CONSTITUTION AND GOVERNANCE

(A) Corporations Established Before 6 May 1992

652. Initial constitution. A higher education corporation[1] established[2] before 6 May 1992[3] was required to consist of not less than 12 and not more than 24 members[4] and the person who was for the time being the principal of the institution[5], unless he chose not to be a member[6]. Of the appointed members:

(1) up to 13 had to be persons appearing to the appointing authority[7] to have experience of, and to have shown capacity in, industrial, commercial or employment matters or the practice of any profession[8];

(2) not less than four and not more than eight had to be persons nominated[9] otherwise than by other members of the corporation[10]; and

(3) at least one and not more than four had to be persons nominated[11] by the members of the corporation who were either independent members or initial nominee members and the principal of the institution (if he was a member)[12].

It was for the appointing authority to determine any question as to whether any person was qualified[13] for appointment as a member of a corporation of any description or category[14].

The provisions described above[15] are subject to the provisions relating to the subsequent determination of membership numbers[16]. The provisions relating to the constitution of higher education corporations[17] do not have effect in relation to a higher education corporation established before 6 May 1992 if an instrument of government[18] for the corporation has effect[19].

1 As to the meaning of 'higher education corporation' see PARA 645.

2 Ie under the Education Reform Act 1988 s 121 (see PARA 646) or s 122 (see PARA 647).

3 Ie the appointed day: see the Education Reform Act 1988 s 123(3), (4) (s 123(3) substituted, s 123(4) added, by the Further and Higher Education Act 1992 s 93(1), Sch 8 paras 27, 32(b)); the Education Reform Act 1988 s 124A(10) (added by the Further and Higher Education Act 1992 s 71(1)); and the Further and Higher Education Act 1992 (Commencement No 1 and Transitional Provisions) Order 1992, SI 1992/831. As to the constitution and government of higher education corporations established after 6 May 1992 see PARA 657 et seq.

4 Ie appointed in accordance with the provisions of the Education Reform Act 1988 Sch 7 paras 3–18 (see the text to notes 5–16; and PARAS 653–656).

5 References, in relation to a corporation, to the institution are references: (1) in relation to any time before the transfer date applicable in relation to the corporation, to the institution the corporation is established to conduct (Education Reform Act 1988 Sch 7 para 1(3)(b)(i)); and (2) in relation to any later time, to any institution for the time being conducted by the corporation in exercise of its powers under the Education Reform Act 1988 (Sch 7 para 1(3)(b)(ii)). As to the meaning of 'the transfer date' see PARA 647 note 7.

6 Education Reform Act 1988 Sch 7 paras 1(3)(a), 3(1). The members of the corporation for the time being were known as the board of governors of the institution: Sch 7 para 3(3).

7 The Secretary of State was the appointing authority for the purposes of the Education Reform Act 1988 Sch 7 in relation to the appointment of the first members of a corporation: Sch 7 para 5(1). As to the Secretary of State see PARA 58.

8 Education Reform Act 1988 Sch 7 para 3(2)(a). These members are known as 'the independent members': see Sch 7 para 3(2)(a). In the case of any corporation, a person who was employed at the institution (whether or not as a teacher), a full-time student at the institution, or an elected member of any local authority, was not eligible for appointment as an independent member or as an additional nominee member (see note 12) of the corporation: Sch 7 para 4(4). For these purposes, a person who was not for the time being enrolled as a student at an institution was to be treated as such a student during any period when he was granted leave of absence from the institution for the purposes of study or travel or for carrying out the duties of any office held by him in the student union at the institution: Sch 7 para 4(5). In Sch 7 para 4, 'local authority' includes a non-metropolitan district council for an area for which there is a county council: Sch 7 para 4(8) (added by SI 2010/1158). As to the meaning of 'local authority' generally see

PARA 25 (definition applied by the Education Reform Act 1988 s 235(7) (amended by the Education Act 1996 s 582(1), Sch 37 para 81(4))).

In determining the number of members to appoint within each 'variable category of members' (ie independent members, initial nominee members and additional nominee members), the Secretary of State was required to secure that at least half of all the members of the corporation as first constituted were independent members: Education Reform Act 1988 Sch 7 paras 2(2), 5(2).

9 Ie in accordance with the Education Reform Act 1988 Sch 7.

10 Education Reform Act 1988 Sch 7 para 3(2)(b). These members, known as 'the initial nominee members', were to consist of at least one and not more than three local authority nominees, one teacher nominee, one general staff nominee, and one student nominee, and could include up to two academic nominees: Sch 7 paras 3(2)(b), 4(1). 'Local authority nominee' means a person, other than a person employed at the institution (whether or not as a teacher) or a student at the institution, nominated by a local authority specified in relation to the corporation in an order made by the Secretary of State; 'teacher nominee' means a teacher at the institution nominated by the teachers at the institution; 'general staff nominee' means a person employed at the institution otherwise than as a teacher and nominated by the persons so employed; 'student nominee' means a student at the institution nominated by the students at the institution; and 'academic nominee' means a teacher at the institution nominated by the academic board: Sch 7 para 4(2). As to the meaning of 'employed' see PARA 301 note 2. Before making an order specifying local authorities in relation to any corporation for the purposes of Sch 7 para 4(1)(a), the Secretary of State was required to consult such associations of local authorities as appeared to him to be concerned: Sch 7 para 4(7). Such orders, being of local effect, are not recorded in this work.

11 Ie in accordance with the Education Reform Act 1988 Sch 7. See also note 8.

12 Education Reform Act 1988 Sch 7 para 3(2)(c). These members are known as 'the additional nominee members', and of those members, the one required by Sch 7 para 3(2)(c) had to be a person who had experience in the provision of education, and the three others permitted by that provision were one person who had such experience and two persons who did not need not to have such experience: Sch 7 paras 3(2)(c), 4(3). See also note 8.

13 Ie in accordance with the Education Reform Act 1988 Sch 7 para 4(1)–(5): see the text to notes 8, 10, 12.

14 Education Reform Act 1988 Sch 7 para 4(6).

15 Ie the provisions of the Education Reform Act 1988 Sch 7 paras 3–4: see the text to notes 1–14.

16 Education Reform Act 1988 Sch 7 para 2(1). The provisions mentioned in the text, relating to the subsequent determination of membership numbers, are those contained in Sch 7 para 6: see PARA 653.

17 Ie the Education Reform Act 1988 Sch 7.

18 Ie an instrument of government made under the Education Reform Act 1988 s 124A: see PARA 657.

19 See the Education Reform Act 1988 s 123(3) (as substituted: see note 3).

653. Membership. Following the appointment by the Secretary of State[1] of the first members of a higher education corporation[2] established[3] before 6 May 1992[4], the corporation was required to make a determination[5] with respect to its membership numbers[6]. Such a determination had to fix the number of members of each variable category[7] of which the corporation was to consist, subject to the applicable limits[8]. In making a determination, the corporation was required to secure that at least half of all the members of the corporation, when constituted in accordance with the determination, would be independent members[9]. A determination could not have effect so as to terminate the appointment of any person who was a member of the corporation at the time when it took effect[10], and could be varied by a subsequent determination[11].

These provisions[12] do not have effect in relation to a higher education corporation established before 6 May 1992 if an instrument of government[13] for the corporation has effect[14].

1 Ie under the Education Reform Act 1988 Sch 7 paras 3–4: see PARA 652. As to the Secretary of State see PARA 58.

2 As to the meaning of 'higher education corporation' see PARA 645.

3 Ie under the Education Reform Act 1988 s 121 (see PARA 646) or s 122 (see PARA 647).
4 Ie the appointed day: see the Education Reform Act 1988 s 123(3), (4) (s 123(3) substituted, s 123(4) added, by the Further and Higher Education Act 1992 s 93(1), Sch 8 paras 27, 32(b)); the Education Reform Act 1988 s 124A(10) (added by the Further and Higher Education Act 1992 s 71(1)); and the Further and Higher Education Act 1992 (Commencement No 1 and Transitional Provisions) Order 1992, SI 1992/831. As to the constitution and government of higher education corporations established after 6 May 1992 see PARAS 657–663.
5 Ie under the Education Reform Act 1988 Sch 7 para 6.
6 Education Reform Act 1988 Sch 7 para 6(1). No member could be appointed to the corporation at any time after the appointment by the Secretary of State of the first members before the first determination of the corporation under Sch 7 para 6 took effect: see Sch 7 para 7(1), (2). As to the qualifications of members and tenure of office see Sch 7 paras 7(5)–(8), 8–10. As to the payment of allowances to members see Sch 7 para 11. As to the election of a chairman see Sch 7 para 12.
7 As to the meaning of 'variable category of members' see PARA 652 note 8.
8 Education Reform Act 1988 Sch 7 para 6(2). The applicable limits are those set out in Sch 7 paras 3–4 (see PARA 652): see Sch 7 para 6(2).
9 Education Reform Act 1988 Sch 7 para 6(3). As to the meaning of 'independent member' see PARA 652 note 8. Where an appointment of an additional independent member of the corporation fell to be made in consequence of a determination under Sch 7 para 6, the appointing authority for the purposes of Sch 7 in relation to the appointment was required to be the corporation if the appointment was made within the period of three months beginning with the date of the determination (Sch 7 para 7(4)(a)) or, if the appointment was not made within that period, was required to be the current independent members of the corporation (Sch 7 para 7(4)(b)). No appointment of an independent member of the corporation by the corporation under Sch 7 para 7(4)(a) could be made unless the appointment had been approved by the current independent members of the corporation: Sch 7 para 7(7).
10 Education Reform Act 1988 Sch 7 para 6(4).
11 Education Reform Act 1988 Sch 7 para 6(5). The subsequent determination referred to in the text is a determination under Sch 7 para 6: see Sch 7 para 6(5).
12 Ie the Education Reform Act 1988 Sch 7.
13 Ie an instrument of government made under the Education Reform Act 1988 s 124A: see PARA 657.
14 See the Education Reform Act 1988 s 123(3) (as substituted: see note 4).

654. The appointing authority. The appointing authority in relation to the appointment of any member (other than an independent member[1]) of a higher education corporation[2] established[3] before 6 May 1992[4], at any time after the appointment by the Secretary of State of the first members[5], is the corporation[6].

These provisions[7] do not have effect in relation to a higher education corporation established before 6 May 1992 if an instrument of government[8] for the corporation has effect[9].

1 As to the meaning of 'independent member' see PARA 652 note 8. Special provision is made as to the appointing authority for the appointment of independent members in the following circumstances:
  (1) where an appointment of an additional independent member falls to be made in consequence of a determination under the Education Reform Act 1988 Sch 7 para 6 (see Sch 7 para 7(4), (7); and PARA 653);
  (2) where a vacancy in the office of an independent member arises on the death of any such member (see Sch 7 para 7(6), (7); and PARA 653);
  (3) where a vacancy in the office of an independent member arises on any existing independent member ceasing to hold office on the expiry of his term of office (see Sch 7 para 7(5), (7); and PARA 653);
  (4) where a vacancy in the office of an independent member arises on any such member resigning his office (see Sch 7 para 7(6), (7); and PARA 653); and
  (5) where a vacancy in the office of an independent member arises on any such member being removed from office by the corporation (see Sch 7 para 7(6); and PARA 653).
  Additionally, if the number of independent members of the corporation falls below the number needed in accordance with its articles of government for a quorum, the Secretary of State or, in relation to Wales, the Welsh Ministers is the appointing authority in relation to the appointment

of such number of independent members as is required for a quorum: Sch 7 para 7(8) (added by the Further and Higher Education Act 1992 s 71(3)(a)). As to the Secretary of State see PARA 58. As to the Welsh Ministers see PARA 59. As to the meaning of 'Wales' see PARA 7 note 3. The functions of the Secretary of State under the Education Reform Act 1988 Sch 7, so far as exercisable in relation to Wales, were transferred to the National Assembly for Wales (see the National Assembly for Wales (Transfer of Functions) Order 1999, SI 1999/672, art 2, Sch 1) and are now vested in the Welsh Ministers (see the Government of Wales Act 2006 s 162(1), Sch 11 para 30).

2   As to the meaning of 'higher education corporation' see PARA 645.
3   Ie under the Education Reform Act 1988 s 121 (see PARA 646) or s 122 (see PARA 647).
4   Ie the appointed day: see the Education Reform Act 1988 s 123(3), (4) (s 123(3) substituted, s 123(4) added, by the Further and Higher Education Act 1992 s 93(1), Sch 8 paras 27, 32(b)); the Education Reform Act 1988 s 124A(10) (added by the Further and Higher Education Act 1992 s 71(1)); and the Further and Higher Education Act 1992 (Commencement No 1 and Transitional Provisions) Order 1992, SI 1992/831. As to the constitution and government of higher education corporations established after 6 May 1992 see PARAS 657–663.
5   Ie under the Education Reform Act 1988 Sch 7 paras 3–4: see PARA 652.
6   Education Reform Act 1988 Sch 7 para 7(1), (3).
7   Ie the Education Reform Act 1988 Sch 7.
8   Ie an instrument of government made under the Education Reform Act 1988 s 124A: see PARA 657.
9   See the Education Reform Act 1988 s 123(3) (as substituted: see note 4).

655.   Committees and proceedings. A higher education corporation[1] established[2] before 6 May 1992[3] may establish a committee for any purpose[4]. The number of members of a committee so established, which may include persons who are not members of the corporation, and the terms on which they are to hold and vacate office, must be fixed by the corporation[5].

The validity of any proceedings of a corporation or of any committee of a corporation is not affected by a vacancy amongst the members or by any defect in the appointment or nomination of a member[6]. In the event of an equality of votes at any meeting of a corporation the chairman of the corporation[7] has a second or casting vote[8].

These provisions[9] do not have effect in relation to a higher education corporation established before 6 May 1992 if an instrument of government[10] for the corporation has effect[11].

1   As to the meaning of 'higher education corporation' see PARA 645.
2   Ie under the Education Reform Act 1988 s 121 (see PARA 646) or s 122 (see PARA 647).
3   Ie the appointed day: see the Education Reform Act 1988 s 123(3), (4) (s 123(3) substituted, s 123(4) added, by the Further and Higher Education Act 1992 s 93(1), Sch 8 paras 27, 32(b)); the Education Reform Act 1988 s 124A(10) (added by the Further and Higher Education Act 1992 s 71(1)); and the Further and Higher Education Act 1992 (Commencement No 1 and Transitional Provisions) Order 1992, SI 1992/831. As to the constitution and government of higher education corporations established after 6 May 1992 see PARAS 657–663.
4   Education Reform Act 1988 Sch 7 para 13(1).
5   Education Reform Act 1988 Sch 7 para 13(2), (3).
6   Education Reform Act 1988 Sch 7 para 14.
7   As to the election of the chairman see PARA 653.
8   Education Reform Act 1988 Sch 7 para 15.
9   Ie the Education Reform Act 1988 Sch 7.
10 Ie an instrument of government made under the Education Reform Act 1988 s 124A: see PARA 657.
11 See the Education Reform Act 1988 s 123(3) (as substituted: see note 3).

656.   Application of seal and proof of instruments. The application of the seal of a higher education corporation[1] established[2] before 6 May 1992[3] must be authenticated by the signature of the chairman[4] of the corporation or of some other member authorised either generally or specially by the corporation to act for that purpose together with that of any other member[5]. Every document purporting to be an instrument made or issued by or on behalf of a corporation and to be duly executed under the seal of the corporation, or to be signed or executed by a person authorised by the corporation to act in that behalf, is to be received in evidence and be treated, without further proof, as being so made or issued unless the contrary is shown[6].

These provisions[7] do not have effect in relation to a higher education corporation established before 6 May 1992 if an instrument of government[8] for the corporation has effect[9].

1 As to the meaning of 'higher education corporation' see PARA 645.
2 Ie under the Education Reform Act 1988 s 121 (see PARA 646) or s 122 (see PARA 647).
3 Ie the appointed day: see the Education Reform Act 1988 s 123(3), (4) (s 123(3) substituted, s 123(4) added, by the Further and Higher Education Act 1992 s 93(1), Sch 8 paras 27, 32(b)); the Education Reform Act 1988 s 124A(10) (added by the Further and Higher Education Act 1992 s 71(1)); and the Further and Higher Education Act 1992 (Commencement No 1 and Transitional Provisions) Order 1992, SI 1992/831. As to the constitution and government of higher education corporations established after 6 May 1992 see PARAS 657–663.
4 As to the election of the chairman see PARA 653.
5 Education Reform Act 1988 Sch 7 para 16.
6 Education Reform Act 1988 Sch 7 para 17.
7 Ie the Education Reform Act 1988 Sch 7.
8 Ie an instrument of government made under the Education Reform Act 1988 s 124A: see PARA 657.
9 See the Education Reform Act 1988 s 123(3) (as substituted: see note 3).

(B) Corporations Established After 6 May 1992 and Other Corporations Constituted by Instruments of Government

657. Instruments of government. For each higher education corporation[1] established[2] on or after 6 May 1992[3] there must be an instrument (known as the 'instrument of government') providing for the constitution of the corporation and making such other provision as is required[4]. The initial instrument of government of a higher education corporation so established must be such as is prescribed by an order of the Privy Council[5]. An order of the Privy Council may: (1) make an instrument of government of any higher education corporation established before 6 May 1992[6] or make a new instrument of government of any higher education corporation in place of the instrument prescribed under the provisions above[7]; or (2) modify[8] an instrument made in pursuance of head (1) above[9].

An instrument of government of a higher education corporation must comply with specified requirements[10] and may make any authorised provision[11] and such other provision as may be necessary or desirable[12].

1 As to the meaning of 'higher education corporation' see PARA 645.
2 Ie under the Education Reform Act 1988 s 122: see PARA 647.
3 Ie the appointed day: see the Education Reform Act 1988 s 124A(10) (s 124A added by the Further and Higher Education Act 1992 s 71(1)); and the Further and Higher Education Act 1992 (Commencement No 1 and Transitional Provisions) Order 1992, SI 1992/831.
4 Education Reform Act 1988 s 124A(1) (as added: see note 3). The provision referred to is that required under s 124A: see s 124A(1) (as so added).
5 Education Reform Act 1988 s 124A(2) (as added: see note 3). An order under s 124A(2) or (3) (see the text to notes 6–7) may make such provision as appears to the Privy Council necessary or desirable to secure continuity in the government of the institution or institutions to which it relates: s 124A(5) (as so added). Such orders, being of local effect, are not recorded in this work.
   A power vested in the Privy Council under Pt II (ss 120–161) may be exercised by any two or more of the Lords and others of the Council: s 124D(1), (2) (ss 124C, 124D added by the Further and Higher Education Act 1992 s 71(1)). An act of the Privy Council is sufficiently

signified by an instrument signed by the clerk of the Council: Education Reform Act 1988 s 124D(3) (as so added). An order or act signified by an instrument purporting to be signed by the clerk of the Council is deemed to have been duly made or done by the Privy Council: s 124D(4) (as so added). An instrument so signed is to be received in evidence in all courts and proceedings without proof of the authority or signature of the clerk of the Council or other proof: s 124D(5) (as so added). As to the Privy Council see CONSTITUTIONAL AND ADMINISTRATIVE LAW vol 20 (2014) PARA 268 et seq.

6   Ie a higher education corporation with respect to which the Education Reform Act 1988 Sch 7 has effect: see PARA 652 et seq. Where an instrument of government is made under s 124A for a higher education corporation with respect to which Sch 7 has effect (s 124C(3) (as so added)), the instrument applies, subject to s 124C(5) below, as if the persons who, immediately before its coming into effect, were the members of the corporation had been appointed in accordance with the instrument for the residue of the term of their then subsisting appointment (s 124C(4) (as so added)). Any local authority nominee, teacher nominee, general staff nominee or student nominee (within the meaning, in each case, of Sch 7: see PARA 652 note 10) ceases to hold office: s 124C(5) (as so added).

7   Education Reform Act 1988 s 124A(3)(a) (as added: see note 3). See also note 5.

8   As to the meaning of 'modify' see PARA 631 note 2.

9   Education Reform Act 1988 s 124A(3)(b) (as added: see note 3).

10 Ie the requirements of the Education Reform Act 1988 Sch 7A (see PARAS 658–662): s 124A(4)(a) (as added: see note 3).

11 Ie any provision authorised by the Education Reform Act 1988 Sch 7A: see PARAS 658–662.

12 Education Reform Act 1988 s 124A(4)(b) (as added: see note 3).

658.   Power to provide for change of name.   The instrument of government[1] of a higher education corporation[2] must empower the corporation to change its name with the consent of the Privy Council[3].

1   Ie an instrument of government made under the Education Reform Act 1988 s 124A: see PARA 657.

2   As to the meaning of 'higher education corporation' see PARA 645.

3   Education Reform Act 1988 Sch 7A para 1 (Sch 7A added by the Further and Higher Education Act 1992 s 71(4), Sch 6)). See further PARA 622.

659.   Membership of the corporation.   The instrument of government[1] of a higher education corporation[2] must make provision for the membership of the corporation[3] whereby the corporation is to consist of not less than 12 and not more than 24 members[4] and the person who is for the time being the principal of the institution, unless he chooses not to be a member[5]. Of the appointed members:

(1)   up to 13 (known as 'independent members') must be persons appearing to the appointing authority[6] to have experience of, and to have shown capacity in, industrial, commercial or employment matters or the practice of any profession[7];

(2)   up to two may be teachers at the institution nominated by the academic board and up to two may be students at the institution nominated by the students[8] at the institution[9]; and

(3)   at least one and not more than nine (known as 'co-opted members') must be persons nominated by the members of the corporation who are not co-opted members[10].

A person (other than a person appointed in pursuance of head (2) above) is not eligible for appointment as a member of the corporation, otherwise than as a co-opted member, if he is employed[11] at the institution (whether or not as a teacher), or is a full-time student at the institution, or is an elected member of any local authority[12]. It is for the appointing authority to determine any question as to whether any person is qualified[13] for appointment as a member of the corporation of any description or category[14].

1 Ie the instrument of government made under the Education Reform Act 1988 s 124A: see PARA 657.

2 As to the meaning of 'higher education corporation' see PARA 645.

3 The instrument must make provision for the membership of the corporation which meets all the requirements of the Education Reform Act 1988 Sch 7A paras 3–5 (see the text to notes 4–12, and PARAS 660, 661): Sch 7A para 2 (Sch 7A added by the Further and Higher Education Act 1992 s 71(4), Sch 6).

4 Ie appointed in accordance with the Education Reform Act 1988 Sch 7A para 3: see Sch 7A para 3(1)(a) (as added: see note 3). The Secretary of State or, in relation to Wales, the Welsh Ministers may by order amend or repeal Sch 7A para 3: s 124A(9) (s 124A added by the Further and Higher Education Act 1992 s 71(1)). As to the Secretary of State see PARA 58. As to the Welsh Ministers see PARA 59. As to the meaning of 'Wales' see PARA 7 note 3. The functions of the Secretary of State under the Education Reform Act 1988 s 124A, Sch 7A, so far as exercisable in relation to Wales, were transferred to the National Assembly for Wales (see the National Assembly for Wales (Transfer of Functions) Order 1999, SI 1999/672, art 2, Sch 1) and are now vested in the Welsh Ministers (see the Government of Wales Act 2006 s 162(1), Sch 11 para 30).

5 Education Reform Act 1988 Sch 7A para 3(1)(b) (as added: see note 3).

6 As to the appointing authority see PARA 661.

7 Education Reform Act 1988 Sch 7A para 3(2)(a) (as added: see note 3).

8 A person who is not for the time being enrolled as a student at the institution must be treated as such a student during any period when he has been granted leave of absence from the institution for the purposes of study or travel or for carrying out the duties of any office held by him in the student union at the institution: Education Reform Act 1988 Sch 7A para 3(5) (as added: see note 3).

9 Education Reform Act 1988 Sch 7A para 3(2)(b) (as added: see note 3).

10 Education Reform Act 1988 Sch 7A para 3(2)(c) (as added: see note 3). The co-opted member required by Sch 7A para 3(2)(c) must be a person who has experience in the provision of education: Sch 7A para 3(3) (as so added).

11 As to the meaning of 'employed' see PARA 301 note 2.

12 Education Reform Act 1988 Sch 7A para 3(4) (as added: see note 3). For these purposes, 'local authority' includes a non-metropolitan district council for an area for which there is a county council: Sch 7A para 3(7) (Sch 7A as so added; Sch 7A para 3(7) added by SI 2010/1158). As to the meaning of 'local authority' generally see PARA 25 (definition applied by the Education Reform Act 1988 s 235(7) (amended by the Education Act 1996 s 582(1), Sch 37 para 81(4)). As to local government areas and authorities in England and Wales see LOCAL GOVERNMENT vol 69 (2009) PARA 22 et seq.

13 Ie in accordance with the Education Reform Act 1988 Sch 7A para 3(1)–(5): see the text to notes 1–12.

14 Education Reform Act 1988 Sch 7A para 3(6) (as added: see note 3).

660. Membership numbers and appointments. The instrument of government[1] of a higher education corporation[2] must make provision for the membership of the corporation[3] whereby the corporation must make a determination with respect to its membership numbers[4]. Such a determination must fix the number of members of each variable category[5] of which the corporation is to consist, subject to the applicable limits[6]. In making such a determination, the corporation must secure that at least half of all the members of the corporation, when constituted in accordance with the determination, will be independent members[7]. Such a determination does not have effect so as to terminate the appointment of any person who is a member of the corporation at the time when it takes effect[8], and may be varied by a subsequent determination[9].

No appointment of members may be made before the first determination of the corporation[10] takes effect[11].

1 Ie the instrument of government made under the Education Reform Act 1988 s 124A: see PARA 657.

2 As to the meaning of 'higher education corporation' see PARA 645.

3   The instrument must make provision for the membership of the corporation which meets all the requirements of the Education Reform Act 1988 Sch 7A paras 3–5 (see the text to notes 4–11, and PARAS 659, 661): Sch 7A para 2 (Sch 7A added by the Further and Higher Education Act 1992 s 71(4), Sch 6).

4   Education Reform Act 1988 Sch 7A para 4(1) (as added: see note 3). The Secretary of State or, in relation to Wales, the Welsh Ministers may by order amend or repeal the Education Reform Act 1988 Sch 7A paras 4, 5, 11: see s 124A(9) (s 124A added by the Further and Higher Education Act 1992 s 71(1)). As to the Secretary of State see PARA 58. As to the Welsh Ministers see PARA 59. As to the meaning of 'Wales' see PARA 7 note 3. The functions of the Secretary of State under the Education Reform Act 1988 s 124A, Sch 7A, so far as exercisable in relation to Wales, were transferred to the National Assembly for Wales (see the National Assembly for Wales (Transfer of Functions) Order 1999, SI 1999/672, art 2, Sch 1) and are now vested in the Welsh Ministers (see the Government of Wales Act 2006 s 162(1), Sch 11 para 30).

5   References in the Education Reform Act 1988 Sch 7A, in relation to a corporation, to a variable category of members are references to any category of members in relation to which the number applicable in accordance with Sch 7A para 3 (see PARA 659) is subject to variation: Sch 7A para 11 (as added: see note 3).

6   Education Reform Act 1988 Sch 7A para 4(2) (as added: see note 3). The applicable limits are those set out in Sch 7A para 3 (see PARA 659): see Sch 7A para 4(2) (as so added).

7   Education Reform Act 1988 Sch 7A para 4(3) (as added: see note 3). As to the independent members of a corporation see PARA 659.

8   Education Reform Act 1988 Sch 7A para 4(4) (as added: see note 3).

9   Education Reform Act 1988 Sch 7A para 4(5) (as added: see note 3).

10   Ie under Education Reform Act 1988 Sch 7A para 4: see the text to notes 1–9.

11   Education Reform Act 1988 Sch 7A para 5(1) (as added: see note 3). This requirement is stated to be subject to s 124C (see PARAS 657 note 6, 661): see Sch 7A para 5(1) (as so added).

661.   The appointing authority. The appointing authority in relation to the appointment of the first members of a higher education corporation[1] established[2] on or after 6 May 1992[3] is the appropriate national authority[4] and, in determining the number of members to appoint within each variable category of members[5], it must secure that at least half of all the members of the corporation as first constituted are independent members[6].

The instrument of government of a higher education corporation must make provision for the membership of the corporation[7] whereby the appointing authority in relation to the appointment of any member (other than an independent member[8]) of the corporation is the corporation[9].

1   As to the meaning of 'higher education corporation' see PARA 645.

2   Ie under the Education Reform Act 1988 s 122: see PARA 647.

3   Ie the appointed day: see the Education Reform Act 1988 s 124A(10) (ss 124A, 124C both added by the Further and Higher Education Act 1992 s 71(1)); and the Further and Higher Education Act 1992 (Commencement No 1 and Transitional Provisions) Order 1992, SI 1992/831.

4   Ie the Secretary of State or, in relation to Wales, the Welsh Ministers. As to the Secretary of State see PARA 58. As to the Welsh Ministers see PARA 59. As to the meaning of 'Wales' see PARA 7 note 3. The functions of the Secretary of State under the Education Reform Act 1988 s 124C, Sch 7A, so far as exercisable in relation to Wales, were transferred to the National Assembly for Wales (see the National Assembly for Wales (Transfer of Functions) Order 1999, SI 1999/672, art 2, Sch 1) and are now vested in the Welsh Ministers (see the Government of Wales Act 2006 s 162(1), Sch 11 para 30).

5   As to the meaning of 'variable category of members' see PARA 660 note 5 (definition applied by the Education Reform Act 1988 s 124C(2) (as added: see note 3)).

6   Education Reform Act 1988 s 124C(1) (as added: see note 3). As to independent members see PARA 659.

7   The instrument must make provision for the membership of the corporation which meets all the requirements of the Education Reform Act 1988 Sch 7A paras 3–5 (see the text to notes 8–9, and PARAS 659, 660): Sch 7A para 2 (Sch 7A added by the Further and Higher Education Act 1992 s 71(4), Sch 6).

8   Special provision is made as to the appointing authority for the appointment of independent members in the following circumstances:

(1)   where an appointment of an additional independent member falls to be made in consequence of a determination under the Education Reform Act 1988 Sch 7A para 4 (see PARA 660), the appointing authority in relation to the appointment is, if the appointment is made within the period of three months beginning with the date of the determination, the corporation (Sch 7A para 5(3)(a) (as added: see note 7)), or, if the appointment is not made within that period, is the current independent members of the corporation (Sch 7A para 5(3)(b) (as so added));

(2)   where a vacancy in the office of an independent member arises on any existing independent member ceasing to hold office on the expiry of his term of office, the appointing authority in relation to the appointment of the member's successor is, if the appointment is made not less than three months before the expiry of that term, the corporation (Sch 7A para 5(4)(b)(i) (as so added)) or, if the appointment is not so made, is the current independent members of the corporation (Sch 7A para 5(4)(b)(ii) (as so added)); and in these circumstances the member's successor must not be appointed more than six months before the expiry of that term (Sch 7A para 5(4)(a) (as so added));

(3)   where a vacancy in the office of an independent member arises on the death of any such member or on any such member ceasing to hold office in accordance with the instrument of government, the appointing authority in relation to the appointment of the member's successor is, if the appointment is made within the period of three months beginning with the date of death or the date on which the office becomes vacant (as the case may be), the corporation (Sch 7A para 5(5)(a) (as so added)), or, if the appointment is not made within that period, is the current independent members of the corporation (Sch 7A para 5(5)(b) (as so added)).

No appointment of an independent member by the corporation in accordance with Sch 7A paras 5(3)(a), (4)(b)(i) or (5)(a) may be made unless the appointment has been approved by the current independent members of the corporation: Sch 7A para 5(6) (as so added). As to the meaning of 'month' see PARA 54 note 26.

Additionally, if the number of independent members of the corporation falls below the number needed in accordance with its articles of government for a quorum, the appropriate national authority is the appointing authority in relation to the appointment of such number of independent members as is required for a quorum: Sch 7A para 5(7) (as so added).

9   Education Reform Act 1988 Sch 7A para 5(2) (as added: see note 7). This provision is stated to be subject to s 124C (see the text to notes 1–6): see Sch 7A para 5(2) (as so added). The appropriate national authority may by order amend or repeal Sch 7A para 5: see s 124A(9) (as added: see note 3).

662.   Procedural requirements.   The instrument of government[1] of a higher education corporation[2] may[3] provide for the eligibility of persons for membership of the corporation and must provide for their period of office and the circumstances in which they are to cease to hold office[4]. The instrument must provide for one or more officers to be chosen from among the members[5] and may provide for the corporation to establish committees and permit such committees to include persons who are not members of the corporation[6]. The instrument may also provide for the corporation to pay allowances to its members[7]; and must provide for the authentication of the application of the seal of the corporation[8].

1   Ie the instrument of government made under the Education Reform Act 1988 s 124A: see PARA 657.
2   As to the meaning of 'higher education corporation' see PARA 645.
3   Ie subject to any other requirements of the Education Reform Act 1988.
4   Education Reform Act 1988 Sch 7A para 6 (Sch 7A added by the Further and Higher Education Act 1992 s 71(4), Sch 6). As to membership of a corporation see PARAS 659–660.
5   Education Reform Act 1988 Sch 7A para 7 (as added: see note 4).
6   Education Reform Act 1988 Sch 7A para 8 (as added: see note 4).
7   Education Reform Act 1988 Sch 7A para 9 (as added: see note 4).
8   Education Reform Act 1988 Sch 7A para 10 (as added: see note 4). As to proof of documents see PARA 663.

663. Proof of documents and validity of proceedings. The validity of any proceedings of a higher education corporation[1] for which an instrument of government has effect[2], or of any committee of such a corporation[3], is not affected by a vacancy amongst the members or by any defect in the appointment or nomination of a member[4]. Every document purporting to be an instrument made or issued by or on behalf of a higher education corporation for which an instrument of government has effect and purporting to be duly executed under the seal of the corporation[5], or to be signed or executed by a person authorised by the corporation to act in that behalf, must be received in evidence and treated, without further proof, as being so made or issued unless the contrary is shown[6]. In relation to a higher education corporation for which an instrument of government has effect, the members of the corporation for the time being are known as the board of governors of the institution conducted by the corporation[7].

1   As to the meaning of 'higher education corporation' see PARA 645.
2   Ie the instrument of government made under the Education Reform Act 1988 s 124A: see PARA 657.
3   As to the power to appoint committees see PARA 662.
4   Education Reform Act 1988 s 124A(6) (s 124A added by the Further and Higher Education Act 1992 s 71(1)). As to membership of a corporation see PARAS 659–660.
5   As to the authentication of documents by the application of the seal of the corporation see PARA 662.
6   Education Reform Act 1988 s 124A(7) (as added: see note 4).
7   Education Reform Act 1988 s 124A(8) (as added: see note 4).

C. POWERS AND DUTIES

664. Conduct of institutions in accordance with articles of government. Any institution conducted by a higher education corporation[1] must be conducted in accordance with articles of government, to be made by the corporation with the approval of the Privy Council[2]. The articles of government:

(1)   must determine the functions[3] to be exercised in relation to the institution by the board of governors[4] of the institution, the principal of the institution and the academic board of the institution[5]; and

(2)   may regulate the constitution and functions of committees of the corporation[6] and of the academic board of the institution and provide for the delegation of functions of the board of governors and the academic board to such committees, to the chairman of the corporation or to the principal[7].

The articles of government must also make provision with respect to the procedure for meetings of the board of governors, of the academic board and of committees of the corporation and the procedure in relation to the appointment of members of the corporation (including in either case quorum and proxies)[8]; and may make provision with respect to:

(a)   procedures for the appointment, promotion, suspension and dismissal of staff[9];

(b)   procedures for the admission, suspension and expulsion of students[10]; and

(c)   the appointment and functions of a clerk to the board of governors[11].

The articles of government may also make provision authorising the board of governors to make rules or byelaws for the government and conduct of the institution[12], including in particular rules or byelaws with respect to the conduct of students and staff (or either of them)[13] and any procedures mentioned in head (a) or head (b) above[14].

The Privy Council may[15] require higher education corporations, any class of such corporations specified in the direction, or any particular higher education corporation so specified, to amend their articles of government, or to secure that any rules or byelaws made in pursuance of their articles of government are amended by the board of governors, in any manner so specified[16].

1 As to the meaning of 'higher education corporation' see PARA 645.
2 Education Reform Act 1988 s 125(1) (s 125(1), (5)–(7) amended by the Further and Higher Education Act 1992 s 71(2)). Articles of government made under the Education Reform Act 1988 s 125 may be varied or revoked by subsequent articles made by the corporation with the approval of the Privy Council: s 125(5) (as so amended). As to the exercise of the powers of the Privy Council under the Education Reform Act 1988 Pt II (ss 120–161) see PARA 657 note 5. As to the Privy Council see CONSTITUTIONAL AND ADMINISTRATIVE LAW vol 20 (2014) PARA 268 et seq.
3 As to the meaning of 'functions' see PARA 590 note 2.
4 As to the board of governors of an institution see PARAS 652 note 6, 663.
5 Education Reform Act 1988 s 125(2)(a).
6 As to the power to establish committees see PARAS 655, 662.
7 Education Reform Act 1988 s 125(2)(b).
8 Education Reform Act 1988 s 125(3). As to the membership of corporations see PARAS 653, 659.
9 Education Reform Act 1988 s 125(3)(a).
10 Education Reform Act 1988 s 125(3)(b).
11 Education Reform Act 1988 s 125(3)(c).
12 Education Reform Act 1988 s 125(4).
13 Education Reform Act 1988 s 125(4)(a).
14 Education Reform Act 1988 s 125(4)(b).
15 Ie by a direction under the Education Reform Act 1988 s 125: see s 125(6) (as amended: see note 2). Before giving such a direction, the Privy Council must consult the board of governors of the higher education corporation or (as the case may be) of each higher education corporation to which the direction applies: s 125(7) (as amended: see note 2). As to the exercise of the duty to consult see JUDICIAL REVIEW vol 61 (2010) PARA 627.
16 Education Reform Act 1988 s 125(6) (as amended: see note 2).

665. **Powers of a higher education corporation.** A higher education corporation[1] may:

(1) provide higher education[2];
(2) provide further education[3];
(3) provide secondary education[4] suitable to the requirements of persons who have attained the age of 14 years[5];
(4) provide education which is secondary education by virtue of the Education Act 1996[6];
(5) participate in the provision of secondary education at a school[7]; and
(6) carry out research and publish the results of the research or any other material arising out of or connected with it in such manner as it thinks fit[8].

A higher education corporation may also do anything which appears to it to be necessary or expedient for the purpose of or in connection with the exercise of any of the powers so conferred, including in particular:

(a) conducting an educational institution for the purpose of carrying on activities undertaken in exercise of any of those powers and, in particular, assuming the conduct as from the transfer date[9] applicable in relation to the corporation of the institution in respect of which the corporation is established and for that purpose to receive any property, rights and liabilities[10] transferred[11] to the corporation[12];

(b) providing facilities of any description appearing to the corporation to be necessary or expedient for the purposes of or in connection with carrying on any such activities (including boarding accommodation and recreational facilities for students and staff and facilities to meet the needs of students having learning difficulties)[13];

(c) supplying goods and services[14];

(d) acquiring and disposing of land[15] and other property[16];

(e) entering into contracts, including in particular contracts for the employment[17] of teachers and other staff for the purposes of or in connection with carrying on any such activities[18] and contracts with respect to the carrying on by the corporation of any such activities[19];

(f) to form, participate in forming or invest in a company for the purpose of carrying on any such activities[20];

(g) to form, participate in forming or otherwise become a member of a charitable incorporated organisation[21] for the purpose of carrying on any such activities[22];

(h) borrowing such sums as it thinks fit for the purposes of carrying on any activities it has power to carry on or meeting any liability transferred to it[23] and, in connection with such borrowing, granting any mortgage, charge or other security in respect of any land or other property of the corporation[24];

(i) investing any sums not immediately required for any of the purposes mentioned in head (h) above[25];

(j) accepting gifts of money, land or other property and applying it, or holding and administering it on trust for, any of those purposes[26]; and

(k) doing anything incidental to the conduct of an educational institution providing higher or further education[27], including in particular power to found scholarships or exhibitions[28] and to make grants and give prizes[29].

1   As to the meaning of 'higher education corporation' see PARA 645.
2   Education Reform Act 1988 s 124(1)(a). As to the meaning of 'higher education' see PARA 24.
3   Education Reform Act 1988 s 124(1)(b). As to the meaning of 'further education' see PARA 22 (definition applied by s 235(7) (amended by the Education Act 1996 s 582(1), Sch 37 para 81(4)).
4   As to the meaning of 'secondary education' see PARA 21 (definition applied by the Education Reform Act 1988 s 235(7) (amended by the Education Act 1996 s 582(1), Sch 37 para 81(4)).
5   Education Reform Act 1988 s 124(1)(ba) (s 124(1)(ba), (bb), (bc) added by the Learning and Skills Act 2000 s 142(2)(a); and the Education Reform Act 1988 s 124(1)(ba) amended by the Education Act 2002 s 215(1), Sch 21 para 8). As to the time at which a person attains a particular age see PARA 7 note 6. A higher education corporation may not provide education of a kind specified in the Education Reform Act 1988 s 124(1)(ba) unless it has consulted such local authorities as it considers appropriate: see s 124(1A) (added by the Learning and Skills Act 2000 s 142(2)(b); and amended by SI 2010/1158). As to the meaning of 'local authority' see PARA 25 (definition applied by the Education Reform Act 1988 s 235(7) (as amended: see note 4). As to the exercise of the duty to consult see JUDICIAL REVIEW vol 61 (2010) PARA 627.
6   Education Reform Act 1988 s 124(1)(bb) (as added: see note 5). The reference to secondary education in the text is a reference to education which is secondary education by virtue of the Education Act 1996 s 2(2B) (see PARA 21): see the Education Reform Act 1988 s 124(1)(bb) (as so added). A higher education corporation may not provide education of a kind specified in s 124(1)(bb) unless it has consulted such local authorities as it considers appropriate: see s 124(1A) (as added and amended: see note 5).

7 Education Reform Act 1988 s 124(1)(bc) (as added: see note 5). As to the meaning of 'school' see PARA 91 (definition applied by the Education Reform Act 1988 s 235(7) (as amended: see note 4).

8 Education Reform Act 1988 s 124(1)(c).

9 As to the meaning of 'transfer date' see PARA 647 note 7.

10 As to the meaning of 'liability' see PARA 84 note 11.

11 Ie under the Education Reform Act 1988 s 126: see PARA 649.

12 Education Reform Act 1988 s 124(2)(a).

13 Education Reform Act 1988 s 124(2)(b) (amended by the Further and Higher Education Act 1992 s 93, Sch 8 paras 27, 33(a); and the Learning and Skills Act 2000 ss 149, 153, Sch 9 paras 1, 15(a), Sch 11). For the purposes of the Education Reform Act 1988 s 124(2)(b) a person has a learning difficulty if he has a significantly greater difficulty in learning than the majority of persons of his age, or he has a disability which either prevents or hinders him from making use of facilities of a kind generally provided by institutions within the higher education sector for persons of his age: s 124(5) (added by the Learning and Skills Act 2000 ss 149, 153, Sch 9 paras 1, 15(a)). However, a person is not to be taken to have a learning difficulty solely because the language (or form of language) in which he is or will be taught is different from a language (or form of language) which has at any time been spoken in his home: Education Reform Act 1988 s 124(6) (added by the Learning and Skills Act 2000 ss 149, 153, Sch 9 paras 1, 15(a)). As to the meaning of 'institution within the higher education sector' see PARA 619. Generally as to learning difficulties under the Children and Families Act 2014 see also PARA 943.

14 Education Reform Act 1988 s 124(2)(c).

15 As to the meaning of 'land' see PARA 84 note 9.

16 Education Reform Act 1988 s 124(2)(d).

17 As to the meaning of 'contract of employment' see PARA 301 note 2.

18 Education Reform Act 1988 s 124(2)(e)(i).

19 Education Reform Act 1988 s 124(2)(e)(ii).

20 Education Reform Act 1988 s 124(2)(f) (s 124(2)(f) substituted, (fa) added, by the Further Education and Training Act 2007 s 26(1), (2)). The reference to investing in a company includes a reference to becoming a member of the company and to investing in it by the acquisition of any assets, securities or rights or otherwise: Education Reform Act 1988 s 124(7) (added by the Further Education and Training Act 2007 s 26(1), (3)).

21 Ie within the meaning of the Charities Act 2011 Pt 11 (ss 204–250): see CHARITIES vol 8 (2015) PARA 226 et seq.

22 Education Reform Act 1988 s 124(2)(fa) (as added (see note 20); and amended by the Charities Act 2011 Sch 7 para 49).

23 Ie under the Education Reform Act 1988 s 126: see PARA 649.

24 Education Reform Act 1988 s 124(2)(g).

25 Education Reform Act 1988 s 124(2)(h).

26 Education Reform Act 1988 s 124(2)(i).

27 Education Reform Act 1988 s 124(2)(j).

28 Education Reform Act 1988 s 124(3)(a).

29 Education Reform Act 1988 s 124(3)(b).

666. Duty to maintain accounts. It is the duty of each higher education corporation[1] to keep proper accounts and proper records in relation to them[2] and to prepare in respect of each financial year[3] of the corporation a statement of accounts[4]. The statement must give a true and fair account of the state of the corporation's affairs at the end of the financial year and of the corporation's income and expenditure in the financial year[5] and must also comply with any directions given by the Higher Education Funding Council[6] as to the information to be contained in the statement, the manner in which the information is to be presented or the methods and principles according to which the statement is to be prepared[7]. The accounts (including any statement in respect thereof) must be audited by persons appointed in respect of each financial year by the corporation[8].

1 As to the meaning of 'higher education corporation' see PARA 645.

2 Education Reform Act 1988 s 124B(1)(a) (s 124B added by the Further and Higher Education Act 1992 s 71(1)); Education Reform Act 1988 Sch 7 para 18(1)(a).

3 For the purposes of the Education Reform Act 1988 s 124B, in relation to a corporation, 'the first financial year' means the period commencing with the date on which the corporation is established and ending with the second 31 March following that date; and 'financial year' means that period and each successive period of 12 months: Education Reform Act 1988 s 124B(7) (as added: see note 2). For the purposes of Sch 7 para 18, 'financial year' means (1) the period commencing with the date on which the corporation is established and ending with the second 31 March following that date; and (2) each successive period of twelve months: Sch 7 para 18(6) (amended by the Local Audit and Accountability Act 2014 s 45, Sch 12, paras 20, 22(c)). The Education Reform Act 1988 s 124B(7) and Sch 7 para 18 have effect subject to the Further and Higher Education Act 1992 s 78: see s 78(2); and PARA 667. As to the date on which a corporation is established see PARAS 646–647. As to the meaning of 'month' see PARA 54 note 26.

4 Education Reform Act 1988 s 124B(1)(b) (as added: see note 2), Sch 7 para 18(1)(b). The corporation must supply a copy of the statement to any person who asks for it and, if the corporation so requires, pays a fee of such amount not exceeding the cost of supply as the corporation thinks fit: s 124B(3) (as so added), Sch 7 para 18(2A) (added by the Further and Higher Education Act 1992 s 71(3)(b)). As to the meaning of 'person' see PARA 7 note 6. As to the inspection of accounts see PARA 667.

5 Education Reform Act 1988 s 124B(2)(a) (as added: see note 2), Sch 7 para 18(2)(a).

6 As to the meaning of references to the Higher Education Funding Council see PARA 691 note 1.

7 Education Reform Act 1988 s 124B(2)(b) (as added: see note 2), Sch 7 para 18(2)(b) (amended by the Further and Higher Education Act 1992 s 93, Sch 8 paras 27, 59(b)(i)).

8 Education Reform Act 1988 s 124B(4) (as added: see note 2), Sch 7 para 18(3). A corporation in Wales must consult, and take into account any advice given by, the Auditor General for Wales before appointing any auditor under the Education Reform Act 1988 s 124B(4) above in respect of its first financial year: s 124B(5A) (added by the Public Audit (Wales) Act 2004 s 66, Sch 2 para 9(1), (3)). As to the Auditor General for Wales see LOCAL GOVERNMENT vol 69 (2009) PARA 796 et seq.

No person is qualified to be appointed auditor under the Education Reform Act 1988 s 124B(4) or Sch 7 para 18(3) except: (1) an individual, or firm, eligible for appointment as a statutory auditor under the Companies Act 2006 Pt 42 (ss 1209–1264) (see COMPANIES vol 15 (2009) PARA 957); (2) a member of the Chartered Institute of Public Finance and Accountancy; or (3) a firm each of the members of which is a member of that institute: Education Reform Act 1988 s 124B(6) (as so added; and amended by the Public Audit (Wales) Act 2004 s 66, Sch 2 para 9(1), (4); SI 2008/948), Education Reform Act 1988 Sch 7 para 18(5) (substituted by the Further and Higher Education Act 1992 s 93, Sch 8 paras 27, 59(b)(ii); and amended by SI 2008/948; and by the Local Audit and Accountability Act 2014 Sch 12 paras 20, 22(b)).

667. Inspection of accounts. The accounts of any higher education corporation[1] are open to the inspection of the Comptroller and Auditor General[2].

1 As to the meaning of 'higher education corporation' see PARA 645. As to the duty to maintain accounts see PARA 666.

2 Education Reform Act 1988 s 135(1)(b). The power conferred by s 135(1) is exercisable only in, or in relation to accounts or other documents which relate to, any financial year in which expenditure is incurred by the corporation in respect of which financial support has been given to it under the Further and Higher Education Act 1992 s 65 (see PARA 701): see the Education Reform Act 1988 s 135(2)(a) (s 135(2) amended by the Further and Higher Education Act 1992 Sch 8 paras 27, 36(b)). The powers under the National Audit Act 1983 s 6 and s 8 (examinations into the economy, efficiency and effectiveness of certain bodies and access to documents and information: see CONSTITUTIONAL AND ADMINISTRATIVE LAW vol 20 (2014) PARA 489) conferred on the Comptroller and Auditor General by virtue of s 6(3)(c) are correspondingly restricted: see the Education Reform Act 1988 s 135(2)(b) (as so amended). As to the Comptroller and Auditor General see CONSTITUTIONAL AND ADMINISTRATIVE LAW vol 20 (2014) PARAS 494–496. As to the meaning of 'financial year' see PARA 628 note 2.

If the Secretary of State or, in relation to Wales, the Welsh Ministers directs that any financial year specified in the direction of the higher education corporations, and subsequent financial years, are to begin with a date specified in the direction, then: (1) the financial year of the corporations immediately preceding the year specified in the direction must end immediately before the date specified in the direction; and (2) the financial year specified in the direction and subsequent financial years must be each successive period of 12 months: Further and Higher Education Act 1992 s 78(1). As to the Secretary of State see PARA 58. As to the Welsh Ministers see PARA 59. As to the meaning of 'Wales' see PARA 7 note 3. The functions of the Secretary of State under the Further and Higher Education Act 1992 s 78, so far as exercisable in relation to Wales, were transferred to the National Assembly for Wales (see the National Assembly for Wales (Transfer of Functions) Order 1999, SI 1999/672, art 2, Sch 1) and are now vested in the Welsh Ministers (see the Government of Wales Act 2006 s 162(1), Sch 11 para 30).

D. CHARITABLE STATUS

668. Higher education corporations as exempt charities. A higher education corporation[1] is a charity[2]. An English[3] higher education corporation is[4] an exempt charity for the purposes of the Charities Act 2011[5]; and a Welsh[6] higher education corporation is[7] excepted from registration under that Act[8].

1　As to the meaning of 'higher education corporation' see PARA 645.
2　Education Reform Act 1988 s 125A (s 125A added by the Teaching and Higher Education Act 1998 s 41(1); and substituted by the Charities Act 2011 Sch 7 para 50). As to the meaning of 'charity' under the Charities Act 2011 see CHARITIES vol 8 (2015) PARA 1.
3　As to the meaning of 'England' see PARA 7 note 3.
4　Ie in accordance with the Charities Act 2011 Sch 3: see CHARITIES vol 8 (2015) PARA 318.
5　Education Reform Act 1988 s 125A(a) (s 125A as added and substituted (see note 2).
6　As to the meaning of 'Wales' see PARA 7 note 3.
7　Ie in accordance with regulations made in compliance with the Charities Act 2011 s 31(3): see CHARITIES vol 8 (2015) PARA 308.
8　Education Reform Act 1988 s 125A(b) (as added and substituted: see note 5).

E. MODIFICATION OF TRUST DEEDS

669. Power of Privy Council to modify trust deeds. An order of the Privy Council[1] may modify[2] any trust deed[3] or other instrument:
  (1)　relating to or regulating any institution conducted by a higher education corporation[4]; or
  (2)　relating to any land or other property held by any person[5] for the purposes of any such institution[6].
Before making any such modifications of any trust deed or other instrument, the Privy Council must, so far as it appears to it to be practicable to do so, consult[7]:
  (a)　the governing body[8] of the institution[9];
  (b)　where that deed or instrument, or any other instrument relating to or regulating the institution concerned, confers power on any other persons to modify or replace that deed or instrument, those persons[10]; and
  (c)　where the instrument to be modified is a trust deed and the trustees are different from the persons mentioned in head (a) or head (b) above, the trustees[11].

1　As to the Privy Council see CONSTITUTIONAL AND ADMINISTRATIVE LAW vol 20 (2014) PARA 268 et seq. As to the exercise of the powers of the Privy Council under the Education Reform Act 1988 Pt II (ss 120–161) see PARA 657 note 5. Orders under s 157, being of local effect, are not recorded in this work.
2　As to the meaning of 'modify' see PARA 631 note 2. Nothing in any provision of the Education Reform Act 1988 or any order made under the Act relating to the trusts subject to which any land or other property or rights transferred thereunder are to be held by the transferee is to be taken as prejudicing any modification of those trusts after that transfer under any provision of the Act or otherwise: s 235(6). As to the meaning of 'land' see PARA 84 note 9.

3　As to the meaning of 'trust deed' see PARA 108 note 6 (definition applied by the Education
　　Reform Act 1988 s 235(7) (amended by the Education Act 1996 s 582(1), Sch 37 para 81(4)).
4　Education Reform Act 1988 s 157(1)(a) (s 157(1)–(3) substituted by the Further and Higher
　　Education Act 1992 s 75). As to the meaning of 'higher education corporation' see PARA 645.
5　As to the meaning of 'person' see PARA 7 note 6.
6　Education Reform Act 1988 s 157(1)(b) (as substituted: see note 4).
7　As to the exercise of the duty to consult see JUDICIAL REVIEW vol 61 (2010) PARA 627.
8　As to the meaning of 'governing body' see PARA 818 note 2.
9　Education Reform Act 1988 s 157(3)(a) (as substituted: see note 4).
10　Education Reform Act 1988 s 157(3)(b) (as substituted: see note 4).
11　Education Reform Act 1988 s 157(3)(c) (as substituted: see note 4).

F. DISSOLUTION

670. Dissolution of higher education corporations. The appropriate national authority[1] may by order[2] provide for the dissolution of any higher education corporation[3] and for the transfer of property, rights and liabilities[4] of the corporation to[5]:

(1)　any person[6] appearing to the appropriate national authority to be wholly or mainly engaged in the provision of educational facilities or services of any description[7];

(2)　any body corporate established for purposes which include the provision of such facilities or services[8];

(3)　a higher education funding council[9]; or

(4)　the Welsh Ministers[10].

Before making such an order the appropriate national authority must consult[11] the corporation[12] and the Higher Education Funding Council[13]. The order may apply the statutory provisions relating to the transfer of staff to higher education corporations[14] with such modifications[15] as the appropriate national authority may consider necessary or desirable[16].

1　Ie the Secretary of State or, in relation to Wales, the Welsh Ministers. As to the Secretary of State
　　see PARA 58. As to the Welsh Ministers see PARA 59. As to the meaning of 'Wales' see PARA 7
　　note 3. The functions of the Secretary of State under the Education Reform Act 1988 s 128, so
　　far as exercisable in relation to Wales, were transferred to the National Assembly for Wales (see
　　the National Assembly for Wales (Transfer of Functions) Order 1999, SI 1999/672, art 2, Sch 1)
　　and are now vested in the Welsh Ministers (see the Government of Wales Act 2006 s 162(1),
　　Sch 11 para 30).
2　Such orders, being of local effect, are not recorded in this work.
3　Education Reform Act 1988 s 128(1)(a). As to the meaning of 'higher education corporation'
　　see PARA 645.
4　As to the meaning of 'liability' see PARA 84 note 11.
5　Education Reform Act 1988 s 128(1)(b). Stamp duty is not chargeable in respect of any transfer
　　effected under or by virtue of s 128(1)(b): see s 230(1) (amended by the Education Act 1993
　　s 307(1), (3), Sch 19 paras 112, 137(a), Sch 21 Pt I; the Education Act 1996 s 582(2), Sch 38
　　Pt I; the Further and Higher Education Act 1992 s 93, Sch 8 paras 27, 55, Sch 9; and the Statute
　　Law (Repeals) Act 2004). This is subject to the requirement that no instrument (other than a
　　statutory instrument) made or executed under or in pursuance of the Education Reform
　　Act 1988 s 128(1)(b) may be treated as duly stamped unless it is stamped with the duty to which
　　it would, but for s 230 (and, if applicable, the Finance Act 1982 s 129 (see STAMP TAXES vol 96
　　(2012) PARA 363)), be liable or it has, in accordance with the Stamp Act 1891 s 12 (see STAMP
　　TAXES vol 96 (2012) PARA 384), been stamped with a particular stamp denoting that it is not
　　chargeable with any duty or that it has been duly stamped: see the Education Reform Act 1988
　　s 230(4) (amended by the Education Act 1993 s 307(1), (3), Sch 19 paras 112, 137(b), Sch 21
　　Pt I).
6　As to the meaning of 'person' see PARA 7 note 6.
7　Education Reform Act 1988 s 128(1)(b)(i). An order under s 128(1)(b)(i) or (ii) (see the text to
　　note 8) must not provide for transferring the property, rights or liabilities of a higher education
　　corporation to any person or body without the consent of that person or body; and, where the

recipient of a transfer under any order under s 128(1)(b) is not an educational charity, any property transferred must be transferred on trust to be used for charitable purposes which are exclusively educational purposes: s 128(2). For these purposes, a charity is an educational charity if the charitable purposes for which it is established are exclusively educational purposes: s 128(3). 'Charitable purposes' has the meaning given by the Charities Act 2011 s 11 (see CHARITIES vol 8 (2015) PARAS 1, 2): Education Reform Act 1988 s 128(5) (amended by the Charities Act 2011 Sch 7 para 51).

8 Education Reform Act 1988 s 128(1)(b)(ii). See also note 7. As to bodies corporate see COMPANIES vol 14 (2009) PARA 2; CORPORATIONS vol 24 (2010) PARA 301 et seq.

9 Education Reform Act 1988 s 128(1)(b)(iii) (substituted by the Further and Higher Education Act 1992 s 93(1), Sch 8 paras 27, 34(a)(i)). As to the meaning of references to a Higher Education Funding Council see PARA 691 note 1.

10 Education Reform Act 1988 s 128(1)(b)(v) (added by the Further and Higher Education Act 1992 s 93(1), Sch 8 paras 27, 34(a)(ii); substituted by the Learning and Skills Act 2000 s 149, Sch 9 paras 1, 16; and amended by SI 2005/3238; and SI 2010/1080). The functions under the Education Reform Act 1988 s 128(1)(b)(v) were vested in the National Assembly for Wales but are now exercisable by the Welsh Ministers by virtue of the Government of Wales Act 2006 s 162(1), Sch 11 paras 30, 32.

11 As to the exercise of the duty to consult see JUDICIAL REVIEW vol 61 (2010) PARA 627.

12 Education Reform Act 1988 s 128(4)(a).

13 Education Reform Act 1988 s 128(4)(b) (substituted by the Further and Higher Education Act 1992 s 93(1), Sch 8 paras 27, 34(b)).

14 Ie the Education Reform Act 1988 s 127: see PARA 648.

15 As to the meaning of 'modifications' see PARA 631 note 2.

16 Education Reform Act 1988 s 128(6) (added by the Further and Higher Education Act 1992 s 93(1), Sch 8 paras 27, 34(c)).

(v) Designated Institutions

671. Designation of institutions. The appropriate national authority[1] may by order[2] designate as an institution eligible to receive support from funds administered by a Higher Education Funding Council[3]:

(1) any institution which appears to the appropriate national authority to be an institution whose full-time equivalent enrolment number[4] for courses of higher education[5] exceeds 55 per cent of its total full-time equivalent enrolment number[6]; and

(2) any institution which is, or is to be, conducted by a successor company to a higher education corporation[7].

1 Ie the Secretary of State or, in relation to Wales, the Welsh Ministers. As to the Secretary of State see PARA 58. As to the Welsh Ministers see PARA 59. As to the meaning of 'Wales' see PARA 7 note 3. The functions of the Secretary of State under the Education Reform Act 1988 s 129, so far as exercisable in relation to Wales, were transferred to the National Assembly for Wales (see the National Assembly for Wales (Transfer of Functions) Order 1999, SI 1999/672, art 2, Sch 1) and are now vested in the Welsh Ministers (see the Government of Wales Act 2006 s 162(1), Sch 11 para 30).

2 Such orders, being of local effect, are not recorded in this work. An order under the Education Reform Act 1988 s 129 in respect of any institution may revoke any order in respect of that institution under the Further and Higher Education Act 1992 s 28 (see PARA 572) (s 74(2)); and an order under s 28 in respect of any institution may revoke any order in respect of that institution under the Education Reform Act 1988 s 129 (Further and Higher Education Act 1992 s 47(4)). An order in force immediately before 6 May 1992 (ie the date on which the Further and Higher Education Act 1992 s 72(1) was brought into force) designating an institution as falling within the Education Reform Act 1988 s 129(3) (repealed) has effect as if made under s 129 as amended by the Further and Higher Education Act 1992 s 72(1): s 72(2). An institution fell within the Education Reform Act 1988 s 129(3) (repealed) if its full-time equivalent enrolment number for courses of advanced further education on 1 November 1985 exceeded 55% of its total full-time equivalent enrolment number on that date and it was on that date either an institution assisted by a local education authority or a grant-aided institution: s 129(3) (repealed).

3 As to the meaning of references to a Higher Education Funding Council see PARA 691 note 1.
4 As to the determination of full-time equivalent enrolment numbers see PARA 651.
5 As to references to courses of higher education see PARA 684.
6 Education Reform Act 1988 s 129(1)(a), (2) (s 129(1), (2) substituted by the Further and Higher Education Act 1992 s 72(1)(a)). As to the meaning of 'total full-time equivalent enrolment number' see PARA 647 note 5.
7 Education Reform Act 1988 s 129(1)(b) (as substituted: see note 6). As to the meaning of 'higher education corporation' see PARA 645. For the purposes of s 129(1)(b), a company is a successor company to a higher education corporation if:
   (1) it is a company limited by a guarantee formed and registered under the Companies Act 2006 (see COMPANIES vol 14 (2009) PARAS 79, 102) (Education Reform Act 1988 s 129(5)(a) (amended by SI 2009/1941));
   (2) at the time when it was formed the persons participating in its formation were all members of a higher education corporation and constituted a majority of the members of that corporation (Education Reform Act 1988 s 129(5)(b));
   (3) its objects are exclusively charitable according to the law of England and Wales and include the conduct of the institution which was at that time conducted by that corporation (s 129(5)(c));
   (4) its articles of association have been approved by the appropriate national authority (s 129(5)(d) (amended by SI 2009/1941)); and
   (5) an order has been made under the Education Reform Act 1988 s 128 (see PARA 670) dissolving the corporation and transferring the property, rights and liabilities of the corporation to the company (whether or not that order has taken effect before the order under this provision is made) (s 129(5)(e)).
   As to the membership of higher education corporations see PARAS 653, 659. As to charitable objects see CHARITIES vol 8 (2015) PARA 2. As to the meaning of 'liability' see PARA 84 note 11.

672. Transfer of property, rights and liabilities to designated institutions.
Where an institution is designated[1] and:
   (1) the order designating the institution so provides[2]; and
   (2) immediately before the date on which the designation takes effect (the 'designation date') the institution is an institution assisted by a local authority ('the former assisting authority')[3],
then, on the designation date in relation to any such institution, specified property, rights and liabilities[4] are transferred to, and by virtue of the Education Reform Act 1988 vested in, the appropriate transferee[5], that is:
   (a) in relation to an institution conducted by a body corporate, that body[6]; and
   (b) in relation to an institution not so conducted, any persons[7] specified in the order designating the institution as persons appearing to the appropriate national authority[8] to be trustees holding property for the purposes of that institution[9].
The property, rights and liabilities in question are all land or other property which, immediately before the designation date, were property of the former assisting authority used or held for the purposes of that institution[10], and all rights and liabilities of that authority subsisting immediately before that date which were acquired or incurred for those purposes[11].

1 Ie by order under the Education Reform Act 1988 s 129: see PARA 671.
2 Education Reform Act 1988 s 130(1)(a).
3 Education Reform Act 1988 s 130(1)(b) (amended by SI 2010/1158). As to the meaning of 'local authority' see PARA 25 (definition applied by the Education Reform Act 1988 s 235(7) (amended by the Education Act 1996 s 582(1), Sch 37 para 81(4)).
4 As to the meaning of 'liability' see PARA 84 note 11.
5 Education Reform Act 1988 s 130(2). Section 130(2) is stated to be subject to s 198 (land and property transfers: see PARA 1330 et seq) and s 130(4): see s 130(2). Section 130(2) does not apply to any liability of the former assisting authority in respect of the principal of, or any interest on, any loan (s 130(4)(a)), or any liability of that authority in respect of compensation

for premature retirement of any person formerly employed by them (s 130(4)(b)). As to the meaning of 'employed' see PARA 301 note 2. As to liabilities of former assisting authorities in respect of loans see PARA 673.

Stamp duty is not chargeable in respect of any transfer effected under or by virtue of s 130 (taken with Sch 10): see s 230(1) (amended by the Education Act 1993 s 307(1), (3), Sch 19 paras 112, 137(a), Sch 21 Pt I; the Education Act 1996 s 582(2), Sch 38 Pt I; the Further and Higher Education Act 1992 s 93, Sch 8 paras 27, 55, Sch 9; and the Statute Law (Repeals) Act 2004). This is subject to the requirement that no instrument (other than a statutory instrument) made or executed under or in pursuance of the Education Reform Act 1988 s 130 may be treated as duly stamped unless it is stamped with the duty to which it would, but for s 230 (and, if applicable, the Finance Act 1982 s 129 (see STAMP TAXES vol 96 (2012) PARA 363)), be liable or it has, in accordance with the Stamp Act 1891 s 12 (see STAMP TAXES vol 96 (2012) PARA 384), been stamped with a particular stamp denoting that it is not chargeable with any duty or that it has been duly stamped: Education Reform Act 1988 s 230(4) (amended by the Education Act 1993 s 307(1), (3), Sch 19 paras 112, 137(b), Sch 21 Pt I).

6   Education Reform Act 1988 s 130(5)(a). As to bodies corporate see COMPANIES vol 14 (2009) PARA 2; CORPORATIONS vol 24 (2010) PARA 301 et seq.

7   As to the meaning of 'person' see PARA 7 note 6.

8   Ie the Secretary of State or, in relation to Wales, the Welsh Ministers. As to the Secretary of State see PARA 58. As to the Welsh Ministers see PARA 59. As to the meaning of 'Wales' see PARA 7 note 3. The functions of the Secretary of State under the Education Reform Act 1988 s 130 and the Further and Higher Education Act 1992 s 84 (see note 10), so far as exercisable in relation to Wales, were transferred to the National Assembly for Wales (see the National Assembly for Wales (Transfer of Functions) Order 1999, SI 1999/672, art 2, Sch 1) and are now vested in the Welsh Ministers (see the Government of Wales Act 2006 s 162(1), Sch 11 para 30).

9   Education Reform Act 1988 s 130(5)(b). Where any persons so specified are the appropriate transferee for the purposes of s 130(2): (1) any land or other property or rights transferred to them under s 130 must be held by them on the trusts applicable under such trust deed relating to or regulating that institution (if any) as may be so specified or, if no such trust deed is so specified, on trust for the purposes of the institution (s 130(6)(a)), although s 130(6)(a) does not apply in relation to any land or other property or rights which immediately before the designation date in relation to the institution concerned were vested in the former assisting authority as trustees for any particular purposes or (as the case may be) for the general purposes of the institution (s 130(7)); and (2) they do not incur any personal liability by virtue of any liability so transferred, but may apply any property held by them on trust for the purposes of the institution in meeting any such liability (s 130(6)(b)). As to the meaning of 'land' see PARA 84 note 9. As to the meaning of 'trust deed' see PARA 108 note 6 (definition applied by s 235(7) (as amended: see note 3).

10   Education Reform Act 1988 s 130(3)(a). Where at any time land is used for the purposes of an institution to which s 130(3)(a) applies, any interest of a local authority in that land subsisting at that time must be taken for the purposes of s 130(3)(a) to be land held for the purposes of that institution (whether or not it is by virtue of that interest that the land is so used): s 138(1)(b), (2) (amended by SI 2010/1158).

Where (apart from the Further and Higher Education Act 1992 s 84) any land or other property of a local authority would on any date ('the date of transfer') be transferred under the Education Reform Act 1988 Pt II (ss 120–161) to the governing body of an institution within the higher education sector, and at any time before that date the authority, the governing body of the institution and the governing body of any other institution which will on that date be an institution within the higher education sector have agreed in writing that the land or property should be transferred on that or a subsequent date to the governing body of that other institution, then, if the appropriate national authority has approved the agreement at any time before the date of transfer, Pt II has effect as if it required the property to be transferred in accordance with the agreement: see the Further and Higher Education Act 1992 s 84(1), (2). References to anything done include anything done before 6 March 1992 (ie the date on which the Education Reform Act 1988 was passed (ie received Royal Assent)): Further and Higher Education Act 1992 s 84(3). For these purposes, 'local authority' includes a non-metropolitan district council for an area for which there is a county council: s 84(4) (added by SI 2010/1158). As to the meaning of 'local authority' generally see PARA 25 (definition applied by the Further and Higher Education Act 1992 s 90(1)). As to the meaning of 'governing body' see PARA 560 note 6. As to the meaning of 'institution within the higher education sector' see PARA 619. As to the meaning of 'writing' see PARA 76 note 8.

11   Education Reform Act 1988 s 130(3)(b).

673. Loan liabilities excepted from transfer. In relation to any institution conducted by a higher education corporation[1] and any designated institution[2], a liability[3] is an 'excepted liability' if it would have been transferred[4] by virtue of the designation but for the statutory exclusion[5] of any such transfer[6].

The amount of any liability of a local authority[7] in respect of the principal of any loan which is an excepted liability in relation to such an institution is to be treated on and after the date on which that liability would have been transferred (the 'operative date')[8] as having been borrowed from that authority by the body of persons[9] to whom the liability would have been transferred (the 'default transferee')[10] on such terms as to repayment and the payment of interest as may be agreed[11] or determined by the Secretary of State[12].

There is a duty to arrive, so far as practicable, at such written[13] agreements as may be necessary for determining the amount of any excepted liability and the terms to apply in relation to the liability imposed on the default transferee by reference to that liability[14].

Notwithstanding any terms so agreed or determined, any liability in respect of any sum treated[15] as having been borrowed from a local authority may at any time be discharged by a single payment of a sum equal to the aggregate of the amount of the principal of the loan outstanding at the time of the payment and the amount of any interest accrued before that time[16].

1 As to the meaning of 'higher education corporation' see PARA 645.
2 Ie any institution designated under the Education Reform Act 1988 s 129 (see PARA 671): see s 199(2).
3 As to the meaning of 'liability' see PARA 84 note 11.
4 Ie under the Education Reform Act 1988 s 130(2): see PARA 672.
5 Ie but for the Education Reform Act 1988 s 130(4)(a): see PARA 672.
6 See the Education Reform Act 1988 s 199(2)(a).
7 As to the meaning of 'local authority' see PARA 25 (definition applied by the Education Reform Act 1988 s 235(7) (amended by the Education Act 1996 s 582(1), Sch 37 para 81(4))).
8 See the Education Reform Act 1988 s 199(2)(b).
9 As to the meaning of 'person' see PARA 7 note 6.
10 See the Education Reform Act 1988 s 199(2)(b).
11 The Education Reform Act 1988 originally referred to agreement made between the Education Assets Board and the authority. The Education Assets Board was renamed the Education Transfer Council by the School Standards and Framework Act 1998 s 136(1) and, by virtue of s 136(2), all statutory references to the Education Assets Board are to be construed as references to the Education Transfer Council. However, the Education Transfer Council was wound up in 2000. See further PARA 1330.
12 Education Reform Act 1988 s 199(1) (amended by the School Standards and Framework Act 1998 s 136(2); and SI 2010/1158). As to the Secretary of State see PARA 58. As to the giving of assistance and advice to the Secretary of State for the purpose of determining any matter under the Education Reform Act 1988 s 199 see s 199(8).
13 As to the meaning of 'written' see PARA 76 note 8.
14 See the Education Reform Act 1988 s 199(3). An agreement made under s 199(3) must be delivered to the default transferee: s 199(9). Any such agreement must be treated as made between the authority and the default transferee: s 199(10). The Secretary of State must be notified if it appears that it is unlikely in the case of any matter on which agreement is required to be reached under s 199(3) that such an agreement will be reached: s 199(5). Where the Secretary of State has received such a notification he may, whether before or after the operative date, give a direction determining the matter, and may include in the direction any provision which might have been included in an agreement under s 199(3): s 199(6). The Secretary of State must consult the authority before giving such a direction: s 199(7).
15 Ie by virtue of the Education Reform Act 1988 s 199(1): see the text to notes 7–12.
16 Education Reform Act 1988 s 199(4).

674. Government and conduct of designated institutions. For each designated institution[1], other than an institution conducted by a company[2], there must be an instrument of government and articles of government[3]. The 'instrument of government' is an instrument providing for the constitution of a governing body[4] of the institution[5]; and the 'articles of government' are the instrument in accordance with which the institution is to be conducted[6]. Each such instrument is required to have been either in force when the designation took effect[7] or made in pursuance of a power under a regulatory instrument[8] or, where no such power exists, made by the body of persons responsible for the management of the institution[9], and must be as approved by the Privy Council[10].

Either of the instrument of government or the articles of government may be modified by order of the Privy Council and no instrument approved by the Privy Council for the purposes of the above provisions may be modified by any other person without the Privy Council's consent[11].

1   'Designated institution' means an institution in relation to which a designation made, or having effect as if made, under the Education Reform Act 1988 s 129 (see PARA 671) has effect, but does not include any institution established by Royal Charter: s 129A(10) (s 129A added by the Further and Higher Education Act 1992 s 73(1)). As to institutions established by Royal Charter see PARA 624 et seq.

2   Education Reform Act 1988 s 129A(1) (as added: see note 1). As to the government of institutions conducted by a company see PARA 675.

3   See the Education Reform Act 1988 s 129A(2) (as added: see note 1).

4   As to the meaning of 'governing body' see PARA 628 note 2.

5   Education Reform Act 1988 s 129A(2)(a) (as added: see note 1).

6   Education Reform Act 1988 s 129A(2)(b) (as added: see note 1).

7   See the Education Reform Act 1988 s 129A(3)(a) (as added: see note 1). If an instrument approved by the Privy Council for the purposes of s 129A falls within s 129A(3)(a) and there is no other power to modify it, the instrument may be modified by the body of persons responsible for the management of the institution: s 129A(6)(a) (as so added). As to the meaning of 'modify' see PARA 631 note 2. As to the meaning of 'person' see PARA 7 note 6.

8   'Regulatory instrument', in relation to an institution, means any instrument of government or articles of government and any other instrument relating to or regulating the institution: Education Reform Act 1988 s 129A(4) (as added: see note 1). If an instrument approved by the Privy Council for the purposes of s 129A was made in pursuance of a power under a regulatory instrument and there is no other power to modify it, the instrument may be modified by the body of persons responsible for the management of the institution: s 129A(6)(a) (as so added).

9   See the Education Reform Act 1988 s 129A(3)(b), (5) (as added: see note 1). An instrument made under s 129A(5) by the body of persons responsible for the management of the institution may replace wholly or partly any existing regulatory instrument: see s 129A(5) (as so added). If an instrument approved by the Privy Council for the purposes of s 129A was made by the body of persons responsible for the management of the institution, the instrument may be modified by those persons: s 129A(6)(b) (as so added).

10 Education Reform Act 1988 s 129A(3) (as added: see note 1). Nothing in s 129A requires further approval for any instrument approved by the Secretary of State for the purposes of s 156 (repealed in relation to designated institutions), and references in s 129A to instruments approved by the Privy Council for the purposes of s 129A include instruments so approved by the Secretary of State: s 129A(9) (as so added). As to the exercise by the Privy Council of its powers under Pt II (ss 120–161) see PARA 657 note 5. As to the Secretary of State see PARA 58. As to the Privy Council see CONSTITUTIONAL AND ADMINISTRATIVE LAW vol 20 (2014) PARA 268 et seq.

11 Education Reform Act 1988 s 129A(7) (as added: see note 1). Before exercising any power under s 129A(7) in relation to any instrument the Privy Council must, so far as it appears to it to be practicable to do so, consult the governing body of the institution, and, where there is such a power as is mentioned in s 129A(3)(b) (see the text to notes 8–9) to modify the instrument and the persons having that power are different from the governing body of the institution, the persons having the power: s 129A(8) (as so added). As to the exercise of the duty to consult see JUDICIAL REVIEW vol 61 (2010) PARA 627.

675.   Instruments of government of designated institutions conducted by companies.   In relation to any designated institution[1] conducted by a company[2], the articles of association of the company[3] must incorporate provision with respect to the constitution of a governing body[4] of the institution (to be known as 'the instrument of government of the institution')[5], and provision with respect to the conduct of the institution (to be known as 'the articles of government of the institution')[6].

The Privy Council[7] may give to the persons[8] who appear to it to have effective control over the company such directions[9] as it thinks fit for securing that the articles of association of the company[10], or any rules or byelaws made in pursuance of any power conferred by the articles of association of the company[11], are amended in such manner as it may specify in the direction[12].

No amendment of the articles of association of the company[13] is to take effect until it has been submitted to the Privy Council for its approval and it has notified its approval to the company[14].

1 As to the meaning of 'designated institution' see PARA 674 note 1.
2 See the Education Reform Act 1988 s 129B(1) (s 129B added by the Further and Higher Education Act 1992 s 73(1)).
3 As to the articles of association of a company see COMPANIES vol 14 (2009) PARA 228 et seq.
4 As to the meaning of 'governing body' see PARA 628 note 2.
5 Education Reform Act 1988 s 129B(2)(a) (as added: see note 2).
6 Education Reform Act 1988 s 129B(2)(b) (as added: see note 2).
7 As to the Privy Council see CONSTITUTIONAL AND ADMINISTRATIVE LAW vol 20 (2014) PARA 268 et seq. As to the exercise by the Privy Council of its powers under the Education Reform Act 1988 Pt II (ss 120–161) see PARA 657 note 5.
8 As to the meaning of 'person' see PARA 7 note 6.
9 Before giving any such directions the Privy Council must consult the persons who appear to it to have effective control over the company: Education Reform Act 1988 s 129B(5) (as added: see note 2). As to the exercise of the duty to consult see JUDICIAL REVIEW vol 61 (2010) PARA 627.
10 Education Reform Act 1988 s 129B(3)(a) (as added (see note 2); and amended by SI 2009/1941).
11 Education Reform Act 1988 s 129B(3)(b) (as added: see note 2).
12 Education Reform Act 1988 s 129B(3) (as added: see note 2).
13 Ie other than one required under the Education Reform Act 1988 s 129B(3)(a); see the text to notes 7–10.
14 Education Reform Act 1988 s 129B(4) (as added (see note 2); and amended by SI 2009/1941).

676. Power of Privy Council to modify trust deeds. An order of the Privy Council[1] may modify[2] any trust deed[3] or other instrument:

(1) relating to or regulating any designated institution[4] other than an institution established by Royal Charter[5]; or

(2) relating to any land or other property held by any person[6] for the purposes of any such institution[7].

Before making any such modifications of any trust deed or other instrument, the Privy Council must, so far as it appears to it to be practicable to do so, consult[8]:

(a) the governing body[9] of the institution[10];

(b) where that deed or instrument, or any other instrument relating to or regulating the institution concerned, confers power on any other persons to modify or replace that deed or instrument, those persons[11]; and

(c) where the instrument to be modified is a trust deed and the trustees are different from the persons mentioned in head (a) or head (b) above, the trustees[12].

1 Such orders, being of local effect, are not recorded in this work. As to the Privy Council see CONSTITUTIONAL AND ADMINISTRATIVE LAW vol 20 (2014) PARA 268 et seq. As to the exercise of the powers of the Privy Council under the Education Reform Act 1988 Pt II (ss 120–161) see PARA 657 note 5.

2 As to the meaning of 'modify' see PARA 631 note 2. Nothing in any provision of the Education Reform Act 1988 or any order made under the Act relating to the trusts subject to which any land or other property or rights transferred thereunder are to be held by the transferee is to be taken as prejudicing any modification of those trusts after that transfer under any provision of the Act or otherwise: s 235(6). As to the meaning of 'land' see PARA 84 note 9.

3 As to the meaning of 'trust deed' see PARA 108 note 6 (definition applied by the Education Reform Act 1988 s 235(7) (amended by the Education Act 1996 s 582(1), Sch 37 para 81(4)).

4 Ie any institution in relation to which a designation made, or having effect as if made, under the Education Reform Act 1988 s 129 (see PARA 671) has effect.

5 See the Education Reform Act 1988 s 157(1)(a), (2)(b) (s 157(1)–(3) substituted by the Further and Higher Education Act 1992 s 75). As to institutions established by Royal Charter see PARA 624 et seq.

6 As to the meaning of 'person' see PARA 7 note 6.

7 Education Reform Act 1988 s 157(1)(b) (as substituted: see note 5).

8 As to the exercise of the duty to consult see JUDICIAL REVIEW vol 61 (2010) PARA 627.

9 As to the meaning of 'governing body' see PARA 628 note 2.

10 Education Reform Act 1988 s 157(3)(a) (as substituted: see note 5).

11 Education Reform Act 1988 s 157(3)(b) (as substituted: see note 5).

12 Education Reform Act 1988 s 157(3)(c) (as substituted: see note 5).

677. Inspection of accounts. The accounts of any designated institution[1] are open to the inspection of the Comptroller and Auditor General[2].

1 Ie within the meaning of the Education Reform Act 1988 s 129A: see PARA 674 note 1.

2 See the Education Reform Act 1988 s 135(1)(c) (substituted by the Further and Higher Education Act 1992 s 93(1), Sch 8 paras 27, 36(a)). As to the Comptroller and Auditor General see CONSTITUTIONAL AND ADMINISTRATIVE LAW vol 20 (2014) PARAS 494–496. The power conferred by the Education Reform Act 1988 s 135(1) is exercisable only in, or in relation to accounts or other documents which relate to, any financial year in which expenditure is incurred by the governing body of the institution in question in respect of which financial support has been given under the Further and Higher Education Act 1992 s 65 (see PARA 701): Education Reform Act 1988 s 135(2)(a) (s 135(2) amended by the Further and Higher Education Act 1992 Sch 8 paras 27, 36(b)). As to the meanings of 'governing body' and 'financial year' see PARA 628 note 2. The powers under the National Audit Act 1983 s 6 and s 8 (examinations into the economy, efficiency and effectiveness of certain bodies and access to documents and information: see CONSTITUTIONAL AND ADMINISTRATIVE LAW vol 20 (2014) PARA 489) conferred on the Comptroller and Auditor General by virtue of s 6(3)(c) are correspondingly restricted: see the Education Reform Act 1988 s 135(2)(b) (as so amended).

(2) OTHER INSTITUTIONS PROVIDING HIGHER EDUCATION

678. Functions of local authorities with respect to higher education. A local authority[1] is no longer under a duty to secure the provision for its area of facilities for higher education[2]. However, a local authority may[3]:

(1) secure the provision for its area of such facilities for higher education as appear to it to be appropriate for meeting the needs of the population of its area[4];

(2) secure the provision of higher education for persons from other areas[5]; and

(3) do anything which appears to it to be necessary or expedient for the purposes of or in connection with such provision[6].

In exercising its power under head (1) above a local authority must have regard to any facilities for higher education provided by institutions within the higher education sector[7] or the further education sector[8] and other bodies which are provided for, or available for use by persons living in, its area[9].

1   As to the meaning of 'local authority' see PARA 25 (definition applied by the Education Reform Act 1988 s 235(7) (amended by the Education Act 1996 s 582(1), Sch 37 para 81(4))).

2   See the Education Reform Act 1988 s 120(1) (amended by SI 2010/1158). As to the meaning of 'higher education' see PARA 24.

3   See the Education Reform Act 1988 s 120(3) (amended by SI 2010/1158).

4   Education Reform Act 1988 s 120(3)(a).

5   Education Reform Act 1988 s 120(3)(b) (amended by the Further and Higher Education Act 1992 s 93(1), Sch 8 paras 27, 30(b)).

6   Education Reform Act 1988 s 120(3)(c).

7   As to the meaning of 'institution within the higher education sector' see PARA 619.

8   As to the meaning of 'institution within the further education sector' see PARA 555.

9   Education Reform Act 1988 s 120(4) (amended by the Further and Higher Education Act 1992 s 93(1), Sch 8 paras 27, 30(c); and SI 2010/1158).

679. Power of governing body of maintained school to provide higher education. Under the Education Act 2002, the governing body of a maintained school[1] has the power to arrange the provision to pupils[2] at the school, whether by teachers at the school or other persons[3], of: (1) courses in preparation for professional examinations at a higher level[4]; or (2) courses[5] providing education at a higher level (whether or not in preparation for an examination)[6]. A governing body may exercise this power in relation to a particular pupil only if it is satisfied that the provision to that pupil of the course in question will not to any significant extent interfere with the other education with which he is being provided at the school[7].

This power to provide higher education has effect notwithstanding the fact that nothing in the Education Act 1996 confers any functions with respect to higher education[8].

1   As to the meaning of 'maintained school' see PARA 103 note 3. As to the governing bodies of maintained schools in England see PARA 150 et seq; and in Wales see PARA 195. As to academies see PARA 345 et seq.

2   As to the meaning of 'pupil' see PARA 20 note 4 (definition applied by the Education Act 2002 s 212(2), (3)).

3   As to the meaning of 'person' see PARA 7 note 6.

4   Ie courses falling within the Education Reform Act 1988 Sch 6 para 1(g): see PARA 684.

5   Ie courses falling within the Education Reform Act 1988 Sch 6 para 1(h): see PARA 684.

6   Education Act 2002 s 28A(1) (s 28A added by the Education Act 2005 s 105). The Welsh Ministers may give, or make arrangements for the giving of, financial assistance to any person in connection with the provision of courses mentioned in the Education Act 2002 s 28A(1) by the governing body of a maintained school in Wales: s 28A(3) (as so added). Sections 15 and 16 (see PARA 78) apply to such financial assistance as they apply to financial assistance given under s 14: see s 28A(4) (as so added). The functions under s 28A in relation to Wales were originally vested in the National Assembly for Wales and are now exercisable by the Welsh Ministers by virtue of the Government of Wales Act 2006 s 162(1), Sch 11 paras 30, 32. As to the Welsh Ministers see PARA 59. As to the meaning of 'Wales' see PARA 7 note 3.

7   Education Act 2002 s 28A(2) (as added: see note 6).

8   See the Education Act 2002 s 28A(5) (as added: see note 6). As to the Education Act 1996 and higher education see s 1(4); and PARA 18.

680. Government of institutions maintained in pursuance of higher education functions. A local authority[1] may, in relation to any institution not within the further education sector[2] or the higher education sector[3] which is maintained by it in the exercise of its further or higher education functions[4]:

(1)   make such provision as it thinks fit in respect of the government of the institution[5]; and

(2)   delegate to the governing body[6] of the institution such functions relating to the management of the finances of the institution, and such other

functions relating to the management of the institution (including the appointment and dismissal of staff), as the authority may determine[7].

1 As to the meaning of 'local authority' see PARA 25 (definition applied by the Further and Higher Education Act 1992 s 90(1) (amended by SI 2010/1158)).
2 As to the meaning of 'institution outside the further education sector' see PARA 555.
3 As to the meaning of 'institution outside the higher education sector' see PARA 619.
4 Further and Higher Education Act 1992 s 85(2) (amended by SI 2010/1158). As to the meaning of 'further education' see PARA 23; and as to the meaning of 'higher education' see PARA 24 (definitions applied by the Further and Higher Education Act 1992 s 90(1)). As to the meaning of 'functions' see PARA 18 note 5 (definition applied by s 90(5) (amended by the Education Act 1996 s 582(1), Sch 37 para 115(3); and the School Standards and Framework Act 1998 s 140(1), Sch 30 para 46(b))).
5 Further and Higher Education Act 1992 s 85(3)(a). The power under s 85(3)(a) includes power to replace any instrument of government or articles of government of an institution made under the Education Reform Act 1988 Pt II Ch III (ss 139–155) (repealed) or s 156 (repealed in relation to designated institutions): see s 85(3)(a).
6 As to the meaning of 'governing body' see PARA 560 note 6.
7 Further and Higher Education Act 1992 s 85(3)(b).

681. Provision of transport. In certain circumstances, a local authority must make arrangements for the provision of transport for the purpose of facilitating the attendance of persons receiving education at any institution maintained or assisted by the authority which provides higher education[1].

1 See, in relation to England, PARAS 464 et seq, 810; and, in relation to Wales, PARAS 469 et seq, 815.

682. Provision of clothing. A local authority may provide such articles of clothing as it may determine suitable for the physical training provided at an institution maintained by the authority which provides higher education[1].

1 See the Education Act 1996 s 510(4); and PARA 482.

683. Institutions ceasing to be maintained by local authority. Where an institution which provides full-time education and is maintained by a local authority[1] in exercise of the authority's further or higher education functions[2] ceases to be maintained by a local authority, any provision of any instrument relating to any land[3] or other property held for the purposes of the institution[4] which:

(1) confers on any person[5] an option to acquire an interest in that land[6] or other property[7]; or

(2) provides (in whatever terms) for the determination or forfeiture of any such interest[8],

has effect, if the institution becomes an institution within the further education sector[9] or an institution within the higher education sector[10] or a grant-aided institution[11], as if the event referred to were the institution's ceasing to be a publicly funded institution[12].

1 As to the meaning of 'local authority' see PARA 25 (definition applied by the Education Reform Act 1988 s 235(7) (amended by the Education Act 1996 s 582(1), Sch 37 para 81(4))).
2 Education Reform Act 1988 s 157(5)(a) (amended by SI 2010/1158). As to the meaning of references to the further or higher education functions of a local authority see PARA 590 note 2.
3 As to the meaning of 'land' see PARA 84 note 9.
4 See the Education Reform Act 1988 s 157(4) (amended by the Further and Higher Education Act 1992 s 93, Sch 8 paras 27, 39(a)(i), Sch 9; and SI 2010/1158).
5 As to the meaning of 'person' see PARA 7 note 6.
6 As to the meaning of references to an interest in land see PARA 84 note 9.
7 Education Reform Act 1988 s 157(4)(a).

8 Education Reform Act 1988 s 157(4)(b).
9 As to the meaning of 'institution within the further education sector' see PARA 555.
10 As to the meaning of 'institution within the higher education sector' see PARA 619.
11 As to the meaning of 'grant-aided institution' see PARA 590 note 11.
12 Education Reform Act 1988 s 157(4) (amended by the Further and Higher Education Act 1992 Sch 8 paras 27, 39(a)(ii), (iii)). 'Publicly funded institution' means an institution which is an institution of any one or more of the following descriptions, that is to say: (1) an institution maintained or assisted by a local authority (Education Reform Act 1988 s 157(6)(a) (amended by SI 2010/1158)); (2) an institution within the further education sector or an institution within the higher education sector (Education Reform Act 1988 s 157(6)(b) (amended by the Further and Higher Education Act 1992 Sch 8 paras 27, 39(c))); and (3) a grant-aided institution (Education Reform Act 1988 s 157(6)(c)).

(3) HIGHER EDUCATION COURSES AND ACADEMIC AWARDS

684. Courses of higher education. Each of the following is a course of higher education[1]:

(1) a course for the further training of teachers or youth and community workers[2];
(2) a post-graduate course (including a higher degree course)[3];
(3) a first degree course[4];
(4) a course for the Diploma of Higher Education[5];
(5) a course for the Higher National Diploma or Higher National Certificate of the Business and Technician Education Council, or the Diploma in Management Studies[6];
(6) a course for the Certificate in Education[7];
(7) a course in preparation for a professional examination at higher level[8];
(8) a course providing education at a higher level (whether or not in preparation for an examination)[9].

1 See the Education Reform Act 1988 s 120, Sch 6; and the Education Act 1996 s 579(1). See also PARA 24. The Secretary of State or, in relation to Wales, the Welsh Ministers may by order amend the Education Reform Act 1988 Sch 6: see s 120(10). At the date at which this volume states the law, no such order had been made. As to the Secretary of State see PARA 58. As to the Welsh Ministers see PARA 59. As to the meaning of 'Wales' see PARA 7 note 3. The functions of the Secretary of State under s 120, so far as exercisable in relation to Wales, were transferred to the National Assembly for Wales (see the National Assembly for Wales (Transfer of Functions) Order 1999, SI 1999/672, art 2, Sch 1) and are now vested in the Welsh Ministers (see the Government of Wales Act 2006 s 162(1), Sch 11 para 30).
2 Education Reform Act 1988 Sch 6 para 1(a).
3 Education Reform Act 1988 Sch 6 para 1(b).
4 Education Reform Act 1988 Sch 6 para 1(c).
5 Education Reform Act 1988 Sch 6 para 1(d).
6 Education Reform Act 1988 Sch 6 para 1(e).
7 Education Reform Act 1988 Sch 6 para 1(f).
8 Education Reform Act 1988 Sch 6 para 1(g). For these purposes, a professional examination is at higher level if its standard is higher than the standard of examinations at advanced level for the General Certificate of Education or the examination for the National Certificate or the National Diploma of the Business and Technician Education Council: Sch 6 para 2.
9 Education Reform Act 1988 Sch 6 para 1(h). For these purposes, a course is to be regarded as providing education at a higher level if its standard is higher than the standard of courses providing education in preparation for any of the examinations mentioned in Sch 6 para 2 (see note 8): Sch 6 para 3.

685. Power to award degrees etc. The Privy Council may by order[1]:

(1) specify any institution which provides higher education[2] as competent to grant[3] either or both of the following: (a) awards[4] granted to persons

who complete an appropriate course of study and satisfy an appropriate assessment[5]; and (b) awards granted to persons who complete an appropriate programme of supervised research and satisfy an appropriate assessment[6];

(2) specify any institution[7] within the further education sector[8] as competent to grant[9] an award[10] of a foundation degree granted to persons who complete an appropriate course of study and satisfy an appropriate assessment[11].

An institution for the time being specified in such an order may grant any award of a kind mentioned in head (1) or (2) above which it is competent to grant by virtue of the order to persons who complete the appropriate course of study or, as the case may be, programme of supervised research on or after the date specified in the order[12]. An institution specified in such an order as competent to grant either or both of the kinds of award mentioned in head (1) above may also[13] grant honorary degrees[14], and grant degrees to members of the academic and other staff of the institution[15]. An institution specified in such an order as competent to grant the kind of award mentioned in head (2) above may also grant honorary foundation degrees[16], and grant foundation degrees to members of the academic and other staff of the institution[17].

It is for the institution to determine, in accordance with any relevant provisions of the instruments relating to or regulating the institution, the courses of study or programmes of research, and the assessments, which are appropriate for the grant of any award and the terms and conditions on which any of the powers to make awards[18] may be exercised[19]. However, an order specifying an institution as competent to grant only the kind of award mentioned in head (2) above may provide that the institution is not to grant such an award to a person unless he was enrolled at the institution at the time he completed the course of study for which the award is granted[20].

1 Such orders, not being made by statutory instrument, and are not recorded in this work. The Education Reform Act 1988 s 124D (see PARA 657 note 5), which regulates the exercise of the Privy Council's powers, applies in relation to orders under the Further and Higher Education Act 1992 s 76(1) as it applies in relation to the exercise of powers for the purposes of the Education Reform Act 1988 Pt II (ss 120–161): see the Further and Higher Education Act 1992 s 76(7). As to the Privy Council see CONSTITUTIONAL AND ADMINISTRATIVE LAW vol 20 (2014) PARA 268 et seq.

2 As to the meaning of 'higher education' see PARA 24 (definition applied by the Further and Higher Education Act 1992 s 90(1)).

3 Ie in pursuance of the Further and Higher Education Act 1992 s 76.

4 'Award' means any degree, diploma, certificate or other academic award or distinction: Further and Higher Education Act 1992 s 76(2) (amended by the Further Education and Training Act 2007 s 19(1), (3)).

5 Further and Higher Education Act 1992 s 76(1)(a), (2)(a) (s 76(1)(a) numbered as such by the Further Education and Training Act 2007 s 19(1), (2)(a)). 'Assessment' includes examination and test: Further and Higher Education Act 1992 s 76(2). Any power conferred on an institution to grant awards in pursuance of s 76 includes power: (1) to authorise other institutions to do so on behalf of the institution (s 76(5)(a)); (2) to do so jointly with another institution (s 76(5)(b)); and (3) to deprive any person of any award granted to him by or on behalf of the institution in pursuance of s 76 (or, in the case of an award granted to him by the institution and another institution jointly, to do so jointly with the other institution) (s 76(5)(c)).

6 Further and Higher Education Act 1992 s 76(1)(a), (2)(b) (s 76(1)(a) as renumbered: see note 5). See also note 5.

7 Where the Privy Council is considering whether to make an order specifying an institution as mentioned in the Further and Higher Education Act 1992 s 76(1)(b), the Privy Council may not make the order unless: (1) the institution gives the Privy Council a statement setting out what it proposes to do as regards making arrangements for securing that any person granted an award under or by virtue of any power that would be conferred on the institution if the order were

made (other than the power described in s 76(4A): see the text to notes 16–17) has an opportunity to progress to one or more particular courses of more advanced study (s 76(2B)(a) (s 76(2B) added by the Further Education and Training Act 2007 s 19(1), (5))); and (2) the Privy Council considers that the proposals are satisfactory and are likely to be carried out (Further and Higher Education Act 1992 s 76(2B)(b) (as so added)).

8   As to the meaning of 'institution within the further education sector' see PARA 555.

9   Ie in pursuance of the Further and Higher Education Act 1992 s 76.

10 An order specifying an institution as competent to grant in pursuance of the Further and Higher Education Act 1992 s 76 only the kind of award mentioned in s 76(2A) may provide that the institution's power to grant such awards does not include the power to authorise other institutions to do so on behalf of the institution: see s 76(5A) (added by the Further Education and Training Act 2007 s 19(1), (10)). See also note 5.

11 Further and Higher Education Act 1992 s 76(1)(b), (2A) (s 76(1)(b) added by the Further Education and Training Act 2007 s 19(1), (2)(b); and amended by the Apprenticeships, Skills, Children and Learning Act 2009 ss 259(1), 266, Sch 16 Pt 11; and the Further and Higher Education Act 1992 s 76(2A) added by the Further Education and Training Act 2007 s 19(1), (4)).

    Within the period of four years beginning with the commencement of the Further Education and Training Act 2007 s 19 (ie 1 May 2008: see the Further Education and Training Act 2007 (Commencement No 1 and Transitional Provisions) Order 2007, SI 2007/3505, art 6) the Secretary of State must lay before Parliament a report about the effect of that section: Further Education and Training Act 2007 s 20. As to the Secretary of State see PARA 58. Within the period of four years beginning with the commencement of the Apprenticeships, Skills, Children and Learning Act 2009 s 259(1) (ie 1 October 2010: see the Apprenticeships, Skills, Children and Learning Act 2009 (Commencement No 2 and Transitional Provisions) (Wales) Order 2010, SI 2010/2413, arts 1(2), 2(c)) the Welsh Ministers must lay before the National Assembly for Wales a report about its effect: Apprenticeships, Skills, Children and Learning Act 2009 s 259(2). As to the Welsh Ministers see PARA 59. As to the National Assembly for Wales see CONSTITUTIONAL AND ADMINISTRATIVE LAW vol 20 (2014) PARA 351 et seq.

12 Further and Higher Education Act 1992 s 76(3) (amended by the Further Education and Training Act 2007 s 19(1), (6)).

13 See the Further and Higher Education Act 1992 s 76(4) (amended by the Further Education and Training Act 2007 s 19(1), (7)).

14 Further and Higher Education Act 1992 s 76(4)(a).

15 Further and Higher Education Act 1992 s 76(4)(b).

16 Further and Higher Education Act 1992 s 76(4A)(a) (s 76(4A) added by the Further Education and Training Act 2007 s 19(1), (8)).

17 Further and Higher Education Act 1992 s 76(4A)(b) (as added: see note 16).

18 Ie conferred by the Further and Higher Education Act 1992 s 76.

19 Further and Higher Education Act 1992 s 76(6) (amended by the Further Education and Training Act 2007 s 19(1), (11)).

20 Further and Higher Education Act 1992 s 76(6A) (added by the Further Education and Training Act 2007 s 19(1), (12)).

686.   Unrecognised degrees.   Any person[1] who, in the course of business, grants, offers to grant or issues any invitation relating to any award[2] which may reasonably be taken to be an award granted or to be granted by a United Kingdom institution[3], and which either is described as a degree[4], or purports to confer on its holder the right to the title of bachelor, master or doctor and may reasonably be taken to be a degree[5], is guilty of an offence[6]. However, this does not apply as respects anything done in relation to any 'recognised award', that is, any award granted or to be granted by a university[7], college or other body which is authorised by Royal Charter or by or under Act of Parliament to grant degrees[8], any award granted or to be granted by any body for the time being permitted by body so authorised to act on its behalf in the granting of degrees[9], or such other award as the appropriate national authority may by order designate as a recognised award for these purposes[10].

1   As to the meaning of 'person' see PARA 7 note 6.

2　The reference to issuing an invitation relating to any award includes, in particular, the issuing of any circular, prospectus or advertisement relating to an award, whether addressed to the public generally, to any section of the public, or to any particular individual or individuals: Education Reform Act 1988 s 214(10)(c).

3　Education Reform Act 1988 s 214(1)(a). 'United Kingdom institution' means any institution established in the United Kingdom, other than one which is, or is affiliated to or forms part of, an institution whose principal establishment is situated outside the United Kingdom: s 214(10)(a). As to the meaning of 'United Kingdom' see PARA 73 note 3. Where in any proceedings for an offence under s 214 it is shown that the defendant granted, offered to grant or issued an invitation relating to an award, and that an address in the United Kingdom was given in any document issued by the defendant certifying the granting of the award or containing the offer or invitation in question, the award must be presumed to fall within s 214(1)(a) unless it is shown that the defendant took reasonable steps to inform the person to whom the award was granted, or any member of the public or particular individual to whom the offer or invitation was addressed that the award was not granted or to be granted by a United Kingdom institution: s 214(4). In any proceedings for an offence under s 214, it is a defence for the defendant to show that the award in question was granted or to be granted by virtue of authority conferred on or before 5 July 1988 by a foreign institution (ie any institution other than a United Kingdom institution: s 214(10)(b)) on the body granting the award (s 214(5)(a)) and that the defendant took reasonable steps to inform the person to whom the award was granted or any member of the public or particular individual to whom the offer was addressed that the award was granted or was to be granted by virtue of authority conferred by a foreign institution (s 214(5)(b)). For the purposes of s 214(5), where on or before 5 July 1988 authority was conferred by a foreign institution on a body to grant awards of any description for a period expiring after that date, and new authority is conferred by the institution (whether before or after the expiry of that period) on the body to grant awards of that description, the new authority is to be taken to have been granted on or before that date: s 214(6). Provision is made for the application of s 214 to Northern Ireland and the Channel Islands: see s 217.

4　Education Reform Act 1988 s 214(1)(b)(i).

5　Education Reform Act 1988 s 214(1)(b)(ii).

6　Education Reform Act 1988 s 214(1). The penalty for such an offence is a fine not exceeding level 5 on the standard scale: see s 214(1). As to the standard scale see SENTENCING AND DISPOSITION OF OFFENDERS vol 92 (2010) PARA 142. As to the enforcement of these provisions see PARA 687. Proceedings for an offence under s 214 may not, in England and Wales, be instituted except by or on behalf of a local weights and measures authority or the chief officer of police for a police area: s 214(8). Where an offence under s 214 which has been committed by a body corporate is proved to have been committed with the consent and connivance of, or to be attributable to any neglect on the part of, any director, manager, secretary or other similar officer of the body corporate, or any person who was purporting to act in any such capacity, he as well as the body corporate is guilty of that offence and is liable to be proceeded against and punished accordingly: s 214(7). As to the meanings of 'England' and 'Wales' see PARA 7 note 3. As to local weights and measures authorities see WEIGHTS AND MEASURES vol 99 (2012) PARA 519. As to chief officers of police see POLICE AND INVESTIGATORY POWERS vol 84 (2013) PARA 112 et seq. A local weights and measures authority must, whenever the appropriate national authority so directs, make to the appropriate national authority a report on the exercise of its functions under s 214 in such form and containing such particulars as the appropriate national authority may direct: see s 215(1). 'Appropriate national authority' means the Secretary of State or, in relation to Wales, the Welsh Ministers. As to the Secretary of State see PARA 58. As to the Welsh Ministers see PARA 59. The functions of the Secretary of State under the Education Reform Act 1988 ss 214, 215, so far as exercisable in relation to Wales, were transferred to the National Assembly for Wales (see the National Assembly for Wales (Transfer of Functions) Order 1999, SI 1999/672, art 2, Sch 1) and are now vested in the Welsh Ministers (see the Government of Wales Act 2006 s 162(1), Sch 11 para 30).

　　Nothing in the Education Reform Act 1988 s 214 applies in relation to the granting of an award to a candidate who before 12 May 1988 began to undertake a course of education approved by the person granting the award in preparation for an examination to qualify for the award, and whether before or after that date, passes the examination; and for these purposes, 'examination' includes any form of assessment, and the reference to passing an examination is to be construed accordingly: s 214(9).

7　As to the meaning of 'university' see PARA 621 note 3.

8　Education Reform Act 1988 s 214(2)(a) (amended by the Further and Higher Education Act 1992 s 93(1), Sch 8 paras 27, 48). For the purposes of the Education Reform Act 1988 s 214 and s 215 (see PARA 687), any body for the time being designated by order made by the appropriate national authority as appearing to it to be a body falling within s 214(2)(a) or (b) (see the text to note 9) (a 'recognised body') must be conclusively presumed to be such a body: s 216(1), (4). As to the bodies designated as recognised bodies see the Education (Recognised Bodies) (England) Order 2013, SI 2013/2992; and the Education (Recognised Bodies) (Wales) Order 2012, SI 2012/1260. The appropriate national authority must compile, maintain and publish by order a list including the name of every body which appears to it for the time being to be a body which is not a recognised body and which either provides any course which is in preparation for a degree to be granted by a recognised body and is approved by or on behalf of the recognised body, or is a constituent college, school or hall or other institution of a university which is a recognised body: Education Reform Act 1988 s 216(2), (3). As to the bodies listed see the Education (Listed Bodies) (England) Order 2013, SI 2013/2993; and the Education (Listed Bodies) (Wales) Order 2012, SI 2012/1259 (amended by SI 2013/2318). Provision is made for the application of the Education Reform Act 1988 s 216 to Northern Ireland and the Channel Islands: see s 217.

9 Education Reform Act 1988 s 214(2)(b). See also note 8.

10 Education Reform Act 1988 s 214(2)(c). An order under s 214(2)(c) may designate as a recognised award either a specified award granted or to be granted by a person named in the order (s 214(3)(a)) or any award granted or to be granted by such a person (s 214(3)(b)). Specified awards are designated under the Education (Recognised Awards) Order 1988, SI 1988/2035 (amended by SI 1989/598; SI 1990/1085; and SI 1993/2828). See also the Education (Recognised Awards) (Richmond The American International University in London) Order 2006, SI 2006/3121.

687. Enforcement of provisions relating to unrecognised degrees. It is the duty of every local weights and measures authority[1] to enforce the provisions with regard to unrecognised degrees[2] within its area[3]. A duly authorised officer of a local weights and measures authority may[4], at all reasonable hours and on production, if required, of his credentials:

(1) for the purpose of ascertaining whether any offence has been committed[5], enter and search any premises[6] which he reasonably believes may be used for or in connection with the carrying on of a business which is concerned with the granting of awards which are not recognised awards[7];

(2) for that purpose, require any person[8] carrying on or employed[9] in connection with any such business to produce any documents or other items[10] relating to the business, and take copies of any such document[11];

(3) require any information which is contained in a computer and is accessible from the premises to be produced in a form in which it can be taken away and in which it is visible and legible if he has reason to believe that it may be evidence of the commission of an offence[12]; and

(4) seize[13] and detain anything which he has reason to believe may be evidence of the commission of such an offence[14].

1 As to local weights and measures authorities see WEIGHTS AND MEASURES vol 99 (2012) PARA 519. Functions under the Education Reform Act 1988 s 215 are 'relevant functions' for the purposes of the Regulatory Enforcement and Sanctions Act 2008 s 4, Sch 3: see LOCAL GOVERNMENT vol 69 (2009) PARA 733.

2 Ie the provisions of the Education Reform Act 1988 s 214: see PARA 686.

3 Education Reform Act 1988 s 215(1). A local weights and measures authority must, whenever the appropriate national authority so directs, make to the appropriate national authority a report on the exercise of its functions under s 215 in such form and containing such particulars as the appropriate national authority may direct: see s 215(1). 'Appropriate national authority' means the Secretary of State or, in relation to Wales, the Welsh Ministers. As to the Secretary of State see PARA 58. As to the Welsh Ministers see PARA 59. As to the meaning of 'Wales' see PARA 7 note 3. The functions of the Secretary of State under the Education Reform Act 1988 s 215, so far as exercisable in relation to Wales, were transferred to the National Assembly for Wales (see the National Assembly for Wales (Transfer of Functions) Order 1999, SI 1999/672, art 2, Sch 1) and are now vested in the Welsh Ministers (see the Government of Wales Act 2006

s 162(1), Sch 11 para 30). Provision is made for the application of the Education Reform Act 1988 s 215 to Northern Ireland and the Channel Islands: see s 217.

4 The Trade Descriptions Act 1968 s 29 (penalty for obstruction of authorised officers: see CONSUMER PROTECTION vol 21 (2011) PARA 523) applies as respects the obstruction of an officer acting in pursuance of the Education Reform Act 1988 s 215 as it applies as respects the obstruction of an officer acting in pursuance of the Trade Descriptions Act 1968, but with the substitution in s 29(1) (1) of a reference to the Education Reform Act 1988 s 215 for the reference to the Trade Descriptions Act 1968 s 28 (Education Reform Act 1988 s 215(7)(a)); and (2) of a reference to the officer's functions under s 215 for the reference to his functions under the Trade Descriptions Act 1968 (Education Reform Act 1988 s 215(7)(b)).

5 Ie under the Education Reform Act 1988 s 214: see PARA 686.

6 If a justice of the peace, on sworn information in writing, is satisfied that there is reasonable ground to believe that any documents or other items which a duly authorised officer has power under this provision to inspect are on any premises and that their inspection is likely to disclose evidence of the commission of an offence under the Education Reform Act 1988 s 214, and is also satisfied either that admission to the premises has been or is likely to be refused and that notice of intention to apply for a warrant under s 215(4) has been given to the occupier, or that an application for admission, or the giving of such a notice, would defeat the object of the entry or that the premises are unoccupied or that the occupier is temporarily absent and it might defeat the object of the entry to await his return, he may by warrant under his hand, which continues in force for a period of one month, authorise an officer of a local weights and measures authority to enter the premises, if need be by force: s 215(4). As to justices of the peace see MAGISTRATES vol 71 (2013) PARA 401 et seq. As to the meaning of 'month' see PARA 54 note 26.

An officer entering any premises by virtue of s 215 may take with him such other persons and such equipment as may appear to him necessary, and on leaving any premises which he has entered by virtue of a warrant under s 215(4) he must, if the premises are unoccupied or the occupier is temporarily absent, leave them as effectively secured against trespassers as he found them: s 215(6).

7 Education Reform Act 1988 s 215(2)(a). As to the meaning of 'recognised award' see PARA 686 (definition applied by s 215(3)).

8 As to the meaning of 'person' see PARA 7 note 6.

9 As to the meaning of 'employed' see PARA 301 note 2.

10 Nothing in the Education Reform Act 1988 s 215 may be taken to compel the production by a solicitor of a document or other item containing a privileged communication made by or to him in that capacity or to authorise the taking of possession of any such item which is in his possession: s 215(8). As to privileged communications between solicitor and client see CONFIDENCE AND INFORMATIONAL PRIVACY vol 19 (2011) PARA 36; LEGAL PROFESSIONS vol 65 (2015) PARAS 538–539.

11 Education Reform Act 1988 s 215(2)(b).

12 Education Reform Act 1988 s 215(2)(c). The offence referred to is one under s 214 (see PARA 686): see s 215(2)(c).

13 An officer seizing any documents or other items in the exercise of his powers under this provision must inform the person from whom they are seized: Education Reform Act 1988 s 215(5).

14 Education Reform Act 1988 s 215(2)(d).

(4) QUALITY AND ASSESSMENT OF HIGHER EDUCATION

688. Assessment of quality of higher education in England. The Higher Education Funding Council for England[1] must:

(1) secure that provision is made for assessing the quality of education provided in institutions for whose activities it provides, or is considering providing, financial support[2]; and

(2) establish a committee, to be known as the 'Quality Assessment Committee', with the function of giving it advice on the discharge of its duty under head (1) above and such other functions as may be conferred on the committee by the Higher Education Funding Council[3].

1 As to the Higher Education Funding Council for England see PARA 691.

2 Further and Higher Education Act 1992 s 70(1)(a) (amended by the Education Act 1994 s 24, Sch 2 para 10(1), (2); and the Further and Higher Education Act 1992 s 70(1) amended by the Higher Education (Wales) Act 2015 Schedule paras 1, 2). The amendment by the Higher Education (Wales) Act 2015 is in force from 1 September 2015: see PARA 721. The Higher Education Funding Council for England currently meets this duty by contracting with the Quality Assurance Agency (QAA) (see PARA 690) to carry out quality assessment reviews.

3 Further and Higher Education Act 1992 s 70(1)(b). See note 2.

The majority of the members of the committee must not be members of the Higher Education Funding Council (s 70(2)(b)) and must be persons appearing to the council to have experience of, and to have shown capacity in, the provision of higher education in institutions within the higher education sector; and, in appointing such persons, the council must have regard to the desirability of their being currently engaged in the provision of higher education or in carrying responsibility for such provision (see s 70(2)(a), (3)).

Schedule 1 applies to the committee as it applies to committees established under Sch 1 para 8 (see PARA 694): s 70(4).

As to the meaning of 'higher education' see PARA 24. As to the meaning of 'institution within the higher education sector' see PARA 619.

689. Assessment of quality of higher education in Wales. Part 3 of the Higher Education (Wales) Act 2015[1] makes provision for the Higher Education Funding Council for Wales[2] to assess, or make arrangements for the assessment of, the quality of education provided by or on behalf of institutions[3] that have a fee and access plan[4], including provision about (1) powers available for the purposes of assessment; and (2) steps that may be taken by the Council in respect of education of inadequate quality[5].

1 Ie the Higher Education (Wales) Act 2015 Pt 3 (ss 17–26). As to the Act generally see PARA 721.
2 As to the Higher Education Funding Council for Wales see PARA 691 et seq.
3 As to higher education institutions see PARA 619 et seq.
4 As to fee and access plans see PARA 721.

5 See the Higher Education (Wales) Act 2015 s 1(4). As to the assessment of quality of education see s 17. As to powers in respect of inadequate education see ss 18–20. As to co-operation with quality assessment etc see s 21. As to supplementary powers for purpose of quality assessment etc see s 22. As to guidance relating to quality of education see ss 23–34. As to advice to the Council about quality assessment functions see s 25. As to the application of Pt 3 where the institution ceases to have an approved plan see s 26. Sections 17–25 are in force from 1 September 2015: see the Higher Education (Wales) Act 2015 (Commencement No 1 Order and Saving Provision) Order 2015, SI 2015/1327; and PARA 721 note 1. The Higher Education (Wales) Act 2015 s 26 is to be brought into force on such day as the Welsh Ministers may appoint by order made by statutory instrument: s 59(2). At the date at which this volume states the law, no such order had been made. See also PARA 721.

690. The Quality Assurance Agency for Higher Education. The Quality Assurance Agency for Higher Education is an independent, non-statutory body established to provide an integrated quality assurance service for the higher education sector[1]. The Agency's principal role is to review the quality and standards of higher education by auditing the way in which each higher education institution manages the overall quality and standards of its educational provision and by reviewing academic standards and the quality of teaching and learning[2]. It also audits academic partnerships with institutions outside the United Kingdom offering teaching leading to the award of United Kingdom degrees and advises Her Majesty's government on applications from higher education institutions for the grant of degree-awarding powers or university status[3]. The Agency publishes the results of its audits and reviews and also publishes a code of practice setting out guidelines on good practice relating to the management of academic quality and standards[4].

Statutory provision is also made for the assessment of matters relating to the arrangements made by institutions within the higher education sector in Great Britain for maintaining academic standards in the institution[5].

1   See further the Quality Assurance Agency for Higher Education website.
2   As to actions following on from such a review see *R (on the application of Interchange Trust) v London Metropolitan University* [2005] EWHC 2841 (Admin), [2006] ELR 308, [2005] All ER (D) 133 (Nov) (university's decision to refuse to continue to run a course provided by the applicant charity was justifiable and sensible, having been part of a separate decision-making process from that of the Quality Assurance Agency, whose review of the course had resulted in a negative report).
3   As to university statutes see PARA 624 et seq. As to the award of degrees see PARA 685 et seq.
4   Publications may be found on the Quality Assurance Agency for Higher Education website: see note 1.
5   A relevant authority must, if directed by the Secretary of State, make provision jointly with another relevant authority or with the Secretary of State for the assessment by a person appointed by them of matters relating to the arrangements made by each institution in Great Britain which is within the higher education sector for maintaining academic standards in the institution: Further and Higher Education Act 1992 s 82(2) (amended by SI 2005/3238; and the Education Act 2011 Sch 12 paras 1, 36). 'Relevant authority' means a higher education funding council, and the Welsh Ministers to the extent that they are discharging their functions under the Learning and Skills Act 2000 Pt 2 (ss 31–41) (see PARA 789 et seq): see the Further and Higher Education Act 1992 s 82(3)(a) (substituted by SI 2005/3238; and amended by SI 2010/1080; the Education Act 2011 Sch 12 paras 1, 36; and the Deregulation Act 2015 Sch 14 paras 36, 39). As to directions see further the Education Act 1996 s 570 (applied by the Further and Higher Education Act 1992 s 89(5) (substituted by the Apprenticeships, Skills, Children and Learning Act 2009 s 125, Sch 8 paras 1, 11(1), (4); and amended by SI 2010/1158)); and PARA 75. As to the meaning of 'person' see PARA 7 note 6. As to the meaning of references to a Higher Education Funding Council see PARA 691 note 1. As to the meanings of 'England' and 'Wales' see PARA 7 note 3. As to the meaning of 'Great Britain' see PARA 73 note 3. As to the meaning of 'functions' see PARA 18 note 5 (definition applied by the Further and Higher Education Act 1992 s 90(5) (amended by the Education Act 1996 s 582(1), Sch 37 para 115(3); and the School Standards and Framework Act 1998 s 140(1), Sch 30 para 46(b))). As to the meaning of 'institution within the higher education sector' see PARA 619.
    The functions of the Secretary of State under the Further and Higher Education Act 1992 s 82(2), so far as exercisable in relation to Wales, were transferred to the National Assembly for Wales (see the National Assembly for Wales (Transfer of Functions) Order 1999, SI 1999/672, art 2, Sch 1) and are now vested in the Welsh Ministers (see the Government of Wales Act 2006 s 162(1), Sch 11 para 30). The functions under the Further and Higher Education Act 1992 s 82(3)(a) now vested in the Welsh Ministers were originally vested in the National Assembly for Wales and are now exercisable by the Welsh Ministers by virtue of the Government of Wales Act 2006 s 162(1), Sch 11 paras 30, 32. As to the Secretary of State see PARA 58. As to the Welsh Ministers see PARA 59.

(5) THE HIGHER EDUCATION FUNDING COUNCILS

(i) Establishment and Constitution of the Higher Education Funding Councils

691.   The Higher Education Funding Council for England and the Higher Education Funding Council for Wales. There are two Higher Education Funding Councils: the Higher Education Funding Council for England and the Higher Education Funding Council for Wales[1].
    The Higher Education Funding Council for England is a body corporate[2] which exercises in relation to England the functions[3] conferred on it[4], and consists of not less than 12 nor more than 15 members appointed by the Secretary of State[5], of whom one must be appointed as chairman[6]. The Higher Education Funding Council for Wales is a body corporate which exercises in

relation to Wales the functions conferred on it[7], and consists of not less than eight nor more than 12 members appointed by the Welsh Ministers[8], of whom one must be appointed as chairman[9].

In appointing the members of the Council, the Secretary of State or as the case may be, the Welsh Ministers must have regard:

(1) to the desirability of including persons who appear to have experience of, and to have shown capacity in, the provision of higher education[10] or to have held, and to have shown capacity in, any position carrying responsibility for the provision of higher education and, in appointing such persons, regard must be had to the desirability of their being currently engaged in the provision of higher education or in carrying responsibility for such provision[11]; and

(2) to the desirability of including persons who appear to have experience of, and to have shown capacity in, industrial, commercial or financial matters or the practice of any profession[12].

One of the members must be the chief officer[13].

The Higher Education Funding Councils are not to be regarded as the servants or agents of the Crown or as enjoying any status, immunity or privilege of the Crown[14], and the property of the Councils is not to be regarded as property of, or property held on behalf of, the Crown[15].

1 In the Education Acts any reference to a higher education funding council: (1) in relation to matters falling within the responsibility of the Higher Education Funding Council for England or to educational institutions in England, is to that council (Further and Higher Education Act 1992 s 62(6)(a)); and (2) in relation to matters falling within the responsibility of the Higher Education Funding Council for Wales or to educational institutions in Wales, is to that council (s 62(6)(b)). As to the meaning of 'the Education Acts' see PARA 1 note 13. As to the meanings of 'England' and 'Wales' see PARA 7 note 3. In the Further and Higher Education Act 1992 Pt II (ss 62–81) references to institutions in England or institutions in Wales: (a) are to institutions whose activities are carried on, or principally carried on, in England or, as the case may be, Wales (s 62(7)(a)); but (b) include, in both cases, the Open University (s 62(7)(b)). In relation to any time before 1 April 1993 (i e the commencement of s 65), references in Pt I (ss 15–61A) and (so far as relating to that Part) Pt III (ss 82–94) to a Higher Education Funding Council are references to the Universities Funding Council established under the Education Reform Act 1988 s 131 (repealed) (which replaced the University Grants Committee) and to the Polytechnics and Colleges Funding Council established under s 132 (repealed): Further and Higher Education Act 1992 s 61(3)(b); Further and Higher Education Act 1992 (Commencement No 1 and Transitional Provisions) Order 1992, SI 1992/831. As to the dissolution of the Universities Funding Council and the Polytechnics and Colleges Funding Council and the transfer of their property, rights and liabilities to the Higher Education Funding Council for England see the Further and Higher Education Act 1992 s 63.
2 As to bodies corporate see COMPANIES vol 14 (2009) PARA 2; CORPORATIONS vol 24 (2010) PARA 301 et seq.
3 As to the meaning of 'functions' see PARA 18 note 5 (definition applied by the Further and Higher Education Act 1992 s 90(5) (amended by the Education Act 1996 s 582(1), Sch 37 para 115(3); and the School Standards and Framework Act 1998 s 140(1), Sch 30 para 46(b))).
4 Further and Higher Education Act 1992 s 62(1)(a). As to the functions of the Higher Education Funding Councils see PARA 698 et seq.
5 As to the Secretary of State see PARA 58.
6 Further and Higher Education Act 1992 s 62(2). As to the tenure of members of the Higher Education Funding Councils see Sch 1 paras 3, 4. As to the payment of salaries, allowances and pensions to members of the Higher Education Funding Councils see Sch 1 para 5.
7 Further and Higher Education Act 1992 s 62(1)(b).
8 The functions of the Secretary of State under the Further and Higher Education Act 1992 s 62 (except those under s 62(8): see PARA 698), so far as exercisable in relation to Wales, were transferred to the National Assembly for Wales (see the National Assembly for Wales (Transfer of Functions) Order 1999, SI 1999/672, art 2, Sch 1) and are now vested in the Welsh Ministers (see the Government of Wales Act 2006 s 162(1), Sch 11 para 30). As to the Welsh Ministers see PARA 59.

9   Further and Higher Education Act 1992 s 62(3). See also note 6.
10 As to the meaning of 'higher education' see PARA 24 (definition applied by the Further and Higher Education Act 1992 s 90(1)).
11 Further and Higher Education Act 1992 s 62(4)(a).
12 Further and Higher Education Act 1992 s 62(4)(b).
13 See the Further and Higher Education Act 1992 Sch 1 para 2(1); and PARA 692.
14 As to the legal status of bodies not to be regarded as the servant or agent of the Crown or as enjoying any status, immunity or privilege of the Crown see CONSTITUTIONAL AND ADMINISTRATIVE LAW vol 20 (2014) PARA 311 et seq.
15 Further and Higher Education Act 1992 Sch 1 para 17. As to Crown property see CROWN AND CROWN PROCEEDINGS vol 29 (2014) PARA 114 et seq.

692. Chief officer. One of the members of the Higher Education Funding Council for England or as the case may be, the Higher Education Funding Council for Wales[1] must be the chief officer[2]. Following the appointment of the first chief officer[3], each subsequent chief officer is to be appointed by the Council with the approval of the appropriate national authority[4] on such terms and conditions, including terms with respect to tenure and vacation of office, as the Council may with the approval of the appropriate national authority determine[5]. On approval by the appropriate national authority of the person to be appointed on any occasion as chief officer of the Council and the terms and conditions of his appointment, the appropriate national authority must:

(1)   if that person is not already a member of the Council, appoint him as a member for the same term as the term of his appointment as chief officer[6]; or

(2)   if he is already such a member but his term of appointment as such ends before the term of his appointment as chief officer ends, extend his term of appointment as a member so that it ends at the same time as the term of his appointment as chief officer[7].

1   As to the Higher Education Funding Councils and membership thereof see PARA 691.
2   Further and Higher Education Act 1992 Sch 1 para 2(1).
3   The first chief officer of each council was appointed by the Secretary of State: see the Further and Higher Education Act 1992 Sch 1 para 2(2). As to the Secretary of State see PARA 58.
4   Ie the Secretary of State or, in relation to Wales, the Welsh Ministers. As to the Welsh Ministers see PARA 59. As to the meaning of 'Wales' see PARA 7 note 3. The functions of the Secretary of State under the Further and Higher Education Act 1992 Sch 1 para 2, so far as exercisable in relation to Wales, were transferred to the National Assembly for Wales (see the National Assembly for Wales (Transfer of Functions) Order 1999, SI 1999/672, art 2, Sch 1) and are now vested in the Welsh Ministers (see the Government of Wales Act 2006 s 162(1), Sch 11 para 30).
5   Further and Higher Education Act 1992 Sch 1 para 2(3).
6   Further and Higher Education Act 1992 Sch 1 para 2(4)(a).
7   Further and Higher Education Act 1992 Sch 1 para 2(4)(b).

693. Staff. Each Higher Education Funding Council[1] may appoint such employees[2] as it thinks fit[3]. Each Council may, with the approval of the appropriate national authority[4], pay to its employees such remuneration and allowances as it may determine[5], and appoint the employees on such other terms and conditions as it may determine[6].

Employment with the Council is included among the kinds of employment to which a scheme under the Superannuation Act 1972[7] can apply[8].

1   Ie each of the Higher Education Funding Council for England and the Higher Education Funding Council for Wales: see PARA 691.
2   As to the meaning of 'employee' see PARA 568 note 9.
3   Further and Higher Education Act 1992 Sch 1 para 7(1). As to the appointment of a chief officer see PARA 692.

4   A determination under the Further and Higher Education Act 1992 Sch 1 para 7(2) or (3) requires the approval of the appropriate national authority: see Sch 1 para 7(4). Any approval of the Secretary of State requires the consent of the Treasury (see Sch 1 para 7(4)), as does any approval of the Welsh Ministers so far as it relates to pensions (see the National Assembly for Wales (Transfer of Functions) Order 1999, SI 1999/672, art 2, Sch 1). 'Appropriate national authority' means the Secretary of State or, in relation to Wales, the Welsh Ministers. As to the Secretary of State see PARA 58. As to the Welsh Ministers see PARA 59. As to the meaning of 'Wales' see PARA 7 note 3. The functions of the Secretary of State under the Further and Higher Education Act 1992 Sch 1 para 7 (except those under Sch 1 para 7(6), (7): see note 8), so far as exercisable in relation to Wales, were transferred to the National Assembly for Wales (see the National Assembly for Wales (Transfer of Functions) Order 1999, SI 1999/672, art 2, Sch 1) and are now vested in the Welsh Ministers (see the Government of Wales Act 2006 s 162(1), Sch 11 para 30). As to the Treasury see CONSTITUTIONAL AND ADMINISTRATIVE LAW vol 20 (2014) PARA 262 et seq.

5   Further and Higher Education Act 1992 Sch 1 para 7(2).

6   See the Further and Higher Education Act 1992 Sch 1 para 7(3).

7   Ie under the Superannuation Act 1972 s 1: see CONSTITUTIONAL AND ADMINISTRATIVE LAW vol 20 (2014) PARA 298.

8   Further and Higher Education Act 1992 Sch 1 para 7(5). A Council must pay to the Treasury, at such times as the Treasury may direct, such sums as the Treasury may determine in respect of the increase attributable to Sch 1 para 7(5) in the sums payable out of money provided by Parliament under the Superannuation Act 1972: Further and Higher Education Act 1992 Sch 1 para 7(6). Where an employee of the Council is, by reference to that employment, a participant in such a scheme and is also a member of the Council, the Treasury may determine that his service as such a member is to be treated for the purposes of the scheme as service as an employee of the Council (whether or not any benefits are payable to or in respect of him by virtue of Sch 1 para 5: see PARA 691): Sch 1 para 7(7). As to membership of the Councils see PARA 691.

694.   Committees. Each Higher Education Funding Council[1] may establish a committee for any purpose[2]. The number of the members of a committee so established, and the terms on which they are to hold and vacate office, are fixed by the Council[3]. A committee may include persons who are not members of the Council[4]. The Council must keep under review the structure of committees so established and the scope of each committee's activities[5].

1   Ie each of the Higher Education Funding Council for England and the Higher Education Funding Council for Wales: see PARA 691.

2   Further and Higher Education Act 1992 Sch 1 para 8(1). As to the appointment by each Council of a Quality Assessment Committee see PARA 688. As to the procedure of committees see PARA 695. As to delegation of functions to committees see PARA 698.

3   Further and Higher Education Act 1992 Sch 1 para 8(2).

4   See the Further and Higher Education Act 1992 Sch 1 para 8(3). As to membership of the Councils see PARA 691.

5   Further and Higher Education Act 1992 Sch 1 para 8(4).

695.   Proceedings. Without prejudice to any other rights, the appropriate national authority[1] may require to be accorded to it as a condition of any grants made[2] to a Higher Education Funding Council[3] under the Further and Higher Education Act 1992[4]:

(1)   a representative of the appropriate national authority to be entitled to attend and take part in any deliberations, but not in decisions, at meetings of the Council or of any committee of the Council[5]; and

(2)   the Council to provide the appropriate national authority with such copies of any documents distributed to members of the Council or of any such committee as it may require[6].

The validity of any proceedings of the Council or of any committee of the Council is not affected by a vacancy among the members or by any defect in the appointment of a member[7]. Subject as otherwise provided[8], a Council may regulate its own procedure and that of any of its committees[9].

1 Ie the Secretary of State or, in relation to Wales, the Welsh Ministers. As to the Secretary of State see PARA 58. As to the Welsh Ministers see PARA 59. As to the meaning of 'Wales' see PARA 7 note 3. The functions of the Secretary of State under the Further and Higher Education Act 1992 Sch 1 paras 11–13, so far as exercisable in relation to Wales, were transferred to the National Assembly for Wales (see the National Assembly for Wales (Transfer of Functions) Order 1999, SI 1999/672, art 2, Sch 1) and are now vested in the Welsh Ministers (see the Government of Wales Act 2006 s 162(1), Sch 11 para 30).
2 Ie under the Further and Higher Education Act 1992 s 68: see PARA 712.
3 Ie the Higher Education Funding Council for England or the Higher Education Funding Council for Wales: see PARA 691.
4 Further and Higher Education Act 1992 Sch 1 para 11.
5 Further and Higher Education Act 1992 Sch 1 para 11(a). As to committees see PARA 694.
6 Further and Higher Education Act 1992 Sch 1 para 11(b).
7 Further and Higher Education Act 1992 Sch 1 para 12. As to the appointment of members of the Councils see PARA 691.
8 Ie subject to the provisions of the Further and Higher Education Act 1992 Sch 1 paras 1–8 (see PARAS 691–694), and Sch 1 paras 11–12 (see the text to notes 1–7).
9 Further and Higher Education Act 1992 Sch 1 para 13.

696. Application of seal and proof of instruments. The application of the seal of each Higher Education Funding Council[1] must be authenticated by the signature of the chairman[2] or of some other person authorised either generally or specially by the Council to act for that purpose, and of one other member[3].

Every document purporting to be an instrument made or issued by or on behalf of the Council and to be duly executed under the seal of the Council, or to be signed or executed by a person authorised by the Council to act in that behalf, is to be received in evidence and treated, without further proof, as being so made or issued unless the contrary is shown[4].

1 Ie each of the Higher Education Funding Council for England and the Higher Education Funding Council for Wales: see PARA 691.
2 As to the chairman of each Council see PARA 691.
3 Further and Higher Education Act 1992 Sch 1 para 14.
4 Further and Higher Education Act 1992 Sch 1 para 15.

697. Accounts. It is the duty of each Higher Education Funding Council[1]: (1) to keep proper accounts and proper records in relation to them[2]; (2) to prepare in respect of each financial year[3] of the Council a statement of accounts[4]; and (3) to send copies of the statement to the appropriate national authority[5] and to the Comptroller and Auditor General[6] or, as appropriate, the Auditor General for Wales[7] before the end of the month of August next following the financial year to which the statement relates[8].

The statement of accounts must comply with any directions[9] given by the appropriate national authority with the approval of the Treasury[10] as to the information to be contained in it[11], the manner in which the information contained in it is to be presented[12], or the methods and principles according to which the statement is to be prepared[13]; and it must contain such additional information as the appropriate national authority may, with the approval of the Treasury, require to be provided for the information of Parliament or, as the case may be, the National Assembly for Wales[14]. The Comptroller and Auditor General or as the case may be, the Auditor General for Wales must examine, certify and report on each statement so received by him and must lay copies of each statement and of his report before each House of Parliament or, as appropriate, the National Assembly for Wales[15].

1 Ie each of the Higher Education Funding Council for England and the Higher Education Funding Council for Wales: see PARA 691.
2 Further and Higher Education Act 1992 Sch 1 para 16(1)(a).
3 For these purposes, 'financial year' means the period beginning with the date on which the Council is established and ending with the second 31 March following that date, and each successive period of 12 months: Further and Higher Education Act 1992 Sch 1 para 16(4). As to the meaning of 'month' see PARA 54 note 26.
4 Further and Higher Education Act 1992 Sch 1 para 16(1)(b).
5 Ie the Secretary of State or, in relation to Wales, the Welsh Ministers. As to the Secretary of State see PARA 58. As to the Welsh Ministers see PARA 59. As to the meaning of 'Wales' see PARA 7 note 3. The functions of the Secretary of State under the Further and Higher Education Act 1992 Sch 1 para 16, so far as exercisable in relation to Wales, were transferred to the National Assembly for Wales (see the National Assembly for Wales (Transfer of Functions) Order 1999, SI 1999/672, art 2, Sch 1) and are now vested in the Welsh Ministers (see the Government of Wales Act 2006 s 162(1), Sch 11 para 30).
6 As to the Comptroller and Auditor General CONSTITUTIONAL AND ADMINISTRATIVE LAW vol 20 (2014) PARAS 494–496.
7 The functions of the Comptroller and Auditor General in the Further and Higher Education Act 1992 Sch 1 para 16 were, in relation to statements of accounts of the Higher Education Funding Council for Wales for financial years beginning in and after 1999, transferred to the Auditor General for Wales: see the National Assembly for Wales (Transfer of Functions) Order 1999, SI 1999/672, art 2, Sch 1. As to the Auditor General for Wales see CONSTITUTIONAL AND ADMINISTRATIVE LAW vol 20 (2014) PARA 400.
8 Further and Higher Education Act 1992 Sch 1 para 16(1)(c).
9 As to directions see the Education Act 1996 s 570 (applied by the Further and Higher Education Act 1992 s 89(5) (amended by the Apprenticeships, Skills, Children and Learning Act 2009 s 125, Sch 8 paras 1, 11(1), (4); and SI 2010/1158)); and PARA 75.
10 As to the Treasury see CONSTITUTIONAL AND ADMINISTRATIVE LAW vol 20 (2014) PARA 262 et seq.
11 Further and Higher Education Act 1992 Sch 1 para 16(2)(a).
12 Further and Higher Education Act 1992 Sch 1 para 16(2)(b).
13 Further and Higher Education Act 1992 Sch 1 para 16(2)(c).
14 See the Further and Higher Education Act 1992 Sch 1 para 16(2); and the National Assembly for Wales (Transfer of Functions) Order 1999, SI 1999/672, Sch 1.
15 See the Further and Higher Education Act 1992 Sch 1 para 16(3); and the National Assembly for Wales (Transfer of Functions) Order 1999, SI 1999/672, Sch 1.

(ii) Functions, Powers and Duties of the Higher Education Funding Councils

A. IN GENERAL

698. Functions of Higher Education Funding Councils. The functions of the Higher Education Funding Councils[1] are principally to administer funds made available by the appropriate national authority[2] for the purpose of providing financial support in connection with the provision of education or carrying out of research by higher education institutions[3] or the provision of higher education by other institutions[4]. The Councils also have certain functions in connection with the funding of teacher training[5]. Additional functions may be imposed[6].

In exercising their functions[7], the Councils must have regard to the requirements of disabled persons[8]. Any dispute as to whether any functions are exercisable by one of the Councils must be determined by the Secretary of State[9].

A Council may authorise the chairman[10], the chief officer[11] or any committee[12] to exercise such of its functions as the Council may determine[13].

1 Ie the Higher Education Funding Council for England and the Higher Education Funding Council for Wales: see PARA 691.
2 Ie the Secretary of State or, in relation to Wales, the Welsh Ministers. As to the Secretary of State see PARA 58. As to the Welsh Ministers see PARA 59. As to the meaning of 'Wales' see PARA 7 note 3.

3 Ie universities, institutions conducted by higher education corporations or designated institutions: see the Further and Higher Education Act 1992 s 65(5).
4 See the Further and Higher Education Act 1992 s 65; and PARA 701.
5 See PARAS 705, 706.
6 See PARA 699.
7 As to the meaning of 'functions' see PARA 18 note 5 (definition applied by the Further and Higher Education Act 1992 s 90(5) (amended by the Education Act 1996 s 582(1), Sch 37 para 115(3); and the School Standards and Framework Act 1998 s 140(1), Sch 30 para 46(b))).
8 Further and Higher Education Act 1992 s 62(7A) (s 62(7A), (7B) added by the Disability Discrimination Act 1995, s 30(5)). 'Disabled persons' means persons who are disabled persons for the purposes of the Equality Act 2010 (see DISCRIMINATION vol 33 (2013) PARA 50 et seq): Further and Higher Education Act 1992 s 62(7B) (as so added; and amended by the Equality Act 2010 Sch 26 para 23).
9 Further and Higher Education Act 1992 s 62(8).
10 As to the chairman of each Council see PARA 691.
11 As to the chief officer of each Council see PARA 692.
12 Ie established under the Further and Higher Education Act 1992 Sch 1 para 8: see PARA 694.
13 Further and Higher Education Act 1992 Sch 1 para 10. See *R (on the application of Queen Mary University of London) v Higher Education Funding Council for England* [2008] EWHC 1472 (Admin), [2008] ELR 540, [2008] All ER (D) 363 (Jun).

699. Power to impose additional functions on Higher Education Funding Councils.

The appropriate national authority[1] may by order[2] confer or impose on a Higher Education Funding Council[3] such supplementary functions relating to the provision of education as the appropriate national authority thinks fit[4]. A function is a 'supplementary function' if it is exercisable for the purposes of:

(1)   the exercise by the appropriate national authority of functions of its under any enactment[5]; or

(2)   the doing by the appropriate national authority of anything it has power to do apart from any enactment[6],

if it relates to, or to the activities of, institutions[7] which are: (a) institutions within the higher education sector[8]; or (b) institutions within the further education sector, or maintained or assisted[9] by local authorities[10], at which prescribed[11] courses of higher education[12] are currently provided[13].

1 Ie the Secretary of State or, in relation to Wales, the Welsh Ministers. As to the Secretary of State see PARA 58. As to the Welsh Ministers see PARA 59. As to the meaning of 'Wales' see PARA 7 note 3. The functions of the Secretary of State under the Further and Higher Education Act 1992 s 69, so far as exercisable in relation to Wales, were transferred to the National Assembly for Wales (see the National Assembly for Wales (Transfer of Functions) Order 1999, SI 1999/672, art 2, Sch 1) and are now vested in the Welsh Ministers (see the Government of Wales Act 2006 s 162(1), Sch 11 para 30).
2 In addition to its other functions the Higher Education Funding Council for England has power to administer on behalf of the Secretary of State any scheme established by him for the payment of grant under the Education (Grant) (Financial Support for Students) Regulations 2001, SI 2001/2894 (see PARA 82) to the governing bodies of institutions within the further education sector (within the meaning of the Further and Higher Education Act 1992 s 91(3): see PARA 555) or to the proprietors of 16 to 19 academies: Higher Education Funding Council for England (Supplementary Functions) Order 2001, SI 2001/2891, art 2 (amended by SI 2012/979). As to the meaning of 'functions' see PARA 18 note 5; and as to the meaning of '16 to 19 academy' see PARA 346 note 13 (definitions applied by the Further and Higher Education Act 1992 s 90(5) (amended by the Education Act 1996 s 582(1), Sch 37 para 115(3); and the School Standards and Framework Act 1998 s 140(1), Sch 30 para 46(b))). See also the Higher Education Funding Council for Wales (Supplementary Functions and Revocation) Order 2012, SI 2012/1904; the Higher Education Funding Council for Wales (Supplementary Functions) Order 2013, SI 2013/1733; and the Higher Education Funding Council for Wales (Supplementary Functions) Order 2014, SI 2014/1464.
3 Ie the Higher Education Funding Council for England and the Higher Education Funding Council for Wales: see PARA 691.

4 Further and Higher Education Act 1992 s 69(5). As to orders made see the Higher Education Funding Council for England (Supplementary Functions) Order 2001, SI 2001/2891; the Higher Education Funding Council for Wales (Supplementary Functions and Revocation) Order 2012, SI 2012/1904; the Higher Education Funding Council for Wales (Supplementary Functions) Order 2013, SI 2013/1733; and the Higher Education Funding Council for Wales (Supplementary Functions) Order 2014, SI 2014/1464. See also note 2.

5 Further and Higher Education Act 1992 s 69(6)(a).

6 Further and Higher Education Act 1992 s 69(6)(b).

7 Further and Higher Education Act 1992 s 69(6).

8 Further and Higher Education Act 1992 s 69(7)(a). As to the meaning of 'institution within the higher education sector' see PARA 619.

9 As to the meaning of 'assisted' see PARA 51 (definition applied by the Further and Higher Education Act 1992 s 90(5) (as amended: see note 2).

10 As to the meaning of 'local authority' see PARA 25 (definition applied by the Further and Higher Education Act 1992 s 90(1)).

11 'Prescribed' means prescribed by regulations made by the appropriate national authority: see the Education Act 1996 s 579(1) (definitions applied by the Further and Higher Education Act 1992 s 90(5) (as amended: see note 2)).

12 As to the meaning of 'course of higher education' see PARA 684 (definition applied by the Further and Higher Education Act 1992 s 90(5) (as amended: see note 2)).

13 Further and Higher Education Act 1992 s 69(7)(b) (amended by SI 2010/1158).

700. Directions. In exercising its functions[1], each Higher Education Funding Council[2] must comply with any directions[3] under the following provisions, and such directions must be contained in an order[4] made by the appropriate national authority[5].

The appropriate national authority may give general directions to a Council about the exercise of its functions[6]. If it appears to the appropriate national authority that the financial affairs of any institution within the higher education sector[7] have been or are being mismanaged it may, after consulting[8] the Council and the institution, give such directions to the Council about the provision of financial support in respect of the activities carried on by the institution as the appropriate national authority considers are necessary or expedient by reason of the mismanagement[9].

1 Ie its functions under the Further and Higher Education Act 1992 Pt II (ss 62–81). As to the meaning of 'functions' see PARA 18 note 5 (definition applied by the Further and Higher Education Act 1992 s 90(5) (amended by the Education Act 1996 s 582(1), Sch 37 para 115(3); and the School Standards and Framework Act 1998 s 140(1), Sch 30 para 46(b))).

2 Ie each of the Higher Education Funding Council for England and the Higher Education Funding Council for Wales: see PARA 691.

3 As to directions see the Education Act 1996 s 570 (applied by the Further and Higher Education Act 1992 s 89(5) (amended by the Apprenticeships, Skills, Children and Learning Act 2009 s 125, Sch 8 paras 1, 11(1), (4); SI 2010/1158)); and PARA 75.

4 At the date at which this volume states the law no such order had been made.

5 Further and Higher Education Act 1992 s 81(1). 'Appropriate national authority' means the Secretary of State or, in relation to Wales, the Welsh Ministers. As to the Secretary of State see PARA 58. As to the Welsh Ministers see PARA 59. As to the meaning of 'Wales' see PARA 7 note 3. The functions of the Secretary of State under the Further and Higher Education Act 1992 s 81, so far as exercisable in relation to Wales, were transferred to the National Assembly for Wales (see the National Assembly for Wales (Transfer of Functions) Order 1999, SI 1999/672, art 2, Sch 1) and are now vested in the Welsh Ministers (see the Government of Wales Act 2006 s 162(1), Sch 11 para 30).

6 Further and Higher Education Act 1992 s 81(2).

7 As to the meaning of 'institution within the higher education sector' see PARA 619.

8 As to the exercise of the duty to consult see JUDICIAL REVIEW vol 61 (2010) PARA 627.

9 Further and Higher Education Act 1992 s 81(3).

701. Administration of funds by Higher Education Funding Councils. Each Higher Education Funding Council[1] is responsible[2] for administering funds made available to the Council by the appropriate national authority[3] and others for the purposes of providing financial support for activities eligible for funding, namely[4]:

(1) the provision of education and the undertaking of research by higher education institutions[5] in the Council's area[6];

(2) the provision of any facilities, and the carrying on of any other activities, by higher education institutions in its area which the governing bodies[7] of those institutions consider it necessary or desirable to provide or carry on for the purpose of or in connection with education or research[8];

(3) the provision by institutions in its area maintained[9] or assisted[10] by local authorities[11], or by such institutions in its area as are within the further education sector[12], of prescribed[13] courses of higher education[14]; and

(4) the provision by any person[15] of services for the purposes of, or in connection with, the provision of education or the undertaking of research by institutions within the higher education sector[16].

Each Council may:

(a) make grants, loans or other payments to the governing body of any higher education institution in respect of expenditure incurred or to be incurred[17] by it for the purposes of any activities eligible for funding by virtue of head (1) or head (2) above[18]; and

(b) make grants, loans or other payments to any persons in respect of expenditure incurred or to be incurred by them for the purposes of the provision as mentioned in head (3) above of prescribed courses of higher education or the provision of services as mentioned in head (4) above[19],

subject in each case to such terms and conditions as the Council thinks fit[20].

Each Council must keep under review activities eligible for funding under these provisions[21].

1 Ie each of the Higher Education Funding Council for England and the Higher Education Funding Council for Wales: see PARA 691.
2 Ie subject to the provisions of the Further and Higher Education Act 1992 Part II (ss 62–81).
3 Ie the Secretary of State or, in relation to Wales, the Welsh Ministers. As to the Secretary of State see PARA 58. As to the Welsh Ministers see PARA 59. As to the meaning of 'Wales' see PARA 7 note 3. The functions of the Secretary of State under the Further and Higher Education Act 1992 s 65, so far as exercisable in relation to Wales, were transferred to the National Assembly for Wales (see the National Assembly for Wales (Transfer of Functions) Order 1999, SI 1999/672, art 2, Sch 1) and are now vested in the Welsh Ministers (see the Government of Wales Act 2006 s 162(1), Sch 11 para 30).
4 See the Further and Higher Education Act 1992 s 65(1).
5 'Higher education institution' means a university, an institution conducted by a higher education corporation or a designated institution: Further and Higher Education Act 1992 s 65(5). As to the meaning of 'university' see PARA 621 note 3. As to the meaning of 'higher education corporation' see PARA 645. In Pt II (ss 62–81), 'designated institution' means an institution in relation to which a designation made, or having effect as if made, under the Education Reform Act 1988 s 129 (see PARA 671) has effect: Further and Higher Education Act 1992 s 72(3).
6 Further and Higher Education Act 1992 s 65(2)(a).
7 As to the meaning of 'governing body' see PARA 560 note 6.
8 Further and Higher Education Act 1992 s 65(2)(b).
9 As to institutions maintained by local authorities see PARA 678 et seq.

10 As to the meaning of 'assisted' see PARA 51 (definition applied by the Further and Higher Education Act 1992 s 90(5) (amended by the Education Act 1996 s 582(1), Sch 37 para 115(3); and the School Standards and Framework Act 1998 s 140(1), Sch 30 para 46(b))).

11 As to the meaning of 'local authority' see PARA 25 (definition applied by the Further and Higher Education Act 1992 s 90(1)).

12 As to the meaning of 'institution within the further education sector' see PARA 555.

13 'Prescribed' means prescribed by regulations made by the appropriate national authority: see the Education Act 1996 s 579(1) (definitions applied by the Further and Higher Education Act 1992 s 90(5) (as amended: see note 10)). As to the regulations made see the Education (Prescribed Courses of Higher Education) Regulations 1993, SI 1993/481 (amended by SI 1998/1970).

14 Further and Higher Education Act 1992 s 65(2)(c) (amended by SI 2010/1158). As to the meaning of 'course of higher education' see PARA 684 (definition applied by the Further and Higher Education Act 1992 s 90(5) (as amended: see note 10)).

15 As to the meaning of 'person' see PARA 7 note 6.

16 Further and Higher Education Act 1992 s 65(2)(d). As to the meaning of 'institution within the higher education sector' see PARA 619.

17 In the application of the Further and Higher Education Act 1992 s 65(3) to any grants, loans or other payments by a Council, the reference to expenditure incurred or to be incurred by the governing body of a higher education institution as mentioned in s 65(3)(a) includes a reference to expenditure incurred or to be incurred by any connected institution to which the governing body proposes, with the consent of the Council, to pay the whole or part of any such grants, loans or other payments: s 65(3A) (s 65(3A), (3B) added by the Teaching and Higher Education Act 1998 s 27). 'Connected institution', in relation to a higher education institution, means any college, school, hall or other institution which the Council in question is satisfied has a sufficient connection with that institution for the purposes of the Further and Higher Education Act 1992 s 65(3A): s 65(3B) (as so added). As to the meaning of 'school' see PARA 91 (definition applied by s 90(5) (as amended: see note 10)).

18 Further and Higher Education Act 1992 s 65(3)(a). Before exercising its discretion under s 65(3)(a) with respect to the terms and conditions (see PARA 702) to be imposed in relation to any grants, loans or other payments, a Council must consult: (1) such bodies representing the interests of higher education institutions as appear to the Council to be concerned; and (2) any such governing body of any particular higher education institution which appears to the Council to be concerned, as appear to the Council to be appropriate to consult in the circumstances: s 66(1). As to the exercise of the duty to consult see JUDICIAL REVIEW vol 61 (2010) PARA 627.

19 Further and Higher Education Act 1992 s 65(3)(b).

20 Further and Higher Education Act 1992 s 65(3). As to the terms and conditions of funding see PARA 702. As to the duty to give reasons for funding decisions based on an informed exercise of academic judgment see *R v Higher Education Funding Council, ex p Institute of Dental Surgery* [1994] 1 All ER 651, [1994] 1 WLR 242, sub nom *R v The Universities Funding Council, ex p The Institute of Dental Surgery* [1994] ELR 506.

21 Further and Higher Education Act 1992 s 69(2).

702. Terms and conditions of funding. The terms and conditions on which a Higher Education Funding Council[1] may make any grants, loans or other payments[2] may in particular:

(1)   enable the Council to require the repayment, in whole or in part, of sums paid by the Council if any of the terms and conditions subject to which the sums were paid is not complied with[3]; and

(2)   require the payment of interest in respect of any period during which a sum due to the Council in accordance with any of the terms and conditions remains unpaid[4],

but must not relate to the application by the body to whom the grants or other payments are made of any sums derived otherwise than from the Council[5].

1   Ie the Higher Education Funding Council for England and the Higher Education Funding Council for Wales: see PARA 691.

2   Ie under the Further and Higher Education Act 1992 s 65: see PARA 701.

3   Further and Higher Education Act 1992 s 65(4)(a). See *R (on the application of Queen Mary University of London) v Higher Education Funding Council for England* [2008] EWHC 1472 (Admin), [2008] ELR 540, [2008] All ER (D) 363 (Jun).

4   Further and Higher Education Act 1992 s 65(4)(b).
5   Further and Higher Education Act 1992 s 65(4).

703. Matters to which Higher Education Funding Councils must have regard in providing funding. In exercising its functions in relation to the provision of financial support for activities eligible for funding[1] a Higher Education Funding Council[2] must have regard to the desirability of not discouraging any institution for whose activities financial support is provided[3] from maintaining or developing its funding from other sources[4]. In exercising those functions a Council must have regard (so far as it thinks it appropriate to do so in the light of any other relevant considerations) to the desirability of maintaining what appears to it to be an appropriate balance in the support given by it as between institutions which are of a denominational character[5] and other institutions[6], and any distinctive characteristics of any institution within the higher education sector[7] for whose activities financial support is provided[8].

1   Ie its functions under the Further and Higher Education Act 1992 s 65: see PARA 701. As to the meaning of 'functions' see PARA 18 note 5 (definition applied by s 90(5) (amended by the Education Act 1996 s 582(1), Sch 37 para 115(3); and the School Standards and Framework Act 1998 s 140(1), Sch 30 para 46(b))).
2   Ie the Higher Education Funding Council for England and the Higher Education Funding Council for Wales: see PARA 691.
3   Ie under the Further and Higher Education Act 1992 s 65: see PARA 701.
4   Further and Higher Education Act 1992 s 66(2).
5   For these purposes, an institution is an institution of a denominational character if it appears to the Council that either: (1) at least one quarter of the members of the governing body of the institution are persons appointed to represent the interests of a religion or religious denomination (Further and Higher Education Act 1992 s 66(4)(a)); (2) any of the property held for the purposes of the institution is held upon trusts which provide that, in the event of the discontinuance of the institution, the property concerned is to be held for, or sold and the proceeds of sale applied for, the benefit of a religion or religious denomination (s 66(4)(b)); or (3) any of the property held for the purposes of the institution is held on trust for or in connection with the provision of education, or the conduct of an educational institution, in accordance with the tenets of a religion or religious denomination (s 66(4)(c)). As to the meaning of 'governing body' see PARA 560 note 6.
6   Further and Higher Education Act 1992 s 66(3)(a).
7   As to the meaning of 'institution within the higher education sector' see PARA 619.
8   Further and Higher Education Act 1992 s 66(3)(b).

704. Payments in respect of persons employed in the provision of higher education. A Higher Education Funding Council[1] has power to make payments, subject to such terms and conditions as the Council thinks fit, to any local authority[2] in its area[3], the London Pensions Fund Authority[4], and the governing body[5] of any designated institution[6], in respect of relevant expenditure[7] incurred or to be incurred by that authority or body of any class or description prescribed[8] for these purposes[9]. Each of those authorities or bodies must give the Council such information as the Council may require for the purposes of the exercise of its power to make such payments[10].

1   As to the meaning of 'higher education corporation' see PARA 645.
2   As to the meaning of 'local authority' see PARA 25 (definition applied by the Education Reform Act 1988 s 235(7) (amended by the Education Act 1996 s 582(1), Sch 37 para 81(4))).
3   Education Reform Act 1988 s 133(1)(a) (s 133(1) substituted by the Further and Higher Education Act 1992 s 67(1); and the Education Reform Act 1988 s 133(1)(a) amended by SI 2010/1158).
4   Education Reform Act 1988 s 133(1)(c) (as substituted: see note 3). The London Pensions Fund Authority was established under the London Government Reorganisation (Pensions etc) Order 1989, SI 1989/1815, art 2: see LONDON GOVERNMENT vol 71 (2013) PARA 149.

5   As to the meaning of 'governing body' see PARA 628 note 2.

6   Education Reform Act 1988 s 133(1)(d) (as substituted: see note 3). A designated institution is an institution designated under s 129 (see PARA 671): see s 133(1)(d) (as so substituted).

7   For these purposes, 'relevant expenditure' means:
    (1)   in relation to a local authority, the London Residuary Body (see note 9) or the London Pensions Fund Authority, expenditure in making payments to or in respect of persons employed or formerly employed at an institution which provides or (in the case of an institution which has ceased to exist since the employment in question came to an end) formerly provided higher education or further education (or both) (s 133(2)(a) (amended by the Further and Higher Education Act 1992 s 67(2); and SI 2010/1158)); and
    (2)   in relation to the governing body of any designated institution, expenditure in making payments to or in respect of persons employed or formerly employed at the institution (Education Reform Act 1988 s 133(2)(b)).
As to the meaning of 'employed' see PARA 301 note 2. As to the meaning of 'higher education' see PARA 24. As to the meaning of 'further education' see PARA 23 (definition applied by s 235(7) (amended by the Education Act 1996 s 582(1), Sch 37 para 81(4)). The reference in the Education Reform Act 1988 s 133(2)(a) to higher education or further education (or both) must be read, in the case of an institution which ceased to exist before 1 April 1989 (ie the date on which s 120 was brought into force: see the Education Reform Act 1988 (Commencement No 4) Order 1988, SI 1988/2271), as a reference to further education within the meaning of the Education Act 1944 s 41 (repealed) as it had effect immediately before that date, and in any other case the reference to further education must be read as a reference to further education within the meaning of s 41 (repealed) as it had effect on that date: Education Reform Act 1988 s 133(3) (amended by the Further and Higher Education Act 1992 s 67(3)).

8   'Prescribed' means prescribed by regulations made by the Secretary of State or, in relation to Wales, the Welsh Ministers: see the Education Act 1996 s 579(1) (definitions applied by the Education Reform Act 1988 s 235(7) (amended by the Education Act 1996 s 582(1), Sch 37 para 81(4)). As to the regulations made see the Education (Polytechnics and Colleges Funding Council) (Prescribed Expenditure) Regulations 1991, SI 1991/2307 (amended by SI 1996/1680; and SI 2000/1410). As to the Secretary of State see PARA 58. As to the Welsh Ministers see PARA 59. As to the meaning of 'Wales' see PARA 7 note 3. The functions of the Secretary of State under the Education Reform Act 1988 s 133, so far as exercisable in relation to Wales, were transferred to the National Assembly for Wales (see the National Assembly for Wales (Transfer of Functions) Order 1999, SI 1999/672, art 2, Sch 1) and are now vested in the Welsh Ministers (see the Government of Wales Act 2006 s 162(1), Sch 11 para 30).

9   Education Reform Act 1988 s 133(1) (as substituted: see note 3). Section 133(1) also provides for payments to be made to the London Residuary Body: see s 133(1)(b) (as so substituted). The Residuary Body was established under the Local Government Act 1985 s 57; it was wound up, and all remaining functions, property, rights and liabilities transferred to and vested in the council of the London Borough of Bromley, on 29 March 1996 (see the Education (London Residuary Body) (Transfer of Functions and Property) (No 2) Order 1992, SI 1992/2257 (amended by SI 1994/580; SI 1997/1990; SI 1998/1129; and SI 2001/3649); and the London Residuary Body (Winding Up) Order 1996, SI 1996/557. See also LONDON GOVERNMENT vol 71 (2013) PARA 5.

10   See the Education Reform Act 1988 s 133(4) (amended by the Further and Higher Education Act 1992 s 67(4); SI 2010/1158).

705. Power to reimburse certain payments to persons formerly employed in teacher training. A Higher Education Funding Council[1] may make payments, subject to such terms and conditions as it thinks fit, to a further education corporation[2] or the governing body of any designated institution[3], in respect of expenditure incurred or to be incurred by that corporation or body in making safeguarded salary payments[4] to a person who in consequence of a direction given by the Secretary of State[5] ceased before 1 April 1989 to be employed in a college for the training of teachers[6], or in a department for the training of teachers in any other establishment of further education[7].

A further education corporation or the governing body of any designated institution must give to a Higher Education Funding Council such information as the Council may require for the purposes of the exercise of its power to make such payments[8].

1   As to the meaning of 'higher education corporation' see PARA 645.
2   As to the meaning of 'further education corporation' see PARA 555 note 3 (definition applied by the Education Act 1994 s 19(5) (amended by the Education Act 1996 s 582(1), Sch 37 para 128)).
3   Ie designated under the Further and Higher Education Act 1992 s 28: see PARA 572.
4   Education Act 1994 s 18(1) (amended by the School Standards and Framework Act 1998 s 140(3), Sch 31). The amount of the safeguarded salary payment is the amount by which, in consequence of the matters mentioned in the Education Act 1994 s 18(2) (see the text to notes 5–7), a person's salary exceeds that which would normally be appropriate to the post held by him: s 18(3).
5   Ie under (1) the Further Education Regulations 1975, SI 1975/1054, reg 3(2) (now revoked); (2) the Education (Schools and Further Education) Regulations 1981, SI 1981/1086, reg 15 (now revoked), being a direction relating to a course for the training of teachers; or (3) reg 16 (now revoked): see the Education Act 1994 s 18(2)(a)–(c). As to the Secretary of State see PARA 58.
6   As to the training of teachers see PARA 1054 et seq.
7   Education Act 1994 s 18(2). As to the meaning of 'further education' see PARA 23 (definition applied by the Education Act 1994 s 19(5) (as amended: see note 2)).
8   See the Education Act 1994 s 18(4).

706.   Higher Education Funding Council for Wales as a funding agency for teacher training.   The Higher Education Funding Council for Wales[1] is responsible for administering funds made available to it by the Welsh Ministers[2] (and others) for the purpose of funding the provision of teacher training (and related activities) by eligible institutions[3].

1   As to the Higher Education Funding Council for Wales see PARA 691.
2   As to the Welsh Ministers see PARA 59.
3   As to the Higher Education Funding Council for Wales as a funding agency for teacher training see PARA 1062 et seq.

C. ANCILLARY POWERS AND DUTIES

707.   Duty to provide information to central government.   Each Higher Education Funding Council[1] must provide the appropriate national authority[2] with such information or advice relating to the provision for its area of higher education[3] as the appropriate national authority may from time to time require[4]; and may provide the appropriate national authority with such information or advice relating to such provision as the Council thinks fit[5]. Information and advice so provided must be provided in such manner as the appropriate national authority may from time to time determine[6].

1   Ie each of the Higher Education Funding Council for England and the Higher Education Funding Council for Wales: see PARA 691.
2   Ie the Secretary of State or, in relation to Wales, the Welsh Ministers. As to the Secretary of State see PARA 58. As to the Welsh Ministers see PARA 59. As to the meaning of 'Wales' see PARA 7 note 3. The functions of the Secretary of State under the Further and Higher Education Act 1992 s 69, so far as exercisable in relation to Wales, were transferred to the National Assembly for Wales (see the National Assembly for Wales (Transfer of Functions) Order 1999, SI 1999/672, art 2, Sch 1) and are now vested in the Welsh Ministers (see the Government of Wales Act 2006 s 162(1), Sch 11 para 30).
3   As to the meaning of 'higher education' see PARA 24 (definition applied by the Further and Higher Education Act 1992 s 90(1)).
4   Further and Higher Education Act 1992 s 69(1)(a).
5   Further and Higher Education Act 1992 s 69(1)(b).

6 Further and Higher Education Act 1992 s 69(1). Section 69(1) does not apply to any information which the Higher Education Funding Council for England receives in its capacity as principal regulator (within the meaning of the Charities Act 2011 s 25: see CHARITIES vol 8 (2015) PARAS 320, 321): Further and Higher Education Act 1992 s 69(1A) (s 69(1A), (1B) added by SI 2010/501; and amended by the Charities Act 2011 Sch 7 para 63). However, this does not prevent the Higher Education Funding Council for England disclosing information under the Charities Act 2011 s 56 or s 57 (see CHARITIES vol 8 (2015) PARA 316): Further and Higher Education Act 1992 s 69(1B) (as so added and amended).

708. General powers. A Higher Education Funding Council[1] may do anything which appears to it to be necessary or expedient for the purpose of or in connection with the discharge of its functions[2], including in particular: (1) acquiring and disposing of land[3] and other property[4]; (2) entering into contracts[5]; (3) investing sums not immediately required for the purpose of the discharge of its functions[6]; and (4) and accepting gifts of money, land or other property[7]. However, a Council may not borrow money[8].

1 Ie the Higher Education Funding Council for England and the Higher Education Funding Council for Wales: see PARA 691.
2 As to the meaning of 'functions' see PARA 18 note 5 (definition applied by the Further and Higher Education Act 1992 s 90(5) (amended by the Education Act 1996 s 582(1), Sch 37 para 115(3); and the School Standards and Framework Act 1998 s 140(1), Sch 30 para 46(b))). As to the functions of the Higher Education Funding Councils see PARA 698 et seq.
3 As to the meaning of 'land' see PARA 568 note 7.
4 Further and Higher Education Act 1992 Sch 1 para 1(1)(a).
5 Further and Higher Education Act 1992 Sch 1 para 1(1)(b).
6 Further and Higher Education Act 1992 Sch 1 para 1(1)(c).
7 Further and Higher Education Act 1992 Sch 1 para 1(1)(d).
8 Further and Higher Education Act 1992 Sch 1 para 1(2).

709. Efficiency studies. A Higher Education Funding Council[1] may arrange for efficiency studies[2] to be promoted or carried out by any person[3] in respect of an institution within the higher education sector[4]. A person promoting or carrying out efficiency studies at the request of a Higher Education Funding Council may require the governing body[5] of the institution concerned:

(1) to furnish the person, or any person authorised by him, with such information[6]; and

(2) to make available to him, or any person so authorised, for inspection its accounts and such other documents[7],

as the person may reasonably require for that purpose[8].

1 Ie the Higher Education Funding Council for England and the Higher Education Funding Council for Wales: see PARA 691.
2 As to the meaning of 'efficiency studies' see PARA 603 note 8.
3 As to the meaning of 'person' see PARA 7 note 6.
4 See the Further and Higher Education Act 1992 s 83(1), (1B) (s 83(1) substituted, (1B) added, by SI 2010/1080; and the Further and Higher Education Act 1992 s 83(1B) amended by the Education Act 2011 Sch 12 para 1, 37). As to the meaning of 'institution within the higher education sector' see PARA 619. As from a day to be appointed, the Further and Higher Education Act 1992 s 83(1B) is further amended: s 83(1B) (prospectively amended by the Higher Education (Wales) Act 2015 Schedule paras 1, 3). At the date at which this volume states the law no such day had been appointed. See generally PARA 721.
5 As to the meaning of 'governing body' see PARA 560 note 6.
6 Further and Higher Education Act 1992 s 83(2)(a).
7 Further and Higher Education Act 1992 s 83(2)(b).
8 See the Further and Higher Education Act 1992 s 83(2) (amended by SI 2010/1080).

D. INFORMATION

710. Duty to give information to Higher Education Funding Councils. A local authority[1], the governing body[2] of any institution within the higher education sector[3], and the governing body of any institution at which prescribed[4] courses of higher education[5] are currently or have at any time been provided[6], must give a Higher Education Funding Council[7] such information as it may require for the purposes of the exercise of any of its functions[8] under the Education Acts[9].

In addition the Higher Education Funding Council for England may direct any exempt charity in relation to which it is the principal regulator[10] to provide it with such information as it considers necessary for the purpose of discharging its duty under the Charities Act 2011[11].

1 Further and Higher Education Act 1992 s 79(a) (amended by SI 2010/1158). As to the meaning of 'local authority' see PARA 25 (definition applied by the Further and Higher Education Act 1992 s 90(1)).
2 As to the meaning of 'governing body' see PARA 560 note 6.
3 Further and Higher Education Act 1992 s 79(b). As to the meaning of 'institution within the higher education sector' see PARA 619.
4 'Prescribed' means prescribed by regulations made by the Secretary of State or, in relation to Wales, the Welsh Ministers: see the Education Act 1996 s 579(1) (definitions applied by the Further and Higher Education Act 1992 s 90(5) (amended by the Education Act 1996 s 582(1), Sch 37 para 115(3); and the School Standards and Framework Act 1998 s 140(1), Sch 30 para 46(b))). As to regulations made see note 6. As to the Secretary of State see PARA 58. As to the Welsh Ministers see PARA 59. As to the meaning of 'Wales' see PARA 7 note 3. The functions of the Secretary of State under the Further and Higher Education Act 1992 s 79, so far as exercisable in relation to Wales, were transferred to the National Assembly for Wales (see the National Assembly for Wales (Transfer of Functions) Order 1999, SI 1999/672, art 2, Sch 1) and are now vested in the Welsh Ministers (see the Government of Wales Act 2006 s 162(1), Sch 11 para 30).
5 As to the meaning of 'course of higher education' see PARA 684 (definition applied by the Further and Higher Education Act 1992 s 90(5) (as amended: see note 4)).
6 Further and Higher Education Act 1992 s 79(c). As to regulations made under s 79(c) see the Education (Prescribed Courses of Higher Education) (Information Requirements) (England) Regulations 2015, SI 2015/225.
7 Ie the Higher Education Funding Council for England or the Higher Education Funding Council for Wales: see PARA 691.
8 As to the meaning of 'functions' see PARA 18 note 5 (definition applied by the Further and Higher Education Act 1992 s 90(5) (as amended: see note 4)).
9 Further and Higher Education Act 1992 s 79. As to the meaning of 'the Education Acts' see PARA 1 note 13. As to the functions of the Higher Education Funding Councils see PARA 698 et seq.
10 Ie within the meaning of the Charities Act 2011 s 25: see CHARITIES vol 8 (2015) PARA 320.
11 See the Further and Higher Education Act 1992 s 79A (added by SI 2010/501; and amended by the Charities Act 2011 Sch 7 para 64). The reference in the text is to the discharge of the duty under the Charities Act 2011 s 26(2): see CHARITIES vol 8 (2015) PARA 320.

E. JOINT EXERCISE OF FUNCTIONS

711. Exercise of functions jointly with other further and higher education bodies. A relevant authority[1] may exercise any of its functions[2] jointly with (1) another relevant authority[3]; or (2) the appropriate national authority[4], where the condition below[5] is met[6]. The condition is that it appears to the persons[7] who are to exercise functions jointly that to do so (a) will be more efficient[8]; or (b) will enable them more effectively to discharge any of their functions[9].

A relevant authority must, if directed[10] to do so by the appropriate national authority, make provision jointly with another relevant authority or with the appropriate national authority for the assessment by a person appointed by them of matters relating to the arrangements made by each institution in Great Britain[11] which is within the higher education sector[12] for maintaining academic standards in the institution[13].

1 'Relevant authority' means a higher education funding council, the Welsh Ministers to the extent that they are discharging their functions under the Learning and Skills Act 2000 Pt II (ss 31–41) (see PARA 789 et seq) or the Scottish Higher Education Funding Council: Further and Higher Education Act 1992 s 82(3)(a) (substituted by SI 2005/3238; and amended by SI 2010/1080; the Education Act 2011 Sch 12 paras 1, 36(1), (4); and the Deregulation Act 2015 Sch 14 paras 36, 39). As to the Higher Education Funding Council for England and the Higher Education Funding Council for Wales see PARA 691. As to the Welsh Ministers see PARA 59. The functions under the Further and Higher Education Act 1992 s 82(3)(a) in relation to Wales were originally vested in the National Assembly for Wales and are now exercisable by the Welsh Ministers by virtue of the Government of Wales Act 2006 s 162(1), Sch 11 paras 30, 32. As to the meaning of 'Wales' see PARA 7 note 3.

2 As to the meaning of 'functions' see PARA 18 note 5 (definition applied by the Further and Higher Education Act 1992 s 90(5) (amended by the Education Act 1996 s 582(1), Sch 37 para 115(3); and the School Standards and Framework Act 1998 s 140(1), Sch 30 para 46(b))).

3 Further and Higher Education Act 1992 s 82(1)(a) (s 82(1) substituted and s 82(1A), (1B) added by the Education Act 2011 Sch 12 paras 1, 36(1), (2)).

4 Ie to the extent that the appropriate national authority is discharging functions under the Education Act 2002 s 14 (see PARAS 78, 615): Further and Higher Education Act 1992 s 82(1)(b) (as substituted: see note 3). The appropriate national authority may exercise functions under the Education Act 2002 s 14 jointly with a relevant authority where the condition in Further and Higher Education Act 1992 s 82(1B) (see the text to notes 7–9) is met: s 82(1A) (as added: see note 3). 'Appropriate national authority' means the Secretary of State or, in relation to Wales, the Welsh Ministers. As to the Secretary of State see PARA 58. The functions of the Secretary of State under the Further and Higher Education Act 1992 s 82, so far as exercisable in relation to Wales, were transferred to the National Assembly for Wales (see the National Assembly for Wales (Transfer of Functions) Order 1999, SI 1999/672, art 2, Sch 1) and are now vested in the Welsh Ministers (see the Government of Wales Act 2006 s 162(1), Sch 11 para 30).

5 Ie the condition in the Further and Higher Education Act 1992 s 82(1B): see the text to notes 7–9.

6 Further and Higher Education Act 1992 s 82(1) (as substituted: see note 3).

7 As to the meaning of 'person' see PARA 7 note 6.

8 Further and Higher Education Act 1992 s 82(1B)(a) (as added: see note 3).

9 Further and Higher Education Act 1992 s 82(1B)(b) (as added: see note 3).

10 As to directions see the Education Act 1996 s 570 (applied by the Further and Higher Education Act 1992 s 89(5) (amended by the Apprenticeships, Skills, Children and Learning Act 2009 s 125, Sch 8 paras 1, 11(1), (4); and SI 2010/1158)); and PARA 75. As to directions as regards the Scottish Higher Education Funding Council see the Further and Higher Education Act 1992 s 82(2A) (added by SI 1999/1756).

11 As to the meaning of 'Great Britain' see PARA 73 note 3.

12 As to the meaning of 'institution within the higher education sector' see PARA 619. As to references to institutions within the higher education sector in Scotland see the Further and Higher Education Act 1992 s 82(3)(b).

13 Further and Higher Education Act 1992 s 82(2) (amended by the Education Act 2011 Sch 12 paras 1, 36(1), (3)).

F. GRANTS

712. Grants to Higher Education Funding Councils, subject to terms and conditions. The appropriate national authority[1] may make grants to each of the Higher Education Funding Councils[2] of such amounts and subject to such terms and conditions as it may determine[3]. The terms and conditions:

(1) may in particular impose requirements to be complied with in respect of every institution, or every institution falling within a class or description specified in the terms and conditions, being requirements to be complied with in the case of any institution to which the requirements apply

before financial support of any amount or description so specified is provided by the Council in respect of activities carried on by the institution[4]; but

(2) must not otherwise relate to the provision of financial support by the Council in respect of activities carried on by any particular institution or institutions[5].

The terms and conditions may not be framed by reference to particular courses of study or programmes of research (including the contents of such courses or programmes and the manner in which they are taught, supervised or assessed) or to the criteria for the selection and appointment of academic staff and for the admission of students[6]; but they may in particular enable the appropriate national authority to require the repayment, in whole or in part, of sums paid by it if any of the terms and conditions subject to which the sums were paid is not complied with[7], and require the payment of interest in respect of any period during which a sum due to the appropriate national authority in accordance with any of the terms and conditions remains unpaid[8].

1 Ie the Secretary of State or, in relation to Wales, the Welsh Ministers. As to the Secretary of State see PARA 58. As to the Welsh Ministers see PARA 59. As to the meaning of 'Wales' see PARA 7 note 3. The functions of the Secretary of State under the Further and Higher Education Act 1992 s 68, so far as exercisable in relation to Wales, were transferred to the National Assembly for Wales (see the National Assembly for Wales (Transfer of Functions) Order 1999, SI 1999/672, art 2, Sch 1) and are now vested in the Welsh Ministers (see the Government of Wales Act 2006 s 162(1), Sch 11 para 30).
2 Ie each of the Higher Education Funding Council for England and the Higher Education Funding Council for Wales: see PARA 691.
3 Further and Higher Education Act 1992 s 68(1).
4 Further and Higher Education Act 1992 s 68(2)(a).
5 Further and Higher Education Act 1992 s 68(2)(b). As to the powers of the Higher Education Funding Councils relating to the funding of higher education see PARA 701 et seq.
6 Further and Higher Education Act 1992 s 68(3).
7 Further and Higher Education Act 1992 s 68(4)(a).
8 Further and Higher Education Act 1992 s 68(4)(b).

G. TRANSFER OF FUNCTIONS IN RELATION TO LAND AND PROPERTY

713. Land and property. Where any land[1] or other property is or was used or held for the purposes of an institution[2], and the appropriate national authority[3] is entitled to any right or interest in respect of the property, or would be so entitled on the occurrence of any event[4], then, if the institution is within the higher education sector[5], the appropriate national authority may direct[6] that all or any of its functions[7] in respect of the property are exercisable on its behalf by a Higher Education Funding Council[8], and the functions must be so exercised in accordance with such directions as the appropriate national authority may give from time to time[9].

1 As to the meaning of 'land' see PARA 568 note 7.
2 Further and Higher Education Act 1992 s 69(4)(a).
3 Ie the Secretary of State or, in relation to Wales, the Welsh Ministers. As to the Secretary of State see PARA 58. As to the Welsh Ministers see PARA 59. As to the meaning of 'Wales' see PARA 7 note 3. The functions of the Secretary of State under the Further and Higher Education Act 1992 s 69, so far as exercisable in relation to Wales, were transferred to the National Assembly for Wales (see the National Assembly for Wales (Transfer of Functions) Order 1999, SI 1999/672, art 2, Sch 1) and are now vested in the Welsh Ministers (see the Government of Wales Act 2006 s 162(1), Sch 11 para 30).
4 Further and Higher Education Act 1992 s 69(4)(b).
5 As to the meaning of 'institution within the higher education sector' see PARA 619.

6 As to directions see the Education Act 1996 s 570 (applied by the Further and Higher Education Act 1992 s 89(5) (amended by the Apprenticeships, Skills, Children and Learning Act 2009 s 125, Sch 8 paras 1, 11(1), (4); and SI 2010/1158)); and PARA 75.

7 As to the meaning of 'functions' see PARA 18 note 5 (definition applied by the Further and Higher Education Act 1992 s 90(5) (amended by the Education Act 1996 s 582(1), Sch 37 para 115(3); and the School Standards and Framework Act 1998 s 140(1), Sch 30 para 46(b))).

8 Ie the Higher Education Funding Council for England or the Higher Education Funding Council for Wales: see PARA 691.

9 Further and Higher Education Act 1992 s 69(4).

(6) STUDENT FEES FOR TUITION ETC, AND FAIR ACCESS TO HIGHER EDUCATION

(i) Fees and Access in England

A. THE DIRECTOR OF FAIR ACCESS TO HIGHER EDUCATION

714. Appointment, status, staffing and remuneration. The Director of Fair Access to Higher Education is appointed by the Secretary of State[1]. The Director is to hold and vacate office in accordance with the terms of his appointment[2], but may not be appointed for a term of more than three years[3]. He may at any time resign by giving written[4] notice to the Secretary of State[5]. The previous appointment of a person as Director does not affect his eligibility for re-appointment[6]. The Director is paid such remuneration and allowances as the Secretary of State may determine[7].

The Director may appoint such staff as he may determine[8], and the remuneration and other conditions of service of any person so appointed are to be determined by the Director[9]. The Director and the Higher Education Funding Council for England[10] may enter into arrangements with each other for the provision to the Director by the Council, on such terms as may be agreed, of staff, accommodation or services[11].

The Director and his staff are not to be regarded as servants or agents of the Crown[12].

1 See the Higher Education Act 2004 s 31(1), (2). As to the Secretary of State see PARA 58. As to the functions of the Director see PARA 715.

2 Higher Education Act 2004 Sch 5 para 2(1).

3 Higher Education Act 2004 Sch 5 para 2(1)(a).

4 As to the meaning of 'written' see PARA 76 note 8.

5 Higher Education Act 2004 Sch 5 para 2(1)(b).

6 Higher Education Act 2004 Sch 5 para 2(2).

7 Higher Education Act 2004 Sch 5 para 3. The Director of Fair Access to Higher Education is eligible to be a member of the schemes made under the Superannuation Act 1972 s 1 (see CONSTITUTIONAL AND ADMINISTRATIVE LAW vol 20 (2014) PARA 298): Sch 1 (amended by SI 2013/1609).

8 Higher Education Act 2004 Sch 5 para 4(1).

9 Higher Education Act 2004 Sch 5 para 4(2).

10 As to the Higher Education Funding Council for England see PARA 691.

11 Higher Education Act 2004 Sch 5 para 5.

12 Higher Education Act 2004 Sch 5 para 1. As to the legal status of bodies not to be regarded as the servant or agent of the Crown see CONSTITUTIONAL AND ADMINISTRATIVE LAW vol 20 (2014) PARA 311 et seq.

715. Functions of the Director of Fair Access to Higher Education. The Director of Fair Access to Higher Education[1] has such functions relating to plans[2] regarding student fees and fair access to higher education[3] as are conferred on him[4]. In addition, the Director may, where he considers it appropriate to do so, identify good practice relating to the promotion of equality of opportunity in connection with access to higher education, whether full-time or part-time[5], and give advice about such practice to publicly-funded institutions[6].

The Director must perform his functions[7] in such a way as to promote and safeguard fair access to higher education, including part-time higher education in so far as his functions are exercisable in relation to it[8]. In the performance of his functions, the Director has a duty to protect academic freedom, including, in particular, the freedom of institutions: (1) to determine the contents of particular courses[9] and the manner in which they are taught, supervised or assessed[10]; and (2) to determine the criteria for the admission of students and apply those criteria in particular cases[11]. The Director must, in the performance of his functions, have regard to any guidance given to him by the Secretary of State[12].

If so requested by the Director, the Higher Education Funding Council for England must provide the Director with any information which is in its possession and is reasonably required by the Director for the purposes of his functions[13]. If so requested by the Higher Education Funding Council for England or the Secretary of State, the Director must provide the Council or the Secretary of State with any information which is in his possession and which is reasonably required by the Council for the purposes of its functions, or the Secretary of State for the purposes of the Secretary of State's functions relating to the training for members of the school workforce[14].

The Director must provide to the Secretary of State, as soon as possible after the end of each financial year[15], a report on how he has performed his functions during that year[16]. The Secretary of State may by direction require the Director, either in such a report or in a special report, to report to him on such matters related to access to higher education as may be specified in the direction[17]. The Secretary of State must lay before each House of Parliament a copy of each report provided to him; and the Director must publish the report once it has been so laid[18].

1   As to the Director of Fair Access to Higher Education see PARA 714.
2   In the Higher Education Act 2004 Pt 3 (ss 22–41), (1) any reference to a 'plan' is a reference to a plan complying with s 33 (see PARA 718) (see ss 22(a), 41(1)); and (2) any reference to an 'English approved plan' is a reference to a plan approved under s 34 (see PARA 719) (see ss 22(b), 41(1) (amended by the Higher Education (Wales) Act 2015 Schedule paras 7, 8, 21)). The amendment by the Higher Education (Wales) Act 2015 is in force from 1 September 2015: see generally PARA 721.
3   'Higher education' is not defined in the Higher Education Act 2004; as to its meaning in the Education Act 1996 see PARA 24.
4   Higher Education Act 2004 s 31(3). As to the functions of the Director see further PARA 717 et seq.
5   Higher Education Act 2004 s 31(4)(a).
6   Higher Education Act 2004 s 31(4)(b). 'Publicly-funded institution' means any institution receiving grants, loans or other payments from the Higher Education Funding Council for England under the Further and Higher Education Act 1992 s 65 (see PARA 701) or financial assistance from the Secretary of State under the Education Act 2002 s 14 (see PARAS 78, 615): Higher Education Act 2004 s 31(5) (amended by the Education Act 2011 Sch 5 paras 18, 24). As to the Higher Education Funding Council for England see PARA 691. As to the Secretary of State see PARA 58. 'Institution' includes any training provider, whether or not the training provider would otherwise be regarded as an institution: Higher Education Act 2004 s 41(1) (definition added by the Education Act 2005 Sch 14 para 35(1), (2)(b)). As to the meaning of 'training provider' see PARA 1059 note 3 (definition applied by the Higher Education Act 2004 s 41(3) (added by the Education Act 2005 Sch 14 para 35(1), (5))).
7   Ie under the Higher Education Act 2004 Pt 3 (ss 22–41).

8   Higher Education Act 2004 s 32(1).

9   In relation to a part-time course that a student begins on or after 1 September 2012, except in such circumstances as may be prescribed, 'course' does not include any postgraduate course other than a course of initial teacher training: Higher Education Act 2004 s 41(1) (definition amended by the Education Act 2011 s 77(1)); Education Act 2011 s 77(2), (3).

10   Higher Education Act 2004 s 32(2)(a).

11   Higher Education Act 2004 s 32(2)(b).

12   Higher Education Act 2004 s 32(3).

13   Higher Education Act 2004 s 40(1) (amended by the Education Act 2011 Sch 5 paras 18, 28(1), (2)). The Higher Education Act 2004 s 40(1) does not apply to any information which the Higher Education Funding Council for England receives in its capacity as principal regulator (within the meaning of the Charities Act 2011 s 25: see CHARITIES vol 8 (2015) PARA 320 321): Higher Education Act 2004 s 40(1A) (s 40(1A), (1B) added by SI 2010/501; and amended by the Charities Act 2011 Sch 7 para 97(a), (b)). However, this does not prevent the Higher Education Funding Council for England disclosing information to the Director under the Charities Act 2011 s 56 or s 57 (see CHARITIES vol 8 (2015) PARA 316): Higher Education Act 2004 s 40(1B) (as so added and amended). The Secretary of State may provide the Director with information for the purposes of the exercise by the Director of the Director's functions: s 40(1C) (added by the Education Act 2011 Sch 5 paras 18, 28(1), (2)).

14   Higher Education Act 2004 s 40(2) (amended by the Education Act 2011 Sch 5 paras 18, 28(1), (4)). The reference in the text is to training for members of the school workforce within the meaning of the Education Act 2005 Pt 3 (ss 84A–100): see PARA 1062 et seq.

     The Higher Education Act 2004 s 40(2) does not apply to information which the Higher Education Funding Council for England requires for the purposes of its functions as principal regulator (within the meaning of the Charities Act 2011 s 25: see CHARITIES vol 8 (2015) PARA 320): Higher Education Act 2004 s 40(3) (added by SI 2010/501; and amended by the Charities Act 2011 Sch 7 para 97(c)).

15   As to the meaning of 'financial year' see PARA 716 note 4.

16   Higher Education Act 2004 Sch 5 para 7(1). See also s 40(1C); and note 13.

17   Higher Education Act 2004 Sch 5 para 7(2).

18   Higher Education Act 2004 Sch 5 para 7(3).

716.   Finance. The Secretary of State[1] may make payments to the Director of Fair Access to Higher Education[2].

It is the duty of the Director: (1) to keep proper accounts and proper records in relation to the accounts[3]; (2) to prepare in respect of each financial year[4] a statement of the accounts in such form as the Secretary of State may direct[5]; and (3) to send copies of the statement to the Secretary of State and the Comptroller and Auditor General[6] before the end of the month of August next following the financial year to which the statement relates[7]. The Comptroller and Auditor General must examine, certify and report on each statement so received by him, and must lay copies of each statement and of his report before each House of Parliament[8].

1   As to the Secretary of State see PARA 58.

2   Higher Education Act 2004 Sch 5 para 6. As to the Director of Fair Access to Higher Education see PARA 714.

3   Higher Education Act 2004 Sch 5 para 8(1)(a).

4   'Financial year' means: (1) the period beginning with the date on which the first Director takes office and ending with the next 31 March; and (2) each subsequent period of 12 months ending with 31 March: Higher Education Act 2004 Sch 5 para 7(4). As to the meaning of 'month' see PARA 54 note 26.

5   Higher Education Act 2004 Sch 5 para 8(1)(b).

6   As to the Comptroller and Auditor General see CONSTITUTIONAL AND ADMINISTRATIVE LAW vol 20 (2014) PARAS 494–496.

7   Higher Education Act 2004 Sch 5 para 8(1)(c).

8   Higher Education Act 2004 Sch 5 para 8(2).

B. STUDENT FEES FOR TUITION ETC

717. Duty of Secretary of State to impose condition as to student fees, etc. A grant made by the Secretary of State[1] to the Higher Education Funding Council for England[2] must be made subject to a condition requiring the Council to impose a condition[3] in relation to any grants, loans or other payments made by the Council[4] to the governing body[5] of a relevant institution[6]. In regard to financial assistance given by the Secretary of State[7] to the governing body of a relevant institution, the terms on which that financial assistance is given must include such a condition[8].

The condition[9] requires the governing body of the relevant institution to:

(1)   secure that, in respect of any qualifying course[10], the qualifying fees[11] in respect of any academic year[12] which begins during the grant period[13] at a time when an English approved plan is in force in relation to the institution do not exceed such limit, not exceeding the higher amount[14], as is provided by the plan for that course and that academic year[15];

(2)   secure that, in respect of any qualifying course, the qualifying fees in respect of any academic year which begins during the grant period at a time when no English approved plan is in force in relation to the institution do not exceed the basic amount[16]; and

(3)   comply with the general provisions[17] of any English approved plan that is in force in relation to the institution during any part of the grant period during which it is in force[18].

Such a condition must provide:

(a)   in the event of a failure by the governing body to comply with the requirement specified in head (1) above:

    (i)   where the qualifying fees do not exceed the higher amount, for the imposition by the funding body[19] on the governing body of any financial requirements required by a relevant direction[20]; and

    (ii)   where the qualifying fees exceed that amount, for the imposition by the funding body on the governing body of any financial requirements required by a relevant direction[21] and where the funding body is the Higher Education Funding Council for England of other financial requirements determined by the Council in accordance with principles specified by the Secretary of State in the condition[22];

(b)   in the event of a failure by the governing body to comply with the requirement specified in head (2) above, for the imposition by the funding body on the governing body of:

    (i)   where the funding body is the Higher Education Funding Council for England, financial requirements determined by the Council in accordance with principles specified by the Secretary of State in the condition[23]; and

    (ii)   where the funding body is the Secretary of State, such financial requirements as the Secretary of State thinks appropriate[24];

(c)   in the event of a failure by the governing body to comply with the requirement specified in head (3) above, for the imposition by the funding body on the governing body of any financial requirements required by a relevant direction[25].

Where such a condition is imposed in connection with any grants, loans or other payments made to the governing body of a relevant institution, and those payments are to any extent made in respect of persons undertaking a course which is provided in whole or part by any other institution, then for these purposes fees payable by such persons to the other institution are to be regarded as fees payable by them to the relevant institution[26].

1 As to the Secretary of State see PARA 58.
2 Ie under the Further and Higher Education Act 1992 s 68: see PARA 712. As to the Higher Education Funding Council for England see PARA 691.
3 Ie under the Higher Education Act 2004 s 24: see the text to notes 9–26. No condition under s 24 applies in relation to any fees which are payable, in accordance with regulations under the Education (Fees and Awards) Act 1983 s 1, by students other than those falling within any class of persons prescribed by such regulations for the purposes of s 1(1) or (2) (see PARA 1111): Higher Education Act 2004 s 29(1). See also note 8.
4 Ie under the Further and Higher Education Act 1992 s 65: see PARA 701.
5 In the Higher Education Act 2004 Pt 3 (ss 22–41), any reference to the 'governing body' of an institution: (1) in relation to any institution except a training provider falling within head (2), has the meaning given by the Further and Higher Education Act 1992 s 90(1), but subject to any provision made by virtue of s 90(2) (see PARA 560 note 6); and (2) in the case of a training provider who but for s 90(1) would not be regarded as an institution, means the training provider: Higher Education Act 2004 s 41(1A) (added by the Education Act 2005 Sch 14 para 35(1), (3)). As to the meaning of 'institution' see PARA 715 note 6 but see also note 6. As to the meaning of 'training provider' see PARA 1059 note 3 (definition applied by the Higher Education Act 2004 s 41(3) (added by the Education Act 2005 Sch 14 para 35(1), (5))).
6 Higher Education Act 2004 s 23(1), (2) (s 23 substituted by the Education Act 2011 Sch 5 paras 18, 19). 'Relevant institution' means (1) in the case of a grant to which the Higher Education Act 2004 s 23(2) applies, an institution specified, or of a class specified, by the Secretary of State in a condition under s 23(2); (2) in the case of financial assistance to which s 23(4) applies (see the text to notes 7, 8), an institution specified, or of a class specified, by order made by the Secretary of State for the purposes of s 23(4): s 23(5) (as so substituted). Nothing in the Further and Higher Education Act 1992, the Education Act 2002 or the Education Act 2005, so far as it imposes any prohibition or other requirement in relation to the imposition of conditions by the Secretary of State or the Higher Education Funding Council for England applies to: (1) any condition or terms imposed by virtue of the Higher Education Act 2004 s 23 by the Secretary of State; or (2) any condition under s 24 (see the text to notes 9–26) imposed by the Higher Education Funding Council for England: s 29(3) (amended by the Education Act 2005 Sch 14 para 29; and the Education Act 2011 Sch 5 paras 18, 23(a), (c), (d), 29(a)).
   As to the provision of financial support for students see PARA 1095 et seq.
7 Ie under the Education Act 2002 s 14: see PARAS 78, 615.
8 Higher Education Act 2004 s 23(3), (4) (as substituted: see note 6). The condition referred to in the text is a condition under s 24: see note 3.
9 Ie under the Higher Education Act 2004 s 24.
10 'Qualifying course' means a course of any description prescribed for the purposes of the Higher Education Act 2004 s 24: s 24(6). As to the meaning of 'course' see PARA 715 note 9. 'Prescribed' means prescribed by regulations made by the Secretary of State: s 24(6). The power to prescribe descriptions of course by virtue of the definition of 'qualifying course' in s 24(6) may not be exercised in such a way as to discriminate: (1) in relation to courses of initial teacher training, between different courses on the basis of the subjects in which such training is given (s 29(2)(a)); and (2) in relation to other courses, between different courses at the same or a comparable level on the basis of the areas of study or research to which they relate (s 29(2)(b)). See also note 6. As to the regulations made under s 24(6) see the Student Fees (Amounts) (England) Regulations 2004, SI 2004/1932 (amended by SI 2007/1865; SI 2010/3020; SI 2010/3021; SI 2011/432; and SI 2012/433); the Student Fees (Qualifying Courses and Persons) (England) Regulations 2007, SI 2007/778 (amended by SI 2007/2263; SI 2008/1640; 2011/87; and SI 2012/1653); the Higher Education (Higher Amount) (England) Regulations 2010, SI 2010/3020 (amended by SI 2012/433; and SI 2013/3106); and the Higher Education (Basic Amount) (England) Regulations 2010, SI 2010/3021 (amended by SI 2012/433; and SI 2013/3106).
   See *R (on the application of Hurley) v Secretary of State for Business, Innovation and Skills* [2012] EWHC 201 (Admin), [2012] ELR 297, [2012] All ER (D) 116 (Feb); and note 11.
11 'Qualifying fees', in relation to a relevant institution, means the fees payable to the institution by a qualifying person in connection with his undertaking a qualifying course; and 'qualifying

person' means a person falling within any class of persons prescribed for the purposes of the Higher Education Act 2004 s 24: s 24(6). As to the regulations made for these purposes see note 10. In Pt 3 (ss 22–41), 'fees', in relation to undertaking a course, means fees in respect of, or otherwise in connection with, undertaking the course, including admission, registration, tuition and graduation fees but excluding: (1) fees payable to an institution for awarding or accrediting any qualification where the institution does not provide the whole or part of the course and is not a publicly-funded institution; (2) fees payable for board or lodging; (3) fees payable for field trips (including any tuition element of such fees); (4) fees payable for attending any graduation or other ceremony; and (5) such other fees as may be prescribed, in relation to England, by regulations made by the Secretary of State: s 41(1) (definition amended by the Higher Education (Wales) Act 2015 Schedule paras 7, 21). This amendment is in force from 1 September 2015: see generally PARA 721. For the above purpose, 'publicly-funded institution' means any university or other institution receiving grants, loans or other payments under the Further and Higher Education Act 1992 s 65 (see PARA 701) or the Education Act 2005 s 86 (see PARA 1062) or financial assistance under the Education Act 2002 s 14 (see PARAS 78, 615), any institution maintained by a local authority in the exercise of its further and higher education functions, any institution receiving a recurrent grant towards its costs under regulations made under the Education Act 1996 s 485 (see PARA 82), or any institution receiving financial resources under the Apprenticeships, Skills, Children and Learning Act 2009 s 100 (see PARA 783) or the Learning and Skills Act 2000 s 34 (see PARA 792): Higher Education Act 2004 s 41(2) (amended by the Education Act 2005 Sch 14 para 35(1), (4); SI 2010/1080; SI 2010/1158; and the Education Act 2011 Sch 5 paras 18, 29, Sch 16 para 22).

An increase in the maximum fees chargeable by universities, alongside measures including making loans available to those who need them, does not amount to an unjustified restriction on the right to education under the Convention for the Protection of Human Rights and Fundamental Freedoms, Protocol 1 (Paris, 20 March 1952; TS 46; Cmnd 9221), art 2: *R (on the application of Hurley) v Secretary of State for Business, Innovation and Skills* [2012] EWHC 201 (Admin), [2012] ELR 297, [2012] All ER (D) 116 (Feb).

12 'Academic year', in relation to a course, means an academic year applicable to the course: Higher Education Act 2004 s 24(6).

13 'The grant period' means the period in respect of which the grants, loans or other payments in question are made: s 24(6) (definition amended by the Education Act 2011 Sch 5 paras 18, 20(1), (4)(a)). For the purposes of the Higher Education Act 2004 s 24(1), an academic year which begins at the same time as the grant period is to be taken to begin during the grant period, and an academic year which begins with the day on which an English approved plan comes into force is to be taken to begin at a time when the plan is in force: s 24(2). As to the meanings of 'plan' and 'English approved plan' see PARA 715 note 2.

14 'The higher amount' means such amount as may be prescribed for the purposes of the Higher Education Act 2004 s 24 as the higher amount: s 24(6). 'The basic amount' means such amount as may be prescribed for the purposes of s 24 as the basic amount: s 24(6). As to the regulations made for these purposes see note 10. Where regulations under s 24(6) have been made prescribing the basic amount and the higher amount for those purposes: (1) no regulations may be made increasing the basic amount unless: (a) the Secretary of State is satisfied that the increase is no greater than is required to maintain the value of the amount in real terms (s 26(2)(a)(i)); or (b) a draft of the regulations has been laid before, and approved by a resolution of, each House of Parliament (s 26(2)(a)(ii)); and (2) no regulations may be made increasing the higher amount unless: (a) the Secretary of State is satisfied that the increase is no greater than is required to maintain the value of the amount in real terms (s 26(2)(b)(i)); or (b) each House of Parliament has at any time after 1 January 2010 passed a resolution that, with effect from a date specified in the resolution, the higher amount should be increased to an amount specified in the resolution, and the increase is an increase to the specified amount with effect from the specified date (s 26(2)(b)(ii)). For the purposes of heads (1) and (2) above, the Secretary of State is to have regard to such index of prices as may be specified in, or determined in accordance with, regulations made by him under s 26(3): s 26(3). As to the regulations made see the Student Fees (Inflation Index) Regulations 2006, SI 2006/507.

15 Higher Education Act 2004 s 24(1)(a).

16 Higher Education Act 2004 s 24(1)(b). Section 24(1)(b) has effect in relation to the qualifying fees payable by a qualifying person in connection with his undertaking a qualifying course ('the relevant course'), even if those fees are payable in respect of an academic year which begins at a time when an English approved plan is in force in relation to the institution, where: (1) the qualifying person had on or before 1 August 2005 received an offer, whether conditional on obtaining specified qualifications or not, of a place on the relevant course or a similar course, and the first academic year of the relevant course begins before 1 September 2007; or (2) the

qualifying person had received an offer of a place on a qualifying course (whether or not at the same institution as the relevant course) the first academic year of which begins before 1 September 2006, he was unable to take up the offer because a specified qualification or grade was not awarded to him, he appealed against the decision not to award him the qualification or grade, the appeal was allowed after the last date on which he could have taken up the offer, and as a result he was offered a place on the relevant course, and the first academic year of the relevant course begins after 31 August 2006 but before 1 September 2007: see s 25(1)–(3). For the purposes of head (1) above, a course ('the original course') is similar to the relevant course if it appears to the governing body of the institution providing the relevant course that the subject matter of the course is in whole or in part the same as the subject matter of the original course, and (except where the original course is no longer being provided) the relevant course is provided by the institution which was to have provided the original course: s 25(4).

17 As to the meaning of 'general provisions' see PARA 718 note 11.

18 Higher Education Act 2004 s 24(1)(c).

19 'Funding body' means (1) in the case of a grant, loan or other payment made under the Further and Higher Education Act 1992 s 65 (see PARA 701), the Higher Education Funding Council for England; (2) in the case of financial assistance given by the Secretary of State under the Education Act 2002 s 14 (see PARAS 78, 615) to the governing body of a relevant institution, the Secretary of State: Higher Education Act 2004 s 24(6) (definition substituted by the Education Act 2011 Sch 5 para 20(1), (4)(a)).

20 Higher Education Act 2004 s 24(3)(a)(i). The direction referred to in the text is a direction under s 37(1)(a) (see PARA 720): see s 24(3)(a)(i).

21 Ie under the Higher Education Act 2004 s 37(1)(a): see PARA 720.

22 Higher Education Act 2004 s 24(3)(a)(ii) (amended by the Education Act 2011 Sch 5 paras 18, 20(1), (2)(a). The condition referred to in the text is the condition under the Higher Education Act 2004 s 23(2) (see the text to notes 1–6): see s 24(3)(a)(ii).

23 Higher Education Act 2004 s 24(3)(b)(i) (s 24(3)(b) amended by the Education Act 2011 Sch 5 paras 18, 20(1), (2)(b)). The condition referred to in the text is the condition under s 23(2) (see the text to notes 1–6): see the Higher Education Act 2004 s 24(3)(b)(i).

24 Higher Education Act 2004 s 24(3)(b)(ii) (s 24(3)(b) as amended: see note 23).

25 Higher Education Act 2004 s 24(3)(c). The direction referred to in the text is a direction under s 37(1)(a) (see PARA 720): see s 24(3)(c). Any financial requirements imposed by virtue of s 24(3)(c) must relate to one or more of the following: (1) the repayment, with or without interest, of the whole or any part of any sums received by the governing body in respect of the grant, loan or other payment in question (s 24(4)(a)); (2) the withdrawal or reduction of any amount that has been awarded but not yet paid in respect of the grant, loan or other payment in question (s 24(4)(b)); or (3) the refusal to award (or to award to the extent expected) any other grant, loan or other payment under the Further and Higher Education Act 1992 s 65 (see PARA 701) or (as the case may be) the Education Act 2002 s 14 (see PARAS 78, 615) in respect of the grant period or any subsequent period (Higher Education Act 2004 s 24(4)(c) (amended by the Education Act 2005 Sch 14 para 26; and the Education Act 2011 Sch 5 paras 18, 20(1), (4)(b)).

26 Higher Education Act 2004 s 24(5).

718. Contents of plans. A plan regarding student fees and fair access to higher education[1] relating to an institution[2] must, in relation to each qualifying course[3] in connection with which fees[4] are to be payable to the institution by qualifying persons[5], specify or provide for the determination of a limit (not exceeding the higher amount[6]) which those fees are not permitted to exceed[7]. Such a plan must also include such provisions relating to the promotion of equality of opportunity[8] as are required by regulations[9] to be included in the plan, and may also include further provisions relating to the promotion of equality of opportunity[10].

The general provisions[11] of such a plan that may be required by such regulations[12] include, in particular, provisions:

(1)   requiring the governing body[13] to take, or secure the taking of, measures to attract applications from prospective students who are members of groups which, at the time when the plan is approved, are under-represented in higher education[14];

(2) requiring the governing body to provide, or secure the provision of, financial assistance to students[15];

(3) requiring the governing body to make available to students and prospective students information about financial assistance available to students from any source[16];

(4) setting out objectives relating to the promotion of equality of opportunity[17];

(5) relating to the monitoring by the governing body of its compliance with the provisions of the plan and its progress in achieving any objectives set out in the plan by virtue of head (4) above[18]; and

(6) requiring the provision of information to the relevant authority[19].

The regulations may not require a plan to include among the general provisions of the plan any provision referring to particular courses[20] or to the manner in which courses are taught, supervised or assessed, or to include any provision relating to the criteria for the admission of students[21].

1   Ie a plan under the Higher Education Act 2004 s 33. As to the meaning of 'plan' see PARA 715 note 2.
2   As to the meaning of 'institution' see PARA 715 note 6.
3   As to the meaning of 'qualifying course' in relation to England see PARA 717 note 10 (definitions applied by the Higher Education Act 2004 s 33(7) (amended by Higher Education (Wales) Act 2015 Schedule paras 7, 13(1), (7)). This amendment is in force from 1 September 2015: see generally PARA 721. As to the meaning of 'England' see PARA 7 note 3.
4   As to the meaning of 'fees' see PARA 717 note 11.
5   As to the meaning of 'qualifying person' in relation to England see PARA 717 note 11 (definitions applied by the Higher Education Act 2004 s 33(7) (as amended: see note 3).
6   'The higher amount' means, in relation to England, the amount from time to time prescribed as the higher amount under the Higher Education Act 2004 s 24(6) (see PARA 717 note 14): s 33(7) (as amended: see note 3).
7   Higher Education Act 2004 s 33(1). As to the approval, duration and variation of plans see PARA 719. As to the enforcement of plans see PARA 720.
8   'Equality of opportunity' means equality of opportunity in connection with access to higher education: Higher Education Act 2004 s 33(7).
9   'Regulations' means regulations made, in relation to England, by the Secretary of State: see the Higher Education Act 2004 s 33(7) (as amended: see note 3). As to the regulations made see the Student Fees (Approved Plans) (England) Regulations 2004, SI 2004/2473 (amended by SI 2012/433; and SI 2012/765). As to the Secretary of State see PARA 58.
10 Higher Education Act 2004 s 33(2) (amended by the Higher Education (Wales) Act 2015 Schedule paras 7, 13(1), (2)).
11 In the Higher Education Act 2004 Pt 3 (ss 22–41), any reference to the 'general provisions' of a plan under s 33 is a reference to the provisions included in the plan by virtue of s 33(2) (see the text to notes 8–10): see ss 33(4), 41(1) (s 33(4) (amended by the Higher Education (Wales) Act 2015 Schedule paras 7, 13(1), (4)). This amendment is in force from 1 September 2015: see generally PARA 721.
12 Ie regulations made by virtue of the Higher Education Act 2004 s 33(2): see the text to notes 8–10.
13 As to the meaning of 'governing body' see PARA 717 note 5.
14 Higher Education Act 2004 s 33(5)(a) (s 33(5) amended by the Higher Education (Wales) Act 2015 Schedule paras 7, 13(1), (5)). This amendment is in force from 1 September 2015: see generally PARA 721.
15 Higher Education Act 2004 s 33(5)(b).
16 Higher Education Act 2004 s 33(5)(c).
17 Higher Education Act 2004 s 33(5)(d) (amended by the Higher Education (Wales) Act 2015 Schedule paras 7, 13(1), (5)). This amendment is in force from 1 September 2015: see generally PARA 721.
18 Higher Education Act 2004 s 33(5)(e).
19 Higher Education Act 2004 s 33(5)(f). 'Relevant authority' means, in relation to England, the Director of Fair Access to Higher Education (see PARA 714): see s 30 (amended by the Higher Education (Wales) Act 2015 Schedule paras 7, 11(1), (2)).
20 As to the meaning of 'course' see PARA 715 note 9.

21　Higher Education Act 2004 s 33(6) (amended by the Higher Education (Wales) Act 2015
　　Schedule paras 7, 13(1), (6)). This amendment is in force from 1 September 2015: see generally
　　PARA 721.

719. Approval, duration and variation of plans. The governing body[1] of any
institution[2] which (1) is or may become eligible to receive grants from the Higher
Education Funding Council for England[3]; or (2) provides higher education[4] and
is or may become eligible to receive financial assistance from the Secretary of
State[5], may apply to the relevant authority[6] for approval of a proposed plan
regarding student fees and access to higher education[7] relating to the institution[8].
The relevant authority may, if it thinks fit, approve the plan[9], and may issue
guidance to such institutions as to the matters to which the relevant authority is
to have regard in deciding whether to approve plans[10]. The relevant authority's
functions in relation to the approval of plans must be exercised in accordance
with regulations[11]. Regulations may, in particular, specify matters to which the
relevant authority is, or is not, to have regard in making any determination
relating to approval[12]; and may require the institution to which any approved
plan relates to publish the plan in the prescribed manner[13].

A plan must specify the period during which it is to be in force[14]. The length
of that period must not exceed such maximum as may be prescribed by
regulations made by the Secretary of State[15]. These provisions[16] do not prevent
the approval of a new plan taking effect on the expiry of a previous plan[17].

Regulations[18] may make provision enabling an English approved plan[19] to be
varied with the approval of the relevant authority[20].

1　As to the meaning of 'governing body' see PARA 717 note 5.
2　As to the meaning of 'institution' see PARA 715 note 6.
3　Ie under the Further and Higher Education Act 1992 s 65 (see PARA 701): see the Higher
　　Education Act 2004 s 34(1)(a) (s 34(1) substituted by the Education Act 2011 Sch 5 paras 18,
　　25; and amended by the Higher Education (Wales) Act 2015 Schedule paras 7, 14(1), (2))). As to
　　the Higher Education Funding Council for England see PARA 691. The amendment by the
　　Higher Education (Wales) Act 2015 is in force from 1 September 2015: see generally PARA 721.
4　'Higher education' is not defined in the Higher Education Act 2004; as to its meaning in the
　　Education Act 1996 see PARA 24.
5　Ie under the Education Act 2002 s 14 (see PARAS 78, 615): see the Higher Education Act 2004
　　s 34(1)(b) (as substituted and amended: see note 3). As to the Secretary of State see PARA 58.
6　'Relevant authority' means, in relation to England, the Director of Fair Access to Higher
　　Education (see PARA 714): see the Higher Education Act 2004 s 30 (amended by the Higher
　　Education (Wales) Act 2015 Schedule paras 7, 11). As to the meaning of 'England' see PARA 7
　　note 3. The amendment by the Higher Education (Wales) Act 2015 is in force from 1 September
　　2015: see generally PARA 721.
7　As to the meaning of 'plan' see PARA 715 note 2. As to the contents of plans see PARA 718. As to
　　the enforcement of plans see PARA 720.
8　Higher Education Act 2004 s 34(1) (as substituted and amended: see note 3).
9　Higher Education Act 2004 s 34(2).
10　Higher Education Act 2004 s 34(3).
11　Higher Education Act 2004 s 34(4). 'Regulations' means regulations made by the Secretary of
　　State: s 34(7) (amended by the Higher Education (Wales) Act 2015 Schedule paras 7, 14(1), (3)).
　　This amendment is in force from 1 September 2015: see generally PARA 721.
　　　　Regulations made by virtue of the Higher Education Act 2004 s 34 or s 36 (see the text to
　　notes 18–20) must include provision: (1) requiring any decision of the relevant authority under
　　s 34 or s 36 affecting the governing body of an institution to have effect in the first instance as
　　a provisional decision (s 39(a)); (2) enabling the governing body of the institution to apply for a
　　review of the provisional decision to a person, or panel of persons, appointed in accordance
　　with the regulations by the Secretary of State (in relation to England) (s 39(b) (s 39(b), (c)
　　amended by the Higher Education (Wales) Act 2015 Schedule paras 7, 19)); (3) enabling the
　　Secretary of State to pay remuneration and allowances to any person so appointed (Higher
　　Education Act 2004 s 39(c) (as so amended)); (4) prescribing the grounds on which an

application for the review of a provisional decision may be made (s 39(d)); and (5) requiring the relevant authority to reconsider its provisional decision having regard to any recommendation of the person or panel (s 39(e)). As to the regulations made under s 34 see the Student Fees (Approved Plans) (England) Regulations 2004, SI 2004/2473 (amended by SI 2012/433; and SI 2012/765). The amendment by the Higher Education (Wales) Act 2015 is in force from 1 September 2015: see generally PARA 721.

12 Higher Education Act 2004 s 34(5). As to the regulations made see note 11.

13 Higher Education Act 2004 s 34(6). As to the regulations made see note 11.

14 Higher Education Act 2004 s 35(1).

15 See the Higher Education Act 2004 s 35(2)(a) (s 35(2) amended by the Higher Education (Wales) Act 2015 Schedule paras 7, 15). As to the regulations made see note 11. The amendment by the Higher Education (Wales) Act 2015 is in force from 1 September 2015: see generally PARA 721.

16 Ie the Higher Education Act 2004 s 35(1), (2): see the text to notes 14–15.

17 Higher Education Act 2004 s 35(3).

18 Ie regulations made, in relation to England, by the Secretary of State: see the Higher Education Act 2004 s 36(2)(a) (s 36(2) amended by the Higher Education (Wales) Act 2015 Schedule paras 7, 16(1), (3)). As to the regulations made see note 11. The amendment by the Higher Education (Wales) Act 2015 is in force from 1 September 2015: see generally PARA 721.

19 As to the meaning of 'English approved plan' see PARA 715 note 2.

20 Higher Education Act 2004 s 36(1) (amended by the Higher Education (Wales) Act 2015 Schedule paras 7, 16(1), (2)). This amendment is in force from 1 September 2015: see generally PARA 721. See also the Higher Education Act 2004 s 39; and note 11.

720. Enforcement of plans. If the Director of Fair Access to Higher Education[1] is satisfied that the governing body[2] of an institution[3] in England[4] which is required[5] to comply with a specified requirement[6] has failed to comply with that requirement[7], the Director may do either or both of the following:

(1) direct the Higher Education Funding Council for England[8] or the Secretary of State[9] (or both) to impose specified financial requirements[10] on the governing body[11]; or

(2) notify the governing body that on the expiry of the existing plan he will refuse to approve a new plan[12] during a specified period[13].

The Secretary of State may by regulations[14] make provision:

(a) as to the matters to which the Director must, or may not, have regard in exercising these powers[15];

(b) as to the procedure to be followed in connection with the giving of any direction or notification under head (1) or head (2) above[16];

(c) as to the financial requirements that may be specified by virtue of head (1) above[17]; and

(d) as to the effect of a notification under head (2) above[18].

1 As to the Director of Fair Access to Higher Education see PARA 714.

2 As to the meaning of 'governing body' see PARA 717 note 5.

3 As to the meaning of 'institution' see PARA 715 note 6.

4 As to the meaning of 'England' see PARA 7 note 3.

5 Ie by virtue of a condition imposed under the Higher Education Act 2004 s 24: see PARA 717.

6 Ie specified under the Higher Education Act 2004 s 24(1)(a) or s 24(1)(c): see PARA 717.

7 The governing body of an institution is not to be regarded for the purposes of the Higher Education Act 2004 s 37(1) as having failed to comply with the requirement specified in s 24(1)(c) (see PARA 717) by reason of its failure to comply with any of the general provisions of an English approved plan, if the governing body shows that it has taken all reasonable steps to comply with that provision: s 37(2) (title to s 37 amended by the Higher Education (Wales) Act 2015 Schedule paras 7, 17). This amendment is in force from 1 September 2015: see generally PARA 721. As to the meaning of 'general provisions' of a plan see PARA 718 note 11. As to the meanings of 'plan' and 'English approved plan' see PARA 715 note 2.

8 As to the Higher Education Funding Council for England see PARA 691.

9 As to the Secretary of State see PARA 58.

10 Ie under the Higher Education Act 2004 s 24(3): see PARA 717.

11 Higher Education Act 2004 s 37(1)(a) (amended by the Education Act 2011 Sch 5 paras 18, 26).
12 Ie under the Higher Education Act 2004 s 34: see PARA 719.
13 Higher Education Act 2004 s 37(1)(b).
14 Regulations made by virtue of the Higher Education Act 2004 s 37(3)(b) must include provision: (1) requiring any decision of the relevant authority under s 37 affecting the governing body of an institution to have effect in the first instance as a provisional decision (s 39(a)); (2) enabling the governing body of the institution to apply for a review of the provisional decision to a person, or panel of persons, appointed in accordance with the regulations by the Secretary of State (in relation to England) (Higher Education Act 2004 s 39(b) (s 39, s 39(b), (c) amended by the Higher Education (Wales) Act 2015 Schedule paras 7, 19)); (3) enabling the Secretary of State to pay remuneration and allowances to any person so appointed (Higher Education Act 2004 s 39(c) (as so amended)); (4) prescribing the grounds on which an application for the review of a provisional decision may be made (s 39(d)); and (5) requiring the relevant authority to reconsider its provisional decision having regard to any recommendation of the person or panel (s 39(e)). As to the regulations made under s 37 see the Student Fees (Approved Plans) (England) Regulations 2004, SI 2004/2473 (amended by SI 2012/433; and SI 2012/765). The amendments by the Higher Education (Wales) Act 2015 are in force from 1 September 2015: see generally PARA 721.
15 Higher Education Act 2004 s 37(3)(a).
16 Higher Education Act 2004 s 37(3)(b).
17 Higher Education Act 2004 s 37(3)(c).
18 Higher Education Act 2004 s 37(3)(d).

(ii) Fees and Access in Wales

721. Fee and access plans. The Higher Education (Wales) Act 2015[1] makes provision for higher education institutions[2] in Wales[3] to have the power to set their own fees, so long as their plans are approved by the Higher Education Funding Council for Wales[4]. The Council is responsible for monitoring the compliance of institutions setting the fees[5].

Part 2[6] of the Higher Education (Wales) Act 2015 makes provision about fee and access plans, and deals with (1) the contents of a fee and access plan, including a fee limit; (2) failure to comply with a fee limit or other requirement included in a fee and access plan; (3) the validity of certain contracts; and (4) the monitoring of fee and access plans[7].

Part 5[8] makes provision for circumstances in which (a) the Council may refuse to approve a new fee and access plan for an institution; and (b) the Council must, or may, withdraw its approval of an institution's fee and access plan[9].

1 The Higher Education (Wales) Act 2015 received Royal Assent on 12 March 2015 and in accordance with s 59(1) the following provisions came into force on Royal Assent: Pt 1 (s 1) (overview), s 55 (regulations), s 56 (directions given by Welsh Ministers), s 57 (interpretation), s 58(3), (4) (certain regulations), s 59 (commencement), s 60 (short title etc). Under s 59(2), (3) other provisions come into force on such day as the Welsh Ministers may appoint by order made by statutory instrument. As to the Welsh Ministers see PARA 59. At the date at which this volume states the law one commencement order has been made: see the Higher Education (Wales) Act 2015 (Commencement No 1 Order and Saving Provision) Order 2015, SI 2015/1327, which brings provisions into force on 19 May 2015, 25 May 2015, 1 August 2015, 1 September 2015 and 1 January 2016. Amongst the amendments brought into force are those in the Higher (Education (Wales) Act 2015 s 58, Schedule paras 1, 2, 7–21, 22, 23, 24–26 on 1 September 2015. In particular it should be noted that the Higher Education Act 2004 ss 27, 28, 38, 40A are repealed as from that day by the Higher (Education (Wales) Act 2015 Schedule paras 9, 18, 20. Certain transitional provisions in the Higher (Education (Wales) Act 2015 Schedule paras 27–31 come into force on 1 August 2015. As to an order made in consequence of the Higher Education (Wales) Act 2015 see the Higher Education (Wales) Act 2015 (Consequential Provision) Order 2015, SI 2015/1353 under which a course run in England by an institution in Wales which provides higher education, and which is a charity, is subject to the same provisions (ie the Higher Education (Wales) Act 2015 ss 5, 10) about fee limits as apply to courses provided by the institution in Wales.

Part 6 (ss 41–46) makes procedural provision about notices and directions given by the Council (including provision about the review of certain notices and directions): s 1(7). See also the Higher Education (Fee and Access Plans) (Notices and Directions) (Wales) Regulations 2015, SI 2015/1485. The Higher Education (Wales) Act 2015 s 41(1)(a) is in force from 1 January 2016, s 41(1)(b), (d), (2) is in force from 1 September 2015 and s 42–46 are fully in force by 1 September 2015 (see note 1).

Part 7 (ss 47–54) makes supplementary provision about functions of the Council, including provision relating to guidance, reports, information and advice: s 1(8). Sections 47–49 are in force from 25 May 2015: see note 1. Section 51(1)(a), (e), (2) in force from 1 September 2015 (see note 1). Section 52(1) is in force for certain purposes from 25 May 2015 and is in force for other purposes from 1 September 2015, s 52(4) is in force from 19 May 2015, s 52(5) is in force from 25 May 2015, ss 52(2), (3), 53, 54(1) are in force from 1 September and s 54(3), (4) is in force from 25 May 2015 (see note 1).

Part 8 (ss 55–60) contains general provisions, including provision about the exercise of powers to make regulations, and the interpretation of terms used in the Act: s 1(9). Part 8 also introduces a Schedule containing amendments to existing enactments and transitional provision: see s 1(10).

2 As to designation of a provider of higher education as an institution for these purposes see the Higher Education (Designation of Providers of Higher Education) (Wales) Regulations 2015, SI 2015/1497. As to higher education institutions generally see PARA 619 et seq.

3 As to the meaning of 'Wales' see PARA 7 note 3.

4 As to the Higher Education Funding Council for Wales see PARA 691 et seq. As to the provision of financial support for students see PARA 1095 et seq.

5 The Council now has a duty to prepare and publish a code relating to the organisation and management of the financial affairs of institutions, and monitors compliance with it: see PARA 722.

6 Ie the Higher Education (Wales) Act 2015 Pt 2 (ss 2–16).

7 See the Higher Education (Wales) Act 2015 s 1(3). As to the application for approval of fee and access plans see ss 2, 3; and the Higher Education (Fee and Access Plans) (Wales) Regulations 2015, SI 2015/1498, reg 3. The Higher Education (Wales) Act 2015 s 2 is fully in force by 1 January 2016 and s 3 is fully in force by 1 September 2015 (see note 1). As to the content of fee and access plans see ss 4–6; and the Higher Education (Fee and Access Plans) (Wales) Regulations 2015, SI 2015/1498, regs 4–6. The Higher Education (Wales) Act 2015 ss 4–6 are fully in force by 1 January 2016 (see note 1). As to the approval etc of a fee and access plan see ss 7–9; and the Higher Education (Fee and Access Plans) (Wales) Regulations 2015, SI 2015/1498, reg 7. The Higher Education (Wales) Act 2015 s 7 is fully in force by 1 January 2016, ss 8, 9 are in force from 19 May 2015 (see note 1). As to publication of an approved fee and access plan see the Higher Education (Fee and Access Plans) (Wales) Regulations 2015, SI 2015/1498, reg 8. As to variation of an approved plan see reg 9. As to the fee limit see the Higher Education (Amounts) (Wales) Regulations 2015, SI 2015/1496; and as to qualifying courses etc in relation to which a fee limit must be set see the Higher Education (Qualifying Courses, Qualifying Persons and Supplementary Provision) (Wales) Regulations 2015, SI 2015/1484. As to compliance with the fee limit see the Higher Education (Wales) Act 2015 ss 10–12; and the Higher Education (Fee and Access Plans) (Notices and Directions) (Wales) Regulations 2015, SI 2015/1485. The Higher Education (Wales) Act 2015 ss 10–12 are fully in force by 1 September 2015 (see note 1). As to compliance with the general requirements of an approved plan see s 13; and as to validity of contracts see s 14. Section 14 is in force from 1 September 2015 (see note 1). As to the Council's duty to monitor and evaluate compliance and effectiveness and the institution's duty to co-operate see ss 15, 16. Sections 15(1)(a), 16 are in force from 1 September 2015 (see note 1).

8 Ie the Higher Education (Wales) Act 2015 Pt 5 (s 37–40).

9 See the Higher Education (Wales) Act 2015 s 1(6). As to refusal to approve new fee and access plan see s 37. Section 37(7) is in force from 19 May 2015 (see note 1). As to the withdrawal of approval of existing fee and access plan see ss 38, 39. Sections 38(2), 39(4) are in force from 19 May 2015 (see note 1). As to the publication of a notice under Part 5 see s 40. Section 40(2) is in force from 19 May 2015 (see note 1).

722. Financial affairs of institutions that have fee and access plans. Part 4 of the Higher Education (Wales) Act 2015[1] makes provision about the duty of the Higher Education Funding Council for Wales[2] to prepare and publish a code relating to the organisation and management of the financial affairs of institutions[3] that have fee and access plans[4], including provision about (1) compliance with the code; and (2) powers available for the purposes of monitoring compliance with the code, and in the case of failure to comply with the code[5].

1 Ie the Higher Education (Wales) Act 2015 Pt 4 (ss 27–36). As to the Act generally see PARA 721.
2 As to the Higher Education Funding Council for Wales see PARA 691 et seq.
3 As to higher education institutions see PARA 619 et seq.
4 As to fee and access plans see PARA 721.
5 See the Higher Education (Wales) Act 2015 s 1(5).
    As to the financial management code, including procedure for approval and monitoring its compliance see ss 27–31. Section 27(1) is in force for certain purposes from 25 May 2015, s 27(2), (3), (7), (8) is in force from 25 May 2015 and s 27(9), 28, 29 are in force from 1 September 2015 (see note 1).
    As to powers in respect of failure to comply with the code see ss 32–34. As to the duty to co-operate with monitoring see s 35. As to the powers of entry and inspection with regard to monitoring compliance see s 36. Sections 32–36 are to be brought into force on such day as the Welsh Ministers may appoint by order made by statutory instrument: s 59(2). At the date at which this volume states the law, no such order had been made. See also PARA 721.

(7) COMPLAINTS BY STUDENTS AGAINST HIGHER EDUCATION INSTITUTIONS

723. Status of students and right of redress, etc. Although a student stands in a contractual relationship with a university whatever the nature of the institution which he attends[1], relevant decisions are still open to judicial review[2]. Also, in relation to issues which do not actually touch upon matters of academic judgment, there is a statutory scheme for the review of complaints made by students or former students at qualifying institutions or by students working towards the grant of one of the qualifying institution's awards[3].

1 See PARA 1089.
2 See PARA 1089 note 2. As to judicial review generally see JUDICIAL REVIEW.
3 As to student complaints see PARA 1089 et seq. In particular as to the Office of the Independent Adjudicator for Higher Education see PARA 1091 note 5.

INDEX

Education

FURTHER EDUCATION
    CORPORATION
meaning 555n³
accounts, inspection of 1283
articles of government—
    initial 563
    provisions in 562
    requirement for 562
    subsequent 564
charitable status 566
collaboration arrangements, entry into
    569
complaints procedures, guidance as to
    618
dissolution 571
governing body: meaning 560n⁶
higher education sector, transfer to 557,
    620
incorporation—
    draft proposals for, publication of
      561
    existing institutions 559
    further institutions 560
    subsequent 564
instruments of government—
    initial 563
    provisions in 562
    requirement for 562
    Wales, consultation in 562
land held by, disposal of 1328
members' liability 565
orders incorporating 560
powers—
    collaboration arrangements, entering
      into 569
    principal 567
    supplementary 568, 594
property transfer 591
secondary education, duty to safeguard
    pupils receiving 595
sixth form college corporation converted
    into—
    Secretary of State's power to make
      order 580
    See further SIXTH FORM COLLEGE
      CORPORATION
supply of goods or services by
    567n¹⁰,¹¹
Wales, guidance as to consultation in
    570

FURTHER EDUCATION INSTITUTION
meaning. See under WORDS AND
    PHRASES
articles of government, requirement for
    573
clothing, provision of 601

FURTHER EDUCATION
    INSTITUTION—*continued*
collective worships, holding of act of
    598
complaints procedures, guidance as to
    618
corporations. *See* FURTHER EDUCATION
    CORPORATION
designation—
    accounts of designated institution,
      inspection of 1283
    institution in Wales conducted by
      company 574
    order as to 572
disabled, access and facilities for 1348
discipline—
    England, prohibited items in—
      alcohol 610n³
      prohibited item: meaning 608n³
      search powers 608
      seizure powers 610
    force, use by staff—
      grounds for 622
      member of staff: meaning 611n¹
      power to use 611
      recording and reporting of 612
    Wales, power to search for weapons
      in 609
discrimination. *See under* FURTHER
    EDUCATION
education at, provision of 555
efficiency studies 603, 787
employment contract, avoidance of
    certain terms 593
England, inspection in—
    action plan—
      area inspection, following 1266
      duty to publish 1264
    area inspection—
      meaning 1265
      action plan following 1266
      education or training the subject
        of 1265n³
      information in connection with,
        provision of 1265
      report following 1265
      request for 1265
    cases in which otherwise not
      required 1263
    documents and other records, right to
      inspect, take away etc 1267
    entry etc powers 1267
    exempt institution, inspection of
      1263
    framework for 1260
    further education and training 1261

References are to paragraph numbers; superior figures refer to notes

References are to paragraph numbers; superior figures refer to notes

References are to paragraph numbers; superior figures refer to notes

INDEPENDENT SCHOOL—*continued*
Education and Skills Act 2008,
　regulation and inspection
　under—*continued*
　independent educational institution
　　standards—
　　meaning 394
　　action plan. *See* action plan *above*
　　regulations 394
　independent inspectorate—
　　powers of 395
　　report on 395
　independent post-16 college—
　　meaning 383n⁴
　　application of provisions 383
　inspection—
　　direction of Secretary of State, on
　　　397
　　entry powers 398
　　fees 399
　　independent inspectorate, by 395
　　prescribed intervals, at 396
　　publication of report of 400
　　records, of 398
　　right of 398
　　Secretary of State's powers 395
　material change—
　　meaning 388
　　application for approval of—
　　　determination 390
　　　inspection and report 389
　　　requirement 388
　　unapproved, deregistration where
　　　391
　notice and other documents, service
　　of 415
　offences—
　　body corporate, by 413
　　proceedings for 412
　　unincorporated body, by 414
　participation in management,
　　prohibition on—
　　appeals 411
　　appropriate authority, direction by
　　　409
　　information, provision of 410
　part-time education, provision of
　　382n⁶
　registration—
　　application for—
　　　determination of 386
　　　procedure 385
　　　proprietor, by 385
　　deregistration 387
　　information, proprietor's duty to
　　　provide 393

INDEPENDENT SCHOOL—*continued*
Education and Skills Act 2008,
　regulation and inspection
　under—*continued*
　registration—*continued*
　　material change. *See* material
　　　change *above*
　　register, duty to keep 384
　　unsuitable person, removal from
　　　register 392
　relevant restriction—
　　imposition of—
　　　meaning 403
　　　emergency, in 404
　　　Secretary of State, by 403
　　　Tribunal, by 408
　　variation or revocation 403
fees 381
individual pupil information, provision
　of 374
National Curriculum, adoption of—
　England, for 859
　Wales, for 873
powers—
　non-maintained schools, provision of
　　education at 371
　Secretary of State—
　　general powers 373
　　performance information, to
　　　require 371
　Welsh Ministers—
　　general powers 373
　　performance information, to
　　　require 371
religious education, preferment of
　teachers willing to give 378
special educational needs in 376
staff at—
　employment of 377
　preferment of teachers willing to give
　　religious education 378
　religious character, certain schools
　　with 379
　suitability etc 377
travelling and subsistence allowances for
　governors 380
Wales, in—
　meaning 9n¹
　regulation and inspection. *See*
　　Education Act 2002, regulation
　　and inspection under *above*
　special educational needs, and 376
welfare of child accommodated in 375

LOCAL AUTHORITY—*continued*

accessibility strategies and plans, duty to implement 11

admission to school. *See* SCHOOL ADMISSION

assistance to school by 51

chief education officer, appointment 57

clothing, power to provide 482

compulsory school age, persons over—
apprenticeship training $32n^4$
education and training for 32
work experience for 33

conferences, organisation etc 53

director of children's services, appointment 57

education—
detention order, persons subject to $27n^6$
functions. *See* education functions *below*
general responsibility for 27
primary schools, as to 31
provision of. *See* education functions *below*
secondary schools, as to 31

education committee—
appointment of members, power to direct 56
regulations as to 56

education functions—
meaning 25
appropriate education, provision of $31n^8$
childcare, provision of 30
Education Act 1996, persons not covered by 46
enforcement by Secretary of State 45, 62
generally 37
higher education, provision of 39, 678
nursery schools, provision of 29
persons over compulsory school age, education and training for 32
persons over 19, as to 36
pupil referral units, provision of education in 37
statutory list of $25n^6$
transfer of local education authority functions 26
welfare of children, and 28
youth detention, persons subject to 38

educational research, powers as to 53

England, in—
meaning 25

LOCAL AUTHORITY—*continued*

England, in—*continued*
annual performance targets 49
core entitlement, duties as to 35
director of children's services, appointment 57
education and training for 16 to 18-year-olds, powers as to 34
high standards and fulfilment of potential, promotion of 43
inspection of. *See under* HER MAJESTY'S CHIEF INSPECTOR OF EDUCATION, CHILDREN'S SERVICES AND SKILLS
persons over compulsory school age 32
relevant education function: meaning $43n^2$
travel arrangements. *See under* SCHOOL ATTENDANCE (travel arrangements)
travel functions $466n^3$
See also education functions *above*

English: meaning $26n^7$

financial statement 329

goods and services, powers as to supply of 54

governors, travelling and subsistence allowances to 52

grant to school or other institution by 51

high standards, duty to promote 43

holidays, fixing dates of 458

information, provision of 48, 605, 940

inspection of—
England, in. *See under* HER MAJESTY'S CHIEF INSPECTOR OF EDUCATION, CHILDREN'S SERVICES AND SKILLS
Wales, in. *See under* HER MAJESTY'S CHIEF INSPECTOR OF EDUCATION AND TRAINING IN WALES

legal proceedings, documentary evidence in 50

loan of money, powers as to 54

maintained school, inspection for specific purpose 1180

medical officer: meaning $50n^5$

non-maintained schools, provision of education at 40

overview and scrutiny committees—
appointment 55
discharge of functions by 55
members' voting powers 55
procedure etc 55
Secretary of State's powers as to 55
Welsh Ministers' powers as to 55

LOCAL AUTHORITY—*continued*
  potential, duty to promote fulfilment
    of 43
  prevention of terrorism, duties as to 8
  primary school, power to establish etc
    41
  pupil referral units, provision of
    education in 37
  revenue accounts etc, duty to keep 54
  scholarships, grant of 483
  school expenses, payment of 483
  school inspection, measures to be taken
    following 1169
  secondary school, power to establish
    etc 41
  Secretary of State—
    performance of functions, power to
      secure 45, 62
    See also SECRETARY OF STATE FOR
      EDUCATION
  special educational needs, persons with.
    See SPECIAL EDUCATIONAL NEEDS
  terms, fixing dates of 458
  vocational qualifications, power to
    award or authenticate 42
  Wales, in—
    meaning 25
    chief education officer, appointment
      57
    complaints and enforcement in 44
    education and training for 16 to
      18-year-olds, powers as to 34
    high standards and fulfilment of
      potential, promotion of 43
    information, duty to provide 67
    inspection of. *See under* HER
      MAJESTY'S CHIEF INSPECTOR OF
      EDUCATION AND TRAINING IN
      WALES
    inspection of schools by. *See* SCHOOL
      INSPECTION (WALES) (local
      authority, by)
    intervention by Welsh Ministers. *See*
      INTERVENTION IN SCHOOLS
      (WALES) (local authority's
      education functions, intervention
      by Welsh Ministers)
    relevant education function: meaning
      $43n^{10}$
    travel arrangements. *See under*
      SCHOOL ATTENDANCE (travel
      arrangements)
    See also education functions *above*
  Welsh: meaning $26n^8$
  youth detention, education for persons
    subject to 38

LOCAL EDUCATION AUTHORITY
  further education functions, institutions
    maintained in exercise of 589
LOCAL WEIGHTS AND MEASURES
  AUTHORITY
  unrecognised degrees, enforcement of
    provisions as to 687
LOOKED AFTER CHILD
  admission to specified school—
    England, in 236, 255
    Wales, in 256
MAINTAINED SCHOOL
  meaning 99
  adjudicator. *See* SCHOOLS ADJUDICATOR
  alteration—
    excluded 132
    prescribed $110n^4$, 132, $133n^2$
    proposals for—
      meaning $135n^1$
      determination by governing body
        134
      implementation 136
      interested bodies, rights of 135
      publication 133
      relevant change in instrument of
        government $133n^{28}$, $134n^6$
    restriction 110
  categories 106
  charges—
    permitted—
      admission, for 334
      board and lodging at boarding
        schools, for 341
      charging policy 340
      generally 338
      information, provision of 342
      list of 338
      regulation of 339
      remissions policy 340
      singing, tuition in $339n^{15}$
      unaffected contributions and
        charges 343
    prohibition—
      admission, for 334
      incidental charges 337
      provision of education, for 335
      public examination, in respect of
        336
      transport 337
  charitable status 102
  community school. *See* COMMUNITY
    SCHOOL
  discontinuance—
    notice by governing body as to 116
    proposals for—
      academy proposals $119n^2$

MAINTAINED SCHOOL—*continued*
  discontinuance—*continued*
    proposals for—*continued*
      adjudicator, reference to 121
      comments 118
      consideration of 119
      determination 122
      implementation—
        community school 125
        community special school 125
        foundation school 126
        foundation special school 128
        maintained nursery school 125
        voluntary aided school 127
        voluntary controlled school 126
      information, provision of 123
      objections 118
      proposers: meaning 120n^2
      publication 115
      requirement to implement 124
      withdrawal 120
    restriction 110
    Secretary of State's power to direct
        117
  establishment—
    new school. *See* new school,
        proposals for *below*
    restriction 110
  exclusion of pupil. *See under* PUPIL
  financing—
    accounts 328
    budget share—
      amount 315
      determination of—
        England, in 317
        regulations, provisions in 316
        Wales, in 318
      funding period: meaning 315n^3
      requirement for 315
    charges. *See* charges *above*
    delegated budget—
      meaning 323
      duty to have 323
      effect of delegation 324
      governing body's right to 323
      new school, commencement date
          323
      property in 323
      restriction on spending 323
      suspension of delegation—
        effect 327
        notice accompanying 325
        reasons for 325
        review 326

MAINTAINED SCHOOL—*continued*
  financing—*continued*
    financial statement from local
        authority—
      England, in 329
      Wales, in—
        certification by Auditor General
            330
        power to call for 329
    free early years provision in England,
        budgetary provision in respect
        of 320
    local authority's financial scheme—
      duty to maintain 321
      inconsistency with rules or
          regulations 321
      publication and revision 322
      scope 321
    recoupment—
      adjustment between local
          authorities 332
      cross-border provisions 333
      excluded pupil, for 331
      provision for education: meaning
          333n^2
    schools budget, schools forum to
        advise on matters relating to 319
  foundation. *See* FOUNDATION SCHOOL
  funding. *See* maintenance and funding
      below
  further education provided by 588
  generally 91
  governing body. *See* GOVERNING BODY
      (MAINTAINED SCHOOL)
  grammar, designation as 101
  infant school: meaning 113n^{13}
  information, provision of 940
  inspection—
    local authority, by, for specific
        purpose 1180
    See also generally under SCHOOL
        INSPECTION (ENGLAND)
  junior school: meaning 113n^{14}
  maintenance and funding—
    community school 107, 306
    community special school 306
    local authority's duty 305
    maintain: meaning 306n^4
    nursery school 306
    See also financing *above*
  new school, proposals for—
    academy proposals 119n^2
    adjudicator, reference to 121
    comments 118
    consideration of 119

MAINTAINED SCHOOL—*continued*
  new school, proposals for—*continued*
    implementation—
      community school 125
      community special school 125
      foundation school 126
      foundation special school 128
      maintained nursery school 125
      voluntary aided school 127
      voluntary controlled school 126
    in Wales, to be maintained by English
        local authority 114
    information, provision of 123
    invitation for 111
    objections 118
    proposers: meaning 120n^2
    publication of—
      governing body, by 115
      Secretary of State's consent to 112
      special cases 113
    requirement to implement 124
    site and buildings for 129
    voluntary aided school—
      assistance for proposers of 131
      grants for certain expenditure 130
    withdrawal 120
  performance targets 939
  premises, provision of 306
  pupil. *See* PUPIL
  rating 1370
  responsible body 12n^{19}
  Secretary of State, communications by
      103
  sex education class, exclusion from 7
  specialist 100
  Sunday school or other place of
      worship, no requirement to attend
      931
  trust deed etc, modification of 146
  voluntary. *See* VOLUNTARY SCHOOL
  voluntary aided. *See* VOLUNTARY AIDED
      SCHOOL
  voluntary controlled. *See* VOLUNTARY
      CONTROLLED SCHOOL
  Wales, in—
    alteration, establishment or
        discontinuance, proposals for—
      approval 143
      consultation 142
      determination 143
      generally 140
      objections 142
      proposer: meaning 140n^{12}
      publication 142
      regulated alteration 143n^3

MAINTAINED SCHOOL—*continued*
  Wales, in—*continued*
    change of category, proposals for—
      approval 143
      consultation 142
      determination 143
      generally 141
      objections 142
      proposer: meaning 140n^{12}
      publication 142
    excessive or insufficient provision,
        directions to make proposals to
        remedy 144
    rationalisation of school places,
        proposals for 145
    School Organisation Code 139
    Welsh Ministers—
      communications by 103
      partnership agreements between local
          authorities and governing bodies
          104
      school places, proposals for
          rationalisation of 145
      transition from primary to secondary
          school, plans to facilitate 105
MARSHALL AID COMMEMORATION
    COMMISSION
  accounts 1114
  annual report by 1114
  constitution 1114
  establishment and functions 1114
MIDDLE SCHOOL
  meaning 91
NATIONAL ASSEMBLY FOR WALES
  education and training matters,
      responsibility for 59n^{24}
NATIONAL COLLEGE FOR TEACHING
    AND LEADERSHIP
  alleged offences, reporting restrictions—
    application to dispense with 1072
    breach—
      defence to charge of 1074
      offence and penalty 1073
    ceasing to apply 1072
    nature of allegations 1072
    provisions, application of 1072
    publication: meaning 1072n^6
    relevant criminal offence: meaning
        1072n^4
  disciplinary cases, investigation of 1068
  guidance document 1066n^7
  information, supply of—
    agency, by 1071
    contractor, by 1071
    employer, by—
      dismissal, following 1070

NATIONAL COLLEGE FOR TEACHING
  AND LEADERSHIP—*continued*
information, supply of—*continued*
  employer, by—*continued*
    resignation, following 1070
    serious misconduct, following
      dismissal etc because of 1070,
      1071
  list of persons prohibited from teaching
    etc 1069
  prohibition order by Secretary of State
    1068
  reporting restrictions as to alleged
    offences. *See* alleged offences,
    reporting restrictions *above*
  responsibility for teacher training 1054
  Secretary of State acting on behalf of
    1066
  teacher misconduct, application of
    statutory provisions 1067

NATIONAL CURRICULUM FOR
  ENGLAND
  assessment arrangements 859, 863
  attainment targets 859, 863
  basic curriculum, as part of 857
  careers education and guidance 858
  constituents of 859
  development work and experiments 866
  EHC plan, pupil with 868
  establishment by order 863
  exceptions and modifications to 867
  foreign language: meaning 861n[13]
  free school, and 368
  general duties as to 856
  home schooling, and 426
  implementation of, duty to secure 864
  independent schools, adoption by 859
  key stages—
    meaning 860
    attainment targets 861
    first, second and third, requirements
      for 861
    fourth, requirements for 862
    generally 860
  modern foreign language: meaning
    861n[15]
  order, Secretary of State's power to
    revise etc by 863
  orders and regulations, procedure for
    making 865
  performance targets 939
  programmes of study 859
  pupil referral unit 430
  revision of 863
  supervision. *See* OFQUAL

NATIONAL CURRICULUM FOR
  ENGLAND—*continued*
  temporary exceptions for individual
    pupils 869

NATIONAL CURRICULUM FOR
  WALES
  assessment arrangements 873
  basic curriculum, as part of 871
  careers education and guidance 872
  constituents 873
  development work and experiments 881
  establishment by order 878
  exceptions and modifications to 882
  foundation phase 873, 874
  free school, and 368
  general duties as to 870
  home schooling, and 426
  implementation of, duty to secure 879
  independent schools, adoption by 873
  key stages—
    meaning 875
    fourth, requirements for 877
    generally 875
    second and third, requirements for
      876
  local—
    meaning 885n[3]
    fourth key stage, pupils in—
      child being registered pupil,
        application of provisions to
        894
      child not being registered pupil,
        application of provisions to
        893
    choice of courses, pupil's 888
    course of study—
      meaning 885n[5]
      learning domain, falling within
        885n[6]
      maximising availability of
        courses 892
      pupil's right to choose 888
    entitlement—
      delivery of, joint working 892
      head teacher's decision as to 889
      head teacher's decision to
        remove 890
    formation 885
    local authority and governing
      bodies working together 892
    local curriculum: meaning 885n[3]
    more than one 885
    planning the curriculum 891
    regulations as to formation 885
    vocational course of study 885n[19]

References are to paragraph numbers; superior figures refer to notes

OFQUAL—*continued*
  regulatory function—
    meaning $851n^2$
    duty to keep under review 851
  research and development programmes
    850
  review of qualifications by 828
  services, provision of 849
  unnecessary burdens, duty not to
    impose or maintain 851

OFSTED
  administration 1128
  changes to education inspection,
    guidance as to $1132n^2$
  Chief Inspector. *See* HER MAJESTY'S
    CHIEF INSPECTOR OF EDUCATION,
    CHILDREN'S SERVICES AND SKILLS
  committees 1128
  common inspection framework—
    application of 1132
    handbook as to $1132n^3$
  complaints against schools 546
  documentary evidence, application of
    legislation 1128
  establishment 1128
  functions—
    assignment by Secretary of State 1129
    general 1129
    performance of 1130
    supplementary powers 1131
  general responsibility for inspections
    1127
  inspectors, appointment etc 1146
  powers, supplementary 1131
  role 1127
  seal, application of 1128
  staff 1128

ORDER
  academy. *See under* ACADEMY
    (conversion of school into)
  education supervision. *See* EDUCATION
    SUPERVISION ORDER
  pay and conditions. *See under* TEACHER
    (pay and conditions)
  school attendance. *See* SCHOOL
    ATTENDANCE ORDER
  service of 76

OXFORD UNIVERSITY
  governance 626
  graduate privileges 643
  jurisdiction privileges over members
    641
  library, rights under copyright
    legislation 642
  publications, privileges regarding 642

OXFORD UNIVERSITY—*continued*
  religious instruction and worship etc
    644

POLITICS
  balanced treatment of political issues,
    duty to secure 909
  political indoctrination, prohibition 908

PRIMARY SCHOOL
  meaning 91
  appropriate education, provision of
    $31n^8$
  establishment 41
  primary education: meaning 20
  provision of, local authority's duty as
    to 31
  rural: meaning $115n^{17}$
  Wales, in, free breakfasts 493
  withdrawal of pupil from, for secondary
    education 438

PRIVY COUNCIL
  higher education corporation's trust
    deed etc, power to modify 669
  higher education institution's trust deed
    etc, power to modify 676
  university, power to confer title on
    institution 621

PUBLIC SCHOOL
  meaning $370n^1$
  chapel 370
  Eton $370n^2$
  generally 370
  headmaster, appointment 370
  income 370
  legislation, application of 370
  teachers, appointment 370

PUPIL
  meaning $20n^4$, $493n^3$
  admission. *See* SCHOOL ADMISSION
  behaviour. *See* good behaviour *below*
  board and lodging, provision for—
    EHC plan, for person with 507
    otherwise than at school 506
    special educational needs, pupil with
      506
  bullying—
    cyberbullying, advice on $509n^{12}$
    guidance for governing bodies $509n^{12}$
    guidance for head teachers $509n^{12}$
    teacher's duty to prevent 1087
  cleanliness—
    cleansing of pupil—
      arrangements for 496
      compulsory, notice for 495
      girl 496
      subsequent offence 495
      suspension pending 497

SCHOLARSHIP
  Commonwealth Scholarship
    Commission. *See* COMMONWEALTH
    SCHOLARSHIP COMMISSION
  industrial 1112
  Marshall Aid Commemoration
    Commission. *See* MARSHALL AID
    COMMEMORATION COMMISSION

SCHOOL
  meaning 91
  absence from, regulations as to 459
  accessibility strategies and plans 11
  adjudicator. *See* SCHOOLS ADJUDICATOR
  admission of pupils. *See* SCHOOL
    ADMISSION
  choice of, dispute between parents as
    to 7n[6]
  complaints against—
    exclusion, as to 546n[24]
    generally 546
    investigation of, in England. *See*
      SCHOOL INSPECTION (ENGLAND)
      (complaints, investigation of)
    Ofqual. *See* OFQUAL
    Ofsted. *See* OFSTED
    procedure 546
    special educational needs, in case of
      546
    type of school, relevance 546
    useful information, availability of 546
  compulsory school age 19
  day, regulations as to duration of 459
  discrimination in—
    accessibility strategies and plans 11
    application of legislation 9n[1]
    detriment: meaning 9n[11]
    disability, contravention of duty as
      to 12
    duty not to discriminate in provision
      of education 9
    single-sex schools turning
      co-educational 10
  equality duties. *See* EQUALITY (schools,
    in)
  governors, travelling and subsistence
    allowances to 52
  independent. *See* INDEPENDENT SCHOOL
  inspection—
    England, in. *See* SCHOOL INSPECTION
      (ENGLAND)
    Wales, in. *See* SCHOOL INSPECTION
      (WALES)
  intervention. *See* INTERVENTION IN
    SCHOOLS (ENGLAND);
    INTERVENTION IN SCHOOLS (WALES)
  maintained. *See* MAINTAINED SCHOOL

SCHOOL—*continued*
  nursery. *See* NURSERY SCHOOL
  primary. *See* PRIMARY SCHOOL
  proprietor: meaning 51n[4]
  responsible body: meaning 9n[1]
  secondary. *See* SECONDARY SCHOOL
  staffing of. *See* SCHOOL STAFF
  trustees of 1303n[7]
  types 91
  year, regulations as to duration of 459

SCHOOL ADMISSION
  appeals—
    excluded children, in relation to 252
    governing body's right to appeal 252
    parents, arrangements for 251
    sixth form children, arrangements
      for 251
  charges for—
    allowed, where 334
    prohibition on 334
  circumstances preventing 224
  code for—
    approval 226
    issue 225
    making of 226
    revision 225
  compulsory school age, children under
    257
  direction to admit child to specified
    school—
    local authority, by—
      conditions to be satisfied 253
      generally 253
      governing body's response 254
      looked after child—
        England, in 255
        Wales, in 256
      power to give 253
      procedure for giving 254
      suitable education: meaning 253n[7]
  discrimination in relation to 233
  England, arrangements in—
    adjudicator—
      decisions of—
        binding nature of 242
        matters relating to 242
        regulations as to 242
      functions 241
      objections referred to 240
      reports by local authorities to 245
      variations referred to 238
    co-ordination of 243
    establishment or expansion,
      restriction or alteration
      following 239

References are to paragraph numbers; superior figures refer to notes

SCHOOL PREMISES—*continued*
approval—
building byelaws, exemption from 1347
need to obtain 1346
building byelaws, exemption from 1347
disabled, access and facilities for 1348
disposal on discontinuance of foundation, voluntary or foundation schools—
foundation body, by—
application to appropriate authority 1320
generally 1320
notice of intention to discontinue 1322
governing body, by—
application to appropriate authority 1320
dissolution of body, transfer of property, rights and liabilities on 1324
generally 1320
notice of intention to discontinue 1322
trustees, by—
application to appropriate authority 1321
generally 1321
notice of intention to discontinue 1323
occupation of existing site, notice terminating 1325
disturbance on 1351
governing body, control of use by—
England, in—
community and community special schools—
occupation and use 1355
transfer of control agreements 1356
foundation and foundation special schools—
occupation and use 1357
transfer of control agreements 1358
voluntary schools—
control of use outside school hours 1361
occupation and use 1359
transfer of control agreements 1360
Wales, in—
community and community special schools—
occupation and use 1362

SCHOOL PREMISES—*continued*
governing body, control of use by—*continued*
Wales, in—*continued*
community and community special schools—*continued*
transfer of control agreements 1363
foundation and foundation special schools—
occupation and use 1364
transfer of control agreements 1365
maintained nursery schools—
occupation and use 1362
transfer of control agreements 1363
voluntary schools—
control of use outside school hours 1368
occupation and use 1366
transfer of control agreements 1367
harmful apparatus and materials, control of 1349
health and safety duties 1353
new—
approval 1346
relaxation of prescribed standards 1345
nuisance on 1351
occupiers' liability 1354
prescribed standards for—
local authority, school maintained by 1344
local authority functions, exercise of 1344
regulations for 1344
relaxation in special cases 1345
School Sites Acts, provision of premises under 1297

SCHOOL SITE
additional, relaxation of prescribed standards 1345
Charity Commission scheme 1297
foundation school, provision for 1295
foundation special school, provision for 1295
local authority, transfer of interest by 1295, 1296
new, relaxation of prescribed standards 1345
School Sites Acts, provision of premises under 1297
site: meaning $1295n^3$

Words and Phrases

Words in parentheses indicate the context in which the word or phrase is used